SECOND EDITION

INTERNATIONAL BUSINESS LAW: A TRANSACTIONAL APPROACH

Larry A. DiMatteo
Associate Professor
Warrington College of Business
University of Florida
J.D., The Cornell Law School
LL.M., The Harvard Law School

Lucien J. Dhooge
Associate Professor
Eberhardt School of Business
University of the Pacific
J.D., University of Denver
LL.M., Georgetown University Law Center

THOMSON
™
WEST

Australia · Canada · Mexico · Singapore · Spain · United Kingdom · United States

THOMSON

WEST

International Business Law: A Transactional Approach, 2nd Edition

Larry A. DiMatteo and Lucien J. Dhooge

VP/Editorial Director
Jack W. Calhoun

Publisher
Rob Dewey

Acquisitions Editor
Steven Silverstein, Esq.

Developmental Editor
Bob Sandman

Editorial Assistant
Brian Coovert

Executive Marketing Manager
Lisa Lysne

Sr. Production Editor
Tim Bailey

Manager of Technology, Editorial
Vicky True

Technology Project Editor
Christine A. Wittmer

Manufacturing Coordinator
Charlene Taylor

Art Director
Michelle Kunkler

Cover and Internal Design
Ramsdell Design/Cincinnati

Cover Image
© Ken Ross/Taxi

Production
Stratford Publishing Services

Printer
Thomson-West

Library of Congress Control Number: 2004112964

For more information about our products, contact us at:

Thomson Learning
Academic Resource Center
1-800-423-0563

Asia (including India)
Thomson Learning
5 Shenton Way
#01-01 UIC Building
Singapore 068808

Australia/New Zealand
Thomson Learning Australia
102 Dodds Street
SouthBank, Victorial 3006
Australia

Canada
Thomson Nelson
1120 Birchmount Road
Toronto, Ontario
M1K 5G4
Canada

Latin America
Thomson Learning
Seneca, 53
Colonia Polanco
11560 Mexico
D.F. Mexico

Thomson Higher Education
5191 Natorp Boulevard
Mason, Ohio 45040
USA

UK/Europe/Middle East/Africa
Thomson Learning
High Holborn House
50/51 Bedford Row
London WC1R 4LR
United Kingdom

Spain (including Portugal)
Thomson Paraninfo
Calle Magallanes, 25
28015 Madrid, Spain

To my heart and my soul: my wife Colleen for her love and support
and my son, Ian, for his inspiration.
L. A. D.

To my wife Julia for her love, support, and patience.
L. J. D.

Brief Contents

Contents

Part 4: Exporting and Importing: The Documentary Transaction and Trade Finance

Part 5: Sales of Services, Licensing of Intellectual Property, and Electronic Transactions

Table of Cases and Laws

United States Statutory Law

English Case Law

English Statutory Law

European Union Law

Other European Laws

Brazilian Law

Canadian Law

Chinese Law

Dutch Law

French Law

German Law

Hungarian Law

ICC Arbitration Cases

Indonesian Law

International Treaties and Conventions

Preface

The international marketplace offers great opportunity for a domestic enterprise seeking to expand. It is also a place where the risks of loss are somewhat unique in character. Accordingly, the American businessperson must become an astute manager of international business risk in order to minimize the chances of financial loss. This book will illuminate the risks of doing business internationally, while providing the student of international business law with tools to help minimize those risks.

The legal issues relevant to international business transactions can be seen as a due diligence checklist. The sophisticated international entrepreneur directly addresses the legal issues discussed in this book before transacting international business. The tremendous expansion of international business is a testament to the fact that the legal issues in international business transactions are discernible. Furthermore, the real world often provides solutions to the risks associated with such issues.

The trend toward increased international trade is likely to continue. It began at the end of World War II with the establishment of the World Bank, International Monetary Fund, United Nations, and the evolution of the General Agreement on Tariffs and Trade (GATT). The trend continued to accelerate with the adoption of the North American Free Trade Agreement (NAFTA), the deepening of the European Union (EU), and the establishment of the World Trade Organization (WTO). It will continue to accelerate with the expansion of the European Union into Eastern Europe, the entry of the People's Republic of China into membership in the WTO, the explosion of e-commerce, and the continuing quest for new international markets.

In order to obtain profits in the international marketplace, small to large size companies will have to develop an "international business strategy" in order to stay competitive. This book provides an introduction to the legal issues that need to be addressed in formulating such a strategy.

Transactional Approach

The subtitle of this book, *A Transactional Approach*, was selected to distinguish it from the more generic texts on International Business Law. As such, it focuses on transactional international business law. The text presents international business transactions with an emphasis on rules *and* practice. The topics of coverage have been selected to place predominant emphasis on matters that most directly impact private business transactions: export-import, licensing and technology transfer, and sales of services. It is the authors' belief that it is these practical legal aspects of international business that are most relevant to today's business student. Therefore, extensive coverage of more "macro" issues like expropriation or nationalization, workings of the United Nations, and international monetary policy are abandoned due to the increasingly minor role they play in today's international business arena. This is not to say that these areas of coverage are not important, but that in a relatively stable free trade environment they are unlikely to be of direct importance to the international entrepreneur. Given the time limitations in a standard college course, it is to the basics of transactional business law that this textbook's coverage is directed.

Managerial Perspective

Throughout the book, capsules and materials will be provided to illustrate the law of international business transactions *as practiced*. A variety of methods will be utilized to provide the student with a real world perspective. These methods include case studies, checklists, forms, tables, and summaries.

Capsules, Exhibits, and Icons

The chapters contain numerous capsules and exhibits that emphasize the transactional and managerial emphasis of the text. The Doing Business Internationally and Focus on Transactions capsules provide checklists and practical information relevant to the international entrepreneur. Comparative Law capsules highlight differences in national legal systems. Exhibits expose the student to the forms used in carrying out international business transactions, along with charts and statistics. International icons alert the reader to coverage in the text of foreign laws.

Special Features

A number of *hot topics* are included to make the textbook more comprehensive and cutting edge. These topics include in-depth coverage of international commercial arbitration; recent interpretations of the United Nations Convention for the International Sale of Goods (CISG); the legal issues of e-commerce and other types of electronic transactions; the expanding recognition of international franchising; the problems of international bribery, including the adoption of the OECD Anti-Corruption Code; the development of international standards such as the International Standards Organization's ISO 9000 and ISO 14000; the unique issues pertaining to joint venturing; the continuing problem of piracy of intellectual property; and changes in international business practices and procedures wrought by the terrorist attacks of September 11, 2001.

Electronic Transactions

The growing importance of electronic means of communicating and contracting in the international business arena is reflected in the allotment of an entire chapter to the topic, along with coverage of electronic developments pertaining to the other substantive topics discussed throughout the book.

Ethics Coverage

Ethical questions in international business can arise in various contexts. These contexts include the ethics of negotiations, disclosure of information, dealing with foreign governments, and the divergence between home country and host country laws. The student will be encouraged to form a mind-set in which ethical behavior will become an inherent part of his or her approach to international business. An entire chapter is devoted to the topic, along with a number of ethics capsules placed throughout the book.

Sources and References

The text reflects an earnest attempt to expose the student to a sampling of foreign law. National laws from approximately two dozen countries are referenced and used for purposes of illustration. There are numerous references throughout the text to a number of primary sources. All references to the Uniform Commercial Code, or UCC, are references to the law of the United States. The book also makes ample use of a variety of European Economic Community (EEC), European Community (EC), and European Union (EU) directives and regulations. This body of law, apologetically, is referred to as EU Regulations. The reader may refer to the footnotes for the proper citations. In order to emphasize the nature of national laws' impact upon international business transactions, the laws of the European Union, the People's Republic of China, and the Russian Federation have been singled out for extra attention. These three bodies of law were also selected because of the importance of these markets in world trade. These bodies of law also provide an excellent comparison between laws pertaining to international business in developed and emerging market economies. Emphasis on the law of the European Union also serves to highlight the difficulties inherent in harmonizing differing national legal systems. The use of national law serves to illuminate the typical issues found in international business transactions.

Case Law

A concerted effort has been made to update the case law in order to provide a more contemporary flavor to the text. Sixty-eight of the cases are from 1990 to the present; of those, 44 cases were decided no earlier than 1997. Of course, some older cases remain because of their power as precedents or as clear illustrations of a given legal principle. Along with a presentation of American law, cases have been selected from Canada, the European Union, Japan, the Netherlands, New Zealand, the Russian Federation and the United Kingdom, along with International Chamber of Commerce Arbitration cases and cases employing the GATT dispute resolution processes.

Style and Structure

A premium has been placed upon readability by the use of clear narrative, carefully edited case summaries and articles, and concise use of tangential materials. Also, in the spirit of the practical-managerial focus of the book, more in-depth insight is offered in certain areas so that the student is exposed not only to the *why* a given rule of law has evolved, but also *how* it is applied in practice. The chapter coverage allows for the use of the chapters as individual modules or as blocks of chapters. The first seven chapters can be viewed as foundational in that they provide the legal environment of international business, including: International Business Risks, International Business Ethics, Strategies for Doing Business Internationally, International Dispute Resolution, National and International Trade Regulation, and International Contract Law. Chapters 8–11 focus upon the legalities of exporting-importing, covering International Sales Law, the Documentary Transaction, Transport of Goods, and International Trade Finance. Chapter 12 provides coverage of the growing area of the international sale of services. Chapters 13 and 14 pertain to the important area of technology transfer and the international licensing of intellectual property rights. Finally, Chapter 15 provides coverage of the evolving area of electronic transactions that cuts across all of the ways of doing business internationally.

Internet Exercises

A number of Internet exercises have been placed in the end-of-chapter problems sections. In addition, relevant Web sites have been inserted in the margins throughout the text. These provide important Web sites that students can use for reference or to answer a question or project posed. The exercises and additional Web site references can be used in individual or group assignments.

Key Terms

Learning the terminology of international business is an important part of any international business law course. The key terms used in the chapters are listed at the end of each chapter. Definitions of terms are provided in the text and in a special glossary found on the book's Web site at *http://dimatteo.westbuslaw.com*.

Case Highlights

Following each case is a capsule listing principles of law, concepts, and business practices highlighted in the case. Some of the highlights summarize the reasons why the case was inserted into the textbook. Other highlights alert the student to the fact that most legal disputes involve multiple issues. Many of these "external" highlights are examined elsewhere in the textbook. The instructor may also use these points as a starting point for a more in-depth discussion of the multiple issues of the case.

Chapter Problems

Each chapter concludes with problems appropriate for classroom discussion. The Instructor's Manual provides the answers and relevant case citations to the problems, along with other ideas for class discussion. The Test Bank included in the Instructor's Manual, provides additional essay questions that provide an additional source for discussions.

Appendices

The Appendices selected are to be actively used by the student. Appendix A provides the text of the Convention for the International Sale of Goods (CISG) and should be referred to in conjunction with Chapter 8's coverage of the law of sales. Appendix B is the Agreement Establishing the World Trade Organization. This is supplemental to the material in Chapters 5 and 6 on trade regulation. Students interested in the WTO should read this foundational document to better understand the scope, governance, and purpose of this international trade organization.

Appendix C is selected provisions of the Agreement on Trade-Related Aspects of Intellectual Property Rights (TRIPS). The TRIPS Agreement is discussed in Chapter 13. A review of TRIPS will help the student better understand the reach of intellectual property law. Finally, the Hague Rules found in Appendix D should be referred to in conjunction with Chapter 10's coverage of carrier liability.

Instructor's Manual and Test Bank (ISBN: 0-324-30369-6)

The Instructor's Manual provides additional source materials including a chapter-by-chapter bibliography, Chapter topics and objectives, lecture outlines, answers to end-of-chapter problems, and additional student in-class and take-home exercises. The Manual also provides supplemental material, such as statutes. These materials can be used in preparation for class or given as handouts. The Test Bank provides short answer (true-false and multiple choice) questions, along with essay questions.

Acknowledgments

We would like to thank the editorial staff at West Legal Studies in Business, especially our editors, Steve Silverstein, Bob Sandman, and Tim Bailey. We are grateful for the help of Angela N. Jones in updating the Instructor's Manual and Test Bank, as well as verifying the Internet sources.

We especially thank the following reviewers whose comments helped us plan this Second Edition:

Mary Ann Donnelly
Le Moyne College

Stephanie Greene
Boston College

James E. Hickey, Jr.
Hofstra University School of Law

Melinda G. Hickman
Lincoln Memorial University

Georgia Holmes
Minnesota State University, Mankato

John Anthony Wrieden
Florida International University

Norman Gregory Young
California State Polytechnic University, Pomona

About the Authors

Larry A. DiMatteo is a Professor of Management & Legal Studies in the Warrington College of Business Administration at the University of Florida. He is a graduate of the Cornell and Harvard Law Schools. He served previously as President of the International Law Section of the *Academy of Legal Studies in Business* and currently is the Senior Articles Editor of the *American Business Law Journal.* He is the author of numerous publications dealing with contract law, contract theory, and international business transactions. His books include *The Law of International Business Transactions* (2002); *Equitable Law of Contracts: Principles and Standards* (2001); The *Law of International Contracting* (2000); and *Contract Theory: The Evolution of Contractual Intent* (1998).

K. Benjamin Simons

Lucien J. Dhooge is an Associate Professor of Business Law at the Eberhardt School of Business at the University of the Pacific where he teaches international business law and the legal and ethical environment of business. He received his J.D. from the University of Denver College of Law and LL.M. in international and comparative law from the Georgetown University Law Center. Professor Dhooge is a four-time recipient of the Ralph C. Hoeber Award granted annually by the Academy of Legal Studies in Business for excellence in research. He was designated the outstanding junior business law faculty member in the United States by the ALSB in 2002.

Laurie Gallant

The purpose of this chapter is to review briefly some of the major topics and issues involved in international business transactions. The remaining chapters of the book will expand on the topics outlined in this chapter. The first part of Chapter One highlights the tremendous growth in international business transactions and some of the causes behind this expansion. One factor that has aided the expansion of international trade is the development of a supranational trade law. Chapter One therefore introduces the reader to the concept of international customary law.

We will examine the ways international business is transacted. The concepts of direct and indirect exporting, licensing, and direct foreign investment will be introduced. This discussion will provide a basic understanding of the perceived advantages and disadvantages of each method of transacting international business. These methods will be explored further in Chapter Three, along with hybrid ways of transacting business, such as franchising and joint venturing.

The second half of Chapter One will focus on the risks involved in international

Chapter 1

Introduction to International Business Transactions

business transactions. The great opportunities presented by international business transactions do not come without risk. Some risks are the same as those in purely domestic transactions; others are unique to the international business environment. First, we will analyze how companies evaluate such risks. Second, we will review the generic risks associated with international business transactions, including risks associated with cultural and language differences, currency risks, legal risks, and political risks. Finally, we will look at the tools that have been developed to minimize and manage such risks. We conclude by discussing strategies for managing international business risks, including the development of an export plan, use of intermediaries, and a form of international business known as countertrade.

Ultimately, the goal of teaching international business law is to sensitize future entrepreneurs to the risks of international business and the ways to manage such risks. A savvy entrepreneur is adept at analyzing risk and is knowledgeable about the techniques to minimize risk. After Chapter One introduces the reader to the risks of international business transactions, the rest of the textbook will explore more fully how such risks are minimized in the areas of exporting, direct foreign investment, and intellectual property transfer.

The Global and Regional Marketplace

The relaxation of international trade barriers after the Second World War has produced a dramatic increase in world trade in goods, services, and technology licensing. A number of factors have facilitated this expansion in international trade including:

- Seven Rounds of General Agreement on Tariffs and Trade (GATT) Negotiations
- The expansion of GATT with the adoption of the 1994 World Trade Organization (WTO) Agreements into other areas, such as trade in services, technology transfer, and foreign investment
- The deepening of regional trading blocks, such as the European Union (EU) and the North American Free Trade Area (NAFTA)
- The disintegration of the Soviet Union and Warsaw Pact and the advent of "emerging economies," many of which have become members of the EU
- Dramatic advances in telecommunications and information technologies
- The development of vibrant international capital markets in Europe and North America
- Economic reform based upon capitalist models currently under way in the People's Republic of China

This list is far from exhaustive, but it illustrates the fact that we live in an age of dynamic global economic development and interdependence. It should be noted that the threat of terrorism worldwide, emphasized by the attack on September 11, 2001, has placed a degree of uncertainty on international trade and travel that is difficult to measure.

The forces listed here have resulted in significant increases in cross-border trade in manufactured goods and services, international joint ventures, mergers, acquisitions, strategic alliances and affiliations, infrastructure projects, privatization, and international direct investment. The liberalization of trade and investment rules has created a "world of opportunities" for the international entrepreneur.[1] The lure of profits from international business transactions has drawn many domestic businesses into the global marketplace. The mobility of goods and services has enabled domestic companies to search the world for new markets to sell their products and to procure component parts used in the manufacture of their products. The producer of goods and services, or the innovator of technology, can maximize profits with a global business strategy. This strategy encompasses not only developing foreign markets for a company's products but also outsourcing materials, labor, and component parts. Even a company that takes a more isolated domestic sales strategy is likely to be affected by international developments.

The best measure of globalization has been the tremendous growth in the international **trade in goods**. Exhibit 1.1 illustrates the trend in world trade over the past few decades and into the early part of the current decade.

A second measure of globalization is **foreign direct investment (FDI)**. FDI represents the capital investments made by companies in other countries. It includes the purchase of real estate, manufacturing plants, service and distribution centers, or foreign businesses. Between 1981 and 1985, total world FDI averaged $98 billion per year. By 1997, FDI had reached $440 billion. According to the United Nations Conference on Trade and Development, foreign direct investment inflows increased to $735 billion in 2001. The increase in world FDI has, much like trade, occurred mostly in the three major regional trade areas of Europe, the Americas, and East Asia. Globalization is likely to expand both at the regional level and at the

http://

U.S. Bureau of Economic Affairs: **http://www.state.gov/e/ eb/tpp.** Information on U.S. trade programs with links to NAFTA and WTO Web sites.

http://

U.S. Department of Commerce Bureau of Economic Analysis: **http://www.bea.doc.gov.** Provides statistics pertaining to economic activity.

---

1. See, generally, Ward Bower, "The Future Structure of the Global Legal Marketplace," The Metropolitan Corporate Counsel (1999).

EXHIBIT 1.1   *Trends in World Trade Integration (trillions of dollars)*

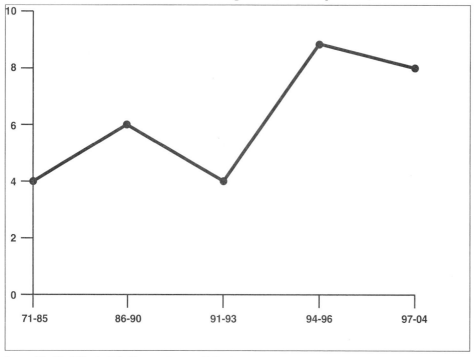

Source: The World Bank, *Global Economic Prospects* 15 (Washington, D.C. 1995). Reprinted with permission. Copyright ©
    1995 by the International Bank for Reconstruction and Development and the World Bank.

worldwide level. The causes of this expected growth include the advance of global
telecommunications and the increased transferability of services and intellectual
property. Service and knowledge industries, such as entertainment, education, and
health care, will benefit from the expansion of the **General Agreement on Tariffs
and Trade (GATT)** into areas other than the sale of goods. The upward trend in
services and intellectual property trade will continue in the next decade and
beyond. The average annual growth rate for trade in commercial services between
1980 and 1993 was 7.7 percent, compared with 4.9 percent for trade in goods. The
dollar value of trade in commercial services grew to $1.6 trillion, with an annual
growth rate of 6 percent by 2002, while the annual growth rate of trade in goods
was 4 percent.

http://

World Bank:
**http://www.
worldbank.org.** Provides
statistics and informa-
tion on international
trade and finance.

Laws of International Business Transactions

International law generally refers to the historically developed transnational rules
and norms that national courts use to regulate three primary relationships: (1)
the relationship between two nations, (2) the relationship between a nation and
an individual, and (3) the relationship between persons or entities from different
countries. This book is primarily concerned with the last type of relationship—
the person-to-person relationship between two parties transacting business across
national borders. The first two types of relationships will be reviewed at times,
however, because of their effect upon private business relationships. Thus, the

regulations promulgated by the World Trade Organization (WTO) will be studied because of their direct impact on the export and import of goods, services, and intellectual property rights.

There are numerous sources of international business law. **Article 38** of the Statute of the **International Court of Justice**[2] lists the sources of international law. In order of superiority, they are (1) international conventions[3] and treaties,[4] (2) international custom or general practice, (3) general principles of law recognized by civilized nations, and (4) judicial decisions and scholarly writings. These are the same sources of law often used by private parties in international litigation or arbitration proceedings.

The primary source of law in international business transactions is, however, the private contract entered into by the business parties. The contract is the first source of law referred to by a court or arbitration panel in resolving a contract dispute. At times, however, the contract may fail to provide a solution, either because it does not deal with the issue in dispute or because the parties interpret the contract differently. It was once said that "no written contract is ever complete; even the most carefully drafted document rests on volumes of assumptions that cannot be explicitly expressed."[5] This quote illustrates that a substantial core of any international business transaction is non-legal in nature. Businesspeople prefer the language of business and are often unconcerned with the legal language of the formal contract document.

Despite this informal attitude, the language of business does tend to be "codified" into legally recognizable customs and trade usage. This transformation is a well-worn tradition that dates back to the medieval *lex mercatoria*.[6] The *lex mercatoria*, or law of merchants, provides the mechanism in which day-to-day uses and practices are recognized by businesspeople, as well as by courts and arbitral tribunals, as international customary law. It has also been said that "the transformation of international business law signifies more than just an incremental normative change; it signifies a quite radical revision in the very prism through which we view transnational deals and disputes."[7] This statement indicates that the latter half of the twentieth century saw a broad transformation in international trade and business. This transformation has resulted in a broad expansion of international business law.

The reality of trade liberalization and the rapid expansion of exporting in services and licensing, combined with the technological enhancement of business relationships, have increased the number of international conventions and supranational responses to globalization. Business students should incorporate these conventions and standards in their perspective of international business transactions because they are often the vehicle for overcoming cultural, language, and legal differences in cross-border transactions.

International Court of Justice: **http://www. icj-cij.org.**

Links to *lex mercatoria* developments: **http://lexmercatoria.net.** This Web site describes itself as a monitor for developments in international customary law and Internet infrastructure.

---

2. The International Court of Justice (ICJ) or World Court is located at The Hague in the Netherlands. Its statute, a part of the United Nations Charter, dictates the jurisdiction and powers of the court.
3. The term *convention* is used in connection with multilateral agreements, as opposed to bilateral arrangements.
4. The Vienna Convention on the Law of Treaties defines a *treaty* as "an international agreement between States and governed by international law." Under U.S. law, a treaty becomes federal law and is binding on federal, state, and local governments.
5. Arthur Rosett, "Critical Reflections on the CISG," 45 *Ohio State Law Journal* 265, 287 (1984).
6. See, generally, R. Goode, "Usage and Its Reception in Transnational Commercial Law," 46 Int'l & Comp. L.Q. 1 (1997); Lord Mustill, "The New Lex Mercatoria: The First Twenty-Five Years," 4 *Arbitration International* 86 (1988).
7. Kenneth C. Randall & John E. Norris, "A New Paradigm for International Business Transactions," 71 *Washington University Law Quarterly* 599, 624 (1993).

The acceptance of generally recognized contract principles, the trend toward economic trade unions, the adoption of international conventions, and the growth of international customary law have all led to common approaches among national legal systems in the area of international contract law. In the long term, international unification and harmonization are likely to reduce transaction costs relating to international contract formation.

International Customary Law

Following standard practices, custom, and trade usage can minimize the risk of legal disputes stemming from contractual misunderstandings. These secondary sources of international business law can be divided into two general groups, the first of which includes international conventions or regional initiatives aimed at harmonizing rules about cross-border transactions. Examples are the Hague Rules[8] on the liability of international carriers of goods by sea and the Agreement on Trade-Related Aspects of Intellectual Property Rights (TRIPS) within the GATT.[9] Regional efforts generally revolve around major free trade areas such as NAFTA and the EU and also include broader-based institutions such as the Organization for Economic Cooperation and Development (OECD).

The second group, the *lex mercatoria* or customary international law, has developed to bridge language, cultural, and legal differences among businesspeople throughout the world. The materials and manuals produced by the **International Chamber of Commerce (ICC)** in Paris illustrate the evolution of the *lex mercatoria*. The ICC was created in 1919 to promote free trade and private enterprise and to represent business interests at the international level. Members include national councils from more than sixty countries. Headquartered in Paris, France, the ICC is a nongovernmental organization whose current mission is to promote world trade, harmonize trade practices, and provide practical services to businesspeople. These services include the International Court of Arbitration in Paris, the Centre for Maritime Cooperation in London, the Counterfeiting Intelligence Bureau in London, and the Institute of International Business Law and Practice in Paris. The ICC's UCP 500 (Uniform Customs and Practices for Documentary Credits)[10] and its INCOTERMS 2000 manual (trade terms) are examples of international trade customs that have risen to near-universal acceptance in the international banking and business communities.

International business transactions require a firm understanding of the substantive laws of the country in which one intends to transact business, and of any relevant international conventions. Clarity of writing will not overcome the immutable (mandatory) rules of a given country or international convention. For example, a clearly written, principal-friendly termination clause in an agency agreement will not survive the **evergreen provisions** found in a number of European countries. An evergreen provision is a statutory preemption of the termination and commission clauses found in agency contracts.

http://
Department of State
Private International
Law Database:
**http://www.state.gov/
s/1/c3452.htm.**
Provides information
on international transactional law compiled
by the Office of Legal
Adviser.

INTERNATIONAL

---

8. The Hague Rules were codified in the United States as the Carriage of Goods by Sea Act (COGSA) in 1936, which applies to an international export or import shipment involving a bill of lading for transport from or to a U.S. port.

9. Agreement on Trade-Related Aspects of Intellectual Property Rights (TRIPS), General Agreement on Tariffs and Trade (GATT), April 15, 1994.

10. The UCP was first published in 1933 and subsequently revised in 1951, 1962, 1974, 1983, and 1993. UCP 500 came into effect on January 1, 1994.

Preventive Contracting and the CISG

Most international business disputes stem from poorly written contracts or the parties' failure to recognize key substantive issues. Given the universal nature of business transactions and the globalization of the marketplace, contractual failures attributable to inherent linguistic and cultural differences have significantly diminished, but when they do occur, they can lead to high transaction costs. Another cause of legal disputes is the existence of fundamental differences in national rules interpreting contractual terms. Thus, a primary way to understand the risk of international business transactions is to review cases and arbitral decisions dealing with contract disputes.

Under the **United Nations Convention on Contracts for the International Sale of Goods (CISG)**,[11] a written contract is not required and a contract may be proved by "any means including witness testimony."[12] In practice, many business transactions are characterized by a high degree of informality. An English court noted in this regard: "One has to bear in mind that commercial men do not look at things from the lawyer's point of view."[13] Despite the informal nature of business contracting and the common use of standard forms, however, it is likely that sophisticated business-people are fully aware of their national rules of contract and the supportive legal sanctions. For that reason, it is recommended that even sale of goods transactions governed by the CISG should be based upon at least a semiformal writing. This seems especially necessary, given the difficulty of procuring reputable business partners in foreign countries and the obstacles of language and culture, including differences in negotiating styles. These factors, and the potential difficulty and expense of obtaining a legal remedy in a foreign country, justify the additional time spent researching legal issues and writing a contract. A carefully written contract often highlights the latent differences of language and law while there is time to reconcile differences before the execution of the contract. Preventive contracting diminishes the likelihood of disputes about contract interpretation.

What are the generally recognized principles of international business law? What are some of the fundamental contract law differences among the major national legal systems of which the U.S. entrepreneur should be aware? What are the typical characteristics of the export or import contract? These questions will be addressed in Chapters Seven and Eight on international contract and sales law.

Behind every business transaction are the fears of nonperformance and of one party's using the law to obtain a legal or equitable remedy. Understanding international contract dispute resolution is important in order to negotiate and draft an effective contract. Just as prenuptial agreements are written in anticipation of a possible divorce, contracts should be written in anticipation of possible contract disputes. What can international businesspeople write into their contracts to make dispute resolution less likely to be needed? What can they write into the contract that would make dispute resolution less painful or costly in the event it is necessary? What can be included in the contract to increase the chances for success in a dispute resolution? These questions will be addressed in Chapter Four on international commercial dispute resolution.

---

11. United Nations Convention on Contracts for the International Sale of Goods, April 11, 1980, U.N. Doc. A/CONF.97/18, Annex I, reprinted in 19 I.L.M. 668.
12. CISG at Article 11.
13. Hugh Beale & Tony Dugdale, "Contracts Between Businessmen: Planning and the Use of Contractual Remedies," 2 *British Journal of Law & Society* 45, 49 (1975).

Scope of International Business Transactions

All business transactions involve considerable risk. The essence of being a businessperson or entrepreneur is a willingness to confront risk of loss, in the search for profits. Profit seeking or risk taking underscores the capitalistic, free-market system. The most consistently successful entrepreneurs are those who take steps to avoid or at least minimize risk, and risk-aversion techniques and strategies have been developed to provide stability and security to business transactions. Risk minimization is essential for both domestic transactions and those that cross national boundaries, but there are profound differences in approach between international and domestic business transactions.

The **basket of risks** associated with an international transaction is different in many ways from that of a U.S. domestic transaction. Businesses' efforts to minimize risk differ, too. Many international risk management devices, although long-standing, are likely to be unfamiliar to the U.S. businessperson on his or her initial foray into exporting, licensing, or direct foreign investment. International dealings are further complicated by the fact that the basket of risks to be confronted is constantly fluctuating, depending on the type of business entity, the type of good or service being sold, the country of the other party, the country of performance, and the means of transportation.

At the broadest level of analysis, the risk characteristics depend largely on the type of transaction. Transactions are categorized under four general groupings: **exporting-importing** (sale of goods), **sale of services** (consulting, distribution, transportation, marketing, sales), **licensing** (technology or intellectual property transfer), and **direct foreign investment** (foreign operations). This classification is overly simplified because many transactions display characteristics of two or more categories. We will examine vehicles of doing business—like franchising, joint venturing, and countertrade—independently of classification, since these three vehicles are hybrids of two or more of the four broader categories. The **franchise** transaction generally involves the contractual transfer or licensing of a bundle of intellectual property rights, know-how, trade secrets, and possibly the sale of goods or services. The **joint venture** is most closely associated with direct foreign investment but may also involve the transfer of goods, services, technology, and capital. **Countertrade** is a form of exporting used to overcome the risks of currency convertibility, local participation requirements, and restrictions against the repatriation of capital, profits, or hard currency. Countertrade can also be used within the framework of a joint venture or technology transfer. These forms of doing business internationally will be more fully explored in Chapter Three on international business strategies.

http://

International Trade Administration: **http://www.trade.gov.** Provides export assistance and information on doing business with foreign countries.

Indirect and Direct Exporting

The most popular method of transacting business internationally remains the export of goods and services, which is generally divided into indirect and direct exporting. The principal advantage of **indirect exporting** for a smaller company is that it provides a way to penetrate foreign markets without the complexities and risks of direct exporting. A number of different kinds of intermediary firms are utilized in the area of indirect exporting. A company may contact **commission agents** or **buying agents** who find foreign firms that want to purchase U.S. products. Such agents seek to obtain the desired items at the lowest possible price and are paid a commission by their foreign clients. In some cases, the agents may be foreign government agencies or quasi-governmental firms empowered to locate and purchase desired goods.

An indirect exporter may also hire an **export management company (EMC)**. An EMC, in essence, acts as the export department for one or several producers of goods or services. It solicits and transacts business in the names of the producers it represents or in its own name for a commission, salary, or retainer plus commission. Some EMCs offer immediate payment for products, either by arranging financing or by directly purchasing products for resale. EMCs usually specialize by product line or by foreign market. The best EMCs know their products and markets very well and usually have well-established networks of foreign distributors already in place. This immediate access to foreign markets is one of the principal reasons for using an EMC. One disadvantage to using an EMC is that a manufacturer may lose control over foreign sales. Control is an important issue for a manufacturer concerned with maintaining its product and company image in foreign markets.

A manufacturer that wants to minimize its involvement may sell its goods to an **export trading company (ETC)**. An ETC takes title to the product and exports for its own account, and for the manufacturer the transaction is essentially a domestic sale. Some special ETCs are organized and operated by producers. These types of ETCs can be organized along multiple- or single-industry lines and can represent producers of competing products. The U.S. Congress has encouraged the growth of ETCs through the enactment of the Export Trading Company Act of 1982, which allows banks to make equity investments in commercial ventures that qualify as ETCs. In addition, the Export-Import Bank (Eximbank) of the United States is allowed to make working capital guarantees to U.S. exporters. The Office of Export Trading Company Affairs (OETCA), within the U.S. Department of Commerce, promotes the formation and use of U.S. export intermediaries and issues export trade certificates that provide limited immunity from U.S. antitrust laws.

An indirect exporting method similar to using an ETC is selling goods to an **export agent** or **remarketer**. Export agents or remarketers purchase products directly from the manufacturer and then pack and mark the products according to their own specifications. They sell overseas through their contacts in their own names and assume all account risks. The U.S. manufacturer relinquishes control over the marketing and promotion of its product, which could have an adverse effect on future sales efforts abroad.

Direct Exporting

A company new to direct exporting generally treats export sales no differently from domestic sales, using existing personnel and organizational structures. However, there are advantages to separating international from domestic business, including centralization of specialized international market skills and focusing of marketing efforts. Regardless of how a company organizes for exporting, it should ensure that the structure facilitates the marketer's job. Experience shows that a company's success in foreign markets depends less on the attributes of its products than on its marketing methods.

Once a company has been organized to handle exporting, it must select the proper channel of distribution in each market. These channels include sales

http://
U.S. government links:
http://firstgov.gov.
Provides links to all relevant government Web sites.

representatives, agents, distributors, retailers, and end users. A **foreign sales representative** is the equivalent of a manufacturer's representative in the United States. The representative uses the company's product literature and samples to present the product to potential buyers; a representative often handles many complementary lines from different manufacturers. The sales representative usually works on a commission basis, assumes no risk or responsibility, and is under contract for a definite period of time. The contract defines territory, terms of sale, method of compensation, reasons and procedures for terminating the agreement, and other details. In contrast, a **foreign agent** normally has authority to make commitments on behalf of the firm he or she represents. Any contract should state whether the representative or agent does or does not have legal authority to obligate the firm.

The **foreign distributor** is a merchant who purchases merchandise from a U.S. exporter, resells it at a profit, and generally provides after-sales support and service. The distributor usually carries an inventory of products and spare parts and maintains adequate facilities and personnel for normal servicing operations. The U.S. exporter must carefully screen all potential representatives, agents, or distributors. The following information should be obtained and reviewed: (1) current status and history, including background on principal officers; (2) personnel and other resources (salespeople, warehouse, and service facilities); (3) sales territory covered; (4) current sales volume; (5) typical customer profiles; (6) methods of introducing new products into the sales territory; (7) names and addresses of U.S. firms currently represented; (8) trade and bank references; and (9), if a foreign company, the company's view of the in-country market potential for the exporter's products. This information is not only useful in gauging how much the representative knows about the exporter's industry but also provides valuable market research in its own right. Credit reports are available from commercial firms and from the Department of Commerce's International Company Profiles program. To protect itself against possible conflicts of interest, a U.S. firm must also learn about other product lines that the foreign firm represents.[14]

Evaluating Risks Through Market Research

To be successful, international entrepreneurs and exporters must assess foreign markets through market research. Exporters engage in market research primarily to identify their marketing opportunities and constraints and also to identify and find prospective customers. A company's market research should determine the largest foreign markets for its products and identify trends, outlook, conditions, practices, and competitors in those markets.

In conducting primary market research, a company collects data directly from the foreign marketplace through interviews, surveys, and other direct contacts with representatives and potential buyers. Primary market research has the advantage of being tailored to a company's needs and answering specific questions, but it is time-consuming and expensive. Because of the expense of primary market research, most firms rely on secondary data sources (see Focus on Transactions: General Sources for Market Research).

---

14. Most of the material in the section on direct exporting was taken from the National Trade Data Bank, a product of STAT-USA, U.S. Department of Commerce.

Focus on Transactions

General Sources for Market Research

- **Export America.** This monthly publication of the U.S. Department of Commerce contains recent news stories, market analyses, technical advice on exporting, trade leads, and success stories of export marketing.
- **FedBizOpps.** FedBizOpps is the self-described "single government point-of-entry for Federal government procurement opportunities over $25,000." FedBizOpps provides government buyers with the ability to publicize opportunities through the direct posting of information on the Internet. In addition, commercial vendors seeking federal markets for their goods and services can utilize the FedBizOpps Web site to "search, monitor and retrieve opportunities solicited by the entire Federal contracting community."
- **Trade Information Center.** A comprehensive source for U.S. companies seeking information on federal programs and activities that support U.S. exports, including information on overseas markets and industry trends, the center maintains a computerized calendar of U.S. government-sponsored domestic and overseas trade events.
- **Export.Gov.** The official export portal for the U.S. government, Export.Gov provides basic information about exporting, partner and trade leads, trade events, export finance, shipping documentation and requirements, and pricing. Of particular importance is the market research provided by the portal. This market research consists of country and industry market reports, trade agreements and statistics, agricultural market research, project feasibility studies, and country-specific quick reference guides.
- **Global Business Opportunities (GLOBUS).** The GLOBUS database provides daily trade leads from the Trade Opportunities Program and the Department of Agriculture, as well as daily summaries of procurement activities from the Defense Logistics Agency, the United Nations, and the Commerce Business Daily leads.
- **Economic Bulletin Board (EBB).** The PC-based EBB is an online source for trade leads as well as the latest statistical releases from the Bureau of the Census, the Bureau of Economic Analysis, the Bureau of Labor Statistics, the Federal Reserve Board, and other federal agencies.
- **National Trade Data Bank (NTDB).** The NTDB contains export promotion and international trade data collected by fifteen U.S. government agencies. Updated each month and released on CD-ROM, the data bank enables access to more than 100,000 documents. The NTDB contains the latest census data on U.S. imports and exports by commodity and country; the complete Central Intelligence Agency (CIA) World Factbook; the complete Foreign Traders Index, which contains more than 50,000 names and addresses of individuals and firms abroad interested in importing U.S. products; and many other data sources.
- **Small Business Administration (SBA).** The SBA markets research-related general resources.

Secondary market research is conducted in three basic ways. The first is by keeping abreast of world events that influence the international marketplace, watching for announcements of specific projects, or simply visiting likely markets. The second is by analyzing trade and economic statistics. Trade statistics are generally compiled by product category and by country. These statistics provide the U.S. firm with information about shipments of products over specified periods of time.

Demographic and general economic statistics such as population size and makeup, per capita income, and production levels by industry can be important indicators of the market potential for a company's products. The third method of secondary market research is obtaining the advice of experts, including those at the U.S. Department of Commerce and other government agencies; attending seminars, workshops, and international trade shows; hiring an international trade and marketing consultant; talking with successful exporters of similar products; and contacting trade and industry association staff.

Working with secondary sources is less expensive and helps the company focus its marketing efforts. However, the most recent statistics for some countries may be more than two years old. Also, statistics on sale of services are often unavailable. Yet, even with these limitations, secondary research is a valuable and relatively easy first step for a company to take (see Doing Business Internationally: A Step-by-Step Approach to Market Research).

A Step-by-Step Approach to Market Research

Doing Business Internationally

1. **Screen potential markets**
   Step 1. Obtain export statistics that indicate product exports to various countries.
   Step 2. Identify five to ten large and fast-growing markets for the firm's product. Examine them over the past three to five years. Has market growth been consistent year to year? Did import growth occur even during periods of economic recession? If not, did growth resume with economic recovery?
   Step 3. Identify some smaller but fast-emerging markets that may provide ground-floor opportunities. If a market is just beginning to open up, there may be fewer competitors. Growth rates should be substantially higher in these countries to qualify as up-and-coming markets, given the lower starting point.
   Step 4. Target three to five of the most statistically promising markets for further assessment. Consult with Department of Commerce district offices, business associates, freight forwarders, and others to help refine targeted markets.

2. **Assess targeted markets**
   Step 1. Examine trends for company products as well as related products that could influence demand. Calculate overall consumption of the product and the amount accounted for by imports. Obtain economic backgrounds and market trends for each country. Demographic information, such as population and age, can be obtained from International Population Reports published by the U.S. Bureau of the Census and the United Nations' Statistical Yearbook.
   Step 2. Ascertain the sources of competition, including the extent of domestic industry production and the countries of origin of the major competitors in each targeted market. Look at each competitor's U.S. market share.
   Step 3. Analyze factors affecting marketing and use of the product in each market, such as end user sectors, channels of distribution, cultural idiosyncrasies, and business practices.
   Step 4. Identify any foreign barriers (tariff or non-tariff) to the product being imported into the country. Identify any U.S. barriers (such as export controls) affecting exports to the country. Country information kits produced by the OPIC can be helpful.
   Step 5. Identify any U.S. or foreign government incentives to promote exporting of the product or service.

continued

A Step-by-Step Approach to Market Research (*continued*)

3. **Draw conclusions**
   After analyzing the data, the company may conclude that its marketing resources would be applied more effectively to a few countries. In general, efforts should be directed to fewer than ten markets if the company is new to exporting; one or two countries may be enough to start with. The company's internal resources should help determine its level of effort.

Source: National Trade Data Bank, a product of STAT-USA, U.S. Department of Commerce.

Risks of International Business Transactions

The numerous risks associated with international business transactions vary, depending on the method of transaction, such as trade, licensing, or direct investment. They also vary by what countries the business parties are located in or what country the transaction is to be performed in. The country where a party is a citizen or national is its **home country**. If a party is transacting business in a foreign country, then that country is referred to as the **host country**. The varieties of risk that exist to some degree for all countries and all methods of transacting business can be grouped into categories. This section will analyze four categories of international business risks: cultural and language, currency, legal, and political.

The types of risks that an international businessperson faces, as well as the methods utilized to minimize such risks, vary from transaction to transaction, depending on a number of variables. Two of the most fundamental variables are the identity of the host country and the type of transaction. In general, the level of risk escalates in the three basic ways of conducting international business, from exporting-importing to licensing and from licensing to direct foreign investment. We will investigate the different types of risks involved in these areas of international business transactions. The importance of assessing host country risk is highlighted by a review of three comparative scenarios (see pages 13–14). In each scenario, representatives of a U.S.-based company must weigh the risks of doing business in two countries by using one of the three basic market entry strategies discussed in the previous section. The *italicized words* represent key concepts that will be defined and explored throughout the textbook.

Using these three scenarios, we can begin to understand the complexity of the risks involved in international business transactions. A successful international businessperson is sophisticated and able to recognize risks and take the appropriate precautions.

Risks in Developing Countries

The level of risk in transacting business in many developing countries is considerably higher than in developed countries. Some countries are marked by

Scenario 1: Sale of Goods to Nigeria and Canada

Nigeria has been rated near the bottom of the recent *International Corruption Perceptions Index* and *Global Corruption Report* published by Transparency International, a non-governmental organization (NGO). It may be difficult to undertake business dealings in Nigeria without being asked to give a bribe. To best understand the risks of doing business with such a country, it is prudent to order a *political risk report* from a professional risk assessment company. It is also advisable to contact the U.S. State Department for information. It is imperative to fully investigate the foreign party, including credit and reference checks. A strong *ethics compliance program* will need to be in place to prevent the giving of bribes in violation of the U.S. *Foreign Corrupt Practices Act*. In addition, the official Nigerian currency unit, the naira, is not *convertible* to a hard currency like the U.S. dollar, European euro, or British pound. Payment in one of these hard currencies is unlikely because of government restrictions against the *repatriation* of such currencies from the country. Thus, the risk of doing business, even in the relatively risk-free method of exporting, may be too great a problem in a place like Nigeria.

Any exporting to such a country needs to be supported by a *confirmed letter of credit* from a reputable international bank. The currency convertibility and repatriation problems could be overcome through a *countertrade* transaction in which goods are exchanged for each other or an export transaction is linked to an import transaction. Another device to eliminate the risk to a company is to find an *export trading company* willing to perform the transaction on its own account. Finally, the costs and feasibility of obtaining political and credit risk insurance should be investigated. The OPIC, *Eximbank*, and the MIGA provide various types of insurance.

In contrast to exporting to Nigeria, exporting to Canada offers a low level of risk. *Country* and *currency risks* are minimal, given that Canada is a stable, industrialized country and a member of the NAFTA. Although currency fluctuations are possible, the Canadian dollar is freely convertible into the U.S. dollar. Currency fluctuation risk may be a concern in a long-term transaction, and both parties may manage that risk through a variety of *hedging* techniques. In a one-shot export transaction, the risk of a dramatic currency rate change is unlikely. The U.S. exporter can eliminate all currency risk by simply requiring payment in U.S. dollars.

Scenario 2: Licensing Technology to the People's Republic of China and France

The licensing of technology and the transfer of *intellectual property rights* present the next level of risk in international business transactions. Whenever a company discloses confidential information and trade secrets to a third party, there is always a risk that the information may be further disclosed to unauthorized parties. The problem is confounded when that disclosure is made in a foreign country that is not protective of intellectual property.

China has acceded to numerous intellectual property rights conventions, such as the *Berne Convention*, but in the past the level of trademark, copyright, and patent infringement through piracy and counterfeiting has been relatively high. Costly and time-consuming legal action to prevent the importation of illegal *gray market* goods has been the only effective countermeasure. It is hoped that China's recent induction into the WTO will result in greater enforcement of intellectual property law. In the meantime, the *licensor* needs to negotiate a *transfer agreement* that includes contractual protections against the misuse of the licensed information. The problem remains whether such protections will be enforced. To reduce the cost of enforcement and increase the likelihood of success, the licensor should consider alternative dispute resolution methods such as *mediation* and *arbitration*. It is also important for the licensor to understand that, unlike in the United States, the licensing agreement may not be a totally private affair. Less developed countries, former communist countries, and China often require government approval and registration of licensing agreements. The contract is likely to be reviewed, and pro-licensor clauses modified. Clauses most susceptible to revision include the *royalty, confidentiality, termination*, and *grant back* clauses.

In contrast to China, France has an established record of intellectual property protection. It is important for the intellectual property owner to register its rights under the patent, copyright, and trademark laws of France before entering any transfer agreement. The license or transfer agreement is generally enforced as written under French law, but superseding *EU Regulations* dealing with licensing of patents and intellectual property must be addressed, and certain provisions that are legal under U.S. laws may be illegal under EU *competition* (antitrust) *law*.

Scenario 3: Purchasing a Company in the Russian Federation and Germany

The riskiest of all international business transactions is direct foreign investment, which can range from opening a branch office to purchasing an existing company or building a manufacturing facility. Foreign direct investment is risky primarily because it makes a company susceptible to a wide range of *host country laws*. These laws cover the areas of employment and labor, environment, health and safety, product liability, and taxation. In considering direct foreign investment, the first decision is what type of legal vehicle should be chosen to operate the foreign enterprise. The most popular way of doing business is to establish an independent subsidiary under the laws of the host country.

In purchasing an existing company in Russia, the greatest risk is the uncertainty in the meaning and enforcement of commercial laws. Most of the current Western-styled laws were enacted following the fall of communism in 1991. The supporting jurisprudence found in Western legal systems has yet to be developed by the Russian courts; in fact, the widespread ineffectiveness of the Russian legal system has been well chronicled. Russia is a country where the use of a *joint venture* with an established Russian partner might be advantageous. A joint partner can share the risks and provide a portion of the capital or offer necessary government contacts and a distribution system. Joint ventures have to be approved or registered with government agencies, and failure to register can lead to severe negative consequences such as the dissolution of the joint venture.

In contrast, purchasing a company in Germany is much the same as buying a company in the United States. There is little likelihood of government *expropriation* or *nationalization* in Germany. Germany's pro-worker labor laws, however, prohibit an acquiring firm from ignoring existing collective bargaining agreements. The employment-at-will doctrine of the United States allows an acquiring firm to downsize the workforce with little legal restraint, but in Germany employment is viewed as a *property right* that must be respected. Any substantial changes in the workforce, such as layoffs or plant closings, must be submitted to a *works council* made up of employees. Finally, the corporation laws in both Russia and Germany should be researched. The limited liability provided by the corporate entity is sacrosanct in U.S. law, but in foreign legal systems an attempt to *pierce the corporate veil* to hold a parent company or a joint venture partner liable is more likely to be successful.

arbitrary government actions, excessive taxation, ineffective legal and dispute resolution systems, and a high degree of corruption. These countries find it difficult to interest foreign investment. Therefore, the best and possibly the only way to conduct business in these countries is by exporting. Some countries have passed laws to assure foreign investors and businesspeople by legally attempting to reduce the risks of doing business. Mexico passed the Foreign Investment Act of 1993 in order to attract and protect foreign investment. It opened large portions of the Mexican market to foreign ownership. However, in certain strategic economic industries, approval of the National Commission of Foreign Investments is needed for foreign ownership of greater than 49 percent, while some industries, such as oil, electricity, and railroads, remain reserved for Mexican nationals. The Foreign Investment Act provides expedited procedures to gain governmental approvals.

Russia has enacted a regulation on hard currency control that attempts to placate foreign investors' fears about the repatriation of hard currencies. The law requires any purchase or sale of foreign currencies to be approved by the Central Bank of the Russian Federation. Currency control is also delegated to the State Customs Committee, the Ministry of Finance, and Inspector of Currency Control. However, Article 8 of the Hard Currency Law recognizes the right of nonresidents

"to freely transfer, export, and transmit hard currency if that hard currency was previously transferred or imported to the Russian Federation." The law mandates strict bookkeeping requirements for all hard currency transactions. Residents and nonresidents must maintain records of their hard currency operations for a period of five years.

In 2004, the National People's Congress, the legislative assembly of the People's Republic of China, voted to amend the national constitution to provide formal governmental guarantee of private property rights. The amendment specifically provided that "legally obtained private property of the citizens shall not be violated." The amendment constitutes a formal renunciation of the Maoist doctrine that condemned private ownership of property and serves to place such ownership on an equal legal footing with state-owned property. Such standing benefits not only the indigenous Chinese business community but also the growing number of foreign entrepreneurs maintaining investments in the country since the initiation of economic reforms in the late 1970s.

INTERNATIONAL

Language and Cultural Risk

In the past, a major obstacle to international business transactions was the transacting parties' differences in language and cultural background. Language difficulties have diminished significantly because of the precipitous rise in foreign language proficiency. Nonetheless, even when dealing with a foreign counterpart who speaks English, misunderstandings can still occur. One device to overcome language differences is to have the contract drawn in the languages of both parties. But the *Falcoal, Inc. v. Kurumu* case that follows illustrates that even this precaution may fail to overcome inconsistencies that may result from translation. The language problem in this case revolves around the

Falcoal, Inc. v. Kurumu
660 F. Supp. 1536 (S.D. Tex. 1987)

David Hittner, District Judge. Plaintiff Falcoal, Inc. is an American corporation having its principal place of business in Houston, Texas. Defendant Kurumu (TKI) is a commercial entity, owned and controlled by the Turkish government. TKI decided to import a portion of Turkey's coal supply. In an attempt to solicit bids, TKI issued a notice announcing a "sartname" ("terms and conditions"). This announcement was made in local Turkish-language publications. The sartname distributed by TKI was issued in Turkish and provided by its terms that any conflicts as to its terms would be settled by reference to the original Turkish language version. Falcoal submitted the bid that was ultimately accepted by TKI. Falcoal's bid was signed and submitted by its authorized agent, Zihni, a Turkish company. The negotiation of the contract took place entirely in Ankara, Turkey.

After the parties had agreed to the terms, Zihni prepared two copies of the contract, an English version and a Turkish version. Although the parties assert that they believed the content of the two versions to be identical, the English contract and the Turkish contract contain forum selection clauses which directly contradict each other. The Turkish-language version provides that "the final jurisdiction for the settlement of any disputes, in the case of the PURCHASER [TKI] submitting a claim, lies within the jurisdiction of the Houston commercial courts and, in the case of the SUPPLIER [Falcoal] submitting a claim lies within the jurisdiction of the Ankara commercial courts." The English-language contract, by contrast, provides that any dispute "shall be finally settled in Houston and submitted to the jurisdiction of the Courts of the U.S.A. if the claim is put forward by Supplier [Falcoal] and in

Ankara, Turkey, and submitted to the Turkish Courts if the claim is put forward by Buyer [TKI]."

Pursuant to the contract, Falcoal was to deliver 100,000 tons of coal to a shipper of TKI's choice. Falcoal agreed to post a performance bond in an amount equal to 10 percent of the contract price and, pursuant to this agreement, Citibank International-Ankara issued a performance bond in favor of TKI in the amount of $400,000. This bond was secured by a letter of credit opened by Falcoal at Citibank International-Dallas. The contract further provided that, to secure payment for the coal, TKI was to open a letter of credit in New York forty-five days before shipment. TKI failed to open this letter of credit. When the coal was not shipped, TKI, allegedly wrongfully and without authorization, drew on Falcoal's performance bond. Falcoal subsequently brought this suit against TKI alleging breach of contract for failing to open the New York letter of credit in Falcoal's favor, conversion and fraud for wrongfully drawing on Falcoal's performance bond, and injury to Falcoal's business reputation. TKI has moved to dismiss, alleging lack of subject matter jurisdiction and lack of personal jurisdiction.

Subject Matter Jurisdiction

TKI asserts that this Court lacks subject matter jurisdiction because TKI, as an entity of the Turkish government, has sovereign immunity under the Foreign Sovereign Immunities Act of 1976 (FSIA), 28 U.S.C. § 1602 *et seq.* However, Falcoal contends that TKI waived sovereign immunity by agreeing to a forum selection clause and falls within the commercial exception of the FSIA. The waiver provision and commercial exception are found in section 1605(a):

Section 1605 (a) A foreign state shall not be immune from the jurisdiction of courts of the United States or of the States in any case-

(1) in which the foreign state has waived its immunity either explicitly or by implication, notwithstanding any withdrawal of the waiver which the foreign state may purport to effect except in accordance with the terms of the waiver;

(2) in which the action is based upon a commercial activity carried on in the United States by the foreign State; or upon an act performed in the United States in connection with a commercial activity of the foreign state elsewhere; or upon an act outside the territory of the United States in connection with a commercial activity of the foreign state elsewhere and that act causes a direct effect in the United States.

This Court would find merit to Falcoal's "waiver" argument, were the English version forum clause the only clause at issue. However, the Court cannot ignore the existence of the Turkish contract, whose forum clause provides for suit in Houston when TKI is the plaintiff. That contract expressly provides for suit *against* TKI in

Turkey. Clearly, under the facts of this case where, as here, there are two contradictory forum clauses and where the issue of which forum clause should control is vigorously contested, the English-language clause cannot be said to constitute a waiver of sovereign immunity.

The Court next reviews Falcoal's argument that TKI's actions place it within the exceptions to sovereign immunity set forth in section 1605(a)(2). Clearly this action is not one "based upon commercial activity carried on [by TKI] in the United States." The FSIA defines such commercial activity as activity "having substantial contact with the United States." The mere provision for payment in the United States, however, is not a "substantial contact" meeting the test for commercial activity under the FSIA. It remains for this Court to determine whether TKI's conduct falls within the third clause of section 1605(a)(2) as to whether the conduct alleged against TKI constitutes "an act outside the territory of the United States in connection with a commercial activity of the foreign state elsewhere" which "causes a direct effect in the United States." At issue is the definition of "direct effect."

TKI asserts, and Falcoal has not shown otherwise, that it has had no contacts with the Texas forum, nor in fact with the United States, other than its involvement in the contract which is the subject of this suit. That contract was solicited, negotiated, drafted, and executed in Turkey and in the Turkish language. The contract itself does not establish minimum contacts with the Texas forum. Nor does TKI's agreement to pay through a letter of credit in New York create personal jurisdiction. Thus, in the instant case the constitutional requirements for exercise of in personam jurisdiction are lacking.

In an effort to resolve the tension between 28 U.S.C. § 1605(a)(2) and 28 U.S.C. § 1330(b), courts have taken two approaches. Some have held that an effect cannot reach the level of "direct" effects described in the statute and thus sovereign immunity cannot be overcome, unless the effect fulfills the "minimum contacts" requirement. Other courts have given "direct effect" its literal meaning and found such an effect when an American corporation has suffered a direct financial injury due to a foreign sovereign's conduct. This Court finds the latter approach to be most reasonable. The Court holds that the conduct of TKI in drawing on Falcoal's performance bond was an action which caused a direct effect in the United States, and thus TKI cannot claim sovereign immunity from this suit. Subject matter jurisdiction, therefore, exists.

Personal Jurisdiction

Constitutionally, this Court cannot exercise personal jurisdiction over TKI unless TKI has taken some action that may be construed as an expression of waiver or implied consent to the exercise of such jurisdiction. Falcoal contends that such an implied consent is found in the forum selection clause of the English version contract. This Court could find waiver, however, only if it were found that the Turkish-language clause is unenforceable and the English version valid. The Court thus faced with the existence of two contradictory clauses, must look to the law of the appropriate forum to determine which clause to enforce. Because the contract was solicited, negotiated and executed in Turkey, Turkish law must apply. Both parties agree that, were Texas law to apply, the existence of contradictory clauses would evidence a lack of meeting of the minds on the issue of forum for suit, and the clause should be dropped from both contracts. However, in the absence of a determination of similar Turkish law, the clauses cannot be eliminated from the contract. Although this Court finds that TKI has been divested of its sovereign immunity to this suit by its actions in Turkey having a direct effect in the United States and, thus, subject matter jurisdiction

exists, the Court finds that it lacks personal jurisdiction over TKI. Motion to Dismiss is GRANTED.

Case Highlights

- Importance of the forum selection clause in international contracts
- Use of letters of credit and performance bonds to secure payments and performances
- Defense of sovereign immunity, along with the waiver and "commercial activity" exceptions
- Determining if a court has personal jurisdiction over the defendant through the "minimum contacts" or "direct effects" standards
- Importance of determining the appropriate law to be applied
- Importance of selecting the language that controls when more than one language contract is executed

pivotal issues of where the parties may sue under the contract's forum selection clause and whether the U.S. court had personal jurisdiction over the foreign defendant.

Risks of Cultural Differences

INTERNATIONAL

Business executives who hope to expand abroad should learn about the history, culture, and customs of the countries to be visited. Business manners and methods, religious customs, dietary practices, humor, and acceptable dress vary widely from country to country. For example, one should never touch the head of a Thai or pass an object over it: the head is considered sacred in Thailand. In addition, one should avoid using triangular shapes in Hong Kong, Korea, and Taiwan: the triangle is considered a negative shape. The number 7 is considered bad luck in Kenya and good luck in Slovakia, and it has magical connotations in Benin. The number 10 is bad luck in Korea, and 4 means death in Japan. Red is a positive color in Denmark, but it represents witchcraft and death in many African countries. A nod means no in Bulgaria, and shaking the head from side to side means yes. The OK sign commonly used in the United States (thumb and index finger forming a circle and the other fingers raised) means zero in France, is a symbol for money in Japan, and carries a vulgar connotation in Brazil. The use of a palm-up hand and moving index finger signals "come here" in the United States and some other countries, but it is considered vulgar in others. In Ethiopia, repeatedly opening and closing the palm-down hand means "come here."

Understanding and heeding cultural variables such as these are critical to success in international business and travel. Lack of familiarity with the business practices, social customs, and etiquette of a country can weaken a company's

http://

Department of State:
http://www.state.gov.
The U.S. State
Department publishes
commercial guides for
numerous foreign
countries. This is a
good place to start to
learn about differences
in culture and business
customs.

position in the market, prevent it from accomplishing its objectives, and ultimately lead to failure. Some of the cultural distinctions that U.S. firms face most often include differences in business styles, attitudes toward development of business relationships, attitudes toward punctuality, negotiating styles, gift-giving customs, greetings, significance of gestures, meanings of colors and numbers, and customs regarding titles. U.S. firms must pay close attention to different styles of doing business and the degree of importance placed on developing business relationships. In some countries, businesspeople have a very direct style; in others, they have a subtler style and value a personal relationship more than most U.S. businesspeople. For example, in the Middle East, engaging in small talk before engaging in business is standard practice.

The U.S. businessperson must also consider foreign customs. For example, attitudes toward punctuality vary greatly from one culture to another and, if misunderstood, can cause confusion. Romanians, Japanese, and Germans are very punctual, whereas people in many of the Latin countries have a more relaxed attitude toward time. The Japanese consider it rude to be late for a business meeting but acceptable, even fashionable, to be late for a social occasion. In Guatemala, on the other hand, one might arrive from ten minutes early to forty-five minutes late for a luncheon appointment.

Proper use of names and titles is often a source of confusion in international business relations. In many countries (including the United Kingdom, France, and Denmark), it is appropriate to use titles until use of first names is suggested. First names are seldom used for doing business in Germany. Visiting businesspeople should use the surname preceded by the title. Titles such as "Herr Direktor" are sometimes used to indicate prestige, status, and rank. In Thailand, people address one another by first names and reserve last names for very formal occasions and written communications. In Belgium, it is important to address French-speaking business contacts as "Monsieur" or "Madame," while Dutch-speaking contacts should be addressed as "Mr." or "Mrs." To confuse the two is a great insult.

INTERNATIONAL

Customs concerning gift giving are extremely important to understand. In some cultures, gifts are expected, and failure to present them is considered an insult, whereas in other countries offering a gift is considered offensive. Business executives also need to know when to present gifts, where to present gifts, what type of gift to present, what color the gift should be, and how many to present. Gift giving is an important part of doing business in Japan, where gifts are usually exchanged at the first meeting. In sharp contrast, gifts are rarely exchanged in Germany and are usually considered inappropriate. Gift giving is not a normal custom in Belgium or the United Kingdom either, although in both countries flowers are a suitable gift when invited to someone's home.

Customs concerning the exchange of business cards vary, too. Although this point seems of minor importance, observing a country's card-giving customs is a key part of business protocol. In Japan, for example, the Western practice of accepting a business card and pocketing it immediately is considered rude. The proper approach is to carefully look at the card after accepting it, observe the title and organization, acknowledge with a nod that the information has been digested, and perhaps make a relevant comment or ask a polite question. In addition, it is essential to understand the importance of rank in the other country, know who the decision makers are, be familiar with the business style of the foreign company, and understand the negotiating etiquette and nature of agreements in the country.[15]

Another facet of international business concerns selling practices. Because cultures vary, there is no single code by which to conduct business. Certain business practices, however, transcend culture barriers: (1) answer requests promptly and clearly; (2) keep promises—a first order is particularly important because it shapes a customer's image of a firm as a dependable or undependable supplier; (3) be polite, courteous, and friendly; and (4) personally sign all letters.

The importance of religious practices should not be underestimated; religious and cultural differences not only directly affect a foreign entrepreneur in the negotiation of a contract but also subsequently affect employees and agents in the performance of the contract. The *Kern v. Dynalectron Corporation* case that follows illustrates the challenges faced by an organization in conducting its business in a foreign country.

Kern v. Dynalectron Corporation
577 F. Supp. 1196 (N.D. Tex. 1983)

Belew, District Judge. Wade Kern filed this religious-discrimination suit pursuant to Title VII of the Civil Rights Act of 1964, 42 U.S.C. § 2000e-2000e-17 (1976) against Dynalectron Corporation. On August 17, 1978, Wade Kern entered into a written contract of employment with the Defendant, Dynalectron Corporation, to perform duties as a helicopter pilot. The work to be performed in Saudi Arabia consisted of flying helicopters over crowds of Moslems making their pilgrimage along Muhammad's path to Mecca. Those pilots who were stationed at Jeddah would be required to fly into the holy area, Mecca. Saudi Arabian law, based upon the tenets of the Islamic religion, prohibits the entry of non-Moslems into the holy area, Mecca, under penalty of death. Thus, Dynalectron, in accordance with its contract with Kawasaki, requires all pilots stationed at Jeddah to be (or become) Moslem. Had Wade Kern continued to work for Dynalectron, he would have been based in Jeddah and, therefore, his conversion from Baptist to Moslem would have been required. Defendant later offered Kern a job as a member of the air crew, a position not requiring his conversion. However, Kern declined to take that job. Kern filed a sworn complaint with the Equal Employment Opportunity Commission alleging that he was denied an employment opportunity with Defendant due to its discrimination against him because of his religious beliefs.

One of the several ways in which the defendant can carry his burden is by establishing that the discrimination was not unlawful since religion may be a bona fide occupational qualification (B.F.O.Q.). The B.F.O.Q. defense is set forth in § 703(a) of Title VII:

Notwithstanding any other provision of this title it shall not be an unlawful employment practice for an employer to hire and employ employees on the basis of religion, sex, or national origin in those certain instances where religion, sex, or national origin is a bona fide occupational qualification reasonably necessary to the normal operation of that particular business or enterprise.

The use of the word "necessary" in section 703(e) requires that we apply a business necessity test, not a business convenience test. There can be no question but that non-Moslem pilots stationed in Jeddah are not safe as compared to Moslem pilots. Therefore, Dynalectron's discrimination against non-Moslems in general, and Wade Kern specifically, is not unlawful since to hire Moslems exclusively for this job "is a bona fide occupational qualification reasonably necessary to the normal operation of that particular business," § 703(a) of Title VII. Notwithstanding the religious discrimination in this case, the Court holds and finds that the B.F.O.Q. exception is properly applicable.

---

15. The material in this section was taken from the National Trade Data Bank, a product of STAT-USA, U.S. Department of Commerce.

In *Fernandez v. Wynn Oil Co.*, 653 F.2d 1273 (9th Cir. 1981), a female plaintiff sued her employer for discriminatorily not promoting her because she was female. The job to which she would have been promoted required her to deal with South American businessmen who preferred not to do business with females. There, the Court stated that the mere fact that it was an international case did not distinguish it from other cases wherein it was held that mere customer preference would not justify the use of the B.F.O.Q. exception. The requirement that an individual be a Moslem to perform the duties of a helicopter pilot in certain portions of Saudi Arabia is a bona fide occupational qualification within the meaning of 42 U.S.C. § 2000e-2(e). Thus, Kern voluntarily and unilaterally rescinded his agreement to work for Defendant and thus breached his obligation under the contract.

Case Update

The district court's decision was upheld by the U.S. Court of Appeals for the Fifth Circuit in *Kern v. Dynalectron Corporation*, 746 F.2d 810 (5th Cir. 1984).

Case Highlights

- The use of a written employment contract to limit the employer's liabilities
- Extraterritorial application of U.S. employment discrimination laws
- The Bona Fide Occupational Qualification defense (B.F.O.Q.) to an employment discrimination claim
- Religion as a B.F.O.Q. in some international business situations

---

Currency Risks

Currency risks are a concern in almost all business transactions that cross national borders. There are three separate risks that relate to currency and international business transactions: **convertibility, repatriation**, and **currency rate fluctuation**. A buyer and a seller in different countries rarely use the same currency. Payment is usually made in either the buyer's or the seller's currency or in a mutually agreed-on currency that is foreign to both parties. Convertibility is the issue of whether one currency is convertible into another currency. Easily convertible currencies are generally referred to as hard currencies. The world's hard currencies include the U.S. dollar, British pound, European euro, Swiss franc, and Japanese yen.

Unlike countries with hard currencies, countries with soft currencies do not possess sizable exchange reserves and surpluses in their balance of payments needed to convert their currencies into hard ones. Russian rubles cannot be converted to U.S. dollars, which leaves the U.S. businessperson with limited options, specifically, reinvest the rubles in the Russian economy or find an alternate means of payment, such as countertrade. An exporter or investor can overcome any convertibility problem by requiring payment in a hard currency.

The second currency risk, repatriation, may present itself when a foreign party attempts to remove hard currency from a host country. Some foreign countries have enacted currency laws that block the movement of hard currencies outside the country. Less developed countries, for example, have limited hard currency reserves and do not allow them to be used for the purchase of private goods. Once again, countertrade may be the only option available to overcome the repatriation risk of doing business in such countries.

The third and broadest type of currency risk is the devaluation of the currency of payment. The relative value between the dollar and the buyer's currency may change between the time the deal is made and the time payment is received. If the U.S. exporter agrees to payment in a foreign currency and is not properly protected, a devaluation of the foreign currency could cause the exporter to lose money in the transaction. One of the simplest ways for a U.S. exporter to avoid this type of risk is to quote prices and require payment in U.S. dollars. Then the burden and risk are placed on the buyer to make the currency exchange. If the buyer asks to make payment in a foreign currency, the exporter should consult an international banker before negotiating the sales contract. International banks can help one hedge against such a risk, if necessary, by agreeing to purchase the foreign currency at a fixed price in dollars regardless of the value of the currency when the customer pays. If this mechanism is used, the fees charged by the bank should be included in the price quotation.

The *Bernina Distributors v. Bernina Sewing Machine Company* case illustrates how a party did not anticipate the risk of a currency rate fluctuation. In this case, a poorly written open price term[16] resulted in significant monetary losses due to an unanticipated currency fluctuation.

A foreign importer or exporter can minimize the risk of a negative currency rate change through techniques of hedging. This is accomplished by entering into forward, future, or option contracts. Some investors specialize in **arbitrage**, which is the simultaneous buying and selling of the same foreign exchange in two or more markets to take advantage of price differentials. A **forward contract** requires two parties to exchange specified amounts of two currencies at some future time. The

---

Bernina Distributors, Inc. v. Bernina Sewing Machine Company

646 F.2d 434 (10th Cir. 1981)

Distributor of sewing machines brought action against importer of sewing machines for breach of contract. Defendant Bernina Sewing Machine Company (Importer), a Utah corporation, imports and supplies Bernina sewing machines to plaintiff Bernina Distributors, Inc. (Distributor). The problems that have arisen relate mostly to pricing and are caused by the fluctuations of exchange rates and decreases in the value of the U.S. dollar versus the Swiss franc. The case involves a long-term supply contract to run for seven years. The contract contained an open price term in which "prices are automatically subject to change when factory costs are increased." Importer is required to pay in Swiss francs. The open price term allowed Importer to increase price as follows: "(a) To the extent of any increase of factory invoice costs to Importer. (b) To the extent of any increase in duty charges. (c) To the extent of increases in insurance, freight, handling, broker and port fees, or other similar charges. Increases to duty or factory invoice costs shall be adjusted as they occur. Increases to all other charges shall be adjusted at the

commencement of each calendar year." But with the precipitous decline of the dollar in relation to the Swiss franc, Importer's costs nearly doubled and thus halved its rate of return per dollar invested.

Logan, Circuit Judge. Importer maintains that the risk of currency fluctuations had not been considered or allocated in the contract and that under the Uniform Commercial Code, this "open price term" should be determined according to what the court finds to be reasonable. We believe that the contract provisions are quite comprehensive and hence, the statutory provision is inapplicable to this case. Thus, we believe the contract places the risk of a diminishing profit margin on the Importer and that the Importer bears the risk of currency fluctuations. The Importer also asserts that the court's interpretation makes the contract impracticable under § 2-615 of the Uniform Commercial Code. The U.C.C. excuses performance under a contract when performance "has been made impracticable by the occurrence of a contingency the nonoccurrence of which was a basic assumption on which the contract was made." In our view the instant

---

16.   Open price term refers to a contract price term that fails to state the price to be paid at a fixed amount. The open price term allows for the adjustment of the amount paid based upon specified variables such as costs of production, changes in freight and insurance rates, and changes in tariff rates.

contract is not one made impracticable by the contingency of the devalued dollar. Comment 8 to § 2-615 states that this excuse does "not apply when the contingency in question is sufficiently foreshadowed at the time of contracting." Also, cost increases alone do not render a contract impracticable. The loss would have to be especially severe and unreasonable. Importer was aware of the possibility of a reduction in profits due to exchange rate fluctuations and could have guarded against this contingency. For example, a cost-plus formula for determining the price could have been utilized. Furthermore, Importer was represented by counsel throughout and should have known that the contract provided for price increases only to the extent of actual cost increases.

To grant relief on this issue would be to disturb an agreed-upon allocation of risk between commercial equals. The district court did not err in prohibiting Importer from charging Distributor under the contract's "open price term" a margin of ten percent on increased cost due to exchange rate fluctuations. Furthermore, the contract was not rendered impracticable due to the increase in costs to the Importer related to the currency fluctuation.

Case Update

The Tenth Circuit Court of Appeals denied Importer's request for a rehearing in *Bernina Distributors, Inc. v. Bernina Sewing Machine Company*, 689 F.2d 903 (10th Cir. 1981).

Case Highlights

- Common practice of entering into long-term supply contracts.
- Use of open price or price escalation clauses to adjust the contract price over the term of the contract.
- A determination that a risk has been allocated to one of the parties defeats demand for a contract adjustment.
- Contract law allows for an excuse from not fulfilling a contract. In the sale of goods, the Uniform Commercial Code § 2-615 grants an excuse for commercial impracticability. The law also allows the parties to write an express excuse or *force majeure* clause.
- An excuse for commercial impracticability will not be granted if the risk was foreseeable or the burden on a party is not unduly severe.
- Since currency fluctuations are foreseeable, courts are likely to view them as allocated risks and not grant an excuse.
- It is important to write clear and detailed clauses, especially in long-term contracts. The Court suggested the use of a "cost-plus" formula in the open price term.

International Finance Corporation: **http://www.ifc.org.** This is the finance arm of the World Bank.

problem with a forward contract is that if the underlying deal falls through, the party is still required to purchase (exchange) the other currency. The **futures contract** is like a bond that can be sold prior to maturity. Either party can avoid their obligations under the contract by selling it in the secondary market.[17] A well-developed futures market provides a high level of liquidity but, just as in the bond market, the value of the futures contract fluctuates, depending on the underlying values of the currencies.

In the *Bernina* case, the importer could have hedged by entering a futures contract to purchase Swiss francs for a fixed amount of dollars. This would have protected it against the subsequent devaluation of the dollar. In fact, the value of the futures contract would have increased in value in the futures market because the contract gives a right to buy Swiss francs at a lower fixed price. Another device used to hedge currency risks is the option contract. A **currency option** gives a party a right, but not the obligation, to buy or sell a currency at a fixed rate in the future; a purchaser and a seller of foreign currencies agree on a specific rate of exchange at a future date. The purchaser may choose to exercise or pass on the option, thus limiting the effect of unfavorable exchange rate

17.   In 1972, the Chicago Mercantile Exchange established the International Monetary Market for trading in currency futures contracts.

fluctuations. The seller is paid a fee for tendering the option. The right to sell a currency in the future is a put option, while the right to buy is a call option. The option is obtained by paying a substantial premium whether the option is exercised or not.

Legal Risk

One of the primary risks in all international business transactions is the application and enforcement of foreign laws. Host country laws may include restrictions on currency conversion and repatriation of profits. If a company is deemed to be doing business in a foreign country, then it may become subject to the legal jurisdiction of a foreign court. Companies that establish a presence in a foreign country must also be concerned with local employment laws. Many countries impose severe restrictions on the termination of employees or agents, such as requiring lengthy notice requirements and substantial severance payments. Other host country laws that should be examined include labeling, marketing, and advertising laws; income and sales tax laws; environmental laws; product and consumer liability laws; health and safety laws; and antitrust or competition laws. In order to decrease the uncertainty due to the risks of foreign laws, the United States has entered into **bilateral investment treaties (BIT)** with many foreign countries. These treaties provide the basic legal framework for a company investing in a foreign country. They generally address issues of convertibility of currency, repatriation of profits, compensation for expropriation, protection of intellectual property, and nondiscriminatory treatment of foreign investors.

Because of differences in language, culture, and legal systems, the intentions of parties in an international transaction may not be easily discernible from their contract. Therefore, it is imperative, more so than in a purely domestic undertaking, for the parties to express carefully intended rights and obligations in a written contract. At the time of execution, the parties must, with the assistance of their lawyers, review each contract clause to make sure all parties understand them.

Of course, such a model approach to contract review is not often practical. For example, in the typical export transaction, there is no single form that both parties read and sign. The parties simply exchange their own forms in order to effect an offer and acceptance. Nonetheless, each party should take the time to carefully review the terms and conditions in the other party's form before entering into the contract. This is especially important if it is the first transaction between the contracting parties. It is also important, particularly in large transactions with a corporation or partnership, to verify the other party's authority to bind the company to a contract.

Often the quality of a contract is evident not in what it says but in what it fails to say, and an international contract is often the product of "studied ambiguity."[18] Vagueness or ambiguity in contractual language is employed to achieve the illusion of agreement. Parties make use of "a kind of Esperanto" in which "parties often draft a contract in ambiguous form in order to achieve agreement."[19] The roots of contract ambiguity come from two sources, the parties negotiating the contract and those charged with its drafting. A common scenario is that the principals negotiate

http://
International Law Dictionary: **http://august1.com/ pubs/dict/** provides definitions or words and phrases used in private and public international law.

---

18.   Johan Steyn, "A Kind of Esperanto?" *The Frontiers of Liability*, Vol. 2. P. B. H. Birks, Ed. New York: Oxford University Press, 1994.
19.   Ibid. p. 13.

the general framework for an agreement and then turn over to their attorneys the task of writing the language of the agreement. Such brief negotiations increase the risk of ambiguity inherent in interpersonal communication, especially within a cross-cultural context.

A key issue for international businesspeople is to determine at what stage they should enlist the services of a lawyer. Businesspeople often do not use lawyers in the negotiation stage of contracting; they view them as obstacles to rather than facilitators of agreement. The businessperson-to-businessperson, face-to-face exchange is a paradigm of how business is done, while lawyers are relegated to the task of writing the formal documents. In international contracting, the businessperson, especially one new to international dealings, would be well advised to enlist an astute international transactional lawyer, along with foreign counsel. The issue of trust aside, international dealings should be evidenced by clearly written and highly negotiated agreements.

Legal systems can differ in substantive laws, procedures, remedies, and levels of enforcement. Although the fundamental legal concepts dealing with business transactions are similar in the civil, common, and socialist legal systems, idiosyncratic differences in the rules can result in unexpected legal liabilities. For example, in Germany the civil law system recognizes the notion of *nachfrist* notice[20] in the area of sale of goods. In U.S. law, a party has the right to strictly enforce the delivery date stated in the contract and can summarily reject a request for more time. In contrast, the civil law concept of *nachfrist* notice dictates that such dates should not be strictly enforced. A request for additional time should be granted unless the non-breaching party can give a commercially viable reason for not granting the requested extension.

Suppose that a U.S. businessperson enters into a contract with a German supplier for delivery of goods on June 1. On May 25, the German supplier sends a letter requesting an extension for delivery to June 30. Under U.S. law, the buyer may simply reject the request and hold the German supplier in breach of contract if the goods are not delivered on June 1. In fact, the U.S. buyer in this instance responds by saying that the contract provides for delivery on June 1 and any delivery beyond that date will not be accepted. On June 1, the goods are not delivered, and the U.S. buyer obtains substituted goods from another supplier. On June 30, the goods are received from the German supplier. The U.S. buyer responds by rejecting the "late" delivery. Under *nachfrist* notice, it is the U.S. buyer and not the German supplier who has breached the contract. Because the U.S. buyer failed to give a commercially viable reason for not granting the additional time, the civil law automatically awards the time extension. Therefore, the delivery on June 30 was timely, and the German can now sue for full contract damages under German law.

In other instances, the rules of law may be similar, but the available procedures and remedies differ significantly. In some countries, the cultural abhorrence to litigation results in difficulty in finding adequate legal counsel and restricted discovery options.[21] The U.S. Federal Rules of Civil Procedure provide a liberal set of rules that allow for full discovery of the other party. Such sweeping discovery techniques may not be available in other countries. Also, the remedies available to the plaintiff may be of

INTERNATIONAL

http://

American Society of International Law: **http://www.asil.org.** Provides information on current developments in international law, along with links to international documents and analysis.

---

20. *Nachfrist* notice is the requirement that a party grant an extension of time to perform the contract upon the request of the other party. *Nachfrist* notice will be examined in Chapter Eight.

21. Discovery is the pretrial process whereby the litigants uncover evidence by questioning the opposing party either in writing (interrogatories) or in person (depositions), examining documents provided by the opposing party, and obtaining the testimony of independent non-party witnesses.

a different order. The U.S. notions of treble (triple) and punitive damages are not found in most foreign legal systems, and the U.S. and common law views that prefer to give monetary damages are not found in civil law countries. In civil law, the plaintiff is allowed the choice of suing for monetary damages or receiving an order of specific performance that forces the other party to honor the contract.

Finally, similarities in the substantive laws of a country may mask differences in the enforcement of those laws. This can be seen in the areas of intellectual property protection and corruption. A number of countries have ratified the primary international property rights conventions, such as the Paris and Berne Conventions, but have been lax in their enforcement. Lax enforcement has resulted in high levels of counterfeiting and piracy of trademarks, patents, and copyrights. Another example is the enforcement of anti-bribery or corruption laws. All countries prohibit bribing government officials, but lack of enforcement in some countries has resulted in a culture where bribery has become common. Such an environment places limitations on U.S. businesspeople prohibited from making illegal payments to foreign officials under the Foreign Corrupt Practices Act.

A number of countries, especially in the developing world, have enacted laws specifically targeted to foreign investment and trade. Examples of such specialized host country laws include laws that protect host country agents and distributors of foreign products from termination without notice or payment. In some countries—notably within the European Union—a foreign exporter or manufacturer may not terminate its host country agent without paying statutorily determined indemnity compensation or damages in concordance with evergreen statutes. Evergreen statutes limit the ability of a principal or employer to discharge an employee or agent.

INTERNATIONAL

Some countries limit the amount of equity ownership that a foreign company may hold in a host country enterprise. These local participation requirements often result in the foreign company creating a partnership or joint venture with nationals of the host country. Because of the limited amount of hard currency in some countries, other laws restrict a foreign investor or exporter from withdrawing or repatriating their profits or royalties from the country.

Another common area of host country intervention is in the area of technology transfers. In some countries, private licensing agreements must be registered and approved by the government. Pro-licensor clauses involving royalty payments, termination, and training may be rewritten to be more favorable to the licensee. These types of specialized host country laws need to be analyzed to determine their impact on a potential foreign investment, export transaction, or intellectual property transfer. Chapter Fourteen will explore these types of laws in more detail.

Political Risk

Political or country risk broadly refers to the negative consequences that stem from a change in government policies. In the area of import-export, **trade barriers** represent the most common risk. The U.S. trade representative classifies trade barriers into seven general categories.

- Import policies, including tariffs and other import charges, quantitative restrictions,[22] and import licensing
- Standards, labeling, testing, and certification

22.   A quota is an example of a quantitative restriction.

- Government procurement restrictions
- Export subsidies
- Lack of intellectual property protection
- Service barriers
- Investment barriers

http://

World Trade
Organization:
http://www.wto.org.
Provides links to all
WTO Agreements.

A number of international agreements address trade barriers. The **Uruguay Round** of the GATT addressed all of these trade barriers in some fashion. GATT negotiations traditionally targeted tariff barriers and quantitative restrictions. The original 1947 GATT contained provisions aimed at "reducing fees and formalities connected with importation and exportation" (Article VIII), "general elimination of quantitative restrictions" (Article XI), and the "publication of trade regulations" (Article X). The WTO Agreements that followed the Uruguay Round of GATT committed the newly formed WTO to a reduction and elimination of all categories of trade barriers. **Non-tariff barriers** include import quotas and other quantitative restrictions, non-automatic import licensing, customs charges and fees, customs procedures, export subsidies, unreasonable standards, discriminatory labeling, and discriminatory government procurement policies.

The 1994 WTO Agreements included a separate Agreement on Import Licensing. **Technical barriers** to trade are addressed by a number of the **WTO Agreements**, including the Agreement on Technical Barriers, Agreement on the Application of Sanitary and Phytosanitary Measures, Agreement on Customs Valuation, and the Agreement on Preshipment Inspection. Restrictions on foreign government procurement are the subject of the Agreement on Government Procurement. Export subsidies were addressed in the 1947 Agreement in Article VI (Antidumping and Countervailing Duties) and Article XXIII (Nullification and Impairment). The 1994 Agreements also included an Antidumping Agreement and an Agreement on Subsidies and Countervailing Measures.

http://

Political Risk
Information:
**http://www.political-
risk.net.** Provides data
and information on
political risk.

Intellectual property protection, barriers to trade in service, and barriers to investment are dealt with directly in separate agreements: the Agreement on Trade-Related Investment Measures (TRIMs), General Agreement on Trade in Services (GATS), and the TRIPS agreement. The Investment Agreement prohibits countries from requiring the purchase of domestically produced products, from conditioning the importation of products on a company's agreement to export products, and from restricting access to foreign exchange. The Agreement on Services prohibits the use of qualification and licensing requirements as barriers to the establishment of a business or the practicing of a profession by a foreign party. Any such requirements are to be based upon "objective and transparent criteria" and must include "adequate procedures to verify the competence of professionals" from foreign countries. The TRIPS Agreement is a comprehensive framework that covers all areas of intellectual property, including copyright, trademark, country of origin indicators, patent, industrial designs, and trade secrets. This agreement will be reviewed in Chapter Thirteen.

A prevalent form of political risk involves changes in government regulation of foreign business activity, sometimes referred to as **creeping expropriation**. This includes changes in formal regulations, licensing procedures, and the enactment of price controls. Creeping expropriation can also be a less legitimate form of interference, such as the extortion of bribes, arbitrary changes in standards and inspection requirements, and the non-enforcement of intellectual property laws. Another major form of political risk is tax calculation and enforcement. A change in the rates, a denial of a tax credit, or a change in accounting rules can be used to manipulate corporate income taxes. Other forms of taxes, such as revenue taxes, can also be manipulated. These taxes are associated with the importation and exportation of goods and include the value-added tax,[23] sales tax, excise tax, and tariffs.

EXPROPRIATION AND NATIONALIZATION

The most extreme forms of political risk are **expropriation** and **nationalization**. Expropriation is a government seizure of individual foreign businesses and assets. Nationalization refers to the seizure of all businesses, foreign and domestic, in a particular industry. Both include some form of compensation, but in the past the compensation has not equaled the value of the lost investments. Fortunately, the threats of a foreign government nationalizing an industry or expropriating a foreign company's assets have severely diminished. The free trade era has made it clear that countries need to attract foreign investment and trade in order to continue to develop. In fact, the opposite of nationalization and expropriation, the **privatization** of government-owned industries, has been the dominant trend over the past few decades.

http://
Information on privatization issues: **http://www. privatization.org.** Privatization.org is a private think tank that provides information on domestic and foreign privatization issues.

To encourage foreign investments, many developing countries and former communist countries have passed laws protecting them. In May 1993, for example, Russia enacted Foreign Economic Activity legislation that states that foreign investments on its territory "shall enjoy full and unconditional legal protection." More specifically, it states that foreign investments "shall not be subject to nationalization or confiscation except when such measures are adopted in the social interests." In case of nationalization or confiscation, Russia states it will give prompt, adequate, and effective compensation to the foreign investor.

In the past, the key area of dispute was not whether a country had the legal right to nationalize or expropriate, but the amount of compensation to be paid. Often, the foreign government was willing to pay only the cost paid by the foreign investor. Russia's foreign investment protection law commits it to pay "the real value of the investments being nationalized." It further requires the government to pay in hard currency and to pay interest in the event of any delay in the making of the payment.

Bilateral investment treaties (BITs) are another avenue by which countries safeguard foreign investment from expropriation and other investment risks. BITs provide that a host country must not discriminate against foreign investors and must agree to pay prompt, adequate, and effective compensation in case of expropriation. They also provide for alternative dispute resolution by way of arbitration with the **International Center for Settlement of Investment Disputes (ICSID)**.

Risk Assessment and Management

Before entering a foreign market, a business should measure the degree and likelihood of political risk by performing a formal risk assessment. This may be done internally through research with materials obtained through the U.S. State Department and the OPIC. Some businesses enlist private companies that specialize in risk

---

23. Value-added tax or VAT is a popular method of taxation in Europe. It imposes a tax on goods and services at each stage of the production process equal to the value added to the product at each stage. It is similar, but not identical, to a sales tax.

assessment. If a project is very large, however, then management should meet with government officials of the foreign country to discuss the company's goals. If possible, a formal **concession agreement** should outline the duties of the foreign government and the rights of the company. It should specify the level of tariffs to be charged, the right of the company to repatriate profits, the host country's commitment to intellectual property protection, the applicable level of taxation, and the government's **transfer pricing** policy.[24] It is also prudent to require the use of mediation and arbitration in case of a dispute.

Managing Risk Through Insurance

http://
Overseas Private
Investment
Corporation:
http://www.opic.gov.

Once the potential risk is assessed, a business can insure against a loss by obtaining political risk insurance. An investor may obtain insurance to protect investments in foreign countries. To encourage U.S. companies to invest in developing countries, the U.S. government established the **Overseas Private Investment Corporation (OPIC)**. The OPIC is a government corporation that assists U.S. private investments in developing countries by providing loans, loan guarantees, investment services, and insurance against political risks. The OPIC provides low-cost expropriation insurance to U.S. companies. The **Export-Import Bank of the United States (Eximbank)** provides financing assistance to U.S. exporters and through the **Foreign Credit Insurance Association (FCIA)** provides different types of insurance coverage. The FCIA works with the Eximbank to provide political and commercial risk insurance to U.S. exporters. Political risk insurance protects against the expropriation of goods, the nonconvertibility of currency, and the inability of a foreign purchaser to obtain an import license, as well as losses arising from political instability and resultant civil strife.

OPIC offers four types of insurance coverage.[25] First, it insures against restrictions on the repatriation of profits. Second, it insures against expropriation and nationalization. Third, it insures against damage to assets due to war or civil strife. Fourth, it provides business interruption insurance for losses of income resulting from political disturbances. The OPIC will also insure banks willing to finance export transactions, enabling a bank to confirm a letter of credit from a risky importer and its bank. OPIC insurance is available only to American investors or exporters undertaking business in a foreign country with which the United States has entered into a BIT. In addition, OPIC is allowed to sue a foreign country because BITs require the foreign country to waive sovereign immunity protection.

An internationally based investment insurance company is the **Multilateral Investment Guarantee Agency (MIGA)**. Established in 1988 as part of the World Bank, MIGA encourages investment in developing countries through the mitigation of noncommercial investment barriers. It provides insurance against expropriation, war, and other noncommercial risks and offers investment guarantees for direct foreign investments, as well as licensing, franchising, and transfers of technology.

The determination of whether political or commercial risk insurance will be needed should be made when the underlying contract is negotiated, and the cost and type of insurance to be procured should be stated in the contract. Insurance

---

24. Transfer pricing is the price that an affiliated company, such as a subsidiary, charges another affiliated company. Manipulation of transfer prices can be used to move profits and costs from a high-tax to a low-tax country.

25. 22 U.S.C. § 2194(a)(1)(A-D) (2000).

procurement may be subject to foreign government regulation. In China, for example, insurance in conjunction with a joint venture must be obtained through a Chinese insurance company.

INTERNATIONAL

The decision to obtain commercial insurance may be dictated by the commercial lender. Provisions in the underlying contract should also be reviewed for their potential impact on subsequent insurance claims. For example, choice of law clauses should be reviewed to determine if there are laws that preclude the insured from making a claim under its insurance policy.

The application for insurance, like the application for a letter of credit, is contractual in nature. The applicant should read the form carefully and answer it as honestly and comprehensively as possible. The general rule is that the applicant must disclose any information that would "materially" influence the insurance company's decision to grant the requested insurance.[26] In the related area of marine insurance, a court stated that "an applicant for a marine insurance policy is bound to reveal every fact within his knowledge that is material to the risk."[27] In that case, an owner of a company failed to disclose that he had previously filed claims for more than two dozen losses at sea. The court found that there was sufficient evidence for fraud in intentionally concealing material facts and allowed rescission of the insurance policy.

Typical provisions found in most insurance contracts include a description of the insured property, a definition of an expropriatory act, a waiting period, notice, warranties, recoveries, duty to minimize loss,[28] and definition and computation of loss.[29] The definition of what expropriatory acts are covered by the expropriation insurance policy should be closely scrutinized. Does the policy cover both partial and total loss or expropriation? A "waiting period" is often required between the expropriatory loss and collecting on the insurance policy. In large projects, the waiting period can be as long as a year. The duties of the insured regarding the preservation of the investment and any claims pertaining to the loss should be clearly defined. A warranty provision often requires the insured to take steps in order to preserve its coverage. For example, the insured may have to certify that it will comply with relevant host country laws and that the uninsured portion of the investment will remain uninsured. Also, rights to recoveries made after payment on the claim should be defined.

Managing Risk Through Intermediaries

Exporting, licensing, and direct foreign investment risks can be reduced by using professional consultants and agents. International specialists such as freight forwarders, customs brokers, political risk analysts, international lawyers, and commercial insurance companies all offer expertise and services.

Customs brokers assist importers with the entry and admissibility of goods, their classification and valuation, and the payment of duties. In the United States, customhouses are licensed pursuant to Title Nineteen of the Code of Federal Regulations in order to transact business with the Customs Service. They can be

---

26. See New York Insurance Law § 3105(b) (McKinney's).
27. *Cigna Property & Casualty Insurance Co. v. Polaris Pictures Co.*, 1998 WL 734391 (9th Cir. 1998).
28. See *Slay Warehousing Company Inc. v. Reliance Insurance Co.*, 471 F.2d 1364 (8th Cir. 1973).
29. S. Linn Williams, "Political and Other Risk Insurance: OPIC, MIGA, EXIMBANK, and Other Providers," 5 *Pace International Law Review* 59, 106–112 (1993).

hired to provide the necessary import and customs documents. Generally, the seller or exporter hires the freight forwarder, while the customs broker is the agent for an importer or purchaser. An "export" freight forwarder must be certified by the Federal Maritime Commission to handle ocean freight.

The **freight forwarder** often arranges all documentation needed to move a shipment from origin to destination and assembles documents for presentation to the bank in the exporter's name. The forwarder arranges for cargo insurance, notifies the buyer of the shipment, and advises the shipper of marking and labeling requirements. In exchange, the forwarder is paid a fee by the exporter and may receive a percentage of the freight charge from the common carrier. The international banker offers financing assistance, provides guarantees of payment, and facilitates the movement of documents between the parties.

Countertrade

Countertrade is used to overcome currency convertibility and repatriation problems or the capital shortcomings of a foreign party.[30] This section will discuss some of the common forms of countertrade, including barter, buy-back, and counterpurchase. A **barter transaction** involves an exchange of goods or services, but barter agreements are not always simple, cashless, single-document arrangements. They sometimes involve two separate documentary sales, often with separate letters of credit. A form of countertrade known as **counterpurchase** is an economic transaction in which one party sells goods to the other party and, in return, the first party agrees to purchase goods from the second party or another party in that country so as to achieve an agreed ratio between the reciprocal performances.[31] This is often done to fulfill a government's requirement that hard currencies being repatriated be offset by an incoming hard currency flow. A variant is the **offset agreement**. "Offsets constitute an agreement by the foreign seller to include as part of the sale in the foreign nation the use of parts or services from local suppliers."[32] An offset satisfies local content requirements where the host country mandates that a certain percentage of a good be a product of local materials and labor. In **buy-back** or compensation transactions, exporters of heavy equipment, technology, or entire manufacturing facilities are allowed to purchase a certain percentage of the output of the facility at a below market price. Many variations of countertrade are described in McVey's "Countertrade: Commercial Practices, Legal Issues, and Policy Dilemmas."

The Department of Commerce can advise and assist U.S. exporters faced with countertrade requirements. The Finance Services and Countertrade Division of the International Trade Administration's Office of Finance monitors countertrade trends, disseminates information, and provides general assistance to enterprises seeking barter and countertrade opportunities. Another source for information and contract clauses dealing with countertrade is the **United Nations Commission on International Trade Law (UNCITRAL)**. It publishes the *Legal Guide on International Countertrade Transactions*, which provides information on how best to

http://
United Nations:
http://www.un.org/law.
Provides links to United Nations initiatives in the area of private international business.

---

30. See, generally, John C. Grabow, "Negotiating and Drafting Contracts in International Barter and Countertrade Transactions," 9 *North Carolina Journal of International Law & Commercial Regulation* 255 (1984).

31. See UNCITRAL, "Preliminary Study of Legal Issues in International Countertrade" (1988).

32. Ralph H. Folsom, Michael Wallace Gordon & John A. Spagnole, Jr., *International Business Transactions* §5.6, at 162 (2d ed. 2001).

Thomas B. McVey, "Countertrade: Commercial Practices, Legal Issues, and Policy Dilemmas"

16 *Law & Policy Int'l Bus.* 1 (1984)

Doing Business Internationally

Countertrade frequently is confused with the concept of barter. Barter is an exchange of goods effectuated without the use of currency. Countertrade is most frequently used to refer to two reciprocal sales transactions in which each party is paid in currency. Despite this technical distinction, most observers view barter transactions as a subcategory of countertrade. The two most common types of countertrade are known as counterpurchase and compensation (buy-back) trade.

Counterpurchase

In a counterpurchase arrangement, a private firm agrees to sell products to a sovereign nation and to purchase from the nation goods which are unrelated to the items which it is selling. For example, in a series of transactions between a major U.S. manufacturer of commercial aircraft and the government of Yugoslavia, the U.S. firm sold jet aircraft to Yugoslavia and agreed to purchase substantial quantities of Yugoslav crystal glassware, cutting tools, leather coats, and canned hams.

In a counterpurchase transaction, each party is paid in currency upon the delivery of its products to the other party. It is common in such transactions for a private firm to be allowed a period of time following the delivery of the goods that it is selling in which to fulfill its purchase obligation. Periods of from three to five years, for example, were not uncommon in counterpurchase obligations imposed by the Soviet Union and Eastern European nations. Often, the parties agree upon a list of goods from which the private firm later will be able to select items to purchase.

Private firms resort to a variety of methods to dispose of goods which they are forced to purchase, but most frequently resell these goods to trading companies or directly to end users, often at a discount or "disagio." Sometimes the private firm will resell the countertraded goods at a price below that which it paid for them, seeking to offset this loss by larger profits generated by the sale of its own product to the nation.

Compensation

The most common form of countertrade is referred to as "compensation" or "buy-back." In a compensation transaction, a private firm will sell equipment, technology, or even an entire plant to a sovereign nation and agree to purchase a portion of the output produced from the use of the equipment or technology. For example, in the celebrated $20 billion Occidental Petroleum ammonia countertrade transaction with the Soviet Union, Occidental assisted the Soviets in constructing and financing ammonia plants and agreed to purchase quantities of ammonia produced in these plants over a twenty-year period.

Compensation transactions frequently involve significantly longer periods of time during which the private firm will be permitted to fulfill its purchase obligation than in counterpurchase. In addition, compensation transactions are generally of larger dollar value than counterpurchase transactions. Unlike counterpurchase transactions, the products which the private firm purchases in compensation are frequently of marketable quality and in demand in the international marketplace. Further, Western firms frequently are able to negotiate a purchase price for the output that is below the world market price so that the firm can earn a profit in reselling the product which it is forced to buy.

Barter

Barter, swap, and other types of noncurrency transactions are frequently viewed as forms of countertrade. In many cases, the sovereign nation will impose a barter requirement in a coercive fashion for purposes of disposing of surplus or low quality goods which it otherwise cannot sell. Barter transactions are frequently utilized in crude oil transfers as a means of conveying crude below official OPEC prices. Similarly, barter is occasionally used as a means of "liberating" blocked currencies or otherwise circumventing foreign exchange controls.

continued

A Step-by-Step Approach to Market Research (*continued*)

Clearing Agreements

Although countertrade is conducted most frequently between a sovereign nation and a private firm, countertrade arrangements also occur between and among sovereign nations. Nations have historically entered into bilateral or multilateral "clearing agreements" under which they agree to purchase equal values of each other's products over a specified period of time. This is a form of reciprocal trading not unlike the private firm–sovereign nation relationships discussed above. When an imbalance develops in an account that a nation cannot rectify, private firms known as "switch trading" firms offer to assist the recalcitrant nation in disposing of the goods which it is required to purchase, usually for a fee.

Framework Agreements

In a countertrade "framework agreement" a private firm establishes a formal, long-term "crediting" mechanism with the host nation under which exports generated by the private firm are routinely credited to the countertrade commitments of numerous third-party firms on an ongoing basis. The key to a framework agreement is that the "crediting" of the offsetting purchases or the escrowing and payment of funds is undertaken on a routine and ongoing basis under a prearranged agreement rather than on the more common case-by-case basis.

"Positive" or "Reverse" Countertrade

In certain instances, private firms prefer countertrade arrangements over conventional transactions. In so-called "positive" or "reverse" countertrade, the private firm views the goods that it will be required to purchase as more valuable than hard currency. This is most often the case when a firm seeks to establish a guaranteed supply of a valuable commodity or production component when it anticipates future shortages of these items. For example, in one of the proposed East-West "gas-for-pipes" transactions, a group of private firms was negotiating with the Soviet Union to transfer equipment and technology for the transportation and production of natural gas to the Soviets in return for guarantees of quantities of natural gas produced through the use of this equipment and technology.

Performance Requirements

A performance requirement is a condition imposed by a sovereign government that requires foreign parties who wish to undertake an investment in that nation to agree to take certain steps to increase exports from the nation. Such steps include the agreement by the foreign investors to export a certain percentage of the output from the investment project, to employ a certain level of local inhabitants in the project, to use a predetermined level of locally produced components in the manufactured product, and to transfer certain technology to the host nation. Performance requirements are distinguishable from other types of countertrade requirements in that the former involve a private firm's investment in the imposing nation rather than its sale of goods to the nation. Both practices involve intervention by the host nation in the free market process, however, and in view of their similarity are frequently treated as the same phenomenon.

Collection-Through-Export Transactions

A major problem for U.S. firms doing business abroad is the collection of overseas funds which have been restricted from repatriation due to foreign exchange controls. In such instances, a private firm might be owed funds by a foreign party as a result of a trade debt or have profits denominated in local currency which are earned by a foreign subsidiary. The private firm will have possession of the local currency in the host country, but due to foreign exchange shortages will be unable to convert this currency into dollars. In a collection-through-export transaction, the firm will use the local currency to purchase locally produced goods, export the goods from the host nation, and sell the goods overseas for dollars or another convertible currency.

structure a countertrade transaction. It also discusses the types of clauses generally found in countertrade contracts. The clauses discussed in the *Guide* include type, quality, and quantity of goods; pricing of goods; participation of third parties; payment; restrictions on resale; liquidated damages; security for performance; failure to perform; choice of law; and settlement of disputes.

Because of the difficulty in finding marketable goods in a foreign country to fulfill a countertrade (counterpurchase) commitment, certain clauses take on added importance. First, an extended period of time should be allotted to the exporter to obtain host country goods to satisfy its countertrade obligations. Second, a broad list of countertrade goods should be negotiated to enhance the exporter's chances of finding marketable goods. Third, because of the poor quality of some foreign goods, the exporter should negotiate broad inspection rights. Also, the costs and uncertainty of the countertrade arrangement may warrant the granting of a *disagio* (discount) of the amount of goods needed to be purchased to fulfill the countertrade commitment.

Another provision included in countertrade contracts is a penalty clause for non-performance of the countertrade (counterpurchase) commitment. In some cases, paying a penalty instead of purchasing unmarketable goods may make better economic sense for the exporter. Of course, the penalty clause should make clear that payment of the penalty releases the exporter from any further liability.[33]

Developing an Export Plan

Before attempting to export, a firm should develop an export plan that answers the following ten questions: (1) What countries are targeted for sales development? (2) What products are selected for export? What modifications, if any, must be made to adapt them for overseas markets? (3) In each country, what is the basic customer profile? (4) What marketing and distribution channels should be used to reach customers? (5) What special challenges pertain to each market (competition, cultural differences, import controls, etc.), and what strategy will be used to address them? (6) How will the product's export sales price be determined? (7) What will be the time frame for implementing each element of the plan? (8) What personnel and company resources will be dedicated to exporting? (9) What will be the cost in time and money for each element? (10) How will results be evaluated and used to modify the plan? The next Focus on Transactions feature provides an outline for a generic export plan.

The way a company chooses to export its products can have a significant effect on its export plan. One goal of the export plan will be to determine whether the firm should export directly or indirectly. The basic distinction between these approaches to exporting relates to a company's level of involvement in the export process. Firms that are new to exporting or are unable to commit staff and funds to complex export activities may find indirect exporting appropriate. Exporting indirectly through intermediaries leaves it to the intermediary firm to find foreign markets and buyers for its products. Export management companies (EMCs), export trading companies (ETCs), international trade consultants, and other intermediaries can give the exporter access to well-established expertise and trade contacts. A firm contemplating a greater involvement in a foreign market will need to seek the expertise of a foreign lawyer.

---

33.   William G. Frenkel, "Legal Protection Against Risks Involved in Doing Business in the Republics of the Former U.S.S.R.," 10 *International Quarterly* 395, 431 (1998).

Focus on Transactions

Sample Outline for an Export Plan[34]

Introduction: Why This Company Should Export

Part I. Export Policy Commitment Statement

Part II. Situation/Background Analysis

- Product or Service
- Operations
- Personnel and Export Organization
- Resources of the Firm
- Industry Structure, Competition, and Demand

Part III. Marketing Component

- Identifying, Evaluating, and Selecting Target Markets
- Product Selection and Pricing
- Distribution Methods
- Terms and Conditions
- Sales Goals: Profit and Loss Forecasts

Part IV. Tactics: Action Steps

- Primary Target Countries
- Secondary Target Countries
- Indirect Marketing Efforts

Part V. Export Budget

- Pro Forma Financial Statements

Part VI. Implementation Schedule

- Follow-up
- Periodic Operational and Management Review (Measuring Results Against Plan)

The direct exporting approach is more ambitious and difficult, because the exporter personally handles every aspect of the exporting process from market research and planning to foreign distribution and collections. Consequently, a significant commitment of management time and attention is required to achieve good results. However, this approach may also be the best way to achieve maximum profits and long-term growth. With appropriate help and guidance from third-party experts, including freight forwarders and international banks, even small or medium-sized firms can export directly if they are able to commit enough staff time to the effort. For those who cannot make that commitment, the services of an EMC, ETC, trade consultant, or other qualified intermediary is indispensable.

A U.S. company may take a multifaceted approach to exporting. For example, it may elect to export directly to nearby markets such as Canada or Mexico, while letting an EMC handle more ambitious sales to Saudi Arabia or China. An exporter may also choose to gradually increase its level of direct exporting, after it has gained experience and sales volume appears to justify added investment.

Finding and Managing Foreign Lawyers

INTERNATIONAL

One of the best ways to find foreign legal counsel is to follow the recommendations of U.S. lawyers or businesspeople with experience in a given country. Other sources for foreign lawyers are national or local bar associations or chambers of commerce. Some foreign bar association rules are more restrictive in the area of advertising. German lawyers, for example, are prohibited from advertising or actively seeking clients. Also, a number of international bar associations and societies publish membership lists.

---

34.   Source: National Trade Data Bank, a product of STAT-USA, U.S. Department of Commerce.

Examples of international law societies include the German-American Lawyers' Association and the German-British Jurists' Association.

    Selecting a foreign legal representative requires considering a number of criteria. Language skills are vital to an effective dialogue; international law directories often list the language capabilities of foreign lawyers. Also, it is important to understand the type of assistance that will be required. In complicated international business transactions, numerous national laws are likely to be applicable. In addition, the timing of commercial transactions is of great importance to the businessperson. Therefore, U.S. businesspeople must clearly communicate the time frame of the transaction to their foreign counsel.

http://

FindLaw's West Legal Directory: **http:// dictionary.lp.findlaw. com.**

KEY TERMS

arbitrage
Article 38
barter transaction
basket of risks
bilateral investment treaty (BIT)
buy-back
buying agent
commission agent
concession agreement
convertibility
counterpurchase
countertrade
creeping expropriation
currency option
currency rate fluctuation
customs broker
direct foreign investment
disagio
evergreen provisions
export agent
Export-Import Bank of the United
  States (Eximbank)
export management company
  (EMC)
export trading company (ETC)

exporting-importing
expropriation
foreign agent
Foreign Credit Insurance
  Association (FCIA)
foreign direct investment (FDI)
foreign distributor
foreign sales representative
forward contract
franchise
freight forwarder
futures contract
General Agreement on Tariffs
  and Trade (GATT)
home country
host country
indirect exporting
International Center for
  Settlement of Investment
  Disputes (ICSID)
International Chamber of
  Commerce (ICC)
International Court of Justice
joint venture
lex mercatoria

licensing
Multilateral Investment Guarantee
  Agency (MIGA)
nationalization
non-tariff barriers
offset agreement
Overseas Private Investment
  Corporation (OPIC)
privatization
remarketer
repatriation
sale of services
technical barriers
trade barriers
trade in goods
transfer pricing
United Nations Commission on
  International Trade Law
  (UNCITRAL)
United Nations Convention
  on Contracts for the
  International Sale of
  Goods (CISG)
Uruguay round
WTO Agreements

CHAPTER PROBLEMS

1. You are a manager at a U.S. company that manufactures moderately priced personal computers. The company is contemplating expanding overseas with an initial emphasis on exporting to Latin America. You have been assigned the task of preparing a preliminary market analysis for the country of Brazil. Using the sources found in the Focus on Transactions feature on page 10, conduct market research. Prepare a report that focuses on the opportunities and pitfalls of exporting to Brazil and offer recommendations.

2. As vice president for foreign operations of a U.S. multinational corporation, you have been asked to prepare a report for the board of directors regarding "doing business" in Germany and Nigeria. Discuss the following in your report: (1) the different ways of "doing business" in foreign countries, (2) the way you would recommend for each of the two countries mentioned, (3) the risks of doing business in these countries, and (4) ways of minimizing those risks.

3. A U.S. businessperson enters into a joint venture with an Italian company in the business of manufacturing and selling agricultural and vegetable products. The joint venture agreement gives the U.S. businessperson a 50 percent equity ownership in the joint venture. The parties also enter into a shareholder agreement that restricts the shareholders' ability to transfer shares without offering the other shareholders the opportunity to purchase the shares and that provides for arbitration of any shareholder disputes in Rome, Italy. The Italian defendant attempted to purchase ownership interest in the joint venture of the Italian company. The U.S. businessperson sues in the United States on the ground of tortious interference with the shareholder agreement. The plaintiff asserts that the tort claim is not subject to the arbitration clause and argues that a tort claim is outside the scope of the arbitration clause because it is restricted to contract claims directly related to the shareholder agreement. Is the plaintiff correct on the issue of arbitrability, or will the plaintiff be forced to arbitrate in Rome, Italy? *Marchetto v. DeKalb Genetics Corp.*, 711 F. Supp. 936 (N.D. Ill. 1989).

4. Your company is contemplating exporting goods to the following countries: France, Croatia, and Nigeria. Research the following: (1) the currency of each country and the current conversion rate into U.S. dollars and (2) restrictions in each country pertaining to the conversion of the national currency into U.S. dollars and any repatriation limitations. Check the U.S. Department of State Country Commercial Guides for each of these countries for relevant information. If the currency risks are severe for any of these countries, what alternatives should you explore in order to do business in these countries?

INTERNET EXERCISES

1. Review the Web site of the International Finance Corporation, the private investment arm of the World Bank, for information on the political risks of doing business in a country from the developing world: **http://www.ifc.org.**

2. Review the online catalog of materials published by International Chamber of Commerce Publishing, SA, at **http://www.iccbooks.com.**

3. Review the Web site of the World Intellectual Property Organization at **http://www.wipo.int** for materials that would be of assistance to someone contemplating the international licensing of intellectual property rights.

4. Review the international trade law database at **http://lexmercatoria.net/.**

5. Search the Web for sites of international law firms that provide assistance to companies undertaking international business transactions. Some of these sites provide interesting articles and links to current developments in the law of international business transactions.

6. Your company manufactures a popular brand of clothing with a world-recognized trademark. You are asked to prepare a political risk report on exporting to two countries in Europe of your choosing. One country is to be a member of the European Union, and the other is not a member of the European Union and is located in the Balkans. Compare the different types of risk for the two countries. Recommend a market entry strategy (exporting, licensing, direct investment) for each country. A good place to start is the U.S. Department of State Country Commercial Guides for each country at **http://www.state.gov.**

This textbook's primary focus is on the *legal* implications of doing business internationally. This chapter emphasizes some of the important *ethical* implications of international business dealings and explores how a multi-national business confronts the issues of transnational ethics. It also discusses various **standards**.

Standards refer to government regulations pertaining to labor, health, safety, and environmental concerns. A variety of "voluntary standards" also exist, advanced by either trade associations or non-governmental organizations. The **International Labor Organization (ILO)** is an example of a non-governmental agency that publishes standards for the workplace.

Most international business decisions have both legal and ethical implications—how to address differences between host country and home country stan-dards, for exam-ple. Generally, the legal answer to this dilemma is quite clear: Because the busi-ness activity tran-spires within the jurisdiction of the host country, then the busi-nessperson need only comply with

http://
International Labor Organization:
http://www.us.ilo.org.

Chapter 2

The Ethics of International Business

the standards of the host country, assuming no extraterritorial application of home country law. The ethical answer is much more complicated. If the host country's standards are lower than those of the home country, is complying with the lesser standards ethical? Most U.S. companies face this question when starting business operations in less developed countries. Answering becomes more difficult if the lower standards are likely to result in harm to people or the environment. Ultimately, a multinational company may be *ethically* required to apply standards higher than those of the host country.

Demarcating the line between law and ethics and accounting for ethical factors in business decisions is crucial to international business transactions. The ethical assessment is complicated by differing cultural and national outlooks on what is ethically appropriate and will be influenced by the nuances of culture, religion, and economics. **Ethical relativism** or **cultural relativism**, which holds that because different countries or cultures have different ethical belief systems there is no supranational way of determining whether an action is right or wrong, is often used to argue that ethical decisions are confined within the boundaries of a given country or culture. Ethical relativism asserts that the correctness of an action is to be measured by whatever a majority within a society believes is morally correct.

The problem of cultural relativism that confronts all multinational enterprises will be examined in the context of five common areas of concern: environment, standards, bribery, advertising, and human rights. Before exploring these issues in detail, an exploration of general ethical schools and approaches will provide insight.

http://
Business Ethics—
Wharton Ethics
Program: **http//ethics.
wharton.upenn.edu/.**

International Business Ethics

http://

For materials on ethical relativism see Ethics Update: **http://ethics.acusd.edu.**

Business managers often do not recognize the ethical implications of their decisions. From the perspective of corporate profits and credibility, a good reputation in the global marketplace has become paramount for most multinational enterprises, partly because bad ethical practices are readily apparent in an increasingly transparent global economy. Multinational companies are often the target of surveillance by the media, government agencies, competitors, private watch groups, and even their own employees. Public relations disasters resulting from unethical practices can be catastrophic.

To better sensitize employees to ethical issues, there must be some agreement on what is right or wrong. Some basic assumptions regarding the rightness of certain practices and activities must be made. These basic assumptions are descriptive, not normative, in nature. For example, the issue will not be whether bribery is wrong but whether Americans or citizens of most civilized nations believe that bribery is wrong. A review of the traditional schools of ethics provides a starting point for the U.S. businessperson's approach to ethical decision making and will enable the businessperson to better apply moral reasoning to ethical problems in the international setting. The ethical schools to be reviewed are utilitarianism, rights and duties, virtue, and ethics of care.

Utilitarianism

http://

For a review of utilitarianism see Ethics Update: **http://ethics.acusd.edu.**

The **utilitarian ethics** approach is teleological in nature. Teleology or consequentialism looks to the consequences of a decision or an action to determine if it was ethically appropriate. There are many different formulations of this approach. Egoism simply determines the rightness of an action, whether it produces more good than bad, for the individual decision maker. In the area of business, egoism is often associated with the economics of Adam Smith, an eighteenth-century Scottish philosopher generally regarded as the father of modern economics. His masterwork, *The Wealth of Nations*, was published in 1776. Smith provided the rationalization for free market economics: Individuals should be allowed to make decisions based on their own narrow self-interests. If not interfered with, according to this position, such rational self-interest will produce an efficient economy that benefits society as a whole. Smith's view of self-interest and the free market has largely been misunderstood, however. Smith's moral philosophy as described in his other masterwork, *A Theory of Moral Sentiments*, saw *rational* self-interest as incorporating many altruistic factors not normally associated with the economic (rational) person of free market theory.

A simplified version of utilitarianism is the economic concept of benefit-cost. **Benefit-cost analysis** attempts to monetize the ethical determination by placing a dollar value on the benefits and costs of an action from the narrow perspective of the decision maker. The danger of this narrow interpretation of utilitarianism was demonstrated in the infamous Pinto automobile case. The decision not to install a relatively inexpensive device to prevent rear-end explosions was based on a narrow dollar calculation, which concluded that the cost to defend and settle personal injury and wrongful death lawsuits was less than the costs of incorporating the safety feature. This analysis raises the questions: Is an examination of benefits and cost performed solely from the perspective of the automobile company ethically sufficient? How does one place a value on human life or well-being? Are certain concerns, such as human life, **dominant considerations** that outweigh the other factors in the benefit-cost equation?

A true utilitarian analysis attempts to weigh all direct and indirect effects from the perspectives of all parties or stakeholders affected and not just from the perspective of the decision maker. It is imperative for the decision maker to continuously expand the utilitarian analysis to take into account as many effects and stakeholders as possible. It is also important to seek out alternatives that would minimize costs (harm) and increase the net benefit. In addition, benefit-cost utilitarianism fails to take into account how the net benefit of an action is distributed. Thus, a multinational company decision that creates a net benefit is unlikely to be ethical if the company retains the entire net benefit and the host country and its people receive none. In some developing countries, a few leaders and their associates might hoard the host country's benefits.

Dominant considerations relate to **incommensurability**. How do we value life, equality, health, and other intangible considerations? We can argue that we make those valuations every day in determining reasonable levels of safety or pollution. A utilitarian would argue that the market establishes society's preference level of safety or pollution. Did the market establish reasonable levels in the Pinto decision, where safety concerns were ignored? Did the individual consumers establish such reasonable levels? Would the actions of the manufacturer have been more ethical if they had disclosed the dangers of rear-end explosions? Would they have been absolved of moral responsibility if they had offered the consumer the option of purchasing the safety device?

The utilitarian calculation should be the first stage in a two-stage process. A second stage would analyze how the net benefits are distributed. This process is associated with the notion of **distributive justice**. The second stage may also weigh the effects of an action from the perspective of individual rights and entitlements. For example, if a net benefit results in the diminishment of basic human rights, then the action would be considered unethical. In essence, certain concerns, such as human rights, would take priority over the results of a purely utilitarian analysis. This idea that certain things are sacrosanct is part of the concept of dominant considerations. Certain negative consequences can preempt the determination that an action creates the "greatest good for the greatest number."

If an action produces the greatest good at the expense of the rights of a minority, then utilitarianism fails in its sanctioning of such an action as ethical. In sum, an international businessperson using a utilitarian approach to decision making should list all those affected by the decision. The businessperson then must value the good and bad consequences of the decision from the perspective of all those on the list. Next, the analysis should be expanded to include any indirect effects not previously considered. In determining the net benefit or cost of a decision, the decision maker should seek out alternatives that would produce greater net benefits. If alternatives are found, then the decision maker should ask some fundamental questions in comparing the alternatives: Which alternative best promotes the common good? Which alternative best respects the rights of the individual? Which alternative best maintains the valuable traits of character espoused in the company's code of conduct? Finally, the decision maker must attempt to uncover any dominant considerations that would preclude the action despite the net benefits.

Rights and Duties

Whereas the utilitarian approach focuses on the net benefits to society, a rights and duties approach views morality from the perspective of the individual. A **moral right** of someone creates a correlative **moral duty** of others not to interfere in the exercise of

that right. John Locke championed the notion of inalienable rights that antecede the social contract that binds people together in a society and binds a people to their government. These inalienable rights, as enunciated in U.S. foundational documents (the Declaration of Independence, the Constitution, and the Bill of Rights) and the French *Rights of Man*, recognize the sanctity of individual autonomy and equality in the pursuit of personal interests. This sanctity of individual freedom is embodied in the U.S. right to vote, right of association, freedom of religion, and right to a free press. In the area of international documents, the **Universal Declaration of Human Rights** adopts a basic rights approach to international human rights concerns (see Comparative Law: Universal Declaration of Human Rights). More recently, the United Nations passed a resolution titled the **Declaration on the Right to Development,**[1] which asserts that every person has a basic human right to development. The declaration places responsibility on individual nations and the international community to ensure that everyone shares in the benefits of development. Article 3 of the declaration states that countries have "the duty to cooperate in ensuring development and eliminating obstacles to development," including the formulation of international development policies that promote the "more rapid development of developing countries." International cooperation is required to provide these countries with "appropriate means to foster their comprehensive development."

The rights approach views morality from the perspective of the individual, whereas utilitarianism measures morality from a societal perspective. Thus, rights

---

Universal Declaration of Human Rights (Adopted by the United Nations General Assembly on December 10, 1948)

COMPARATIVE LAW

Article 2 states that "everyone is entitled to certain rights and freedoms, without distinction of any kind, such as race, color, sex, language, religion, political or other opinion, national or social origin, property, birth, or other status." This nondiscrimination principle applies to the enumerated rights listed in the declaration. Article 3 provides the general recognition that "everyone has the right to life, liberty, and security of person." Other articles provide specific rights, including the right to be free from torture or degrading treatment (Article 5), right to recognition everywhere as a person under the law (Article 6), right to an effective remedy for acts violating fundamental rights (Article 8), right to a fair and public hearing by an impartial tribunal (Article 10), freedom of movement (Article 13), right to own property (Article 17), freedom of religion (Article 19), right to take part

in government (Article 21), and the right to social security, including "the economic, social, and cultural rights indispensable for his dignity" (Article 22). In the area of nondiscrimination, Article 7 states that "all are entitled to equal protection against discrimination." Article 23 provides that "everyone, without any discrimination, has the right to equal pay for equal work." Quality of life and a living wage are considered fundamental human rights. Article 23 states that everyone has a right to work, to just and favorable working conditions, and to a just remuneration, ensuring for himself and his family "an existence worthy of human dignity." Article 25 further defines just remuneration as one that provides a "standard of living adequate for health and well-being, including food, clothing, housing and medical care and necessary social services, and the right to security in the event of unemployment, sickness, disability, or old age."

---

1.   United Nations General Assembly Resolution 41/128 (December 16, 1986).

can be seen as dominant considerations that trump a strictly utilitarian calculation of net benefits. Because of the firm belief in individual rights in U.S. political culture, a U.S. corporation will always have difficulty doing business in a culture that openly discriminates against women or minority groups. The developmental benefits of a foreign investment must be weighed against the need to honor and protect the rights of the individual. Ethical issues like this often surface because of the **conflict of relative development**,[2] which questions the appropriateness of considering whether a certain standard is acceptable in the home country of the multinational company. Instead, it suggests considering whether the practice or standard would have been acceptable at the time the home country was at a similar stage of development. Past sins, however, may not be sufficient to justify contemporary practices. Sometimes a host country's standards can be considered inadequate for any level of development. This is the issue in the ethics of wage determination. Do foreign workers have a moral right to a subsistence wage that is likely to be above the market rate in most developing countries? Is it right for a foreign company to pay a wage far below those paid in its home country and one that fails to improve the standard of life in the impoverished host country?

Another conflict that produces ethical concerns is the **conflict of cultural tradition**,[3] in which an unethical practice in a home country is considered ethically proper in the host country. How does a company contend with the low "glass ceiling" against women that is an overt part of Saudi Arabian culture and religious beliefs? How did the open discrimination against blacks under South African apartheid law influence U.S. investment in that country? The initial response to the subjugation of blacks in South African society was not to boycott foreign investment. Instead, multinational corporations (MNCs) agreed as a group to do business in South Africa but to openly defy the apartheid laws. The hope was that the MNCs could do more good in overturning apartheid by working within the system than by outside pressure. Although this approach was eventually abandoned in favor of boycott and embargo, it is an example of moral imagination that overcame the bipolar all-or-nothing approach. It also demonstrates the power of concerted acts of moral behavior. Because the Western companies agreed to defy the laws as a group, the government of South Africa elected not to enforce the laws and punish them.

INTERNATIONAL

INTERNATIONAL

A form of a rights approach to ethics is **Kantian ethics**. Like the rights approach, this school is deontological in nature. It is premised on the belief that there are absolute duties (or rights) that cannot be changed despite the consequences created by such a duty. Immanuel Kant constructed an ethical system that recognized the existence of absolute moral duties or laws that he referred to as **categorical imperatives**. These duties were non-negotiable and were a priori to any utilitarian calculation. One common formulation of the categorical imperative is that human beings can never be used as a "means to an end." All individuals are to be recognized as equal, rational persons. It is thereby wrong to subject anyone to a risk without that person's informed consent. Thus, the MNC that constructs a hazardous chemical plant in a developing country has a moral duty to fully disclose the health risks to its host country, the local community, and its foreign workers. The problem with disclosure is that the low level of economic development and per capita income may render the information meaningless. Does the foreign company have to do more than disclose and obey

http://

For materials on Kantian ethics see Ethics Update: **http://ethics.acusd.edu.**

---

2.   Thomas Donaldson, "Values in Tension: Ethics Away from Home," *Harvard Business Review* (Sept.–Oct. 1996).

3.   Ibid.

whatever host country regulations may apply? Kantian ethics would hold that we have a universal duty to not intentionally harm one another.

The categorical imperative requires that the MNC do more than merely disclose or comply with host country regulations. Thus, Union Carbide of America's arguments that it was not morally responsible for the Bhopal disaster is difficult to support under the duty not to harm.[4] Union Carbide said that it lacked control over the safety and operations of the Indian plant. It argued that its independent subsidiary, which was 49 percent owned by the Indian government and citizens, was responsible for the plant. Furthermore, it claimed that it had no responsibility for the safety of the plant because all management and safety personnel were Indian and because the Indian government controlled safety inspections and standards. In fact, the blueprints for the Bhopal plant provided by Union Carbide were rejected by the government of India in favor of an Indian-designed alternative. Does the forced abdication of all control by Union Carbide to the Indian government absolve it of moral responsibility for the accident, or is it simply an excuse used by the parent company to avoid liability? (See Focus on Transactions: Ethical Issues Raised by the Bhopal Disaster.) Critics would argue that such companies have a moral responsibility not to locate hazardous plants in a foreign country unless they retain sufficient control. Should the fact that the pesticides produced by the Bhopal plant helped feed millions of Indians be entered into this ethical equation?

Virtue Ethics

Virtue ethics[5] focuses not on the morality of an action but on the moral character or motivation of the actor. It separates motives into virtues and vices. Vices are seen

---

Focus on Transactions

Ethical Issues Raised by the Bhopal Disaster

- To what extent should multinational companies maintain identical standards at home and abroad, regardless of how lax laws are in the host country?
- How wise are laws that require plants to be staffed entirely by local employees?
- What is the responsibility of corporations and governments in allowing the use of otherwise safe products that become dangerous because of local conditions (e.g., proximity of residences in Bhopal)?
- Should certain kinds of plants not be located in developing nations?
- Was the true moral responsibility for Bhopal that of the Indian government, because of its local participation and management requirements (which reduce parent company control and the flow of technical expertise)?
- Did the parent company have an ethical responsibility to protect workers and the public? Does this responsibility have priority over the duty to earn a profit?
- Does the absence of sufficient government regulations excuse the parent company from any legal responsibility?
- Did the parent company have a social responsibility not to locate a plant in a foreign country where it did not have sufficient control? Should a parent company be held liable as parents are held liable for the damage done by their children?

---

4. *In re Union Carbide Corp. Gas Plant Disaster at Bhopal*, 809 F.2d 195 (2d Cir. 1987).
5. See generally Alasdair MacIntyre, *After Virtue: A Study in Moral Theory* (1984). See also Aristotle, *Nicomachean Ethics*.

as destructive to human relationships and include selfishness, deceptiveness, and unfairness. In contrast, Aristotle saw virtues as acquired moral traits that allow a person to act according to right and practical reason. This approach is useful in understanding the importance of corporate culture. Clearly, a corporate culture that emphasizes profit at any cost is not conducive to encouraging moral business virtues among the company's employees.

http://
For a fuller analysis of virtue ethics see Ethics Update: **http://ethics. acusd.edu.**

Ethics of Care

The **ethics of care**[6] approach focuses on the importance of preserving a web of relationships. A company's weighting of the benefits and costs of a decision should take into account certain concrete relationships. It is ethically appropriate, for example, for a company to place greater weight on the benefits and costs of a decision to its workers and community as compared to a foreign community. Utilitarian, deontological, and justice approaches to ethics emphasize the impartiality and equality of all parties. The ethics of care recognizes that we owe an obligation to some more than to others.

The potential influence of this approach can be illustrated by the typical case of plant relocation. The board of directors must decide whether to relocate a long-established and aging plant in its country to a more economically friendly location in a developing country. A utilitarian approach would justify the move purely on efficiency grounds. The rights perspective would recognize the right of an owner to move the business to maintain the financial viability of the company. Furthermore, under the employment at will doctrine prevalent in the United States, an employer owes no duty of continued employment to workers. Finally, because business and corporations are organized under the fairly enacted laws of a country, they are entitled to respect as artificial beings, and their fairly arrived-at decisions should not be subject to interference. In contrast, the ethics of care would recognize the special obligation a company has to its workers and community. Then the cost of the relocation to the company's workers and community may override the determinations made under the other ethical approaches.

Integrative Approach to International Business Ethics

The different ethical approaches to business decision making all offer insight into how to decide or act. An **integrative approach**, incorporating the best of each, is especially prudent in international business dealings, given the problem of ethical and cultural relativism. Such an approach would weigh the benefits and harms of a decision and compare them with alternatives (utilitarian). It would take into account whether a given action would disrespect the basic rights of persons (rights). It would also judge the distributive effects of the decision and see how the benefits and burdens are ultimately distributed (justice). Finally, it would weigh the impact of the decision upon those who have a concrete relationship with the company (care). The integrative approach would help ensure a fuller stakeholder analysis of international business decisions. The concerns of individuals (rights) and society (utilitarian) are considered both impartially (justice) and preferentially (care).

http://
Code of Ethics Online Project, Center for Study of Ethics in the Professions, Illinois Institute of Technology: **http://www.iit.edu/ departments/csep/ PublicWWW/codes.** Database with over 850 corporate, professional, and government codes of ethics.

---

6.   See generally Carol Gilligan, *In a Different Voice: Psychology Theory and Women's Development* (1982).

Such an approach can be found in many **corporate codes of conduct** and related initiatives. These initiatives have been dubbed "human rights entrepreneurialism," which is defined as "efforts by companies to compete with one another for consumers or investors through a commitment to human rights."[7] The primary focus of such entrepreneurialism is known as triple bottom line, which has been defined as "a business philosophy that focuses on economic prosperity, environmental quality, and social justice."[8] National governments and international organizations have also become involved in these efforts.[9] The number of such initiatives continues to increase in the United States, as does the number of companies involved in compliance and monitoring efforts.[10]

An examination of Unocal Corporation's code of conduct illustrates the uses of the various approaches to ethics. The reader can see in its mandates the influences of utilitarian, rights, justice, and virtue-based approaches to ethical decision making. Unocal's code (see Doing Business Internationally) states that the company "strives

---

Doing Business Internationally

Unocal's Approach to Ethical Decision Making

Unocal Corporation's Language	Ethical Approach
"Unocal believes that we have a responsibility to *society*, especially in relation to the *impact* of our operations."	Utility Calculation & Expanded Utilitarian
"All employees must respect the *dignity* of others."	Justice & Fairness
"We will respect *human rights* in all our activities."	Rights
"We recognize there are *no globally accepted legal or ethical standards* for business operations and activities."	Duties/Relativism
"[High standards of business and personal ethics] means behaving *honestly* and with *integrity* at all times."	Virtues

---

7. Ralph G. Steinhardt, "Litigating Corporate Responsibility," *Global Dimensions* 2 (2001).
8. Canadian Business for Social Responsibility, *GoodCompany Guidelines for Corporate Social Performance* 11 (2002).
9. One example of a private industry initiative is the Voluntary Principles on Security and Human Rights. Adopted in 2000, these principles establish a code of conduct for U.S. and British companies engaged in the energy and extractive industries. The principles were the result of consultations between U.S. and British-based oil, gas, and mining companies; nongovernmental organizations; corporate responsibility groups; labor organizations; and the U.S. and British governments. Examples of initiatives by international organizations include the International Labor Organization's Tripartite Declaration of Principles Concerning Multinational Enterprises and Social Policy (establishing voluntary standards with respect to employment promotion, equality of opportunity, treatment, security, training, wages, benefits, conditions of work, and industrial relations) and the Organization for Economic Cooperation and Development's Declaration on International Investment and Multinational Enterprises (establishing voluntary standards for employment, industrial relations, and environmental and consumer protection).
10. Forty-five percent of the *Fortune* global top 250 companies issue annual environmental, social, or sustainability reports, in addition to their financial reports, according to a survey completed by KPMG in 2002.

to achieve standards consistent with its Vision and Values in all its operations." In achieving this goal, Unocal promises to "be sensitive to the culture, context and needs of local communities and strive to make the community a better place to live and conduct business." At the same time, Unocal is "committed to complying with the laws, rules and regulations applicable to the conduct of our business wherever we operate." However, cross-cultural misunderstandings still limit the ability of multinational companies to fashion a code of ethics that can be internationally understood and applied.[11] Abstract terms, such as *human rights* or *bribery*, have various connotations that depend on cultural values and local customs. In fact, corporate codes of ethics are not as prevalent in many countries of the world.

Even when a code of ethics is implemented, cross-cultural misunderstandings can occur between managers in a host country and those in the home office. Unocal attempts to strike a balance between respecting the customs and laws of a host country and remaining true to its own code of ethics and that of its home country. The issue of cross-cultural morality as represented in the divergence between host and home country standards will be more fully addressed later in this chapter.

Codes of conduct have also been criticized for other perceived shortcomings.[12] They have been subject to criticism for failing to include important protections, such as the right to organize, or focusing exclusively on one issue, such as child labor, to the exclusion of other concerns. Another important shortcoming of many codes is their lack of implementation and independent monitoring of compliance. As a result, companies may succumb to the temptation to portray their actions in a more positive light than warranted by on-the-ground realities. The multitude of codes, programs, initiatives, and related efforts, each with its own scope and characteristics, has resulted in a cacophony of principles, which often defy standardization and comparative measurement. These inadequacies have fueled renewed efforts to draft mandatory codes of conduct governing transnational operations. One example in this regard is the French Parliament's adoption in 2002 of regulations requiring all French corporations to report on the sustainability of their social and environmental performance, including human resources utilization, community relations and initiatives, and labor standards.[13]

INTERNATIONAL

The Amoral International Businessperson

Nobel laureate Milton Friedman wrote in 1970 that the only social responsibility of business is to increase profits.[14] Under Friedman's analysis, corporations have no social conscience and should not be concerned with being good "corporate citizens." In his view, it is wrong for a corporation to spend its profits on social or charitable concerns because the practice of social responsibility applies only to individuals and not to corporations. It is the prerogative of individual stockholders to voluntarily spend their share of the corporate profits on behalf of social ends. From an ethical perspective, corporations need conform only to the **moral minimum**.

11.   See generally Warren A. French & John Granrose, *Practical Business Ethics*, 165–169 (1994).
12.   See Mark B. Baker, "Tightening the Toothless Vise: Codes of Conduct and the American Multinational Enterprise," 20 *Wisconsin International Law Journal* 89 (2001).
13.   See Law No. 2001-420 of May 15, 2001, art. 116. See also Decree No. 2002-221 of Feb. 20, 2002, art. 148-2.
14.   Milton Friedman, "The Social Responsibility of Business Is to Increase Profits," *New York Times Magazine* (1970).

The moral minimum, according to Friedman, is simply obeying the "basic rules" or laws of society in the pursuit of greater profits. What are the "basic rules" of society? Should the definition of basic rules be restricted to the mandatory laws of the country? Do you agree with Friedman that a corporation has no social conscience and should not promote desirable "social ends"?

One approach to reconciling these questions is the **myth of the amoral businessperson**. It asserts that good ethics is consistent with the pursuit of profits. Moreover, this school of business argues that good ethical business practices are necessary for long-run profitability. Francis Fukuyama, in his study of why some societies were more prosperous than others, isolated the notion of trust as the crucial factor.[15] Under his notion of trust, business is essentially a cooperative venture whose very existence requires ethical behavior. The rational self-interest depicted in Adam Smith's economic man results in uncooperative behavior. In fact, the nature of business shows that even people motivated solely by self-interest still have good reason to be ethical in their business dealings.

Merck, an international pharmaceutical company, sees its reputation for ethical behavior as a competitive advantage. Merck's code of ethics is a clear rejection of the amoral businessperson perspective. Instead, it views one of its functions as a corporation is to be a good corporate citizen. In short, profits are important, but not necessarily the determinant factor in corporate decision making. Merck's motto, as espoused by its founder, states: "We try never to forget that medicine is for people. It is not for profits. The profits follow, and if we remember that, they have never failed to appear. The better we have remembered that, the larger they have been." The next section focuses on the special problems of accountability in the organizational setting.

Organizational Ethics

Organizational ethics is a serious problem for the multinational enterprise. How do moral standards, developed in conjunction with personal will or responsibility, apply to corporations? Assuming that organizations are morally responsible, what individuals within the organization should be held accountable for violations of the corporation's moral duties? The traditional view is that those who *knowingly* partake in unethical actions should be held accountable. In the case of insider trading, for example, all those who knowingly give and use inside information are morally responsible. The problem is the fragmentation of responsibility in large organizations. An unethical action may be performed by many loosely connected actors. Some may simply be following organizational rules and may be unaware of the outcome of their contribution to the process; their ignorance may absolve them of moral responsibility.

The problem of **subordinate responsibility** was documented by Hannah Arendt in her 1963 work, *Eichmann in Jerusalem: A Report on the Banality of Evil*. Adolf Eichmann was a typical middle-level bureaucrat in charge of the trains carrying Jews to the death camps. His response to the morally reprehensible nature of his behavior was that he was "just following orders." Eichmann seemed to possess no ill will toward Jews but was incapable of thinking from the perspective of another

http://

Web sites discussing corporate social responsibility: Web Watch—Resources for Corporate Social Responsibility at **http://www.csreurope. org/default.aspx** or Business for Social Responsibility at **http://www.bsr.org** or Corporate Social Responsibility in Europe at **http://www.ebnsc.org.**

http://

Organizational Ethics: Ethics Resource Center at **http://www.ethics.org.** For an interesting avenue for exploring the ethics of a company's corporate culture scroll to "Ethical Effectiveness Quick Test."

http://

Database of 326 links on ethics including business and environmental ethics, see Markkula Center for Applied Ethics: **http://www.scu.edu/ ethics.** Click on "Ethical Links," then on "Browse Ethical Links."

---

15. Francis Fukuyama, *Trust: The Social Virtues and the Creation of Prosperity* (1995).

person. His "inability to think [ethically]" was as dangerous as someone acting with evil intent. Viewing an action from the perspectives of different stakeholders inside and outside the organization will sensitize corporate decision makers to ethically relevant issues.

In 1994, a group of business leaders introduced the **Caux Round Table Principles for International Business**, which blend the Western concept of the dignity of all human beings with the Japanese concept of *kyosei*—that a primary value of society is working together for the common good. The Caux Principles list the factors companies should take into account when making business decisions. Principle One makes it the responsibility of business to go *beyond shareholders toward stakeholders*. Businesses should take into consideration not only the well-being of their shareholders but also that of their customers, employees, suppliers, competitors, and communities.

Principle Two deals specifically with companies transacting business in a foreign country. It requires directing the social and economic impact of business at advancing *innovation, justice, and world community*. Businesses in foreign countries should create productive employment and raise the standard of living of its citizens.

Principle Three admonishes that it may not be appropriate for a company to enforce its rights strictly under the law. In the area of intellectual property rights, disclosure of some information demonstrates a concern for the long-term development of an impoverished country. Principle Three is closely related to Principle Four, which requires respect for applicable international and national rules of law but recognizes that some behavior, although legal, may have adverse consequences.

Principle Six makes *respect for the environment* a moral minimum for all international businesses. Environmental protection includes improving the environment, promoting sustainable development, and avoiding the wasteful use of natural resources.

Principle Seven targets bribery and corruption and their damaging effect on a country's development.

Finally, Section Three of the Caux Principles recognizes MNCs as "global corporate citizens" that are under an obligation to "contribute to such forces of reform and human rights as are at work in the communities in which [they] operate."

As previously noted, the assumption that corporations have social and environmental responsibilities has been recognized by international organizations such as the ILO and the Organization for Economic Cooperation and Development (OECD). Another example in this regard is the United Nations' Global Compact. Launched by Secretary-General Kofi Annan in July 2000, the Global Compact is a voluntary corporate citizenship initiative designed to "advance responsible corporate citizenship so that business can be part of the solution to the challenges of globalization." The Global Compact brings private industry together with U.N. agencies, labor, and civil society to support nine principles relating to human rights, labor, and the environment. The mainstreaming of these principles into daily business activities ultimately seeks to achieve the Secretary-General's vision of "a more sustainable and inclusive global economy."[16] One final example worthy of mention is the Global Sullivan Principles. Initially created by the Reverend Leon H. Sullivan, a member of the board of directors of General Motors Corporation, to promote racial equality and improve the quality of life of nonwhite populations in South Africa, the Sullivan Principles are based on the fundamental principles of nonsegregation, equal treatment, fair employment practices, equal pay for equal

http://
The Caux Round Table: **http://www. cauxroundtable.org.**

http://
For additional materials on environmental ethics, see Environmental Ethics at **http://www.cep.unt. edu/enethics.html** or International Society for Environmental Ethics at **http://www.cep.unt. edu/ISEE.html.**

---

16.   See United Nations Global Compact Organization, *What Is the Global Compact?* (2000).

work, the initiation and development of training programs, the promotion of nonwhites to managerial positions, and improvement of the quality of employees' lives outside the work environment.[17]

Environmental Ethics

INTERNATIONAL

As illustrated previously by the Bhopal tragedy, rapid economic development and industrialization may come at a price: harm to the local and world environments. It is important to balance the goals of industrialization with environmental protection. For the least developed nations, assistance from the developed world is imperative. Those countries that have successfully evolved from a poor country to a developed country or one considered an emerging economy must themselves ensure a healthy environment for their citizens. The Republic of Korea is one such country. Thirty years ago, Korea's gross domestic product per capita was comparable to poorer states in Asia and Africa. Korea is now the twelfth largest trading nation in the world, with a gross domestic product eighteen times that of its North Korean counterpart and an annual growth rate that averaged above 7 percent between 1999 and 2002. This growth has been brought about by rapid industrialization at the expense of the environment. In one of its largest industrial centers, there is a monument to the country's drive toward industrialization that bears the inscription: "Dark smoke arising from factories are symbols of our nation's growth and prosperity."[18]

http://

Envirolink: **http:// envirolink.org/ envirohome.html** provides environmental news and links.

Because of environmental neglect, environmental protection became an important political issue beginning in the 1980s. By 1997, more than 300 non-governmental organizations (NGOs) had been established, including the Korean Environmental Preservation Association and the Korea Action Federation for the Environment. Eventually, the government began to respond to the people's increased sensitivity to environmental concerns. The country had never had a separate agency assigned to the enforcement of environmental laws. In 1979, the government established the Environmental Administration (EA) to monitor environmental enforcement and duties. This was followed by an amendment to the Korean Constitution giving all citizens a right to a clean and healthy environment. Beginning in the 1990s, Korea began to model its environmental laws after those in the United States. This began with the enactment of the Basic Environmental Policy Act (BEPA) in 1990. At the same time, the EA was elevated to cabinet level as the Ministry of Environment.

The Korean experience shows the importance of public awareness of environmental problems and the instrumental role of NGOs in pressuring the government to act. Economic development and the emergence of strong democratic principles allowed public awareness to flourish. However, major shortcomings remain in Korea's environmental laws. Economic development has been successful in raising the Korean standard of living and in supporting the creation of democratic principles but at a cost to the environment. The current issue is whether a sufficient amount of the monies produced by its economic expansion will be used to more fully modernize its environmental laws.

The Korean experience is also relevant to other rapidly industrializing states. For example, in its 1997 report on the status of environmental protection in China entitled "Clear Water, Blue Skies: China's Environment in the New Century," the World Bank

---

17.   See Sullivan Principles Organization, Global Sullivan Principles (1977).
18.   See Hong Sik Cho, "An Overview of Korean Environmental Law," 29 *Environmental Law* 501 (1999). (This article was drawn upon in this chapter's discussion of Korean environmental laws.)

estimated that each year, 178,000 Chinese living in major urban areas suffer early death as a result of atmospheric pollution, primarily from coal- and biomass-fueled industrial operations. The World Bank further found that air pollution–related health impacts resulted in the loss of 7.4 million person work years annually. Water pollution has contaminated 52 of the 135 sections of urban rivers monitored in the country. Acid rain originating from coal-fueled industrial operations in southern and southwestern China may damage more than 10 percent of the surrounding land areas and reduce annual agricultural and forestry productivity by 3 percent. The World Bank estimates the cost of air and water pollution damage in China at $54 billion annually. It remains to be seen whether environmental damage will continue unabated or result in environmental protection efforts similar to the Korean model.

Host-Home Country Standards

A multinational enterprise is confronted with different standards in the various countries where it does business, and it must resolve whether to apply host or home country standards to a foreign operation. It can choose among three approaches. First, it may decide that a company is ethically and legally obligated to apply only host country standards to its activities within that country. One exception is made for home country laws that apply extraterritorially, such as the **Foreign Corrupt Practices Act (FCPA)**[19] and U.S. antitrust laws. This approach is closely associated with the moral minimum school of business ethics, in which complying with applicable law is a company's only moral imperative.

Second, the company may determine that an ethical company should apply the higher standards of its home country's laws and regulations, critical in areas where harm is a foreseeable consequence of the activity. This approach requires that the more stringent environmental, health, and safety regulations found in U.S. law should be used in foreign operations.

The third approach is a variation of the second. This approach asserts that, although higher standards are preferred, they may not be ethically required in all instances. This approach allows a U.S. company to take into account the stage of development of the host country. Using this approach, an ethical company must answer the following question: Will the application of the more stringent requirements of the home (developed) country be harmful to the host (developing) country or its development? An alternative formulation of this question is whether good consequences from a corporate presence in a country override the application of lower national standards. For example, can the economic benefits of a corporate operation in an impoverished country justify operation in a country that openly discriminates against groups within the population?

There are a number of ways to answer these questions. One utilizes ethical relativism. It holds that ethics is culture bound and thus the ethical determination of the host country should be honored. However, doing something Americans consider ethically repugnant is problematic for a U.S. company. A second way has been labeled the "righteous American" perspective, dictating the use of U.S. rules and standards in foreign business operations. The danger of such an approach is that it may diminish the importance of respecting local culture and

http://
"Ethical Considerations in International Start-up Companies" at Babson College—Business Ethics Program: **http://roger.babson.edu/ethics/entrepre.htm.**

---

19. The Foreign Corrupt Practices Act prohibits U.S. individuals, companies, and direct foreign subsidiaries of U.S. companies from offering, promising, or paying anything of value to any foreign government official in order to obtain or retain business. See 15 U.S.C. §§78dd-1-78ff (2000).

lifestyles. A third and more radical perspective is that international companies need not follow any ethical rules. Because their competitors may not do so, following high ethical standards would place them at a competitive disadvantage. This perspective was advanced by those critical of the Foreign Corrupt Practices Act.

Foreign Corrupt Practices Act

http://

Legislative history of FCPA at Justice Department Web site: **http://www.usdoj.gov/ criminal/fraud/fcpa. html.**

The Foreign Corrupt Practices Act (FCPA) was intended to have and has had a major impact on the way U.S. companies do business overseas. Since the passage of the FCPA, several firms convicted of bribing foreign officials have been subject to criminal and civil enforcement actions, resulting in large fines, exclusion from federal government contracts, and jail terms for employees and officers. The antibribery provisions of the FCPA make it illegal for a U.S. person or company to make corrupt payments to a foreign official for the purpose of obtaining business (see Comparative Law: FCPA Bribery Provisions and Focus on Transactions: Five Elements of a FCPA

COMPARATIVE LAW

Foreign Corrupt Practices Act: Bribery Provisions

(a) It shall be unlawful for any issuer of securities or for any officer, director, employee, or agent of such issuer or any stockholder thereof acting on behalf of such issuer, to make use of any instrumentality of interstate commerce corruptly in furtherance of an offer, payment, promise to pay, or authorization of the payment of any money, or **offer, gift, promise to give**, or **authorization** of the giving of **anything of value** to—(1) any foreign official, (2) any foreign political party or official thereof or any candidate for foreign political office, (3) any person, while knowing that all or a portion of such money or thing of value will be offered, given, or promised, directly or indirectly, to any foreign official for purposes of—

(A) influencing any act or decision of such foreign official in his official capacity

(B) inducing such foreign official to use his influence with a foreign government or instrumentality thereof, in order to assist such issuer in **obtaining or retaining business** for or with, or directing business to, any person;

(b) Exception for **routine governmental action**. Subsection (a) shall not apply to

any facilitating or expediting payment to a foreign official, political party, or party official the purpose of which is to expedite or to secure the performance of a routine governmental action by a foreign official, political party, or party official.

(c) **Affirmative defenses.** It shall be an affirmative defense to actions under subsection (a) that—

(1) the payment, gift, offer, or promise of anything of value that was made, was **lawful under the written laws** and regulations of the foreign official's, political party's, party official's, or candidate's country; or

(2) the payment, gift, offer, or promise of anything of value that was made, was a reasonable and **bona fide expenditure**, such as travel and lodging expenses, incurred by or on behalf of a foreign official, party, party official, or candidate and was directly related to—

(A) the promotion, demonstration, or explanation of products or services; or

(B) the execution or performance of a contract with a foreign government or agency thereof.

Five Elements of a FCPA Offense

Focus on Transactions

Who

The FCPA potentially applies to any individual, company, officer, director, employee, or agent of a company and any stockholder acting on behalf of a U.S. controlled company. U.S. parent companies may be held liable for the acts of foreign subsidiaries if they authorized, directed, or controlled the activity in question, as can U.S. citizens or residents who were employed or acting on behalf of such foreign-incorporated subsidiaries.

Corrupt Intent

The person making or authorizing the payment must have corrupt intent and must have intended to induce the recipient to misuse his official position.

Corrupt Act

The FCPA prohibits paying, offering, promising to pay, or authorizing to pay or offer money or anything of value.

Recipient

The prohibition extends to corrupt payments to a foreign official, a foreign political party or party official, or any candidate for foreign political office.

Business Purpose

The FCPA prohibits only payments to assist the firm in obtaining or retaining business or directing business to any person.

Offense). The FCPA also requires companies whose securities are traded in the United States to meet strict accounting provisions. These provisions require corporations to make and keep books and records that accurately reflect the transactions of the corporation and to devise an adequate system of internal accounting controls.

The international entrepreneur should always be cautioned against activities that involve the corruption of a foreign official. Most national laws outlaw the payment of bribes in order to obtain a service, contract, license, approval, or other regulatory consideration from a government official. Unfortunately, anticorruption laws in some countries are not enforced and bribes are openly solicited. **Transparency International**, a non-governmental group of business leaders and former government officials, is dedicated to promoting international business ethics and eliminating corruption. Its primary concern is the damage that bribery causes to the economic and democratic progress of developing countries.

http://
Transparency
International: **http://
www.transparency.org.**

Transparency International has used statistics to link corruption with lost development opportunities such as foreign direct investment. Nevertheless, the definition and practice of bribery vary significantly across cultures. For example, in the Indonesian concept of *sharism*, a bribe is shared and loses the character of a bribe in the traditional sense. The Indonesian bribe is best understood as an "express fee" to move requests to a higher level in order to get them processed more expeditiously. The amount is usually reasonable and somewhat standardized, and the money does not remain with the official who received it. Rather, it is shared with others in the office. It has been argued that, in Latin America, low ethical standards in politics have had a strong impact on individuals, companies, and the economic systems. "Deception, bribery, fraud, and dishonest negotiations have been means to succeed in private and public organizations in Latin American countries."[20]

INTERNATIONAL

---

20.   M. Cecilia Arruda, "Business Ethics in Latin America," 16 *Journal of Business Ethics* 1597 (1997).

The implication is that to level the competitive playing field, the foreign businessperson will need to make facilitation payments or bribes.

The pressure to give bribes is especially troublesome for the U.S. businessperson because of the severe civil and criminal penalties available through the FCPA.[21] The act applies extraterritorially to foreign activities of U.S. citizens and companies and to the foreign entities controlled by them. Furthermore, U.S. companies are liable for bribes made by its foreign agents. Actual knowledge of the bribery is not required. Prosecutors need only prove that the firm should have been aware of a high probability that bribery would occur. Incorporated within the act are stringent accounting provisions that require companies doing business abroad to maintain records and auditing controls that provide reasonable assurances that bribery is not occurring. A company is liable for violating the accounting provisions even if no illegal bribery has occurred. Violations of the statute can result in large fines and imprisonment for up to five years for an individual.

Because of the vagaries of the FCPA, Congress sought to clarify some of its provisions and meanings to provide additional guidance, and the **Foreign Corrupt Practices Act Amendments of 1988** added more detailed definitions of some of the crucial terms of the FCPA. Of foremost importance, it gave examples of expenditures that would be considered "routine government expenditures." Fees paid to an official for an action "ordinarily" done in the performance of official duties are exempted: obtaining permits, licenses, or other official documents to qualify a person to do business in a foreign country; processing governmental papers, such as visas and work orders; providing police protection, mail pickup and delivery, or scheduling inspections associated with contract performance or inspections related to transit of goods across the country; providing phone service, power, and water supply; loading and unloading cargo or protecting perishable products or commodities from deterioration; or actions of a similar nature.

The question remains as to what other payments will be allowed for "actions of a similar nature." The 1988 Amendments provide a possible solution to such uncertainty by allowing a private party to obtain an **Attorney General Opinion**. The attorney general, after consultation with appropriate U.S. departments and agencies and after obtaining the views of all interested persons through public notice and comment procedures, is required to establish a procedure to provide responses to inquiries concerning conformance of an action with the Department of Justice's enforcement policy regarding the FCPA. The attorney general is required to issue an opinion within thirty days after receiving a request. The crucial distinction for the determination of whether a payment is "routine" is that between a discretionary act and a clerical one. Therefore, the term "routine governmental action" does not include any decision by a foreign official about whether, or on what terms, to award new business. These types of decisions are discretionary in nature, and the payment would be considered a bribe.

The 1988 Amendments state that a minor payment made to "any employee of a foreign government or any department, agency, or instrumentality thereof whose duties are essentially ministerial or clerical" would not be considered a bribe under the FCPA. What is considered a minor payment remains to be determined on a case-by-case basis. As we are about to see, a Federal Appeals Court in *Lamb v. Philip Morris, Inc.*[22] ruled that the FCPA does not provide a private right of action. Thus,

---

21. The Foreign Corrupt Practices Act was amended in 1988 and again in 1998. See Foreign Corrupt Practices Act Amendments, Public Law No. 100-418 (1988). See also International Anti-Bribery and Fair Competition Act, Public Law No. 105-366 (1998).

22. 915 F.2d 1024 (6th Cir. 1990).

Lamb v. Philip Morris, Inc.

915 F.2d 1024 (6th Cir. 1990)

Guy, Circuit Judge. Since we find that no private right of action is available under the Foreign Corrupt Practices Act of 1977 (FCPA), we affirm the dismissal of the plaintiffs' FCPA claim. On May 14, 1982, a Philip Morris subsidiary known as C.A. Tabacalera National and a B.A.T. subsidiary known as C.A. Cigarrera Bigott, SUCS, entered into a contract with La Fundacion Del Niño (the Children's Foundation) of Caracas, Venezuela. The agreement was signed on behalf of the Children's Foundation by the organization's president, the wife of the then President of Venezuela. Under the terms of the agreement, the two subsidiaries were to make periodic donations to the Children's Foundation totaling approximately $12.5 million dollars. In exchange, the subsidiaries were to obtain price controls on Venezuelan tobacco, elimination of controls on retail cigarette prices in Venezuela, tax deductions for the donations, and assurances that existing tax rates applicable to tobacco companies would not be increased. In the plaintiffs' view, the donations promised by the defendants' subsidiaries amount to unlawful inducements designed and intended to restrain trade. The plaintiffs further assert that the district court erred in prohibiting them from pursuing a private cause of action under the FCPA.

Although the Foreign Corrupt Practices Act was enacted more than a decade ago, the question of whether an implied private right of action exists under the FCPA apparently is one of first impression at the federal appellate level. The Supreme Court recently explained that: In determining whether to infer a private cause of action from a federal statute, our focal point is Congress' intent in enacting the statute. Our central focus is on congressional intent, "with an eye toward" four factors: (1) whether the plaintiffs are among "the class for whose especial benefit" the statute was enacted; (2) whether the legislative history suggests congressional intent to prescribe or proscribe a private cause of action; (3) whether implying such a remedy for the plaintiff would be consistent with the underlying purposes of the legislative scheme; and (4) whether the cause of action is one traditionally relegated to state law.

First, the defendants contend, and we agree, that the FCPA was designed with the assistance of the Securities and Exchange Commission (SEC) to aid federal law enforcement agencies in curbing bribes of foreign officials. The authorization of stringent criminal penalties amplifies the foreign policy and law enforcement considerations underlying the FCPA. As such, individual private citizens are not part of a class for whose "especial benefit" the statute was enacted. Second, the availability of a private right of action apparently was never resolved (or perhaps even raised) at the conference that ultimately produced the compromise bill passed by both houses and signed into law. Third, recognition of the plaintiffs' proposed private right of action, in our view, would directly contravene the carefully tailored FCPA scheme presently in place. Congress recently expanded the Attorney General's responsibilities to include facilitating compliance with the FCPA. Because this legislative action clearly evinces a preference for compliance in lieu of prosecution, the introduction of private plaintiffs interested solely in post-violation enforcement, rather than pre-violation compliance, most assuredly would hinder congressional efforts to protect companies and their employees concerned about FCPA liability.

Finally, because the potential for recovery under federal antitrust laws in this case belies the plaintiffs' contention that an implied private right of action under the FCPA is imperative, we attach no significance to the absence of state laws proscribing bribery of foreign officials. We AFFIRM the district court's dismissal of the FCPA claim.

Case Update

The U.S. Supreme Court refused to grant certiorari and hear the case in *Lamb v. Philip Morris, Inc.* 498 U.S. 1086 (1991).

Case Highlights

- The main statutory purpose of the FCPA is pre-violation compliance and not post-violation prosecution.
- There is no implied private cause of action permitted under the FCPA.
- The Justice Department and the SEC are solely responsible for the enforcement of the FCPA.

businesspeople cannot bring a lawsuit against a competitor for obtaining a contract in violation of the FCPA. They are limited to bringing the alleged violation to the attention of the Justice Department.

Two other important definitional changes were made by the 1988 Amendments. First, the definition of "foreign official" was broadened to include "any officer or employee of a public international organization." Second, the "knowing" requirement for criminal liability under the FCPA was substantially modified. Actual knowledge of a bribe is not required. Instead, the government needs to prove only that a party had reason to know that some of its money would be used to bribe a foreign official. A party can be found guilty of bribery if a person is aware that another person is "engaging in such conduct, that such circumstance exists, or that such result is substantially certain to occur." When knowledge of the existence of a particular circumstance is required for an offense, such knowledge is established if a person is "aware of a high probability of the existence of such circumstance."

The issue remains what is evidence of "substantial certainty" or "high probability." The court in *United States v. Liebo*[23] found that evidence of knowledge of bribery can be proven circumstantially. It held that giving airline tickets as a "gift" to a cousin of a foreign official was sufficient to sustain conviction of a business executive when the foreign official's approval was necessary to obtain contracts. This case illustrates two provisions of the FCPA. First, third-party bribery is just as illegal as "direct" bribery. Second, the minor payment or expenditure exception is to be narrowly construed.

United States v. Liebo
923 F.2d 1308 (8th Cir. 1991)

Gibson, Circuit Judge. Richard H. Liebo appeals from his convictions for violating the bribery provisions of the Foreign Corrupt Practices Act and making a false statement to a government agency. The background leading to Liebo's conviction has all the earmarks of a modern fable. Between January 1983 and June 1987, Liebo was vice-president in charge of the Aerospace Division of NAPCO International, Inc., located in Hopkins, Minnesota. NAPCO's primary business consisted of selling military equipment and supplies throughout the world. Liebo flew to Niger to get the President of Niger's approval of a supply contract. He flew to Niger and met with Captain Ali Tiemogo. Tiemogo was the chief of maintenance for the Niger Air Force. Tiemogo testified that during the trip, Liebo told him that his company would make "some gestures" to him if he helped get the contract approved. When asked whether this promise played a role in deciding to recommend approval of the contract, Tiemogo stated, "I can't say 'no,' I cannot say 'yes,' at that time," but "it encouraged me." Following Tiemogo's recommendation that the contract be approved, the President signed the contract.

Tahirou Barke, Tiemogo's cousin and close friend, testified that in August 1985 he returned to Niger to be married. After the wedding, he and his wife honeymooned in Paris, Stockholm, and London. He testified that before leaving for Niger, he informed Liebo of his honeymoon plans, and Liebo offered to pay for his airline tickets as a gift. Liebo paid for the tickets, which cost $2,028. Barke testified that he considered the tickets a "gift" from Liebo personally.

Over a two-and-a-half-year period beginning in May 1984, NAPCO made payments totaling $130,000 to three "commission agents." The practice of using agents and paying them commissions on international contracts was acknowledged as proper, legal, and an accepted business practice in third-world countries. NAPCO issued commission checks to "agents," identified as Amadou Mailele, Tiemogo's brother-in-law, and Fatouma Boube, Tiemogo's sister-in-law. At Tiemogo's request, both Mailele and Boube set up bank accounts in Paris. Evidence at trial established that NAPCO's corporate president, Henri Jacob, or another superior of Liebo's, approved these "commission payments." To obtain foreign military sales

23. 923 F.2d 1308 (8th Cir. 1991).

financing, NAPCO was required to submit a Contractor's Certification and Agreement with the Defense Security Assistance Agency. In the Contractor's certification submitted in connection with the third Niger contract, Liebo certified that "no rebates, gifts or gratuities have been given contrary to United States law to officers, officials, or employees" of the Niger government. Following a three-week trial, the jury acquitted Liebo on all charges except the count concerning NAPCO's purchase of Barke's honeymoon airline tickets and the related false statement count.

Liebo first argues that his conviction for violating the bribery provisions of the Foreign Corrupt Practices Act by giving Barke airline tickets for his honeymoon should be reversed. First, Liebo contends that there was insufficient evidence to show that the airline tickets were "given to obtain or retain business." Second, he argues that there was no evidence to show that his gift of honeymoon tickets was done "corruptly." We believe that there is sufficient evidence that the airplane tickets were given to obtain or retain business. The relationship between Barke and Tiemogo could have allowed a reasonable jury to *infer* that Liebo made the gift to Barke intending to buy Tiemogo's help in getting the contracts approved. Accordingly, a reasonable jury could conclude that the gift was given "to obtain or retain business."

Next, Liebo contends that his conviction should be reversed because the court erred in the giving of jury instructions distinguishing a "gift or gratuity" from a bribe. Here, the court instructed the jury that the term "corruptly" meant that "the offer, promise to pay, payment or authorization of payment, must be intended to induce the recipient to misuse his official position or to influence someone else to do so," and that "an act is 'corruptly' done if done voluntarily and intentionally, and with a bad purpose of accomplishing either an unlawful end or result, or a lawful end or result by some unlawful method or means." We agree. A jury may infer a corrupt intent if a payment is given voluntarily or intentionally. AFFIRMED

Case Highlights

- Third-party bribery under the FCPA includes the use of agents to make payments to government officials and indirect payments to persons associated with a government official.
- Merely classifying something as a gift (as in *United States v. Liebo*) or a donation (as in *Lamb v. Philip Morris*) is not conclusive in assessing whether it constitutes a bribe.
- Direct evidence of actual intent to give a bribe is not required under the FCPA. Rather, intent may be inferred from circumstantial evidence.
- Despite the multimillion-dollar size of the government contracts, two airline tickets satisfies the "anything of value" requirement and is not considered a "minor expense."

The *Liebo* case illustrates the concept of **third-party bribery**. In that case, should Liebo have been concerned by the fact that the "commission agents" were related to the government official or that monies were being deposited into foreign bank accounts? Third-party bribery exists when a company hires another and has "reason to know" that a portion of the money would be used to bribe. A third party may be a joint venture partner or an agent. How can one determine if one has "reason to know" of a bribe made by a third party?

The type of circumstantial evidence that can be used to satisfy the "reason to know" requirement was illustrated in *SEC v. Tesoro Petroleum Corporation.*[24] In this case, a company was prosecuted even though it did not directly pay or authorize any bribes. It hired a foreign agent to obtain contracts from a foreign government. It was alleged to have been guilty of third-party bribery. The evidence included the payment of a commission considerably larger than the market rate, a disproportionately small contract price compared with the commission paid, and substantial secrecy, including the use of Swiss bank accounts. No written contract was entered into with the foreign agent. U.S. companies are expected to exercise *due diligence* and take steps to ensure they have formed a business relationship with a reputable partner or representative. These

24. 2 FCPA Rep. (D.D.C. 1980).

http://

Lay-Person's Guide to
the FCPA: **http://www.
usdoj.gov/criminal/
fraud/fcpa.html.**

parties should be investigated to determine if they are qualified, whether they have ties
to the government, the number and reputation of their clients, and their reputation
with the U.S. Embassy, local bankers, and other business associates.

The *Tesoro* and *Liebo* cases show that any company's FCPA compliance program
needs to address a number of red flags, especially where express and direct bribery
are not present. Red flags include paying a commission substantially higher than
the going rate, the existence of family or business ties between an agent and government officials, and commission payments made in a third country. Are there any
other red flags that may indicate the potential for third-party bribery? A company's
compliance program should require any potential agent to disclose past or current
ties to government officials, a report on the agent's character by way of reference
checks, and a carefully worded written agreement with the agent. The written
agreement should expressly state that the agent is working as an independent agent
and is not authorized to make any illicit payments on behalf of the principal. It
should contain FCPA-oriented clauses, including one that requires the agent to
comply with all laws and regulations of both the home and host countries.

Whether a U.S. parent company is liable for the acts of a foreign subsidiary
depends on the degree of ownership and control exerted by the parent over its
foreign subsidiary. The benchmark for degree of ownership is whether the U.S.
company is a majority or minority owner. If it is a majority owner, then it is vicariously liable for the violations of its subsidiary. If it owns less than 50 percent, then
it need only make a good-faith effort to have its subsidiary comply with the FCPA.
Finally, the FCPA does not distinguish between violations involving direct bribery,
third-party bribery, and bribery committed by a controlled subsidiary. In fact, the
1988 Amendments stiffened the fines for violations of any of the bribery provisions.
Currently, the FCPA provides for individual criminal fines of $100,000 and impris-
onment of up to five years. A company may be fined up to $2 million per violation.
The amendments also implemented an individual civil fine of $10,000, which
cannot be reimbursed by the company.

FCPA Accounting Provisions

Section 102 of the FCPA requires anyone covered by the act to "make and keep
records in reasonable detail that accurately and fairly reflect the transactions and
dispositions of assets." Failure to do so subjects that person or company to the same
types of fines as imposed under the bribery provisions. In other words, a company
can violate the FCPA without committing any acts of bribery. The problem with the
accounting requirements is that the original act did not define what is meant by
"reasonable." It does not provide a materiality standard to assist in the determination of what needs to be reported.

The 1988 Amendments defined *reasonableness* as that exhibited by the "prudent
person." Therefore, a company is not expected to show an unrealistic degree of
exactitude. Implied in the notion of the prudent person is the use of a benefit-cost
approach. Therefore, the accounting requirements are satisfied if the system of
internal accounting controls is sufficient to provide reasonable assurance that
(1) transactions are executed in accordance with management's specific authorizations, (2) transactions are recorded to permit preparation of financial statements
in conformity with generally accepted accounting principles, (3) access to assets is
permitted only with specific management authorization, and (4) accountability for
assets is reviewed at reasonable intervals. Under the original act, a company could

technically be held criminally liable for inadvertent errors. The 1988 Amendments limits criminal liability under the accounting provisions to those who *knowingly* falsify records.

OECD Convention on Combating Bribery

The magnitude of foreign bribery has resulted in some recent movement at the international and regional levels. In 1988, the U.S. Congress directed the president to commence negotiations in the **Organization for Economic Cooperation and Development (OECD)** to obtain agreement among its members on antibribery provisions. The OECD, a Paris-based organization with thirty member countries, was formed after World War II to help build a new economic system based on free international trade.[25] On February 15, 1999, the OECD Convention on Combating Bribery of Foreign Public Officials in International Business Transactions went into effect. The OECD Convention sets forth the following goals:

INTERNATIONAL

- To achieve the highest sustainable economic growth and employment and a rising standard of living in member countries, while maintaining financial stability, and to contribute to the development of the world economy
- To contribute to sound economic expansion in member countries as well as nonmember countries in the process of economic development
- To contribute to the expansion of world trade on a multilateral and nondiscriminatory basis in accordance with international obligations

The OECD provides a venue for countries to develop economic and social policies. Even though all countries have laws that make the bribery of officials a crime, only the FCPA is applied extraterritorially to the bribery of foreign officials. The relative success of the FCPA, the growth of the global marketplace, and the recognition of the economic costs to the bribe giver and to foreign economies provided the impetus for the OECD Convention.

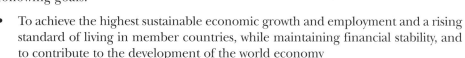
For information on the OECD Convention on Combating Bribery of Foreign Public Officials and its implementation: **http://www.oecd.org** then click on "By Topic" and then click on "Corruption."

Before the adoption of the OECD Convention on Bribery, a number of predecessor acts were adopted. In 1996, for example, the OECD passed a resolution on the tax deductibility of bribes to foreign public officials. Incredibly, countries such as France, Germany, Norway, and Denmark had previously allowed for the deductibility of bribes paid as a cost of doing business. To study issues of corruption, the OECD has established the Development Centre on Corruption. Its major focus is to assist developing countries in the fight against corruption.

INTERNATIONAL

The convention provides a framework and guidance to signatories regarding the steps to be taken to combat bribery of their public officials. It defines public officials broadly to include public agencies, public enterprises, and public international organizations. Like the FCPA, it adopts the extraterritorial approach to the international bribery of foreign government officials. It mandates that countries prosecute their nationals for offenses committed abroad. In the accounting area, it

25.   The thirty members of the OECD are Australia, Austria, Belgium, Canada, the Czech Republic, Denmark, Finland, France, Germany, Greece, Hungary, Iceland, Ireland, Italy, Japan, Korea, Luxembourg, Mexico, Netherlands, New Zealand, Norway, Poland, Portugal, the Slovak Republic, Spain, Sweden, Switzerland, Turkey, United Kingdom, and the United States. Along with the OECD members, a number of nonmember countries have also signed, specifically, Argentina, Brazil, Bulgaria, Chile, and Slovenia.

requires that each signatory enact "dissuasive civil, administrative, or criminal penalties for such omissions and falsifications in respect of the books, records, accounts, and financial statements" of companies subject to the signatory's laws and regulations regarding the maintenance of books and records, financial statement disclosures, and accounting and auditing standards.

The United States is a member of the OECD and is bound by the bribery convention. The 1998 Amendments to the FCPA recognize the OECD Convention on Combating Bribery. The amendments require the Secretary of Commerce to submit an annual report to Congress of the following information: (1) a list of the countries that have ratified the convention, the dates of ratification by such countries, and the entry into force for each country; (2) a description of domestic laws enacted by each party to the convention that implement commitments under the convention; (3) an assessment of the measures taken by each party to the convention during the previous year to fulfill its obligations under the convention; and (4) an explanation of the domestic laws enacted by each party to the convention that would prohibit the deduction of bribes in the computation of domestic taxes. Under item 3, foreign countries are to be evaluated by the degree to which they enforce their domestic antibribery laws, their efforts to promote public awareness of the evils of corruption, and their effectiveness in monitoring and enforcement.

U.S. Federal Sentencing Guidelines

The U.S. **federal sentencing guidelines**, which became effective on November 1, 1991, fundamentally altered the approach to organizational accountability. Previously, enforcement actions relating to crimes committed in the corporate context were directed only against the employees responsible for the act. Under the guidelines, the corporate or organizational entity can be held vicariously liable for the criminal acts of its employees. The guidelines also allow for the mitigation of fines for those companies that demonstrate **due diligence** in attempting to prevent misconduct. They provide for more lenient treatment of corporate executives who had implemented an ethics program.

For an excellent overview of the Organizational Guidelines go to the Web site of the U.S. Sentencing Commission: **http://www.ussc.gov/org guide.htm.** See "Overview" in the section on Organizational Guidelines and Compliance.

The importance of these guidelines has increased with a 1996 Delaware court decision that held that corporate directors could be personally liable for subordinates' wrongdoing if they had failed to establish an ethics program.[26] In short, the guidelines "reward organizations for establishing a legal and ethical compliance program."[27] By law, a company's penalties for violating the law are adjusted based on the degree of cooperation the company exhibits during the government investigation. The penalties can also be reduced if the company had an existing compliance program (see Focus on Transactions: Designing an Effective Compliance Program), along with exhibiting due diligence in policing the program. It is in a company's best interest to develop a compliance program in such areas as the FCPA, export regulations, environmental compliance, and health and safety laws.

---

26.   See *In re Caremark International, Inc. Derivative Litigation,* 698 A.2d 959 (Del. Ch. 1996).

27.   O. C. Ferrell, Debbie Thorne LeClair& Linda Ferrell, "The Federal Sentencing Guidelines for Organizations: A Framework for Ethical Compliance," 17 *Journal of Business Ethics* 353, 354 (1998).

Designing an Effective Compliance Program

Features

- Implementation of codes of conduct
- Custom-designed standards and procedures
- Compliance supervised by high-level managers or by an ethics officer
- Employee education publications and training
- Effective reporting procedure
- Development of monitoring and auditing procedures
- Infractions appropriately disciplined
- Annual reviews and amendments to program

- Reporting violations to appropriate authorities
- Compensation adjusted for effective compliance

Other Techniques

- Compliance programs required for suppliers and business associates
- Third-party verification: compliance audit performed by independent third party

The base or minimum fines to be assessed under the guidelines range from $5,000 to $72.5 million. The levels of base fines are based on two calculations: the seriousness of the offense and the culpability of the organization. The offenses targeted by the guidelines include customs violations, bid rigging, fraud, antitrust violations, transportation of hazardous materials, environmental crimes, commercial bribery, and copyright infringement. Culpability factors include history of past infractions and the rank of the employees within the company implicated in the wrongdoing. Specifically, the organization's culpability increases as higher ranking employees are involved. The guidelines also expressly recognize mitigating factors that can lessen the punishment: implementing an effective compliance program, self-reporting infractions, and cooperating with government investigators.

In the area of labor-management relations, an example of the use of an effective compliance system would be improving a company's global working conditions. The compliance program would specifically state the criteria to be addressed, such as the nonuse of forced labor, controlled use of child labor, the implementation of minimum health and safety standards, maximum working hours, payment of a "living wage," and antidiscrimination policies. Customized standards and third-party verification are essential to a compliance program with these types of objectives.

International Standards

Standards to ensure adequate levels of quality, labor, and environmental sensitivity in the production and marketing of goods and services are important and evolving. The wide variety of national standards in these areas produces a number of problems. First, it promotes the lowest common denominator in the production of goods. Companies that are motivated only by short-term profits will attempt to cut costs by searching for countries with the most lax environmental and labor laws. Second, a company seeking to market its products internationally has to contend with differing standards that may act as barriers to importing a company's goods into various countries. One solution to both problems has been the development of international standards, which can both reduce barriers to trade and ensure minimum levels of quality, labor standards, and environmental compliance.

A non-governmental organization established in 1947, the **International Organization for Standardization (ISO)**, is a worldwide federation of national standards bodies from 146 countries, and includes one representative from each country. The mission of ISO is to promote the development of standardization and related activities in the world to facilitate the international exchange of goods and services and to develop cooperation in the spheres of intellectual, scientific, technological, and economic activity.[28] International standardization is well established for many technologies in such diverse fields as information processing and communications, textiles, packaging, distribution of goods, energy production and utilization, shipbuilding, banking, and financial services. It will continue to grow in importance for all sectors of industrial activity for the foreseeable future.

The ISO has developed international codes for country names, currencies, and languages that have helped to eliminate duplication and incompatibilities in the collection, processing, and dissemination of information. As resource-saving tools, universally understandable codes play an important role in both automated and manual documentation. The ISO and many of its members are actively involved in consulting and training services, including seminars on the application of standards in quality assurance systems, technical assistance to exporters concerning standards requirements in other countries, workshops on consumer involvement in standardization, and conferences and symposia covering recent developments in testing and certification.

The most recognized international standard is the **ISO 9000**. The purpose of the ISO 9000 standard is to facilitate international commerce by providing a universally recognized and respected set of quality standards. The ISO 9000 standards apply to all types of organizations in all kinds of areas. The ISO provides guidelines for developing a quality management system. If ISO auditors like what they see, they certify that a company's quality system has met ISO's requirements. They then issue an official certificate and record the company's name in their registry. The company can then promote the quality of its products and services as ISO 9000 certified.

http://
International
Organization for
Standards: **http://
www.iso.ch/iso/en/
ISOOnline.frontpage.**

The ISO's most recent effort, **ISO 14000**, is a series of international, voluntary environmental management standards. The ISO 14000 series of standards effectively addresses the needs of organizations worldwide by providing a common framework for managing environmental issues. ISO 14000 standards require a company to establish an environmental management system (EMS), which enables an organization of any size or type to control the impact of its activities, products, or services on the natural environment. The benefits of installing an EMS include (1) assuring customers of a commitment to demonstrable environmental management, (2) maintaining good public and community relations, (3) obtaining insurance at reasonable cost, (4) reducing incidents that result in liability, and (5) facilitating the attainment of permits and authorizations. The standards in the ISO 14000 series fall into two major groups: organization-oriented standards and product-oriented standards. Organization-oriented standards provide comprehensive guidance for establishing,

---

28.　*ISO* is derived from the Greek *isos*, meaning "equal," which is the root of the prefix "iso-" that occurs in *isometric* (of equal measure or dimensions) and *isonomy* (equality of laws, or of people before the law), among others.

maintaining, and evaluating an EMS. Product-oriented standards are concerned with determining the environmental impacts of products and services over their life cycles and include the use of environmental labels and declarations. Product-oriented standards help an organization communicate specific environmental information to consumers and other interested parties.

The ISO has been successful in raising the level of awareness in areas of product quality and the environment. Its certifications under ISO 9000 and ISO 14000 provide both practical and ethical benefits to companies. From a practical perspective, products with these certifications are likely to find fewer obstacles in the area of importation. Most countries recognize the significance of the ISO certifications. From an ethical perspective, companies can use these certifications as evidence of their commitment to producing high-quality products and to being an environmentally conscious company.

The Council on Economic Priorities Accreditation Agency has used the ISO model to develop the **Social Accountability Standard**. The SA 8000 standard ensures that a company and its suppliers provide an equitable and safe workplace for their employees. The SA 8000 certification requires a company to restrict the use of child or forced labor, to respect the right of workers to unionize, to limit the workweek to forty-eight hours, to provide a safe working environment, and to pay a living wage that meets the basic needs of the workers. The SA 8000 allows companies to demonstrate a commitment to international human rights standards. Firms that wish to avoid bad publicity should adopt the SA 8000 standards as a preventive measure.

The activities of the European Union (EU) deserve special attention. EU requirements include the placement of a **CE mark** by the manufacturer on all regulated products. Importers who obtain the CE mark will be guaranteed access to the markets of all EU members. The CE mark asserts that the product meets the mandatory health, safety, and environmental requirements of the EU. A more recent development is the establishment of a voluntary mark known as the **EU Ecolabel**. Products without the Ecolabel may still enter the EU, but the label, if used, replaces the existing national equivalents. To obtain an Ecolabel, the manufacturer must show that its products are less harmful to the environment than other similar products.

INTERNATIONAL

The Ethics of Advertising

How a company markets its products internationally will play a major role in whether it is successful. Failure to take into account the differences in national cultural and legal approaches to advertising is a recipe for failure. Internationally, the development of supranational rules of advertising has been sporadic. The best example of a multinational effort is the International Consumer Protection and Enforcement Network. The United States and twenty-nine other countries have agreed to cooperate in resolving advertising disputes that cross national boundaries. At the regional level, the European Union has enacted two directives aimed at harmonizing European law on misleading and **comparative advertising**.[29] Before the 1997 Directive 97/55/EC on Comparative Advertising was enacted, such advertising was banned in Italy, Belgium, and Luxembourg and highly restricted in such

INTERNATIONAL

29. Directive 84/450/EEC (1984) ("Misleading Advertising Directive") and Directive 97/55/EC (1997) ("Comparative Advertising Directive").

countries as Germany and France. In contrast, in the United States more than 25 percent of all advertising is comparative.[30]

The 1997 Directive legalizes the use of comparative advertising that is defined as "any advertising which explicitly or by implication identifies a competitor or goods or services offered by a competitor." However, comparative advertising is permitted only if (1) it does not mislead; (2) it compares goods or services meeting the same needs or serving the same purpose; (3) it objectively compares one or more material, relevant, verifiable, and representative features of the goods and services; (4) it does not create confusion in the marketplace between the advertiser and a competitor or with the competitor's trademarks or trade names; (5) it does not discredit or denigrate the trademarks, trade names, goods, or services of a competitor; (6) for products with designation of origin, it relates in each case to products with the same designation; and (7) it does not present goods or services as imitations or replicas of trademarked goods or services.

The EU directive also requires the advertiser to demonstrate promptly the accuracy of its comparative claim. In contrast, the U.S. Federal Trade Commission requires only proof of a *reasonable basis*. The use of subjective features such as taste or feel is permitted in the United States. Under the EU Directive's requirement of objective proof, such comparative advertising is prohibited. Specifically, "Comparison on the basis of subjective factors, and opinion-based puffery are . . . prohibited [including] it seems . . . the use of objectively administered consumer preference tests." Thus, the U.S. exporter should not assume that its comparative advertisements are automatically legal under the directive, especially in countries that have traditionally prohibited such forms of advertising.

Professional Standards of International Advertising

http://

For a menu of ICC advertising codes:
http://www.iccwbo.org/ home/menu_advert_ marketing.asp.

The International Chamber of Commerce (ICC) has sponsored a number of ethical codes relating to international advertising and marketing, including codes regarding advertising practices, sales promotion, direct marketing, environmental advertising, sponsorship, and the ICC/ESOMAR International Code of Marketing and Social Research Practice. The ICC International Code of Advertising Practice was first issued in 1937 and was last revised in 1997. The main principles contained in the ICC code on advertising are summarized in the Comparative Law feature that follows. The ICC code applies to advertising in *any* medium for the sale of goods *or* services.

The introduction to the code describes it as a voluntary, self-regulating ethical code but noted its use in a legal proceedings: "The Code is designed primarily as an instrument of self-discipline but it is also intended for the use of the courts as a reference document within the framework of applicable law."[31] The underlying principle of the code is that "all advertising should be legal, decent, and truthful." Articles 3 through 17 provide some details regarding the meaning of "decent and truthful." Article 18 allots responsibilities to any professional advertising agency and any firm or company that advertises. Furthermore, anyone employed

---

30.   Paul Spink & Ross Petty, "Comparative Advertising in the European Union," 47 *International & Comparative Law Quarterly* 855 (1998). See also Ross D. Petty, "Advertising Law in the United States and European Union," 16 *Public Policy & Marketing* 2 (1997).

31.   ICC, *International Code of Advertising Practice*, Introduction (1997 edition).

ICC International Code of Advertising Practice

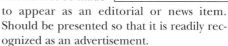

COMPARATIVE LAW

Article 2: Decency
Should not offend prevailing standards of decency.

Article 3: Honesty
Should not exploit consumers' lack of experience or knowledge.

Article 4: Social Responsibility
Should not condone any form of discrimination, play on fear, or play on superstition.

Article 5: Truthful Presentation
Should not mislead with regard to characteristics, value, terms of guarantee, intellectual property rights, or official recognition or approval and should not misuse research results.

Article 6: Comparisons
Comparison to other products should be based on facts that can be substantiated and should not be unfairly selected.

Article 7: Denigration
Should not denigrate any firm, organization, profession, or product.

Article 8: Testimonials
No use of personal testimonials or endorsements unless genuine, verifiable, relevant, and based upon personal experience or knowledge. Testimonials that have become obsolete should not be used.

Article 10: Exploitation of Goodwill
Should not infringe upon intellectual property or goodwill.

Article 11: Imitation
Should not imitate other advertisements or unduly imitate others' advertising campaigns in other countries.

Article 12: Identification
Should not be made to appear as an editorial or news item. Should be presented so that it is readily recognized as an advertisement.

Article 13: Safety and Health
Should not, without reason justifiable on educational or social grounds, contain any visual presentation or any description of dangerous practices or of situations that show a disregard for safety or health.

Article 14: Children
Applies to children defined as minors under applicable national laws. Should not exploit their inexperience or give unreal perception of the true value of the product. For example, the use of the word *only* should be avoided. Should not directly appeal to children to persuade their parents to buy the advertised products.

Article 15: Guarantees
Should not contain any reference to a guarantee that does not provide the consumer with rights additional to those provided by law.

Article 17: Environmental Behavior
Should not approve or encourage actions that contravene the law, self-regulating codes, or generally accepted standards of environmentally responsible behavior.

Article 21: Substantiation
Descriptions, claims, or illustrations relating to verifiable facts should be capable of substantiation.

Source: International Chamber of Commerce, International Code of Advertising Practice (1997), http://www.iccwbo.org/home/statements_rules/rules/1997/advercod.asp

within these companies or agencies shall be liable to "a degree of responsibility commensurate with their positions." This liability is levied against both the selling company and its advertising agency, along with responsible officers and employees.

Human Rights Considerations

That human rights standards are applicable to the operations of MNCs is beyond serious disagreement. The preamble of the Universal Declaration of Human Rights states that "*every individual and every organ of society . . .* shall strive by teaching and education to promote respect for [human] rights and freedoms and by progressive measures, national and international, to secure their universal and effective recognition and observance." The placement of these responsibilities upon MNCs recognizes that the economic aspects of globalization must also include social and ethical dimensions. Although international trade agreements and institutions, most notably the General Agreement on Tariffs and Trade and the World Trade Organization, provide a legal framework for the economic aspects of trade liberalization, human rights standards provide balance by creating a legal framework for the associated social and ethical dimensions. The language of the preamble of the Universal Declaration also recognizes the growing role of the private sector "to resolve problems of human welfare, often in response to conditions generated by international and national financial markets and institutions."[32]

INTERNATIONAL

As MNCs have become more aware of the social and environmental impact of their operations, so, too, have the states in which they operate. As a result, an increasing number of states are attempting to control the activities of MNCs within their boundaries. Examples of this emerging trend remain haphazard but present nonetheless throughout the developing world. For example, Belize, Brazil, and Ecuador have acted to slow the progress of deforestation, and Bolivia has committed $90 million to efforts to eradicate child labor. In Asia, Thailand has adopted legislation to protect women from sexual harassment and increased enforcement of prohibitions on child labor and environmental degradation, and Cambodia imposed criminal sanctions on illegal logging operations. In Nigeria, a country with a long history of human rights violations, the government has directed MNCs engaged in the petroleum industry to submit reports on pipeline maintenance and plans to combat pollution associated with their operations.

Increasing awareness of human rights is also a result of the evolving legal environment in the United States, which is best exemplified by the dramatic increase in litigation against U.S.-based MNCs pursuant to the **Alien Tort Claims Act (ATCA)**.[33] This litigation consists of three distinct types of cases. The initial category of cases alleges complicity by MNCs in violations of non-labor-related human rights, such as torture and arbitrary detention. The second category of cases alleges violations of labor rights by MNCs, such as efforts to discourage unionization and utilization of forced labor. The third category of cases consists of claims of environmental degradation. The following opinion of the Federal District Court in the *Doe v. Unocal Corporation* exemplifies recent trends in ATCA litigation against MNCs.

There has also been increased interest in the topic of socially responsible investing in recent years. Shareholders have attempted to address social and environmental issues through the introduction of corporate resolutions at annual shareholders' meetings. Alternatively, shareholders may choose to divest themselves of ownership of shares of companies whose practices violate human rights standards or who maintain facilities in countries that tolerate such violations. Although divestment by individual

---

32.   Maastricht Guidelines on Violations of Economic, Social and Cultural Rights (1997), § I(2).

33.   See 28 U.S.C. § 1350 (2000) (providing federal jurisdiction for "any civil action by an alien for a tort only, committed in violation of the law of nations or a treaty of the United States").

shareholders may have no appreciable impact, such action by institutional investors would undoubtedly cause consternation in the boardrooms of many MNCs.

A recent example in this regard is the investment policy adopted by the California Public Employees Retirement System (CalPERS). CalPERS is the largest public pension fund in the United States, with assets in excess of $150 billion. Adopted in February 2002 and implemented five months later, the CalPERS criteria rate investments in emerging markets according to an analysis of country and market factors.[34] Relevant country factors include political stability, transparency, and productive labor practices. Relevant market factors include liquidity and volatility, the regulatory and legal environment, investor protection, the openness of capital markets, and transaction costs. Although the impact of the CalPERS approach remains to be determined,

---

Doe v. Unocal Corporation
963 F. Supp. 880 (C.D. Cal. 1997)

Paez, District Judge. Doe plaintiffs, farmers from the Tenasserim region of Burma, bring this class action against defendants Unocal Corporation (Unocal), Total, S.A. (Total), the Myanma Oil and Gas Enterprise (MOGE), the State Law and Order Restoration Council (SLORC), and individuals John Imle, President of Unocal, and Roger C. Beach, Chairman and Chief Executive Officer of Unocal. According to plaintiffs' complaint, SLORC is a military junta that seized control in Burma in 1988, and MOGE is a state-owned company controlled by SLORC that produces and sells energy products.

Plaintiffs contend that in or before 1991, several international oil companies, including Unocal and Total, began negotiating with SLORC regarding oil and gas exploration in Burma. As a result of these negotiations, the Yadana gas pipeline project was established to obtain natural gas and oil from the Andaman Sea and transport it, via a pipeline, across the Tenasserim region of Burma. In July of 1992, Total and MOGE signed a production-sharing contract for a joint venture gas drilling project in the Yadana natural gas field. In early 1993, Unocal formally agreed to participate in the joint venture drilling project.

Plaintiffs allege on information and belief that the parties agreed that SLORC, acting as an agent for the joint venture, would clear forest, level ground, and provide labor, materials and security for the Yadana pipeline project. Plaintiffs also contend, on information and belief, that Unocal and Total subsidized SLORC activities in the region. According to plaintiffs, when Unocal and Total entered into the agreement by which SLORC undertook to clear the pipeline route and provide security for the pipeline, defendants knew or should have known that SLORC had a history of human rights abuses violative of customary international law, including the use of forced relocation and forced labor. Plaintiffs assert, on information and belief, that defendants Unocal and Total were aware of and benefited from, and continue to be aware of and benefit from, the use of forced labor to support the Yadana gas pipeline project.

Unocal moves to dismiss plaintiffs' complaint for lack of subject-matter jurisdiction.

Jurisdiction may be premised on the Alien Tort Claims Act (ATCA) which provides that the district courts shall have original jurisdiction of any civil action by an alien for a tort only, committed in violation of the law of nations or a treaty of the United States. 28 U.S.C. §1350. Thus, the ATCA requires (1) a claim by an alien, (2) alleging a tort, and (3) a violation of international law. Here, plaintiffs are aliens, and they assert tort claims. However, the parties dispute whether plaintiffs may assert claims based on violations of international law against the private defendants.

To the extent a state action requirement is incorporated into the ATCA, courts look to the standards developed under 42 U.S.C. § 1983. "A private individual acts under color of law within the meaning of section 1983 when he acts together with state officials or with significant state aid." Under the joint action approach, private actors can be state actors if they are "willful participants in joint action with the state or its agents." An agreement between government and a private party can create joint action. Here, plaintiffs allege that SLORC and MOGE are agents of the private defendants; that the defendants are joint venturers, working in concert with

---

34.   For a complete discussion of the CalPERS investment formula and its application, see generally Wilshire Associates, *Permissible Equity Markets Investment Analysis* (2002).

one another; and that the defendants have conspired to commit the violations of international law alleged in the complaint in order to further the interests of the Yadana gas pipeline project. Additional factual inquiry is not necessary. Plaintiffs have alleged that the private plaintiffs were and are jointly engaged with the state officials in the challenged activity, namely forced labor and other human rights violations in furtherance of the pipeline project. These allegations are sufficient to support subject-matter jurisdiction under the ATCA.

Moreover, the private actors may be liable for violations of international law even absent state action. [I]ndividual liability remained available, in the face of the 19th century trend toward statism, for a handful of private acts, including piracy and slave trading. The allegations of forced labor in this case are sufficient to constitute an allegation of participation in slave trading. Although there is no allegation that SLORC is physically selling Burmese citizens to the private defendants, plaintiffs allege that, despite their knowledge of SLORC's practice of forced labor, both in general and with respect to the pipeline project, the private defendants have paid and continue to pay SLORC to provide labor and security for the pipeline, essentially treating

SLORC as an overseer, accepting the benefit of and approving the use of forced labor. These allegations are sufficient to establish subject-matter jurisdiction under the ATCA.

Case Highlights

- The ATCA grants subject matter jurisdiction to U.S. district courts with respect to claims asserted by aliens that multinational corporations have committed torts in violation of internationally recognized human rights standards.
- Subject-matter jurisdiction exists pursuant to the ATCA when alien plaintiffs allege that multinational corporations acted in concert with host governments with respect to activities that result in violations of internationally recognized human rights standards.
- Subject-matter jurisdiction exists pursuant to the ATCA for a handful of private acts, including piracy and slave trading, even in the absence of state action.

---

the size of the investment fund and its resultant significance to investment markets cannot escape the attention of MNCs with operations in countries maintaining questionable human rights credentials.

Finally, there is a growing awareness of the link between social responsibility, including respect for human rights, and profitability. In addition to enhancing corporate image, advocacy of human rights promotes much needed integrity in national legal and fiscal systems. In turn, this integrity creates a secure investment environment for MNCs by discouraging arbitrary decisions, protecting intellectual property rights, and ensuring economic stability, thereby fostering an atmosphere conducive to future growth.

KEY TERMS

Alien Tort Claims Act (ATCA)
Attorney General Opinion
benefit-cost analysis
categorical imperatives
Caux Round Table Principles for
    International Business
CE mark
comparative advertising
conflict of cultural tradition
conflict of relative development
corporate code of conduct
cultural relativism

Declaration on the Right to
    Development
distributive justice
dominant considerations
due diligence
ethical relativism
ethics of care
EU Ecolabel
federal sentencing guidelines
Foreign Corrupt Practices
    Act (FCPA)
Foreign Corrupt Practices Act

Amendments of 1988
incommensurability
integrative approach
International Labor
    Organization (ILO)
International Organization for
    Standardization (ISO)
ISO 9000
ISO 14000
Kantian ethics
moral duty
moral minimum

moral right
myth of the amoral businessperson
Organization for Economic
    Cooperation and Development
    (OECD)

organizational ethics
Social Accountability Standard
standards
subordinate responsibility
third-party bribery

Transparency International
Universal Declaration of Human
    Rights
utilitarian ethics
virtue ethics

CHAPTER PROBLEMS

1. How can a parent company insulate itself from liability under the Foreign Corrupt Practices Act for acts of its foreign subsidiaries, affiliates, and partners? See H. Lowell Brown, "Parent-Subsidiary Liability Under the Foreign Corrupt Practices Act," 50 *Baylor Law Review* 1 (1998).

2. Devise a program for your company to ensure compliance with the Foreign Corrupt Practices Act. What is the importance of *corporate culture* to any such compliance program? See Daniel L. Goelzer, "Designing an FCPA Compliance Program: Minimizing the Risks of Improper Foreign Payments," 18 *Northwestern Journal of International Law & Business* 282 (1998). See also Patrick J. Head, "The Development of Compliance Programs: One Company's Experience," 18 *Northwestern Journal of International Law & Business* 535 (1998).

3. What is the difference between a bribe and a facilitation fee? Does it make a difference if payments or bribes are a crime in a foreign country, but laws against them are not enforced? If such payments are not considered illegal in a foreign country, is it proper to make such payments? From an ethical point of view, should the FCPA be read broadly or narrowly? Is giving a bribe a victimless crime? Does bribe giving affect the free market system? How? Do you believe that the FCPA places U.S. companies at a competitive disadvantage?

4. Your company has been trying for more than a year to obtain the assets of a formerly government-owned petroleum business. However, the approval process and review of the contract documents have been held up for months in the government bureaucracy. An official approaches your vice president of acquisitions and suggests that, if your company pays the expenses for a ten-day "negotiating" trip for himself and his family to Disney World and Miami, the approval process could be completed within one week. Should your company authorize the expenditure? Would your answer be different if it were a $200 "fee" to expedite the importation of your company's products into the country?

5. You have obtained a U.S. government grant to help train physicians in a developing country on new techniques for fighting AIDS. While working within the developing country's Ministry of Disease Control, you have uncovered evidence that certain monies received through the International Red Cross had been misappropriated by

certain officials in the ministry. The money was to be used to test and ensure the safety of the country's blood supply. Instead, it seems that the money was used to buy new ambulances for some of the country's hospitals. Should you report this transgression? Do you have any legal duty to report? Do you have an ethical duty to report? If so, to whom? Does the fact that such reporting may jeopardize your relationship with members of the ministry and the U.S. agency that hired you enter into your decision? Does the FCPA apply to this case? How can materials on whistle blowing be applied to this hypothetical incident? Do you have an obligation to obtain a sufficient amount of evidence before reporting?

6. Your company transfers you to a foreign subsidiary as an assistant manager of operations. The purpose of the assignment is to be trained by one of the company's "top managers." Soon after arriving, you discover that the manager had instituted an unusual accounting system. You have no real evidence, but the talk around the office is that the manager's success is due to his payments to his government connections. It is also rumored that some of the hidden transactions have profited the manager personally. The subsidiary remains one of the most profitable of your company's foreign operations. What do you do?

7. Lord Coke had this to say about bribery: "Though the bribe be small, yet the fault is great." Do you agree that the size of the bribe is unimportant in determining legal or ethical wrongdoing?

8. What are the elements of an effective ethics or environmental compliance program? How would you develop an ethics or environmental compliance program that would satisfy the dictates of the federal sentencing guidelines? See Paul E. Fiorelli, "Fine Reduction Through Effective Ethics Program," 56 *Albany Law Review* 403 (1992); Paul E. Fiorelli, "The Environmental Sentencing Guidelines for Business Organizations," 22 *Boston College Environmental Affairs Law Review* 481 (1995).

9. It is currently estimated that only 13 percent of middle managers posted overseas by U.S. companies are women, even though women make up nearly half of the middle managers at these companies. What do you think are the reasons for such an imbalance? At the same time, a poll of human resources executives shows that 80 percent of them believed that global work experience was essential for advancement. Can this be seen as the potential for creating a global glass ceiling? What can companies do to overcome such bias?

10. In 1971, John Rawls published his masterwork, *A Theory of Justice.* Simply stated, he equated justice with notions of procedural fairness. Rawlsian justice judges a decision or rule on whether it was arrived at through a process of procedural fairness. Thus, a decision is just or ethical if it was fairly made. A decision or rule is fairly made if each person affected by it is given the most extensive basic liberties compatible with the similar rights of others. Furthermore, social and economic inequalities are arranged to the greatest benefit of the least advantaged persons, and such inequalities are attached to positions open to all under conditions of fair equality of opportunity. Although Rawls's approach is targeted at political and not moral theory, its use in dealing with the least advantaged countries of the world may be productive. These rules are to be applied behind a *veil of ignorance,* where the parties are unaware of their status or positions. How can this approach be used to ethically judge dealings between developed and developing countries? If these rules were applied behind such a veil, then would such dealings be likely to result in more equitable transactions?

11. One of the negative by-products of the corporate ethics movement is a decrease in employee privacy. To ensure ethical compliance in the workplace and discourage misbehavior, employers have begun to monitor employee use of the company's e-mail system to discourage its use for personal purposes and as a vehicle of sexual harassment. Some companies have installed video cameras to monitor employee movements. How should companies balance their ethics monitoring with employee privacy concerns? Need they fully disclose to their employees the extent of their monitoring practices?

12. Unocal's Code of Conduct clearly prohibits the company from engaging in the conduct alleged by the plaintiffs to have occurred in the *Doe v. Unocal Corporation* litigation. However, did the alleged retention of the Burmese military to provide security for the Yadana natural gas pipeline project violate Unocal's Code of Conduct? Are the duties and obligations set forth in the code of conduct applicable to entities with which Unocal enters into agreements, such as the Burmese military? Should it be applicable to such contractors? Furthermore, Unocal's Statement on International Political Neutrality establishes that its participation in energy development projects "is based on resource potential, business economics and technical expertise—not political motivations." The statement consequently prohibits company or employee "participation, support and public or private alliances with foreign political parties, opposition movements or other political organizations engaged in the domestic political affairs of a foreign country." Does the security arrangement with the Burmese military as alleged by the plaintiffs violate Unocal's Statement of Political Neutrality?

INTERNET EXERCISES

1. Review the Corruption Perception Index published by Transparency International at **http://www.transparency.org/**.

2. Review the Web site of Sweatshop Watch for recent developments involving the problem of low labor standards in the international production of goods: **http://www.sweatshopwatch.org.**

A U.S. company must develop a strategy or business plan to establish a foreign business operation. A foreign business strategy encompasses activities like hiring foreign employees, establishing a foreign office, and acquiring foreign business assets, such as acquisition of companies or the incorporation of a subsidiary. The factors that affect planning foreign operations, like the risks of international business transactions, vary according to the country, type of industry, size of operation, and legal issues such as foreign regulations and taxation.

As discussed in Chapter One, the first major decision is whether entry into a foreign country should be through a direct or indirect presence. The most indirect form of foreign entry is exporting goods or licensing technology. These transactions can involve little direct contact or the use of surrogates or agents within the country. A company that wants to do more than just sell to a foreign importer but does not want a direct presence within a country will often hire agents or independent contractors to help market, sell, and distribute its products. These agents are generally hired as independent contractors and not as direct employees. The

Chapter 3

Strategies for International Business

next two sections review the ways a foreign company can conduct business in the United States and the ways a U.S. company can operate internationally.

Strategies for Doing Business in the United States

The various forms of doing business in the United States are organized and controlled under state laws. Although there are technical variations among such laws, the common forms of doing business are similar in all the states. A foreign company planning to do business in the United States may do so through a **branch office**. Generally, the only formal procedure required of a branch is to register to do business with the appropriate state regulatory agency. The branch is considered simply an extension of the foreign corporation, and the corporation is liable for the debts of the branch under U.S. common law.

Alternatively, the foreign corporation may elect to operate one of a number of independent entities recognized under state laws, including the joint venture, general partnership, limited partnership, corporation, and limited liability company. The **joint venture** is a hybrid that forms either a partnership or a corporation. A joint venture can be loosely defined as an association between two or more parties with an agreement to share the profits and often the management of a particular project. In the United States, the joint venture is commonly treated as a partnership, especially for tax purposes. In this common method for international business investment, a foreign company seeks out a domestic company in order to penetrate the host country's market. The advantages of joint venturing will be discussed in greater detail later in the chapter.

http://

For general information
on U.S. business law,
including the laws of
partnership and corpo-
rations, see "Business
Law" at U.S. Small
Business Administration:
**http://www.
businesslaw.gov.**

http://

Materials on corporate
law: FindLaw Corporate
Law at **http://www.
findlaw.com/01topics/
08corp** or Hieros
Gamos Corporate Law
at **http://www.hg.org/
corp.html** or Cornell at
**http://www.law.cornell.
edu/topics/
corporations.html.**

In a **general partnership**, all the partners are jointly and severally liable for partnership debts. Unlike a joint venture, a partnership mandate is more flexible and ongoing. Whereas a joint venture is established to accomplish a narrow business objective, a general partnership typically envisions a long-term evolution of the business, including the development of goals not contemplated by the partners at the time of inception. In a partnership, as in the partnership-style joint venture, the losses and profits of the business *pass through* directly to the partners for purposes of taxation. This avoids the problem of double taxation most closely associated with the corporation.

The **limited partnership** couples the pass-through feature of a general partnership with the concept of limited liability found in a corporation. Limited liability is achieved through the division of the partners into two classes: general and limited partners. The general partner has unlimited liability, but the limited partners are liable only up to the amount of their capital contributions. A limited partnership, however, is a statutorily created mode of doing business. Unlike the general partnership, which originates in common law, the limited partnership must fulfill a state's limited partnership statute requirements. In contrast, the general partnership is formed simply through the agreement, express or implied, of the partners. The benefit of limited liability comes at a price; state law requires that a limited partner be a silent or passive investor. A limited partner who becomes involved in the day-to-day management of the business acquires by law the status of a general partner and, as a general partner, incurs unlimited liability for the debts of the partnership.

A more recent development is the **limited liability company (LLC)**. Established under specific state statutes, these entities take various forms. The greatest advantage of LLCs is that they provide limited liability without the formalism of the corporation. In some instances, an LLC may be an alternative to a joint venture or limited partnership, offering both the flexibility of a partnership and the limited liability of the corporation. Types of limited liability companies vary by state law.

The most common form of doing business for the foreign investor is the **corporation**, whereby an investor purchases shares in an existing or newly formed entity. As a shareholder, the investor's liability is limited to the amount paid for the shares of stock. The corporation is created when the shareholders file a *certificate of incorporation* with one of the fifty secretaries of state. In the past, Delaware was the most popular state of incorporation because of its liberal corporate laws. Today, most states have simplified their laws to make it easier for corporations to conduct business. Once incorporated, a business is required to file annual reports or pay state franchise taxes. Most states do not differentiate between corporations owned by residents or by foreign nationals. Once a corporation receives its charter from the state, other parties are prohibited from using its corporate name when doing business in that state.

Strategies for Entering a Foreign Market

A U.S. company that wants a direct foreign presence has a number of options, including establishing a representative office, beginning a joint venture with an established company, setting up a branch office, or forming a full-scale foreign subsidiary. Forming a foreign subsidiary requires deeper business and legal involvement than establishing a representative office. A **representative office** is established for limited purposes, such as undertaking market analysis and product promotion.

Host country laws dictate what types of activities a representative office may pursue. For example, a representative office may obtain leads of potential customers but cannot negotiate or enter into contracts, tasks reserved to the parent company in the home country. The advantage of operating a representative office is that the company is not considered to be *doing business* in the foreign country, so it avoids host country regulations and is not subject to foreign taxation. Such offices are relatively inexpensive and the easiest to establish.

To have a full-time presence and transact business, a company needs to establish an operation to do business within a foreign country. The joint venture vehicle allows a company to share expertise and risks with a **local partner**, who often brings benefits such as customer and distribution networks, existing contacts with important government officers, and knowledge of the host country's legal and regulatory system. A joint venture may also be the only option in a country that prohibits wholly owned foreign subsidiaries. A joint venture is usually a partnership but can also be undertaken by establishing a corporation or limited liability company, with each party owning a portion of the equity. These types of enterprises are referred to as **equity joint ventures**.

A third option, in which the parties agree to perform certain tasks without forming a new entity, is a **contractual joint venture**. In 1988, China enacted the Law on Chinese-Foreign Contractual Joint Ventures. Last amended in 2000, this law allows the parties to operate as separate companies and may not require a minimum capital contribution from the foreign investor under certain circumstances. Factors like taxation, liability, and host country commercial and corporate laws, however, influence the form of the joint venture. China has enacted separate laws to regulate different types of joint ventures. Equity joint ventures are governed by the Chinese-Foreign Equity Joint Venture Law, most recently amended in 2001. This law requires the establishment of a Chinese limited liability company, for which the foreign participant must provide a minimum of 25 percent of the capital. In addition, the ownership rights of the foreign investor are transferable but only with the consent of the other parties to the equity joint venture. The parties to a joint venture will need to research whether the joint venture can be formed under U.S. law, the law of the host country, or the laws of a third country, as well as which will be the most favorable.

Another means of entering a foreign market is the **foreign subsidiary** or **affiliate**. A company may elect to establish an independent foreign subsidiary or an affiliate. An affiliate is a business enterprise located in one country that is directly or indirectly owned or controlled by a company located in another country. Ownership of 10 percent of its voting securities is generally considered "control." The subsidiary is generally established under the laws of the foreign country and pays taxes on the profits it earns in the foreign country, but the parent company's income is not subject to host country taxation. Companies with foreign subsidiaries often attempt to reduce the enterprise's overall tax liability through **transfer pricing**, in which one subsidiary of an enterprise charges another for goods or services. Companies manipulate these transfer prices to move profits to countries with lower tax rates. Foreign subsidiaries may be heavily regulated in some countries; some host countries require that a portion of the subsidiary be locally owned and that the board of directors include nationals of the host country. In some countries, the establishment of a wholly owned foreign subsidiary may not be possible.[1] Also,

http://

Chinese Foreign Equity Joint Venture Law: **http://www.qis.net/ chinalaw/prclaw11.htm.**

INTERNATIONAL

http://

http://www.state.gov: For tips and general information on doing business in foreign countries click on "Countries and Regions" and then click on "Country Background Notes."

---

1.   For example, Chinese Law Concerning Enterprises with Sole Foreign Investment permits such an enterprise only
     if it uses advanced technologies or markets its products outside China.

http://
Information and links
about market access and
foreign government
regulations: **http://www.
mac.doc.gov.**

INTERNATIONAL

foreign corporation laws may not be as friendly as U.S. law in limiting the liability of the parent company. In certain countries, a creditor is allowed to *pierce the corporate veil* more easily to sue the parent company. The crucial advantages of a foreign subsidiary over the branch office are that the parent company has limited liability and is able to carry on a broad range of business activities.

No matter what type of enterprise is selected, joint venture or foreign subsidiary, a company must submit to a vigorous approval process in countries like China. China has a dual approval process, whereby the enterprise or venture must first be approved by the Minister of Foreign Trade and Economic Cooperation and then registered with the Administration of Industry and Commerce, which reviews financing and debt-equity guidelines. Upon approval, the foreign enterprise is issued a business license to conduct business in China. The use of a Chinese consultant familiar with the approval process and having *quanxi* (connections) with central and local government authorities is essential.

Foreign Corporation Law

The roles and duties played by different constituent groups, such as the shareholders and board of directors, vary under foreign corporate laws (see Comparative Law: Corporate Governance in the United States, Germany, and Japan). Japanese

---

COMPARATIVE LAW

Corporate Governance in the United States, Germany, and Japan[2]

Corporate Goals and Objectives

What differentiates the governance structures of the United States, Japan, and Germany are the roles the various stakeholders play in monitoring and controlling the firm. For example, in the United States, the primary stakeholder has been the shareholder, whereas in Japan and Germany labor historically has also had a relatively strong voice. The American Law Institute asserts that a corporation's primary objective should be "corporate profit and shareholder gain." Traditionally, Japanese corporations have operated to benefit a small group of owners, rather than to maximize shareholder value. Its corporate governance system emphasizes the protection of employees and creditor interests as much or more than shareholder interests. Management has had few direct incentives to enhance share-

holder value. German law clearly defines the goals of German corporations. Its business corporation statute states that "the managing board, on its own responsibility, is to manage the corporation for the good of the enterprise and its employees, the common weal of society, and the State." German law dictates that managers operate the firm for the benefit of multiple stakeholders, not just shareholders.

Management Structure

In the United States, shareholders typically elect directors at annual shareholder meetings. Labor is rarely involved in the corporate governance system. Japan, like the United States, uses a single-tier board structure. Traditionally, Japanese boards have been large, with some of the largest firms having more than fifty directors. Most typically, board members are current or former senior and middle management. The mixing of

continued

---

2. Excerpted from Timothy L. Fort and Cindy A. Schipani, "Corporate Governance in a Global Environment: The Search for the Best of All Worlds," 33 *Vanderbilt Journal of Transnational Law* 829 (2000).

Corporate Governance in the United States, Germany, and Japan (*continued*)

management and director roles in Japanese corporate governance is in stark contrast to the separate, independent roles encouraged in U.S. corporate governance law. The system used in Germany is significantly different from those in either the United States or Japan. In large German firms, employees select half the board of directors. This practice is known as *codetermination*. Modern German corporations with more than 500 employees have a two-tiered board structure. A supervisory board performs the strategic oversight role, while a management board performs the operational and day-to-day management role. In firms with more than 2,000 employees, employees must comprise half of the supervisory board; shareholder representatives make up the other half. Supervisory boards also may include representatives of firms with whom the corporation has vertical relationships, such as suppliers and customers. The supervisory board appoints and oversees the management board. The German board structure thus functions to explicitly represent the interests of nonshareholder constituents and ensures that major strategic decisions are not made without the consent of employees and their representatives.

corporate law is strikingly similar to U.S. corporate law: A single board of directors is elected by the shareholders, and the directors owe the traditional duties of loyalty and care to the corporation and its shareholders. Securities laws in Japan, however, do not play the central role that they play in the United States. Bank financing, not security offerings, remain the fundamental vehicle for financing corporate expansion in Japan. Because corporate capital is largely privately funded, the need for disclosure, as mandated under U.S. securities laws, is not as important in Japan as it is in the United States.

INTERNATIONAL

In contrast, the corporate laws of Germany,[3] China, and France reflect fundamentally different views of the objectives of the board of directors and the role of the corporation in society. Germany mandates a two-tiered board of directors: the supervisory board and the management board. The employees and the shareholders each elect half of the supervisory board, which then appoints the management board members. The **supervisory board** oversees the management board and approves the financial statements and major corporate decisions. The **management board** carries out the strategic objectives established by the supervisory board and makes the day-to-day decisions in managing the company. The German corporate structure places a primary emphasis on the interests of the employees and a secondary emphasis on shareholder interests.

INTERNATIONAL

In China, shareholders' interests are the dominant vehicle for corporate decision making. Unlike in the United States, shareholder power pervades the day-to-day operation of the company. The Chinese Company Law requires large companies to establish a **supervisory committee** of shareholders that has the power to investigate and supervise the financial affairs of the company. Furthermore, shareholders are authorized to pass their own resolutions that must be implemented by the board of directors. Business plans and investment decisions are formulated by the board of directors but must be submitted to the shareholders for approval.

INTERNATIONAL

3. It is important to note that there are no European Union directives that require any particular corporate form. Corporate law is found solely in the individual national laws of the members of the EU.

INTERNATIONAL

French corporate law is unique because it provides alternate governance structures for the public corporation, or S.A.[4] The articles of incorporation may select a management structure that is headed by a U.S.-style board of directors or one with a management committee or executive board and a **shareholders' council**. The latter form acts in many ways like the two-tiered system in Germany. The shareholders' council possesses most of the powers that are delegated to the board of directors under U.S. corporate law.

Piercing the Corporate Veil

U.S. corporate law and practice is considered to be corporation friendly. The limitation on personal liability offered by the corporate form is highly guarded by U.S. courts. The formation of a corporation with minimal capitalization is sufficient to shield the corporate shareholders from personal liability for the debts and obligations of the corporation. This protection is given whether the shareholder is an individual or a parent corporation. Thus, a corporation may use an independent incorporated subsidiary to shield itself from liability. However, U.S. law does allow a court to disregard the corporate form through the doctrine of **piercing the corporate veil**. If the corporate form is considered a sham, U.S. courts may allow the shareholders to be sued personally for the debts of the disregarded corporation.

The case of *Raven Metal Products v. McGann*[5] illustrates some of the factors a court assesses to decide if a corporate entity should be disregarded and the entity's owners exposed to personal liability. Raven Metal brought suit for breach of contract for nonpayment for materials delivered to Northeast Trailer, Inc. Brenda McGann was the sole director, officer, and shareholder of Northeast Trailer. Northeast held no corporate meetings, and no corporate records existed. McGann used corporate funds to pay personal expenses. The court stated that there are two general elements that must be met to pierce the corporate veil. First, the owners must exercise complete domination of the corporation in respect to the transaction being attacked. Second, such domination is used to commit a fraud or wrong against the plaintiff. The court refused to pierce the corporate veil because there was no wrongful act, and despite the domination of McGann over Northeast, there was no evidence of actual fraud. Furthermore, the court noted that the corporate money used to pay personal expenses was not in excess of what McGann's services were worth to the corporation. This case illustrates the U.S. view in favor of upholding the limited liability of the corporate form.

The *Finnish Fur Sales v. Shulof* case shows that the U.S. presumption against piercing the corporate veil is not held as strongly in other countries. The case also introduces the bill of exchange instrument and the law of negotiable instruments as separate vehicles of liability. This area of law will be more fully explored in Chapter Eleven, International Trade Finance.

Another method used to pierce the corporate veil is **enterprise liability**. Although this theory has been widely rejected by U.S. courts, some foreign courts recognize it. Enterprise liability looks at affiliated companies as an enterprise to be held liable individually or as a whole. A parent company may be held liable for the acts of its subsidiaries, or a franchisor may be held liable for the acts of its

---

4. S.A. stands for *Sociedad Anonyme*.
5. 699 N.Y.S.2d 503 (N.Y. Sup. Ct.1999).

Finnish Fur Sales Co., Ltd. v. Juliette Shulof Furs, Inc., George Shulof and Juliette Shulof

770 F. Supp. 139 (S.D.N.Y. 1991)

Leisure, District Judge. This is an action to collect sums allegedly owed in connection with furs purchased at two auctions in Vantaa, Finland. Plaintiff Finnish Fur Sales Co., Ltd. ("FFS"), asserts its claim of failure to pay for and clear 2,469 fox pelts against defendants Juliette Shulof Furs, Inc. ("JSF"), and George Shulof. Plaintiff Okobank Osuuspankkien Keskuspankki Oy ("Okobank") asserts its claim of failure to honor a bill of exchange against defendants JSF and George Shulof. FFS is a limited company organized under Finnish law, which sells fur pelts raised by Finnish breeders at public auctions held several times each year. The auctions are conducted under certain Conditions of Sale ("Conditions"), which are listed in the auction catalogue, a copy of which is given to each prospective bidder in advance of the auction. A one-page English translation of the Conditions appears on the inside cover of the catalogue.

JSF is a New York corporation that has conducted a fur business for approximately 15 years. George Shulof, an officer of JSF, has been in the fur business since 1935. Mr. Shulof attended the FFS auctions held in Vantaa, Finland, in January and May 1987. He purchased over $500,000 worth of skins at the January auction, and some $700,000 worth of skins at the May auction. FFS claims that, in addition to the liability of JSF, Mr. Shulof is personally liable for this debt, based on Finnish law, the custom and practice of the fur trade, and the provisions of section 4 of the Conditions. Section 4 provides: "Any person bidding at the auction shall stand surety as for his own debt until full payment is made for purchased merchandise." George Shulof denies any personal liability on the grounds, *inter alia*, that the provision is unenforceable under both New York and Finnish law. JSF made a cash down payment and accepted a bill of exchange (the "Bill of Exchange") for $30,328.39. According to plaintiffs, in January 1989, Okobank became holder in due course of the Bill of Exchange, which was presented for collection on or about February 7, 1989, at Bank Leumi in New York, but was dishonored. The Bill of Exchange was signed "Juliette A. Shulof" above the printed name "Juliette Shulof Furs Inc."

Liability of George Shulof

In this case, application of New York choice of law analysis is required. Section 15 of the Conditions provides that "these conditions are governed by Finnish law." Choice of law clauses are routinely enforced by

the courts of this Circuit "if there is a reasonable basis for the choice." Finland's contacts with the transactions at issue are substantial, rendering the choice of law clause enforceable unless a strong public policy of New York is impaired by the application of Finnish law. Mr. Shulof also argues that, under New York law, Section 4 of the Conditions would be invalid as contravening New York's policy against imposing personal liability on corporate officers.

It is also well-established under New York law, as under Finnish law, that "the owner of property offered for sale at auction has the right to prescribe the manner, conditions and terms of sale. The conditions of a public sale, announced by the auctioneer at the time and place of the sale, are binding on the purchaser, whether or not he knew or heard them." In the case at bar, George Shulof contends that the provisions of Section 4 are unconscionable and would not be enforced by a New York court. Nevertheless, a perusal of the Conditions reveals that their entire text is only a single page long, and that all of the Conditions, including Section 4, are printed in the same size print, which, although small, is legible. Under these circumstances, it seems unlikely that a New York court would refuse to enforce Section 4 in an arm's-length commercial transaction involving a sophisticated defendant accustomed to bidding at fur auctions.

Given the lack of a clear conflict with either New York law or policy, this Court concludes that a New York court would apply Finnish law to the issue before the Court. The Court also notes that a similar result has often been reached under New York conflicts rules even in the absence of a contractual choice of law clause. Thus, Mr. Shulof must be held jointly and severally liable with JSF for any damages owed to FFS for the furs purchased at its 1987 auctions.

Liability of Juliette Shulof

The parties agree that New York law governs the issue of the liability of Juliette Shulof on the Bill of Exchange, which was executed and payable in New York. The parties do not dispute that the Bill of Exchange is a negotiable instrument, and therefore subject to the provisions of Article 3 of the Uniform Commercial Code, as adopted by the state of New York. The relevant section of the Code is § 3-403, which governs signatures by authorized representatives. Under subsection (2), an authorized representative who signs his own name to an instrument:

(a) is personally obligated if the instrument neither names the person represented nor shows that the representative signed in a representative capacity;

(b) except as otherwise established between the immediate parties, is personally obligated if the instrument names the person represented but does not show that the representative signed in a representative capacity, or if the instrument does not name the person represented but does show that the representative signed in a representative capacity.

An Official Comment to this section offers examples of signatures and the legal implication of each type of signature. An authorized representative will not be personally bound by the following: a signature in the name of the represented party; "Peter Pringle by Arthur Adams, Agent"; or "Arthur Adams, Agent" (assuming that the principal is named in the instrument). In the case of a signature such as "Arthur Adams, Agent," or "Peter Pringle Arthur Adams," parol evidence may be offered in litigation between the immediate parties to prove representative capacity.

In the case at bar, Mrs. Shulof signed as "Juliette A. Shulof" above a typed name of "Juliette Shulof Furs Inc.," which had been typed in by the preparer of the instrument, FFS. The cases interpreting signatures of this type demonstrate the special treatment of negotiable instruments under New York law. As reflected in the discussion in an earlier section of this opinion, New York has, as a general rule, a policy against imposing personal liability on corporate officers if the circumstances are ambiguous. However, this policy gives way before the policy considerations underlying N.Y.U.C.C. § 3-403, which "aims to foster certainty and definiteness in the law of commercial paper, requirements deriving from the' 'necessity for takers of negotiable instruments to tell at a glance whose obligation they hold.' "

It is undisputed that Okobank never dealt with either of the Shulofs or JSF. Mrs. Shulof offers no evidence sufficient to raise a triable issue of fact as to either Okobank's status as a *holder in due course* or her allegations of fraud in the inducement on the part of FFS. Accordingly, the Court finds that Mrs. Shulof's signature on the Bill of Exchange did not give notice that she signed in a representative capacity only, and therefore she is personally liable for the amount of the bill. SO ORDERED.

Case Highlights

- There is a strong public policy in U.S. corporate law against imposing personal liability on corporate officers for actions performed on behalf of the corporation.
- It is customary under Finnish law for an agent to be held personally liable as a surety for goods purchased at an auction.
- A corporate officer who signs a bill of exchange or draft must state she signs *only* in a representative capacity in order to avoid personal liability.
- The public policy underlying negotiable instrument law is that a *holder in due course* may collect against the signer of the instrument.
- A choice of law clause in a contract will be enforced if there is a reasonable connection between the choice and the transaction, unless a strong public policy of the forum court is threatened.
- Owners at an auction have the right to prescribe the manner, conditions, and terms of sale.

---

franchisees. Taken to an extreme, each individual subsidiary or franchisee can be held liable for the acts of other subsidiaries or franchisees. This theory has also been widely rejected by the courts in many developed countries.[6]

Establishing a Business in a Foreign Country

The requirements for establishing a business or an office in a foreign country vary dramatically from one country to the next. The least level of involvement in entering a foreign market is hiring a foreign sales representative or agent. Some countries, however, limit foreign companies to hiring nationals as sales representatives

---

6. See OECD, *The Responsibility of Parent Companies for Their Subsidiaries* ¶¶ 65–70 (1980). See also P. T. Muchlinski, *Multinational Enterprises and the Law* 328 (1995).

or agents. The foreign exporter, however, can exert substantial control over its agents through **management agreements**. Such agreements do not *establish* the foreign exporter for purposes of tax liability; the tax liability of the foreign company is generally restricted to the income of any expatriates assigned to the representative office.

The next level of entry into a foreign market is the establishment of a representative or branch office. With a branch office, the parent company establishes any type of operation—sales office, manufacturing plant, or distribution facility—without setting up an independent legal entity. The branch office generally operates under the trade name of the parent company. Advantages of such an operation include ease in establishment, central management, and fewer required disclosures of confidential information to third parties. The major disadvantages are the risk of host country taxation and unlimited liability for the activities of the branch office, such as product liability. A business permit is required in most countries, and in some countries registering to establish a foreign office entails multiple filings with multiple agencies. In Indonesia, the activities of a representative office are limited to signing sales contracts, collecting payments, and other general business activities. In other countries, other activities are also limited.

An important issue in entering a foreign market is the protection of the company's trade name. In the United States, corporate and trade names are protected under the individual states' incorporation statutes. Once a business name is reserved, all other persons or companies are precluded from using that or a similar name. In many foreign countries, the only avenue of protection for a business name is for a company to register it as a foreign trademark.

Companies planning a permanent presence in a foreign country may choose to establish an independent subsidiary or purchase an existing company. The corporate entity is recognized in almost all countries in the world, but names and abbreviations for corporations vary in different legal systems. In the United States, a corporation is signified by the use of "Inc." after the company's name to indicate that it is an "incorporated" entity. The term "Limited" or "Ltd." is used in Canada and Great Britain. "S.A." for *Sociedad Anonyme* is the corporate designation in France and Spain, "SpA" or *Societa per Azioni* is the Italian symbol for corporation, and "Y.K." or *Yugen-Kaisha* is the Japanese designation for a corporation. The number of options for establishing a business in a given country can be staggering. In Russia, for example, the 1990 Law on Enterprises recognized no fewer than ten forms of business enterprises.[7]

The number of recognized enterprises in Russia was subsequently reduced by the 1994 Civil Code.[8] Even though the nomenclature is similar to that found in the United States, there are key differences in the Russian forms of enterprise. The Russian partnership is considered a separate entity for purposes of taxation, and therefore does not benefit from the pass-through feature of U.S. partnerships. Double taxation, at the partnership and individual levels, is the result.

Another variation not found in U.S. law is the limited liability company *with additional liability*. The standard Russian limited liability company, like those in the

http://

http://www.export. gov/tcc/ provides links to topics pertaining to foreign employment and labor laws.

INTERNATIONAL

INTERNATIONAL

INTERNATIONAL

---

7.   These included the state enterprise, municipal enterprise, individual or family private enterprise, full partnership, mixed partnership, closed joint stock company or limited liability partnership, open joint stock company, association of enterprises, branch of an enterprise, and labor collective enterprise.

8.   The Civil Code recognizes the individual partnership (general and limited), limited liability company (ordinary or additional liability), joint stock company (open and closed), and the industrial or unitarian enterprise (state or municipal).

United States, limits the owners' liability for the debts of the company to the value of their contributions. The limited liability company with additional liability makes the owners liable for a pro rata share of the company's debts in bankruptcy. This form is intended to provide additional security to creditors.

INTERNATIONAL

The **joint stock company** is the Russian form of corporation and is regulated under the 1996 Law on Enterprises. Under this law, a joint stock company may be open or closed. The closed version is limited to no more than fifty shareholders, who can maintain their ownership interests through a preemptive right to purchase a pro rata share of any subsequent issuances of stock. Unlike U.S. laws, this Russian law grants subsidiaries express rights that can be used against the parent company. The parent company is jointly and severally liable for any orders it gives to its subsidiaries. It is also liable for the insolvency of a subsidiary due to the parent's fault. Finally, shareholders of the subsidiary have the right to sue the parent company for losses caused by the fault of the parent company.[9]

Foreign Competition Law

INTERNATIONAL

If the market entry strategy decided upon is the purchase of an existing foreign company, then the legalities of acquiring a company under host country laws must be thoroughly researched, particularly whether the acquisition conforms to the host country's **competition law**.[10] The European Union provides one example of an advanced competition law system. To purchase a company situated in a European Union country, a purchaser must obtain clearance from Directorate IV of the European Commission. The following *Commission Decision of 17/11/1999* provides insight into the nuances of European competition law.

Commission Decision of 17/11/1999

(1999 OJ C 357) (Case No IV/M.1652)

On October 14, 1999, the Commission received a notification of proposed concentration pursuant to Article 4 of Council Regulation (EEC) No 4064/89 of the acquisition by the Belgian company, s.a. D'Ieteren n.v. ("D'Ieteren"), of sole control over the South African company, Plate Glass & Shatterprufe Industries Limited ("PGSI"). Following examination of the notification, the Commission has concluded that the notified operation falls within the scope of Council Regulation (EEC) No 4064/89 and does not raise serious doubts as to its compatibility with the common market and with the EEA Agreement.

D'Ieteren is involved in a range of business activities in the automotive sector, comprising broadly: i) wholesale and retail motor vehicle distribution, ii) servicing and repair and the supply of spare parts for motor vehicles, iii) short term car rental, and iv) long term car rental and financing. D'Ieteren has practically no activities outside the EU, and within the EU some 70% of its turnover is achieved in Belgium. PGSI is a group involved in the manufacture, distribution, repair, and replacement of glass and board products. It has activities in South Africa, Central Africa, the United States, Australia, New Zealand, and Brazil, as well as in the EU.

The transaction consists of a number of steps through which D'Ieteren will acquire sole control of PGSI. D'Ieteren will carry out these steps through a joint venture company, S.A. Dicobel ("Dicobel"), in which it will hold 70% of the shares. The remaining 30% are held by S.A. Copeba Novo ("Copeba"), a Belgian listed holding company. In the Shareholders' Agreement of Dicobel, Copeba's role is stated to be that of "financial partner" and provision is made for a majority representation by

---

9.   This material was taken from Edward C. Vandenberg, "The Evolution of Russian Forms of Business Enterprise," 28 *Ottawa Law Review* 343 (1996–1997).

10.   Competition law in the United States is referred to as antitrust law.

D'Ieteren on the Board, whose majority will make the strategic decisions of the company. Dicobel will, in turn, acquire the majority shareholding of each of three companies, namely, Old Belron Rest of the World, HoldCo Southern Africa, and Glass SA, which between them comprise the PGSI group of companies. Through its majority presence on the Boards of these companies and the arrangements for strategic decision-making, Dicobel will enjoy sole control over PGSI. Thus D'Ieteren, through its sole control of Dicobel, will have sole control of PGSI.

Concentration of a Community Dimension

The operation constitutes an acquisition by D'Ieteren of sole control of PGSI, and is, therefore, a concentration within the meaning of Article 3.1.b. of the Merger Regulation. D'Ieteren and PGSI have a combined aggregate worldwide turnover in excess of EUR 2,500 million. In each of three member states their combined aggregate turnover is more than EUR 100 million. The operations have, therefore, a Community dimension.

Relevant Product Markets

The activities of D'Ieteren and PGSI, through its subsidiary, Belron International n.v., overlap in two areas, in themselves vertically related, i.e., i) the supply of automotive glass to the independent aftermarket, consisting of independent car dealerships, garages, and bodyshops ("IAM"), which the Commission has already considered to constitute a product market in itself, and ii) the repair and replacement of automotive glass, which would constitute another product market.

Relevant Geographic Markets

The IAM market has already been considered of a Community-wide geographic scope by the Commission and this definition is retained in the present case. With regard to the repair and replacement of automotive glass, D'Ieteren submitted that the existence of national distribution networks with national pricing and single (free call) telephone numbers indicated a national geographic scope for this market. Other characteristics, such as different suppliers in different member states and appreciable price differences from one member state to another, can be considered further indicators of a national scope for the market for these services. However, given that the operation does not raise any serious concerns, either at a national or wider level (D'Ieteren does not have these activities outside of Belgium), the Commission does not need to define the geographic

scope of the market for the repair and replacement of automotive glass more precisely in the present case.

Assessment: The Repair and Replacement of Automotive Glass

The repair and replacement of automotive glass would constitute an affected market in Belgium, due to the addition of PGSI/Belron's share of some 39% to D'Ieteren's own share of some 1%. D'Ieteren's activities have been limited to services provided in its own car dealerships situated in the Brussels area, whereas PGSI/Belron operates from a network of 40 branches throughout Belgium, replacing the glass at the branches or at the location chosen by the customers. Although the operation strengthens considerably D'Ieteren's market share, the actual change brought about in the overall structure of supply in the market is very small indeed, given D'Ieteren's very limited share. Furthermore, D'Ieteren has indicated that it will be confronted with competition from a variety of competitors, including: (i) independent service providers who market as a single source and supply a network assistance of the type provided by PGSI/Belron, which between them enjoy some 5%–15% of the market, (ii) independent car dealerships who as a block account for some 25%–35%, and (iii) bodyshops and garages who make up the remaining 15%–25% or so of the market. The Commission's market investigation did not result in the expression of any significant concerns by the other players with regard to the competitive impact of the operation. In the circumstances and in the light of the factors mentioned above, i.e., the marginal change in market structure and the range of competitors, the Commission considers that the operation will not lead to the creation or strengthening of a dominant position in the repair and replacement of automotive glass in Belgium.

For the above reasons, the Commission has decided not to oppose the notified operation and to declare it compatible with the common market and the EEA Agreement.

Case Highlights

- Directorate IV of the European Commission is responsible for the enforcement of EU Competition Law.
- Before acquiring a European company, a foreign investor should *notify* (consult with) Directorate IV.
- Factors used to determine whether an acquisition or merger will create a dominant *position* (monopoly) subject to abuse include whether the acquisition has a community dimension, the relevant product markets, the geographic scope of the market, and the market shares of the companies.

Foreign Trade Zones

http://

Directorate IV of the
European Commission
regarding EU competi-
tion law: **http://
europa.eu.int/comm/
competition/index_en.
html.**

A foreign or free trade zone can minimize legal exposure in a foreign country. Foreign and domestic merchandise may enter the designated foreign trade zones without a formal customs entry. Therefore, importation into the zone and subsequent reexportation are not subject to customs duties or excise taxes. While in the trade zone, the merchandise may be:

• Stored	• Tested
• Sampled	• Displayed
• Relabeled	• Repackaged
• Repaired	• Cleaned
• Assembled	• Manufactured
• Processed	• Mixed

If the final product is exported, no customs duty or excise tax is levied. If the final product is imported into the country, then customs duties and excise taxes are due at the time of *transfer* from the foreign trade zone and formal entry into the country. The fact that duties are due only at the time merchandise is transferred out of the trade zone can be used by foreign exporters to improve their cash flow by shortening the time between paying customs duties and receiving income from the sale of goods. A foreign exporter may ship unsold goods into a trade zone for storage purposes without incurring the costs of duties or formal entry. The goods may be transshipped without penalty; prospective buyers can inspect goods, and rejected goods can be transferred out or destroyed duty-free. Foreign free trade zones are found in many countries in the world and conform to the free trade principles of GATT.

International Taxation

No matter what vehicle is chosen to transact foreign business operations, the foreign investor is subject to the tax ramifications of doing business across national borders. International taxation is one of the most complicated issues of doing business internationally, because taxation is dealt with differently among the countries of the world. In the United States, for example, citizens or resident aliens must pay federal income tax on their worldwide income. International tax treaties and federal statutes grant certain exemptions, deductions, and credits to protect people against being taxed by more than one country on the same income. Nonresident aliens are taxed only on their U.S. source business income. A nonresident alien providing services within the United States for either a foreign or U.S. employer must pay U.S. income tax on wages or compensation received for services. In contrast, resident aliens in the United States are taxed the same as U.S. citizens on their worldwide income.

Joint Ventures and Franchising

An international joint venture or franchising arrangement is attractive for a number of reasons.[11] First, they allow a party to utilize the partner's or franchisee's

---

11. See generally Karen J. Hladik, *International Joint Ventures* (1985); Robert Radway, "Overview of Foreign Joint Ventures," 38 *Business Lawyer* 1040 (1983); Susan Goldenberg, *Hands Across the Ocean: Managing Joint Ventures with a Spotlight on China & Japan* (1988).

local expertise, marketing skills, and established lines of distribution. Joint ventures and franchises are well suited for entry into a foreign market through the use of a host country national familiar with the local language, law, and culture. Second, a joint venture or franchise may provide a means to avoid host country protectionist trade requirements. Joint ventures, for example, are used to provide technology to a foreign partner who has production facilities and access to the local market.

Joint Ventures

International joint ventures are used in a wide variety of manufacturing, mining, and service industries and are frequently undertaken in conjunction with technology licensing by the U.S. firm to the joint venture. The host country may require that a certain percentage, often 51 percent, of manufacturing or mining operations be owned by nationals of that country, thereby obligating U.S. firms to operate through joint ventures. In addition, U.S. firms may find it desirable to enter into a joint venture with a foreign firm to spread the high costs and risks frequently associated with foreign operations. Moreover, the local partner may bring to the joint venture its knowledge of the customs and tastes of the people, an established distribution network, and valuable business and political contacts. Having local partners also decreases the foreign status of the firm and may provide some protection against discrimination or expropriation, should conditions change.

There are, of course, possible disadvantages to international joint ventures. A major potential drawback to joint ventures, especially in countries that limit foreign companies to 49 percent or less participation, is the loss of effective managerial control, which can result in reduced profits, increased operating costs, inferior product quality, and exposure to product liability and environmental litigation and fines. U.S. firms that wish to retain effective managerial control will incorporate this issue in negotiations with the prospective joint venture partner and frequently the host government.

Like technology licensing agreements, joint ventures can raise U.S. or foreign antitrust issues in certain circumstances, particularly when the prospective joint venture partners are major existing or potential competitors in the affected national markets. Firms may wish to consider applying for an **export trade certificate of review** from the Department of Commerce or a **business review letter** from the Department of Justice when significant U.S. antitrust issues are raised by the proposed international joint venture.

U.S. firms contemplating international joint ventures should also consider retaining experienced legal counsel in the host country. It may be disadvantageous for a U.S. firm to rely on its potential joint venture partner to negotiate approvals and advise on legal issues, because its prospective partner's interests may not always coincide with its own. Qualified foreign counsel can be very helpful in obtaining government approvals and providing ongoing advice regarding the host country's patent, trademark, copyright, tax, labor, corporate, commercial, antitrust, and exchange control laws.[12]

---

12. See generally National Trade Data Bank, a product of STAT-USA, U.S. Department of Commerce.

THE JOINT VENTURE AGREEMENT

A simple definition of joint venture[13] is "a contract that creates a partnership for the purpose of performing some kind of business operation."[14] It is a business collaboration in which the joint venture participants share resources, risks, and profits. Joint ventures often involve joint management and are established for a specific objective and sometimes for a fixed duration. For a joint venture to succeed, it must be carefully thought out and researched by all the prospective partners. "Feasibility studies are undertaken, confidential information is exchanged, and huge amounts of money are committed"[15] before parties enter a joint venture contract. The parties must move cautiously to gain the trust of other participants; the parties' capacities, motives, prior relationships, and project objectives should be fully discussed during the preliminary stage of the negotiations.

A joint venture is an elastic vehicle for doing business that can take numerous forms. For example, the parties can enter into an agreement to work together to achieve certain business goals as joint venturers, or they can agree to create an entirely separate entity, such as a corporation, to transact business. Two of the common uses of the joint venture in conducting international business are the single project and business alliance joint ventures.[16] The **single project venture** exists when a number of parties or companies agree to enter into a partnership to develop specific business opportunities with a single, identifiable goal. These single project joint ventures generally have a relatively short life span. An example would be a joint venture for a single construction project. The **business alliance venture** envisions a more fluid, long-term business relationship.

Under U.S. law, a joint venture is generally considered a general partnership. The core issues in the partnership agreement include the scope of the business enterprise, the capitalization of the venture, the organization and management of the venture, and the termination of the business. A major concern in most joint venture agreements is providing the mechanisms for decision making. The joint venturers may disagree on how best to deal with post-formation events. It is important, especially in the long-term joint venture agreement, to provide a mechanism to prevent decisional deadlock.

In negotiating and structuring joint ventures, proper attention should be given to the issues of share allocation, enterprise financing, minority interests' protection, confidentiality, and the transfer and continuation of the business.[17] Shares may be allocated based on each party's contribution, or joint venturers may authorize different classes or types of shares to attract other investors, such as venture capitalists. Funding decisions have a direct impact on the location of profits for tax purposes.[18] Investors may structure their contributions as either equity contributions or loans,

---

13. The term *joint venture* is not legally defined in many foreign legal systems. (One important exception is the European Union, which has adopted rules for joint ventures.) Therefore, there is often no foreign joint venture law. It is important to research foreign law to become familiar with the forms of doing business recognized under the national law that can be utilized to approximate the joint venture concept.

14. William F. Fox Jr., *International Commercial Agreements: A Primer on Drafting, Negotiating and Resolving Disputes* 79 (1992).

15. Denis Philippe, "Drawing Up a Joint Venture Contract," 20 *The Comparative Law Yearbook of International Business* 25, 27 (1998).

16. See Mark Pery-Knox-Gore, *Joint Ventures in Structuring International Contracts* 87 (ed. Dennis Campbell 1997).

17. See generally Michael E. Hooton, "Structuring and Negotiating Joint Ventures," 27 *Creighton Law Review* 1013 (1994).

18. See D. Kevin Dolan, "Special Issues in Structuring International Joint Ventures," 22 *Tax Management International Journal* 51 (1993).

and they should give full consideration to all accounting and tax ramifications. For example, investors would like to avoid the European Union's 1 percent duty on company capital.

The **purpose clause**, which maps the scope and goals of the business enterprise, is crucial for maintaining the long-term viability of the joint venture arrangement.[19] Scope should be defined along three parameters: geography, products and services, and duration. A careful balance must be struck between a clause that is precise but restricts future expansion and one that allows the venture to develop in different directions, because an overly specific statement of the venture's purpose can lead to an undesirable termination. This can be accomplished by a specific purpose clause coupled with an **exceptions clause** that allows for adjustments to the purpose clause along prescribed parameters. An alternative provision would allow a periodic review of the purpose clause with a renegotiation requirement.

Joint venturers must also establish the initial level of capitalization, including the amount and form of currency to be invested by each partner and a method for adjusting foreign currency differences. If noncurrency contributions are contemplated, the agreement should specify a valuation method. Also, the parties should expressly agree to the adoption of accounting standards, such as U.S. or European Union accounting standards and practices. The agreement should also specify the level and type of indebtedness the venture is authorized to undertake. Establishing an acceptable debt-to-equity ratio for the venture is prudent.

A successful joint venture agreement provides the means to make future funding decisions. The most likely cause of joint venture failure is the parties' disagreement regarding future capital infusions. If external funding is likely to be sought in the future, an agreement is needed as to whether the joint venture partners will provide guarantees to procure external financing. The joint venture agreement should also have a counterindemnity clause, in which the joint venture partners agree to be responsible on multiple-party guarantees only to the proportion of their shareholdings.

If the joint venture is between numerous parties, then provisions to protect minority interests may be necessary. One way to protect minority interests is to categorize decisions as "ordinary" or "extraordinary." Extraordinary decisions would require a supermajority vote for approval; for example, a two-thirds or 75 percent vote would be required to approve extraordinary decisions. Extraordinary decisions could include:

- Capital expenditures in excess of a certain amount
- Borrowings in excess of a certain amount
- Increasing of share capital
- Issuance of new stock or admittance of a new joint venture partner
- Giving guarantees; appointment or removal of directors
- Setting employee remuneration above a certain level
- Material changes in the business operation or nature of the business
- Sale or transfer of assets
- Making contracts with principals of the joint venture
- Approval of budgets

19. A number of valuable suggestions for those considering a joint venture contract are in Steven R. Salbu & Richard A. Brahm, "Strategic Considerations in Designing Joint Venture Contracts," *Columbia Business Law Review* 253 (1992).

In case of a deadlock regarding an important decision, a party may be offered the right to leave the joint venture; a provision should address the transfer or sale of ownership to the other partners. Share price should be fair and determined by an independent accounting firm. The shares being sold should be offered to all remaining partners in proportion to their existing ownership interests. The agreement should also provide whether, in the event of termination, the joint venture partners have the right to continue in the same business after the termination.

Strict confidentiality and noncompetition provisions are also necessary. The partners may be prohibited from competing with the joint venture by stipulations that include being unable to hire employees of the joint venture for a period of time, maintaining the secrecy of all confidential information, and not soliciting customers of the joint venture. Of course, these restrictions must be reasonable, or they will be subject to challenge as illegal restraints of trade.

Another crucial set of provisions to ensure the ongoing viability of the venture is the management provisions. *Double parenting* is a pervasive problem in which both joint venturers attempt to assert independent control over the joint venture. The degree of managerial control to be placed with the different joint venturers should be carefully delineated in the agreement. Will the owner of the greater share have greater managerial control? Will a local minority partner be allowed a degree of control greatly exceeding its proportional ownership? Other issues to be dealt with by management clauses include: (1) Should veto power be given to the partners, including minority partners, for particular classes of important decisions? (2) How will the selection of the top manager and management team be decided? (3) What reporting and information systems will be used to communicate between the joint venture and its owners?[20] Ultimately, these provisions will reflect the essential nature of the joint venture as one controlled by a dominant parent or as one with a shared management structure.

Finally, the joint venture should have a detailed termination provision, stating the events that allow the parties to terminate their involvement. The following list suggests the types of considerations that should be discussed in drafting a termination clause:[21]

- Failure of a participant to make required capital contributions
- Failure of a participant to obtain necessary government approvals
- Failure of the venture to reach a pre-agreed level of profitability
- Management deadlock
- Failure of one partner to purchase the shares of another (breach of buy-sell agreement)
- An adverse and debilitating change in the law
- Bankruptcy or insolvency of one of the participants

The termination clause should also describe how unforeseeable or force majeure events will affect a termination of the joint venture.

---

20.   Ibid. at 292–294.
21.   Taken from William G. Frenkel, "Legal Protection Against Risks Involved in Doing Business in the Republics of the Former U.S.S.R.," 10 *International Quarterly* 395, 467 (1998).

ANCILLARY AGREEMENTS

The joint venture agreement is probably only one of a number of documents to be prepared for a well-planned joint venture undertaking. Other documentation commonly includes a formal business plan, distribution agreement, intellectual property transfer or licensing agreement, management agreement, service contracts, and secondment agreements. A carefully written business plan is vital to maintaining cordial relationships among the joint venture partners. It should be sufficiently long-term in nature, set realistic revenue and profit goals, and provide for a "cushion" in capital and time in meeting the plan's objectives. The business plan should include other necessary studies, such as a long-term strategic plan and a marketing plan.

Secondment agreements are used to require the "lending" of employees of the joint venture partners to the joint venture. It is important to determine whether these employees are to be treated as independent contractors or as employees of the joint venture. From the point of view of the joint venture, treatment as independent contractors is preferred. The joint venture partner would then remain primarily obligated to the employees being lent. Service contracts between the partners and their joint venture could also be utilized in the management of the joint venture enterprise.

Sometimes, one of the joint venture partners is given the formal responsibility to manage the joint venture. In that case, the managing partner should enter into a formal management agreement with the joint venture. The management agreement, among other things, should outline the allocation of costs between the partner's core business and the joint venture business. Often one of the contributions of a joint venture partner is its expertise in its home country regarding the distribution of goods or services. An express **distribution agreement** should be entered into between that partner and the joint venture. The distribution agreement's termination provisions should be tied to those in the joint venture agreement. This point may be important if the distributor is removed as a joint venture partner.

International joint ventures may include the use of the know-how or intellectual property rights of one of the joint venture partners. In such a situation, an independently negotiated **intellectual property transfer** or licensing agreement is necessary and should deal with the withdrawal of the licensor-partner. A name change of the joint venture may be required if the existing name is associated with the intellectual property of the withdrawing partner. The licensor-partner may demand a provision that makes the licensing of intellectual property rights "coterminous with the licensor's involvement in the joint venture."[22]

FOREIGN GOVERNMENT REGULATION

Foreign governments commonly regulate joint venture transactions. The most common restrictions are foreign participation requirements in which control of the enterprise must vest in a local company. The trend, however, has been toward a liberalization of such participation requirements. The first Doing Business Internationally feature summarizes the practice and law of joint venturing in Indonesia. Note that it is now possible for a foreign investor to obtain almost total ownership of an Indonesian joint venture.

---

22. Pery-Knox-Gore, *supra* note 16, at 99.

Joint Ventures and Licensing in Indonesia[23]

Doing Business Internationally

Since 1994, the government has removed most requirements for domestic equity and joint ventures. However, foreign investors who opt for 100 percent initial ownership are obligated to divest to Indonesians some share—even as little as 1 percent—after 15 years. This can be accomplished through the stock market. This requirement is too new to have been tested yet. As a practical matter, a local joint venture partner is often essential for success in this market, for the same reason that an active Indonesian agent or distributor has advantages over a foreign trade representative office. The choice of an Indonesian joint venture partner is critical for many reasons, especially for knowledge of the local scene and contacts, which are important for successful operations. A partnership in Indonesia is difficult to dissolve, however. Consequently, the first choice has to be the correct choice. Business sense is crucial to any commercial endeavor; "contacts" alone, although important, cannot substitute for business skills in an Indonesian partner. Because Indonesians place great importance on personal relationships and mutual understanding, partnerships tend to be based primarily on genuine accord, with the written contract playing a less significant role. It is therefore important that any agreement be well understood by both sides. A contract over which there are conflicting interpretations is certain to cause future problems. In any case, a soundly written legal agreement is strongly encouraged, despite the weakness of the Indonesian legal system to enforce such contracts.

http://

World Trade Organization links to foreign investment laws: **http://www.wto.org.**

INTERNATIONAL

Unique types of government regulations can be found on a country-by-country basis. The list in the second Doing Business Internationally feature demonstrates that governmental regulation is pervasive in the establishment and operation of a joint venture in China. The joint venture laws are merely frameworks or enabling statutes. Detailed regulations must be consulted before establishing a joint venture. Also, ancillary laws must be reviewed in conjunction with the operation of the joint venture. For example, Chinese law states that "matters such as the recruitment and

Approval and Establishment of a Joint Venture in China

Doing Business Internationally

Step One. Signing of cooperative joint venture contract

Step Two. Submission of joint venture contract and articles of association for examination and approval to the State Council department in charge of foreign economic relations and trade or a department or local government authorized by the State Council (The approval authority must render a decision within forty-five days.)

Step Three. Application for registration (to appropriate industry and commerce agency, within thirty days of receipt of approval certificate from approval authority)

continued

---

23.   U.S. Department of State Country Commercial Guide for Indonesia (2004).

Approval and Establishment of a Joint Venture in China (*continued*)

Step Four. Receipt of business license (date of establishment)

Step Five. Register venture with appropriate tax authority within thirty days of the date of establishment

Step Six: Postestablishment Concerns

Any "major amendments" in the joint venture contract must be submitted to the approval authority. Any transfers of rights and obligations under the cooperative joint venture contract must be approved by the approval authority.

Any changes in the management and operation of the joint venture (to a party not an original partner) must be by unanimous vote of the board of directors and with the approval of the approval authority.

Record keeping and certifications must be verified by an accountant registered in China. The joint venture must establish and support a labor union to represent its employees.

Open a foreign exchange account.

---

dismissal of employees, remuneration, welfare benefits, labor protection and labor insurance shall be stipulated in contracts signed in accordance with the law." In fact, a foreign investor is required to enter into a labor contract as a condition for joint venture approval. The labor contract must be submitted to the labor administration department of the appropriate municipal or provincial government for approval. Furthermore, the labor-management relationship is regulated throughout the term of employment. Most workers are hired from a pool of workers provided by the local government labor department. They are to be selected for employment through an approved examination. Finally, any discharge of an employee must be reported to the labor management department for approval. Anyone contemplating a joint venture in China ought to obtain copies of form contracts (available in English) used by Chinese enterprises and consult with the Chinese Ministry of Foreign Trade and Economic Cooperation created in 1982 to expedite foreign trade contracts.

Franchising

Though franchising is an attractive arrangement, it does pose some problems. Franchising is a uniquely U.S. form of doing business. Franchising is allowed in most countries of the world, but many foreign laws do not expressly recognize the franchise form of business. For example, even though franchises have been registered in Germany and there are currently 760 franchise operators with 41,000 outlets throughout the country, franchising itself has not been explicitly codified in German law. As a result, more general bodies of law, such as licensing or partnership law, are used by analogy to regulate the franchise relationship. In Germany, franchises are regulated through application of German commercial, trademark, competition, and consumer credit laws.

Because the franchise is not expressly recognized in some countries, imposing exclusive franchise territories is susceptible to attack under foreign competition or antitrust laws. In Europe, an EU **block exemption** that provides a general exemption from the ban on cartels for franchise arrangements has alleviated the problem. Because of the EU block exemption, the franchise industry in Europe is primarily

http://

For an informative article on joint venturing in the People's Republic of China see "Establishing A Joint Venture with the People's Republic of China: A Guide for American Businesses" in the *New England International and Comparative Law Annual*: **http://www.nesl.edu/intl journal/vol5/rice.htm.**

http://

http://www.jus.uio.no/ lm/china.laws/index. html. gives texts of the commercial laws of the People's Republic of China including trade law, labor law, company law, and "foreign contract law."

INTERNATIONAL

INTERNATIONAL

self-regulated. The European Franchise Federation acts as an umbrella organization for the different national franchise associations, guiding those promoting franchise operations. The European Franchise Federation has issued a code of ethics that should be reviewed by a foreign party intending to franchise in Europe. National franchise associations have also issued guidelines, such as the German Franchise Association's Pre-Contract Disclosure Requirements.

INTERNATIONAL

Before entering into a franchising contract with a foreign entity, an investor must thoroughly research the investment climate in the host country. For example, in Indonesia, franchising became a popular vehicle for foreign entry until the devaluation of the rupiah in 1997. The depreciation of the rupiah made the payment of franchise royalties in foreign exchange difficult.[24] Aside from the convertibility issue, Indonesia places no major restrictions on the repatriation of profits and maintains no capital controls, and foreign exchange may flow freely in and out of the country. Foreign investors have the right to repatriate capital and profits at the prevailing rate of exchange.

The U.S. State Department's *Commercial Guide for Indonesia* summarizes the law pertaining to franchising as follows:

With the release of the Government Regulation No. 16 of 1997, dated June 18, 1997, the Indonesian franchise industry had—for the first time—a foundation in Indonesian law. This regulation, which was complemented by the issuance of a Decree of the Ministry of Industry and Trade No. 259/MPP/Kep/7/1997, was designed to promote an orderly climate for franchise businesses as well as to provide guidance and protection for both franchisers and franchisees.

The regulation, which contains a description of the franchiser-franchisee relationship, states that a franchise agreement between a franchiser and a franchisee must be written in Indonesian and be subject to Indonesian law. The Government of Indonesia has limited the operation of large franchise businesses to provincial capitals. Only small and medium-scale enterprises, or licensed non-small-scale entrepreneurs, may operate franchise businesses in smaller cities or rural areas. This regulation was designed to insulate indigenous small and medium-size companies against competition from foreign franchisers, and to encourage local companies to develop their own franchise concepts.

The regulation obligates every franchise business to obtain a registration certificate, namely the STPUW (Surat Tanda Pendaftaran Usaha Waralaba or Foreign Business Registration Certificate), from the Ministry of Industry and Trade. The registration should be made at least thirty working days from the date of the franchising agreement, which shall be valid for at least five years, takes effect. The regulation further stipulates that priority should be given to the use of domestic goods and/or products as long as they meet the required quality standards.

Given these restrictions, the foreign franchisor should exercise considerable caution in utilizing its own standard franchise form agreements.

The State Department Guide notes that joint venturing with an established Indonesian company is the preferred method of market entry. This means of market entry has been enhanced by recent developments. First, in 1994, the Indonesian government removed most local participation requirements. Second, a number of firms will provide background and credit checks on Indonesian firms. Third, an Indonesian company can provide the necessary knowledge and contacts with the local market. One drawback to establishing an Indonesian franchise relationship is the difficulty of dissolving a joint venture or franchise partnership

24.   Ibid.

under Indonesian law. Therefore, careful background research, prior dealings, and a clear, comprehensive agreement are necessary.

Other areas of interest for those contemplating franchising, licensing, or joint venturing in a foreign country include the protection of intellectual property rights, the use of a local attorney, transferability of ownership interests, and expropriation and dispute settlement policies. Intellectual property protection, for example, is wanting in Indonesia. As a result, U.S. companies may utilize a strategy to identify counterfeiters and then sign them as legal licensees of their products.[25] Nonetheless, it is important to register intellectual property as soon as possible and to challenge any unauthorized registrations. The commercial guide suggests acquiring a local partner as the best way to defend against the infringement of intellectual property rights.

The Indonesian record for the enforcement of foreign arbitration awards has been uneven. In the area of dispute resolution, Indonesia is a party to the New York Convention on the enforcement of foreign arbitration awards, but because an Indonesian court is more likely to enforce an award issued by an Indonesian arbitration panel, the guide suggests an arbitration clause that designates Indonesia as the place of arbitration.[26] Enforcement of international arbitration awards was within the jurisdiction of the Supreme Court, which was slow to issue decisions. In August 1999, Indonesia's Parliament passed Arbitration Law Number Thirty, which granted the power to enforce international arbitration awards to the District Court of Central Jakarta. Law Number Thirty has greatly reduced instances where district courts fail to act or enforce international arbitration awards, and the enforcement of such awards has been expedited since the adoption of the law. Nevertheless, since its adoption of the New York Convention in 1981, fewer than two dozen foreign arbitration awards have been registered with Indonesian courts. The transfer and expropriation policies of the Indonesian government are conducive to foreign entry. Foreign investors have the right to repatriate capital and profits, and no permits are required to transfer foreign exchange.

FRANCHISE LAW

The advantage of franchising is aptly stated as its method for facilitating "the transfer of know-how and managerial expertise to the franchisee companies while simultaneously allowing the franchisor to quickly establish a presence in the country. Under a typical franchising agreement, the franchisor receives royalties and fees as stipulated in the contract. In exchange, the franchisee has the right to use (and manufacture) copyrighted, patented, or service-marked materials identifying the enterprise. The franchisor typically provides training and organizational guidance in return for a guarantee that the franchisee will follow these operational directions."[27]

---

25. Ibid.
26. "Because Indonesia's legal system is currently being overhauled and modernized, firms are strongly advised to locate and retain a local attorney early in the investment process. In the event of a commercial dispute, one should first attempt to reach consensus through negotiation, using a mediator acceptable to both parties if necessary. If deliberation fails to achieve consensus, then companies may enter into arbitration. To prepare for this eventuality, an arbitration clause should be included in any commercial contract with Indonesia chosen as the site of arbitration. This is recommended because foreign arbitral awards have proven difficult to enforce locally. Badan Arbitrase Nasional Indonesia (BANI) is the local arbitration board and companies may employ BANI or select their own arbitration vehicle and procedures (i.e., ICC or UNCITRAL). Only when arbitration fails should companies consider litigation. The Indonesian court system has proven to be an ineffective means of recourse for American companies." U.S. Department of State, Country Commercial Guide for Indonesia (2004).
27. Ibid.

http://

Franchise and distribution law—recent legal developments: **http://www.franchise distriblaw.net.**

The expertise of the franchisor is reflected in areas of the franchise contract such as the opening and financing of the franchise, along with the means and content of advertisement. Contractual clauses pertaining to the franchisor's assistance in obtaining financing and opening the franchise should state specific obligations. In the area of advertisement, the clause should state the franchisor's control over the content and placement of advertisements. Also, it may mandate a minimum level of franchisee expenditures on advertisements.

Some franchise agreements provide for a pool of funds contributed by franchisees that the franchisor then uses to place advertisements. The franchise agreement should detail how advertising monies are to be spent by the franchisor. The franchisees may request a clause allocating advertising monies between a national or international campaign and local advertisement. The *Broussard v. Meineke Muffler Shops* case involves a dispute over such an advertisement provision. It illustrates some of the nuances of U.S. franchise law and how courts are reluctant to pierce the limited liability protection that franchising offers to the franchisor.

Broussard v. Meineke Discount Muffler Shops

155 F.3d 331 (4th Cir. 1998)

Wilkinson, Chief Judge. This case is a study in the tensions that can beset the franchisor-franchisee relationship. Ten owners of Meineke Discount Muffler franchises sued franchisor Meineke Discount Muffler Shops, Inc. ("Meineke"), Meineke's in-house advertising agency New Horizons Advertising, Inc. ("New Horizons"), three officers of Meineke, and Meineke's corporate parents GKN and GKN Parts Industries Corporation ("PIC"). Plaintiffs claimed that Meineke's handling of franchise advertising breached the Franchise and Trademark Agreements ("FTAs") that Meineke had entered into with every franchisee. Plaintiffs also advanced a raft of tort and statutory unfair trade practices claims arising out of the same conduct. Plaintiffs won a $390 million judgment against Meineke and its affiliated parties.

Under all versions of the FTA, each franchisee was to pay Meineke an initial franchise fee and thereafter some percentage of its weekly gross revenue (generally 7%–8%) as a royalty. Franchisees also paid Meineke 10 percent of weekly revenues to fund national and local advertising. Initially, franchisees made these advertising contributions directly to a third-party advertising agency, M&N Advertising ("M&N"), which placed ads on a commission basis. In 1982, franchisees paid their 10 percent contributions to a central account maintained by Meineke, the Weekly Advertising Contribution ("WAC") account.

Franchise advertising is addressed in two sections of the FTAs. All versions of the FTA oblige Meineke "to purchase and place from time to time advertising promoting the products and services sold by FRANCHISEE." The FTAs provide that "all decisions regarding whether to utilize national, regional, or local advertising, or some combination thereof, and regarding selection of the particular media and advertising content, shall be within the sole discretion of MEINEKE and such agencies or others as it may appoint." Three categories of disbursements from the WAC account, totaling approximately $32.2 million, are at the heart of this lawsuit. At a dealers' meeting in April 1993, a Meineke official read from a December 1992 Uniform Franchise Offering Circular ("UFOC") that disclosed New Horizons' 5%–15% commission rates. Plaintiffs knew before the meeting that New Horizons took commissions from WAC funds but claim they were unaware that its rates were so high.

The jury returned a verdict against Meineke for breach of contract and against Meineke and New Horizons for breach of fiduciary duty, negligence, and unjust enrichment. The jury found that GKN and PIC had utilized Meineke and New Horizons as mere instrumentalities, and that PIC was merely an instrumentality of GKN, which justified piercing the corporate veil and imposing vicarious liability on GKN. Along with Meineke and New Horizons, GKN, PIC, and three officers of Meineke were found to have committed fraud, and of making negligent misrepresentations. The jury awarded plaintiffs $196 million in compensatory damages, which, over Meineke's objection, was not allocated among the various theories of liability or among defendants. The jury awarded a total of $150 million in punitive damages: $70 million against Meineke; $7 million against New Horizons; $1.8 million against PIC; $70 million against GKN; and $1.2 million total against the three Meineke officers.

The district court erred by allowing plaintiffs to advance their claims for breach of fiduciary duty when there is no indication that North Carolina law would recognize the existence of a fiduciary relationship between franchisee and franchisor. "Rather," in North Carolina "parties to a contract do not thereby become each others' fiduciaries; they generally owe no special duty to one another beyond the terms of the contract and the duties set forth in the U.C.C." Though plaintiffs would portray franchisees as helpless Davids to the franchisor's Goliath, size, as that story teaches, is not a reliable indicator of strength or influence. Our hesitation is strengthened by the refusal of courts in many other jurisdictions to superimpose fiduciary duties on a franchisor-franchisee relationship.

Furthermore, shareholders who take an active interest in the affairs of the corporation are "non-outsiders" and thus protected from tortious interference claims by the same qualified privilege that protects directors and officers of the corporation. And if those shareholders do not completely dominate the affairs of the corporation, the corporate veil will not be pierced and they will be shielded from vicarious liability. Setting up such a safe harbor preserves

the advantages of limited liability while encouraging shareholders to actively monitor corporate affairs.

REVERSED AND REMANDED

Case Highlights

- The franchise arrangement is contractual in nature; however, U.S. regulations require certain disclosures through a Uniform Franchise Offering Circular (UFOC).
- Because of the contractual nature of the franchise arrangement, the franchisor does not owe a fiduciary duty to its franchisees.
- Note the size of the punitive damages component of the jury award. Punitive damages are unique to American law and generally are not found in foreign legal systems.
- Note also that the corporate veil will be pierced to hold shareholders or a parent corporation vicariously liable only when the shareholders or parent exercises complete *domination* over the corporation or its subsidiary, or if they fail to observe corporate formalities.

The franchise relationship is a uniquely American creation. According to the International Franchise Association, there are 1,500 franchise companies operating 320,000 outlets in the United States. One in twelve retail businesses in the United States is a franchise operation. These businesses generate in excess of $1 trillion in annual sales. The United States has developed an extensive body of law regulating the franchise relationship. For example, the Federal Trade Commission's (FTC) Franchise Rule imposes six different requirements in connection with the "advertising, offering, licensing, contracting, sale or other promotion of a franchise in or affecting commerce."[28] These requirements mandate the franchisor to disclose to prospective franchisees the basis for earnings and advertising claims, provide of a copy of the franchise agreement prior to its execution, and give the franchisee the right to demand a refund of deposits and payments. Remedies that may be sought by the FTC in the event of a violation of the rule include injunctions, asset freezes, civil penalties of up to $11,000 per violation, and investor and consumer redress that is not subject to monetary limitations. However, the FTC does not require registration, filing, review, or approval of disclosures, advertising, or agreements by franchisors prior to their utilization. The following opinion of the U.S. Court of Appeals in *Nieman v. Dryclean U.S.A. Franchise Company, Inc.* resolves the issue of the applicability of the FTC franchise rule to an agreement between a U.S.-based franchisor and a franchisee located in Argentina.

In addition to FTC regulation, a large number of states regulate the offer and sale of franchises. Many state laws require franchisors to register a detailed offering

---

28. Federal Trade Commission, Franchise Rule, 16 C.F.R. § 436.1 (2004).

Nieman v. Dryclean U.S.A. Franchise Company, Inc.

178 F.3d 1126 (11th Cir. 1999)

Smith, Senior Circuit Judge. This case arises out of negotiations between Dryclean U.S.A. Franchise Company, Inc. (DUSA) and Mario Nieman, an Argentine citizen, concerning the possible opening of dry-cleaning franchises in Argentina. Nieman sought a master franchise agreement which would give him the right to sell franchises throughout Argentina. In February 1994, the parties executed a letter agreement. Nieman signed the agreement in Argentina, then mailed it back to DUSA in Florida, where DUSA's representative signed it. Under the terms of the agreement, Nieman gave DUSA a $50,000 non-refundable deposit in exchange for DUSA's agreement not to negotiate with others regarding the Argentine master franchise agreement for sixty days. In effect, Nieman bought a sixty-day option to purchase the master franchise agreement.

Nieman intended to use the sixty-day period to arrange financing, but ultimately failed to raise the necessary capital. DUSA kept the non-refundable deposit and Nieman sued for its return under the Florida Deceptive and Unfair Trade Practices Act (DUTPA). The basis of Nieman's suit was that DUSA had failed to make the disclosures required under the DUTPA and under the Federal Trade Commission (FTC) Franchise Rule. DUSA defended on the ground that the DUTPA and the Franchise Rule do not apply because this transaction took place in Argentina and the DUTPA and the Franchise Rule have no extraterritorial application. DUSA did not dispute that it failed to make the relevant disclosures.

The District Court for the Southern District of Florida granted summary judgment to Nieman. The court held that the DUTPA applied to this transaction because "Congress has the power to prevent unfair trade practices in foreign commerce by citizens of the United States, although some acts are done outside the territorial limits of the United States." The court ordered DUSA to refund the full amount of Nieman's $50,000 deposit. DUSA appeals.

In order to provide a basis for a *foreign* franchisee to sue in regard to a *foreign* franchise deal, the Franchise Rule would have to apply extraterritorially. An agency regulation has the force and effect of law only if it is authorized by congressional grant of authority; it is therefore subject to limitations imposed by Congress. The Franchise Rule was promulgated by the FTC under the authority of the Federal Trade Commission Act. Thus, for the Franchise Rule to have extraterritorial application, Congress must have intended the FTC Act to apply extraterritorially.

It is undisputed that Congress has the power to regulate the extraterritorial acts of U.S. citizens. Whether Congress has chosen to exercise that authority, however, is an issue of statutory construction. "It is a longstanding principle of American law 'that legislation of Congress, unless a contrary intent appears, is meant to apply only within the territorial jurisdiction of the United States.'" *EEOC v. Arabian Am. Oil Co.*, 499 U.S. 244, 248 (1991). This presumption "serves to protect against unintended clashes between our laws and those of other nations which could result in international discord." *Arabian Am. Oil Co.*, 499 U.S. at 248.

The presumption against extraterritoriality can be overcome only by clear expression of Congress' intention to extend the reach of the relevant Act beyond those places where the United States has sovereignty or has some measure of legislative control.

The FTC Act provides that "unfair or deceptive acts or practices in or affecting commerce are hereby declared unlawful." 15 U.S.C. § 45(a)(1). The Act defines "commerce" to mean "commerce among the several States or with foreign nations." 15 U.S.C. § 44. Based upon these passages, Nieman argues that, by defining commerce to include foreign commerce, Congress showed that it intended the FTC Act to apply extraterritorially.

We agree with DUSA that the language of the FTC Act does not clearly indicate that Congress intended the Act to apply extraterritorially. The provisions in the FTC Act that Nieman points to as supporting extraterritorial application of the Act are at best ambiguous and, more importantly, are virtually identical to those that the Supreme Court found *not* to support extraterritorial application of Title VII of the Civil Rights Act of 1964. See *Arabian Am. Oil Co.*, 499 U.S. at 249–251.

Further, even if Congress intended the unfair trade provisions of the FTC Act to give the FTC the authority to apply regulations extraterritorially, the evidence does not suggest that the FTC exercised such authority. Rather, the evidence shows that the FTC did not intend its Franchise Rule to apply to a U.S. franchisor in its dealings with foreign franchisees with respect to franchises to be located in a foreign country.

First, the Franchise Rule was not intended to protect franchisees in foreign countries. When it was promulgated, the Rule was accompanied by a Statement of Basis and Purpose that reviewed the history of franchising in the United States and discussed measures that had been taken by various U.S. federal agencies and state governments to address unfair franchising practices. The Statement of Basis and Purpose is silent regarding the history or problems of franchising in other countries.

Second, the provisions of the Rule itself reveal a purely domestic focus. For example, the rule addresses potential conflicts with state law but does not mention foreign law.

Third, the FTC has never indicated that the Franchise Rule was intended to apply to foreign franchisees. For example, the Final Interpretive Guides devote a section to potential conflicts between the Franchise Rule and state and local laws, but are silent with regard to foreign laws.

Finally, the FTC recently issued an Advance Notice of Proposed Rulemaking, proposing to modify the Rule to "clarify" that it does not apply to the sale of franchises to be located outside the United States. Although the FTC has not issued a formal modification of the Franchise Rule, the Federal Register notices are evidence that extraterritorial application of the Rule was not contemplated at the time it was promulgated.

DUSA's failure to comply with the disclosure requirements of the Franchise Rule does not provide Nieman with a cause of action to seek refund of his non-refundable deposit.

REVERSED

Case Update

The U.S. Supreme Court subsequently refused to grant certiorari to review the decision of the Eleventh Circuit Court of Appeals.

Case Highlights

- There is a presumption against the extraterritorial application of U.S. law, including the FTC's Franchise Rule.
- The presumption against extraterritoriality may only be overcome by a clear expression of Congress's intention. In any event, such application may extend only to those areas where the United States has sovereignty or has some measure of legislative control.
- Broad grants of authority to regulate commerce, including foreign commerce, contained in federal statutes do not necessarily demonstrate an intent to grant the statute extraterritorial application.
- The interpretation of the reach of a federal statute by the agency responsible for its enforcement is relevant to the inquiry with respect to the statute's territorial reach.

---

before being able to solicit franchisees. Some statutes provide the franchisee with a right to cure any of its defaults under the franchise agreement and grant a minimum notice period prior to termination by the franchisor. The popularity of franchising in the United States, along with increased governmental regulation, has produced a number of franchise clauses that are commonly used and recognized in the franchise industry. The next section will review some of the clauses commonly found in the franchise agreement.

THE FRANCHISE AGREEMENT

The following commonly used clauses place various obligations upon the franchisor and the franchisee. These clauses should be completely understood in the negotiation of a franchise agreement. A **site selection clause** delineates the franchisor's responsibilities in the site selection process. Such clauses range from placing an affirmative duty on the franchisor to find an appropriate site to simply requiring the franchisor's approval. An approval clause should state the criteria for the franchisor's disapproval of a site. In *Brennan v. Carvel Corp.*[29] the court went outside the boundaries of the franchise site selection clause in finding that the franchisor had failed to meet its obligations in the site selection process. The court found that the franchisor's deposit agreement stated that the franchisor would expend a "substantial amount of time and effort in seeking, surveying, and showing locations available for a store." This case illustrates the importance in reviewing

---

29. 929 F.2d 801 (1st Cir. 1991).

all franchise documentation for consistency. A *merger clause*[30] in the final franchise agreement is unlikely to prevent courts from reviewing preliminary agreements, ancillary agreements, promotional materials, and governmental filings for purposes of clarification or to substantiate a claim of misrepresentation.

Physical layout and signage, along with operational standards, are important areas of control for the franchisor. Clauses relating to these matters are essential to maintain systemwide integrity and uniformity of standards. Most retail franchises utilize layouts that maintain the uniformity of appearance at all franchise locations. "The design or display *package* may be in conjunction with the trademarks and service marks provided by the franchisor or as part of the advertising controls."[31] Failure of the franchisee to adhere to these and other operational standards generally provides the franchisor with good cause for termination of the franchise operation. Most layout clauses give the franchisor the absolute right of approval.

An **operational standards clause** provides a detailed description of quality standards and operational goals. It generally refers to an operating manual provided by the franchisor. To defend a decision to terminate, the franchisor should ensure that the franchise agreement has a clear notice provision and provides a reasonable period of time to cure deficiencies. An associated concern is the training of the franchisee and its employees, because training and consultation provided by the franchisor are the heart of many franchise arrangements. Key employees of the franchisee are trained in all facets of the business. Consultation involves dealing with problems that occur from time to time. A franchisor's failure to provide adequate training and consultation under these clauses would be grounds for a lawsuit by the franchisee.

Most franchise systems are premised on uniform treatment between the franchisor and all its franchisees. However, franchisors sometimes incorporate a clause in their franchise agreements that allows them to vary contractual terms among their different franchisees. Such clauses have been grounds for claims of discriminatory treatment. Other common clauses include those on territorial exclusivity and protection, noncompetition, transfers and assignments, terminations, and nonrenewals and those pertaining to pricing, purchase of supplies, hours of operation, franchisor's rights of inspection, and audits. **Territorial clauses** grant the franchisee an exclusive territory within which the franchisor is barred from competing. The problem with such clauses is that the franchisor and franchisee may disagree regarding the scope of expansion of franchise operations within the territory. An alternative is to give the franchisee a period of time to fully develop the franchise territory. After the expiration of that time, the franchisor is then allowed to further develop the territorial market. The franchisee is protected somewhat by being granted a right of first refusal for any new locations within the territory.

The termination of the franchise by the franchisor, either for cause or nonrenewal, is the action most likely to lead to litigation. Most franchise agreements contain a clause that allows the franchisor to terminate for any violation, but most courts will not view favorably termination for a minor breach. Likewise, the **renewal clause** often provides an absolute right of the franchisor not to renew. Instead of absolute rights to

---

30. A merger clause states that the express terms of the written contract may not be varied or modified by prior oral or written statements or agreements. The court is to render a decision based on its review of the four-corners of the final contract. See, Uniform Commercial Code §2–202.

31. Robert W. Emerson, "Franchise Contract Clauses and the Franchisor's Duty of Care Toward Its Franchisees," 72 *North Carolina Law Review* 905, 909 (1994). (hereinafter "Franchise Contract Clauses").

terminate or not to renew, termination or nonrenewal clauses should specify the violations or reasons that are considered material for termination and grounds for nonrenewal. Appropriate grounds for termination or nonrenewal include the loss of a lease, failure to operate the business, franchisee insolvency, denial of franchisor access to inspect, and repeated violations of quality standards.[32] Internationally, termination without good cause or without a reasonable period to correct deficiencies will be vulnerable to legal challenge. For example, Japanese law requires that the franchisor provide the franchisee with formal notice of a breach of the franchise agreement and the opportunity to remedy deficiencies within a reasonable time prior to termination.[33] Unreasonably short periods of time granted to a franchisee for the correction of deficiencies are legally inoperative. In the United States, nineteen states require good cause for the termination of franchises.[34] The following opinion of the Judicial Committee of the Privy Council of New Zealand in *Dymocks Franchise Systems Pty Ltd. v. Todd* demonstrates the difficulties surrounding the implied obligation of the parties to a franchise agreement to act in good faith in the course of their relationship.

INTERNATIONAL

Dymocks Franchise Systems (NSW) Pty Ltd v. Todd
Judicial Committee of the Privy Council [2002] I NZLR 289

Lord Browne-Wilkinson. This was an appeal by Dymocks Franchise Systems (NSW) Pty Ltd, the appellant, from the decision of the Court of Appeal. This appeal relates to franchises to sell books at three stores in New Zealand granted by the appellant to the respondents. The case is complicated but in general terms the appellant contends that the respondents breached the franchise agreements in a manner which justified the appellant summarily terminating them. The respondents contend that there was no justification for such summary termination by the appellant which, conversely, was itself a repudiation by the appellant. After a trial lasting some seven weeks and in a judgment running to 66 printed pages Hammond J. held in favour of the appellant that the summary termination was justified. On appeal, the Court of Appeal reversed that decision and held that the appellant not the respondents had repudiated the franchises.

The Dymock group of companies is a long-established retail bookseller in Australia. During the 1980s it started to operate a franchising system through the appellant company, Dymocks Franchise Systems (NSW) Pty Ltd (Dymocks). Initially, all the franchises were in Australia. But in 1994 Dymocks expanded its franchising operation to New Zealand.

Dymocks entered into three franchise agreements with the respondents, Mr. and Mrs. Todd and their companies Bilgola Enterprises Ltd and Lambton Quay Books Ltd (together called "the Todds"). The three Todd franchises together were responsible for approximately 70 per cent of Dymocks' turnover in New Zealand.

The contractual documents in this case are very long and in some respects complicated. Each of the Todd franchises is regulated by a formal contract extending to over 50 pages which incorporates as part of the contractual documents Dymocks' confidential operations manual running to a further 250 pages. The operations manual is a hotchpotch document dealing with a wide range of different topics stretching from the laying down of mandatory contractual requirements for forfeiture at one end to detailed provisions covering every aspect of running the book-selling shop and business down to the state of the premises, the way in which they are to be presented and so on. The operations manual is expressly incorporated into each of the contractual documents by clause 11H of the franchise agreement. All three agreements regulating each of the three stores are in, for practical purposes, identical terms. Clause 11L provides that the governing law is the law of New South Wales.

---

32. See *Dayan v. McDonald's Corp.*, 466 N.E.2d 958 (Ill. 1984).

33. See Mark Abell & Lisa Sen, *Franchising in India* 243 (1998).

34. See Robert W. Emerson, "Franchising and the Collective Rights of Franchisees," 43 *Vanderbilt Law Review* 1503, 1511, n. 27 (1990). Good cause for the termination of franchise agreements is required in Arkansas, California, Connecticut, Delaware, Hawaii, Illinois, Indiana, Iowa, New Jersey, Michigan, Minnesota, Mississippi, Missouri, Nebraska, North Dakota, South Dakota, Virginia, Washington, and Wisconsin.

As has been said, the operations manual forms part of the contractual documents. The manual appears in some places to modify the terms of the main agreement. Clause 9 of the main agreement provides for summary termination of the franchise in the event of the specified breaches, some of which are of minor importance. However, the manual provides:

"If we believe you have gone beyond the constraints of our Franchise Agreement we will give you fair notice, verbally and in writing, before resorting to legal action and every opportunity will be given to you to rectify the matter. Some of the significant areas of infringement which could give rise to the termination of the Franchise Agreement are [and then certain specific instances are mentioned]."

A central issue in the case relates to certain negotiations between the Todds and Blue Star Consumer Retailing Ltd (Blue Star). Blue Star was the main competitor of Dymocks in the New Zealand market and the negotiations took place unknown to Dymocks between November 1997 and early 1998. They related to a possible joint venture between the Todds and Blue Star (the Blue Star affair). Because these negotiations were covert and concealed by Mr. Todd from Dymocks, the facts concerning them did not become known to Dymocks until after they had determined the contracts with the Todds on other grounds.

The Todds' trading for the first two years was reasonably successful. However, by late 1996 the results were falling off. There was a difference of opinion as to the reason for this. Dymocks thought it was due to inefficient management by the Todds involving the payment of seriously excessive costs. The Todds on the other hand attributed the fall-off to a failure by Dymocks to achieve a "critical mass" of Dymocks shops in consequence of which the Dymocks franchise was unable to secure large enough discounts from suppliers. The Todds further considered that Dymocks had failed to build up quickly enough to prevent another chain of "premium" bookshops establishing itself.

On 9 February 1998 Dymocks served formal notices on the Todds terminating the three franchise agreements inter alia on the grounds [of] . . . failure to operate the business in accordance with the manual by failing to do certain things required by the manual, most of which were minor but included refusing to participate in group buying. On 13 February 1998 the Todds responded by alleging that the notices of termination themselves constituted repudiation by Dymocks and accepting such repudiation. Shortly thereafter these proceedings were started.

The Blue Star Affair

Blue Star conducted the largest book-selling business in New Zealand although hitherto it had not traded in the "premium" end of the market. It was rumoured at this time that it was about to enter the premium book sector. On 8 September 1997 Mr. Todd and his general manager went to a meeting with the chairman of Blue Star who raised the possibility of a joint venture with the Todds. Mr. Todd's reaction was that he was not free to enter such a venture because of his obligations to Dymocks. However, there was a further meeting on 14 November 1997 at which a joint venture was again discussed between Mr. Todd and Mr. Ferrand of Blue Star but the proposal was described as "speculative" until the Todds could obtain a release from their agreement with Dymocks. Mr. Ferrand produced a draft confidentiality agreement previously prepared which was signed by both Dymocks and Blue Star. It recited that the parties had agreed to disclose information (described as being "of a secret and confidential nature . . . of commercial value to the party providing this information") and to "explore the various advantages of the parties entering into a joint venture agreement." It restricted the use of the information to the purposes for which it was provided. Mr. Todd then provided an analysis of key performance indicators; sales figures for the stores; gross margins; some information on set-up costs; employment costs; fees information; and the consolidated statement of the financial position of Bilgola as at 30 September 1997. It is not clear when discussions between the Todds and Blue Star ended. Amongst the papers produced by Mr. Ferrand under subpoena were sales figures for the three stores for the months November and December 1997 and January 1998. The information disclosed was commercially valuable to Blue Star.

The termination action was fought throughout with great elaboration and proliferation of issues. As to the termination action, the Judge started by considering broadly the extent to which a duty of good faith in franchise contracts was recognised in North American law, Australian law and the common law generally. He held that Australian law, at least to some extent, was developing conceptions of good faith. After these prefatory remarks on good faith the Judge turned to consider the termination by Dymocks on the grounds of specific breaches of contract alleged in the notice of the termination. He held that Dymocks could not summarily terminate the contracts without notice on those grounds for two reasons. First, the passage from the operations manual quoted above required notice to be given and secondly, on the expert evidence the law of New South Wales required in a case such as this that powers of termination be exercised in good faith, that is, reasonably. Having reached that conclusion the Judge seems to have been of the view that he had disposed of all Dymocks' claims save the claim based on breach of an obligation of good faith based on the Blue Star affair.

The Judge considered that the Blue Star affair provided grounds for the termination. The Judge then went on to hold that this breach of the implied duty of confidentiality inherent in the franchise was such as to justify summary termination of the franchise agreement. To sum up, Dymocks' claims to terminate the franchise agreement before the Judge failed on all points save one, namely the Judge's finding of a breach of an implied obligation of good faith in the franchise agreement.

The Court of Appeal upheld the Judge's decision on all points save the one on which the Judge had held in Dymocks' favour, that is, the Court of Appeal held the judge had erred in holding that there was in New South Wales law an obligation of good faith and confidentiality implied in the franchise agreements. Accordingly, the appeal was allowed since Dymocks by giving notice of termination had themselves wrongfully repudiated the agreements.

On the appeal, Dymocks contends that the Judge's decision on [good faith and confidentiality] should be restored and the Court of Appeal's view rejected. The difficulty in this case is to determine whether the Judge had before him sufficient evidence of New South Wales law to justify his finding of such an obligation of good faith in this case.

Three distinguished experts on New South Wales law gave evidence. It was on the basis of such evidence and the evidence of Professor John Carter that the Judge held that, under the law of New South Wales, a power to terminate had to be exercised reasonably. Once the Blue Star facts had emerged, not surprisingly Dymocks sought to rely on a requirement of good faith in the franchise agreements. But the experts were not recalled to give evidence. Apparently counsel for both parties told the Judge that he was just as able to read and apply the relevant authorities as the experts in New South Wales law. On that basis the Judge made widespread findings as to the requirements of good faith in the New South Wales law of contract affecting this case. It was on that ground that the Court of Appeal reversed the Judge's decision on this issue of good faith.

Their Lordships are in complete agreement with the Court of Appeal that this was an unsuitable case for a Judge to seek to ascertain foreign law without the assistance of expert testimony. Throughout the common law world it is a matter of controversy to what extent obligations of good faith are to be found in contractual relationships. The expert evidence shows that the legal analysis of an implied obligation of good faith in New South Wales is far from clear.

Since the decision of the learned Judge there have been further decisions in Australia, particularly that of the Court of Appeal of New South Wales in *Burger King Corporation v Hungry Jack's Pty Ltd*. In that case a franchise agreement was apparently treated as being a contract of a kind which by operation of law gives rise to a general duty of good faith. However, even after this decision, in further affidavits giving evidence of New South Wales law put before Their Lordships, the experts are not agreed. Mr. Bathurst QC and Sir Laurence Street consider that such an implication of good faith into franchise agreements is now established. Professor Carter, the distinguished contract lawyer, disagrees. He says: "In my opinion, Australian law has not yet reached the stage where it can be said that all contracts (or all franchise contracts) contain a term—implied in law—

subjecting the parties to a duty to exercise good faith in the performance of their obligations."

Their Lordships therefore agree with the Court of Appeal that the Judge erred in the exercise of his discretion in seeking to determine this difficult question of New South Wales law without proper expert evidence. In view of the continuing disagreement between the experts as to whether or not there is an obligation of good faith in a case such as the present, Their Lordships prefer the course of prudence and do not seek to answer the question.

However, before leaving this issue Their Lordships wish to say a word or two about the Court of Appeal judgment on it. Although the Court of Appeal decided the point on the ground that the necessary expert evidence was not before the Court, they made a number of comments suggesting that "there is no room" for superimposing a general duty of good faith, that to do so conflicts with requirements of certainty in commercial contracts, and that franchise agreements are not analogous to employment contracts (where duties of good faith are implicit). These comments suggest that, in their view, the development of the law so as to make an obligation of good faith implicit in the relationship between franchisor and franchisee (as in the case of partnership and other joint venture agreements) is not desirable. Their Lordships propose to express no concluded view on these comments and wish to reserve their opinion on the suggestion that the implication of an obligation of good faith in the relationship between franchisor and franchisee would be an undesirable development.

The Judicial Committee held nevertheless that Dymocks was justified in terminating the agreement on the basis of Defendants' failure to remit franchise fees and refusal to participate in Dymocks' activities, including the group buying program.

APPEAL ALLOWED.

Case Highlights

- A choice of law clause in a franchise agreement will govern its interpretation, including the existence of an implied obligation of the parties to act in good faith.
- National courts may be reluctant to impose an implied obligation upon the parties to a franchise agreement to act in good faith in the absence of clear evidentiary support by expert witnesses. Given this reluctance, the parties should expressly provide for such an obligation in their franchise agreement.
- Franchisors should carefully delineate the franchisee's obligations with respect to the maintenance of confidentiality with respect to sensitive financial information exchanged in the course of the franchise relationship.

Other provisions deal with the mechanics of the franchise relationship. Foremost is the franchise fee or **royalties clause**. The franchise agreement commonly requires that an initial fee be paid for the right to obtain a franchise and then payment of royalties based upon a percentage of gross or net sales. The agreement should provide a commencement and expiration date. One common means of fixing the dates is to provide for expiration in a certain number of years from commencement or the date the franchise opens for business. Because most franchise arrangements include the transfer of intellectual property rights, the agreement should expressly retain the title to those rights to the franchisor. The following Comparative Law feature illustrates a franchise clause dealing with the transfer of trade secrets and intellectual property. The clause makes clear that the franchisor owns the intellectual property being licensed and that on the franchise's termination all property rights return to the franchisor.

The final two clauses to be discussed are the insurance and the franchisee review clauses. It is prudent for the franchisor, especially in the international setting, to require the franchisee to maintain certain types and amounts of insurance. The franchisee can be required to carry specific amounts of comprehensive general liability and products liability insurance. The contract should provide that the franchisor should be an "additional endorsee" on all such policies. The **insurance clause** should be coupled with a *hold harmless clause* that requires the franchisee to defend the franchisor against any liability claims arising from or related to its operation of the franchise.

The **franchisee review clause** is used to combat future claims of misrepresentation or overbearing by the franchisor. They generally incorporate a number of provisos, including "a statement that the franchisee has received no guarantees, representations, warranties or the like as to the profitability of the franchise being purchased

---

COMPARATIVE LAW

Intellectual Property Transfer Clause

FRANCHISEE acknowledges that ownership of all right, title, and interest to the ABC franchise system and its marks are and shall remain vested solely in the franchisor, and the FRANCHISEE disclaims any right or interest therein or the goodwill derived therefrom. FRANCHISEE agrees that all materials loaned or otherwise made available to him by the franchisor at any time before or during the term of this Agreement relating to the franchise system, including, without limitation, the Manual in its entirety, financial information, marketing strategy, and programs are to be considered trade secrets of the franchisor and shall be kept confidential and used by FRANCHISEE only in connection with the franchise operation. FRANCHISEE agrees not to divulge any of the trade secrets to any person other than its employees and then only to the extent necessary for the operation of the franchise and, specifically, that FRANCHISEE will not, nor permit anyone to, reproduce, copy, or exhibit any portion of the Manual or any other trade secrets of the franchisor. FRANCHISEE shall immediately notify franchisor of all infringements or limitations of franchisor's marks which come to its attention.[35]

---

35.   Emerson, "Franchise Contract Clauses," *supra* note 31, at 958.

and that the franchisee has conducted its own independent investigation of the merits of the investment."[36] Another clause vital to the franchisor's defense against misrepresentation is the merger clause. The merger clause attempts to prevent the entry of any parol evidence in a subsequent adversarial proceeding. The role of parol evidence in contract disputes will be discussed in Chapter Seven, International Contract Law, and Chapter Eight, International Sales Law.

UNIDROIT GUIDE TO INTERNATIONAL MASTER FRANCHISING

One way to avoid entering multiple franchise agreements with individual franchisees in a foreign country is the **master franchise** arrangement. In the master franchise arrangement, the franchisor enters into an agreement with a subfranchisor or master franchisee to develop an entire franchise territory. The subfranchisor is entitled to establish individual franchise locations or to find subfranchisees to operate within its territory. The contractual relationship may run between the subfranchisee and the subfranchisor or, most commonly, between the subfranchisee and the franchisor. In this way, the franchisor can directly exercise control over the individual franchise operations.

The International Institute for the Unification of Private Law (UNIDROIT) has published an elaborate document titled *UNIDROIT Guide to International Master Franchise Arrangements*. It provides an array of information, along with standard clauses to be used in the drafting of a master franchise contract. The approach of the publication is to provide clauses that are fair to all parties concerned and based on *best practices*. Some of the issues addressed are the types of franchising arrangements available, the relationship between the franchising agreement and other types of agreements (commercial agency, license, technology transfer, distribution), and the differences in the franchisor-franchisee and subfranchisor-subfranchisee relationships. The contract issues discussed include the nature and extent of the rights granted (e.g., exclusivity of rights granted to subfranchisor); duration of agreement and provisions for renewal; alternative fee structures; calculation of payments (timing, accounting, currency, tax issues); costs and control of advertising; supply of equipment, products, and services; the transfer and protection of intellectual property (confidentiality clauses, noncompetition clauses, grant-back clauses, post-termination clauses); assignment and transfer; indemnification and insurance (franchisor liability to third parties); remedies for breach; and termination.

http://
UNIDROIT: **http://www.unidroit.org.**

INTERNATIONAL FRANCHISING

Principles recognized under U.S. franchise law do not always translate well into other legal systems.[37] For example, previous editions of the U.S. State Department's *Country Commercial Guide for Russia* downplayed the use of franchising as a viable option in entering the Russian market and noted that the concept was little understood in the country. In support of these conclusions, the guide cited the failure of early attempts to establish franchise distribution due to confusion regarding ownership and the responsibilities of the parties to a franchise agreement. The most recent edition of the guide concluded that "the conditions that would support a rapid growth in the [franchise] sector have been created only recently."[38] Despite this optimism, the guide also notes that domestic franchisors still outnumber

http://
International Franchise Association: **http://www.franchise.org.**

INTERNATIONAL

---

36. Ibid.
37. See generally Philip F. Zeidman & Michael Avner, "Franchising in Eastern Europe and the Soviet Union," 3 *DePaul Business Law Journal* 307 (1991).
38. U.S. State Department's Country Commercial Guide for Russia (2004).

foreign franchisors operating in the country. The Federal District Court in *McAlpine v. AAMCO Automatic Transmission, Inc.*, described the synergy of franchising and the inherent seeds for its own destruction:

The franchise arrangement starts as a mutually advantageous business relationship. Both the franchisor and the franchisee contribute to this arrangement in order to obtain benefits they could not obtain independently. The franchisor's contribution is a combination of factors: trademark, recognized product or service, experience, advertising, and management support. The franchisee's contribution is capital, day-to-day management and the payment of franchise fees. The franchisor benefits from the use of franchisee capital, fees, and lower-level management, for it allows the franchise organization to expand more rapidly. As the franchise becomes successful, the partnership arrangement which seemed reasonable at its inception begins to appear burdensome to the franchisee who comes to regard the payment of franchise fees as restricting its profitability.[39]

To further illustrate the point, the *Dayan v. McDonald's Corp.* case exemplifies the two major risks of international franchising, namely, loss of control over franchise operations and inability to terminate the franchise relationship.

Another issue especially important for franchising in a foreign country is to provide the appropriate means of protecting the franchisor's **trade secrets**. There is no generally accepted definition of trade secrets. It is a much broader concept than statutorily protected intellectual property rights (patent, copyright, trademark). The Uniform Trade Secrets Act offers this definition:

"Trade Secret" means information, including a formula, pattern, compilation, program, device, method, technique, or process, that: (i) derives independent economic value, actual or potential, from not being generally known to, and not being readily ascertainable by proper means by other persons who can obtain economic value from its disclosure or use, and (ii) is the subject of efforts that are reasonable under the circumstances to maintain its secrecy.[40]

The franchisor should determine if the information being given is a trade secret. If so, it should expressly list in the franchise agreement the information that it intends to treat as trade secrets. The agreement may list information not

Dayan v. McDonald's Corporation

466 N.E.2d 958 (Ill. App. 1984)

This appeal arises out of a suit brought to enjoin McDonald's Corporation from terminating Raymond Dayan's restaurant franchise in Paris, France. Other issues relating to this controversy have been considered twice before by this court. After a 65-day trial, the circuit court of Cook County denied plaintiff's request for a permanent injunction. The trial court issued a 114-page memorandum and an order terminating plaintiff's franchise to operate McDonald's restaurants in and around Paris.

This case has a lengthy legal and historical background involving prior litigation. Dayan originally filed an action against McDonald's in 1970 alleging the defendant corporation had breached a prior agreement giving Dayan the right to purchase certain franchises and to develop and operate certain restaurants in Paris. The unique character of the 1971 license agreement was a key factor at trial. The record reveals that the terms of this agreement were the subject of extensive negotiations between McDonald's and Dayan and differed substantially from McDonald's standard licensing agreement. McDonald's submitted three alternate proposals to Dayan. Proposal 1 was McDonald's standard license agreement with a 3% royalty fee on gross receipts, real estate to be bought and developed by McDonald's with

---

39.   461 F. Supp. 1232, 1238–39 (E.D. Mich. 1978).
40.   Uniform Trade Secrets Act § 1(4), 14 U.L.A. 541 (1980).

rental rates comparable to U.S.A. leases. Proposal 2 was a joint venture with McDonald's and Dayan each owning 50% equity. Proposal 3 was a developmental license similar to the original Canadian franchises and provided for a 1% royalty fee, Dayan to develop his own real estate, and no McDonald's service except as ordered and paid for by Dayan. Under the standard McDonald's license embodied in proposal 1, McDonald's would be obligated to provide extensive services to Dayan in all areas of restaurant operations and Dayan would pay a correspondingly higher royalty fee. Dayan insisted upon the 1% developmental license.

The necessity of maintaining the Quality, Safety, and Cleanliness (QSC) standards is explicitly recognized in the Master License Agreement (MLA). It recites the rationale for maintaining QSC standards—"departure of Restaurants anywhere in the world from these standards impedes the successful operation of Restaurants throughout the world, and injures the value of its [McDonald's] Patents, Trademarks, Trade name, and Property." In addition, the individual operating license agreements (OLA) included the following termination provision:

Licensee acknowledges that uniform quality and taste of food, excellence of service, cleanliness, appearance, and general performance are of the utmost importance to the successful operation of the business venture of the Licensee and of all other Licensees using said System. The Licensee agrees that any violation of this paragraph shall be deemed to be a substantial breach of this Agreement and shall give the Licensor the right to terminate this Agreement.

Witnesses called by McDonald's testified as to the deplorable condition of Dayan's restaurants. In particular, their testimony revealed that Dayan was not using approved products; he used no pickles; he charged extra for catsup or mustard; he hid straws and napkins under the counter; he refused to take a refresher course at McDonald's "Hamburger University"; the stores were filthy and without many items of necessary equipment; the store crews were poorly trained and frequently out of uniform, and customer complaints were numerous. Barnes, the president of McDonald's international division, testified that in June 1976 he informed Dayan that he would be given six months to bring his restaurants up to standard and at the end of this period McDonald's would exercise its right to formal inspection. The inspectors found gross violations of McDonald's QSC standards at all the stores they visited. In July 1977, a stern warning letter was sent to Dayan advising him that the number, variety, and severity of QSC deficiencies justified a default declaration but that such declaration would be held in abeyance for six months to "give you an opportunity to take immediate corrective action." Ultimately, McDonald's brought suit in Paris to terminate the MLA,

which resulted in Dayan filing the present suit in Illinois to enjoin termination.

In Illinois, as in the majority of American jurisdictions, a *covenant of good faith* and *fair dealing* is implied in every contract absent express disavowal. Problems relating to good faith performance typically arise where one party to the contract is given broad discretion in performance. The dependent party must then rely on the party in control to exercise that discretion fairly. It remains to be seen, however, what limitation the implied covenant of good faith imposes on franchisor discretion in terminating a franchise agreement. A Utah Supreme Court held that the implied covenant of good faith limited the power of the franchisor to terminate a franchise agreement without good cause. The court stated that "when parties enter into a contract of this character, and there is no express provision that it may be cancelled without cause, it seems fair and reasonable to assume that both parties entered into the arrangement in good faith, intending that if the service is performed in a satisfactory manner it will not be cancelled arbitrarily." These cases reflect judicial concern over longstanding abuses in franchise relationships, particularly contract provisions giving the franchisor broad unilateral powers of termination at will. Taken collectively, they stand for the proposition that the implied covenant of good faith restricts franchisor discretion in terminating a franchise agreement to those cases where good cause exists. However, plaintiff would have us go further and argues that even if McDonald's had good cause for termination, if it also had an improper motive the termination would be a breach of the implied covenant of good faith. Dayan would attribute to McDonald's a desire to recapture the lucrative Paris market as an impermissible motive. We cannot agree. As a general proposition of law, it is widely held that where good cause exists, motive is immaterial to a determination of good faith performance.

Our review of the evidence admits of no doubt; the trial court properly resolved this issue in favor of McDonald's. To characterize the condition of Dayan's restaurants as being in substantial noncompliance with McDonald's QSC standards is a profound understatement. Throughout trial the various witnesses struggled to find the appropriate words to describe the ineffably unsanitary conditions observed in these restaurants, as did the trial court in its memorandum opinion. Terms describing the uncleanliness—such as "indescribable," "extremely defective sanitary conditions," "filthy, grimy, cruddy," "deplorable," "significantly unsanitary," "contaminated," "unsanitary," "very dirty," "very, very dirty," "disgusting," "abundance of filth," "pig pens"—tell only part of the story. The accuracy of these epithets is supported by voluminous, detailed testimonial evidence which consumed many weeks of trial and thousands of pages of transcript and is also corroborated by over 1,000 photographs admitted in evidence at trial. Dayan also argues that McDonald's was obligated to provide him with the operational assistance necessary to enable him to meet the QSC standards. As the trial court correctly realized: "It does not take a McDonald's trained French speaking operational man to know that grease dripping from the vents must be stopped and not merely collected in a cup hung from the ceiling, that dogs are not permitted to defecate where food is stored, that insecticide is not blended with chicken breading, that past-dated products should be discarded, that a potato peeler should be somewhat cleaner than a tire-vulcanizer and that shortening should not look like crank case oil."

Contrary to plaintiff's contention, the MLA negotiated by him explicitly stated what he had to do if he wished such assistance; he had to request it in writing and pay for it. Accordingly, we reject Dayan's argument that he was entitled to the same operational assistance prior to termination as the standard licensee. The judgment of the trial court denying plaintiff's request for a permanent injunction and finding that McDonald's properly terminated the franchise agreement is AFFIRMED.

Case Highlights

- Note the length and complexity, and ultimately the costs, of the litigation pertaining to this termination of a franchise agreement.
- A master license agreement (MLA) is often used to develop an entire territory, and each franchise location is also governed by individual operating license agreements (OLA).
- Under U.S. law, the franchisor's right to terminate a franchise is limited by the duty of good faith and fair dealing, along with individual state statutes.
- Standards relating to quality, safety, and cleanliness (QSC) are vital to maintaining the integrity and reputation of the franchise system as a whole.

---

generally considered trade secrets and expressly state that the information is to be deemed "secret and confidential." For example, customer lists provided by the franchisor have been held to be legally protected trade secrets. A trade secret designation in the agreement is enhanced if the information is not readily obtainable through alternative sources and the franchisor treats the lists as "secret and confidential." The agreement can further protect the franchisor with a separate confidentiality clause and a noncompetition clause. The **noncompetition clause** should balance the goal of protecting the franchisor with the need to devise reasonable restrictions regarding scope, duration, and territory. Overly restrictive noncompetition clauses are likely to be reviewed and modified by most courts.

A franchise agreement that provides for a large amount of franchisor control may create problems under host country regulation. For example, "excessive control or the public appearance of such control may give rise to an agency relationship between the franchisor and the franchise" under foreign law.[41] If viewed as a dependent agency relationship, as discussed in Chapter Twelve, the franchisor may become susceptible to the tax and labor laws of the host country, as well as become vulnerable to lawsuits such as products liability claims. The next section briefly reviews foreign regulation of franchising with a focus on EU Regulations.

FOREIGN REGULATION OF FRANCHISING: EU REGULATION

http://

Franchise law in Ontario, Canada: **http://www.trytel.com/ &sim~pbkerr/ franchise.html.**

A number of restrictions on franchising can be found in U.S. and foreign laws. For example, in the United States a number of state franchise statutes limit the ability of the franchisor to terminate the franchise at will. Internationally, some countries offer a less friendly environment for franchising than that of the United States. Host

---

41.   Ralph H. Folsom, *International Business Transactions* 96 (2d ed. 2002).

country laws vary significantly—from laws that do not even recognize the franchise form of business to laws that limit the types of contract provisions that will be enforced. The effectiveness of using model forms is limited by the fact that vast differences in contractual issues occur from industry to industry and under host country laws.

Before contemplating franchising in Europe, a franchisor will need to review EU franchise regulations for purposes of negotiating legally enforceable franchise agreements. The regulations offer insight about what types of clauses can be incorporated into an international franchise agreement. The European Union (EU) places limits on franchises so that they conform to its competition law.[42] Franchises operating in the EU were previously subject to specific and detailed regulation of their relationship. **EU Regulation 4087/88** provided an exemption from the application of EU competition law in Article 81 of the Treaty of Rome. This regulation recognized that some restrictions on the rights of the franchisee were needed to maintain the "homogeneity of the network and the constant cooperation between franchisor and franchisees [in order to] ensure a constant quality of the products and services" being provided. The regulation provided a list of clauses that, although restrictive of competition, had a strong nexus to these philosophical goals, the so-called *white list*. They allowed the development of exclusive franchise territories and prohibited franchisees from actively seeking customers outside the franchise territory and selling the goods or services of a competitor. By contrast, prohibited clauses included those that restricted a franchisee from purchasing from another franchisee, from filling orders from parties outside its territory that were not actively sought, unduly limiting the franchisee's choice of suppliers or customers, and restrictions on pricing, otherwise known as the *black list*. The regulation was widely followed in drafting European franchise agreements.

INTERNATIONAL

In 1999, the EU adopted **Regulation 2790/1999**, the so-called vertical agreements regulation.[43] This regulation superseded Regulation 4087/88 and is applicable to agreements containing such restraints entered into as of June 1, 2000. Agreements entered into prior to the effective date became subject to the new regulation on January 1, 2002. The term "vertical restraints" is broadly defined and undoubtedly includes most franchising arrangements, including those based on agency relationships and selective distribution arrangements. Regulation 2790/1999 provides an automatic exemption from EU competition law for such agreements for firms with less than 30 percent market shares. Under such circumstances, there is no need for the involvement of the EU Commission. Rather, the contract is valid and can be enforced in the national courts of the member states without further institutional intervention. In this regard, the regulation has been described as "more economic and less formalistic."[44] By contrast, companies whose market share exceeds 30 percent are subject to an analysis by the Commission pursuant to EU competition laws, the results of which determine whether the agreement is entitled to an exemption. In any event, certain restraints, such as resale price maintenance, clauses resulting in market allocation, and exclusive dealing covenants in excess of five years, are prohibited in all vertical restraint agreements, including franchise documents.[45]

42. See Dieter A. Schmitz & Alain Van Hamme, "Franchising in Europe: The First Practical EEC Guidelines," 22 *The International Lawyer* 717 (1988).

43. Commission Regulation (EU) No. 2790/1999 of 22 December 1999.

44. Folsom, *International Business Transactions, supra* note 41, at 103.

45. For a fuller explanation of how Regulation 2790/1999 relates to franchising in the EU, see Joanna Goyder, *EU Distribution Law* (3d. ed. 2000).

KEY TERMS

affiliate
block exemption
branch office
business alliance venture
business review letter
competition law
contractual joint venture
corporation
distribution agreement
enterprise liability
equity joint venture
EU Regulation 4087/88
exceptions clause
export trade certificate of review
foreign subsidiary

franchisee review clause
general partnership
insurance clause
intellectual property transfer
joint stock company
joint venture
limited liability company (LLC)
limited partnership
local partner
management agreements
management board
master franchise
noncompetition clause
operational standards clause
piercing the corporate veil

purpose clause
Regulation 2790/1999
renewal clause
representative office
royalties clause
secondment agreement
shareholders' council
single project venture
site selection clause
supervisory board
supervisory committee
territorial clause
trade secrets
transfer pricing

CHAPTER PROBLEMS

1. Read the following articles and do a comparative analysis: Ronald J. Gilson & Mark J. Roe, "Lifetime Employment: Labor, Peace and the Evolution of Japanese Corporate Governance," 99 *Columbia Law Review* 508 (1999); Mark J. Roe, "German Codetermination and German Securities Markets," 1998 *Columbia Business Law Review* 167 (1998); Mark J. Roe, "Some Differences in Corporate Structure in Germany, Japan, and the United States," 102 *Yale Law Journal* 1927 (1993).
2. Select two of the following countries: China, United States, Japan, Germany. Compare and contrast corporate

law in the two countries you have selected. Discuss how corporate law reflects society's fundamental view of the role of the corporation.
3. What does the phrase "piercing the corporate veil" mean? When might the corporate veil be pierced? How does this philosophy compare with that of many U.S. trading partners?
4. What are some of the issues that potential joint venture partners need to discuss in detail before entering into an agreement? Discuss some of the contractual clauses that can be incorporated into an agreement to minimize potential conflict.

INTERNET EXERCISES

1. Research a foreign country or countries for opportunities and restrictions on the different ways of transacting business discussed in this chapter by using the U.S. Department of State's country commercial guides. Individual country commercial guides can be obtained at **http://www.state.gov.**
2. Research the status of franchising in a foreign country. A good place to start is the Web site for the International

Franchise Association at **http://www.franchise.org.** A growing number of national franchise associations, along with the European Franchise Federation, can also be assessed.
3. Compare the Contractual Joint Venture Law of the People's Republic of Korea at **http://210.145.168.243/pk/** (under "Economy" click on "Foreign Trade Laws") with the Chinese Foreign Equity Joint Venture Law at **http://www.qis.net/chinalaw/prclaw11.htm.**

The cost and uncertainty of potential litigation with a foreign citizen or company can act as a deterrent to international business transactions. The prospect of having to pursue a claim or to defend a claim in a foreign court using foreign law may prove too risky for some businesspeople. At the least, anyone contemplating a business transaction with a foreign entity should ask the following questions: (1) What are the alternatives to transnational litigation? (2) Where will a future dispute be argued or settled? (3) What country's law would be applied to such a dispute? (4) Will a settlement or decision be enforceable in a foreign country? These questions should be discussed during the earlier stages of contract negotiation, and an international contract should expressly answer these questions through the use of forum selection, choice of law, and alternative dispute resolution clauses. The answer to question (1) is that international commercial arbitration is a popular alternative to international litigation. The contractual devices represented by choice of law and forum selection clauses provide the avenue for dealing with questions (2) and (3). Finally, a review of national laws and international conventions will help answer question (4).

Chapter 4

International Commercial Dispute Resolution

International Litigation

Anyone seeking to undertake international litigation faces three areas of concern. First, how does one properly begin a lawsuit against a foreign company? Second, once the litigation begins, how do the parties gather evidence in foreign countries? Third, if successful in the litigation, how does one enforce a judgment in a foreign country?

To bring a lawsuit against a foreign company, one must properly serve process. **Service of process** is the formal notification of defendants to defend themselves in court. Proper service of process is necessary for a court to obtain **personal jurisdiction** over the defendant. Failure to obtain legally sufficient service of process is likely to result in the nonenforceability of any *default judgment* obtained in the event that the defendant fails to appear. To require a foreign party to defend itself in a suit brought in the United States, the service of process should meet the requirements of both the United States and the country of the party being served. This is especially crucial if the judgment will need to be enforced in a foreign country. Service of process requirements, however, vary widely throughout the world. The U.S. Federal Rules of Civil Procedure state that service in a foreign country may be made "by any form of mail, requiring a signed receipt, to be addressed and dispatched by the clerk of the court to the party to be served." In contrast, service by mail is generally not recognized by foreign court systems.

http://
International Bar Association—Sections on business law and legal practice: **http://www.ibanet.org.**

http://
Text of Hague Service Convention: **http://hcch.e-vision.nl/index_en.php?act=conventions.listings.**

Adoption of the Convention on the Service Abroad of Judicial and Extrajudicial Documents in Civil or Commercial Matters, or the **Hague Service Convention**, is one response to the problem of international service of process. The Hague Service Convention provides a government means to ensure effective and recognizable service of process. The signatory countries to the convention are required to establish a central authority for processing foreign plaintiffs' service of process requests. The central authority serves the defendant directly or arranges to have it served by the appropriate government agency. Fifty-five states have adopted the Hague Service Convention, including the United States, Japan, China, France, Germany, Great Britain, Italy, Spain, and Canada. In countries not party to the convention, **dual service** of process is recommended. Dual service aims to satisfy the service requirements of the country of the forum court and the country of the defendant in order to enhance the enforceability of any future judgment.

Service of process in conformity with international and national rules only partially addresses the issue of the ability of national courts to exercise authority over foreign defendants. Courts must also possess **jurisdiction** to enter a judgment binding upon the parties appearing before them and subject to enforcement abroad. Jurisdiction is the power of a court to hear a case. There are two types of jurisdiction. **Subject matter jurisdiction** is the power of the court over the type of case pending before it. It may be based on the type of case, such as civil, criminal, probate, or domestic relations, or on the amount of money at issue. Personal jurisdiction is the power of the court over the people appearing before it. U.S. courts exercise two different types of personal jurisdiction. *General personal jurisdiction* permits courts to adjudicate any claims against a defendant regardless of whether the claims have any relation to the forum court. For a court to exercise general jurisdiction, the defendant must have a significant presence in the forum. This presence may premised upon nationality, residence, or organization within the United States, or it may consist of a "continuous and systematic presence" within the forum.[1] *Specific personal jurisdiction* permits courts to adjudicate only those claims arising from or relating to the defendant's activities in the forum. For a court to exercise specific personal jurisdiction, the defendant must purposefully avail itself of the protections of the forum.[2] Merely placing a product into the stream of commerce is insufficient unless the product was specifically designed for the forum or the defendant provided regular advice or service to customers in the forum or maintained a distributor in the forum. Furthermore, the forum must be a reasonable location for the conduct of the litigation. To determine the reasonableness of the forum, the court must balance the burden on the defendant, the interest of the selected forum in resolving the dispute, the plaintiff's interest in obtaining relief in the forum, and applicable foreign policy concerns, if any, arising from the exercise of jurisdiction. The issue of personal jurisdiction over a foreign defendant is discussed in *Alpine View Company, Ltd. v. Atlas Copco AB*.

There are a number of defenses to the exercise of jurisdiction, even when such would be proper under the requirements of due process. The U.S. Code grants **sovereign immunity** to foreign states (Foreign Sovereign Immunities Act or FSIA) and their political subdivisions, agencies, and instrumentalities.[3]

---

1. See *Helicopteros Nacionales de Colombia v. Hall*, 466 U.S. 408 (1984).
2. See *Asahi Metal Industries v. Superior Court*, 480 U.S. 102 (1987).
3. See 28 U.S.C. §§ 1602–07 (2000). For the English law counterpart (State Immunity Act of 1978) see Chapter 33, 17 I.L.M. 1123 (1978).

Alpine View Company, Ltd. v. Atlas Copco AB
205 F.3d 208 (5th Cir. 2000)

King, Chief Judge. This case arises out of an alleged breach of a 1992 Intentional Agreement ("1992 Agreement") between Alpine View Company, Limited ("Alpine View"), and Uniroc AB ("Uniroc"), a wholly-owned subsidiary of the Swedish holding company, Atlas Copco AB ("ACAB"). In 1989, Bjorn Hansen, the president of Alpine View, was granted exclusive worldwide rights to the distribution and sale of offshore drill bits manufactured by Shanghai Machinery & Equipment Import/Export Corporation ("SMEC"), a Chinese company.

To facilitate the sale of these products, Hansen sought an established distributor, and eventually executed the 1992 Agreement with Uniroc. Under the 1992 Agreement, Uniroc was to purchase drill bits from Bjorn Hansen A/S, and eventually become the exclusive distributor of those products in certain specified sectors of the world market. Uniroc was to pay Alpine View a commission based on net sales to users and distributors outside the Atlas Copco Group, which comprises ACAB and its 71 subsidiaries. To enhance its ability to deal directly with SMEC, Uniroc was also to enter into a separate distributorship agreement with that company. The existence of the separate distributorship agreement was a precondition for the effectiveness of the 1992 Agreement. Alpine View is incorporated under the laws of the British Virgin Islands and Hansen is a resident of Norway. Compressors and Comptec are each Delaware corporations, with Compressors having its principal place of business in Massachusetts and Comptec having its in New York. Robbins is a Washington corporation and has its principal place of business in that state. Compressors, Comptec, and Robbins are all subsidiaries of ACAB.

Dismissal for Lack of Personal Jurisdiction

We review *de novo* a district court's dismissal for want of personal jurisdiction. The Due Process Clause permits the exercise of personal jurisdiction over a nonresident defendant when (1) that defendant has purposefully availed himself of the benefits and protections of the forum state by establishing *minimum contacts* with the forum state; and (2) the exercise of jurisdiction over that defendant does not offend traditional notions of fair play and substantial justice. Minimum contacts can be established either through contacts sufficient to assert specific jurisdiction, or contacts sufficient to assert general jurisdiction. *Specific jurisdiction* over a nonresident corporation is appropriate when that corporation has purposefully directed its activities at the forum state and the "litigation results from alleged injuries that arise out of or relate to those activities." *General jurisdiction*, on the other hand, will attach where the nonresident defendant's contacts with the forum state, although not related to the plaintiff's cause of action, are "continuous and systematic."

I. Specific Jurisdiction and the Stream-of-Commerce Theory

The Supreme Court stated that the "foreseeability that is critical to due process analysis is that the defendant's conduct and connection with the forum State are such that he should reasonably anticipate being haled into court there." Appellants rely heavily on the stream-of-commerce theory. In support of their argument that the *stream-of-commerce theory* is applicable to cases other than those involving products liability, Appellants point to courts applying the theory to cases raising antitrust or intellectual property related claims. When a nonresident's contact with the forum state stems from a product, sold or manufactured by the foreign defendant, which has caused harm in the forum state, the court has specific jurisdiction if it finds that the defendant delivered the product into the stream of commerce with the expectation that it would be purchased by or used by consumers in the forum state. However, delivery of products into the stream of commerce does not support assertion of specific jurisdiction over ACAB and Robbins. Appellants argue that putting products into the stream of commerce with the expectation that Texans will purchase or use those products suffices to establish jurisdiction with respect to "any claims." This is more akin to a general jurisdiction argument than to a specific jurisdiction argument. Appellants make no attempt to link Appellees' contacts with Texas and the instant litigation. This is a link that specific jurisdiction requires. Appellants have not asserted that the alleged misdeeds occurred in Texas, or that the 1992 Agreement was negotiated or executed in Texas. Neither Alpine View nor Hansen is considered a Texas resident.

2. General Jurisdiction and the Alter-Ego Doctrine

Appellants also challenge the district court's conclusion that they had not shown that assertion of general jurisdiction was proper in this case. To make a *prima facie* showing of general jurisdiction, Appellants must produce evidence that affirmatively shows that ACAB's and Robbins' contacts with Texas that are unrelated to the litigation are sufficient to satisfy due process requirements. Those unrelated contacts must be substantial, continuous, and systematic. Examining the submitted evidence, it is clear that Appellants have not demonstrated that Robbins' direct contacts with Texas during the relevant period were sufficient to establish general jurisdiction. The evidence shows, at best, that Robbins sold, on isolated occasions, products to entities located in Texas and that Robbins' personnel made field service visits to Texas. These contacts are neither substantial, continuous, nor systematic.

The same conclusion is compelled with regard to ACAB. Appellants rely on evidence that indicates that the products of ACAB's subsidiaries are sold in Texas. However, "a foreign parent corporation is not subject to the jurisdiction of a forum state merely because its subsidiary is present or doing business there; the mere existence of a parent-subsidiary relationship is not sufficient to warrant the assertion of jurisdiction over the foreign parent." Appellants must make a *prima facie* showing that ACAB so controls other organizations that the activities of those organizations may be fairly attributed to ACAB for purposes of asserting jurisdiction over it. Under Texas law, the *alter-ego doctrine* applies when there is such unity between the parent corporation and its subsidiary that the separateness of the two corporations has ceased and holding only the subsidiary corporation liable would result in injustice. We have said, however, that "100% stock ownership and commonality of officers and directors are not alone sufficient to establish an *alter-ego* relationship between two corporations." Instead, "the degree of control exercised by the parent must be greater than that normally associated with common ownership and directorship." Such control has not been indicated here. The existence of intercorporate loans does not establish the requisite dominance, and in fact,

interest-bearing loans suggest separation of corporate entities. We conclude that the district court did not err in dismissing Appellants' claims against Robbins and ACAB for lack of personal jurisdiction.

Case Highlights

- International litigation is often complex because of the diversity of the parties. In this case, the parties were from China, Sweden, Norway, the British Virgin Islands, and the states of New York, Massachusetts, Washington, and Delaware.
- Under the due process clause of the U.S. Constitution, personal jurisdiction over a defendant must be based on either "minimum contacts" for purposes of gaining specific jurisdiction or "substantial, continuous, and systematic" contacts for purposes of gaining general jurisdiction.
- Specific jurisdiction requires a nexus between the minimum contacts and the injuries claimed, whereas general jurisdiction allows for lawsuits on unrelated claims.
- The stream-of-commerce theory is applicable only if the defendant delivers a product into the stream of commerce with the expectation that it would be purchased in the forum state.
- A foreign parent company does not become subject to the jurisdiction of a foreign court simply because its subsidiary is amenable to that state's jurisdiction.
- The alter-ego theory allows jurisdiction over a parent company if the parent company "dominates" the activities of a subsidiary that has sufficient contacts with the forum court.

Foreign states are immune from lawsuits, and federal courts lack subject matter jurisdiction over claims against foreign states unless an enumerated exception is applicable. Once a defendant establishes that it is a foreign state, the burden of production shifts to the plaintiff to offer evidence that an exception is applicable. There are several potential exceptions to sovereign immunity. A commonly utilized exception is for commercial activities. This exception covers a commercial activity carried on in the United States by the foreign state, an act performed in the United States in connection with a commercial activity of the foreign state elsewhere, or an act outside the United States in connection with a foreign commercial activity that causes a direct effect in the United States.

A *commercial activity* is defined as a regular course of commercial conduct or a particular commercial transaction. The U.S. Supreme Court has elaborated on this term by noting that "when a foreign government acts, not as a regulator of a market, but in the manner of a private player within it, the foreign sovereign's actions are' 'commercial' within the meaning of the FSIA."[4] The activity must be within the power of private citizens rather than those reserved exclusively for sovereigns. The problem with this type of categorization of activities is that government procurement has become increasingly commercialized, making the distinction between sovereign and commercial activities difficult to define. The gravity of this problem becomes apparent in developing countries, where almost by necessity a governmental entity is involved with international transactions. For example, a government partner is common in joint venture undertakings in developing countries. It is important in such dealings to negotiate a contract clause in which the governmental entity *waives* its sovereign immunity defense.

INTERNATIONAL

Furthermore, a judicial determination of the exercise of sovereign power or commercial activity may not characterize an entire transaction, and the two can coexist in a set of interrelated transactions. For example, in *Kuwait Airways Corporation v. Iraq Airways Corporation*, the British House of Lords found that the seizure of civilian aircraft owned by Kuwaiti Airways by the Iraqi military and their removal from the country at the direction of the Iraqi government during the invasion of Kuwait in August 1990 were sovereign acts entitled to immunity pursuant to the State Immunity Act of 1978.[5] However, subsequent government orders dissolving Kuwaiti Airways and transferring its assets to Iraq Airways violated international law and were not exercises of sovereign authority subject to state immunity. As such, these orders were subject to challenge before appropriate English judicial authorities. The *Parex Bank v. Russian Savings Bank* case further elaborates upon the commercial activity exception to foreign sovereign immunity.

Courts have developed numerous doctrines outside the statutory framework by which they may refuse to exercise jurisdiction in a given case. The **act of state doctrine** has been described as "a non-jurisdictional, prudential doctrine based on the notion that the courts of one country will not sit in judgment on the acts of the government of another [state], done within its own territory."[6] In *Sabbatino*, the U.S. Supreme Court delineated a three-part test to assist courts in determining whether the act of state doctrine bars consideration of specific claims. This test consists of balancing the degree of codification or consensus concerning the particular area of international law at issue, the implications of judicial resolution of the issue for U.S. foreign relations, and whether the government whose actions are at issue remains in existence at the time of the court's decision.

The **political question doctrine** provides that a political question is not subject to review by courts. The doctrine precludes a court from hearing a case involving one or more of the following factors: (1) a constitutional commitment of the issue to a coordinate political department, (2) a lack of judicially discoverable and manageable standards for resolving it, (3) the impossibility of deciding without an initial policy determination of a kind clearly for nonjudicial discretion, (4) the impossibility of a court's undertaking independent resolution without expressing lack of the respect due coordinate branches of government, (5) an unusual need for unquestioning adherence to a political decision already made, or (6) the potentiality of embarrassment from multifarious pronouncements by various departments on one question.[7] A broader international principle that courts use to rationalize decisions to honor

4. *Republic of Argentina v. Weltover, Inc.*, 504 U.S. 607, 614 (1992).
5. 2 Lloyd's Rep. 317 (H.L. 1995).
6. *Underhill v. Hernandez*, 168 U.S. 250, 252 (1897). See also *Banco Nacional de Cuba v. Sabbatino*, 376 U.S. 398, 428 (1964).
7. See *Baker v. Carr*, 369 U.S. 186, 217 (1962).

Parex Bank v. Russian Savings Bank

116 F. Supp.2d 415 (2000)

Sweet, District Judge. Defendant Russian Savings Bank ("Sberbank") moves to dismiss the complaint filed by Plaintiff Parex Bank ("Parex"). Parex is a financial institution organized and existing under the laws of Latvia. Sberbank is an open joint-stock company organized under the laws of the Russian Federation. Its majority shareholder is the Central Bank of the Russian Federation, and its principal place of business is Moscow.

The dispute arose out of Sberbank's alleged failure to honor a nondeliverable forward exchange contract ("NDF contract") between the parties in the aftermath of Russia's 1998 financial crisis. On March 11, 1998, a Parex trader in Riga, Latvia telephonically initiated a contract for a nondeliverable forward transaction with Sberbank in Moscow. The parties agreed to exchange rubles for dollars at the currency exchange rate as of March 9, 1999. At the time the contract was entered into, the value of the Russian ruble was determined by the MICEX exchange and fluctuated based on market trading within a trading band set by the Russian government. To the extent that the exchange rate moved unfavorably for a party, the contract required that party to pay the other party the difference between the MICEX dollar-ruble exchange rate on March 9, 1999 and the agreed amount of 6.9 multiplied by 5,362,318.84. The difference was to be transferred in dollars into the other party's Bank of New York account.

Five months after the NDF contract was negotiated, Russia suffered a financial crisis that fundamentally altered its financial landscape. Like other emerging world markets, Russia's financial system collapsed after violence erupted in Indonesia in May 1998. In August of 1998, Russia's Central Bank enacted emergency measures to counteract the country's serious liquidity problem. On August 17, the Russian Government announced a package of severe economic measures: First, it raised the trading band, which allowed the ruble to devalue; second, it ordered a 90-day moratorium on the repayment of foreign debt by banks; and third, it announced the restructuring of ruble-denominated debt. Russian citizens withdrew their savings from banks en masse and stores closed. In late August of 1998, the ruble-dollar trading on the MICEX exchange was temporarily suspended. From August to the beginning of September, the ruble lost a significant portion of its face value.

In early September, due to the combination of the economic crisis, the nonexistence of any MICEX exchange rate on which to assess the NDF contract, and the moratorium on paying back foreign debt, Sberbank representatives contacted Parex in an attempt to settle the NDF contract. Sberbank offered to settle at a rate equivalent to the ceiling for rubles set by the Russian government in 1998, 7.15 rubles per dollar. Parex objected to what it viewed as Sberbank's altering the terms of the NDF contract. The ensuing negotiations took place either in Moscow or by telephone between Riga and Moscow through February of 1999, and failed to produce a settlement.

On the value date of March 9, 1999, Parex demanded that Sberbank transfer $3,755,642.01 to Parex's Bank of New York account in satisfaction of the contract. Parex filed this action in the New York Supreme Court three months later, and Sberbank properly removed it to this Court on August 9, 1999. Sberbank filed the instant motion to dismiss on March 24, 2000.

Where a case is brought against a "foreign state," the Foreign Sovereign Immunities Act ("FSIA") provides that personal jurisdiction exists where there is both subject matter jurisdiction and proper service. This Court concluded in a prior opinion that Sberbank, as an instrumentality or agency of the Russian State, qualifies as a "foreign state" under the FSIA. The FSIA is the only basis for the subject-matter jurisdiction of the United States courts. Under the FSIA, foreign states are immune from suit in the United States unless one of several exceptions applies.

The most relevant exception to foreign sovereign immunity is the "commercial activity" exception, which provides that a foreign state is not immune from suit in any case in which the action is based upon . . . an act outside the territory of the United States in connection with a commercial activity of the foreign state elsewhere and that act causes a direct effect in the United States. 28 U.S.C. § 1605(a)(2). A state is involved in "commercial activity" under the FSIA when it functions like an actor in the private marketplace rather than in a governmental or public capacity. See *Hanil Bank v. PT Bank Negara Indonesia*, 148 F.3d 127, 130 (2d Cir. 1998). An act is made "in connection" with commercial activity if there is a "substantive connection" or "causal link" between the act and the commercial activity.

The "act" at issue here, Sberbank's failure to deposit funds into Parex's Bank of New York account, arises out of a deal transacted outside of the United States, in Moscow and Riga.

Despite the fact that one of the parties to the exchange was a foreign state, the rubles for dollars exchange at issue here was conducted as a private transaction rather than as a public service, and as such constitutes "commercial activity." See *Republic of Argentina v. Weltover, Inc.*, 504 U.S. 607 (1992).

The only issue remaining to establish whether the Court has subject matter jurisdiction over this case is whether Sberbank's failure to deposit funds into Parex's Bank of New York account caused a "direct effect" in the United States.

The Second Circuit requires that the conduct having a direct effect in the United States be "legally significant" in order for the commercial activity exception to apply. Employing this test, the Second Circuit recently held that an Indonesian state bank's failure to pay on a letter of credit owed to a Korean bank for deposit in New York caused a direct effect in the United States. *Hanil Bank*, 148 F.3d at 133. As here, the contract had been entered into out of the United States, and the only connection to the United States was the bank account into which the funds were to have been deposited. By contractually consenting to pay the funds into the plaintiff's New York account and then failing to do so, the Court held, the Indonesian bank caused a legally significant direct effect in New York.

Under this reasoning, there is subject matter jurisdiction over the instant dispute. As in *Weltover* and *Hanil Bank*, neither party here is a citizen of the United States, and one of them is a foreign state. The parties contracted at a location outside the United States that a monetary deposit would be made by one party into the other party's New York bank account. And, as in both *Weltover* and *Hanil Bank*, "money that was supposed to have been delivered to a New York bank for deposit was not forthcoming." Under the law of this Circuit, Sberbank's failure to deposit

dollars into Parex's Bank of New York account caused a legally significant direct effect in the United States. Therefore, every element of FSIA § 1605(a)(2) has been met, and this Court has subject-matter jurisdiction over the case.

Case Highlights

- Sovereign immunity, as provided for under the Foreign Sovereign Immunity Act, is reserved for foreign states and the agencies or instrumentalities of a foreign state.
- Foreign agencies or instrumentalities may lose their sovereign immunities if they engage in commercial activities in a fashion similar to activities engaged in by private people.
- For the commercial activity exception to apply to transactions occurring outside the United States, the activity must have a significant direct effect in the United States.
- A significant direct effect occurs when a foreign sovereign enters into a contract to deposit funds into a bank account located in the United States and then fails to do so in contravention of the agreement.
- Events in distant locations (such as Indonesia in this case) can have significant effects on economies throughout the world.

---

or enforce acts of another country is the principle of **comity**. It is defined as "the recognition which one nation allows within its territory to the legislative, executive or judicial acts of another nation."[8]

U.S. courts have also developed a general discretionary principle known as the *forum non conveniens* **doctrine**. The *forum non conveniens* doctrine can be applied to any case if the court determines that there is a more convenient forum to hear the case.[9] Courts engage in a two-step process in deciding whether to dismiss a claim based on *forum non conveniens*. The first step is determining if an adequate alternative forum exists. If such a forum exists, then the court must balance a series of factors involving the private interests of the parties and the public interest in maintaining the litigation in the selected forum. Public interest factors include court congestion, the unfairness of imposing jury duty on a community with no relation to the litigation, the interest of the community in having localized controversies decided at home, and avoidance of problems associated with conflict of laws and the application of foreign law. Private interest factors include ease of access to

---

8. *Hilton v. Guyot*, 159 U.S. 113, 164 (1895).
9. See *Piper Aircraft Co. v. Reyno*, 454 U.S. 235, 254 n.22 (1981). See also *Gulf Oil Corp. v. Gilbert*, 330 U.S. 501, 506–09 (1947).

evidence, the cost for witnesses to attend trial, the availability of compulsory process, and other factors that might shorten the trial or make it less expensive. The plaintiff's choice of forum is subject to judicial deference, and the burden of demonstrating the existence of an adequate alternative forum and that the balance of private and public interests favor trial in the foreign forum rests with the defendant. The *Capital Currency Exchange* case examines some of the nuances of this judge-made doctrine.

A final consideration is **venue**. Venue refers to the issue of choosing between different courts that all possess jurisdiction (personal and subject matter) over the case. Venue is concerned with ascertaining the court that possesses the most appropriate or best geographical location to hear a case. This concern relates to the appropriate judicial district in the U.S. federal judicial system and the appropriate county in U.S. state judicial systems. With respect to federal litigation, the Alien Venue Statute provides that aliens may be sued in any federal judicial

Capital Currency Exchange v. National Westminster Bank and Barclays Bank

155 F.3d 603 (2d Cir. 1998)

McLaughlin, Circuit Judge. Capital Currency Exchange, N.V. ("CCE"), is a financial company organized under the laws of the Netherlands Antilles. CCE and its affiliates are engaged principally in two kinds of international financial transactions: (1) retail currency exchange and (2) money transfers from the United States to England. CCE and its affiliates had a longstanding banking relationship with Barclays UK. In 1991, CCE, on behalf of Worldcash, sought a New York State money transmission license. To qualify for this license, Worldcash had to post a $500,000 bond in favor of the New York State banking authorities. CCE arranged with Barclays UK's New York office to issue an irrevocable letter of credit as security for the bond. In May 1995, for reasons that the parties dispute, Barclays UK told CCE to find another banker. In August 1995, NatWest UK declined to provide CCE with banking services. CCE maintains that NatWest UK and Barclays UK conspired to drive CCE out of the money transfer business by depriving it of banking services in violation of the antitrust laws, specifically Sections 1 and 2 of the Sherman Act. On November 6, 1996, defendants moved to dismiss the complaint under the *forum non conveniens* doctrine.

In a *forum non conveniens* analysis, a court must determine that an adequate alternative forum exists. An alternative forum is adequate if: (1) the defendants are subject to service of process there; and (2) the forum permits "litigation of the subject matter of the dispute." We believe there is an adequate, alternative forum. Plaintiffs may challenge defendants' allegedly anticompetitive actions under Articles 85 and 86 of the Treaty of Rome, which English courts are bound to enforce. Although English courts have not yet awarded damages in an antitrust case, it appears that English courts have the power to do so. It is well established, however, that the unavailability of treble damages does not render a forum inadequate. Thus, suits brought under the Sherman Act are subject to dismissal under the *forum non conveniens* doctrine.

AFFIRMED.

Case Update

The U.S. Supreme Court denied certiorari and refused to hear the case in *Capital Currency Exchange v. National Westminster Bank and Barclays Bank*, 526 U.S. 1067 (1999).

Case Highlights

- For a court to dismiss a case under the *forum non conveniens* doctrine, it must determine that an adequate alternative forum exists.
- The unavailability of certain remedies under the laws of the alternative forum does not render that forum inadequate.

district with the exception of suits against foreign sovereigns, which may be initiated only in U.S. District Court for the District of Columbia.[10]

International Discovery

Once the defendant is properly served and personal jurisdiction is obtained, the next issue is the ability to pursue **discovery** against the defendant. Discovery is the process of gathering evidence from one's adversary and from third parties. Discovery is often the most difficult and costly part of international litigation. The U.S. Federal Rules of Civil Procedure allow for numerous and broad methods of discovery. Other countries with less liberal discovery methods are less receptive to requests for the discovery of their nationals. The purpose of the Convention on the Taking of Evidence Abroad in Civil or Commercial Matters (**Hague Evidence Convention**) is to facilitate the discovery of foreign parties. This convention provides for the use of *letters of request* that require foreign courts to perform the discovery process. It also provides for the "taking of evidence by diplomatic officers, consular agents and commissioners."

A number of factors limit the effectiveness of the convention. First, although the United States has ratified the convention, only thirty-one other states, very few of which are located outside Western Europe, have adopted the convention. Second, a foreign court may reject a letter of request if the court deems it to be in violation of its national laws. Nonetheless, a U.S. plaintiff having problems with foreign discovery should seek the help of the U.S. State Department in gathering evidence through the Hague Evidence Convention.

http://
Text of Hague Evidence Convention: **http://hcch.e-vision.nl/ index_en.php?act= conventions. textscid=82.**

Enforceability of Judgments

After obtaining a judgment in an international litigation, the winning party often needs to enforce the judgment in a foreign country. This is likely when the foreign defendant does not possess enough assets in the forum court to satisfy the judgment. International litigation judgments are more difficult to enforce than arbitral awards. In *Hilton v. Guyot*,[11] the Supreme Court held that a foreign judgment is entitled to enforcement if the defendant had an opportunity for a fair trial. A fair trial is predicated on the foreign court possessing personal and subject matter jurisdiction, conducting trials using *regular* procedures, and acting "under a system of jurisprudence likely to secure an impartial administration of justice." Despite this embrace of international comity, however, the court in *Hilton* failed to enforce a French judgment under a **rule of reciprocity**. The rule of reciprocity holds that a country will not enforce judgments rendered in a foreign country that does not likewise enforce its judgments. Because of the convergence of national legal systems and the U.S. recognition of other legal systems, the rule of reciprocity has rarely been used in recent years as a defense to the enforcement of a foreign judgment. However, the rule of reciprocity retains an important role in legal systems outside the United States. For example, many Asian states, such as China, Indonesia, Japan, Korea, Malaysia, and Taiwan, as well as Mexico and many African states, require

INTERNATIONAL

10.   See 28 U.S.C. § 1391(d) (2000).
11.   159 U.S. 113 (1895).

reciprocity prior to the enforcement of a foreign judgment.[12] By contrast, some states, most notably Argentina, Brazil, and India, have abolished the reciprocity requirement.

The court in *Hunt v. BP Exploration Ltd.*[13] reviewed U.S. law on the enforcement of foreign judgments. The case involved the enforcement of a British judgment against a U.S. defendant. The court recognized that *Hilton* was still good law. Therefore, the most effective grounds for attacking a foreign judgment is to argue that a defendant

---

Nelson Bunker Hunt v. BP Exploration Company (Libya) Ltd.

492 F. Supp. 885 (N.D. Tex 1980)

Higginbotham, District Judge. This parallel London/Dallas litigation stems from a relationship between BP and Hunt with respect to an oil field located in Libya. In 1957, Libya granted Hunt Concession No. 65 in the province of Cyrenaica. In June 1960, Hunt entered into a letter agreement as to Concession No. 65 with BP accompanied by an Operating Agreement. The 1960 Agreement provided that Hunt would convey to BP an undivided one-half interest in Concession No. 65. On May 2, 1975, BP instituted suit in England, relying primarily on Section 1(3) of the Frustrated Contracts Act, 1943 ("Act"). BP's claim under the Act was that its contract with Hunt was frustrated when BP's interest in the concession was expropriated, and that, because of BP's contractual performance before expropriation, Hunt obtained a valuable benefit. Hunt declined to accept service of the writ issued on May 2, 1975, through agents and solicitors in the U.K. and attempts to serve him personally during a short visit also proved unsuccessful.

On June 19, 1975, the High Court of Justice, Queen's Bench Division, Commercial Court, granted BP's request for service by mail. On June 30, 1978, Mr. Justice Goff entered judgment against Hunt, and held that the counterclaim under the Act failed. On March 26, 1979, an English court awarded BP $15,575,823 and $8,922,060. Both Hunt and BP appealed but the Court of Appeals in England has not yet decided the appeals.

The Law of Recognition

Hilton v. Guyot is the leading American decision on the recognition and enforcement of foreign country judgments. The Supreme Court held that:

Where there has been opportunity for a full and fair trial abroad before a court of competent jurisdiction, conducting the trial upon regular proceedings, after due citation or voluntary appearance of the defendant, and under a system of jurisprudence likely to secure

an impartial administration of justice between the citizens of its own country and those of other countries, and there is nothing to show either prejudice in the court, or in the system of laws under which it is sitting, or fraud in the procuring of the judgment, or any other special reason why the comity of this nation should not allow it full effect, the merits of the case should not, in an action brought in this country upon the judgment, be tried afresh, as on new trial or an appeal, upon the mere assertion of the party that the judgment was erroneous in law or in fact.

Applying the *Hilton v. Guyot* principles of comity in order to determine whether a foreign country judgment should be recognized presents difficult social and public policy judgments. Comity is a recognition which one nation extends to the legislative, executive, or judicial acts of another. It is not a rule of law, but one of practice, convenience, and expediency. It is a nation's expression of understanding that demonstrates due regard both to international duty and convenience and the rights of persons protected by its own laws. Comity should be withheld only when its acceptance would be contrary or prejudicial to the interest of the nation called upon to give it effect.

In this case, Hunt cannot seriously assert that there was not timely notice and opportunity to defend, that fraud was involved, or that the proceedings were not rendered according to a civilized jurisprudence. Hunt asserts, correctly, that if the English court had no personal jurisdiction over him, the judgment should not be recognized. The record reflects, however, that the English court did have jurisdiction over Hunt. This court turns to a minimum contacts analysis in order to determine if the English court's exercise of jurisdiction comports with our own notions expressed in due process terms. Hunt's contacts with England are of such an extent and of such nature that the maintenance of this suit does not offend fair play and substantial justice. Hunt has engaged in much purposeful activity in England. The contract was

---

12. See Louis Garb & Julian Lew, *Enforcement of Foreign Judgments* (2003).
13. 492 F. Supp. 885 (N.D. Tex. 1980).

executed in England, Hunt has personally traveled to England to participate in meetings with BP, he had agents resident in England to represent his interests, and BP's principal place of business was in London.

Public Policy

Hunt's argument that an American judgment would not be recognized in England and so should not, on public policy grounds, be recognized here is in essence an assertion that reciprocity is an essential element of recognition. The court disagrees. Though the *Hilton* case required reciprocity as a condition of recognition, American decisions since *Hilton* have moved "decisively away from the requirement of reciprocity as a condition of recognition." Indeed, the draftsmen of the Uniform Foreign Money-Judgment Recognition Act consciously rejected reciprocity as a factor to consider in recognizing foreign money judgments.

Effect of the Appeal

Hunt next argues that the English judgment is not entitled to recognition because it is now on appeal; and the decision of the Court of Appeal will be subject to review by the House of Lords. Existing precedent on comity, the principle under which foreign country judgments are recognized, lends support to this assumption. The Uniform Foreign Money-Judgments Recognition Act provides that "if the defendant satisfies the court either that an appeal is pending or that he is entitled and intends to appeal from the foreign judgment, the court may stay the proceedings until the appeal has been determined or until the expiration of a period of time sufficient to enable the defendant to prosecute the appeal." Therefore, it is necessary for this court to stay the proceedings until a final determination of the proceedings in England.

Case Highlights

- Comity is a recognition that one nation extends to the legislative, executive, or judicial acts of another.
- Reciprocity is no longer a factor considered in the recognition of a foreign judgment.
- A foreign judgment is not due recognition while it is in the process of being appealed.

---

did not have an opportunity for a fair trial. These arguments are procedural ones centered on due process and public policy concerns. In *Hunt*, the court held that, given the historical deference received by British judgments, the *Hilton* due process standards were met, given the similarities of the legal systems.

However, major substantive differences in the laws of the court rendering judgment and the enforcing court will also be scrutinized during the enforcement stage. For example, U.S. courts will generally not enforce foreign country's penal and tax judgments.[14] The court in *Hunt v. BP Exploration* did not enforce the British judgment, pending its appeal in the English court system. It cited the Uniform Foreign Money-Judgments Recognition Act, which states that "if the defendant satisfies the court either that an appeal is pending or that he is entitled and intends to appeal from the foreign judgment, the court may stay the proceedings until the appeal has been determined or until the expiration of a period of time sufficient to enable the defendant to prosecute the appeal."[15] The decision in *Yahoo!, Inc. v. La Ligue Contre Le Racisme et L'Antisemitisme* provides another example of a U.S. court refusing to enforce a foreign judgment on public policy grounds, specifically, the guarantee of free speech contained in the First Amendment to the U.S. Constitution.

http://

The Hague Conference on private International Law has begun work on a new judgment convention—Hague Convention on International Jurisdiction and Foreign Judgments in Civil and Commercial Matters: **http://www.cptech. org/ecom/jurisdiction/ hague.html.** The proposed Convention would likely also deal with issues of Internet jurisdiction.

---

14. See, e.g., *Republic of Honduras v. Philip Morris Company*, 341 F.3d 1253 (11th Cir. 2003); *Attorney General of Canada v. R.J. Reynolds Tobacco Holdings, Inc.*, 268 F.3d 103 (2d Cir. 2001); *Nicor Int'l Corporation v. El Paso Corporation*, 292 F. Supp.2d 1357 (S.D. Fla. 2003); *European Community v. Japan Tobacco, Inc.*, 186 F. Supp.2d 231 (E.D.N.Y. 2002).

15. The Uniform Foreign Money-Judgments Recognition Act, §6, 13 Uniform Laws Annotated (U.L.A.) 263 (1962). The shortcoming of the act is that it has not received a significant degree of international adoption.

A number of international conventions have been promulgated to help enforce judgments internationally. Three are regional in nature: Members of the European Union can use **Regulation No. 44/2001 on Jurisdiction and the Recognition and Enforcement of Judgments in Civil and Commercial Matters**. The **Lugano Convention** applies to all countries in the European Free Trade Area. Finally, the **Inter-American Convention on the Extraterritorial Validity of Foreign Judgments** applies to members of the Organization of American States. The only truly "international" convention, the **Hague Convention on the Recognition and Enforcement of Foreign Judgments in Civil and Commercial Matters**, has been accepted by only three states and has failed to be effective in facilitating the enforcement of foreign judgments.

In contrast, the United Nations Convention on the Recognition and Enforcement of Foreign Arbitral Awards or **New York Convention** has been widely accepted and is

---

Yahoo!, Inc. v. La Ligue Contre Le Racisme et L'Antisemitisme

169 F. Supp.2d 1181 (N.D. Cal. 2001)

Fogel, District Judge. Plaintiff moves for summary judgment. Defendants oppose the motion. For the reasons set forth below, the motion will be granted. Defendants La Ligue Contre Le Racisme Et l'Antisemitisme ("LICRA") and L'Union Des Etudiants Juifs De France, citizens of France, are non-profit organizations dedicated to eliminating anti-Semitism. Plaintiff Yahoo!, Inc. ("Yahoo!") is a corporation organized under the laws of Delaware with its principal place of business in Santa Clara, California. Yahoo! is an Internet service provider that operates various Internet websites and services that any computer user can access at the Uniform Resource Locator ("URL") http://www.yahoo.com. Yahoo! provides a variety of means by which people from all over the world can communicate and interact with one another over the Internet. Any computer user with Internet access is able to post materials on many of these Yahoo! sites, which in turn are instantly accessible by anyone who logs on to Yahoo!'s Internet sites. As relevant here, Yahoo!'s auction site allows anyone to post an item for sale and solicit bids from any computer user from around the globe. Yahoo! records when a posting is made and after the requisite time period lapses sends an e-mail notification to the highest bidder and seller with their respective contact information. Yahoo! is never a party to a transaction, and the buyer and seller are responsible for arranging privately for payment and shipment of goods. Yahoo! monitors the transaction through limited regulation by prohibiting particular items from being sold [but] does not actively regulate the content of each posting, and individuals are able to post, and have in fact posted, highly offensive matter, including Nazi-related propaganda and Third Reich memorabilia, on Yahoo!'s auction sites.

On or about April 5, 2000, LICRA sent a "cease and desist" letter to Yahoo!'s Santa Clara headquarters informing Yahoo! that the sale of Nazi and Third Reich related goods through its auction services violates French law. LICRA threatened to take legal action unless Yahoo! took steps to prevent such sales within eight days. Defendants subsequently filed a civil complaint against Yahoo! in the Tribunal de Grande Instance de Paris (the "French Court").

The French Court found that approximately 1,000 Nazi and Third Reich related objects, including Adolf Hitler's *Mein Kampf, The Protocol of the Elders of Zion* (an infamous anti-Semitic report produced by the Czarist secret police in the early 1900's), and purported "evidence" that the gas chambers of the Holocaust did not exist were being offered for sale on Yahoo.com's auction site. Because any French citizen is able to access these materials on Yahoo.com directly or through a link on Yahoo.fr, the French Court concluded that the Yahoo.com auction site violates Section R645–1 of the French Criminal Code, which prohibits exhibition of Nazi propaganda and artifacts for sale. On May 20, 2000, the French Court entered an order requiring Yahoo! to (1) eliminate French citizens' access to any material on the Yahoo.com auction site that offers for sale any Nazi objects, relics, insignia, emblems, and flags; (2) eliminate French citizens' access to web pages on Yahoo.com displaying text, extracts, or quotations from *Mein Kampf* and *Protocol of the Elders of Zion*; [and] (3) post a warning to French citizens on Yahoo.fr that any search through Yahoo.com may lead to sites containing material prohibited by Section R645–1 of the French Criminal Code, and that such viewing of the prohibited material may result in legal action against the Internet user. The order subjects Yahoo! to a penalty of 100,000 Euros for each day that it fails to comply with the order. Yahoo! subsequently posted the required warning and prohibited postings in violation of Section R645–1 of the French Criminal Code from appearing on Yahoo.fr. Yahoo! also amended the auction policy of Yahoo.com to prohibit individuals from auctioning: Any item that promotes, glorifies, or is directly associated with groups or individuals known principally for hateful or violent positions or acts, such as Nazis or the Ku Klux Klan. Official government-issue stamps and coins are not prohibited under this policy. Expressive media, such as books and films, may be subject to more permissive standards as determined by Yahoo! in its sole discretion. Notwithstanding these actions, the Yahoo.com auction site still offers certain items for sale (such as stamps, coins, and a copy of *Mein Kampf*) which appear to violate the French Order.

Yahoo! claims that because it lacks the technology to block French citizens from accessing the Yahoo.com auction site to view materials which violate the French Order or from accessing other Nazi-based content of websites on Yahoo.com, it cannot comply with the French order without banning Nazi-related material from Yahoo.com altogether. Yahoo! contends that such a ban would infringe impermissibly upon its rights under the First Amendment to the United States Constitution. Accordingly, Yahoo! filed a complaint in this Court seeking a declaratory judgment that the French Court's orders are neither recognizable nor enforceable under the laws of the United States.

As this Court and others have observed, the instant case presents novel and important issues arising from the global reach of the Internet. Indeed, the specific facts of this case implicate issues of policy, politics, and culture that are beyond the purview of one nation's judiciary. Thus it is critical that the Court define at the outset what is and is not at stake in the present proceeding.

This case is *not* about the moral acceptability of promoting the symbols or propaganda of Nazism. Most would agree that such acts are profoundly offensive. By any reasonable standard of morality, the Nazis were responsible for one of the worst displays of inhumanity in recorded history. This Court is acutely mindful of the emotional pain reminders of the Nazi era cause to Holocaust survivors and deeply respectful of the motivations of the French Republic in enacting the underlying statutes and of the defendant organizations in seeking relief under those statutes. Vigilance is the key to preventing atrocities such as the Holocaust from occurring again.

Nor is this case about the right of France or any other nation to determine its own law and social policies. A basic function of a sovereign state is to determine by law what forms of speech and conduct are acceptable within its borders. In this instance, as a nation whose citizens suffered the effects of Nazism in ways that are incomprehensible to most Americans, France clearly has the right to enact and enforce laws such as those relied upon by the French Court here.

What *is* at issue here is whether it is consistent with the Constitution and laws of the United States for another nation to regulate speech by a United States resident within the United States on the basis that such speech can be accessed by Internet users in that nation. In a world in which ideas and information transcend borders and the Internet in particular renders the physical distance between speaker and audience virtually meaningless, the implications of this question go far beyond the facts of this case. The modern world is home to widely varied cultures with radically divergent value systems. There is little doubt that Internet users in the United States routinely engage in speech that violates, for example, China's laws against religious expression, the laws of various nations against advocacy of gender equality or homosexuality, or even the United Kingdom's restrictions on freedom of the press. If the government or another party in one of these sovereign nations were to seek enforcement of such laws against Yahoo! or another U.S.-based Internet service provider, what principles should guide the court's analysis?

The Court has stated that it must and will decide this case in accordance with the Constitution and laws of the United States. It recognizes that in so doing, it necessarily adopts certain value judgments embedded in those enactments, including the fundamental judgment expressed in the First Amendment that it is preferable to permit the non-violent expression of offensive viewpoints rather than to impose viewpoint-based governmental regulation upon speech. The government and people of France have made a different judgment based upon their own experience. In undertaking its inquiry as to the proper application of the laws of the United States, the Court intends no disrespect for that judgment or for the experience that has informed it.

No legal judgment has any effect, of its own force, beyond the limits of the sovereignty from which its authority is derived. However, the United States Constitution and implementing legislation require that full faith and credit be given to judgments of sister states, territories, and possessions of the United States. The extent to which the United States, or any state, honors the judicial decrees of foreign nations is a matter of choice, governed by "the comity of nations." *Hilton v. Guyot*, 159 U.S. 113, 163 (1895). Comity "is neither a matter of absolute obligation, on the one hand, nor of mere courtesy and good will, upon the other." *Hilton*, 159 U.S. at 163–64. United States courts generally recognize foreign judgments and decrees unless enforcement would be prejudicial or contrary to the country's interests.

As discussed previously, the French order's content and viewpoint-based regulation of the web pages and auction site on Yahoo.com, while entitled to great deference as an articulation of French law, clearly would be inconsistent with the First Amendment if mandated by a court in the United States. What makes this case uniquely challenging is that the Internet in effect allows one to speak in more than one place at the same time. Although France has the sovereign right to regulate what speech is permissible in France, this Court may not enforce a foreign order that violates the protections of the United States Constitution by chilling protected speech that occurs simultaneously within our borders. The reason for limiting comity in this area is sound. "The protection to free speech and the press embodied in [the First] amendment would be seriously jeopardized by the entry of foreign judgments granted pursuant to standards deemed appropriate in [another country] but considered antithetical to the protections afforded the press by the U.S. Constitution." Absent a body of law that establishes international standards with respect to speech on the Internet and an appropriate treaty or legislation addressing enforcement of such standards to speech originating within the United States, the principle of comity is outweighed by the Court's obligation to uphold the First Amendment.

Yahoo! seeks a declaration from this Court that the First Amendment precludes enforcement within the United States of a French order intended to regulate the content of its speech over the Internet. Yahoo! has shown that the French order is valid under the laws of France, that it may be enforced with retroactive penalties, and that the ongoing possibility of its enforcement in the United States chills Yahoo!'s First Amendment rights. Yahoo! also has shown that an actual controversy exists and that the threat to its constitutional rights is real and immediate. Defendants have failed to show the existence of a genuine issue of material fact or to identify any such issue the existence of which could be shown through further discovery. Accordingly, the motion for summary judgment will be granted.

Case Highlights

- Businesses operating in the international market-place must remain constantly vigilant with respect to the social policies, cultural sensitivities, and moral acceptability of their business practices in the states in which they conduct their operations.
- The global reach and largely unregulated nature of the Internet continues to present novel and important legal issues for states, businesses, and consumers.
- U.S. courts generally recognize foreign judgments and decrees unless enforcement would be prejudicial or contrary to the country's interests.
- Absent international standards with respect to speech on the Internet, such as may be contained in a treaty or national legislation addressing such speech originating within the United States, the interests represented by the First Amendment outweigh the principle of comity to the judgments of foreign courts.

INTERNATIONAL

enforced by 134 states. Thus, the enforcement of a judgment in a foreign country is dependent on the nuances of enforcement in that particular country. For example, France and Switzerland refuse to enforce a foreign judgment against their nationals unless there is a clear indication that the national voluntarily intended to submit to the jurisdiction of the foreign court. Many countries will not enforce U.S. judgments that are contrary to their public policy. For example, foreign courts are unlikely to enforce punitive and treble damage awards because there are no such remedies recognized under their laws. Punitive damages are awarded in the relatively few states whose legal systems originated in the common law tradition, such as Australia, Canada, India, Ireland, New Zealand, and the United Kingdom. In any event, no country rivals the United States in the number of instances when such awards are made available. Faced with such obstacles, a plaintiff may choose to file suit directly in the country of the defendant or to arbitrate the claim.

Choice of Law

How do courts determine which national laws apply in a given case? Generally, absent a **choice of law clause** in which the parties to a contract expressly state the law that will govern any disputes, the law of the country most *closely connected* to the agreement will govern. Sometimes the courts may apply the principle of *depecage* to apply different governing laws to different parts of the contract. In short, different parts of the contract may have closer connections to different countries. The country of closest connection is often the country of the residence of the performing party.

Courts have fashioned **conflict of law rules** to assist them in making choice of law decisions. These rules are essentially a list of factors used to determine the country with the closest connection to the case. Under the *Restatement (Second) of the Conflict of Laws*,[16] the law of the jurisdiction with the "most significant contacts" governs both tort and contract claims. In evaluating tort claims, the following four factors are relevant: (1) the domicile, place of incorporation, and place of business of the parties; (2) the place where a tort occurred; (3) the place where the relationship of the parties is centered; and (4) the place where the injury occurred. With respect to contract claims, the factors are (1) the place of contracting, (2) the place of negotiation, (3) the place of performance, (4) location of the subject matter of the contract, and (5) the domicile, place of incorporation, and place of business of the parties. Other factors considered include the place the contract was signed and the place the breach occurred. The Restatement also states that if the place of negotiating the contract and the place of performance are in the same country, the law of that country will usually be applied. If a specific contract clause or issue is invalid in a country with a close connection to the contract, then that country's laws may be deferred to because of its strong interest in enforcing its laws and public policies.

Before a contract and a choice of law clause are drafted, the conflict of law rules in the national law of the other party should be researched. This will help determine whether an express choice of law clause is needed and, if so, the factors the foreign country will use in assessing the enforceability of the choice of law selection. The conflict of law rules found in Hungarian law are shown in the following Comparative Law capsule.[17]

Hungarian Conflict of Law Rules

Specific Rules

Sale/purchase contracts: Law of the country of the seller

Lease contracts: Law of the country of the lessor

Banking/credit contracts: Law of the country of the financial institution

Employment contracts: Law of the country in which the services are performed

When the services are to be performed in more than one country, then the law of the country of the employer is applicable.

General Default Rule

If specific rules are not applicable: Law of the country of the party performing the principal obligation.

COMPARATIVE LAW

---

16. See Restatement (Second) of the Conflict of Laws § 187 (1971).

17. See Articles 25–29 & 51–52 of Law Decree No. 13 of 1979 on Private International Law. See also Ferenc Mádl & Lajos Vékás, *The Law of Conflicts and of International Economic Relations* 375, 459–65 (1998).

One principle used in determining the law to be applied by the forum court is that, absent sufficient proof to establish with reasonable certainty the substance of the foreign principles of law, the court should apply the law of its country. A court is not expected to decide a case based on incomplete and frequently confusing explanations of foreign law. In *Banque Libanaise Pour Le Commerce v. Khreich,*[18] the Federal Circuit Court stated that it was the plaintiff's "burden to provide the legal pigment and then paint the district court a clear portrait of the relevant foreign (Abu Dhabi) law." It affirmed the right of the lower court to apply Texas law to what was primarily a foreign transaction.

Judicial Abrogation of Choice of Law Clauses

Internationally, courts and arbitration tribunals have generally enforced contractual choice of law clauses. Courts, however, usually require that the choice of law have some connection to the parties or the contract. Arbitration tribunals, on the other hand, are more likely to enforce a reasonable choice of law selection, even if the law chosen is not connected to the contract or the transaction. Arbitrators may see an unconnected choice of law selection as a fair compromise, given the international nature of the transaction, especially if the parties' choice is the laws of one of the more popular neutral countries, such as Great Britain, the United States, Switzerland, or Germany. For example, in an arbitration enforcing an English choice of law clause in a contract for the sale of seed potatoes between a Dutch seller and a Mozambique buyer, an **International Chamber of Commerce (ICC)** arbitration panel held that "the parties to transnational contracts enjoy a large degree of autonomy in selecting the proper law of their contract."[19] This selection was subject to arbitral deference, especially when the selected law was that of a country to which the contract bore some connection or was the law of a country selected for reasons of its expertise (such as English law in maritime matters) or neutrality (such as Swedish or Swiss law). The panel concluded that it could disregard the parties' selection only if there was an indication that English law was selected for the express purpose of avoiding a mandatory provision of the laws of the Netherlands or Mozambique.

INTERNATIONAL

At times, statutory mandates may preempt this reasonableness inquiry. For example, the *English Unfair Contract Terms Act of 1977* adopts a presumption of unreasonableness for indemnity clauses by which a consumer is "made to indemnify another person in respect of liability that may be incurred by the other for negligence or breach of contract."[20] For international sales contracts, the act voids any choice of law clause whose purpose is the avoidance of the Unfair Terms Act.

Courts have used a number of factors in scrutinizing choice of law clauses. The following excerpts from the *Restatement (Second) of the Conflict of Laws* provide the rationale for the need for such rules and the factors that courts review in deciding whether to honor a choice of law selection.

---

18.   915 F.2d 1000 (5th Cir. 1990).
19.   Claimant: Buyer (Mozambique) v. Defendant: Seller (The Netherlands), International Chamber of Commerce, Case No. 5505, ¶ 17 (1987).
20.   Unfair Contract Terms Act § 4(1) (as amended 2003).

SECTION ONE: REASON FOR THE RULES OF CONFLICT OF LAWS

The world is composed of territorial states having separate and differing systems of law. Events and transactions occur, and issues arise, that may have significant relationships to more than one state, making necessary a special body of rules and methods for their ordering and resolution.

SECTION SIX: CHOICE OF LAW PRINCIPLES

The factors relevant to the choice of law include:
   (a) the needs of the international system,
   (b) the relevant policies of the forum,
   (c) the relevant policies of other interested states and the relative interests of those states in the determination of the particular issue,
   (d) the protection of justified expectations,
   (e) the basic policies underlying the particular field of law,
   (f) certainty, predictability, and uniformity of result, and
   (g) ease in the determination and application of the law to be applied.

In weighing these factors, the modern judicial trend is to give great deference to the choice made by the parties in their contractual choice of law clause. As noted by one commentator, "[i]n the area of contracts, where choice-of-law rules are uncertain, some measure of predictability and certainty is achieved by allowing the parties, within broad limits, to select the law to govern the validity and effect of their contract."[21] This deference also advances the policy goal of protecting "the justified expectations" of the contracting parties.

The Restatement also provides two grounds for abrogating the parties' choice of law clause. First, the chosen law has no substantial relationship to the parties or the transaction, and there is no reasonable basis for the parties' choice. Second, application of the law of the chosen state would be contrary to a fundamental policy of a country that has a materially greater interest than the chosen state in the determination of the particular issue. A forum court is unlikely to enforce a choice of law under such circumstances. *Milanovich v. Costa Crociere, S.p.A.* addresses the unique instance when a party to a contract seeks to set aside its own choice of law provision on the basis that it violates public policy.[22]

Milanovich v. Costa Crociere, S.p.A.
954 F.2d 763 (D.C. Cir. 1992)

Wald, Circuit Judge. Appellants Gregory Milanovich and Marjorie Koch-Milanovich, a husband and wife residing in the District of Columbia, booked passage for a one-week Caribbean cruise on an Italian flag vessel owned by appellee Costa Crociere, S.p.A. The cruise disembarked from San Juan, Puerto Rico on February 6, 1988. On the morning of February 7, while the ship was in international waters, the deck chair upon which Mr. Milanovich was sitting collapsed, allegedly causing him serious injury.

---

21.   Willis Reese, "Conflict of Laws and the Restatement Second," 28 *Law & Contemporary Problems* 679 (1963).
22.   954 F.2d 763 (D.C. Cir. 1992).

On March 31, 1989, appellants filed a personal injury action in the United States District Court for the District of Columbia. The suit was filed one year and fifty-three days after the date of the accident. The cruise company promptly moved for summary judgment claiming that the suit was time-barred by a provision of the passage ticket establishing a one-year time limit for bringing personal injury actions. Appellants opposed summary judgment arguing that another provision of the ticket invoked Italian law as the "ruling law of the contract," and that under Italian law the one-year limitation was unenforceable. They submitted uncontroverted expert testimony that under Articles 1341 and 1342 of the Italian Civil Code, provisions expressly referenced in the passage ticket, liability limiting provisions in certain kinds of "adhesion" contracts, of which a passenger ticket is one, are unenforceable against the nondrafting party unless that party gives specific written assent to such provisions. Without such written approval, they contended, the one-year limitation period in this case was unenforceable.

The district court disagreed. Because of the preponderance of U.S. contacts—appellants are U.S. citizens, the cruise was advertised in the U.S., the tickets were purchased and delivered in the U.S., and the ship left from and returned to a U.S. port—the court held that U.S. law, not Italian law, provided the rule of decision regarding the validity of the one-year limitation clause. Applying U.S. law, the court found that this provision had been effectively incorporated into the contract and was legally enforceable. On appeal, the Milanoviches challenge the district court's refusal to enforce the choice-of-law provision contained in their passage ticket. The question we ultimately face is whether a provision of that contract limiting the time for suit was validly incorporated and is legally enforceable. The resolution of those questions depends, however, on the body of contract law with which we examine the contract.

The contract contains a provision purporting to adopt Italian law as the law of the contract, but to follow that direction and use Italian contract law to decide whether the provision telling us to use Italian law is valid would obviously be "putting the barge before the tug." *DeNicola v. Cunard Line Ltd.*, 642 F.2d 5, 7 n.2 (1st Cir. 1981) What law should govern whether a choice-of-law provision is a valid part of a maritime contract is a difficult question, but one we need not decide because both parties here have assumed that American contract law principles control.

Under American law, contractual choice-of-law provisions are usually honored. Restatement (Second) of Conflict of Laws § 187 (1971). The district court here, however, ignored the choice-of-law clause, reasoning that *The Bremen* case, in which the Supreme Court enforced a similar clause, was distinguishable because it involved commercial parties of equal bargaining strength. Appellees, in turn, argue that the district court properly disregarded the choice-of-law clause—a clause that *they* drafted and included in this adhesion contract—because a contractual choice-of-law clause is only one factor to be considered in a court's choice-of-law analysis. We find neither argument persuasive.

First, while there are indeed statements by some district courts that a choice-of-law clause is only one factor in determining the applicable law, they appear to express mainly the courts' understandable reluctance to automatically enforce the terms of these adhesion contracts against the passenger. While these concerns warrant heightened judicial scrutiny of choice-of-law provisions in passage tickets, they do not sanction their utter disregard, especially where there are no countervailing polices of the forum implicated and where it is the nondrafting party that seeks enforcement of the choice-of-law provision.

Second, the district court's conclusion that the reasoning of *The Bremen* is limited to the commercial context has been undermined by the Supreme Court's recent decision in *Carnival Cruise Lines, Inc. v. Shute*, 113 L. Ed. 2d 622, 111 S. Ct. 1522 (1991), in which the Court extended the logic of *The Bremen* to contracts governing pleasure cruises. In *Carnival Cruise*, an injured cruise ship passenger filed suit in his home state despite a stipulation in the passage ticket requiring all suits to be filed in Florida. The Court recognized that the choice-of-forum clause was not the subject of bargaining, but nonetheless considered whether it was "reasonable" and therefore enforceable under American law. The Court noted that "forum-selection clauses contained in form passage contracts are subject to judicial scrutiny for fundamental fairness," *id.* at 1528, but concluded that this particular choice-of-forum clause was reasonable and that the plaintiff had failed to satisfy the "'heavy burden of proof'" required to set aside the clause on grounds of inconvenience. *Id.* at 1528 (quoting *The Bremen*, 407 U.S. at 17).

Under *The Bremen* and *Carnival Cruise* decisions, then, courts should honor a contractual choice-of-law provision in a passenger ticket unless the party challenging the enforcement of the provision can establish that "enforcement would be unreasonable and unjust," "the clause was invalid for such reasons as fraud or overreaching," or "enforcement would contravene a strong public policy of the forum in which suit is brought." *The Bremen*, 407 U.S. 1, 15, 32 L. Ed. 2d 513, 92 S. Ct. 1907 (1972); *see also Carnival Cruise*, 111 S. Ct. at 1528.

Appellees do not argue that enforcement of the choice-of-law provision would be unreasonable or unjust, or that they have been the victim of fraud, bad faith or overreaching; after all, *appellees* drafted the choice-of-law provision and included it in the form passage contract. Instead, appellees argue that a particular policy of the forum would be contravened by enforcement of the contractual choice-of-law clause. Under 42 U.S.C. § 183b(a), they say, it is unlawful for the . . . owner of any sea-going vessel . . . transporting passengers . . . from or between ports of the United States and foreign ports to provide . . . a shorter period for . . . the institution of suits on [claims for loss of life or bodily injury] than one year.

Appellees argue that this provision implicitly sanctions a maximum limitation period of one year and was enacted "to provide uniformity of treatment and predictability of outcome for American passengers" regardless of the nationality of the carrier. Enforcing a choice-of-law clause that will permit suit beyond one year from the date of the accident, appellees argue, would contravene this public policy. The plain language of 42 U.S.C. § 183b, however, reveals that the provision seeks only to prevent time limitations of *less* than one year. Enforcing the choice-of-law clause here obviously does not contravene that policy. To the extent there is an affirmative forum policy regarding time bars to suit, it is embodied in 46 U.S.C. § 763a, which provides for a three-year statute of limitations for maritime torts. Enforcing the choice-of-law clause here would clearly not undermine that policy.

The Milanoviches' passage ticket designates Italian law as the ruling law of the contract. Appellees, the parties opposing enforcement of that provision, have not demonstrated that the choice-of-law clause is unjust or unreasonable or that its enforcement would violate American public policy. We therefore see no reason to deny enforcement of this express provision of the Milanoviches' passage ticket. Under Italian law, as it was explained by appellants' expert without contradiction by appellees, the contract's one-year limitation on suit is invalid, and thus appellants' action was timely filed. The summary judgment of the district court is vacated and the case is remanded for further proceedings to adjudicate appellants' personal injury claim.

Case Highlights

- Choice of law provisions are enforceable in tickets for pleasure cruises as well as commercial maritime contracts.
- Choice of law provisions contained in tickets for pleasure cruises are enforceable in the absence of unreasonableness, injustice, fraud, bad faith, overreaching, or contravention of a strong public policy of the forum.
- A party challenging the enforceability of a choice of law provision in a U.S. court bears a "heavy burden of proof," especially when the challenging party is the author of the clause.
- Contracting parties should exercise due care in the preparation of a choice of law provision, including significant research of the substantive provisions of the selected law prior to its incorporation into the contract.

Arbitration of Disputes in International Transactions

The simplest solution to a contract dispute is to contact and negotiate with the other party. With patience, understanding, and flexibility, one can often resolve conflicts to the satisfaction of both sides. If, however, negotiations fail and the sum involved is large enough to warrant the effort, a company should obtain the assistance and advice of its legal counsel and other qualified experts. If both parties can agree to take their dispute to an arbitration agency, this step is preferable to legal action, because arbitration is often faster and less costly. The ICC handles the majority of international arbitrations and is usually acceptable to foreign companies because it is not affiliated with any single country.

Litigation is the less preferred method of dispute resolution in many countries. It is seen in some countries, most notably in Japan, as a failure of the businessperson qua businessperson. (See Doing Business Internationally: The Role of Alternative Dispute

http://
ICC International Court of Arbitration— International Dispute Resolution Center: **http://www.iccwbo.org/ index_court.asp.** Provides links to ICC rules and model clauses.

Doing Business Internationally

The Role of Alternative Dispute Resolution in Japan[23]

The Japanese have characteristically been reluctant to litigate disputes. The Japanese litigation system promises up to a ten-year wait before a controversy is resolved. There is a cultural aversion to conflict based on ingrained notions of *wa* or peace and harmony. Informal resolution usually preserves the relationship between the parties. It removes the stigma of blame or fault associated with one who is found guilty or liable. The Japanese attitude toward compromise, conciliation, and arbitration is discussed here.

- *Compromise.* Compromise or *wakai* differs from out-of-court settlement negotiations in that it involves a judge. In *benron-ken wakai* the parties present their cases orally before the judge and, with the judge, explore areas of compromise. In *soshjno wakai* or "compromise before the court," after thorough discussions with both parties, the judge generates compromise proposals. Compromise offers obvious benefits not found in traditional litigation. A compromise may preserve peace and the status quo and come at the expense of the legitimate expectations of one of the parties; unlike in a court of law, the judge in compromise proceedings is free to disregard the legal merits and standing of the parties in order to settle the dispute equitably and restore a sense of harmony between the parties. As a ruler under Confucian principles, the judge is bound to act with compassion and benevolence. The compromise proceedings are confidential. The compromise agreement represents a voluntary contract; parties are always free to refuse a judicially sponsored

settlement, but the same judge presiding over the compromise proceedings would also hear the case at trial.

- *Conciliation.* Conciliation or *chtei* may be initiated by application of the parties or by the court and may occur while a lawsuit is pending. Unlike with court-sponsored compromise, a court appoints a conciliation committee. A conciliation commissioner must be a lawyer, must have expert knowledge and experience useful in settling disputes, and must possess "rich knowledge and experience in public life." There is, however, no guarantee that the outcome will reflect the legal merits of the case. Indeed, it has been described as "OK, OK (*maamaa*)" or "fifty/fifty (*seppan*)" conciliation because of the overriding emphasis placed on settling the dispute and restoring harmony.

- *Arbitration.* Japanese arbitration or *chsai* can be divided into two categories: arbitration conducted between two Japanese parties and arbitration conducted between a Japanese party and a foreign party. Arbitration has not been favored as a method of dispute resolution among the Japanese because, like litigation, arbitration involves the "imposition" of a settlement by a third party and therefore cannot restore the harmony disrupted by the dispute. Arbitration has, however, gained widespread acceptance as a means of resolving disputes in international business transactions between Japanese and foreign parties. Arbitration allows Japanese concerns to negotiate "equitable positions as opposed to purely legal technicalities" and to avoid extensive pretrial discovery battles that serve only to "exacerbate the conflict."

Resolution in Japan.) In such cultures, arbitration may prove "a' 'face-saving' approach to dispute resolution."[24] From a more practical perspective, litigation is an expensive process likely to permanently damage the business relationship and is inherently unpredictable as to result. International litigation is often unduly delayed because of

23.   Andrew M. Pardieck, "Virtuous Ways and Beautiful Customs: The Role of Alternative Dispute Resolution in Japan," 11 *Temple International & Comparative Law Journal* 31, 33, 37–42, 44–45, 55 (1997).

24.   Steven C. Nelson, "Alternatives to Litigation of International Disputes," 23 *International Lawyer* 187, 199 (1989).

a lack of uniformity in procedural rules. For example, the liberalized nature of U.S. discovery rules often meets with hostility in foreign courts.

The uncertainty of dispute resolution in a foreign country is generally more manageable through arbitration than through the national court system. This is especially true in former Soviet bloc countries and developing countries, where the enforcement of new substantive laws is uncertain and uneven. Furthermore, even when enforced, the remedies granted may be insufficient to fully protect the contract and property rights of the foreign party. In general, arbitral awards rendered in countries party to the New York Convention are readily enforceable in all other signatory countries.[25]

Arbitration is appealing for a variety of reasons. Frequently cited advantages over conventional litigation include potential savings in time and expense, confidentiality, and expertise of the arbitrators. For export transactions, in which the parties to the agreement are from different countries, additional advantages are neutrality, the avoidance of either party's domestic courts, and ease of enforcement. In an agreement to arbitrate, usually consisting of a clause inserted in the contract, the parties also have broad powers to specify many significant aspects of the arbitration. The arbitration clause may appoint an arbitration institute and may name the arbitration location, the law and rules that will govern, qualifications of the arbitrators, and the language in which the arbitral proceedings will be conducted.

For an international arbitration to work effectively, the national courts in the countries of both parties to the dispute must recognize and support arbitration. Should one party attempt to avoid arbitration after a dispute has arisen, the other party must be able to rely on the judicial system in either country to enforce the agreement to arbitrate. In addition, the party that prevails in the arbitration proceeding must be confident that the national courts will enforce the decision of the arbitrators. The federal policy of the United States is to approve and support resolution of disputes by arbitration. Through the New York Convention, which the United States ratified in 1970, 134 countries have undertaken international legal obligations to recognize and enforce arbitral awards. (See Comparative Law: Convention on the Recognition and Enforcement of Foreign Arbitral Awards.) The New York Convention is by far the most

---

Convention on the Recognition and Enforcement of Foreign Arbitral Awards (June 10, 1958)[26]

COMPARATIVE LAW

Article I

When signing, ratifying or acceding to this Convention any State may on the basis of reciprocity declare that it will apply the Convention to the recognition and enforcement of awards made only in the territory of another Contracting State. It may also declare that it will apply the Convention only to differences arising out of legal relationships, whether contractual or not, which are considered as commercial under the national law of the State making such declaration.

Article II

Each Contracting State shall recognize an agreement in writing under which the

continued

25. Pardieck, *supra* note 23, at 58.
26. Title 9 U.S.C. §§ 1–16, 201–07 & 301–06 codify the United States Arbitration Act, the Convention on the Recognition and Enforcement of Foreign Arbitral Awards, and the Inter-American Convention on International Commercial Arbitration, respectively.

Convention on the Recognition and Enforcement of Foreign Arbitral Awards (June 10, 1958) (*continued*)

parties undertake to submit to arbitration all or any differences which have arisen or which may arise between them in respect of a defined legal relationship, whether contractual or not, concerning a subject matter capable of settlement by arbitration.

The term "agreement in writing" shall include an arbitral clause in a contract or an arbitration agreement, signed by the parties or contained in exchange of letters or telegrams.

Article III
Each Contracting State shall recognize arbitral awards as binding and enforce them in

accordance with the rules of procedure of the territory where the award is relied upon, under conditions laid down in the following articles.

Article IV
To obtain the recognition and enforcement mentioned in the preceding article, the party applying for recognition and enforcement shall, at the time of the application, supply a duly authenticated original award or certified copy.

---

important international agreement on commercial arbitration and may be credited for much of the explosive growth of arbitration in international business disputes.

The convention provides for the full recognition of contract arbitration clauses and outlines a narrow set of grounds for the nonenforcement or vacating of an arbitration award: (1) where an award was procured by corruption, fraud, or undue means; (2) where there was evident partiality or corruption in the arbitrators; (3) where the arbitrators were guilty of misconduct in refusing to postpone the hearing or in refusing to hear evidence pertinent and material to the controversy; (4) where the arbitrators exceed their powers; (5) where there was evident miscalculation of figures; and (6) where the arbitrators have awarded upon a matter not submitted to them. The *Iran Aircraft Industries* case examined the issue of the enforceability of a foreign arbitration award.

Iran Aircraft Industries v. Avco Corporation
980 F.2d 141 (2d Cir. 1992)

Lumbard, Circuit Judge. The district court declined to enforce an award of the Iran–United States Claims Tribunal which resulted in an award of $3,513,086 due from Avco to the Iranian parties. The Iranian parties contend that the Award is enforceable under the United Nations Convention on the Recognition and Enforcement of Foreign Arbitral Awards (the "New York Convention").

The New York Convention

Avco argues that the district court properly denied enforcement of the Award pursuant to Article V(1)(b) of the New York Convention because it was unable to present

its case to the Tribunal. Article V(1)(b) of the New York Convention "essentially sanctions the application of the forum country's standards of due process." The New York Convention, however, provides for nonenforcement where: "The party against whom the award is invoked was not given proper notice of the appointment of the arbitrator or of the arbitration proceedings or was otherwise unable to present his case." In this case, Avco was not made aware that the Tribunal required actual invoices to substantiate its claim. Having thus led Avco to believe it had used a proper method to substantiate its claim, the Tribunal then rejected Avco's claim for lack of proof. We believe that by so misleading Avco the Tribunal denied Avco the opportunity to present its claim in a meaningful manner. Accordingly, Avco was "unable to present its case" within the meaning of Article V(1)(b), and enforcement of the Award was properly denied.

AFFIRMED.

Cardamone, Circuit Judge, dissenting. The New York Convention obligates U.S. courts to enforce foreign arbitral awards unless certain defenses provided in Article V(1) of the Convention are established. The specific defense with which we deal in the case at hand appears in article V(1)(b). That section states that enforcement of an arbitral award may be denied if the court is satisfied that the party against whom the award is sought to be enforced was unable to present its case before the arbitration panel. The standard, as the majority points out, essentially involves a due process inquiry to see whether the party against whom enforcement is sought has been put on notice and has had an opportunity to respond.

Avco was not denied due process before the Iran–U.S. Claims Tribunal. The ruling by the Hague Tribunal in the instant matter was not high-handed or arbitrary. A reading of prior cases reveals that they involved arbitration hearings actually cut short and not completed before an award was rendered. The present picture is vastly different. Avco had a full opportunity to present its claims, and was on notice that there might be a problem with its proof. Accordingly, I dissent and vote to enforce the award.

Case Highlights

- The New York Convention requires U.S. courts to enforce foreign arbitration awards.
- Enforcement of an arbitration award may be withheld if the losing party was denied due process.
- Due process requires the defendant be given proper notice and an opportunity to be heard.

An arbitration clause does not and should not completely separate the arbitration from the court system. At least in two instances, the court system is crucial to the vitality of the arbitration process. The first is the most obvious: The arbitration award must be enforced through the court system. An unenforceable award renders the arbitration process a meaningless exercise. Fortunately, the New York Convention has provided security of enforcement in many national jurisdictions. Nonetheless, the arbitration clause should expressly state that the parties consent to the jurisdiction of any competent court for purposes of the enforcement and satisfaction of any award. Establishing an escrow account before arbitration commences will make enforcement less problematic and court-dependent. The parties can be required to deposit money, letters of credit, or insurance bonds. The arbitration clause should then provide that the arbitrator is empowered to release the funds held in escrow to satisfy any award.

A second role for the court system is in granting injunctive relief pending the outcome of the arbitration. The arbitration clause may provide that the parties can apply to the arbitrators for injunctive relief, but the arbitrator's ability to restrain the parties may be legally ineffective. Thus, the clause should also allow the parties to resort to the court system. This provision is especially important in the area of intellectual property, where the critical need to restrain the release of confidential information and trade secrets makes injunctive relief a necessity. It is important for the aggrieved party to maintain the status quo pending the outcome of the arbitration process.

The sensitivity of the information may also dictate a clause that restrains the release of information within the arbitration process. First, the clause should reiterate that all information provided in the arbitration is to remain private and confidential. Release of such information by one of the parties would be a ground for a separate claim. Second, the clause should provide that information is to be provided to the arbitrators during the resolution process and not during the selection process. The next section discusses the parameters for negotiating a proper arbitration clause.

Arbitration and Mediation Clauses

Arbitration is the most common vehicle for dispute resolution in international commercial transactions.[27] It can be institutionalized through the use of standard rules provided by such organizations as the **American Arbitration Association (AAA)** or the ICC, or it can be done on an ad hoc basis.[28] Arbitration offers the potential for a shortened, cost-effective, confidential, and hopefully more amicable means to resolve a dispute. It allows the parties to select arbitrators with the necessary expertise to understand the technicalities of the issues in dispute. Also, an unusual choice of law is more likely to be sustained by a panel of arbitrators than by national courts of law. Unlike courts, arbitrators' primary mandate comes from the contractual arbitration clause and not national public policy concerns.

Confidentiality, especially in areas involving sensitive information, and the finality of arbitration awards (compared with the multiple appeals common in litigation) make alternative dispute resolution the preferred means for solving contractual disputes. Most courts honor the dictates of an arbitration clause. The *Farrel Corporation* case demonstrates, however, that there are some instances when a court will ignore such a clause.

http://

American Society of International Law's Guide to Electronic Resources for International Law (section on International Settlement Dispute): **http://www.asil.org/.** Includes a database with 61 national arbitration statutes. Click on "Dispute Resolution."

Farrel Corporation v. International Trade Commission

949 F.2d 1147 (Fed. Cir. 1991)

Michel, Circuit Judge. Farrel manufactures and distributes worldwide heavy machinery used in mixing rubber and plastics. Pomini, an Italian company, also sells imported rubber and plastics processing machinery in competition with Farrel. From 1957 until 1986, Farrel and Pomini entered into a series of licensing agreements allowing Pomini to manufacture, using Farrel's technology, and sell a line of rubber and plastics mixing machines worldwide, with the exceptions of the United States, the United Kingdom and Japan.

The agreements included provisions requiring that Pomini return all designs, specifications, and other materials on the expiration of the contractual relationship. Each of the licensing agreements contained an arbitration clause requiring that "all disputes" be resolved by arbitration under the International Chamber of Commerce ("ICC"): "All disputes arising in connection with the present Agreement shall be finally settled by

arbitration. Arbitration shall be conducted in Geneva, Switzerland, in accordance with the rules of Arbitration of the International Chamber of Commerce. Judgment upon the award rendered may be entered in any Court having jurisdiction, or application may be made to such Court for a judicial acceptance of the award and an order of enforcement, as the case may be."

On January 1, 1986, in accordance with the license provisions, Farrel terminated Pomini's rights to use or to retain Farrel technology. Approximately seven months later, Pomini announced that it planned to enter the U.S. market and supply American customers with internal mixing devices and components it manufactured in Italy. Farrel later alleged that Pomini was only able to do this by using trade secrets that Pomini had misappropriated from Farrel. Farrel filed a complaint against Pomini in the Tribunal of Busto Arsizio, an Italian civil court, alleging the misappropriation of trade secrets and infringement of

27. "When businesses enter into transnational relationships such as contracts for the sale of goods, joint ventures, construction projects, or distributorships, the contract typically calls for arbitration in the event of any dispute." Yves Dezalay & Bryant Garth, "Merchants of Law as Moral Entrepreneurs: Constructing International Justice from the Competition for Transnational Business Disputes," 29 *Law & Society Review* 27, 30 (1995). Compare Christina S. Romano, "1996 Brazilian Commercial Arbitration Law," 5 *Annual Survey of International & Comparative Law* 27 (1999) (Brazil was slow in accepting the desirability of international commercial arbitration).

28. Dezalay & Garth ("Merchants of Law," at 31) note that the arbitration rules of the United Nations Commission on International Trade Law are often used for ad hoc arbitration. To find the UNCITRAL arbitration rules, see 31 U.N. GAOR, Supp. No. 17, Doc. A/31/17 at 33 (1976), reprinted in 15 I.L.M. 701 (1976).

various patents and trademarks registered in Italy. A similar suit was filed in the Scottish Court of Sessions, in which Farrel alleged that Pomini infringed certain of its patents and trademarks registered in the United Kingdom. In both suits, Pomini asserted, as an affirmative defense, the "existence of binding arbitration agreements between the parties requiring that all disputes be resolved by an arbitration panel of the ICC."

Meanwhile, on July 24, 1990, Farrel filed a complaint against Pomini with the Commission. It alleged that Pomini violated 19 U.S.C. § 1337(a) in the importation and sale of internal mixing machines and their components by misappropriating trade secrets, committing trademark infringement, and falsely representing the manufacturers' source. Farrel petitioned for an immediate cease and desist order under 19 U.S.C. § 1337(f) and a limited permanent exclusion order forbidding entry into the United States of Pomini's internal mixing devices. On October 3, 1990, the administrative law judge ("ALJ") assigned to the case issued an initial determination terminating the investigation based on the existence of the arbitration clauses in the technology licensing agreements.

We have jurisdiction over appeals from the International Trade Commission. The Commission has exclusive authority to investigate, either on the basis of a complaint or on its own initiative, allegations that foreign importers are engaging in unfair methods of competition and unfair acts in the importation of articles. The ITC, through its staff, conducts the investigations. Farrel contends that the Commission, by relying on a private contractual arbitration agreement to terminate its investigation, acted contrary to its authority. We conclude that the Commission acted contrary to law by terminating its investigation on the basis of an arbitration agreement without first determining whether a violation existed as required under Section 1337. The Commission's decision terminating the instant investigation is REVERSED AND REMANDED.

Case Update

The U.S. Supreme Court denied certiorari and refused to hear the case in *Farrel Corporation v. International Trade Commission*, 504 U.S. 913 (1992).

Case Highlights

- The existence of an arbitration clause in a contract provides an affirmative defense against a party's commencement of litigation.
- The U.S. International Trade Commission (ITC) has exclusive jurisdiction over the issuance of cease and desist orders, preventing infringing foreign goods from being imported into the United States.
- The ITC must research the merits of any claims of violations of the Tariff Act or intellectual property laws, despite the existence of an arbitration agreement.

THE CUSTOM ARBITRATION CLAUSE

A vague, simple arbitration clause is often not worth the paper it is printed on, because issues it does not deal with will probably need to be resolved in court. An arbitration clause should state the specific rules to be applied, such as the rules of the ICC[29] or the AAA. The AAA's standard clause states: "Any controversy or claim arising out of or relating to this contract, or the breach thereof, shall be settled by arbitration administered by the American Arbitration Association in accordance with its applicable rules and judgment on the award rendered by the arbitrator may be entered in any court having jurisdiction thereof." This clause makes clear that *all* issues pertaining to the contract are to be arbitrated, and it provides a complete set of rules and procedures in referencing the AAA rules of arbitration. The *entry of judgment* language ("may be entered in any court") is essential to show intent that any arbitration award is to be final and binding. In short, in international contracting it is important "to make absolutely clear in the contract that both parties desire arbitration, are willing to accept judgment of an award, and are willing to accept judgment in any jurisdiction."[30]

---

29.   International Chamber of Commerce, Rules of Arbitration (1998), available at http://www.iccwbo.org.
30.   James H. Davis, Kenneth E. Payne & John R. Thomas, "Drafting the Technology License Agreement," 13 *ALI-ABA Course Materials Journal* 27 (1996).

http://

American Arbitration
Association:
http://www.adr.org.

The AAA standard clause does not provide for mediation or conciliation[31] as a means to resolve a dispute before a formal arbitration. It is highly recommended that a **med-arb clause** be utilized in most contracts. Conciliation or mediation as a required precursor to any arbitration is generally advantageous to both parties. First, mediation has been shown to be highly successful in resolving disputes promptly and preserving the long-term solidarity of the contractual relationship. Second, if mediation is unsuccessful, the parties will have a better understanding of the issues in dispute, which is likely to lead to a more efficient arbitration. Mediation may be more appealing if the clause states that the arbitrators may include mediation costs in their arbitration award. The downside of mediation is minimal, because either party retains the power to end the mediation at any time in order to proceed to arbitration.

The standard arbitration clause can be transformed easily into a med-arb clause by inserting the following language: "The parties agree first to attempt to settle the dispute through mediation administered by the AAA and its Commercial Mediation Rules or ICC ADR Rules before resorting to arbitration." Conciliation makes sense in an international business dispute because of the increased chance that misunderstandings are due to cultural and language differences.[32] Unfortunately, international mediation or conciliation is an underutilized dispute resolution device. Therefore, the arbitration clause should state expressly that the parties have agreed to submit voluntarily to conciliation before they proceed with a formal arbitration.

http://

Mediation Information
and Resource Center:
http://www.mediate.com
or ADR and Mediation
Resources: **http://
adrr.com.**

To stimulate interest in conciliation, the ICC adopted its ADR Rules, which became effective on July 1, 2001. The ICC ADR Rules, discussed in the next section, are made up of seven concise articles intended to encourage simplicity, flexibility, timeliness, cost savings, and confidentiality in the conciliation process. In practice, it is best for the parties to negotiate a custom clause. The additional time spent negotiating and drafting the clause will be well spent, given the costs of international dispute resolution. Focus on Transactions: A Checklist for the Drafter lists issues that should be addressed in negotiating a custom arbitration clause.

ICC ADR RULES

The ICC ADR rules simplify the process of beginning alternative dispute resolution. Any party seeking alternative dispute resolution simply submits a request for ADR, along with a $1,500 application fee. Unless provided by an agreement, the ICC, through an ICC National Committee, appoints a single individual, known as a *neutral*, to facilitate the process. The neutral then seeks an agreement on the type of alternative dispute resolution to be used. If the parties are unable to reach an agreement, the neutral is authorized to utilize mediation as the preferred mode of dispute resolution. Flexibility is enhanced by the fact that the rules place few restraints on the neutral, other than to be guided by "principles of fairness and impartiality and by the wishes of the parties." The ICC's position regarding costs is that they should be considerably less than the costs of arbitration. Administrative expenses are set in the ICC's discretion but, in any event, cannot exceed $10,000. The neutral's fee is set at an hourly rate fixed by the ICC in consultation with the

---

31. Some commentators distinguish between mediation and conciliation. Because there is no generally accepted definition upon which to base any such differences, the two words will be used interchangeably. Mediation or conciliation refers to the use of a third party to negotiate a settlement of a dispute. The mediation is a nonbinding proceeding. The mediator has no power to issue a binding ruling.
32. Eric A. Schwartz, "International Conciliation and the ICC," 5 *The ICC International Court of Arbitration Bulletin* 5, 6 (Nov. 1994).

A Checklist for the Drafter[33]

It is not enough to state that "disputes arising under the agreement shall be settled by arbitration." Although that language indicates the parties' intention to arbitrate and may authorize a court to enforce the clause, it leaves many issues unresolved. Issues such as when, where, how, and before whom a dispute will be arbitrated are subject to disagreement once a controversy has arisen, with no way to resolve them except to go to court.

Some of the more important elements a practitioner should keep in mind when drafting, adopting, or recommending a dispute resolution clause follow:

- The clause might cover all disputes that may arise or only certain types.
- It could specify only arbitration—giving a binding result—or also provide an opportunity for nonbinding negotiation or mediation.
- The arbitration clause should be signed by as many potential parties to a future dispute as possible.
- To be fully effective, "entry of judgment" language in domestic cases is important.
- It is normally a good idea to state whether a panel of one or three arbitrators is to be selected and to include the place where the arbitration will occur.
- If the contract includes a general choice of law clause, it may govern the arbitration proceeding. The consequences should be considered.
- Consideration should be given to incorporating the AAA's Procedures for Large, Complex Disputes for potentially substantial or complicated cases.
- The drafter should keep in mind that the AAA has specialized rules for arbitration in the construction, patent, securities, and certain other fields. If anticipated disputes fall into any of these areas, the specialized rules should be considered for incorporation in the arbitration clause. An experienced AAA administrative staff manages the processing of cases under AAA rules.
- The parties are free to customize and refine basic arbitration procedures to meet their particular needs. If the parties agree on a procedure that conflicts with otherwise applicable AAA rules, the AAA will almost always respect the wishes of the parties.

Focus on Transactions

parties and the neutral. The fee must be reasonable, based on the complexity of the dispute and other relevant circumstances.

Concerns for confidentiality are emphasized in the rules' general mandate that the confidential nature of the process shall be respected in the absence of an agreement of the parties or if such confidentiality is prohibited by law. Statements made in the course of the proceedings cannot be used as evidence in subsequent proceedings between the parties, and the neutral cannot be called to testify as a witness at such proceedings.

Legality of Arbitration and Forum Selection Clauses

A well-written arbitration clause answers not only the question of how a contract dispute is to be resolved but also where the dispute is to be resolved. In the latter sense, an arbitration clause acts as a forum selection clause. In the past, U.S. courts often

---

33.   Drafting Dispute Resolution Clauses: A Practical Guide (2004), available at http://www.adr.org.

voided forum selection clauses as usurping the court's jurisdiction. One of the public policy concerns was to preserve the U.S. plaintiff's right to bring a lawsuit in a U.S. court. However, the U.S. Supreme Court in the *Bremen v. Zapata Off-Shore Company*[34] case held that a forum selection clause should be voided only in unusual cases. The court determined that forum selection clauses are to be enforced fully unless the attacking party meets "the heavy burden of showing that its enforcement would be unreasonable, unfair, or unjust." The court explained that the challenging party needed to show that the "contractual forum will be so gravely difficult and inconvenient" that the plaintiff will, for all practical purposes, be deprived of the right to proceed with the claim. The court's stated rationale was that the expansion of U.S. business would be retarded if "we insist on a parochial concept that all disputes must be resolved under our law and in our courts." Furthermore, it reasoned that the security and predictability of international contracts and contract dispute resolution must be ensured. "The elimination of uncertainties by agreeing in advance on a forum acceptable to both parties is an indispensable element in international trade and contracting." The *Tennessee Imports, Inc.* case explores the issues of the arbitrability of specific issues and the enforceability of arbitration clauses.

Forum selection and arbitration clauses should be as carefully drafted as any other provision within a contract. Failure in this regard may result in unnecessary lawsuits or litigation in multiple jurisdictions. Particular attention should be paid to the clear designation of a forum and the applicability of the clause to all claims that may arise from the terms of the contract. In addition, the clause should include language mandating the utilization of the designated forum rather than merely providing the parties with the option of submission of claims to the forum.

Tennessee Imports, Inc. v. Pier Paulo

745 F. Supp. 1314 (M.D. Tenn. 1990)

Nixon, District Judge. Plaintiff, Tennessee Imports, Inc., brought this action for breach of contract and tortious interference with contract against defendant Prix Italiais an Italian corporation with its principal place of business in Venice, Italy. The contract provided that "should any dispute arise between the contractual parties or in connection with the relations stipulated by this contract and no settlement can be achieved, then both parties agree to the competence of the Arbitration Court of the Chamber of Commerce in Venice, Italy." Tennessee Imports argued that enforcement of this provision would result in substantial inconvenience and would deny it effective relief. Furthermore, that the tortious interference claim is not within the scope of the forum selection clause. The defendants have responded to the plaintiff's arguments as follows: (1) That the Arbitration Court referred to in Article 8 is the Arbitration Court of the International Chamber of Commerce, a well-recognized and competent arbitral body which may conduct proceedings in

Venice, (2) That the contract between Prix and Tennessee Imports was the result of "arms length negotiations by experienced and sophisticated business entities," and (3) That, because of the expansion of American trade and commerce in world markets, public policy now supports upholding forum selection clauses.

A. The Federal Arbitration Act

Because the forum selection clause at issue is also an arbitration clause found in the contract involving international commerce, its validity, interpretation, and enforcement are governed by the Federal Arbitration Act, 9 U.S.C. § 1 et seq. Congress enacted the Arbitration Act in 1924 "to ensure judicial enforcement of privately made agreements to arbitrate." The Act sets up "a presumption in favor of arbitration," and requires that courts "rigorously enforce agreements to arbitrate." In the field of international commerce, this presumption in favor of arbitration was

---

34.   407 F. 1 (1971).

strengthened by adoption of the United Nations Convention on the Recognition and Enforcement of Foreign Arbitral Awards ("New York Convention"). The United States ratified the Convention on September 30, 1970, with certain reservations as allowed by Article I (3) of the Convention. These reservations include the following: "The United States of America will apply the Convention, on the basis of reciprocity, to the recognition and enforcement of only those awards made in the territory of another Contracting State." Italy ratified the Convention on January 31, 1969, without reservations.

The language of the Convention contemplates a very limited inquiry by the courts in determining the enforceability of arbitration clauses found in international commercial agreements. In making this determination, the Court must first address three questions: (1) Is there an agreement in writing to arbitrate the subject of the dispute?, (2) Does the agreement provide for arbitration in the territory of a signatory country?, and (3) Does the agreement arise out of a legal relationship, whether contractual or not, which is considered as commercial? In the case of narrow arbitration clauses, the court will determine if issues fall within the scope of an arbitration clause before referring them to arbitration.

In the case of broad arbitration clauses, arbitrability of issues arguably falls within the scope of the clause and it will be left to the arbitrators to determine whether an issue falls within the scope of a clause. Nevertheless, in certain cases, a stay or preliminary injunction may be a more appropriate solution. A court may issue a preliminary injunction if it deems preliminary injunctive relief necessary to ensure that the arbitration process remains a meaningful one.

B. The Enforceability of the Arbitration Clause

Each of the two parties is incorporated and has their principal place of business in different countries that are signatories to the New York Convention. The sales contract contains an express agreement to arbitrate and provides for arbitration in Italy. Thus, if the disputes between these parties fall within the scope of their arbitration agreement, this Court must enforce that agreement unless the Court finds that it falls within the Tennessee Imports' claim of inducing and procuring breach. A party cannot tortiously induce a breach of its own contract. Tennessee Imports

cannot escape arbitration merely by characterizing these claims as sounding in tort. Courts have consistently held that broad arbitration clauses encompass contract-based tort claims.

Tennessee Imports argues that Prix used its superior economic power to obtain Tennessee Imports' assent to the arbitration clause without negotiation and, as such, it is adhesive and unconscionable. The Uniform Commercial Code addresses the subject of unconscionability in §2–302. It states that "the basic test is whether, in the light of the general commercial background and the commercial needs of the particular trade or case, the clauses involved are so one-sided as to be unconscionable under the circumstances existing at the time of the making of the contract and not of disturbance of allocation of risks because of superior bargaining power." The clause is not hidden in the small print boilerplate of a standard form contract. It is not the product of a battle of forms. It is not buried among the provisions of a lengthy and complex sales agreement. On its face, the contract appears to be one specifically drawn to define the relationship between these two parties. Tennessee Imports appears to have had ample opportunity to examine the contract before executing it. Having made its choice, Tennessee Imports must now abide by it.

The parties are hereby REFERRED to arbitration.

Case Highlights

- Arbitration clauses that state the place for arbitration also serve as forum selection clauses.
- In a case involving a "narrow" arbitration clause, the court will determine if issues fall within the scope of an arbitration clause before referring them to arbitration.
- In case of "broad" arbitration clauses, the arbitrators will generally determine the arbitrability of an issue.
- A court may issue a preliminary injunction if it deems preliminary injunctive relief necessary to ensure that the arbitration process remains a meaningful one.
- Courts are not receptive to attacks on the enforceability of an arbitration clause on grounds of unconscionability, especially when both parties are merchants.

The potential dangers of inexact drafting of forum selection clauses and resultant multitudinous litigation are demonstrated in *Frediani & Del Greco S.p.A. v. Gina Imports, Ltd.*[35] In this case, Frediani & Del Greco, an Italian corporation, brought an action in an Illinois court against Gina Imports, Ltd., an Illinois corporation, for collection of

---

35.   870 F. Supp. 217 (N.D. Ill. 1994).

unpaid invoices relating to the delivery of olive oil. The terms and conditions stated on the invoices provided, in part, "For any controversy, the only competent forum will be Lucca." In granting Gina Import's motion for summary judgment, the District Court held that, although the clause may have lost some meaning in its translation from Italian to English and could have been clearer in any event, it nonetheless constituted an exclusive forum selection agreement. The court held that use of the term *any controversy* encompassed litigation, arbitration, and other forms of dispute resolution. The term *forum* referred to a location, of which Frediani & Del Greco's home city of Lucca qualified. As for exclusivity, the court noted that the language used was "will be" and not the usual mandatory language "shall." Nevertheless, other words clarified that the clause was mandatory. Specifically, the term *forum* was limited by *only competent.* The court concluded that the word *only* in particular made the clause mandatory and exclusive. As a result, the plaintiff was not permitted to disregard the forum selection clause within its own invoice and was required to commence proceedings in Italy.

In the area of consumer purchases, some courts continue to void arbitration clauses. In a 1999 case, a New York court voided an arbitration clause as unconscionable under Section 2–302 of the Uniform Commercial Code. *Bower v. Gateway*[36] involved the sale of a Gateway computer. After receiving an order either by mail, phone, or Internet, Gateway mailed its "Standard Terms and Conditions of Agreement." The standard terms stated that any dispute would be resolved under the arbitration rules of the International Chamber of Commerce. The court in *Bower* held that the high cost of arbitration would unconscionably deter the purchaser from invoking a claim.

In contrast, arbitration is accepted without question in most international business settings. The court in *Europcar Italia, S.P.A. v. Maiellano Tours, Inc.*[37] held that any party to a foreign arbitration award may seek confirmation in a U.S. court within three years after the award was made.[38] The case involved the enforcement of an award made through an informal procedure in Italy. The U.S. Court of Appeals for the Second Circuit held that "in light of the differences in arbitration among the signatory countries, the New York Convention should be read broadly to cover both formal and informal arbitration. A stay of confirmation should not be lightly granted lest it encourage abusive tactics by the party that lost in arbitration."[39]

The next two sections examine two clauses, force majeure and liquidated damages, which should also be analyzed in conjunction with the dispute resolution clause. The **force majeure clause** provides excuses against breach of contract claims. The occurrence of a force majeure event precludes the nonbreaching party from pursuing litigation or arbitration against the breaching party. The **liquidated damages clause**, by which the parties agree in advance to damages in the event of breach, may make litigation or arbitration unnecessary.

Force Majeure Clause

A force majeure (superior force) clause allows a party to terminate its obligations under a contract because of the occurrence of something described in the clause. Force majeure events include wars, blockades, strikes, governmental interference or

---

36. 676 N.Y.S.2d 569 (App. Div. 1999).
37. 156 F.3d 310 (2d Cir. 1998).
38. 9 U.S.C. § 207 (2000).
39. See also *Fertilizer Corporation of India v. IDI Management, Inc.*, 517 F.Supp. 948 (S.D. Ohio 1981).

approval, fire, transportation problems, and others. Any event expressly designated by the parties will be given force majeure effect. Often overlooked, a force majeure clause should be custom drafted to take into account the type of industry, the countries, and type of carriage involved.

The force majeure clause that excuses a breaching party from liability for non-performance is common under most national legal systems. Force majeure refers to "extraordinary events independent of the parties' will that cannot be foreseen or averted by them with due diligence, being beyond their control and preventing the contracting party from fulfilling the obligation undertaken in the contract."[40] Most force majeure events require four criteria to satisfy the requirements of most national laws: (1) The event must be external to the transaction and the parties, (2) it must render the performance radically different from that originally contemplated, (3) it must have been unforeseeable (objectively), and (4) its occurrence must be beyond the control of the party concerned.[41]

In *Harriscom Svenska*[42] the force majeure clause enabled a seller to avoid liability for not performing on a contract. An Iranian distributor filed a breach of contract claim against a manufacturer of radio communications products. The manufacturer claimed an excuse under the agreement's force majeure clause. It claimed that the U.S. government prohibition on all sales to Iran of goods categorized as military equipment was a force majeure event. The U.S. State Department began a commodity jurisdiction proceeding, authorized by the *Arms Export Control Act*, to decide whether the radio was a military product that should be on the government's munitions list. Placement on the list would require the manufacturer to obtain export licenses for all its sales of the radio, not just those to Iran. The manufacturer negotiated a compromise in which it agreed to "voluntarily withdraw from further sales to the Iranian market." In exchange, the government agreed that the radio was not subject to the stringent export controls of munitions list products.

One of the issues before the court was whether the manufacturer's failure to ship spare radio parts was a voluntary act or a force majeure. Other issues included whether the defendant was released under the force majeure clause that excused performance under circumstances of governmental interference, whether the voluntary nature of defendant's compliance negated the excuse, and whether the defendant was required to give substituted performance through its Indian licensee. Despite the voluntary nature of the defendant's actions, the court held that the government had undoubted power to compel compliance. Like commercial impracticability, a force majeure clause excuses nonperformance when circumstances beyond the control of the parties prevent performance. The court held that the governmental interference in this case was such a circumstance.

The importance of a well-drafted force majeure clause is illustrated by the case of *Bende & Sons, Inc. v. Crown Recreation, Inc.*[43] In that case, a U.S. seller of combat boots sought an excuse for nonperformance because of the derailment of the train transporting the boots. It sought the excuse of commercial impracticability under Section 2–615 of the Uniform Commercial Code. Section 2–615 provides for an excuse for nonperformance when performance is "made

40. Theo Rauh, "Legal Consequences of *Force Majeure* Under German, Swiss, English, and United States' Law," 25 *Denver Journal of International Law & Policy* 151 (1996).
41. Ibid. at 152.
42. 3 F.3d 576 (1993).
43. 548 F. Supp. 1018 (E.D. Louisiana 1982).

impracticable by the occurrence of a contingency the nonoccurrence of which was a basic assumption on which the contract was made." Surprisingly, the court rejected the defense, holding that the derailment was an allocated risk because "common sense dictates that they could easily have foreseen such an occurrence."[44]

In *Phillips Puerto Rico Core, Inc. v. Tradax Petroleum*,[45] liability rested upon the interpretation of a standard force majeure clause in relationship to a trade term. The clause in question read as follows:

FORCE MAJEURE: In the event of any strike, fire or other event falling within the term Force Majeure preventing or delaying shipment or delivery of the goods by the seller . . . then the contract period of shipment or delivery shall be extended by 30 days on telex request made within seven days of its occurrence. Should shipment or delivery of the goods continue to be prevented beyond 30 days, the unaffected party may cancel the unfulfilled balance of the contract. Should the contract thus be cancelled and/or performance be prevented during any extension to the shipment or delivery period neither party shall have any claim against the other.[46]

The trade term in the contract provided was cost and freight (C & F) for products to be shipped from Algeria to Puerto Rico. The U.S. Coast Guard unexpectedly detained the ship while in transit. The purchaser brought suit against the seller for breach of contract, and the seller claimed an excuse by invoking the force majeure clause. The court held that the defense was not necessary because, under the C & F term, the risk of loss had already passed to the purchaser at the port of shipment. Therefore, the purchaser no longer had a claim of nonperformance against the seller. A more detailed force majeure clause could have provided that the purchaser was not obligated on the purchase if the goods were detained prior to actual delivery at the port of destination.

The force majeure clause should be a highly negotiated, customized provision dealing with the particulars of the specific parties and specific type of contract. Unfortunately, most contracts, domestic and international, utilize vaguely worded standard excuse or exemption clauses. In the most recent edition of "*Force Majeure* and Hardship," the ICC provides an elaborate force majeure clause.[47] The ICC model clause includes a long list of traditional force majeure events, such as hostilities between states, civil disorder, natural disasters, and compliance with applicable national laws. However, the ICC also includes less apparent events, such as prolonged failure of telecommunications, which may absolve a party from performance of its contractual obligations. Parties may be excused from their contractual obligations upon the occurrence of one of these events if it is beyond the party's "reasonable control." The failure of third parties upon whom performance of the contract depends may also relieve a contracting party of its obligations. It also provides that, in any event, a party seeking relief pursuant to a force majeure

---

44. Ibid. at 1022.
45. 782 F.2d 314 (1985).
46. This clause does possess a number of good features, even though it does not adequately define the term *force majeure*. It does define the responsibilities of the party attempting to declare force majeure. It also provides an automatic thirty-day performance extension before allowing the purchaser to cancel the contract. A graduated response to a force majeure event should be considered in drafting a force majeure clause. The drafter should attempt to define not only the events to be considered as force majeure but also the relative duties and rights of each party stemming from such an event.
47. ICC, Publication No. 650, "*Force Majeure* and Hardship" (2003).

clause must undertake "all reasonable means to limit the effect of the impediment or event upon its performance of its contractual duties."

The concept of force majeure or excuse has been incorporated in Article 79 of the Convention for the International Sale of Goods (see Chapter Eight). Article 79 refers to a force majeure event as an **impediment**. The impediment must be reasonably unforeseeable because technically everything is foreseeable. Foreseeable impediments cannot serve as an excuse for nonperformance. Foreseeable impediments or events are occurrences "a party could reasonably be expected to take into account and to make contingency plans for when entering into the contract." Work stoppages or strikes at a supplier or subcontractor are generally not sufficient causes. This presumption may be overcome if, for example, the contract specifies the use of a particular supplier or subcontractor.

Impediment does not mean inconvenient, or more costly, or difficult to perform. Because the force majeure clause generally does not recognize changes in circumstances that result in mere hardship, the parties may expand the clause to include events that make performance not impossible but unduly costly. Such a clause is referred to as a **hardship clause**. The most recent edition of the ICC's "*Force Majeure* and Hardship" manual obligates parties to negotiate "alternative contractual terms" in the event continued performance of the contract becomes "excessively onerous" because of an unforeseeable event beyond the reasonable control of the parties. The party invoking the hardship clause may terminate the contract in the event it is unable to negotiate satisfactory alternative terms with the other contracting party. The parties may avoid the uncertainty associated with the vagueness of these terms by providing specific examples within their contract. However, caution should be exercised in this regard, as any listing will be incomplete by necessity, given the unforeseeable nature of many hardships. Furthermore, any list of such occurrences may be deemed exclusive without language indicating that they are only demonstrative rather than exhaustive.

Another force majeure type of clause that can be considered is the **government approval clause**. If some government permit, license, or approval is required to perform under the contract, then the parties may elect to have the approval be a *condition precedent* to the contract. This type of provision is especially appropriate in an intellectual property transfer transaction in a country where government approval is required. A simple government approval clause in an export contract would read: "Seller shall obtain all necessary permits, licenses, or permissions to export the goods. Buyer shall obtain all necessary permits, licenses, or permissions to import the goods. This contract is not fully executed and enforceable until such permissions have been received."[48]

Liquidated Damages Clause

Liquidated damages clauses state in advance the damages that the parties agree to voluntarily pay upon breaching the contract, technically eliminating the need for a court action or arbitral proceeding. These clauses, however, also known as penalty clauses, are not uniformly enforced under all national legal systems. This section compares substantive differences in liquidated damages law among different legal systems.

---

48.   William F. Fox Jr., *International Commercial Agreements: A Primer on Drafting, Negotiating and Resolving Disputes* 168 (3rd ed. 1998).

INTERNATIONAL

The common law system requires courts to void liquidated damages clauses that act as penalties. A *penalty* is defined as an inflated amount aimed at punishing the breaching party. Courts are required simply to set aside a clause that is found to impose a true penalty in such jurisdictions. This voiding of penalties is a minority approach under most national laws. The French Civil Code deals directly with the issue of liquidated damages or penalty clauses. Article 1152 allows the courts to provide alternative relief if the stipulated amount is "obviously excessive." It expressly grants courts the authority to reduce the penalty under such circumstances. In Japan, there is a strong presumption that penalty clauses are enforceable, but Article 420(1) of the Japanese Civil Code precludes a court from changing (reforming) the penalty amount.

The laws of Denmark, Sweden, Finland, and Norway allow either the voiding or reformation of a penalty clause deemed unreasonable. The Russian Civil Code grants courts the right to reduce a penalty payable pursuant to a written contractual clause in the event that it is "clearly incommensurate to the consequences of the violation of the obligation." In contrast, Anglo-American common law simply allows for the voiding of a penalty clause when the stipulated amount is considered unreasonably large.

INTERNATIONAL

To provide some uniformity between common law and civil law, the Council of Europe adopted *Resolution (78) 3 on Penal Clauses in the Civil Law.*[49] It adopts the civil law approach that the "sum stipulated may be reduced by the court when it is manifestly excessive." In its explanatory memorandum, the Committee on Legal Cooperation explained that some penal clauses are "*stricto sensu* whose main purpose is to act as a threat to induce the promisor to perform," whereas others are "a genuine preassessment of damages or liquidated damages." However, unlike in the common law, the clauses that are *stricto sensu* are not invalid per se under the civil law. In short, it is acceptable under the civil law for a liquidated damages clause to serve as not only a means for just compensation but also as an incentive (threat) to induce performance.

INTERNATIONAL

A further review of foreign national laws demonstrates that the common law approach to liquidated damages is not the only viable alternative. For example, Article 114 of the Contract Law of the People's Republic of China provides that a contract may include a liquidated damages clause (*weiyue jin*) payable in the event of breach by one of the parties. The amount of damages set forth in the clause may be increased or decreased, depending on the losses sustained by the innocent party. Alternatively, Article 115 allows the parties to use deposits as a way of securing an obligor's performance. The deposit becomes nonrefundable upon a breach of performance by the obligor. Conversely, if the obligee fails to perform, then it must return twice the amount of the deposit. This concept of deposit forfeiture mimics the doctrine of *arrhes* in Section 1590 of the French Civil Code. Under the doctrine of *arrhes*, a deposit is forfeited when the deposit giver cancels a contract. If the deposit holder cancels the contract, then that party must refund twice the amount of the deposit. The rules embodied in the doctrine of *arrhes* can be understood as the use of deposits as liquidated damages. Furthermore, the potentially penal nature of retaining the entire deposit or doubling the amount refunded is deemed irrelevant under this doctrine.

49.　Adopted by the Committee of Ministers on January 20, 1978, at the 281st meeting of the Ministers' Deputies.

KEY TERMS

act of state doctrine
American Arbitration Association (AAA)
choice of law clause
comity
conflict of law rules
discovery
dual service
force majeure
forum non conveniens doctrine
government approval clause
Hague Convention on the Recognition and Enforcement of Foreign Judgments in Civil and Commercial Matters

Hague Evidence Convention
Hague Service Convention
hardship clause
impediment
Inter-American Convention on the Extraterritorial Validity of Foreign Judgments
International Chamber of Commerce (ICC)
jurisdiction
liquidated damages clause
Lugano Convention
med-arb clause
New York Convention
personal jurisdiction

political question doctrine
Regulation No. 44/2001 on Jurisdiction and the Recognition and Enforcement of Judgments in Civil and Commercial Matters
rule of reciprocity
service of process
sovereign immunity
subject matter jurisdiction
venue

CHAPTER PROBLEMS

1. Abraham Lincoln once gave this advice relating to litigation: "Persuade your neighbors to compromise whenever they can. Point out to them how the nominal winner is often the real loser—in fees, expenses, and waste of time. As a peacemaker, the lawyer has a superior opportunity of being a good man." The Roman philosopher Cicero once admonished that "the litigious spirit is more often found with ignorance than with knowledge of law." Do you agree with this view of litigation? Do you believe that alternative dispute resolution is adequately used by U.S. business enterprises? What would you recommend for improving the U.S. dispute resolution system?

2. Several securities investors who were customers of a broker signed a standard agreement that included a clause requiring the arbitration of any controversies relating to their accounts. When the investments turned sour, the investors sued the broker and the broker's principal in the U.S. District Court for the Southern District of Texas under the 1933 Securities Act. The defendant moved that the claims be submitted to arbitration, under the agreement. Should the plaintiffs be forced to arbitrate their federal securities law claims? Does the public policy of full enforcement of the securities laws prevail over the public policy favoring arbitration? *Rodriguez de Quijas v. Shearson/American Express, Inc.*, 490 U.S. 477 (1989).

3. Your son has been killed in a car accident in a foreign country. You believe a U.S. agency is holding information that may provide insight into the cause of the accident. You file a motion to compel the agency to comply with your subpoena requesting certain documents. Will the court compel the agency to comply with the subpoena? Does the notion of sovereign immunity enter into the court's determination? *In re Application of Mohamed al Fayed*, 92 F.Supp.2d 137 (D.D.C., 2000).

4. Pursuant to a request by a foreign court, a legal alien resident of the United States is asked to testify about his activities during World War II and his immigration to the United States. Can he be compelled to testify against himself? Does the Fifth Amendment's privilege against self-incrimination extend to the fear of being prosecuted by a foreign nation? *United States v. Balsys*, 524 U.S. 666 (1998).

5. A U.S. seller and an English purchaser of services enter into a contract for servicing heavy machinery at the purchaser's factory. The service contract included an exculpatory clause that relieved the seller of all liability relating to his work. U.S. law generally enforces such clauses, and English law often voids such clauses. The choice of law clause in the contract provided that U.S. law would apply to the contract. Soon after the U.S. seller serviced the machinery, it malfunctioned, injuring two workers and causing substantial property damage to the English company's factory. The English party brought suit in an English court. The U.S. company seeks a dismissal citing the exculpatory clause. What factors will the English court look at in determining the validity of the choice of law clause as it relates to the issues of this case?

INTERNET ACTIVITIES

1. Review the model arbitration and mediation clauses published by the International Chamber of Commerce at **http://www.iccwbo.org/index_court.asp.**

2. Review the index of the Hague Conference international conventions sponsored by the Hague Conference on Private International Law at **http://hcch.e-vision.nl/index_en. php?act = conventions.listings.**

This chapter is the first of two covering regulation of international trade. We will first look at the world trading system as it has evolved under the General Agreement on Tariffs and Trade (GATT). The postwar success of GATT has led to the establishment of a permanent international institution, the World Trade Organization (WTO). Its primary purpose is the removal of barriers to international free trade. This chapter reviews the WTO and the agreements it has been empowered to enforce. International trade has also been affected by the development of strong regional trading blocs. Two of the more successful attempts at regional trade integration, the European Union (EU) and the North American Free Trade Agreement (NAFTA), will be examined.

Extending the coverage of trade regulation to the national level, Chapter Six will examine the relationship between national trade regulation and the world trading system, particularly export and import regulations. Topics include import requirements, the assessment of tariff duties, country of origin rules, marking requirements, and national standards regulations. Chapter Six concludes with an

Chapter 5

International Trade Regulation

examination of the U.S. export regulation system. It is advisable to read Chapter Six only after becoming familiar with the requirements of the WTO system presented in this chapter.

World Trading System

The multilateral trading system known as the **General Agreement on Tariffs and Trade (GATT)** is one of the legacies of the Great Depression and World War II, along with such institutions as the United Nations, the International Bank for Reconstruction and Development (World Bank), and the International Monetary Fund. Originally conceived as a temporary measure to preserve some of the free trade ideals of the failed Havana Charter and the institution it was intended to create (the International Trade Organization), the GATT entered force on January 1, 1948. The United States was one of the original twenty-three signatories to what was referred to as GATT 1947. The principles set forth in GATT 1947 and its successors were accepted by the United States as binding legal obligations, despite the absence of congressional ratification.

There have been eight subsequent rounds of GATT negotiations since its creation in 1947. As a result of these negotiations, by 2003 tariff rates among the industrial countries have fallen to an average rate of 3.8 percent. This can be compared with the tariff rates enacted by the United States in the Smoot-Hawley **Tariff Act of 1930**, which was passed in the protectionist atmosphere that characterized the United States in the post–World War I era and imposed tariffs ranging from 50 percent to 100 percent.

http://
For information on the GATT Agreements see **http://www.ciesin.org/ TG/PI/TRADE/ gatt.html.**

Promising not to raise a trade barrier is as important as lowering one. Under GATT, when countries agree to open their markets, they are required to bind their commitments. In the area of tariffs, bindings amount to placing ceilings on customs tariff rates. Countries may reduce their tariff rates below the bound rates but may not exceed them. One of the achievements of the final rounds of GATT was to increase the amount of trade covered by **binding commitments**:

Increased Bindings Due to Uruguay Round

Percentages of tariffs bound	Before 1986	After 1994
Developed Countries	78	99
Developing Countries	21	73
Transition Economies	73	98

All agricultural products are now subject to bound tariffs. Expansion of binding commitments has resulted in a tremendous increase in market stability and security.

Because of the great success of reducing tariffs, the eighth round of GATT, the **Uruguay Round**,[1] expanded for the first time into nontariff areas, such as services and intellectual property. The U.S. Department of Commerce now defines trade barriers to include not only tariffs but also quantitative restrictions, import licensing, and customs barriers; standards, testing, labeling, and certification; government procurement; export subsidies; service barriers; lack of intellectual property protection; and investment barriers. Most important, the Uruguay Round culminated with the establishment of a permanent body to oversee the implementation of GATT principles and agreements—the **World Trade Organization (WTO)**. Other WTO agreements produced by the Uruguay Round relate to agriculture, textiles, customs valuation, import licensing procedures, government procurement, and numerous other topics. The agreements relating to sanitary and phytosanitary measures, safeguards, dumping, subsidies, and dispute resolution will be discussed in this chapter. Two of these agreements relate to topics previously unaddressed within the GATT, specifically, services and intellectual property rights. These agreements, the **General Agreement on Trade in Services (GATS)** and the **Agreement on Trade-Related Aspects of Intellectual Property Rights (TRIPS)**, will be discussed in Chapters Twelve and Thirteen, respectively.

http://
World Trade
Organization: **http://
www.wto.org.**

GATT Principles

The four founding principles of GATT are the elimination of quantitative restrictions on imports, the most-favored-nation principle (now known as normal trade relations), the national treatment principle, and the principle of transparency. All four are aimed at advancing the notion of nondiscrimination, by which countries are mandated not to discriminate among different foreign trading partners or between domestic goods and imported goods.

GATT Article XI prohibits the imposition of **quantitative restrictions** upon imports and exports other than through duties, taxes, and other charges. As a general principle, members of the WTO are prohibited from adopting quotas,

1. The participation of the United States in the Uruguay Round was implemented by the U.S. Congress in December 1994. See Uruguay Round Agreements Act, 19 U.S.C. §§ 3501–3624 (2000).

licensing schemes, and other measures that prohibit or restrict the importation of any product from other WTO members or the exportation or sale for export of any product to other WTO members.

Article I of the GATT sets forth the **normal trade relations** or most-favored-nation principle. This principle requires that members of the WTO offer all other members their most favorable tariff rates. If a country grants benefits to a trading partner through a bilateral agreement, then it must also grant those benefits to all other members of the WTO. Thus, when a country lowers a trade barrier or opens up a domestic market, it must do so for all its trading partners.

There are three major exceptions to the most-favored-nation principle. First, a country can raise barriers to the importation of goods from specific countries that have violated the principles of GATT. These punitive barriers are generally enacted when a foreign government gives illegal **subsidies** or when a foreign exporter is accused of **dumping** goods on a foreign market. A subsidy is a financial contribution made by the government that benefits a domestic enterprise or industry. This financial contribution can take many different forms, including direct transfers of funds (such as loans, grants, and equity infusions), loan guarantees, tax credits, and price supports. Article VI of the GATT and the *Agreement on Subsidies* and *Countervailing Measures* requires the member seeking to impose a **countervailing duty** to first prove that the entry of the subsidized goods into the territory of a WTO country will cause or threaten to cause material injury to an established domestic industry. Particularly noteworthy in this regard are subsidies payable upon export performance and the purchase or utilization of domestically manufactured goods or input over imported goods or input. In such a circumstance, the injured state is permitted to impose a countervailing duty on the subsidized goods in an amount equal to the illegal subsidy. The procedure by which a WTO member may impose countervailing duties on illegally subsidized goods is discussed later in this chapter.

An example of an illegal subsidy may be found in WTO opinions relating to U.S. tax treatment of foreign sales corporations.[2] The foreign sales corporation program was designed to promote U.S. exports by granting favorable tax treatment to such entities, which were controlled by U.S.-based parent companies. In October 1999, a WTO dispute resolution panel concluded that the foreign sales corporation program constituted an illegal export subsidy. The panel agreed with the European Union's contention that the program granted subsidies contingent upon export performance and the use of domestic over imported goods. The panel recommended the abolition of the program by October 1, 2000. In response to this ruling, President Clinton signed the Extraterritorial Income Exclusion Act (ETI) in November 2000. However, the ETI still permitted U.S. taxpayers to exclude earnings of qualifying foreign trade income from gross income. As a result, the ETI was again challenged by the European Union. In January 2002, the WTO held that the ETI also constituted a prohibited export subsidy. In May 2003, the WTO endorsed the European Union's request for the imposition of countermeasures in an amount equal to the estimated annual subsidy, specifically, $4 billion. The European Union delayed imposition of these countermeasures until March 2004, when it announced additional customs duties of 5 percent on specified U.S. products, to be followed by monthly increases of

---

2. See, e.g., United States Tax Treatment for Foreign Sales Corporations: Recourse to Article 21.5 of the DSU by the European Communities, AB-2001-8, WT/DS108/AB/RW (adopted by the Dispute Settlement Body, 29 January 2002).

1 percent up to a ceiling of 17 percent, to be reached by March 2005 in the event that compliance had not occurred by that time. Legislative efforts to comply with the WTO's ruling remained bogged down in Congress in late 2004.

Another area where additional duties are assessed is when there is proof of illegal dumping. Dumping occurs when a foreign company sells its product overseas for less than the price charged for the same or comparable goods in the company's home market or for less than the cost of production. Article VI of the GATT and the Agreement upon Implementation of Article VI prohibit such practices if they cause or threaten material injury to an established industry or materially retard the establishment of domestic industry in a WTO member. States are permitted to impose **antidumping duties** on goods sold in their territories under such circumstances. The antidumping duties are set at an amount necessary to offset the benefits received by the foreign company from the unfair price. The procedure by which a WTO member may impose antidumping duties on dumped products originating in another WTO member is discussed later in this chapter.

The second major exception to the most-favored-nation principle is safeguard measures. GATT Article XIX and the Agreement on Safeguards provide that a WTO member may undertake emergency action if a product is imported into its territory "in such increased quantities and under such conditions as to cause or threaten serious injury to domestic producers of like or directly competitive products." In such circumstances, the WTO member is permitted to undertake emergency action to prevent or remedy such injury. Such emergency action is known as a **safeguard measure**. Safeguard measures usually take the form of temporary tariff increases. Unlike dumping and subsidies, no GATT violation is necessary for a state to adopt a safeguard measure.

GATT places numerous limitations on safeguard measures. Safeguard measures may be utilized only if a product is being imported in such increased quantities as to cause serious injury to a domestic industry that produces like or directly competitive products. *Serious injury* is defined as a significant and imminent overall impairment in the position of the affected domestic industry as a whole. In the event of such injury, safeguard measures may be imposed for only a limited period of time, not to exceed four years (with one four-year extension). Such measures must be lifted as conditions improve in the affected domestic industry. Such measures must also apply to all such imports, regardless of their source of origin, in order to comply with the mandates of normal trade relations.

In addition, safeguard measures may be imposed only after the completion of a public administrative investigation that evaluates the affected industry and the economic factors relevant to the industry's performance and determines that the increased level of imports is the cause of the injury. In the United States, this administrative procedure is set forth in Section 201 of the *Trade Act of 1974*.[3] The **International Trade Commission (ITC)**, an independent federal administrative agency, may conduct an investigation of increases in imports and their effect on a designated industry at the request of private industry, trade and labor associations, the U.S. Congress, or the president, or at the ITC's own volition. This investigation must determine the existence of serious injury to a domestic industry caused by an increase in imports. In addition to determining the existence of an increase in imports and its causal link to industry performance, the ITC may examine numerous relevant

---

3. See 19 U.S.C. §§ 2251–54 (2000).

economic indicators in the course of its investigation. These indicators include the idling of productive facilities, the inability of the industry to earn a reasonable profit or generate capital, unemployment or underemployment, the status of inventories, and declines in sales, market share, production, wages, and employment. The president may adopt the ITC's conclusions and impose a safeguard measure only if it will "facilitate efforts by the domestic industry to make a positive adjustment to import competition and provide greater economic and social benefits than costs." Remedies available to the president include tariff increases of up to 50 percent, quotas (although these are not favored by the WTO), tariff rate quotas (which allow a certain number of articles to be imported at one tariff rate while excess amounts are permitted to enter at higher tariff rates), and trade adjustment assistance to workers in the affected industry, as well as the industry itself. The steel safeguards case in the following Comparative Law section demonstrates the strict standards applicable to the imposition of safeguard measures and the consequences for ignoring them.

The Steel Safeguards Case

COMPARATIVE LAW

The U.S. steel industry has suffered from many problems in the past thirty-five years. For example, the global steel market has experienced massive overproduction, as exemplified by the production of 747 million tons in 2001—a global record. Furthermore, foreign competitors that pay lower wages, provide fewer (if any) benefits, use newer technology that reduces labor costs, and receive government subsidies have also had an impact on U.S. steel producers. Finally, U.S. minimills utilizing electric furnace technology, paying lower wages, and operating without unions present formidable competition to traditional domestic steel producers. As a result, there were thirty-one bankruptcies in the U.S. steel industry between 1998 and 2002.

On October 22, 2001, the International Trade Commission found that twelve of the thirty-three domestic steel lines in the United States had suffered serious injury as a result of increased imports. These twelve lines constitute 79 percent of all steel produced in the United States. President George W. Bush accepted these conclusions and, on March 4, 2002, imposed tariffs of up to 30 percent on the majority of steel entering the United States for a period of three years. Steel originating from states with free trade agreements with the United States—specifically, Canada, Israel, Jordan, and Mexico—were exempted from the tariff increases.

Foreign reaction to the imposition of this safeguard measure was harsh. EU Trade Commissioner Pascal Lamy remarked, "The international market isn't the Wild West where everyone acts as he pleases." German chancellor Gerhard Schroeder condemned the tariffs as contrary to free markets, and French president Jacques Chirac characterized them as "serious and unacceptable." Even the United Kingdom, the United States' closest ally, expressed displeasure with the decision to increase tariffs. Patricia Hewitt, the minister of trade and industry, asked, "Why should developing countries commit to free and open markets when the United States closes its domestic market to address a problem which many see as largely of the U.S. industry's own making?" Trade ministers in Japan, Korea, and the People's Republic of China also expressed displeasure with the U.S. safeguard measure.

Many states increased their own tariffs on imported steel in response to the U.S. action and in order to prevent a flood of imported steel diverted from the U.S.

continued

The Steel Safeguards Case (*continued*)

market. On March 25, 2002, the EU imposed tariffs on steel imports of up to 26 percent to protect its steel manufacturers from the anticipated dumping of Asian steel in the European market. The cost of the increase in these duties was estimated at $355 million. Japan and the People's Republic of China followed suit with significant tariff increases on imported steel in May 2002.

In addition, the EU, joined by Brazil, Japan, Korea, New Zealand, and Switzerland, asked the World Trade Organization to declare that the U.S. steel safeguard measure violated the GATT. In addition to defending against this action, the United States responded by granting exemptions to the increased tariffs. By August 2002, the United States had granted 727 of the 1,200 filed requests for exemption.

The Dispute Settlement Body of the World Trade Organization issued its preliminary report, finding the safeguard measure to be in violation of the GATT on March 26, 2003. The final report was issued on July 11, 2003. The 968-page ruling concluded that the United States failed to prove that steel imports had increased or that such increases, if any, caused serious harm to the U.S. steel industry and that it had further violated the GATT by granting exemptions to Canada, Israel, Jordan, and Mexico. An appeal of the Dispute Settlement Body's ruling was rejected on November 10, 2003.

The EU consequently called for an immediate end to the tariffs and threatened retaliation through the imposition of 100 percent tariffs totaling $435 million by mid-December 2003. This retaliation was to be directed at politically important states such as Florida, California, and the Carolinas. President Bush subsequently lifted the tariffs on December 4, 2003. In so doing, he cited a September 2003

report of the International Trade Commission concluding that the safeguard measure generated $650 million in increased tariff revenues as compared with a $30.4 million decline in gross domestic product. The president also noted that the industry had engaged in significant restructuring in the twenty-one months when the safeguards had been in place. As such, the president concluded: "These safeguard measures have now achieved their purpose, and as a result of changed economic circumstances, it is time to lift them."

U.S. trade partners welcomed the termination of the safeguard measures. Patricia Hewitt noted, "We in Europe, by standing together, by using the WTO and saying 'we're going to uphold the rules of world trade,' we've played our hand very, very effectively indeed." The reaction was less positive in the United States. Senator Robert Byrd (Democrat, West Virginia) remarked that the decision to lift the tariffs "shattered any credibility [the Bush administration] ever had with the steel industry in West Virginia and across this country." While praising the removal of the tariffs, Senator Charles Grassley (Republican, Iowa) noted, "The tariffs may have helped some sectors of the economy, but they certainly hurt others."

These sentiments were echoed by industry members. For example, Thomas Usher, the chief executive officer of U.S. Steel Group, noted, "The tariffs were working as planned and have been instrumental in bringing about the improvements in the industry that we've seen over the last two years. This decision will complicate the historic restructuring that is ongoing in the industry." Leo Gerard, the president of the United Steelworkers of America, characterized the removal of the safeguards as "capitulating to European blackmail and a sorry betrayal of American steelworkers and steel communities."

The third major exception to the most-favored-nation principle is countries' formation of regional free trade areas whose agreements do not apply to goods from outside the regional group. The countries within the group may lower barriers among themselves without having to grant the reduced barriers to other WTO countries. Thus, the trade agreements embodied in the **European Union (EU)**[4] and the **North American Free Trade Agreement (NAFTA)**[5] do not violate the WTO Agreements. These regional trading blocs will be discussed later in this chapter.

The **national treatment principle** applies only once goods enter a foreign market. Once a product, intellectual property right, or service enters a foreign market, it must receive the same treatment given to domestically produced goods, services, and intellectual property rights, even though it can be treated differently at the time of importation. Therefore, charging customs duties on imported goods is not a violation of the national treatment principle. On the other hand, import requirements that are disguised trade barriers are subject to attack as a violation of national treatment. For example, it is illegal to require foreign goods to satisfy higher standards or to pass more rigorous testing or inspection than domestic goods. The *Italian Discrimination Against Imported Agricultural Machinery* case that follows illustrates the GATT's prohibition on discrimination between domestic and imported products in the context of a government financing program.

Italian Discrimination Against Imported Agricultural Machinery
GATT Report L/833–7S/60 (1958)

1. The Panel for Conciliation examined with the representatives of the United Kingdom and Italy the complaint of the United Kingdom Government that certain provisions of chapter III of Italian Law No. 949 of 25 July 1952, which provides special credit facilities to some categories of farmers or farmers' co-operatives for the purchase of agricultural machinery produced in Italy, were inconsistent with the obligations of Italy under Article III of the General Agreement and that the operation of this Law impaired the benefits which should accrue to the United Kingdom under the Agreement. The panel heard statements from both parties and obtained additional information from them to clarify certain points. It also heard a statement by the observer of Denmark recording his Government's interest as an exporter of agricultural machinery, especially of reaper binders, in the United Kingdom complaint. On the basis of these statements the Panel considered whether the provisions of the Italian Law of 25 July 1952 concerning the granting of special facilities for the purchase of domestic agricultural machinery had effects which were inconsistent with the provisions of the General Agreement. It considered further whether and to what extent the operation of these provisions impaired the benefits accruing directly or indirectly to the Government of the United Kingdom

under the General Agreement. Finally, the Panel agreed on a recommendation which, in its opinion, would assist the Italian and United Kingdom Governments in arriving at a satisfactory adjustment of the case submitted by the United Kingdom to the CONTRACTING PARTIES.

2. In accordance with the Law of 25 July 1952, the Italian Government established a revolving fund which enabled the Ministry of Agriculture and Forestry to grant special credit terms *inter alia* for the purchase of Italian agricultural machinery. To this fund are allocated by budgetary appropriations 25 thousand million lire a year for five fiscal years starting with the year 1952–53; out of these 25 thousand million lire, the Law provides that 7.5 thousand million would be assigned for the purchase of agricultural machinery, an amount which may be modified by the Italian authorities. The loans are granted at 3 per cent, including fees to the Credit Institute, for a period of five years to finance up to 75 per cent of the cost of the machinery. The interest and repayments of the loans are paid into the revolving fund and may be used for further loans. The revolving fund will remain in existence until 1964. Eligible purchasers may benefit from these favourable terms when they buy Italian agricultural machinery; if, on the other hand, they wish to buy foreign machinery

---

4. The members of the European Union are Austria, Belgium, Cyprus, the Czech Republic, Denmark, Estonia, Finland, France, Germany, Greece, Hungary, Ireland, Italy, Latvia, Lithuania, Luxembourg, Malta, Netherlands, Poland, Portugal, Slovakia, Slovenia, Spain, Sweden, and the United Kingdom.
5. The members of NAFTA are the United States, Canada, and Mexico.

on credit the terms would be less favourable. The United Kingdom delegation indicated that loans on commercial terms were presently available at the rate of about 10 per cent while the Italian delegation stated that farmers could obtain from agricultural credit institutions five-year loans on terms substantially more favourable than 10 per cent.

3. The Italian delegation estimated that during the period 1952–1957 the purchasers of about half of the Italian tractors sold in Italy (i.e. about one-third of all tractors sold in the country) benefited from the credit facilities provided under Law No. 949.

5. The United Kingdom delegation noted that Article III:4 of the General Agreement provided that products imported into the territory of any contracting party "shall be accorded treatment no less favourable than that accorded to like products of national origin in respect of all laws, regulations and requirements affecting their internal sale, offering for sale, purchase, transportation. . . ." As the credit facilities provided under the Italian Law were not available to the purchasers of imported tractors and other agricultural machinery these products did not enjoy the equality of treatment which should be accorded to them. The fact that these credit facilities were reserved exclusively to the purchasers of Italian tractors and other agricultural machinery represented a discrimination and the operation of the Law involved an inconsistency with the provisions of Article III of the General Agreement which provides that laws, regulations and requirements affecting internal sale should not be applied to imported products so as to afford protection to domestic producers. The United Kingdom would not challenge the consistency with the General Agreement of subsidies which the Italian Government might wish to grant to domestic producers of tractors and other agricultural machinery in accordance with the terms of paragraph 8 (b) of Article III. However, in the case of the Italian Law the assistance by the State was not given to producers but to the purchasers of agricultural machinery, a case which is not covered by the provisions of paragraph 8 (b). Even in the case of subsidies granted to producers the rights of the United Kingdom under Article XXIII of the General Agreement would be safeguarded as was recognized by the CONTRACTING PARTIES in paragraph 13 of the report on other barriers to trade which they approved during the course of the Review Session.

6. The Italian delegation considered that the General Agreement was a trade agreement and its scope was limited to measures governing trade; thus the text of paragraph 4 of Article III applied only to such laws, regulations and requirements which were concerned with the actual conditions for sale, transportation, etc.,

of the commodity in question and should not be interpreted in an extensive way. In particular, the Italian delegation stated that the commitment undertaken by the CONTRACTING PARTIES under that paragraph was limited to qualitative and quantitative regulations to which goods were subjected, with respect to their sale or purchase on the domestic market.

8. Moreover the Italian delegation considered that the text of Article III:4 could not be construed in such a way as to prevent the Italian Government from taking the necessary measures to assist the economic development of the country and to improve the conditions of employment in Italy.

11. The Panel agreed that the question of the consistency of the effects of the Italian Law with the provisions of the General Agreement raised a problem of interpretation. It had the impression that the contention of the Italian Government might have been influenced in part by the slight difference of wording which existed between the French and the English texts of paragraph 4 of Article III. The French text which had been submitted to the Italian Parliament for approval provided that the imported products *ne seront pas soumis à un traitement moins favorable* whereas the English text read "the imported product shall be accorded treatment no less favourable." It was clear from the English text that any favourable treatment granted to domestic products would have to be granted to like imported products and the fact that the particular law in question did not specifically prescribe conditions of sale or purchase appeared irrelevant in the light of the English text. It was considered, moreover, that the intention of the drafters of the Agreement was clearly to treat the imported products in the same way as the like domestic products once they had been cleared through customs. Otherwise indirect protection could be given.

12. In addition, the text of paragraph 4 referred both in English and French to laws and regulations and requirements *affecting* internal sale, purchase, etc., and not to laws, regulations and requirements governing the conditions of sale or purchase. The selection of the word "affecting" would imply, in the opinion of the Panel, that the drafters of the Article intended to cover in paragraph 4 not only the laws and regulations which directly governed the conditions of sale or purchase but also any laws or regulations which might adversely modify the conditions of competition between the domestic and imported products on the internal market.

15. The Panel also noted that if the Italian contention were correct, and if the scope of Article III were limited in the way the Italian delegation suggested to

a specific type of laws and regulations, the value of the bindings under Article II of the Agreement and of the general rules of non-discrimination as between imported and domestic products could be easily evaded.

16. The Panel recognized—and the United Kingdom delegation agreed with this view—that it was not the intention of the General Agreement to limit the right of a contracting party to adopt measures which appeared to it necessary to foster its economic development or to protect a domestic industry, provided that such measures were permitted by the terms of the General Agreement. The GATT offered a number of possibilities to achieve these purposes through tariff measures or otherwise. The Panel did not appreciate why the extension of the credit facilities in question to the purchasers of imported tractors as well as domestically produced tractors would detract from the attainment of the objectives of the Law, which aimed at stimulating the purchase of tractors mainly by small farmers and co-operatives in the interests of economic development. If, on the other hand, the objective of the Law, although not specifically stated in the text thereof, were to protect the Italian agricultural machinery industry, the Panel considered that such protection should be given in ways permissible under the General Agreement rather than by the extension of credit exclusively for purchases of domestically produced agricultural machinery.

25. In the light of the considerations set out above the Panel suggests to the CONTRACTING PARTIES that it would be appropriate for them to make a recommendation to the Italian Government in accor-

dance with paragraph 2 of Article XXIII. The Panel considers that the recommendation should draw the attention of the Italian Government to the adverse effects on United Kingdom exports of agricultural machinery, particularly tractors, of those provisions of Law No. 949 limiting the prescribed credit facilities to purchasers of Italian produced machinery and suggest to the Italian Government that it consider the desirability of eliminating within a reasonable time the adverse effects of the Law on the import trade of agricultural machinery by modifying the operation of that Law or by other appropriate means.

Case Highlights

- GATT's national treatment principle requires that foreign firms be afforded the same competitive opportunities, including market access, that are available to domestic parties.

- GATT's national treatment principle is applicable to internal conditions of sale, including laws modifying conditions of competition between imports and domestic goods.

- Economic development initiatives are not exempt from the national treatment principle, especially where there are less restrictive means to foster such development.

- Dispute settlement bodies will not permit states to "easily evade" principles of the GATT, including national treatment.

The **transparency principle** is the fourth founding principle of GATT. The transparency principle prohibits a country from making its import standards and requirements secretive. It also precludes a country from constantly changing import requirements without reason. Most WTO agreements require governments to fully disclose import policies and practices publicly, including formally notifying the WTO of any changes. Disguised barriers often violate both the national treatment and transparency principles.

The WTO Agreements

The 1980s and 1990s witnessed a tremendous liberalization of international trade law. The breadth of this liberalization was evident in the successful conclusion of the Uruguay Round of GATT. The expansion beyond GATT's traditional mandate

http://

Harvard Law School— WTO documents and press releases: **http:// www.law.harvard. edu/library/services/ research/guides/ international/world_ trade.php.**

of tariff reduction shows how pervasive the free trade movement has become. Its side agreements on investment, services, technology protection, and government procurement, along with the creation of the WTO, indicate that the internationalization of business transactions will continue. Tariffs of 5 percent or less have become common. A number of provisions, mostly of a technical nature, of immediate importance to international exporters and importers include the Agreement on the Application of Sanitary and Phytosanitary Measures, Agreement on Technical Barriers to Trade, Customs Valuation Code, Agreement on Preshipment Inspection, Agreement on Rules of Origin, and Agreement on Import Licensing Procedures.

The **Agreement on the Application of Sanitary and Phytosanitary Measures (SPS)** is aimed at promoting international standards for import restrictions to protect human, animal, and plant life and health. As defined in GATT's Agreement on Technical Barriers to Trade (Standards Code), a standard is a technical specification contained in a document that specifies the characteristics of a product, such as levels of quality, performance, safety, or dimensions. Standards may include terminology, symbols, testing, packaging, marking, or labeling requirements.

SPS mandates that countries not use such measures or restrictions "as disguised devices" to restrict the importation of goods. States must "accept one another's measures as equivalent; but the exporting country may need to demonstrate that its measures achieve the importing country's SPS protection level and for this purpose to give the importing country access for inspection, testing, and similar procedures."[6] The parallel Agreement on Technical Barriers to Trade requires that the importing country allow importers access to its testing and certification standards and procedures. Parties to this agreement are to "use international standards wherever possible; maintain transparency through publication and notification of all relevant information . . . through 'enquiry points' established in each country."[7] The problems of conflicting national standards, the role of such standards as disguised restrictions on imports, and conformity to GATT principles are addressed in the U.S. Trade Representative's summary of the opinion of the WTO Dispute Settlement Body in the box WTO Hormones Report Confirms U.S. Win.

Other agreements are also directly related to national import requirements. The **Customs Valuation Code** attempts to standardize country challenges to the valuations placed on goods being imported. It places the burden of proof on the importer to provide additional evidence of valuation. However, a country must give the importer adequate opportunity to respond to the country's challenge. An associated accord, **Agreement on Preshipment Inspection**, pertains to an importing country's right to preshipment inspection. This right to preinspect goods for quality, quantity, and value is afforded only to developing countries. Because of the limited resources of developing countries, GATT recognizes their right to hire private companies to inspect the goods in the country of export. The **Agreement on Import Licensing Procedures** is based on the principle that application procedures should be made as simple as possible. Finally, the work

---

6. John Kraus, *The GATT Negotiations: A Business Guide to the Results of the Uruguay Round*, ICC Pub. No. 533 (E) 18 (1994).
7. Ibid. at 22.

WTO Hormones Report Confirms U.S. Win[8]

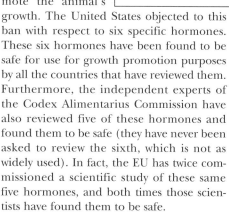

COMPARATIVE LAW

The World Trade Organization (WTO) released to the public today the final dispute settlement panel report on the European Union's import ban on meat produced using growth-promoting hormones. The WTO panel's findings, which uphold the claims of the United States, were issued confidentially to the concerned governments on June 30, 1997. This was the first dispute involving the SPS agreement.

"This final report confirms the value of the new WTO Agreement on the Application of Sanitary and Phytosanitary Measures in distinguishing legitimate food safety requirements from unscientific and unjustified barriers to U.S. exports," U.S. Trade Representative Charlene Barshefsky said. "I am pleased that the WTO agreed that the EU has no scientific basis for blocking the sale of American beef in Europe. This is a sign that the WTO dispute settlement system can handle complex and difficult disputes where a WTO member attempts to justify trade barriers by thinly disguising them as health measures. I am pleased that the panel affirmed the need for food safety measures to be based on science, as they are in the United States."

The WTO report finds that Europe's ban on the use of six hormones to promote the growth of cattle is inconsistent with the EU's obligations under the WTO Agreement on the Application of Sanitary and Phytosanitary Measures (SPS Agreement). In particular, the panel's report affirms that the EC's ban is not based on science. It was not based on a risk assessment or on the relevant international standards, and the EC has arbitrarily or unjustifiably distinguished between its policy for the hormones and other substances, resulting in discrimination or a disguised restriction on trade.

Background
On January 1, 1989, the EU imposed a ban on imports of animals and meat from animals treated with hormones to promote the animal's growth. The United States objected to this ban with respect to six specific hormones. These six hormones have been found to be safe for use for growth promotion purposes by all the countries that have reviewed them. Furthermore, the independent experts of the Codex Alimentarius Commission have also reviewed five of these hormones and found them to be safe (they have never been asked to review the sixth, which is not as widely used). In fact, the EU has twice commissioned a scientific study of these same five hormones, and both times those scientists have found them to be safe.

Three of the hormones at issue are naturally present in all meat and in all people. The hormone level in beef from animals to which these hormones have been administered to promote growth are well within the normal levels. In fact, the levels in beef are far less than, for example, the level of these hormones found in a single egg. (For example, an average adult would need to eat 169 pounds of beef from animals to which one of these hormones has been administered in order to equal the amount of that hormone in one egg.)

The U.S. challenge to the EU import ban was based primarily on arguments that the ban breaches provisions of the WTO Agreement on the Application of Sanitary and Phytosanitary Measures ("SPS Agreement"). This was the first dispute involving the SPS Agreement. That agreement clearly preserves the right of governments to apply food safety measures to protect human life and health, but at the same time it requires that such measures must in fact be for that purpose and not for protectionist purposes.

The SPS Agreement establishes rules for determining whether import bans and other

continued

---

8.   Press Release, Office of the United States Trade Representative, "WTO Hormones Report Confirms U.S. Win" (August 18, 1997).

WTO Hormones Report Confirms U.S. Win (*continued*)

trade-restrictive actions that governments may characterize as food safety measures protect public health or provide a competitive advantage for domestic producers. In particular, the SPS Agreement relies on science to distinguish legitimate food safety measures from disguised protectionism. The SPS Agreement provides dispute settlement panels with clear guideposts for their review. It provides that measures must be based on scientific principles, must not be maintained without sufficient scientific evidence, must be based on a scientific assessment of whether there are any risks to human life or health, must not be more trade-restrictive than required to achieve the appropriate level of protection from such risks, and must be based on international standards, guidelines or recommendations, where they exist, except where a more stringent standard is deemed appropriate in order to achieve a different level of protection or where there is a scientific justification.

The SPS agreement also encourages dispute settlement panels to seek advice on scientific issues from experts chosen by the panel in consultation with the parties to the dispute. In making its findings in this dispute, the panel sought the advice of independent scientific experts, the first time a WTO panel has made use of this procedure. The panel report summarizes the advice received from the experts and includes the transcript of the panel's meeting with the experts.

In this case the EU's import ban ignores a vast body of scientific evidence—including evidence produced by the EU's own reviews—that it is safe to consume meat from animals to which these drugs have been administered in accordance with good animal husbandry practice.

During the WTO legal proceedings the EU claimed that its ban is based on health concerns. However, when it was first put in place, the EU acknowledged that the ban served the purpose of eliminating competition from imports of hormone-fed beef in EU markets and of leveling the competitive playing field in Euroqe where, prior to the EU ban, some countries allowed the use of growth hormones for farm animal production and others did not. The United States argued that U.S. meat treated with these six growth promoting hormones is safe and that the EU's attempt to protect domestic production from more competitive imports (and intra-EU competition) is trade protectionism, not protection of health and safety.

This dispute has a long history. The 1989 EU ban cut off U.S. beef exports to the Community valued then at approximately $100 million annually. The United States tried to challenge the EU measures under the dispute settlement procedures available at the time, but the EU refused to allow a technical experts group to review the case. In response to the EU's blockage of dispute settlement procedures, the United States increased duties on certain products of the EU, pursuant to section 301 of the Trade Act of 1974. The increased U.S. duties remained in effect until the United States succeeded in having a WTO panel established to examine the EU hormone ban.

After the World Trade Organization (WTO) was created, the United States invoked the new WTO dispute settlement procedures to challenge the EU ban. Under the new WTO procedures, the EU cannot block the process, as it was able to do under the prior procedures.

The United States requested consultations with the EU in late January 1996, and in May 1996 the WTO Dispute Settlement Body established a panel to hear the case. Canada later brought a parallel action to challenge the EU ban, and the same panelists were assigned to hear the Canadian case. The panel has issued its final report with similar findings with respect to the challenge by Canada.

Case Update
The WTO Appellate Body affirmed the dispute settlement panel's opinion on January 15, 1998.

on developing uniform **country of origin rules** is ongoing and should be monitored in the future.

WTO Dispute Settlement System

The member countries of the WTO have agreed that if they believe that another member country has violated trade rules, they will use the WTO system of resolving disputes instead of taking unilateral action. The **WTO Dispute Settlement Understanding (DSU)**, enacted in 1994, provides for the prompt handling of international trade disputes. Its procedures for settling disputes provide fixed time periods for prompt resolution. In urgent cases, the rules provide for a final decision within three months. In cases that use the maximum time periods and that are appealed, the dispute resolution process should not take more than fifteen months. The settlement system provides the following maximum time periods: sixty days for consultation and mediation, forty-five days for the appointment of the dispute panel, six months for the panel to issue its decision and report, three weeks for the submission of the report to WTO members, and sixty days for the Dispute Settlement Body to adopt the report. In case of an appeal, the WTO Appellate Body has ninety days to issue its report, and the Dispute Settlement Body has thirty days to adopt the appeals report.

The **Dispute Settlement Body (DSB)** is the sole authority for appointing the panel of experts to decide cases. Before taking any formal action, the disputing countries must consult with each other in an attempt to settle the dispute. They can also ask the WTO director-general to mediate the dispute. Upon the failure of consultation, the complaining country can request that a panel be established to hear the dispute. **WTO Panels** are like tribunals, usually consisting of three to five experts. The two countries usually agree on the panel members. If they cannot agree, then the director-general appoints the panelists. The activities of the panel are confidential. Before the hearing, each side prepares its case in writing. At the first hearing, both parties present, along with any other country that voices an interest in the case. At a second hearing, both parties submit written rebuttals and present oral arguments. The panel may also consult experts or appoint an advisory group of experts to prepare a report.

The panel prepares a first-draft report and submits it to both parties for comments. It then submits an interim report of its findings and conclusions, allowing either party one week to request a review. If a review is requested, the panel has two weeks to hold additional meetings with the parties. The panel then submits a *final report*, which becomes the ruling of the DSB unless it is rejected. However, the final report can be rejected only by a unanimous vote of the DSB. The losing party then must prepare and submit a proposal to implement the ruling within a reasonable period of time. If the losing party fails to implement the ruling within a reasonable period of time, the parties must negotiate compensation pending a full implementation. If the parties do not agree on compensation, then the Dispute Settlement Body authorizes measures of retaliation for the prevailing country. These sanctions usually entail withholding or suspending tariff concessions previously mandated under GATT. The WTO's dispute resolution process, including appeals to the Appellate Body, is further discussed in the Comparative Law highlight. The next section illustrates the WTO Dispute Settlement System at work in the famous U.S.-EU Bananas Dispute.

COMPARATIVE LAW

Understanding the WTO: Settling Disputes[9]

Dispute settlement is the central pillar of the multilateral trading system, and the WTO's unique contribution to the stability of the global economy. Without a means of settling disputes, the rules-based system would be less effective because the rules could not be enforced. The WTO's procedure underscores the rule of law, and it makes the trading system more secure and predictable. The system is based on clearly-defined rules, with timetables for completing a case. First rulings are made by a panel and endorsed (or rejected) by the WTO's full membership. Appeals based on points of law are possible.

However, the point is not to pass judgment. The priority is to settle disputes, through consultations if possible. By May 2003, only about one third of the nearly 300 cases had reached the full panel process. Most of the rest have either been notified as settled out of court or remain in a prolonged consultation phase, some since 1995.

Disputes in the WTO are essentially about broken promises. WTO members have agreed that if they believe fellow-members are violating trade rules, they will use the multilateral system of settling disputes instead of taking action unilaterally. That means abiding by the agreed procedures, and respecting judgments.

A dispute arises when one country adopts a trade policy measure or takes some action that one or more fellow-WTO members considers to be breaking the WTO agreements, or to be a failure to live up to obligations. A third group of countries can declare that they have an interest in the case and enjoy some rights.

A procedure for settling disputes existed under the old GATT, but it had no fixed timetables, rulings were easier to block, and many cases dragged on for a long time inconclusively. The Uruguay Round agreement introduced a more structured process with more clearly defined stages in the procedure. It introduced greater discipline for the length of time a case should take to be settled, with flexible deadlines set in various stages of the procedure. The agreement emphasizes that prompt settlement is essential if the WTO is to function effectively. It sets out in considerable detail the procedures and the timetable to be followed in resolving disputes. If a case runs its full course to a first ruling, it should not normally take more than about one year—15 months if the case is appealed. The agreed time limits are flexible, and if the case is considered urgent (e.g. if perishable goods are involved), it is accelerated as much as possible.

The Uruguay Round agreement also made it impossible for the country losing a case to block the adoption of the ruling. Under the previous GATT procedure, rulings could only be adopted by consensus, meaning that a single objection could block the ruling. Now, rulings are automatically adopted unless there is a consensus to reject a ruling—any country wanting to block a ruling has to persuade all other WTO members (including its adversary in the case) to share its view.

Although much of the procedure does resemble a court or tribunal, the preferred solution is for the countries concerned to discuss their problems and settle the dispute by themselves. The first stage is therefore consultations between the governments concerned, and even when the case has progressed to other stages, consultation and mediation are still always possible.

Settling disputes is the responsibility of the Dispute Settlement Body (the General Council in another guise), which consists of all WTO members. The Dispute Settlement Body has the sole authority to establish panels of experts to consider the case, and to accept or reject the panels' findings or the results of an appeal. It monitors the

continued

---

9.   World Trade Organization, "Understanding the WTO: Settling Disputes," available at **http://www.wto.org**.

Understanding the WTO: Settling Disputes (*continued*)

implementation of the rulings and recommendations, and has the power to authorize retaliation when a country does not comply with a ruling.

First stage: consultation (up to **60 days**). Before taking any other actions the countries in dispute have to talk to each other to see if they can settle their differences by themselves. If that fails, they can also ask the WTO director-general to mediate or try to help in any other way.

Second stage: the panel (up to **45 days** for a panel to be appointed, plus 6 months for the panel to conclude). If consultations fail, the complaining country can ask for a panel to be appointed. The country "in the dock" can block the creation of a panel once, but when the Dispute Settlement Body meets for a second time, the appointment can no longer be blocked (unless there is a consensus against appointing the panel).

Officially, the panel is helping the Dispute Settlement Body make rulings or recommendations. But because the panel's report can only be rejected by consensus in the Dispute Settlement Body, its conclusions are difficult to overturn. The panel's findings have to be based on the agreements cited.

The panel's final report should normally be given to the parties to the dispute within six months. In cases of urgency, including those concerning perishable goods, the deadline is shortened to three months.

The agreement describes in some detail how the panels are to work. The main stages are:

Before the first hearing: each side in the dispute presents its case in writing to the panel.

First hearing: the case for the complaining country and defense: the complaining country (or countries), the responding country, and those that have announced they have an interest in the dispute, make their case at the panel's first hearing.

Rebuttals: the countries involved submit written rebuttals and present oral arguments at the panel's second meeting.

Experts: if one side raises scientific or other technical matters, the panel may consult experts or appoint an expert review group to prepare an advisory report.

First draft: the panel submits the descriptive (factual and argument) sections of its report to the two sides, giving them two weeks to comment. This report does not include findings and conclusions.

Interim report: The panel then submits an interim report, including its findings and conclusions, to the two sides, giving them one week to ask for a review.

Review: The period of review must not exceed two weeks. During that time, the panel may hold additional meetings with the two sides.

Final report: A final report is submitted to the two sides and three weeks later, it is circulated to all WTO members. If the panel decides that the disputed trade measure does break a WTO agreement or an obligation, it recommends that the measure be made to conform with WTO rules. The panel may suggest how this could be done.

The report becomes a ruling: The report becomes the Dispute Settlement Body's ruling or recommendation within 60 days unless a consensus rejects it. Both sides can appeal the report.

Either side can appeal a panel's ruling. Sometimes both sides do so. Appeals have to be based on points of law such as legal interpretation—they cannot reexamine existing evidence or examine new issues.

Each appeal is heard by three members of a permanent seven-member Appellate Body set up by the Dispute Settlement Body and broadly representing the range of WTO membership. Members of the Appellate Body have four-year terms. They have to be individuals with recognized standing in the field of law and international trade, not affiliated with any government.

continued

Understanding the WTO: Settling Disputes (*continued*)

The appeal can uphold, modify or reverse the panel's legal findings and conclusions. Normally appeals should not last more than 60 days, with an absolute maximum of 90 days.

The Dispute Settlement Body has to accept or reject the appeals report within 30 days, and rejection is only possible by consensus.

Even once the case has been decided, there is more to do before trade sanctions (the conventional form of penalty) are imposed. The priority at this stage is for the losing defendant to bring its policy into line with the ruling or recommendations. The dispute settlement agreement stresses that "prompt compliance with recommendations or rulings of the DSB [Dispute Settlement Body] is essential in order to ensure effective resolution of disputes to the benefit of all Members."

If the country that is the target of the complaint loses, it must follow the recommendations of the panel report or the appeals report. It must state its intention to do so at a Dispute Settlement Body meeting held within 30 days of the report's adoption. If complying with the recommendation immediately proves impractical, the member will be given a "reasonable period of time" to do so. If it fails to act within this period, it has to enter into negotiations with the complaining country (or countries) in order to determine mutually-acceptable compensation—for instance, tariff reductions in areas of particular interest to the complaining side.

If after 20 days, no satisfactory compensation is agreed, the complaining side may ask the Dispute Settlement Body for permission to impose limited trade sanctions (suspend concessions or obligations) against the other side. The Dispute Settlement Body must grant this authorization within 30 days of the expiry of the "reasonable period of time" unless there is a consensus against the request.

In principle, the sanctions should be imposed in the same sector as the dispute. If this is not practical or if it would not be effective, the sanctions can be imposed in a different sector of the same agreement. In turn, if this is not effective or practicable and if the circumstances are serious enough, the action can be taken under another agreement. The objective is to minimize the chances of actions spilling over into unrelated sectors while at the same time allowing the actions to be effective.

In any case, the Dispute Settlement Body monitors how adopted rulings are implemented. Any outstanding case remains on its agenda until the issue is resolved.

THE UNITED STATES–EU "BANANAS DISPUTE"

On January 14, 1999, the United States requested the DSB, as required by the DSU of the WTO, to authorize the suspension of existing tariff concessions to the EU in the amount of $520 million. A WTO Dispute Resolution Panel on May 22, 1997, decided that the EU had illegally placed restrictions on the importation of bananas into EU countries. The panel upheld the claims of the United States, Ecuador, Guatemala, Honduras, and Mexico that the EU's distribution of import licenses for Latin American bananas to French and British companies deprived U.S. companies of a major part of the banana distribution business they had developed in the previous century. The distribution business of U.S. companies was further injured by the EU's grant of import licenses for Latin American bananas to European banana-ripening firms that had not historically imported bananas. The EU also violated the GATT by imposing more burdensome licensing requirements on imports originating from Ecuador, Guatemala, Honduras, and Mexico than those applied to other countries' bananas. Finally, the panel held that the EU's licensing scheme discriminatorily allocated access to European markets not based on past levels of trade, which served to create trade distortions in violation of the GATT. The panel's decision was affirmed by the Appellate Body on September 9, 1997.

The EU objected to the amount of the **suspension** as not being equivalent to the level of **nullification** or **impairment** of benefits suffered by the United States and submitted the amount of the suspension for arbitration. Pursuant to the DSU, the level of suspension is to be determined by the following principles: (1) the complaining party should first seek suspension of benefits in the *same sector* as that in which the impairment or nullification was found; (2) if this is not practical, then it should seek suspension or concessions "in other sectors under the same agreement"; and (3) if that is not practical, then it should seek a suspension under another covered agreement.[10] The basic rationale of these principles is to ensure that suspensions or concessions across different sectors remain the exception and not the rule. It would seem that sector-specific concessions or suspensions are preferred to prevent an escalation of animosities and a broader trade war.

The panel issued its decision on April 19, 1999. The panel held that the EU import regime pertaining to bananas violated both the GATT and the GATS. The United States had requested the suspension only after it had won the dispute before the WTO panel and the EU had failed to abide by the panel's decision. The revised import regime instituted by the EU in response to the decision continued to place tariff quotas on bananas imported from the Caribbean and Central and South America. This violated the national treatment principle of GATT and GATS, in which like products are to be treated equally, irrespective of their origin. To show violation of this nondiscrimination principle, two elements must be proved. First, the services or goods at issue must be sufficiently alike. Second, the imported goods or services are treated less favorably than those of domestic origin. The arbitration panel held that the revised bananas import regime of the EU continued to violate the national treatment principle. It was a "continuation of nullification or impairment of United States benefits" found under the previous EU regime.

The arbitration panel then turned to the remaining issue of whether the concessions the United States requested ($520 million) were appropriate. In determining the level of concessions, the WTO panel may consider both direct and indirect benefits. Consideration of *indirect benefits* was especially important in this case, because the United States is not an exporter of bananas. Instead, the United States argued that the restrictions on Latin American banana exports indirectly impaired U.S. exports. For example, the United States exports farm products, such as fertilizers, used in the production of bananas that would have been exported to the EU. The arbitration panel ultimately decided that the concessions requested were excessive, even with the consideration of indirect benefits. It reduced the concession amount to $191.4 million. The United States lifted its sanctions on July 1, 2001, after the EU agreed to adopt a new licensing system for bananas.

The settlement of the U.S.-EU "Bananas Dispute" demonstrates the problems associated with member states ignoring WTO dispute resolution decisions. Why do states comply with the results of the dispute settlement process? Certainly, the threat of economic sanctions (especially for smaller states and economies) looms large in

---

10.   For example, in the area of services, the WTO has developed a "Services Sectoral Classification List" that identifies
        service sectors.

the decision to comply. States may also have reciprocity concerns. The failure of a state to comply with a WTO decision may encourage other states to disregard their free trade obligations pursuant to the GATT. A state may also wish to preserve its international reputation and not be known as one that disregards its international obligations. Compliance may also serve as a tool to rebut opposing domestic interests, such as labor and trade unions and environmental groups. However, not all DSB opinions have resulted in compliance or a negotiated settlement. For example, the EU has failed to comply with the opinions of the DSB and Appellate Body in the previously-discussed EC Measures Concerning Meat and Meat Product (Hormones) case. As a result, the United States applied for and received approval from the WTO to impose sanctions in May 1998. Sanctions commenced in 1999 and totaled $116.8 million annually.

Antidumping and Subsidies Procedures

The GATT system of enforcement does allow for retaliation at the national level for violations of the GATT agreements. The most common trade violation is dumping goods on foreign markets. As previously noted, dumping occurs when a foreign exporter sells goods below the price at which it sells them in its home country or below the cost of production. Article VI of the GATT and the Agreement on the Implementation of Article VI require states to conduct a formal administrative investigation prior to the imposition of antidumping duties. This administrative procedure has two prongs in the United States.[11] The **International Trade Administration (ITA)** within the Department of Commerce is responsible for determining whether dumping has occurred and its extent, and the International Trade Commission (ITC) is responsible for determining the existence of material injury. Injury due to goods imported at "less than fair value" can be proven by showing one of the following: (1) sales lost to imports sold at "less than fair value," (2) suppression of export prices through underselling, (3) lost profits, (4) reduced employment or capacity utilization, (5) declining sales, (6) growth of imports, (7) reduced product development abilities, or (8) magnitude of the dumping margin. If the ITA finds a case of dumping and the ITC finds material injury, then the ITA issues an antidumping order that fixes the duties to be levied against the foreign exporters. The antidumping duty is assessed on an entry-by-entry basis in an amount equal to the difference between the U.S. price of the good and the foreign market value of similar goods. Antidumping duties can be as high as 400 percent of the value of the goods being imported and can be assessed for periods of up to twenty years. The Department of Commerce may adjust the antidumping duty on an annual basis. The decisions of the ITA and ITC with respect to the determination of dumping, the existence of material injury, and the imposition of antidumping duties are reviewable by the **U.S. Court of International Trade**. Decisions of this court are subject to review by the **U.S. Court of Appeals for the Federal Circuit** and, potentially, the U.S. Supreme Court.

The GATT requires a similar procedure prior to the imposition of countervailing duties for actionable subsidies. As discussed earlier in the chapter, the primary types of actionable subsidies are those based on export performance or requiring the utilization of domestically produced goods rather than foreign goods. Article VI of the

http://
Text of WTO codes and agreements: **http:// www.wto.org/english/ docs_e/docs_e.htm.**

---

11. The definition of dumping is set forth in 19 U.S.C. § 1677(34–35) (2000). Antidumping procedures are set forth in 19 U.S.C. § 1673–1673h (2000).

GATT and the Agreement on Subsidies and Countervailing Measures prohibit the imposition of a countervailing duty upon the entry of subsidized goods into the territory of a WTO member unless the subsidy causes or threatens to cause material injury to an established domestic industry. In the United States, the ITA determines if a subsidy exists, and the ITC determines the existence of material injury.[12] In the event an actionable subsidy is deemed to exist, a countervailing duty may be imposed. The amount of the countervailing duty is based on (1) the volume of the subsidized imports; (2) the effect of imports on domestic prices for like or directly competitive products; (3) the impact of imports on domestic industry, including actual or potential declines in output, sales, market share, profits, productivity, return on investments, and capacity; and (4) the actual and potential effect of the subsidized import on cash flow, inventories, employment, wages, growth, investments, and the ability to raise capital. As in the area of dumping, ITA and ITC determinations with respect to actionable subsidies are subject to judicial review by the U.S. Court of International Trade and the U.S. Court of Appeals for the Federal Circuit. The *Delverde USA v. United States* case that follows explores the meaning of an illegal foreign subsidy and the assessment of a countervailing duty by the Department of Commerce.

Delverde USA, Inc. v. United States
202 F.3d 1360 (Fed. Cir. 2000)

Lourie, Circuit Judge. Delverde, SrL ("Delverde") and Delverde USA, Inc., appeal from the September 25, 1998, decision of the United States Court of International Trade affirming the Department of Commerce's ("Commerce's") countervailing duty determination. Because Commerce's methodology for determining whether Delverde indirectly received countervailable subsidies from the Italian government is inconsistent with § 771(5) of the Tariff Act of 1930 ("Tariff Act"), as amended by the Uruguay Round Agreements we vacate and remand. In 1995, Commerce launched a countervailing duty investigation of certain non-egg dry pasta in packages of five pounds or less imported in 1994 from Italy. Upon investigation of 17 Italian manufacturer-importers, Commerce discovered that, in 1991, Delverde purchased certain corporate assets, namely, a pasta factory and related production assets, name, and trademark, from a private company that had previously received several nonrecurring countervailable subsidies from the Italian government from 1983 to 1991.

First, when Commerce determines that a company has received a *nonrecurring subsidy*, Commerce divides the amount of that subsidy by the number of years equal to "the average useful life of renewable physical assets in the industry concerned" and allocates an amount to each year accordingly. Second, Commerce assumes that when a company sells "productive assets" during "the average useful life," a *pro rata* portion of that subsidy "passes through" to the purchaser at the time of the sale. Commerce then quantifies the assumed "pass through" amount, makes adjustments based on the purchase price, allocates an amount to the year of investigation, and calculates the *ad valorum* subsidy rate. In Delverde's case, Commerce determined that the average useful life of renewable physical assets in the food processing industry was 12 years. Commerce thus held Delverde responsible for a *pro rata* portion of the nonrecurring subsidies that were granted to the former owner between 1983 and 1991 because they fell within that 12-year period.

The Tariff Act of 1930 defines a subsidy as including "financial contributions" and "benefits" conferred and defines them as follows:

A "financial contribution" includes:

(i) the direct transfer of funds, such as grants, loans, and equity infusion, or the potential direct transfer of funds or liabilities, such as loan guarantees,

(ii) foregoing or not collecting revenue that is otherwise due, such as granting tax credits or deductions from taxable income,

(iii) providing goods or services, other than general infrastructure, or

(iv) purchasing goods.

---

12.   The definition of subsidies is set forth in 19 U.S.C. § 1677(5–6) (2000). Procedures to countervail actionable subsidies are set forth in 19 U.S.C. § 1671-1671h (2000).

A "benefit" shall normally be treated as conferred where there is a benefit to the recipient, including

(i) in the case of equity infusion, if the investment decision is inconsistent with the usual investment practice of private investors, including the practice regarding the provision of risk capital, in the country in which the equity infusion is made,

(ii) in the case of a loan, if there is a difference between the amount the recipient of the loan pays on the loan and the amount the recipient would pay on a comparable commercial loan that the recipient could actually obtain on a market,

(iii) in the case of a loan guarantee, if there is a difference, after adjusting for any difference in guarantee fees, between the amount the recipient of the guarantee pays on the guaranteed loan and the amount the recipient would pay for a comparable commercial loan if there were no guarantee by the authority, and

(iv) in the case where goods or services are provided, if such goods or services are provided for less than adequate remuneration, and in the case where goods are purchased, if such goods are purchased for more than adequate remuneration.

A change in ownership of all or part of a foreign enterprise or the productive assets of a foreign enterprise does not by itself require a determination by an administering authority that a past countervailable subsidy received by the enterprise no longer continues to be countervailable, even if the change of ownership is accomplished through an arm's length transaction.

We conclude that the statute does not contemplate any exception to the requirement that Commerce determine that a government provided both a financial contribution and benefit to a person, either directly or indirectly, by one of the acts enumerated, before charging it with receipt of a subsidy, even when that person bought corporate assets from another person who was previously subsidized. In other words, the Change of Ownership provision does not change the meaning of "subsidy." A subsidy can only be determined by finding that a person received a "financial contribution" and a "benefit" by one of the acts enumerated in §§ 1677(5)(D) and (E).

Having determined that the meaning of the statute is clear, we need only determine whether Commerce's methodology is in accordance with the statute. We have concluded that it is not. Nowhere following its methodology did Commerce determine whether Delverde

directly or indirectly received a financial contribution and benefit from one of the acts enumerated. Rather, Commerce's methodology conclusively presumed that Delverde received a subsidy from the Italian government—i.e., a financial contribution and a benefit—simply because it bought assets from another person who earlier received subsidies.

Lastly, an "effect" of a subsidy may be a competitive advantage that the subsidy recipient obtained from the subsidies. A subsidy may enable a recipient to manufacture and sell products at lower price due to the subsidies it received. The issue here, however, is not whether Delverde was able to produce and sell pasta products at lower price, but whether it received a subsidy in the first place. It is undisputed that Delverde was not the direct recipient of any subsidy. The question is whether Delverde was an indirect recipient by having purchased assets from a company that did directly receive one. As we stated earlier, the statute does not permit Commerce simply to assume that Delverde received a *pro rata* portion of those subsidies.

Commerce's methodology for determining whether Delverde received a countervailing subsidy is invalid as being inconsistent with 19 U.S.C. § 1677(5). For the reasons stated above, the decision of the Court of International Trade is VACATED and REMANDED.

Case Highlights

- An illegal subsidy given by a foreign government can be attributed to the purchaser of the company that had received the subsidy.
- The Department of Commerce cannot assume that when a company sells "productive assets" during "the average useful life," a pro rata portion of the subsidy used to purchase those assets "passes through" to the purchaser at the time of the sale.
- The Department of Commerce must show that an illegal subsidy was given and that the purchaser of the company at least indirectly benefited from the earlier subsidy before assessing a countervailing duty.

U.S. procedures for the assessment of antidumping and countervailing duties have been the subject matter of a recent WTO dispute settlement action. In October 2000, the United States adopted the *Continued Dumping and Subsidy Offset Act*.[13] Adopted in October 2000 as part of a fiscal year 2001 agriculture appropriations bill, the act provided that antidumping and countervailing duties would be distributed by the U.S. Commissioner of Customs on an annual basis to petitioning companies

---

13.   The Continued Dumping and Subsidy Offset Act of 2000 can be found at 19 U.S.C. § 1675c(a-e) (2000).

that had suffered losses as a result of the dumping of imports or maintenance of the actionable subsidy. These petitioners were referred to as "affected domestic producers." This statute resulted in the payment of hundreds of millions of dollars to U.S. companies. A WTO dispute resolution panel created at the request of Australia, Brazil, Canada, Chile, the EU, India, Indonesia, Japan, Korea, Mexico, and Thailand concluded that the act was a nonpermissible specific action against dumping and subsidies. In addition, the panel concluded that the act provided an improper financial incentive to U.S. companies to initiate and support antidumping and countervailing duty investigations. The panel's report was affirmed by the Appellate Body on January 16, 2003.[14] Despite assurances by President Bush that he would seek its repeal, the act remained in force and effect as of late 2004.

The next two sections discuss the unilateral statutory devices in Section 301 and Section 337 of the Smoot-Hawley Tariff Act of 1930, which a U.S. party can use to combat unfair trade practices of foreign competitors.

Section 301

The Office of the **U.S. Trade Representative (USTR)** is authorized by statute to retaliate against activities of other countries that are deemed to violate U.S. rights under international trade agreements. The USTR coordinates the development of U.S. trade policy, leads activity on U.S. international trade regulations, and seeks to expand U.S. exports by promoting the removal of foreign trade barriers and the procurement of rights to foreign markets. USTR retaliation is popularly referred to as Section 301 sanctions.[15] (See Doing Business Internationally: Applying Section 301.) A business that is being unfairly treated in a foreign market may petition the USTR to intervene in the matter under Section 301 of the Trade Act of 1974.

http://

U.S. International Trade Administration: **http:// www.ita.doc.gov/.**

Applying Section 301[16]

Actionable practices under Section 301 are acts or policies engaged in by U.S. trading partners that violate a trade agreement, or are found to be unjustifiable, unreasonable, or discriminatory, and burden or restrict U.S. commerce:

(a) **Trade Agreement Violations:** Where a country violates the terms of a bilateral or multilateral agreement with the United States, or acts in a manner that effectively denies the benefit of the agreement to the United States, Section 301

can be invoked to impose sanctions against imports of that country.

(b) **Unjustifiable, Unreasonable, and Discriminatory Practices:** An act, policy, or practice is regarded as "unjustifiable" if it denies most-favored-nation treatment to U.S. exports or national treatment to U.S. business interests, if it fails to protect U.S. intellectual property rights, if it denies U.S. businesses the

Doing Business Internationally

continued

---

14.   See United States: Continued Dumping and Subsidy Offset Act of 2000, WT/DS217/234/AB/R (adopted by the WTO Appellate Body 16 January 2003).

15.   Section 301 retaliation is found in 19 U.S.C. §§ 2411–20 (2000).

16.   Peter B. Feller & Vincent M. Routhier, "Invoking Section 301 to Overcome Foreign Trade Barriers," *The Metropolitan Corporate Counsel* (October 2000) 138.

Applying Section 301 (*continued*)

right of establishment in the foreign country concerned, or if it is otherwise inconsistent with the international rights of the United States. The term "unreasonable" refers to acts, policies, or practices that are "unfair and inequitable," even though they may fall short of violating the international legal rights of the United States. If any country treats U.S. products, services, or investments less favorably than those supplied by domestic or third-country sources, that country could become the subject of a "discriminatory practices" determination. A determination that a foreign practice is unjustifiable, unreasonable, or discriminatory is not *per se* sufficient to trigger retaliatory authority under Section 301. The USTR must also determine that the practice burdens or restricts U.S. commerce.

(c) **Burdens or Restricts U.S. Commerce:** The term "U.S. commerce" refers to the transnational flow of U.S. goods, as well as trade-related services and investments. It includes U.S. exports to countries other than the one whose practice is being questioned. As a general proposition, it can be said that a foreign practice "burdens or restricts" U.S. commerce if it causes immediate harm to U.S. interests in some significant and measurable way, or forecloses future market opportunities that would otherwise be available.

Retaliation and Settlement. Section 301 provides that, before any trade sanctions may be imposed, the USTR must consult with the government of the country charged with an offending practice. Where a trade agreement that is the subject of a Section 301 action contains provisions governing the resolution of disputes, such dispute resolution mechanisms must be utilized within 150 days if consultations have not produced an accord. These requirements apply even when retaliation is mandatory. Thus, in every Section 301 action the USTR's first

step is to discuss the problem with the country involved, with a view toward a negotiated settlement of the dispute. This process often results in elimination or satisfactory codification of the practice in question or in an agreed compensation package. It is only when this process fails that retaliatory steps are taken.

Since the enactment of Section 301, 90 cases have been initiated by the USTR. While most of the cases were settled without resort to sanctions, the threat that U.S. market access could be reduced or eliminated was often instrumental in achieving an agreement under Section 301. Moreover, since 1995, Section 301 has gained increased importance as a means of enforcing the results of binding dispute settlement before the WTO: countries that fail to implement the recommendations of WTO panels can face trade retaliation. In the United States such retaliation is implemented through Section 301. Written in broad terms, Section 301 gives the USTR considerable discretion to investigate virtually any type of foreign trade practice. The types of unfair trade practices found actionable include:

Discriminatory Government Procurement Practices: USTR initiated several investigations concerning discrimination by the Japanese government involving outright prohibitions on the procurement of foreign satellites or certain Japanese exclusionary practices such as technical standards favoring Japanese producers.

Quotas, Tariffs and Licensing Schemes: Section 301 was also invoked in the celebrated bananas case. In April 1999, retaliatory tariffs were imposed as a result of the EU's failure to modify its banana quotas and import licensing schemes. The dispute originated with a section 301 petition filed by Chiquita Brands International, Inc., alleging discriminatory treatment against U.S. commercial interests in certain banana-producing countries.

Section 301 provides a means to counter a broad range of unfair foreign practices, including discriminatory rules of origin, discriminatory government procurement, licensing systems, quotas, exchange controls, restrictive business practices, discriminatory bilateral agreements, taxes that discriminate against U.S. products, discriminatory product standards, and nonenforcement of intellectual property rights protections. After the conclusion of the Uruguay Round, "Section 301 has assumed greater importance as a compliance tool for USTR to assure that U.S. commercial interests can realize the benefits promised by our trading partners."[17]

Section 301 investigations are initiated by the USTR on its own initiative or in response to an interested party's petition. The USTR allows U.S. businesses to approach it on an informal and confidential basis with pertinent information. This confidential alternative diminishes the risk that a foreign country will seek retribution against the party for instigating a Section 301 proceeding. Whether by formal or informal means, the interested party seeking to invoke Section 301 must provide detailed information on both the foreign trade practice complained of and its impact on U.S. commerce.

The deadline for completing Section 301 investigations involving rights under a trade agreement is eighteen months, and investigations of alleged unreasonable, discriminatory, or unjustified practices must be completed within twelve months. An expedited investigation, not exceeding six months, is undertaken when there are allegations that a foreign country has failed to provide adequate and effective intellectual property rights protection. Once an investigation has been initiated, the USTR is obligated to pursue bilateral negotiations with the offending country and, if necessary, institute a formal dispute resolution proceeding with the WTO. If the dispute remains unresolved, the USTR is authorized to impose *unilateral* trade restrictions equal to the amount of burden placed on U.S. commerce. The sanctions available to the USTR include imposition of additional duties or restrictions on imports from the offending country, suspension of trade agreement concessions, and imposition of fees or restrictions on services and service sector authorizations. Section 407 of the *Trade and Development Act of 2000* requires the USTR to revise the list of products subject to retaliatory tariffs 120 days after their initial imposition and every 180 days thereafter.[18] This procedure serves to expand the scope of the retaliation by rotating its effects throughout numerous sectors of the offending country's economy.

In 1999, the European Union challenged the unilateral nature of Section 301 as a violation of the WTO Agreements. It alleged that the speed of retaliation under Section 301 violated the WTO Dispute Settlement Understanding. On January 27, 2000, the WTO Dispute Settlement Body accepted the findings of the WTO panel's report that held the rights of the United States under Section 301 did not violate the WTO Dispute Settlement Understanding.[19] The practice of the USTR to consult with the foreign government to resolve the dispute before authorizing sanctions, strictly adhere to the requirements of the Dispute Settlement Understanding, and retaliate only if authorized by the Dispute Settlement Body satisfied the requirements of the WTO. As such, although Section 301 could be utilized to violate WTO obligations, it did not preclude the United States from acting consistently with such obligations.

http://
International Trade
Law Monitor: **http://
www.jus.uio.no/lm/
international.economic.
law/itl.html.**
(Lex Mercatoria)

---

17.   Ibid.
18.   The Trade and Development Act of 2000 can be found at 19 U.S.C. § 2416(b)(2)(A-F) (2000).
19.   See United States-Sections 301–310 of the Trade Act of 1974, WT/DS152/R (Report of the Panel, 22 December 1999).

Despite this decision, the use of Section 301 remains controversial, especially among developing states that may not possess the economic leverage to sustain a challenge to its utilization in the WTO.

Section 337 of the Tariff Act

Section 337 of the Tariff Act of 1930 provides for relief to be given by the International Trade Commission for "unfair methods of competition" in the importation or sale of imported goods.[20] Section 337 does not define "unfair competition," but patent, copyright, and trademark infringement are all considered unfair competition. Proof of infringement of intellectual property rights relating to the imported goods is usually sufficient to prove injury. Section 337 is most commonly used to prevent the importation of illegal pirated or counterfeited goods or *gray market* goods, those produced and sold abroad by a licensee of an intellectual property right and then imported into the United States for sale in competition with the U.S. licensor (and in violation of restrictions in the license). Standing to seek relief from the ITC requires showing some use of an intellectual property right in the United States. Ownership of a U.S. trademark or patent, without use in the United States, is not sufficient. Furthermore, Section 337 does not apply to unfair methods of competition occurring exclusively overseas with no U.S. nexus.

The ITC must conduct a formal evidentiary hearing before an administrative law judge prior to the imposition of penalties pursuant to Section 337. The hearing may occur as a result of a complaint by an injured company or on the ITC's own initiative. The ITC may adopt, modify, or reverse the administrative law judge's decision. The administrative law judge's decision is deemed adopted if the ITC does not review it. The ITC's order becomes final within sixty days of its issuance, unless the president disapproves it for public policy reasons.

The sole remedy under Section 337 is the exclusion of the goods from the United States. No damages can be granted. A **permanent exclusion order** prohibits entry of any of the specified goods produced by the named foreign producer or importer into the United States. A party may also obtain a **cease and desist order** prohibiting future imports by the accused importer or distributor. The minimum daily penalty for violating an exclusion or a cease and desist order is $100,000 or twice the domestic value of the imported goods. An investigation may be opened upon petition from a domestic producer. Any decision of the ITC may be appealed to the Court of Appeals for the Federal Circuit.

http://
To check results of Fourth Ministerial Conference in Doha, Qatar, November 9–13, 2001, go to: **http://www.wto.org** and click on "Ministerial Conferences."

The Future of Global Trade Negotiations

In November 2001, the WTO commenced the latest round of GATT negotiations, the **Doha Round**. This round of WTO negotiations began less than two years after the

---

20.   Section 337 of the Smoot-Hawley Tariff Act of 1930 can be found at 19 U.S.C. § 1337 (2000).

failure of the attempt to start the Millennium Round in Seattle in December 1999. The Doha Round is centered on the Doha Declaration, which has numerous focal points, including agriculture, antidumping and actionable subsidies procedures, competition law, dispute resolution, electronic commerce, government procurement, intellectual property protections, services, and tariffs on industrial products, to name but a few. According to the World Bank, successful completion of negotiations on these issues could raise global income by $500 billion annually by 2015, with 60 percent of these gains accruing to the developing world.

However, negotiations stalled in 2002 and came to a complete standstill at the WTO's ministerial meeting in Cancún, Mexico, in September 2003. The breakdown of negotiations at Cancún was accompanied by considerable acrimony and demonstrated deep divisions between members of the developed world, a block of developing countries known as the G-21, and African states.[21] The primary stumbling blocks concerned agriculture (with particular emphasis on subsidies), market access for industrial products, and the so-called Singapore Issues of competition, investment, transparency in government procurement, and trade facilitation. The failure of the Cancún summit also revealed divisions between members of the developed world, with the United States, the EU, and Japan espousing different viewpoints with respect to these issues.

However, in July 2004, the WTO member states reached a framework for the resumption of negotiations of the Doha Round. This framework called for reform of global agricultural trade (including the elimination of export subsidies), the broadening of market access for manufactured goods through tariff cuts, harmonization and the reduction of nontariff barriers, and intensified negotiations to open global services markets.[22] Nevertheless, despite this recent effort, the likelihood of completion of negotiations by the January 1, 2005, deadline set forth in the Doha Declaration appears remote at best.

Opposition to the WTO continues among many public interest, environmental, consumer, and labor groups. Labor groups protested the alleged dumping of foreign products, a lack of international labor standards, and the movement of production to countries with lower standards. Environmental groups have accused the WTO of not considering the environmental impacts of its decisions. Consumer and public interest groups protest the WTO's failure to give product and food safety priority over trade. These groups also protested the secretiveness of WTO decision making and the undemocratic nature of WTO decisions that override local and national rules.[23] Comparative Law: Criticism of the WTO develops the parameters of the prevailing controversies surrounding the WTO.

---

21. The G-21 consists of Argentina, Bolivia, Brazil, Chile, China, Colombia, Costa Rica, Cuba, Ecuador, Egypt, Guatemala, India, Indonesia, Mexico, Nigeria, Pakistan, Paraguay, Peru, the Philippines, South Africa, Thailand, and Venezuela. African states that took a particularly active role at the Cancún meeting were referred to as the "West African Four": Benin, Burkina Faso, Chad, and Mali.

22. For additional information on the framework, *see* Press Release, U.S. Trade Representative, Charting a Course to Prosperity (July 31, 2004).

23. For a review of the criticisms of the WTO lodged by these groups and possible solutions see, Larry A. DiMatteo, Kiren Dosanjh, Paul L. Frantz, Peter Bowal, & Clyde Stoltenberg, "The Doha Declaration and Beyond: Giving a Voice to Non-Trade Concerns Within the WTO Trade Regime," 36 *Vanderbilt Journal of Transnational Law* 95 (2003). This article examines the relationship between the WTO and environmental, consumer protection, and labor policy, as well as the implications of WTO membership on national sovereignty.

Criticism of the WTO

COMPARATIVE LAW

Excerpts from *Whose Trade Organization?*[24]

For Richer or Poorer: Facts and Fiction About Trade and Economic Gains in the Developed World and Economic Results of the WTO in the United States

In the early 1990s, many economists argued that the opening of foreign markets for U.S. exports under NAFTA and the WTO would create jobs and increase income in the U.S. As Congress was considering the WTO and other Uruguay Round agreements in 1994, the President's Council of Economic Advisers claimed that the adoption of the package would increase annual U.S. GDP by $100–200 billion over the next decade. Others claimed that its adoption would lead to a decline in the U.S. trade deficit. President Clinton even went so far as to promise that the average American family would gain $1700 annually from the WTO's adoption. The growth projections were revised drastically downward shortly after the WTO came into effect. By 2002, the U.S. trade deficit has grown to more than four times its pre-WTO size, and millions of U.S. jobs—including almost two million manufacturing jobs—have been lost during the era of the WTO. Annual average U.S. family income did not increase by $1700 in *any* year since the WTO passed, much less in each year. Indeed, as this chapter describes, one cannot prove, either using trade theory models or empirically, that most Americans have benefited from the WTO—yet it can be shown that the economic well-being of many has declined. In short, few of the claims made about the benefits that would flow from greater trade liberalization can be shown to have been even remotely accurate. This, however, has not stopped another round of ridiculous projections and promises regarding the economic benefits that would follow if a "Doha Round" is launched.

Warning: The WTO Can Be Hazardous to Public Health

Corporate-driven globalization under the WTO has sharply increased income disparity, which the World Health Organization has identified as one of the key correlates of a country's health status. Trade liberalization is producing greater income inequality between and within nations, which in turn, has led to greater disparities in public health conditions and outcomes. In the area of public health, WTO challenges—or even threatened challenges—have already been used to undermine important public health policies on the grounds that they constrain or interfere with trade.

The WTO on Agriculture: Food as a Commodity, Not a Right

Farmers in rich and poor countries have only seen their incomes decline, with many losing farms and livelihoods under the WTO regime. In the developing world, the combination of sharply lower prices and the effects of WTO rules regarding the patenting of seeds and plants under the WTO agreement on Trade-Related Aspects of Intellectual Property have led to increased hunger in many nations. In a perverse twist—which actually demonstrates how the WTO's Agreement on Agriculture rules are not about "free Trade"—while prices paid farmers have plummeted, consumer food prices have not declined and in many instances, have risen. Meanwhile, the WTO has forced the elimination of domestic policies aimed at ensuring food sovereignty and security in developing countries and of policies aimed at supporting small farmers in rich countries. These changes have greatly benefited multinational commodity trading and food processing companies who, in the absence of government price and supply management programs, have been able to manipulate the markets to keep prices paid to farmers low at the same time as they have kept consumer prices for food steady or rising.

The WTO's Coming to Dinner and Food Safety Is Not on the Menu

The WTO's relentless drive toward the "harmonization" of food, animal and plant regulations based on low, industry-preferred

continued

24.   Lori Wallach & Patrick Woodall, *Whose Trade Organization?: Field Guide to the World Trade Organization* (New Press, 2004).

Criticism of the WTO (*continued*)

international standards endangers human health and sharply curtails the ability of elected governments to protect the health of their citizens in this critically important area. WTO-approved standards are generally set in private-sector bodies which do not permit consumer or health interests to participate and which make decisions without complying with domestic regulatory procedures for openness, participation or balance. Even if a country's domestic food safety law treats domestic and foreign products identically, if the policy provides greater consumer protection than the WTO-named international standard, it is presumed to be a WTO violation. WTO obligations to declare exporting nations' meat inspection systems "equivalent" has allowed meat that does not meet U.S. safety standards to enter the U.S. market and appear in stores with USDA labels. Meanwhile, countries' attempts to regulate for emerging health threats (such as "Mad Cow" disease) or to regulate products whose health effects are uncertain (such as genetically modified foods and artificial hormone residues in meat), are characterized as trade barriers in the WTO. The World Health Organization has recognized the globalization of the food supply as a major threat to international public health.

The WTO's Controversial Dispute Settlement Procedure

With the exception of the North American Free Trade Agreement, the WTO contains the most powerful enforcement procedures of any international agreement now in force. The remarkably broad reach of WTO rules and their implications for a wide variety of domestic policies, many with only a passing connection to trade, makes the WTO's system a particular threat because it ensures strong enforcement of inappropriately expansive and biased rules. Unlike the GATT, which required consensus to bind any country to an obligation, the WTO is unique among international agreements in that its panel rulings are automatically binding and only the unanimous consent of all WTO nations can halt their implementation, which are backed up

by trade sanctions which remain in place until a WTO-illegal domestic policy is changed.

The WTO and the Developing World: Do as We Say, Not as We Did

During the Uruguay Round GATT negotiations, developing countries raised concerns about the expansive set of seventeen new international commercial agreements to be enforced by a global commerce agency, the WTO. Rich countries and the GATT Secretariat staff promised developing countries that they would experience major gains as industrialized countries lowered and eventually eliminated tariffs on such items as textiles and apparel and cut agricultural subsidies that had enabled large agribusinesses to dominate world commodity markets. Think tanks, public opinion-makers and newspaper editorials have continued to relentlessly promote this notion of developing countries being the primary beneficiaries of the WTO and globalization—despite a paucity of evidence to support such contentions and a growing record proving the opposite. After nearly nine years of the WTO, few if any of the promised economic benefits materialized for developing countries and for many, poverty has worsened. The number of people living on less than $1 a day (the World Bank's definition of extreme poverty) has risen since the WTO went into effect.

The WTO's Environmental Impact: First, Gattzilla Ate Flipper

Over its almost nine years of operation, the WTO's anti-environmental rhetoric has been replaced by more politic pronouncements even as it has systematically ruled against every domestic environmental policy that has been challenged and has eviscerated exceptions that might have been used to safeguard such laws. Instead of seeking to resolve conflicts between commercial and environmental goals, the WTO's largely ineffectual Committee on Trade and the Environment has become a venue mainly for identifying green policies that violate WTO rules.

Regional Expansion of Free Trade

The regionalization of trade, as evidenced by the European Union (EU) and the North American Free Trade Agreement (NAFTA), has removed trade barriers and created larger markets for foreign goods. Regional trading blocs can help overcome the obstacles of nontransparent and different national standards. The GATT encourages trade liberalization on a regional level by allowing for such agreements in Article XXIV.

There are two basic types of regional trade agreements. A **free trade agreement** is defined as a group of two or more states where tariffs and other trade barriers are reduced and eliminated. The North American Free Trade Agreement is a regional free trade agreement. By contrast, a **customs union** is a free trade area with the additional feature of a common external tariff on products originating from outside the union. The European Union is a customs union.

North American Free Trade Agreement (NAFTA)[25]

The North American Free Trade Agreement of the United States, Canada, and Mexico creates a free trade area with more than 425 million people and $11 trillion in combined gross domestic product. It also serves to unite important trade partners. Canada is the United States' largest trade partner, with two-way trade totaling $371 billion in 2002. Mexico is the United States' second largest trade partner, with two-way trade of $231 billion in 2002.

http://

NAFTA Secretariat—rules, decisions, status reports, text of all 22 chapters of NAFTA: **http://www.nafta-sec-alena.org.**

NAFTA had its origins in the United States–Canada Free Trade Agreement, which became effective on January 1, 1989. The United States opened free trade negotiations with Mexico later in 1989, and Canada subsequently joined these discussions. Agreement between the parties was reached in 1993, and NAFTA became effective on January 1, 1994. NAFTA was implemented in the United States by the adoption of the NAFTA Implementation Act on December 8, 1993.[26] The *Made in*

Made in the USA Foundation v. United States

56 F. Supp. 2d 1226 (N.D. Alabama 1999)

Propst, District Judge. In 1990 the United States, Mexico, and Canada initiated negotiations with the intention of creating a "free trade zone" through the elimination or reduction of tariffs and other barriers to trade. After two years of negotiations, the leaders of the three countries signed the North American Free Trade Agreement ("NAFTA" or the "Agreement") on December 17, 1992. Congress approved and implemented NAFTA on December 8, 1993, with the passage of the NAFTA Implementation Act ("Implementation Act").

The President purportedly negotiated and concluded NAFTA pursuant to his constitutional responsibility for conducting the foreign affairs of the United States and in accordance with the Omnibus Trade and Competitiveness Act of 1988 under the so-called "fast-track" procedure. Congress then approved and implemented NAFTA by enacting the Implementation Act, pursuant to its power to legislate in the areas of tariffs and domestic and foreign commerce. The plaintiffs contend that this failure to go through the Treaty Clause in Article II, Section 2, of the

25.   The enumerated goals of NAFTA are to (1) eliminate trade barriers, (2) promote conditions of fair competition, (3) increase investment opportunities, (4) provide adequate protection for intellectual property rights, (5) establish effective procedures for its implementation and application, and (6) provide for the resolution of disputes among the parties to the agreement. See generally Bernard D. Reams Jr. & Jon S. Schultz, eds. *The North American Free Trade Agreement* (1994).

26.   The NAFTA Implementation Act can be found at 19 U.S.C. §§ 3301–3624 (2000).

U.S. Constitution renders the Agreement and, apparently, the Implementation Act, unconstitutional.

The issues are the following:

(1) Do NAFTA and the Implementation Act constitute a "treaty" as contemplated by Article II, Section 2, of the Constitution?
(2) Even if NAFTA and the Implementation Act constitute a "treaty" as contemplated by Article II, Section 2, of the Constitution, was the making and implementation of NAFTA authorized under other provisions of the Constitution?

Remarkably, in the over two hundred years of this nation, the Supreme Court of the United States has not specifically and definitively decided the principles applicable to these issues.

The Constitutionality of NAFTA

The Treaty Clause states that the President "shall have the Power, by and with the Advice and Consent of the Senate, to make Treaties, provided two-thirds of the Senators present concur." The plaintiffs' ultimate argument in this case is that the Treaty Clause should be read as an exclusive grant of power with respect to those international agreements that may be called "treaties," and that NAFTA falls within the bounds of the proper definition of the term. The plaintiffs acknowledge that the text of the Constitution fails to establish a test for determining when an international agreement is a "treaty" as opposed to some other type of agreement.

It is also clear that under international law the Agreement would be considered to be a treaty and there is no clear distinction between what constitutes a treaty under international law as opposed to a treaty "in the constitutional sense." While NAFTA is likely a treaty, it may not be a "treaty," as contemplated by the Treaty Clause. Nevertheless, I will assume that it is such. The most significant issue before the court is whether the Treaty Clause is an exclusive means of making an international agreement under the circumstances of this case.

The fact that the President has the power to make treaties by and with the advice and consent of the Senate is not saying that agreements with foreign nations cannot otherwise be made and implemented. However, it should be noted that the Supreme Court has upheld the power of Congress to delegate to the President the ability to negotiate and conclude agreements with foreign nations or to implicitly approve the President's actions with respect to such agreements. Under such circumstances, the President is said to "exercise not only his powers but also those delegated by Congress," and has been allowed to conclude international agreements settling claims of United States citizens. I hold that the President had the authority to negotiate and conclude NAFTA pursuant to his executive authority and pursuant to the authority granted to him by Congress in accordance with the terms of the Omnibus Trade and Competitiveness Act of 1988.

Case Highlights

- The treaty clause of the U.S. Constitution grants the president the power to make treaties with the advice and consent of the Senate.
- NAFTA is considered a treaty according to international law.
- Congress may also delegate additional powers to negotiate international agreements to the president, as it did under its "fast track" legislation.

---

the USA Foundation v. United States case addresses the constitutionality of the U.S. adoption of NAFTA and serves to illustrate the comparative powers of the U.S. president and Congress in the area of international trade agreements.

The substantive provisions of NAFTA in many ways mirror those set forth in the GATT. For example, NAFTA members are required to accord one another's products national treatment. NAFTA also mandates the eventual elimination of tariffs and nontariff barriers. Its members have been more successful in eliminating tariffs than nontariff barriers. For example, by 2003, 90 percent of all tariffs applicable to goods traded between the United States, Canada, and Mexico had been eliminated. The remaining tariffs average 1 percent and are to be eliminated by 2008. The complete elimination of tariffs is likely to harm some domestic industries in the short term, so NAFTA contains **snapback provisions** that allow for the reinstitution of previous tariff levels at times to alleviate short-term negative impacts on industry and business. By contrast, the NAFTA members have failed to meet the 1999 deadline for the elimination of all nontariff barriers to trade. In addition, NAFTA also addresses numerous specific industries and goods in a manner similar to the GATT. Examples in this regard include agriculture, services, and textiles.

NAFTA enacted a series of complicated rules of origin that the North American businessperson must master to earn the lower NAFTA tariff rates. Goods must be certified as **regional goods** to cross NAFTA borders freely. The traditional test of **substantial transformation**[27] (where a good or material is further processed), which usually results in a tariff classification change for the goods, is not sufficient when certain goods are imported from outside NAFTA and then moved within NAFTA. For example, textile products must go through a *triple transformation* to obtain regional goods status. Other products, like automobiles, electronics, and machinery, have to pass stringent *cost tests*. Depending on the good, somewhere between 50 percent and 62.5 percent of the good's costs must be regional in origin.

NAFTA's ultimate long-term impact on trade is more likely to come in its nontariff provisions, which include an agreement to reduce barriers to direct foreign investment, eliminate performance standards, ensure the free flow of capital, offer expropriation assurances, and institute a dispute resolution mechanism. The breadth of NAFTA and its potential impact on regional trade can be seen in the following list of some of the committees and groups authorized by NAFTA articles[28] (references to NAFTA articles are in brackets):

- Working Group on Rules of Origin [513]
- Working Group on Customs [513(6)]
- Working Group on Agricultural Subsidies [705(6)]
- Working Group on Trade and Competition [1504]
- Committees: Trade in Goods [316]
- Sanitary and Phytosanitary Measures [722]
- Financial Services [1412]
- Private Commercial Disputes [2022(4)]
- Land Transportation Standards [913(5)]
- Telecommunications Standards [913(5)]
- Automotive Standards [913(5)]
- Small Business [1021]

It remains to be seen if the standing committees and working groups will produce harmonization or mutual recognition of national rules and standards. Such efforts should be closely monitored by the businessperson operating within the NAFTA countries.

Despite their similarities, NAFTA differs from the GATT in several important provisions. For example, NAFTA's provisions with respect to the imposition of safeguard measures are similar to those contained within the GATT but impose stricter obligations on the member states. To impose safeguards pursuant to NAFTA, a member state must demonstrate that increased imports of a good are the substantial cause of serious injury, or threat thereof, to a domestic industry producing a like or directly competitive product. However, unlike the GATT, the state seeking to impose the safeguard measure must agree with the state against which such action is taken on the payment of trade compensation. Furthermore, in the event

---

27. Substantial transformation will be discussed more fully in Chapter Six.
28. See Leonard Waverman, "Post-NAFTA: Can the United States, Canada, and Mexico Deepen their Economic Relationships?" in *Integrating the Americas: Shaping Future Trade Policy*, Sidney Weintraub, ed. (1994).

the United States, Canada, or Mexico applies a safeguard measure pursuant to the GATT, it may be applied only to goods coming from its other NAFTA trade partners if the import of the affected good from such partner is a significant share of the total imports of the good.

Another distinction between NAFTA and the GATT is in the area of cross-border investments. NAFTA affords several rights to investors from member states: (1) easing of requirements for the establishment of companies within member states; (2) national treatment and most-favored-nation status for foreign investors; (3) the relaxation of foreign exchange rules; (4) prohibition of expropriation of foreign property in the absence of a public purpose, conducted in accordance with due process of law and upon payment of just compensation; (5) the elimination of employment preferences for nationals; and (6) the elimination of domestic content and purchasing requirements. Member states are free to exclude designated industries from inclusion in these provisions. For example, the United States has made exceptions for the nuclear power, broadcasting, mining, and air transportation industries, as well as those industrial activities deemed crucial to national security.

However, unlike the GATT, these protections are enforced through an investor-state dispute resolution procedure that grants standing to injured private investors to seek monetary damages directly from the member state acting in violation of these protections. This grant of standing has proven very controversial, as it derogates to private investors the right to protest traditionally reserved to states and, arguably, grants them a right to veto domestic legislation that negatively affects their investments.

NAFTA also addresses environmental and workers' rights issues. With respect to the environment, NAFTA members pledge to cooperate in protecting the environment and developing common standards through the North American Agreement on Environmental Cooperation. These activities are coordinated by the Commission for Environmental Cooperation. NAFTA also recognizes basic labor rights in the North American Agreement on Labor Cooperation. This agreement recognizes (1) freedom of association, (2) the right to engage in collective bargaining and strikes, (3) prohibitions upon forced labor and child labor, (4) freedom from employment discrimination, (5) the right to receive equal pay for work of equal value, and (6) the right to minimum working conditions and occupational safety and health.

Another significant difference between NAFTA and the GATT is in the area of dispute resolution. Dispute resolution under NAFTA is subject to oversight by the *Fair Trade Commission.* Disputes between NAFTA members are initially to be resolved through negotiated settlements. In the event of failure of such negotiations, either of the disputing states may request the Fair Trade Commission to authorize the formation of a dispute resolution panel. The dispute resolution panel of five members is empowered to decide whether a violation of NAFTA has occurred and propose a solution. Panels specifically lack jurisdiction to order a state found to be in violation of its NAFTA obligations to change its laws. However, the state must take affirmative steps to implement the panel's decision or reach an agreement with respect thereto within thirty days. Failure to implement a panel's recommendations in a timely fashion may result in the authorization of retaliation by the panel against the violating state.

Despite these differences with GATT, NAFTA has proven to be equally controversial. Many of the previously noted objections to the GATT have also been raised with respect to NAFTA. The primary objection raised to NAFTA has been the purported loss of jobs to Mexico. Critics contend that NAFTA has encouraged U.S. companies to relocate plants across the border in Mexico to take advantage of cheaper labor costs and lax environmental and labor standards. Finished products from these plants, called **maquiladoras**, may be subsequently imported into the United States duty-free. Maquiladoras now number in the thousands and are the second largest source of revenue in Mexico after the oil industry. However, the operation of maquiladoras has been accompanied by many problems, such as environmental degradation, labor exploitation, and social dislocation, as Mexican workers migrate north looking for work in factories. Critics argue that these developments have, in turn, weakened environmental and labor protection laws in the United States as well as in Mexico.

Other U.S. Free Trade Initiatives

The United States has been a world leader in forging greater regional economic integration. In addition to its NAFTA partners, the United States has signed free trade agreements with seven states, dating back to the U.S.-Israel Free Trade Agreement of 1985. The negotiation of bilateral free trade agreements accelerated during the George W. Bush administration. The United States entered into free trade agreements with Jordan in December 2001 and Chile and Singapore in 2003. By mid-2004, the United States had also finalized similar agreements with Australia, Bahrain, and Morocco.

U.S. free trade efforts have also extended to the proposal and creation of several new multilateral and regional trade agreements. In March 1996, the Asia Pacific Economic Group, consisting of the United States and twenty other states, issued the Bogor Declaration, in which they committed to free trade among all members by 2020.[29] In May 2003, the United States announced an initiative to implement a regional free trade agreement in the Middle East by 2013. The Middle East Free Trade Agreement is to be initially based on the negotiation of **Trade and Investment Framework Agreements (TIFA)** with potential member states. The goals of TIFAs are to forge closer economic ties between the signatories, promote free trade and investment, and foster transparency and economic reform. The United States has entered into TIFAs with Algeria, Egypt, Kuwait, Qatar, Saudi Arabia, Tunisia, the United Arab Emirates, and Yemen. TIFA negotiations were underway with Oman in mid-2004. In June 2003, the U.S Trade Representative announced that the United States had entered negotiations for the purpose of reaching a multilateral free trade agreement with the Southern African Customs Union, consisting of Botswana, Lesotho, Namibia, South Africa, and Swaziland. In May 2004, the United States signed the Central American Free Trade Agreement (CAFTA) with Costa Rica, El Salvador, Guatemala, Honduras, and Nicaragua. Negotiations were underway in mid-2004 to add the Dominican Republic as a party to this agreement. The CAFTA requires the elimination of 80 percent of tariffs imposed on U.S. consumer and industrial products exported to the Central American signatories by 2014. Seventy-five percent of exports from these states to the United States are or will become duty-free. The United States has also initiated negotiations for the formation of a multilateral free trade agreement with Colombia, Ecuador, and Peru.[30]

29. The members of the Asia Pacific Economic Group are Australia, Brunei Darussalam, Canada, Chile, the People's Republic of China, Hong Kong, Indonesia, Japan, Korea, Malaysia, Mexico, New Zealand, Papua New Guinea, Peru, the Philippines, Russia, Singapore, Chinese Taipei, Thailand, the United States, and Vietnam.

30. Additional information on U.S. bilateral free trade agreements and regional initiatives is available at the Web site of the U.S. Trade Representative (**www.ustr.gov**).

The most ambitious regional free trade initiative in which the United States is participating is the ongoing negotiations to draft the **Free Trade Agreement of the Americas (FTAA)**. If negotiations are successfully concluded, the FTAA will become the world's largest free trade agreement by uniting thirty-four states in the Western Hemisphere with a combined population of 800 million people and a gross domestic product in excess of $13 trillion.[31] Under the FTAA, 65 percent of U.S. exports of consumer and industrial goods not covered by NAFTA would become duty-free, with all tariffs eliminated by 2015. Exports of chemicals, construction and mining equipment, energy and environmental products, information technology, medical equipment, nonwoven fabrics, paper, steel, and wood products would become duty-free immediately throughout the member states. Fifty-six percent of agricultural products would also be entitled to immediate duty-free treatment, with the remainder of agricultural tariffs phased out over a number of years. Textiles would be entitled to duty-free treatment in five years. The FTAA would also contain provisions relating to investments, government procurement, and trade in services. FTAA negotiations were stalled in mid-2004, and it appears highly unlikely that the parties will reach agreement by their self-imposed deadline of January 1, 2005.[32]

Other Regional Trade Agreements

There are numerous other models of regional free trade and economic integration in the international arena. Three of these models are discussed next.

THE EUROPEAN UNION

The European Union has been defined as a loose association of states with a basis in international law, formed for the purpose of forging closer ties among the peoples of Europe.[33] The modern EU had its inception in three treaties from the 1950s. The Treaty of Paris of 1952 between Belgium, France, Italy, Luxembourg, the Netherlands, and West Germany integrated the coal and steel industries through the creation of the European Coal and Steel Community. The EURATOM Treaty of 1958 between the same states accomplished the same purpose with respect to the civilian use of nuclear power. The **Treaty of Rome** of the same year between these states eradicated internal tariffs and restrictions, created a common external tariff for goods originating in nonmember states, and strove to create a common market through the free movement of people, services, goods, and capital.

http://

Europa—The European Union Online: **http://europa.eu.int** or European Union Internet Resources—University of California, Berkeley: **http://www.lib.berkeley.edu/GSSI/eu.html.**

Four rounds of expansion occurred between 1972 and 1995. Denmark, Ireland, and the United Kingdom were added as a result of expansion in 1972 and 1973. The second expansion in 1979 through 1981 added Greece, and the third expansion in 1985 and 1986 extended membership to Portugal and Spain. Austria, Finland, and Sweden became members in 1994 and 1995.

Recent EU treaties have proven as ambitious in their goals as their predecessors. Adopted in 1993, the Treaty on European Union, the so-called **Treaty of Maastricht**, changed the name of the association from the European Economic

---

31. The states involved in the negotiation of the Free Trade Agreement of the Americas are the thirty-four democratically elected governments in the Western Hemisphere. Cuba has been excluded from participation in these negotiations.
32. Additional information on the Free Trade Agreement of the Americas is available at its Web site **(http://www.ftaa-alca.org/ALCA_E.asp)**.
33. Additional information on the European Union is available at its Web site **(http://europa.eu.int)**.

Community to EU. The Treaty of Maastricht also established the framework for the creation of the European Central Bank and the introduction of the European currency unit, the *euro*, which became the exclusive national currency of twelve of the member states on February 22, 2002.[34] More ambitious still was the **Treaty of Nice** of 2000, which served to expand the EU to include Cyprus, the Czech Republic, Estonia, Hungary, Latvia, Lithuania, Malta, Poland, Slovakia, and Slovenia. These states joined the EU effective May 1, 2004. This expansion created the largest regional trading bloc in the world, more than 440 million people. The most ambitious EU initiative to date, the **Constitution for Europe**, remains under negotiation. EU leaders reached an agreement on a draft of the Constitution in June 2004. It will restructure the institutions responsible for EU governance, create the new office of EU foreign minister to coordinate foreign affairs, and enshrine numerous personal freedoms and rights applicable to all *eurocitizens* residing within the member states.

The EU presently has four principal institutions. The Council of Ministers has one representative from each member state. The presidency of the council currently rotates every six months among the member states. The council serves as the chief legislator and coordinator of economic cooperation and foreign affairs. The second institution is the European Commission, twenty-seven members appointed by the council to serve four-year terms. The commission is responsible for enforcing and implementing EU treaties and legislation, determining the legal bases for legislation enacted pursuant to treaties, and coordinating integration among the member states. The European Parliament has 732 representatives directly elected from member states for a term set by state law. The number of parliamentarians allocated to each state is based on population. The Parliament has the right to be consulted about legislation before its implementation and occasionally has the right to veto proposed legislation. The Parliament also approves the appointment of commission members by the council. Finally, the European Court of Justice serves as the guardian of the treaties and integrator by jurisprudence. It has twenty-five judges representing each member state and appointed by the council for six-year terms.

The primary law of the EU is found in the provisions of the treaties themselves. There are four separate types of secondary law. Secondary law in the EU is legislation enacted pursuant to the treaties that serves to implement them. **Regulations** are statements of law binding in their entirety on member states. Regulations immediately become part of the national law in all member states and are superior to inconsistent national laws. By contrast, **directives** are binding on member states as to the result to be achieved but leave the means of implementation to the member states. As such, directives require the passage of implementing legislation by each member state. **Decisions** are a type of legislation specifically applicable to member states and individuals, binding in their entirety and requiring no implementing legislation. Finally, recommendations are nonbinding policy statements.

Three primary principles underlie all EU law. The **supremacy doctrine** provides that EU law preempts inconsistent national laws in fields where transfer of power and integration have occurred. National law governs in fields where no transfer of authority to the EU has occurred. A related doctrine is the **principle of subsidiarity**. This principle recognizes national sovereignty by providing that the EU will act only in those areas that are appropriate for community-level action. The **direct effects**

---

34. Denmark, Sweden, and the United kingdom elected not to participate in monetary union.

doctrine allows individuals to claim rights created by specific provisions of the treaties and implementing legislation before national courts.

Numerous issues confronting the EU will determine its ultimate future success. Expansion has raised the issue of whether the EU has become too large to be governable. There remain unresolved questions with respect to funding the multitude of EU institutions, the inordinate amount of which falls upon wealthy states such as Germany. Economic issues, such as immigration and labor policies, monetary policy, and the future viability of the euro, also loom large. There are also concerns that the new member states may result in environmental degradation and strain the EU's ability to comply with international environmental treaties. Social issues may arise as a result of efforts to integrate the highly diverse populations of twenty-five member states. Only time will tell if the EU ultimately fulfills its expectations and potential as the most ambitious economic integration plan of the twentieth century.

MERCOSUR

Mercosur, otherwise known as the "Southern Common Market," was created in 1991 between Argentina, Brazil, Paraguay, and Uruguay.[35] The original purpose of Mercosur was the creation of a free trade area between these states. In 1994, this goal was transformed into the goal of creating a customs union. Attempts to achieve this goal in the past decade have been uneven. Mercosur has succeeded in eliminating approximately 95 percent of the tariffs assessed on goods traded between the member states. As a result, trade between the member states has increased by more than 200 percent in the past decade. The member states have also established a common external tariff of 12 percent on goods originating from nonmember states. However, closer integration has been hindered by many factors, including the absence of central enforcement mechanisms to ensure the compliance of member states with their commitments and the economic difficulties associated with the regional recession and currency devaluations of the late 1990s.

THE AFRICAN UNION

Created by the *Sirte Declaration* of September 1999, the African Union is the successor to the Organization for African Unity.[36] The fifty-three member states of the African Union have agreed to continue the mission of the previous organization in forging closer ties among the peoples of Africa and overcoming the lingering economic vestiges of colonialism on the African continent. However, the African Union has a more ambitious economic agenda than its predecessor. One of the goals set forth in the Sirte Declaration is the greater socioeconomic integration of African peoples and the establishment of "the necessary conditions which enable the continent to play its rightful role in the global economy." These goals are to be achieved, in part, through the establishment of the African Central Bank, the African Investment Bank, and the African Monetary Fund. Whether the member states will be able to fully implement the Sirte Declaration and whether the new organization can overcome the numerous political, social, and economic problems that plague the African continent remain to be determined.

---

35. Additional information on Mercosur in English is available at the Web site of the Organization of American States (**www.sice.oas/agreemts/Mercin_e.asp#MERCOSUR**).

36. Additional information on the African Union is available at its Web site (**http://www.africa-union.org**).

KEY TERMS

Agreement on Import Licensing
   Procedures
Agreement on Preshipment
   Inspection
Agreement on the Application
   of Sanitary and Phytosanitary
   Measures (SPS)
Agreement on Trade-Related
   Aspects of Intellectual Property
   Rights (TRIPS)
antidumping duty
binding commitments
cease and desist order
Constitution for Europe
countervailing duties
country of origin rules
customs union
Customs Valuation Code
decisions
direct effects doctrine
directives
Dispute Settlement Body
Doha Round
dumping

European Union (EU)
free trade agreement
Free Trade Agreement of the
   Americas (FTAA)
General Agreement on Tariffs
   and Trade (GATT)
General Agreement on Trade in
   Services (GATS)
impairment
International Trade
   Administration (ITA)
International Trade Commission
   (ITC)
maquiladoras
national treatment principle
normal trade relations principle
North American Free Trade
   Agreement (NAFTA)
nullification
permanent exclusion order
principle of subsidiary
quantitative restrictions
regional goods
regulations

safeguard measure
snapback provisions
subsidies
substantial transformation
supremacy doctrine
suspension
Tariff Act of 1930
Trade and Investment Framework
   Agreement [TIFA]
Treaty of Maastricht
Treaty of Nice
Treaty of Rome
transparency principle
U.S. Court of Appeals for the
   Federal Circuit
U.S. Court of International Trade
U.S. Trade Representative
   (USTR)
Uruguay Round
World Trade Organization
   (WTO)
WTO Dispute Settlement
   Understanding (DSU)
WTO panels

CHAPTER PROBLEMS

1. How can the free trade mandate of the World Trade Organization be reconciled with the concerns of labor, environmental, and consumer groups? What is meant by the word *free* in the term *free trade*? Does free mean no restrictions on the flow of labor, capital, goods, services, and technology? Should free trade be limited by other concerns, such as local disruption? Should local cultural concerns be a limitation on the nonregulation of trade? How can the WTO dispute resolution and enforcement process be reconciled with a country's assertion of national sovereignty over its national laws and regulations?

2. In its Least Developed Countries Report for 2004, the United Nations Conference on Trade and Development (UNCTAD) asserts that international trade has not played a major positive role in reducing poverty in the least developed countries. As a result, UNCTAD concluded, "If past trends persist, the LDCs are likely to become the major locus of extreme poverty in the world economy by 2015." What can be done to improve the effect of free trade on these impoverished countries? Should the WTO take a greater role in obtaining preferential tariff treatment for goods exported from these

countries? How can developed countries continue to justify protection of domestic industries such as agriculture and textiles through granting subsidies?

3. How can one reconcile restrictive immigration policies with the notion of free trade? Why should goods, services, and capital be allowed to move freely and not people? How do the restrictive immigration laws sanctioned under NAFTA compare with the EU's "Four Freedoms" of goods, services, capital, and people and the EU's movement toward EU passports and citizenship? How does one reconcile U.S. interests in "border control" with its own liberal democratic principles? How does one reconcile the call to "regain control of our borders" with the government's policy to not harass employers of illegal aliens in industries where their labor is needed? What are the ethical arguments against proposals to prohibit undocumented immigrants from receiving emergency medical care or public schooling? One argument can be found in the U.S. Constitution, where no distinction is made between legal and illegal immigrants in the admonition that "all [people] are endowed by their Creator with inalienable rights."

4. One can argue that regional trade areas like the European Union work like "mini-GATTS." In such systems, it is inevitable that national concerns and sovereignty will conflict with the free trade dictates of the union. National subsidies traditionally given to domestic agricultural industries are one instance. France has a long-standing policy of granting aid to olive growers. Can France continue to give such aid under the auspices of the European Union? If so, does it need the permission of the EU? Are regional trade areas such as the EU and the North American Free Trade Agreement consistent with the GATT's mandate of free trade on a global scale? Do such agreements make the achievement of this goal more difficult by dividing the world into regional blocs and diverting attention from the achievement of GATT's global aspirations?

5. Ralph Nader and Lori Wallach had this to say about the World Trade Organization: "The binding provisions that define the WTO's functions and scope do not incorporate any environmental, health, labor, or human rights considerations. There is nothing in the institutional principles of the WTO to inject any procedural safeguards of openness, participation, or accountability. The WTO 'dispute resolution system' is the mechanism that enforces WTO control over democratic governance. WTO panel members are selected from qualifications that produce panelists with a uniformly protrade perspective. The new rules favor the largest, most developed nations. Unlike the old GATT rules, the new WTO requires all members to agree to be bound by all Uruguay Round accords. The rule forces many countries, usually small ones, to accept trade in areas that might be undesirable in the long run. WTO rules are now enforceable as regards all existing federal, state, and local laws. In effect, countries have voluntarily sacrificed their own sovereignty. The WTO's rules and powerful enforcement mechanism promote downward harmonization of wages, environmental, worker, and health standards. Some international trade is useful, whereas other global trading favors corporate advantages over those of workers, consumers, and the environment. Concentrating power in international organizations, as trade pacts do, tends to remove critical decisions from citizen control."[37] Do you agree with Nader and Wallach's assessment of the dangers of the WTO? Do you think the dangers outweigh the benefits? What role should governments play in balancing the promotion of free trade through organizations like the WTO and the concerns addressed in this quote?

INTERNET EXERCISES

1. Review recent developments in the area of trade law by reviewing the following websites: **http://www.jus. uio.no/lm/international.economic.law/itl.html** (International Trade Law) and **http://www.ita.doc.gov/** (U.S. International Trade Administration).

2. Read the overview of the WTO and GATT at **http://www.wto.org/.**

3. Review recent WTO decisions that highlight the intersection between free trade and environmental issues. See, for example, **http://www.lib.uchicago.edu/~llou/wto/** and **http://www.worldtradelaw.net.**

---

37.   Ralph Nader & Lori Wallach, "GATT, NAFTA, and the Subversion of the Democratic Process" in *The Case Against the Global Economy*, Jerry Mander & Edward Goldsmith, eds.

Countries' export and import regulations have a direct impact on an exporter or importer's ability to undertake profitable international trade transactions. National regulations may keep an exporter from honoring a contract if the exporter is precluded from exporting the goods. The cost of importing can dramatically change if the duties assigned to a transaction through customs regulations are different from the importer's expectations. This chapter addresses the relationship between U.S. customs regulations and private business transactions. Does the typical U.S. exporter need to be concerned with violating U.S. export regulations? What do U.S. export regulations demand of the exporter? What are the consequences of violating the regulations?

In importing, the assessment of duties and marking requirements are crucial. A miscalculation of duty owed to the government of import could convert an otherwise profitable import transaction into a loss. In addition to duties, penalties for violating the customs laws can be substantial. Failure to conform to a country's marking or country of origin requirements can bar the goods from importation. We will discuss import regulations first and then review the export regulations of the United States.

Chapter 6

National Import and Export Regulation

Import Requirements and Duties

To import goods into a foreign country, the importer must satisfy a number of requirements. The three basic types of laws that regulate the importation of goods are the assessment of duties, marking requirements, and standards requirements. Unlike export regulation, which tends to be more country-specific, there is general agreement among most countries on how to classify goods and assess import duties. The fundamental factors used to determine the customs duties are classification, valuation, and country of origin. Duties vary with the type of goods, their value, and where they originated.

Most countries have enacted a uniform classification system, the **harmonized tariff schedule (HTS)**.[1] The U.S. version is published by the U.S. International Trade Commission. In 1989, the new HTS replaced older schedules in more than fifty countries, including the United States.[2] Versions of the HTS are currently in use in 179 countries representing 98 percent of world trade. The HTS classification involves selecting the HTS product classification that best describes the goods being imported. This classification determines the duty rate to be applied. The goods must then be valued to determine the amount of duty owed. The duty owed is usually the

http://
Harmonized Tariff Schedule: **http:// hotdocs.usitc.gov/ tariff_chapters_ current/toc.html.**

---

1. The U.S. Harmonized Tariff Schedule can be found at **http://hotdocs.usitc.gov/tariffs_chapters_current/toc.html**.
2. The U.S. statute adopting the Harmonized Tariff Schedule can be found at 19 U.S.C. § 1202 (2000).

value of the goods multiplied by the duty rate provided by the classification. The **country of origin** determines if the goods are subject to a normal trade relations rate, a NAFTA (or other free trade agreement) rate, or a rate provided by the **generalized system of preferences (GSP)**.

The GSP is a framework under which developed countries give preferential tariff treatment to manufactured goods imported from designated developing countries.[3] The GSP program assists the economic development of certain developing countries by permitting designated products to enter developed countries at reduced duty rates or duty-free. GSP is expressly authorized by the GATT as an exception to the normal trade relations principle. In the United States, nations eligible for GSP treatment are referred to as designated beneficiary developing countries or least-developed beneficiary countries. Products originating in designated beneficiary developing countries receive reduced rates of duty, and products originating from least-developed beneficiary countries receive duty-free treatment. There are more than 140 countries, nonindependent territories, and associations of states that receive GSP status in the United States, with 41 countries designated as least-developed beneficiary countries. U.S. law provides that all developing states are eligible for such status unless they participated in an oil embargo against the United States, fail to cooperate with the United States in the enforcement of narcotics trafficking laws, support international terrorism, expropriate property of U.S. citizens without the payment of compensation, do not adhere to the New York Convention with respect to the enforcement of arbitration clauses and awards, or maintain a communist form of government.[4] States that are ineligible according to these criteria include Cuba, Iran, Libya, Myanmar (Burma), North Korea, and Sudan. The developing state "graduates" from the GSP program for all products imported into the United States when it reaches a per capita gross national product of $8,500. Examples of states that have "graduated" from the program include South Korea and Singapore. The developing state may lose its GSP status with respect to a single product when more than half of total U.S. imports of the product originate from that state or when imports of the product from the state exceed limits set by the U.S. Congress. This method by which a developing state may lose its eligibility for GSP treatment does not apply to states located in sub-Saharan Africa.

In some circumstances, no duties may be owed, or the duties payable may be deferred to some future time. For instance, goods placed in a government **bonded warehouse** or entered into a **foreign trade zone** are not subject to duties until they officially enter into the country. A bonded warehouse is more limited in scope than the free trade zone: Duty is deferred until the goods are formally entered into United States commerce, but manufacturing is not permitted unless the goods are subsequently exported. Foreign trade zones, free ports, and similar customs-privileged facilities are now in operation in almost every country. U.S. regulations define a *foreign trade zone* as a "restricted-access area, in or adjacent to a Customs port of entry."[5] Customs duty is not due when goods enter into the foreign trade zone, only when they enter the commerce of the United States. The importer pays customs on the lower value of the finished goods after assembly or manufacture in the zone or of the imported parts and components. Many U.S. manufacturers and their distributors

http://

USTR-General System of Preferences: **http://www.ustr.gov/.** Under the Trade and Development tab click Preference Programs, then click Generalized Systems of Preferences, then U.S. Generalized System Preferences Guidebook.

---

3. The GSP system in the United States can be found at 19 U.S.C. §§ 2461-67 (2000). The most recent iteration of the European Union's GSP system is set forth in Regulation 2501/2001/EC adopted on December 10, 2001.
4. See 19 U.S.C. § 2462(b)(1-2) (2000).
5. U.S. law with respect to the creation and operation of foreign trade zones is set forth at 19 U.S.C. § 81a-81u (2000). See also 15 C.F.R. § 400.2(e) (2004).

use free ports or free trade zones for receiving shipments of goods that are then reshipped in smaller lots to customers throughout the surrounding areas.

Bonded warehouses are also found in many locations. Here, goods can be warehoused without duties being assessed. Once goods are released, they are subject to duties. An importer may use a free trade zone to assemble or manufacture a product from imported components to take advantage of duty preferences or store finished products in a bonded warehouse for a period of time if the importer expects duty rates to decrease.

The customs and tariff laws of the United States are enforced by the **Bureau of Customs and Border Protection** (Customs), the successor to the U.S. Customs Service formerly housed within the Department of Treasury. Customs is now an agency within the Department of Homeland Security, a cabinet-level department formed in April 2003 in the aftermath of the terrorist attacks of September 11, 2001. Customs is headed by the commissioner of customs and border protection, who reports to the secretary for homeland security. Customs was created through the merger of its border control functions with those from the Department of Agriculture, the Immigration and Naturalization Service, and the U.S. Border Patrol. Customs primarily operates as a law enforcement agency. It serves two functions in this regard. Initially, Customs has considerable responsibility in the enforcement of laws governing U.S. trade, including the collection of tariff revenue, enforcement of customs laws, exclusion of goods violating U.S. intellectual property laws, supervision of exports, and administration of foreign trade zones. Its security responsibilities include border security, narcotics interdiction, and the prevention of terrorists from entering the United States.

http://
World Customs
Organization: **http://
www.wcoomd.org.**

When importing into the United States, an importer must classify the goods, subject to review by Customs, by selecting a category from the HTS. The HTS used in the United States is taken from an international classification scheme administered by the **World Customs Organization (WCO)**. HTS classification is a series of numbers that identify categories of goods, beginning with broad categories. As numbers are added, the description becomes increasingly more specific. The HTS uses the following groupings: section, chapter, heading, and subheading. Twenty-two sections broadly cover products from different industries, and ninety-nine chapters group products by industry, ranging from agricultural and component products to finished products. Each grouping is represented by a series of numbers. The first six digits of a tariff classification, uniform for all countries using the WCO system, represent the chapter and heading levels. The first two digits refer to the chapter and the next four to the heading and subheadings. Countries may add more detail by using an additional four digits. In the United States, digits seven and eight denote tariff items and digits nine and ten are used for statistical purposes.

Exhibit 6.1, from the HTS, gives the tariff rates for a number of leather products. The general rate of duty is that provided to WTO members under the normal trade relations principle. The success of GATT in reducing the overall level of world tariff rates is apparent. The WTO rates in this excerpt range from zero to 6 percent. The "2" rates of duty column shows applicable rates according to the Tariff Act of 1930—the rate that would be applied if the United States removed normal trade relations status from the imports of a certain country. Most of the rates in this column are between 30 and 45 percent. Elsewhere in the HTS, rates chargeable pursuant to the Tariff Act of 1930 reach as high as 90 percent. These exorbitant rates are meant to punish an exporting country and effectively prevent the importation of goods from that country. These rates also demonstrate the importance of normal trade relations status.

EXHIBIT 6.1   *Excerpt from Harmonized Tariff Schedule*

Harmonized Tariff Schedule of the United States (2004)
Annotated for Statistical Reporting Purposes

VIII
42-11

Heading/ Subheading	Stat. Suf- fix	Article Description	Unit of Quantity	Rates of Duty 1 General	Rates of Duty 1 Special	Rates of Duty 2
4203		Articles of apparel and clothing accessories, of leather or of composition leather:				
4203.10		Articles of apparel:				
4203.10.20	00	Of reptile leather	No.	4.7%	Free (A,CA,CL,E, J,IL,JO,MX,SG)	35%
4203.10.40		Other	. . . .	6%	Free (CA,D,IL,J+, JO,MX,R) 4.5% (CL,SG) 4.8% (E)	35%
		Coats and jackets:				
	10	Anoraks	No.			
		Other:				
	30	Men's and boys'	No.			
	60	Women's, girls' and infants'	No.			
		Other:				
	85	Men's and boys'	No.			
	95	Women's, girls' and infants'	No.			
		Gloves, mittens and mitts:				
4203.21		Specially designed for use in sports:				
		Baseball and softball gloves and mitts (including batting gloves):				
4203.21.20	00	Batting gloves	No.	3%	Free (A*,CA,CL,E, IL,J,JO,MX,SG)	30%
4203.21.40	00	Other	No.	Free		30%
		Ski or snowmobile gloves, mittens and mitts:				
4203.21.55	00	Cross-country ski gloves, mittens and mitts	prs.	3.5%	Free (A*,CA,CL,E, IL,J,JO,MX,SG)	45%
4203.21.60	00	Other	prs.	5.5%	Free (A*,CA,CL,E, IL,J,JO,MX) 4.1% (SG)	45%
4203.21.70	00	Ice hockey gloves	prs.	Free		30%
4203.21.80		Other		4.9%	Free (A*,CA,CL,E, IL,J,JO,MX,SG)	30%
	30	Golf gloves	doz.			
	60	Other	X			

Source: Chapter 42 at http://hotdocs.usitc.gov/tariff_chapters_current/toc.html

General Rules of Interpretation

Despite the more than 5,000 tariff classifications in the HTS, there is often no exact fit between the good being imported and any HTS tariff classification. In selecting a tariff classification, an importer should consult the **General Rules of Interpretation** at the beginning of the HTS. When more than one tariff selection is possible, the rules are the means by which the importer and Customs make the final selection. When a good is subject to more than one section or chapter heading number, then the General Rules of Interpretation are applied to determine the appropriate classification number.

http://

U.S. Bureau of Industry and Security: **http:// www.bxa.doc.gov.**

The primary rule of interpretation is the **rule of specificity**. It requires the use of a heading that provides a more specific description of the good over one that gives a more general description. If neither description is considered more specific, then the heading for the material, component, or function that provides the **essential character** of the good is to be used. Terms contained within the HTS are to be given their common and popular meaning unless a commercial meaning was clearly intended. The opinion of the Court of Appeals for the Federal Circuit in *Rollerblade, Inc. v. United States* demonstrates the application of the common and popular meaning rule. In the event that neither the rule of specificity nor the essential character rule determines a classification, then the heading that occurs last in numerical order applies. The **Customs Electronic Bulletin Board** provides information on classification rulings, quotas, currency conversion rates, customs valuation provisions, and directives.[6]

Over time, as more headings are added to the HTS, the rule of specificity and the essential character rule may result in a change of classification for a specific product and therefore a different duty rate, so importers must keep up to date on changes or

---

Rollerblade, Inc. v. United States

282 F.3d 1349 (Fed. Cir. 2002)

Rader, Circuit Judge. Rollerblade, Inc. (Rollerblade) appeals from a summary judgment of the United States Court of International Trade affirming the United States Customs Service (Customs) classification of imported in-line roller skating protective gear under subheading 9506.99.6080 (99.6080) of the Harmonized Tariff Schedules of the United States (HTSUS). Because Customs correctly classified the imports, this court affirms.

The imports in this case are in-line roller skating protective gear, such as knee pads, elbow pads, and wrist guards. Customs classified the imported protective gear as residual "other" sports equipment under subheading 99.6080 of the HTSUS, which carries a duty rate of 4% ad valorem. Rollerblade appealed to the Court of International Trade, arguing that Customs should have classified the protective gear as "accessories" under subheading 9506.70.2090. HTSUS subheading 70.2090 carries a 0% duty rate. Rollerblade sought this "accessory" classification because the protective gear was designed, tested, manufactured and marketed solely for use with in-line roller skates.

The Court of International Trade affirmed the Customs classification based primarily on its interpretation of the dictionary meaning of the term "accessory." According to the trial court, an accessory under subheading 70.2090 must be "of" or "to" the article (roller skates) listed in the heading, not "of" or "to" the activity (roller skating) for which the article is used. The trial court found that the protective gear had a direct relationship to the activity of

roller skating, but not to the HTSUS heading, namely roller skates. Hence, the trial court affirmed Custom's refusal to classify Rollerblade's protective gear under subheading 70.2090 as an "accessory" to roller skates. Moreover, on summary judgment, the Court of International Trade concluded that Customs properly classified the protective gear under the residual "other" [sports equipment] subheading 99.6080.

Classification of goods under the HTSUS entails both ascertaining the proper meaning of specific terms in the tariff provision and determining whether the merchandise subject to tariffs comes within the description of those HTSUS terms. When reviewing whether the imports fit within those terms, this court uses a clear error standard. *Universal Elecs., Inc. v. United States*, 112 F.3d 488, 491 (Fed. Cir. 1997).

When the HTSUS does not define a tariff term, the term receives its "common and popular meaning." *E.M. Chems. v. United States*, 920 F.2d 910, 913 (Fed. Cir. 1990). To determine a term's common meaning, a court may consult "dictionaries, scientific authorities, and other reliable information sources." *C.J. Tower & Sons v. United States*, 69 C.C.P.A. 128, 673 F.2d 1268, 1271 (CCPA 1982).

Like the trial court, this court also observes that HTSUS offers no definition for the term "accessory." Thus, the trial court correctly consulted the common (dictionary) meaning of the term. As the Court of International Trade found, dictionary definitions

---

6.   The Customs Electronic Bulletin Board can be found at **http://www.cebb.customs.treas.gov/public/default.htm.**

indicate that an "accessory" must bear a direct relationship to the primary article that it accessorizes. In this case, under subheading 70.2090, the article accessorized is roller skates, not the general activity of roller skating. Moreover, as found by the trial court, the protective gear lacks a direct relationship to the roller skates. The protective gear does not directly act on the roller skates at all. Unlike a roller skate part or accessory, the protective gear does not directly affect the skates' operation. Thus, based on the common meaning of "accessory" and the language of subheading 70.2090, this court sustains the trial court's conclusion that Rollerblade's imported protective gear is not a roller skate accessory.

Rollerblade argues that the protective gear is, alternatively, "parts" of the roller skates. Rollerblade would classify the protective gear as roller skate parts because it contributes to the safe and effective operation of the skates and functions by design solely with the skates.

A "part" is "an essential element or constituent; integral portion which can be separated, replaced, etc." *Webster's New World Dictionary* 984 (3d College Ed. 1988). Thus, based on the common meaning, the term "part," like the term "accessory," must have a direct relationship to the primary article, rather than to the general activity in which the primary article is used. Again, the protective gear in this case has a relationship to the activity of roller skating, and not directly to the roller skates.

Rollerblade's imported protective gear protects the wearer from injuries related to an activity using the article. The imports do not attach to or contact in any way the subheading article, namely roller skates. The imports are not necessary to make the skates themselves work, nor are they necessary to make the skates themselves work efficiently or safely. At best, the protective gear adds to the comfort and convenience of the wearer while roller skating. In other words, the roller skates

work in the same manner whether the skater wears the protective gear or not. Concurrent use of the protective gear with the roller skates no doubt reduces injuries to the skater from the activity of roller skating, but this observation does not make the protective gear "parts" of the roller skates.

In this case, the most applicable heading is 9506, entitled "articles and equipment for general physical exercise ... gymnastics, athletics, other sports." Subheading 99.6080, entitled "other," is the so-called catch-all for this provision. The definition offered for "equipment" includes those articles that are necessary and specifically designed for use in athletics and other sports. Rollerblade's imported protective gear fits within this category because it is "equipment" specifically designed for use in the sport of roller skating.

In sum, the Court of International Trade did not err in its determination that Customs properly classified Rollerblade's imported protective gear under the residual subheading 99.6080.

AFFIRMED.

Case Highlights

- As a general rule, U.S. courts defer to Customs' interpretation of terms contained within the HTS.
- Undefined terms in the HTS will be given their "common and popular meaning" as set forth in "dictionaries, scientific authorities, and other reliable information sources."
- Accessories and parts must have a direct relationship to the primary article, rather than to the general activity in which the primary article is used.

---

additions to the HTS. The need for additions to tariff classifications is especially apparent in the area of technology products. On December 13, 1996, the first ministerial meeting of the World Trade Organization issued the Declaration on Trade in Information Technology Products (ITA), which established a framework for expanding world trade in information technology products and enhancing market access opportunities for such products. To implement that declaration, forty-two WTO members and governments agreed on the common objective of achieving, where appropriate, a common classification of such goods for tariff purposes within the existing nomenclature of the Harmonized Commodity Description and Coding System (HS). It further called for a future joint session with the WCO to update existing HS nomenclature.

The general rule-making authority in customs classification and assessment of duties in the United States is vested in Customs. U.S. courts generally defer to Customs' rule-making authority when the underlying statutes are unclear. The

Supreme Court in the *United States v. Haggar Apparel Company* case that follows held that the courts will grant deference to Customs when it writes regulations that clarify parts of the tariff statutes that are unclear as to particular goods or services. So long as Customs is reasonable in its interpretation, its rules should stand. The *Haggar* case also introduces the reader to Section 9802 of the HTS, which provides a special exemption from tariff duties for items temporarily exported for assembly and then returned to the United States.

The *United States v. Haggar* case dealt with the relationship between an executive branch agency (Customs) and the courts. Another issue is the ability of individual states to enact laws that may affect international trade. State governments retain

---

United States v. Haggar Apparel Company

526 U.S. 380 (1999)

Justice Kennedy. This case concerns regulations relating to the customs classification of certain imported goods issued by the United States Customs Service. The question is whether these regulations are entitled to judicial deference in a refund suit brought in the Court of International Trade. Contrary to the position of that Court and the Court of Appeals for the Federal Circuit, we hold the regulation in question is subject to the analysis required by *Chevron U.S.A. Inc. v. Natural Resources Defense Council, Inc.*, and that if it is a reasonable interpretation and implementation of an ambiguous statutory provision, it must be given judicial deference.

Respondent Haggar Apparel Co. designs, manufactures, and markets apparel for men. This matter arises from a refund proceeding for duties imposed on men's trousers shipped by respondent to this country from an assembly plant it controlled in Mexico. The fabric had been cut in the United States and then shipped to Mexico, along with the thread, buttons, and zippers necessary to complete the garments. There the trousers were sewn and reshipped to the United States. If that had been the full extent of it, there would be no dispute, for if there were mere assembly without other steps, all agree the imported garments would have been eligible for the duty exemption which respondent claims.

Respondent, however, in the Government's view, added one other step at the Mexican plant: permapressing. Permapressing is designed to maintain a garment's crease in the desired place and to avoid other creases or wrinkles that detract from its proper appearance. The Customs Service claimed the baking was an added process in addition to assembly, and denied a duty exemption; respondent claimed the baking was simply part of the assembly process, or, in the words of the controlling statute, an "operation incidental to the assembly process." After being denied the exemption it sought for the permapressed articles, respondent brought suit for refund in the Court of International Trade. The court declined to treat the regulation as

controlling. The court ruled in favor of respondent. On review, the Court of Appeals for the Federal Circuit declined to analyze the regulation under *Chevron*, and affirmed.

The statute on which respondent relies, Section 9802, provides importers a partial exemption from duties otherwise imposed. The relevant regulation interpreting the statute with respect to permapressed articles provides as follows:

Any significant process, operation, or treatment other than assembly whose primary purpose is the fabrication, completion, physical or chemical improvement of a component, or which is not related to the assembly process, whether or not it effects a substantial transformation of the article, shall not be regarded as incidental to the assembly and shall preclude the application of the exemption to such article. The following are examples of operations not considered incidental to the assembly:

(4) Chemical treatment of components or assembled articles to impart new characteristics, such as showerproofing, permapressing, sanforizing, dying or bleaching of textiles.

The Customs Service (which is within the Treasury Department) is charged with the classification of imported goods under the proper provision of the tariff schedules in the first instance. In addition, the Secretary is directed by statute to "establish and promulgate such rules and regulations not inconsistent with the law . . . as may be necessary to secure a just, impartial and uniform appraisement of imported merchandise and the classification and assessment of duties thereon at the various ports of entry."

For the reasons we have given, the statutes authorizing customs classification regulations are consistent with the usual rule that regulations of an administering agency warrant judicial deference. We turn to respondent's second major contention, that the statutes governing the reviewing authority of the Court of International Trade in classification cases displace this customary framework. The Court of Appeals held in this case, and in previous cases presenting the issue, that these regulations were not entitled to deference because the Court of International Trade is charged to "reach the correct decision" in determining the proper classification of goods. The whole point of regulations such as these, however, is to ensure that the statute is applied in a consistent and proper manner. Deference to an agency's expertise in construing a statutory command is not inconsistent with reaching a correct decision. If the agency's statutory interpretation fills a gap or defines a term in a way that is reasonable in light of the legislature's revealed design, we give that judgment controlling weight.

The customs regulations may not be disregarded. Application of the *Chevron* framework is the beginning of the legal analysis. Like other courts, the Court of International Trade must, when appropriate, give customs regulations *Chevron* deference. The judgment is VACATED and the case is remanded for further proceedings consistent with this opinion.

Case Update

Upon remand, the U.S. Court of Appeals for the Federal Circuit deferred to Customs' interpretation of an "operation incidental to the assembly process." The Federal Circuit determined that it was reasonable to conclude that this term did not apply to permapressing, which involved oven-baking that caused chemical changes in the fabric. See *United States v. Haggar Apparel Company*, 222 F.3d 1337 (Fed. Cir. 2000). The U.S. Supreme Court refused to grant certiorari to rehear the case, and the Court of International Trade entered judgment on the Federal Circuit's opinion. See *United States v. Haggar Apparel Company*, 532 U.S. 906 (2001). See also *United States v. Haggar Apparel Company*, 133 F. Supp.2d 695 (Ct. Int'l Trade 2001).

Case Highlights

- The Court of International Trade is the U.S. court that has jurisdiction over any civil matters against the United States arising out of federal laws governing import transactions. The court hears cases dealing with antidumping, product classification, valuation, and countervailing duty matters.
- Permapressing clothes is not assembly under Section 9802 or an "operation incidental to the assembly process."
- Merely because a process, operation, or treatment fails to produce a substantial transformation does not automatically result in a duty exemption under Section 9802.
- The Customs Service has been delegated the authority to promulgate rules for the classification of imported goods and assessment of duties.
- Courts must give deference to the regulations published by the Customs Service.

---

significant authority with respect to adoption of laws designed to protect the health, safety, welfare, and morals of their citizens, the so-called police powers. This authority may at times conflict with the U.S. Constitution's grant of primary authority over matters relating to foreign relations and commerce to the federal branch of government. For example, Article I, Section 8 of the Constitution confers the power to regulate commerce, including commerce with foreign nations, upon the U.S. Congress. This grant of authority prohibits state governments from adopting laws that place a substantial burden on interstate and foreign commerce. Another example is the Import-Export Clause in Article I, Section 10. This clause prohibits states from taxing imports and exports. Furthermore, the grant of authority to the executive branch with respect to foreign affairs set forth in Article II is extremely broad and subject to deference because of the president's role as the chief representative of the United States abroad and commander in chief of the armed forces.[7] In any event, Article VI provides that the U.S. Constitution, federal law adopted pursuant thereto, and treaties are the "supreme Law of the Land." This clause has been interpreted to require that federal law should prevail over conflicting state law when the U.S. Congress either expresses the intention that federal law prevail or such a result is implicit in the legislation. The *Crosby v. National Foreign Trade Council* case deals with the interaction of a state statute limiting the procurement of goods from companies transacting business with the country of Myanmar with federal authority with respect to foreign commerce.

---

7. See *United States v. Curtiss-Wright Exp. Co.*, 299 U.S. 304 (1936).

Crosby v. National Foreign Trade Council

530 U.S. 363 (2000)

Justice Souter. The issue is whether the Burma law of the Commonwealth of Massachusetts, restricting the authority of its agencies to purchase goods or services from companies doing business with Burma, is invalid under the Supremacy Clause of the National Constitution owing to its threat of frustrating federal statutory objectives. We hold that it is.

In June 1996, Massachusetts adopted "An Act Regulating State Contracts with Companies Doing Business with or in Burma (Myanmar)." The statute generally bars state entities from buying goods or services from any person (defined to include a business organization) identified on a "restricted purchase list" of those doing business with Burma.

In September 1996, three months after the Massachusetts law was enacted, Congress passed a statute imposing a set of mandatory and conditional sanctions on Burma. The federal Act has five basic parts, three substantive and two procedural. First, it imposes three sanctions directly on Burma. It bans all aid to the Burmese Government except for humanitarian assistance, counternarcotics efforts, and promotion of human rights and democracy. The statute instructs United States representatives to international financial institutions to vote against loans or other assistance to or for Burma, and it provides that no entry visa shall be issued to any Burmese government official unless required by treaty or to staff the Burmese mission to the United Nations. These restrictions are to remain in effect "until such time as the President determines and certifies to Congress that Burma has made measurable and substantial progress in improving human rights practices and implementing democratic government." Second, the federal Act authorizes the President to impose further sanctions subject to certain conditions. He may prohibit "United States persons" from "new investment" in Burma, and shall do so if he determines and certifies to Congress that the Burmese Government has physically harmed, rearrested, or exiled Daw Aung San Suu Kyi (the opposition leader selected to receive the Nobel Peace Prize), or has committed "large-scale repression of or violence against the Democratic opposition." Third, the statute directs the President to work to develop "a comprehensive, multilateral strategy to bring democracy to and improve human rights practices and the quality of life in Burma." As for the procedural provisions of the federal statute, the fourth section requires the President to report periodically to certain congressional committee chairmen on the progress toward democratization and better living conditions in Burma as well as on the development of the required strategy. And the fifth part of the federal Act authorizes the President "to waive, temporarily or permanently, any sanction [under the federal Act] . . . if he determines and certifies to Congress that the application of such sanction would be contrary to the national security interests of the United States."

On May 20, 1997, the President issued the Burma Executive Order No. 13047. He certified that the Government of Burma had "committed large-scale repression of the democratic opposition in Burma" and found that the Burmese Government's actions and policies constituted "an unusual and extraordinary threat to the national security and foreign policy of the United States," a threat characterized as a national emergency. The President then prohibited new investment in Burma "by United States persons."

Respondent National Foreign Trade Council (Council) is a nonprofit corporation representing companies engaged in foreign commerce; 34 of its members were on the Massachusetts restricted purchase list in 1998. In April 1998, the Council filed suit in the United States District Court for the District of Massachusetts, seeking declaratory and injunctive relief against the state officials charged with administering and enforcing the state Act. The District Court permanently enjoined enforcement of the state Act, holding that it "unconstitutionally impinged on the federal government's exclusive authority to regulate foreign affairs." The United States Court of Appeals for the First Circuit affirmed on three independent grounds. It found the state Act unconstitutionally interfered with the foreign affairs power of the National Government, violated the Foreign Commerce Clause and was preempted by the congressional Burma Act.

Congress clearly intended the federal Act to provide the President with flexible and effective authority over economic sanctions against Burma. Within the sphere defined by Congress, then, the statute has placed the President in a position with as much discretion to exercise economic leverage against Burma, with an eye toward national security, as our law will admit. It is simply implausible that Congress would have gone to such lengths to empower the President if it had been willing to compromise his effectiveness by deference to every provision of state statute or local ordinance that might, if enforced, blunt the consequences of discretionary Presidential action.

And that is just what the Massachusetts Burma law would do in imposing a different, state system of economic pressure against the Burmese political regime. The state statute penalizes some private action that the federal Act may allow, and pulls levers of influence that the federal Act does not reach. But the point here is that the state sanctions are immediate and perpetual, there being no termination provision. This unyielding application undermines the President's intended statutory authority by making it impossible for him to restrain fully the coercive power of the national economy when he may choose to take the discretionary action open to him, whether he believes that the national interest requires sanctions to be lifted, or believes that the promise of lifting sanctions would move the Burmese regime in the democratic direction. Quite simply, if the Massachusetts law is enforceable the President has less to offer and less economic and diplomatic leverage as a consequence.

The State has set a different course, and its statute conflicts with federal law at a number of points by penalizing individuals and conduct that Congress has explicitly exempted or excluded from sanctions. It restricts all contracts between the State and companies doing business in Burma. It prohibits contracts between the State and United States persons for goods, services, or technology, even though those transactions are explicitly exempted from the ambit of new investment prohibition when the President exercises his discretionary authority to impose sanctions under the federal Act.

As with the subject of business meant to be affected, so with the class of companies doing it: the state Act's generality stands at odds with the federal discreteness. The Massachusetts law directly and indirectly imposes costs on all companies that do any business in Burma. It sanctions companies promoting the importation of natural resources controlled by the government of Burma, or having any operations or affiliates in Burma. The state Act thus penalizes companies with pre-existing affiliates or investments, all of which lie beyond the reach of the federal act's restrictions on "new investment" in Burmese economic development. The state Act, moreover, imposes restrictions on foreign companies as well as domestic, whereas the federal Act limits its reach to United States persons.

Finally, the state Act is at odds with the President's intended authority to speak for the United States among the world's nations in developing a "comprehensive, multilateral strategy to bring democracy to and improve human rights practices and the quality of life in Burma." Again, the state Act undermines the President's capacity, in this instance for effective diplomacy. It is not merely that the differences between the state and federal Acts in scope and type of sanctions threaten to complicate discussions; they compromise the very capacity of the President to speak for the Nation with one voice in dealing with other governments.

While the threat to the President's power to speak and bargain effectively with other nations seems clear enough, the record is replete with evidence to answer any skeptics. First, in response to the passage of the state Act, a number of this country's allies and trading partners filed formal protests with the National Government. Second, the EU and Japan have gone a step further in lodging formal complaints against the United States in the World Trade Organization (WTO), claiming that the state Act violates certain provisions of the Agreement on Government Procurement, and the consequence has been to embroil the National Government for some time now in international dispute proceedings under the auspices of the WTO. Third, the Executive has consistently represented that the state Act has complicated its dealings with foreign sovereigns and proven an impediment to accomplishing objectives assigned it by Congress. This evidence in combination is more than sufficient to show that the state Act stands as an obstacle in addressing the congressional obligation to devise a comprehensive, multilateral strategy.

Because the state Act's provisions conflict with Congress's specific delegation to the President of flexible discretion, with limitation of sanctions to a limited scope of actions and actors, and with direction to develop a comprehensive, multilateral strategy under the federal Act, it is preempted, and its application is unconstitutional, under the Supremacy Clause.

The judgment of the Court of Appeals for the First Circuit is affirmed.

Case Update

President Clinton's 1997 executive order did not prove effective in ending human rights abuses in Burma or in fostering democratization. On July 29, 2003, President George W. Bush issued Executive Order No. 13310 blocking assets of Burmese financial institutions and government officials and banning the exportation of U.S. financial services to Burma and the importation of any Burmese product into the United States. President Bush's executive order was based, in part, on authority granted to him pursuant to the Burmese Freedom and Democracy Act adopted by the U.S. Congress in July 2003.

Case Highlights

- A state law that imposes a sanctions regime upon a foreign sovereign and those conducting business with it is an unconstitutional intrusion on federal government powers, especially if the state sanctions regime differs from the federal regime.
- State action that compromises the ability of the president to speak for the United States with one voice in dealing with foreign governments is unconstitutional.
- State action that conflicts with a specific congressional delegation of power to the president for conduct of foreign affairs is preempted by the supremacy clause of the U.S. Constitution.

Assessment of Duties

The assessment of import tariffs or duties is a product of three variables: (1) classification of the goods being imported, (2) valuation of the goods, and (3) the country of origin. Focus on Transactions: The Dutiable Status of Goods outlines the factors involved in applying these three variables in U.S. import or customs law.

The viability of export contracts, especially long-term supply contracts, revolves around the parties' abilities to quantify and predict costs. The amount of customs duties to be paid is an important factor that must be analyzed before any long-term contract is signed. An import duty is a tax imposed on imports by a customs authority. Duties are generally based on the value of the goods (**ad valorem** **duties**), other factors such as weight or quantity (**specific duties**), or a combination (compound duties). *Ad valorem* literally means "according to value" and refers to any charge, duty, or tax that is applied as a percentage of value. The classification of goods will determine the specific ad valorem tariff rate. The value of the goods is influenced by many factors. It would be prudent for an exporter to obtain an official ruling on the customs classification of, tariff rate for, and other import fees applying to a specific product before entering into a contract.

The Dutiable Status of Goods

Focus on Transactions

CLASSIFICATION	+ VALUATION	+ COUNTRY-OF-ORIGIN
The Harmonized Tariff Schedule Rules of Interpretation:	**Transaction Value**	**"Rules-of-Origin"**
Common/Commercial Meaning	Price Paid	Grown, mined, produced, or manufactured
Rule of Relative Specificity	Packing Costs	"Substantial Transformation Test"
		• new article
Essential Character Principle	Commissions (by buyer)	• value added
		• process/assembly
Principal Use Rule	Value of "Assists"	• consumer good
Latest Entry Rule	Royalties/Fees (by buyer)	
Doctrine of the Entireties	Proceeds of Resale (accruing to seller)	
Chief Weight Rule (Textiles)		

Dutiable Status is the Customs Service determination of the amount of money or duty owed by the importer. These three columns summarize the factors used in calculating the duty owed. Column 1 (Classification) and Column 3 (Country-of-Origin) determine the rate (%). Column 2 (Valuation) determines the value of the imported goods. The value of the goods is then multiplied by the rate to determine the amount of duty (tax) owed.

Section 9802

The *United States v. Haggar* case introduced **Section 9802**, which allows importers to deduct the value of assembly from duty assessment. This exemption is given for "articles assembled abroad in whole or in part of fabricated components that are products of the United States." It also extends the exemption to any advancement in value or improvement in condition that is a result of "operations incidental to the assembly process such as cleaning, lubricating, and painting." This exemption has resulted in the creation of a corridor of assembly plants, popularly known as maquiladoras, along the U.S.-Mexican border. Maquiladora or "in-bond" industry allows foreign importers to ship components into Mexico duty-free for assembly and reexport. The key issue of contention between Customs and importers is the definition of "fabrication."

In the *Samsonite Corporation v. United States* opinion that follows, Customs successfully challenged an importer's deduction for the value of assembling luggage

http://

Mexico Maquiladora Information: **http://www.mexicomaquila.com/mi.htm** or U.S. Department of Labor: An Overview of the Maquiladora Program: **http://www.dol.gov/ilab/media/reports/nao/maquilad.htm.**

Samsonite Corporation v. United States
889 F.2d 1074 (Fed. Cir. 1989)

Friedman, Senior Circuit Judge. This is an appeal from a judgment of the United States Court of International Trade upholding the denial by the Customs Service of a deduction from assessed duties of the cost of an item that had been manufactured in the United States and, after undergoing certain changes in Mexico, was incorporated into the finished product shipped from Mexico to the United States. The Court of International Trade described the metal strips and Samsonite's use of them in assembling the luggage, as follows: "When they left Tuscon [*sic*], the strips were straight, approximately 1-7/8 inches wide and 55 inches long. After arrival at plaintiff's assembly facility in Nogales, the strips were bent by machine into a squared-sided form and riveted on the open outsides to sheets of plastic, which thereby became the bottom plates of completed frame assemblies."

The Customs Service classified the imported merchandise as luggage under Item 706.62 of the Tariff Schedules of the United States and assessed the 20 percent *ad valorem* duty that that item provides, less the cost or value of certain components of the luggage that had been manufactured in the United States. The latter deduction was made pursuant to Item 807.00 of those schedules. The Customs Service denied a deduction from the value of the luggage for the cost of the steel strips. The Court of International Trade upheld Customs' denial of the deduction.

The court held that the steel strips "were not exported in condition ready for assembly." It found that the "bending process" to which the strips were subjected "did more than' 'adjust' the article. The process created the component to be assembled, the essence of which is

its configuration. Without the resultant shape, the plastic plate could not be attached so as to constitute the bottom, and the completed frames could not be inserted into plaintiff's bags, thereby imparting the intended overall form and structural stability of the finished luggage."

To obtain a deduction for American-fabricated articles assembled abroad, the components (a) must have been exported from the United States "in condition ready for assembly without further fabrication," (b) not have lost their physical identity in the articles by change in form, shape, or otherwise, and (c) not have been advanced in value or improved in condition "except by being assembled" and except "by operations incidental to the assembly process such as cleaning, lubricating, and painting." The critical inquiry is whether the bending and shaping that the strips underwent constituted "fabrication" or mere assembly and operations incidental to the assembly process. We hold that what was done to the strips in Mexico was fabrication and not mere assembly. The judgment of the Court of International Trade dismissing the action is AFFIRMED.

Case Highlights

- To obtain the duty exemption for offshore assembly in Section 9802, the exported items must be ready for assembly without further fabrication.
- The "bending process" to which the strips were subjected in *Samsonite* "did more than 'adjust' the article" and thereby constituted further fabrication.

in Mexico. Steel strips were produced in the United States and then sent to the company's assembly plant in Mexico. The case involved the deductibility of the costs of the steel strips upon importation into the United States. The Court agreed with the Customs Service that shaping the steel strips before placing them within the luggage constituted a further fabrication and not mere assembly.

Transaction Value

http://

Legal Information Institute-Tariff Act of 1930: **http://www4.law. cornell.edu/uscode/ unframed/19/ch4.html.** See also, International Trade Data System-Major Trade Laws Since 1930: **http://www. itds.treas.gov/trade laws.html.**

Section 402 of the Tariff Act of 1930 provides the basic method for determining the value of goods for customs purposes. U.S. Customs law has subsequently enacted the GATT Valuations Code, which uses the concept of **transaction value**[8] as the basis of customs valuation. Transaction value requires that the value of imported goods be determined on a *commercially realistic basis*. This means goods must be priced at a value that would be the result of a sale between two unrelated parties in the ordinary course of business. The valuation of goods is based upon the calculation of transaction value—namely, the costs of the goods to the importer. It is in the interest of the importer to keep the transaction value as low as possible, and so conflict may arise over what items of costs should be included in the transaction values. Those items most contested include commissions paid by the buyer,[9] royalties or fees paid by the buyer after importation,[10] the value of *assists*[11] (material, equipment, or services provided to the seller by the buyer), and resale proceeds paid to the original seller. Note that the **Agreement on Customs Valuation** adopted in the Uruguay Round of GATT recognizes transaction value as the internationally preferred means of calculating dutiable value.

Transaction value in a transaction occurring partly in a free trade zone may be difficult to determine because the import transaction is not the product of an arm's-length sale, as would be the case, for example, for a transfer of raw materials or inventory between affiliated companies. The Tariff Act provides four alternative valuation methods when an arm's-length transaction is not present.[12] The most preferred method is to use the transaction value of identical goods, the price charged by the same manufacturer or importer to an unrelated customer. If there is no such information available, then the transaction value of similar goods is used. This is the price charged for nearly identical goods sold by the same manufacturer.

The third preferred alternative value is the use of the **deductive value** of the goods. The deductive value is the price that the goods being imported are ultimately sold for in the United States. The importer is allowed to *deduct* a number of costs from that price, including international freight, duties, and certain commissions. For example, foreign inland freight costs can be deducted but only if they are separately invoiced. Purchasing goods using the "ex-factory" trade term will remove the costs of inland shipment.[13] Although selling commissions are included in determining dutiable value, commissions paid by the buyer are not dutiable. Therefore,

---

8. See 19 U.S.C. § 1401a (a)(1)(A) (2000).
9. See ibid. § 1401a (b)(1)(B). See also *Rosenthal-Netter, Inc. v. United States,* 861 F.2d 261 (Fed. Cir. 1988); *Monarch Luggage Co. v. United States,* 715 F.Supp. 1115 (1989).
10. See 19 U.S.C. § 1401a (b)(1)(D) (2000).
11. See ibid. § 1401a (b)(1)(C) & (h)(1)(A-B). See also *Texas Apparel Co. v. United States,* 698 F. Supp 932 (Ct. of Int'l Trade 1988), *aff'd* 883 F.2d 66 (Fed. Cir. 1989), *cert. denied,* 493 U.S. 1024 (1990).
12. See 19 U.S.C. § 1401a(c-e) (2000).
13. Trade terms are explained in Chapter Nine.

by proving that any middleman is acting as the buyer's purchasing agent, the buyer's commission can be excluded from the valuation.

To reduce the transaction value and hence the amount of tariff duties, a sophisticated importer will attempt to *unbundle* the import transaction into dutiable and nondutiable parts. If goods are purchased on credit that requires interest payments, the importer should separate the credit part of the sale from the sale of goods. If the price of goods reflects the interest charged by the seller, then the interest becomes part of dutiable value. In contrast, interest alone is not dutiable. Another example of unbundling is when an import contract provides for an inspection of goods at the port of shipment. If the seller obtains and pays for an inspection certificate as part of the documentary transaction, those costs are included in the transaction value, but inspection services paid for by the buyer are not part of the transaction value.

The final, least-preferred alternative valuation method is the **computed value** of the goods. This value is fabricated by adding the manufacturer's actual labor and material costs, along with an estimate of its general expenses and profits. The *Orbisphere Corporation v. United States* case that follows explores the concept of deductive value and the types of expenses that may be deducted before duties are assessed.

Orbisphere Corporation v. United States

765 F. Supp. 1087 (Ct. Int'l Trade 1991)

Musgrave, Judge. Plaintiff contests certain aspects of the Customs Service's valuation of plaintiff's products. Plaintiff alleges that in revaluing its merchandise on the basis of the "deductive value" of that merchandise, as ordered by the Court and as opposed to the earlier valuation on the basis of "transaction value," Customs improperly failed to subtract from the deductive value amounts of certain commissions, profits, and expenses involved in the sales as required by statute. Defendant argues that its failure to subtract those amounts was justified because the three items at issue—commissions, profits, and expenses—did not qualify as deductible under the applicable statute.

A. Controlling Statutes

Section 1401a(d)(2)(A)(i), under which the merchandise was appraised pursuant to the earlier opinion, defines "deductive value" as "the unit price at which the merchandise concerned is sold in the greatest aggregate quantity at or about the date of importation." Paragraph (3)(A) of that section prescribes a number of downward adjustments to the unit price stated above, including the following at issue in this case: "The price determined under paragraph (2) shall be reduced by an amount equal to any commission actually paid or agreed to be paid, or the addition usually made for profit and general expenses, in connection with sales in the United States of imported merchandise that is of the same class or kind,

regardless of the country of exportation." Paragraph 3 also provides that "the deduction made for profit and general expenses shall be based upon the importer's profit and general expenses, unless such profits and general expenses are inconsistent with those reflected in sales in the United States of imported merchandise of the same class or kind, in which case the deduction shall be based on the usual profit and general expenses reflected in such sales, as determined from sufficient information." The principal question concerning this section in the present case is what kind of connection must be shown between the items of expenses or profits to be deducted and the U.S. sales of the imported merchandise.

The rule emanating from these decisions concerning the requisite connection between the expenses to be deducted from the import sales price and the underlying sales transactions appears to be that an importer may not prove that connection by merely multiplying the amount of its total expenses by the percentage that its sales of the subject merchandise make up of its total sales. It requires a specific listing of expenses involved in, and added in the price of, sales of the particular products or line at issue. Subparagraph (B) of paragraph (3) further provides, for purposes of applying the above adjustment that "the deduction made for profit and general expenses shall be based upon the importer's profits and general expenses, unless such profits and general expenses are inconsistent with those reflected in sales in the United States of imported merchandise of the same class or kind, in which case the deduction shall be based on the usual profit and general expenses reflected in such sales, as determined from sufficient information."

The disputed expenses in the present case are:

1. salary and expenses for travel;
2. costs for "U.S. accounting services";
3. costs for "U.S. legal services";
4. director's fees and expenses for travel to Geneva.

Accordingly, the Court orders that the deductive value computed by Customs for this merchandise be reduced by the amount of those expenses. The deduction for profits is provided not based on where the profits end up but in order to provide a value of the goods sold in the United States that approximates the cost of the goods before shipment, resale, and expenses associated therewith. Accordingly, it is clear that in this case plaintiff's profits on the sales in question should have been deducted from the deductive value of the merchandise. Therefore, Customs

is hereby ordered to amend its previous calculation of the deductive value of the subject merchandise by subtracting therefrom amounts equal to plaintiff's expenses and profits discussed herein.

Case Highlights

- Items relating to imported goods, such as profits and expenses, occurring within the United States should be subtracted in using the deductive method of calculating value for purposes of duty assessment.
- Other items that may be deducted from the value of imported goods include the cost of legal services, travel expenses, and accounting costs.
- The importer of goods must show the connection between the items being deducted and the U.S. sale of the imported goods.

Customs Valuation in the European Union

EU Taxation and Customs Union-Taric: **http://europa.eu.int/comm/taxation_customs/databases/taric_en.htm.**

INTERNATIONAL

The European approach to customs valuation is similar to that of the United States. EU Regulation 2913/92, as amended, established the **European Union's Customs Code**, which bases the valuation of imported goods on the notion of transaction value or the "price actually paid."[14] Article 29 provides that transaction value must be adjusted for any proceeds of subsequent sales that are remitted by the buyer to the exporter, directly or indirectly. Article 32 provides a list of the types of charges that must be included in transaction value. Customs value includes the costs of packing, commission and brokerage, and royalty and license fees. Items that are not included in the customs valuation include freight charges; charges incurred subsequent to import; buying commissions; charges for construction, erection, assembly, maintenance, and technical assistance; and finance charges. However, these items are excludable only if they are separately listed and actually paid. One advantage of the EU tariff is that it is fully harmonized in the area of import licensing. The single tariff structure known as *Taric* provides rules for determining whether an import license is required for a particular good.[15] Note that most EU members also maintain their own country lists of goods requiring an import license.[16]

Drawback of Customs Duties

Drawback is a form of tax relief in which a lawfully collected customs duty is refunded or remitted wholly or in part because of the particular use made of the

---

14. See EU Regulation 2913/92, arts. 29–33.
15. *Taric* is the abbreviation for "Tarif Intégré de la Communauté" or "Integrated Tariff of the Community."
16. Information on import forms for the European Union is contained in Title VII of EU Regulation 2454/93 and Title III of EU Regulation 2913/92.

commodity on which the duty was collected. U.S. firms that import materials or components that they process or assemble for reexport may obtain drawback refunds of all duties paid on the imported merchandise, less 1 percent to cover customs costs. This practice encourages U.S. exports by permitting exporters to compete in foreign markets without the handicap of including in their sales prices the duties paid on imported components.

The U.S. **Trade and Tariff Act of 1984** revised and expanded drawbacks.[17] Under existing regulations, several types of drawback have been authorized, but only three are of interest to most manufacturers. First, if articles manufactured in the United States by using imported merchandise are exported, then the duties paid on the imported merchandise used may be refunded as a drawback. Second, if both imported merchandise and domestic merchandise of the same kind and quality are used to manufacture articles, some of which are exported, then duties paid on the imported merchandise are refundable as a drawback, regardless of whether that merchandise was used in the exported articles.

Finally, if articles of foreign origin imported for consumption are exported from the United States or are destroyed under the supervision of Customs within three years of the date of importation, in the same condition as when imported and without being "used" in the United States, then duties paid on the imported merchandise are refundable as a drawback. Incidental operations on the merchandise, such as testing, cleaning, repacking, or inspection, are not considered "uses" of the article. To obtain drawback, the U.S. firm must file a claim at a Customs port office with a drawback unit. The claim and all supporting documentation generally must be filed within three years of exportation or destruction of the goods.[18]

U.S. Foreign Trade Zones

Exporters should also consider the customs privileges of U.S. foreign (free) trade zones. These zones are domestic U.S. sites that are considered outside U.S. customs territory and are available for activities that might otherwise be carried on overseas for customs reasons. For export operations, the zones offer accelerated export status for purposes of excise tax rebates and customs drawback. For import and reexport activities, no customs duties, federal excise taxes, or state or local ad valorem taxes are charged on foreign goods moved into foreign trade zones unless and until the goods, or products made from them, are officially moved into the United States. This means that the use of zones can be profitable for operations involving foreign dutiable materials and components being assembled or produced here for reexport. In addition, quota restrictions do not ordinarily apply.

There are now 240 approved foreign trade zones in port communities throughout the United States. The value of the merchandise utilizing these zones exceeds $225 billion. These facilities are available for operations involving storage, repacking, inspection, exhibition, assembly, manufacturing, and other processing.

http://
List of world's free trade zones with links to government agencies: **http://www. escapeartist.com/ftz/ ftz_index.html.**

---

17.   See 19 U.S.C. § 1313 (2000). See also 19 C.F.R. §§ 191.21-191.28 & 191.71-191.76 (2004).
18.   For a thorough discussion of drawbacks and procedures applicable to the filing of drawback claims, see generally U.S. Customs Service, *Drawback: A Refund for Certain Exports* (2002).

Information about the zones is available from the Foreign-Trade Zones Board of the International Trade Administration.

Country of Origin

The modern trend is to use resources in a number of locations in the manufacture of goods. The global marketplace includes the global manufacture of goods. Globalization presents problems in determining the country of origin for a good that is a product of processes that take place in different countries. The country of origin of a good is used to determine the applicable tariff rate and whether any quantitative restrictions are relevant. For example, a product of a less developed country is often given a reduced tariff rate under the GSP. Lower tariffs and restrictions are also available for goods produced within a free trade area. Thus, the NAFTA provides a unique set of "country of origin" rules to determine if a good is to be considered a North American product.

Country-specific or industry-specific restrictions like antidumping duties, quotas, and voluntary restraint agreements depend on the determination of the country of origin. Unfortunately, country of origin determinations can be complicated and uncertain for a number of reasons. First, country of origin rules generally come from national import laws. Thus, individual countries have used different criteria and have varied in their interpretations. Second, the rise of the global marketplace for goods, services, and raw materials, along with the development of global corporations, has resulted in products being manufactured in different stages in different countries with component parts coming from all over the world. The true country of origin is often difficult to determine.

Country of origin rules are also used to conform to import laws pertaining to the labeling of products manufactured, produced, assembled, or made from materials from different countries. A number of methods have been developed to make this determination. **Substantial transformation** is considered the primary test in country of origin determinations and is the one adopted under U.S. law. Under this approach, the country of origin is the last country in which a good or product was substantially transformed. A substantial transformation occurs when a product is changed into a new or different product. For example, if a good has changed from a producer good to a consumer good, a substantial transformation has occurred.

Substantial transformation has been defined as a transformation in which a good is "manufactured into a new and different article, having a distinctive name, character, or use from that of the original article."[19] Factors often utilized in applying this test include whether the good went through a tariff classification change, the irreversibility of the transforming process and the length of time that it will last, the amount of value added because of the transformation, and the complexity of the processing operation (including changes in mechanical and chemical properties). For example, the greater the value added, the more likely that a substantial transformation has occurred.

http://

NAFTA Secretariat: **http://www.nafta-sec-alena.org/DefaultSite/index.html.** See also NAFTA Customs Web site: **http://www.customs.ustreas.gov/nafta/.** Click the "United States link for information on rules of origin and valuation matters."

---

19.   *Ferrostaal Metals Corp. v. United States*, 664 F. Supp. 535, 537 (Ct. Int'l Trade 1987) (quoting *Anheuser-Busch Brewing Corp. v. United States*, 207 U.S. 556 (1908)).

An alternative method to determine country of origin is to perform a value-added analysis. The **value-added test** is based on the use of percentages, either of the value added or percentage of component parts coming from imported materials, to determine the country of origin. Used in the European Union, this method was adopted under NAFTA for goods transported from one NAFTA country to another. NAFTA's country of origin rules use the value-added test as part of a multi-step approach, depending on the type of product being imported. In general, nonregional (non-NAFTA) materials or components need to be sufficiently transformed to result in a tariff classification change.

In some areas, not only do nonregional goods have to be substantially transformed but also the final end product needs to contain a specified percentage of regional (NAFTA) content (value-added). The value-added percentage applied under NAFTA varies according to the type of good. Automobiles, for example, are required to have a regional content equal to 62.5 percent or more of NAFTA-originating materials and labor. A number of problems are associated with the value-added method. First, it penalizes lesser-developed countries because of their low costs of labor and raw materials. Second, multinational enterprises may manipulate transfer pricing among their affiliated companies to reduce the value of imported materials in order to avoid tariff duties or to ensure a certain country of origin designation.[20]

The **specified processes test** expressly lists the types of processes or operations that are considered to confer country of origin status. However, this test has not been used comprehensively. Instead, it has been used in a piecemeal fashion, primarily by the European Union, Japan, Norway, and Switzerland, to target certain products.

The final method of origin determination is the **change in tariff classification** approach. This test bases country of origin status upon any change in a product that results in a change in its tariff classification. Tariff classifications are almost universally affixed with the Harmonized Commodity Description and Coding System. This classification system has been enacted in the United States in the Harmonized Tariff Schedule. The most recent attempt at harmonizing country of origin rules is the **Agreement on Rules of Origin** of GATT. This agreement adopts the change in tariff classification as the primary method to determine origin. However, negotiations are ongoing, and no final agreement with respect to the harmonization of the rules of origin of WTO members has yet been reached.

In conjunction with the Origin Agreement, the WCO **Technical Committee on Rules of Origin** and the WTO **Committee on Rules of Origin** have been established to interpret the rules. The Origin Agreement also emphasizes the importance of transparency. It requires all WTO countries to publish their nation's origin rules and applications of their rules. It also requires members to give a **binding assessment** to anyone who requests an advanced determination of origin. The binding assessment must then be honored for a period of three years for all comparable goods or imports.

U.S. Customs administers a number of laws that revolve around the country of origin of imported goods. These laws include those relating to marking requirements,

---

20. See Joseph A. LaNasa III, "Rules of Origin and the Uruguay Round's Effectiveness in Harmonizing and Regulating Them," 90 *American Journal of International Law* 625 (1996).

qualification for trade preferences under a free trade agreement, application of antidumping duties and quota restrictions, and granting of a special duty status for tariff reductions. The country of origin determinations may vary under the different statutes. Therefore, the same good can be considered from Country A for purposes of marking and from Country B for purposes of assessing a duty. The next section explores the application of country of origin rules to national marking requirements.

Marking Requirements

U.S. law requires that the country of origin must be marked on all imported goods. This **marking requirement** is found in Section 304(a) of the Tariff Act of 1930. It states that "every article of foreign origin imported into the United States shall be marked in a conspicuous place in such manner as to indicate to an ultimate purchaser the English name of the country of origin."[21] Civil actions pertaining to marking requirements are heard in the Court of International Trade. There are exceptions to the marking requirements. For example, goods that are incapable of being marked, such as crude substances, personal goods, and goods not native to the United States, need not be marked.

A key issue in determining the type of marking necessary to comply with the Act is defining the **ultimate purchaser**. Customs regulations define the ultimate purchaser as "the last person in the United States who will receive the article in the form in which it is imported."[22] Therefore, if the imported item is used in a manufacturing process, then the manufacturer is the ultimate purchaser. The manufacturing process must result in a substantial transformation of the article for this to be the case. If the identity of the article remains essentially the same after the manufacturing process, then the user or consumer who uses the article after the process is regarded as the ultimate purchaser. The Tariff Act provides severe punishment, including fines and imprisonment, for anyone destroying, removing, or altering any mark required under the Act. In addition, anyone importing unmarked items is subject to civil penalties, including an additional 10 percent ad valorem duty.[23]

Marking requirements vary widely from country to country. NAFTA, for example, includes a number of marking provisions. Formulas are provided to determine whether a good was produced in a NAFTA country in order to take advantage of the lower tariff rates between the United States, Canada, and Mexico. The labeling of a product regarding its country of origin may mean different things, depending on the law or the test being applied. The use of the label "Made in the USA" may vary, depending on the appropriate regulations. NAFTA defines something made in a NAFTA country, whether in the United States, Canada, or Mexico, as something in which at least 55 percent of the labor and component parts were supplied by a NAFTA country.[24] In contrast, the U.S. Federal Trade Commission states that the "Made in the USA" label should be used in advertising only when the product is "whole or in substantial part of domestic origin."[25]

21. 19 U.S.C. § 1304(a) (2000).
22. 10 C.F.R. § 134.1(d) (2003).
23. See 19 U.S.C. § 1304(i) (2000).
24. NAFTA's marking requirements are set forth in Annex 311 to the agreement.
25. 15 U.S.C. § 45a (2000).

Customs Modernization Act

The **Customs Modernization and Informed Compliance Act** has implemented a number of changes to U.S. customs law.[26] Prior to its enactment, Customs was primarily responsible for classifying and valuing imported products. Legal responsibility in these areas is now entirely upon the importer of the goods. The importer is under a duty of *reasonable care* to correctly classify and value the goods being imported. This duty cannot legally be delegated to a customs broker. The importer remains liable for any misclassification or undervaluation.

The necessity of accuracy on the part of the importer in the classification and valuation of products cannot be overstated. U.S. law provides that an importer who fails to exercise reasonable care to ensure the accuracy of disclosures with respect to these variables in its importation documentation may be penalized in an amount equal to twice the lost duty (but no more than the domestic value of the goods at issue) or, if no duty was lost as a result of the misstatement, an amount up to 20 percent of the dutiable value of the goods. Penalties for more serious misconduct are substantially higher. For example, an importer who acts in a grossly negligent manner in wanton disregard of the accuracy of the disclosures with respect to these variables may incur penalties in an amount double to those imposed for merely negligent conduct. Importers engaging in actual fraud—specifically, intentional misstatements of material facts—may incur fines up to 100 percent of the value of the goods in question and potential criminal liability of up to two years in prison for each violation.[27]

The importer's secondary responsibility under the Modernization Act is to implement a proper record-keeping system.[28] Although U.S. law requires Customs to determine the duties to be assessed on imports, the process known as liquidation, within one year of their entry, importers are required to maintain records of import transactions for five years after entry and produce such documents to Customs on demand.[29] Failure to maintain adequate records that substantiate the importer's customs declarations can result in substantial penalties. Willful violations are punishable by fines equal to the lesser of $100,000 or 75 percent of the value of the merchandise. Negligent failure to comply with the record-keeping requirement is punishable by a fine equal to the lesser of $10,000 or 40 percent of the value of the imports.[30]

Another recent innovation is the development and implementation of the **Automated Commercial Environment (ACE)**. The current Customs import system, the Automated Commercial System, was designed in 1984. Customs determined that the system could not meet the requirements placed on it by the increase in trade and began work on ACE in August 2001. Development and implementation of ACE became more urgent with Customs' increased responsibilities as a result of its reorganization and relocation within the Department of Homeland Security. When fully implemented, ACE will provide the international trade community, including Customs officials, importers, distributors, and financial institutions, with an integrated and fully automated information system to collect, process, and analyze import and export data. ACE's goals include greater efficiency and lower costs in the entry of goods into the United States as Customs ends its port-by-port processing program.

http://
United States Automated Export System at U.S. Customs Web site: **http://www.customs.treas.gov.**

---

26.   Pub. L. No. 103-182, 107 Stat. 2170 (1993).

27.   See 19 U.S.C. § 1592(a-f) (2000).

28.   See ibid. § 1508(a).

29.   The U.S. statute requiring Customs to liquidate imports can be found at 19 U.S.C. § 1504(a) (2000). The statute requiring document retention by importers can be found at 19 U.S.C. § 1508(c)(1) (2000).

30.   See ibid. § 1509(g)(2)(A-B) (2000).

EXHIBIT 6.2   *Overview of ACE (Automated Commercial Environment)*

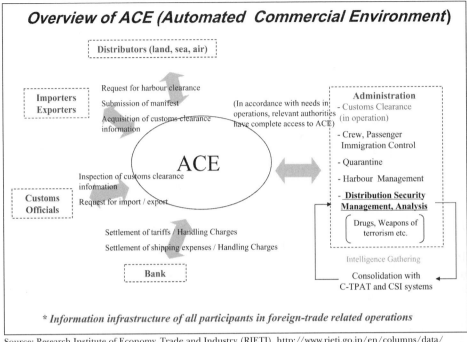

Source: Research Institute of Economy, Trade and Industry (RIETI), http://www.rieti.go.jp/en/columns/data/a01_0085_01.pdf

According to Customs, ACE will enhance border security, increase access to data, reduce paperwork, increase the flow of trade, simplify and expedite the release of cargo, and provide interested parties with convenient online access to data. Exhibit 6.2 provides an overview of ACE's operation upon its implementation.

Foreign National Import Restrictions, Requirements, and Standards

http://
U.S. State Department-
Country Commercial
Guides: **http://www.
state.gov.**

A good source for general information on import restrictions and requirements of foreign countries is the country commercial guides published by the U.S. and Foreign Commercial Service and the U.S. Department of State. The 2004 country guide for Mexico, for example, provides information on tariffs and import licenses and documentation. It notes that Mexico embarked on a progressive and scheduled reduction of tariffs when the NAFTA took effect on January 1, 1994. As a result, the average tariff on U.S. goods entering Mexico is 0.1 percent, with 80 percent of such goods entering the country duty-free.

However, the guide also identifies numerous obstacles and expenses U.S. importers will encounter in attempting to enter the Mexican marketplace. For example, NAFTA's duty-free benefits to U.S. importers are somewhat blunted by the fact that Mexico has free trade agreements with thirty-two other states, including the European Union and ten states in Latin America. Free trade negotiations are ongoing with several other states, including Argentina, Brazil, Panama, and, most notably, Japan. NAFTA's benefits are further impaired by the Sectoral Promotion Program (PROSEC), which reduces tariffs to between zero and 5 percent on a wide range of imports deemed necessary to the growth of Mexico's export manufacturing sector. Twenty different industrial sectors and 16,000 tariff line items are affected by

PROSEC. As a result of these free trade agreements and PROSEC, many of U.S. companies' strongest international trade competitors enjoy equal or nearly equal access to the Mexican market.

In addition, Mexico imposes a value-added tax on most sales transactions, including sales of foreign products. This tax ranges from 10 percent for products remaining in border regions to 15 percent for products destined for Mexico's interior. Luxury goods are subject to an additional 5 percent tax. Finally, special taxes as high as 110 percent are imposed on certain products such as alcoholic beverages, tobacco products, and nonalcoholic beverages containing sweeteners other than cane sugar. These additional costs must be factored into all decisions regarding entry and participation in the Mexican marketplace.

Given these taxes, the calculation of transaction value for imports is crucial. Mexico adheres to the NAFTA rule that calculates import duty on the basis of the U.S. plant value of the product as stated in the invoice, plus U.S. freight charges to the border and any other separately listed costs paid by the importer, such as packing. However, 200 specially identified products are subject to "minimum estimated prices" to combat fraudulent undervaluation for customs purposes. These products include alcoholic beverages, apparel, chemicals, footwear, steel, appliances, and some agricultural products. Importers of such products must post a guarantee representing any difference in duties and taxes if the declared customs value is less than the established reference price. Guarantees are usually in the form of cash deposits or lines of credit established with authorized banks. These banks charge significant fees to open, manage, and close accounts. Mexican customs authorities have six months to determine whether to release the guarantee or initiate a formal investigation of the declared customs value. Exemptions exist for highly capitalized importers. Those importers not qualifying for an exemption may nonetheless expedite the entry process by obtaining certification of their invoices by their local chamber of commerce.

The country commercial guide for Mexico also identifies necessary documentation to be completed during the course of the importation process. These documents include the basic Mexican import document, the *pedimiento de importacion*, as well as a commercial invoice in Spanish, a bill of lading, other customs valuation documents if necessary, and documents evidencing compliance with Mexican product safety and performance regulations. Products qualifying for duty-free treatment pursuant to NAFTA must use the NAFTA certificate of origin to receive preferential treatment. In addition, an import license may be necessary for certain sensitive products such as weapons, ammunition, leather and fur products, meat products, medical equipment, pharmaceuticals, and processed foods. The country commercial guide identifies the appropriate Mexican government agencies responsible for the issuance of licenses with respect to these products. In any event, the guide advises potential importers that the participation of a professional customs broker is required unless the importer possesses such accreditation. The guide warns potential importers that Mexican customs laws are strictly enforced, and errors in paperwork may result in fines and potential confiscation of merchandise as contraband.

Standards Requirements

The existence of nonharmonized standards for similar products or technologies in different countries or regions can contribute to "technical barriers to trade." Standards are technical specifications or other precise criteria to be used as rules, guidelines, or definitions of characteristics to ensure that materials, products, processes, and services are fit for their intended purposes. All countries have enacted requirements that certain goods or services must meet their standards before being allowed entry. These country-specific standards are not always transparent and in the past may have acted as barriers to trade.

In more recent times, there have been regional efforts to harmonize product standards. In the European Union, standards harmonization has allowed free movement of goods within the Union. In 1992, the European Union developed voluntary standards that allow companies to affix an **eco-label** to their products. An eco-label is a voluntary mark awarded by the European Union to producers who can show that their products are significantly less harmful to the environment than similar products. Several products are eligible for eco-labels, including cleaning products, dishwashers, footwear, personal computers, televisions, textiles, and washing machines. In 1993, the EU developed the **CE Mark**. This "umbrella" label warrants that the good bearing the mark meets all relevant EU directives relating to health, safety, and environmental protection for that type of product. All manufacturers in the EU and abroad must meet the CE Mark requirements to market their products in the Union. Once a manufacturer has received a CE Mark for a given product, it may market the product with the attached mark throughout the EU without further modifications. One of the difficulties confronting importers is the absence of a comprehensive list of products subject to the CE Mark requirement.

The harmonization of product standards is also a goal of NAFTA. Chapter IX of NAFTA permits the United States, Canada, and Mexico to adopt national standards, including protective measures relating to human, animal, or plant life or health, the environment, and consumers. However, these standards must be designed to achieve the states' legitimate objectives and cannot create unnecessary obstacles to trade. NAFTA members are encouraged to adopt international standards where available. In any event, the United States, Canada, and Mexico are to accord national treatment with respect to the application of standards to imported goods.

The application of these rules has met with mixed success. Standards organizations in the United States and Canada have developed joint standards in several areas. For example, the Canadian Standards Association (CSA) and the U.S. Air Conditioning and Refrigeration Institute have harmonized performance requirements for air conditioners and numerous types of heat pumps. CSA and Underwriters Laboratories have developed common electrical safety standards for these products, as well as for refrigerant motor-compressors. Underwriters Laboratories has also received accreditation in Canada. Finally, the CSA has been recognized by the U.S. Occupational Safety and Health Administration as a nationally recognized testing laboratory. As a result of this recognition and the recognition of U.S. testing and certification organizations by Canada's national standards organization, the Standards Council of Canada, U.S. manufacturers can gain product approval for the United States and Canada from one source. This cooperation eliminates the time and expense of pursuing separate certification for each market.

By contrast, the United States has not been as successful in harmonization of its standards with Mexico. Poorly drafted regulations, inadequate communication between responsible government agencies, and the lack of transparency have created barriers to the entry of U.S. products into the Mexican marketplace. Mexico currently maintains an estimated 730 Normas Oficiales Mexicanas (NOMs) utilizing the harmonized tariff system. Compliance with NOMs is mandatory, and importers must obtain a certificate of compliance prior to the introduction of their products into the country.

Furthermore, Mexico maintains in excess of 6,000 voluntary product standards known as Normas Mexicanas (NMXs). Although voluntary, as their name implies, NMXs become mandatory if they are mentioned in a NOM. This system has caused confusion, delay, and expense among importers seeking access to the Mexican marketplace and has complicated efforts to achieve harmonization. As noted in Mexico's country commercial guide, although the number of trade disruptions concerning standards has decreased in the past six years, "serious disruptions still occur."

Internationally, the 1994 WTO Agreements include a framework for the harmonization of some health and safety standards. The two framework agreements are the WTO Agreement on Technical Barriers to Trade (TBT) and the WTO Agreement on Sanitary and Phytosanitary Measures (SPS). The TBT defines technical regulations as laws establishing product standards that must be met prior to sales within the enacting state. Although permissible, the TBT prohibits the application of these regulations in a manner that violates normal trade relations or national treatment. Furthermore, all technical regulations must have an underlying scientific basis. The process by which technical regulations are proposed and adopted must be transparent, and affected companies must be granted a reasonable time to adapt to changes in standards prior to their effective date. WTO member states are urged to utilize internationally recognized standards whenever possible and are encouraged to continue negotiations to achieve harmonization of technical regulations.

By contrast, the SPS applies to laws designed to protect human, animal, and plant life. SPS requires that all such laws be applied only to the extent necessary to accomplish this goal and not serve as disguised restrictions on trade. Sanitary measures must not be applied in a manner as to defeat the principles of normal trade relations or national treatment. Furthermore, as in the TBT, the SPS requires that all sanitary measures be based on scientific evidence. Inspections conducted by states to ensure compliance with applicable sanitary measures must be performed in a fair, reasonable, and timely manner.

In the area of service standards, the General Agreement on Trade in Services (GATS) requires that all countries review their laws so that "qualification requirements and procedures, technical standards, and licensing requirements do not constitute unnecessary barriers to trade in services." Any such requirements should be "based on objective and transparent criteria." In the area of professional services, each country "shall provide for adequate procedures to verify the competence of professionals" of any other country.

Historically, the International Labor Organization (ILO) has been active in developing international labor standards. The ILO was established in 1919 and became a specialized agency of the United Nations in 1946. It seeks to promote social justice in areas such as employment, pay, health, working conditions, and freedom of association among workers. It is headquartered in Geneva, Switzerland.

http://
European Commission-
Standards: **http://www.
europa.eu.int/comm/
dgs/health_consumer/
library/surveys/sur16_
en.html.**

Export Regulations

The primary federal law concerning exports is the **Export Administration Act (EAA)**.[31] Adopted in 1979, the purpose of the EAA was to balance the need to facilitate growth in export trade with national security interests. The EAA provides two

http://
Bureau of Industry
and Security: **http://
www.bxa.doc.gov.**

---

31. See 50 U.S.C. App. §§ 2401-20 (2000).

reasons for the need for U.S. export controls. Initially, export controls are to be implemented to prevent significant contributions to the military potential of any state that would prove detrimental to U.S. national security interests. Second, export controls are to further U.S. foreign policy objectives or fulfill international obligations.

The EAA expired on June 30, 1994. Its substantive provisions and related regulations were extended in Executive Order 12924, issued on August 19, 1994, by President Clinton, who concluded that the expiration of the EAA and resultant absence of export controls presented an unusual and extraordinary threat to U.S. national security, foreign policy, and the economy. President George W. Bush extended the EAA and its regulations by Executive Order 13222, issued on August 17, 2001. The EAA is now extended annually by presidential notice published in the *Federal Register.*

The EAA and its regulations are applicable to four separate types of transactions. Initially, the EAA applies to the export of commodities and technical data from the United States. Second, the EAA is applicable to the reexport of U.S.-origin commodities and technical data to foreign countries. The export and reexport from a foreign country of products with U.S.-origin parts is also subject to the EAA. Finally, the export and reexport from a foreign country of products based on U.S. technical data is governed by the EAA.

The EAA establishes several grounds for the imposition of export controls.[32] For example, the president may impose export controls for national security reasons. The president enjoys broad discretion in this regard, and his decision does not need to satisfy mandatory criteria or be based on extensive findings of fact. The president may also impose export controls for foreign policy reasons. To impose an export control on the basis of foreign policy considerations, the president must demonstrate that (1) the control is likely to achieve its intended foreign policy purpose, (2) the control is compatible with U.S. foreign policy objectives, (3) the reaction of other countries is not likely to render the control ineffective, (4) the effect of the control on U.S. industry does not exceed the foreign policy benefits, (5) the control is capable of effective enforcement, (6) adequate consultation has occurred with industry, Congress, and U.S. allies, and (7) all less restrictive alternatives have been exhausted. The president may also impose export controls to prevent the excessive drain of scarce materials. Export controls are also available as tools in antiterrorism and nuclear nonproliferation efforts.

The EAA also makes it illegal for U.S. companies to comply with or support any boycott, primary or secondary, fostered or imposed by a foreign country against a U.S. ally. A primary boycott is a refusal to engage in direct trade with a target state. By contrast, a secondary boycott is a refusal to engage in trade with states that directly trade with a target state.

Primary responsibility for the administration and enforcement of U.S. export controls resides with the **Bureau of Industry and Security (BIS)**. Located within the Department of Commerce, BIS is the successor to the former Bureau of Export Administration, which it replaced in April 2002. The mission of BIS is to "advance U.S. national security, foreign policy and economic interests." This mission is advanced, in part, through regulating the export of sensitive goods and

---

32. See ibid. §§ 2404-07.

technologies and the enforcement of export control and antiboycott laws. BIS has four separate bureaus. Export Administration has four offices: nonproliferation and treaty compliance, national security and technology transfer, exporter services, and strategic industry and economic security. Export Enforcement also has four offices: export enforcement, intelligence and field support, analysis, and antiboycott compliance. Other BIS offices include the Office of Chief Counsel for Industry and Security and the Office of International Programs.

The first question every U.S. exporter must answer is whether the merchandise it seeks to send abroad requires a BIS export license. Licenses are necessary for a relatively small percentage of exports. License requirements are dependent upon the technical characteristics of the merchandise, its destination, its end use, and the identity of the end user. The exporter must determine whether the merchandise has a specific **Export Control Classification Number (ECCN)**. The ECCN describes a particular good or type of good and shows the controls imposed on its export. ECCNs are set forth on the **Commerce Control List**, which has ten broad categories of goods: nuclear materials, materials, chemicals, microorganisms and toxins, materials processing, electronics, computers, telecommunications, sensors and lasers, and navigation, marine, and propulsion systems. These ten categories are further subdivided into five product groups: equipment, assemblies and components; test, inspection, and production equipment; material; software; and technology.

Once the exporter has obtained an ECCN, the merchandise must be cross-referenced with the **Commerce Country Chart**. The ECCN and Commerce Country Chart define goods subject to export controls based on technical specifications and the country of ultimate destination. Even assuming that the goods do not normally require a license, based on the ECCN and Commerce Country Chart, a license may still be required, depending on the identity of the ultimate recipient. Certain individuals and organizations may be prohibited from receiving U.S. exports entirely or may receive them only if they possess an appropriate license. So that exporters can identify these entities and individuals, BIS maintains the Treasury Department's Specially Designated Nationals and Blocked Persons List and an unverified list of firms for which BIS was unable to complete an end-use check.

Finally, the exporter must determine the end use of the product. Some end uses are permissible, but others may require a license or are prohibited. For example, exports of items for purposes associated with the proliferation of weapons of mass destruction and related missile technology are prohibited without express authorization.

The United States controls the exportation of goods by issuing three types of export licenses. The **general license** is a grant of authority to all exporters for certain types of goods. Exporters do not have to apply for a general license because authorization to export is automatically granted through the EAA and its associated administrative regulations.[33] Goods qualifying for a general license are exported under the designation "no license required" (NLR). This designation is applicable when the goods are not on the Commerce Control List or are on the list but not required to be licensed upon application of the Commerce Country Chart. However, the exporter will have to provide a **Shipper's Export**

---

33. See ibid. § 2403(a)(3).

Declaration (SED) (Exhibit 6.3) and may have to provide a **Destination Control Statement**. Exporters are required to place this statement on commercial invoices and bills of lading for most export sales. These statements alert foreign

EXHIBIT 6.3 *Shipper's Export Declaration*

U.S. DEPARTMENT OF COMMERCE – Economics and Statistics Administration – U.S. CENSUS BUREAU – BUREAU OF EXPORT ADMINISTRATION

FORM **7525-V** (7-18-2003) **SHIPPER'S EXPORT DECLARATION** OMB No. 0607-0152

1a. U.S. PRINCIPAL PARTY IN INTEREST (USPPI)(Complete name and address)

ZIP CODE

2. DATE OF EXPORTATION

3. TRANSPORTATION REFERENCE NO.

b. USPPI'S EIN (IRS) OR ID NO.

c. PARTIES TO TRANSACTION ☐ Related ☐ Non-related

4a. ULTIMATE CONSIGNEE *(Complete name and address)*

b. INTERMEDIATE CONSIGNEE *(Complete name and address)*

5a. FORWARDING AGENT *(Complete name and address)*

5b. FORWARDING AGENT'S EIN (IRS) NO.

6. POINT (STATE) OF ORIGIN OR FTZ NO.

7. COUNTRY OF ULTIMATE DESTINATION

8. LOADING PIER *(Vessel only)*	**9.** METHOD OF TRANSPORTATION *(Specify)*	**14.** CARRIER IDENTIFICATION CODE	**15.** SHIPMENT REFERENCE NO.
10. EXPORTING CARRIER	**11.** PORT OF EXPORT	**16.** ENTRY NUMBER	**17.** HAZARDOUS MATERIALS ☐ Yes ☐ No
12. PORT OF UNLOADING *(Vessel and air only)*	**13.** CONTAINERIZED *(Vessel only)* ☐ Yes ☐ No	**18.** IN BOND CODE	**19.** ROUTED EXPORT TRANSACTION ☐ Yes ☐ No

20. SCHEDULE B DESCRIPTION OF COMMODITIES *(Use columns 22–24)*

D/F or M (21)	SCHEDULE B NUMBER (22)	QUANTITY – SCHEDULE B UNIT(S) (23)	SHIPPING WEIGHT (Kilograms) (24)	VIN/PRODUCT NUMBER/ VEHICLE TITLE NUMBER (25)	VALUE (U.S. dollars, omit cents) (Selling price or cost if not sold) (26)

27. LICENSE NO./LICENSE EXCEPTION SYMBOL/AUTHORIZATION

28. ECCN *(When required)*

29. Duly authorized officer or employee

The USPPI authorizes the forwarder named above to act as forwarding agent for export control and customs purposes.

30. I certify that all statements made and all information contained herein are true and correct and that I have read and understand the instructions for preparation of this document, set forth in the **"Correct Way to Fill Out the Shipper's Export Declaration."** I understand that civil and criminal penalties, including forfeiture and sale, may be imposed for making false or fraudulent statements herein, failing to provide the requested information or for violation of U.S. laws on exportation (13 U.S.C. Sec. 305; 22 U.S.C. Sec. 401; 18 U.S.C. Sec. 1001; 50 U.S.C. App. 2410).

Signature	**Confidential –** Shipper's Export Declarations (or any successor document) wherever located, shall be exempt from public disclosure unless the Secretary determines that such exemption would be contrary to the national interest (Title 13, Chapter 9, Section 301 (g)).
Title	Export shipments are subject to inspection by U.S. Customs Service and/or Office of Export Enforcement.
Date	**31.** AUTHENTICATION *(When required)*
Telephone No. (Include Area Code)	E-mail address

Clear fields 1 to 19

Clear Fields 20 to 26

Clear Fields 27 to 31

Clear all fields

This form may be printed by private parties provided it conforms to the official form. For sale by the Superintendent of Documents, Government Printing Office, Washington, DC 20402, and local Customs District Directors. The **"Correct Way to Fill Out the Shipper's Export Declaration"** is available from the U.S. Census Bureau, Washington, DC 20233.

EXHIBIT 6.3   *(continued)*

1. **(a) U.S. Principal Party In Interest (USPPI)**—Provide the name and address of the USPPI. The USPPI is the person in the United States that receives the primary benefit, monetary or otherwise, of the export transaction. Generally that person is the U.S. seller, manufacturer, order party, or foreign entity.

   (b) USPPI Employer Identification Number (EIN) or ID Number—Enter the USPPI's Internal Revenue Service Employer Identification Number (EIN) or Social Security Number (SSN) if no EIN has been assigned. If an EIN or SSN is not available a border crossing number, passport number, or a Customs identification number must be reported.

   (c) Parties To Transaction—Indicate if this is a *related* or *non-related* party transaction. A related party transaction is a transaction between a USPPI and a foreign consignee, (e.g., parent company or sister company), where there is at least 10 percent ownership of each by the same U.S. or foreign person or business enterprise.

2. **Date of Exportation**—Enter the date the merchandise is scheduled to leave the United States for all methods of transportation.

3. **Transportation Reference Number**—Report the booking number for ocean shipments. The booking number is the reservation number assigned by the carrier to hold space on the vessel for the cargo being shipped. For air shipments the air waybill number must be reported.

4. **(a) Ultimate Consignee**—Enter the name and address of the foreign party actually receiving the merchandise for the designated end-use or the party so designated on the export license.

   (b) Intermediate Consignee—Enter the name and address of the party in a foreign country who makes delivery of the merchandise to the ultimate consignee or the party so named on the export license.

5. **Forwarding Agent**—Enter the name and address of the forwarding or other agent authorized by a principal party in interest.

   (b) Forwarding Agent Employer Identification Number (EIN) or ID Number—Enter the forwarding agent's Internal Revenue Service Employer Identification Number (EIN).

6. **Point (State) of Origin or Foreign Trade Zone (FTZ) Number**

   (a) If from a FTZ enter the FTZ number for exports leaving the FTZ, otherwise enter the:

   (b) two-digit U.S. Postal Service abbreviation of the state in which the merchandise actually starts its journey to the port of export, or

7. **Country of Ultimate Destination**—Enter the country in which the merchandise is to be consumed, further processed, or manufactured; the final country of destination as known to the exporter at the time of shipment; or the country of ultimate destination as shown on the export license. Two-digit (alpha character) International Standards Organization (ISO) codes may also be used.

8. **Loading Pier**—(For vessel shipments only) Enter the number or name of the pier at which the merchandise is laden aboard the exporting vessel.

9. **Method of Transportation**—Enter the method of transportation by which the merchandise is exported (or exits the border of the United States). Specify the method of transportation by name, such as, vessel, air, rail, truck, etc.

10. **Exporting Carrier**—Enter the name of the carrier transporting the merchandise out of the United States. For vessel shipments, give the name of the vessel.

11. **Port of Export**
    For Vessel and Air Shipments—Enter the name of the U.S. Customs port where the merchandise is loaded on the carrier (airplane or ocean vessel) that is taking the merchandise out of the United States.

12. **Foreign Port of Unloading**—For vessel shipments between the United States and foreign countries, enter the foreign port and country at which the merchandise will be unloaded from the exporting carrier.

13. **Containerized**—(For vessel shipments only) Check the **YES** box for cargo originally booked as containerized cargo and for cargo that has been placed in containers at the vessel operator's option.

14. **Carrier Identification Code**—Enter the 4-character Standard Carrier Alpha Code (SCAC) of the carrier for vessel, rail and truck shipments, or the 2- or 3-character International Air Transport Association (IATA) Code of the carrier for air shipments. In a consolidated shipment, if the ultimate carrier is unknown, the consolidator's carrier ID code may be reported.

15. **Shipment Reference Number**—Enter the unique reference number assigned by the filer of the SED for identification purposes. For example, report an invoice number, bill of lading or air waybill number, internal file number or so forth.

16. **Entry Number**—Enter the Import Entry Number when the export transaction is used as proof of export for import transactions, such as In-Bond, Temporary Import Bond or Drawbacks and so forth.

17. **Hazardous Materials**—Check the appropriate "Yes" or "No" indicator that identifies the shipment as hazardous as defined by the Department of Transportation.

18. **In Bond Code**—Report one of the 2-character In-Bond Codes listed in Part IV of Appendix C of the FTSR (15 CFR Part 30) to indicate whether the shipment is being transported under bond.

19. **Routed Export Transaction**—Check the appropriate "Yes" or "No" indicator that identifies the transaction as a routed export transaction. A routed export transaction is where the foreign principal party in interest authorizes a U.S. forwarding or other agent to export the merchandise out of the United States.

20. **Schedule B Description of Commodities**—Enter a sufficient description of the commodity as to permit verification of the Schedule B Commodity Number or the commodity description as shown on the validated export license. Include marks, numbers, or other identification shown on the packages and the numbers and kinds of packages (boxes, barrels, baskets, etc.)

21. **"D" (Domestic), "F" (Foreign) or M (Foreign Military Sales)**

    (a) *Domestic exports* (D)—merchandise that is grown, produced, or manufactured in the United States.

    (b) *Foreign exports* (F)—merchandise that has entered the United States and is being re-exported in the same condition as when imported.

    (c) *Foreign Military Sales* (M)—exports of merchandise that are sold under the foreign military sales program.

22. **Schedule B Number**—Enter the commercial description of the commodity being exported and the ten-digit commodity number as provided in Schedule B-Statistical Classification of Domestic and Foreign Commodities Exported from the United States.

23. **Quantity**—Report whole unit(s) as specified in the Schedule B commodity classification code.

24. **Shipping Weight** (kilograms)—(For all methods of transportation) Enter the gross shipping weight in kilograms

25. **VIN/Product Number/Vehicle Title Number**—(For used self-propelled vehicles only).

26. **Value** (U.S. dollars)—Enter the selling price or cost if not sold, including freight, insurance, and other charges to U.S. port of export, but excluding unconditional discounts and commissions (nearest whole dollar, omit cents).

27. **License No./License Exception Symbol/Authorization**—*Whenever a SED or AES record is required*:

    (a) Enter the license number on the SED or AES record when you are exporting under the authority of a Department of the Treasury, Office of Foreign Assets Control (OFAC) license or any other export license number issued by a Federal government agency.

EXHIBIT 6.3   *(continued)*

(b) Enter the correct License Exception symbol (e.g. LVS, GBS, CIV) on the SED or AES record when you are exporting under the authority of a License Exception. See § 740.1, § 740.2, and § 758.1 of the Export Administration Regulations (EAR).

(c) Enter the "No License Required" (NLR) designator when you are exporting items under the NLR provisions of the EAR when the items being exported are subject to the EAR but not listed on the Commerce Control List (CCL).

28. Export Control Classification Number (ECCN)—Whenever SED or AES record is required, you must enter the correct Export Control Classification Number (ECCN) on the SED or AES record for all exports authorized under a license or License Exception.

29. Duly authorized officer or employee—Provide the signature of the USPPI authorizing the named forwarding or agent to effect the export when such agent does not have a formal power of attorney or written authorization.

30. Signature/Certification—Provide the signature of the USPPI or authorized forwarding or other agent certifying the truth and accuracy of the information on the SED.

31. Authentication—For Customs use only.

buyers of goods and documents that diversion contrary to U.S. law is prohibited. In addition, the exporter must complete all necessary U.S. Postal Service forms if the goods are to be exported through the Postal Service.[34]

In limited instances and depending upon the applicability of the ECCN, commerce control list, and commerce country guide, an exporter must obtain an **individually validated license (IVL)** for certain products and for export to certain countries.[35] An IVL grants authority to a specific exporter to export specific products to a specific destination for a limited period of time (usually two years). BIS also may grant a **special comprehensive license (SCL)** to exporters it deems to be experienced and knowledgeable. The SCL substitutes for an IVL for shipments by exporters who participate in export and reexport transactions on a routine basis. An exporter must have adequate safeguards in place to ensure that each export and reexport meets the terms of the SCL and the requirements of the EAA. The severity of punishment for failing to obtain the appropriate export license is demonstrated in *United States v. Shetterly*.

United States v. Donald Shetterly

971 F.2d 67 (7th Cir. 1992)

Kanne, Circuit Judge. After a jury trial, Donald Shetterly was convicted of attempting to export a controlled microwave amplifier to (then) West Germany without an export license in violation of § 2410(a) of the Export Administration Act of 1979, and was sentenced to 41 months imprisonment. He now appeals his conviction and sentence.

Mr. Shetterly was introduced to Karl Mann, a West German businessman. From 1987 through 1989, Mr. Shetterly sent electronic equipment, including micro-wave amplifiers and computer software, to Mr. Mann in West Germany. In October 1988, Mr. Mann sent a letter to Mr. Shetterly requesting him to purchase an amplifier from Berkshire Technologies, Inc., of Oakland, California. Mr. Shetterly called Berkshire to inquire about the amplifier and spoke with William Lum, the president of Berkshire. The amplifier was on the Department of Commerce's **commodity control list** and therefore a validated license was required for its exportation out of the United States. Export licenses are required for exporting

---

34. To mail goods through the U.S. Postal Service, Postal Service Form 2976-A needs to be completed. It is a two-part document incorporating a "customs declaration" and "dispatch note." It requests the seller's address, addressee's address, list of contents, quantity, value, and net weight. It allows the sender to classify the materials as a commercial sample, documents, gift, or merchandise. The sender must certify the accuracy of the list of contents and that the item "does not contain any dangerous article prohibited by postal regulations." Therefore, the sender must be familiar with both U.S. export regulations and postal regulations. The "dispatch note" portion requires the declaration of customs duty and a customs stamp. The form must be filled out in English but advises that the sender "may add a translation of the contents to facilitate Customs treatment in the destination country." It also states that one's signature is a "guarantee that the particulars given are correct."

35. See 50 U.S.C. App. § 2403(a)(1-2)(2000).

certain commodities under the Export Administration Act. A general license merely requires that the commodity meets certain standards—no license application is necessary and no license document is issued.

A validated license requires the exporter to file a license application before exporting commodities that cannot be exported under a general license or with other authorization by the Office of Export Licensing. Such commodities are included in the Department of Commerce's commodity control list. See 15 C.F.R. § 799.1 Supp. 1. At the time of the offense, a validated license was required for exportation of the Berkshire amplifier because its value exceeded $5,000.00.

This case arose prior to the breakup of the former Soviet Union. In line with cold war attitudes, Mr. Lum testified that he was suspicious that the destination of the amplifier was overseas because he "had become aware of significant attempts by the Soviets to obtain the amplifier." Mr. Shetterly argues that the statement was improper because it implied that his goal was to supply technology to the Soviet Union. However, there was evidence that the technology involved was already known to the Soviets; therefore, any error was harmless.

50 U.S.C. § 2410(a) states that one who "knowingly violates or conspires to or attempts to violate any provision of the Export Administration Act, or any regulation, order or license issued thereunder" commits a crime. Mr. Shetterly contends that an exportation or attempted exportation of a controlled commodity without a license becomes a crime under § 2410(a) only when the exporter knows that a license is required. We agree with the government's assertions that specific intent is not required for a violation of § 2410(a). In order to establish that Mr. Shetterly violated § 2410(a), the government was required to prove beyond a reasonable doubt that Mr. Shetterly knowingly exported or attempted to export a controlled commodity, without obtaining the appropriate export license, in violation of 15 C.F.R. § 799.1 Supp. 1 (the commodities control list).

Finally, Mr. Shetterly argues that the district court misapplied the Sentencing Guidelines by refusing to depart below the Guidelines. Mr. Shetterly was sentenced pursuant to Guideline § 2M5.1, which provides for a base offense level of 22 "if national security or nuclear proliferation controls were invaded." One of the bases of the Export Administration Act is to protect national security. See 50 U.S.C. § 2402. Accordingly, the district judge sentenced Mr. Shetterly to 41 months of imprisonment, the minimum sentence in the applicable Guideline range. Mr. Shetterly alleges that trial counsel's petition to depart downward from the Guidelines was inadequate, and that the district court erred in failing to consider the implication of Application Note 2 of Guideline § 2M5.1, whereby a court can consider the degree to which the violation threatened a security interest of the United States, the volume of commerce involved, the extent of planning or sophistication, and whether there were multiple occurrences in determining a sentence within the Guidelines. Therefore, we must review the record to determine whether the district judge exercised his discretion in refusing to depart from the Guidelines or whether he felt that he lacked authority to depart.

The district judge's statements indicate he considered that it would no longer be illegal to export the Berkshire amplifier out of the country without a license. It is clear that the judge used his discretion in refusing to depart. Therefore, we have no jurisdiction to review his refusal to depart. AFFIRMED.

Case Highlights

- Export licenses are required for exporting certain commodities under the Export Administration Act.
- A general license requires merely that the commodity meets certain standards: No license application is necessary, and no license document is issued.
- A good that is on the Department of Commerce's Commodity Control List requires a validated license.
- Knowingly exporting or attempting to export a controlled commodity without a license is a crime.

If an export license is required, exporters must complete Form BIS-748P, a multipurpose application form, and submit it to BIS for approval.[36] The application form can be used to request authority to export or reexport or to request BIS to classify merchandise on behalf of the exporter. Export applications can be submitted online through BIS's **Simplified Network Application Process (SNAP)**. BIS reviews the merchandise in question, its destination, its end use,

---

36. See ibid. § 2409.

and the reliability of each party to the transaction. BIS may also send the application out for review by other federal agencies. The Focus on Transactions: U.S. Government Agencies with Export Control Responsibilities box lists federal agencies that may become involved in the export process and the types of goods for which they are responsible.

To expedite the application process, the exporter may have to obtain an international import certificate and/or a **Statement of Ultimate Consignee and Purchaser** (Exhibit 6.4). The former is issued by the government of importation and certifies that the goods will be disposed of in the designated country. The latter is an assurance from the purchaser that the goods will not be resold or disposed of contrary to the requirements of the export license.

A freight forwarder or customs broker may assist the exporter in preparing documentation, including these forms. However, the exporter is ultimately

http://

Tradeport is a comprehensive site on international shipping and trade: **http://www. tradeport.org.**

Focus on Transactions

U.S. Government Agencies with Export Control Responsibilities

Agency	Types of Goods
Department of Defense, Defense Threat Reduction Agency	Defense-related and dual-use technology
Department of Energy, Office of Arms Control and Nonproliferation	Nuclear technology and technical data
Department of Energy, Office of Fuels Program	Natural gas and electric power
Department of State, Directorate of Defense Trade Controls	Defense services and articles
Department of the Interior, Division of Management Authority	Endangered species
Department of the Treasury, Office of Foreign Assets Control	Enforcement of trade sanctions
Drug Enforcement Administration, International Chemical Control Unit	Chemicals used to produce controlled substances
Drug Enforcement Agency, International Drug Unit	Controlled substances
Environmental Protection Agency, Office of Solid Waste	Toxic waste
Food & Drug Administration, Import/Export	Drugs
Food & Drug Administration, Office of Compliance	Medical devices
Nuclear Regulatory Commission, Office of International Programs	Nuclear material and equipment
Patent & Trademark Office, Licensing and Review	Patent filing data

EXHIBIT 6.4   *Statement by Ultimate Consignee and Purchaser*

FORM **BIS-711** FORM APPROVED UNDER OMB CONTROL NO. 0694-0021, 0694-0093	U.S. DEPARTMENT OF COMMERCE BUREAU OF INDUSTRY AND SECURITY Information furnished herewith is subject to the provisions of Section 12(c) of the Export Administration Act of 1979, as amended, 50 U.S.C. app 2411(c) and its unauthorized disclosure is prohibited by law.	DATE RECEIVED (Leave Blank)

STATEMENT BY ULTIMATE CONSIGNEE AND PURCHASER

1. ULTIMATE CONSIGNEE	CITY	
ADDRESS LINE 1	COUNTRY	
ADDRESS LINE 2	POSTAL CODE	TELEPHONE OR FAX

2. DISPOSITION OR USE OF ITEMS BY ULTIMATE CONSIGNEE NAMED IN BLOCK 1

We certify that the items: *(left mouse click in the appropriate box below)*

A. ☐ Will be used by us (as capital equipment) in the form in which received in a manufacturing process in the country named in Block 1 and will not be reexported or incorporated into an end product.

B. ☐ Will be processed or incorporated by us into the following product (s) _____
to be manufactured in the country named in Block 1 for distribution in _____

C. ☐ Will be resold by us in the form in which received in the country named in Block 1 for use or consumption therein.
The specific end-use by my customer will be_____

D. ☐ Will be reexported by us in the form in which received to _____

E. ☐ Other (describe fully)_____

NOTE: If BOX (D) is checked, acceptance of this form by the Bureau of Industry and Security as a supporting document for license applications shall not be construed as an authorization to reexport the items to which the form applies unless specific approval has been obtained from the Bureau of Industry and Security for such export.

3. NATURE OF BUSINESS OF ULTIMATE CONSIGNEE NAMED IN BLOCK 1

A. The nature of our usual business is_____

B. Our business relationship with the U.S. exporter is _____

and we have had this business relationship for _____ year(s).

4. ADDITIONAL INFORMATION

5. ASSISTANCE IN PREPARING STATEMENT

STATEMENT OF ULTIMATE CONSIGNEE AND PURCHASER

We certify that all of the facts contained in this statement are true and correct to the best of our knowledge and we do not know of any additional facts which are inconsistent with the above statement. We shall promptly send a supplemental statement to the U.S. Exporter, disclosing any change of facts or intentions set forth in this statement which occurs after the statement has been prepared and forwarded, except as specifically authorized by the U.S. Export Administration Regulations (15 CFR parts 730-774), or by prior written approval of the Bureau of Industry and Security, we will not reexport, resell, or otherwise dispose of any items approved on a license supported by this statement (1) to any country not approved for export as brought to our attention by means of a bill of lading, commercial invoice, or any other means, or(2) to any person if we know that it will result directly or indirectly, in disposition of the items contrary to the representations made in this statement or contrary to Export Administration Regulations.

6. SIGNATURE OF OFFICIAL OF ULTIMATE CONSIGNEE	**7.** NAME OF PURCHASER
NAME OF OFFICIAL	SIGNATURE OF PURCHASER
TITLE OF OFFICIAL	NAME OF OFFICIAL
DATE *(mmmm,dd,yyyy)*	TITLE OF OFFICIAL
CERTIFICATION FOR USE OF U.S. EXPORTER - We certify that no corrections, additions, or alterations were made on this form by us after the form was signed by the (ultimate consignee)(purchaser).	DATE *(mmmm,dd,yyyy)*
8. NAME OF EXPORTER	SIGNATURE OF PERSON AUTHORIZED TO CERTIFY FOR EXPORTER
NAME OF PERSON SIGNING THIS DOCUMENT	TITLE OF PERSON SIGNING THIS DOCUMENT	DATE *(mmmm,dd,yyyy)*

We acknowledge that the making of any false statements or concealment of any material fact in connection with this statement may result in imprisonment or fine, or both and denial, in whole or in part, of participation in U.S. exports and reexports.

Public reporting burden for this collection of information is estimated to average 15 minutes per response plus one minute for recordkeeping, including the time for reviewing instruments, searching existing data sources, gathering and maintaining the data needed, and completing and reviewing the collection of information. Send comments regarding this burden estimate or any other aspect of this collection of information, including suggestions for reducing this burden, to the Director of Administration, Room 3889, Bureau of Industry and Security, U.S. Department of Commerce,

Washington, DC 20230, and to the Office of Management and Budget Paperwork Reduction Project (0694-0021, 0694-0093), Washington, D.C. 20503. Notwithstanding any other provision of law, no person is obligated to respond to nor shall a person be subject to a penalty for failure to comply with a collection of information subject to the Paperwork Reduction Act unless that collection of information displays a currently valid OMB Control Number.

responsible for the accuracy of all the export documents. To protect itself from violations of government reexport restrictions, the exporter should ensure that an export prohibition clause is written into the export contract. The clause should state the country of importation and prohibit the purchaser-importer from selling, delivering, or reexporting the goods to another country.

Licenses are granted on a case-by-case basis that may cover a single transaction or multiple transactions. BIS reviewed 10,767 license applications with a total value of $16.8 billion in fiscal year 2002. It approved 8,735 of these applications, returned 1,826 applications without action, and denied 206 applications. The average processing time for these applications was thirty-nine days. Despite these improvements in efficiency, the *Daedalus Enterprises v. Baldridge* case illustrates that the process for obtaining a license may be costly and time-consuming.

As previously noted, exporters must always be wary of the possibility of **diversion**. Diversion is the illegal placement of goods or commodities into the hands of individuals for whom an export license would not be granted because of the country group or the characteristics or end use of the product. Exporters should protect themselves from the possibility of diversion by consulting the BIS red flag indicators listed in the box feature Doing Business Internationally: Red Flag

---

Daedalus Enterprises, Inc. v. Baldridge

563 F. Supp. 1345 (D.C. 1983)

Parker, District Judge. Export license applicant brought suit to enjoin the Department of Commerce's noncompliance with the Export Administration Act's timetable for processing applications for export licenses. Section 10 of the Export Administration Act of 1979 provides for a timetable that governs the Department of Commerce's processing of applications for certain export licenses. Plaintiff, Daedalus Enterprises, Inc. ("Daedalus"), brings this suit to enjoin the Department of Commerce's noncompliance with the Export Administration Act's timetable. Under the authority of the Export Administration Act of 1979 ("the Act"), the Department of Commerce ("the Department") administers export controls in consultation with other United States agencies and departments. Under Section 10(h), whenever the export license being sought implicates national security, the application for the export license—after being referred to the other agencies and departments—is referred by the Secretary for multilateral review to the Coordinating Committee ("COCOM"), which includes representatives of the NATO countries plus Japan, less Iceland.

Daedalus engages in research, development, manufacture, and service in the field of remote sensing of the environment. Within this field, Daedalus specializes in airborne infrared and visual line-scanning devices and associated data analysis equipment. Daedalus manufactures infrared equipment, conducts surveys using such equipment, and analyzes data derived therefrom for governmental and commercial clients. An integral component of the Daedalus system is a magnetic instrumentation tape recorder. Daedalus entered into an agreement with Romania whereby Romania agreed to purchase a Daedalus multispectral airborne scanner. Soon after entering into the agreement, Daedalus filed an application with the Department for a license to export the scanner. Some 29 months after the filing of the first license application, and some 21 months after

the filing of the second application, the Secretary has not reached a final decision to grant or deny the licenses.

The Secretary's strongest argument is that plaintiff has not exhausted the statutorily prescribed administrative remedies. Under the Act, an applicant may file a petition with the Secretary requesting compliance with the time periods established by the Act. Nonetheless, the fact that Daedalus failed to submit a written petition does not bar its claim here. The doctrine of exhaustion is intended, in part, to afford the administrative agency the first opportunity to correct any error. When the agency has already made it abundantly obvious that it would not correct the error and would not conform its actions with the strictures of the Act, it would be meaningless to compel the hapless plaintiff to pursue further administrative remedies simply for form's sake. Here, plaintiff sought repeatedly to ascertain the status of the application. The Court will not force plaintiff to submit to the futile formality of petitioning the same officials yet again.

Case Highlights

- The Export Administration Act vests authority and discretion in the Secretary of Commerce in the processing of export license applications. However, this discretion is limited.
- The doctrine of exhaustion of remedies found in administrative law requires an applicant to follow all administrative appeals processes before seeking judicial relief.
- The Secretary of Commerce cannot unduly delay a decision on an export license application and then receive a dismissal based on the exhaustion of remedies doctrine.

Red Flag Indicators: Things to Look for in Export Transactions

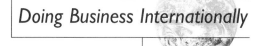
Doing Business Internationally

Use the following as a checklist to discover possible violations of the Export Administration Regulations.

- The customer or its address is similar to one of the parties on the Bureau of Industry and Security list of denied people.
- The customer or purchasing agent is reluctant to offer information about the end use of the item.
- The product's capabilities do not fit the buyer's line of business, such as an order for sophisticated computers for a small bakery.
- The item ordered is incompatible with the technical level of the country to which it is being shipped, such as semiconductor manufacturing equipment being shipped to a country that has no electronics industry.
- The customer is willing to pay cash for a very expensive item when the terms of sale would normally call for financing.

- The customer has little or no business background.
- The customer is unfamiliar with the product's performance characteristics but still wants the product.
- The customer declines routine installation, training, or maintenance services.
- Delivery dates are vague, or deliveries are planned for out-of-the-way destinations.
- A freight-forwarding firm is listed as the product's final destination.
- The shipping route is abnormal for the product and destination.
- Packaging is inconsistent with the stated method of shipment or destination.
- When questioned, the buyer is evasive and especially unclear about whether the purchased product is for domestic use, for export, or for reexport.

Indicators: Things to Look for in Export Transactions. The presence of one or more of these red flags in a transaction should alert an exporter of the possibility of diversion.

An exporter is liable for diversion if it had reason to know that the end user was going to direct the exported product to a prohibited destination. As a general rule, the exporter has a duty to conduct itself in a reasonable manner. Furthermore, the duty to become and remain informed with respect to the ultimate disposition of exported products remains with the exporter.

There are serious penalties for diversion.[37] An exporter found responsible for diversion may be assessed a penalty equal to the greater of five times the value of the exports or $50,000. This penalty increases to five times the value of the exports or $1 million for companies and $250,000 for individuals in the event that the diversion is deemed willful. In addition, individual violators may receive jail sentences of up to ten years. Civil penalties may also be assessed. A civil penalty of $10,000 per violation may be assessed except if the violation endangers national security, in which case the penalty is increased to $100,000 per violation. The goods, property used to commit the violation, and property derived from proceeds of the violation are subject to forfeiture. Violators may also be disqualified from obtaining export licenses in the future.

37. See ibid. § 2410 (a-c), (g).

KEY TERMS

ad valorem duties
Agreement on Customs Valuation
Agreement on Rules of Origin
Automated Commercial
    Environment (ACE)
binding assessment
bonded warehouse
Bureau of Customs and Border
    Protection
Bureau of Industry and Security
    (BIS)
CE Mark
change in tariff classification test
Commerce Control List
Commerce Country Chart
Committee on Rules of Origin
commodity control list
computed value
country of origin
Customs Electronic Bulletin Board

Customs Modernization and
    Informed Compliance Act
deductive value
Destination Control Statement
diversion
drawback
eco-label
essential character
European Union's Customs Code
Export Administration Act (EAA)
Export Control Classification
    Number (ECCN)
foreign trade zone
general license
General Rules of Interpretation
generalized system of preferences
    (GSP)
harmonized tariff schedule (HTS)
individually validated license (IVL)
marking requirement

rule of specificity
Section 9802
Shipper's Export Declaration (SED)
Simplified Network Application
    Process (SNAP)
special comprehensive license (SCL)
specific duties
specified processes test
Statement of Ultimate Consignee
    and Purchaser
substantial transformation
Taric
Technical Committee on Rules of
    Origin
Trade and Tariff Act of 1984
transaction value
ultimate purchaser
value-added test
World Customs Organization
    (WCO)

CHAPTER PROBLEMS

1. Customs classified aluminum ingots that were shipped to the United States from Canada as not of Canadian origin. The ingots contained less than 1 percent materials from countries other than Canada. Customs imposed a tariff of 0.19 percent on aluminum ingots imported from Canada. The Court of International Trade ruled in favor of Customs, finding that the aluminum underwent "substantial transformation" because a foreign-origin substance (grain refiner) was mixed with the aluminum to make the ingots less likely to crack and therefore worked a substantial transformation. Alcan protested that the tariff should be the 0.038 percent that would apply under NAFTA if the ingots had not undergone "substantial transformation" with goods that originated from outside of Canada. Do you think that the Court's decision was correct? *Alcan Aluminum Corp. v. United States*, 165 F.3d 898 (Fed. Cir. 1999)

2. William C. Dart sought to overturn a decision by the Secretary of Commerce imposing civil sanctions for violations of the Export Administration Act. The act precludes judicial review of such fines under its so-called finality clause. What are the competing concerns of the person fined and the limited appeal procedure provided in the act? Has the world changed in a way that has changed the balance between these concerns? *Dart v. United States*, 848 F.2d 217 (D.C. Cir. 1988)

3. Import documentation requirements and other regulations imposed by foreign governments vary from country to country. It is vital that exporters be aware of the regulations that apply to their own operations and transactions. Many governments, for instance, require consular invoices, certificates of inspection, health certification, and various other documents. Select a country and research its basic documentary requirements for the importation of goods.

4. Export controls remain a controversial topic, even in light of concerns about the proliferation of nuclear technology to Iran and North Korea and other sensitive products and information to terrorist organizations. Export controls have been criticized as inadequate to prevent hostile and potentially hostile countries from obtaining sensitive technology. Critics have also contended that some export controls are overly broad and thus unduly restrictive. Export controls lacking multilateral support may be ineffective. The imposition of controls under such circumstances serves to divide allies and undermine the chances of establishing effective multilateral controls when necessary. Finally, critics contend that export controls weaken the U.S. economy and give domestic producers a reputation for being unreliable. Do you agree with this statement? What arguments support the continuation of export controls? What interests are represented on each side of this controversy? What interests should prevail in the resolution of this controversy?

INTERNET EXERCISES

1. You are an importer of synthetic sails used for recreational sailboats. You import the sails from the People's Republic of China. Look at the Harmonized Tariff Schedule to determine the rate of duty that will be charged for the sails. The HTS can be accessed at **http://hotdocs.usitc.gov/tariff_chapters_current/toc.html** and **http://www.itds.treas.gov/HTSindex.html.**

2. Research the customs laws of Japan and compare them to those of the United States. To compare the customs laws of another country see the Web site for Japanese Customs at **http://www.customs.go.jp/index_e.htm.**

3. You have completed an export contract and need to ship goods from Miami, Florida, to Buenos Aires, Argentina. Determine which shipping lines are available for such a shipment and research the documentation needed for such a shipment. See the following Web sites: **http://www.mglobal.com** (Maritime Global Net) and **http://www.tradeport.org** (Tradeport is a comprehensive site on international shipping and trade).

A thorough knowledge of substantive law rules and principles is imperative in drafting a good contract. For U.S. businesspeople, a working knowledge of the **Uniform Commercial Code (UCC)** provides a solid foundation for drafting a sales contract. At the international level, however, the general principles of contract law are less specific and are applied sporadically by national courts. Knowing the law of the country of your foreign contracting party may be necessary to avoid misunderstandings. Cultural and language differences, however, may prevent a contract from ever being formed. Knowledge of the other party's culture and negotiating style is important if an initial inquiry is to develop into a long-term contractual relationship.

Business behavior differs among cultures. Some cultures focus on the importance of developing a contractual and social relationship and not on the importance of the deal, as is prevalent in the United States. Many cultures view a formal, detailed contract as unnecessary and hindering a good faith, evolving contractual relationship in which the parties mutually work through problems. For example, in many Asian cultures, "the contract may not represent finality but a starting point of a relationship. It is assumed that the contract will be reexamined, reinterpreted, or renegotiated if conditions change. In these more traditional cultures, negotiators seek mainly broad-based agreements that are general, flexible, and implicit."[1] In contrast, U.S. businesspeople view a contract as the operative tool for ensuring full and complete performance—something that should be honored at any cost.

Many foreign cultures view the negotiation phase of contracting as one in which a relaxed development of the relationship should be pursued. This is in opposition to the U.S. "time is money" approach. Without a firm understanding of the cross-cultural differences in negotiating styles, the likelihood of successful completion of the negotiations is greatly diminished. This chapter reviews some of the cultural nuances in negotiating a contract in an international setting, with a focus on Japan. It then shifts focus to the nuances of substantive contract law at the national and international levels, with a particular emphasis on the area of pre-contractual liability.

Chapter 7

International Contract Law

INTERNATIONAL

Negotiating an International Contract

The substantive laws and commercial means of doing business are amazingly similar among the world's different legal systems, but the differences in negotiating styles and contract customs are profound. For example, even though the importance of a written contract is universally recognized in principle, executing

---

1. Claude Cellich, Review of *Cross-Cultural Business Negotiations* by Donald W. Hendon, Rebecca A. Hendon, & Paula Herbig, 10 *Journal of International Consumer Marketing* 120 (1998).

a long, detailed contract may be frowned upon in some countries. Requiring the execution of such a contract may impair trust in the relationship and render the agreement invalid.[2]

International contract negotiation is a very difficult and complicated affair. The nuances of language and culture make it risky for the unsophisticated importer or exporter. The negotiation of an international contract is generally more time-consuming than in a domestic transaction because foreign contractors need to develop a trust in their U.S. counterpart before entering into a contract. It is important for the U.S. businessperson to understand these cultural differences.

The added time invested to negotiate an international contract carefully will provide significant dividends in the long term. First, an agreement that successfully overcomes language, cultural, and legal differences will better reflect basic under-standings and minimize misunderstandings. For example, it is difficult for U.S. businesspeople "to realize that in some countries, especially in Asia, it is character-istic for a businessperson to speak in vague terms with nuances that only experience can help decipher."[3] Second, the trust developed early in a contractual relationship helps to ensure a long-term international business contact.

INTERNATIONAL

The following excerpt discusses some of the nuances associated with Japanese negotiators and business practices:

The authority of the Japanese negotiator is not clear. No clear mandate or instruction is given to the negotiator. Since no one in a Japanese corporation can make decisions by himself but must gain the consent from various groups, even an executive does not have the authority to bind the corpo-ration without clearance of a decision making procedure called ringi. . . . After commencement of the negotiation, the negotiator has to report the negotiation in detail to all the departments and organizations concerned and then seek their comments. . . . Almost always, unanimous consent is necessary. . . . This constant effort to obtain consent and approval from all people concerned requires enormous energy and time. . . . To get consent of all people concerned using various skills is called "nemawashi." When negotiation comes to the final stage, the terms and conditions agreed by the negotiators should also have been approved by all people concerned as above. Then the gen-eral manager of the business department will prepare a circulation proposal of the transaction called a "ring-sho" or proposal paper. It will be circulated to all departments concerned within the corporation. Heads of the relevant departments will put their seals on the covering page of the ring-sho as an indication of approval.[4]

Effects of Ringi Decision Making on Japanese Negotiation Style

Lengthy Negotiations

Since the negotiators have to persuade a large number of people, decision making takes time. . . . The Japanese negotiators are always conducting two way negotiations; one with the opposite party to the transaction and another internal one with people in relevant departments and organiza-tions. Unanimous decision making in Japanese corporations delays negotiations considerably. This difficulty is offset by the fact that if a substantial majority approves a proposal, it becomes very difficult to raise objections because of tacit pressure to follow the majority.

2. See Magoroh Maruyama, "Contracts in Cultures," 10 *Human Systems Management* 33 (1991).
3. Warren A. French & John Granrose, Practical Business Ethics 166 (1995).
4. Noboru Kashiwagi & E. Anthony Zaloom, "Contract Law and the Japanese Negotiation Process," in The Business Guide to Japan, pp 89–101, Gerald Paul McAlinn, ed. (Singapore: Reed Academic Publishing Asia, 1996).

Quick Implementation

At the performance stage of contracts, implementation by Japanese corporations is said to be quick because all people concerned know the details of the project and they approved the contract. . . . It is impossible to raise objections at the performance stage.

Relative Inflexibility

Because of the number of people whom the Japanese negotiator must persuade and the enormous amount of energy expended, the negotiator cannot change the basic structure or policy of the proposed transaction quickly. . . . It follows that if counsel to a Japanese corporation, or the other side in the negotiations, comes up with an excellent idea in the middle of the negotiation stage which may save tax or other transactional costs, but may require a fundamental change of transactional structure, the negotiator would not accept the idea even though she understands its merits. . . .

Simple Negotiation Tactics

Japanese negotiators may not freely use negotiation tactics like bluff or threat because they have to answer to too many people and departments. The Japanese negotiators' first offer would not be far more than what they expect because overly aggressive proposals may be considered greedy. Usually, they do not have alternatives, because discussion and review of alternatives in the other relevant departments and organizations need further time and energy. Thus, it invites other departments and organizations to determine the best proposal and to concentrate on pursuing that best proposal. . . .

Preference for Simple Legal Structures

The Japanese do not like complicated or sophisticated legal structures for transactions. Such structures may seem technical and may easily be interpreted by judges, government officials and scholars as a means of evasion of tax or other regulations. Also a complicated legal structure would hinder the persuasion process.[5]

INTERNATIONAL

http://

International Trade Administration— Information on foreign culture and customs: **http://www.ita.doc.gov/ td/tic.**

Such cultural differences have crucial practical importance in the negotiation and formation of a contract. The Confucian influence of harmony permeates contracting in Japan, and the U.S. style of hard bargaining and pressure tactics is likely to meet with failure. It is important to state a position firmly and at the same time not disturb the *wa* or harmony of the negotiation. The Japanese aversion to litigation stems from their belief in a societal "duty to avoid discord."[6] Interestingly, the Japanese also dislike arbitration. They believe that parties should negotiate directly in resolving disputes. In case of failure in negotiating a solution, the Japanese prefer the use of conciliation or *chotei*.[7]

---

5. Noboru Kashiwagi & E. Anthony Zaloom, "Contract Law and the Japanese Negotiation Process," in *The Business Guide to Japan* 89–101 (Gerald Paul McAlinn, ed., 1996).
6. Comment, "'Working It Out:' A Japanese Alternative to Fighting It Out," 37 *Cleveland St. Law Review.* 149, 157 (1989).
7. Ibid. at 164. See generally Kawashima Takeyoshi, "Dispute Resolution in Contemporary Japan," *Law in Japan* 42 (1963); Dan F. Henderson, *Conciliation and Japanese Law* (1965).

The *wa* concept is reflected in the Japanese approach to negotiation as the process of developing a trusting business relationship (*shinrai kankei*) and not the simple formation of a contract. (See Doing Business Internationally: Contract Characteristics in Japan.) From a practical perspective, this results in Japanese contracts that are simple, short, and vague. All problems are to be dealt with through acts of conciliation. All questions are to be answered through a process of *reconcilement*, whereby "parties in the dispute confer with each other and reach a point at which they come to terms and restore *harmonious* relationships."[8] The contract provides a basic framework that allows for modification and flexibility. Performance standards are not defined restrictively. Thus, U.S. businesspeople may have to modify their proclivity for long, detailed agreements.

Cultural differences can have a profound impact on new business relationships. The U.S. exporter should be careful in approaching a prospective contact in Japan. The Japanese place a high premium on personal contact, and a Japanese importer may not respond to written inquiries. Therefore, any initial inquiry should be followed by a personal contact. The best approach is to ask to be introduced by an intermediary known to the other party.[9]

Another possible conflict resulting from cultural differences comes from the U.S. businessperson's propensity to send a written agreement when negotiations have entered into their final stages. A U.S. businessperson may ask an attorney to confirm the terms discussed and agreed upon before the negotiations are complete. The lawyer may respond by sending a letter or a proposed agreement to the other party. However, the letter may not elicit a response

---

Contract Characteristics in Japan

Doing Business Internationally

- "Contract" assumes not opposition of parties but cooperation.
- Parties attach more importance to establishing a collaborative human relationship than to preparing a highly formal, legalistic written contract.
- Contract provisions are written not to be rigid but to be flexible and changeable.
- Parties prefer clauses that, in case of changed circumstances, require the parties to act in good faith to renegotiate the term, rather than including detailed clauses to cover anticipated disputes.
- Contracts generally are simple, consisting of a few short clauses.
- There is an implied understanding that clauses are to be applied leniently in the area of performance and nonperformance.
- In case of dispute, the preferred means of resolution is the giving of mutual concessions and not litigation.
- To conclude a negotiation often means not to sign a written contract, but to establish a personal and cordial relationship.

Source: Shoji Kawami, "Japan" in *Precontractual Liability* 215 (Ewoud H. Hondius, ed. 1991).

---

8. *supra* note 5, at 163.
9. See Elliot Hahn, "Negotiating Contracts with the Japanese," 14 *Case Western Reserve Journal International Law* 377 (1982).

"because the unexpected arrival of a contract probably appears abrupt and possibly coercive to a foreign recipient."[10] To avoid cultural faux pas, one attorney gives this advice:

Do some reading on the country—at least you'll know where it is. Know something of the history. Talk to someone who's done business there, an American businessman or someone from the Department of Commerce—find out who the trade specialist is in that country and talk to that person. And once you get there, don't hop off the plane and set up meetings. . . . Don't do the trilogy of hotels, restaurants, and office buildings. Instead of staying in your hotel room answering e-mail, get up in the morning and walk around.[11]

A number of criteria must be satisfied for cross-cultural contract negotiations to conclude successfully. First, the negotiations should lead to a written contract that is enforceable in the countries of both parties. Second, conflicts that result from cross-cultural misunderstandings should be avoided through a carefully negotiated and written contract that informs both parties of their rights and duties. A full understanding of rights and duties provides the basis for the development of a strong business relationship. Third, dispute resolution should be completely and fairly addressed in the contract. Because of the cost, inconvenience, and uncertainty of transnational litigation, the contract should outline cost-effective and relationship-preserving means of dispute resolution. Some countries, such as China and Japan, have long emphasized conciliation without resort to litigation as the preferred manner of dispute resolution.

The risks of international business dealings addressed in Chapter One should be minimized by appropriate contract provisions. Special attention should be devoted to the issue of "changed circumstances," because various legal and business cultures deal with this issue differently. U.S. culture places a premium on the strict enforcement of contractual rights and duties, regardless of circumstance. In contrast, some other cultures will not strictly enforce a contract if there has been a change in circumstances. Therefore, the contract should deal carefully with issues of renegotiation and modification of the contract in the event of such changes.

Principles of International Contract Law

Despite the differences in how foreign laws and culture deal with the negotiation, interpretation, and enforcement of contracts, there are similarities among different legal systems in how the law supports commercial transactions. For example, the civil law and common law legal systems provide similar mechanisms for facilitating business transactions. Most differences are a matter of style and not substance.

Additionally, there is a trend toward developing a unified body of international business law that can be seen at work on a number of different levels. First, the growth of **customary international business law** is shown by the almost universal adoption of the **International Chamber of Commerce (ICC)** standards in the area of trade terms (INCOTERMS) and letters of credit (Uniform Customs and Practices for Documentary Credits or UCP). Second, the increased publication and citation of international commercial arbitration decisions are evidence of the development of an international commercial jurisprudence not directly tied to national laws.

---

10. See Dan F. Henderson, "The Role of Lawyers in U.S.-Japanese Business Transactions," 38 *Washington Law Review* 1 (1963).
11. Laurel-Ann Dooley, "Culture Clashes Hinder Deals," *National Law Journal* B1, B4 (September 13, 1999).

Finally, there have been important developments in the enactment of international treaties and conventions unifying international business law. (See Comparative Law: International Commercial Law Conventions.) The clearest example of this trend was the ratification of the United Nations **Convention on Contracts for the International Sale of Goods (CISG)** on January 1, 1988. This pioneering effort to unify international sales law will be the subject of Chapter Eight.

For links to "modern"
lex mercatoria: **http://**
www.lexmercatoria.org.

Customary International Law (Lex Mercatoria)

It is impossible to adequately draft a contract without knowledge of substantive contract law. The need is compounded in drafting an international contract, where there are at least three possible sources of law—the national laws of each of the parties and international contract law or the *lex mercatoria*. The *lex mercatoria* or "law of merchants" refers to business customs or trade usage developed by businesspeople throughout the world to facilitate business transactions. Some degree of *harmonization* has been achieved through the adoption of international conventions. These conventions often become enacted into national law or become a part of the *lex mercatoria*. The ideal situation for the international businessperson is to have a working knowledge of the domestic laws of the seller and buyer, along with any relevant trade usage and international conventions.

Even when contract writers attempt to reduce their need to know a foreign law by using a choice of law clause, they still must be knowledgeable about the mandatory or immutable rules and regulations found in the foreign law. Also, arbitrators often resort to a supranational law or *lex mercatoria* in place of a full application of

International Commercial Law Conventions (1954–Present)

- United Nations Convention on the Recognition and Enforcement of Foreign Arbitral Awards (New York Convention) (1958)
- United Nations Convention on the Limitation Period of the International Sale of Goods (1974)
- United Nations Convention on Carriage of Goods by Sea (1978)
- Uniform Rules Concerning the Contract for International Carriage of Goods by Rail (1980)
- United Nations Convention on Contracts for the International Sale of Goods (CISG) (1980)
- United Nations Convention on Multimodal Transport (1980)
- UNIDROIT Convention on Agency in the International Sale of Goods (1983)

- Convention on the Law Applicable to Contracts for the International Sale of Goods (1985)
- UNIDROIT Convention on International Factoring (1988)
- United Nations Convention on International Bills of Exchange and International Promissory Notes (1988)
- United Nations Convention on the Liability of Operators of Transport Terminals in International Trade (1991)
- United Nations Convention on Independent Guarantees and Stand-By Letters of Credit (1996)
- Uniform Rules Concerning the Contract of International Carriage of Goods by Rail (1999)

a national law designated by a choice of law clause. Danish professor Ole Lando listed the following seven sources[12] of the *lex mercatoria* that can be used in the interpretation of contracts:

- *Public International Law:* There are provisions in the Vienna Convention on the Law of Treaties that can be applied to private international contracts.
- *Uniform Laws:* The Hague Rules (codified as the Carriage of Goods by Sea Act or COGSA) and the CISG are examples of successful attempts at uniform international laws.
- *General Principles of Contract Law:* The best example of a general principle of contract law in most national legal systems is *pacta sunt servanda,* or what is referred to in the common law as *sanctity of contract.*
- *Rules of International Organizations:* Courts may look to nonbinding rules published by such international organizations as the United Nations, the Organization for Economic Cooperation and Development (OECD), and the International Institute for the Unification of Private Law (UNIDROIT).
- *Custom and Usage:* The clearest examples of custom and usage or *customary international law* that has reached a level of almost universal acceptance are the standards and rules published by the International Chamber of Commerce, such as INCOTERMS and the UCP.
- *Standard Form Contracts:* Once again, the ICC is a good source for standard form contracts and standard clauses. For example, the ICC publishes standard or model forms of distribution and agency agreements. They also publish a manual to be used in the drafting of force majeure and hardship clauses.
- *Arbitral Decisions:* Although not widely reported, arbitral decisions provide an outstanding resource for principles.

Generally recognized international contract principles have a direct bearing on how one approaches the drafting of an international contract. These principles are used by courts and arbitration panels in the interpretation of contracts. They are also used to determine the parties' rights and duties regarding performance and subsequent requests for adjustments in the contract. The general principle is that contracts should prima facie be enforced according to their terms under the doctrine of **pacta sunt servanda**. However, *pacta sunt servanda* is also qualified by the concept of **abus de droit**—the rule that unfair or unconscionable contracts and clauses should not be enforced.

INTERNATIONAL

The general duty of good faith in international contracting is a more expanded version of the good faith requirement found in the United States. The U.S. concept of good faith is applied only to the area of performance and enforcement of contractual obligations. In contrast, the civil law concept *culpa in contrahendo* requires that the parties negotiate in good faith.[13] Thus, in international contracting, there is a possibility of liability before the conclusion of a contract. The civil law concept of *culpa in contrahendo* is fully explored later in the chapter's coverage of precontractual liability. The civil law also, at times, extends

12. Ole Lando, "The *Lex Mercatoria* in International Commercial Arbitration," 34 *International & Comparative Law Quarterly* 747 (1985).
13. See Friedrich Kessler & Edith Fine, "*Culpa in Contrahendo,* Bargaining in Good Faith, and Freedom of Contract: A Comparative Study," 77 *Harvard Law Review* 401 (1964). For an analysis of the ethics of negotiation, see Gerald B. Wetlaufer, "The Ethics of Lying in Negotiations," 75 *Iowa Law Review* 1219 (1990).

the principle of good faith to include a duty to adjust the contract in the event of unforeseen circumstances.

The notion of good faith should guide the U.S. businessperson's response to all communications from a foreign party. For example, in some legal systems failure to respond to a letter or request is often regarded as evidence of assent to its terms. This concept can be seen at work in the CISG's adoption of the civil law concept of *nachfrist* **notice**, in which a party makes a request for additional time to perform. In the event that the receiving party fails to respond and fails to give a commercially viable reason for a denial of the request, then the extension is automatically granted.[14] There is no counterpart to this notion in the common law. It is important for the international businessperson, and her lawyer, to understand these principles when drafting and performing a contract.

INTERNATIONAL

http://

UNIDROIT—menu of sponsored conventions: **http://www.unidroit.org.**

Some contract codes, like the CISG, can be used to create a checklist of issues or clauses that should be dealt with in an international contract. The Focus on Transactions: Checklist of Important International Contract Clauses box is an ICC checklist that illustrates how a substantive body of law or principles may be utilized as a checklist in the drafting of a contract. This checklist includes issues covered in the **UNIDROIT Principles of International Commercial Contracts**. The material in parentheses refers to the relevant articles of the *UNIDROIT Principles*.

General principles of international contracting are important for reasons other than drafting and performing contracts. Foreign courts and arbitration panels use these principles of international contracting in interpreting an ambiguity in a contract. The next section examines the process of contract interpretation that is pivotal to the resolution of contract disputes.

Checklist of Important International Contract Clauses

Focus on Transactions

- Exclusion of trade usage (Articles 1.9 and 4.3(f))
- Four corners clause (integration or merger clause) (Articles 2.1.17 and 2.1.18)
- Time of performance, early performance, late performance (Articles 6.1.1, 6.1.5, and 7.1.5)
- Order of performance (Article 6.1.4)
- Place of performance, place of payment (Article 6.1.6)
- Form of payment (Articles 6.1.7 and 6.1.8)
- Currency of payment (Article 6.1.9)
- Transportation costs, other expenses (Article 6.1.11)
- Government approvals (Articles 6.1.14–6.1.17)
- Hardship clause (Articles 6.2.1–6.2.3)
- Force majeure clause (Article 7.1.7)
- Termination clause, notice provisions (Articles 7.3.1 and 7.3.2)
- Forum selection and arbitration clauses (Article 7.3.5(3))
- Limitation of liability clause (Article 7.1.6)
- Interest on delinquent payments (Article 7.4.9)
- Damages, liquidated damages clause (Articles 7.4.1–7.4.4 and 7.4.13)

---

14.   See CISG Articles 47–48, 63. See also Chapter Eight.

Contract Interpretation

An important part of contract law pertains to the rules or standards used by courts in the interpretation of contracts. In U.S. contract law, the standard of review is embedded in the reasonable person approach. In the United States, the imprimatur of the reasonable person approach can be seen throughout the **Restatement (Second) of Contracts (Restatement)** and the Uniform Commercial Code. It can be seen whenever reference is made to the fact that a party had reason to know or should have known something. There is *reason to know* if a person "has information from which a person of similar intelligence would infer that the fact in question does or will exist." The line between *reason to know* and actual knowledge is often nonexistent. *Reason to know* is a factual determination based on the circumstances and information available to the parties. In contrast, *should know* is generally associated with a legal duty to know. The "should know" standard "imports a duty to ascertain the facts."[15] Thus, *should know* is relatively unconcerned with actual knowledge.

The determination of whether a party had *reason to know* is accomplished through the **totality of the circumstances analysis**.[16] This analysis takes into account all the circumstances of the contract, including the contract itself, prior dealings between the parties, how the parties performed the contract, subsequent modification to the contract, and relevant business customs and trade usage. *Should know* is more a judicial reflection regarding what is reasonable, given the parties and the circumstances. The difference is that *reason to know* is more a party-specific analysis. In contrast, *should know* is community focused; that is, it determines what a reasonable interpretation or result is, based on business or community standards.[17]

Modern contract law has witnessed an increasing preemption by statutory law of contract interpretation. The **English Unfair Contract Terms Act of 1977** adopts a presumption of unreasonableness for indemnity or exculpatory clauses that "by reference to any contract term a party is made to indemnify another party in respect of liability for negligence or breach of contract."[18] For international sales contracts, it voids any choice of law clause whose purpose is the avoidance of the Unfair Contract Terms Act.[19] This statute is an example of how mandatory rules preempt a court's search for the contractual intent of the parties. The parties' intent regarding such a clause becomes irrelevant because the statute invalidates the clause.

Customary law, the examining of current business customs and trade usage, has often been the vehicle by which the common law has applied the reasonable person standard in interpreting contracts. Justice Turley in the 1842 case of *Jacob v. State* convincingly stated this grassroots metamorphosis: "Common law sources are to be found in the usage, habits, manners, and customs of a people. The common law of a country will be modified, and extended by analogy, *construction, and custom*, so as to embrace

http://

United Kingdom Department of Trade and Industry—English unfair terms in consumer contracts regulations: **http://www.hmso.gov.uk/si/si1999/19992083.htm.**

INTERNATIONAL

---

15. Restatement (Second) of Contracts (1981), § 19, Comment *b.*
16. See generally Larry A. DiMatteo, "The Counterpoise of Contracts: The Reasonable Person Standard and the Subjectivity of Judgment," 48 *South Carolina Law Review* 293, 318 (1997).
17. For example, "what is reasonable depends on the circumstances; it may be reasonable to hold a non-merchant to mercantile standards if he is represented by a mercantile agent." Restatement (Second) of Contracts (1981), § 221, Comment *b.*
18. Unfair Contract Terms Act § 4(1) (1977). An exculpatory clause is a provision in a contract that absolves one of the parties from responsibility for all damages, injuries, or losses, including those (negligently) caused by that party.
19. See ibid. § 27(2)(a-b).

new relations, springing up from time to time, from an amelioration or change of society."[20] The courts use the reasonable person standard to discourage unconscionable practices and encourage the development of judicially approved standards of reasonableness.

Convergence and Divergence of National Laws

The interrelationship between national and international legal systems is critical to the entrepreneur in assessing the legal risks of a transaction. One commentator stated that "with the world so interrelated, economic relations and their international aspects are influenced by the interests of and relations between subjects of commercial law from various countries."[21] Even without the development of uniform international laws like the CISG, there has been a significant convergence of contract law between the different legal systems.

Council of Europe:
http://www.coe.int.

INTERNATIONAL

The differences in contract law between the common law and civil law systems are more style than substance. The next Comparative Law feature is taken from a resolution of the **Council of Europe** pertaining to the enforceability of **penal clauses**, or what U.S. legal practitioners call **liquidated damage clauses**.

Penal Clauses in Europe and the United States

COMPARATIVE LAW

Council of Europe Resolution (78)3 on Penal Clauses in Civil Law
Considering that the aim of the Council of Europe is to achieve greater unity between its members, in particular the adoption of common rules in the field of law and considering that it is necessary to provide judicial control over penal clauses in civil law in appropriate cases where the penalty is manifestly excessive.

Article 2
The promisee may not obtain concurrently performance of the principal obligation, as specified in the contract, and payment of the sum stipulated in the penal clause unless the sum was stipulated for delayed performance.

Article 7
The sum stipulated may be reduced by the court when it is manifestly excessive.

Explanatory Memorandum
The legal systems of member states have devised various means to enable courts to exercise a certain control over penal clauses, although the circumstances under which this control can be exercised differ considerably from one state to another. It is one of the essential aims of the present resolution to contribute towards a *harmonisation* of the laws of the member states.

It is left to each legal system to determine under what precise circumstances the sum concerned is manifestly excessive. It is suggested that in a given case the courts may have regard to a number of factors such as:

i. comparing the damage preestimated by the parties at the time of contracting and the damage actually suffered by the promisee.

continued

---

20.   22 Tenn. 493, 514–15 (1842) (emphasis added).

21.   Tsvetana Kamenova, "Civil Law in Bulgaria: The Relationship Between International and Domestic Law and the Impact on Civil Law," in George Ginsburgs, Donald D. Barry, & William B. Simons, *The Revival of Private Law in Central and Eastern Europe* 541 (1996).

Penal Clauses in Europe and the United States (*continued*)

ii. the legitimate interests of the parties including the promisee's nonpecuniary interests.

iii. the category of contract and the circumstances under which it was concluded, in particular the relative social and economic position of the parties, or the fact that the contract was a standard form contract.

iv. the reason for the failure to perform, in particular the good or bad faith of the promisor.

United States
Uniform Commercial Code, Section 2-718(1): Liquidation or Limitation of Damages
Damages for breach by either party may be liquidated in the agreement but only at an amount which is reasonable in the light of the anticipated or actual harm caused by the breach, the difficulties of proof of loss, and the inconvenience or nonfeasibility of otherwise obtaining an adequate remedy. A term fixing unreasonably large liquidated damages is void as a penalty.

Restatement (Second) of Contracts, Section 356(1) and Comment b
(1) Damages for breach by either party may be liquidated in the agreement but only at an amount that is reasonable in the light of the anticipated or actual loss caused by the breach and the difficulties of proof of loss. A term fixing unreasonably large liquidated damages is unenforceable on grounds of public policy as a penalty.
Comment b. A determination whether the amount fixed is a penalty turns on a combination of these two factors. If the difficulty of proof of loss is great, considerable latitude is allowed in the approximation of anticipated or actual harm. If, on the other hand, the difficulty of proof of loss is slight, less latitude is allowed in that approximation.

First, take note that the Council of Europe's membership includes both common law and civil law countries.[22] Therefore, the resolution is itself an example of contract law convergence in Europe. Second, the similarities between the resolution and U.S. law, as described in the excerpts from the Uniform Commercial Code and the Restatement, are further evidence of convergence.

Despite the growing similarities among the different legal systems, significant divergence remains. There are concepts within the civil law systems simply not found in common law. A review of the following provisions taken from the **French Civil Code** demonstrates that there are foreign contract law principles that have no American law counterpart.

French Civil Code Section 1590

If the promise to sell was made with payment of a deposit (arrhes), *each of the contracting parties is at liberty to withdraw. The one who paid the deposit, on forfeiting it, and the one who received it, on returning twice the amount.*

---

22. The Council of Europe consists of forty-five states. The member states are Albania, Andorra, Armenia, Austria, Azerbaijan, Belgium, Bosnia & Herzegovina, Bulgaria, Croatia, Cyprus, the Czech Republic, Denmark, Estonia, Finland, France, Georgia, Germany, Greece, Hungary, Iceland, Ireland, Italy, Latvia, Liechtenstein, Lithuania, Luxembourg, Malta, Moldova, the Netherlands, Norway, Poland, Portugal, Romania, the Russian Federation, San Marino, Serbia & Montenegro, Slovakia, Slovenia, Spain, Sweden, Switzerland, the former Yugoslav Republic of Macedonia, Turkey, Ukraine, and the United Kingdom. Belarus and Monaco are currently candidates for membership. Canada, the Holy See, Japan, Mexico, and the United States have observer status.

Section 1587

With respect to wine, oil, and other things which it is customary to taste before buying, there is no sale so long as the buyer has not tasted and accepted them.

Section 1674

Where a seller has suffered a loss greater than seven-twelfths of the price of an immovable, he is entitled to apply for the rescission of the sale even though he may have expressly renounced in the contract the faculty of applying for that rescission.

Section 1681

In the case where the action for rescission is entertained, the purchaser has the choice, either to return the thing while taking back the price which he paid for it, or to keep the tenement while paying the balance of the fair price, after deducting one-tenth of the total price.

Note the differences between the **doctrine of *arrhes***, as described in Section 1590 of the French Civil Code, and the normal deposit given in U.S. business transactions. Does the doctrine of *arrhes* invite either party to breach the contract if they change their minds? Can the doctrine of *arrhes* be used as an implicit liquidated damages or penalty clause? Why are the inspection rights for wine and other similar products so different from what is found in most sales of goods transactions? Sections 1674 and 1681 reflect the influence of medieval just price theory that allowed a party to rescind a contract if the price paid or received was considered unjust. Why do you think the just price provision allows the buyer to retain 10 percent of the value of the goods?

Another area of concern for the international entrepreneur is the difference between "law in books" and "law in action." A number of countries have enacted modern, Westernized commercial codes, but uniformity in their interpretation and application is somewhat lacking. An example is the law of many Islamic countries by which there is a direct interrelationship between religious and secular codes. The main body of law, the **Shari'a**, comprises religious, social, and legal mandates. The main body of this source of law was completed by the early tenth century, at least as practiced by the majority Sunni. Beginning with the Ottoman Empire in the nineteenth century, however, "the Shari'a lost its exclusivity as the governing law of contracts to a combination of sacred and secular laws."[23]

INTERNATIONAL

The secular laws have included a modern codification of contract and commercial law with which a Western businessperson would be quite comfortable. For example, Saudi Arabia has enacted a set of regulations governing commercial law, negotiable instruments, and corporate law. The problem for an outside businessperson is that the principles of the Shari'a still take precedence over these secular statutes. Most of the judges in the secular court system have religious training, and their decisions are reviewed by a commercial board that ensures conformity with the dictates of the Shari'a.[24] The application and intrusion of religious principles into commercial law disputes is sporadic, yet a party may seek to overcome a decision based on the commercial codes by resorting to Shari'a principles. In such cases, the

INTERNATIONAL

23.   Nabil Saleh, "The Law Governing Contracts in Arabia," 38 *International & Comparative Law Quarterly* 761, 763 (1989).
24.   Ibid. at 765–766.

Shari'a "becomes a means of perverting the course of justice by allowing the strongest party in a dispute to select among the components of the law of contract those legal provisions which will settle that dispute on the most favorable terms."[25]

National Contract Codes

Those attempting to do business in a foreign country should make a good faith effort to acquaint themselves with that country's contract and sales laws. A thorough examination is not possible here, but the existence of statutory or commercial codes will allow a cursory review. Even a cursory review will highlight some of the similarities and differences in foreign contract laws in the case of the **Russian Civil Code**, the **Unified Contract Law of the People's Republic of China**, and the **Principles of European Contract Law**. The first two are examples of transitional economies enacting Western-style codes compatible with their emerging market status. The latter example more closely resembles a "restatement" of general principles taken from the underlying national contract law systems.

Russian Civil Code

INTERNATIONAL

A special concern in international contracting is the problem of assessing the laws in the countries of the former Soviet bloc and those countries that remain under a centrally planned economy or socialistic legal regime, such as the People's Republic of China. The enormous change in the legal systems of the former Soviet bloc countries often means that the substantive and procedural laws are still in flux and that their enforcement is uncertain. A brief look at selected provisions of the Russian Civil Code will illustrate some of the similarities and differences between this first-generation commercial statute and U.S. contract law. Chapter Thirteen's coverage of intellectual property law will illustrate not only some of the substantive differences but also the problems with the legal enforcement of these new laws.

The most obvious observation in reviewing the contract provisions of the Russian Civil Code is how similar the rules are to U.S. law. For example, Article 158 allows silence as a means of acceptance only if there was a prior agreement of the parties. Article 160 defines the requirements of the written form, or what is known under U.S. law as the **statute of frauds**, more broadly and is more modern than the definition currently found in Article 2 of the UCC. For example, Article 160(2) states that "the use when concluding a transaction of a facsimile reproduction of a signature with the assistance of mechanical or other means of copying, electronic-cypher signature, or other analogue of a signature in one's own hand shall be permitted in the instances and procedure provided by a law, other legal acts, or by agreement of the parties." However, this modernity is muted by Article 162, which expressly notes that foreign economic transactions are invalid unless in writing. Although oral contracts are recognized in some instances, the Russian Civil Code places strong emphasis on formalities, including the written form, notarial certifications, and in some cases, governmental registration. As a general rule, a foreign party should not contemplate moving forward on a business transaction without

---

25.   Ibid. at 786–787.

a formal written contract. It is also good practice, even if not technically required in a given transaction, for the parties' signatures to be notarized.

Article 428 recognizes the U.S. notion of the **contract of adhesion**, whereby a party signs the contract form provided by the other party on a take-it-or-leave-it basis. It grants the signing party the right to demand dissolution under such circumstances. Thus, a term that is not contrary to the law may be voided if it deprives the adhering party of the rights "usually granted under contracts of that type, or excludes or limits the responsibility of the other party or contains other terms clearly burdensome for the adhering party, that it, on the basis of its reasonably understood interests, would not have accepted if it had the possibility of participating in the determination of the terms of the contract." The importance of disclosure as a means to preclude the right to demand dissolution is also recognized. Dissolution cannot be demanded if the adhering party "knew or should have known on what conditions the contract is concluded." The general mandate against the enforcement of unfair terms in an adhesion contract can be contrasted with the **European Union Directive on Unfair Terms** in consumer contracts. (See Comparative Law: EU Council Directive 93/13/EEC on Unfair Terms in Consumer Contracts.) This directive is much narrower in scope in that it invalidates only certain types of exculpatory clauses.

Despite the overall similarities between the Russian Civil Code and U.S. contract law, there are some unique provisions in the Russian Code with which foreign businesspeople should become familiar. An example is the types of contracts that need to be in written form. Contracts of a certain amount need to be in writing. The threshold when the contracting parties are individuals is an amount exceeding "not less than ten times the minimum amount of payment of labor." Article 162 expressly states that in an international business transaction "the failure to comply with the simple written form of a foreign economic transaction shall entail the invalidity of the transaction."

INTERNATIONAL

EU Council Directive 93/13/EEC on Unfair Terms in Consumer Contracts (1993)

COMPARATIVE LAW

Article 3

A contractual term which has not been individually negotiated shall be regarded as unfair if, contrary to the requirement of good faith, it causes a significant imbalance in the parties' rights and obligations arising under the contract, to the detriment of the consumer.

Article 4

[T]he unfairness of a contractual term shall be assessed, taking into account the nature of the goods or services for which the contract was concluded and by referring, at the time of conclusion of the contract, to all the circumstances attending the conclusion of the contract and to all the other terms of the contract or of another contract on which it is dependent.

Assessment of the unfair nature of the terms shall relate neither to the definition of the main subject matter of the contract nor to the adequacy of the price and remuneration, on the one hand, as against the services or goods supplied in exchange, on the other, in so far as these terms are in plain intelligible language.

Article 5

In the case of contracts where all or certain terms offered to the consumer are in writing, these terms must always be drafted in plain, intelligible language. Where there is doubt about the meaning of a term, the interpretation most favorable to the consumer shall prevail.

Furthermore, some types of contracts require a notary's certification, and some international contracts need to be registered with government agencies. Failure to do so also results in the contract being invalidated. If the contract is executory or yet to be performed, then failure to register renders it null and void. However, in a partially performed or concluded contract, the court has the option of enforcing the contract by ordering the parties to register the contract.

Of critical importance to the foreign contracting party are the provisions dealing with preliminary contract, changes of circumstances, and quality of goods. Article 451 recognizes an excuse for a "material change of circumstances." Article 451(2) lists four conditions or requirements similar to those found in U.S. excuse doctrines: (1) the contract was premised on the change of circumstances not occurring, (2) the party could not avoid the occurrence even when using reasonable care, (3) the occurrence materially alters the contract, and (4) it was not an allocated risk under the contract or through industry custom. The subject of excuse will be studied more fully in Chapter Eight.

Article 429 recognizes the preliminary contract, which is not recognized under U.S. law. The parties have an affirmative obligation to conclude the contract under the Russian notion of preliminary contract. If the parties fail to state a time for concluding the contract, then the law provides that it should be concluded within one year from the conclusion of the preliminary contract. Thus, the potential for precontractual liability seems to be much greater under the Russian Civil Code than under U.S. law. Of course, "preliminary contract" can be a misnomer if the preliminary agreement is considered a contract unto itself.

The final topic to be examined is the recognition of implied warranties. Article 469(2) adopts the language but not the nomenclature of the UCC's warranties of merchantability and fitness. The code, however, offers a broader selection of remedial options to the receiving party. As under the CISG,[26] Article 475 grants the buyer a price reduction option. Under the UCC, the buyer must pay in full and then make a claim for damages under a breach of warranty cause of action. In contrast, the price reduction remedy allows the buyer to unilaterally reduce the price based on the diminished value caused by the defect. Article 475 also allows the buyer the option to demand specific performance by requiring "the replacement of the good of improper quality by a good corresponding to the contract." Under U.S. law, specific performance is only ordered when the goods are considered unique.

China's Unified Contract Law

Another interesting codification of contract law aimed at facilitating international trade is the People's Republic of China's Contract Law, otherwise known as the Unified Contract Law (UCL).[27] The UCL was adopted by the National People's Congress in March 1999 and became effective on October 1, 1999. The law is divided into twenty-three chapters. The first eight chapters are labeled as general principles. These chapters set forth rules on contract formation, validity, performance, alteration and assignment, termination, and breach. Chapters Nine through Twenty-Three establish rules with respect to specific types of contracts, such as those relating to sales, leases, gifts, loans, public utilities, transportation,

http://
Overview of the Russian Civil Code: **http://www. russianembassy.org/ RUSSIA/civil_code.htm.**

http://
Foreign Economic Contract Law of PRC: **http://www.qis.net/ chinalaw/prclaw20.htm.**

INTERNATIONAL

---

26.   See CISG Article 50.
27.   For an excellent commentary on the UCL, see Patricia Pattison & Daniel Herron, "The Mountains are High and the Emperor is Far Away: Sanctity of Contract in China, 40 *American Business Law Journal* 459 (2003).

construction, technology, and services. Articles 123 and 124 of the UCL provide that Chapters Nine through Twenty-Three are applicable to these specific contracts. The principles set forth in Chapters One through Eight apply to all other types of contracts, as well as serve as "gap fillers" in the absence of specific provisions in Chapters Nine through Twenty-Three.

A reading of the UCL reveals a great many similarities with U.S. law. For example, Articles 68 and 69 contain a version of the U.S. concepts of *anticipatory repudiation* and *adequate assurance.* Upon providing "reliable evidence" of the probable inability of a party to perform its obligations, a party to a contract may, upon immediate notice, suspend performance. This suspension must be lifted where the other party provides an "appropriate guarantee."[28] The contract may be dissolved if the other party does not regain its ability to perform its obligations or provide an appropriate guarantee.

INTERNATIONAL

Article 113 adopts the common law's foreseeability limitation on damages enunciated in *Hadley v. Baxendale.*[29] Under the rules of *Hadley,* damages are not to exceed those that could have been foreseen at the time of contract formation by the party breaching the contract. Articles 114 through 116 adopt the U.S. law of liquidated damages. Article 114 provides that contracting parties "may agree that when one party breaches the contract, that party shall pay the other party a penalty of a specified amount depending on the nature of the breach." The parties may also agree on the method by which this amount is to be calculated. However, there are some differences between the UCL and U.S. law in this regard. One immediate difference is the use of the term *penalty,* which has a negative connotation in U.S. law and may defeat the application of an otherwise enforceable liquidated damages clause.[30] Second, Article 114 provides that an injured party may request that a court or arbitration body increase the penalty when it is less than the losses sustained as a result of the breach. The court or arbitration body may also decrease the penalty when it is "excessively high compared with the losses sustained."

Article 115 provides that the parties may agree to the provision of a deposit providing security for contractual performance. This deposit may be utilized in addition to the penalty provision set forth in Article 114. In the event of a breach, the injured party may choose to invoke either the penalty or retain the deposit under Article 115. Article 119 adopts the common law principle of mitigation. The nonbreaching party "should take appropriate measures to prevent any increases in the losses sustained." A breaching party is not liable for increases in losses sustained by an injured party that fails to undertake such measures.

Articles 117 and 118 recognize the excuse of **force majeure** ("superior force"). A force majeure event is some unforeseeable happening that prevents one party from performing on the contract. The law will generally excuse the nonperforming party from the contract without liability. The requirements for a force majeure event are outlined in Article 117. *Force majeure* is defined as "a situation which, on an objective view, is unforeseeable, unavoidable and is not able to be overcome." Article 118 requires that the party unable to perform its obligation must immediately notify the other party in order to reduce potential losses and provide evidence of the force majeure within a reasonable time.

Articles 10 through 12 establish requirements for the format of contracts. Article 10 recognizes oral and written contracts but mandates that contracts be in writing

28.   Unfortunately, the terms *reliable evidence* and *appropriate guarantee* are not defined in the law.
29.   156 Eng. Rep. 145 (Ct. Ex. 1854).
30.   See U.C.C. § 2-718(1).

when required by applicable laws or administrative regulations. An example is Articles 79 through 90, which establish written requirements for the assignment of contractual obligations. The "written form" of a contract refers to those documents setting forth the content of the contract and include instruments, correspondence, and electronic communications (such as telegrams, telexes, facsimiles, and electronic mail).

The UCL also requires that contracts display a degree of certainty with respect to specifically designated terms. Article 12 states that contracts shall contain the following provisions:

- the title, name, and residence of each party
- the subject matter
- the quantity and quality of the subject matter
- the price or remuneration
- the period, place, and methods of contractual performance
- liability for breach
- the methods of dispute resolution

These provisions show that Chinese contract law emphasizes the need for a more comprehensive written contract then is required under the UCC.

Although not mandating alternative dispute resolution, Article 128 encourages the use of conciliation or mediation. If such processes are unsuccessful, the parties may then institute arbitration pursuant to any preexisting agreement between the parties. The parties may file suit in the people's court if there is no preexisting agreement or such agreement is invalid. Article 129 provides a general statute of limitations[31] period of four years for bringing a lawsuit or applying for arbitration. The period begins from the "date on which the party knows or ought to know that there has been an infringement of its rights."

Principles of European Contract Law

http://

The Principles of European Contract Law may be accessed at: **http://www.jus.uio.no/ lm/eu.contract. principles.1998/or http://www.storme.be/ PECL2en.html.**

INTERNATIONAL

In 1999, the European Union's Commission on Contract Law published its revised *Principles of European Contract Law* (European Principles).[32] The stated purpose of the European Principles was to respond to a need for a Community-wide (European) infrastructure of contract law to consolidate the rapidly expanding volume of EU law regulating specific types of contracts. Article 1.101(2–3) states that the European Principles will apply to a contract dispute in two main scenarios: when the parties select them as their choice of law and when the contract is to be governed by general principles of law or the *lex mercatoria*. The former scenario is likely to occur when the contracting parties are in disagreement over the application of a given national law. The European Principles, like the CISG, serve as a broad, fairly written compromise choice of law. The CISG applies only to sale of goods transactions, whereas the European Principles apply to all types of contracts. The second scenario is likely to occur in the setting of international arbitration. Arbitrators, at times, want to avoid the application of a harsh national law in favor

---

31. A statute of limitations establishes a period of time from the accrual of a cause of action (as upon the occurrence or discovery of a breach of contract) within which a litigation or arbitration must begin.

32. For a brief overview of the Principles of European Contract Law, see Larry A. DiMatteo, "Contract Talk: Reviewing the Historical and Practical Significance of the Principles of European Contract Law," 43 *Harvard International Law Journal* 569–81 (2002).

of a "fairer" general principle from international customary law. In time, arbitrators may recognize the European Principles as evidence of customary international law as has been done with the CISG.[33]

A review of the European Principles demonstrates extensive similarity with the U.S. common law of contracts and the UCC. It also shows significant differences that could potentially lead to unexpected liabilities for one who is familiar with only U.S. law. The following review outlines some of the differences and notes comparable provisions in the CISG. One caveat should be noted: The U.S. businessperson will find much more common ground than differences between the European Principles and U.S. contract law. Understanding the differences is important, however, to avoid certain liabilities. For example, the European Principles adopt the CISG's approach to formalities. Article 2.101 is almost identical to Article 11 of the CISG, which provides that "[a] contract of sale need not be concluded in or evidenced by writing and is not subject to any other requirement as to form [and] may be proved by any means, including witnesses." In contrast, the UCC requires all contracts for goods of $500 or more to be in writing.

The European Principles go further than even the CISG[34] in rejecting provisions that reduce the admissibility of evidence in a contract dispute. The enforceability of common contract clauses, such as written modification and merger clauses, is jeopardized under Articles 2.105 and 2.106. Under these articles, a **written modification clause** that requires a writing to make any changes to the contract provides only a presumption.[35] The other party may still introduce evidence to rebut the presumption. The articles further state that "a party may by its statements or conduct be precluded from asserting such a clause."[36] In contrast, American courts are more likely to enforce such a clause and bar admission of extrinsic evidence.[37] In addition, a **merger clause** found in a standard form or in the general conditions[38] section of a contract does not fare very well under the European Principles. The standard merger clause states that the document into which it is incorporated is a final integration of the parties' agreement and supersedes all other statements, writings, or correspondences. A merger clause that is *individually negotiated* will be enforced; otherwise, the clause establishes only a presumption. However, even when fully negotiated, a merger clause can be voided in the case of ambiguity in the contract or on grounds of waiver. Article 2.105(3) states that "the parties' prior statements may be used to interpret the contract." In contrast, there is a strong presumption in American law of enforcing merger clauses to prevent the admission of evidence of prior oral or written statements to contradict the written contract. Regarding subsequent statements and conduct, it provides that such statements and conduct may preclude a party "from asserting a merger clause to the extent that the other party has reasonably relied upon the subsequent statements or conduct."

---

33. See, e.g., International Chamber of Commerce Case No. 5713 of 1989 discussed in section titled "Choice of Law and Conflicts of Law" in Chapter Eight
34. See CISG Article 29(2).
35. See European Principles Article 2.106(1).
36. Ibid. at Article 2.106(2).
37. Extinsic or parol evidence includes oral statements or conduct that is offered to contradict a term in a contract; in this case to avoid enforcement of a clause requiring a writing to modify the contract.
38. The following definition of general conditions is provided in the European Principles' Article 2.209(3) (Conflicting General Conditions): "General conditions of contract are terms which have been formulated in advance for an indefinite number of contracts of a certain nature, and which have not been individually negotiated between the parties."

In the area of **notice,** the European Principles state that notice becomes effective "when it reaches the addressee." It qualifies this rule by stating that a properly dispatched notice of nonperformance, which is subsequently lost or delayed in transmission, "shall have effect from the time at which it would have arrived under normal circumstances."[39] Notice plays a much larger role in the actual negotiation of contract terms under the European Principles than it does under the common law system. Article 2.104(1) states that "contract terms which have not been individually negotiated may be invoked against a party who did not know of them only if the party invoking them took reasonable steps to bring them to the other party's attention before or when the contract was concluded." In contrast, Section 2-207 of the UCC allows for the enforcement of additional terms in the fine print of a contract between merchants even if they were not negotiated or no steps were taken to bring them to the attention of the other party. Note that the individual negotiation rule in the European Principles is not confined to standard form contracting transactions. Article 4.110(1) allows a party to void an unfair term that was not individually negotiated. It defines *unfair* as causing "a significant imbalance in the parties' rights and obligations."[40]

A number of rules in the area of **offer** should be noted. First, exporters should be aware that a circular, advertisement, or proposal they consider as an invitation to offer may be construed as a standing offer under the European Principles. Article 2.201(3) states that "a proposal to supply goods or services at stated prices made by a professional supplier in a public advertisement or a catalogue, or by a display of goods, is *presumed* to be an offer to sell or supply at that price until the stock of goods, or the supplier's capacity to supply the service, is exhausted." In contrast, such advertisements or catalogues would generally not be considered as offers under U.S. contract law.

Second, the **firm offer rule** is expanded to further restrict the offeror's ability to revoke the offer. Unlike Section 2-205 of the UCC, the offer need not be from a merchant, be in writing, be signed, or be for a period less than three months. An offer may not be revoked if it indicates that it is irrevocable or fixes a time for acceptance. Thus, a statement that the offeree must accept within ninety-five days will be interpreted as a firm offer for ninety-five days. Under U.S. law, the offer would self-terminate after three months (ninety days), and nothing prevents the offeror from revoking the offer prematurely; to be considered a firm offer, the offer must expressly assure the receiving party that the offer will remain open for a fixed period of time. More important, under the European Principles any offer may be recognized as a firm offer if it is "reasonable for the offeree to rely on the offer being irrevocable and the offeree has acted in reliance on the offer." Thus, the offer need not give any assurance that it is to remain open.[41] The CISG adopts an approach identical to the European Principles.[42]

In the area of **acceptance,** not surprisingly, the common law's dispatch or **mailbox rule** is rejected for the civil law's receipt rule. Under the European Principles, a contract is concluded when the acceptance reaches the offeror.[43] It would seem that the receipt rule for acceptance would provide the offeror with an

---

39. Article 1.303(4) (Notice).
40. Article 4.110 makes an exception for terms that provide the "main subject matter of the contract" and are provided in "plain and intelligible language." Also, the adequacy of value exchanged between the parties is not a ground for voiding a term. See Article 4.110(2)(a-b) (Unfair Terms Not Individually Negotiated).
41. See also CISG Article 16.
42. See CISG Article 16(2).
43. See European Principles, Article 2.205(1) (Time of Conclusion of the Contract).

additional period to revoke the offer. But like Article 18 of the CISG, the right to revoke an offer is frozen when the acceptance is dispatched,[44] even though the acceptance is not effective until receipt. In the event that the acceptance does not reach the offeror within a reasonable time, then the revocation would be unfrozen and preclude the formation of a contract. If a revocation has not already been sent, a late acceptance due to problems of transmission gives the offeror the option to reject the acceptance by informing the offeree, "without delay," that the offer has lapsed.[45]

The **battle of forms** scenario[46] commonly found in international sale of goods transactions is dealt with in Article 2.208, titled "Modified Acceptance," and Article 2.209, titled "Conflicting General Conditions." The offeree's form that gives a definite assent (acceptance) to the offer creates a contract unless it possesses additional or different terms that materially alter the offer. Article 2.208 recognizes that the parties can include contract language to control the battle of the forms scenario. The offeror may incorporate a clause in its offer to the effect that it "expressly limits acceptance to the terms of the offer."

The offeree may condition its acceptance upon the offeror's assent to its additional terms. Article 2.208 requires that the offeror must expressly agree to the additional terms in order for the conditional acceptance to effectuate a contract. An agreement to the additional terms can be obtained by the offeree requiring the offeror to sign and return the conditional acceptance. A conditional acceptance will be treated as a rejection if the offeror's assent to the additional or different terms "does not reach the offeree within a reasonable time." Article 2.209 provides that the fine print terms in offer and acceptance forms will generally be considered as "general conditions" and that only the general conditions that are "common in substance" become a part of the contract. Thus, conflicting general conditions would not become a part of the contract.

The European Principles also recognize a general area of **precontractual liability** and the duty of good faith negotiation not recognized under U.S. contract law. The very real possibility of unexpected liability is discussed later in this chapter in the section on Precontractual Instruments. For current purposes, note that parties have a general duty to negotiate in good faith. Failure to do so, such as never intending to enter into a contract, is grounds for a claim of damages. Thus, terminating a negotiation without giving a viable reason is not an appropriate approach. A party can be held liable for losses caused to the other party by breaking off negotiations.[47]

Article 2.302, titled **Breach of Confidentiality,** recognizes an affirmative duty not to disclose confidential information obtained in the course of negotiations. Statements made during the negotiations may also provide separate grounds for an action. Article 6.101(2) ("Statements Giving Rise to Contractual Obligation") states that if a professional supplier gives information about the quality or uses of services or goods when marketing or advertising or otherwise before a contract is concluded, then the "statement is to be treated as giving rise to a contractual obligation." This precontractual line of obligation is further extended to agents of the supplier. The supplier is contractually liable for statements made "by a person

---

44. See ibid. Article 2.202(1) (Revocation of an Offer). See also Chapter Eight.
45. European Principles, Article 2.207(2) (Late Acceptance).
46. Compare U.C.C. § 2-207 and CISG Article 19.
47. See European Principles, Article 2.301 (Negotiations Contrary to Good Faith).

in *earlier links* of the business chain."[48] To avoid such liability, the exporter-supplier must review advertisements, promotional brochures, and the practices of its foreign sales representatives.

A unique feature of the European Principles is its coverage of the **agency** relationship. Because the agency relationship is common in international transactions, as in hiring a foreign sales representative or distributor, the section on agency law is of crucial importance. Its coverage of the agency contract is limited to the relationship between third parties and the principal or agent. It does not govern the relationship between the principal and the agent. The rules on agency are divided into those governing **direct representation** and those governing **indirect representation**. In direct representation, the agent acts in the name of the principal. In contrast, indirect representation is when a third party is unaware that the agent is acting as an agent.

The agency rules in the European Principles are consistent with most of the agency rules in common law. A number of its specific rules are of note, however. First, if the agent indicates it is acting as agent, it must identify the principal within a reasonable time of entering into the contract upon the request of the third party. If the agent unduly delays disclosing the principal, then the agent becomes personally bound by the contract.[49] Second, if the third party doubts the authority of the agent, "it may send a written confirmation to the principal or request ratification" from the principal.[50] If the principal fails to respond in a timely fashion, the agent's act is considered authorized.

In the area of **genuineness of assent**, the European Principles recognize many of the same contract-voiding events found in common law. The terminology in parentheses is the common law equivalent to the invalidating rule found in the European Principles. A party has the right to void a contract due to: Mistake as to Facts or Law (unilateral mistake),[51] Mutual Mistake,[52] Fraud,[53] Threats (duress),[54] Unfair Advantage (undue influence),[55] and Unfair Terms (unconscionability).[56] In the area of mutual mistake, the court is charged directly with adapting (reforming) the contract rather than rescinding the agreement. If both parties made the same mistake, the court may, at the request of either party, bring the contract into accordance with what might reasonably have been agreed, had the mistake not occurred.

The notion of **economic duress** is placed not under the threats (duress) umbrella but within the notion of unfair advantage (undue influence). A party may avoid a contract if at the time of contracting "it was dependent on or had a relationship of trust with the other party, was in *economic distress* or had urgent needs, was improvident, ignorant, inexperienced, or lacking bargaining skills." In contrast, the notion that the party had "no reasonable alternative" is in the article on threats. The article on fraud recognizes a substantial duty to disclose information. The general duty of good faith and fair dealing is also applied to require a duty to disclose under certain circumstances. Factors to be considered in determining the need for

---

48.   Ibid. Article 6.101(3).
49.   See ibid. Article 3.203 (Unidentified Principal).
50.   Ibid. Article 3.208 (Third Party's Right with Respect to Confirmation of Authority).
51.   See ibid. Article 4.103 (Mistake as to Facts or Law).
52.   See ibid. Article 4.105(3) (Adaptation of Contract).
53.   See ibid. Article 4.107 (Fraud).
54.   See ibid. Article 4.108 (Threats).
55.   See ibid. Article 4.109 (Excessive Benefit or Unfair Advantage).
56.   See ibid. Article 4.110 (Unfair Terms Which Have Not Been Individually Negotiated).

disclosure include whether one of the parties had "special expertise," the cost of obtaining the information, whether the other party could reasonably have acquired the information independently, and whether the information would have been material to the decision maker.[57]

The European Principles adopt the civil law notion of *nachfrist* notice.[58] The nonperforming party may obtain an extension of the time of performance by giving notice to the other party. Generally, the extension must be given unless the nonbreaching party gives a commercially viable reason for not granting the extension. After the expiration of the extension, the nonbreaching party may terminate the contract even for minor breaches. There is no such provision for requesting or granting additional time in U.S. law.

In the area of contractual excuse for breach, the European Principles adopt civil law rules consistent with common law contracts. Article 8.108 recognizes the notion of **impediment** as a ground to excuse a breaching party for nonperformance. The test of impediment is similar to that in the common law excuse doctrines (impossibility, frustration). The impediment must not have been "reasonably expected" and must be beyond the control of the nonperforming party to prevent or avoid.[59] The nonperforming party must give prompt notice of the impediment or be liable for damages resulting from the nonreceipt of the notice. In the event that the impediment is perceived to be temporary in nature, the nonperforming party is not excused from the contract but is granted a temporary suspension of performance.

There are two fundamental differences between the European Principles and U.S. law in the area of remedies. First, a unique remedy of **price reduction** is given to the buyer of nonconforming goods. Under the UCC, the buyer may reject nonconforming goods under the **perfect tender rule**[60] or may accept the goods, pay in full, and make a breach of warranty claim. The price reduction remedy in the European Principles, also found in the CISG,[61] allows the buyer to reduce unilaterally the price paid for the goods based on the diminution of value due to the nonconformity. Second, the right to **specific performance** is not considered an extraordinary remedy. Article 9.102(1) of the European Principles states simply that "the aggrieved party is entitled to specific performance, including the remedying of a defective performance." In contrast, the UCC adopts the common law rule that specific performance is warranted only when the goods are *unique*.[62]

UNIDROIT Principles of International Commercial Contracts

UNIDROIT is a specialized agency of the United Nations that promotes the unification of law. In May 1994, it published *Principles of International Commercial Contracts* (UNIDROIT Principles). The UNIDROIT Principles were most recently revised in April 2004. Its primary differences from the CISG are threefold. First,

---

57. See ibid. Article 4.107(3) (Fraud).
58. See CISG Articles 47 & 63.
59. See European Principles, Article 8.108(1) (Excuse Due to an Impediment). Compare U.C.C. § 2-615 (impracticability) and CISG Article 74.
60. See U.C.C. § 2-601 (Perfect Tender Rule).
61. Compare European Principles, Article 9.401, and CISG Article 50.
62. See U.C.C. § 2-716(1) (Buyer's Right to Specific Performance).

it is not for adoption as a domestic law of international contracts. It is intended merely to provide neutral principles acceptable for guidance for lawyers and businesspeople from different legal systems. Second, it provides a set of general principles applicable to all types of contracts. In contrast, the CISG applies only to the commercial sale of goods and supplies a number of specific rules for that type of transaction. Third, the UNIDROIT Principles cover contract negotiations, whereas the CISG deals merely with the mechanics of formation (offer and acceptance rules).

Businesspeople writing an international contract of any type may want to review the UNIDROIT Principles. Although they are nonbinding, courts have applied them as the law governing an international contract and as a means of interpreting and supplementing international uniform law instruments and domestic law.[63] In this regard, one U.S. federal court has expressed the opinion that the UNIDROIT Principles represent an authoritative expression of international commercial law.[64]

Among the features of the UNIDROIT Principles that should be noted are those involving the formation of contracts.

- There is no writing requirement. The UNIDROIT Principles simply state that a contract "may be proved by any means, including witnesses."[65] Representations made during the negotiation stage may be entered into evidence even if they conflict with the written contract.
- International trade usage is recognized. The parties are "bound by a usage that is widely known to and regularly observed in international trade by parties in the particular trade concerned except where the application of such a usage would be unreasonable."[66]
- Article 2.1.16 recognizes a duty of confidentiality for information obtained during the course of negotiations.
- Article 2.1.20, titled "Surprising Terms," provides a means for a party to void fine print terms in a standard form contract. Terms that a party "could not reasonably have expected" will not be enforced. A conspicuous and clearly written but unusual term is, however, enforceable.

The UNIDROIT Principles expressly cover precontractual liability for conduct during the negotiation phase. Along with the potential of liability for bad faith negotiation, the UNIDROIT Principles acknowledge the fine line between negotiation and contract in three ways. First, a contract does not require an agreement on all details of the transaction. The fact that no agreement needs to be reached on all details of a transaction implies that parties may not know exactly when they enter into a transaction. Article 2.1.13 suggests that if a party wants to avoid being "dragged" into a contract by surprise, it must specify in advance that agreement on an issue it considers important has to be reached. If no agreement on that specific item is reached, there will be no contract.

Second, sometimes negotiations are not actually finished when one of the parties starts to perform. For instance, the legal departments of the two companies

---

63. See Michael J. Bonell, "UNIDROIT Principles 2004: The New Edition of the Principles of International Commercial Contracts," at **http://www.unidroit.org/english/principles/contracts/principles2004/2004-1-bonell.pdf.**

64. See *Ministry of Defense and Support for the Armed Forces of the Islamic Republic of Iran v. Cubic Defense Systems, Inc.*, 29 F. Supp.2d 1168, 1173 (S.D. Cal. 1998).

65. Compare UNIDROIT Principles Article 1.2 and U.C.C. §§ 2-201 & 2-202.

66. Compare UNIDROIT Principles Article 1.9(2) and U.C.C. § 1-205.

may still be discussing the contract terms when the sales department of the seller begins delivery of goods or services. In such a situation, the shipment of the goods or delivery of services can be considered as acceptance of the offer. Thus negotiations can be overtaken by contract performance. Third, sometimes parties to a contract intentionally leave **open terms**—terms to be agreed on in future negotiations. In such a case, a contract is formed with the open terms inserted in the future by agreement of the parties or implied by a court or arbitration panel.

The UNIDROIT Principles provide a number of standards for conducting negotiations. Article 2.1.15(2) states that "a party who negotiates or breaks off negotiations in bad faith is liable for the losses caused to the other party." In addition, Article 2.1.16 makes a party liable when it discloses or improperly uses confidential information obtained in the course of negotiations. Breach of confidentiality may entitle the injured party to compensation based on the benefit the party in breach received by disclosing the information.[67] The UNIDROIT Principles are indicative of how most civil law legal systems are likely to affix liability in the negotiation stage. Parties are generally required to act in good faith during the negotiation phase. For example, a termination of lengthy negotiations, without a justified reason, will be considered bad faith and subject the party to a suit for damages or expenses. Such precontractual liability may include claims for expenses directly related to the negotiations, including travel, research, and consulting costs. It may also support a claim for indirect damages, such as lost profits from other potential deals that the innocent party gave up to pursue negotiations with the terminating party.[68] German, French, Italian, and Belgian laws have elaborate rules on precontractual liability and the conducting or terminating of negotiations. In contrast, U.S. law does not require that negotiations be conducted in good faith. The differences between the civil and common laws in the area of negotiations will be discussed in the next section's coverage of precontractual liability.

INTERNATIONAL

In the area of performance, the UNIDROIT Principles include a section on **hardship,** defined as "where the occurrence of events fundamentally alters the equilibrium of the contract."[69] To claim a hardship, a party must show that the event causing the hardship could not reasonably have been taken into account at the time of contracting, that the event was beyond the party's control, and that the risks were not assumed by the party in the contract.[70] Hardship allows the party to "request negotiations."[71] In the event that the parties do not agree to an adjustment or settlement, the court is instructed to either terminate the contract or adjust the contract to restore its equilibrium.[72] The next Focus on Transactions feature provides practical tips for international contracting.

---

67.   See UNIDROIT Principles Article 2.1.16.

68.   The civil code countries make a distinction between mere negotiations and preliminary agreement. The line between the two is a very subtle one. In addition, the civil code countries provide for extended periods of time for bringing lawsuits. Under the Italian Civil Code, the statute of limitations to bring a breach of the duty of good faith negotiations is five years, extended to ten years for a breach of contract. In contrast, there is no cause of action in the United States for bad faith negotiation, whereas the statute of limitations under Section 2-725(1) of the Uniform Commercial Code is four years, and the contracting parties are authorized to reduce the period to as little as one year.

69.   Compare UNIDROIT Principles Article 6.2.2 and U.C.C. § 2-615.

70.   See UNIDROIT Principles, Article 6.2.2(a-d).

71.   Ibid. Article 6.2.3(1).

72.   See ibid. Article 6.2.3(4)(a-b).

Focus on Transactions

Practical Tips for International Contracting

Tip 1 : Even if not legally required to, put the contract in writing!

Tip 2 : Negotiate a choice of law clause.

Tip 3 : Custom design a forum selection or arbitration clause.

Tip 4 : Negotiate a specific force majeure clause.

Tip 5 : Expressly allocate the risk of currency exchange rate fluctuations.

Tip 6 : For a long-term or multiple installments contract, negotiate a detailed price escalation clause.

Tip 7 : Assure payment and performance through third-party devices such as confirmed letters of credit, standby letters of credit, performance bonds, and bank guarantees.

Tip 8 : Seek the expert advice of international lawyers, foreign legal counsel, international bankers, freight forwarders, customs brokers, insurance brokers, and governmental agencies.

Precontractual Liability

Under U.S. common law, a negotiating party owes no duty of good faith to the other party.[73] One may terminate negotiations in bad faith and not be liable for the other party's expenses, with one major exception. *Reliance theory* may be used to extend contractual liability to protect someone who reasonably relied on the promise or assurance of the other party that it would conclude a final agreement. Section 90(1) of the Restatement, often referred to as **promissory estoppel**, allows a court to give a remedy if a person's promise, such as a promise to conclude negotiations, is reasonably relied on and injustice can be prevented only by the enforcement of the promise.

The court in *Nimrod Marketing v. Texas Energy Corporation*[74] held that a purchasing agent who expended money in reliance of obtaining a contract from one of its clients could sue for damages when the client hired another subcontractor. The client had sent a letter to the agent that stated: "Acting pursuant to your responsibilities as our purchasing agent, it is our hope to begin construction of the housing project shortly upon obtaining a contract with the foreign government." The court ruled that based on the doctrine of promissory estoppel, the agent had reasonably relied on the assurance in the letter. See Focus on Transactions: Reliance Factors (Liability for Oral Statements and Informal Business Letters).

INTERNATIONAL

Examining the legal system of France allows us to see how other legal systems deal with the potential liability of precontractual correspondences and instruments. French law is less dependent than U.S. law on the literal designation of writings or instruments as legal or nonlegal. For example, Article 1135 of the French Civil Code provides that agreements "are binding not only as to what is therein expressed, but also as to all the consequences which equity, usage or statute give to the obligation according to its nature." This willingness to go beyond the writings

---

73.   For an analysis of precontractual liability in conjunction with the CISG, see Michael Joachim Bonnell, "Formation of Contracts and Precontractual Liability Under the Vienna Convention on International Sale of Goods," in *Formation of Contracts and Precontractual Liability* 175 (Paris: ICC Publishing, S.A. 1990).

74.   769 F.2d 1076 (5th Cir. 1985).

Reliance Factors (Liability for Oral Statements and Informal Business Letters)[75]

Focus on Transactions

1. Does the language in the statement or letter border on a promise or a guarantee?
2. Is there a disclaimer of liability in the statement or letter?
3. Does the statement or letter invite one of the parties to take steps to ensure performance of an underlying obligation?
4. What was the intent of the party giving the statement or letter?
5. Did either party receive legal advice as to the legality of the statement or letter?
6. What was the relative sophistication of the parties regarding the purpose or legality of the statement or letter?
7. What were the prior dealings between the parties regarding such letters or statements?
8. What is the custom or practice in that particular business or industry regarding the purpose and legality of such statements or letters?
9. What was the length of negotiations pertaining to the statement or letter?
10. Was there actual reliance upon the statement or letter?

of the parties is further elaborated upon in Article 1156: "One must in agreements seek what the common intention of the contracting parties was, rather than pay attention to the literal meaning of the terms."

This informality provides parties greater flexibility in structuring transactions. French courts look to the purpose of a letter or a writing to determine if it creates an enforceable contractual obligation. One might argue that even informal business letters, seemingly not binding on the surface, are more likely to have legal consequences under this purpose-oriented approach to enforceability. The presumption is that most businesspeople would not spend time negotiating and drafting letters and documents unless they believed them to be legally binding. French courts often ask the following question when reviewing an instrument for enforceability purposes: Would two sophisticated commercial entities spend time to create a meaningless, unenforceable instrument?

The *R.G. Group, Inc. v. Bojangles'* case provides an example of negotiations and preliminary writings that do not lead to contractual liability. It also introduces the concepts of the statute of frauds and promissory estoppel. The former is an obstacle to contract formation, and the latter is an alternative avenue of liability.

As the *R.G. Group, Inc.* case demonstrates, contractual liability under U.S. law becomes possible only when the parties move beyond mere negotiations. The importance of the line between negotiations and contract has been explored in recent cases. In *Novecon Ltd. v. Bulgarian-American Enterprise Fund,* a federal appeals court held that no contract was formed when one party responded to a letter from a second party by stating that it agreed to the terms of the second party's proposal.[76] The case involved Novecon, a company that develops business projects in Bulgaria. Novecon proposed a joint venture for a construction project in Sofia on land

75. See Larry A. DiMatteo & Rene Sacasas, "Credit and Value Comfort Instruments: Crossing the Line from Assurance to Legally Significant Reliance and Toward a Theory of Enforceability," 47 *Baylor Law Review* 357 (1995).
76. 190 F.3d 556, 564 (D.C. Cir. 1999), *cert. denied*, 529 U.S. 1037 (2000).

R.G. Group, Inc. v. Bojangles' of America, Inc.

751 F.2d 69 (2d Cir. 1984)

Pratt, Circuit Judge. Plaintiff R.G. Group, Inc., claim to have made an oral agreement with the defendants, Bojangles' of America, Inc., and its parent corporation, The Horn & Hardart Company, in which plaintiff gained the exclusive right to develop and operate some twenty "Bojangles' Famous Chicken 'N Biscuits" fast-service restaurants. Sometimes an oral promise or handshake is all that is needed, but when substantial sums of money are at stake it is neither unreasonable nor unusual for parties to require that their contract be entirely in writing and signed before binding obligations will attach. This case does not even present much of a cautionary tale. Its lesson is simply that when experienced businessmen and lawyers are told explicitly and clearly that a major and complex agreement will be binding only when put in writing, then they should be rather cautious about assuming anything different.

Bojangles' gave Gillman of R.G. Group a copy of its standard form development franchise agreement. Its general provisions include requirements that the entire agreement, and any modifications, be in writing and signed by the parties: "This Development Franchise Agreement together with all the Appendices and Exhibits annexed hereto contain the entire agreement and understanding between the parties hereto with respect to the subject matter hereof and supersedes all prior negotiations and oral understandings between the parties hereto, if any. There are no agreements, representations, or warranties other than those set forth, provided for or referred to herein." Gillman testified that he had asked Bojangles' representative Schupak over the telephone, "Do we have a handshake deal?" Schupak's answer, according to Gillman, was "Yes, we have a handshake deal today and right now." The agreement, however, was never signed. On December 14, 1982, Schupak called Gillman and told him that Bojangles' franchise committee had refused to approve the application put together by Gillman.

A. Was There a Contract?

Under New York law, if parties do not intend to be bound by an agreement until it is in writing and signed, then there is no contract until that event occurs. This rule holds even if the parties have orally agreed upon all the terms of the proposed contract. On the other hand, where there is no understanding that an agreement should not be binding until reduced to writing and formally executed, and "where all the substantial terms of a contract have been agreed on, and there is nothing left for future settlement," then an informal agreement can be binding even though the parties contemplate memorializing their contract in a formal document. The point of these rules is to give parties the power to contract as they please, so that they may, if they like, bind themselves orally or by informal letters, or that they may maintain "complete immunity from all obligation" until a written agreement is executed. Hard and fast requirements of form are out of place.

Freedom to avoid oral agreements is especially important when business entrepreneurs and corporations engage in substantial and complex dealings. In these circumstances there are often forceful reasons for refusing to make a binding contract unless it is put in writing. The actual drafting of a written instrument will frequently reveal points of disagreement, ambiguity, or omission which must be worked out prior to execution. Details that are unnoticed or passed by in oral discussion will be pinned down when the understanding is reduced to writing. These considerations are not minor; indeed, above a certain level of investment and complexity, requiring written contracts may be the norm in the business world, rather than the exception.

To begin with, it is not surprising that considerable weight is put on a party's explicit statement that it reserves the right to be bound only when a written agreement is signed. A second factor of major significance is whether one party has partially performed, and that performance has been accepted by the party disclaiming the contract. A third factor is whether there was literally nothing left to negotiate or settle, so that all that remained to be done was to sign what had already been fully agreed to. A fourth factor is whether the agreement concerns those complex and substantial business matters where requirements that contracts be in writing are the norm rather than the exception. In the present case the evidence on each of these factors unequivocally supports Bojangles' position. There was, first of all, the explicit wording of the development franchise agreement itself, which declared on its face that "when duly executed" it would set forth the parties' rights and obligations.

Here there was no performance, partial or otherwise, by either party. The third factor—whether there was literally nothing left to agree to—supports defendants' position as well. Winarick, RG Associates' chief operating officer, admitted in a deposition that the unresolved territory issue was an important one. The fourth factor concerns the extent to which, as a practical business matter, the agreement involved a scale of investment and complexity such that a writing requirement would be expected. Certainly this is the kind of agreement where it would be unusual to rely on an oral understanding. Bojangles' franchise contracts run for twenty years and cover detailed matters of capital structure for franchisees, purchase and development of real estate, construction of stores, trade secrets, transfers of interest, and rights on termination or default.

B. The Statute of Frauds.

The district court also decided that even if there had been an oral agreement, it would be rendered void by the New York statute of frauds. That statute provides in relevant part: "Every agreement, promise, or undertaking is void, unless it or some note or memorandum thereof be in writing, if such agreement, promise, or undertaking by its terms is not to be performed within one year from the making thereof." The required memorandum may consist of several documents, only some of which are signed, provided that they clearly refer to the same transaction.

Plaintiff argues that four documents, taken together, contain all the terms of the alleged contract. The writings put forward by plaintiffs, however, contradict the alleged oral agreement. Although plaintiffs rely in part on the standard form development franchise agreement to satisfy the statute, that agreement states that it is effective only when signed, that any modification or amendment to it must be in writing, and that any agreement concerning its subject matter must be in writing and signed. Our conclusion, therefore, is that the district court was correct in holding that there is no triable issue concerning plaintiffs' failure to satisfy the statute of frauds.

C. Promissory Estoppel.

Plaintiff also argues for recovery on the basis of promissory estoppel. In New York a claim for promissory estoppel requires "a clear and unambiguous promise; a reasonable and foreseeable reliance by the party to whom the promise is made; and an injury sustained by the party asserting the estoppel by reason of his reliance." However, there never was "a clear and unambiguous promise" to plaintiff that the development franchise was theirs. Plaintiff's counsel admitted in hearings before the district court that "the vast bulk" of plaintiffs' expenditures were made prior to December 3, the date of the alleged promise. Hence the district court was correct in rejecting the promissory estoppel claim both for lack of a clear promise and for lack of reliance. AFFIRMED.

Case Highlights

- If parties do not intend to be bound by an agreement until it is in writing and signed, then there is no contract until that event occurs.
- An informal agreement can be binding, even though the parties contemplate memorializing their contract in a formal document.
- It is good business practice to place an agreement in writing because writing frequently reveals points of disagreement, ambiguity, or omission that should be worked out before entering a contract.
- A court will weigh a number of factors to determine whether the parties intended to be bound before entering into a formal written contract, including whether one party reserved the right to be bound prior to a formal agreement, whether there has been a partial performance, whether there were still outstanding issues, and the complexity of the agreement.
- The statute of frauds requires any contract that cannot be performed within one year to be in a signed writing.
- Promissory estoppel is not available to recover expenses incurred before the making of a promise.

---

owned by Batsov, which was to get a share of the project for contributing land. A construction loan was to come from Bulgarian-American Enterprise Fund (BAEF). There were four letters between Novecon and BAEF concerning who would have what responsibility for the project. BAEF's last letter said that there were unresolved issues with Batsov that had to be settled before the matter could be finalized. Novecon replied that it accepted the terms of the offer and that it understood that BAEF would resolve matters with Batsov.

Negotiations between BAEF and Batsov did not go well, and BAEF withdrew from the project. Novecon sued for breach of contract. The court granted BAEF summary judgment. It stated that "for an enforceable contract to exist there must be both (1) agreement as to all material terms and (2) intention of the parties to be bound." The court held that there was no contract by reasoning that BAEF merely extended an offer to negotiate when it said that matters with Batsov needed to be resolved as a necessary part of any agreement. Parties "will not be bound to a preliminary agreement unless the evidence presented clearly indicates that they intended to be bound at that point." The exchange of communications did not constitute an agreement but were merely a part of the preliminary negotiations.

The federal district court's opinion in *Fairbrook Leasing, Inc. v. Mesaba Aviation, Inc.* provides a comparison to the opinions in *R.G. Group, Inc.* and *Novecon*. In that case, the court was confronted with the parties' failure to reach a final agreement with respect to the leasing of aircraft. The issue for resolution was whether the parties' admittedly preliminary agreement and subsequent performance pursuant thereto were sufficient bases upon which to find an enforceable contract.

Fairbrook Leasing, Inc., v. Mesaba Aviation, Inc.

295 F. Supp. 2d 1063 (D. Minn. 2003)

Rosenbaum, District Court Judge. Plaintiffs Fairbrook Leasing, Inc. ("FLI"), Lambert Leasing, Inc. ("LLI"), and Swedish Aircraft Holdings AB ("Swedish Holdings") lease aircraft. Defendant Mesaba Aviation, Inc. ("Mesaba") operates a regional airline under an airline services agreement ("code sharing agreement") with Northwest Airlines ("Northwest"). In the course of that business, Mesaba leased Saab aircraft through FLI, LLI, and Swedish Holdings.

On March 7, 1996, Mesaba, FLI, and Saab Aircraft of America, Inc. ("SAAI"), executed a "Term Sheet Proposal for the Acquisition of Saab 340 Aircraft by Mesaba Aviation, Inc." ("Term Sheet"). The Term Sheet provided that FLI deliver to Mesaba, and Mesaba shall sublease from FLI, twenty 340A Aircraft. At FLI's option, the term of each Sublease was between 72 and 96 months. The Term Sheet set the basic rent as $44,000 per aircraft, per month. The Term Sheet stated that it "is to be governed in all respects" by New York law.

In May, 1996, while negotiations on final documents continued, FLI began to deliver the 340A aircraft. The Term Sheet called for an April 15, 1996, deadline, at which time the parties were to deliver definitive documentation. This deadline was extended in writing several times, but finally expired on August 30, 1996. Notwithstanding the absence of a finalized agreement, Mesaba continued to accept planes under short-term leases.

Negotiations ultimately ceased in December, 1998. Mesaba continued to operate the 23 Saab 340A aircraft throughout 1998, 1999, 2000, and 2001, and continued its lease payments. In 2001, Mesaba declared it would begin to return some of the leased aircraft. FLI protested that the aircrafts' lease duration, as established under the Term Sheet, had not expired. In October, 2002, Mesaba ceased making lease payments for several of the Saab 340A aircraft. This action ensued.

Under New York law, a preliminary agreement will not ordinarily bind parties who contemplate further negotiation and the execution of a formal instrument. Notwithstanding this general principle, preliminary agreements may be found binding in appropriate circumstances. New York law recognizes two types of binding preliminary agreements. The first, ("Type I"), arises when the parties agree on "all the points that require negotiation" and is preliminary only as to form. The parties have the right to demand performance of the transaction. The second, ("Type II"), establishes a framework for agreement, and binds the parties to negotiate in good faith within that framework. The parties are free to walk away once they have made a good faith effort to close the deal and have not insisted on conditions that do not conform to the preliminary writing.

To assess whether the parties have demonstrated an intent to be bound by a Type I agreement, a court considers: (1) the language of the agreement; (2) the existence of open terms; (3) whether there has been partial performance; and (4) whether the agreement is of the type usually committed to writing. For a Type II agreement, a court considers the same four factors, plus a fifth—the context of the negotiations resulting in the preliminary agreement.

The Court finds the Term Sheet's language indicates the parties have reached a Type I agreement. The Term Sheet unambiguously states that, "By signing this Term Sheet, SAAI, FLI and Mesaba evidence their agreement to negotiate, execute and deliver definitive documentation." This language does not indicate a qualification or hesitation concerning the existence of an agreement; it merely indicates that scrivener (lawyer) work—"definitive documentation"—remains to be done. The parties carefully avoided making the Term Sheet effective on the execution of formal documentation. The Court does not consider it trivial that even though a final document was never created, the parties actively engaged in millions of dollars of aircraft delivery and lease payments for those planes. Finally, although the Term Sheet sets a deadline for drafting formal documents, the Term Sheet never suggests the parties have not closed their deal.

Partial performance is an unmistakable signal that one party believes there is a contract; and the party who accepts performance signals, by that act, that it also understands a contract to be in effect. The Court finds this factor strongly supports the conclusion that the Term Sheet is a binding contract. Plaintiffs delivered, and defendant paid for, 23 aircraft, even in the absence of final documents. This occurred using only the Term Sheet. The parties' performance continued, even recognizing that other collateral matters might remain.

This case arises not in the context of a law school examination, but in the real world. Plaintiffs had airplanes for sale and lease, and Mesaba needed those planes to transport its customers. It is clear to the Court that the parties found having planes in Mesaba's hands, and plaintiffs receiving a cash flow, to be more important than having a bunch of written documents. In a perfect world, the final documents would have been exchanged and signed, but neither the parties nor this Court occupy that world. This does not mean the parties did not have a contract; they did—the Term Sheet.

Even assuming there is no Type I agreement, the Term Sheet satisfies the requirements of a Type II agreement. The factors above, plus the overall context of negotiations, favor a conclusion that Mesaba and FLI bound themselves at a minimum to a framework within which to negotiate open terms in good faith.

The Term Sheet is explicit: "By signing this Term Sheet, SAAI, FLI and Mesaba evidence their agreement to negotiate, execute and deliver definitive documentation in substantially the form" of earlier drafts. Because the Term Sheet language controls subsequent drafts, the framework is clear. The Term Sheet reflects agreement on all "major terms" of a lease: the identity of lessor and lessee, the number of planes, the rent for each, the configuration of each plane, the delivery schedule, and the lease term. Here, FLI and Mesaba performed the major terms as they continued to negotiate the minor ones.

The overall context of the negotiations supports a conclusion that a Type II agreement existed. Mesaba needed planes to fulfill its route obligations under a ten-year Northwest code-sharing agreement which was up for renewal in the summer of 1997. All of Mesaba's business derives from this code-sharing agreement, and presumably, it would have been of some concern to Northwest if Mesaba did not have enough planes to fly its routes. Yet the record does not reflect that Mesaba either had, or was pursuing, any other long-term contracts to obtain a supply of Saab 340A planes in 1997. Mesaba needed plaintiffs' performance to fulfill its obligations.

For all the foregoing reasons, plaintiffs' motion for summary judgment is granted.

Case Highlights

- A preliminary agreement will not ordinarily bind parties who contemplate further negotiation and the execution of a formal instrument.
- A court may enforce a preliminary agreement when the parties demonstrate an intent to be bound based upon consideration of the language of the agreement, the existence of open terms, whether there has been partial performance, and whether the agreement is of the type usually committed to writing.
- A court may enforce a preliminary agreement when it determines that the agreement establishes a framework for agreement based upon the context of the negotiations. Under such circumstances, the parties are bound to negotiate in good faith within the framework and may abandon the negotiations once they have made a good faith effort to finalize the transaction.

Culpa in Contrahendo

The famous case of *Texaco v. Pennzoil*[77] illustrates that simply knowing the black-letter rules of contract law may not be enough to avoid liability. In this case, Getty and Pennzoil reached an "agreement in principle" and held a news conference

---

77. 729 S.W.2d 768 (Tex. Ct. App. 1987), *cert. dismissed*, 485 U.S. 994 (1988).

announcing the tentative agreement. Before the parties entered a formal agreement, Getty entered into a formal contract to sell to Texaco. Industry custom indicated that the term *agreement* in "agreements in principle" is different than the term *contract*. Thus, such agreements were generally considered preliminary and conditional on the signing of a formal contract. Nonetheless, the jury found there was a contractual "meeting of the minds" and that, but for the interference by Texaco, the parties would have signed a formal contract. Texaco was held liable for **tortious interference of contract** for its attempt to buy Getty. A jury awarded Pennzoil $7.53 billion in compensatory damages and an additional $3 billion in punitive damages. Texaco subsequently filed for bankruptcy protection before settling out of court.

INTERNATIONAL

The *Texaco* case also serves to illustrate the importance of contract negotiations and the dangers of acting in bad faith during those negotiations. Unlike in the United States, the idea of precontractual liability is accepted in most of the world's national legal systems. In civil law, one form of precontractual liability, **culpa in contrahendo**, has long been a part of its contract and tort laws. This liability is generally premised on the implied duty of the parties to act in good faith during the negotiations of a contract. In contrast, the UCC mandates good faith only during the performance and enforcement of contracts. Good faith under the civil law system means more than not breaking off negotiations in bad faith. Numerous duties are assigned to the negotiating parties. Under Dutch law, there are duties to disclose essential information, to investigate in order to obtain necessary information, and to refrain from negotiating with third parties. A Dutch court in *Plas v. Valburg*[78] divided precontract negotiations into three different stages.

The result in *Plas v. Valburg* was based on the Dutch court's conclusion that the parties had reached a "continuing stage" of negotiations, in which termination required compensation for expenses. These expenses could include all costs directly connected to the negotiations, including travel and estimating expenses and possibly damages that result from the fact that the prejudiced party was not able to conclude a contract with another party during the negotiations. However, the court concluded that the parties had not reached the third stage, in which the injured party is entitled to reimbursement of expenses incurred as well as profits (expectancy or

Plas v. Valburg

18-6 Nederlandse Jurisprudentie 723 (1983)

A construction firm, Plas, submitted a tender or bid to build a municipal swimming pool in the Town of Valburg. Its proposal was considered to be the best one by the Mayor and his municipal councilors agreed to the plan. The proposal was within the budget made available for the project. However, the City Council rejected the recommended bid in favor of an alternative tender by another company at a lower price. Plas sued for expenses and damages.

The court held that there are three steps in most contract negotiations that result in the creation of numerous rights and duties. During the initial stage of negotiations either party is free to break off negotiations without any liability to the other party. The next stage or "continuing stage" of negotiations allows either party to break off negotiations, but the breaking off party remains obligated to compensate the other party for at least some of its expenses. These types of

78.   This case was extracted from Michael Tegethoff, "*Culpa in Contrahendo* in German and Dutch Law: A Comparison of Precontractual Liability," 5 *Maastricht Journal of European & Comparative Law* 341, 347 (1998).

damages are grounded upon Dutch tort law. In short, the breaking off of negotiations is deemed to be a tortious act.

During the third and final stage of negotiations the parties are not free to break off negotiations. To do so would be considered within the doctrine of *culpa in contrahendo* or an infringement of the rules of good faith. This stage is entered into when the parties mutually and reasonably expect that in any case a contract of some kind would result from the negotiations. The breaking off party is obligated to pay for the expectancy damages of the other party. These damages include any expenses incurred and, if deemed appropriate, the profits that would have been made by that party.

Decision. The parties had not entered into the third or final stage of negotiations. Therefore, it is inappropriate to award Plas damages for lost profits. The negotiations had entered into the second or continuing stage

and therefore, Plas is awarded damages to cover the expenses incurred in preparing its bid proposal.

Case Highlights

- Dutch law divides contract negotiations into three stages.
- The preliminary or initial stage of negotiations results in no legal liability.
- Bad faith termination during the second or continuing stage of negotiations results in a claim for out-of-pocket expenses or what in U.S. contract law are referred to as reliance damages.
- The parties are prohibited from terminating negotiations during the third or final stage of negotiations without being liable for full contract damages, known under U.S. law as expectancy damages.

---

contract damages) that would have accrued as a result of completion of the contract. The bases for awarding expectancy or contract damages when there is an infringement of the obligation of good faith negotiations is explored in *Min v. Mitsui Bussan K.K.* in the context of Japanese contract law.[79]

INTERNATIONAL

Min v. Mitsui Bussan K.K.
Tokyo High Court (March 17, 1987)

Beginning in August 1973, Plaintiff Min, a Malaysian politician and businessman, conducted negotiations with Mitsui Bussan K.K., a Japanese general trading company (Mitsui), concerning a joint venture project to log and develop a forested area in Indonesia (the Project). Min and the employees of the Lumber Division of Mitsui had several conferences in both Tokyo and Singapore in the course of the negotiations, more than half of the conferences being held in Tokyo. In January 1974, Min and the manager of the Lumber Division reached the following basic understanding at a conference held in Tokyo:

(1) For the price of U.S. $4,000,000, Mitsui shall purchase from Min 50% of the shares of a certain Brunei corporation which holds a majority of the shares in a certain Indonesian corporation that has lumbering rights in Indonesia.

(2) Mitsui shall pay the share purchase price to Min on April 30, 1974.

(3) By the end of February 1974, Mitsui and Min shall enter into a basic contract covering the matters necessary for the Project.

After this conference, the Manager sent Min a letter dated January 29, 1974 (the Letter) to confirm these understandings, and on February 6, 1974, Min responded with his own letter, which stated that he accepted the offer made in the Letter. From February 21 to February 27, 1974, Min and the employees in charge at Mitsui held a conference in Singapore at which they completed a draft of the contract between Min and Mitsui for the sale and purchase of the shares in the Brunei corporation and a draft of a basic contract between Min and Mitsui concerning the Project. Min and employees of Mitsui also agreed that Min should rent an office in Singapore to proceed with the Project, and in April 1974 Min began to rent such an office.

---

79. This case was extracted from Kenneth L. Port & Gerald Paul McAlinn, *Comparative Law: Law and the Legal Process in Japan* 484–489 (2003). The original translation appeared in *Law and Investment in Japan* (Yanagi et al., eds. 1994).

By the April 30, 1974 deadline, however, Mitsui neither signed the draft contracts nor paid to Min the U.S. $4,000,000 purchase price for the shares in the Brunei corporation. Instead, Mitsui continued negotiations with Min. In July 1974, Mitsui proposed to Min a loan of U.S. $4,000,000, rather than proceeding with the purchase of the shares in the Brunei corporation. Mitsui suspended the offer of the loan when Min was arrested and detained by Malaysian authorities in October 1974 under the Public Security Maintenance Regulations (an arrest that Min claims was politically motivated).

After Min's arrest, Mitsui maintained contact with representatives of Min, and in July 1975 Mitsui agreed with them that, after Min's release, it would make its best efforts to execute the loan it had suspended. Min was released on January 31, 1976, and requested Mitsui to proceed with the suspended loan. Mitsui refused and in May 1976 told Min that it had no legal obligation to him.

Min brought suit against Mitsui, raising both contract and tort claims. The District Court rejected Min's contract claims, stating that . . . the Letter should not be regarded as an offer to enter into the alleged Share Purchase Contract. With respect to Min's tort claim, however, the court held in favor of Min, finding that Mitsui was liable to Min for Min's expenses in preparation for the Project and for his attorney's fees. Mitsui appealed the finding of its tort liability.

In light of the negotiations toward the conclusion of an agreement, Min came to have a right of expectation of, or an interest in, the conclusion of the agreement. Mitsui was thus obligated under the principle of good faith to make efforts to enter into the agreement in order not to infringe upon Min's right or interest. Nonetheless, Mitsui failed to perform its duty and, despite its repeated assurances that it would enter into and perform the agreement, it later reversed its course and concluded that entering into the agreement would be impossible, thereby injuring the said interest of Min.

In the modern world, the principles of good faith and trust govern not only contractual relationships, but also relationships under private law, and such principles thus apply not only after conclusion of an agreement but also at the stage of preparations toward conclusion of an agreement. In the event that preparation between two parties progresses toward conclusion of an agreement and the first party comes to expect that the agreement will surely be concluded, the second party becomes obligated under the principles of good faith and trust to try to conclude the agreement, in order not to injure the expectation of the first party. Therefore, if the second party, in violation of its obligation, concludes that the agreement is undesirable, it is liable for damages incurred by the first party as the result of its illegal acts.

In this case, we find that the Letter sent by Mitsui and Min's response, to which Mitsui offered no subsequent objection, caused Min to expect that the agreement would be concluded. Mitsui, therefore, should be considered to have become obligated from that time to make good faith efforts, under the principles of good faith and trust, to conclude the agreement. Absent special circumstances that justified suspension of efforts to conclude the agreement, Mitsui should not have been allowed unilaterally and unconditionally to suspend performance of its obligations. Mitsui should thus be found liable to Min for any damages incurred by Min due to such suspension.

Case Highlights

- The principles of good faith and trust govern the contractual relationship as well as the preparations toward conclusion of an agreement.
- Advanced negotiations may create in one party a right of expectation of, or an interest in, the conclusion of the agreement, thereby obligating the other party to the negotiations under the principle of good faith to make efforts to enter into the agreement.
- The failure of the parties to reach an enforceable contract does not relieve the parties of potential tort liability for violation of the principles of good faith and trust in the negotiation process.

One of the most common and important contracts that an exporter or manufacturer enters is with a foreign distributor for its products. This contract and relationship is vital to the successful marketing, sales, and distribution of products into a foreign market. The *SA Pasquasy v. Cosmair* case that follows deals with the negotiation of an exclusive distribution agreement.

SA Pasquasy v. Cosmair, Inc.

[1989] ECC 508

A party to negotiations with a view to entering an exclusive distributorship agreement, without valid reason breaks off negotiations just as they are about to be completed, is at fault and incurs liability in damages. This is especially the case where the party knowingly allows the other party to incur considerable expense in order to be ready to perform his side of the contract and where both parties had clearly expressed their intention to enter into a permanent relationship. The facts of the case showed that the final version of the distribution agreement was at the point of being signed and that the correspondence between the parties showed that there was consensus on the essential elements of the agreement.

We find for the plaintiff on the tort claim of *culpa in contrahendo*. Furthermore, we hold L'Oreal to be jointly liable with its subsidiary, despite the fact that it took no part in the negotiations itself, because the facts show that it induced its subsidiary to break off the talks. The plaintiff claims the following damages: (1) advertising expenses incurred in the promotion of defendant's products, (2) investments related to carrying out the expected contract, and (3) loss of opportunity. We find that the advertising expenses were reasonable and necessary because the products in question were unknown in Belgium and Luxembourg.

The plaintiff claims that it purchased a building, along with office equipment and a new computer system, in order to service the new distributorship agreement. It seeks to recover three years of the depreciation value (term of the distributorship) of these investments. Claims for damages are restricted by two principles. First, the damages must be assessed *in concreto* (certain, not speculative). Second, the victim is obligated to do everything to keep his damages to a minimum (duty to mitigate). The facts indicate that the plaintiff had acquired other distributorships that are also serviced by the new investments. We hold that the expenses in question do not appear to constitute injury having a necessary causal connection with the defendants' fault. Also, by acquiring new distributorships the plaintiff has been able to make a profit on its investment and therefore there is no damage.

Finally, plaintiff claims the loss of the opportunity of obtaining the profit anticipated by the grant of the distributorship for three years. In conformity with the prospective agreement and during the negotiations sales had already commenced over a period of ten months. The plaintiff estimates that its minimum loss profit amounts to 15 percent of the planned sales quota for the three years. We believe that 8 percent is more realistic because the plaintiff agreed to bear a number of expense items. Also, the profit would have accrued over the three-year period of the agreement. Therefore, the total amount of the calculated profits should be reduced by two-fifths. Judgment for the plaintiff for 8,864,788 Belgian francs.

Case Highlights

- Elements that favor an award in *culpa in contrahendo* include the suddenness of the termination, the finality of the negotiations, and knowingly allowing the other party to incur expenses.
- The nonterminating party is entitled to expenses and investments incurred in preparing to perform the contract, along with damages related to lost opportunity or profits.
- The nonterminating party's claims for damages are limited to losses that are provable with certainty and by its duty to mitigate.

U.S. businesspeople must understand the potential for precontractual liability in international business dealings. First, there is no true counterpart to such liability in the common law system. Thus, what are considered *mere negotiations* in U.S. law can lead to unexpected legal liability in an international business negotiation. Second, the effect of damages granted for a bad faith termination of negotiations can be catastrophic. Under the doctrine of *culpa in contrahendo*, a court has the authority to grant full contract damages, including lost profits.

Precontractual Instruments

This section reviews the legal significance of preliminary writings, correspondences, and precontractual instruments. Precontractual instruments are used in most areas of trade and finance. Examples include letters of intent, letters of support, and letters of assurance. For want of a better term, they will be referred to as **comfort instruments.**[80] Comfort instruments are generally given to encourage another party to enter into a contractual obligation. They may be made in conjunction with the negotiations between the parties or by a third party to the negotiations. For example, a parent company may send a letter of assurance or support "encouraging" a bank to lend money to its subsidiary. The issue becomes whether such informal letters can lead to contractual liability.

INTERNATIONAL

The potential for contractual liability lies in the internal inconsistency of many of these instruments. The typical comfort instrument tries to offer a guaranty type of assurance without the resultant guaranty type of liability. The 1923 English case of *Rose & Frank Company v. Crompton* is one of the earliest instances of a court coming to terms with a comfort instrument's internal contradiction.[81] The Court determined that the operative phrase in the letter was that it was a *contract of honor* and that mere loss of honor is not a basis for contractual liability. The line between contract and noncontract remains ambiguous.

Judge Vaisey in *Chemco Leasing SpA. v. Rediffusion Plc.* sarcastically framed the issue of comfort instrument enforceability. It is a "*gentlemen's agreement* which is not an agreement, made between two persons neither of whom is a gentlemen, whereby each expects the other to be strictly bound without himself being bound at all."[82] If this is true, then there is little ground for enforcement under either the express intent of the promisor or reliance by the promisee. On its face, the instrument's ambiguous nature would make it difficult to find the requisite intent, subjectively or objectively. The recipient of the comfort instrument would be hard-pressed to prove justifiable reliance.

INTERNATIONAL

Internationally, courts have been more likely to enforce such instruments. The civil law system, for instance, seems to place less weight on the semantic labeling of instruments when determining the existence of a legally enforceable obligation. The lack of dependency on legal literalism, both in the labeling of instruments and in the words of art used within the instruments, allows greater flexibility in affixing contractual liability than is found in the common law system. For example, in Germany there are no specific provisions in the civil or commercial codes concerning the giving of contractual guarantees. U.S. contract law would hold that comfort instruments are unenforceable because they lack clear contractual intent. French jurisprudence renders a contrary presumption, finding that such comfort instruments possess an implied intent to be binding **obligations de faire** (contracts). The presumption is grounded in the belief that parties generally do not intend to create meaningless contractual types of documentation.[83]

---

80.   See generally Larry A. DiMatteo & Rene Sacasas, "Credit and Value Comfort Instruments," 47 *Baylor Law Review* 357 (1995).
81.   1924 All E.R. 245, 255 (Ct. App. 1923).
82.   LEXIS Enggen library, Cases file (Q.B. July 19, 1985), *aff'd*, LEXIS Enggen library, Cases file (Eng. C.A. Dec. 12, 1986).
83.   "There is a normal assumption that a business transaction is not meaningless and that the words have a purpose" (*Chelsea Industries, Inc. v. Accuray Leasing Corp.*, 699 F.2d 58, 60 (1st Cir. 1983)). See also *Cincinnati Enquirer, Inc. v. American Security & Trust Co.*, 160 N.E.2d 392, 398 (Ohio 1958).

KEY TERMS

abus de droit
acceptance
agency
battle of forms
breach of confidentiality
comfort instruments
contract of adhesion
Convention on Contracts for the
    International Sale of Goods
    (CISG)
Council of Europe
culpa in contrahendo
customary international business law
direct representation
doctrine of *arrhes*
economic duress
English Unfair Contract Terms Act
    of 1977
European Union Directive on
    Unfair Terms
firm offer rule

force majeure
French Civil Code
genuineness of assent
hardship
impediment
indirect representation
International Chamber of
    Commerce (ICC)
lex mercatoria
liquidated damage clause
mailbox rule
merger clause
nachfrist notice
notice
obligations de faire
offer
open terms
pacta sunt servanda
penal clause
perfect tender rule
precontractual liability

price reduction
Principles of European
    Contract Law
promissory estoppel
Restatement (Second) of Contracts
    (Restatement)
Russian Civil Code
Shari'a
specific performance
statute of frauds
tortious interference of contract
totality of the circumstances analysis
UNIDROIT
UNIDROIT Principles of
    International Commercial
    Contracts
Unified Contract Law of the
    People's Republic of China
Uniform Commercial Code (UCC)
wa
written modification clause

CHAPTER PROBLEMS

1. Justice Cardozo noted a profound change in the law of contracts and the reduced role of formality as a requirement for contractual liability in the following quote: "The law has outgrown its primitive stage of formalism when the precise word was the talisman, and every slip was fatal. It takes a broader view today. A promise may be lacking, and yet the whole writing may be *instinct with an obligation,* imperfectly expressed" (*Wood v. Duff-Gordon,* 222 N.Y. 88 (1917)). If this is true, what are the consequences for precontractual liability? Do contracts have to be very detailed to be enforceable?

2. Two firms work together to prepare a complex bid for a buyer. One firm (Company A) drops the other (Company B) before getting the bid. After working for some time on specifications, negotiating with the buyer, and being chosen as a final candidate for the job, Company A told Company B that it was disappointed with Company B's behavior and obtained the contract on its own, with minor modifications from the joint proposal submitted previously. Company B sued Company A for breach after Company A subcontracted the work to another firm. Because there was no formal subcontract, what theory of recovery can Company B allege? What types of damages, if any, may Company B claim? See *TACS Corp. v. Trans World Communications, Inc.,* 155 F. 3d 659 (3d Cir.1998).

3. Review the *Bojangles, Plas, Min,* and *SA Pasquasy* cases on preliminary agreements and *culpa in contrahendo* and answer the following questions: What could the party being sued have done differently to avoid liability? Would your answer be different under U.S. as compared with civil law?

INTERNET EXERCISES

1. Review and compare the United Kingdom Department of Trade and Industry English unfair terms in consumer contracts regulations at **http://www.hmso.gov. uk/si/si1999/19992083.htm/** with the European Union Directive on Unfair Contract Terms at **http://europa.** **eu.int/comm/consumers/cons_int/safe_shop/unf_cont _terms/index_en.htm.**

2. Review the European Commission's home page for Consumer Affairs at **http://europa.eu.int/comm/ consumers/index_en.html.** What types of consumer protection initiatives has the EU undertaken? What areas in the subject index would be a concern for an international businessperson?

3. For a good review and explanation of Chinese commercial law, see **http://www.jus.uio.no/lm/china.laws/.**

4. Read the "overview" of the Council of Europe, along with the different subject areas within the organization and associated links: **http://www.coe.int.**

5. For a more extensive review of the Russian Civil Code see: **http://www.russianembassy.org/RUSSIA/civil_code.htm.**

6. Review the site of the Commission on European Contracts for recent developments on the principles of European contract law at **http://www.storme.be/PECL2en.html.**

The success of international customary law or trade usage provided a strong foundation for an international convention on sales law. Examples of the expansion of international customary law in the area of commercial transactions are the universal acceptance of the International Chamber of Commerce's INCOTERM (glossary of trade terms) and its regulations relating to international letters of credit (Uniform Customs and Practices for Documentary Credits or UCP). The major area lacking uniformity was the law covering the underlying transaction—the sales contract. The **United Nations Convention on Contracts for the International Sale of Goods (CISG)** has been the most successful attempt to fill this gap. The CISG may become the foundation for a uniform international law of sales for the twenty-first century.

This chapter reviews the CISG in detail to explain this important international document and to review the major issues of international sales law. The CISG is compared with the U.S. **Uniform Commercial Code (UCC)**. Most recently revised in 2001, the UCC is the product of the National Conference of Commissioners on Uniform State Laws and the American Law Institute. These

Chapter 8

International Sales Law

organizations have collaborated on numerous uniform codes. The UCC is their most successful collaboration to date and has been adopted by all fifty states and the District of Columbia. The UCC covers many different topics, including sale of goods, commercial paper, and secured transactions. Those areas not within the scope of the UCC, such as real estate and service contracts, are left to the common law.

This chapter highlights the differences between the CISG and the UCC. These differences are most likely to result in unexpected legal liability for the U.S. businessperson. An in-depth review serves two major purposes. First, it familiarizes the reader with major sales law issues common to all legal systems. Second, this review allows a closer analysis of how these issues are treated differently among nations.

International Sales Law

Most legal issues in international trade are settled by application of domestic national laws. At the beginning of the twenty-first century, however, it is appropriate to discuss the emergence of a truly international law of sales or a new *lex mercatoria*. *Lex mercatoria*, or law of merchants, refers to a system of rules of law created by international merchants, independent of any national legal system, for the purpose of governing international business transactions. The adoption in 1980 of the CISG marked a milestone in the development of the new *lex mercatoria*.[1] E. Allan Farnsworth,

http://

General coverage of the *lex mercatoria*: **http://www.lexmercatoria.com.**

---

1. See generally Albert H. Kritzer, *Guide to Practical Applications of the United Nations Convention on Contracts for the International Sale of Goods* (Kluwer 1989); Symposium, "Convention on the International Sale of Goods," 21 *Cornell International Law Journal* 419–589 (1988).

the reporter of the Restatement (Second) of Contracts, has predicted that the CISG will become the governing law of most export and import of goods transactions.

The CISG went into effect in the United States on January 1, 1988.[2] Thus, the United States has two laws of contracts for the sale of goods: the UCC and the CISG. If two contracting parties are residents of the United States and another CISG country, a U.S. court will apply the CISG rather than the UCC. The CISG, however, is an optional law, and the parties may *opt out* of it through a choice of law clause in their contract. As of late-2004, the United Nations Treaty Section reported that sixty-three countries have adopted the CISG. (See Comparative Law: Contracting Parties to the CISG.) The list of the contracting states includes most of the major U.S. trading partners, including Australia, Canada, China, France, Germany, Israel, Italy, Korea, Mexico, and Russia. Countries that have not adopted the CISG include Japan, Britain, and Brazil.

The coverage of the CISG can be grouped into three broad areas: substantive coverage, jurisdiction, and types of transactions. The CISG covers most substantive issues of contract law. There are, however, areas of law not covered under the CISG, including products liability, the legality of a contract, the capacity of the parties to contract, and whether the nonbreaching party is entitled to specific performance.

http://

For an update on recent signatories and international case and arbitral law on the CISG refer to the following Web site: **http://cisgw3.law.pace. edu.**

COMPARATIVE LAW

Contracting Parties to the CISG

Argentina	Australia	Austria	Belarus
Belgium	Bosnia-Herzegovina	Bulgaria	Burundi
Canada	Chile	China	Colombia
Croatia	Cuba	Czech Republic	Denmark
Ecuador	Egypt	Estonia	Finland
France	Georgia	Germany	Greece
Guinea	Honduras	Hungary	Iceland
Iraq	Israel	Italy	Korea
Kyrgyzstan	Latvia	Lesotho	Lithuania
Luxembourg	Mauritania	Mexico	Moldova
Mongolia	Netherlands	New Zealand	Norway
Peru	Poland	Romania	Russian Federation
Saint Vincent	Singapore	Slovakia	Slovenia
Spain	Sweden	Switzerland	Syria
Uganda	Ukraine	United States	Uruguay
Uzbekistan	Yugoslavia	Zambia	

Source: United Nations Treaties at **http://www.untreaty.un.org.**

---

2.   See 15 U.S.C. App. at 49 (2000).

These substantive areas are decided under a national law of contract. The national law to be applied is determined by applying the forum courts' conflict of law rules. The next section reviews the area of conflict of laws and its impact on the applicability of the CISG.

Choice of Law and Conflict of Laws

A **choice of law clause** used to avoid application of the CISG must be carefully drafted. For example, the parties may intend the UCC to be the law of the transaction. To that end, the parties negotiate the following choice of law clause: "the law of the State of New York shall apply to any disputes." Under Article 1(1)(a) of the CISG, however, the law of New York is the CISG if the two parties are from different CISG countries. To avoid such a quagmire, clear choice of law clauses should be drafted. For example, the previous choice of law clause should specify that the "Uniform Commercial Code of the State of New York" is the applicable law.

The CISG has three areas of **jurisdiction**. Article 1 of the CISG states that unless there is an express choice of law clause in the contract, the CISG will be the law of dispute in two situations. First, CISG will apply if the two parties have their places of business in countries that have ratified the CISG. Article 10(a) of the CISG offers guidance about how to determine **place of business** for multinational enterprises by providing: "If a party has more than one place of business, the place of business is that which has the closest relationship to the contract and its performance." Therefore, if a foreign subsidiary of a corporation enters into a contract, the place of business for determining the jurisdiction of the CISG is the location of the subsidiary and not of the parent company.

The second ground for CISG jurisdiction is when only one of the parties is from a CISG country. In that event, the court or arbitral tribunal is instructed to use its **conflict of law rules** to determine the law of the dispute. If the conflict of law rules direct the court or tribunal to the party whose country has ratified the CISG, then the CISG becomes the law of the dispute. Note, however, that the United States opted out of the second ground for jurisdiction. A U.S. court or arbitral tribunal will apply the CISG only when both parties are from different CISG countries.

A third ground for the use of the CISG in a dispute is based in customary international law. An arbitral panel or a court may use the CISG as evidence of trade usage instead of applying the law of an individual country. This is exactly what happened in *International Chamber of Commerce Arbitration Case No. 5713 of 1989*. In that case, the contract contained no provisions regarding the substantive law (no choice of law clause). Under such circumstances, the arbitrators usually apply the law designated as the proper law by applying conflict of law rules that they deem appropriate. The law of the country of the seller appeared to be the proper law governing the contract. Instead, the tribunal found that there is no better source to determine the prevailing trade usage than the terms of the CISG. This was so even though neither the country of the buyer nor the country of the seller was a party to the CISG. The issue in the case was the length of time a purchaser had to give notice of defect. The arbitration tribunal disregarded the domestic law's shorter statute of limitations period in favor of the two-year period provided in the CISG. In short, the arbitral tribunal used the CISG as evidence of international trade usage to avoid what it deemed to be an unfair domestic law. The arbitrator's decision stated that "as the applicable provisions of the law of the country where

http://

Contracting Parties to the CISG Table **http://cisgw3.law.pace.edu/cisg/countries/cntries.html**

http://

Department of State, Office of Legal Adviser—Private international law database: **http://www.state.gov/s/l/c3452.htm.** Click on "Transactions Law."

the seller had his place of business appeared to deviate from the generally accepted trade usage as reflected in the CISG in that it imposed extremely short and specific requirements in respect of the buyer giving notice to the seller in case of defects, the tribunal elects to apply the CISG."

This voluntary application of the CISG as evidence of customary international law should not come as a surprise. Because the CISG is the product of compromise between the world's major legal systems it possesses a universal appeal that many arbitrators find beneficial in their search for a *lex mercatoria* type of justification for their awards. The clear and nonlegal language of the CISG provides arbitrators a good source of supranational rules of commerce.[3]

Commercial Sale of Goods

The CISG covers only transactions for the sale of goods. Sales of services and transfers of intellectual property rights do not come under the jurisdiction of the CISG. In addition, Article 2(a-f) excludes certain types of goods from coverage, including goods purchased for personal, family, or household use; goods purchased at auction; electricity; securities; and ships, vessels, and aircraft. Many transactions, however, include more than one subject matter. For example, the sale of computer software is often a **mixed sale** involving the sale of a tangible item, like a disk or a CD-ROM, along with a service or technical assistance agreement and a license pertaining to intellectual property rights. Is this type of transaction covered by the CISG? Article 3 provides a two-part test to distinguish a service contract from a sale of goods. First, a contract is not for the sale of goods if the buyer provides a substantial part of the materials used in the production of the goods. This would be considered a contract for labor or assembly services. Second, a preponderant part of the contract must not be for the supply of labor or services.

The problem of mixed sales has previously been addressed in the application of the UCC. In *Micro Data Systems, Inc. v. Dharma Systems*,[4] the court held that labor can be considered as a component part of a good when determining the applicability of the UCC to a mixed sale transaction. In that case, the buyer agreed to pay $125,000 for software and $125,000 for services necessary to adapt the system to the buyer's needs. The court ruled that the "services" were not services to be rendered directly to the buyer but merely the labor to be extended in producing the modified software. As a result, the court concluded that the transaction was a sale of goods.

A **computer software sale** normally mixes the characteristics of a sale of goods, a sale of services, and a lease or license of technology, because software possesses both tangible and intangible elements. According to Article 3's second test, a software sale will be considered within the scope of the CISG only if a preponderant part of the transaction is for tangible goods. If, for example, a company contracts for software to computerize its inventory, the court may look to the allocation of the price within the contract among the different components. Thus, if the contract

---

3. See generally Larry A. DiMatteo, "The CISG as Source of International Customary Law," American Arbitration Association, *Dispute Resolution Journal* (1998).
4. 148 F.3d 649 (7th Cir. 1998).

provided for $20,000 worth of database software and $15,000 worth of support service and labor for data entry, the contract would be considered predominantly one for the sale of goods and covered by the CISG.

One suggested resolution for the intangibility of technology and software is to treat such items as **virtual goods**,[5] the approach taken in applying the UCC to software products. Virtual goods are treated just like conventional goods for purposes of UCC and possibly CISG applications. Article 2 of the UCC covers "transactions in goods." Therefore, its coverage is limited not to sales but by the word *transactions.* In contrast, the CISG expressly uses the term *sales* in defining its coverage. Its definition of goods is based primarily upon the concept of *movability.* Software clearly satisfies the requirement of movability.

The crucial determination of CISG applicability is if the sale of a copy of software, along with a license for its use, is considered a "sale of goods." Generally, the transfer of items by way of license are considered not to be sale of goods. Software licensing agreements, however, often have the characteristics of sale of goods transactions. If the copy being licensed is one for perpetual use for which the licensee pays a one-time licensing fee, then the software is essentially being sold, even though the licensor retains title to the software. In short, even though ownership of the technology is retained by the licensor, the licensee becomes the owner of the copy. Thus, the CISG is likely to cover sales of "off the shelf" software.

Parol Evidence Rule and CISG

The UCC requires that "some writing sufficient to indicate that a contract of sale has been made" must evidence any sale of goods for a price of $5,000 or more.[6] This same section of the UCC requires that the party against whom enforcement is sought must have signed the writing. In contrast, the CISG applies the view of many civil law countries that a writing is not required to enforce an agreement. By its adoption of the common law's **parol evidence rule**, the UCC writing requirement or **statute of frauds** also prevents the admission of evidence that contradicts the writing.[7] The parol evidence rule protects the sanctity of an unambiguous written contract intended to be the final agreement or integration of agreements of the parties. The rule prevents admitting into evidence any prior or contemporaneous oral statements or writings that contradict the contract.

UCC Section 2-201 also lists exceptions, including the **written confirmation rule**, an order for **specially manufactured goods**, and cases in which the parties' conduct has overtaken the lack of a sufficient writing, such as when payment or receipt of goods has occurred. The written confirmation rule is available only in commercial transactions because it requires that both parties be merchants. It states that a writing sent by one of the parties confirming the conclusion of a contract is sufficient to satisfy the writing requirement. The other party need not sign or acknowledge receipt of the confirmation to be bound by it. Section 2-201 does

5. See Marcus Larson, "Applying Uniform Sales Law to International Software Transactions," 5 *Tulane Journal of International & Comparative Law* 445 (1997).
6. UCC § 2-201(1). The amount requirement has been increased under Revised Article 2 (2002 Draft) so that only contracts involving values of $5,000 or more need be evidenced by a writing or record. Existing Article 2 sets the amount at $500.
7. See ibid. § 2-202.

allow the receiving party to object to the confirmation and thus prevent the formation of a contract. The notice of objection must be given within ten days of the receipt of the written confirmation.

The parol evidence rule seeks to preserve the integrity of unambiguous written contracts by refusing to allow the admission of oral statements or previous correspondence to contradict the written agreement. Under this rule, when parties place their agreement in writing, all previous oral and written documents merge into the final written agreement. However, such final written agreements may be explained or supplemented by prior dealings, trade usage, or course of performance information. **Prior dealings** include prior contracts and performances between the parties that establish a common basis for understanding and for interpreting subsequent contracts. **Trade usage** refers to the customs and practices regularly observed in a given trade or business. These usages "furnish the background and give meaning to the language used by merchants in that trade."[8] **Course of performance** is premised on the fact that the parties' conduct in performing under the contract is a good indication of what they believe to be its meaning. Section 2-208 of the UCC states that "any course of performance accepted or acquiesced in without objection shall be relevant to determine the meaning of the agreement."[9]

Unlike the UCC, Article 11 of the CISG states that a "contract need not be concluded in or evidenced by writing." In addition, a contract and its terms may be proven "by *any* means," including witness testimony. Therefore, the potential for liability for representations made during the negotiation stage is greater under the CISG. The UCC's parol evidence rule allows a party to avoid liability for statements made during the negotiations if those statements are not placed within the final written contract. Under the CISG, prior oral statements regarding anything, including quality and performance, are potentially enforceable. An unknowing American businessperson could be charged with unexpected liability for oral statements or representations made in informal correspondence. The CISG's lack of a writing requirement and of a parol evidence rule gives the recipient of a letter or documents a strategic advantage in proving enforceability. Also, oral assurances given to persuade another party to enter into a contract may be used to prove intent.

INTERNATIONAL

INTERNATIONAL

The CISG's lack of a writing requirement is further complicated by Articles 12 and 96, which allow contracting states to *opt out* of Article 11's lack of a writing requirement. Some countries, mostly the countries of the former Soviet Union and socialist law countries, have opted out in favor of domestic laws that require a writing. These countries include Russia, Ukraine, Belarus, Estonia, and Hungary.[10] The following opinion of the High Arbitration Court of the Russian Federation demonstrates the implementation of a writing requirement for contracts and provides a useful comparison to the statute of frauds set forth in the UCC.

The absence of a required writing is also an issue in states that have not adopted the CISG. For example, a contract is considered to be a consensual act pursuant to the Japanese Civil and Commercial Codes. As such, there is no requirement that a contract be committed to writing for it to be deemed effective. Formality requirements inherent in the UCC, such as the writing requirement, are alien to the law of contracts in Japan as expressed in these codes.

8. Ibid. § 1-205, Comment 4.
9. Ibid. § 2-208(1).
10. See, e.g., *Adamfi Video v. Alkotók Studiósa Kisszövetkezet*, Metropolitan Court of Budapest, Case No. AZ 12.G.41.471/1991 (March 24, 1992), available at **http://www.unilex.info/case.cfm.**

High Arbitration Court of the Russian Federation
Resolution No. 4670/96 (1997)

The Presidium of the Supreme Arbitration Court of the Russian Federation has reviewed the protest of the Deputy Chairman of the Supreme Arbitration Court of the Russian Federation on the Decision of the Arbitration Court for the City of Moscow of February 15, 1996 on case No. 60-409.

The joint stock company "Electrim" (Poland) filed a lawsuit against the private joint-stock company "Firma Kosmos" with the Arbitration Court for the City of Moscow seeking damages for the cost of a party of onions shipped under the contract No. PL 000144058/24–5155, dated May 11, 1994, as well as for the annual interest and court expenses in the total amount of U.S. $304,072.80. On February 25, 1996, the court reached its decision to satisfy the claim in the amount of U.S. $304,072.80 and U.S. $151,576.12 in interest.

In his protest, the Deputy Chairman of the Supreme Arbitration Court of the Russian Federation has suggested that the decision should be reversed and remanded. After reviewing the protest, the Presidium finds no ground for reversal.

In accordance with contract No. PL 000144058/24-5155 of May 11, 1994, the joint-stock company "Electrim" was obliged to deliver onions CIF Novorossiysk. On May 30, 1994, the first load of goods (500 tons) was shipped on the said terms.

In a fax dated June 24, 1994, the seller offered the buyer to change the terms of delivery to FOB Alexandria (Egypt) for the second load of onions. Pursuant to the International Trade Terms (Incoterms-1990), the CIF term of delivery means that the seller has to contract for carriage, whereas the FOB term of delivery means that the seller hands over the goods to the carrier contracted by the buyer.

The buyer chartered a ship and sent it to the port of loading (Alexandria). Besides, the parties modified Provision Four of the contract deducting the cost of freight from the price of goods. On arrival of the goods, their improper quality was determined. It served as a reason for the total refusal to pay for that load of goods.

When resolving the dispute, the court reasonably applied the Vienna United Nations Convention on Contracts for the International Sale of Goods of April 11, 1980. However, it wrongfully applied Articles 11 and 29 of the Convention which allowed modifications of a contract to be made in any form.

However, when joining the mentioned Convention, the USSR—whose obligations have passed to the Russian Federation—made a declaration that Article 12 was applicable. Article 12 establishes that a contract of sale shall be made or modified in writing.

The court's conclusion, that the modification of the contract price by means of its reducing for the cost of freight was, in fact, a written agreement between the parties to modify the terms of delivery, is correct. The assessment of the buyer to modify the contract is also evidenced by his chartering a ship and paying the cost of freight. Besides, an agent of the buyer in the port of loading signed a certificate of acceptance of August 5, 1994 which reflected the proper quality of the goods.

In these circumstances, the refusal to pay for the goods shall be held unreasonable and, therefore, the court has correctly ordered to uphold the claims in relation to the debt and interest.

The Decision of the Arbitration Court for the City of Moscow of February 15, 1996 on case No. 60-409 is affirmed.

Case Highlights

- Article 12 of the CISG permits contracting states to opt out of Article 11 and require that contracts be memorialized in writing.
- The Russian Federation, through obligations that passed to it from the former Soviet Union, has opted out in favor of domestic laws that require written contracts.
- The writing necessary to meet the requirement of Russian domestic law may be informal, such as a facsimile or similar document.
- The signature of a party to a contract modification is not necessary to meet the requirements of Russian law but rather may be evidenced by partial performance by the party sought to be charged.

The importance of the parol evidence rule to contract disputes is discussed in the following *MCC-Marble Center* case. This is a recent U.S. case involving the interaction of the CISG with other U.S. law. The court was asked to determine if the U.S. parol evidence rule is to be applied to cases involving the CISG.

MCC-Marble Ceramic Center v. Ceramica Nuova D'Agostino, S.P.A.

144 F. 3d 1384 (11th Cir. 1998)

"MCC" is a Florida corporation engaged in the retail sales of imported tiles. "D'Agostino" is an Italian manufacturer of tiles. At a trade show they orally agreed on a sale of tiles. The agreed terms were placed on one of D'Agostino's standard preprinted order forms. The executed forms were printed in Italian. MCC brought suit claiming a breach of the requirements contract when D'Agostino failed to satisfy a number of orders. D'Agostino responded that it was under no legal obligation to fill the orders because MCC had defaulted on payment for previous shipments. MCC responded that the earlier tiles they received were of a lower quality than contracted for and that it was entitled to reduce payment in proportion to the defects. D'Agostino replied that Clause 4 on the reverse side of the purchase order form required that all complaints for defects must be made in writing not later than 10 days after receipt of merchandise and this had not been done by MCC. MCC argued that the parties never intended the terms and conditions printed on the reverse of the order form to apply to their agreement.

Birch, Circuit Judge. Article 8 of the CISG provides: "For purposes of this Convention statements made by and other conduct of a party are to be interpreted according to his intent where the other party knew or should have been aware what that intent was. Due consideration is to be given to *all* relevant circumstances of the case including negotiations." The plain language of the Convention, therefore, requires an inquiry into a party's subjective intent as long as the other party to the contract was aware of that intent. MCC argues that it did not intend to be bound by the terms on the manufacturer's form since it was entirely in Italian. We find it nothing short of astounding that an individual, purportedly experienced in commercial matters, would sign a contract in a foreign language and expect not to be bound simply because he could not comprehend its terms. The general proposition is that they will bind parties who sign contracts regardless of whether they have read them or understand them. Nonetheless, Article 8(1) of the CISG requires a court to consider evidence of the parties' subjective intent. Affidavits of agents of MCC acknowledged that D'Agostino's representatives were aware of MCC's subjective intent not to be bound by the fine print terms.

The issue of whether the parol evidence rule applies to the CISG is a question of first impression in this circuit. It is important to whether the testimony of MCC's subjective intent and D'Agostino's awareness of it will be admitted to

contradict or vary the terms of the written contract. We begin by observing that the parol evidence rule, contrary to its title, is a substantive rule of law, not a rule of evidence. The Uniform Commercial Code includes a version of the parol evidence rule that states that "a writing intended by the parties as a final expression of their agreement may not be contradicted by evidence of any prior agreement or contemporaneous oral agreement." The CISG contains no express statement on the role of parol evidence. Moreover, Article 8(3) [of the CISG] expressly directs the courts to give "due consideration to all relevant circumstances of the case including the negotiations." It is a clear instruction to admit and consider parol evidence regarding the negotiations to the extent they reveal the parties' subjective intents.

Another court, however, appears to have arrived at a contrary conclusion. In *Beijing Metals & Minerals Import/Export Corp. v. American Bus. Ctr., Inc.*, 993 F.2d 1178 (5th Cir. 1993), a defendant sought to avoid summary judgment on a contract claim by relying on evidence of negotiated oral terms that the parties did not include in their written agreement. The court held that the parol evidence rule would apply regardless of whether Texas law or the CISG governed the dispute. We find the Beijing opinion is not particularly persuasive on this point. Moreover, the parties in the present case have not cited to us any persuasive authority from the courts of other States party to the CISG.

Our reading of Article 8(3) as a rejection of the parol evidence rule, however, is in accordance with the great weight of academic authority. Furthermore, a wide number of the other States that are parties to the CISG have rejected the rule in their domestic jurisdictions. One of the primary factors motivating the negotiation and adoption of the CISG was to provide parties to international contracts for the sale of goods with some degree of certainty as to the principles of law that would govern potential disputes. Courts applying the CISG cannot, therefore, upset the parties reliance on the Convention by substituting familiar principles of domestic law [such as the parol evidence rule] when the Convention requires a different result. Moreover, to the extent parties wish to avoid parol evidence problems they can do so by including a merger clause in their agreement that extinguishes any and all prior agreements and understandings not expressed in the writing.

What a judge or jury does with the parol evidence once it is entered into evidence is within their discretion as the weighers of the evidence. A reasonable finder of fact is free to disregard the parol evidence that conflicts with the written contract. Thus, it may disregard testimony that sophisticated international merchants signed a contract without intending to be bound as simply too incredible to believe and hold MCC to the conditions printed on the reverse side of the contract. However, this is for the trier of fact to determine. Moreover, because Article 8 requires a court to consider any "practices which the parties have established between themselves, usage, and any subsequent conduct of the parties" in interpreting contracts, whether the parties intended to adhere to the ten day limit for complaints of defects, as stated on the reverse of the contract, will have an impact on whether MCC was bound to adhere to the limit in order to preserve its warranty claims.

The CISG precludes the application of the parol evidence rule, which would otherwise bar the consideration of evidence concerning a prior or contemporaneously negotiated oral agreement. Since material issues of fact remain, we cannot affirm the district court's summary judgment in D'Agostino's favor.

Case Update

- The U.S. Supreme Court denied certiorari to review the decision of the Eleventh Circuit Court of Appeals in *MCC-Marble Ceramic Center v.*

Ceramica Nuova D'Agostino, S.P.A., 526 U.S. 1087 (1999).

- The Eleventh Circuit Court of Appeals' reasoning in *MCC-Marble Ceramic Center* has been cited in more recent court opinions as "highly persuasive." See *Mitchell Aircraft Spares, Inc. v. European Aircraft Service AB*, 23 F. Supp.2d 915, 919 (N.D. Ill. 1998).

Case Highlights

- The court suggests that the use of a merger clause would be an effective means to prevent parol evidence from being admitted. A merger clause is a statement that the final written contract is the only evidence of the parties' agreement.
- Because the CISG has been adopted in numerous countries, any previous foreign decisions on a particular issue should be reviewed to obtain uniform interpretations of the CISG.
- The two-year period found in Article 39 of the CISG is the outside limit for giving a notice of defect. A party must give notice within a reasonable time, which normally means within days of finding the defect. In addition, the parties can agree to a shorter notice period.

CISG and Uniform Commercial Code

This section focuses primarily on the substantive provisions of the CISG in order to demonstrate the potential for unintended legal liability for American businesspeople in international contracting. These substantive provisions are compared with relevant provisions in the UCC (see Comparative Law: Selective Comparison of CISG and UCC).[11] Although the UCC was a blueprint for the drafting of the CISG, the U.S. exporter must be cognizant of the fundamental differences between the two laws. Sixteen years after its implementation in the United States, the CISG remains a complete unknown to many businesspeople and lawyers. The CISG must be understood and applied effectively by U.S. exporters and importers because it not only places some unique responsibilities on sellers and buyers of goods but also provides a number of rights and remedies not found in U.S. law. In addition, this section emphasizes relevant differences in legal systems that have not ratified the CISG with the example of the Japanese Civil and Commercial Codes.

http://
Uniform Commercial Code: http://www.law.cornell.edu/ucc/ucc.table.html.

---

11.   See generally Henry Gabriel, Practitioner's Guide to the CISG and UCC (1994); William Hancock, ed., Guide to the International Sale of Goods (1986). See also B. Blair Crawford, "Drafting Considerations Under the 1980 United Nations Convention on Contracts for the International Sale of Goods," 8 *Journal of Law & Commerce* 187 (1988).

COMPARATIVE LAW

Selective Comparison of CISG and UCC

CISG Description	CISG Articles	UCC Description	UCC Sections
Writing Requirement	11, 13, 14	Statute of Frauds	2-201
Parol Evidence Rule	8, 9	Parol Evidence Rule	2-202
Formation	14, 19–21, 23	Formation	2-204
Obligation of Good Faith	None	Obligation of Good Faith	1-202
Revocability of Offer	16	Firm Offer Rule	2-205
Acceptance upon Receipt	18	Mailbox Rule	2-206
Battle of the Forms	14, 19	Additional Terms	2-207
Fixing Price Term	14, 55, 56	Open Price Term	2-305
Fixing Place of Delivery	57	Place for Delivery	2-308
Time for Delivery; *Nachfrist*	33, 63	Time for Delivery, Performance	2-309
Place of Payment	57	Time for Payment	2-310
Avoidance; Rejection	81, 86	Manner of Rejection	2-602
Limited Right to Reject Goods	49	Perfect Tender Rule	2-601
Warranty Against Third Party	41, 42	Warranty of Title	2-312
Warranties	35	Warranties	2-313-16
Inspection	38	Right to Inspection	2-513
Nonconformity; Nondelivery	36, 49, 51	Rights on Improper Delivery	2-601
Notice of Avoidance	49	Failure to Particularize	2-605
Failure to Notify	49	Acceptance of Goods	2-606
Particularized Notice of Defect	39	Generalized Notice of Defect	2-607(3)(a)
Fundamental Breach; Notice	25, 49, 73, 81–82	Revocation of Acceptance	2-608
Anticipatory Breach	71–73	Anticipatory Repudiation	2-609-10
Price Reduction Remedy	50	Not Available	
Nachfrist Notice	47, 48, 63	Not Available	
Impediment Exemption	79	Commercial Impracticability	2-615
General Notice	27	Notice of Excuse	2-616

Mechanics of Formation

The CISG can be divided into four groups: **general provisions** (Articles 1–13), **contract formation** (Articles 14–24), **rights and obligations** (Articles 25–88), and **ratification** (Articles 89–101). This section examines the group dealing with contract formation, along with articles in the ratification group that bear on formation. All legal systems recognize the formation of a contract when an **offer** and an **acceptance** are exchanged. The key issue is determining the exact time of formation in order to decide the effectiveness of attempted **revocations** by the **offeror** and attempted **rejections** (subsequent to the sending of an acceptance) by the **offeree**. The offeror is the party making an offer to contract; the offeree is the party that receives an offer and is empowered to create a binding contract through an acceptance of the offer. A contract may be formed when the offer invites the offeree to accept by the commencing of performance and then performance begins. Commencement of performance may not be sufficient, however. Most legal systems require the offeree to notify the offeror within a reasonable time that performance has commenced. Section 2-206(2) of the UCC states: "Where the beginning of a requested performance is a reasonable mode of acceptance an offeror who is not notified of acceptance within a reasonable time may treat the offer as having lapsed before acceptance."

The common law rule known as the dispatch or **mailbox rule** holds that a contract is formed upon the sending of the acceptance by placing it into a reasonable means of transmission. Almost all other legal systems of the world, and the CISG, find a contract to come into existence only when and if the acceptance or notice of the acceptance is received by the original offeror. For example, Article 1326 of the Italian Civil Code provides that a contract is formed "at the moment the offeror has knowledge of the offeree's acceptance." Furthermore, an acceptance must be communicated to the offeror within "the time set by the offeror or within that time ordinarily necessary according to the nature of the transaction or usage."

Other legal systems outside the United States reach a similar result. For example, China's Unified Contract Law (UCL) provides that a contract is formed at the time an acceptance takes place. In a manner similar to that provided in the CISG, an acceptance does not occur until notice reaches the offeror.[12] Furthermore, an acceptance must reach the offeror within the time period specified by the offer. If the offer does not specify a time period for acceptance, the UCL requires immediate acceptance for oral offers and communication of acceptance of written offers within a "reasonable time period."[13] However, unlike the CISG, the UCL provides an exception for late acceptances if such acceptance would, under normal circumstances, arrive promptly but was delayed. Under such circumstances, the acceptance is effective unless the offeror promptly notifies the offeree that the offeror will not accept the purported acceptance on account of the expiration of time.[14]

One exception to this trend in legal systems outside the United States is in the Japanese Civil Code. As a general rule, it provides that a contract between persons at a distance comes into existence at the time of dispatch of the purported acceptance.[15] However, the code also provides that an acceptance is not effective if it is not received by the offeror within the time, if any, specified in the offer.[16] This apparent conflict has been interpreted by scholars to provide an exception to the dispatch rule for an offer containing a specific time for acceptance. However, there are no reported cases addressing this contradiction. These examples demonstrate the necessity of familiarity with basic rules of contract formation for the U.S. businessperson.

http://
Pace University Institute of International Commercial Law— recent cases and developments interpreting the CISG: **http://www. cisg.law.pace.edu.**

INTERNATIONAL

INTERNATIONAL

INTERNATIONAL

---

12. Compare CISG, Article 18(2) and People's Republic of China Contract Law, Articles 25–26.
13. Compare CISG, Article 18(2) and People's Republic of China Contract Law, Article 23(1–2).
14. See People's Republic of China Contract Law, Article 29.
15. See Japan Civil Code, Article 526(1).
16. See ibid. Article 521(2).

Most international commercial transactions involve long-term negotiations, along with numerous exchanges of correspondence and documents. It is often the difficult task of a court or arbitral tribunal to analyze the numerous exchanges to determine if and when a contract was formed. Articles 14–24 of the CISG, similar to those found in U.S. law, outline a number of offer and acceptance rules to be used to resolve formation issues. The following Hungarian court decision, *Pratt & Whitney v. Malev*, was one of the first to apply the CISG offer-acceptance rules.

Pratt & Whitney Corp. v. Malev Hungarian Airlines
Metropolitan Court of Budapest, 13 Bp. P.O.B. 16 (1991)

Malev Airlines (defendant) entered into negotiations with Pratt & Whitney (plaintiff) to supply it with jet engines to be installed on jumbo jets that defendant was purchasing from Boeing Aircraft or Airbus of France. After carrying on thorough negotiations, Pratt & Whitney sent a meticulously written proposal of 15 pages to defendant on December 14, 1990, with a deadline for the proposal of December 21, 1990. Defendant accepted the proposal on December 21, 1990. After numerous other discussions and correspondences, defendant informed plaintiff in a March 25, 1991 letter that it no longer planned on buying plaintiff's engine. The issues for the court included whether the proposal without a fixed price or quantity was an offer, whether the defendant's response was an acceptance, and whether aircraft parts were covered under the CISG.

Hungarian Court. The applicable law of this case is the Vienna Sales Convention (CISG). Article 2 of the CISG excludes from coverage the sale of "ships, vessels, hovercraft, or aircraft." Does this exclusion include aircraft engines and parts? We believe that such component parts are covered as contracts relating to the production of goods as defined in Article 3 of the Convention. The defendant argues that Plaintiff's proposal of December 14, 1990, was of a general informative character, not an offer, but only a letter of intent. Furthermore, there were further discussions regarding the equipment after the December 14, 1990, proposal and the merchandise was not properly defined in that proposal.

According to Article 14 of the CISG, a proposal to be an offer need only be addressed to one or more definite persons, be adequately specified, and indicate the offerer's intention to bind itself in case of its acceptance. A proposal is adequately defined if it indicates the goods and fixes the quantity and price expressly or contains provisions for their definition. We hold that

the proposal leaves no doubt about its subject, that it indicates unambiguously the goods subject of the sale. Because it leaves to the buyer the exact engine to be purchased along with the quantity of the order is not critical. The number of engines will be decided based upon the number of airplanes the defendant decides to buy in the future. The proper indication of the goods is not affected by the condition that according to the proposal the buyer could choose from among the enumerated engines. Therefore, plaintiff's proposal of December 14, 1990, was a legal offer under the CISG.

The next issue was whether defendant's response of December 21, 1990, was an acceptance under Article 18 of the CISG. It is noted that the offer contained the language that the defendant's "acceptance of this proposal is conditional upon the approvals of the governments of Hungary and the United States." This condition does not prevent the formation of a contract. Article 23 of the CISG states that a contract becomes valid when the offeror receives a notification of acceptance. We believe that defendant's response of December 21, 1990, established a valid agreement. The court finds the defendant in breach of contract under the CISG.

Case Highlights

- Although ships, vessels, and aircraft are excluded from the CISG, a sale of parts for such items is covered by the CISG.
- An offer is sufficient even if it allows the offeree to fix the quantity term at some later date.
- A conditional acceptance does not prevent the formation of a contract.

Battle of the Forms

Most international export transactions make use of standard forms to expedite the negotiation and conclusion of contracts. Exhibits 8.1 and 8.2 show a standard purchase order and the fine print or **boilerplate** found on the reverse of a pro forma invoice. Either one of such forms, along with others such as price quotes or written confirmations, may act as the offers and acceptances in the contract formation process. The chronological order of communication determines, for example, if a purchase order acts as an offer or as an acceptance.

Most exporters and importers review the front page of the other party's form (see Exhibit 8.1: Purchase Order). Few take the time to read and understand the terms and conditions on the reverse. Failure to read and understand the boilerplate is dangerous because the terms on the reverse side of each party's respective forms are often in conflict or contain terms that the other party would not have agreed to if it was aware of them at the time of formation. For example, Paragraphs One through Three of the "Terms and Conditions" in Exhibit 8.2 Pro Forma Invoice absolve the seller of any responsibility for the goods when they are delivered to any third party, such as a freight forwarder or common carrier. This term may conflict with the trade terms on the face of the form.

Paragraph Four in Exhibit 8.2 makes the seller's quotations as to freight and insurance *nonbinding*. Paragraph Five limits seller's liability for its own negligent acts to $50 per shipment. Paragraph Six requires the buyer to notify seller of any defects in the goods within sixty days of the date of exportation or lose its right to sue for breach of warranty. Paragraph Seven allows the seller to retain a lien on the goods for "all charges or expenses incurred by the Seller in connection with the shipment to the Purchaser." Paragraph Eight absolves seller from any governmental requirements pertaining to the shipment of the goods, including marking and health regulations. Paragraph Nine mandates that any dispute must be settled in a court near the seller (City of Miami) and using the law of the seller's place of business (State of Florida). Paragraph Ten passes the costs of any litigation brought by the seller, including attorneys' fees, to the purchaser. The one-sided nature of these terms will become important only if the parties are involved in a contract law dispute, but by the time of a dispute, it may be too late for the purchaser to object to the onerous terms. Exchanging forms with conflicting or varying terms is referred to as the **battle of the forms**.

A U.S. businessperson familiar only with the UCC will be exposed to unexpected consequences under the CISG in a battle of the forms scenario. Section 2-207 of the UCC provides that, between merchants, additional terms contained within a purported acceptance become part of the contract unless "the offer expressly limits acceptance to the terms of the offer, they materially alter [the terms of the offer] or notification of objection to them has already been given or is given within a reasonable time after notice of them is received."[17]

Article 19 of the CISG resolves a conflict in the exchange of forms differently than does Section 2-207 of the UCC. Article 19 provides two methods by which additional terms contained within a purported acceptance do not become part of the completed contract. First, the offeror may prevent incorporation of additional terms in the contract by providing an oral or written objection to the offeree "without undue delay."[18] In addition,

http://

Guide to the CISG:
**http://www.
businesslaws.com/
toc44.htm.**

---

17.   UCC § 2-207(2)(a-c).
18.   CISG, Article 19(2).

EXHIBIT 8.1   *Purchase Order*

PURCHASE ORDER

(ORDEN DE COMPRA)

January 15, 2005

No. 7777895

To: Latin America Exporting Co.
P.O. Box 54321
Miami, Florida 33152
USA

Date Required: March 15, 2005

Deliver to: Compania Mundial

Mexico City, Mexico

Payment: Irrevocable LOC

Terms of Payment

CASH AGAINST DOCUMENTS

Payment Against the Following Documents:

Commercial Invoice	( )	Packing List	( )
Insurance Certificate	( )	Bill of Lading	( )
Quality Certificate	( )	Airway Bill	( )
Forwarders Receipt	( )		

Shipped By: _____

Final Destination: _____

Forwarders Insurance Taken By:

_____

_____

Trade terms governed by INCOTERMS 1990 CIF Mexico City

Identifying Marks	Quantity	Description	Unit Price	Amount
C&M "Made in USA"	350	Model #345 HTS # 8059101345	US $45.99	$
C&M "Made in USA"	150	Model #198 HTS # 8059101152	US $74.50	$
			Total	$

Packing: Each in Cardboard Box,144 per double export carton,
weighing 14 & 16 kilograms and measuring 25x25x10 cm.

Shipment: via M/V Hathaway from Port of Miami

Payment: Irrevocable Letter of Credit for 110% of CIF value at sight,
through Banco de Mexico to Nations Bank, Miami, Florida

Notify Party: Towers of Mexico Customs Broker

Confirmed By: _____

a purported acceptance that contains material alterations of the original offer serves as a rejection of the offer and constitutes a counteroffer. Unlike the UCC, the CISG defines materiality to include, among other things, "additional or different terms relating to the price, payment, quality and quantity of the goods,

EXHIBIT 8.2   *Pro Forma Invoice—Terms and Conditions*

Pro Forma Invoice
Terms and Conditions
(Please read carefully.)

1. <u>Services by Third Parties:</u> Unless the Company carries, stores, or otherwise physically handles the shipment, and the loss, damage, or delay occurs during such activity, the Company assumes no liability as a carrier, but undertakes only to use reasonable care in the selection of carriers, truckmen, lightermen, forwarders, customhouse brokers, warehousemen, and others to whom it may entrust the goods for delivery unless a separate bill of lading or other contract of carriage is issued by the Company, in which event the terms thereof shall govern.

2. <u>Liability Limitations of Third Parties:</u> The Company is authorized to select all necessary third parties as required to transport the goods, all of whom shall be considered as the agents of the Purchaser and subject to all conditions as to limitation of liability and to all rules and regulations and conditions appearing in bills of lading or receipts issued by such third parties. The Company shall not be liable for any loss, damage, expense, or delay to the goods for any reason whatsoever when the goods are in the possession of third parties.

3. <u>Choosing Routes or Agents:</u> Unless specified by the Customer in writing, the Company has complete freedom in choosing the means, route, and procedure to be followed in the handling, transportation, and delivery of the goods.

4. <u>Quotations Not Binding:</u> Quotations as to fees, rates of duty, freight charges, insurance premiums, or other charges are for informational purposes only and are subject to change without notice unless the Company in writing specifically undertakes the transportation of the shipment at the specified rate.

5. <u>Limitation of $50 per Shipment:</u> The Customer agrees that the Company shall in no event be liable for any loss, expense, or delay to the goods resulting from the negligence or fault of the Company for any amount in excess of $50 per shipment.

6. <u>Presenting Claims:</u> In no event shall the Company be liable for any act or omission or default unless the claim is presented to it at its office within 60 days from the date of exportation of the goods in a written statement to which sworn proof of claim shall be attached.

7. <u>General Lien on Any Property:</u> The Company shall have a general lien on any and all property and documents relating thereto of the Purchaser in its possession or en route, for all claims for charges, expenses or advance incurred by the Company in connection with any shipments to the Purchaser, and if such claims remain unsatisfied for a period of thirty days, the Company may sell at public auction or private sale, and apply the net proceeds of the sale to the payment of the amount due Company. The Purchaser remains liable for any deficiency in the sale.

8. <u>No Responsibility for Governmental Requirements:</u> It is the responsibility of the Purchaser to know and inform the Company of the marking requirements of the country of importation, and all other safety and health regulations, and all other requirements of law or official regulations. The Company shall not be responsible for action taken or fines or penalties assessed by any governmental agency against the shipment.

9. <u>Construction of Terms and Venue:</u> The foregoing terms and conditions shall be construed according to the laws of the State of Florida. Unless otherwise consented to in writing by the Company, no legal proceeding against the Company may be instituted by either the Purchaser, its assigns or subrogee, except in the City of Miami, Florida.

10. <u>Costs of Collection:</u> Purchaser shall pay all costs, charges, and expenses including attorney's fees, reasonably incurred or paid by the Company (including attorney's fees for any appeals taken) because of the failure of the Purchaser to perform and comply with the terms and conditions of this agreement including payment of monies due and every such payment shall bear interest from the date at the highest rate permitted by law.

place and time of delivery, extent of one party's liability to the other or the settlement of disputes."[19]

For example, a seller responds to a purchase order ("the offer") with a confirming invoice ("the acceptance"). The confirming invoice, however, includes an **additional term** that limits purchaser's ability to make a claim for breach of warranty by providing a short notice period. What is the legal effect of the additional notice requirement? If construed as a nonmaterial modification, the CISG and the UCC would acknowledge the contract formation, incorporating the additional term. Article 19(3) of the CISG, however, broadly defines material to include the "extent of one party's liability to the other." In essence, the CISG adopts the old common law **mirror image rule**, in which the acceptance must be a mirror image of the offer. Thus, under the CISG, the additional term converts the attempted acceptance into a counteroffer, resulting in a finding of no contract. The following opinion of the U.S. Court of Appeals for the Ninth Circuit in *Chateau des Charmes Wines Ltd. v. Sabate USA, Inc.* demonstrates the operation of the materiality provisions of the CISG.

Chateau des Charmes Wines Ltd. v. Sabate USA, Inc.

328 F.3d 528 (9th Cir. 2003)

Per Curiam. Chateau des Charmes Wines, Ltd. ("Chateau des Charmes"), a Canadian company, appeals the dismissal of its action for breach of contract and related claims arising out of its purchase of wine corks from Sabate, S.A. ("Sabate France"), a French company, and Sabate USA, Inc. ("Sabate USA"), a wholly owned California subsidiary. Sabate France manufactures and sells special wine corks that it claims will not cause wines to be spoiled by "cork taint," a distasteful flavor that some corks produce. It sells these corks through a wholly owned California subsidiary, Sabate USA.

In February 2000, after some preliminary discussions about the characteristics of Sabate's corks, Chateau des Charmes, a winery from Ontario, Canada, agreed by telephone with Sabate USA to purchase a certain number of corks at a specific price. The parties agreed on payment and shipping terms. No other terms were discussed, nor did the parties have any history of prior dealings. Later that year, Chateau des Charmes placed a second telephone order for corks on the same terms. In total, Chateau des Charmes ordered 1.2 million corks.

Sabate France shipped the corks to Canada in eleven shipments. For each shipment, Sabate France also sent an invoice. Some of the invoices arrived before the shipments, some with the shipments, and some after the shipments. On the face of each invoice was a paragraph in French that specified that "Any dispute arising under the present contract is under the sole jurisdiction of the

Court of Commerce of the City of Perpignan." On the back of each invoice a number of provisions were printed in French, including a clause that specified that "any disputes arising out of this agreement shall be brought before the court with jurisdiction to try the matter in the judicial district where Seller's registered office is located." Chateau des Charmes duly took delivery and paid for each shipment of corks. The corks were then used to bottle Chateau des Charmes' wines.

Chateau des Charmes claims that, in 2001, it noticed that the wine bottled with Sabate's corks was tainted by cork flavors. Chateau des Charmes filed suit in federal district court in California against Sabate France and Sabate USA alleging claims for breach of contract, strict liability, breach of warranty, false advertising, and unfair competition. Sabate France and Sabate USA filed a motion to dismiss based on the forum selection clauses. The district court held that the forum selection clauses were valid and enforceable and dismissed the action. This appeal ensued.

The question before us is whether the forum selection clauses in Sabate France's invoices were part of any agreement between the parties. The disputes in this case arise out of an agreement for a sale of goods from a French party and a United States party to a Canadian party. Such international sales contracts are ordinarily governed by a multilateral treaty, the United Nations Convention on Contracts for the International Sale of

---

19. Ibid. Article 19(3).

Goods (CISG), which applies to "contracts of sale of goods between parties whose places of business are in different States . . . when the States are Contracting States." The United States, Canada, and France are all contracting states to the CISG. Accordingly, the Convention governs the substantive question of contract formation as to the forum selection clauses.

Under the CISG, the oral agreements between Sabate USA and Chateau des Charmes as to the kind of cork, the quantity, and the price were sufficient to create binding contracts. The terms of those agreements did not include any forum selection clause. Indeed, Sabate France and Sabate USA do not contend that a forum selection clause was part of their oral agreements, but merely that the clauses in the invoices became part of a binding agreement. The logic of this contention is defective. Under Article 29(1) of the CISG, a "contract may be modified or terminated by the mere agreement of the parties." However, Article 19(3) of the CISG states that "[a]dditional or different terms relating, among other things, to . . . the settlement of disputes are considered to alter the terms of the offer materially." There is no indication that Chateau des Charmes conducted itself in a manner that evidenced any affirmative assent to the forum selection clauses in the invoices. Rather, Chateau des Charmes merely performed its obligations under the oral contract.

Nothing in the Convention suggests that the failure to object to a party's unilateral attempt to alter materially the terms of an otherwise valid agreement is an "agreement" within the terms of Article 29. Here, no circumstances exist to conclude that Chateau des Charmes's conduct evidenced an "agreement." We reject the contention that because Sabate France sent multiple invoices it created an agreement as to the proper forum with Chateau des Charmes. The parties agreed in two telephone calls to a purchase of corks to be shipped in eleven batches. In such circumstances, a party's multiple attempts to alter an agreement unilaterally do not so effect.
REVERSED and REMANDED.

Case Highlights

- U.S. courts will apply the CISG in accordance with its terms to contracts for the sale of goods between parties whose places of business are in different states that are parties to the CISG.
- Under the CISG, contracts may be modified or terminated by the mere agreement of the parties without further formalities.
- The CISG provides that additional or different terms relating to the settlement of disputes are considered material alterations to the terms of an offer.
- Nothing in the CISG provides that the failure to object to a party's unilateral attempt to materially alter the terms of an agreement is itself an agreement to such alterations.

Similar results as dictated by Article 19 of the CISG may occur in legal systems outside the United States that have adopted the CISG. For example, Article 30 of China's UCL provides that material alterations contained within a purported acceptance constitute a counteroffer. Material alterations are defined as alterations to the "subject matter of the contract, quantity, quality, price or remuneration, time limits on contractual performance, the place and methods of contractual performance, liability for breach of contract and methods of dispute resolution."[20] By contrast, nonmaterial alterations become part of the contract unless the offeror "immediately expresses its opposition or the offer clearly stipulates that the offeree may not in its acceptance make any alterations to the contents of the offer."[21]

INTERNATIONAL

Although it has not adopted the CISG, a similar result is reached in Japan. Acceptance (*shodaku*) in Japanese law constitutes a declaration by the offeree to reply to and be bound by a specific offer to enter into a contract. A reply that purports to act as an acceptance but contains new or additional terms is regarded by the Japanese Civil Code as a counteroffer.[22]

INTERNATIONAL

20.   People's Republic of China Contract Law, Article 30.
21.   Ibid. Article 31.
22.   See Japan Civil Code, Article 528.

The impact of the CISG's adoption of the mirror image rule may be profound. The use of standard forms in the formation of modern contracts is a universal practice. Invariably, whenever seller's and buyer's forms are exchanged, there will be conflicting terms in the fine print that neither party is likely to read unless a dispute arises. Under the CISG's broad materiality standard, the agreements thus formed are technically unenforceable.

However, two German courts seemed to recognize the reality of standard form contracting and ignored the broad materiality definition in Article 19(3). They held that a forum selection clause and a restrictive notice provision pertaining to claims of defects were not material terms.[23] These provisions seem to come within the purview of Article 19(3) as terms relating to the "extent of one party's liability to the other party or the settlement of disputes." The German courts' decisions demonstrate that until there are enough cases interpreting the CISG, contracting parties are likely to be surprised by some of the decisions national courts produce by applying the CISG. One way to avoid a battle of the forms is to use a single or model contract that both parties sign.

The battle of the forms scenario is further illustrated in *Filanto, S.P.A. v. Chilewich International Corp.* In this case, one of the parties attempted to incorporate another document by reference in its offer. A belated acceptance attempted to delete the reference in order to avoid an arbitration clause. The issues for the court were whether a contract had been formed and, if so, under whose terms.

Filanto, S.P.A. v. Chilewich International Corp.

789 F. Supp. 1229 (S.D.N.Y. 1992)

An Italian footwear manufacturer brought action against New York export-import firm, alleging breach of contract. This case is a striking example of how a lawsuit involving a relatively straightforward international commercial transaction can raise an array of complex questions. Defendant Chilewich signed a contract with a Russian importer for a long-term supply of footwear. This "Russian Contract" contained an arbitration clause: "All disputes are to be settled by the Arbitration tribunal of the Chamber of Commerce in Moscow, Russia."

Chilewich then entered into negotiations with Filanto, an Italian manufacturer, to supply the shoes needed for the Russian contract. After a negotiation meeting, Chilewich sent Filanto a letter, dated July 27, 1989, that stated: "Attached please find our contract to cover the purchases from you. Same is governed by the conditions which are enumerated in the standard contract in effect with the Russian buyers, copy of which is also enclosed." Subsequently, Chilewich procured a letter of credit to the benefit of Filanto as required under the contract. Soon thereafter, Filanto began to perform on the contract.

On September 2, 1989, Chilewich received a letter from Filanto that included the following statement: "Returning back the enclosed contracts signed for acceptance, if we do not misunderstand, regarding the Russian contract, we have to respect only the following points: Packing and marking, way of shipment, delivery." After its Russian buyer rejected an earlier shipment of shoes, Chilewich never purchased a subsequent order of 90,000 pairs of boots. It is Chilewich's failure to do so that forms the basis of this lawsuit. Chilewich commenced an arbitration action in Moscow. Filanto moved to enjoin the arbitration, or alternatively, for an order directing that arbitration be held in New York rather than Moscow because of unsettled political conditions in Russia.

Brieant, Chief Judge. The facts indicate that when Filanto thought it was desirable to do so, it recognized that it was bound by the incorporation by reference of portions of the Russian contract. Also, Chapter 2 of the Federal Arbitration Act comprises the Convention on the Recognition and Enforcement of Foreign Arbitral Awards. The Arbitration Convention requires courts to

---

23. See Federal Supreme Court of Germany, BGH VIII ZR 304/00, Jan. 9, 2002 (F.R.G.), available at **http://www.cisg.law.pace.edu/cisg/wais/db/cases2/020109g1.html**; see also Amtsgericht [Petty Court] [AG] Kehl 3 C 925/93, Oct. 6, 1995 (F.R.G.), available at **http://www.cisgw3.law.pace.edu/cases/951006g1.html**.

recognize "any agreement in writing under which the parties undertake to submit to arbitration." The term "agreement in writing" is defined as "an arbitral clause in a contract or an arbitration agreement, signed by the parties or contained in an exchange of letters or telegrams." The threshold question is whether these parties actually agreed to arbitrate their disputes. The Federal Arbitration Act controls this determination.

The "federal law of contracts" to be applied in this case is found in the United Nations Convention on Contracts for the International Sale of Goods (CISG). The parties offer varying interpretations of the numerous letters and documents exchanged between them. There simply is no satisfactory explanation as to why Filanto failed to object to the incorporation by reference of the Russian contract in a timely fashion. Chilewich had in the meantime commenced its performance under the Agreement by furnishing a letter of credit to Filanto. An offeree who, knowing that the offeror has commenced performance, fails to notify the offeror of its objection to the terms of the contract within a reasonable time will be deemed to have assented to those terms. The August 7, 1990, acceptance, noting its objection to the arbitration clause, to Chilewich's March 13, 1990, Memorandum Agreement was untimely due to Filanto's awareness of Chilewich's commencement of performance. Furthermore, Filanto's June 21, 1991, letter makes reference to the "Master Purchase Contract" (the Russian contract). This letter comes within CISG Article 8(3) directive that "in determining the intent of a party due consideration is to be given to any *subsequent conduct* of the parties."

Heeding the presumption in favor of arbitration, which is even stronger in the context of international commercial transactions, the Court holds that Filanto is bound by the terms of the March 13 Memorandum Agreement and so must arbitrate its dispute in Moscow. SO ORDERED.

Case Update

The U.S. Court of Appeals for the Second Circuit dismissed an appeal of the district court's opinion in *Filanto, S.P.A. v. Chilewich International Corp.*, 984 F.2d 58 (2d Cir. 1993).

Case Highlights

- The Federal Arbitration Act requires courts to enforce reasonable arbitration clauses. Any state law that restricts the federal policy in favor of arbitration is preempted.
- The ability of one party to add or delete contract terms in the battle of the forms scenario is lost if the party delays its response beyond a reasonable time or after the other party begins performance.
- A court will take into consideration the conduct of the parties following the formation of the contract (course of performance) when interpreting a contract.

Contract Interpretation

A famous case of contract interpretation involved the judicial attempt to define the word *chicken*. The *Frigaliment Importing Co. v. B.N.S. International Sales Corp.* case illustrates how a court attempts to define terms in a contract through its reading of the contract itself and its use of evidence of prior dealings, course of performance, and trade usage. It also introduces a number of important legal concepts, including the **four-corner analysis**, the **totality of the circumstances**, and the **reasonable person standard**.

The *Frigaliment* case illustrates a hierarchy of tools that courts use in interpreting contracts. The first level is studying the language of the contract to determine its meaning. This is sometimes referred to as four-corner analysis or the plain meaning rule. If the language is unclear, the court proceeds to the next level: analyzing the relationship and actions of the contracting parties. First, it will look at evidence of "course of performance" of the parties for the contract in dispute to judge by the postformation conduct of the parties what the parties believed that contract meant. If the meaning is still unclear, the court will study any prior contracts or dealings between the parties to infer a previously established meaning. The final level of analysis is to infer a meaning from outside the contract by using trade usage or

Frigaliment Importing Co. v. B.N.S. International Sales Corp.

190 F. Supp. 116 (S.D. N.Y. 1960)

Action by buyer of fresh frozen chicken against seller for breach of warranty. Two contracts are in suit. In the first, a New York sales corporation confirmed the sale to plaintiff, a Swiss corporation, of: "US fresh Frozen Chicken, Grade A, Government Inspected, 2½ to 3 lbs. each, all chickens individually wrapped, packed in secured fiber cartons suitable for export." The second contract was identical save that only 50,000 lbs. of the heavier "chicken" were called for. When the initial shipment arrived in Switzerland, plaintiff found that the birds were not young chickens suitable for broiling and frying but stewing chickens or "fowl." Protest ensued. Nevertheless, shipment under the second contract was made again being stewing chickens. The issue is: What is a chicken?

Friendly, Circuit Judge. Plaintiff says "chicken" means a young chicken, suitable for broiling and frying. Defendant says "chicken" means any bird of the genus that meets contract specifications on weight and quality, including what it calls "stewing chicken" and plaintiff pejoratively terms "fowl." To support its claim, plaintiff sends a number of volleys over the net; defendant essays to return them and adds a few serves of its own. Assuming that both parties were acting in good faith, the case nicely illustrates Oliver Wendell Holmes's remark "that the making of a contract depends not on the agreement of two minds in one intention, but on the agreement of two sets of external signs—not on the parties' having *meant* the same thing but on having *said* the same thing." Since the word "chicken" standing alone is ambiguous, I turn first to see whether the contract itself offers any aid to its interpretation.

Plaintiff's first contention hinges on an exchange of cablegrams which preceded the formal contracts. After testing the market price, plaintiff accepted, and sent defendant a confirmation. These and subsequent cables between plaintiff and defendant, which laid the basis for the additional quantities under the first and for all of the second contract, were predominantly in German, although they used the English word "chicken." Defendant's agent testified that when asked plaintiff's agent what kind of chicken were wanted, received the answer "any kind of chickens." Defendant relies on conduct by the plaintiff after the first shipment had been received. Defendant argues that if plaintiff was sincere in thinking it was entitled to young chickens, plaintiff would not have allowed the shipment under the second contract to go forward.

Plaintiff's next contention is that there was a definite trade usage that "chicken" meant "young chicken." Here there was no proof of actual knowledge of the alleged usage; indeed it is quite plain that defendant's belief was to the contrary. Plaintiff endeavored to establish such a usage by the testimony of witnesses. However, one witness stated that a careful businessman protected himself by using "broiler" when that was what he wanted and "fowl" when he wished older birds. An employee of a company that publishes a daily market report on the poultry trade gave his view that the trade meaning of "chicken" was "broilers and fryers." Defendant provided a witness that said that in the trade, "chicken" would encompass all the various classifications of chicken. Defendant also provided a regulation of the Department of Agriculture that defined "chickens" as various classes including "*Broiler or fryer,* Roaster, Capon, Stag, Hen or *stewing* chicken or *fowl.*"

When all the evidence is reviewed, it is clear defendant believed it could comply with the contracts by delivering stewing chickens. Plaintiff asserts that it is equally plain that plaintiff's own subjective intent was to obtain broilers and fryers. Because plaintiff has the burden of showing that "chicken" was used in the narrower rather than in the broader sense, and this it has not sustained, judgment shall be entered dismissing the complaint.

Case Highlights

- A four-corners analysis requires a court or arbitral panel to find the answer to the issue in dispute within the contract.
- In a totality of the circumstances analysis, the court or arbitrator looks outside the contract to interpret its meaning.
- In performing a totality of the circumstances analysis, a court will apply the reasonable person standard.
- Under the reasonable person standard, the contract is interpreted from the perspective of a reasonable person in that particular trade or business.

custom. In *Frigaliment*, none of these levels of analysis provided a clear meaning for the word *chicken*. As a result, the plaintiff lost because of its failure to meet its burden of proof regarding the meaning of the word.

The second and third levels of analysis are referred to as a totality of the circumstances analysis. The courts often look to the circumstances surrounding the execution of a written contract to find the parties' intent. Lord Wilberforce in *Reardon Smith Line, Ltd.*[24] defined the totality of the circumstances analysis as the need in "commercial contracts for the court to know the commercial purpose of the contract. This presupposes knowledge of the genesis of the transaction, background, context, and the market in which the parties were operating." The background and context include oral negotiations, prior dealings, trade usage, and custom.

The common law has long used the reasonable person standard as an aid in interpreting and enforcing contracts. The reasonable person standard reflects the totality of the circumstances analysis because it is often constructed from the usages, customs, and practices of businesspeople in a particular trade. The role of the reasonable person standard has become more important because of the modern innovation of standard forms, in that most terms of standard forms are not the product of negotiations and conscious agreement. The reasonable person standard is used to interpret the so-called fine print or boilerplate terms to see if the terms meet the measure of commercial reasonableness.

The traditional approach to contract interpretation held that the act of signing a standard form was evidence that the signer intended to accept all of its terms. This approach became increasingly untenable as it became apparent that, in reality, there was no such actual consent. Instead, at least one of the parties does not read or understand the fine print of the preprinted form. The role of the reasonable person standard was thus expanded to determine what terms would be excluded.

Karl Llewellyn[25] devised two roles for the reasonable person standard in the area of standard form contracts: (1) to interpret the meaning of the terms expressly negotiated by the parties and (2) to determine what nonnegotiated terms are to be reconstructed or expelled because of unreasonableness. The reasonable person standard is also used to determine what terms are to be implied to fill gaps in the contract. For purposes of determining reasonableness, the standard looks to the terms generally found in such contracts. The reasonable person standard is used to conform the boilerplate terms to the spirit of the contract as represented by the negotiated terms and the type of transaction being undertaken.[26]

Duty to Inspect and Proper Notice

A purchaser receiving defective goods must give timely and effective notice of nonconformity. What are the buyer's responsibilities when receiving noncomforming goods under the CISG? The buyer has three duties. First, Article 38 (1) requires the buyer to inspect the goods "within as short a period as is practicable."

http://

"The Aftermath of *MCC-Marble*. Is this the Death Knell for the Parol Evidence Rule?" **http://cisgw3.law.pace.edu/cisg/biblio/torzilli.html** or "The U.N. Sales Convention (CISG) and *MCC-Marble Ceramic Center, Inc. v. Ceramica Nuova D'Agostino, S.P.A.*: The Eleventh Circuit Weighs in on Interpretation, Subjective Intent, Procedural Limits to the Convention's Scope, and the Parol Evidence Rule. **http://cisgw3.law.pace.edu/cisg/biblio/flechtner1.html**.

24. *Reardon Smith Line, Ltd. v. Yngvar Hansen-Tangen* [1976] 1 W.L.R. 989, 996 (Eng. H.L.).
25. Karl Llewellyn was the reporter and chief architect of the UCC.
26. See generally Larry A. DiMatteo, "The Counterpoise of Contracts: The Reasonable Person Standard and the Subjectivity of Judgment," 48 *South Carolina Law Review* 293, 338–341 (1997).

http://

United Nations
Commission on
International Trade Law
(UNCITRAL)—
abstracts of foreign case
law on CISG (CLOUT):
**http://www.uncitral.org/
en-index.htm.**

INTERNATIONAL

INTERNATIONAL

INTERNATIONAL

Second, the buyer must inform the seller of the nonconformity "within a reasonable time after he has discovered it or ought to have discovered it."[27] Any claim for nonconformity is time barred if not reported within two years of delivery to the buyer.[28] Third, the notice to the seller must specify the nature of the nonconformity.[29]

A German court dealt with the notion of due diligence in the inspection of goods, specifically, shoes. Following customer complaints about measurements, sewing quality, and color fading, a German retailer attempted to cancel a second order with the Italian manufacturer. The goods were shipped nonetheless. The retailer inspected only a selected sample of the shoes and failed to detect any nonconformities. Following additional customer complaints, the retailer attempted to reject the order on account of nonconformity. The court found in favor of the seller, holding that the expiration of sixteen days rendered the buyer's notice as untimely.[30] The court's rationale was based on due diligence: Because the buyer was aware of nonconformities stemming from the first order, it should have performed a more detailed inspection of the shoes in the second order. The court presumed that such an inspection would have uncovered the nonconformity at an earlier date.

This result is consistent with rules in states that have not adopted the CISG. For example, Article 121 of Japan's Commercial Code provides that, in transactions between merchants, the buyer must inspect the goods without delay and report any defect immediately to the seller. Failure to comply with these requirements prevent the buyer from rescinding the contract or reducing the price paid for the goods. In the event that the defects are not immediately discoverable (latent defect), the buyer has six months within which to discover defects and notify the seller. The passage of this time without a notice of defects to the seller prohibits the buyer from rescinding the contract or reducing the price paid for the goods.

In numerous cases, buyers have lost their rights to reject goods because their notices lacked specificity. A German court held that a notice provided by a German clothing retailer to an Italian seller of fashion goods, stating that the goods failed to conform because of "poor workmanship and improper fit," was ineffective because of its lack of specificity.[31] Another German court refused to give effect to a notice that informed the seller of flowers that its goods were of "bad quality" and "poor appearance."[32] Similarly, German and Italian courts have deemed notices stating that the goods are "defective" or "present problems" as lacking sufficient specificity to be effective pursuant to Article 39.[33] A Swiss court refused to give effect to a notice to an Italian seller that its furniture had "wrong parts" and was

27.   CISG, Article 39(1).

28.   See ibid. Article 39(2).

29.   See ibid. Article 39(1).

30.   See Landgericht Stuttgart, 3 KFh O 97/89, Aug. 31, 1989 (F.R.G.), available at **http://www.cisgw3.law.pace.edu/cases/ 890831g1.html.**

31.   See Landgericht München, 17 HKO 3726/89, July 3, 1989 (F.R.G.), available at **http://www.cisgw3.law.pace.edu/cases/ 890703g1.html.**

32.   See Oberlandgericht Saarbrücken, 1 U 703/97–143, June 3, 1998 (F.R.G.), available at **http://www.cisg.law.pace.edu/ cisg/wais/db/cases2/980603g1.html.**

33.   See Landgericht Erfurt, 3 HKO 43/98, July 29, 1998 (F.R.G.), available at **http://www.cisg.law.pace.edu/cisg/wais/db/ cases2/980729g1.html** (soles of shoes). See also Tribunal di Vigevano, July 12, 2000, n. 405 (It.), available at **http://www. cisg.law.pace.edu/cisg/wais/db/cases2/000712i3.html** (vulcanized rubber to be utilized for shoes).

"full of breakages."[34] These results are consistent with the Japanese Commercial Code, which requires buyers to inform sellers of the type and extent of defects in goods tendered pursuant to sales contracts.

The specificity required under the UCC, however, is less demanding than that required under the CISG. Initially, the rejecting party need only state in general terms the reason for the rejection. Comment One states that it is the policy of this section to permit the "buyer to give a quick and informal notice of defects in a tender without penalizing him for omissions in his statement."[35] There is one exception to the general character of the UCC notice requirement. Where the defect in a tender could have been cured by the seller, a buyer who merely rejects without stating the objections is deemed to be acting in commercial bad faith. Except when the seller has the ability and right to cure, this clarification indicates that a general notice and not a particularized one is sufficient to meet the dictates of the UCC.

Nachfrist *Notice*

Another concept foreign to Anglo-American contract law is the civil law notion of *nachfrist* **notice**. The underlying premise behind this concept is that a delay in performance does not in itself constitute a material breach of the contract. The notion allows a buyer or seller to fix an additional time for performance beyond what is specified in the contract. The additional time must be of a reasonable duration. The reasonableness of the time extension depends on the nature, extent, and consequences of the delay, along with the importance to the buyer of prompt delivery.

The civil law's ability to affix additional time was adopted in Articles 47 through 49 and 63 of the CISG. The buyer may give notice to the seller that delivery will be accepted beyond the time prescribed. The buyer is then enjoined from taking legal action during the *nachfrist* period and must accept any proper tender of performance during that period. If the seller makes a request for a *nachfrist* extension, then the buyer is obligated to respond to the request. Failure to do so results in the automatic granting of the additional time. The failure of the breaching party to perform during the extension allows the other party to declare an immediate voiding of the contract. (See Comparative Law: A *Nachfrist* Case Study.)

U.S. businesspeople unaware of the practice of *nachfrist* notice will be subject to unintended liabilities. They may mistake a *nachfrist* notice as a meaningless, nonlegal request for more time. Failure to respond in a proper way will result in an unintended granting of additional time and a freezing of their legal options. This is likely to be compounded by their rejecting delivery of goods during the *nachfrist* period as untimely, resulting in liability for the purchase price, along with possible additional freight and storage costs. The existence of an express "time of the essence" clause is unlikely to provide a party any further protection from the use of *nachfrist* notice. Businesspeople must realize that the receipt of seemingly meaningless communications should be fully investigated for legal consequences.

http://
"*Nachfrist* Notice and Avoidance Under the CISG": **http://www.cisg. law.pace.edu/cisg/ biblio/kimbel.html.**

---

34.   Kantonsgericht [District Court] [KG] Nidwalden, 15/96 Z, Dec. 3, 1997 (Switz.), available at **http://www.cisgw3.law. pace.edu/cisg/wais/db/cases2/971203sl.html.**

35.   UCC § 2-605, Comment 1.

COMPARATIVE LAW

A *Nachfrist* Case Study

A contract between an Italian clothing manufacturer and a German retailer provided for a schedule of delivery dates stating that the clothes were "autumn goods, to be delivered July, August, September, plus or minus." *Municipal Court of Holstein, 5 C 73/89, CLOUT Case No. 7.* The first delivery of the goods was made on September 26. The retailer rejected the delivery of the goods as untimely. The court rejected the buyer's argument that the term "autumn goods" envisioned delivery of three equal shipments for the months of July, August, and September. Such misunderstandings are common, given the problems of linguistic and cultural differences, along with the tendency of businesspeople toward brevity in business communiqués. *What could the German importer have done differently to avoid such a misunderstanding?* First, it should have defined "autumn goods" more carefully to ensure timely and qualitatively effective delivery of the goods. Second, as suggested by the German court, they could have made use of the *nachfrist* notice provision in the CISG. The purchaser should have sent notice pursuant to Article 47 of the CISG. Article 47(1) states that the "buyer may fix an additional period of time of reasonable length for performance by the seller." Article 48(2) allows a seller to "request" additional time for performance. Such notice of the granting of additional time to perform is normally given in conjunction with a fixed and known delivery date. The German court held that "the buyer did not effectively void the contract by refusing acceptance of the goods *without fixing an additional period* in the previous cases of nondelivery."

The implications of this decision could support a number of interpretations. First, the use of *nachfrist* notice in this situation would have been evidence that the parties had indeed intended multiple delivery dates throughout July, August, and September. Second, the decision holds the possibility that *nachfrist* notice may be used to fix an unspecified delivery date. At the minimum, it would have placed a burden on the exporter to respond to the request for delivery. The failure of the exporter to respond would have allowed the German importer to declare the contract as voided and to seek substituted goods elsewhere. Article 49 provides that the "buyer may declare the contract voided in the case of nondelivery, if the seller does not deliver goods within the additional period of time fixed by the buyer."

Seller's Right to Cure

The seller's **right to cure** defective goods under the CISG is similar to that offered in the UCC. Section 2-508(1) of the UCC allows a seller to cure the delivery of defective goods if the time for performance has not expired. Article 48(1) of the CISG allows the seller to cure after the contract date for delivery unless such late delivery would cause the buyer "unreasonable inconvenience or uncertainty." The buyer retains the right to sue for damages and expenses caused by the delay or by the initial delivery of nonconforming goods.[36]

36. However, an ICC Tribunal held that a seller who is guilty of a fundamental breach has no right to cure beyond the due date in the contract without the buyer's consent (ICC Case No. 7531 of 1994).

Anticipatory Breach and Adequate Assurance

Anticipatory breach is a concept of Anglo-American legal derivation. The civil law does not recognize the right of a party to avoid or suspend their contract obligation in anticipation of a breach by the other party.[37] Contract avoidance is permitted only at the time of breach or by way of a court order. Article 71(1) of the CISG allows a party to suspend its performance if it becomes clear that the other party will not perform. It gives two broad grounds for anticipatory breach. The first basis is that the other party has become seriously deficient in its ability to perform or in its creditworthiness. The second basis is the other party's preparation or lack of preparation or insufficiency of its performance to date, which calls into question its ability or willingness to perform under the contract. When one party anticipates a breach of the other party and suspends performance, it must give immediate notice of the suspension. Regardless of what basis a party may claim, anticipatory repudiation pursuant to the CISG requires evidence that a party intended to breach the contract prior to the date for performance and that such breach was fundamental.[38]

The suspending party must lift its suspension in the event that the other party provides **adequate assurance** that it will perform as contracted. Section 2-609(1) of the UCC provides a similar device for suspending performance. It states that when reasonable grounds for insecurity arise with respect to performance, the concerned party "may in writing demand adequate assurance of due performance" and may suspend performance until such assurance is given. Failure to give adequate assurance within a reasonable time, not exceeding thirty days, results in a repudiation of the contract.

Damages

The CISG damage provisions are in Articles 74 through 77. Article 74 provides the general measure of damages. It adopts the common law rule that damages should be limited to those that were foreseeable at the time of contract formation—what is popularly known as the rule of *Hadley v. Baxendale*.[39] The damages that can be collected are restricted in three ways. First, only foreseeable **consequential damages** related to the breach may be recovered. Article 74 states that "damages may not exceed the loss which the party in breach foresaw or ought to have foreseen at the time of the conclusion of the contract." Second, damages will be limited to those that are provable with some degree of certainty. Therefore, purely speculative damages may not be collected.

Third, Article 77 provides that even if the loss was foreseeable and its amount is certain, the nonbreaching party will be limited in the recovery in the event the party failed to **mitigate** the damages. Article 77 provides that if the nonbreaching party "fails to take such measures to mitigate the loss, the party in breach may claim

---

37. For example, in Japan, a seller of goods may not accept a buyer's declaration that he or she will not accept the goods prior to their delivery and consequently not pay the purchase price. Rather, the seller must wait until the time for performance arrives, tender the goods, and demand payment.
38. See *Magellan International Corp. v. Salzgitter Handel GmbH*, 76 F. Supp.2d 919, 925–26 (N.D. Ill. 1999).
39. 156 Eng. Rep. 145 (Ct. Ex.1854).

a reduction in damages in the amount by which the loss should have been mitigated." For example, the buyer who has a source for substituted goods must make efforts to obtain those substituted goods. Otherwise, the buyer will be precluded from collecting full loss of profits. This is similar to the rule adopted in Section 2-715(2)(a) of the UCC that holds the breaching party liable for all damages that *could not reasonably be prevented*. In the case of a fundamental breach, Article 75 allows the nonbreaching party to void the contract. It also authorizes the nonbreaching party to obtain substituted goods. The nonbreaching party may then sue the breaching party for the difference between the contract price (of the voided contract) and the price, if higher, of the substituted goods. If the nonbreaching party elects not to procure substituted goods, it may as an alternative sue for lost opportunity damages. Article 76(1) of the CISG allows the nonbreaching party to recover for the difference between the contract price and the market price at the time of avoidance.

The *Delchi Carrier v. Rotorex* case that follows examines the different types of damages available in a typical breach of contract case. The case involves delivery of defective goods—component parts used by the buyer in the production of air conditioning units. The court assessed the damages that the buyer may collect when the delivery of defective goods results in a production slowdown at its plant. The court also decided on the types of out-of-pocket expenses the buyer could collect against the seller.

Unlike the UCC, the CISG does not allow for recovery for breach of warranty that results in injury to people or property. Article 5 of the CISG states that it does not cover claims resulting from the "liability of the seller for death or personal injury caused by the goods to any person." Therefore, **products liability** remains to be determined under national laws. In contrast, Section 2-715(2)(b) of the UCC allows recovery of consequential damages stemming from the seller's breach due to "injury to person or property proximately resulting from any breach of warranty."

Delchi Carrier, S.P.A. v. Rotorex Corp.

71 F.3d 1024 (2d Cir. 1995)

The case involved a warranty dispute between a U.S. seller of compressors ("Rotorex") and an Italian purchaser ("Delchi"). The trial court determined that the compressors failed to conform to the specifications provided in the contract or the sample provided by Rotorex to Delchi. After Rotorex failed to cure the defects, Delchi brought suit for breach of contract and recovery of damages, including consequential damages for lost profits. The lost profits were allegedly due to lost volume caused by a closing of the assembly line for four days until the compressors were repaired. They also sued for incidental damages such as the cost to repair the compressors, the cost of storage, and the costs of expediting substitute goods.

Winter, Circuit Judge. The governing law of this case is the CISG. Article 74 allows for Delchi to collect monetary damages that are equal to its loss, including lost profits. Those damages are limited, however, to damages foreseeable at the time of the formation of the contract. Its first claim of damages is the cost of repairing the nonconforming compressors. These damages are recoverable because they were a foreseeable result of Rotorex's breach. Hence, Delchi is entitled to expenses for repairing the units including labor cost, costs of extraordinary inspections, and testing of the units. Pursuant to Article 77 of the CISG Delchi attempted to mitigate its losses by expediting a shipment of previously ordered Sanyo compressors. The expedited shipment cannot be considered as cover under Article 75, because they were previously ordered. Nonetheless, Delchi's actions in expediting the shipment were both commercially reasonable and reasonably foreseeable. Therefore, Delchi is entitled to recover the additional cost of air shipment over the cost of ocean shipment. Delchi is also entitled to the incidental costs of handling and storage of the rejected compressors.

The CISG permits recovery of lost profits resulting from a diminished volume of sales. In conformity to the common law, to recover for lost profit under CISG, a party must provide sufficient evidence to estimate the amount of damages with reasonable certainty. Delchi proved with sufficient certainty a total lost profit of 546,377,612 lire. Delchi did not prove with sufficient certainty lost sales from "anticipated profits." Delchi's claim of 4,000 additional lost sales in Italy is supported only by speculative testimony of Italian sales agents who stated they would have ordered if more were available. Delchi provides no documentation of additional lost sales in Italy and that Delchi's inability to fill those orders was directly attributable to Rotorex's breach.

Delchi is entitled to compensatory damages for those expenses incurred in repairing nonconforming goods, obtaining substituted goods, storage of rejected goods, and reasonably certain lost profits. Lost profits do not include profits that arise from anticipated sales that cannot be determined by reasonable certainty.

Case Highlights

- Article 74 of the CISG allows a party to collect any foreseeable damages incurred because of a breach of contract.
- Article 77 of the CISG requires the plaintiff to mitigate its damages. Expenses incurred in mitigating damages, such as expediting shipment of substitute goods, are recoverable against the breaching party.
- The plaintiff may also collect incidental damages, such as costs incurred in repairing, storing, and protecting the defective goods.
- A plaintiff may collect lost profits caused by delivery of defective goods, but only those profits that can be proven with reasonable certainty.
- In sum, under the CISG and the UCC, damages are restricted by three principles: (1) they must have been foreseeable at the time that the contract was signed, (2) they were not caused by the plaintiff's failure to mitigate, and (3) they must be proven with reasonable certainty and are not merely speculative.

Warranty Provisions

The CISG's warranty provisions mimic the warranty provisions in the UCC. The warranties that are of concern to most seller-exporters are any implied warranties that a court may use to hold the seller liable for nonconforming goods. Section 2-314 of the UCC recognizes the two common law implied warranties of merchantability and particular purpose (see Comparative Law: UCC Section 2-314(2)). A sale of fungible commodities is normally governed by the **implied warranty of merchantability**. Section 2-314(2)(c) states it is implied that for the goods to be merchantable they must be "fit for the ordinary purposes for which such goods are used." The **implied warranty for a particular purpose** entails conveying specific requirements from the buyer to the seller. This communication is generally done to take advantage of the seller's superior knowledge or expertise in selecting or producing the product.

Article 35(2)(a) of the CISG recognizes the implied warranty of merchantability through its provision that goods do not conform to contractual requirements unless they are "fit for the purposes for which goods of the same description would ordinarily be used." The implied warranty for a particular purpose is recognized in Article 35(2)(b), which states that goods are to conform to "any purpose expressly or impliedly made known to the seller" at the time of the formation of the contract. Warranties may also arise from the use of samples or models. Specifically, Article 35(2)(c) requires sellers under such circumstances to provide goods of equivalent quality to the sample or model

COMPARATIVE LAW

UCC Section 2-314(2)

Goods to be *merchantable* **must be at least such as:**

(a) pass without objection in the trade under the contract description; and

(b) in the case of fungible goods, are of fair average quality within the description; and

(c) are fit for the ordinary purposes for which such goods are used; and

(d) run, within the variations permitted by the agreement, of even kind, quality, and quantity within each unit and among all units involved; and

(e) are adequately contained, packaged, and labeled as the agreement may require; and

(f) conform to the promises or affirmations of fact made on the container or label if any.

Comment 2: The question when the warranty is imposed turns on the meaning of the terms of the agreement as recognized in the trade. Goods delivered under an agreement made by a merchant in a given line of trade must be of a quality comparable to that generally acceptable in that line of trade under the description of the goods used in the agreement.

Comment 8: Fitness for the ordinary purposes for which goods of the type are used is a fundamental concept of the present section and is covered in paragraph (c). As stated above, merchantability is also a part of the obligation owing to the purchaser for use. Correspondingly, protection, under this aspect of the warranty, of the person buying for resale to the ultimate consumer is equally necessary, and merchantable goods must therefore be *honestly* resalable in the normal course of business because they are what they purport to be.

upon which the contract was formed. A breach of warranty also occurs pursuant to Article 35(2)(d) in the event that the goods are inadequately packaged for shipment.

The *T.J. Stevenson* case that follows discusses the warranty of merchantability and the importance of giving notice upon receiving defective or nonconforming goods. Failure to give timely notice results in buyers losing their right to remedies, including the right to reject the defective goods and the right to sue for damages.

Often a seller attempts to disclaim all warranties, express or implied, or wants to limit its liability through a **limited express warranty**. The UCC allows such a **disclaimer** only by the use of clear and conspicuous language.[40] Language such as the "purchaser takes as is" is considered clear disclaimer language. In addition, the disclaimer must be conspicuous. Specifically, it must be easily noticeable in reviewing the contract. It cannot be fine print on a page filled with fine print terms. In contrast, the CISG provides no formal requirements for disclaimers. Any form of disclaimer is enforceable under the CISG. This informality is consistent with the laws in many civil law jurisdictions. For example, Article 1487 of the Italian Civil Code simply provides that the contracting parties "can increase or decrease the effects of the warranty and can also agree that the seller not be subject to any warranty." The U.S. District Court's opinion in *Supermicro Computer, Inc. v. Digitechnic, S.A.* addresses the lack of formal rules in the CISG with respect to disclaimers.

---

40.   See UCC § 2-316(2).

T.J. Stevenson & Co. v. 81,193 Bags of Flour
629 F.2d 338 (5th Cir. 1980)

An *in rem* action, stemming from insect infestation of wheat flour, was brought by an ocean carrier which claimed a lien on the cargo for freight, detention, and expenses, and also sought recovery of damages from milling company (seller) and shipper consignee (buyer), the Republic of Bolivia. The miller filed counterclaims against Bolivia and the carrier and Bolivia counterclaimed for breach of warranty. The Republic of Bolivia had entered into a contract for the purchase of 26,618 metric tons of flour from ADM Milling Co. The contract contained the following delivery term: "Delivery of goods by SELLER to the carrier at point of shipment shall constitute delivery to BUYER." Upon satisfactory delivery, the price was payable by irrevocable letter of credit. The contract also contained an express warranty of merchantability: "Seller warrants that the product sold shall be of merchantable quality." The warranty clause contained the following notice requirements: "BUYER hereby waives any claim based on the quality of the goods unless, within twenty days of the arrival of goods at destination, BUYER sends SELLER a letter by registered mail specifying the nature of the complaint."

Brown, Circuit Judge. With this decision we hopefully end, in all but a minor respect, an amphibious imbroglio and commercial law practitioner's nightmare involving a shipload of flour. Without pause to reflect on the complications that simple insects—confused flour beetles or otherwise—can create in the lives of men and Courts, we proceed to explain our decision. One issue permeates this case: What was the source of the flour infestation? The District Judge rightly concluded that infestation began either on the rail cars or at the mill supplying the flour. Neither the warehouses nor the ships were the source of any significant infestation.

The Warranty

The District Judge rightly held that the flour failed to meet the express warranty provision of the contract. The issue being, infestation and all, whether the flour was of merchantable quality. The Uniform Commercial Code Section 2-314(2) defines merchantable as goods that "are fit for the ordinary purposes for which such goods are used." Official Comments 2 and 8 provide helpful clues to divining the parties' intent. Comment 2: "Goods delivered under an agreement made by a merchant in a given trade *must be of a quality comparable to that generally acceptable in that line of trade.*" Comment 8:

"Merchantable goods must be *honestly resalable in the normal course of business because they are what they purport to be.*" We have often recognized that no food is completely pure. The FDA has long permitted very small amounts of insect fragments and other *dead* infestation in food products.

Here the question is: How much live infestation renders consumer-destined flour unfit for the ordinary purposes for which it is used? The evidence indicates that consumer-intended flour containing substantial amounts of live infestation is not merchantable under prevailing standards. Trade usage and course of dealing point to but one conclusion: Although flour may be "fit for human consumption" in the sense that it can be eaten without causing sickness, it is nonetheless not of merchantable quality.

Risk of Loss

Since it has been established that consumer-intended flour containing substantial amounts of live infestation is unmerchantable and the infestation in this case began before the flour reached the State Docks warehouses, we are confronted with the issue of which party is to be responsible for the further infestation of the flour as it stood in the warehouses or lay in Stevenson's ships. The delivery term in the contract read as follows: "F.A.S. MOBILE, ALABAMA for export." Section 2-509(1) of the Uniform Commercial Code reads that where there is no breach and where the contract requires the seller to ship the goods by carrier then: "if it does not require him to deliver at a particular destination, the risk of loss passes to the buyer when the goods are duly delivered to the carrier." However, Section 2-510(1) provides that in case of breach "where a tender or delivery of goods so fails to conform to the contract as to give a right of rejection the risk of their loss remains on the seller until cure or acceptance." Since it was materially nonconforming at the time it arrived in Mobile, Bolivia could have rejected the flour at that time. We therefore conclude that under Section 2-510(1)'s plain language, the risk of loss of the infested flour remained on the seller.

Breach of Warranty Claim

In order for Bolivia to win on its warranty claim it must satisfy the relevant notice requirements. Section 2-607(3)(a) of the UCC states that "the buyer must within a reasonable time after he discovers or should have discovered any breach notify the seller of breach or be barred from any remedy." Furthermore, the contract added the contractual requirement that notice must be in writing "within twenty days after arrival of the goods." ADM contends that under Section 2-607(3)(a) and the contract provision, it never received adequate notice of the defects. The facts show that there were informal communications throughout the time there were problems with the flour. The parties were in "continuous communication" with one another from the time the infestation problems were found. Also, Bolivia telexed ADM that no further payments would be permitted under the "irrevocable" letter of credit. From this view of the parties' course of conduct, one may infer that ADM was aware of Bolivia's dissatisfaction with the flour. Its awareness operated as a waiver of the specific notice provisions of the contract. ADM's reply to the telex as well as its informal communications dealt with the substance of Bolivia's complaint and did not fault Bolivia for failing to comply with the contract's notice requirements. ADM's responses to Bolivia's initial complaints established a course of performance in which the registered mail requirement of the contractual notice provision could be disregarded.

Defendant (seller) was liable for breach of warranty and its argument that it did not receive adequate notice is rejected.

Case Highlights

- Under the UCC, any defect is ground for rejection. The CISG gives a right of rejection only if there is a fundamental breach.
- The court disregarded the specific notice requirements of the contract by imputing actual notice from the actions and correspondence between the parties after the goods were delivered.
- FAS stands for Free Alongside Ship. Under this term, the risk of loss to the goods is transferred to the buyer when the goods are delivered to the port of shipment and ready for loading onto the ship. However, the court found that because the goods were defective upon delivery to the ship, the risk of loss never passed to the buyer. FAS is a trade term that will be discussed in detail in Chapter Nine.
- If nonconforming goods can be resold for another purpose, then a court is likely to find that the breach did not constitute a fundamental breach. In such a case, the buyer has no right to reject the goods. Instead, the buyer may make use of the price reduction remedy provided for in the CISG. Under this remedy, the buyer can unilaterally reduce the price of the goods by the difference in value between the goods in their defective condition and the value of conforming goods.

Supermicro Computer, Inc. v. Digitechnic, S.A.
145 F. Supp. 2d 1147 (N.D. Cal. 2001)

Legge, District Court Judge. Supermicro Computer, Inc. (Supermicro) is a California corporation that manufactures computer parts. Digitechnic, S.A. (Digitechnic) is a French corporation that assembles and sells computer network systems. Digitechnic made fourteen purchases of computer parts from Supermicro between May 1996 and December 1997. In each of the transactions, Digitechnic placed an order with Supermicro via phone or e-mail, and Supermicro shipped the goods to France. Supermicro included a sales invoice and a user's manual with each shipment. The sales invoice and user's manual contained certain terms and conditions, including a limited warranty and limitations of liability.

Beginning in 1998, Digitechnic allegedly experienced electrical problems with some of the parts that it

had purchased from Supermicro; specifically, some of the parts caught fire. Digitechnic demanded $200,400 in replacement costs, and consequential damages of approximately $6,000,000. Supermicro rejected the demand and claimed that, based on the limited warranty contained in the sales invoices and the consequential damages waiver found in the user's manual, Digitechnic's sole remedy was the repair and replacement of any malfunctioning parts.

In December 1998 Digitechnic filed an action in France in the Tribunal de Commerce de Bobginy (French Commercial Court) The French case has been ongoing since that time and Supermicro has been participating in it. Supermicro filed this action on January 20, 2000, more than a year after the French action began.

The complaint seeks a declaration that: (1) the computer parts were not defective; (2) the parts failed as a result of Digitechnic's misuse, and (3) even if Supermicro were at fault, Digitechnic's sole remedy is for repair or replacement.

Supermicro now moves for partial summary adjudication, solely on the issue of what remedy is available to Digitechnic. Digitechnic opposes the motion for partial summary adjudication, and moves for a stay or dismissal based on the first-filed French case.

The parties agree that the United Nations Convention on Contracts for the International Sale of Goods (CISG) governs their transactions. The case law interpreting and applying the CISG is sparse. As one court which wrestled with the treaty put it, "despite the CISG's broad scope, surprisingly few cases have applied the Convention in the United States." See *MCC-Marble Ceramic Center, Inc., v. Ceramica Nuova D'Agostino, S.p.A.*, 144 F.3d 1384, 1389 (11th Cir. 1998).

Application of the CISG here requires a court to resolve an issue of first impression. To wit, the court must determine whether a warranty disclaimer in a purchase order is valid under the CISG. The court has no controlling authority on this issue. Supermicro contends that Article 35 of the CISG permits warranty disclaimers such as the one at issue. Article 35 however, deals with a seller's obligation to deliver conforming goods. It does not discuss disclaimers. If anything, a disclaimer in this case might not be valid because the CISG requires a "mirror-image" approach to contract negotiations that allows the court to inquire into the subjective intent of the parties. Here, Digitechnic has submitted evidence that it was not aware of the disclaimer and that it would not have purchased the goods had it been aware of the disclaimer. If Digitechnic was not aware of the disclaimer, then it may not have been valid. Given that this issue of law is unsettled, this factor weighs against this court exercising its discretion to hear the matter in favor of the French court that already has the issue before it.

Supermicro does not explain why, after participating in the French proceeding for more than one year, a declaratory relief action here is necessary. Digitechnic has adduced evidence which demonstrates that it does not intend to bring an action in the United States. Moreover, there is additional evidence that Supermicro filed this action after receiving an adverse preliminary ruling in the French case. All of this indicates that Supermicro, after participating in the foreign action, initiated this proceeding in the hopes of obtaining a more favorable result in its home forum.

The French Commercial Court is a court of competent jurisdiction to hear this dispute and render an enforceable final judgment. French Commercial Courts hear disputes between merchants concerning transactions governed by commercial law. French Commercial Court proceedings can result in a final, enforceable judgment. Its judgments can be appealed. It is clear that the French court has made a substantial investigation into the facts of this dispute. It would be unnecessarily duplicative for this court to rule on issues already addressed by the French court.

Issuing the declaratory judgment requested by Supermicro would not "settle all aspects of the controversy" pending in the French case. Such a judgment could also lead to conflicts between the French and U.S. legal systems if the parties attempt to enforce inconsistent judgments.

This court has the discretion to either stay or dismiss the action. A dismissal without prejudice is the preferable course here. If either party ultimately prevails in France, as appears likely, then no action in this forum will be necessary. For the reasons discussed, Supermicro's motion for partial summary adjudication is DENIED, and Digitechnic's motion to dismiss is GRANTED. The action is dismissed without prejudice.

Case Highlights

- Article 35 of the CISG deals exclusively with the seller's obligation to deliver conforming goods and does not address disclaimers of warranties.
- The CISG provides no formal requirements for disclaimers.
- Provisions in a sales contract purporting to constitute a disclaimer are subject to the CISG's "mirror image" requirement with respect to the intent of the parties.
- U.S. courts may abstain from deciding a case arising pursuant to the CISG and defer to a determination of a foreign tribunal when: (1) the foreign tribunal possesses jurisdiction, (2) the foreign tribunal can render an enforceable final judgment, (3) the foreign tribunal has made a substantial investigation into the facts of the dispute, (4) it would be unnecessarily duplicative for a U.S. court to rule on issues already addressed by the foreign tribunal, (5) intervention by the U.S. court would not settle all aspects of the controversy between the parties, and (6) intervention by the U.S. court could lead to a conflict with the foreign tribunal due to potentially inconsistent judgments.

Focus on Transactions: Limited Liability and Disclaimer in Software Contracts was taken from a joint publication of the American Bar Association and the American Law Institute.[41] It illustrates the disclaimer language merchants often use. Some of the language in the software licensing agreement is printed in capital letters. This capitalization is meant to satisfy U.S. law that requires disclaimers of

---

Limited Liability and Disclaimer in Software Contracts

Focus on Transactions

5. Warranty

5.1 *Limited Warranty.* Licensor warrants that the Programs licensed to Licensee hereunder, if properly installed and used, shall materially conform to the specifications set forth in the accompanying Documentation for a period of three (3) months from the date of shipment of the Software to Licensee (hereinafter the "Warranty Period"). Licensee shall promptly notify Licensor in writing upon the discovery of any non-conformance. Licensor shall correct any such non-conformance of which it has been properly notified within the Warranty Period, through the means it determines to be most appropriate. Any replacement of Software shall be effected only after the return of the non-conforming Software to Licensor.

5.2 Notwithstanding the warranty provisions above, Licensor shall have no warranty obligations with respect to any part or parts of the Software which have been damaged in transit or by improper installation or operation, or by misuse, abuse, or negligent use or repair or alteration or improper storage or which have been damaged by use which does not conform to the specific or general instructions of the Licensor or to the provisions of the Documentation, or if Licensee or any third party has modified or attempted to modify the Software or if the damage has occurred due to causes external to the Software, or if the Software has been subject to an extreme power surge or electromagnetic field, whether or not through the fault of the Licensee, or if Licensee has refused to implement software changes recommended by Licensor.

5.3 The warranty set forth above shall be exclusive and in lieu of all other liabilities, obligations, conditions and/or warranties, expressed or implied (including, but not limited to any implied and/or statutory warranties or conditions of MERCHANTABILITY, noninfringement and fitness for a PARTICULAR PURPOSE, as well as any implied and/or statutory warranties arising from the course of performance, course of dealing, or usage of trade), and Licensee hereby waives all other rights, obligations and/or warranties and assumes all risks and liabilities in respect thereof. Licensor makes no warranty that the operation of the software will be error free or without interruption. Licensor does not warrant that the software shall operate with any hardware or software other than as specified in the documentation.

6. Limitation of Liability.

In no event shall Licensor be liable for any loss of or damage to revenues, profits, or goodwill, or other special, incidental, indirect, and CONSEQUENTIAL DAMAGES of any kind, resulting from its performance or failure to perform pursuant to the terms of this agreement or any of the attachments hereto, or resulting from the furnishing, performance, or use or loss of any software or other materials delivered to Licensee hereunder, including without limitation any interruption of business, whether resulting from breach of contract or breach of warranty or otherwise, even if Licensor has been advised of the possibility of such damages.

---

41.   Lisa Wannamaker & E. Gail Gunnells, "Negotiating and Drafting International Software License Agreements," 46 *The Practical Lawyer* 45–48 (June 2000).

implied warranties to be conspicuously stated so as to alert a buyer of the existence of the disclaimer. There is no conspicuousness requirement in the CISG. Therefore, a disclaimer may be placed within the fine print terms. The final sentence of the disclaimer is an example of a merger clause. It is meant to bar the buyer from claiming that the seller gave a different warranty through oral representations or other documents. However, under the CISG, this other evidence may be admitted because the CISG states that a contract "may be proved by any means, including witnesses."

Contractual Excuses

All legal systems provide relief for someone who, despite good faith intentions, is unable to perform. Despite the technical breach of the contract, the court will excuse the breaching party from claims of damages. The common law created the **doctrine of impossibility** and the **doctrine of frustration**. The former requires the contracting party to be objectively prevented from performing and generally entails the destruction of the subject matter of the contract. Under the doctrine of frustration, the performance may still be objectively possible, but the reason for the performance has ceased. For example, a hotel charges five times its normal rate for the weekend of the Super Bowl. Because of the threat of a hurricane, the Super Bowl is postponed. The purpose for renting a room at the exorbitant rate has been frustrated. The booking agent or renter will be relieved of its obligations to pay for the room.

INTERNATIONAL

The availability of contractual excuses in the civil law countries varies. In France, *pacta sunt servanda* or sanctity of contract generally prevails over any request for an excuse. If the contract does not provide an excuse through a force majeure clause, then the contract will be enforced without any modification to its terms. This is reflected in Article 1134 of the French Civil Code, which provides for the revocation of contracts only upon mutual consent or for causes authorized by law. These causes are enumerated in Article 1234 and include payment, novation, voluntary release, setoff, merger, loss of the subject matter, nullity or rescission, and expiration of the statute of limitations.

INTERNATIONAL

By contrast, other civil law jurisdictions are more liberal with respect to requests for excuse. In Germany, Section 313 of the Civil Code permits the "adaptation" (adjustment or reformation) of a contract if a material change occurs such that the parties would not have concluded the contract or would have done so on different terms if they foresaw the change or it is unreasonable to bind a party to the unaltered form of the contract. The disadvantaged party may terminate the contract if adaptation is impossible or cannot be reasonably imposed. Italian law recognizes total and partial impossibility. Specifically, total impossibility requires the court to restore the parties to their precontractual state.[42] By contrast, partial impossibility may result in corresponding reductions in the performances required by the contracts or in withdrawal from the contract if there is a lack of appreciable interest in partial performance.[43] The Japanese Civil Code recognizes the concept of impossibility of performance (*riko funo*). Impossibility of performance discharges an obligor from performance, assuming that the cause is not attributable to the

INTERNATIONAL

INTERNATIONAL

---

42.   Italian Civil Code, Article 1463.
43.   See ibid. Article 1464.

obligor.[44] Japanese law also recognizes the principle of changed circumstances (*jijo henko*). This doctrine permits rescission or modification of a contract in the event of a drastic change in circumstances that cannot be attributed to the contracting parties and would result in unfairness and violation of good faith if enforced without modification.

The UCC and the CISG possess their own excuse provisions. The UCC provision found in Section 2-615(a) is popularly referred to as the **doctrine of impracticability**. It excuses a party from performing if the performance has been "made impracticable by the occurrence of a contingency the nonoccurrence of which was a *basic assumption*" of the contract. Article 79(1) of the CISG allows for an excuse if nonperformance is due to an **impediment** that is beyond the control of the breaching party and was not foreseeable at the time of contract formation. However, the excuse is not permanent. Performance is suspended only for the duration of the impediment. The person attempting to exercise an Article 79(1) impediment must give prompt notice of the impediment to the other party. Failure to do so exposes the party to damages resulting from not giving notice.

Parties should also be aware that national courts have been reluctant to excuse a party for an impediment to performance pursuant to Article 79. Businesspeople cannot rely on this article merely on the ground that performance has become unforeseeably more difficult or unprofitable. Circumstances where parties were not granted an excuse under Article 79 include the buyer's inability to obtain foreign currency, substantial increases in the cost of goods, inability to deliver goods because of emergency production stoppage, and financial difficulties of the seller's main supplier. Shortages may not serve as a basis for avoidance of performance unless goods of equal or similar quality are no longer available on the market. The following *International Chamber of Commerce Arbitration Case No. 6281* involves a seller's attempt to excuse performance as a result of an increase in the market price of steel. As can be seen from this case, the CISG establishes a high standard for parties seeking to excuse their contractual performances.

All the excuse doctrines revolve around all or some of the following parameters: unforeseeability, undue hardship, and events beyond the party's control. Most excuse doctrines require that the changed circumstances be **objectively unforeseeable** at the time of contract formation. If they were foreseeable, then the losses resulting from the breach will be considered as allocated risk. The breaching party will be susceptible to full contract damages. **Undue hardship** generally means more than a mere loss. The fact that the contract becomes unprofitable for one of the parties is insufficient; the loss must be nearly catastrophic. Beyond control means the event is a type of force majeure or superior force occurrence. There are no feasible alternatives for the party to perform on the contract. The UNIDROIT Principles summarize these factors:[45]

- the events occur or become known to the disadvantaged party after the conclusion of the contract;
- the events could not reasonably have been taken into account by the disadvantaged party at the time of the conclusion of the contract;
- the events are beyond the control of the disadvantaged party; and
- the risk of the events was not assumed by the disadvantaged party.

http://
UNIDROIT (The International Institute for the Unification of Private Law): **http:// www.unidroit.org.**

---

44. See Japan Civil Code, Articles 415, 534, & 536.
45. UNIDROIT Principles, Article 6.2.2 (a-d).

International Chamber of Commerce
Case No. 6281 of 26 August 1989

On August 20, 1987, the parties entered into a contract for the sale of 80,000 metric tons of steel bars at a price of $190 per ton with delivery to a port in Yugoslavia. The contract provided the buyer with an option to purchase an additional 80,000 metric tons. On November 27, 1987, the buyer informed seller that it would exercise the option. The seller requested $215 per ton for the additional delivery. On January 26, 1988, the buyer purchased 80,000 tons from another supplier at a price of $216 and brought suit against seller for the difference between the original contract price and the price spent for the substituted goods.

Paris, France. The arbitrator decided that Yugoslav law was applicable. The arbitrator noted that Article 133 of the Yugoslav Law on Obligations allowed for a rescission of a contract due to "changed circumstances." The seller argues that it should be released from the contract due to changed circumstances, namely the increase in the market price of steel. Article 133 does list "economic events, such as extremely sudden and high increases or decreases of prices" as one of the reasons resulting in a frustration of a contract. However, a party cannot make such a claim if he should have taken such circumstances into account at the time of contracting. The world market prices of products, such as steel, fluctuate, as is known from experience. Also, the amount of damage must exceed a reasonable entrepreneurial risk. An increase in market prices from $190 to $215 amounts to slightly less than 13.16%. This increase is well within the customary margin. Furthermore, the development was also predictable. A reasonable seller had to expect that steel prices might go up further.

The buyer's purchase from another supplier, however, cannot be interpreted as a substitute purchase because he had failed to inform the seller of his intention to do so. Thus buyer's damage is limited to the difference between the $190 and $215 and not the $216 replacement price. It should be remarked in passing that the outcome would have been the same under Articles 74 to 77 of the CISG.

AWARD: Seller shall reimburse the buyer in the amount of $2,000,000 (80,000 × $25).

Case Highlights

- Most price or cost increases will not be considered the type of unforeseeable event that excuses a party for breaching a contract.
- Losses due to cost increases, market price changes, or currency fluctuations are considered allocated risks and are to be borne by the party that is allocated the risk in the contract.
- The nonbreaching party may have to agree to a price increase under the duty to mitigate damages. It would then be able to recoup the price increase by suing for damages.

Frustration

In some countries, such as the United Kingdom, the excuse of commercial frustration remains the primary excuse doctrine. The parties are relieved of their contractual obligations as of the date of frustration, and the courts do not have the authority to modify or reform the contract. Commercial frustration does not require that the subject matter of the contract has become objectively impossible to perform. Instead, because of changed circumstances, the purpose or the value of the subject matter of the contract has been severely diminished.

The modern doctrine of frustration in the United Kingdom had its origin in the House of Lords' opinion in *Fibrosa Spolka Akcyjna v. Fairbairn Lawson Combe Barbour Ltd.*[46] In this case, a contract for a British company to provide machinery to a Polish company was frustrated by the outbreak of war. The Polish company had already paid a deposit and sought its recovery on the basis of frustration. Such recovery was

INTERNATIONAL

---

46.   1943 App. Cas. 32 (H.L.).

prohibited under English precedent that provided that the losses "lie where they fall" in frustrated contracts. In ordering the return of the deposit, the House of Lords held that if there was a total failure of consideration, there may be an obligation owed by one party to make restitution to another party. This decision was subsequently enshrined in the Law Reform (Frustrated Contracts) Act of 1943.

The Force Majeure Clause

http://

Examples of *force majeure* clauses— licensing digital information: **http:// www.library.yale.edu/ ~llicense/forcecls.**

The force majeure clause lists the type of events that excuse the parties from the performance of their contracts. Force majeure events may include wars, blockades, strikes, governmental interference or approval, fire, and transportation problems. The parties are free to recognize any event as one to be given force majeure effect. A force majeure clause should be custom drafted to take into account the type of industry, the countries, and the type of carriage involved. The discussion of the *Harriscom v. Svenska* case and other materials in Chapter Four illustrated the importance of a properly drafted force majeure clause for avoiding liability.

Limitation Periods

Another important contract law issue is the statute of limitations or warranty period that will be applied to any future claims of the parties. It is always advisable for the parties to agree on a reasonable limitation period, but what is a reasonable limitation period? When does the limitation period commence? Should there be any instances when the limitation period should be stopped or tolled? The United Nations' sponsored **Convention on the Limitation Period in the International Sale of Goods**[47] provides uniform rules governing the period of time within which a party may bring a claim in conjunction with an international sale of goods. As of mid-2004, there were eighteen contracting parties to the convention.[48] The Convention entered into force in the United States on December 1, 1994.[49]

The Convention prescribes a four-year limitation period for most claims.[50] Article 2(a) defines an international sale as one in which "the buyer and seller have their places of business in different states." Article 22(1) states that the limitation period cannot be modified through contract. However, Article 22(3) does make an exception for arbitral proceedings by providing: "The provisions of this Article shall not affect the validity of a clause in the contract of sale which stipulates that arbitral proceedings shall be commenced within a shorter period of limitation." The four-year limitation period, even if applicable, can be shortened through the adoption of restrictive notice provisions. Article 1(2) states that "this Convention shall not affect a particular time-limit within which one party is required, as a condition for the acquisition or exercise of his claim, to give notice to the other party or perform

---

47. The Convention on the Limitation Period in the International Sale of Goods was concluded in New York on June 14, 1974. An amendment to the Convention, known as the 1980 Protocol, was concluded in Vienna on April 11, 1980. Both instruments entered into force on August 1, 1988.

48. The contracting parties to the Convention are Argentina, Belarus, Cuba, the Czech Republic, Egypt, Guinea, Hungary, Mexico, Moldova, Paraguay, Poland, Romania, Slovakia, Slovenia, Uganda, the United States, Uruguay, and Zambia.

49. See U.S.C.S. International Agreements 445 (1995).

50. See Convention on the Limitation Period in the International Sale of Goods, Article 8.

any act other than the institution of legal proceedings." Additionally, the convention does not apply to certain types of claims. For example, Article 4(a-f) exempts certain sales of goods such as those purchased for personal, family, or household use; at auction; and on execution or by authority of law; as well as sales of commercial paper, ships, aircraft, and electricity. Article 5(a-f) provides that claims for personal injury caused by defective products and claims on bills of exchange or drafts are not governed by the Convention. The Convention is also not applicable if the preponderant part of the contract is the supply of labor or other services.[51]

The Convention outlines rules for the determination of the commencement of the limitation period and when the period is to be tolled. Article 9(1) provides the general rule that the limitation period commences on the date that the "claim accrues." This date is further defined in Article 10(1) as the date when a breach of contract occurs. Other commencement dates are provided for acts of fraud and claims of defects. For example, a claim arising from "a defect or other lack of conformity" accrues on the date when the "goods are handed over to or their tender is refused by the buyer." The period for a claim of fraud commences on the date when the fraud was discovered or "reasonably could have been discovered."

A temporary suspension of the limitation period, otherwise known as tolling, is granted when there is a submission to arbitrate the claim. Article 14(1) states that when the parties submit a claim to arbitration in accordance with an arbitration clause "the limitation period shall cease to run." Other tolling provisions for specific types of claims and events are provided elsewhere in the Convention. For example, Article 15(a-c) provides for a tolling of the limitation period when a creditor asserts a claim in conjunction with the death or incapacity of the debtor or a dissolution or bankruptcy proceeding. Article 18(1) provides for a further tolling when there are multiple debtors. It states that "where legal proceedings have been commenced against one debtor, the limitation period prescribed in this Convention shall cease to run against any other party jointly and severally liable." This tolling of the limitation period is granted, "*provided that the creditor informs such party in writing within that period that the proceedings have been commenced.*" Note the importance of notifying all potential debtors.

The Convention does place an outer limit for the tolling of the limitation period through these provisions. Article 23 states that "notwithstanding the provisions of this Convention, a limitation period shall in any event expire no later than ten years from the date on which it commenced."

It is important to ascertain national limitation periods, given the relatively small number of states that are contracting parties to the Convention. Associated limitation periods vary greatly from country to country and from cause of action to cause of action. For example, European Union law provides for a ten-year statute of limitation for products liability claims, accruing from the date the actual product is placed in the stream of commerce.[52] However, this limitation period shrinks to three years from the date the plaintiff became aware or should reasonably have become aware of the damage, the defect, and the identity of the producer.[53] In comparison, the limitation period for warranty claims is two years starting from the date of delivery.[54]

INTERNATIONAL

51.   See ibid. Article 6(1).
52.   See EU Directive 85/374, Article 11.
53.   See ibid. Article 10(1).
54.   See EU Directive 99/44, Article 5(1).

Limitation periods are somewhat different in Asian countries. For example, China's UCL provides a four-year time limit for filing a lawsuit or initiating arbitration in relation to disputes arising from international sale of goods contracts, accruing from the date that the injured party knew or should have known of the violation of its rights.[55] Parties doing business in Japan have two separate limitation periods of which to be aware. Initially, a limitation period (*shometsu jiko*) provides relief from contractual obligations as a result of the passage of specific periods of time as prescribed by law. General civil obligations (*minji saiken*) are subject to a ten-year limitation period , and commercial obligations (*shoji saiken*) are subject to a five-year limitation period.[56] These periods of time are subject to interruption by intervening events. In addition, businesspeople must be aware of time limitations (*joseki kikan*) that serve to extinguish obligations and are not subject to interruption by intervening events. For example, the civil code grants purchasers of defective products one year from the date they became aware of the existence of the defect to institute proceedings seeking rescission or monetary compensation.[57]

KEY TERMS

acceptance	four-corner analysis	prior dealings
additional term	impediment	products liablity
adequate assurance	implied warranty for a particular	ratification
anticipatory breach	purpose	reasonable person standard
battle of the forms	implied warranty of merchantability	rejection
boilerplate	jurisdiction	revocation
choice of law clause	*lex mercatoria*	rights and obligations
computer software sale	limited express warranty	right to cure
conflict of law rules	mailbox rule	specially manufactured goods
consequential damages	mirror image rule	statute of frauds
contract formation	mitigate	totality of the circumstances
Convention on the Limitation	mixed sale	trade usage
Period in the International Sale	*nachfrist* notice	undue hardship
of Goods	objectively unforeseeable	Uniform Commercial Code (UCC)
course of performance	offer	United Nations Convention on
disclaimer	offeree	Contracts for the International
doctrine of frustration	offeror	Sale of Goods (CISG)
doctrine of impossibility	parol evidence rule	virtual goods
doctrine of impracticability	place of business	written confirmation rule

CHAPTER PROBLEMS

1. Compare the Uniform Commercial Code's treatment of anticipatory repudiation and adequate assurance in Sectoins 2-609 and 2-610 with the CISG's treatment in Articles 71–73. Can you find any significant differences?

2. In many transactions involving technology transfer, the contract provides for the sale of both goods and services. Does the CISG apply to such contracts?

3. How do courts determine which national laws apply in a given case?

---

55. See People's Republic of China Contract Law, Article 129.
56. See Japan Civil Code, Article 167. See also Japan Commercial Code, Article 522.
57. See Japan Civil Code, Articles 566(3) & 570.

4. Section 2-205 of the Uniform Commercial Code provides an exception to the rule that an offeror is the "master of the offer" or has a right to revoke the offer at any time. It provides that "an offer given by a *merchant* in a *signed writing* which gives *assurance* that it will be held open is not revocable, but in no event may such period of irrevocability exceed three months." The CISG's firm offer rule is found in Article 16. It provides that an offer cannot be revoked "if it indicates that it is irrevocable or if it was reasonable for the offeree to rely on the offer being irrevocable and the offeree has acted in reliance on the offer." Do you see any significant differences between these two versions of the firm offer rule? Which version is broader? Why?

5. (A) As a seller and exporter of goods, you are negotiating a long-term (three-year) installment contract. Because of the length of the contract, an open price term needs to be negotiated. Write a clause that anticipates the risks involved in entering a long-term supply contract. What cost factors should be described in detail? Also, how would you interrelate the open price term with a force majeure clause?

(B) You are negotiating a contract for the shipment of goods from Miami to the Middle East. The risks and costs of the shipment will be yours to the point of destination. Draft a force majeure clause. What events would you want to be considered as force majeure? Should some occurrences provide for an excuse (termination) and others for suspension?

(C) In a "battle of forms" situation, the additional terms in the acceptance often become a part of the contract. Assuming that you are the offeror, draft language for your offer that would preclude those additional terms from entering the contract. Assuming that you are the offeree, draft a clause for your acceptance that would make it clear that there is no contract unless it is on the terms of the acceptance (counteroffer).

6. A business manager who corresponds with numerous contacts in the international business world sends letters and faxes to agents, customers, suppliers, distributors, lenders, and many others. Most U.S. businesspeople have been educated to believe that they would expose their companies to liability if and only if they enter into a formal written contract. The formal written contract is a product of the company's lawyers. They are also aware that under the UCC's statute of frauds they are not liable for oral promises. They further (incorrectly) rationalize that the statute of frauds requires a fully negotiated, written agreement signed by both parties. Therefore, they often say or write things aimed at encouraging another party to take some action. They converse and write letters under the assumption that they would not be held liable until they enter a formal agreement. How have these assumptions changed with the enactment of the CISG? Can businesspeople be held liable for promises or assurances made in simple business letters? How can a manager avoid such unintended liability?

7. The European Union has a directive pertaining to warranties in consumer transactions. Compare the selected provisions of Directive 99/44/EC with the warranty provisions found in the UCC and CISG. Note that the European word for "warranty" is *guarantee*.

8. Review the purchase order in Exhibit 8.1 and answer the following questions:

(a) Why is payment by "Irrevocable LOC"? What does LOC signify?

(b) What is the importance of the term "Cash Against Documents"? Is this considered to be advance payment or payment through a documentary transaction?

(c) Of the documents listed for possible delivery, which is absolutely needed for purposes of a documentary transaction?

(d) Why is the letter of credit amount based on "CIF plus 10%"?

(e) What does CIF signify? What does "INCOTERMS" refer to?

(f) What is wrong with the designation "CIF Mexico City"?

(g) What does the acronym "HTS" represent?

(h) What does "M/V Hathaway" represent?

(i) Who is the "notify party"? Can the common carrier deliver the goods to the notify party?

(j) What is the importance of the notation "at sight"?

(k) What roles do the Banco de Mexico and Nations Bank of Miami play? What are these banks called?

INTERNET EXERCISES

1. Review the latest revision to Article 2 of the Uniform Commercial Code to see if any changes make it more similar or dissimilar to the CISG. You can use Comparative Law: Selective Comparison of CISG and UCC, page 260, to look up relevant sections. The recent revised drafts of Article 2 can be accessed at **http://www.law.upenn.edu/bll/ulc/ulc_frame.htm.**

2. Review how Islamic law deals with sale of goods and commercial law. See Centre of Islamic and Middle Eastern Studies at **http://www.soas.ac.uk/Centres/IslamicLaw/Materials.html.**

3. Select a country and research its sales law by using the Cornell Law School Legal Information Institute at **http://www.law.cornell.edu.** Select "Law by Source or Jurisdiction" and then "Law from Around the World."

The two fundamental risks of international exporting are the seller's payment risk and the buyer's delivery risk. The seller fears relinquishing control over its goods before receiving payment, and the buyer fears making payment before obtaining possession of the goods. The method of payment agreed to by the parties determines who will bear the burden of these two risks. For sales within the United States, if the buyer has good credit, sales are usually made on open account; if not, cash in advance is required. For products sold abroad, there are several basic methods of payment. As with domestic sales, a major factor that determines the method of payment is the seller's level of trust in the buyer's ability and willingness to pay. This chapter begins with a review of the different methods of payment utilized in the sale of goods. It then focuses on the most common method of payment in international transactions—the documentary collections transaction.

Chapter 9

The Documentary Transaction

Methods of Payment

The common methods of payment in international trade, ranked in order from the least secure for the exporter-seller, are (1) open account and consignment sales, (2) documentary collection, (3) documentary credit, and (4) cash in advance. Exhibit 9.1: Methods of Payment Risk Scale lists the different methods of payments on a risk scale from the perspective of the exporter-seller and importer-buyer.

Because getting paid in full and on time is of utmost concern, exporters should carefully weigh these different methods of payment. For example, the buyer would much prefer an open account transaction in which payment does not have to be made until sometime after the delivery of the goods. In an **open account** transaction, the exporter simply bills the customer, who is expected to pay under agreed terms at a future date. Open account sales do pose risks. The exporter may have to pursue collection abroad, which can be difficult and costly. Receivables may be harder to finance, because drafts or other evidence of indebtedness are unavailable. In a foreign transaction, an open account is a satisfactory method of payment if the buyer is well established, has demonstrated a long and favorable payment record, or has been thoroughly checked for creditworthiness. In contrast, **cash in advance** before shipment is the most desirable method from the perspective of the seller. The seller is relieved of all collection problems and has immediate use of the money, especially if a wire transfer is used.

The other methods of payment lie between the two extremes of open account and cash in advance. The two most common may be labeled documentary transactions. **Documentary collections** and **documentary credit transactions** are the two forms of documentary transactions. The documentary collections transaction is the focus of this chapter. The documentary credit transaction, which utilizes letters of credit to guarantee payment to the seller, will be the subject of Chapter Eleven. Both methods involve the use of documents to ensure the

http://

International Trade Data System— "International Trade Terms": **http://www.itds.treas.gov/glossaryfrm.html.** This site provides a comprehensive glossary of legal and business terms, many of which appear in the next three chapters.

EXHIBIT 9.1   *Methods of Payment Risk Scale*

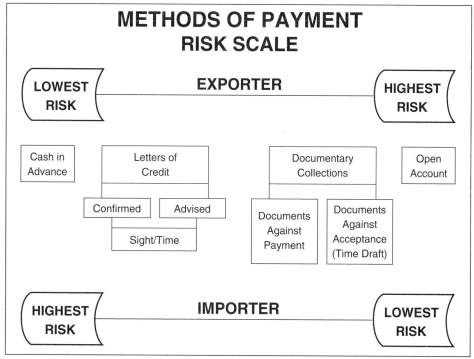

passage of title to the goods to the buyer and payment to the seller while the goods are in transit.

In a documentary collections transaction, the buyer is obligated to pay on delivery of documents rather than on delivery of goods. The documentary credit transaction also requires payment on delivery of documents, but that payment is further guaranteed by a commercial bank through the issuance of a letter of credit. The seller receives payment through the letter of credit upon presentation of documents to the bank.

Another intermediate method of payment is the **consignment sale**. In international consignment sales, the buyer receives use of the goods, but title remains with the seller until the goods are sold to a third party. This method is most common when goods are shipped to a foreign distributor to be sold on behalf of the exporter. The exporter retains title to the goods until the distributor sells them. Once the goods are sold, payment is sent to the exporter. With this method, the exporter accepts a great deal of risk and loss of control over the goods and may have to wait an extended period of time for payment. When this type of sale is contemplated, it may be wise to consider some form of risk insurance.

The Sales Contract and Documentary Transaction

Before exporting to or entering a foreign market, an analysis of the factors that relate to the profitability of such an entry should be undertaken. Many new exporters calculate their export price by the **cost-plus method** alone. In the cost-plus method of calculation, the exporter starts with the domestic manufacturing cost and adds administration, research and development, overhead, freight forwarding, distributor margins, customs charges, and profit. The net effect of this pricing approach may be that the export price escalates into an uncompetitive range.

A more competitive method of pricing for market entry is what is termed **marginal cost pricing**. This method considers the direct, out-of-pocket expenses of producing and selling products for export as a floor beneath which prices cannot be set without incurring a loss. For example, products may have to be modified for the export market to accommodate different sizes, electrical systems, or labeling requirements. Changes of this nature may increase costs. On the other hand, the export product may be a stripped-down version of the domestic product and therefore cost less. If additional products can be produced without increasing fixed costs, the incremental cost of producing additional products for export should be lower than the average production costs for the domestic market only.

In addition to production costs, overhead, and research and development, other costs should be allocated to domestic and export products in proportion to the benefit derived from those expenditures. Additional costs often associated with export sales include (1) market research and credit checks; (2) business travel; (3) international postage, cable, and telephone rates; (4) translation costs; (5) commissions, training charges, and other costs involving foreign representatives; (6) consultant and freight forwarding costs; and (7) product modification and special packaging.

As in the domestic market, demand in the foreign market is a key to setting prices. What will the market bear for a specific product or service? For most consumer goods, per capita income is a good gauge of a market's ability to pay. Per capita income for most of the industrialized nations is comparable to that of the United States. For the rest of the world, it is much lower. In lower per capita income markets, simplifying the product to reduce the selling price may be the answer. The exporter must also keep in mind that currency valuations alter the affordability of the goods. Thus, pricing should accommodate fluctuations in currency and the relative strength of the dollar. Few companies are free to set prices without carefully evaluating their competitors' pricing policies. Where many competitors are servicing a particular foreign market, the exporter may have little choice but to match the going price in order to establish a market share. If the exporter's product or service is new to a particular foreign market, it may actually be possible to set a higher price than is normally charged domestically. Only after it has estimated the cost, demand, and competition for its goods is the exporter-seller ready to prepare a *pro forma* **invoice** and enter into an export contract.

http://
International Trade Administration—sample export quotation worksheet: **http://www.unzco.com/basicguide/figure10.html.**

Pro Forma Invoice

The prudent exporter realizes the importance of entering into a well-defined agreement. When the parties are from different countries, setting up the transaction in advance is vital. First, the imposition of larger geographical distances, along with customs regulations and special documentary requirements, makes the international sale of goods transaction more complicated. Second, the exporting and importing transaction requires the use of various third parties, such as commercial banks, international common carriers, custom brokers, and freight forwarders. Thus, before entering into an international sales contract, the seller should consider the costs associated with these two factors. The form that describes the allocation of these costs between the seller and the buyer is the seller's pro forma invoice.

Many export transactions, particularly for first-time exporters, begin with the receipt of an inquiry from abroad, followed by a request for a quotation or a pro forma invoice. The pro forma invoice is provided by a seller prior to the shipment of

http://
International Trade Administration—example of *pro forma* invoice: **http://www.unzco.com/basicguide/figure11.html.**

goods, informing the buyer of the kinds and quantities of goods and their costs. It is generally the basis for the formation of the sales contract, along with the buyer's purchase order. A pro forma invoice describes the product, states a price for it, sets the time of shipment, and specifies the sale and payment terms. Before preparing the pro forma invoice, the prudent exporter or importer should develop a checklist of the important terms and documentary requirements that need to be incorporated. An example is provided in Focus on Transactions: International Shipping Checklist. Most of the documents in the feature are explained in detail later in this chapter.

Because the foreign buyer may not be familiar with the product, the description of it in the pro forma invoice must be more detailed than it would be in a domestic quotation. The description should include (1) buyer's name and address; (2) buyer's reference number and date of inquiry; (3) list of requested products and brief description; (4) price of each item (it is advisable to indicate whether items are new or used and to quote in U.S. dollars to reduce foreign-exchange risk); (5) gross and net shipping weight (in metric units where appropriate); (6) total cubic volume

International Shipping Checklist

Commercial Invoice

- Will a commercial invoice suffice or is a customs or consular invoice required?
- Are all charges in accord with the original quotation?
- Are terms of delivery clear? Was *INCOTERMS 2000* used?
- Are terms of payment and currency of payment clearly stated?
- Are unit descriptions, measures, and prices recorded the same way as on all other documents? Are they exactly as required by the letter of credit?
- Is a destination control statement required?

Packing List

- Are shipper and consignee clearly identified?
- Are all item descriptions and units of measure per the commercial invoice and the letter of credit?
- Are carton marks and numbers accurate?
- Does the packing list conform to the importing country's requirements?

Shipper's Export Declaration (SED)

- Is a SED required?
- Has the correct export license designation been used? Is an individual validated export license required?

- Have the commodity, consignee, and destination country been reviewed for export controls?

Bills of Lading

- Are the consignee, shipper, and notify party clearly identified?
- Do descriptions, marks, and numbers match the commercial invoice and packing list?
- Are ocean bills of lading marked "On Board," if required by a letter of credit?
- If freight charges are included on the commercial invoice, is the bill of lading marked "Prepaid"?
- Are any of the items classifiable as hazardous materials?

Certificate of Origin

- Is an origin certificate required by the letter of credit or by the destination country?

Miscellaneous Documents

- Preshipment inspection certificate?
- Insurance certificate?
- Manufacturer's certificate?
- Phytosanitary inspection certificate?
- Weight certificate?

and dimensions (in metric units where appropriate) packed for export; (7) trade discount, if applicable; (8) delivery point; (9) terms of sale; (10) terms of payment; (11) insurance and shipping costs; (12) validity period for quotation; (13) total charges to be paid by customer; (14) estimated shipping date from factory or U.S. port; and (15) estimated date of shipment arrival.

The pro forma invoice should not be confused with the commercial invoice. Pro forma invoices (see Exhibit 9.2) are not for payment purposes but are essentially

EXHIBIT 9.2   *Sample* Pro Forma *Invoice*

Tech International
1000 J Street, N.W.
New York, New York 20005
Telephone: 202-555-1212
Fax: 202-555-1111

Date: Jan. 12, 2005

To: Gomez Y. Cartagena
Bogota, Colombia

Our Reference: Col. 91-14
We hereby quote as follows:

Terms of Payment: Letter of Credit

Terms of Sale: CIF Buenaventura, Colombia

QUANTITY	MODEL	DESCRIPTION	UNIT	EXTENSION
3	2-50	Separators in accordance with attached specifications	$14,750.00	$44,250.00
3	14-40	First-stage Filter Assemblies Per attached specifications	$1,200.00	$3,600.00
3	custom	Drive Units—30 hp each (for operation on 3-phase 440 v., 50 cy. current) complete with remote controls	$4,235.00	$12,705.00

Total FOB New York, New York, domestic packed...$60,555.00

Export processing, packaging, prepaid inland freight to JFK International Airport

& forwarder's handling charges FOB Dulles Airport, Virginia......................................$63,670.00

Estimated air freight and insurance..$2,960.00

Estimated CIF Buenaventura, Colombia..$66,630.00

Estimated gross weight 9,360 lbs.; Estimated cube 520 cu. ft.

Export packed 4,212 kg.; Export packed 15.6 cu. meters

1. All prices quoted herein are U.S. dollars.

2. Prices quoted herein for merchandise only are valid for 60 days from this date.

3. Any changes in shipping costs or insurance rates are for account of the buyer.

4. We estimate ex-factory shipment approximately 60 days from receipt here of purchase order and letter of credit.

Source: National Trade Data Bank, a product of STAT-USA, U.S. Department of Commerce.

quotations in an invoice format. The invoice should be conspicuously marked "pro forma invoice." The price quotations must state explicitly that they are subject to change without notice. If a specific price is agreed on or guaranteed by the exporter, the precise period during which the offer remains valid should be specified.

The Documentary Transaction

To alleviate the seller's risk of not being paid or the buyer's risk of not receiving the goods after making payment, most export contracts require a documentary transaction. The sale of goods contract is converted into a sale of documents contract. The buyer contracts to buy documents, and the seller promises to provide conforming documents to the buyer while the goods are in transit. In the documentary transaction, the seller is paid and the buyer receives title to the goods while the goods are in transit to the port of destination. In this way, the buyer's delivery and seller's payment risks are diminished. Upon receiving the documents, the buyer is in a position to resell the goods to downstream buyers or to use the documents as collateral to obtain financing. In the event that the buyer refuses to pay for the documents, the seller still retains title and control of the goods. Selling the goods to someone else through negotiation of the documents can then mitigate the losses.

The documentary collections transaction requires drafts to be paid either when presented for payment or at a date after the buyer receives the goods. A draft or **bill of exchange**[1] is analogous to a foreign buyer's check. Drafts that are paid upon presentation or demand are called **sight drafts**. Drafts that are payable at some time after presentation of the documents are called **time drafts**. Like checks used in domestic commerce, drafts sometimes carry the risk that they will be dishonored. A sight draft is used when the seller wishes to retain title to the shipment until receipt of payment.

Banks use these instruments to effectuate payment to the seller upon the presentation of the documents. A draft is a written, unconditional order for payment from the **drawer** (seller) to the **drawee** (buyer). It directs the drawee to pay a specified sum of money, in a given currency, on a specific date to the payee (seller). The documentary transaction allows the buyer to take possession either by making payment upon the presentation of the draft or by acceptance of the draft. The first type of documentary collections transaction is called **cash against document** and is the ordinary means of processing a documentary collections transaction.

The second type is referred to as **documents against acceptance**. The cash against document transaction requires the buyer to sign a sight draft before receiving the necessary documents. The sight draft is then processed through the banking system for immediate payment to the seller. In the documents against acceptance transaction, instructions are given by the seller to a bank, indicating that the documents transferring title to the goods should be delivered to the buyer-drawee upon the buyer's acceptance of the attached time draft. The buyer's signature indicates its guarantee to pay the draft at some future time. The function of drafts as means of payment and as used for purposes of financing are discussed in detail in Chapter Eleven.

For an exporter or importer to understand its responsibilities in a documentary transaction, it is advisable to develop an export-import checklist. The Focus on Transactions: Checklist for Export-Import Transactions box provides an example of

http://
United States Department of Commerce—guide to international trade: **http://www.unzco.com/ basicguide.** Provides information on all aspects of documentary transactions.

---

1. The term *draft* is used commonly in the United States, and *bill of exchange* is the term used in the United Kingdom and some other Commonwealth countries.

Focus on Transactions

Checklist for Export-Import Transactions

- Enter into a sales contract (1)
- Obtain letter of credit (if required) (2)
- Obtain confirmation of letter of credit (3)
- Hire carrier for transport of goods (4)
- Obtain necessary insurance policies (5)
- Arrange inspection of goods prior to shipment (6)
- Prepare goods for shipment: packing, marking (7)

- Deliver to carrier (8)
- Obtain shipping documents (9)
- Transmit shipping documents (10)
- Obtain payment under letter of credit (11)
- Entry and customs clearance in the country of delivery (12)
- Final liquidation of customs duties and delivery to importer (13)

such a checklist. The numbers to the right of the checklist items refer to the description that follows.

Enlisting the services of commercial banks to provide letters of credit (2 and 3) and to transfer documentation (10) is a common requirement of the standard sales contract (1). Following receipt of the letter of credit, the seller prepares the goods for shipment (7) and obtains an insurance policy to cover the risk of loss of the goods while they are being transported to the buyer (5). To diminish the risk of fraudulent documentation, a prudent buyer negotiates for inspection rights (6). The inspection of the goods will take place before the goods are loaded at the port of shipment. The inspection company issues an inspection certificate that the seller sends to the buyer, along with the other required documents. The buyer will be able to review the inspection report before paying for the documents and taking possession of the goods at the port of destination.

The international sales contract almost always provides for transit of the goods by ocean carriage. Under the standard **CIF** (cost, insurance, freight) contract, for example, the seller must ship the goods by obtaining the services of a freight forwarding company and a common carrier to transport the goods to the buyer (4). The contract will require the seller to obtain a bill of lading from the common carrier to prove that the goods have been sent as dictated by the contract (8 and 9). The seller will not be able to receive payment unless it delivers to the bank for transmission to the buyer a conforming bill of lading, along with the other documents stated in the sales contract (10). After the bank reviews the documents, the seller receives payment (11). Upon receipt of the bill of lading and other documents, the buyer is then able to take delivery of the goods for import into the country (12 and 13).

The Documentary Collections Transaction

As discussed in the previous section, the seller in a documentary collections transaction is required to present a number of conforming documents as required in the sales contract to receive payment. The required documents are generally attached to a draft or bill of exchange. The seller draws the draft on the account of the buyer and makes it payable to the seller. Unlike with a standard check or bank draft, the seller is both the drawer and payee of the documentary draft. To better reduce the payment risk, the seller (exporter) will want to negotiate a sight draft so that it will receive payment immediately upon the presentation of the documents. Some exporters, however, will agree to wait for payment, especially when doing business with an established customer. In such cases, a time draft is utilized that provides for payment within a set number of days after presentment or from shipment. In that case, the buyer should be required to sign and note "accepted" on the time draft before obtaining possession of the documents.

The typical documentary collections transaction proceeds along a chronological timeline as shown in Exhibit 9.3: Documentary Collections Flowchart. It begins with the negotiation and execution of a sales contract (1). The sales contract is usually formed by the exchange of a pro forma invoice or price quotation from the seller and a purchase order from the buyer. The seller often contacts a freight forwarder to obtain freight quotes and insurance information before drafting the pro forma invoice. After the contract is formed, the seller contacts the freight forwarder to book shipment on a common carrier (2A and 2B). The freight forwarder coordinates the movement of the goods, submits the export documentation to U.S. Customs and Border Protection, obtains the bill of lading from the carrier, and compiles other required documents.

The **bill of lading** is a title document that allows the goods to be transferred while they are in transit to the port of destination. Without the bill of lading, or similar title document, the documentary transaction would not be possible. The bill of lading allows a sale of goods transaction to be converted to a sale of documents. Upon receiving the bill of lading, the buyer becomes the owner of the goods. Any dispute over the ownership of goods will be resolved in favor of the party in possession of the bill of lading and not the party in the actual possession of the goods. The functions and characteristics of the bill of lading are reviewed in detail later in this chapter.

EXHIBIT 9.3   *Documentary Collections Flowchart*

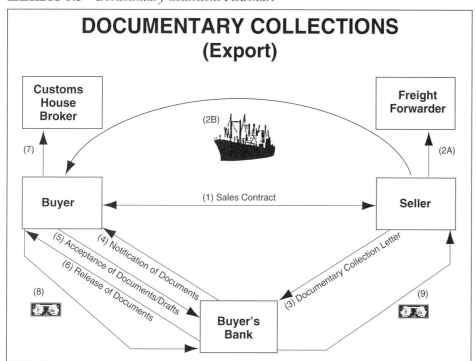

To obtain the bill of lading, the goods are delivered to the common carrier. The bill of lading is endorsed by the shipper and sent via the shipper's bank to the buyer's bank or to another intermediary, along with a sight draft, invoices, and other supporting documents specified by the buyer, such as packing lists, consular invoices, and insurance certificates. The seller usually does not submit the documents and draft directly to the buyer's bank. Instead, it uses a local bank to transmit the documents through its corresponding relations to the buyer's bank. These documents are presented to the buyer's bank, along with a documentary collections letter or order (3). The collection letter or order includes a draft drawn on the buyer's account either payable at sight or at a future time.

The buyer's bank acts as the collecting bank for purposes of transmitting payment to the seller. It notifies the buyer of the receipt of the documents and collects payment on the draft (sight draft) or notifies the seller of the buyer's acceptance of the draft (time draft) (4 and 5). Following the payment or acceptance, the bill of lading and other documents are released to the buyer (6). Before the cargo can be released, the original ocean bill of lading must be properly endorsed by the buyer and surrendered to the carrier, because it is a document that evidences title. Air waybills of lading, on the other hand, do not need to be presented for the buyer to claim the goods. The buyer transmits the shipping documents to its customs broker (7). The customs broker clears the goods through customs at the port of importation and arranges inland transport to the buyer's warehouse. Finally, funds are wired through the banking system to the seller's account (8 and 9). If the sales contract requires the purchaser to guarantee payment through a letter of credit, then the first step in the process is the procurement by the buyer of a letter of credit. The role of letters of credit in international business transactions will be examined in Chapter Eleven.

Documentation

Several documents are commonly used in exporting. Of course, the documents actually used in each case depend on the requirements of the exporting and importing countries. First, as in a domestic transaction, the **commercial invoice** is a bill for the goods prepared by the seller (see Exhibit 9.4). A commercial invoice contains basic information about the transaction, including a description of the goods, the address of the buyer and seller, and the delivery and payment terms. The buyer needs the invoice to prove ownership and to arrange payment. Some governments use the commercial invoice to place a value on the goods in assessing customs duties.

Second, bills of lading are contracts between the owner of the goods and a common carrier. A negotiable or shipper's order bill of lading can be bought, sold, or traded while goods are in transit and is used for letter-of-credit transactions. A straight bill of lading is nonnegotiable. The customer usually needs the original bill of lading to take possession of the goods.

Third, certain countries require a **consular invoice**, which is used to control and identify goods. The consular invoice is purchased from the consulate of the country to which the goods are being shipped and usually must be prepared in the language of that country. Fourth, some countries require a signed statement as to the origin of the export item. Such **certificates of origin** are usually obtained through a semiofficial organization, such as a local chamber of commerce.

Fifth, some purchasers and countries may require a **certificate of inspection** attesting to the specifications of the goods shipped. Inspection certificates are often

http://

International Trade Administration— sample of a straight bill of lading: **http://www. unzco.com/basicguide/ figure3.html.**

EXHIBIT 9.4   *Commercial Invoice*

Invoice	**Shipper Information:**

Invoice

Date: _____

Bill of Lading / Air Waybill No.:_____

Invoice Number: _____

Purchase Order No.:_____

Terms of Sale (Incoterm): _____

Reason for Export: _____

Shipper Information:
Tax ID/VAT No.: _____
Contact Name: _____
Company Name: _____
Company Address: _____
_____
City: _____
State/Province: _____
Postal Code: _____
Country: _____
Telephone No.: _____
E-Mail ID: _____

Ship To:
Tax ID/VAT No.: _____
Contact Name: _____
Company Name: _____
Company Address: _____
_____
_____
City: _____
State/Province: _____
Postal Code: _____
Country: _____
Telephone No.: _____
E-Mail ID: _____

Sold To:
Tax ID/VAT No.: _____
Contact Name: _____
Company Name: _____
Company Address: _____
_____
_____
City: _____
State/Province: _____
Postal Code: _____
Country: _____
Telephone No.: _____
E-Mail ID: _____

No. Units	Unit of Measure	Description of Goods (include Harmonized Tariff Number If known)	Country of Origin	Unit Value	Total Value

Additional Comments:

Invoice Line Total:	
Discount/Rebate:	
Invoice Sub-Total:	
Freight Charges:	
Insurance:	
Other (Specify Type)_____:	
Invoice Total Amount:	
Currency Code:	

Declaration Statement:

Shipper Signature / Title   **Date:**

_____

Total Number of Packages:_____

Total Weight (indicate LBS or KGS):_____

These commodities, technology, or software were exported from the United States in accordance with the Export Administration Regulations. Diversion contrary to U.S. law prohibited.

obtained from independent testing organizations. Sixth, the seller who provides insurance must provide an **insurance certificate** or binder stating the type and amount of coverage. This insurance certificate is negotiable so that it can be transferred along with the bill of lading.

Seventh, the United States requires a **Shipper's Export Declaration (SED)**. The preparation and submission of the SED was discussed in Chapter Six. Chapter Six also discussed the eighth requirement, specifically, obtaining a general or an individually validated **export license**. Ninth, an export **packing slip** or list itemizes the material in each individual package being shipped. It gives the individual and

http://
International Trade Administration— sample packing list: **http://www.unzco.com/ basicguide/figure7. html.**

gross weights and measurements for each package, along with the package markings. The packing list is attached to the outside of a package in a waterproof envelope marked "packing list enclosed." It allows the shipper or forwarding agent to determine the total shipment weight and volume, and whether the correct cargo is being shipped. In addition, customs officials use the list to check the cargo. The more common documents used in the documentary transaction are further defined in Doing Business Internationally: List of Export Documents.

List of Export Documents

Doing Business Internationally

Bill of Lading
A title document issued by a shipping company. It also serves as a formal receipt of the goods and a carriage contract. The holder of the bill of lading has a right to claim delivery of the goods from the shipping company at the port of destination. The most common bill of lading in international transport is the ocean bill of lading. A multimodal transport bill of lading may be used when more than one form of transport is being used.

Letter of Credit
A document issued by the importer-purchaser's bank to guarantee the payment of the draft to the exporter for the purchase of the goods or upon the presentation of documents by the exporter. A transferable letter of credit allows the exporter (beneficiary) to make the credit payable to others (suppliers).

Letter of Indemnity
This document allows a carrier to release goods to the consignee not yet in possession of the bill of lading. It is a guarantee to indemnify the carrier from all liability related to the release. It is also called a "steamer guarantee."

Export License
A government-issued document granting permission to export the specific commodity to a specific country.

Dock Receipt
This document certifies the receipt of the goods by a carrier at the port of shipment.

Warehouse Receipt
Acknowledges receipt of the goods by a warehouse operator. A "dock warrant" not only acknowledges receipt but also is a document of title.

Commercial Invoice
This document is prepared by the exporter and lists and describes the goods. It generally also gives the prices, discounts, quantities, and delivery and payment terms. It is used by governments to place a valuation of the goods for the assessment of customs duties.

Consular Invoice
An invoice certified by the consul of the country of import. It is used by customs officials to verify the value, quantity, and quality of the goods. The consul may compare the export price with the market price in the exporting country to determine if dumping is evident.

Certificate of Inspection
An inspection certificate is issued by an independent inspection company to assure the purchaser of the quantity and quality of the goods being shipped. Preshipment inspection is a requirement for importation of goods into many developing countries.

Certificate of Origin
This document may be required by the country of import. It is provided by a third party, such as an official of the local chamber of commerce or an official of the consular office.

Bill of Exchange or Draft
An order addressed to the importer or the importer's bank for the payment of a fixed sum at sight or in the future (time draft).

continued

List of Export Documents (*continued*)

ATA Carnet
An international customs document for the temporary duty-free import of goods into a country for display, demonstration, or other purposes. A carnet is usually good for one year from the date of issuance. Generally, a bond or cash deposit of 40 percent of the value of the goods is required. Carnets are sold in the United States by the U.S. Council for International Business, 1212 Avenue of the Americas, New York, New York 10036, (212) 354–4480.

ISO 9000 Certificate
International quality standards that certify the exporter meets certain minimum requirements of quality.

Marine Insurance Certificate or Binder
Generic form of insurance available even in multimodal transport.

The number of documents the exporter must deal with varies, depending on the destination of the shipment. Because each country has different import regulations, the exporter must be careful to provide proper documentation. Exporters should seriously consider having the freight forwarder handle the documentation. Much of the documentation is routine for freight forwarders or customs brokers acting on the firm's behalf, but the exporter is ultimately responsible for the accuracy of the documentation.

Bill of Lading

The bill of lading is the traditional transport document and serves three functions: (1) carriage contract between the ship owner and the shipper, (2) evidence of receipt that the goods were delivered to the ship, and (3) document of title (see Exhibit 9.5: Bill of Lading).[2] Its function as a title document allows for the sale, transfer, and "collateralization" of the goods while in transit. Lord Mustill, in discussing the third function of the bill of lading, states that "it is a symbol of constructive possession of the goods which can transfer possession by endorsement and transfer; it is a transferable *key to the warehouse.*"[3] Although the bill of lading generally serves as a document of title, receipt, and carriage contract, other agreements may preempt its role in one of these areas. For example, a prior agreement, such as a freight or booking contract, may control the contractual relationship between the shipper and the common carrier. In *M & Z Trading Corporation v. Cargolift Ltd,*[4] the shipper argued that a prior freight agreement governed, while the common carrier contended that its bill of lading constituted the contract. The court reasoned that the resolution of such disputes turns on factual and legal issues relating to, for example, the parties' negotiations, the documents generated during those negotiations, and the status and legal effect of the bill of lading. By the express terms of the prior agreement, the carrier's general

---

2. See generally Georgios Zekos, "The Contractual Role of Bills of Lading Under Greek Law"; "The Contractual Role of Bills of Lading Under United States Law"; and "The Contractual Role of Bills of Lading Under English Law," 39 *Managerial Law* Nos. 3–5 (1997).

3. *Enichem Anic S.P.A. v. Ampelos Shipping Co. (The Delfini),* 1 Lloyd's Rep. 252, 268 (C.A. 1990).

4. No. 98-56887, 2000 U.S. App. LEXIS 11573 (9th Cir. May 1, 2000).

EXHIBIT 9.5   *Bill of Lading*

Any Container Line	BILL OF LADING

SHIPPER/EXPORTER

BOOKING NUMBER

BILL OF LADING NUMBER

EXPORT REFERENCES

CONSIGNEE

FORWARDING AGENT   FMC NO.
                       CHB NO.

NOTIFY PARTY

ALSO NOTIFY - ROUTING & INSTRUCTIONS

VESSEL	VOYAGE	FLAG	PLC OF RECEIPT BY PRECARRIER	RELAY POINT	POINT AND COUNTRY OF ORIGIN OF GOODS
			PORT OF LOADING	LOADING PIER	TYPE OF MOVE
PORT OF DISCHARGE			PLACE OF DELIVERY BY ON CARRIER	ORIGINALS TO BE RELEASED AT	

PARTICULARS FURNISHED BY SHIPPER

MARKS & NO'S/CONTAINER NO'S	NO.OF PKGS.	DESCRIPTION OF GOODS	WEIGHT	MEASUREMENTS

FREIGHT CHARGES	RATED AS	PER	RATE	TO BE PREPAID IN U.S. DOLLARS	TO BE COLLECTED IN U.S. DOLLARS	FOREIGN CURRENCY

SUBJECT TO SECTION 7 OF CONDITIONS, IF SHIPMENT IS TO BE DELIVERED TO THE CONSIGNEE WITHOUT RECOURSE ON THE CONSIGNOR, THE CONSIGNOR SHALL SIGN THE FOLLOWING STATEMENT; 'THE CARRIER SHALL NOT MAKE DELILIVERY OF THIS SHIPMENT WITHOUT PAYMENT OF FREIGHT AND OTHERLAWFUL CHARGES.'   **TOTALS**

IN WITNESS WHEREOF THE CARRIER BY ITS AGENT HAS SIGNED

SIGNATURE OF CONSIGNOR

RECEIVED THE GOODS OR PACKAGES SHIPPER'S LOAD AND COUNT GOODS HEREINAFTER MENTIONED IN APPARENT GOOD ORDER AND CONDITION UNLESS OTHERWISE INDICATED TO BE RELAYED AS HEREIN PROVIDED, THE RECEIPT, CUSTODY, CARRIAGE, DELIVERY, AND TRANSSHIPPING OF THE GOODS ARE SUBJECT TO THE TERMS APPEARING ON THE FACE AND BACK HEREOF, AND CARRIER'S TARIFFS ON FILE WITH THE INTERSTATE COMMERCE COMMISSION AND/OR THE FEDERAL MARITIME COMMISSION, WASHINGTON, D.C

LIABILITY LIMITED TO AMOUNT SPCIFIED IN SEC 16 UNLESS INCREASED VALUE DECLARED BY SHIPPER AS SPECIFIED BELOW;

ORIGINAL BILLS OF LADING ALL OF THE SAME TENOR AND DATE ONE OF WHICH BEING ACCOMPLISHED THE OTHERS TO STAND VOID.

DECLARED VALUE

BY _____ CARRIER

*APPLICABLE ONLY WHEN USED AS A THROUGH BILL OF LADING AFTER MENTIONED IN APPARENT GOOD ORDER AND CONDITION UNLESS
**INDICATE WHETHER ANY OF THE CARGO IS HAZARDOUS MATERIAL UNDER DOT, IMCO,OR OTHER REGULATIONS AND INDICATE THE CORRECT COMMODITY NUMBER IN DESCRIPTION OF PACKAGES AND GOODS ABOVE.

BY _____ FOR SHIPPER
DATE

obligations began upon the initial pickup of the goods in Canada and continued until final delivery in Russia. The court held that the bill of lading could have only, at most, supplemented the parties' prior agreement, unless the parties clearly agreed otherwise. Therefore, the bill of lading did not nullify the lengthy course of negotiations that culminated in the prior freight agreement.

Documentary practice may be transformed in the near future by the development of **electronic data interchange (EDI)**. EDI had its genesis in the mid-1980s with the development of the Rules for Electronic Bills of Lading by the Comité Maritime International. Under these rules, the right to control goods and transfer possession was based on the possession of a "private key" made available by the carrier upon the shipper's receipt of goods. This private key could be construed "in any technically appropriate form the parties could agree upon for securing the authenticity and integrity of the electronic transmission."[5] Although the system failed to gain widespread acceptance, it did cause the United Nations Commission on International

---

5.   Jan Ramberg, *ICC Guide to Incoterms 2000: Understanding and Practical Use* 30 (1999).

Trade Law (UNCITRAL) to develop the 1996 Model Law for Electronic Commerce. The model law recognizes that the primary functions of a bill of lading are to evidence an agreement, give a party the legal right to claim goods from a carrier, and transfer rights to goods in transit. The model rules conclude that these functions can be provided in a medium other than a paper document, specifically, an electronic exchange of messages or **electronic bill of lading**.

The most recent effort in this regard is the development of a system named BOLERO. This system was developed and is administered by Bolero International, Ltd., a company created in April 1998 by the Society for Worldwide Interbank Financial Telecommunication and the Through Transport Club. The BOLERO system is designed to be utilized by all parties in the trade process, including importers, exporters, freight forwarders, port authorities, inspection agencies, carriers, customs agencies, and financial institutions. BOLERO is based on a core messaging platform that enables users to exchange electronic trade documents through the Internet. These documents are received and sent through a so-called trusted third party. The authenticity of electronic messages is secured by digital signatures. These signatures also serve to exclude the possibility that the transmitters will change the content of their messages once they have been sent. The BOLERO bill of lading generated by this process has the advantages of increased speed, diminished cost, and greater efficiency through the elimination of errors and lost data.

Another example of electronic international commerce is Paction, a Web-based application that permits parties to prepare, negotiate, and complete contracts for the international purchase and sale of goods on line. The contracts resulting from the process are based on the model international sales contract developed by the **International Chamber of Commerce (ICC)**. Paction was developed and is administered by Allagraf Limited. Paction provides access to the ICC's standard terms of contract, as well as specific text, thereby permitting the parties to prepare customized contracts specifically applicable to the particular transaction at hand. The application is designed for smaller companies new to international trade and provides extensive online assistance to subscribers. The acceptance of such services as Paction and BOLERO in the international business community remains to be determined, but the increasingly electronic nature of commercial transactions throughout the world bodes well for their future.[6]

Characteristics of Bills of Lading

The standard documentary sales contract requires an **on-board bill of lading**. The on-board bill of lading warrants that the cargo has been placed aboard a named vessel and is signed by the master of the vessel. This type of bill ensures the buyer that the goods are indeed on the ship in transit to the port of destination. A **received-for-shipment bill of lading** recognizes only the delivery of the goods to the common carrier; it does not warrant that the goods have been placed upon the ship.

If the sales contract is silent regarding the type of bill of lading, must the buyer accept a received-for-shipment bill of lading when presented with the documents? The answer for the U.S. exporter is different, depending on whether the UCP 500[7]

---

6. Additional information regarding BOLERO can be found at **http://www.bolero.net.** Additional information regarding Paction can be found at **http://paction.modelcontracts.com.**

7. See *Uniform Customs and Practices for Documentary Credits* as published by the International Chamber of Commerce. See Chapter Eleven.

or Article 5 of the Uniform Commercial Code (UCC) is applied. Section 1-201(15) of the UCC defines a document of title simply as a "bill of lading." It does not differentiate between "on-board" and "received-for-shipment." Section 1-201(6) further defines bill of lading as "a document evidencing the receipt of goods for shipment issued by a person engaged in the business of transporting or forwarding goods." Section 2-323 specifically authorizes the use of a "received-for-shipment" bill of lading in CIF or C & F contracts.[8] In contrast, Article 23 of the UCP states that "banks will, unless otherwise stipulated in the Credit, accept a document which: (ii) indicates that the goods have been loaded on board, or shipped on a named vessel."

Bills of lading are contracts between the owner or shipper of goods and the carrier. They do not affect the contractual relationship between the seller and the buyer. The person or firm named in a bill of lading to which goods are to be turned over is the **consignee**. A **straight bill of lading** is nonnegotiable. Such a bill allows only for delivery to the named consignee in the bill. A negotiable or **order bill of lading** can be bought, sold, or traded while the goods are in transit. The order bill is also used for many types of financing transactions.[9] The owner needs the original bill of lading to take possession of the goods. A **clean bill of lading** is a receipt for goods issued by a carrier with an indication that the goods were received in "apparent good order and condition." In letter of credit transactions, a "clean, on-board, order bill of lading" is necessary for the shipper to obtain payment from the bank.

Air Waybill

Most transport of goods is performed through ocean carriage. In the event of transit by air, however, the operative transport document is the **air waybill** (Exhibit 9.6). The air waybill is a bill of lading that covers both domestic and international flights that transport goods to a specified destination. It is a nonnegotiable instrument that serves as a receipt for the shipper. Unlike the ocean bill of lading, the air waybill does not act as a document of title. Therefore, it merely serves as a contract of carriage and a receipt for goods.

The front of the air waybill makes a number of important representations. First, unless noted otherwise, the "goods are accepted in apparent good order and condition." Second, the shipper is directed to the reverse of the form for an explanation of the carrier's "limitation of liability." Third, the shipper is provided with notice of the right to increase carrier's liability by "declaring a higher value for carriage and paying a supplemental charge." A space is provided for the "amount of insurance" requested by the shipper. Above the signature line, shippers are notified that they are certifying that the goods are not dangerous unless described as such. If dangerous by nature, then the shipper certifies that the goods are in "proper condition for carriage by air according to the applicable dangerous goods regulation."

---

8. Section 2-323(1) of the UCC provides: "Where the contract contemplates overseas shipment and contains a term CIF or C & F or FOB vessel, the seller unless otherwise agreed must obtain a negotiable bill of lading stating that the goods have been loaded on board or, in the case of a term CIF or C & F, received for shipment."
9. See Chapter Eleven.

EXHIBIT 9.6   *Air Waybill*

Shipper's Name and Address	Shipper's Account Number	Not negotiable
		Air Waybill *

issued by

Copies 1, 2 and 3 of this Air Waybill are originals and have the same validity.

| Consignee's Name and Address | Consignee's Account Number | It is agreed that the goods described herein are accepted in apparent good order and condition (except as noted) for carriage SUBJECT TO THE CONDITIONS OF CONTRACT ON THE REVERSE HEREOF. ALL GOODS MAY BE CARRIED BY ANY OTHER MEANS INCLUDING ROAD OR ANY OTHER CARRIER UNLESS SPECIFIC CONTRARY INSTRUCTIONS ARE GIVEN HEREON BY THE SHIPPER, AND SHIPPER AGREES THAT THE SHIPMENT MAY BE CARRIED VIA INTERMEDIATE STOPPING PLACES WHICH THE CARRIER DEEMS APPROPRIATE. THE SHIPPER'S ATTENTION DRAWN TO THE NOTICE CONCERNING CARRIER'S LIMITATION OF LIABILITY. Shipper may increase such limitation of liability by declaring a higher value for carriage and paying a supplemental charge if required. |

Issuing Carrier's Agent Name and City

Accounting information

Agent's IATA Code   Account No.

Airport of Departure (Addr. of first Carrier) and requested Routing

| to | By first Carrier | Routing and Destination | to | by | to | by | Currency | Chgs Code | WT/VAL | | Other | | Declared Value for Carriage | Declared Value for Customs |
| --- | --- | --- | --- | --- | --- | --- | --- | --- | PPD | COLL | PPD | COLL | | |

Airport of Destination	Flight/Date	For Carrier Use only	Flight/Date	Amount of Insurance	INSURANCE – If carrier offers insurance, and such insurance is requested in accordance with the conditions thereof, indicate amount to be insured in figures in box marked "Amount of Insurance".

Handling Information

These commodities licensed by the U.S. for ultimate destination   Diversion contrary to U.S. law prohibited.

No. of Pieces RCP	Gross Weight	kg lb	Rate Class / Commodity Item No.	Chargeable Weight	Rate / Charge	Total	Nature and Quantity of Goods (incl. Dimensions or Volume)

Prepaid	Weight Charge	Collect	Other Charges
	Valuation Charge		
	Tax		
	Total other Charges Due Agent		Shipper certifies that the particulars on the face hereof are correct and that insofar as any part of the consignment contains dangerous goods, such part is properly described by name and is in proper condition for carriage by air according to the applicable Dangerous Goods Regulations.
	Total other Charges Due Carrier		
			Signature of Shipper or his Agent
Total prepaid	Total collect		
Currency Conversion Rates	cc charges in Dest. Currency		Executed on (Date) at (Place) Signature of Issuing Carrier or its Agent
For Carriers Use only at Destination	Charges at Destination	Total collect Charges	

Source: *A Basic Guide to Exporting*, U.S. Department of Commerce in cooperation with Unz & Co., Inc. (1999).

Trade Terms

The insertion of a **trade term** into the sales contract allows the parties to designate the point at which the costs and risks of transport are divided between the seller and buyer. The **risk of loss** allocation determines who has the responsibility for any loss or damage to the goods while they are in transit. The generic costs allocated by the trade term are the costs of freight and insurance. As a practical matter, the trade term also allocates other responsibilities, including customs clearance, payment of duties, and the loading-unloading of the goods from the common carrier. The trade term is an element in the contract of sale and can normally be found in the pro forma invoice. The importance of the trade term and other **risk-shifting clauses**[10] in the international sales contract is explained in the following excerpt:

The Export-Import Contract

Many of the risks inherent in an international transaction can be allocated by the importer and exporter through their contract of sale, under familiar principles of contract law. . . . Out of the price-delivery term, and especially out of the term "CIF" which is probably the most widely used term in international trade contracts, has come a great deal of law. The price-delivery term defines the title to the goods, time and place of delivery, time and place of payment, importer's right of inspection, the risk of loss or damage to the goods in transit, and the cost of transportation.

***

An international sales contract typically contains other risk-shifting clauses. Force majeure and other contingency clauses are added to escape liability where unforeseen circumstances prevent performance of an assumed obligation. Choice of law, choice of forum, and arbitration clauses seek to avoid the vagaries, uncertainties, and delays of foreign litigation. The tendency to spell out in detail such matters as inspection rights and remedies for breach may also be an attempt to substitute the law of the contract for that of any national legal system.

***

Destination and Shipment Contracts

An importer may ask his foreign supplier to place the goods on board a vessel bound for the country of destination and to bear the risks of the voyage. Such a contract is called a "destination contract." . . . "Shipment contracts" cast the risk of loss upon the purchaser from the moment of loading or shipment. The seller typically agrees to place the goods on board or alongside the vessel, but the risks of transit are shifted to the buyer. Typical shipment contracts include FAS, FOB, CIF, and CFR.[11]

http://

International Chamber of Commerce: **http:// www.iccwbo.org.**

The trade term controls the parties' respective obligations regarding contracting for shipping and insurance services. The trade term is also important in determining the conformity of documents in the documentary transaction. A trade term, whether taken from the international trade terms manual (*INCOTERMS*) as published by the ICC or the UCC, is a three-letter acronym that allocates the cost, risk of loss, and responsibilities of transporting the goods between the seller and buyer.

    In addition, the trade term affects documentary requirements. For example, the **FOB** (free on board) trade term generally dictates that the bill of lading need not show that the freight has been paid because freight costs and shipping arrangements are delegated to the buyer in an FOB contract. There are some variations recognized by most parties. For instance, the buyer can negotiate an additional services clause into a FOB contract. This clause often requires the seller to secure liner space and an insurance certificate as agent for the buyer. This type of clause acts as a compromise for the seller who wants to avoid the risk of paying for any escalation in insurance or freight costs. Additionally, such a clause benefits the buyer who is willing to incur such costs but finds it difficult to book a ship or insurance at the port of shipment.

---

10.   Examples of risk-shifting clauses include arbitration, forum selection, choice of law, force majeure, and liquidated damages clauses.
11.   Harold J. Berman, The Law of International Commercial Transactions (Lex Mercatoria), 2 *Journal of International Dispute Resolution* 245–248, 276 (1988).

In selecting trade terms, the parties should also be concerned with any conflicts between the chosen trade term and other terms in the contract. For example, a CIF contract shifts the risk of loss to the buyer at the port of shipment. If the contract provides that the seller guarantees a certain weight or quality at arrival, then the risks of loss below that weight would seem to shift back to the seller. What term will dictate liability for loss during transit? Harold J. Berman notes: "The tendency of courts (in the United States) has been to subordinate conflicting terms to the CIF term."[12] Under the UCC, a guarantee of quality clause is likely to be construed only as a guarantee of "ordinary deterioration, shrinkage, and the like in transportation."[13] All other causes of loss or damage remain with the buyer. Furthermore, an occurrence within the "quality clause" does not provide the buyer with a right of rejection but only a right of adjustment. Berman notes that comments to UCC Section 2-321(3) make such a presumption.

The express language used in an agreement is frequently a precautionary, fuller statement of the normal CIF terms and hence not intended as a departure or variation from them. Moreover, the dominant outlines of the CIF term are so well understood commercially that any variation should, whenever reasonably possible, be read as falling within those dominant outlines rather than as destroying the whole meaning of a term which essentially indicates a contract for proper shipment rather than one for delivery at destination.[14]

Nonetheless, it is important for contracting parties not to vary recognized trade terms. In international contracting, the trade terms as defined in **INCOTERMS 2000** should be used.[15] The dangers of varying the standard trade terms are illustrated by *Kumar Corporation v. Nopal Lines, Ltd.*[16] Kumar entered into a contract to sell goods to Nava in Venezuela on a consignment basis. Consignment is the delivery of goods from an exporter (consignor) to an agent (consignee) under agreement that the agent sells the goods on the account of the exporter. The consignor retains title to the goods until sold. The consignee sells the goods for commission and remits the net proceeds to the consignor. The contract trade term was CIF. Unfortunately, the goods were stolen while in possession of the common carrier at the port of shipment. Because payment was not due until a resale of the goods in Venezuela, Nava was under no obligation to pay against documents. In bringing suit against the common carrier, Kumar had to overcome the defense that under the CIF term, risk of loss had passed to the buyer and, therefore, Kumar had no standing to sue. Failure to overcome that defense would have resulted in Kumar not having any recourse except for a claim under an applicable insurance policy.[17]

International sale of goods contracts are defined as either **shipment** or **destination contracts**. Whether a contract is described as a shipment or destination contract depends on when the risk of loss passes from the seller to the buyer. In a shipment contract, the risk of loss passes to the buyer at the point of shipment. In contrast, in a destination contract, the risk of loss passes to the buyer at the point of destination.

12.   Ibid. at 250. Berman notes a more drastic example of inconsistency, when a CIF term is coupled with a "no arrival, no sale" clause. "With full risk of loss on the seller, it makes no sense for the buyer to have the right to the insurance proceeds." Ibid. at 251.

13.   Ibid. at 253, citing UCC § 2-321(2).

14.   UCC § 2-320, Comment 14.

15.   *INCOTERMS 2000* may be found at *ICC GUIDE TO INCOTERMS 2000*, ICC Pub. No. 620 (1999).

16.   462 So.2d 1178 (Fl. Ct. Appeals 1985), *petition for review denied, S.E.L. Maduro (Florida), Inc. v. Kumar Corp.*, 476 So.2d 675 (Fla. 1985).

17.   Ironically, Kumar's negligence in not procuring insurance coverage enabled it to sue the common carrier. The court held that because Kumar had failed to obtain insurance as required by the CIF term, the risk of loss remained with Kumar. Thus, Kumar had the requisite standing to sue the common carrier.

The risk of loss refers to which party will suffer the loss of damaged or lost goods. For example, if the risk of loss has passed to the buyer and the goods are subsequently lost at sea, then the buyer will have to pay for goods it will never receive. The party that has the risk of loss is liable for any damages to the goods that occurred while it retained the risk. The trade term, among other things, allocates the risk of loss. If the contract fails to use a trade term, then generally the risk of loss passes at the time the seller delivers the goods to the carrier.[18] Thus, the presumption is in favor of a shipment contract. To avoid risk of loss and performance disputes, the contract should use accepted trade terms to clearly state whether it is a shipment or destination contract.

It is important, as discussed in *Phillips Puerto Rico v. Tradax Petroleum* in Chapter Three, to examine the interrelationship between the trade term and other terms in the contract, especially if other language in the contract can be construed as modifying the trade term. This was the issue in *Warner Brothers & Company v. Israel*.[19] This case involved the purchase of Philippine sugar for shipment to New York City. The trade term in the contract stated "Philippines-C.I.F. Terms." Another provision in the contract said the seller was to deliver sugar of a "net delivered weight." The sugar was delayed entry into the United States because of the imposition of a government sugar quota. The buyer attempted to avoid payment by arguing that the "net delivered weight" language converted the contract to a delivery or destination contract. It argued that the net delivered weight could be determined only at the port of destination.

The court rejected the argument, holding that it was a CIF contract by which the purchaser must pay upon the presentation of documents. It held that the "net delivered weight" language referred to the adjustment of the price based on the weight of the sugar actually delivered, but it was not enough to convert the express trade term into a destination contract. It further noted the general proposition that a delivery term (to be delivered to New York City) does not change an express trade term. The court found: "Under the ordinary CIF contract, delivery of the goods would not be a condition precedent to be performed at the risk of the seller. . . . Nor is it made so merely because the obligation to contract for the carriage is expressed in the form of the delivery of the goods at a designated place."[20] The result may be different, however, if the destination term is included in the same provision as the trade term. Therefore, it is important to use the trade term without further explanation and to make sure that other terms in the contract do not expressly conflict with the term chosen.

The contract of carriage (bill of lading) should be consistent with the allocation of responsibilities provided by the trade term in the sales contract. A misunderstanding regarding the trade or delivery term is likely to prevent exporters from meeting contractual obligations or make them responsible for shipping costs they sought to avoid. Trade terms must be understood and used correctly. The trade terms in international business transactions often sound similar to those used in domestic business, but they frequently have very different meanings.[21] For this reason, the exporter must

---

18. See CISG Article 67 ("handing the goods over to the first carrier") when the contract envisions carriage of goods and Article 69 (when contract requires buyer to pick up goods at seller's place of business); UCC § 2-503 (risk passes at seller's place of business upon notification to buyer if the contract does not require sending the goods) and § 2-504 (when contract envisions "shipment by seller," risk passes when placed in possession of carrier). See generally Harold J. Berman & Monica Ladd, "Risk of Loss or Damage in Documentary Transactions Under the Convention on the International Sale of Goods," 21 *Cornell International Law Journal* 423 (1988).

19. 101 F.2d 59 (2d Cir. 1939).

20. Ibid. at 61.

21. For example, compare *INCOTERMS 2000 with* Sections 2-319 ("F.O.B. and F.A.S."), 2-320 and 2-321 ("C.I.F. and C. & F."), and 2-322 ("Delivery Ex Ship") of the Uniform Commercial Code.

know the terms before preparing a quotation or a pro forma invoice. A few of the more common terms used in international trade include:

- CIF (cost, insurance, freight) to a named overseas port of import. Under this term, the seller quotes a price for the goods, including insurance and all transportation charges to the point of debarkation from the vessel.
- CFR (cost and freight) to a named overseas port of import. Under this term, the seller quotes a price for the goods that includes the cost of transportation to the named point of debarkation. The buyer pays the cost of insurance.
- CPT (carriage paid to) and CIP (carriage and insurance paid to) a named place of destination. These terms are used in place of CFR and CIF, respectively, for shipment by modes other than water.
- EXW (ex works) at a named point of origin, such as the seller's factory, mill, or warehouse. Under this term, the price quoted applies only at the point of origin, and the seller agrees to place the goods at the disposal of the buyer at the specified place on the specified date. The buyer pays all charges for transport and insurance.
- FAS (free alongside ship) at a named port of export. Under this term, the seller quotes a price for the goods that includes charges for delivery of the goods alongside a vessel at the port. The buyer handles the cost of loading, ocean transportation, and insurance.
- FCA (free carrier) to a named place. This term replaces the former "FOB named inland port" to designate the seller's responsibility for the cost of loading goods at the named shipping point. It may be used for any mode of transport, including multimodal.
- FOB (free on board) at a named port of export. The seller quotes the buyer a price that covers all costs up to and including delivery of goods aboard an overseas vessel.
- DES (delivered ex ship) to a named place of destination. The DES term requires the seller to pay the cost of transport and insurance to the port of destination. The buyer is responsible for unloading the ship and for clearing the goods through customs.

The exporter should quote CIF whenever possible, because it has meaning abroad. It shows the foreign buyer that the seller will bear the cost of shipping the product to the port in the country of importation. If assistance is needed in figuring the CIF price, an international freight forwarder can help. If at all possible, the exporter should quote the price in U.S. dollars. Doing so eliminates the risk of possible exchange rate fluctuations and the problems of currency conversion. *INCOTERMS 2000*, a booklet issued by the ICC and the most accepted source of international trade terms, is the subject of the next section.

INCOTERMS 2000

The rules for interpreting a trade term are of primary importance in international sale of goods transactions. Trade terms allocate the costs of freight and insurance, along with stating the time that the risk of loss passes to the purchaser. The rules of interpretation for trade terms also determine who is responsible for dealing with customs agents and the payment of tariffs. Traditionally, national laws provide the rules of

http://

Company Guide to Shipping includes materials on INCOTERMS, bills of lading, shipping documents, and a glossary. **http://www.yellowglobal.com/resources/index.jsp.**

interpretation.[22] In international trade, trade terms as defined in the *INCOTERMS 2000 Manual*, published by the ICC, have obtained almost universal acceptance.[23] (See Focus on Transactions: Incoterms.) The word *Incoterm* is an abbreviation of "international commercial terms." A selected Incoterm becomes part of an international sales contract between a seller and a buyer. A key advantage in using Incoterms is that they are updated every ten years to reflect contemporary commercial practices.[24] *INCOTERMS 2000* provides thirteen terms categorized into four groups. The first group is the E Group, which has one trade term (EXW). The second group is the F Group, signifying that the seller must hand over the goods to a designated carrier free of risk and expense to the buyer. This group has three trade terms (FCA, FAS, and FOB). The C Group, signifying that the seller must bear certain costs even after risk of loss or damage to the goods has passed, has four trade terms (CFR, CIF, CPT, and CIP). Finally, the D Group of five trade terms (DAF, DES, DEQ, DDU, and DDP) requires that the goods arrive at a stated destination. Along with selecting an Incoterm, the parties should detail any rights and obligations associated with the shipment of the goods, including any special marking, packaging, inspection, and testing requirements.

Focus on Transactions

Incoterms

Ex Works (. . . named place)

"Ex works" means that the seller delivers when it places the goods at the disposal of the buyer at the seller's premises or another named place not cleared for export and not loaded on any collecting vehicle. The buyer has to bear all costs and risks involved in taking the goods from the seller's premises. If the parties wish the seller to be responsible for the loading of the goods on departure and to bear the risks and all of the costs of such loading, this should be made clear by adding explicit wording to this effect in the contract for sale. This term should not be used when the buyer cannot carry out the export formalities directly or indirectly. In such circumstances, the FCA term should be used, provided the seller agrees to load at its cost and risk.

FCA Free Carrier (. . . named place)

"Free carrier" means that the seller delivers the goods, cleared for export, to the carrier nominated by the buyer at the named place. If delivery occurs at the seller's premises, the seller is responsible for loading. If delivery occurs at any other place, the seller is not responsible for unloading. The term may be used irrespective of the mode of transport, including multimodal transport. "Carrier" means any person who, in a contract of carriage, undertakes to perform or to procure the performance of transport by rail, road, air, sea, or inland waterway or by a combination of such modes. If the buyer nominates a person other than a carrier to receive the goods, the seller is deemed to have fulfilled the obligation to deliver the goods when they are delivered to that person.

FAS Free Alongside Ship (. . . named port of shipment)

"Free alongside ship" means that the seller delivers when the goods have been placed alongside the vessel at the named port of shipment. This means that the buyer has to bear all costs and risks of loss of or damage to

continued

---

22. See, e.g., Uniform Commercial Code §§ 2-319-22.
23. Ramberg, *supra* note 5, at 69-171.
24. As a result, the CISG elected not to provide any competing terms, and the most recent revision of Article 2 of the Uniform Commercial Code eliminated its provisions dealing with trade terms.

Incoterms (*continued*)

the goods from that moment. The FAS term requires the seller to clear the goods for export. If the parties wish the buyer to clear the goods for export, this should be made clear by adding explicit wording to this effect in the contract of sale. This term can be used only for sea or inland waterway transport.

FOB Free on Board (. . . named port of shipment)

"Free on board" means that the seller delivers when the goods pass the ship's rail at the named port of shipment. This means that the buyer has to bear all costs and risks of loss or damage to the goods from that point. The FOB term requires the seller to clear the goods for export. This term can be used only for sea or inland waterway transport. If the parties do not intend to deliver the goods across the ship's rail, the FCA term should be used.

CFR Cost and Freight (. . . named port of destination)

"Cost and freight" means that the seller delivers when the goods pass the ship's rail in the port of shipment. The seller must pay the costs and freight necessary to bring the goods to the named port of destination, but the risk of loss or damage to the goods, as well as any additional costs due to events occurring after the time of delivery, are transferred from the seller to the buyer. The CFR term requires the seller to clear the goods for export. This term can be used only for sea and inland waterway transport. If the parties do not intend to deliver the goods across the ship's rail, the CPT term should be used.

CIF Cost, Insurance, and Freight (. . . named port of destination)

"Cost, insurance, and freight" means that the seller delivers when the goods pass the ship's rail in the port of shipment. The seller must pay the costs and freight necessary to bring the goods to the named port of destination, but the risk of loss or damage to the goods, as well as any additional costs due to events occurring after the time of delivery, are trans-ferred from the seller to the buyer. However, in CIF the seller also has to procure marine insurance against the buyer's risk of loss or damage to the goods during the carriage. The seller contracts for insurance and pays the insurance premium. The buyer should note that under the CIF term the seller is required to obtain insurance only on minimum cover-age. The buyer who wishes to have the protec-tion of greater coverage would either need to agree expressly with the seller or make extra insurance arrangements. The CIF term requires the seller to clear the goods for export. The term can be used only for sea and inland waterway transport. If the parties do not intend to deliver the goods across the ship's rail, the CIP term should be used.

CPT Carriage Paid To (. . . named place of destination)

"Carriage paid to" means that the seller deliv-ers the goods to the carrier it nominates but that the seller must in addition pay the cost of carriage necessary to bring the goods to the named destination. This means that the buyer bears all risks and any other costs occurring after the goods have been so delivered. "Carrier" means any person who, in a contract of carriage, undertakes to perform or to pro-cure the performance of transport, by rail, road, air, sea, or inland waterway or by a com-bination of such modes. If subsequent carriers are used for the carriage to the agreed desti-nation, the risk passes when the goods have been delivered to the first carrier. The CPT term requires the seller to clear the goods for export. This term may be used for any mode of transport, including multimodal transport.

CIP Carriage and Insurance Paid To (. . . named place of destination)

"Carriage and insurance paid to" means that the seller delivers the goods to the carrier it nominates but that the seller must in addition pay the cost of carriage necessary to bring the goods to the named destination. This means that the buyer bears all risks and any addi-tional costs occurring after the goods have

continued

Incoterms (*continued*)

been so delivered. However, in CIP the seller also has to procure insurance against the buyer's risk of loss or damage to the goods during the carriage. The seller contracts for insurance and pays the insurance premium. The buyer should note that under the CIP term the seller is required to obtain insurance only on minimum coverage. Having the protection of greater coverage would require the buyer to either agree expressly with the seller or to make extra insurance arrangements. "Carrier" means any person who, in a contract of carriage, undertakes to perform or to procure the performance of transport, by rail, road, air, sea, or inland waterway or by a combination of such modes. If subsequent carriers are used for the carriage to the agreed destination, the risk passes when the goods have been delivered to the first carrier. The CIP term requires the seller to clear the goods for export. This term may be used for any mode of transport, including multimodal transport.

DAF Delivered at Frontier (. . . named place)

"Delivered at frontier" means that the seller delivers when the goods are placed, not unloaded, at the disposal of the buyer on the arriving means of transport, cleared for export but not cleared for import at the named point and place at the frontier, before the customs border of the adjoining country. The term *frontier* may be used for any frontier, including that of the country of export. Therefore, it is of vital importance that the frontier in question be defined precisely by always naming the point and place in the term. If the parties wish the seller to be responsible for unloading the goods from the arriving means of transport and to bear the risks and costs of unloading, this should be made clear by adding explicit wording to this effect in the contract of sale. The term may be used irrespective of the mode of transport when goods are to be delivered at a land frontier. When delivery takes place in the port of destination, on board a vessel or on the quay (wharf), the DES or DEQ terms should be used.

DES Delivered Ex Ship (. . . named port of destination)

"Delivered ex ship" means that the seller delivers when the goods are placed at the disposal of the buyer on board the ship not cleared for import at the named port of destination. The seller has to bear all the costs and risks involved in bringing the goods to the named port of destination before discharging. If the parties wish the seller to bear the costs and risks of discharging the goods, then the DEQ term should be used. This term can be used only when the goods are to be delivered by sea or inland waterway or by multimodal transport on a vessel in the port of destination.

DEQ Delivered Ex Quay (Duty Paid) (. . . named port of destination)

"Delivered ex quay" means that the seller delivers when the goods are placed at the disposal of the buyer not cleared for import on the quay (wharf) at the named port of destination. The seller has to bear the costs and risks involved in bringing the goods to the named port of destination and discharging the goods on the quay (wharf). The DEQ term requires the buyer to clear the goods for import and pay for all formalities, duties, taxes, and other charges upon import. If the parties wish to include in the seller's obligations all or part of the costs payable upon import of the goods, this should be made clear by adding explicit wording to this effect in the contract of sale. This term can be used only when the goods are to be delivered by sea or inland waterway or by multimodal transport on discharging from the vessel onto the quay (wharf) in the port of destination. However, if the parties wish to include in the seller's obligations the risks and costs of the goods from the quay to another place in or outside the port, the DDU or DDP terms should be used.

DDU Delivered Duty Unpaid (. . . named place of destination)

"Delivered duty unpaid" means that the seller delivers the goods to the buyer, not cleared for import and not unloaded from any arriving

continued

Incoterms (*continued*)

means of transport at the named place of destination. The seller has to bear the costs and risks involved in bringing the goods thereto, other than any "duty" (which term includes the responsibility for and the risks of carrying out customs formalities and the payment of formalities, customs duties, taxes, and other charges) for import in the country of destination. Such "duty" has to be borne by the buyer, as well as any costs and risks caused by the buyer's failure to clear the goods for import in time. However, if the parties wish the seller to carry out customs formalities and bear the costs and risks resulting from it, as well as some of the costs payable upon import of the goods, this should be made clear by adding explicit wording to this effect in the contract of sale. This term may be used irrespective of the mode of transport, but when delivery is to take place in the port of destination on board the vessel or on the quay (wharf), the DES or DEQ term should be used.

DDP Delivered Duty Paid (. . . named place of destination)
"Delivered duty paid" means that the seller delivers the goods to the buyer, cleared for import and not unloaded from any arriving means of transport at the named place of destination. The seller has to bear all the costs and risks involved in bringing the goods thereto, including any "duty" (which term includes the responsibility for and the risk of carrying out customs formalities and the payment of formalities, customs duties, taxes, and other charges) for import in the country of destination. This term should not be used if the seller is unable directly or indirectly to obtain the import license. However, if the parties wish to exclude from the seller's obligations some of the costs payable upon import of the goods, this should be made clear by adding explicit wording to this effect in the contract of sale. If the parties wish the buyer to bear all risks and costs of the import, the DDU term should be used. This term may be used irrespective of the mode of transport, but when delivery is to take place in the port of destination on board the vessel or on the quay (wharf), the DES or DEQ term should be used.

When using an Incoterm, the parties should always cite to the *INCOTERMS* manual. Thus, in selecting an Incoterm, the parties should identify the three-letter trade term, such as CIF, FOB, or DES, "as defined in *INCOTERMS 2000.*"[25] The thirteen Incoterms provide a broad range of options regarding the relative responsibilities of the exporter and importer. Variations of the terms should be explicitly set forth in the parties' agreement. The burden placed on a party seeking to modify Incoterms explicitly set forth in a sales contract was addressed by the court in *St. Paul Guardian Insurance Company v. Neuromed Medical Systems & Support GmbH.*[26]

Some of the terms are to be used only for certain modes of transportation, whereas others can be used for all modes of transportation. The FAS, FOB, CFR, CIF, DES, and DEQ terms are used for carriage of goods by sea. The EXW, FCA, CIP, CPT, DAF, DDU, and DDP terms can be used generally, including for multimodal means of shipment.

---

25.   The material in this paragraph was taken from ICC, "The ICC Model International Sale Contract," Pub. No. 556(E) (1997) at 30–31.
26.   No. 00 Civ. 9344 (SHS), 2002 U.S. Dist. LEXIS 5096 (S.D.N.Y. Mar. 26, 2002).

St. Paul Guardian Insurance Company v. Neuromed Medical Systems & Support, GmbH

No. 00 Civ. 9344 (SHS), 2002 U.S. Dist. LEXIS 5096 (S.D.N.Y. Mar. 26, 2002)

Stein, District Court Judge. Plaintiffs St. Paul Guardian Insurance Company and Travelers Property Casualty Insurance Company have brought this action as subrogees of Shared Imaging, Inc., to recover $285,000 they paid to Shared Imaging for damage to a mobile magnetic resonance imaging system ("MRI") purchased by Shared Imaging from defendant Neuromed Medical Systems & Support GmbH ("Neuromed").

Shared Imaging, an American corporation, and Neuromed, a German corporation, entered into a contract of sale for a Siemens Harmony 1.0 Tesla mobile MRI. According to the complaint, the MRI was loaded aboard the vessel "Atlantic Carrier" undamaged and in good working order. When it reached its destination of Calumet City, Illinois, it had been damaged and was in need of extensive repair, which led plaintiffs to conclude that the MRI had been damaged in transit.

The one page contract of sale contains nine headings. Under "Delivery Terms" it provides, "CIF New York Seaport, the buyer will arrange and pay for customs clearance as well as transport to Calumet City." Under "Payment Terms" it states, "By money transfer to one of our accounts, with following payment terms: US $93,000—downpayment to secure the system; US $744,000—prior to shipping; US $93,000—upon acceptance by Siemens of the MRI system within 3 business days after arrival in Calumet City." In addition, under "Disclaimer" it states, "system including all accessories and options remain the property of Neuromed till complete payment has been received." Neuromed contends that because the delivery terms were "CIF New York Seaport," its contractual obligation, with regard to risk of loss or damage, ended when it delivered the MRI to the vessel at the port of shipment and therefore the action must be dismissed because plaintiffs have failed to state a claim for which relief can be granted.

The parties concede that pursuant to German law, the U.N. Convention on Contracts for the International Sale of Goods ("CISG") governs this transaction. INCOTERMS are incorporated into the CISG through Article 9(2) which provides that:

The parties are considered, unless otherwise agreed, to have impliedly made applicable to their contract or its formation a usage of which the parties knew or ought to have known and which in international trade is widely known to, and regularly observed by, parties to contracts of the type involved in the particular trade concerned.

At the time the contract was entered into, Incoterms 1990 was applicable. INCOTERMS define "CIF" (named port of destination) to mean the seller delivers when the goods pass "the ship's rail in the port of shipment." The seller is responsible for paying the cost, freight and insurance coverage necessary to bring the goods to the named port of destination, but the risk of loss or damage to the goods passes from seller to buyer upon delivery to the port of shipment.

Plaintiffs' legal expert contends that INCOTERMS are inapplicable here because the contract fails to specifically incorporate them. Nonetheless, the German Supreme Court—the court of last resort in the Federal Republic of Germany for civil matters—concluded that a clause "fob" without specific reference to INCOTERMS was to be interpreted according to INCOTERMS "simply because the [INCOTERMS] include a clause' 'fob'." The use of the "CIF" term in the contract demonstrates that the parties "agreed to the detailed oriented [INCOTERMS] in order to enhance the Convention." Thus, pursuant to CISG Article 9(2), INCOTERMS definitions should be applied to the contract despite the lack of an explicit INCOTERMS reference in the contract.

Plaintiffs argue that Neuromed's explicit retention of title in the contract to the MRI machine modified the "CIF" term, such that Neuromed retained title and assumed the risk of loss. INCOTERMS, however, only address passage of risk, not transfer of title. Under the CISG, the passage of risk is likewise independent of the transfer of title. Pursuant to the CISG, "the risk passes without taking into account who owns the goods. The passing of ownership is not regulated by the CISG according to Article 4(b)." Moreover, according to Article 67(1), the passage of risk and transfer of title need not occur at the same time, as the seller's retention of "documents controlling the disposition of the goods does not affect the passage of risk."

German law also recognizes passage of risk and transfer of title as two independent legal acts. In fact, it is standard "practice under German law to agree that the transfer of title will only occur upon payment of the entire purchase price, well after the date of passing of risk and after receipt of the goods by the buyer." Accordingly, pursuant to INCOTERMS, the CISG, and specific German law, Neuromed's retention of title did not thereby implicate retention of the risk of loss or damage.

Plaintiffs next contend that even if the "CIF" term did not mandate that title and risk of loss pass together, the other terms in the contract are evidence that the parties' intention to supercede and replace the "CIF" term such that Neuromed retained title and the risk of loss. That is incorrect.

Citing the "Delivery Terms" clause in the contract, plaintiffs posit that had the parties intended to abide by the strictures of INCOTERMS there would have been no need to define the buyer's obligations to pay customs and arrange further transport. Plaintiffs' argument, however, is undermined by Incoterms 1990, which provides that "it is normally desirable that customs clearance is arranged by the party domiciled in the country where such clearance should take place." The "CIF" term as defined by INCOTERMS only requires the seller to "clear the goods for export" and is silent as to which party bears the obligation to arrange for customs clearance. The parties are therefore left to negotiate these obligations. As such, a clause defining the terms of customs clearance neither alters nor affects the "CIF" clause in the contract.

Plaintiffs also cite to the "Payment Terms" clause of the contract, which specified that final payment was not to be made upon seller's delivery of the machine to the port of shipment, but rather, upon buyer's acceptance of the machine in Calumet City. These terms speak to the final disposition of the property, not to the risk for loss or damage. INCOTERMS do not mandate a payment structure, but rather simply establish that the buyer bears an obligation to "pay the price as provided in the contract of sale." Inclusion of the terms of payment in the contract does not modify the "CIF" clause.

The terms of the contract do not modify the "CIF" clause in the contract such that the risk of loss remained with Neuromed. Thus, because (1) Neuromed's risk of loss of, or damage to, the MRI machine under the contract passed to Shared Imaging upon delivery of the machine to the carrier at the port of shipment and (2) it is undisputed that the MRI machine was delivered to the carrier undamaged and in good working order, Neuromed's motion to dismiss for failure to state a claim is hereby granted.

Case Update

The opinion of the U.S. District Court for the Southern District of New York was affirmed by the U.S. Court of Appeals for the Second Circuit in *St. Paul Guardian Insurance Company v. Neuromed Medical Systems & Support, GmbH,* 53 Fed. Appx. 173 (2d Cir. 2002).

Case Highlights

- Pursuant to CISG art. 9(2), Incoterms, definitions should be applied to an international sales contract despite the lack of an explicit Incoterms reference in the contract.
- *INCOTERMS 1990 (2000)* defined "CIF" to mean the seller delivers when the goods pass "the ship's rail in the port of shipment." The seller was responsible for paying the cost, freight, and insurance coverage necessary to bring the goods to the named port of destination, but the risk of loss or damage to the goods passed from seller to buyer upon delivery to the port of shipment.
- Payment terms and retention of title contained within the sales contract does not modify the application of Incoterms, which are concerned with the passage of risk of loss.
- Any variation of the meaning of an Incoterm must be explicitly provided in the sales contract.

INCOTERMS 2000 made a number of changes to *INCOTERMS 1990*. The most important differences in substance concern:

- placing the export clearance obligation under FAS on the seller (previously on the buyer).
- the specification of the seller's obligation to load the goods on the buyer's collecting vehicle and the buyer's obligation to receive the seller's arriving vehicle unloaded under FCA.
- the placing of the import clearance obligation under DEQ on the buyer (previously on the seller).
- the suggestion that instead of relying on the "crossing the ship's rail" standard found in the FOB, CFR, and CIF terms, the parties are invited to choose such terms as FCA, CPT, and CIP, in which delivery of the goods is connected to the handing over of the goods to the carrier.

Given these changes, the seller and the buyer in an international sales transaction must specify that the provisions of *INCOTERMS 2000*, rather than an earlier version, are applicable to their contract.

The "crossing the ship's rail" standard shifts the risk of loss to the buyer when the cargo passes an imaginary line above the ship's rail. This murky standard is likely to produce dispute in the event that the goods are damaged while in possession of the carrier prior to loading, while the goods are being loaded on the ship, or when the goods arrive in an unsatisfactory condition after incurring damage at an indeterminate time. An example in this regard is the following opinion in *BP Oil International, Ltd. v. Empresa Estatal Petroleos de Ecuador.*[27] Despite the court's opinion in this case, note that the seller remains liable if it intentionally concealed the nonconformity or should have known of such nonconformity and failed to disclose the same to the buyer.

INCOTERMS 2000 lists obligations that the terms allocate, including:

- obtaining necessary export licenses and government authorizations
- satisfying import requirements and formalities
- giving notice regarding a vessel hired for transport
- giving notice of delivery to the common carrier
- checking, packaging, and marking goods
- obtaining transport and other documents

The notice of the hiring of a vessel is normally the responsibility of the buyer under the FOB, FAS, and FCA terms. Notice of delivery to the common carrier is the responsibility of the seller. The next few sections provide an overview of the various Incoterms.

BP Oil International, Ltd. v. Empresa Estatal Petroleos de Ecuador

332 F.3d 333 (5th Cir. 2003)

Smith, Circuit Judge. Empresa Estatal Petroleos de Ecuador ("PetroEcuador") sent BP Oil International, Ltd. ("BP") an invitation to bid for supplying 140,000 barrels of unleaded gasoline deliverable "CFR" to Ecuador. "CFR," which stands for "Cost and Freight," is one of thirteen International Commercial Terms ("Incoterms") designed to "provide a set of international rules for the interpretation of the most commonly used trade terms in foreign trade." Incoterms are recognized through their incorporation into the Convention on Contracts for the International Sale of Goods ("CISG").

BP responded favorably to the invitation, and PetroEcuador confirmed the sale on its contract form. The final agreement required that the oil be sent "CFR La Libertad-Ecuador." A separate provision, paragraph 10, states, "Jurisdiction: Laws of the Republic of Ecuador." The contract further specifies that the gasoline have a gum content of less than three milligrams per one hundred milliliters, to be determined at the port of departure. PetroEcuador appointed Saybolt, Inc. ("Saybolt"), a company specializing in quality control services, to ensure this requirement was met.

To fulfill the contract, BP purchased gasoline from Shell Oil Company and, following testing by Saybolt, loaded it on board the M/T TIBER at Shell's Deer Park, Texas, refinery. The TIBER sailed to La Libertad, Ecuador, where the gasoline was again tested for gum content. On learning that the gum content now exceeded the contractual limit, PetroEcuador refused to accept delivery. Eventually, BP resold the gasoline to Shell at a loss of approximately two million dollars.

BP sued PetroEcuador for breach of contract. The district court determined that Ecuadorian law governed. BP argued that the term "CFR" demonstrated the parties' intent to pass the risk of loss to PetroEcuador once the goods were delivered on board the TIBER. The district court disagreed and held that under Ecuadorian law, the seller must deliver conforming goods to the agreed destination, in this case Ecuador. The court granted summary judgment for PetroEcuador.

BP and PetroEcuador dispute whether the domestic law of Ecuador or the CISG applies. After recognizing that federal courts sitting in diversity apply the choice of law rules of the state in which they sit, the district court applied

---

27.   332 F.3d 333 (5th Cir. 2003).

Texas law, which enforces unambiguous choice of law provisions. Paragraph 10, which states "Jurisdiction: Laws of the Republic of Ecuador," purports to apply Ecuadorian law. Though the court correctly recognized that federal courts apply the choice of law rules of the state in which they sit, it overlooked its concurrent federal question jurisdiction that makes a conflict of laws analysis unnecessary. The general federal question jurisdiction statute grants subject matter jurisdiction over every civil action that arises, *inter alia*, under a treaty of the United States. 28 U.S.C. § 1331(a). The CISG, ratified by the Senate in 1986, creates a private right of action in federal court. The treaty applies to "contracts of sale of goods between parties whose places of business are in different States . . . when the States are Contracting States." CISG art. 1(1)(a). BP, an American corporation, and PetroEcuador, an Ecuadorian company, contracted for the sale of gasoline; the United States and Ecuador have ratified the CISG.

A signatory's assent to the CISG necessarily incorporates the treaty as part of that nation's domestic law. BP's expert witness as to Ecuadorian law observed that "the following source of *Ecuadorian law* would be applicable to the present case: (i) United Nations Convention on the International Sale of Goods. . . ." PetroEcuador's expert did not disagree with this assessment. Given that the CISG *is* Ecuadorian law, a choice of law provision designating Ecuadorian law merely confirms that the treaty governs the transaction.

The CISG incorporates Incoterms through article 9(2), which provides [that] "[t]he parties are considered, unless otherwise agreed, to have impliedly made applicable to their contract or its formation a usage of which the parties knew or ought to have known and which in international trade is widely known to, and regularly observed by, parties to contracts of the type involved in the particular trade concerned." Even if the usage of Incoterms is not global, the fact that they are well known in international trade means that they are incorporated through article 9(2).

The final agreement, drafted by PetroEcuador, specified that the gasoline be sent "CFR La Libertad-Ecuador" and that the cargo's gum content be tested pre-shipment. Shipments designated "CFR" require the seller to pay the costs and freight to transport the goods to the delivery port, but pass title and risk of loss to the buyer once the goods "pass the ship's rail" at the port of shipment. The goods should be tested for conformity before the risk of loss passes to the buyer. In the event of subsequent damage or loss, the buyer generally must seek a remedy against the carrier or insurer.

In light of the parties' unambiguous use of the Incoterm "CFR," BP fulfilled its contractual obligations if the gasoline met the contract's qualitative specifications when it passed the ship's rail and risk transferred to PetroEcuador. Indeed, Saybolt's testing confirmed that the gasoline's gum content was adequate before departure from Texas. Having appointed Saybolt to test the gasoline, PetroEcuador "ought to have discovered" the defect before the cargo left Texas. Permitting PetroEcuador now to distance itself from Saybolt's test would negate the parties' selection of CFR delivery and would undermine the key role that reliance plays in international sales agreements. Nevertheless, BP could have breached the agreement if it provided goods that it "knew or could not have been unaware" were defective when they "passed over the ship's rail" and risk shifted to PetroEcuador.

Therefore, there is a fact issue as to whether BP provided defective gasoline by failing to add sufficient gum inhibitor. The district court should permit the parties to conduct discovery as to this issue only. The judgment dismissing PetroEcuador is REVERSED and REMANDED for proceedings consistent with this opinion.

Case Highlights

- The CISG incorporates Incoterms through article 9(2), which incorporates usages into contracts that "the parties knew or ought to have known and which in international trade is widely known to, and regularly observed by, parties to contracts of the type involved in the particular trade concerned."
- Shipments designated CFR pass title and risk of loss to the buyer once the goods pass the ship's rail at the port of shipment.
- The goods should be tested for conformity before the risk of loss passes to the buyer. In the event of subsequent damage or loss, the buyer generally must seek a remedy against the carrier or insurer rather than the seller.
- The seller cannot avoid liability through utilization of the CFR designation if it provided goods that it knew or could not have been unaware were defective when they passed over the ship's rail and risk shifted to the buyer.

The E Term

The **ex works** term is the most pro-seller trade term. It represents the seller's minimum obligation. The seller's obligation to deliver is fulfilled by notifying the buyer that the goods are available at the seller's factory, warehouse, or office. The seller is not responsible for loading the goods on the vehicles provided by the buyer or for clearing the goods for export. The buyer bears all the costs and risks of transport from seller's place of business to the point of destination. Only an expert importer willing to undertake satisfying export formalities in a foreign country should use this term.

The F Terms

Under the F terms, the seller is responsible for arranging the necessary precarriage to reach the agreed location for handing over the goods to the carrier. It is the buyer's responsibility to arrange and pay for the main carriage of the goods to their final destination. **FCA** (free carrier) is the main F term because of its applicability to all modes of transport. This term should be used when handing over to the carrier is not completed alongside a ship or over the ship's rail. Under the FCA term, the seller's primary duties are to deliver the goods at the named point, provide the buyer with evidence of delivery of the goods to a carrier, and arrange export clearance. The buyer's primary duty is to designate and contract with a carrier for transport of the goods to their final destination. Risk of loss transfers from the seller to the buyer upon delivery of the goods to the carrier.

If the goods are to be transported by sea or inland waterway, the parties may elect to utilize the **FAS** (free alongside ship) or FOB terms. FAS requires the seller to deliver the goods alongside the ship, provide a receipt evidencing such delivery, and facilitate export clearance. The buyer bears all costs and risks from the moment the goods are placed alongside the vessel. The buyer's obligation is to designate and contract with a carrier for transport of the goods to their final destination. Under FOB (free on board), the seller must deliver conforming goods on board the vessel named by the buyer at the stipulated time and must give notice to the buyer of the delivery. The seller bears all costs up to the passing of the ship's rail at the port of shipment, including exportation fees, the packing and checking of the goods. The seller is also obligated to arrange for export clearance. The buyer bears all risks upon the goods' passage of the ship's rail. The buyer's primary duty is once again to designate and contract with a carrier to transport the goods to their final destination. Both terms may be only used for sea and inland waterway transport.

The C Terms

There are two groups of C terms. **CFR** (cost and freight) and **CIF** (cost, insurance, and freight) are used only when the goods are carried by sea or inland waterway. The other two C terms, **CPT** (carriage paid to) and **CIP** (carriage and insurance paid to), are more flexible, as they can be used with respect to any form of transportation.

The CFR term requires the seller to contract for carriage, deliver the goods on board, provide a clean transport document (such as a bill of lading), arrange for export clearance, and pay the unloading costs for the seller's account under the contract of carriage. As such, liability for costs transfers at the port of destination.

However, risk of loss transfers to the buyer when the goods pass the ship's rail. The buyer's duties are to accept delivery from the seller, receive the goods from the carrier, and remit such costs as are not for the seller's account pursuant to the contract for carriage. The CFR term is also referred to in the United States as the C & F term. It is essentially the same as the CIF term, except that the responsibility to obtain and pay for the marine insurance is shifted to the buyer. It remains the responsibility of the seller to clear the goods through customs at the place of shipment or exportation. It is important to understand that the C terms are "shipment contracts" and not "arrival or destination contracts." The risk of loss is transferred, as in the F terms, at the port of shipment. Risk of loss in a C & F sales contract is discussed in the following opinion of the U.S. district court in *International Commodities Export Corporation v. North Pacific Lumber Company.*[28]

The seller's obligations under the CIF term are identical to those under the CFR term, with the exception that the seller must arrange and pay for insurance. In this regard, the seller is required to provide the buyer with a cargo insurance policy or certificate. The buyer's duties, risk transfer, and cost transfer are identical to those under the CFR term.

CPT and CIP terms can be used for any form of transport. Under the CPT term, the seller's primary duties are to contract for carriage, deliver the goods to the first carrier, pay loading and unloading costs (if for the seller's account under the contract of carriage), and arrange for export clearance. The buyer must accept delivery of the goods from the seller, receive the goods from the carrier, and pay such costs as are not for the seller's account under the contract for carriage. Risk transfers to the buyer when the goods are delivered to the initial carrier. Liability for additional costs passes at the place of destination. The duties of the parties and transfers of risk and cost are

---

International Commodities Export Corporation v. North Pacific Lumber Company

764 F. Supp. 608 (D. Or. 1991)

Redden, District Court Judge. A two-day court trial was held beginning on March 22, 1991 to resolve this dispute.

Findings of Fact

On or about August 2–4, 1988, plaintiff International Commodities Export Corporation (ICEC), prepared sales contract no. L35701 which memorialized the final agreement reached regarding the sale of 230 metric tons of Chinese small white beans to defendant North Pacific Lumber Company (North Pacific). The parties' agreement included the following terms: (a) the beans were to conform to sample PC-16; (b) shipment was to be "C. & F. liner terms" Portland, Oregon; (c) North Pacific would pay ICEC $570 per metric ton for 230 metric tons of beans; and (d) payment would be made by North Pacific to ICEC "NCRI/Documents" (net cash receipt of invoice and documents). The documents ICEC was to deliver to

North Pacific included a weight certificate, quality certificate, certificate of origin, and bills of lading.

On or about August 26, 1988, six separate containers of beans (approximately 2,100 bags) were loaded on board the vessel "Jian He" at the port of Hong Kong. The "Jian He" sailed on or about August 26, 1988 and arrived in Portland on or about September 18, 1988. On or about September 4, 1988, seven containers of beans (approximately 2,433 bags) were loaded on board the vessel "Tokyo Maru" at the port of Hong Kong. The "Tokyo Maru" sailed on or about September 4, 1988, and arrived in Portland on or about September 25, 1988.

The certificates of quality were prepared by an independent marine and cargo surveyor, Andrew & Paulmann (H.K.) Ltd. These inspection certificates of quality verified that the surveyor had opened at random three percent of the total consignment and found the

---

28. 764 F. Supp. 608 (D. Or. 1991).

bean quality to be in conformity with the description of the goods as stipulated in the shipper's invoice.

On October 4, 1988, the Food and Drug Administration (FDA) collected a twenty pound sample of beans from the "Jian He" shipment. After inspecting the beans, on October 15, 1988, the FDA detained the shipment concluding they "contained filth." On October 12, 1988, the FDA collected a twenty pound sample of beans from the "Tokyo Maru" shipment. After inspecting the beans, on November 1, 1988, the FDA detained the shipment concluding they were "unfit for food in that [the beans had a] musty/moldy odor, moldy beans present."

North Pacific sought to obtain the FDA's approval of a plan to recondition the beans in order to bring them up to import standards. Since their arrival, the beans have been stored in a warehouse in Portland, Oregon under federal government detention. Despite substantial efforts by North Pacific to propose a plan in an attempt to cleanse the beans, the government has refused to lift the detention order. After exhaustive efforts in Portland to secure the release of the beans, by letter dated July 3, 1989, North Pacific rejected the shipments for failure to conform with Sample PC-16 as warranted by ICEC. North Pacific sold the beans to a buyer in South Africa per North Pacific's "Order Acceptance" dated January 15, 1990.

Conclusions of Law

Defendant accepted the goods when, after a reasonable opportunity to inspect the goods, it signified to plaintiff that it would take or retain them in spite of their alleged nonconformity. Defendant failed to make an effective rejection of the goods until July 3, 1989, at which time the rejection was not timely. This failure constitutes an acceptance of the goods. I find no language by defendant of clear and unequivocal rejection of the beans in any of the communications between the parties up until the July 3, 1989 letter.

Once the defendant accepted the beans, the burden is on the defendant to establish any nonconformity of the goods to the contract. Upon the presentation of documents in good order at the place of shipment (Hong Kong), title to the goods passed from plaintiff and the risk of deterioration or loss shifted to defendant. Under a C. & F. contract, whatever happened to the beans on board the vessel or after delivery to defendant at the port of destination was not the responsibility of plaintiff. That was a risk expressly assumed by the defendant under a C. & F. shipment contract.

The "Inspection Certificate of Quality," conducted and prepared by Andrew & Paulmann (H.K.) Ltd., concluded that the "quality [of the beans] was in conformity with [the] description of goods as stipulated in shipper's invoice." These documents are *prima facie* evidence of the fulfillment of plaintiff's obligation under the contract.

The defendant failed to revoke its acceptance of the goods until July 3, 1989 at which time the revocation was not timely. Defendant failed to comply with the notice requirements of revocation of acceptance. The official comment to U.C.C. § 2-608 states that the content of the notice required to be given to a seller is governed by considerations of good faith, prevention of surprise, and reasonable adjustment. *More will generally be necessary than the mere notification of breach.* . . . U.C.C. § 2-608, comment 5 (emphasis added).

Up until July 3, 1989, the defendant exercised ownership of the goods and performed acts inconsistent with plaintiff's alleged ownership of the goods. The defendant continued to attempt to sell the beans for nine months after the beans arrived in Portland and prior to rejecting the beans on July 3, 1989. Throughout those nine months, defendant exercised dominion and control over the beans and at no time did defendant tender ownership or control of the beans to plaintiff. Even after the FDA's inspection and detention of the beans on October 15, 1988 and November 1, 1988, plaintiff continued to exercise dominion and control over the beans by attempting to sell them and by creating and proposing various plans to recondition the beans to the FDA.

Conclusion

I find that plaintiff's contractual obligations were fulfilled when it delivered the beans, certified by an independent surveyor as conforming to contract specifications, into the hold of the chartered vessels. I award plaintiff declaratory relief finding that plaintiff's obligations have been fulfilled and that no sums are due or other liability has accrued to defendant.

Case Highlights

- The burden is on the buyer to establish any nonconformity of the goods to the contract once the goods have been accepted.
- Under a C & F shipment contract, the buyer assumes the risk of loss of the goods while in transit and after delivery at the port of destination.
- The UCC provides that the notice to revoke acceptance requires more than mere notification of breach and is governed by considerations of good faith, prevention of surprise, and reasonable adjustment.
- The buyer's exercise of dominion over the goods and performance of other acts inconsistent with the seller's continued ownership interest defeat a buyer's attempts to revoke acceptance.

identical in the CIP contract, with the exception of the seller's obligation to obtain insurance and provide the buyer with a cargo insurance policy or certificate.

The D Terms

The D group terms (DAF, DES, DEQ, DDU, DDP) are the only terms that are considered to be destination contracts. The **DAF** (delivered at frontier) term requires the seller to clear the goods for export and deliver the goods to the border of an adjoining country. The buyer's primary duties are to take delivery of the goods at the frontier (or assume responsibility for on-carriage) and arrange for import clearance. Risk and cost transfer from the seller to the buyer when the goods have been delivered to the frontier. This term is used primarily in conjunction with rail or road transport but may also be used for ocean carriage. The frontier needs to be expressly defined because it can mean either the border of the country of import or export.

The **DES** (delivered ex ship) term is the most long-standing of the D terms. DES obligates the seller to bear the costs and risks of shipment to the port of destination. The seller's responsibilities end when the goods have been made available to the buyer on board the ship at the port of destination. The seller must also provide a document enabling the buyer to take delivery from the ship and arrange export clearance. It is the buyer's responsibility to unload the goods from the ship and clear the goods through customs in the country of delivery. This term, along with the **DEQ** (delivered ex quay) term, are to be used only for water transport.

The DEQ term gives the seller the added responsibility of unloading the goods and makes the goods available to the buyer at the wharf (quay). Risk and cost transfer from the seller only upon the placement of the goods at the buyer's disposal on the quay. The buyer remains responsible for arranging import clearance.

The remaining D terms, **DDU** (delivered duty unpaid) and **DDP** (delivered duty paid), are similar to DAF to the extent that they can be used in association with any mode of transport, including ocean, rail, and truck. The DDU term requires the seller to deliver the goods at the named destination and arrange for export clearance. The buyer's duties are to take delivery of the goods at the destination and arrange for import clearance. Risk and cost transfer from the seller to the buyer when the goods are made available to the buyer at the destination.

Whereas ex works signifies the seller's minimum obligation, the DDP term denotes the seller's maximum obligation. The seller's duties are identical to those contained in the DDU term, with the additional obligation of obtaining import clearance. The buyer's sole duty is to take delivery of the goods from the named place of destination. Risk and cost transfers are identical to those under the DDU term.

The traditional prevalence of the FOB, CFR, and CIF terms is likely to give way to increased use of the CPT, CIP, and FCA terms. The traditional supremacy of FOB, CFR, and CIF contracts was due to the central importance of marine carriage. The advent of modern containerization and multimodal transport will probably result in these terms yielding to the FCA, CPT, and CIP terms, simply because the traditional function of the ship's rail as the dividing point between sellers' and buyers' functions has been replaced by other points, such as cargo terminals or other reception facilities. This change has also influenced documentation and reduced significantly the use of on-board bills of lading. Thus, even in the carriage of goods by sea, nonnegotiable sea waybills have increasingly replaced bills of lading.[29]

The Future of INCOTERMS

Despite its status as the embodiment of generally recognized international trade customs, Incoterms face some obstacles. As noted by the ICC itself, "commercial practice is not the same in all parts of the world."[30] As a result, Incoterms cannot reflect worldwide practices or what actually happens with respect to the loading and unloading of cargo and conclusion of carriage contracts. To its credit, *INCOTERMS 2000* attempts to assist users by introducing more flexibility into its terms. As can be seen from the summary of Incoterms in the previous Focus on Transactions section, *INCOTERMS 2000* permits the parties to modify the parties' duties with respect to arrangement for carriage, responsibility for loading and unloading, the procurement of insurance, and the arrangement of import and export clearance. These modifications recognize the diversity of practices prevalent among different locations and participants in the global economy.

Despite commending these innovations as reflective of what actually occurs at ports throughout the world, commentators have expressed some concern that the decennial revision of *Incoterms* may detract from its mission of providing a uniform standard of global terms of trade. For example, failure of the parties to designate which version of *Incoterms* is incorporated into their agreement may cause confusion and foster disputes. This failure may be the result of poor draftsmanship, a lack of understanding of *Incoterms*, or lack of awareness of changes from one edition to its successor. One commentator noted that "fundamental changes to the rules, if not properly introduced, could endanger the status of Incoterms as a generally recognized international custom of the trade."[31]

In any event, contracting parties are strongly advised to refrain from blind reliance upon *Incoterms*. Rather, the parties must ascertain the particular customs of the locations where the goods they sell and purchase are transferred. Although broad in its reach, *Incoterms* cannot be expected to supplant all traditional practices throughout the world. As has been noted more than once throughout the previous chapters, parties to international business transactions are best served by obtaining as much information as possible about the places, parties, and practices surrounding the transactions in which they become involved.

KEY TERMS

air waybill	CFR	consular invoice
bill of exchange	CIF	cost-plus method
bill of lading	CIP	CPT
cash against document	clean bill of lading	DAF
cash in advance	commercial invoice	DDP
certificate of inspection	consignee	DDU
certificate of origin	consignment sale	DEQ

---

29. Jan Ramberg, "Novel Features of the ICC Incoterms 1990" in *United Nations Uniform Commercial Law in the Twenty-First Century* 80 (1992).
30. Ramberg, *supra* note 5, at 14.
31. Ibid. at 10.

DES	FAS	packing slip
destination contract	FCA	*pro forma* invoice
documentary collections transaction	FOB	received-for-shipment bill of lading
documentary credit transaction	*INCOTERMS 2000*	risk of loss
documents against acceptance	insurance certificate	risk-shifting clause
drawee	International Chamber of	shipment contract
drawer	Commerce (ICC)	Shipper's Export Declaration (SED)
electronic bill of lading	marginal cost pricing	sight draft
electronic data interchange (EDI)	on-board bill of lading	straight bill of lading
export license	open account	time draft
ex works	order bill of lading	trade term

CHAPTER PROBLEMS

1. A buyer and seller entered into a contract for the sale of widgets "CIF Omaha." A further provision stated that delivery was to be at a "factory in Omaha, Tulsa, or Kansas City, to be designated by the buyer." The widgets were lost in transit. The buyer refused to pay on the presentation of the documents, arguing that the additional provision had converted the shipment contract to a destination contract. What type of contract was this and why? What advice would you give someone regarding the use of trade terms?

2. You are the purchasing agent for a U.S. luggage manufacturer. You are asked to outsource some of the components, including steel strips used in the fabrication of the structural frames of the larger pieces of luggage. Your company's manufacturing plant is located in Peoria, Illinois. Your research finds that the companies best able to supply the strips are located in Windsor, Canada; São Paulo, Brazil; and Padang, Indonesia. In asking for price quotations, what types of documents should you require? From your perspective, which trade term should be used in the price quotations?

3. You are a manufacturer of precision industrial tools and parts based in Ithaca, New York. You have been contacted by a manufacturer in Budapest, Hungary, to begin supplying it with an assortment of your products. Using

INCOTERMS, prepare a pro forma invoice with three different shipping options. For each option (INCOTERM), itemize the costs and relative responsibilities of the two parties. Consider how you will get the goods from Ithaca to Budapest. What modes of transport will need to be utilized? Whom can you contact for information needed to prepare the invoice?

4. An export contract required that the seller provide: "A full set of 3 original clean on-board bills of lading." Instead, the seller presented a full set of 3 clean on-board bills of lading but only one was marked "Original." The other two bills of lading were marked "Duplicate" and "Triplicate." Can the buyer reject the bills of lading as not conforming to the documentary requirements of the contract?

5. A foreign buyer negotiates with a foreign exporter for goods to be shipped out of a foreign port. To protect itself from fraud in the transaction, the buyer requires that the exporter provide an inspection certificate as one of the documents to be presented for payment. When the documents were presented for payment, the buyer noticed that the date on the inspection certificate was later than the shipment date on the bill of lading. The certificate failed to state when the inspection occurred. Can the buyer refuse payment because of this discrepancy?

INTERNET EXERCISES

1. You are unsure of what trade term to use in negotiating an export contract. You are willing to be responsible for the loading and shipping costs to the port of destination, along with the cost of unloading, but do not want to be responsible for import and customs clearance. What INCOTERM would best serve your needs? See **http://www.itds.treas.gov/incoterms.html.**

2. Select a country and research the documentary requirements for the importation of goods into that country. Such information can be obtained from the following sources: (1) U.S. Department of Commerce; (2) foreign government Web sites, especially consulate sites; (3) Bureau of National Affairs Export Shipping Manual; and (4) National Council on International Trade Development (NCITD).

http://

The Freight Detective's
Transportation
Reference Desk for
information on
Transportation Law:
**http://www.cargolaw.
com/d2.
referencedesk.html**

I n transporting goods throughout the world, different types of **common carriers** are utilized. A common carrier is a company that contracts with the public for transportation of goods or people; commercial airlines, overnight courier services, and international shipping lines are all examples of common carriers. Each type of common carrier or carriage contract is governed by its own **unimodal transport convention**. The most important international transport conventions are listed in Doing Business Internationally: International Transport Conventions.

The application of different carriage liability regimes in an international transport of goods transaction is potentially overwhelming. The leg of transport (land, rail, ocean) in which the loss-inducing event occurs determines the convention to be applied. Determining liability is further complicated by the existence of different legal regimes for a given mode of transport. For example, in ocean carriage there

Chapter 10

Transport of Goods

are three alternative legal regimes: the International Convention for the Unification of Certain Rules Relating to Bills of Lading (**Hague Rules**) adopted in 1924, the Brussels Protocol Amending the Hague Rules (**Hague-Visby Rules**) adopted in 1968, and the United Nations Convention on the Carriage of Goods by Sea (**Hamburg Rules**) adopted in 1978. (See Comparative Law: International

---

International Transport Conventions

Doing Business Internationally

Carriage by Air
Convention for the Unification of Certain Rules Relating to International Carriage by Air (Warsaw Convention) (1929)

Hague Protocol to Amend the Convention for the Unification of Certain Rules Relating to International Carriage by Air (The Hague Protocol) (1955)

Convention Supplementary to the Warsaw Convention for the Unification of Certain Rules Relating to International Carriage by Air performed by a Person other than the Contracting Carrier (1961)

Protocol to Amend the Convention for the Unification of Certain Rules Relating to International Carriage by Air (Guatemala Protocol) (1971)

Protocols 1–4 to Amend the Convention for the Unification of Certain Rules Relating to International Carriage by Air (1975)

Convention for the Unification of Certain Rules for International Carriage by Air (1999) (Montreal Protocol or Convention)

Carriage by Rail
Uniform Rules concerning the Contract for International Carriage of Goods by Rail (CIM) (1980)

continued

International Transport Conventions (*continued*)

Uniform Rules concerning the Contract for International Carriage of Goods by Rail (CIM) (1999)

Carriage by Road
Convention on the Contract for the International Carriage of Goods by Road (CMR) (1956)

Carriage by Sea
International Convention for the Unification of Certain Rules Relating to Bills of Lading (Hague Rules) (1924)

Brussels Protocol Amending the Hague Rules Relating to Bills of Lading (Hague-Visby Rules) (1968)
United Nations Convention on the Carriage of Goods by Sea (Hamburg Rules) (1978)

Multimodal Transport
United Nations Convention on International Multimodal Transport of Goods (1980)
UNCTAD/ICC Rules for Multimodal Transport Documents (1991)

Ocean Carriage of Goods Conventions.) If a loss is sustained during an ocean voyage, then it must be determined which ocean carriage convention is applicable.

This task is made more difficult by the fact that not all states are parties to all of these conventions. As of late 2004, the Hague Rules had been ratified by fifty states, including Argentina, Israel, the Netherlands, Turkey, and the United States.

INTERNATIONAL

International Ocean Carriage of Goods Conventions

COMPARATIVE LAW

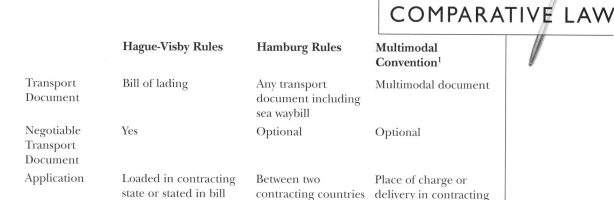

	Hague-Visby Rules	Hamburg Rules	Multimodal Convention[1]
Transport Document	Bill of lading	Any transport document including sea waybill	Multimodal document
Negotiable Transport Document	Yes	Optional	Optional
Application	Loaded in contracting state or stated in bill of lading	Between two contracting countries	Place of charge or delivery in contracting country; two different modes

continued

1.   To date, this convention has been ratified by only ten states and has not come into force. It is placed here to illustrate what a future multimodal convention may look like.

International Ocean Carriage of Goods Conventions (*continued*)

Basis of Carrier's Liability	Due diligence in providing seaworthy ship; not liable for exceptions	Liable unless it proves it took all reasonable measures	Multimodal transport operator liable unless it proves it took all reasonable measures
Limitation of Carrier's Liability	666.67 units of account/package or 30 units of account/Kg^2 of gross weight whichever is higher	835 SDR^3 per package or 2.5 SDR per Kg of gross weight	920 SDR per package or 2.75 per Kg or the higher amount provided under national law for a particular mode or leg of the transit
Limitation Period for Legal Action	1 year	2 years	2 years but notice must be given within 6 months of delivery

The Hague-Visby Rules have been ratified by twenty-four states, including Australia, Belgium, Canada, France, Italy, Japan, New Zealand, Singapore, and the United Kingdom. By contrast, the Hamburg Rules have been adopted by twenty states, including Chile and Mexico.

The most established and important of the international carriage conventions is the Hague Rules. The Hague Rules have been enacted into law in the United States as the **Carriage of Goods by Sea Act** (**COGSA**).[4] Most international transport of goods necessarily includes ocean carriage, and despite the increased use of multimodal transport documents, the **ocean bill of lading** remains the paramount title document. This chapter focuses on the legal regime instituted by the Hague Rules. The chapter concludes with a review of the related topic of marine insurance. The first section of this chapter is, however, devoted to air carriage, including the premier air carriage convention—the Convention for the Unification of Certain Rules Relating to International Carriage by Air (**Warsaw Convention**).

Air Waybill and the Warsaw Convention

http://
Text of the Warsaw Convention: **http:// www.forwarderlaw.com/ archive/warsaw.htm**

As a contract of carriage, the **air waybill** incorporates by reference the pertinent international carriage convention, namely, the Warsaw Convention. The Warsaw Convention is the most important multilateral treaty governing the liability of air carriers. As of late 2004, it had been ratified by 145 states, including almost all those in the developed world. As noted in the previous Doing Business Internationally box,

---

2. Under the Hague Rules and COGSA, the per-package limitation is fixed at $500. See COGSA, 46 U.S. App. § 1304(5) (2000). The Hague-Visby Rules per-package limitation translates to $1,000. See Hague-Visby Rules, art. IV(5)(a).

3. SDR is the acronym for "special drawing rights," a standard of value based on the rates of a basket of different national currencies.

4. COGSA is located at 46 U.S.C. App. §§ 1300-15 (2000).

the Warsaw Convention has been amended numerous times since its creation in 1929. The most recent amendment is the Convention for the Unification of Certain Rules for International Carriage by Air (**Montreal Convention**) adopted in 1999. The Montreal Convention has been adopted by more than thirty states, including Canada, Japan, Mexico, and the United States. Unlike the Warsaw Convention, which had as its purpose the protection of the fledging air transport industry, the Montreal Convention is focused on the protection of air travelers. For example, the Montreal Convention provides for electronic waybills and tickets, as well as amending the previous limitations on liability for death and bodily injury to passengers. For the purposes of this chapter, the most important provisions relate to the liability of air carriers for cargo losses.

Like the Hague Rules, the Warsaw Convention limits liability for the common carrier. The standard terms and conditions of the air waybill generally state that the liability limitation is "250 French Francs per kilogram unless the consignor has made, at the time the package was handed over to the carrier, a special declaration of the value at delivery and has paid a supplementary sum if the case so requires."[5] Under such circumstances, the carrier is liable in an amount up to the declared sum unless it can prove that the sum is greater than the value to the consignor at delivery. The carrier is also liable for delays in transporting cargo unless it proves that it took reasonable measures to avoid the damage or that such measures were impossible to undertake. The Warsaw Convention limits the forum where lawsuits may be initiated, including states that are parties to the convention and where the carrier is incorporated or has its principal place of business. In any event, the carrier must be notified immediately with respect to damaged cargo and no more than fourteen days after receipt. Claims for damages arising from delays in the transportation of cargo must be made in writing within twenty-one days from the date on which the cargo was delivered. The Warsaw Convention places a two-year limitation period on the filing of claims against carriers.

International Ocean Carriage Conventions

Liability of common carriers is fixed by a combination of international conventions and national laws. National laws define issues of title and negotiability, whereas the international conventions impose the minimum duties of the carriers and provide limits to carrier liability. This was not always the case. Carriers, at one time, were able to shield themselves from liability by incorporating broad limitation of liability or **exculpatory clauses**. After many disputes with shippers, a compromise on issues of liability was reached in the Hague Rules. The Hague Rules established a number of carrier responsibilities, such as the requirement to undertake due diligence in providing a seaworthy ship, to not deviate materially from the carriage contract, and to provide shippers with the opportunity to declare a higher value for their goods. In return, the shipping companies are provided a limitation of liability to cap their potential liabilities, along with a number of exemptions from liability.

As previously mentioned, three international conventions regulate the liability of common carriers in the international transport of goods by sea: the Hague Rules, the Hague-Visby Rules, and the Hamburg Rules. There was, however, a predecessor

http://
Megalaw.com—
Admiralty/Maritime
law: **http://www.
megalaw.com/top/
admiralty.php.** Provides
links to all of the major
maritime laws in the
United States, including the Harter Act.

---

5. Warsaw Convention, art. 22(2).

to these international conventions, the U.S. **Harter Act of 1893**.[6] The primary objective of the Harter Act was to prohibit clauses whereby carriers attempted to eliminate their liability for acts of negligence. The Harter Act prohibited the enforcement of broad exculpatory clauses incorporated into the standard bills of lading by the shipping industry. It did not, however, attempt to regulate the relationships between carriers and shippers comprehensively. The Harter Act remains in force for goods shipped from one U.S. port to another U.S. port.

The Hague-Visby Rules updated the Hague Rules, but some countries, including the United States, have failed to ratify the update. The liability of the carrier and associated companies is directly affected by which version is applied. Under the Hague-Visby Rules, the limit of liability is significantly increased. The Hamburg Rules are more pro-shipper than the Hague and Hague-Visby Rules. However, carrier liability protections are automatically extended to the servants or third-party contractors of the carriers under the Hamburg Rules.

The *Prima U.S. v. M/V Addiriyah* case that follows illustrates a number of points. First, it provides an introduction to the different third parties involved in the international shipment of goods, including the common carrier, stevedores, freight forwarder, nonvessel operating common carrier, and the custom broker. Second, it analyzes the importance of being designated a common carrier under the various carriage conventions, along with the potential liabilities of the freight forwarder.

Prima U.S. Inc. v. M/V Addiriyah

223 F.3d 126 (2d Cir. 2000)

McLaughlin, Circuit Judge. The Westinghouse Electric Corporation ("Westinghouse") contracted in writing with Panalpina, Inc. ("Panalpina"), a "freight forwarder," for the transportation and shipment of an electric transformer from the manufacturer in Italy to the ultimate consignee, the 3M Corporation in Iowa. Panalpina, as freight forwarder, was to oversee all of the transportation for the transformer, both on land and over sea. Panalpina's obligations under the contract included ensuring that the transformer was properly secured and lashed onto a flat-rack for ocean shipment. As is the industry custom, Panalpina did not issue a bill of lading for the shipment.

Pursuant to the standard terms and conditions listed on the reverse side of its contract, Panalpina undertook to exercise "reasonable care" in the selection of those who would actually carry, store, or otherwise handle the goods. The standard terms also limited Panalpina's liability for losses to $50 per shipment, and they disclaimed liability for all consequential or special damages in excess of this amount. These were the same terms utilized in the prior ten-year course of dealing involving more than 1,000 transactions between Westinghouse and Panalpina. When the time came to ship the transformer, Panalpina

arranged for it to be picked up at a factory in Melegano, Italy, and brought to the Port of Genoa for an ocean trip.

In Genoa, Panalpina hired Ligure Toscano, a customs broker, to coordinate the movement of the transformer through the Genoa Port. Because the transformer was oversized, it had to be secured to a forty-foot "flat-rack" container for ocean shipment. Through Toscano, Panalpina hired CSM, a local stevedore, to load the transformer onto the appropriate container, and to lash it securely for the trip. The transformer, on its flat-rack, was loaded aboard the M/V *Addiriyah* for the voyage to the United States.

During the ocean voyage, the M/V *Addiriyah* encountered heavy seas and the transformer, which CSM had negligently lashed to its flat-rack, broke loose, crushing a laser cutting machine owned by Prima (U.S.A), Inc. ("Prima"). Prima, via its subrogated insurer, filed a complaint against Westinghouse and Panalpina. Prima sought damages for the loss of its laser. A third-party action was then filed by Westinghouse against Panalpina for indemnification. The district court went on to find Panalpina liable to Westinghouse, in indemnity. Panalpina now appeals, challenging the district court's decision that it must indemnify Westinghouse for CSM's negligent

---

6. 46 U.S.C. App. §§ 190-96 (2000).

actions. Panalpina asserts that it is only a freight forwarder, and hence, should not be made to indemnify Westinghouse.

Panalpina was a freight forwarder, not a carrier

The job of a "non-vessel operating common carrier" (NVOCC) is to consolidate cargo from numerous shippers into larger groups for shipment by an ocean carrier. An NVOCC issues a bill of lading to each shipper. If anything happens to the goods during the voyage the NVOCC is liable to the shipper because of the bill of lading that it issued. A freight forwarder like Panalpina, on the other hand, simply facilitates the movement of cargo to the ocean vessel. The freight forwarder secures cargo space with a steamship company, gives advice on governmental licensing requirements, proper port of exit and letter of credit intricacies, and arranges to have the cargo reach the seaboard in time to meet the designated vessel.

Unlike a carrier, a freight forwarder does not issue a bill of lading, and is therefore not liable to a shipper for anything that occurs to the goods being shipped. As long as the freight forwarder limits its role to arranging for transportation, it will not be held liable to the shipper. By analogy, Panalpina was hired to act as a "travel agent" for the transformer: it set things up and made reservations, but did not engage in any hands-on heavy lifting.

Of course, a party that calls itself a freight forwarder might in fact be performing the functions of a carrier in which case function would govern over form. But the burden of demonstrating any deviation from what freight forwarders normally do in the maritime context must rest, and heavily so, on the party who would show such deviation. Moreover, when a freight forwarder selects someone to perform transportation services, that selection fulfills the forwarder's obligations in the absence of proof that the selection itself was negligent. We REVERSE the district court's order that Panalpina indemnify Westinghouse.

Case Highlights

- The "non-vessel operating common carrier" (NVOCC) consolidates cargo from numerous shippers into larger groups for shipment by an ocean carrier.
- Unlike a carrier, a freight forwarder does not issue a bill of lading and is not liable for damage to the goods while in the possession of a carrier.
- The freight forwarder is liable if it negligently selects a third party, such as a common carrier or customs broker, who proves to be incompetent.

COGSA

The Carriage of Goods by Sea Act or COGSA is the U.S. domestic version of the Hague or Hague-Visby Rules. Most of the major maritime nations of the world have adopted one of these two conventions into their national laws. The U.S. Carriage of Goods by Sea Act is modeled after the Hague Rules; the United Kingdom's is modeled on the Hague-Visby Rules.

The application of COGSA in the United Kingdom differs from its counterpart in the United States in two fundamental ways. First, Hague-Visby Rules apply to any shipments *from* a port in the United Kingdom. This differs in application from the Hague Rules as adopted in the United States. COGSA in the United States applies to all shipments *from* and *to* U.S. ports. In the United Kingdom, COGSA does not automatically apply to shipments from a foreign port to the United Kingdom. Second, COGSA does apply to shipments *from* one port in the United Kingdom to another such port. In contrast, the Harter Act covers shipments from one U.S. port to another U.S. port, unless the parties expressly agree that COGSA is to be the governing law. All future references in this chapter will be to COGSA as the codified version of the Hague Rules.

COGSA applies only to shipments evidenced by a bill of lading. COGSA states that it applies only to carriage of goods by sea where the carriage contract

http://
English Carriage of Goods Act of 1971: **http://www.jus.uio.no/ lm/england.carriage.of. goods.by.sea.act.1971/ doc.html.** For a complete version of Hague-Visby Rules select "Schedule of The Hague-Visby Rules."

INTERNATIONAL

http://

Recent Developments—
the need to change
COGSA: **http://www.
forwarderlaw.com/
archive/arch2.htm**
or **http://www.
forwarderlaw.com/
archive/arch2.htm.** For
a bibliography of
articles by Professor
Sturley of the University
of Texas Law School
analyzing the proposed
changes to COGSA:
**http://www.utexas.edu/
law/faculty/msturley/
publist.html.**

provides for "a bill of lading or any similar document of title."[7] The carriage contract is the bill of lading that is issued by either a common carrier or a charter party. A **charter party** is one who leases the entire ship from the ship's owner. COGSA would apply if the charter party then enters into carriage contracts with third parties and issues bills of lading in conjunction with these contracts.

The period of coverage under COGSA is limited to "the time when the goods are loaded on to the time they are discharged from the ship."[8] Therefore, unless the bill of lading extends the period of coverage, COGSA does not cover the period of time when the goods are in the possession of the common carrier before loading and after discharge. Bills of lading generally incorporate a marine extension or **warehouse-to-warehouse clause** to extend the period of coverage.

In addition, specialized companies, such as stevedore companies, are used by the common carrier to move the goods to and from the ship and to load and off-load the goods. COGSA protection is extended to these third-party companies through the use of a **Himalaya clause**. The third party need not be specifically named in the Himalaya clause for the protection of a carriage convention to be extended. General language, for example, is sufficient to extend defenses under the bill of lading to stevedores.[9] The following provision is an example of a typical Himalaya clause:

No servant or agent of the Carrier (including every independent contractor from time to time employed by the Carrier) shall in any circumstances whatsoever be under any liability whatsoever to the Merchant (shipper). Every right, exemption, defense and immunity of whatsoever nature applicable to the Carrier shall also be available and shall extend to protect every such servant or agent of the Carrier.[10]

This clause was held to be sufficient to extend coverage to a stevedore company and a consultant hired to supervise the stowage of the cargo. Almost any company working in conjunction with the common carrier is extended the same COGSA protections. For example, marine terminal operators have been extended protection under a general Himalaya clause.[11]

The primary objective of COGSA is to limit the liability of the common carrier while ensuring a claim for damages by shippers. COGSA limits the liability of the common carrier to $500 (Hague Rules) or $1,000 (Hague-Visby Rules) per package. It also provides seventeen exemptions that fully exempt the common carrier from all liability for damage to or loss of the goods. If the losses relate to a number of enumerated duties, however, the **per-package limitation** and seventeen exemptions are removed, and the common carrier becomes liable for all damages. These duties are the carrier's failure to perform **due diligence** in providing a seaworthy ship, the carrier's commission of a **material deviation**, and the failure of the carrier to provide a **fair opportunity** for the shipper to declare a value above the per-package limitation.

---

7.   Hague Rules, art. I(b); COGSA, 46 U.S.C. App. §§ 1300, 1301(b) (2000).
8.   Hague Rules, art. I(e); COGSA, 46 U.S.C. App. § 1301(e) (2000).
9.   See *Secrest Machine Corp. v. S.S. Tiber*, 450 F.2d 285 (5th Cir. 1971).
10.   *General Elec. Co. v. Inter-Ocean Shipping*, 862 F. Supp. 166, 169 (S.D. Tex. 1994).
11.   See *Wemhoener Pressen v. Ceres Marine Terminals, Inc.*, 5 F.3d 734 (4th Cir. 1993).

Carrier Liability

The primary grounds for common carrier liability are outlined in a single paragraph, Section 1304 (5), of COGSA. The numbers within the paragraph that follows signify important liability issues that are then explained.

§1304 (5):

Neither the carrier nor the ship shall in any event be or become liable for any loss or damage to or in connection with the transportation of goods in an amount exceeding $500 per package (1) lawful money of the United States, or in case of goods not shipped in packages, per customary freight unit (2) or the equivalent of that sum in other currency, unless the nature and value of such goods have been declared by the shipper before shipment and inserted in the bill of lading (3). This declaration, if embodied in the bill of lading, shall be prima facie evidence, but shall not be conclusive on the carrier. In no event shall the carrier be liable for more than the amount of damage actually sustained (4).[12]

The carrier's liability under COGSA is determined in one of two ways. First, an amount (not to exceed $500) per package is multiplied by the number of packages listed or described in the bill of lading (1). Alternatively, the carrier's liability may be based on the amount declared by the shipper on the bill of lading (3). The per-package limitation is the default provision, meaning that if the shipper fails to declare a higher amount, then the carrier's liability is automatically capped at $500 per package.

Some types of goods, however, are not packaged for shipment. There are, therefore, no packages available for the purposes of calculating the carrier's liability. In such cases, COGSA provides an alternative known as the **customary freight unit (CFU)** to determine the number of packages (2). For example, in *Caterpillar Overseas, S.A. v. Marine Transport, Inc.*, the court determined that each tractor in a shipment of tractors was a CFU.[13] Other examples are measurements used for bulk goods, such as tons (coal), cubic yards (wheat), or barrels (oil). Note that the $500 per package amount is an upper limit. If the goods have a value of less than $500 per package, then the carrier is liable only for the lesser amount (4).[14] The Hague Rules and COGSA provide that the actual loss figure is to be determined based on the value of the goods at the time and place of discharge. In this regard, the loss is determined by the difference in market value of the goods in sound condition at the point of destination and the fair market value of the goods in their damaged state. By contrast, the Hague-Visby Rules offer three sources for the determination of value: commodity exchange price, current market price, or "the normal value of goods of the same kind and quality."[15]

As discussed previously, the cap of $500 per package or CFU is overridden by any higher value declared by the shipper on the bill of lading. There is a correlative duty of the carrier to provide an opportunity for such a declaration. The carrier is liable for an undeclared higher value if it failed to give the shipper "a *fair opportunity* to choose a higher liability by paying a corresponding greater charge."[16] Common carriers generally honor their duty to provide fair opportunity to declare a higher

http://

The text of the United States Carriage of Goods by Sea Act: **http://www.access.gpo. gov/uscode/title46a/ 46a_22_.html.**

---

12.   Hague Rules, art. IV(4); COGSA, 46 U.S.C. App. § 1304(5) (2000).
13.   900 F.2d 714 (4th Cir. 1990).
14.   The same is true if the shipper declares a higher value. If the value of the goods is less than the amount declared, then the carrier is liable only for the true value.
15.   See Hague-Visby Rules, art. IV(5)(a).
16.   *Cincinnati Milacron Ltd. v. M/V American Legend*, 784 F.2d1161 (4th Cir. 1986).

value by providing notice and a space to declare a higher value on the face of the bill of lading. Although good practice, some courts have held placing a space on the face of the bill of lading is not required. Language found in the fine print on the back of the bill of lading form may be sufficient.[17]

Carrier Duties

The Hague Rules and COGSA not only restrict the common carrier's ability to limit its liabilities but also set out a number of mandatory responsibilities.[18] COGSA lists a number of duties of the carrier that pertain to its issuance of bills of lading. First, there is a general duty on the carrier to issue a bill of lading when receiving goods from the shipper. Second, the bill must include basic information, including "leading marks" provided by the shipper for the identification of the goods; the number of packages or pieces, the quantity, or the weight as furnished by the shipper; and the apparent order or condition of the goods. Any such statements regarding these requirements are prima facie evidence that the goods were so delivered to the carrier. Thus, the carrier becomes a guarantor of the information provided by the shipper and placed on the bill of lading.

If the goods delivered are not in the condition stated on the bill of lading or there is a **shortage** as to quantity, then the shipper or the party receiving goods meets its burden of proof by providing the bill of lading as evidence. However, a party's right to make claim against the carrier is limited by two procedural requirements. First, the receiving party must give notice of loss either at the port of discharge or at the time of receiving the goods from the carrier. If the loss is not apparent at the time of receiving the goods, then notice must be given in writing within three days. Failure to give notice is prima facie evidence that the goods received were as indicated on the bill of lading. On giving the required notice of loss, COGSA provides a one-year **statute of limitations**. The party suffering a loss must commence suit within one year of the delivery of the goods.

COGSA prohibits any attempts by the carrier to insert into its bill of lading more restrictive procedural requirements or attempts to limit its duties and liabilities. COGSA states that "any clause, covenant or agreement in a contract of carriage relieving the carrier or the ship from liability for loss or damage to or in connection with the goods, arising from negligence, fault or failure in the duties and obligations or lessening such liability shall be null and void and of no effect."[19] The question has arisen whether an arbitration clause in the bill of lading is subject to challenge under this limitation. The Supreme Court in *Vimar Seguros y Reaseguros, S.A. v. M/V Sky Reefer*[20] found that an arbitration clause in the bill of lading was not subject to attack under COGSA. The Court referred to the **Federal Arbitration Act**[21] for the general premise that arbitration is a favored means of dispute resolution in the United States. Regarding COGSA, it held that

17. See, e.g., *Mori Seiki USA, Inc. v. M/V Alligator Triumph*, 990 F.2d 444 (9th Cir. 1993).
18. See Hague Rules, art. III(3–8); see also COGSA, 46 U.S.C. App. § 1303(3-8) (2000).
19. 46 U.S.C. App. § 1303(8) (2000).
20. 515 U.S. 528 (1995).
21. 9 U.S.C. §§ 1-3, 10 (2000).

an arbitration clause is not to be considered as a type of disclaimer or limitation of liability that is generally prohibited under COGSA.

The arbitration clause was held not to lessen the liability of the common carrier by increasing the costs of obtaining relief. The added cost argument pertained not so much to the fact that arbitration was mandated but that the arbitration was to be held in Tokyo, Japan. The lessening of liability argument was not strengthened by the fact that both Japanese and American laws were based upon the Hague Rules. The Court did outline one exception to the enforcement of arbitration clauses in bills of lading: if a forum selection clause and a choice of law clause are used in tandem to prevent a shipper from pursuing its statutory remedies under COGSA.

A clause limiting carrier liability that is generally recognized by the courts is the **force majeure clause**. The force majeure clause is a standard clause in a marine contract exempting the parties from liability for nonperformance resulting from a condition beyond their control, such as government interference, wars, and "acts of God." The next part of the chapter analyzes more fully the carrier's duty to shippers and its liabilities for failing to perform those duties.

Seaworthiness

In order to gain the protections of COGSA, the common carrier must undertake due diligence in the preparation and inspection of the ship to ensure its **seaworthiness**. The due diligence undertaking is to be performed before the ship departs from the port of shipment. The seaworthiness determination is done at the time of departure. In the event that the ship becomes unseaworthy after it leaves the port of shipment, the common carrier remains protected under COGSA.

Four parameters must be met for a ship to be considered seaworthy under COGSA. First, the ship used must be appropriate for the type of carriage. Factors in making this determination include the type of goods transported and the anticipated route of transit.[22] A ship that may be seaworthy for lake or river travel may be unseaworthy for ocean carriage, and a ship that may be seaworthy for the carriage of containers may not be seaworthy for the shipment of bulk goods. Second, the ship must be properly equipped for the "reception, carriage, and preservation" of the goods. Thus, all mechanical devices such as fire suppression equipment and refrigeration units must be properly maintained and functioning.

Third, the common carrier must staff the vessel with a competent crew, properly trained to operate the ship and its equipment. Fourth, the carrier must "properly and carefully load, handle, stow, keep, and discharge the goods carried."[23] Proper **stowage** varies according to the types of goods transported. Goods that are susceptible to motion must be properly lashed or secured in the hull of the ship. The *Manifest Shipping* case that follows focuses on the "equipment" and "competency" of the crew elements of seaworthiness.

22.   See *Marine Office of America Corp. v. Lilac Marine Corp.*, 296 F. Supp.2d 91, 103 (D.P.R. 2003).
23.   COGSA, 46 U.S.C. App. § 1303(2) (2000).

Manifest Shipping v. Uni-Polaris Insurance Co.

1 Lloyd's L. R. 651 (Q.B. 1995)

Justice Tuckey. *Star Sea* had an engine room and cargo holds that were protected from fire by a full flood carbon dioxide extinguishing system. It also had an electrically powered fire pump in the engine room and an emergency fire pump in the forepeak. While in transit from Brazil with a load of bananas she was inspected by the Belgian port authority and found to have a nonworking emergency fire pump. The chief engineer in repairing the pump cut the suction pipe. The emergency fire pump was repaired but the cut pipe was never repaired. On the return trip to South America a fire started in the engine room. The shipowner filed a claim under its marine insurance policy for a constructive total loss. The insurance company denied liability contending that the ship had been sent to sea in an unseaworthy state. The lower court held that the cut pipe made the vessel unseaworthy; however, as the fire involved electrical cables, the fact that the emergency pipe was not working would not have materially affected the spread of the fire.

The present court holds that the ship was unseaworthy on another matter. The ship was unseaworthy pertaining to this claim because of the incompetence of the ship's master. The master's conduct demonstrated a massive ignorance of the working of the carbon dioxide fire suppression system. Furthermore, this incompetence is attributable to the ship's owner because it looked to the maintenance of the fire equipment and the training of the master with a blind eye.

The essence of this allegation is that the master was unaware of the need to use the carbon dioxide system as soon as he realized that the fire could not be fought in any other way. Instead the system was not discharged until at least two and one-half hours after the fire had started. I have no doubt that this was negligent, but does it indicate that the master was incompetent so as to render the ship unseaworthy? I accept that just because the master made a mistake or mistakes, it does not follow that he was incompetent. In fact, given the master's years of experience, I do not doubt his general competence. However, since he did not undergo fire training when he was first certified his competence regarding the particular fire suppression system is in doubt. The master's conduct demonstrates a massive ignorance of its essentials which can only be characterized as incompetence. Due to this incompetence I find that the vessel was unseaworthy. Judgment is REVERSED.

Case Highlights

- Under COGSA, for a ship to be seaworthy, its equipment must be in good working order, and the crew must be competent in operating the equipment.
- A nonoperational fire suppression system will generally render a ship unseaworthy.
- A ship's captain or master may possess general competence but still be judged incompetent regarding the operation of the ship's equipment.

Per-Package Limitation

Section 1304(5) of COGSA, as discussed earlier, provides a liability limitation to the common carrier of $500 per package. An issue often litigated is the definition of a "package" for purposes of calculating damages. Congress did not define the term *package* in COGSA. Clearly, cargo fully boxed or crated is a "package," particularly "where the mode of packaging conceals the identity of the goods being shipped." Similarly, freestanding cargo not enclosed in a box or crate clearly constitutes "goods not shipped in a package." But what about cargoes where some preparation for transportation has been made but the mode of packaging does not completely conceal or enclose the goods? The answer is not always obvious.

In *Institute of London Underwriters v. Sea-Land Service, Inc.,*[24] the court held that a yacht shipped in an on-deck cradle constituted a package. In comparison, another

24. 881 F.2d 761, 768 (9th Cir. 1989).

court held that a transformer to which a wooden skid was attached did not constitute a package. A package is likely to be presumed if the cargo fits a plain, ordinary definition of "package." In short, if the cargo could not have been simply dumped in a hold, then it is likely to have been carried with some sort of packaging. Also, most courts will give great weight to the designation of the cargo as packages in the bill of lading.

A common problem is the existence of a number of different "packages" for a court to choose from in assessing COGSA damages. The different means of quantifying a shipment of goods may stem from how the goods are packaged or how they are described in the bill of lading. In *Sony Magnetic Products Inc. v. Merivienti*,[25] Sony packed a standard cargo container with videocassette tapes. Sony first placed the tapes into 1,320 cardboard cartons and then strapped the cartons onto fifty-two wooden pallets. The carrier issued Sony a bill of lading with the following description: "Description of Packages and Goods, 1 × 40 foot container STC [said to contain]: 1,320 Ctns." The bill of lading did not reserve space for designating the value of the cargo, but the attached export certificate showed a value of $424,765.44. The court found that each of the 1,320 cartons was a "package" for purposes of COGSA, capping liability at $660,000, and then awarded $424,765.44, the actual damages sustained by Sony as evidenced by the invoice value of the tapes.

Previously, the court in *Vegas v. Compania Anonima Venzolana de Navegacion*[26] decided that an ambiguity on a bill of lading regarding the number of COGSA packages should be resolved in favor of the shipper. Like the shipper in the *Sony* case, Vegas had consolidated cartons of goods onto pallets and informed the carrier on the bill of lading of the number of individual cartons. Unlike the shipper in *Sony*, however, Vegas not only disclosed the number of cartons but also disclosed that they had been consolidated onto pallets. The *Vegas* court resolved the ambiguity, a stated number of cartons and a lesser number of pallets, on the bill of lading in favor of the shipper. Note that the *Sony* court used only the value listed in the export certificate as evidence of value. It did not hold that the value of the goods listed on the attached export certificate was a declaration of a higher value for purposes of COGSA. Section 1304(5) expressly requires that any declared value be "inserted in the bill of lading." The *Groupe Chegaray /V. de Chalus v. P&O Containers*

Groupe Chegaray/V. de Chalus v. P&O Containers
251 F.3d 1359 (11th Cir. 2001)

Oakes, Circuit Court Judge. This case involves an eight-ton, 40-foot container filled with perfumes and cosmetics shipped from France to Florida that mysteriously disappeared while in a marine terminal at Port Everglades, Florida. In resolving this dispute, this Court once again navigates through the muddy waters of determining the meaning of "package" under the Carriage of Goods by Sea Act ("COGSA" or the "Act"). Subsection 1304(5) limits carrier liability to $500 "per package," but fails to define the term "package."

Parbel Inc. is a Florida company that imports *L'Oreal* products from France. In 1992, Parbel ordered a shipment consisting of four containers from Parfums Et Beaute International Et Cie ("Parfums"), which shipped the order on the Nedlloyd Holland, a ship operated by P&O Containers, Ltd. ("P&O"). P&O contracted to deliver the shipment from LeHavre, France, to Parbel's warehouse in Miami, Florida. After the Nedlloyd Holland arrived at Port Everglades in Ft. Lauderdale, Florida, the containers were off-loaded from the ship and

---

25.   An excerpt of this case is used in this chapter because it pertains to the enumerated exemption of "latent defect."
26.   720 F.2d 629 (11th Cir. 1983).

stored in a container yard operated by Sea-Land Service, Inc. ("Sea-Land") until delivery to the consignee in Miami. Sometime between December 26 and December 28, 1992, one of the containers mysteriously disappeared.

The perfumes and cosmetics in the missing container were packed into a total of 2,270 shoebox-sized corrugated cardboard cartons. These small cartons were then consolidated into 42 larger units, which were bound together with plastic wrap and packed onto 42 pallets, with two cartons remaining.

Groupe Chegaray/V. De Chalus ("Groupe Chegaray"), Parbel's subrogated insurer, paid for the loss under a cargo insurance policy and brought a subrogation action against P&O and Sea-Land. The district court found that the number of packages under COGSA was 2,270 and that appellants were jointly and severally liable for Groupe Chegaray's damages up to $1,134,000.

In addition to the lack of statutory guidance, unforeseeable technological strides in the shipping industry since 1936 have contributed to the frustration of many courts attempting to define a COGSA package. Traditionally, shipments were made by "breakbulk," whereby goods were packaged into parcels which could be hand-loaded into a vessel's cargo-hold. The advent of the container in the 1960s revolutionized the shipping industry by enabling the shipment of massive metal boxes filled with goods that were often concealed and/or not divided into breakbulk size. Modern containers are able to hold hundreds of "packages" as the term was probably understood in 1936. Thus, if ever the meaning of a "package" was self-evident, the container turned it into a puzzle.

In order to determine what constitutes the COGSA package, we begin by looking at the bill of lading.

P&O's ON BOARD bill of lading states:

CONTAINERS: 4 UNITS
    138 PACKAGES COSMETICS
    AS DETAILED ON THE ATTACHED RIDER

The rider describes the missing container as follows:

1 40' DRY VAN S.T.C. said to contain
    31 PACKAGES NOS. 43/73 ORDER 70187 × COSMETICS
    11 PACKAGES + 2 CTNS ORDER 70188A COSMETIC
    ———— *UNIT TOTALS* ————
    42 PACKAGES STC 2268 CARTONS + 2 CTNS

Appellants argue that the number of COGSA packages is four because "4" is listed in the bill of lading under the heading "NO. OF PKGS." In the alternative, they argue that the 42 pallets plus two cartons are the COGSA packages because they are described as such in the bill of lading. Groupe Chegaray, on the other hand, contends that because the bill of lading is ambiguous regarding the number of COGSA packages, we are required to resolve the

ambiguity in their favor and affirm the district court's finding that the 2,270 cartons constitute the COGSA packages. We believe that the 42 pallets, described as "packages" in the bill of lading, plus the two cartons, represent the accurate number of COGSA packages.

In this Circuit, "we approach any attempt to define a container as a COGSA package with great reluctance. Moreover, our inquiry into the matter does not end . . . at a quick glance at the 'number of packages' column on the bill of lading." *Fishman & Tobin, Inc. v. Tropical Shipping & Constr. Co.*, 240 F.3d 956, 964 (11th Cir. 2001)

Because neither the statute nor its legislative history is particularly helpful in defining a COGSA package, this Court has adopted a family of principles for the task. We begin by assuming "that Congress intended to vest the word with its plain, ordinary meaning." We elaborated upon this assumption by endorsing the Second Circuit's definition of a COGSA package in *Aluminios Pozuelo, Ltd. v. S.S. Navigator* as "a class of cargo, irrespective of size, shape or weight, to which some packaging preparation for transportation has been made which facilitates handling, but which does not necessarily conceal or completely enclose the goods." More recently, we listed four additional principles to determine a COGSA package: (1) the court should look to the parties' contractual agreement in the bill of lading; (2) a COGSA package is the result of some amount of preparation for the purpose of transportation, which also facilitates handling; (3) a container can be considered a COGSA package only in light of a clear agreement to that effect; and (4) when goods are placed in containers without being described as separately packaged, they are classified as "goods not shipped in packages" for COGSA purposes, absent an agreement otherwise. Finally, when a bill of lading is ambiguous regarding what constitutes the COGSA package, then, in light of the widely accepted understanding that the original purpose of § 1304(5) was to protect shippers against carriers, the ambiguity is resolved against the carrier.

Applying these principles, we believe that the district court was correct to find that the container did not constitute the COGSA package and that the bill of lading was not ambiguous. But we find that the court was incorrect not to accord greater weight both to the description of the pallets as packages in the bill of lading and to the fact that the shipper chose to package and wrap the 2,270 carton boxes onto 42 separately numbered pallets.

Here, the bill of lading could not have been more clear. It described the pallets in plain language as "packages." Groupe Chegaray can point to no case where the bill of lading was not found to be ambiguous, that finds a unit explicitly referred to as a "package" to not be the COGSA package.

Parbel chose to incur the expense of packaging the 2,270 shoebox-sized cartons onto a total of 42 pallets. While Groupe Chegaray is correct to point out that the record is not explicit regarding whether the 42 plastic-wrapped units containing the cartons were themselves each plastic-wrapped onto the pallets or just plastic-wrapped together and moved around with pallets, we find this consideration to be immaterial. The 42 units of plastic-wrapped cartons clearly facilitated the efficient transport of the individual cardboard boxes, and reduced any safety or damage risks that may have been involved in handling them. The fact that Parbel chose to package the cartons in these manageable units instead of shipping them loose supports our conclusion that they represent the COGSA package.

For the foregoing reasons, we find that the correct number of COGSA packages is 44, representing the 42 pallets plus the two outstanding cartons. Accordingly, we VACATE the district court's judgment and REMAND for further proceedings. On remand, the district court must apply the $500 liability limitation to each of the 42 pallets and each of the two cartons.

Case Highlights

- Although the bill of lading is important for determining the number of packages pursuant to COGSA, the court must make inquiry beyond merely noting the number of packages listed on the document.
- In determining what a package is for purposes of COGSA, the court will examine the bill of lading and the amount of preparation for the purpose of transportation. There is also a presumption against a container being a package in the absence of clear agreement to that effect, and when goods are placed in containers without being described as separately packaged, they are classified as "goods not shipped in packages" for COGSA purposes, absent an agreement otherwise.
- When a bill of lading is ambiguous regarding what constitutes the COGSA package, then the ambiguity is resolved against the carrier.

---

case that follows addresses the issue of the number of packages for purposes of COGSA through examination of the bill of lading.

Once it is determined that goods have been lost or damaged, any prospective plaintiff must face procedural issues. First, who has the burden of proving damages and how can such proof be rebutted? Second, what parties have standing to sue the carrier? The *Polo Ralph Lauren v. Tropical Shipping* case that follows reviews these different procedural issues relevant to all claims under COGSA.

Polo Ralph Lauren, L.P. v. Tropical Shipping & Construction Co.

215 F.3d 1217 (11th Cir. 2000)

Kravitch, Circuit Judge. This appeal centers on what recourse, if any, an owner of goods lost at sea has against the carrier when the owner of the goods is not a named party to the bill of lading. Plaintiff Polo Ralph Lauren, L.P. ("Polo"), seeks damages for cargo lost overboard while in transport with Tropical Shipping & Construction Company ("Tropical"). Polo apparently entered into a bailment contract with Drusco, Inc. ("Drusco") for the manufacture and delivery of 4,643 pairs of pants.

Under the terms of this agreement, Polo sent fabric to Drusco in Florida, which Drusco cut and preassembled before shipping the fabric pieces to the Dominican Republic to be sewed into finished pants. Drusco entered into similar arrangements with several other clothing

manufacturers and combined the pants from all of the manufacturers into two large sealed containers that it delivered to Tropical. Drusco also arranged for the return shipment of the finished trousers to Florida where it would add designer accoutrements before returning them to the manufacturers for sale to retailers.

While en route from the Dominican Republic to Florida, the container containing Polo's cargo was lost overboard in rough seas. Polo asserted claims for breach of contract, bailment, and negligence. The district court dismissed the contract claim on the ground that Polo did not have standing because it was not named in the bills of lading. The court also granted summary judgment to Tropical on the bailment and negligence claims as preempted by COGSA.

COGSA: An Exclusive Remedy

COGSA, enacted in 1936, governs "all contracts for carriage of goods by sea to or from ports of the United States in foreign trade." The purpose of COGSA was to achieve international uniformity and to redress the edge in bargaining power enjoyed by carriers over shipper and cargo interests by setting out certain duties and responsibilities of carriers that cannot be avoided even by express contractual provision. Plaintiff states a *prima facie* claim under COGSA by demonstrating delivery of goods in sound condition to a carrier and their subsequent receipt in damaged condition. The burden then shifts to the carrier to establish that the damage was not caused by its negligence.

We conclude that because COGSA applies in this case, it provides Polo's exclusive remedy and preempts Polo's tort claims. We have found no cases in which a court has allowed a tort claim to proceed when COGSA applies. Polo's complaint therefore should have stated a single COGSA claim instead of three separate causes of action. Many courts have recognized that a COGSA claim against a negligent carrier for lost or damaged goods comprises elements of both contract, arising from the breach of the contract of carriage, and tort, issuing from the breach of the carrier's duty of care.

Although recognizing the COGSA claim's hybrid nature, these cases do not stand for the proposition that COGSA provides various causes of action, both contract and tort, from which a plaintiff may choose in seeking redress from a negligent carrier. Nothing in the language of COGSA or the cases interpreting it leads us to believe otherwise. We therefore conclude that COGSA affords one cause of action for lost or damaged goods. The district court properly granted summary judgment on Polo's actions in bailment and negligence.

Polo's Standing to Bring a COGSA Claim

The district court rejected Polo's argument that it was a third-party beneficiary to the bills of lading and granted summary judgment. Polo is not named in the bills of lading. Contracts bind only named parties unless both parties to the contract clearly express a mutual intent to benefit a third party. This rule of strict construction applies with equal force in contracts of carriage. The third party need not be mentioned by name as long as the contract refers to a "well-defined class of readily identifiable persons" that it intends to benefit.

Polo argues that the inclusion of the "owner of the goods" in the bills of lading evinces a clear intent to benefit that class of persons. The back of the bills of lading uses the phrase "shipper, consignee, or owner of the goods" repeatedly in defining the conditions of the contract of carriage. The final clause of the bills iterates that the "Shippers, Consignees, and Owners of the goods and the Holder of the Bill of Lading" expressly agree to all its terms. Polo argues that these recurring references to the "owner of the goods" intend to benefit Polo.

In *All Pacific Trading, Inc. v. Vessel M/V Hanjin Yosu*, 7 F.3d 1427 (9th Cir.1993), the court considered a consolidated action brought by nine owners of damaged goods and their insurers. Eight of the nine plaintiffs delivered their goods to different non-vessel-operating common carriers ("NVOCCs") who issued bills of lading to the shippers and then delivered the goods to the carrier, who in turn executed separate bills of lading with the NVOCCs. The cargo owners were not named in the bills of lading with the carrier. The court rejected the carrier's argument that the plaintiff cargo owners lacked standing to sue because it found that the cargo owners were actual parties to the bills of lading. As with the bills of lading before us, those bills of lading contained a clause obligating the "owner of the goods" to their terms.

The bills of lading between Tropical and Drusco recurrently refer to the "owner of the goods" and specifically bind the "owner of the goods" to its terms and obligations, creating the possibility that Polo would have standing to sue as owner of the goods or as a third-party beneficiary to the bills of lading. There was sufficient evidence before the district court of Polo's ownership to render improvident its grant of summary judgment on Polo's COGSA claim.

AFFIRMED in part; REVERSED in part.

Case Highlights

- COGSA governs all contracts for carriage of goods by sea to or from ports of the United States in foreign trade.
- The initial burden of proof is on the shipper to prove that the goods delivered to the carrier were in sound condition. This burden is met by providing a "clean" bill of lading. The burden then shifts to the carrier to prove that the damage was not caused by its negligence.
- A party does not have to be named in the bill of lading to have standing to sue the carrier if it is a member of a class of people that were intended to benefit from the carriage contract.

COGSA Coverage

COGSA[27] is more comprehensive than the Harter Act in regulating the carrier-shipper relationship. The Hamburg Rules are even more so. All three provide a relatively fair allocation of liability between the carrier and the shipper. There are some important differences, however, between the different carriage conventions. For example, COGSA limits the liability of the carrier to the time frame represented from "tackle to tackle," or from time of loading to time of discharge. It does not take into account the time when the goods are in the control of the carrier before the loading and after the unloading of the cargo.

The Hamburg Rules extend the period of responsibility to include when the goods are in the control of the carrier but not on the ship. Article 7 of the Hague Rules (COGSA) allows the parties to agree to extend the period of application to the period "prior to the loading, and subsequent to the discharge."[28] This is generally done through the insertion of a warehouse-to-warehouse clause into the bill of lading. The *Mori Seiki USA, Inc. v. M/V Alligator Triumph* case that follows reviews the "tackle to tackle" coverage of COGSA and the use of the Himalaya clause to extend COGSA to third parties.

http://

Text of Hamburg Rules: **http://www.jus.uio.no/ lm/un.sea.carriage. hamburg.rules.1978/ doc.html.**

Mori Seiki USA, Inc. v. M/V Alligator Triumph

990 F.2d 444 (9th Cir. 1993)

Hug, Circuit Judge. Appellant, Mori Seiki USA, Inc. ("Mori Seiki"), was the consignee of a precision lathe that was damaged while being transported from Nagoya, Japan to Houston, Texas. The lathe was damaged after it was unloaded from an ocean vessel at the Port of Los Angeles, but before it was released from the seaport. Mori Seiki filed suit in district court seeking damages from the ocean carrier (Mitsui), the ship (M.V. *Alligator Triumph*), the seaport operator (Trans Pacific Container), and the stevedore services firm which unloaded and handled its lathe (Marine Terminals Corporation).

Applicability of COGSA After Discharge

COGSA applies to all cargo shipments carried by sea, to or from the United States. By its own terms, COGSA limits liability for cargo damage to $500, if the damage occurs between the time the cargo is loaded on to the

ship and the time it is discharged from the ship ("tackle to tackle"). Parties to a shipping agreement, however, may contractually extend the limitation period.

The bill of lading at issue in this case stated that "with respect to loss or damage occurring during the period from the time when the Goods arrived at the sea terminal at the port of loading to the time when they left the sea terminal at the port of discharge the carrier shall be responsible for such loss or damage to the extent prescribed by the Hague Rules (COGSA)." The plain meaning of this language is that COGSA's liability limitation would extend to the period after the lathe was discharged from the ship, but before it was released from the sea terminal. Although it is true that a bill of lading is a contract of adhesion, which is "strictly construed against the carrier," and that "any ambiguity in the bill of lading must be construed in favor of the shipper and against the carrier," we are not persuaded that such an ambiguity exists here. The bill of lading extended COGSA's $500 liability limitation to the period during which the lathe was damaged.

---

27.   In the United States, see Article 7 of the Uniform Commercial Code for domestic transactions. For international transactions involving bills of lading, refer to the Pomerene Bills of Lading Act, 49 U.S.C. §§ 80101-16 (2000).

28.   See also COGSA, 46 U.S.C. App. § 1307 (2000).

Extension of Liability Limitation Under the Himalaya Clause

Mitsui's bill of lading included a so-called "Himalaya clause," which is commonly used to extend a carrier's defenses and liability limitations to certain third parties performing services on its behalf. The district court concluded that the seaport operator and the stevedore services company were covered by the Himalaya clause in Mitsui's bill of lading. We conclude, therefore, that the Himalaya clause extended Mitsui's COGSA defenses, including the $500 package liability limitation, to Marine Terminal Corporation. AFFIRMED.

Case Highlights

- COGSA covers only the "tackle to tackle" portion of the carriage unless contractually extended in the bill of lading.
- The Himalaya clause is commonly inserted in the freight contract to extend a carrier's defenses and liability limitations (COGSA) to third parties performing services on its behalf, such as a stevedore company.

Carrier is defined more broadly by the Hamburg Rules. It is "any person by whom a contract of carriage of goods by sea has been concluded with a shipper."[29] By not referring to "carrier," as COGSA does, the Hamburg Rules apply to parties such as freight forwarders and terminal or nonvessel common carriers. COGSA applies only to shipments covered by a bill of lading. In contrast, the Hamburg Rules apply to any contracts of carriage by sea, such as straight or nonnegotiable bills of lading and electronic documents.

In addition, the Hamburg Rules provide specific rules for carriage above deck, whereas the Hague Rules exclude deck carriage from their application. COGSA does permit the parties to agree to above-deck carriage. This is done through the incorporation of a **clause paramount** into the bill of lading. The burden of proof is on the shipper under COGSA to prove that any loss was due to the fault of the carrier. The burden is satisfied generally by the presentment of a *clean* bill of lading. In contrast, carrier fault is presumed under the Hamburg Rules. Article 5(1) of the Hamburg Rules states that "the carrier is liable for loss of or damage to the goods, as well as from delay in delivery, if the occurrence which caused the loss, damage or delay took place while the goods were in his charge." The carrier may still avoid liability if it can demonstrate it took "all measures that could reasonably be required to avoid the occurrence and its consequences."[30]

A still unresolved issue is how best to deal with combined or **multimodal transport** contracts. The Hague Rules and COGSA were enacted prior to the advent of **containerization**. Containerization allows a single container to be used in different modes of transit.[31] A container can be attached to a truck, placed on the bed of a railroad car, and loaded on a ship. The current approach is the recognition that the different unimodal conventions form a network of liability. Each segment of the transport is governed by the convention applicable to that type of transportation.

http://

The ICC also works to uncover and prevent maritime crimes (and fraud) through its International Maritime Bureau: **http:// www.iccwbo.org/ccs/ menu_imb_bureau.asp.**

29.   Hamburg Rules, art. 1(1).
30.   Ibid. art. 5(1).
31.   A *container* is a uniform, reusable metal box in which goods are shipped by vessel, truck, or rail. Standard lengths include ten, twenty, thirty, and forty feet (forty-foot containers generally hold about 40,000 pounds of cargo). See generally Seymour Simon, "The Law of Shipping Containers," *Journal of Maritime Law & Commerce* 507 (1974); Tallman Bissel, "The Operational Realities of Containerization and Their Effects on the 'Package' Limitation and the 'On-Deck' Prohibition: Review and Suggestions," 45 *Tulane Law Review* 902 (1971); Laurence B. Alexander, "Containerization, the Per Package Limitation, and the Concept of 'Fair Opportunity,'" 11 *The Maritime Lawyer* 123 (1986).

Under the International Chamber of Commerce's **Rules for Multimodal Transport Documents**, the carrier must prove during which stage of the multimodal transport the damage occurred. It also places a presumption in favor of the shipper in the event that the carrier does not meet its burden. If the stage during which the damage occurred cannot be established, "the system of liability most favorable to the claimant of the relevant modes of transport is deemed to apply."[32]

Containerization poses a number of concerns as it relates to the application of COGSA. First, multimodal transport raises questions about the continued relevancy and importance of the traditional ocean bill of lading, given that newer multimodal transport documents have become increasingly popular. Second, can a container filled with packages of goods be itself considered a single package for purposes of calculating per package liability? The Hague-Visby Rules provide guidance in defining the word *package*. It states that "where a container, pallet, or similar article of transport is used to consolidate goods, the number of packages or units enumerated in the bill of lading as packed in such article of transport shall be deemed the number of packages or units."[33] Courts, in order to protect shippers, have generally held that a container cannot be considered a package. This is especially true when the bill of lading lists a more specific number of units or packages. The more specific description prevails over any general statement referring to the number of "containers."

The court in *Marcraft Clothes, Inc. v. M/V Kurobe Maru*[34] held that multimodal containers are generally not to be considered as packages for the calculation of COGSA liability of the common carrier. The enumeration on the bill of lading that the container was filled with 4,400 men's suits made each suit a "package" for purposes of COGSA liability. The issue remains, however, whether the common carrier can expressly designate the container as the package for purposes of COGSA's per-package limitation. Generally, courts have rejected the notion that a container can be designated as a package to limit the carrier's liability to $500 for the entire shipment.

In *All Pacific Trading v. Vessel M/V Hanjin Yosu*,[35] the carrier inserted the following clause into the bill of lading: "Where the cargo has been packed into containers it is expressly agreed that the number of such containers shown on the face hereof shall be considered the number of packages for the purpose of the application of the limitation of liability provided for herein." The carrier further argued that the container was the proper package because the rate agreement was determined by the number of containers and not by the number of packages within the containers. The court rejected the carrier's arguments that the containers were indeed the "packages." It focused on the fact that elsewhere on the bill of lading there was a listing of the number of packages in each container.[36]

---

32. Frank G. M. Smeele, "The Contract of Carriage" in *International Contracts: Aspects of Jurisdiction, Arbitration and Private International Law* 257 (Marieele Koppenol-Laforce, ed. 1996).

33. Hague-Visby Rules, art. IV(5)(c).

34. 575 F. Supp. 239 (S.D.N.Y. 1983).

35. 7 F.3d 1427 (9th Cir. 1993).

36. See also *Universal Leaf Tobacco Co. v. Companhia De Navegacao Maritima Netumar*, 993 F.2d 414 (4th Cir. 1993) (courts will not consider a container as a package if the bill of lading discloses the number of packages within the container); *Cia Panameña de Seguros, S.A. v. Prudential Lines, Inc.*, 416 F. Supp. 641 (D.C. 1976) (court rejected bill of lading definition of container as package).

The law on this topic remains unsettled, as indicated by the court in *St. Paul Insurance Co. v. Sea-Land Service*.

The court notes with some trepidation that it is its view that the determination that the $500 per package or per customary freight unit limitation should not apply to a container said to contain packages should be re-examined. Cases seeking to apply the limitation to containers pursuant to bills of lading are all too common particularly because carriers have drafted bills of lading with all sorts of terms relating to its applicability to container shipments. Furthermore, because of reasons of reductions of cost and prevention of theft or damage, containers have become a customary freight unit, if not the customary freight unit recognized by COGSA.[37]

To avoid the classification of a container as a COGSA package, the shipper should request a detailed description in the bill of lading expressly stating the number of packages within each container.

Material Deviation

The next three sections explore areas of carrier fault that result in the removal of a carrier's liability limitation under the per-package rule. The three areas where the common carrier is held to be fully liable for all damages are material deviation, failure to give fair opportunity to declare a higher value, and **misdelivery**. The first of these three areas of full carrier liability is reviewed in this section. Material deviation claims can generally be divided into two groups: those involving the above-deck carriage of goods and those involving a change in the expected route of the ship.

Above-deck carriage has historically been considered a material deviation, but this claim has severely diminished in modern times. The advent of containerization and more powerful ships has made above-deck carriage commonplace, in that containers help protect the cargo from the adverse conditions of sea travel. As a result, on-deck carriage of containerized cargo is not a deviation if the carrier proves an established custom of such storage. On-deck storage of containers may also be deemed reasonable and therefore not a material deviation. Furthermore, modern ships allow for larger cargo capacity by stacking containers below and above the deck. For this reason, ocean carriage has become more efficient and reasonable. Most bills of lading now reflect the practice of above-deck carriage by the incorporation of a clause paramount.

The court in *DuPont de Nemours International v. Mormacvega*[38] recognized an implied exception to the COGSA principle that carriage on the deck of the ship is a material deviation. It held that it is not an unreasonable deviation from the carriage contract to carry the goods above deck if the ship is one designed for above-deck containerized carriage. This can be seen as judicial recognition of the technological developments since the writing of the Hague Rules.

The common carrier generally prevents a material deviation claim for above-deck carriage by inserting a clause paramount in the bill of lading. In essence, the shipper agrees to allow the common carrier to decide whether the goods are to be carried below or above deck. The clause asserts that the Hague Rules (COGSA) or

---

37.   745 F. Supp. 186, 189 (S.D.N.Y. 1990).
38.   493 F.2d 97 (2d Cir. 1974). See also *Electro-Tec Corp. v. S.S. Dart Atlantica*, 598 F. Supp. 929 (D. Md. 1984).

other pertinent convention will apply to goods stowed above deck. The following clause is an example of a clause paramount.

http://

For an example of a more expansive clause paramount:
http://www.oocl.com/ BL/Terms_p3.htm.

The bill of lading shall have effect subject to all the provisions of the Carriage of Goods by Sea Act of the United States, as approved on April 16, 1936. The defenses and limitations of said Act shall apply to goods whether carried on or under the deck, to carriage of goods between U.S. ports, or between non-U.S. ports, before the goods are loaded on and after they are discharged from the vessel, and throughout the entire time the goods are in the actual custody of Carrier, whether acting as carrier, bailee, or stevedore. Carrier shall be entitled to the full benefit of all rights and immunity under and all limitations and exemptions from liability contained in any law of the United States or any other place whose law shall be compulsorily applicable. If any term of this bill of lading be repugnant to the Carriage of Goods by Sea Act or any other law compulsorily applicable, such term only shall be void. This bill of lading shall be construed and the rights of the parties determined according to the laws of the United States.[39]

This clause does more than simply extend COGSA to above-deck carriage. It also extends COGSA's coverage beyond tackle-to-tackle to the entire period that the goods are in the possession of the carrier. Some courts have recognized this extension of COGSA even when the bill of lading fails to incorporate such a clause.[40] It also extends COGSA protection to all third parties involved with the transport of the goods by sea including stevedores and preempts the application of the Harter Act extending coverage to shipments between U.S. ports. Finally, it selects U.S. law as the law to be used to interpret the carriers' obligations and liabilities under the bill of lading. The *American Home Assurance Co. v. M/V Tabuk* case that follows reviews the material deviation doctrine with respect to above-deck storage.

American Home Assurance Co. v. M/V Tabuk

170 F. Supp.2d 431 (S.D.N.Y. 2001)

Marrero, District Court Judge. American Home Assurance Company ("American Home") brings this action, pursuant to the Carriage of Goods by Sea Act ("COGSA"), seeking recovery of the value of certain cargo lost during trans-Atlantic transport by defendants United Arab Shipping Company (S.A.G.) and M/V TABUK (hereinafter collectively referred to as "United Arab"). Prior to the start of the bench trial in this action, the Court granted judgment to American Home on the issue of liability and thereafter conducted a trial limited to the issue of damages. The Court now sets forth its findings of fact and conclusions of law.

Plaintiff American Home was the marine cargo insurer of certain cargo described below and is subrogated to the rights of Raytheon Systems Company ("Raytheon"),

the beneficiary of Hughes Aircraft Systems International ("Hughes"). Defendant TABUK is a ship employed in the common carriage of merchandise by water for hire, and United Arab is the owner of the TABUK.

On or about February 12, 1999, Hughes delivered one hundred Tow 2A missiles (the "Cargo")—manufactured by Raytheon—to defendants at the port in Wilmington, North Carolina for delivery to the Kuwait National Guard. The Cargo was placed into nine pallets; eight pallets contained twelve missiles, and one pallet contained four missiles. The nine pallets were loaded into a 20-foot ocean shipping container for transport. The bill of lading provides that goods "may be carried on deck at the ocean carrier's option and if carried on deck shall not be required to specifically note, mark or stamp any statement

---

39.   This clause was taken from *St. Paul Fire & Marine Insurance v. Sea-Land Service, Inc.*, 745 F.Supp. 186, 188 (S.D.N.Y. 1990).

40.   See, e.g., *Binladen BSB Landscaping v. M.V. Nedlloyd Rotterdam*, 759 F.2d 1006 (2d Cir. 1985), *cert. denied*, 474 U.S. 902 (1985).

of on-deck carriage on this bill of lading any custom to the contrary notwithstanding."

United Arab undertook to transport the Cargo to Kuwait aboard the TABUK and stowed the Cargo on-deck. On or about February 15, 1999, the container with the Cargo was lost overboard during a storm while the TABUK was traveling in the North Atlantic Ocean.

Raytheon had insured the Cargo with American Home. As a result of the loss of the Cargo, Raytheon submitted a claim to American Home for $2,560,250.00. American Home paid the claim and now seeks recovery of this amount in damages from United Arab.

In this case, American Home has contended that stowage of the Cargo on the TABUK's deck constitutes a deviation. At trial, American Home argued that the deviation in this case was unreasonable because (1) stowage did not conform with the ship's Cargo Securing Manual; (2) the total number of containers on deck exceeded the figure represented in the Lloyd's Register of Shipping and in the TABUK's own brochure as the number of containers that could be safely loaded on deck; and (3) the chain used to secure the Raytheon container was deficient in terms of its safe working load.

In opposition, while United Arab concedes that even if stowage on deck is a deviation, United Arab had expressly reserved the discretion in the bill of lading to employ such stowage, and that it was reasonable to do so because of safety and commercial concerns. United Arab further argues it does not lose its limitation even if it was negligent, grossly negligent or reckless in connection with stowage of the Cargo.

To the extent American Home argues that carriers should not benefit from the limitation because they were negligent, such culpability is not an unreasonable deviation. Mere negligence, lack of due diligence, or a failure to properly handle, stow, care, or deliver cargo, never has constituted deviation.

Moreover, even if stowage on deck had been a contractual deviation, it would have been a reasonable one. In *Du Pont de Nemours Int'l S.A. v. S.S. Mormacvega*, 493 F.2d 97 (2d Cir. 1974), the Second Circuit observed that "technological innovation and vessel design may justify stowage other than below deck" and affirmed a trial court's determination that on-deck stowage of a container on a specially designed container ship constituted a reasonable deviation. Since Du Pont, courts have held as a matter of law that on-deck stowage on container ships designed for such stowage is reasonable. Here, the Court finds that the TABUK was modified to carry containers on its deck, and that the modifications permitted the safe carriage of such goods on deck.

Moreover, the Court understands that hazardous materials like the Cargo are usually stored on deck; that it is not safe to store such materials below deck because it is more difficult to fight and contain a fire below deck and because the potential damage from fire and explosions are vastly greater below deck; and that for these reasons all other hazardous materials were stored on-deck. In addition, the Court finds that deck stowage was used before on TABUK voyages. For these reasons, the Court concludes that any deviation here was reasonable.

American Home argues that it is entitled to recover approximately $2,560,250.00 which represents the value of the 100 rockets at the time of loss. United Arab argues that the carrier may limit liability to $500 per package in accordance with the provisions of COGSA and suggests that its liability is either $4,500 (9 packages) or $50,000 (100 packages), depending on whether the number of COGSA packages are the number of pallets shipped (9) or the number of boxes shipped (100). The Court has reviewed the bill of lading which contains a reference to 100 rockets but does not refer to packages of any kind. Accordingly, the Court finds that United Arab is liable for the 100 packages lost at sea and is directed to pay $50,000.00 to American Home.

Case Highlights

- A carrier's negligence, lack of due diligence, or failure to properly handle, stow, care, or deliver cargo does not constitute a deviation.
- On-deck stowage on container ships designed for such stowage is reasonable and does not constitute a material deviation.
- On-deck stowage for the purpose of safety is reasonable and does not constitute a material deviation.

The second ground for a claim of material deviation is an unreasonable route change. If the common carrier fails to follow a customary or reasonable shipping route, then it will be liable for damages resulting from late delivery. A defense to a material deviation in the route would be a change resulting from an emergency, such as mechanical failure or governmental intervention. For example, it would be reasonable for the common carrier to follow instructions to dock at a port for required government inspection or to change route to avoid hostilities. Courts have been reluctant to extend the material deviation doctrine beyond on-deck stowage and route changes. This reluctance is addressed in the *SPM Corporation v. M/V Ming Moon* case that follows.

SPM Corp. v. M/V Ming Moon
965 F. Supp. 1297 (3d Cir. 1992)

Becker, Circuit Court Judge. SPM Corporation ("SPM") was the owner and importer of certain plastic injection molding machines that were shipped from Yokohama, Japan, to Norfolk, Virginia, in June 1988. The shipment consisted of three crates; the one that was eventually damaged weighed 20,400 kilograms. SPM had purchased the machinery for $243,000, and had arranged to resell it to a third party, Canon USA, Inc., for $255,000.

The manufacturer and shipper of the machines, Sumitomo Heavy Industries ("SHI"), engaged Blue Anchor Line ("Blue Anchor") to arrange for transport of the machines. Blue Anchor issued an ocean bill of lading for the shipment, which was negotiated to SPM, the consignee. Blue Anchor never actually handled the cargo, and instead subcontracted with Yangming Marine Transport Corporation ("Yangming") to perform the actual ocean carriage on board the *Ming Moon*, a container vessel. Yangming issued its own ocean bill of lading to Blue Anchor's agent in Japan.

The *Ming Moon* followed its published itinerary and put in at Los Angeles, California, and Savannah, Georgia, before stopping on July 8, 1988 at another intermediate port, Port Elizabeth, New Jersey. At Port Elizabeth, Maher Terminals, Inc. ("Maher"), Yangming's contract stevedore there, restowed SPM's cargo. More specifically, pursuant to Yangming's instructions, Maher's employees removed SPM's cargo from the vessel in order to stow other cargo in the lower hold of the *Ming Moon*, and reloaded SPM's cargo on board the ship. Yangming ordered the restowage to make room for other cargo on the return trip to Japan and to have SPM's oversized cargo relocated so that it would remain accessible for discharge at Norfolk. According to the district court's finding of fact, restowage is a common practice in the maritime trade.

During this restowage, one of SPM's packages was damaged due to negligence by Maher's employees. After the cargo was delivered in Norfolk, the damaged package was declared a constructive total loss. SPM recovered approximately $15,000 in salvage parts, but suffered a net loss of approximately $228,000. SPM then sued Blue Anchor, Yangming, and Maher, seeking recovery of its damages.

The case was tried to the district court. SPM has appealed from the court's order dated August 26, 1991, which found Blue Anchor, Yangming, and Maher liable to SPM, but only in the amount of $500 each, plus pre-judgment interest.

SPM argues that no liability limitation should apply as to any of the defendants because the restowage of its cargo by Yangming and Maher constituted a "deviation" from the carriage agreement that converted the carriers into quasi-insurers liable in full for any damage incurred as a result. The defendants counter that the harsh doctrine of deviation should be limited to carriers' geographical departures from course and to unauthorized on-deck stowage of cargo, and should not be extended to a customary practice such as restowage at an intermediate port.

COGSA recognizes that unreasonable deviations can violate the Act, and most courts have held that an unreasonable deviation also lifts a carrier's liability limitations, including the $500 per package limitation. COGSA affirmatively provides, however, that reasonable deviations do not oust the contract of carriage (or COGSA limitations on liability), and the statute gives courts guidance on which deviations should be considered reasonable.

Unfortunately, COGSA does not define "deviation" itself, which is a predicate for reaching the distinct issues of reasonableness and the consequences of an unreasonable deviation. Lacking a statutory definition of "deviation," courts have offered various definitions of their own. Analysts distinguish between geographic deviations and other, "quasi-deviations." In this case, there was no geographical deviation: the *Ming Moon* followed its advertised course of voyage. SPM's only serious claim is that restowage of cargo at an intermediate port constitutes a quasi-deviation.

Quasi-deviation is a doctrine seemingly entrenched in the law, but not, apparently, expanding in scope. The usual example has been unauthorized on-deck stowage of cargo. Plaintiffs have frequently pressed for expansion beyond that class of cases, but in recent years courts of appeals have generally declined to do so. We agree with our sister circuits that the doctrine of quasi-deviation should not be viewed expansively in the post-COGSA era. Although COGSA did not abolish the doctrine of deviation, the statute's very existence and broad scope obviate the need for an expansive concept of deviation to protect shippers, and the statutory limitation on deviations suggests that courts should construe the doctrine narrowly. At all events, in this case we need not decide that quasi-deviations can never encompass more than unauthorized on-deck stowage because SPM's claim would be an unprecedented expansion of the doctrine.

We refuse to declare the intentional restowage of SPM's cargo at an intermediate port a quasi-deviation. Conduct that is customary in the trade is not a deviation from the contractual voyage because such contracts ordinarily presume that the parties will follow the customs and usages of the maritime trade. Here the district court has found that intermediate port restowage is customary, and that finding is not clearly erroneous. Therefore, the district court properly concluded that no quasi-deviation deprived the defendants of their contractual and statutory limits on liability.

We conclude that the district court correctly held that negligent restowage of cargo at an intermediate port is not a deviation that abrogates contractual and statutory limitations on liability. Accordingly, the district court properly limited the liability of Yangming and Maher to SPM to $500.

Case Highlights

- The doctrine of deviation is limited to carriers' geographical departures from course.
- The doctrine of quasi-deviation is limited to unauthorized on-deck stowage of cargo and cannot be extended to conduct that is customary in the trade, such as restowage at an intermediate port.
- COGSA's breadth serves to narrow the concept of deviation.

Fair Opportunity

The per-package limitation afforded to carriers has a limited number of exceptions. One exception is when the shipper is not given a fair opportunity to declare a higher per-package value for the goods. Courts will carefully examine the bill of lading itself in deciding whether the common carrier has fulfilled its fair opportunity responsibilities. The court in *Komatsu, Ltd. v. States Steamship Co.*[41] held that common carriers' fair opportunity obligations are satisfied when they incorporate the language of Section 1304(5) on the *face* of the bill of lading. The *Travelers Indemnity Co. v. Waterman Steamship Corp.* case that follows further explores the nuances of the carrier's duty to provide an opportunity to declare a higher value.

Travelers Indemnity Co. v. Waterman Steamship Corp. ("The Vessel Sam Houston")

26 F.3d 895 (9th Cir. 1994)

Wiggins, Circuit Judge. This action arose when a barge owned and operated by Waterman sank in the inner harbor of Alexandria, Egypt. The barge was carrying machinery and materials for appellant's assured. The shipment consisted of steel, valves, pumps, and other materials to be used in the erection of sewage treatment plants and elevated water tanks. Travelers sustained a loss of $1,174,876 when a portion of the cargo was lost or damaged. Travelers brought suit against Waterman in federal district court. The district court found that the $500 per package or per customary freight unit limitation on liability, set forth in the Carriage of Goods by Sea Act (COGSA), controlled. In addition, the district court found that 77 "packages" were damaged or lost. Thus, the district court entered final judgment for $38,500.

---

41.   674 F.2d 806 (9th Cir. 1982).

COGSA regulates the liability of international carriers for loss or damage to cargo. Specifically, Section 4(5) of COGSA provides that a carrier is liable for $500 per package or per customary freight unit. 46 U.S.C. § 1304(5). The shipper may increase the carrier's liability, however, by declaring on the bill of lading the nature and value of the goods shipped and paying a higher freight rate. A carrier may take advantage of COGSA's $500 per package or per customary freight unit limitation on liability "only if the shipper is given a 'fair opportunity' to opt for a higher liability by paying a correspondingly greater charge."

The fair opportunity requirement is meant to give the shipper notice of the legal consequences of failing to opt for a higher carrier liability. Thus, the carrier must "bear an initial burden of producing *prima facie* evidence that demonstrates that it provided notice of a choice of liabilities and rates to the shipper." Normally, the carrier can meet this initial burden by showing that the language of COGSA Section 4(5) is contained in the bill of lading. Travelers offered two pieces of evidence. First, L.A. Water submitted to Waterman prior to shipment the export declaration it prepared for customs. This export declaration reported the value of the total cargo to be $6,000,000. Second, Waterman's bill of lading did not contain a designated space in which to declare a higher value. Travelers noted that the *Nemeth* court considered "the fact that the bill of lading contains no designated place for an excess value declaration" to be evidence that the shipper did not have a fair opportunity to opt out of COGSA's liability limitation.

The export declaration does not, in fact, constitute evidence that the shipper "would have opted for a higher liability had it been given a fair opportunity to do so." The party in this case was a sophisticated shipper of goods. And it had shipped its goods with Waterman on several previous occasions. Thus, the shipper was familiar with Waterman's shipping procedures and its bill of lading. Second, a designated place for an excess value declaration is not mandatory. AFFIRMED.

Case Highlights

- A common carrier can take advantage of the $500 per package limitation only if it gives the shipper a "fair opportunity" to declare a higher value.
- A common carrier generally meets its burden to provide a fair opportunity to declare a higher value by incorporating the language of Section 4(5) of COGSA into the bill of lading.
- Designating a space on the front of the bill of lading to declare a higher value is not required by COGSA.
- A statement of higher value in a document other than the bill of lading, even if provided to the common carrier, is of no consequence.

Misdelivery of Goods

Under COGSA, the carrier is obligated to deliver the goods to the holder, and only the holder, of the bill of lading. A cause of action accrues to the shipper in the event that delivery is made to someone not holding the bill of lading. The common carrier is liable for misdelivery, even after the goods are discharged from its ship, because the carrier remains a **bailee** of the goods until they are delivered to the holder of the bill of lading. The *law of bailment* places special duties of care on a party (bailee) who is entrusted with the goods of another party.

The special status of the common carrier under the law of bailment is explored in the *Allied Chemical International Corp. v. Companhia de Navegacao Lloyd Brasileiro* case. In addition, the case illustrates that even though the bill of lading is the universally accepted document of title, national maritime customs and shipping practices need to be understood to protect against misdelivery. Misdelivery can occur when a country's import documentation allows for such a release or when the receiving party and the common carrier make alternative arrangements.

Alternative arrangements are sometimes made for delivery to someone not holding a bill of lading. In one common practice, the common carrier agrees to release the goods to a consignee, not in possession of the bill of lading, upon the presentment of a bank guarantee. The bank guarantee absolves the carrier from

Allied Chemical International Corp. v. Companhia de Navegacao Lloyd Brasileiro

775 F.2d 476 (2d Cir. 1985)

Meskill, Circuit Judge. Companhia de Navegacao Lloyd Brasileiro (Lloyd), an ocean carrier, appeals from a judgment of the United States District Court for the Southern District of New York finding Lloyd liable to Allied Chemical International Corporation (Allied), a shipper, for the misdelivery of goods to the consignee, Banylsa Tecelagem do Brasil S.A. (Banylsa). The carrier caused the goods to be delivered without requiring Banylsa to produce the original order bill of lading.

Allied, an exporter of chemical products, received from Banylsa an order for a quantity of caprolactam, a crystalline cyclic amide used in the manufacture of nylon. The sale was to be in two lots of 6,000 bags on terms of sight drafts against documents through Banco Bamerindus do Brasil S.A. of Sao Paulo, Brazil (Brazilian bank). Lloyd's vessel arrived at the Port of Salvador and in accordance with local custom and usage, the carrier unloaded the caprolactam at a warehouse under the control of the Administration of the Port of Salvador, an agency of the Brazilian government.

Banylsa requested and received from Lloyd in accordance with Brazilian import regulations a "carta declaratoria," a letter declaring that the freight had been paid at the port of origin and that the Merchant Marine Renewal Tax had been paid in Salvador. By virtue of the *carta declaratoria*, Banylsa was able to obtain possession although it had not paid for the goods and it was not in possession of the bill of lading. Soon thereafter, Banylsa filed a voluntary receivership proceeding in the Civil Court of the District of Salvador, Brazil. Allied made a demand on Lloyd for losses incurred as a result of the carrier's failure to request proper documentation before authorizing the release of the caprolactam.

The liability question in this case inextricably involves the critical importance of the documentary transaction in overseas trade. The documentary sale enables the distant seller to protect himself from an insolvent or fraudulent foreign buyer by ensuring that the buyer ordinarily cannot take possession of the goods until he has paid for them. It accomplishes this rather simply. The seller tenders shipping documents, including a negotiable bill of lading, rather than goods to the buyer. By paying for the documents, the buyer gets possession of the original bill of lading.

Possession of the bill of lading entitles the holder to possession of the goods; it represents the goods and conveys title to them. Most likely, the bill will be an order bill of lading, made to the order of or endorsed to the buyer. The carrier, the issuer of the bill of lading, is responsible for releasing the cargo only to the party who presents the original bill of lading. Delivery to the consignee named in the bill of lading does not suffice to discharge the carrier where the consignee does not hold the bill of lading. If the carrier delivers the goods to one other than the authorized holder of the bill of lading, the carrier is liable for misdelivery.

Lloyd contends that clauses 1 and 12 of the bill of lading absolve it from liability. Clause 1 provides that "the Carrier shall not be liable in any capacity whatsoever for any delay, nondelivery or misdelivery, or loss of or damage to the goods occurring while the goods are not in the actual custody of the Carrier." Clause 12 provides that "the responsibility of the Carrier, in any capacity, shall altogether cease and the goods shall be considered to be delivered and at their own risk and expense in every respect when taken into the custody of customs or other authorities." However, when Lloyd discharged the cargo, it assumed the status of a bailee. A bailee is absolutely liable for misdelivering cargo. Therefore, under COGSA, the Harter Act (which still governs the periods prior to loading and after the goods are discharged until proper delivery is made), and the law of bailment, Lloyd is liable for misdelivery. The judgment of the district court is AFFIRMED.

Case Update

The U.S. Supreme Court declined to grant certiorari to hear the case in *Allied Chemical International v. Companhia de Navegacao Lloyd Brasileiro*, 475 U.S. 1099 (1986).

Case Highlights

- The issuer of the bill of lading is responsible for releasing the cargo only to the party who presents the original bill of lading.
- A common carrier is considered as a *bailee* of the goods put in its charge. Therefore, it may be liable in the law of bailment even after it discharges its obligations under COGSA.
- Despite the protections provided under COGSA and other carriage conventions, it is important to know the local customs and practices of the country of importation.

any liability for misdelivery. Note that the carrier remains liable for misdelivery under COGSA but is able to seek indemnification through the guarantee.

In *C-Art, Ltd. v. Hong Kong Islands Line America, S.A.*,[42] the parties' prior course of dealing allowed the importer to present a bank guarantee, rather than wait to receive the bill of lading. However, instead of presenting its normal bank guarantee, the buyer presented a corporate guarantee and received a release of the goods. The court held the carrier liable for misdelivery by reasoning that "the carrier, the issuer of the bill of lading, is responsible for releasing the cargo only to the party who presents the original bill of lading."[43] Even if the importer had presented a bank guarantee or indemnity, the carrier still remains liable to the shipper for misdelivery unless the shipper-seller expressly agreed to such a delivery arrangement.

COGSA Exemptions

If the carrier fulfills its obligations as outlined previously, then its liability is limited to not more than $500 per package. In addition, it obtains the protection of **seventeen COGSA exemptions** (see Comparative Law: The Seventeen COGSA Exemptions). There are sixteen enumerated exemptions and one catchall, the **Q-clause exception**. The enumerated exemptions include losses due to errors in navigation and management of the ship, fire, perils of the sea, acts of God, war, acts of public enemies, government seizure, quarantine restrictions, act or omission of the shipper, strikes, wastage due to inherent vice, insufficiency of packing, and latent

---

The Seventeen COGSA Exemptions

COMPARATIVE LAW

Neither the carrier nor the ship shall be responsible for loss or damage arising or resulting from:

(a) Act, neglect, or default of master or employees in the navigation or in the management of the ship.
(b) Fire.
(c) Perils of the sea.
(d) Act of God.
(e) Act of war.
(f) Act of public enemies.
(g) Arrest or restraint or seizure under legal process.
(h) Quarantine restrictions.
(i) Act or omission of the shipper or owner of the goods or their agents or representatives.

(j) Strikes, lock-outs, or stoppage of labor.
(k) Riots and civil commotions.
(l) Saving or attempting to save life or property at sea.
(m) Wastage in bulk or weight or any other loss arising from inherent defect, quality or vice of the goods.
(n) Insufficiency of packing.
(o) Insufficiency of marks.
(p) Latent defects not discoverable by due diligence.
(q) Any other cause arising without actual fault or privity of the carrier, but the burden of proof shall be on the person claiming the benefit of this exception.

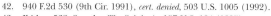

42.   940 F.2d 530 (9th Cir. 1991), *cert. denied*, 503 U.S. 1005 (1992).
43.   Ibid. at 532. See also *The Caledonia*, 157 U.S. 124 (1895).

defects. Perils of the sea include violent or catastrophic storms but not normal storms at sea. Latent defects are those defects not discoverable by due diligence.

The courts have narrowly interpreted most of the exemptions in order to allow shippers to collect on their claims. For example, the latent defect exception has not provided carriers much protection, even when they perform due diligence inspections and testing. The Q-clause exception grants the carrier a general exemption for any damages that arise from a cause that was not the actual fault of the carrier or those of the agents or servants of the carrier. However, COGSA states that the burden of proof is on the carrier to prove that its fault or negligence had not contributed to the loss or damage. Courts have rarely granted an exemption from liability under the Q clause. If there is any possibility that the loss or damage occurred while the goods were in the possession of the carrier, no matter how remote, then the court will probably rule against the carrier's claim of a Q-clause exemption.

Damage to goods attributable to one of these seventeen causes, nonetheless, relieves the carrier of *all* liability. In contrast, the Hamburg Rules eliminate these exceptions and provide a presumption of carrier liability for loss except when occasioned by a fire. In addition, COGSA requires the consignee to make a notice of loss "before or after the time of the removal of the cargo, if apparent."[44] It further provides a limitation period of one year for any claims of loss. The Hamburg Rules allow a claim of loss within one working day after delivery to the consignee. The limitation period is extended to two years. COGSA provides for liability when goods are lost or damaged but makes no mention of liability for a delay in delivery.[45] The Hamburg Rules designate "delay" as an equal ground for recovery.[46]

The *Sony Magnetic Products Inc. v. Merivienti* case that follows further elaborates on the shifting burden of proof between the carrier and the shipper. It also serves to highlight the enumerated exemption of latent defect. Then the *Lamb Head Shipping v. Jennings* case reviews the perils of the sea exemption and how it interrelates with the carrier's duty of due diligence.

Sony Magnetic Products Inc. v. Merivienti

863 F.2d 1537 (11th Cir. 1989)

Kravitch, Circuit Judge. Sony Magnetic Products, Inc., of America contacted Page & Jones, a freight forwarder with offices in Mobile, Alabama, to arrange for the transportation of a container of video cassette tapes to England. Page & Jones reserved space for Sony's cargo with Atlantic Cargo Services on board the *Finnhawk*. Sony packed its cargo of video cassette tapes into a standard shipping container, measuring 40 feet long by 8 feet wide by 8 feet high. As the *Finnhawk's* deck crane was lifting the container of Sony's tapes up to the vessel's cargo deck, the hydraulic motor of the crane exploded causing the container to drop approximately 60 feet to the concrete loading deck below.

The first issue on appeal is whether the district court properly imposed liability on the defendants under COGSA for the damage to Sony's video cassette tapes. A shipper establishes a *prima facie* case under COGSA by proving that the carrier received the cargo in good condition but unloaded it in a damaged condition. A carrier can rebut a shipper's *prima facie* case by establishing either that

---

44. COGSA, 46 U.S.C. App. § 1303(6) (2000).
45. But see *B.F. McKernin & Co. v. United States Lines, Inc.*, 416 F. Supp. 1068 (S.D.N.Y. 1976) (awarding damages for delay in the delivery of goods equal to the price the goods actually brought and the price they would have brought had they been sold on the day that they should have arrived); see also *Santiago v. Sea-Land Service, Inc.*, 366 F. Supp. 1309 (D.P.R. 1973) (awarding damages for delay in the delivery of goods equal to the fair market value on the day goods were to be delivered and the day the goods were actually delivered).
46. See *Hartford Fire Ins. Co. v. Novocargo USA, Inc.*, 257 F. Supp.2d 665, 671–72 (S.D.N.Y. 2003).

it exercised due diligence to prevent the damage to the cargo by properly handling, stowing, and caring for it in a seaworthy ship or that the harm resulted from one of the excepted causes listed in section 1304(2). If the carrier is able to rebut the shipper's *prima facie* case, the burden then shifts back to the shipper to show that the carrier's negligence was, at the least, a concurrent cause of the loss.

The defendants attempted to establish that the accident that caused the damage to Sony's cargo was the result of a latent defect in the motor of the *Finnhawk's* crane, one of the enumerated exceptions. In addition, crew members of the *Finnhawk* maintained that there had been no complaints about or problems with the crane and that it had always been properly maintained and inspected. In pertinent part, § 1304 of COGSA provides as follows:

(2) Neither the carrier nor the ship shall be responsible for loss or damage arising or resulting from—(p) Latent defects not discoverable by due diligence. A latent defect is one that could not be discovered upon reasonable inspection or by any known and customary test.

The district court concluded, as a matter of law, that the defendants had not sustained their burden of proving

that Sony's loss was caused by a latent defect. For the foregoing reasons, the judgment of the district court is AFFIRMED.

Case Highlights

- The bill of lading is often prepared by the freight forwarder, on behalf of the shipper, and submitted to the carrier for signature.
- Presenting a clean bill of lading satisfies the shipper's initial burden of proving that it had delivered cargo in good condition to the carrier.
- A carrier can rebut a shipper's *prima facie* case by establishing either that it exercised due diligence to prevent the damage to the cargo by properly handling, stowing, and caring for it in a seaworthy ship or that the harm resulted from one of the enumerated exemptions or causes.
- The carrier has a heavy burden in proving that the loss was due to a "latent defect."

Lamb Head Shipping v. Jennings
1 Lloyd's L. R. 624 (C.A. 1994)

The *Marel* sailed from Greece to Ghent with a load of Greek corn. While in route it encountered adverse weather conditions with the wind reaching NE force 7 with a swell of about two or three metres. According to the evidence, witnesses felt a "bump" sufficient to cause the crew to be thrown off balance. Less than one hour later the ship sank. The plaintiffs claimed under their marine hull insurance contending that the vessel was lost due to *perils of the sea* which was covered under the policy. The sole issue was whether the loss was caused by perils of the sea.

Justice Dillon. The burden of proving on the balance of probabilities that a vessel was lost by perils of the sea was on the owners. It is not sufficient for the owners merely to prove the incursion of seawater into the insured vessel. In fact, *Marel* was not overwhelmed by exceptionally bad weather. It is very nearly impossible that the only form of unidentified object that was suggested as a possibility, a derelict container, caused the casualty. The crucial question is how the flooding of the engine room came about. The plaintiffs assert that it came about by perils of the sea. "Perils of the sea" does not include the ordinary action of wind and waves.

The primary submission for the plaintiff was that *Marel* had hit a floating container that had fallen from some other ship. However, there was no evidence that there had been any report of any container having been lost in the vicinity. The lower court accordingly found that it was wholly improbable that entry of seawater was due to a collision. Though the general condition of the vessel was good for her age, there had been various botched repairs and the owners were not enthusiastic about spending money unnecessarily. We therefore AFFIRM the lower court's dismissal.

Case Highlights

- The ship owner has the burden to prove a loss due to a "peril of the sea" in making a claim under its marine insurance.
- Perils of the sea do not include the ordinary action of wind and waves.
- Failure to properly repair a ship opens the ship owner to a charge of a lack of due diligence in maintaining the seaworthiness of the vessel.

Freight Forwarders and Multimodal Transport Operators

http://

The role of the freight forwarder and the law of freight forwarding: http://www.itds.treas.gov/freight.html; http://www.unzco.com/basicguide/c10.html; and http://www.forwarderlaw.com.

The final two parts of this chapter focus on the roles and duties of other essential third parties in the transport of goods. These third parties include the **freight forwarder**, **multimodal transport operator**, and **marine insurance company**. The freight forwarder serves three vital functions for importers and exporters by (1) arranging for the shipment of goods with carriers,[47] (2) acting as a freight consolidator, and (3) processing required documentation.

In arranging for the shipment, the forwarder negotiates a freight rate with the carrier as an agent for the shipper. The negative repercussion of the role of the freight forwarder as agent is that it may bind the shipper to modifications made by the carrier to the standard carriage contract. The *Constructores Tecnicos v. Sea-Land Service* case that is next, for example, examines the ability of a freight forwarder to

---

Constructores Tecnicos v. Sea-Land Service, Inc.

945 F.2d 841 (5th Cir. 1991)

King, Circuit Judge. The Honduran government awarded Constructores Tecnicos (Contec), a Honduran company, a contract for the construction of 20 testing wells and 13 water wells in Honduras. In order to perform the work, Contec purchased a Ford LT 9000 Tandem Chassis diesel truck and various drilling accessories, including a portable drilling rig unit from JWS Equipment, Inc., of Moore, Oklahoma. Contec partner Julio Pineda contacted Charles Pagan of Golden Eagle International Forwarding Co. (Golden Eagle), a freight forwarder, and requested that Golden Eagle arrange for transportation of the truck from Oklahoma to Puerto Cortes, Honduras.

Pagan made the transportation arrangements through Sea-Land Service, Inc. (Sea-Land). He filled out a Sea-Land bill of lading, listing the cargo to be shipped but leaving the space for the freight rate blank. The bill of lading did not indicate whether the cargo was to be stowed on deck or below deck. Pagan then delivered the draft bill of lading to Sea-Land's office. The truck and equipment were loaded on the M/V *Vermillion Bay*, a vessel chartered by Sea-Land. The truck and some of the equipment were secured to a flatrack, a form of open container, by chain lashings and stowed on deck.

The M/V *Vermillion Bay* encountered severe weather in the Gulf of Mexico on the fringes of Hurricane Gilbert. During the storm, nearby containers broke free of their lashings causing severe damage to the truck. The ship changed course and docked at Port Everglades,

Florida, where the truck was unloaded and deemed a constructive total loss. Contec brought suit against Golden Eagle, Sea-Land, and International Cargo and Surety Insurance Co. (International Cargo).

COGSA limits an ocean carrier's liability for lost or damaged cargo to $500 per package. A carrier loses this protection, however, if a deviation from the specifications contained in its contract of carriage with the shipper amounts to more than a reasonable deviation. The district court held that a clean bill of lading entitles the shipper to presume below-deck stowage. The lower court, citing a line of authority dating back to the late 19th century, described the legal effect of a clean bill of lading: "A clean bill of lading imports that the goods are to be safely and properly stowed under deck. Absent an express agreement to the contrary or a port custom permitting on-deck stowage, a shipper may presume that a clean bill of lading will result in carriage of the cargo below deck."

The appellants argue that Contec had not dealt directly with the carrier, but rather through an intermediary freight forwarder who had the power to bind the shipper to on-deck shipment. We disagree with appellants' suggestion that there is a hard and fast rule deeming freight forwarders to be agents of shippers. In regard to the shipper's selection of the forwarder, obviously this is an indication that the forwarder's actions can be attributed to the shipper. Control of the manner in

---

47.   The freight forwarder reserves space on the carrier well before the actual shipment date by entering into a *booking contract.*

which the forwarder performs his duties, however, rather than selection, has been the more important factor in deciding the agency question. It is undisputed that the shipper did not control the forwarder's actions in booking cargo. The forwarder was free to select the carrier or line on which to ship the goods and the shipper had little knowledge of the manner in which the forwarder performed its duties, much less controlled the forwarder's performance.

Appellants correctly argue from these facts that Golden Eagle "entered into the contract of carriage on behalf of the shipper," but the conclusion it believes follows—that Golden Eagle's knowledge concerning Sea-Land's practices may be imputed to Contec as a result of an agency relationship—is incorrect without the missing link of control by the shipper over the forwarder's actions. The legal relationship of agency is the threshold question. Only then could the agent's knowledge of the carrier's usual custom of storing oversized containers on deck be deemed sufficient to bind the shipper to a contract in which the shipper consented to on-deck stowage.

If the shipper has in no way consented to on-deck stowage, and cannot be deemed to have done so through a freight forwarder acting as its agent, the law's concern is with the shipper's expectations. WE AFFIRM the judgment awarding damages in excess of the COGSA limitation of liability.

Case Highlights

- The freight forwarder acts as agent for the shipper in selecting a common carrier and booking cargo space.
- The freight forwarder's knowledge of a common carrier's practices that would be deemed to be material deviations is not imputed to the shipper.
- An express provision in the bill of lading or port custom may overcome the presumption in favor of below-deck stowage.

---

bind the shipper to a material deviation. It addresses the question of whether the forwarder acts as an agent for the shipper for purposes of imputing the forwarder's knowledge to the shipper.

It has become common practice for the forwarder to issue carrier-type documents such as the **forwarder's bill of lading** or receipt. In such cases, the forwarder assumes the liability of a carrier or possibly of a multimodal transport operator. Carrier liability, therefore, may extend not only to the actual carriers but also to *contractual* carriers. The freight forwarder also serves the important function of consolidating the shipments of a number of shippers to fill all available space offered by the carrier in order to reduce the freight costs to the individual shippers. Finally, the freight forwarder provides assistance in preparing the necessary documentation needed for customs clearance. **Customs brokers** also deal with customs authorities and help shippers comply with customs regulations.[48]

Multimodal transport operators (MTOs), also known as combined transport operators, arrange for the shipment of goods via different modes of transport, such as sea, rail, road, and air. They enter into separate contracts with the individual carriers. The major benefit to the shipper is that the MTO issues a single transport document for the entire transport. The shipper may make a claim for loss against the MTO, no matter where the loss occurs during the transport.

Because of the increased use of MTOs and freight forwarders as common carriers, the **through bill of lading** has become a more commonly used document of title. The through bill of lading and the liabilities that emanate from it are explained in the *Mannesman Demag Corp.* case that follows. The case also explains

---

48. See Chapter Six, National Export and Import Regulation.

how containerization has transformed the shipping industry and its legal regimes, along with the continued use of the Harter Act to fill gaps in coverage before and after the goods are loaded or discharged from a ship.

Mannesman Demag Corp. v. M/V Concert Express

225 F.3d 587 (5th Cir. 2000)

Smith, Circuit Judge. This case arises from damage sustained to an oxygen compressor owned by Mannesman while in transport from Bremerhaven, Germany, to Terre Haute, Indiana. Atlantic carried the goods from Bremerhaven to the Port of Baltimore, Maryland, aboard the M/V *Concert Express.* Trism carried the goods from Baltimore to Terre Haute. While in route from Baltimore to Terre Haute, the goods were damaged when Trism's trailer overturned.

There was only one bill of lading for the entire transportation, issued by Atlantic, reflecting an agreement to transport the goods from Bremerhaven, Germany, to the midwestern United States. The bill is what is called a "through bill of lading." A through bill of lading is one by which an ocean carrier agrees to transport goods to their final destination. Someone else (e.g., railroad, trucker, or air carrier) performs a portion of the contracted carriage. The bill obligates the common carrier to transport the cargo "through" the port to its ultimate destination.

This case presents an issue of first impression regarding the applicability of federal maritime statutes to inland transport under a through bill of lading. Until the advent of the containerization of cargo, the cargo owner typically would enter into a new shipment contract with a new carrier each time the mode of transport changed. An inland carrier—a railroad, trucker, or, in some cases, an inland barge operator—would carry the goods to a seaport under one contract of carriage. There someone, usually a "freight forwarder" acting on behalf of the cargo owner, would arrange to place the goods in the hands of a steamship line. Different legal regimes arose to govern the parties' rights and liabilities, depending upon the mode of shipment. If the railroad did the damage, then the rules of liability governing railroads would apply. Maritime law would govern the liability of the steamship or ocean leg of the transport.

Along came multimodal or intermodal shipping containers and everything changed. Now, the same steel cargo container can move freely between different modes of transport. Ocean carriers began to offer "door to door" service. Rail carriers, truckers, or other transporters now contract, not with the owner of the goods, but as a subcontractor to the steamship line who

has offered a complete transport package. The U.S. Carriage of Goods by Sea Act (COGSA) governs the liability of an ocean carrier on an international through bill of lading. COGSA contains important benefits to the carrier. Inland carriers frequently attempt to take advantage of the benefits afforded by COGSA.

One of COGSA's most important provisions limits a carrier's liability to five hundred dollars ($500) per package unless a higher value is declared by the shipper. COGSA also contains a one-year limitation for cargo claims. By its terms, COGSA applies "tackle-to-tackle" only; it does not extend to losses that occur prior to loading or subsequent to discharge from a vessel. A Period of Responsibility Clause can be used to extend COGSA's application to the entire time the goods are within the carrier's custody.

Atlantic's bill references two statutes, the Carriage of Goods by Sea Act (COGSA) and the Harter Act. Under COGSA, a carrier of goods in international commerce must "properly and carefully load, handle, stow, carry, keep, care for, and discharge the goods carried." The Harter Act imposes a duty of "proper loading, stowage, custody, care, and proper delivery." Although the Harter Act's applicability to international commerce was partially superseded by COGSA, COGSA is applicable only from the time goods are loaded onto the ship until the time the cargo is released from the ship's tackle at port. Therefore, the Harter Act applies to the period between the discharge of the cargo from the vessel and "proper delivery."

Atlantic's bill of lading provides that, to the extent the Harter Act is compulsorily applicable, the Carrier's "responsibility shall be subject to COGSA." It further states that "where COGSA applies, the Carrier shall not be or become liable for any loss or damage in an amount per package or unit in excess of $500." Therefore, if the Harter Act is compulsorily applicable to Trism's inland transport, the court correctly limited Atlantic's liability to $500 per package. The Harter Act is at its core a maritime law; the Court is unwilling to rule that simply because private parties enter an intermodal agreement federal maritime legislation is thus extended far beyond its congressionally intended bounds. The Harter Act is designed solely to regulate the liability of seagoing carriers. That said, the Court finds that the Harter Act does reach to the point at which goods are loaded onto the vehicles of an inland trucker, whether hired by the shipper or the carrier.

In this age of "containerized" cargoes subject to "multimodal" bills of lading, it is often difficult to locate precisely the points of legal delivery. Increasing efficiency and integration in cargo transport continues to blur the lines separating sea carrier responsibilities from those of others. The Court finds it advisable to keep sea carriers to the standards imposed by the Harter Act until goods are in the hands of land carriers and actually leaving the maritime arena. With COGSA covering carriers' legal responsibilities through discharge, Harter fills a potential gap between discharge and inland transit in those situations where goods, though on the dock, are still within the control and responsibility of the sea carrier.

Case Highlights

- A through bill of lading is one by which an ocean carrier or MTO agrees to transport goods to their final destination.
- The Harter Act fills a potential gap between discharge and inland transit in those situations where goods, though on the dock, are still within the control and responsibility of the sea carrier.
- The Harter Act does reach the point at which goods are loaded onto the vehicles of an inland trucker, whether hired by the shipper or by the carrier.

Marine Insurance

Under international conventions, such as the Hague Rules and Warsaw Convention, a common carrier's liability is frequently limited. Buyers or sellers of goods protect themselves from carrier liability limitations by making arrangements for cargo insurance against losses due to damage or delay in transit. If the buyer or seller neglect to obtain coverage or obtains too little, damage to the cargo may cause a major financial loss. Therefore, even if the terms of sale make the foreign buyer responsible, the exporter should still contemplate obtaining insurance on its own behalf.

Because of the advent of containerization, an insurance policy or policies have to cover multiple modes of transportation. Shipping goods across national boundaries—from one inland destination to a port of shipment, then to a port of destination and the inland point of destination—involves different types of insurance, including marine, war risk, comprehensive general liability, protection and indemnity, and excess insurance. A further complication is that insurance providers often distribute the risk through reinsurance.[49]

To deal with these different issues of coverage, the transit insurance industry has produced a host of standard forms and clauses. The existence of such standardization, however, should not cloud the fact that the transit insurance policy is often a very specific custom contract. Despite the increasing utilization of form policies, "there are inevitable variations negotiated by the parties. There is simply no substitute for a thorough review of the particular insurance contract in the manner of its negotiation and placement."[50]

---

49. Marine insurance is a contractual relationship between an underwriter and the insured (shipper), whereas reinsurance is a contract between different underwriters. As a general rule, the insurer may not reinsure on broader terms than are found in the underlying policy.
50. Raymond P. Hayden & Sanford E. Balick, "Marine Insurance: Varieties, Combinations, and Coverages," 66 *Tulane Law Review* 311, 313 (1991). Most of the information in this section was gleaned from this article. See generally Arthur E. Brunck, *Ocean Marine Insurance* (1988).

http://

Definitions of
Inchmaree clause and
other cargo insurance
terms: **http://www.
tsbic.com/cargo/
glossary.htm.**

Highly specialized, the marine insurance industry provides a variety of insurance policies, including hull, cargo, and liability policies. These policies protect ship and cargo owners from an assortment of exposures, including damage to goods, damage to the ship, damage to others' property, and liability for injury and death. The most common property coverage is provided by **hull insurance**. The owner or charter party of a vessel generally obtains hull insurance to protect the owner or charter party from losses due to damage to the vessel or its equipment. War risk coverage is ordinarily excluded from the standard hull and cargo policies. The hull policy is a perils-only type of policy in that the insured may collect only for losses resulting from expressly listed causes. Therefore, clauses that extend coverage should be carefully considered.

The two most popular extensions are through the **Inchmaree clause** and the **running down clause**. The Inchmaree or additional perils clause extends the list of covered perils, usually to include losses due to negligence of the crew and damage arising from a latent defect. This clause is also commonly inserted in cargo insurance policies. The running down clause provides protection from liability for damages to another vessel caused by a collision with the insured ship. The best sources for hull insurance forms and clauses are Lloyd's of London and the American Institute's Hull Clauses.

Liability coverage is provided through protection and indemnity insurance, offered through associations of shipping companies popularly known as P & I clubs. The **protection and indemnity (P & I) policy** provides two broad categories of protection: third-party liability and contractual liability protection. Third-party liability coverage protects against damages caused to others on account of marine collision. Contractual liability coverage includes protection against passenger liability, liability for lost and damaged cargo, pollution, and general average. Thus, when a cargo owner or its insurance company sues the common carrier for cargo damage, the carrier's insurance company will be required to defend or pay the claim.

http://

Insurance Services
Office, Inc.: **http://
www.iso.com/.**

With the advent of container transport, the **through-transport policy** form of P & I insurance has become popular. A through-transport policy provides indemnification for third-party damage caused during inland transit. Indemnity policies become operative only upon payment by the insured. Another popular policy is **comprehensive general liability (CGL) coverage**. The **Insurance Services Office (ISO)**, a private trade association, introduced this policy in 1986.[51] The most salient features of CGL policies are their comprehensiveness and their broad duty on the part of the insurer to defend. Thus, the insured is provided with the luxury of having legal services paid for by the insurance company, even on claims where insurance coverage is suspect.

Shippers also commonly obtain umbrella or **excess insurance**. Insurance is often multilayered because the underlying insurance provider may be unwilling to provide the amount of coverage requested by the insured. The insured may further limit its exposure by obtaining excess coverage for claims that exceed the amount of the underlying policies. The excess insurance policy incorporates one of a number of popular clauses that control when that coverage becomes operational. These clauses relate the excess coverage to the coverage provided by underlying policies. For example, an escape clause precludes any recovery if the type of claim is covered under an existing policy, even if that claim exceeds the amount of coverage provided by the underlying policy. An **excess clause** covers all claims outside the

---

51. Ibid. at 339.

coverage of the underlying policy. The **pro rata clause** proportions the amount paid under the policy, based on the limits provided by all relevant policies.[52]

Marine Cargo Insurance

The most relevant policy for exporters and importers of goods is the **cargo policy** (see Exhibit 10.1: Sample Insurance Certificate). The restrictions on coverage in cargo insurance revolve around three factors: (1) the causes of loss that it protects

EXHIBIT 10.1   *Sample Insurance Certificate*

SAMPLE INSURANCE CERTIFICATE

FIREMAN'S FUND INSURANCE COMPANY
SAN FRANCISCO, CALIFORNIA
ATLANTIC DIVISION, 110 WILLIAMS STREET
NEW YORK, NEW YORK 10038

SHIPPER/EXPORTER CALIFORNIA CITRUS EXPORT CO. 100 ORANGE GROVE DRIVE SANTA PAULA, CALIFORNIA 93060 U.S.A.	DOCUMENT NO.	CERTIFICATE NO. 999999999
	EXPORT REFERENCES 61102 SHIPPER'S REF # 681038	
CONSIGNEE (Not negotiable unless consigned to order) NAGOYA IMPORT COMPANY HAMAMATSUCHO OFFICE CENTER 2-4-1, SHIBAKOUEN, MINATO-KU NAGOYA, JAPAN	FORWARDING AGENT-REFERENCES FAR EAST FORWARDERS, Inc. FMC 690 25 OCEAN DRIVE TORRANCE, CALIFORNIA 90501	
	POINT AND COUNTRY OR ORIGIN OF GOODS CALIFORNIA, U.S.A.	
NOTIFY PARTY SAME AS CONSIGNEE	DOMESTIC ROUTING/EXPORT INSTRUCTIONS CALIFORNIA FREIGHT COMPANY 21 RIVER ROAD SANTA PAULA, CALIFORNIA 90501	
PIER OR AIRPORT PIER 24 OAKLAND MARINE TERMINAL		
OCEAN VESSEL/VOY. NO. PACIFIC PACER V-71	PORT OF LOADING OAKLAND, CA	INSURED DESTINATION NAGOYA, JAPAN
PORT OF DISCHARGE NAGOYA, JAPAN	FOR TRANSSHIPMENT TO NONE	

PARTICULARS FURNISHED BY SHIPPER

Container No.; Seal No.; Marks & Nos.	No. of Containers or Packages	TYPE OR KIND OF CONTAINERS OR PACKAGES - DESCRIPTION OF GOODS	GROSS WEIGHT	MEASUREMENT
TRIU855204-0	1 x 40'	SHIPPER'S LOAD AND COUNT CY/CY. FREIGHT PREPAID. MAINTAIN TEMPERATURE AT 37 DEG. F. HC REEFER CONTAINER STC: 1001 CARTONS FRESH VALENCIA ORANGES AGREED WEIGHT IS 17.9 KGS/CTN	17935 KGS 39450 LBS	35.431 CM 1251 CFT

DATE OF POLICY Aug. 11, 2005	SUM INSURED $15,837	AMOUNT IN WORDS Fifteen thousand eight hundred and thirty seven dollars

Insured against all risks of physical loss or damage from any external cause irrespective of percentage, but excluding the risks excluded by the F.C. & S and or S.R. &C.C. warranties on the reverse side of this policy except to the extent that such risks may be specifically covered by endorsement; also warranted free from any claim arising out of the inherent vice of the goods insured or consequent upon loss of time or market.

This insurance attaches from the time the goods leave the warehouse at the place named in the policy for the commencement at the transit and continues during the ordinary course of transit until the goods are delivered to the final warehouse at the destination named in the policy.

It is a condition of this insurance that there shall be no interruption or suspension of transit unless due to circumstances beyond the control of the Assured.

The risks covered by this policy include loss, damage or expense resulting from explosion howsoever or wheresoever occurring irrespective of percentage, but it is especially understood and agreed that this wording is not intended to cover any of the risks excluded by the F. C. & S. and/or S.R. & C.C. Warranties set forth elsewhere in this policy.

This insurance is subject to the American Institute Marine Extension Clauses (1943) and the following American Institute Clauses as if the current form of each were endorsed hereon:
South America 60-Day Clause   S.R. & C.C. Endorsement   War Risk Insurance

It is hereby understood and agreed that in the cases of loss or damage to the property insured under this policy, same shall be immediately reported as soon as the goods are landed, or the loss known as expected, to the nearest agent of this Company as designated on the reverse side hereof.

(See reverse side for further terms and conditions which are hereby made a part of the Policy.)

Note: – It is necessary for the assured to give prompt notice to underwriters when he becomes aware of an event for which he is "held covered" under this policy and the right to such cover is dependent on compliance with this obligation.

In witness whereof the company named above has caused this policy to be signed by its duly authorized officers, but this policy shall not be valid unless countersigned by an authorized representative of this Company of the Assured.

Secretary   President

ENDORSEMENT   Countersigned at _____

_____   By _____

---

52.   Ibid. at 357.

against, (2) the amount of coverage, and (3) the duration of the coverage. The first factor determines whether to obtain perils or an all-risk policy. The second factor affects the decision to insure against only a total loss, known as free of particular average, or to insure against partial losses, or *with* average. The third factor involves the incorporation of clauses in the marine insurance that would extend the duration of coverage to periods when the goods are on the shore or in a warehouse. These **extension clauses** include warehouse-to-warehouse, shore, and marine extension clauses.

There are two general types of marine insurance policies: (1) the **perils only policy** and (2) the **all risks policy**. The most common form of cargo insurance is the perils only policy that pays only for losses due to expressly enumerated perils or causes (see Exhibit 10.2: The Standard Perils Only Policy, ILU's Cargo B Clause).

The burden is on the cargo owner to prove that the loss was due to one of the listed perils.[53] Thus, under the perils only policy, a loss caused by an unforeseen event or occurrence would be borne by the owner of the goods. In contrast, broader coverage is available through the all risk policy. The all risk policy covers any losses except those expressly excepted in the policy. The burden to prove that the loss was due to an excluded clause is placed on the insurance company. Standard cargo policies, both of the perils only and all risk varieties, do not cover risks associated with war, revolution, riot, or strikes. These areas of loss are exempted by the **F.C. & S. clause** (free of capture and seizure) and the **S.R. & C.C. clause** (strikes, riots, and civil commotion). The F.C. & S. clause has been interpreted to exclude any losses due to war or civil strife, including rebellion and revolution. Coverage may be requested through an endorsement on the underlying policy or through a separate war risk policy. This decision is likely to be based on the particular places of shipment and destination, along with the expected route of transport and the types of goods being transported.

EXHIBIT 10.2   *The Standard Perils Only Policy (Institute of London Underwriters, Cargo B Clause)*

Risks Covered

This insurance covers:

(1) loss or damage to the subject-matter insured reasonably attributable to:

    (a) fire or explosion

    (b) vessel or craft being stranded, grounded, sunk, or capsized

    (c) overturning or derailment of land conveyance

    (d) collision or contact of vessel, craft or conveyance with any external object other than water

    (e) discharge of cargo at a port of distress

    (f) earthquake, volcanic eruption, or lightning

(2) loss or damage to the subject-matter insured caused by:

    (a) general average sacrifice

    (b) entry of sea, lake, or river water into vessel or place of storage

    (c) jettison or washing overboard

(3) total loss of any package lost overboard or dropped while loaded on to, or unloaded from, vessel or craft.

---

53. Additional coverage can be added through a war and riot risk clause and an Inchmaree clause.

Marine insurance policies also generally specify whether they cover less than total losses, known as **with average**, or whether they cover only total losses, **free of particular average (FPA)**.[54] The more comprehensive policy is one *with average*. This policy protects for partial as well as total losses. However, most with average policies restrict the coverage for partial losses to those losses that exceed 3 percent of the value of the goods. The free of particular average clause states that the insurance company does not have to pay the insured (or "assured") who suffers less than a total loss. This type of limited coverage is not favored.

Marine cargo insurance traditionally covers only the period that the goods are on the ship. Primarily because of the importance of the bill of lading and the use of multimodal containers, the cargo policy is often made to cover risk of loss for periods of time before the loading and after the unloading of the goods. This is generally done by incorporating a warehouse-to-warehouse or **marine extension clause** in the insurance policy that protects the shipper from the start in the exporter's country until received in the importer's country. (See Exhibit 10.3: ILU's Warehouse-to-Warehouse Clause.) The marine extension or warehouse-to-warehouse clause extends the standard marine coverage to the period before the loading of the goods and the period between offloading and delivery to the consignee. The insured must make sure that the clause does not limit the extended coverage through a time limit provision. The best way to ensure this is to provide that the policy remains in operation until the goods are delivered to the consignee.

The *Shaver Transportation Co. v. Travelers Indemnity Co.* case is an excellent review of some of the standard clauses found in most marine insurance policies. Marine insurance policies are directed at one of two intended beneficiaries: the shipper and the common carrier. The clauses reviewed in *Shaver Transportation* apply equally to both perils only and all risk insurance policies. The clauses in the marine

---

EXHIBIT 10.3   *Warehouse-to-Warehouse Clause (Institute of London Underwriters, Clause A)*

Duration

This insurance attaches from the time the goods leave the warehouse or place of storage at the place named herein for the commencement of the transit, continues during the ordinary course of transit and terminates either

(1) on delivery to the Consignee's or other final warehouse or place of storage at the destination named herein,

(2) on delivery to any warehouse or place of storage, whether prior to or at the destination named herein, which the Assured elects to use either

    (i) for storage in the ordinary course of transit, or

    (ii) for allocation or distribution, or

(3) on the expiry of 60 days after the completion of discharge overside of the goods from the oversea vessel at the final port of discharge, whichever shall occur first.

This insurance shall remain in force (subject to termination as provided for above) during delay beyond the control of the Assured, any deviation, forced discharge, reshipment or transshipment and during any variation of the adventure arising from the exercise of a liberty granted to shipowners or charterers under the contract of affreightment (carriage).

---

54.   The marine term for loss is the word *average*.

Shaver Transportation Co. v. The Travelers Indemnity Co.

481 F. Supp. 892 (D. Or. 1979)

Skopil, District Judge. Shaver Transportation Company (Shaver), a barge company, contracted with Weyerhaeuser Company (Weyerhaeuser) to transport caustic soda from Weyerhaeuser plants to a buyer of the soda, GATX. Following the terms of the agreement, Shaver arranged for marine cargo insurance with Travelers. Shaver decided on "Free from Particular Average" and "standard perils" provisions supplemented with "specially to cover" clauses. Upon delivery to GATX, it was determined that the soda had been contaminated with tallow.

The parties agree that contamination occurred as Shaver was loading the caustic soda aboard the barge. The barge had previously carried a load of tallow, and Shaver had not thoroughly cleaned the barge input lines. Shortly thereafter Travelers notified Shaver that the contamination did not represent a recoverable loss under the defendant's marine open cargo policy. There is only one major issue in the case: Are the losses incurred by the plaintiffs the consequences of an insured event under the marine cargo insurance policy? Plaintiffs have meticulously examined the policy and argue for recovery under several theories.

I. Recovery under Perils of the Sea clause and Free from Particular Average clause

The Perils clause, almost identical to ancient perils provisions dating back several hundred years, defines the risks protected by the policy. In addition to a long list of "perils of the sea," the clause includes "all other perils, losses, and misfortunes, that have or shall, come to the hurt, detriment, or damage to the said goods and merchandise." Plaintiff argues that the "forced" disposition of the caustic soda was like jettison (an enumerated peril) and is covered by the concluding language of the clause.

The contamination of the cargo occurred at the time of loading. Therefore, the plaintiffs cannot recover under the Perils clause of the policy. The term "jettison" also appears in the Free from Particular Average clause. If jettison did occur, this clause affords coverage regardless of the amount of cargo damage. However, I find that a jettison did not occur in this instance.

II. Recovery under Warehouse-to-Warehouse clause; Marine Extension clause; Shore Coverage clause

These clauses do not define the nature of the risks covered by the policy but merely define where physically the coverage extends. To recover under either the Warehouse-to-Warehouse or the Marine Extension clause the plaintiffs must show that an insured peril existed and the damage was proximately caused by that peril. The shore coverage clause provides coverage for enumerated risks occurring on shore. Plaintiffs argue that contamination while loading is a shore accident. However, since the contamination occurred within the barge's intake lines, the incident arose "on board." Therefore shore coverage does not apply. Even if it were to apply, contamination of cargo is not within the enumerated risks covered by the shore coverage clause.

III. Recovery of Extraordinary Expenses under Landing and Warehousing clause; Extra Expenses clause; Sue and Labor clause

Under these provisions the insured is entitled to recover expenses associated with losses incurred as a result of an insured peril. I find that the losses suffered by plaintiffs were not caused by a peril covered by the policy. Recovery under these provisions is therefore precluded.

IV. Recovery under Inchmaree clause

The purpose of the Inchmaree clause is to expand the coverage of the policy beyond the perils provision. It allows a vessel owner to become exempt from liability for fault or error in navigation or management of the ship. In contrast, the shipowner must retain liability for negligence in the care and custody of the cargo. The Ninth Circuit, noting that no precise definitions exist, advocates a case-by-case determination using the following test: "If the act in question has the primary purpose of affecting the ship, it is 'in navigation or in management'; but if the primary purpose is to affect the cargo, it is not 'in navigation or in management.'" Using this test, I find that the contamination of the cargo in this case was caused by fault in the care, custody, and control of the cargo.

V. Recovery under Negligence clause

The Negligence clause provides coverage against losses due to enumerated perils caused by the unseaworthiness of the vessel. To recover under this clause plaintiffs must show that the barge was unseaworthy. This unseaworthiness must then cause a loss through one of the enumerated perils: "sinking, stranding, fire, explosion, contact with seawater, or by any other cause of the nature of any of the risks assumed in the policy." "Seaworthiness" depends on such factors as the type of vessel, character of the voyage, reasonable weather, navigational conditions, and type of cargo.

A vessel is unseaworthy if she is not reasonably fit to carry cargo she has undertaken to transport. I find Shaver's barge unseaworthy as a result of improper loading of cargo. Plaintiffs must demonstrate that the unseaworthiness of the barge caused a loss to cargo by one or more of the enumerated perils. Since contamination is not an enumerated peril, no recovery is possible under the Negligence clause of this policy.

Even assuming that a peril existed, defendant claims that contribution cannot be requested when the vessel owner was at fault in creating the situation. Vessel owners have long placed in bills of lading a provision incorporating the protections of the Harter Act and Carriage of Goods by Sea Act. This provision, known as the Jason clause entitles shipowners to contribution notwithstanding negligence in creating the general average situation. However, the shipowner must comply with 46 U.S.C.

§ 1303(1) (a) requiring due diligence to make the vessel seaworthy. The burden of proving "due diligence" in making the vessel seaworthy falls on the vessel owner. I find that Shaver did not meet this burden. Shaver failed to properly clean or inspect the barge's input lines. Shaver failed to use due diligence to make the barge seaworthy. Judgment shall be entered for the defendant.

Case Highlights

- Warehouse-to-warehouse and shore clauses do not define the nature of the risks covered by the policy but merely define where the coverage physically extends.
- The Inchmaree clause allows a vessel owner to become exempt from liability for fault or error in navigation or management of the ship. In contrast, the ship owner must retain liability for negligence in the care and custody of the cargo (stowage).
- A vessel is unseaworthy if it is not reasonably fit to carry the cargo it has undertaken to transport.
- Because contamination is not an enumerated peril, no recovery is possible under the negligence clause.
- The Jason clause allows ship owners to collect general average damages, notwithstanding their negligence in creating the general average situation (see the next section on general average).

---

insurance policy that are referred to in the case have been excerpted and placed in Focus on Transactions: Standard Marine Insurance Clauses. Refer to these clauses in reading the case.

Cargo insurance can be obtained for a single voyage or a fixed period of time. The most common form in exporting is the open or **general cover** form of insurance policy, which is not limited to a specific shipment, but covers numerous shipments for a fixed period of time or until terminated by notice given by the shipper (insured) or the insurance company. The premium is calculated on the basis of the values declared by the shipper on the certificates issued for each shipment. A variant of the open cover policy is the **blanket policy**, in which the shipper is not required to declare the individual values of each shipment. Each shipment is covered up to the maximum amount of the policy.

Marine insurance policies have been standardized through the use of common clauses published by one of a number of associations. An example is the **International Underwriting Association (IUA)**. Founded in 1998, through a merger of the Institute of London Underwriters (ILU) and the London International Insurance and Reinsurance Market Association (LIRMA), the IUA is an association of marine insurance companies that publishes a manual of

http://
American Institute of Marine Underwriters: **http://www.aimu.org** and Institute of London Underwriters: **http://www.iua.co.uk.**

Standard Marine Insurance Clauses (from *Shaver*)

Focus on Transactions

PERILS CLAUSE. Touching the adventures and perils which the said Assurers[55] are contented to bear, and take upon themselves, they are of the seas and inland waters, man of war, fires, enemies, pirates, rovers, assailing thieves, jettisons,[56] letters of mart,[57] reprisals, taking at sea, arrests, restraints and detainments of all kings, princes of people of what nation, condition or quality whatsoever, barratry of the master and mariners,[58] and all other perils, losses and misfortunes, that have or shall come to the hurt, detriment or damage to the said goods and merchandise, or any part thereof.

FREE OF PARTICULAR AVERAGE CLAUSE. Other shipments covered hereunder are insured: Free of Particular Average unless caused by the vessel and/or interest insured being stranded, sunk, burst, on fire or in collision with another ship or vessel or with ice or with any substance other than water, but liable for jettison and/or washing overboard, irrespective of percentage.

WAREHOUSE-TO-WAREHOUSE CLAUSE. This insurance attaches from the time the goods leave the Warehouse and/or Store at the place named in the policy for the commencement of the transit and continues during the ordinary course of transit, including customary transshipment if any, until the goods are discharged overside from the overseas vessel at the final port. Thereafter the insurance continues whilst the goods are in transit and/or awaiting transit until delivered to final warehouse at the destination named in the policy or until the expiry of 15 days (or 30 days if the destination to which the goods are insured is outside the limits of the port) whichever shall first occur. The time limits referred to above to be reckoned from midnight of the day on which the discharge overside of the goods hereby insured from the overseas vessel is completed. Held covered at a premium to be arranged in the event of transshipment, if any, other than as above and/or in the event of delay in excess of the above time limits arising from circumstances beyond the control of the Assured.

MARINE EXTENSION CLAUSE. This policy is extended to cover all shipments which become at risk hereunder in accordance with the following clauses:

I.   This insurance attaches from the time the goods leave the warehouse at the place named in this policy . . . and continues until the goods are delivered to the final warehouse.

II. This insurance specially to cover the goods during deviation, delay, forced discharge, reshipment, and transshipment.

III. This insurance shall in no case be deemed to extend to cover loss, damage, or expense proximately caused by delay or inherent vice or nature of the subject-matter insured.

SHORE COVERAGE CLAUSE. Including while on docks, wharves or elsewhere on shore and/or during land transportation, risks of collision, derailment, fire, lightning, sprinkler leakage, cyclones, hurricanes, earthquakes, floods, the rising of navigable waters, or any accident to the conveyance and/or collapse and/or subsidence of docks and/or structures, and to pay loss or

continued

---

55. *Assured* refers to the party insured by the policy. *Assurer* refers to the insurance company.
56. Cargo may be voluntarily sacrificed by jettison in the common good, giving rise to a general average loss.
57. Letters of mart or marque are government authorizations to commit piracy against a designated state or person.
58. Barratry is fraud or criminal conduct performed by the captain or the crew.

Standard Marine Insurance Clauses (from Shaver) (*continued*)

damage caused thereby, even though the insurance be otherwise F.P.A.

LANDING AND WAREHOUSING CLAUSE. Notwithstanding any average warranty contained herein, these Assurers agree to pay landing, warehousing, forwarding or other expenses and/or particular charges should same be incurred, as well as any partial loss arising from transshipment. Also to pay the insured value of any package, piece, or unit totally lost in loading, transshipment, and/or discharge.

EXTRA EXPENSES CLAUSE. Where, by reason of a peril insured against under this policy, extra expenses are incurred to destroy, dump, or otherwise dispose of the damaged goods, or where extra expenses are incurred in discharging from the vessel and/or craft and/or conveyance, such expenses will be recoverable in full in addition to the damage to the insured interest.

SUE AND LABOR CLAUSE. In case of any loss or misfortune, it shall be lawful and necessary to and for the Assured, his or their factors, servants and assigns, to sue, labor, and travel for, in, and about the defense, safeguard, and recovery of the said goods and merchandise, or any part thereof without prejudice to this insurance; nor shall the acts of the insured or insurers, in recovering, saving, and preserving the property insured, in case of disaster, be considered a waiver or an acceptance of abandonment; to the charges whereof the said Assurers will contribute according to the rate and quantity of the sum herein insured.

INCHMAREE CLAUSE. This insurance is also specially to cover any loss of or damage to the interest insured hereunder, through the bursting of boilers, breakage of shafts or through any latent defect in the machinery, hull, or appurtenances, or from faults or errors in the navigation and/or management of the vessel by the Master, Mariners, Mates, Engineers, or Pilots; provided, however, that this clause shall not be construed as covering loss arising out of delay, deterioration or loss of market, unless otherwise provided elsewhere herein.

NEGLIGENCE CLAUSE. The Assured are not to be prejudiced by the presence of the negligence clause and/or latent defect clause in the bills of lading and/or charter party and/or contract of affreightment. The seaworthiness of the vessel and/or craft as between the Assured and Assurers is hereby admitted, and the Assurers agree that in the event unseaworthiness or a wrongful act or misconduct of shipowner, charterer, their agents or servants, shall, directly or indirectly, cause loss or damage to the cargo insured by sinking, stranding, fire, explosion, contact with seawater, or by any other cause of the nature of any of the risks assumed in the policy, the Assurers will (subject to the terms of average and other conditions of the policy) pay to an innocent Assured the resulting loss. With leave to sail with or without pilots, and to tow and assist vessels or craft in all situations and to be towed.

standard clauses. The sophisticated international exporter or importer should be familiar with the standard forms and clauses published by the ILU, the **American Institute of Marine Underwriters (AIMU)**, and Lloyd's of London. An example of such publications is the manual on cargo clauses published by the AIMU and most recently revised in June 2004. Familiarization with the standard forms is important because underwriters often create their own policies by using clauses found in the standard forms. The standard clauses may be "used as building blocks in custom policies."[59] In addition, there are also standard terms utilized in policies for particular trades.

General Average

http://

Text of the York-Antwerp Rules—1994 Edition: **http://www. jus.uio.no/lm/cmi.york. antwerp.rules.1994/ doc.html.**

http://

The Association of Average Adjusters of the United States: **http://www. usaverageadjusters.org/ Yorkantwerp.htm.**

General average is a venerable doctrine of maritime law that dates back 2,800 years. It provides that when a portion of a ship's cargo is sacrificed to save the rest from a real and substantial peril, each owner of property saved contributes ratably to make up the loss of the sacrificed property's owners. The U.S. Supreme Court in *Barnard v. Adams*[60] described three events that create a general average situation: (1) a common danger to which ship, cargo, and crew are all exposed and which is imminent; (2) a voluntary sacrifice of a part for the benefit of the whole; and (3) successful avoidance of the peril.

Modern law has eased the imminent requirement by demanding only that a peril be real and substantial. Two classes of general average claim exist, specifically, those that arise from sacrifices of part of a ship or cargo made to save the whole venture and those that arise out of **extraordinary expenses** incurred by the ship owner for the joint benefit of ship and cargo. Thus, general average claims are available to both ship owners and cargo owners. The international convention that governs the calculation of general average losses is the **York-Antwerp Rules** of 1994. The *Folger Coffee Co. v. Olivebank* case involves a claim for general average by a common carrier against cargo owners.

Folger Coffee Co. v. Olivebank
201 F.3d 632 (5th Cir. 2000)

Farris, Circuit Judge. In this admiralty and maritime appeal, Folger Coffee Co. and its insurer, Gulf Insurance Company, seek to reverse the district court's judgment that (1) the vessel M/V *Olivebank* is entitled to use general average on a salvage lien and (2) that Folger Coffee and Gulf Insurance owe their proportional share to the general average fund. The M/V *Olivebank* left the Port of Durban, South Africa, with cargo that included granite blocks, steel wire, and earth-moving equipment.

During the voyage the vessel encountered severe weather and extremely rough seas that caused seawater to come over the deck. The vessel's emergency electrical system, required by the Safety of Life at Sea Convention of 1974, should have provided emergency lighting from batteries, followed by the automatic startup of the emergency generator to provide electrical services for steering. The batteries failed and the emergency generator was ultimately started manually. The parties dispute the exact means by which the seawater reached the alternator room. It is, however, undisputed that a skylight, or raised hatch, nine feet above deck and two levels above the alter-

nators was open at some point during the relevant period. It is also undisputed that outside deck-level vent covers to the exhaust vents were open and that these vents lead to the alternator room.

The captain of the vessel put out a Mayday. He entered into a salvage agreement with Pentow Marine, Ltd., a salvage tug, pursuant to a Lloyd's Open Form. The salvors arrived in the late afternoon. The main engines were ultimately started prior to the arrival of the salvors, and, after waiting out the storm, the M/V *Olivebank* sailed to a port of refuge on its own power. The salvors exercised their salvage lien by threatening arrest of the cargo and/or the ship.

The owners of the M/V *Olivebank* declared general average, forcing the cargo interests to provide general average bonds and guarantees. Folger Coffee and Gulf Insurance filed actions in district court seeking a declaration that the vessel was not entitled to general average and recovery for damage to cargo. The district court found that the loss of power was caused by a fortuitous combination of events and that the vessel was seaworthy when it left port.

---

59. Hayden & Balick, *supra* note 50, at 325.
60. 51 U.S. 270 (1850).

Folger Coffee and Gulf Insurance maintain that the M/V *Olivebank* was not entitled to general average because the vessel was unseaworthy under the Carriage of Goods at Sea Act, 46 U.S.C. §§ 1300–1315. The parties do not dispute that the bill of lading covering the cargo aboard the M/V *Olivebank* required general average contribution. Under COGSA, once the vessel establishes that a general average act occurred, the cargo owner might avoid liability only by establishing that the vessel was unseaworthy at the start of the voyage and that the unseaworthiness was the proximate cause of the general average event. If the cargo owner proves unseaworthiness, the vessel may still prevail by proving that it exercised due diligence to make the vessel seaworthy prior to the voyage.

The district court held that the evidence did not support the proposed finding that the vessel was unseaworthy due to a defective emergency electrical system. The district court found that the failure of the batteries and emergency system was due to the same intervening event that caused the primary alternators to fail (entry of seawater) and that the collapse of both systems at the same time was fortuitous. The district court held that the M/V *Olivebank* was seaworthy when it left port and that the open skylight and the vent covers were not an issue of seaworthiness but a management decision. The district court did not commit clear error by finding the vessel seaworthy despite the entry of seawater. It found that the water came onto the ship over the stern in a storm with force 11 winds. This finding has support in the record.

Folger Coffee and Gulf Insurance also contend that the conditions of the skylight, or hatch, and vent covers and the fact that these items were not closed made the vessel unseaworthy. The district court found that the most likely explanation for the entry of water into the alternator room was through the hatch and the exhaust vents and that the vessel was relieved of liability because the decision not to close the skylight or the vent covers was a management decision.

COGSA "excepts the carrier for liability from damage caused by 'act, neglect, or default of the master, mariner, pilot, or the servants of the carrier in the navigation or in the management of the ship.'" Failure to detect a flaw prior to sailing constitutes a failure to exercise due diligence and not an error of management. There is a fine line between actions that constitute errors in management and inaction that constitutes a lack of due diligence. Folger Coffee and Gulf Insurance have misconstrued the district court's use of the phrase "management decision." Neglect by management also relieves liability under COGSA. AFFIRMED.

Case Highlights

- Under COGSA, once the vessel establishes that a general average act occurred, the cargo owner might avoid liability only by establishing that the vessel was unseaworthy at the start of the voyage and that the unseaworthiness was the proximate cause of the general average event.
- There is a fine line between actions that are errors in management, for which the carrier is exempted, and inaction, which is lack of due diligence.

KEY TERMS

air waybill
all risks policy
American Institute of Marine Underwriters (AIMU)
bailee
blanket policy
cargo policy
Carriage of Goods by Sea Act (COGSA)
charter party
clause paramount
common carrier
comprehensive general liability (CGL) coverage
containerization
customary freight unit (CFU)

customs brokers
due diligence
excess clause
excess insurance
exculpatory clause
extension clause
extraordinary expenses
fair opportunity
F.C. & S. clause
Federal Arbitration Act
force majeure clause
forwarder's bill of lading
free of particular average (FPA)
freight forwarder
general average
general cover

Hague Rules
Hague-Visby Rules
Hamburg Rules
Harter Act of 1893
Himalaya clause
hull insurance
Inchmaree clause
Insurance Services Office (ISO)
International Underwriting Association (IUA)
marine extension clause
marine insurance company
material deviation
misdelivery
Montreal Convention
multimodal transport

multimodal transport operator	Rules for Multimodal Transport	stowage
ocean bill of lading	Documents	through bill of lading
perils only policy	running down clause	through-transport policy
per-package limitation	seaworthiness	unimodal transport convention
pro rata clause	seventeen COGSA exemptions	warehouse-to-warehouse clause
protection and indemnity	shortage	Warsaw Convention
(P & I) policy	S.R. & C.C. clause	with average
Q-clause exception	statute of limitations	York-Antwerp Rules

CHAPTER PROBLEMS

1. A shipper obtains a marine (cargo) insurance policy for $25,000 on goods that had a real or market value of $8,000. If the goods are lost at sea, is the insurance company liable for $25,000, $8,000, or nothing?

2. An exporter takes out a marine insurance policy on $50,000 worth of goods but fails to disclose its previous claims history. In fact, the insured had filed claims for loss on eight previous policies covering transport of goods. Can the insurance company avoid making payment for loss of the insured goods?

3. A shipper obtains a cargo insurance policy on 400 sealed crates of "Grade A" industrial grinding wheels. In fact, the grinding wheels were secondhand stock and packaged in 400 burlap sacks. Does such a variation in the description of the insured goods jeopardize the shipper's coverage?

4. Your goods are jettisoned from a ship as a general average act. You file a claim against your marine insurance policy and receive full payment. Does the marine insurance company have a claim for general average against the ship owner and the other cargo owners?

5. During a time of hostilities, a ship owner hires a tug to tow the ship to lessen the danger from enemy submarines. Can the ship owner make a general average claim by arguing that the towing costs are extraordinary expenses incurred for the benefit of the ship and its cargo?

6. Plaintiff Tseng boarded an international flight from New York to Tel Aviv. Before being allowed to board, she was subjected to an intrusive security search. Tseng sued the airline in state court in New York for the torts of assault and false imprisonment. The Warsaw Convention does not address such an injury. Will Tseng be allowed to continue her action under New York law? *El Al Israel Airlines, Ltd. v. Tseng*, 525 U.S. 155 (1999).

7. The plaintiffs are Dutch importers of commodities that included industrial leather gloves. Four shipments of gloves were made in 1982 and 1983. The insurance contract contained the following clause: "This insurance shall in no case be deemed to extend to cover loss damage or expense proximately caused by *inherent vice* or nature of the subject matter insured." The plaintiff claimed that the dropping of water from a source external to the goods damaged the gloves. The defendant asserted that the goods deteriorated as a result of their natural behavior. In short, the goods were damaged because the plaintiff did not properly dry the leather. Is this a case of inherent vice? *Noten v. Harding*, 2 Lloyd's Law Report 283 (English Court of Appeal 1990).

INTERNET EXERCISES

1. Review the Web site of the International Maritime Bureau: **http://www.iccwbo.org/ccs/menu_imb_bureau.asp**. What types of services does this organization provide to international shippers?

2. Research the status of the BOLERO Project in the development of electronic documentation for the shipment of goods at **http://www.bolero.net**.

3. Your company has just entered into an export contract with a company in Chile. It is your job to arrange transport from the Port of Miami to Santiago, Chile. Review shipping schedules to determine the best and fastest transit route at Maritime Global Net: **http://www.mglobal.com**.

Financing export transactions is a crucial part of most export and import businesses. Financing can be obtained in one of two ways. The first, external to the transaction, is when one of the parties obtains a general loan from a commercial bank or a government agency. The second method, internal to the transaction, is facilitated by two documents found in most export transactions: the bill of lading and the **letter of credit**. The importance of the bill of lading as a document of title was discussed in Chapter Nine. A negotiable bill of lading allows the transfer of the goods while they are in transit. Because it is negotiable, it can be used as collateral to secure a loan.

The letter of credit is the main topic of this chapter. The letter of credit is a commercial bank guarantee of either payment by the buyer (letter of credit) or performance by one of the parties (standby letter of credit). Its secondary purpose is to allow the seller to finance the production and export of the goods.

Chapter 11

International Trade Finance

As discussed in Chapter Nine, to lower the risk of nondelivery or nonpayment, the parties often agree to require payment against collection of documents. In the **documentary collections transaction**, the seller does not give up control of the goods until the buyer purchases the documents, minimizing the seller's risk of nonpayment. At the same time, the buyer's nondelivery risk is minimized because, with the documents, it obtains legal control over the goods in transit. The buyer's only remaining risk is fraud, where the documents do not reflect the true shipment. Requiring preshipment inspection minimizes this risk. One risk for the seller remains: the risk that the buyer will dishonor its obligation to purchase the documents. In that case, the seller retains control over the goods, but the goods are in transit to a distant port. The cost of returning or transshipping the goods or finding an alternative buyer is likely to be substantial.

The risk of nonpayment is removed through the use of a **documentary credit transaction**. In such a transaction, the buyer obtains a letter of credit from a bank that guarantees payment to the seller. Substituting the credit or guarantee of a bank for that of the buyer eliminates the risk of nonpayment.[1] This chapter examines three uses of letters of credit in international transactions. First, the letter of credit is used as a device to guarantee a payment obligation in a documentary transaction. Second, the letter of credit is used as a *standby* to guarantee a performance obligation. Three, the letter of credit is used to help finance the exporting or importing of goods.

---

1. See *Voest-Alpine Trading Co. v. Bank of China*, 167 F. Supp.2d 940, 943 (S.D. Tex. 2000), *aff'd*, 288 F.3d 262 (5th Cir. 2002); see also *In re* Sanders-Langsam Tobacco Co., 224 B.R. 1 (E.D.N.Y. 1998).

Letters of Credit

http://
Dictionary of banking
terms: **http://www.
ubs.com/1/e/about/
bterms.html.**

Letters of credit have been called the lifeblood of commerce. They have a long history in international transactions. There is evidence that bankers used letters of credit in Renaissance Europe, imperial Rome, ancient Greece, Phoenicia, and even early Egypt. These simple instruments have survived because of their inherent reliability, convenience, economy, and flexibility. Letters of credit serve three important functions in international business transactions: payment instrument (transfer of documents and collection of funds), guarantee instrument (performance guarantee), and finance instrument (negotiation and collateral).

Between trusted parties, when a letter of credit is not cost-effective, alternatives may be sought to secure payment. The documentary transaction without a letter of credit, in which payment is through a **sight** or **time draft**, is utilized. A draft is simply a check drawn on the account of the purchaser. A sight draft allows the seller to "cash" the draft immediately on presenting the documents to the bank or purchaser. A time draft, like a postdated check, can be cashed only some time after the presentation of the documents, most commonly thirty, sixty, or ninety days. The draft may be sued upon, independent of the underlying export contract. The following is a sample acceptance and payment clause relating to a time draft:

Buyer shall pay for the goods ordered by means of a documentary collection whereby Seller shall draw a time draft which shall be accepted by buyer against buyer's receipt of documents (specify documents) not less than sixty days after shipment, and payable sixty days after such acceptance. Payment of the draft shall be made by buyer's bank upon presentation at bank located (near seller) as shall be designated by buyer's bank and acceptable to seller.[2]

In initial transactions with a new or unknown business party, however, securing payment is a crucial concern. A letter of credit adds a bank's promise to that of the foreign buyer to pay the exporter when the exporter has complied with all the terms and conditions of the letter of credit. The buyer applies for issuance of a letter of credit to the exporter and therefore is called the applicant or **account party**; the exporter is called the **beneficiary party** (see Focus on Transactions: Definitions of Key Letter of Credit and Finance Terms). Payment under a documentary letter of credit is based on documents, not on the terms of sale or the condition of the goods sold. Before payment, the bank responsible for making payment verifies that all documents are exactly as required by the letter of credit. When they are not as required, a discrepancy exists, which must be cured before payment can be made.

A letter of credit may be irrevocable or revocable. The **irrevocable letter of credit** is the one used most commonly in export transactions. A revocable letter of credit does not provide the seller with much security, given the fact that the bank can revoke it at any time. A change to a letter of credit is best performed by a formal **amendment** issued by the bank and signed by all parties. Because changes can be time-consuming and expensive, every effort should be made to get the letter of credit right the first time.

http://
Wachovia corporate and
institutional letters of
credit: **http://www.
wachovia.com/corp_
inst/page/0,,14_2300_
4695_4701,00.html.**

---

2. Dennis J. Murphy, "How to Document International Commercial Transactions," *International Law Quarterly* 70, 85 (1985).

Definitions of Key Letter of Credit and Finance Terms

Focus on Transactions

Account Party
The party requesting or applying for the letter of credit from a bank.

Advising Bank
A bank in the beneficiary's country through which the issuing bank communicates the credit to the beneficiary—sometimes referred to as the correspondent bank.

Back-to-Back Letter of Credit
At the request of the beneficiary, a third bank agrees to issue a second letter of credit, using the first letter of credit as collateral. The second letter of credit is often used to pay or secure the beneficiary's suppliers.

Beneficiary Party
The party for which favor the letter of credit is issued, such as the exporter (seller) in an international sale of goods transaction.

Confirming Bank
The bank in the beneficiary's country that further guarantees the issuing bank's commitment to pay the letter of credit.

Documentary Collection
The use of the banking system for an exporter to transfer documents to a purchaser and to receive payment. The bank is required to not transfer the documents to the purchaser unless the purchaser makes payment or accepts a bill of exchange (draft). The bank does not act as a guarantor of payment as in the documentary credit transaction.

Documentary Credit (Letter of Credit)
An instrument requiring a bank to pay a sum of money to the beneficiary against the presentation of documents stipulated in the letter of credit. It is used most commonly as a payment mechanism for export sales.

Factoring
The exporter sells to a factoring company its rights to receive payment. The factoring company discounts the amount of the payment owed to the exporter in order to produce the desired rate of return. It is used in short-term financing.

Forfaiting
The use of a draft or promissory note given by the purchaser (guaranteed by purchaser's bank) to the exporter to obtain nonrecourse financing. The terms are negotiated in advance so that the exporter is assured of payment before shipping the goods. The importer assumes the costs of discounting the note or draft. It is used in long-term financing.

Nominating Bank
A bank designated by the issuing bank to which the beneficiary party can present documents and obtain payment (may or may not be the advising or confirming bank).

Open Account Transaction
The seller does not require payment until some time after the purchaser receives the goods or documents. This is usually an unsecured type of financing offered by an exporter to a trusted customer.

Red Clause Financing
The seller-exporter is allowed to receive an advance on the letter of credit prior to presenting the required documents. The red clause represents a form of unsecured financing offered by the purchaser to a trusted exporter.

Standby Letter of Credit
A type of credit issued as a guarantee against default by one of the parties to the contract. Generally used to guarantee the performance (not payment) of one of the parties and paid only upon default (nonperformance), it acts as a "standby." Alternative devices that serve the same purpose are the bank guarantee and the performance bond.

continued

Definitions of Key Letter of Credit and Finance Terms (*continued*)

Transferable Credit

A transferable credit can be transferred by the beneficiary party in whole or part to secondary beneficiaries. An exporter may transfer the credit to finance the manufacture or purchase of the goods to be exported. The UCP requires that the original credit expressly provide for transferability. If it does not, the credit is presumed to be nontransferable.

Uniform Commercial Code Article 5

Provides the basic rules for letter of credit transactions within the United States.

Uniform Customs and Practices for Documentary Credits (UCP)

The international rules for letters of credit published by the International Chamber of Commerce in Paris. The current version is known as the UCP 500.

The letter of credit (bank guarantee) requirement in an export contract produces a number of contractual relationships. The purchaser enlists the services of its commercial bank by way of a letter of credit application (see Exhibit 11.1: Letter of Credit Application). If the bank accepts the application, it issues the letter of credit. The application forms the basis of the contract between the applicant or account party (buyer) and the **issuing bank**. The bank, upon issuing the letter of credit, forms a contract with the beneficiary party (seller) to pay the contract price upon the presentation of the required documents. The letter of credit itself fixes the issuing bank's obligations to the beneficiary party. These contractual relationships are independent of one another. As such, claims between the seller and buyer with respect to the sales contract are separate and apart from claims between the beneficiary party and the issuing bank regarding payment pursuant to the terms of the letter of credit.[3]

The International Chamber of Commerce (ICC) has developed a number of standard documentary credit forms, along with "guidance notes" for their proper use.[4] The ICC forms incorporate the requirements of the Uniform Customs and Practices for Documentary Credits (UCP). The UCP is a set of rules published by the ICC applicable to letters of credit to guarantee payment or performance. A review of the ICC forms and guidance notes will help the purchaser draft instructions to the issuing bank and help the beneficiary (seller) prepare the stipulated documents. For example, the letter of credit applicant should understand the repercussions of using broad terminology to describe items of value or amounts of something. The use of words like *approximate* in association with the amount of the credit or the quantity or unit price of the goods will be automatically fixed under Article 39(b) of the UCP. The buyer, for example, will have to accept documents that vary the amount of goods in the range of 5 percent more or less. To avoid such a variance, the applicant should state a specific number of packing units, or words to the effect that "the quantity of the goods specified must not be exceeded or reduced."

A balance should be struck between filling out the letter of credit application completely and avoiding excessive detail. In drafting the instructions to the bank,

http://

International Chamber of Commerce: **http://www.iccwbo.org.**

---

3. See *In re* Papio Keno Club, Inc., 262 F.3d 725 (8th Cir. 2001).
4. See generally ICC, *The New Standard Documentary Credit Forms for the UCP 500*, No. 516 (Charles del Busto, ed., 1993). See also James E. Byrne "Fundamental Issues in the Unification and Harmonization of Letter of Credit Law," 37 *Loyola Law Review* 1 (1991).

EXHIBIT 11.1   *Letter of Credit Application*

APPLICATION FOR
IRREVOCABLE COMMERCIAL LETTER OF CREDIT

PREFERRED BANK

L/C NO. _____

(FOR BANK USE ONLY)

DATE: _____

Please issue for our account an irrevocable Letter of Credit as set forth below by:

☐ AIRMAIL   ☐ AIRMAIL, WITH SHORT PRELIMINARY CABLE ADVICE   ☐ FULL CABLE

ADVISING BANK (If bank, use your correspondent bank)	APPLICANT
BENEFICIARY	AMOUNT
	EXPIRATION DATE

AVAILABLE BY DRAFTS AT _____ DRAWN, AT YOUR OPTION, ON YOU OR YOUR CORRESPONDENT
                                            PLEASE INDICATE SIGHT OR TENOR

FOR _____ % OF THE INVOICE VALUE.

WHEN ACCOMPANIED BY THE FOLLOWING DOCUMENTS, AS CHECKED: *(CHECK REQUIRED DOCUMENTS)*
          ☐ COMMERCIAL INVOICE
          ☐ CUSTOMS INVOICE
          ☐ INSURANCE POLICY AND OR CERTIFICATE COVERING THE FOLLOWING RISKS: (MARINE, WAR RISK, ETC.) _____

                                            IF OTHER INSURANCE IS REQUIRED, PLEASE STATE RISKS
          ☐ PACKING LIST
          ☐ OTHER DOCUMENTS   _____

          ☐ AIR WAYBILL CONSIGNED TO   _____
          ☐ ON BOARD OCEAN BILL OF LADING (IF MORE THAN ONE ORIGINAL HAS BEEN ISSUED ALL ARE REQUIRED)
                    ISSUED TO ORDER OF   _____ **PREFERRED BANK**
                    MARKED: NOTIFY: _____
                                                                                        FREIGHT: COLLECT/PAID

COVERING: Merchandise described in the invoice as: (Mention commodity only in generic terms omitting details as to grade, quality, etc.)
_____

CHECK ONE: ☐ FAS   ☐ FOB   ☐ C & F   ☐ CIF   ☐ C & I   ☐ OTHER

SHIPMENT FROM:	PARTIAL SHIPMENTS	TRANSSHIPMENTS
TO:	☐ PERMITTED	☐ PERMITTED
LATEST:	☐ NOT PERMITTED	☐ NOT PERMITTED

(PLEASE CHECK APPLICABLE BOXES)

☐ Documents must be presented to negotiating by paying bank within _____ days after the date of issuance of documents evidencing shipment or dispatch or taken in charge (shipping) (documents) but within validity of letter of credit.

☐ Insurance effected by ourselves. We agree to keep insurance coverage in force until this transaction is completed.

☐ Special Instructions: _____

DISPOSITION OF DOCUMENTS   ☐ TO US   ☐ OTHER
PLEASE DATE AND OFFICIALLY SIGN THE AGREEMENT ON THE REVERSE OF THE THIS APPLICATION
(SEE REVERSE)
(THE FOLLOWING IS TO BE EXECUTED IF THE APPLICANT IS NOT ALSO THE ACCOUNT PARTY)

be simple, clear, and precise. Excessive detail in the letter of credit application may lead to unnecessary confusion, given the different cultures represented in many international transactions. An overly detailed letter of credit is apt to result in an increased likelihood of documents being rejected that would have ultimately been acceptable to the account party (purchaser). The ICC manual makes these simple suggestions when filling out a letter of credit application:

* Do not call for documents that the Beneficiary cannot obtain. Article 13 (c) of the UCP deals harshly with such instructions by providing that "[i]f a Credit contains conditions without stating the documents to be presented in compliance therewith, banks will deem such conditions not stated and will disregard them."

* Do not state conditions whose observance cannot be ascertained from the face of a document.

Most often, an intermediary bank located near the seller or the port of shipment processes the documents. If that bank confirms the letter of credit, then two additional contractual relationships are formed: between the **confirming bank** and the beneficiary and between the confirming bank and the issuing bank. If the intermediary bank elects not to confirm or guarantee the letter, then it is referred to as an **advising bank**. It acts merely as a conduit for transmitting documents and payments. It has no independent legal obligation to the beneficiary party. A corresponding bank that confirms the letter of credit is independently liable for its payment. See Exhibit 11.2 for an example of a bank letter "confirming" a letter of credit. It lists the required documents, which are more fully detailed in the actual letter of credit. The important legal language is the statement that the bank "confirms and undertakes to honor each draft." In contrast, an advising bank is not liable for the dishonoring of the credit by the issuing bank.

The secondary role of the advising bank to the underlying transaction is reflected in the concomitant lack of liability. As such, advising banks should be aware that their relationships with the beneficiary and the issuing bank may be governed by laws of the country that had the most significant relationship to the transaction. This law is generally the law applicable to the issuing bank, which may lead to the unexpected application of law completely foreign to the advising bank. For example, in *Averbach v. Vnescheconobank*, the U.S. federal court applied the law of Russia to a dispute between the beneficiary, the issuing bank, and an advising bank located in California.[5] The court concluded that the choice of law was to be the local law of the state that had the most significant relationship to the transaction in dispute. Russian law was the suitable choice in this instance, as the issuing bank was located in Russia, the place of performance of the contract was in Russia, and the California bank merely acted as an advising bank with no liability for the dishonoring of the credit.

EXHIBIT 11.2   *Confirmation Letter*

Confirmed Irrevocable Straight Credit

Original Invoices in Duplicate Covering 1000 Cartons of Fashion Clothes (Ladies and Mens) per Pro-Forma
Invoice 63421.
Full Set, Clean On-Board, Original Ocean Bills of Lading, Marked Freight Prepaid and Evidencing Shipment from New York Port to Fortuga.
Full Set Insurance Policy for 110% CIF Value Including War Risk and All Risk Clauses.

Expiring This Office July 4, 20–

We Confirm and Hereby Undertake to Honor
Each Draft and Presented as Above Specified.

Signed

W. W. Smith

---

5.   280 F. Supp.2d 945, 951–52 (N.D. Cal. 2003).

The Letter of Credit Transaction

The typical letter of credit transaction follows this chronology. Each step in the chronology is discussed in the remainder of this section.

- After the U.S. exporter (seller) and buyer agree on the terms of a sale, the buyer arranges for its bank to open a letter of credit.
- The buyer's bank prepares an irrevocable letter of credit, including all instructions to the seller concerning the shipment.
- The buyer's bank sends the irrevocable letter of credit to a U.S. bank, requesting confirmation.
- The U.S. bank prepares a letter of confirmation to forward to the exporter, along with the irrevocable letter of credit.
- The exporter arranges with the freight forwarder to deliver the goods to the appropriate port or airport.
- When the goods are loaded, the forwarder completes the necessary documents.
- The exporter presents to the U.S. bank documents indicating full compliance.
- The bank reviews the documents. If they are in order, the documents are airmailed to the buyer's bank for review and transmitted to the buyer.
- The buyer gets the documents that may be needed to claim the goods.
- A draft, which accompanies the letter of credit, is paid by the exporter's bank at the time specified or may be discounted at an earlier date.

The typical scenario in an export transaction is that the seller and buyer negotiate a contract in which the buyer agrees to provide the seller with a letter of credit. Prior to signing a contract, the importer may seek advice from a **customs broker** regarding import regulations and the documents that it should require from the seller for import purposes. After the execution of the contract, the buyer places an application for the letter of credit with the prospective issuing bank. Following credit approval, the bank issues the original letter of credit, using the details supplied in the letter of credit application.

The original letter of credit is forwarded (mail, telex, or SWIFT)[6] to the exporter's bank. The exporting bank then advises the exporter (beneficiary party) that the letter of credit has been issued. If required, the exporter's bank may also confirm the letter of credit. To ensure that the letter of credit is to be confirmed by a local bank, the exporter should negotiate clear language in the contract. The following clause provides for an irrevocable, confirmed letter of credit:

The Letter of Credit is to be drawn in IRREVOCABLE form and be subject to the Uniform Customs and Practices for Documentary Credits (UCP) as published and updated from time to time by the International Chamber of Commerce. The Letter of Credit must be advised through and CONFIRMED by a bank located at the port of shipment acceptable to the seller. It must be PAYABLE AT THE COUNTERS OF THE CONFIRMING BANK.

This clause expressly makes the UCP the choice of law and requires payment upon presentation of the documents to the confirming bank. This point is especially important to the exporter wanting to receive payment as soon as practicable.

---

6. SWIFT is an industry-owned cooperative supplying messaging services to 7,600 financial institutions in 200 countries. The SWIFT network was created in 1973 to provide banks with a means of handling interbank transactions, including bank transfers and foreign exchange confirmations. In addition to banks, SWIFT provides messaging services to broker/dealers and investment managers.

The UCP is incorporated by reference into most banks' application and letter of credit forms. Letters of credit in the United States are generally regulated under Article 5 of the Uniform Commercial Code.

Upon receiving a letter of credit, the exporter should carefully compare the letter's terms with the terms of the exporter's pro forma invoice or price quotation. The exporter must provide documentation showing that the goods were shipped by the date specified in the letter of credit, or it risks not being paid. Exporters should check with their freight forwarders to make sure that no unusual conditions may arise that would delay shipment. In addition, documents must be presented by the date specified in the letter of credit.

Following approval by the beneficiary, the bank is instructed to send the letter of credit to the freight forwarder with instructions to book shipment. The **freight forwarder** coordinates the movement of the goods, secures the bill of lading, and completes other documentation as required in the letter of credit. Generally, to initiate a relationship with a freight forwarder, the exporter completes a **power of attorney** form. The power of attorney allows the freight forwarder to complete documents in the name of the exporter. The form must be signed by an authorized signatory of the exporter and witnessed.

The original letter of credit and the shipping documents are presented to the advising or confirming bank. If the bank has confirmed the letter of credit, then it will review the documents and pay the exporter. The documents are then sent to the issuing bank with a claim for reimbursement. Upon its approval of the documents, the issuing bank will debit the importer's account for the amount of the letter of credit and any charges due. Following payment, the importer may instruct the bank to forward the documents to a customs broker. The customs broker secures the release of the goods by clearing them through customs. The customs broker will require, among other items, a commercial invoice and a properly endorsed bill of lading for import clearance purposes.

An exporter is often not paid until the advising or confirming bank receives the funds from the issuing bank. To expedite the receipt of funds, wire transfers may be used. Bank practices vary, however, and the exporter may be able to receive funds by discounting the letter of credit at the bank, which involves paying a fee to the bank. Exporters should consult with their international bankers about bank policy.

The *Voest-Alpine International v. Chase Manhattan Bank* case that follows describes a typical letter of credit transaction and introduces the **rule of strict compliance**. The rule of strict compliance is the standard by which banks review documents presented for payment under a letter of credit. Banks must ensure that documents submitted by the beneficiary strictly comply with the letter of credit.[7] The UCP allows a bank to reject any nonconformity or discrepancy between the document being reviewed and the letter of credit requirements. Rejection is warranted for the slightest of discrepancies.[8] Similar documents or documents that would serve the same purpose are to be deemed unacceptable to the issuing bank. The rule of strict compliance should not be confused with the independence principle or **facial compliance rule**. The facial compliance rule refers to the principle that a bank's only obligation in a letter of credit transaction is to review documents. Under the facial compliance rule, a bank is free to disregard any information, even about a fraud in the transaction,

http://

Example of "Draft Transmittal Letter": **http://www.unzco.com/ basicguide/figure12. html.** Click on "Figure 12."

---

7. See *Oei v. Citibank, N.A.*, 957 F. Supp. 492, 503 (S.D.N.Y. 1997).
8. See *Creaciones Con Idea, S.A. v. MashreqBank PSC*, 51 F. Supp.2d 423, 427 (S.D.N.Y. 1999).

Voest-Alpine International v. Chase Manhattan Bank

707 F.2d 680 (2d Cir. 1983)

Cardamone, Circuit Judge. Originally devised to function in international trade, a letter of credit reduced the risk of nonpayment in cases where credit was extended to strangers in distant places. Interposing a known and solvent institution's (usually a bank's) credit for that of a foreign buyer in a sale of goods transaction accomplished this objective. A typical letter of credit transaction, as the case before us illustrates, involves three separate and independent relationships—an underlying sale of goods contract between buyer and seller, an agreement between a bank and its customer (buyer or account party) in which the bank undertakes to issue a letter of credit, and the bank's resulting engagement to pay the beneficiary (seller) providing that certain documents presented to the bank conform ["strict compliance rule"] with the terms and conditions of the credit issued on its customer's behalf.

Significantly, the bank's payment obligation to the beneficiary is primary, direct, and completely independent of any claims that may arise in the underlying sale of goods transaction. Further, employing concepts which underlie letters of credit in non–sale of goods transactions, enables these devices to serve a financing function. And it is this flexibility that makes letters of credit adaptable to a broad range of commercial uses.

Since the great utility of letters of credit arises from the independent obligation of the issuing bank, attempts to avoid payment premised on extrinsic considerations—contrary to the instruments' formal documentary nature—tend to compromise their chief virtue of predictable reliability as a payment mechanism. Viewed in this light it becomes clear that the doctrine of strict compliance with the terms of the letter of credit functions to protect the bank that carries the absolute obligation to pay the beneficiary. Adherence to this rule ensures that banks, dealing only in documents, will be able to act quickly, enhancing the letter of credit's fluidity. Literal compliance with the credit therefore is also essential so as not to impose an obligation upon the bank that it did not undertake and so as not to jeopardize the bank's right to indemnity from its customer. Documents nearly the same as those required are not good enough.

Metal Scrap Trading Corporation (MSTC) is an agency of the Indian government that had contracted to buy 7,000 tons of scrap steel from Voest-Alpine International Corporation (Voest), a trading subsidiary of an Austrian company. In late 1980 MSTC asked the Bank of Baroda to issue two letters of credit in the total amount of $1,415,550—one for $810,600 and the other

$604,950—to Voest to assure payment for the sale. The credits were expressly made subject to the Uniform Customs and Practice for Documentary Credits. The parties originally contemplated that Chase Manhattan Bank, N.A. (Chase or Bank), would serve as an advising bank in the transaction. As such, Chase was to review documents submitted by Voest in connection with its drafts for payment. Amendments to the letters of credit increased Chase's responsibilities and changed its status to that of a confirming bank, independently obligated on the credit to the extent of its confirmation.

The terms and conditions of the credits required proof of shipment, evidenced by clean-on-board bills of lading; certificates of inspection indicating date of shipment; and weight certificates issued by an independent inspector. Sometime between February 2 and February 6 (beyond the January 31 deadline), the cargo was partially loaded aboard the M/V Atra at New Haven. Unfortunately, the Atra never set sail for India. A mutiny by the ship's crew disabled the ship and rendered it unseaworthy. The scrap steel was later sold to another buyer for slightly over a half million dollars, nearly a million dollars less than the original contract price.

On February 13, two days before the expiration date of the credits, Voest presented three drafts with the required documentation to Chase. The bills of lading indicating receipt on board of the scrap metal were signed and dated January 31 by the captain of the Atra. The weight and inspection certificates accompanying the drafts revealed, however, that the cargo was loaded aboard the Atra sometime between February 2 and February 6. Despite this glaring discrepancy Chase advised the Bank of Baroda on February 25 that the drafts and documents presented to it by Voest conformed to the terms and conditions set forth in the letters of credit.

The Bank of Baroda apparently looked at the documents with more care than Chase. It promptly advised Chase that the documents did not comply with the requirements of the letters of credit, that it would therefore not honor the drafts, and that it would hold the documents at Chase's disposal. When Voest presented the drafts for payment on July 30 Chase refused to honor them. Voest thereupon instituted the present suit. It asserted that Chase waived the right to demand strict compliance with the terms of the credits and therefore wrongfully dishonored the drafts. Voest further alleged that regardless of whether the documents conformed to the letters of credit Chase was liable on the drafts because it accepted them.

II. Acceptance

Claims by a beneficiary of a letter of credit that a bank has waived strict compliance with the terms of the credit should generally be viewed with a somewhat wary eye. Acceptance is the drawee's signed engagement to honor the draft as presented and that it "must be written on the draft." By requiring written acceptance on the draft Section 3-410 of the Uniform Commercial Code impliedly eliminated oral acceptances as well. The present record is silent as to whether Chase actually accepted the drafts by proper notation on them.

III. Fraud

Presentation of fraudulent documents to a bank by a beneficiary subverts not only the purposes which letters of credit are designed to serve in general, but also the entire transaction at hand in particular. Falsified documents are the same as no documents at all.

We AFFIRM the judgment in favor of the Bank of Baroda. All parties have acknowledged that the documents tendered Chase did not conform to the established terms and conditions of the letters of credit. The Bank of Baroda, as the issuing bank, was entitled to strict compliance and there is no claim that it waived that right.

Case Highlights

- A typical letter of credit transaction comprises a number of contractual relationships, including between the buyer (account party) and its bank (issuing bank), between the issuing bank and the seller (beneficiary), and between the issuing bank and a corresponding bank (confirming bank).
- A confirming bank owes an independent obligation to the beneficiary party.
- The rule of strict compliance protects banks by allowing them to reject documents because of discrepancies.
- A bank is liable for payment if it "accepts" a draft. However, legal acceptance of a draft may be done only by a written endorsement on the draft (Uniform Commercial Code § 3-410).

---

originating from a source outside the documents. The rule of strict compliance is simply the standard by which the banks review documents.

The rule of strict compliance has been subject to recent judicial criticism. In *E&H Partners v. Broadway National Bank*, the U.S. District Court for the Southern District of New York refused to excuse the dishonor of a letter of credit when the bills of lading and invoices submitted to the issuing bank did not contain identical descriptions of the goods.[9] Rather, the court held that the two descriptions were consistent and did not justify dishonor when the item numbers and quantity numbers stated on the bills of lading and invoices matched. One year later, in *Creaciones Con Idea, S.A. v. MashreqBank, PSC*, the same court held that an exception to the strict compliance rule occurs with respect to insignificant variations in the documents, including when a word in the document is clear despite a typographical error or when the beneficiary provides only five copies rather than six copies of a required document.[10] The federal court's opinion in *Voest-Alpine Trading Company v. Bank of China* that follows examines other discrepancies between the required documents and those that were presented by the beneficiary. The opinion also elaborates upon alternatives to the strict compliance rule.

Two additional rules with respect to the dishonor of letters of credit merit discussion. Initially, an issuing bank is not free to dishonor its obligations at will. Rather, the bank must provide specific reasons for its decision to dishonor. Failure to provide such notice to the beneficiary bars reliance on such grounds

---

9. 39 F. Supp.2d 275, 283 (S.D.N.Y. 1998).
10. 51 F. Supp.2d 423, 427 (S.D.N.Y. 1999).

Voest-Alpine Trading USA Corp. v. Bank of China

167 F. Supp.2d 940 (S.D. Tex. 2000)

Gilmore, District Court Judge. On June 23, 1995, Plaintiff Voest-Alpine Trading USA Corporation ("Voest-Alpine") entered into a contract with Jiangyin Foreign Trade Corporation ("JFTC") to sell JFTC 1,000 metric tons of styrene monomer at a total price of $1.2 million. To finance the transaction, JFTC applied for a letter of credit through Defendant Bank of China. The letter of credit provided for payment to Voest-Alpine once the goods had been shipped to Zhangjiagang, China and Voest-Alpine had presented the requisite paperwork to the Bank of China as described in the letter of credit. The letter of credit was issued by the Bank of China on July 6, 1995 and assigned the number LC9521033/95. In addition to numerous other typographical errors, Voest-Alpine's name was listed as "Voest-Alpine USA Trading Corp." instead of "Voest-Alpine Trading USA Corp" with the "Trading USA" portion inverted. The destination port was also misspelled in one place as "Zhangjiagng," missing the third "a". The letter of credit did indicate, however, that the transaction would be subject to the Uniform Customs and Practice ("UCP 500").

By the time the product was ready to ship, the market price of styrene monomer had dropped significantly from the original contract price between Voest-Alpine and JFTC. Although JFTC asked for a price concession in light of the decrease in market price, Voest-Alpine declined and, through its agents, shipped the styrene monomer on July 18, 1995. All required inspection and documentation was completed. On August 1, 1995, Voest-Alpine presented the documents specified in the letter of credit to Texas Commerce Bank, the presenting bank. Texas Commerce Bank found discrepancies between the presentation documents and the letter of credit which it related to Voest-Alpine. Because Voest-Alpine did not believe that any of the noted discrepancies would warrant refusal to pay, it instructed Texas Commerce Bank to forward the presentation documents to the Bank of China.

Texas Commerce Bank sent the documents to the Bank of China on August 3, 1995. According to the letter of credit, Voest-Alpine, the beneficiary, was required to present the documents within fifteen days of the shipping date, by August 2, 1995. As the documents were presented on August 1, 1995, they were presented timely under the letter of credit. Bank of China received the documents on August 9, 1995.

On August 11, 1995, the Bank of China sent a telex to Texas Commerce Bank, informing them of seven alleged discrepancies between the letter of credit and the documents Voest-Alpine presented, six of which are the subject of this action. The Bank of China claimed that 1) the beneficiary's name differed from the name listed in the letter of credit, as noted by the presenting bank; 2) Voest-Alpine had submitted bills of lading marked "duplicate" and "triplicate" instead of "original"; 3) the invoice, packing list and the certificate of origin were not marked "original"; 4) the date of the survey report was later than that of the bill of lading; 5) the letter of credit number in the beneficiary's certified copy of the fax was incorrect, as noted by the presenting bank; and 6) the destination was not listed correctly in the certificate of origin and the beneficiary's certificate. The Bank of China returned the documents to Voest-Alpine and did not honor the letter of credit.

Section 13(a) of the UCP 500 provides:

Banks must examine all documents stipulated in the Credit with reasonable care, to ascertain whether or not they appear, on their face, to be in compliance with the terms and conditions of the Credit. Compliance of the stipulated documents on their face with the terms and conditions of the Credit shall be determined by international standard banking practice as reflected in these Articles. Documents which appear on their face to be inconsistent with one another will be considered as not appearing on their face to be in compliance with the terms and conditions of the Credit.

The UCP 500 does not provide guidance on what inconsistencies would justify a conclusion on the part of a bank that the documents are not in compliance with the terms and conditions of the letter of credit or what discrepancies are not a reasonable basis for such a conclusion. The UCP 500 does not mandate that the documents be a mirror image of the requirements or use the term "strict compliance."

The Court notes the wide range of interpretations on what standard banks should employ in examining letter of credit document presentations for compliance. Even where courts claim to uphold strict compliance, the standard is hardly uniform. The first and most restrictive approach is to require that the presentation documents be a mirror image of the requirements. Second, there are also cases claiming to follow the strict compliance standard but support rejection only where the discrepancies are such that would create risks for the issuer if the bank were to accept the presentation documents. A third standard, without much support in case law, is to analyze the documents for risk to the applicant.

The mirror image approach is problematic because it absolves the bank reviewing the documents of any responsibility to use common sense to determine if the documents, on their face, are related to the transaction or even to review an entire document in the context of the others presented to the bank. On the other hand, the second and third approaches employ a determination-of-harm standard that is too unwieldy. Such an analysis would improperly require the bank to evaluate risks that it might suffer or that might be suffered by the applicant and could undermine the independence of the three contracts that underlie the letter of credit payment scheme by forcing the bank to look beyond the face of the presentation documents.

The Court finds that a moderate, more appropriate standard lies within the UCP 500 itself and the opinions issued by the International Chamber of Commerce ("ICC") Banking Commission. One of the Banking Commission opinions defined the term "consistency" between the letter of credit and the documents presented to the issuing bank as used in Article 13(a) of the UCP to mean that "the whole of the documents must obviously relate to the same transaction, that is to say, that each should bear a relation (link) with the others on its face." The Banking Commission rejected the notion that "all of the documents should be exactly consistent in their wording."

A common sense, case-by-case approach would permit minor deviations of a typographical nature because such a letter-for-letter correspondence between the letter of credit and the presentation documents is virtually impossible. While the end result of such an analysis may bear a strong resemblance to the relaxed strict compliance standard, the actual calculus used by the issuing bank is not the risk it or the applicant faces but rather, whether the documents bear a rational link to one another. In this way, the issuing bank is required to examine a particular document in light of all documents presented and use common sense but is not required to evaluate risks or go beyond the face of the documents. The Court finds that in this case the Bank of China's listed discrepancies should be analyzed under this standard by determining whether the whole of the documents obviously relate to the transaction on their face.

First, the Bank of China claimed that the beneficiary's name in the presentation documents differed from the letter of credit. While it is true that the letter of credit inverted Voest-Alpine's geographic locator, all the documents Voest-Alpine presented that obviously related to this transaction placed the geographic locator behind "Trading", not in front of it. Furthermore, the addresses corresponded to that listed in the letter of credit and Texas Commerce Bank's cover letter to the Bank of China identified Voest-Alpine Trading USA as the beneficiary in the transaction with JFTC. The letter of credit with the inverted name bore obvious links to the documents presented by Voest-Alpine Trading USA. This is in contrast to a misspelling or outright omission.

The inversion of the geographic locator here does not signify a different corporate entity.

Second, the Bank of China pointed out that the set of originals of the bill of lading should have all been stamped "original" rather than "original," "duplicate" and "triplicate." It should be noted that neither the letter of credit nor any provision in the UCP 500 requires such stamping. In fact, the ICC Banking Commission expressly ruled that "duplicate" and "triplicate" bills of lading did not need to be marked "original" and that failure to label them as originals did not justify refusal of the documents. Int'l Chamber of Commerce, Banking Comm'n, Publication No. 565, *Opinions of the ICC Banking Comm'n 1995–1996* 38 (Gary Collyer ed. 1997). While it is true that this clarification by the ICC came after the transaction at issue in this case, it is clear from the face of the documents that these documents are three originals rather than one original and two copies. The documents have signatures in blue ink vary slightly, bear original stamps oriented differently on each page and clearly state on their face that the preparer made three original bills. While the "duplicate" and "triplicate" stamps may have been confusing, stamps do not make obviously original documents into copies.

Third, the Bank of China claimed that the failure to stamp the packing list documents as "original" was a discrepancy. Again, these documents are clearly originals on their face as they have three slightly differing signatures in blue ink. There was no requirement in the letter of credit or the UCP 500 that original documents be marked as such. The ICC's policy statement on the issue provides that, "banks treat as original any document that appears to be hand signed by the issuer of the document." Int'l Chamber of Commerce, Comm'n on Banking Technique and Practice, *The determination of an "Original" document in the context of UCP 500 sub-Article 20(b)* July 12, 1999). The failure to mark obvious originals is not a discrepancy.

Fourth, the Bank of China argues that the date of the survey report is after the bill of lading and is therefore discrepant. A careful examination of the survey report reveals that the survey took place "immediately before/after loading" and that the sample of cargo "to be loaded" was taken. The plain language of the report reveals that the report may have been issued after the bill of lading but the survey itself was conducted before the ship departed. The date does not pose a discrepancy.

Fifth, the Bank of China claims that the letter of credit number listed in the beneficiary's certified copy of fax is wrong. The letter of credit number was listed as "LC95231033/95" on the copy of fax instead of "LC9521033/95" as in the letter of credit itself, adding an extra "3" after "LC952." However, adding the letter of credit number to this document was gratuitous and in the numerous other places in the documents that the letter of credit was referenced by number, it was incorrect only in one place. Moreover, the seven other pieces of information contained in the document were correct. The document checker could have easily looked to any other document to verify the letter of credit number, or looked to the balance of the information within the document and found that the document as a whole bears an obvious relationship to the transaction.

Finally, the Bank of China claims that the wrong destination is listed in the certificate of origin and the beneficiary's certificate. The certificate of origin spelled Zhangjiagang as "Zhangjiagng" missing an "a" as it is misspelled once in the letter of credit, making it consistent. The beneficiary's certificate, however, spelled it "Zhanjiagng," missing a "g" in addition to the "a", a third spelling that did not appear in the letter of credit. There is no port in China called "Zhangjiagng" or "Zhanjiagng." "Gng" is a combination of letters not found in Romanized Chinese, whereas "gang" means "port" in Chinese. The other information contained in the document was correct, such as the letter of credit number and the contract number, and even contained the distinctive phrase "by courie lukdtwithin 3 days after whipment", presumably meaning by courier within three days after shipment, as in the letter of credit. The document as a whole bears an obvious relationship with the transaction. The misspelling of the destination is not a basis for dishonor of the letter of credit where the rest of the document has demonstrated linkage to the transaction on its face.

Based on the foregoing, the Court finds in favor of the plaintiff, Voest-Alpine.

Case Update

The district court's opinion was upheld on appeal in *Voest-Alpine Trading Corporation v. Bank of China*, 288 F.3d 262 (5th Cir. 2002).

Case Highlights

- Banks must examine all documents stipulated in the letter of credit with reasonable care to ascertain whether they appear, on their face, to be in compliance with the terms and conditions of the letter of credit.
- Courts have taken three different approaches with respect to ascertaining whether documents produced by a beneficiary are in compliance with a letter of credit: the mirror image rule, a rule whereby rejection is permitted only where the discrepancies are such that would create risks for the issuer if the bank were to accept the presentation documents, and an approach that analyzes the documents for risk to the applicant.
- The UCP does not mandate that the documents be a mirror image of the requirements or use the term "strict compliance."
- Courts may determine the consistency between the letter of credit and the documents presented to the issuing bank by deciding whether the documents obviously relate to the same transaction, specifically, that each document bears a relation with the other documents on their face.

---

in the initial and future instances of dishonor. The following opinion in *Hamilton Bank, N.A. v. Kookmin Bank* illustrates the consequences of failure to provide adequate notice of the grounds for an issuing bank's dishonor of its letter of credit.

Second, most international export transactions have a number of expiration dates. Initially, the beneficiary must submit the necessary documents before the expiration of the letter of credit. The UCP also provides another type of expiration date. The **21-day rule** states that the bill of lading, and accompanying documents, must be presented to the bank within twenty-one days from their procurement. If the exporter obtains the bill of lading and delays presentation past the 21 days, then the letter of credit expires, even though the expiration date on the letter has not passed. However, the parties are free to avoid this provision through express terms in the letter of credit. The following opinion in *Heritage Bank v. Redcom Laboratories, Inc.* discusses the circumstances under which parties may avoid the 21-day rule.

Hamilton Bank, N.A. v. Kookmin Bank

44 F. Supp.2d 653 (S.D.N.Y. 1999)

Kaplan, District Court Judge. Kookmin Bank ("Kookmin"), which is organized in the Republic of Korea ("Korea"), presented a draft for payment under a letter of credit (the "L/C") issued by Hamilton Bank, N.A. ("Hamilton"), a national bank with its principal office in Florida. Hamilton refused to pay because a required document was missing. Hamilton, however, failed to notify Kookmin by telecommunication of the reason for its refusal as required by the Uniform Customs and Practice for Documentary Credits (the "UCP"), which governed the L/C. Hamilton brought this action for a declaratory judgment and for damages. Kookmin has counterclaimed to recover the $1.5 million allegedly due on the L/C.

On June 11, 1996, Hamilton issued a letter of credit in the amount of $1,500,000 on behalf of Sky Industries Corporation ("Sky") for the benefit of Sung-Jin Trading Co. ("Sung-Jin") in connection with a proposed transaction in which Sky would purchase leather sport shoes from Sung-Jin. By the original terms of the L/C, payment would be made on a draft upon presentation of (1) a bill of lading, (2) a commercial invoice, (3) a packing list, and (4) a "copy of authaenticated [sic] telex from issuing bank to advising bank, indicating quantity to be shipped, destination, and nominating transporting company" (the "Authenticated Telex"). No draft would be honored until Sky first deposited and pledged funds backing the total amount of the L/C.

The L/C was amended three times, the only relevant amendment being the third which stated in pertinent part "on additional conditions add: No further Amendments of this L/C will be issued by applicant. Any other condition should be in accordance with 'Option Contract' signed by applicant and beneficiary dated May 31, 1996. All other terms remain unchanged." The L/C and each of its amendments stated it was governed by the UCP.

J.G. Kim, the president of Sung-Jin, attempted to negotiate a draft drawn on the L/C to Kookmin's Pusan branch in June 1996. Taek Su Jun, a Kookmin manager, refused to negotiate the draft because the Authenticated Telex was not included among the documents presented. On July 12, Kim allegedly attempted to negotiate a draft drawn on the L/C at Pusan Bank. That same day, Pusan Bank sent a message to Hamilton through SWIFT seeking approval to negotiate the draft without the Authenticated Telex. On July 17, Hamilton responded via SWIFT notifying Pusan Bank that it was not permitted to do so.

On July 13, prior to obtaining a response from Pusan Bank, Kim attempted once again to negotiate his draft to Kookmin. This time, in response to Jun's request for the Authenticated Telex, Kim presented to Kookmin two documents: one entitled "special instructions," purportedly from Sky Industries to Sung-Jin, dated July 2, 1996, and the other a copy of an option contract dated May 31, 1996 between Sung-Jin and Sky Industries which contained a reference to the special instructions. According to Jun, Kim explained that the combination of the option contract and the special instructions obviated the need for the Authenticated Telex. Evidently assuming that the L/C requirements had been satisfied, Kookmin negotiated the draft and remitted $1.5 million to Sung-Jin.

Kookmin sent to Hamilton the documents it obtained from Kim along with a request for payment of $1.5 million. Hamilton received the documents on July 22, 1996 and returned them to Kookmin via courier on July 24 with an accompanying letter stating that they were being returned because presentment was "not in compliance with the terms and conditions of the credit." On August 2, Kookmin again presented the documents to Hamilton. Four days later, Hamilton again returned the documents to Kookmin and sent a message through SWIFT the same day stating that Hamilton was returning them because Kookmin had not presented the Authenticated Telex as required by the L/C.

UCP Article 14

It is undisputed that Kookmin never presented an Authenticated Telex and that the conditions to payment on the L/C therefore were not satisfied fully. Kookmin nevertheless claims that Hamilton is precluded under the UCP from relying on this deficiency because it did not (a) notify Kookmin via telecommunication of the specific reason for its refusal to pay; and (b) state all discrepancies in respect of which the bank refused the documents.

UCP Article 14, "Discrepant Documents and Notice," provides that an issuing bank may refuse documents presented to it for the purpose of drawing on a letter of credit if it "determines that the documents appear on their face not to be in compliance with the terms and conditions of the Credit." If the issuing bank does so, "it must give notice to that effect by telecommunication . . . no later than the close of the seventh banking day following the day of receipt of the documents." Moreover, "such notice must state all discrepancies in respect of which the bank refuses the documents. . . . " Failure to act in accordance with these provisions "precludes the issuing bank from claiming that the documents are not in compliance with the terms and conditions of the Credit." This preclusion, furthermore, is strict. Under Florida law, "a bank will be estopped from subsequent reliance on a ground for dishonor if it did not specify that ground in its initial dishonor." The provisions of Article 14 thus "have been interpreted to incorporate a penalty against an issuing bank that does not assert the noncompliance of documents in a timely fashion."

It is undisputed that Hamilton did not communicate its rejection via telecommunications. It replied via DHL courier. Nor did Hamilton's initial rejection of Kookmin's tender state specific reasons for its action, asserting only that the documents were "not in compliance with the terms and conditions of the Credit." This was not sufficiently specific for purposes of Article 14(d), which requires, *inter alia*, that the issuing bank "must state all discrepancies" for rejecting the documents.

Hamilton contends first that Kookmin had notice of its rejection of the discrepant documents when Hamilton rejected Pusan Bank's attempted presentation. Even assuming, without deciding, that notice of a previous rejection is enough to meet Article 14's required statement of reasons for rejection, this claim is unsupported. First, Hamilton did not send notice to Pusan Bank of its rejection until July 17—four days after Kim negotiated his draft to Kookmin. Second, there is no allegation that Kookmin actually was aware of that rejection. Hamilton next asserts that its second rejection on August 6 via SWIFT fulfilled the Article 14 requirements. But it is mistaken. Not only was this rejection beyond the seven day limit prescribed by Article 14, but the Eleventh Circuit

has held that "a bank will be estopped from subsequent reliance on a ground for dishonor if it did not specify that ground in its initial dishonor." In consequence, Hamilton did not meet the requirements of Article 14.

Conclusion

For the foregoing reasons, Kookmin shall have judgment against Hamilton for $1.5 million plus interest thereon at the rate of 9 percent from July 22, 1996 to the date of judgment.

Case Highlights

- An issuing bank that dishonors a letter of credit must give notice by telecommunication within seven days following receipt of the documents from the beneficiary, which notice must identify all discrepancies in respect of which the bank refuses the documents.
- The failure of the issuing bank to specifically identify discrepancies in the documents precludes it from claiming that the documents are not in compliance with the terms and conditions of the letter of credit.
- The failure of the issuing bank to specifically identify discrepancies in the documents presented by the beneficiary in its initial notice of dishonor serves to estop the bank from reliance on these discrepancies in a subsequent dishonor.

Heritage Bank v. Redcom Laboratories, Inc.

250 F.3d 319 (5th Cir. 2001)

Mith, Circuit Court Judge. Heritage Bank issued a letter of credit to Fiber Wave Telecom, Inc. ("Fiber Wave"), which used it to purchase electronics from Redcom Laboratories, Inc. ("Redcom"), which delivered the goods and made presentment to the bank for payment. Fiber Wave believed the goods defective and successfully petitioned a Texas court to enjoin the bank from honoring Redcom's presentment. Redcom made another demand on the bank during the pendency of the injunction, but the bank refused to honor the presentment and sought a declaratory judgment exonerating it from liability.

Redcom sued the bank for wrongful dishonor, and the district court granted summary judgment for Redcom.

The bank appeals, arguing that the court erred in granting summary judgment. Finding no reversible error, we affirm.

On February 3, 1998, the bank issued Irrevocable Commercial Letter of Credit No. 9518 for $215,729 to Fiber Wave, naming Redcom as the beneficiary. The letter of credit was subject to the Uniform Customs and Practice for Documentary Credits ("UCP"), and was good for one year. It had no special conditions or unusual provisions. Redcom shipped goods to Fiber Wave on March 27, 1998, and made a presentment on April 24, 1998, which the bank received on May 1.

Before the bank determined whether the presentment complied with the letter of credit, Fiber Wave sued the bank and Redcom in state court and obtained a temporary restraining order ("TRO") that enjoined the bank from honoring the presentment. On May 6, the bank, because of the TRO, dishonored the presentment. On June 5, the state court converted the TRO into a temporary injunction.

On November 20, while the injunction was in effect, Redcom made another presentment to the bank for payment under the letter of credit. On November 25, the bank again dishonored the presentment, citing the injunction. The letter of credit expired on February 3, and on March 3, Redcom made another demand to the bank for payment. The bank filed a declaratory judgment action against Fiber Wave and Redcom in state court, and Redcom removed the action to federal court.

The bank contends that the court erred in granting summary judgment for Redcom on the wrongful dishonor claim. The bank argues that Redcom made an untimely, deficient presentment. The bank claims that Redcom did not present its documents within twenty-one days after the date of shipment as required by article 43(a) of the UCP 500. The goods were shipped to Fiber Wave on March 27, 1998. Redcom made a deficient presentment on April 24, twenty-eight days after the date of shipping, and a corrected presentment on November 20, which was 200 days after the shipment. If the twenty-one-day provision applies, Redcom's presentment seems both deficient and untimely. An untimely presentment is an incurable defect, and the bank had no duty to notify Redcom of it. Thus, if the April 24 presentment was untimely, Redcom could make no subsequent presentment that would trigger the bank's payment, and a finding that Redcom failed to make a proper presentment in a timely fashion under the UCP would dispose of the case.

Redcom argues that the parties specifically contracted around the twenty-one-day provision, which says that the bank will honor any proper presentment "on delivery of documents as specified if presented at our counters on or before the expiration date." The bank suggests that this language may be interpreted merely to affirm the period for which the credit was good. A significant showing would have to be made before parties to a letter of credit governed by the UPC would be found to have waived its express terms. The terms of the letter of credit and the actions of the parties suggest that the parties intended to contract around the UPC default rule. The bank notified Redcom after the April 24 and the November 20 presentment that it planned to dishonor it because of the injunction. Even though the bank need not have notified Redcom of the deficiency of untimeliness, it seems surprising that, if the UCP applied, it chose to use the injunction rather than the UCP as the basis for dishonor. Based on its own actions, the bank apparently believed that the letter of credit overrode the UCP's requirements. Therefore, Redcom made a timely presentment.

AFFIRMED.

Case Highlights

- An untimely presentment is an incurable defect, and no subsequent presentment can trigger the issuing bank's payment obligation.
- The issuing bank and the beneficiary are free to contractually avoid the UCP's 21-day presentment rule.
- The agreement to avoid the UCP's 21-day rule may be implied from the parties' actions evidencing their interpretation of the requirements surrounding presentment pursuant to the letter of credit.

The previously discussed *Voest-Alpine v. Chase Manhattan* case also references the **bill of exchange** or **draft**.[11] The draft was previously discussed in Chapter Nine but will be briefly reviewed again here. The draft is a collections instrument that acts very much like a check. It is the mechanism for payment through the banking system. When a seller presents documents for payment on a letter of credit, it presents the bank with a draft drawn on the letter of credit. The draft is an order to the drawee (bank or account party) to pay. The difference between a draft and an ordinary check is that in the documentary draft the seller acts as both the drawer and the payee. The **Convention Providing a Uniform Law for Bills of Exchange and Promissory Notes** of 1930 states that "a bill of exchange or draft contains an

---

11.   The terms *draft* and *bill of exchange* can be used interchangeably. The term used in the United Kingdom is *bill of exchange*; the term used in the United States is *draft*.

unconditional order to pay a determinate sum of money; the name of the person who is to pay (*drawee*); a statement of the time of payment; a statement of the place where payment is to be made; the name of the person to whom or to whose order payment is to be made (*payee*); a statement of the date and of the place where the bill is issued; and the signature of the person who issues the bill (*drawer*)."[12]

The two general types of drafts used in export transactions are the sight draft and the time draft. A sight draft requires payment immediately upon the presentation of the documents. A draft that does not specify the time of payment is deemed payable at sight. Exhibit 11.3 provides an example of a sight draft. Note that if a period of time was entered in the blank following "Sight Days After," then the draft would be converted into a time draft.

If the exporter wants to extend credit to the buyer, a time draft can be used to state that payment is due within a certain time after the buyer accepts the draft and receives the documents. By signing and writing "accepted" on the draft, the buyer is formally obligated to pay within the stated time. When this is done, the draft is called a **trade acceptance** and can be either kept by the exporter until maturity or sold to a bank at a discount for immediate payment. **Acceptance** creates an independent obligation on the acceptor (drawee). The independence of the acceptance obligation means that the obligation "can be enforced by subsequent holders of the instrument without regard to the buyer's rights under the sales contract."[13] In short, the acceptance converts the draft into a negotiable instrument.[14] When a bank accepts a draft, the draft becomes an obligation of the bank and a negotiable instrument known as a **banker's acceptance**. A banker's acceptance can be sold to a bank at a discount for immediate payment. The following excerpt from the *Interpane Coatings v. Australia & New Zealand Banking Group* case describes the use of time drafts and the importance of acceptance.

http://
United Nations Convention on International Bills of Exchange and International Promissory Notes: **http://www. UNCITRAL.org** (follow links from "Adopted Texts" to "International Payments").

EXHIBIT 11.3   *Sight Draft*

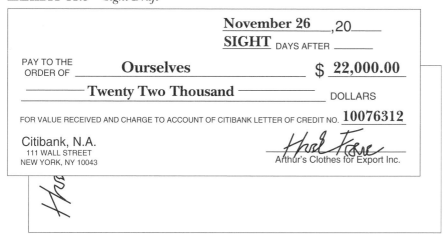

November 26 ,20____

SIGHT DAYS AFTER _____

PAY TO THE ORDER OF _____ **Ourselves** _____ $ **22,000.00**

_____ **Twenty Two Thousand** _____ DOLLARS

FOR VALUE RECEIVED AND CHARGE TO ACCOUNT OF CITIBANK LETTER OF CREDIT NO. **10076312**

Citibank, N.A.
111 WALL STREET
NEW YORK, NY 10043

Arthur's Clothes for Export Inc.

---

12. Convention Providing a Uniform Law for Bills of Exchange and Promissory Notes, art. 1(2–8).

13. John O. Honnold & Curtis R. Reitz, *Sales Transactions: Domestic and International Law* (2001). This casebook provides a good summary of sales law, including the documentary transaction and letters of credit.

14. In the United States, Article 3 of the UCC governs the liabilities of the acceptor (drawee-buyer) and the drawer (seller).

Interpane Coatings v. Australia & New Zealand Banking Group

732 F. Supp. 909 (N.D. Ill. 1990)

Kocoras, District Judge. Underlying this litigation is an international sale of goods run amuck. Interpane, a Wisconsin corporation and the seller in this transaction, delivered the goods to an Australian buyer who then did not pay despite having accepted the goods as well as having endorsed three bills of exchange. In this action, Interpane seeks to hold ANZ, the designated collecting bank in the transaction, liable for its failure to obtain the money from the buyer.

The relevant facts are as follows: Interpane and an Australian entity named McDowell Pacific Pty., Ltd., entered into a contract for the sale of goods whereby Interpane was to ship goods to Australia and McDowell was to pay for them. As is usual in such cases where delivery and payment are to occur at a distant point, the seller used bills of exchange and bills of lading rather than simply shipping the goods to the buyer in Australia with an invoice (open account).

By using this procedure, Interpane reduced the critical transactional points of tender and acceptance to a mere documentary transfer that made acceptance of the bills of exchange a condition precedent to tender. But to do so required the aid of middlemen in the form of banks. The banks involved in the transaction were ANZ and the Chicago branch of Swiss Bank Corporation. ANZ, McDowell's bank, was to act as the presenting and the collecting bank. Swiss Bank was designated Interpane's local representative, forwarding and receiving the relevant documents on behalf of Interpane. It was also the named payee on the bills of exchange. Under the documentary procedure used in this case, Interpane sent ANZ three bills of exchange accompanied by three bills of lading. The bills of exchange were all time drafts with payment to be due 60 days from McDowell's "seeing" them; such bills are called time drafts in order to distinguish them from sight drafts which are actually payable on sight.

There are two principal types of collection orders, those that require mere acceptance by the drawee/buyer and those which require actual payment. If acceptance is required, the collecting bank need only obtain the endorsement of the drawee/buyer before releasing the title documents. By accepting the bills of exchange, the drawee acknowledges the debt and commits to making payment as required by the bill of exchange (in this case 60 days from sight). As the designated collecting bank, ANZ had a contractual duty to follow Interpane's collection orders. Interpane alleges that ANZ breached this contractual duty by not obeying its special instructions, which it alleges required ANZ to endorse the bills of exchange as a guarantor, thus converting them into banker's acceptances, before releasing the title documents to McDowell.

[Case dismissed on procedural grounds (*forum non conveniens*) not related to the bank's obligations under the letter of credit.]

Case Highlights

- Banks play an intermediary role in effecting the transfer of documents and payments in an export transaction.
- Documentary collection transactions condition the release of documents on acceptance or payment of the documentary draft by the buyer.
- Bills of exchange or drafts are the means by which an exporter obtains payment in an international sale of goods transaction.
- Bills of exchange or drafts are orders by the drawer (exporter) to the buyer or buyer's bank (drawee) to pay the exporter (payee). It differs from a check only in that the drawer and the payee are the same party (exporter).
- A time draft is a bill of exchange that requires payment sometime after the buyer accepts the documents.

Uniform Customs and Practices for Documentary Credits

The UCP is a set of rules published by the International Chamber of Commerce, the most recent compilation of which is the **UCP 500**. The UCP applies to letters of credit used to guarantee payment to an exporter in a documentary transaction. They may also be used in conjunction with standby letters of credit used to guarantee a performance. As mentioned earlier, the UCP is incorporated in most international letter of credit transactions by references in the application forms supplied by commercial banks (see Exhibit 11.1: Letter of Credit Application). Letters of credit used to guarantee payment to an exporter are called documentary credits. This name refers to the fact that payment under the letter of credit is contingent upon the exporter's presentation of documents.

As discussed earlier, banks have the duty to use reasonable care in examining documents for conformity to the requirements of the letter of credit. If the documents are in facial compliance, then the bank pays the beneficiary party (exporter) through the letter of credit. The issuing bank must examine the documents within a reasonable time and notify the parties promptly of any nonconformity. The documents must comply strictly with the requirements of the letter of credit. Banks are not liable for accepting forged or false documents. The letter of credit instructions of the account party (buyer) should give precise details of the documents required. For example, a bill of lading must indicate that the goods have been loaded on board the named vessel. Insurance documents must be dated prior to the loading of the goods on board the ship. The description of the goods in the commercial invoice must be the same as the one contained in the letter of credit.

The sophisticated importer-purchaser should become familiar with the requirements and rules of the UCP 500.[15] These rules have a direct bearing on how the applicant completes a letter of credit application. If the applicant places a noncustomary term or instruction in the application, the banks often disregard that instruction in favor of a default rule found in the UCP 500. The following list is a sampling of some of the more important UCP 500 rules:

- Care in selecting an expiration date avoids the bother of obtaining extensions. An unnecessarily prolonged expiration date incurs additional bank charges.
- For a letter of credit to be transferable, the applicant must request such designation. Article 48 of the UCP should be carefully reviewed before making such a request. This article provides that transferring banks are under no obligation to effect a transfer except to the extent and in the manner expressly consented to by the parties. A letter of credit is not deemed transferable merely by inclusion of such terms as *divisible, fractionable, assignable,* and *transferable* without a manifestation of the express consent of the parties as to its transferability.[16]
- Under Article 9 of the UCP, the applicant must request that the letter be confirmed. The applicant may designate the confirming bank or leave it to the discretion of the issuing bank. It is best for the applicant and the beneficiary to agree on the identity of the confirming bank before the credit application is submitted.
- The currency of the letter of credit should be designated by using the ISO currency codes such as USD (U.S. dollar) and GBP (pounds sterling).
- The applicant should designate the bank or banks (nominated banks) at which the credit will be available. An alternative is to insert "freely negotiable by any bank" or "freely negotiable credit." This designation allows the beneficiary to negotiate the documents at any bank willing to negotiate. However, it is desirable for the applicant to limit the free negotiability to a specific country or city.

---

15. For detailed discussion of the requirements of UCP 500, see ICC, *Documentary Credits: UCP 500 & 400 Compared,* No. 511 (Charles del Busto, ed., 1993).
16. UCP 500, art. 48(b).

- The applicant should clearly instruct whether the credit will be made available for partial shipments ("partial shipments allowed" or "partial shipments not allowed"). Shipments by preagreed installments should also be clearly stipulated on the credit application.
- The applicant should provide transport details, including where the shipment is to be "taken in charge, dispatched, or loaded on board" and to where the shipment must be made, whether "at the place of unloading, delivery, or final destination." The applicant should also state the latest date for shipment, dispatch, or taking in charge under the space next to the phrase "not later than" on the credit application. Otherwise, the time limit will be the date of expiration as provided in Article 44 of the UCP. If the applicant uses the phrase "on or about," Article 46(c) of the UCP defines an acceptable period as five days before or after the specified date. Abbreviations for geographical designation should be avoided. Full names should be used for all cities, states, provinces, and countries.

As previously discussed, under the rule of strict compliance, banks are authorized to reject documents even if they are technically in conformity. The use of abbreviations or acronyms in the description of goods may make strict compliance problematic. People in the industry may use such devices in corresponding among themselves, but banks are not required to know or investigate trade custom or usage. This was the situation in the English case of *J.H. Rayner & Co. v. Hambros Bank, Ltd.*,[17] in which the bank rejected a bill of lading that used the notation "C.R.S." in describing the goods. In the nut industry, C.R.S. is the abbreviation for "Coromandel ground nuts." The letter of credit required that the bill of lading state "Coromandel ground nuts." The accompanying commercial invoice did use the full name. Nonetheless, the court upheld the bank's right to reject the documents. Two rationales were given. First, "that even though the description of the goods in the bill of lading was correct in accordance with the custom of trade, the bank could not be held to be affected with a knowledge of the customs of the various trades in which its customers might be concerned." Second, even if the bank possessed knowledge of the trade custom or usage, it must do exactly what its customer requires it to do. There may be some unknown reason why the account party (importer) wants the documents to be detailed in a certain way. It is not for the bank to impose common sense to abrogate a specific instruction in the letter of credit.

The *Rayner* case also demonstrates that although the strict compliance rule has been criticized in the United States, it remains important in transactions to which the law of other countries may be applicable. The parties to the letter of credit transaction are thus well advised to be precise in the drafting of the underlying documentation. In addition, the description of the goods should generally be as brief as possible. In *Rayner*, the result would have been different under the UCP if the letter of credit had not specifically stated that the bill of lading should have that particular description. The UCP requires only that the commercial invoice reflect the description found on the letter of credit. Article 37(c) states that "the description of the goods in the commercial invoice must correspond with the description in the Credit. In all other documents, the goods may be described in general terms not inconsistent with the description of the goods in the Credit." Therefore, it is advisable to keep the description simple and clear.

---

17.   112 K.B. 27 (1943).

In listing documents other than transport documents, insurance documents, and commercial invoices, the applicant should specifically state the issuing entity and what the content of the documents should entail. This is required under Article 21 of the UCP.

Articles 23 through 30 of the UCP should be reviewed in determining the transport documents that will be required. The rules pertaining to two of the more common transport documents, the ocean bill of lading and a bill of lading issued by a freight forwarder, are found in Articles 23 and 30. If the shipment entails the use of more than one mode of transportation, then the applicant should require a multimodal transport document, as described in Article 26.

The content of insurance documents is addressed in Articles 34 through 36 of the UCP. If the applicant fails to state the amount of the insurance to be procured, then Article 34(f)(ii) of the UCP requires an amount equal to CIF value plus 10 percent.

The applicant should specify the time by which the documents need to be presented following shipment of the goods. If a period is not stipulated, then Article 43 (a) of the UCP sets the period as 21 days from the date of shipment. The applicant who wants to allow for presentation irrespective of the date of shipment must so state in the space provided for "Additional Instructions."

In amending an irrevocable letter of credit, it is advisable to use the standard "Irrevocable Documentary Credit Amendment Form." Focus on Transactions: Ten Rules Pertaining to International Letters of Credit further summarizes the rules governing letters of credit.

Rule Six in the Focus on Transactions feature notes that banks have a reasonable time to review documents, not to exceed seven business days, under the

---

Ten Rules Pertaining to International Letters of Credit

Focus on Transactions

Rule 1
Rule of Facial Compliance: Banks are required only to review documents and compare them with the letter of credit's requirements for conformity (not liable for "fraud in the transaction").

Rule 2
Banks are not required to know or to investigate trade or business usage, custom, or practices.

Rule 3
Rule of Strict Compliance: Banks may reject documents for *any* discrepancy.

Rule 4
A letter of credit must have an expiration date to be enforceable.

Rule 5
UCP 500 21-Day Rule: The beneficiary party must deliver documents within 21 days of receipt (21 days from receipt of bill of lading).

Rule 6
Bank's Period of Review: Banks have a *reasonable period* to review documents, not to exceed seven business days (three days pursuant to Article 5 of the UCC or seven days pursuant to UCP 500).

Rule 7
Presumption of Irrevocability: UCP 500 and UCC Article 5 presume that a letter of credit is irrevocable unless it clearly states on its face that it is revocable.

continued

Ten Rules Pertaining to International Letters of Credit (*continued*)

Rule 8
Insurance Certificate: Must not be dated later than date of loading and should be in the amount of CIF plus 10 percent.

Rule 9
Commercial Invoice: Must include the exact description found in the letter of credit.

(Other documents may use general descriptions not inconsistent with one found in the letter of credit.)

Rule 10
A letter of credit is not transferable unless it specifically states that it is a transferable credit.

Uniform Commercial Code[18] and seven days under UCP 500. If the bank accepts nonconforming documents, then it may sue the beneficiary party if it proceeds in a timely fashion. This was the issue in *Habib Bank Ltd. v. Convermat Corp.*[19] In that case, the bank paid on documents that included a bill of lading with a discrepancy in the shipping date. The account party subsequently rejected the documents. The bank waited a month before making a claim against the beneficiary party. The court held that the claim was not made in a timely fashion and dismissed the action. This duty of the bank to act quickly is implied from Article 14 of the UCP. Article 14(d)(i) requires the bank to give notice "by expeditious means." Furthermore, as previously noted in the *Hamilton Bank* case, such notice "must state all discrepancies in respect of which the bank refuses the documents."[20]

Standby Letters of Credit

The Federal Reserve of the United States defines **standby letter of credit** as a letter of credit that "represents an obligation to the beneficiary on the part of the issuer: (1) to repay money borrowed by or advanced to or for the account of the customer (account party); (2) to make payment on account of any evidence of indebtedness undertaken by the account party; or (3) to make payment on account of any default by the party procuring the issuance of the letter of credit in the performance of an obligation."[21] As a general rule, standby letters of credit are distinguishable from documentary letters of credit on the basis that they are traditionally drawn on only in the event that the applicant fails to perform an obligation to the beneficiary, usually a failure to make a payment.[22] Nevertheless, the UCP has been applied to both documentary credits and standby letters of credit. However, on January 1, 1999, new **International Standby Practices (ISP98)** governing standby letters of credit took effect.[23] ISP98 establishes ten separate rules with respect to standby letters of credit, including defining the obligations of the parties, presentation, examination, notice and disposition of documents, transfer and assignment, cancellation, and reimbursement.

---

18.   See U.C.C. § 5-108(b).
19.   554 N.Y.S.2d 757 (N.Y. Sup. Ct. 1990).
20.   UCP 500, art. 14(d)(ii).
21.   12 C.F.R. § 208.24(a)(1-3) (2004).
22.   See *Brenntag International Chemicals, Inc. v. Bank of India*, 175 F.3d 245, 251 (2d Cir. 1999).
23.   See ICC, *International Standby Practices*, No. 590 (1998).

Standby letters of credit can be used to help secure a variety of contractual obligations associated with the export transaction. In addition to performance guarantees often associated with construction projects, standby letters have been used to guarantee warranties, to support borrowers under international loans, to ensure availability of suppliers, to secure countertrade commitments, and to act as deposits in the sale of goods and as prepayment of fees for services.[24] *Itek Corp. v. First National Bank of Boston* illustrates the use of standby letters of credit to guarantee performance of a construction project and for the return of monies paid by the foreign buyer.

Itek Corp. v. First National Bank of Boston
730 F.2d 19 (1st Cir. 1984)

Breyer, Circuit Judge. The First National Bank of Boston ("FNBB"), at the request of Itek Corp., issued several letters of credit running in favor of Bank Melli Iran ("Melli"). Melli demanded payment from FNBB of the money that the letters promised. Itek obtained a federal district court injunction prohibiting FNBB from paying Melli. The basic question that Melli's appeal presents is whether its effort to obtain the money by calling the letters is "fraudulent."

The letters of credit arise out of promises made in a 1977 contract between Itek and Iran's Imperial Ministry of War. The contract provided that Itek would make and sell high-technology optical equipment to the War Ministry at a price of $22.5 million. Iran was to make a 20 percent down payment. It would pay Itek 60 percent of the total price ($13.5 million) as work progressed; it would pay the remaining 20 percent upon satisfactory completion. The contract required Itek to provide two types of bank guarantees. The first, the *down payment guarantee*, was to give the Ministry the right to obtain return of the down payment until Itek produced work of sufficient value. The second, the *good performance guarantee* was for $2.25 million, 10 percent of the contract price. Its object was to protect the Ministry against a breach of contract. The Ministry could call for payment under the guarantees simply by submitting a written request for payment to the bank.

Bank Melli, an instrumentality of the Iranian government, issued the guarantees. Melli required Itek to provide it with similar "standby" letters of credit, issued by an American bank in Melli's favor. The underlying contract provided that if the contract "is cancelled due to *Force Majeure*, all Bank Guarantees of good performance of work will be immediately released." The contract defines *Force Majeure* to include cancellation by the United States

of necessary export licenses. Itek's work proceeded uneventfully until Iran's government collapsed in early 1979. In April 1979 the United States suspended Itek's export license. Itek then proceeded to cancel the contract in accordance with the *force majeure* provisions. At that point, Melli demanded payment on the letters of credit.

Section 5-114(2)(b) of the Uniform Commercial Code authorizes a court to enjoin payment on a letter of credit when it finds "fraud in the transaction." It states that:

(2) Unless otherwise agreed when documents appear on their face to comply with the terms of a credit but a required document is forged or fraudulent or there is fraud in the transaction:

(a) the issuer must honor the draft . . . if honor is demanded by . . . a holder in due course and

(b) in all other cases as against its customer, an issuer acting in good faith may honor the draft or demand for payment despite notification from the customer of fraud, forgery or other defect not apparent on the face of the documents but a court of appropriate jurisdiction may enjoin such honor.

The basic legal question in this case is whether the circumstances surrounding Melli's calls on FNBB's letters of credit establish "fraud in the transaction." We answer this question fully aware of the need to interpret the "fraud" provision narrowly. The very object of a letter of credit is to provide a near foolproof method of placing money in its beneficiary's hands when he complies with the terms contained in the letter itself-when he presents, for example, a shipping document that the letter calls for or (as here) a simple written demand for payment. Despite these reasons for hesitating to enjoin payment of a letter of credit, the need for an exception is apparent. Thus, in a leading case, a seller, contractually committed to ship

24. See Gordon B. Graham & Benjamin Geva, "Standby Credits in Canada," 9 *Canadian Business Law Journal* 180 (1982).

bristles to a buyer, shipped rubbish instead. The court refused to allow the seller to call the letter, put the money in his pocket, and let the buyer sue him, for in the court's view, the seller did not even have a colorable claim that he had done what the contract called for as a precondition to obtaining the money, namely, ship the bristles. *Sztejn v. J. Henry Schroder Banking Corp.*, 31 N.Y.S.2d 631 (Sup. Ct. 1941). If Melli has no plausible or colorable basis under the contract to call for payment of the letters, its effort to obtain the money is fraudulent and payment can be enjoined.

For these reasons, we find adequate support for the district court's conclusions that Melli was without a plausible legal basis for calling the letters of credit and that its call upon them, in the circumstances revealed in this record, constituted "fraud." The injunction therefore was properly issued. And the district court's order is AFFIRMED.

Case Highlights

- A letter of credit that is used to guarantee a performance or return of a deposit is called a standby letter of credit.
- A bank *may* honor a letter of credit when documents comply on their face, even if notified that the documents are forgeries or that there is fraud in the transaction.
- The account party can enjoin the bank from honoring a letter of credit by obtaining a court order (injunction).
- A force majeure clause describes events that allow a party to be excused from performing a contractual obligation.

The *Itek Corp. v. First National Bank of Boston* case notes that under the Uniform Commercial Code, a court may enjoin a bank from honoring the demand for payment when the bank has been notified of fraud in the transaction. The "fraud" exception to the traditional reluctance of courts to interfere with commercial letters of credit and guarantees has been liberally construed in the decisional law both before and after the adoption of the code. However, in most export transactions, an injunction may not be a practical alternative because of the time it takes to obtain such an order.

Alternative Methods of Guaranteeing Performance

http://

World Bank—links to Multilateral Investment Guarantee Agency (MIGA), International Development Association (IDA), and International Finance Corporation (IFC): **http://www. worldbank.org.**

Besides the standby letter of credit, there are other methods of guaranteeing a performance or ensuring the return of monies. A **performance bond** minimizes the buyer's risk of nonperformance by the seller in the export transaction or nonperformance by a contractor in a construction project. The performance bond is a guarantee from an insurance company to pay the insured in case of default (nonperformance). It serves the same function as a standby letter of credit. **Bid bonds** insure against the risk that a bidder may not honor its bid. These are usually required to bid on government procurement contracts.

A **credit surety** guarantees repayment to a bank or lender who finances an export transaction or development project. These sureties generally take the form of a payment guarantee from a state agency, such as the **Export-Import Bank (Eximbank)**, or from a development bank, such as the **World Bank**. A surety may also be in the form of a corporate guarantee from the parent company. A **retention fund** is not a third-party guarantee but an arrangement between the principal parties. In large projects or government procurement contracts, a percentage of the monies is deducted from each payment due the supplier or contractor and is retained in a fund pending the completion of the contract or the expiration of a warranty period.

The bank guarantee or **demand guarantee** is a popular means of guaranteeing performance. A demand guarantee is defined as "any guarantee, bond or other payment undertaking by a bank, insurance company or other body or person given in writing for the payment of money on presentation in conformity with the terms of the undertaking of a written demand for payment and such other documents as may be specified in the Guarantee."[25] Like the standby credit, the demand guarantee secures performance of a nonmonetary obligation. It serves as a default device when performance is not satisfactory. Whereas a bank pays a documentary letter of credit only if things go right, a bank will be called upon to pay a demand guarantee or standby letter only if things go wrong.[26] A special concern of demand guarantees is that the lack of rigid documentation requirements allows for the possibility of unfair calls.[27] Often all the beneficiary is required to do is make a written demand for payment. Both the ICC and UNCITRAL have developed rules to govern these types of instruments. The ICC has published the **Uniform Rules for Demand Guarantees** (Uniform Rules),[28] which has twenty-eight articles addressing issues such as definitions, liabilities and responsibilities, demands, expiration, and governing law and jurisdiction.[29] To discourage unfair calls on demand guarantees, Article 20(a)(ii) of the Uniform Rules requires from the beneficiary a statement describing the way in which the principal is in breach. UNCITRAL has also released its **Convention on Independent Letters of Guarantee and Standby Credits**. However, this convention has been adopted by only six states and has thus proven ineffective.[30]

Sources of Trade Finance

Exporters naturally want to get paid quickly, and importers usually prefer to delay payment at least until they have received and resold the goods.[31] Because of the intense competition for export markets, being able to offer good payment terms is often necessary to make a sale. Exporters should be aware of the many financing options open to them. In some cases, the exporter may need financing to produce goods that have been ordered or to finance other aspects of a sale, such as promotion and selling expenses, engineering modifications, and shipping costs.

Various financing sources are available to exporters, depending on the specifics of the transaction and the exporter's overall financing needs. Variables to assess before making a decision on export or import financing are (1) the cost of financing, (2) the length of the financing, and (3) the risks of financing. The impact on price and profit of different methods of financing should be well understood before a *pro forma* **invoice** is submitted to the buyer.

The greater the risks associated with the transaction, the greater the costs of financing and the more difficult financing will be to obtain. The creditworthiness

---

25. ICC, *Guide to the ICC Uniform Rules for Demand Guarantees,* No. 510 (Roy Goode, ed., 1992).
26. Roy Goode, "Abstract Payment Undertakings in International Transactions," 22 *Brooklyn Journal of International Law* 1, 15 (1996).
27. See ibid. (noting that "the documentation required for a claim on a demand guarantee is skeletal in the extreme, entailing in most cases presentation of no more than the written demand itself").
28. See ICC, *supra* note 25.
29. See ibid.
30. The UNCITRAL Convention on Independent Letters of Guarantee and Standby Credits had been adopted by Belarus, Ecuador, El Salvador, Panama, Kuwait, and Tunisia by late 2004.
31. The material in this section was gleaned from the National Trade Data Bank, a product of STAT-USA, U.S. Department of Commerce.

of the buyer directly affects the probability of payment to the exporter, but it is not the only factor of concern to a potential lender. The political and economic stability of the buyer's country also can be a factor. To provide financing for either accounts receivable or the production or purchase of the product for sale, the lender may require more secure methods of payment, such as a letter of credit or export credit insurance. If a lender is uncertain about the exporter's ability to perform, or if additional credit capacity is needed, a government guarantee program may enable the lender to provide additional financing. The best place to begin, however, is by researching the services provided by commercial banks. Because of their international banking connections and expertise in international business transactions, commercial banks are great sources for information.

Commercial Banks

Most large banks in major U.S. cities have an international department and specialists familiar with particular foreign countries and different types of commodities and transactions. These banks maintain correspondent relationships with smaller banks throughout the country. Larger banks also maintain correspondent relationships with banks in most foreign countries or operate their own overseas branches that provide a direct channel to foreign customers. International banking specialists are generally well informed about export matters. If they are unable to provide direct guidance or assistance, they may be able to refer inquirers to other specialists who can. Banks frequently provide consultation and guidance free of charge to their clients, because they derive income primarily from loans to the exporter and from fees for special services.

Finally, large banks often conduct seminars and workshops on letters of credit, documentary collections, and other banking subjects of concern to exporters. Among the many services a commercial bank may perform for its clients are (1) exchange of currencies; (2) assistance in financing exports; (3) collection of foreign invoices, drafts, and letters of credit; (4) transfer of funds to other countries; and (5) credit information on potential representatives or buyers overseas.

Export Financing

A logical first step in obtaining financing for an exporter is approaching its local commercial bank. If the exporter already has a loan for domestic needs, then the lender already has experience with the exporter's ability to perform. Many lenders, therefore, would be willing to provide financing for export transactions, given a reasonable certainty of repayment. By using letters of credit or export credit insurance, an exporter can reduce the lender's risk. A government guarantee program may offer a lender greater assurance than is afforded by the transaction, enabling the lender to extend credit to the exporter. When selecting a bank, the exporter should ask the following questions: (1) What are the charges for confirming a letter of credit, processing drafts, and collecting payment? (2) Does the bank have foreign branches or correspondent banks? Where are they located? (3) Does the bank have experience with U.S. and state government financing programs that support small business export transactions?

A time draft under an irrevocable letter of credit, confirmed by a U.S. bank, presents relatively little risk of default. To convert these instruments to cash immediately, an exporter must obtain a loan by using the draft as collateral or sell the draft to an investor or a bank for a fee. When the draft is sold to an investor or bank, it is sold at a discount. Banks or other lenders may be willing to buy time drafts that a creditworthy foreign buyer has accepted or agreed to pay at a specified future date. These endorsed drafts or bills of exchange were previously described in this chapter as trade acceptances.

In some cases, banks agree in advance to accept the obligations of paying a draft, usually of a customer, for a fee. As discussed previously, the banker's acceptance is a draft drawn on and accepted by a bank (see Exhibit 11.4: Banker's Acceptance). Depending on the bank's creditworthiness, the acceptance becomes a financial instrument that can be discounted and sold before maturity. The exporter receives an amount less than the face value of the draft so that when the draft is paid at its face value at the specified future date, the investor or bank receives more than it paid to the exporter. The difference between the amount paid to the exporter and the face amount paid at maturity is called a discount, which represents the fees or interest the investor or bank receives for holding the draft until maturity. The bank often discounts drafts **without recourse** to the exporter in case of default by the drawee. Other drafts may be discounted with recourse to the exporter, in which case the exporter must reimburse the investor or bank if the party obligated to pay the draft defaults.

Factoring and Forfaiting

Factoring is the discounting of foreign account receivables without a draft. The exporter transfers title to its account receivables to a factoring company at a discount. These houses specialize in the financing of account receivables by giving cash at a discount from the face value. Although factoring is often done without recourse to the exporter, the exporter should verify the specific arrangement. The factoring company assumes the financial risk of nonpayment and handles the collections on the receivables. Export factoring allows an exporter to sell on **open account**, by which goods are shipped without a guarantee of payment such as a letter of credit.

Forfaiting is the selling at a discount of longer-term account receivables or the promissory notes of the foreign buyer. This is a form of supplier credit in which the exporter turns over export receivables, usually guaranteed by a bank in the importer's country, by selling them at a discount to a forfaiter. This arrangement is generally

EXHIBIT 11.4   *Banker's Acceptance*

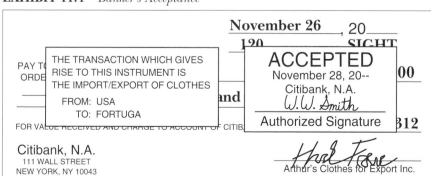

agreed to in advance before the conclusion of the sales contract. The exporter is thus able to incorporate the discount (costs) into the selling price. Forfaiters usually deal in bills of exchange or promissory notes that can be sold on the secondary market. Both U.S. and European forfaiting houses are active in the U.S. market.

Buyer and Supplier Financing

To produce the goods under an export contract, the seller often needs to obtain financing. This financing will at times come from the buyer or from the seller's suppliers. One form of buyer financing is a letter of credit that allows progress payments. Under a progress payment, the bank is authorized by the buyer to pay the seller on inspection by the buyer's agent or receipt of a statement by the seller that a certain percentage of the product has been completed. This type of partial payment under a letter of credit is known as a **red clause** advance. Under the red clause, the seller may demand a partial payment under the letter of credit before the presentation of documents. It is called a red clause because of the danger associated with it. The buyer is at risk for any red clause payments. If the seller subsequently fails to produce the goods or provide conforming documents, then the buyer must reimburse the bank for any red clause advances. Red clause payments are simply unsecured loans from the buyer to the seller.

Supplier financing is generally obtained through the supplier's selling materials to the exporter on account. Generally, the seller produces the goods needed to fulfill the export contract and pays its suppliers before the due date out of the proceeds from the export contract. Suppliers want some sort of collateral or security for selling materials on account, however. Two methods of providing such security are the **transferable credit** and the **back-to-back letter of credit** (see Exhibit 11.5).

Under the transferable credit arrangement, suppliers accept assignment of a part of the letter of credit that the seller receives from the buyer in the export transaction. If it is agreeable to the bank, a documentary letter of credit can be

EXHIBIT 11.5   *Back-to-Back Letter of Credit*

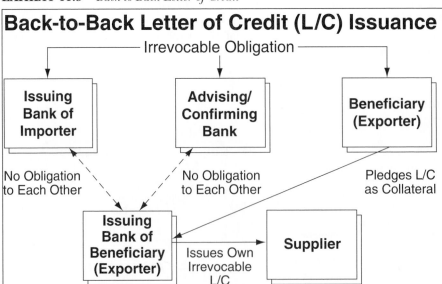

made expressly transferable. It can then be divided and transferred to numerous suppliers of the exporter in order to guarantee payment to them upon the payment of the underlying letter of credit. Otherwise, some banks allow only a single transfer or assignment of a letter of credit.

The seller arranges the back-to-back letter of credit without the assistance of the buyer or issuing bank. The seller makes arrangements with a third-party bank to take the letter of credit from the export transaction as collateral for a new letter of credit. The third-party bank in partial amounts issues a new letter of credit to the suppliers of the seller. Thus, unlike the transferable credit arrangement, the back-to-back letter of credit scenario involves two separate letters of credit. The documentary letter of credit simply acts as collateral for the second letter of credit. The back-to-back letter of credit highlights the importance of the documentary letter of credit in both guaranteeing payments and in financing international trade.

Exhibit 11.6 summarizes the times of payment and risks pertaining to the different types and uses of letters of credit reviewed in this chapter.

EXHIBIT 11.6   *Letter of Credit-Payment and Risks*

Type	Time of Payment	Goods Available to Importer	Risk to Exporter (seller)	Risk to Importer (buyer)
Irrevocable (confirmed letter of credit)	At sight of presentation of documents to bank or within specified number of days after acceptance	After payment	Provides most security	Fraud in the transaction
Revocable	Same as confirmed	After payment	Provides least security	Easier for issuing bank to cancel if evidence of fraud
Sight Draft	When shipment is made	After payment	Risk lies with confirming bank	Assured shipment is made but relies on exporter to ship goods as described in documents
Time Draft	At maturity of draft	Usually before payment	Loses control over goods	Assured shipment is made but relies on exporter to ship goods as described in documents
Red Clause	A percentage of total amount of letter of credit before shipment	After payment	Risk to confirming and issuing banks	The percentage of payment in advance is at total risk
Standby Letter of Credit	At time shipment is received	Usually before payment	Delay in payment	None
Back-to-Back Letter of Credit	Same as irrevocable	After payment	None	None
Transferable Letter of Credit	Same as irrevocable	After payment	Same as irrevocable	None

Government Assistance Programs

Several U.S. government agencies, as well as a number of state and local ones, offer programs to assist exporters with their financing needs. Some are guarantee programs that require the participation of an approved lender; others provide loans or grants to the exporter or to a foreign government. Government guarantee and insurance programs are used by commercial banks to reduce the risk associated with loans to exporters.

Initially created in 1934 and granted status as an independent federal agency in 1945, the Eximbank is the U.S. government's general trade finance agency, offering numerous programs to address a broad range of export needs.[32] Eximbank offers four separate programs designed to benefit U.S. exports. Initially, Eximbank's working capital financing program assists U.S. exporters in obtaining loans to produce or purchase goods or services for export. This financing is extended by commercial lenders to eligible exporters for 1 to 3 years and is guaranteed by Eximbank in an amount equal to 90 percent of the loan amount. This program is often referred to as "pre-export financing." Eximbank also offers a direct loan program with fixed-rate financing to eligible and credit-worthy international buyers of U.S. exports. These loans may be extended to private and public sector institutions. Loans extended pursuant to this program usually involve amounts in excess of $10 million. Eligible borrowers may receive the lesser of 85 percent of the value of the goods or services they are purchasing or 100 percent of the U.S. content of such goods or services. Repayment terms are usually in excess of 7 years. Eximbank's loan guarantee program serves a similar purpose by assisting eligible international buyers in obtaining private financing for the purchase of U.S. goods and services. Eximbank guarantees repayment of 100 percent of such financing. There is no minimum or maximum amount necessary for eligibility for the program. The usual repayment term for the underlying guaranteed obligation is between 5 and 10 years. Finally, Eximbank offers export credit insurance covering such risks as buyer nonpayment for commercial risks (such as bankruptcy) and political risks (such as war and currency inconvertibility). Exporters may obtain short-term or medium-term policies ranging in time from 180 days to 5 years and providing coverage between 85 and 100 percent. Lenders may also purchase insurance protecting against losses attributable to financing of U.S. exports and purchases thereof and financing of export-related accounts receivable. To date, the Eximbank has supported more than $400 billion in U.S. exports.

Insurance may also be purchased through the **Foreign Corporation Insurance Agency (FCIA)**.[33] The FCIA was created in 1962 as an association of fifty insurance companies in conjunction with the Eximbank for the purpose of promoting U.S. exports through the extension of credit insurance. It became a private entity in 1992. FCIA's principal is the Great American Insurance Company of Cincinnati, Ohio. The FCIA offers numerous types of credit insurance policies with respect to exports. These policies usually provide coverage between 90 and 95 percent. Covered occurrences include commercial risks

---

32.   Information on Eximbank's products and services may be found at **http://www.exim.gov.**
33.   Information on the FCIA's products and services may be found at **http://www.fcia.com** and **http://www. exportinsurance.com.**

(such as bankruptcy, insolvency, protracted default, and breach of contract) and political risks (such as war, embargoes, riots and civil commotion, strikes, currency inconvertibility, expropriation, nationalization, and contract frustration). The FCIA also offers marine insurance coverage for losses attributable to physical loss or damage to goods in transit.

The **Overseas Private Investment Corporation (OPIC)** is a U.S. government development agency formed in 1971 for the purpose of facilitating the participation of U.S. private capital in the economic development of less developed countries.[34] OPIC's primary mission is to provide political risk insurance to U.S. companies and financing through direct loans and guarantees. OPIC's political risk insurance provides coverage to U.S. investors in foreign countries against losses associated with currency inconvertibility, expropriation, and political violence, including hostile actions undertaken by national or international forces, civil war, revolution, insurrections, terrorism, and sabotage. OPIC usually provides insurance for a 20-year term in an amount equal to 90 percent of the eligible investment. OPIC coverage for equity investments usually equals 270 percent of the initial investment, with 90 percent allocable to the original investment and 180 percent to cover future earnings. OPIC's loan program offers numerous options to U.S. businesses operating overseas. The loan program is divided into three separate categories designed to meet the needs of small businesses, small and medium enterprises, and structured finance. Since 1971, OPIC has facilitated $145 billion worth of investments in hundreds of projects throughout the world that have generated in excess of $11 billion in host government revenues and created more than 680,000 host country jobs. These investments also have supported more than 254,000 American jobs and $65 billion in U.S. exports.

The **Small Business Administration (SBA)** provides three separate programs related to exports.[35] The Export Working Capital Program encourages private lenders to extend export working capital financing to U.S. businesses by guaranteeing repayment in an amount of $1 million or 90 percent of the loan, whichever is less. The term of this guarantee is 1 year and may be utilized with respect to loans for the acquisition of inventory, payment of manufacturing costs or acquisition of goods destined for export, and payment of costs associated with service contracts with foreign buyers. This program also supports standby letters of credit used in performance bonds and the financing of foreign accounts receivable. The SBA's International Trade Loan Program supports medium- and long-term working capital loans by providing guarantees of up to $1.25 million. Proceeds of these loans are to be used to expand existing export markets, develop new export markets, or assist small businesses adversely affected by imports. Guarantees extended pursuant to this program may be for a term of up to 25 years. Finally, SBA's Export Express program encourages lenders to expedite loan review and approval processes for SBA-guaranteed loans of up to $150,000. Loan proceeds may be used for market development activity (such as foreign trade missions), transaction-specific financing, lines of credit for export activities and working capital, and fixed asset financing.

http://
Small Business Administration Office of International Trade: **http://www.sba.gov/oit/**. Links to SBA exporting guide and trade finance program.

---

34. Information on OPIC's products and services may be found at **http://www.opic.gov**.
35. Information on the SBA's products and services may be found at **http://www.sba.gov**.

KEY TERMS

21-day rule	demand guarantee	performance bond
acceptance	documentary collections transaction	power of attorney
account party	documentary credit transaction	*pro forma* invoice
advising bank	draft	red clause
amendment	Export-Import Bank (Eximbank)	retention fund
back-to-back letter of credit	facial compliance rule	rule of strict compliance
banker's acceptance	factoring	sight draft
beneficiary party	Foreign Corporation Insurance	Small Business Administration
bid bond	Agency (FCIA)	(SBA)
bill of exchange	forfaiting	standby letter of credit
confirming bank	freight forwarder	time draft
Convention on Independent Letters	International Standby Practices	trade acceptance
of Guarantee and Standby	(ISP98)	transferable credit
Credits	irrevocable letter of credit	UCP 500
Convention Providing a Uniform	issuing bank	Uniform Rules for Demand
Law for Bills of Exchange and	letter of credit	Guarantees
Promissory Notes	open account	without recourse
credit surety	Overseas Private Insurance	World Bank
customs broker	Corporation (OPIC)	

CHAPTER PROBLEMS

1. A recent topic of interest, given China's emergence into the global economy, is its treatment of letters of credit. Chinese issuers have been known to reject a letter of credit on the minutest of discrepancies. There are now reports that in certain instances the scrutiny has gotten even worse. One person related that a letter of credit was rejected because it was signed in blue ink instead of black. Several people theorized that the reason for the increased inspection is the cash flow problems in certain provinces. What can be done to overcome this problem of overly strict review and enforcement of documentary requirements?

2. Should the parties to a documentary credit include a dispute resolution clause in their letters of credit or allow disputes to be resolved through litigation? Are there any alternatives to arbitration that could minimize the time and cost of litigation or arbitration?

3. A company engaging in the manufacture and sale of telecommunications equipment entered into an agreement with the "Imperial Government of Carpathia" to install and maintain certain telecommunications equipment. As a condition of the contract and to secure the advance payment, the company was required to guarantee its performance by obtaining two irrevocable letters of credit in amounts equal to the advance payments made by Carpathia. Subsequently, a revolution occurred in Carpathia, and the company was at least temporarily prevented from finishing the contract. The company was

concerned that a new government would "arbitrarily" demand payment on the letters of credit. In light of the foregoing, the company sought a preliminary injunction to prevent the bank from making payment on the letters of credit without first giving the company an opportunity to prove lack of authenticity or the fraudulent nature of the demand. Should the court grant a preliminary injunction? *Stromberg-Carlson Corp. v. Bank Melli Iran*, 467 F. Supp. 530 (S.D.N.Y. 1979).

4. The terms and conditions of a letter of credit state that the beneficiary party (seller) is to provide a certificate of origin listing the goods as originating from "NAFTA Countries." The certificate of origin did state "NAFTA Countries," but the commercial invoice stated only "NAFTA." The issuing bank rejected the documents because the declaration of origin in the commercial invoice was inconsistent with the declaration in the certificate of origin. The beneficiary party bank sues the issuing bank for wrongfully dishonoring the letter of credit. Under the UCP, who wins? Why?

5. A letter of credit is issued with the following terms and conditions: "(1) The beneficiary party must present a full set of clean-on-board bills of lading evidencing shipment from Port A to Port B and (2) documents must arrive at the offices of the issuing bank before arrival of the ship at Port B." The issuing bank rejected the documents for the following reasons: "(1) The bill of lading does not indicate that the goods were placed on board, but instead states that they were taken in charge at Container Freight Yard and (2) the documents were untimely because they were presented to the bank one day after the arrival of the ship." Were the two discrepancies appropriate for rejecting the documents?

6. Test your knowledge of trade finance terminology. Match the term with its definition.

(A) Irrevocable	(1) A letter of credit that does not require the presentation of specified documents. It is extremely risky for the purchaser in an export transaction.	(G) Documentary Credit	(7) Permits the accompanying drafts or bills of exchange to be transferred. This allows for the negotiation of a draft at other banks. The issuing bank is required to reimburse any bank that negotiates the letter of credit.
(B) Negotiable	(2) The letter of credit used in an export transaction that requires the seller to present specified documents to receive payment under the letter.	(H) Standby	(8) A second bank endorses the letter of credit, indicating that it will also guarantee payment upon the presentation of the required documents. In an export transaction, the exporter's bank is generally that bank.
(C) Transferable	(3) A draft or bill of exchange that requires the bank to pay under the letter of credit at the time the documents are presented.	(I) Sight Bill	(9) Permits the beneficiary to negotiate the letter of credit to secondary beneficiaries. The original letter of credit must expressly state that it is transferable.
(D) Confirmed	(4) A letter of credit in which the buyer is named as beneficiary. It is used to guarantee performance on a contract and the return of a deposit or installment payments.	(J) Time Bill	(10) The buyer provides the seller with a letter of credit. That credit is used as collateral by the seller to obtain a second letter of credit. The second provides a guarantee to the seller's suppliers and finances the acquisition of the materials needed by the seller to produce the goods.
(E) Clean	(5) Cannot be revoked without beneficiary's consent. Most common form used in international transactions because it provides greatest security against nonpayment.	(K) Red Clause	(11) Generally granted by commercial banks to large importers. The buyer is allowed to reuse the credit after the bank is reimbursed.
(F) Revolving	(6) The provision in a letter of credit that allows the advancement of monies prior to the seller presenting the required documents. This is a means by which a buyer can provide financing to the seller. It is very risky because it is unsecured, and the buyer is responsible to reimburse the bank whether the seller performs or not.	(L) Back-to-Back	(12) A draft or bill of exchange that orders the bank to pay on the letter of credit only after passage of a certain amount of time following the presentation of the documents. This allows the buyer to resell the goods or obtain financing before being required to pay the seller.

INTERNET EXERCISES

1. Research the availability and requirements of the Small Business Administration's Trade Finance Program at **http://www.sba.gov/oit.**

2. Take a self-guided tour from a Canadian perspective of an international trade transaction at **http://www.rbcglobalservices.com/tmt/trade/services.html.**

3. The U.S. Eximbank is the largest U.S. export financing agency. Explore **http://www.exim.gov** to see how its programs benefit U.S. exporters.

Traditionally, international business law courses have focused on the sale of goods rather than the sale of services. However, a growing portion of U.S. exports falls in the areas of sale of services and the licensing of technology. This chapter highlights the former; Chapters Thirteen and Fourteen will review the latter. Because of the breadth of the topic, instead of providing cases for illustrative and pedagogical purposes, this chapter's coverage is more descriptive. The focus is on the practical issues that an individual or company faces in hiring foreign personnel. It includes an extensive review of the legalities associated with employment and agency contracts.

Sales of services are generally effectuated through employment and consulting contracts, which would seem to indicate that such transactions are purely private in nature. This is generally true in a domestic sale of services contract in the United States, but a host of restrictions and regulations are imposed on the international sale of services. Unlike the United States, some countries have developed an entire regulatory scheme that covers such transactions. The international employer, principal, agent, consultant, and employee must become familiar with these foreign regulations.

Chapter 12

Sale of Services

This chapter reviews the generic ways people sell services, namely, the employment, foreign sales representation, and commercial agency contracts. The distinction between employment and independent contracting is examined in conjunction with these three ways of selling services. This material can be applied to sales of services in any type of industry and business. This material is also relevant to previous chapters, as a number of service industries make the sale of goods transaction possible. This chapter concludes with a review of some specific service areas, including logistics, advertising, security offerings, and accounting.

Almost all industries and businesses use service contracts. An exact definition of sale of services is difficult to fashion because services comprise a broad range of activities. One way of defining a sale of services is by comparing it with the other two modes of international trade: sale of goods and licensing. A good is something tangible and movable. Sale of goods transactions include the sale of raw materials, component parts, equipment, and consumer products. Licensing is less than the total transfer of ownership found in the sale transaction. Licenses generally pertain to intangible items such as technology, know-how, trade secrets, and intellectual property rights (trademarks, patents, copyrights). As discussed in Chapter Eight, many transactions are **mixed sales** that include two or all of the three modes of doing business. A technology transfer, for example, may include a sale of goods (software or computer equipment), a license (right to use the software), and a sale of services (technical assistance and training).

International Sale of Services

The **Organization for Economic Cooperation and Development (OECD)** has estimated that between 60 and 70 percent of the business sector in OECD countries[1] relates to the sale of services. The United States is the largest producer and exporter of services in the world.[2] In 2002, U.S. service exports totaled $255 billion, 17 percent of the global total. According to the Department of Commerce, the principal markets for U.S. services were Canada ($24 billion), Japan ($30 billion), and the European Union ($96 billion). Service exports to these three destinations alone accounted for 54 percent of all U.S. service exports for the year. Mexico is the largest emerging market for U.S. services ($16 million in imports in 2002), but significant growth has occurred across the globe, including Central and South America, the Pacific Rim, Eastern Europe, and the Middle East. In 2002, South Africa became the first African country to import more than $1 billion in services from the United States. After deducting service imports, the United States registered a $74 billion services trade surplus, which was a significant offset to its substantial trade deficit in the goods.

> Organization for Economic Cooperation and Development (OECD): **http://www.oecd.org.**

The service sector accounts for two-thirds of the U.S. gross domestic product (GDP), including government. This amount grows to 75 percent when the private sector GDP is considered by itself. Furthermore, service industries account for nearly 80 percent of nonfarm employment in the United States, specifically 86 million jobs. Many industries account for these jobs, including retail trade (23 million), education (12 million), health services (11 million), finance, insurance, and real estate (8 million), wholesale trade (7 million), social services (6 million), transportation (4 million), entertainment (3 million), and telecommunications (1 million), as well as a host of other industries from accounting to utilities. Internationally, a similar change has taken place, with world trade in services growing to $1.5 trillion in 2002.

Service industries span a wide variety of enterprises, from hamburgers to high technology. The means for selling services internationally include international consulting, services related to the export of goods, electronic transfers of knowledge and data, licensing agreements, franchising services, and tourism services. There has been rapid growth in many service sectors, including transport, communications, finance, and business services, along with knowledge-intensive services, such as computing and consultant services. Advances in innovation, information, knowledge, and communications technologies have driven increased productivity in all segments of business.

The rules-based multilateral trading system so successful in reducing barriers to trade in goods is now being expanded in the area of trade in services. A number of WTO agreements, starting with the **General Agreement on Trade in Services**

---

1. OECD member countries include Australia, Austria, Belgium, Canada, Czech Republic, Denmark, Finland, France, Germany, Greece, Hungary, Iceland, Ireland, Italy, Japan, Korea, Luxembourg, Mexico, Netherlands, New Zealand, Norway, Poland, Portugal, Slovak Republic, Spain, Sweden, Switzerland, Turkey, United Kingdom, and United States. The forerunner of the OECD was the Organization for European Economic Cooperation, which was formed to administer U.S. and Canadian aid under the Marshall Plan for reconstruction of Europe after World War II.

2. The statistics in this section of the text are derived from the U.S. Department of Commerce, International Trade Administration, *Services Exports and the U.S. Economy* (2003).

(GATS) that was concluded during the Uruguay Round of GATT, are targeted to reducing obstacles to trade in services. Services are also subject to regional trade agreements. For example, Chapters Twelve, Thirteen, and Fourteen of the North American Free Trade Agreement (NAFTA) establish standards applicable to cross-border trade in services, telecommunications, and financial services, respectively. At the bilateral level, the United States and the European Union and the European Union and Japan have reached a number of **Mutual Recognition Agreements (MRA)**[3] aimed at reducing trade barriers in specific industries. Trade barrier reduction is to be achieved through the mutual recognition of each other's product testing and certification procedures. At the nongovernmental level, the agenda of the **Trans-Atlantic Business Dialogue (TABD)** includes service-related initiatives such as expansion of GATS, greater coordination of government regulations applicable to service industries, and the development of international accounting standards.[4]

In view of the shift toward services both domestically and internationally and the substantial competitive advantage of the United States in the services field, liberalization in the trade for services has become an important U.S. policy objective. This is evidenced by the fact that the United States was a major promoter of the GATS. Most business services can be exported, especially the highly innovative, specialized, or technologically advanced services that are efficiently performed in the United States. The following sectors have particularly high export potential for U.S. service providers: (1) construction, design, and engineering; (2) banking and financial services; (3) insurance services; (4) legal and accounting services; (5) computer and data services; (6) teaching services; (7) management consulting services; and (8) telecommunications services.

Important features differentiate exporting services from exporting products:

- Services are less tangible than products, providing little in terms of samples that can be seen by the potential foreign buyer. Consequently, communicating a service offer is much more difficult than communicating a product offer. Much more attention must be paid to translating the intangibility of a service into a tangible and saleable offer.
- The intangibility of services makes financing more difficult. Frequently, even financial institutions with international experience are less willing to provide financial support for service exports than for product exports, because the value of services is more difficult to monitor.
- Selling services is more personal than selling products, because it quite often requires direct involvement with the customer. This involvement demands greater cultural sensitivity when services are being provided across national borders.
- Services are much more difficult to standardize than products. Service activities must frequently be tailored to the specific needs of the buyer. This need for adaptation often necessitates the service client's direct participation and cooperation in the service delivery. This inability to standardize services also creates

3. See Charles O. Verrill Jr., Peter S. Jordan, and Timothy C. Brightbill, "International Trade," 32 *International Lawyer* 319, 326 (1998); see also European Commission, Directorate-General for Trade, *A Guide to the Mutual Recognition Agreement Between the European Community and Japan* (2003).
4. See Trans-Atlantic Business Dialogue, TABD Policy Issues 1–2 (2004).

difficulties in measuring and regulating the quality of services. Furthermore, government attempts to regulate services may be viewed as intrusive, given their often personal nature.

- Free trade in services heightens the concern of less developed states about being overrun by service providers from the developed world with superior technical skills and greater numbers of trained professionals. Conversely, free trade in services heightens concerns regarding labor and immigration in the developed world, as such trade creates greater mobility and a resultant migratory labor force.

Demand for certain services is often related to product exports. Many merchandise exports from the United States would not take place if they were not supported by service activities such as banking, insurance, and transportation. For example, U.S. accounting firms have expanded into the customs compliance area. Spurred by globalization and stricter compliance by the U.S. Customs and Border Protection Agency, the accounting firms now offer specialized services to help companies comply with customs regulations. Since enactment of the **Customs Modernization and Informed Compliance Act of 1993**, importers and exporters are required to submit to periodic customs audits and to comply with strict record-keeping requirements.[5] The accounting firms have expanded their services to include advising exporters and importers on how to minimize payment of duties and value-added tax, as well as on handling transfer-pricing and international tax issues. They also offer consulting in valuation, sourcing, trade strategies, logistics, trade process management, and information technology.

In recognition of the increasing importance of service exports, the U.S. Department of Commerce has made the **Office of Service Industries, Tourism, and Finance (OSITF)** responsible for analyzing and promoting services trade. The OSITF is located within the International Trade Administration of the Department of Commerce and provides information on opportunities and operations of services abroad. A number of its divisions focus on specific industry sectors including information, transportation, tourism, marketing, finance, and management.

General Agreement on Trade in Services

The World Trade Organization's General Agreement on Trade in Services (GATS) is a **framework agreement** containing basic obligations that apply to all member countries. It is built of national schedules of commitments and specific goals for continuing liberalization. In addition, a number of annexes to it address individual services sectors. Although the GATS is merely a framework agreement, it is important nonetheless for several reasons. Initially, the GATS provides a benchmark by which future agreements on trade in services may be evaluated. The GATS represents an excellent start to reducing barriers to trade in services. Finally, the commitments of the parties to the GATS prevent backsliding by creating a baseline for trade in services, below which the parties may not fall.

---

5. Pub. L. No. 103-182, 107 Stat. 2170 (1993).

Part I of the basic framework agreement defines the types of services that are covered:

- services supplied from the territory of one party to the territory of another
- services supplied in the territory of one party to the consumers of any other (for example, tourism)
- services provided through the presence of service-providing entities of one party in the territory of any other (for example, banking)
- services provided by nationals of one party in the territory of any other (for example, construction projects or consultancies)

Part II sets out general obligations and disciplines. A **most-favored-nation** obligation states that each party "shall accord immediately and unconditionally to services and service providers of any other member country, treatment no less favorable than that it accords to like services and service providers of any other country."[6] **Transparency** requirements include publication of all relevant laws and regulations pertaining to providing services by foreign individuals or companies.[7] Because domestic regulations and not cross-border rules provide the most significant influence on services trade, provisions spell out that all such measures of general application should be administered in a reasonable, objective, and impartial manner. The agreement contains obligations with respect to **recognition requirements** for the purpose of securing authorizations, licenses, or certification to provide a service. These types of requirements pertain mostly to professional trades, including legal, engineering, medical, insurance, and accounting.

http://

The International Initiatives Program: **http://www.acenet. edu/programs/ international/gats/ 2004-update.cfm.** Information on GATS.

Part III contains provisions on market access and **national treatment** as listed in national schedules. For example, national restrictions on the kind of legal entity or joint venture through which a service is provided or any foreign capital limitations must be eliminated. The national-treatment provision contains the obligation to treat foreign service suppliers and domestic service suppliers in the same manner. Part IV of the agreement establishes the basis for progressive liberalization in the services area through successive rounds of negotiations and the development of national schedules. Part V of the agreement contains institutional provisions, including consultation and dispute settlement and the establishment of a **Council on Services**.

The first annex to the GATS concerns the movement of labor. It permits parties to negotiate specific commitments applying to the movement of people providing services under the GATS. The annex would not apply to measures affecting employment, citizenship, residence, or employment on a permanent basis. It also relates to membership or participation in self-regulatory bodies and securities or futures exchanges. The annex on telecommunications relates to measures that affect access to and use of public telecommunications services and networks. In particular, it requires that such access be accorded to foreign parties on reasonable and nondiscriminatory terms. The annex also encourages technical cooperation to help developing countries strengthen their own domestic telecommunications sectors. The Doing Business Internationally box on the Doha Development Agenda summarizes the process by which expansion of the GATS is to occur.

---

6.   GATS, art. II.
7.   See ibid. art. III.

Doha WTO Ministerial 2001: Ministerial Declaration[8]

Doing Business Internationally

Article 15. The negotiations on trade in services shall be conducted with a view to promoting the economic growth of all trading partners and the development of developing and least-developed countries. We recognize the work already undertaken in the negotiations, initiated in January 2000 under Article XIX of the General Agreement on Trade in Services, and the large number of proposals submitted by members on a wide range of sectors and several horizontal issues, as well as on movement of natural persons. We reaffirm the Guidelines and Procedures for the Negotiations adopted by the Council for Trade in Services on March 28, 2001 as the basis for continuing the negotiations, with a view to achieving the objectives of the General Agreement on Trade in Services, as stipulated in the Preamble, Article IV and Article XIX of that Agreement. Participants shall submit initial requests for specific commitments by June 30, 2002 and initial offers by March 31, 2003.

[To date, thirty-nine members have submitted initial offers, but the pace of discussions with respect to the expansion of GATS remains glacial.]

Services and the Internet

An evolving issue is the role of e-commerce and how the GATS commitments can be responsive to new opportunities for providing services over the Internet. In nearly all sectors, there will be increasing pressure to allow services to be provided across borders. For example, in the case of financial services, regulators will be challenged to justify the requirement to provide these services through a local subsidiary when the service can be provided more efficiently from abroad. However, there is also the possibility that nations and free trade areas will respond with specialized laws aimed at controlling cross-border transactions over the Internet. Consumer protection laws are likely to be tailored to protect nationals engaged in Internet transactions with foreign sellers. An example of such a law is the **EU Directive on Distance Contracts**, which is described in the following Comparative Law feature.

EU Directive 97/7/EC of February 17, 1997 on Protection of Consumers in Distance Contracts[9]

COMPARATIVE LAW

Prior to the conclusion of any distance contract, the consumer must be provided with clear and comprehensible information concerning:

*   the identity and the address of the supplier in cases of contracts requiring payment in advance;

*   the characteristics of the goods or services and their price;
*   delivery costs;
*   the arrangements for payment, delivery, or performance;

continued

8.   World Trade Organization, Doha WTO Ministerial 2001, Ministerial Declaration, Doc. No. WT/MIN(01)/DEC/1, art. 15 (Nov. 14, 2001).

9.   This directive applies to sales of both goods and services through distance contracts such as mail order, telephone communications, or other means of telecommunications.

EU Directive 97/7/EC of February 17, 1997 on Protection of Consumers in Distance Contracts (*continued*)

- the existence of a right of withdrawal;
- the period for which the offer or the price remains valid and the minimum duration of the contract, where applicable;
- the cost of using the means of distance communication.

This information must comply with the principles of good faith in commercial transactions and the principles governing the protection of minors. In the case of telephone calls, the caller's identity and commercial purpose must be made clear at the beginning.

The consumer must receive written confirmation or confirmation in another durable medium (electronic mail) at the time of performance of the contract. The following information must also be given in writing:

- arrangements for exercising the right of withdrawal;
- place to which the consumer may address complaints;
- information relating to after-sales service;
- conditions under which the contract may be rescinded.

The consumer has a right of withdrawal. Where the supplier has met his obligations relating to the provision of information, the consumer has at least seven working days to cancel the contract without penalty.

Where the supplier has failed to meet his obligations as regards information, this period is extended to three months. The supplier is obliged to repay the amounts paid by the consumer within thirty days.

Where the supplier fails to perform his side of the contract, the consumer must be informed and any sums paid refunded. In some cases, it is possible to supply an equivalent good or service.

Where unsolicited goods are supplied, the consumer's failure to reply does not constitute consent.

The use by the supplier of automatic calling devices or faxes requires the prior consent of the consumer.

The Member States must ensure that consumers are allowed judicial or administrative redress so that they are not deprived of protection under the law of a non-Member country.

The Member States may adopt more stringent provisions, provided that these are compatible with the Treaty, such as a ban on the marketing of certain goods and services through distance contracts.

INTERNATIONAL

As in most consumer protection statutes, the EU Directive on Distance Contracts requires the (foreign) seller to disclose certain types of information: location of seller, price and additional costs, and the minimum length of time that the consumer will be bound to the contract. The directive allows the seller to solicit over the telephone, but a follow-up written confirmation is required. An e-mail confirmation does satisfy the writing requirement. The statute mandates a consumer right of withdrawal. The consumer has up to seven days to cancel the contract and receive a full refund of any monies paid. The right of withdrawal is extended to three months in the event that the seller has failed to provide the information required by the directive. This consumer right is akin to the right of rescission found in some federal and state consumer protection statutes in the United States.[10]

---

10.   See, e.g., 15 U.S.C. § 1635 (a-i) (2000). By comparison, California law identifies thirty-five separate contracts subject to specific statutory cancellation rights, as well as thirteen general grounds for cancellation. See California Department of Consumer Affairs, Consumer Transactions with Statutory Contract Cancellation Rights, at **http://www.dca.ca.gov/legal/k-6.html**.

The next to last paragraph of the directive is important. It prevents the seller from avoiding the dictates of the statute by inserting a choice of law clause to select a country outside the EU. Therefore, a choice of law clause selecting the State of California as the law of the contract would be ignored in a dispute pertaining to issues covered by the directive. California law would still apply, however, to contract disputes not covered under the directive. Finally, the statute does not prevent member countries of the EU from enacting more stringent consumer protection legislation. The U.S. exporter, unfortunately, will not only have to satisfy the dictates of the directive but also have to research the consumer protection requirements of each EU country to which it chooses to export.

Hiring Foreign Personnel

Any company seeking to sell its products internationally will need foreign representation. It will be forced to enter the market for services. For example, exporters contemplating an initial penetration into a foreign market have three alternatives for entry. First, it may elect to use employees, whether those already in place or new foreign hires. Second, it may elect to hire independent contractors to provide the needed services. The most common form of service provided by independent contractors is sales representation. Third, it may elect to enter into a distribution relationship with a foreign distributor.

A **foreign sales representative** is an agent who distributes, represents, services, or sells goods on behalf of foreign sellers. The foreign sales representative, also known as a "commission agent," "uses the company's product literature and samples to present the product to potential buyers."[11] The representative forwards orders for goods directly to the seller upon receipt. The representative does not take title to the goods and is usually paid in some combination of salary and commissions on completed sales. Other than the potential loss of a commission, the representative does not bear the risk that the buyer will not pay for the goods. Representatives are appointed through a mutual written contract between the seller and the representative that sets forth the terms of the parties' agreement, including compensation, territory, terms of sale, and termination. The contract should expressly state whether the representative has been retained on an exclusive or nonexclusive basis. The contract should also state whether the representative may bind the seller and, if so, under what terms. This is especially important because the power of representatives to bind their foreign sellers may vary from country to country. As a result of this confusion, many sellers have stopped using the term *agent* to refer to their foreign sales representatives for fear that the term implies more than was intended by the parties.

The following sections focus on the differences between the employment and independent contractor relationships, why those differences are important, and the law pertaining to the use of foreign sales representatives and distributors. Although employment and **independent contractor** relationships are largely matters of private contracting, foreign laws heavily affect the classification of a given relationship. Specifically, once a relationship is designated as an employment or

11.   Unz & Company, *A Basic Guide to Exporting*, Chapter Four (1998); see also Ralph H. Folsom, Michael Wallace Gordon, and John A. Spanogle Jr., *International Business Transactions* 174–75 (6th ed. 2003).

independent contractor relationship, host country laws regulate areas such as notice, termination, and remuneration.

The terminology of agency, employment, and independent contractor as used in the United States may differ from the way it is used in other countries. For example, the general meaning of **agent** may differ from country to country.[12] Generally, an agent denotes the person being hired, whereas the party doing the hiring is referred to as the **principal**. The term *agent* encompasses both dependent and independent agents. An employee is a **dependent agent**. A mixture of employment and agency law governs the employer-employee relationship. In contrast, an independent contractor, such as a consultant, is an **independent agent**. Agency law governs the principal-agent relationship between the hiring company and the consultant.

INTERNATIONAL

By contrast, Mexican law recognizes three different types of representatives.[13] In the mediation contract (*contrato de mediación*), the mediator does not represent the principal but rather distributes information about the principal and its products to potential purchasers. In the commission contract (*contrato de comisión*), the representative receives a mandate from the principal to accomplish a given task (a commission) in return for the payment of compensation (usually in the form of a commission). The term *agency* is reserved for the commission agent (*comisión mercantile*) whose contract with the principal serves as a general power of attorney with respect to commercial acts. In addition, in some foreign legal systems, this relationship is subject to a significant amount of statutory control. The next two sections examine the general nature of the employment and independent contractor relationships.

The Employment Relationship

The philosophical foundation of the U.S. employment relationship, the **employment at will doctrine**, provides that, except for express employment contracts, the employment relationship may be terminated at the will of either party. To prevent employee-generated lawsuits for wrongful termination, companies should avoid the use of employment contracts and make clear at the time of hiring that the employment is "at will." A U.S.-based company's employment manual should emphasize this point. The manual also should state that the general employment policy applies to all subsidiaries. Of course, the "at will" concept may be defined differently in other legal systems.

Second, the employment manual should clearly state that "all employees are hired as at will employees." The employer's code of conduct (ethics code) should also delineate prohibited areas of conduct such as:

- rude or discourteous behavior
- theft or personal dishonesty
- use or possession of alcohol or controlled substances on company premises
- maintenance of inappropriate files on the company's internal network
- transmission of confidential information over the e-mail system

---

12. See Folsom, Gordon, and Spanogle, *International Business Transactions*, at 230.
13. The materials on the agency relationship in Mexico were derived from the remarks of Ignacio Gómez-Palacio appearing in "Establishing an Agency or Distributorship in Mexico," 4 *U.S.-Mexico Law Journal* 72 (1996).

- disclosing nonpublic information, including trade secrets
- duplicating software products
- engaging in any act of harassment or discrimination

The U.S. employer should pay special attention to the last item. Laws and cultural attitudes vary widely among countries. Therefore, a clear policy on sexual harassment should be developed with the international employee in mind. Doing Business Internationally: Standard Sexual Harassment Policy provides a common format for developing a company's **sexual harassment policy**. At the minimum, a policy should state the company's general policy, provide workable definitions of inappropriate conduct, and provide a user-friendly complaint procedure.

The problems of cultural or ethical relativism were discussed in Chapter Two and are very relevant to the discussion of harassment. For example, traditional Japanese culture has emphasized the subordination of women in the workplace.[14] As a result, female employees are routinely placed in auxiliary positions and assigned menial tasks. These positions offer low wages, few benefits, and little, if any, job security and opportunity for advancement. The few women who succeed in reaching management positions are often viewed with suspicion and remain responsible for performing traditional female tasks, such as serving tea. Incidences of sexual harassment (*sekusharu harasumento*) in this environment were commonplace. In an effort to reduce gender discrimination, Japan adopted the Equal Employment Opportunity Law in 1985. Astonishingly, this law did not

INTERNATIONAL

Standard Sexual Harassment Policy

Doing Business Internationally

Three typical sections of a sexual harassment policy include:

General Policy
Management personnel are responsible for maintaining a harassment-free environment and are strictly prohibited from stating or in any way implying that submitting or refusing to submit to sexual advances will have any effect upon an individual's hiring, placement, compensation, training, promotion, or any other term or condition of employment.

Definition
All employees are prohibited from making offensive remarks or engaging in unwelcome overtures, either verbal or physical. Such prohibited conduct includes, but is not limited to, offensive and unwelcome flirtations, advances, or propositions; verbal abuse of a

racial, ethnic, religious, or sexual nature; graphic or degrading comments about an individual or his or her appearance; the display of sexually suggestive objects or pictures; or any offensive or abusive physical contact. Acts of harassment by any employee are strictly prohibited and will result in disciplinary action that may include termination of employment.

Complaint Procedure
When a complaint is received the company's ethics officer or human resources department will conduct an immediate impartial and confidential investigation. At the conclusion of the investigation, the officer or representative of Human Resources will advise the employee of the results.

---

14. The materials in the discussion of sexual harassment in Japan may be found in Galen T. Shimoda, "Japan's New Equal Employment Opportunity Law: Combating Sexual Harassment in the Workplace," 16 *Transnational Lawyer* 215 (2002).

contain a provision directly addressing sexual harassment. Japanese law did not expressly recognize the right of women to work in a harassment-free environment until 2000, when a new equal employment opportunity law entered force and effect. The new law also defines the scope of harassment and creates procedures for employers to follow to address the problem. Given these differences, should a U.S. company tailor a policy or modify its existing policy to take into account different cultural and legal standards of sexual harassment? How can such modifications be justified?

INTERNATIONAL

Culturally and legally, the employment relationship is viewed differently throughout the world. Three areas of employment law in the United States and other countries exemplify these differences. The first area is the employment contract itself. Civil law countries in Europe do not recognize the "at will doctrine" and require a written employment agreement. For example, German law requires employees have a written contract reflecting important aspects of the relationship such as the parties, the work to be performed, salary and benefits, vacation, starting date, place of performance, and notification periods. The same general requirements are applicable in France and Italy pursuant to their respective labor codes. The writing requirement is not, however, unique to Western Europe. For example, the Labor Code of the Russian Federation, which became effective in February 2002, requires that a written agreement must be executed with every employee no later than three days after the employee commences work. Similar requirements are imposed by the Labor Code of the People's Republic of China. Employment contracts in China must be in writing and are required to include provisions relating to the term of the agreement, labor protections and conditions, remuneration, disciplinary procedures, conditions relating to termination, and responsibility for breach of contract. Freedom of contract is limited in all of these examples, as the written contract must conform to the requirements of the applicable labor code.

INTERNATIONAL

The second topic of comparison is the term of employment. The laws of many countries discourage temporary employment agreements. For example, in Germany, temporary employment agreements are permitted for a period not to exceed two years. Employers seeking to utilize such agreements in excess of two years must demonstrate good cause for the deviation from German law. The failure to demonstrate such cause converts the temporary employment relationship into a permanent relationship, with all of the protections accruing to such employees in the country. In Italy, fixed terms of employment set forth in contracts are valid in very limited circumstances. Temporary employment contracts must be in writing and may be extended only once, for a period not exceeding the original term. The extension must commence at the time of the expiration of the original term, must be for the identical job performed during the original term, and must be with the employee's consent. Any failure to conform to these requirements converts the relationship into a permanent employment contract. Temporary employment is similarly limited in the Russian Labor Code. However, by contrast, China's Labor Code recognizes that the term of the employment agreement may be "fixed, flexible or set according to a certain amount of work to be fulfilled."

INTERNATIONAL

The most significant difference between the employment at will doctrine in the United States and other legal systems is in the area of termination. The perspective of legal status of the employee varies from **employment as a property right** in Germany to **lifetime employment** in Japan. Understanding these differences is vital to the U.S. manufacturer that contemplates hiring foreign nationals. The decision to hire foreign employees should be made with full knowledge of the obstacles the employer has to overcome to terminate the relationship. Some of these obstacles are discussed in the following text.

Germany significantly amended its **Termination Protection Act** effective January 2004.[15] Nevertheless, the ability of employers to terminate the employment relationship remains severely limited. In the absence of behavior detrimental to the interests of the employer (such as theft or fraud), employees of "works" with more than ten employees can be terminated only if the termination is "socially justified." "Works" are operating units within a company or facility. This requirement also applies to "works" of more than five employees if the workers were employed prior to the increase in the threshold to ten employees effective on January 1, 2004. Unlike the previous law, the determination of social justification is now limited to consideration of four factors, specifically, the employee's years of service, age, number of dependents, and disability. Notice of such termination must be given, and it ranges from four weeks to seven months, depending on the employee's length of service. Dismissals are permitted only following consultation with statutorily mandated **works councils**. This requirement is significant as, although work councils are present in only 10 percent of all business establishments in Germany, the businesses that have such councils employ half of the entire German workforce. As of January 1, 2004, terminated employees may accept a severance payment in lieu of suing for wrongful dismissal. The amount of the severance payment is half a month's gross salary for every year of service. Employees seeking to challenge their dismissal must file within three weeks of their receipt of the notice of termination.

Similar worker protections exist pursuant to the **French Labor Code**.[16] Termination of the employment relationship on grounds other than *faute grave* requires written notice in the French language, a pretermination meeting with the employee, and statutorily required waiting periods. These requirements make immediate termination impossible in France. Layoffs for economic reasons (otherwise known as **redundancies**) are subject to separate procedural and substantive requirements, especially in the case of multiple dismissals. Amendments to the French Labor Code in 2002 require severe economic constraints prior to multiple dismissals on the basis of redundancy. In addition, a number of French governmental agencies are entitled to receive notice of proposed dismissals and may intervene in the process. Dismissed employees may initiate litigation alleging wrongful termination against a former employer in special labor relations courts (*Conseils de Prud'hommes*). These courts have lay judges elected from employer and employee organizations. As noted by one commentator with respect to wrongful dismissal litigation in these courts, "It is rare that the plaintiff be other than an employee and just as rare that claims be dismissed with no award whatsoever being made against the employer."[17]

INTERNATIONAL

Termination of the employment relationship in Italy is lawful only if it meets one of three requirements.[18] Initially, termination is valid for cause (*giusta causa*). Cause exists where the employee's actions constitute such a dereliction of duty as

INTERNATIONAL

---

15. The materials on the termination of the employment relationship in Germany were derived from Jones Day, *German Labor and Employment News* (2004) and Hale and Dorr, *Features of German Labor and Employment Law* (2003).

16. The materials on the termination of the employment relationship in France were derived from Triplet and Associates, *Layoffs and Redundancies in France: Dismissals on Economic Grounds* (2004).

17. Triplet and Associates, *French Employment Law: Dismissing Employees in France* (2004).

18. The materials on termination of the employment relationship in Italy were derived from Michele Bignami, "What Renders Dismissal Unlawful?" *Personnel Today* (Nov. 2000).

to "undermine the very root of the fiduciary relationship between the parties." Termination may also be justified if it is for a subjective justified reason (*giustificato motivo soggettivo*). This standard requires a serious breach by the employee of the employment contract. Finally, termination may be justified if there is an objective, justified reason (*giustificato motivo oggettivo*). This reason relates to redundancies arising from the employer's business operations. To avail itself of this reason, the employer must demonstrate that there was an objective reason for the redundancy directly connected to economic factors (such as economic savings or reorganization to enhance efficiency), and the terminated employee could not be redeployed because of the absence of a suitable alternative position. Complaints alleging wrongful dismissal are resolved through alternative dispute resolution, arbitration courts, or specialized labor courts. The usual sanction for wrongful termination is payment of damages equivalent to two to six months' salary. Employers of more than fifteen people must reemploy wrongfully terminated people and pay their salary as if the termination never occurred. The employee may convert this right to reemployment into a fixed payment equal to fifteen months' salary. Separate rules relate to mass firings and the termination and wrongful dismissal of senior executives (*dirigenti*).

INTERNATIONAL

Termination of the employment relationship outside Western Europe is equally subject to strict regulation. For example, the **Russian Labor Code** contains an extensive list of grounds for the unilateral termination of the employment relationship.[19] However, the grounds are very narrow, to the extent that they require some actionable misconduct by the employee, such as disclosure of trade secrets, falsification of documents or information related to the formation of the employment agreement, and the exercise of powers not delegated to the employee if such action results in damage to the employer.

INTERNATIONAL

In China, an employer may dissolve an employment contract after consultation for serious violations of applicable workplace rules and regulations, serious dereliction of duty, or accusations of criminal conduct. By contrast, employment contracts may be rescinded upon thirty days' advance written notice where an employee becomes unable to perform the original work duties or another job arranged by the employer because of illness or a work-related injury, where the employee proves to be incompetent to perform the job, or as a result of major changes to the objective conditions underlying the employment agreement that cannot be rectified through amendment or consultation. Employers are also permitted to terminate employment contracts if there is a "genuine need to reduce staff" as a result of "being on the verge of bankruptcy or due to major difficulties in production and business operations." Termination on this basis requires thirty days' advance written notice to all affected employees and trade unions. Reductions may only occur after the opinions of the trade union and affected workers have been solicited and a report filed with the labor administration department of the state council. Terminated workers have priority for new positions if the employer engages in recruiting for new hires within six months of terminating employees for economic reasons. In any event, the employer must pay "appropriate compensation" to the employee upon the rescission of the employment contract or termination for economic reasons. Aggrieved workers may apply

---

19. The materials on termination of the employment relationship in Russia were derived from Baker and McKenzie, *The New Russian Federation Labor Code: Highlights of the New Provisions* (2002).

for conciliation or arbitration, file suit in the People's Court, or settle the dispute through consultation. Trade unions and the labor administration department of the state council may intervene if wrongful termination is alleged.[20]

International Labor Standards

Labor regulation has become a controversial issue in both the regional and global contexts. In the global arena, national and international labor groups have criticized the World Trade Organization (WTO) for its narrow mandate of fostering free trade. These groups believe that free trade agreements should be made conditional on respect for labor standards. Thus far, the WTO has rejected demands to adopt standards for the regulation of labor.

Historically, the **International Labor Organization (ILO)** has been associated primarily with the development of international norms applicable to labor issues. The Treaty of Versailles established the ILO in 1919 with the stated principle that "labor should not be regarded merely as a commodity or article of commerce." A common device used to advance labor standards is the inclusion of **labor clauses** in trade agreements (see Focus on Transactions: ILO Labor Clauses in Public Contracts). This was expressly done in regional free trade agreements such as the North American Free Trade Agreement (NAFTA) and more specifically in EU legislation but was rejected in the enactment of the WTO agreements.

The **ILO Declaration on Fundamental Principles and Rights at Work** has enumerated a number of "core labor standards," including:

- freedom of association and the right to collective bargaining
- elimination of all forms of forced or compulsory labor
- abolition of child labor
- elimination of discrimination with respect to employment and occupation[21]

There is a close relationship between these core labor rights or standards and the basic human rights discussed in Chapter Two. Currently, U.S. law reflects this commitment to core labor rights. For example, a developing country may lose preferential tariff rates for violating labor rights. The General System of Preferences (GSP) law states that reduced tariff rates are to be removed if a country has not taken steps to

http://
International Labor
Organization:
http://www.ilo.org.

ILO Labor Clauses in Public Contracts

Contractor agrees to ensure working conditions not less favorable than those established for work of the same character in the trade or industry where the work is carried on by collective agreement or other recognized machinery of negotiations between employers and workers. Where such agreements are not in existence, then those working conditions that are at "the general level observed in the trade or industry in which the contractor is engaged by employers whose general circumstances are similar."

Focus on Transactions

---

20. See People's Republic of China, Labor Law, arts. 24–30.
21. See ILO Declaration on Fundamental Principles and Rights at Work, art. 2 (a-d) (1998).

http://

The Apparel Industry
and Codes of Conduct:
A Solution to the
International Child
Labor Problem?:
**http://www.dol.gov/
ilab/media/reports/
iclp/apparel/main.htm.**
U.S. U.S. Department
of Labor, "By the Sweat
and Toil of Children:
Efforts to Eliminate
Child Labor":
**http://www.dol.gov/
ilab/media/reports/
iclp/sweat5/welcome.
html.**

afford "internationally recognized worker rights" to its workers.[22] Section 1307 of the Tariff Act of 1930 prohibits the importation of goods produced with prison or indentured labor. In 1997, Section 1307 was amended to include goods produced by using forced or indentured labor, including such labor provided by children. The sporadic implementation of these provisions has been an issue for debate.

The EU has addressed labor standards on a piecemeal basis by incorporating them into agreements on specific activities. For example, EU directives require the insertion of labor clauses in public procurement contracts. Another pro-labor device recognized in Europe is the works council discussed earlier. These employee councils require a company to provide information and seek consultation with its workers on plant and workforce relocations. In 1993, Hoover Europe announced the closing of a plant in France, resulting in the loss of 600 of 700 existing jobs. Partially in response to the public outcry, the EU approved a **European Works Council Directive**[23] that requires large companies, mostly multinational corporations, to establish European Works Councils (EWC). That directive is estimated to cover about 1,500 multinational companies operating in Europe.[24]

The Independent Contractor Contract

The designation of a foreign agent as an employee, partner, or independent contractor is crucial. If the foreign agent is hired as an independent contractor, then the employment regulations just discussed do not apply to the relationship. Furthermore, the principal is not liable for the acts of the independent contractor, as it would be for the acts of an employee or partner.

Independent contractor status must be preserved both in any written contract and in the actual carrying out of the contractual relationship. In the United States, the Internal Revenue Service has devised a seventeen-factor test for determining whether a worker is an employee or an independent contractor.[25] The independent contractor agreement should also include a **nonpartnership clause** to prevent the principal from being vicariously liable under agency principles. A typical nonpartnership clause states that "the party being hired is to perform as an independent contractor and nothing contained herein should be construed as creating a partnership between the parties to this agreement."

In addition, a **work for hire clause** should be inserted into any employment or independent contractor agreement in which the employee or independent contractor is being paid to develop new technology or to perform research and development. This clause makes it clear that all rights to the research and intellectual property rights

22. 19 U.S.C. § 2462(c)(7) (2000).
23. See EU Directive 94/45 (1994).
24. See Brian Bercusson, "Labor Regulation in a Transnational Economy," 6 *Maastricht Journal of European and Comparative Law* 244 (1999).
25. See Revenue Ruling 87-41, 1987-1 C.B. 296, 298. Factors relevant to the creation of an employer-employee relationship may be summarized as follows: (1) the requirement to comply with the employer's instructions with respect to the performance of the work; (2) the existence and need for training; (3) the integration of the worker's services into the business; (4) the requirement of personal rendition of services; (5) the identity of the person responsible for hiring, supervising, and paying subagents; (6) the length of the relationship; (7) the setting of hours of work by the employer; (8) the absence of freedom to work for others; (9) the location where the work is performed; (10) the employer's control of the sequencing of the work; (11) the requirement to submit regular reports; (12) the payment of a salary or lump sum at the end of the job; (13) the reimbursement of business expenses by the employer; (14) the furnishing of tools by the employer; (15) the furnishing of facilities by the employer; (16) the retention of the right to discharge by the employer; and (17) the right of the worker to terminate the relationship.

are to revert to the employer. A typical work for hire clause reads that "all inventions, creations, and research of the employee (or independent contractor) during the term of his employment shall be work for hire and shall be the property of the employer, and that all rights to the intellectual property shall be assigned by the employee (or independent contractor) to the employer."

The Foreign Sales Representative

The most common use of the independent contractor vehicle for transacting business is to hire a foreign sales representative. This relationship has been defined as the hiring of an agent "to prospect for and visit customers with a view to negotiating and, when appropriate, concluding sales agreements in the name and for account of the exporter of goods, services, technology."[26] This relationship is also referred to as a **commercial agency** arrangement.

The following excerpt from the U.S. State Department's country commercial guide for Indonesia illustrates some of the nuances in hiring foreign sales representatives and agents:

INTERNATIONAL

Foreign companies wishing to sell their products in Indonesia are required to appoint an Indonesian agent or distributor pursuant to Government Regulation No. 36/1977. While registration of an Indonesian agent or distributor with the Directorate of Business Development and Company Registration at the Department of Industry and Trade is still voluntary, an agent or distributor wishing to participate in Government procurements should register and obtain a license from the Department of Industry and Trade. Since 1980, the Government began to pressure foreign firms into dealing through an Indonesian agent, rather than third-country middlemen. The predilection of some foreigners for regional representatives, often based in Singapore, rather than Indonesian-based representatives, is particularly unwelcome by the government although it is not prohibited by law. Appointment of the Indonesian agent (or distributor) requires care, since it is difficult to get out of a bad relationship. Indonesian law allows the severance of an agency agreement only by mutual consent or if a clause permitting the severance is contained in the original agency agreement. As in many countries, the Indonesian's network of contacts and personal power dictates what it costs to buy oneself out of a bad agency agreement.[27]

A subsequent determination or conversion, by a foreign government, of an independent sales agent to employment status subjects the exporter to a wide array of foreign laws, including tax and labor laws. An employment designation may also "establish" the company for purposes of personal jurisdiction in the courts of that country. Thus, the structuring and wording of the services contract as one of independent agency, and not dependent agency, is crucial for avoiding such host country laws. The profound differences in the area of agency law between civil law and common law countries require the advice of foreign legal counsel before entering such a relationship.

Before hiring a foreign sales agent or representative, a company should develop a checklist of factors for selection. Each company's checklist should be tailored to reflect the types of products or services to be sold and the differences between targeted countries. The following Focus on Transactions feature suggests the type of questions and factors to be considered in hiring a foreign agent.

---

26. ICC, *The ICC Agency Model Contract: A Commentary*, No. 512 (Fabio Bortolotti, ed., 1993).
27. U.S. State Department's country commercial guide for Indonesia (2004).

Focus on Transactions

Factors to Consider When Choosing a Foreign Representative or Distributor[28]

Size of Sales Force

- How many field salespeople does the representative or distributor have?
- What are the company's short- and long-range expansion plans, if any?
- Would it need to expand to accommodate your account properly? If so, would it be willing to do so?

Sales Record

- Has its sales growth been consistent? If not, why not? Try to determine its sales volume for the past five years.
- What is the average sales volume per outside salesperson?
- What are its sales objectives for next year? How were they determined?

Territorial Analysis

- What sales territory does it now cover?
- Is it consistent with the coverage you desire? If not, is it able and willing to expand?
- Does it have any branch offices in the territory to be covered?
- If so, are they located where your sales prospects are greatest?
- Does it have any plans to open additional offices?

Product Mix

- How many product lines does it represent?
- Are these product lines compatible with yours?
- Would there be any conflict of interest?
- Does it represent any other U.S. firms? If so, which ones?
- If necessary, would it be willing to alter its present product mix to accommodate yours?
- What would be the minimum sales volume needed to justify its handling of your lines? Do its sales projections reflect the minimum figure? From what you know of the territory and the prospective representative or distributor, is the projection realistic?

Facilities and Equipment

- Does it have adequate warehouse facilities?
- What is its method of stock control?
- Does it use computers? Are they compatible with yours?
- What communications facilities does it have?
- If your product requires servicing, is it equipped and qualified to do so? If not, is it willing to acquire the needed equipment and arrange for necessary training? To what extent will you have to share training cost?
- If necessary and customary, is it willing to inventory repair parts and replacement items?

Marketing Policies

- How is its sales staff compensated?
- Does it have special incentive or motivation programs?
- Does it use product managers to coordinate sales efforts for specific product lines?
- How does it monitor sales performance?
- How does it train its sales staff?
- Would it pay or share expenses for sales personnel to attend factory-sponsored seminars?

Customer Profile

- What kinds of customers is it currently contacting?
- Are its interests compatible with your product line?
- Who are the key accounts?
- What percentage of the total gross receipts do these key accounts represent?

continued

28. Unz & Company, *A Basic Guide to Exporting*, at table 3.

Factors to Consider When Choosing a Foreign Representative or Distributor *(continued)*

Principals Represented

- How many principals is it currently representing?
- Would you be its primary supplier?
- If not, what percentage of the total business would you represent? How does this percentage compare with other suppliers?

Promotional Thrust

- Can it help you compile market research information to be used in making forecasts?

- What medium does it use, if any, to promote sales?
- How much of its budget is allocated to advertising? How is it distributed among various principals?
- Will you be expected to contribute funds for promotional purposes?
- How will the amount be determined?
- If it uses direct mail, how many prospects are on the mailing list?
- What type of brochure does it use to describe the company and the products that it represents?
- If necessary, can it translate your advertising copy?

After developing a hiring checklist, a company's next step is to negotiate the foreign representation or agency agreement. The next section reviews some of the issues relevant to the negotiation of a commercial agency contract.

The Commercial Agency Contract

Provisions related to the termination of the agreement are the most important part of an international agency contract[29] because host country laws restrict a foreign company's right to terminate an agency agreement. These laws, popularly referred to as **evergreen statutes**, are dealt with in the next section. Because of these statutes, the agency contract should include an escape or **termination clause** in the agreement that allows the exporter or principal to end the relationship. The contract should spell out exactly what constitutes *just cause* for ending the agreement. The following list illustrates the legal questions that should be considered in negotiating a termination clause in an agency contract.

- How far in advance must the representative be notified of the exporter's intention to terminate the agreement? (Three months satisfies the requirements of most countries.)
- What is just cause for terminating a representative? (Specifying causes for termination in the written contract usually strengthens the exporter's position.)
- Which country's laws will govern a contract dispute? (Laws in the representative's country may forbid the representative from waiving its nation's legal jurisdiction.)

---

29.   Pursuant to U.S. law, the label "agency contract" is broad enough to include a wide variety of contracts, including sales representation, distribution, consulting, advertising, and transportation agreements.

- What compensation is due the representative on dismissal? (Depending on the length of the relationship, the added value of the market the representative has created for the exporter, and whether termination is for just cause as defined by the foreign country, the U.S. exporter may be required to pay damages or an indemnity.)
- What must the representative give up if dismissed? (The contract should specify the return of patents, trademarks, name registrations, customer records, and promotional materials.)
- Should the representative be referred to as an agent? (The contract may need to specify that the representative is not a legal agent with power of attorney.)
- In what language should the contract be drafted? (English should be the official language of the contract in most cases.)

The Focus on Transactions section that follows provides a summary of the issues that an international agency contract should address.

ICC Commercial Agency Guide[30]

Focus on Transactions

- **Independent Contractor Status:** The heading of the agreement should clearly state that it is a commercial agency contract.
- **Definitions:** All terms, especially terms of art, should be defined in the agreement or through reference to internationally recognized definitions.
- **Identity and Capacity of Parties:** The nationality and legal form of each party should be stated, along with the foreign entity's capacity to act as a commercial agent. For example, in some countries, only nationals may act as agents and in others commercial agents must be registered with the government.
- **Products:** The contract should be clear regarding the products that are to be sold on behalf of the principal. If the principal produces different classes of products, then the contract should state which classes are subject to the agency contract. The contract should also address the issue of the development of new products or subsequent improvements of the products listed in the contract.

- **Services to Be Performed by the Agent:** This portion of the agreement should provide a detailed description of the expected duties of the agent.
- **Agency Territory:** The contract should precisely delineate the sales territory that is being given to the agent. The agreement should specify whether this grant of territory to the agent is exclusive or nonexclusive. Restrictions may be placed upon sales to third parties who are likely to export the goods to another territory. Such restrictions are needed to prevent the gray market problem discussed in Chapters Thirteen and Fourteen. Host country laws should be reviewed to see if territorial restrictions will violate competition (antitrust) laws.
- **Solicitation of Customers:** The parties should agree to the groups to be targeted by the agent as potential customers.
- **Sales Provisions:** The agreement should specify any sales targets and the chronological basis upon which such targets are to be determined (daily, weekly,

continued

---

30. This list is derived from ICC, *The ICC Agency Model Contract*, pages 9–107; and Ralph H. Folsom, *International Business Transactions* 182–90 (2d ed. 2002).

ICC Commercial Agency Guide (*continued*)

monthly, or annually). The principal may want to negotiate that the agent is required to meet certain minimum sales levels. It should specify the consequences for the failure to meet sales quotas such as termination, reduction of territory, or loss of exclusivity. This section of the agreement may also require the agent to determine and certify the solvency of customers whose orders he transmits to the principal.

- **Acceptance of Orders:** The agreement should clearly state whether the agent has the authority to bind the principal. Under some foreign laws, agency authority to bind its principal may result in the loss of independent contractor status.
- **Advertising and Marketing Materials:** The contract should stipulate whether the principal is to provide any samples or advertising materials, and which party is to pay the costs of such materials. The contract should make clear whether the principal has the right of prior consent for any materials or advertising produced by the agent.
- **Parts and Service:** The obligations of the agent should be detailed with regard to providing after-sales service and spare parts.
- **Best Efforts Provision:** The principal will want to negotiate a clause that requires the agent to use "best efforts" in marketing and selling the principal's products. The agreement should attempt to define the meaning of "best efforts," such as tying them to generally accepted business practices.
- **Noncompetition Clause:** This provision prohibits the agent from selling the products of a competitor. This clause should be narrowly constructed so as to not violate national laws that view such restrictions harshly.
- **Confidentiality:** The agreement should require the agent to maintain the secrecy of the principal's trade secrets even after the termination of the relationship.

- **Compensation, Payments, and Commissions:** The basis of calculation and the rate of commissions should be clearly stated. If the net amount is used as a basis, then the deductions (e.g., freight, insurance, discounts, taxes, and packing) should be stated. Other compensation and reimbursement for expenses incurred by the agent should also be specified.
- **Duty to Keep Informed:** The agreement should place a duty upon both parties to keep one another informed of material information that may have an effect upon the performance of the agency. From the perspective of the agent, this may include customer complaints, changes in national laws or regulations relating to technical requirements, labeling, and customs regulations, and the existence of any national requirement to register the agency contract. From the perspective of the principal, this may include changes in price lists and advertising materials, all communications with customers, and the status of customer orders, including refusal or inability to fulfill any such order.
- **Intellectual Property Rights Infringement:** The relative responsibilities of the parties as to infringement of intellectual property rights should be defined. For example, the agent's responsibility to notify the principal of any such infringements should be detailed. In order to protect its rights, the principal should register its intellectual property rights in the host country prior to entering any agency relationship.
- **Assignments:** If the parties intend to allow assignment, the contract should state the conditions and procedure for assignments.
- **Subagents:** The agreement should state whether the agent is authorized to employ subagents. If the agent is so empowered, the agreement should

continued

ICC Commercial Agency Guide (*continued*)

provide that the agent is solely responsible for the activities of his subagents.

- **Good Faith and Fair Dealing:** The parties agree that they will act in accordance with good faith and fair dealing and that the terms of the agreement and their conduct pursuant thereto shall be interpreted in good faith.
- **Agreement is the Full Agreement:** The agreement should contain a provision that the parties concur that the written agreement represents the full agreement between the parties.
- **Language of the Contract:** If the contract is written in two languages, it should state which language is to control in the enforcement of the contract.
- **Duration:** The agreement should establish a period of time during which it is in effect. A short and definite duration may be preferable as it allows the principal to consider nonrenewal for legitimate purposes. However, such provision may be unenforceable in some countries which discourage temporary employment. Principals should also exercise care as the agreement and their conduct pursuant thereto may unwittingly create permanent employment under the laws of some countries.
- **Termination:** The contract may be for a fixed period or an indefinite time period subject to reasonable notice. Some national laws require that the notice be of a certain length of time. It may be stipulated that certain events, such as bankruptcy, merger, assignment, or resignation of a key employee, give a party the right to terminate. The rights of the parties upon termination should be set forth as well as a waiver by the agent of termination rights pursuant to applicable national law. It is important to keep in mind that such a waiver may prove unenforceable. Upon termination, the agent should be required to return all documents and samples utilized during the course of the agency to the principal. The termination provision should also deny the agent any further rights with respect to the importation of the product upon termination of the agreement and while any claims for compensation are pending.
- **Force Majeure:** The agreement should include a provision that allows suspension or termination of any obligations to provide products to fulfill orders when the U.S. government imposes restrictions on exports for any reason whatsoever.
- **Choice of Law and Forum Selection Clauses:** The parties should agree on the law that will apply to any disputes. It should also select the court or arbitration panel in which such disputes are to be brought.

Evergreen Statutes

The most difficult laws to avoid are national agency termination laws, popularly referred to as evergreen statutes. These laws often impose minimum notice requirements for terminating an agent or require the payment of an indemnity upon termination unless the termination is based on a just cause. These laws are different than the employment regulations discussed earlier in the chapter. Unlike employment regulations, evergreen statutes do apply to agents acting as independent contractors.

Many European countries grant the agent a right upon the termination of the agency relationship to either an indemnity payment, based on the length of the relationship and the level of past or anticipated payments, or a claim for damages attributed to the termination. A decision not to renew an agency contract is construed as a termination requiring remuneration. **EU Directive 86/653** states that agency contracts should provide for a minimum notice of termination. A reasonable notice period is one month for the first year of service, two months for the second year commenced, and three months for all subsequent years commenced at a minimum.[31] A commercial agent will be owed an indemnity upon termination to the extent that the person has brought new customers to the principal or significantly increased the principal's volume of business.[32]

INTERNATIONAL

The directive also allows national laws to provide for a damage claim to the agent, especially if at the time of termination the agent had not completely amortized the costs and expenses relative to the representation.[33] The best approach is to enter into a fixed-term contract with no renewal options. As stated earlier, the contract should provide a detailed list of performance standards on which termination for just cause may be based. The principal should also be aware that in some countries, as in Belgium (*représentants de commerce*) and France (*représentants placiers*), the agent is presumed to be an employee, even if the contract designates the agent as an independent contractor. Therefore, the easiest way to avoid this presumption is to deal with agents who are artificial entities (corporations).[34]

National labor and employment laws must be checked for obligations of the principal pertaining to social security and other "employment-related" statutory requirements. Under Italian law, the principal and the agent each have a duty to pay a percentage of all commissions to the national agency (ENASARCO) as social security contributions. The principal is legally obligated to withhold the agent's contribution and remit it to the agency, along with an amount to be used toward the **severance indemnity**. A certain percentage is paid on a sliding scale, based on the amount of the commissions paid.

INTERNATIONAL

A **foreign consultant** is a variation of the foreign sales representative. The same issues of host country labor laws and agency termination laws apply to the consulting relationship. The **consulting contract** should be specific as to the scope of the engagement, and it should emphasize the independent status of the consultant. A separate "independent contractor status clause" should be incorporated into the agreement. The previously mentioned seventeen factors the U.S. Internal Revenue Service uses to determine the existence of the independent contractor relationship provide an excellent starting point for emphasizing the independent status of the consultant.

The Distribution Agreement

The distribution agreement is a type of commercial agency relationship. It is also an example of a common form of service contract. A foreign distributor is defined as "a merchant who purchases goods from a U.S. exporter and resells them for a profit. The foreign distributor generally provides support and service for the product and usually carries an inventory of products and a sufficient supply of

31.   See EU Directive 86/653, art. 15(2) (1986).

32.   See ibid. art. 17(2).

33.   See ibid. at art. 17(3). The agent must notify its principal of a claim for indemnity or damages within one year from the date of termination. See ibid. at art. 17(5).

34.   For example, in Belgium if the contract subordinates the agent to the authority of the principal, then there is a legal presumption that an employment relationship has been formed. However, this presumption can be overcome if the agent is a corporate entity.

spare parts and also maintains adequate facilities and personnel for normal servicing operations."[35] Unlike a sales representative, a foreign distributor takes title to the goods and offers them for resale. As such, the foreign distributor assumes the risk of being unable to resell the goods. Engaging the services of a foreign distributor is the most important decision that an exporter of goods will make. Importing goods to a foreign country is of little benefit unless the goods can be sold and delivered to consumers in an efficient manner. It is the job of the foreign distributor to get the goods to market.

Because of the differences in language, culture, and the legal treatment of foreign distributor relationships, it is important to negotiate a foreign distribution agreement that details the respective duties and responsibilities of the parties. Unlike the standard agency relationship, in which the sales contract is between the principal and the purchaser (consumer), the distributor generally sells the goods on its own account. The sales contract is between the distributor and the purchaser. Because of this, the foreign distributor is by necessity an independent contractor in relationship to the exporter or manufacturer.

The selection of a competent and trustworthy foreign distributor or agent is crucial. The U.S. Department of Commerce provides information on foreign distributors and agents through **agent-distributor searches (ADS)**. The U.S. International Trade Administration offers a fee-based service that locates foreign import agents and distributors on behalf of U.S. exporters. It also provides customized market analysis (CMA) reports that identify potential representatives.

The International Chamber of Commerce's **Model Distributorship Contract**[36] outlines the basic framework of the distribution relationship. The contract provides a guide to the underlying risks of the relationship and methods to minimize such risks in the distribution contract. The contract then presents eleven annexes of clauses dealing with the topics of products and territory, commissions, representation, names of existing customers, advertising, conditions of sale, minimum sales targets, inventory and spare parts, after-sales service, changes in control and ownership of the distributor, and termination. *Distributor* is defined in the contract as "not an intermediary or broker but rather a dealer who buys goods in order to resell them in its own name or on its behalf, even if the distributor is often called an 'agent' in business practice."[37] Thus, calling a distributor an agent is a misnomer. In contrast, an agent is generally an independent contractor owing certain fiduciary obligations to the principal. Note, however, that a distributor might act as both an agent and a distributor.

The distributor's relationship with the manufacturer-exporter is purely contractual and is very much akin to a sale of goods transaction. However, it is a special kind of sales relationship because (1) the distributor often deals with the promotion and organization of distribution within its contractual territory; (2) generally the contractual territory is exclusive to the distributor; (3) the transaction is not a single occurrence but lasts for a certain duration; (4) there exists a certain level of loyalty, namely, an obligation to refrain from competition; and (5) the relationship almost always relates to the distribution of brand-name products.

---

35.   Unz & Company, *A Basic Guide to Exporting*, at chapter 4.
36.   ICC, *The ICC Model Distributorship Contract*, No. 518 (1993).
37.   Ibid. at VI.

Before entering into an international distribution agreement, it is imperative to research the law of the distributor's country in order to comply with mandatory legal provisions. Some countries such as Saudi Arabia require distributors to be nationals or wholly owned Saudi companies and to register as distributors with the government. Some countries, by statute or case law, require that the distribution agreement provide the distributor some minimal level of protection regarding issues of termination and compensation. In France, the case law is rich with instances where judges have ordered the principal to pay additional compensation when severing a distribution relationship. Germany recognizes a **goodwill indemnity** that is owed to the distributor upon the termination of the distribution agreement.

INTERNATIONAL

The exporter should include a clause requiring the distributor to use its best efforts to achieve maximum sales. The best efforts provision may also provide minimum sales quotas in order to meet the best efforts obligation. The "minimum sales quota" might trigger an exporter option to terminate the contract or to preclude a renewal of the contract. The exporter may want to place a clause in the agreement that assigns the risk of products liability claims to the distributor, but foreign national law may impose that liability on both the manufacturer-exporter and the distributor. The parties may, instead, agree to obtain a prescribed level of insurance to protect them both against products liability risks.

Often the manufacturer wants to ensure that each of its distributors offers the same conditions of sale to their customers, especially regarding guarantees and after-sales service, but the validity of clauses that appear to entail restrictions on the types of customers to be solicited, resale pricing, and territorial restrictions is questionable under some national laws. For example, the laws of France, Germany, the United Kingdom, and the Scandinavian countries should be closely checked, especially with regard to the area of retail price maintenance.

The distribution agreement must also deal with the issue of changes in **key personnel**. If certain employees are considered essential, they should be recognized in the contract. The contract can then provide for termination in the event that essential people cease to be associated with the distributor. In addition, to avoid the reach of evergreen statutes, the contract should specify exact commencement and expiration dates. Setting a fixed term for the agreement minimizes the chances of large indemnity payments being owed under certain national laws. Renewals should be kept to a minimum. To minimize the size of indemnity payments, it is better to enter into an entirely new contract at the expiration of the first contract.

Foreign Competition Law

Most distribution agreements provide exclusive territories to the distributor. These provisions prohibit the exporter from selling products to customers who are likely to import them into the distributor's territory. The distributor is also prohibited from selling the products outside its exclusive territory. Developing countries are skeptical of these restrictions and generally will not enforce such contractual provisions in their courts. Most developed countries allow the contracting parties full freedom to contract and enforce most restrictive clauses. Under antitrust or competition laws, some forms of exclusivity may be deemed to be anticompetitive, and certain restrictions will be scrutinized.

An example of the interplay between distribution agreements and competition law may be found in **EU Regulation 2790/1999**. This regulation provides a general exemption for vertical distribution agreements, as long as the supplier has less than 30 percent of the relevant market that is the subject matter of the agreement. The **block exemption**[38] for such agreements permits restrictions on sales by one distributor in territory granted exclusively to another distributor, sales to unauthorized distributors, and maximum resale prices. However, the regulation prohibits minimum resale price maintenance and certain distribution agreements between competitors. Perhaps most important, the regulation permits member states to disregard the block exemption if they determine that the exemption does not result in greater economic efficiency.

Price-fixing and **tying clauses** are most likely to be held as illegal pursuant to applicable competition laws. For example, many national laws prohibit the principal or licensor from setting pricing guidelines, especially at the retail level. Tying clauses that require the distributor to purchase other items along with the licensed product are generally unenforceable. One exception is when these tied or tying products or services are needed to ensure the quality of the licensed or distributed product. In such cases, a requirement that the licensee purchase materials from certified suppliers is likely to be enforced.

Noncompetition clauses are also susceptible to nonenforcement. Generally, a distribution contract cannot prohibit the agent or representative from also selling the products of another company. The one major exception is that U.S. courts will allow such clauses in cases involving patented property rights where the distributor is given an exclusive license. Thus, one strategy to increase the chances of enforceability is to tie exclusivity to noncompetition. For example, the distributor can be given the right to sell the goods of a competitor but in doing so converts the distribution agreement from exclusive to nonexclusive.

Logistical Services

An exporter must comply with foreign packing, labeling, and documentation requirements. Because of the complexity of these requirements, most exporters enlist the services of freight forwarders and customs brokers. **Freight forwarders**[39] act as agents of the exporter and importer in transporting cargo worldwide and importing goods into a given country. Freight forwarders are familiar with import and export regulations, methods of shipping, and documentation requirements. They are also a good source for freight and insurance cost information. In a documentary transaction, the freight forwarder can be enlisted to review the letter of credit, bill of lading, and other documents. The freight forwarder can also help in the packaging and marking of the goods for transport. The freight forwarder will be aware of the internationally recognized symbols for handling and shipping products of all kinds.

---

38. A block exemption is simply a statutory recognition that certain types of business practices are to be permitted even though they technically violate EU competition (antitrust) law.
39. Most of the information that follows also applies to customs brokers. However, the services of the freight forwarder are broader in that a freight forwarder provides services pertaining to export requirements, transportation, and importation. The customs broker's expertise generally revolves around the government requirements for the importation of goods.

Law of Freight Forwarding

The freight forwarder plays a crucial role in the transportation of products under an international sales contract. The services provided by the freight forwarder and, to some extent, the customs broker have expanded in modern times. Traditionally, they are engaged to assist merchants in preparing and booking the cargo for carriage. In some cases, freight forwarders act as agents for carriers, particularly liner shipping companies for carriage of goods by sea. Freight forwarding services normally include the clearance of goods for export and import. Freight forwarders also have cooperating partners in other countries to whom instructions are given for the receipt of the cargo and for customs clearance.[40]

The freight forwarder also plays the important role of **cargo consolidator**. Most exporter shipments require booking only a portion of a ship's cargo space. The freight forwarder can obtain more reasonable shipment rates by consolidating the cargo of a number of its clients. In addition, the demands of international **multimodal transport**[41] have transformed the freight forwarder from a mere agent of the shipper to that of an operator with carrier liability. The role of the freight forwarder as a common carrier is recognized in Article 30 of the UCP 500. It allows freight forwarders to issue bills of lading if they are acting as a carrier or multimodal transport operator.

The multiple roles played by the freight forwarder lead to some ethical concerns. As the agent of the shipper, the freight forwarder is supposed to work on the shipper's behalf as an unbiased advisor,[42] but its multiple roles may generate temptations to give preferential treatment to certain customers or to work more in favor of the transport companies than the shipper. Thus, the shipper ought to perform independent checks on the services being provided.

Advertising Services and Law

National laws dealing with deceptive advertising vary in scope and enforcement. Cultural differences may result in an advertising campaign that is legal in one country but deemed illegal in another. Almost all developed countries possess laws that make misleading advertising illegal. Advertising laws are policed by administrative agencies, through private litigation, and via industry self-regulation. These three means of enforcement vary dramatically throughout the world. All three are utilized in the United States.

The **Federal Trade Commission (FTC)** regulates virtually all forms of advertising in the United States. It is empowered to prevent "unfair and deceptive practices."[43] Section 43(a) of the **Lanham Act**[44] created a private cause of action for anyone injured by false advertising.[45] There are also many examples of industry and

INTERNATIONAL

---

40. See Jan Ramberg, *Unification of the Law of Freight Forwarding* (1998), at **http://www.unidroit.org.**
41. For a discussion of "multimodal transport" see Chapter Ten.
42. See Paul R. Murphy and James M. Daley, "Ethics and the International Freight Forwarder: User Perspectives," 65 *Journal of Transportation Law, Logistics & Policy* 95 (1998); see also Paul R. Murphy, James M. Daley, and Patricia K. Hall, "Transportation Ethics: A Comparison of Shipper and Carrier Perspectives," 63 *Journal of Transportation Law, Logistics & Policy* 370 (1996).
43. 15 U.S.C. § 45(a)(1)(2000).
44. Ibid. § 1125(a)(1)(A-B).
45. See generally Ross D. Petty, "Supplanting Government Regulation with Competitor Lawsuits: The Case of Controlling False Advertising," 25 *Indiana Law Review* 351 (1991).

media self-regulation. One example is the National Advertising Division of the Better Business Bureau. In contrast, there is no national self-regulation in Saudi Arabia. Instead, a number of agencies, including the Ministry of Information, screen advertisements for conformity to moral and religious standards.[46] In Italy, "industry self-regulation deals with most of the country's advertising disputes."[47]

Civil law countries, including Germany, "rely on advertising law that authorizes private litigation to control misleading advertising."[48] The Scandinavian countries make use of the consumer ombudsman to enact advertising guidelines and to resolve disputes.[49] Because of the vast differences in advertising law enforcement, the international entrepreneur should seek local counsel before embarking on a marketing campaign. The local counsel can provide information on the substantive law of advertising. However, most exporters use private advertisement agencies to handle their marketing campaigns. At a minimum, the prospective agency should be a member of that country's professional advertisement association. For example, in Chile most advertising agencies are members of the *Asociacion Chilena de Agencias de Publicidad* (Chilean Association of Advertising Agencies or ACHAP).

Businesses may attempt to minimize the risks of false or improper advertising through insurance. Although insurance is unlikely to protect from government prosecution, it minimizes their exposure to private litigation. The *Heritage Mutual Insurance* case that follows illustrates some of the issues created by the intersection of advertising and insurance law. This case explains the important concepts of **advertising injury** and the **duty to defend**.

Heritage Mutual Insurance Co. v. Advanced Polymer Technology, Inc.

97 F. Supp. 2d 913 (S.D. Ind. 2000)

Barker, Chief Judge. This case represents another installment in the ongoing debate about the meaning of "advertising injury," a popular phrase used to describe a type of insurance coverage provided in standard versions of commercial general liability insurance policies issued since the 1970s. Plaintiff, Heritage Mutual Insurance Company ("Heritage"), filed a complaint seeking a declaratory judgment that it has no duty to defend or to indemnify its insured, Advanced Polymer Technology (APT). The policy at issue here, known as the Commercial General Liability ("CGL") form, represents a 1986 version written by the Insurance Services Organization ("ISO"), a for-profit private trade organization that generates standard

insurance forms for use by its clients, mainly insurance companies.

While some insurers may alter the forms they receive from ISO and tailor the standard language based upon the unique coverage requested by their insured, insurers often adopt the ISO forms verbatim. ISO periodically revises and clarifies the coverage offered by its standard insurance forms and alters, deletes or adds language accordingly. For instance, the 1998 ISO CGL policy form modified the 1986 version. Coverage "B" of the CGL policy, entitled "Personal and Advertising Injury Liability," provided in its "Insuring" clause that Heritage would insure APT for any "advertising injury caused by an offense committed in the course of advertising APT's goods, products or services." The policy

46. See U.S. State Department's country commercial guide for Saudi Arabia (2004); see also Mushtaq Luqmani, "Advertising in Saudi Arabia: Content and Regulation," 6 *International Marketing Review* 59 (1989).

47. Ross D. Petty, "Advertising Law and Social Issues: The Global Perspective," 17 *Suffolk Transnational Law Review* 309, 319 (1994).

48. Ibid. at 318; see also Warren S. Grimes, "Control of Advertising in the United States and Germany: Volkswagen Has a Better Idea," 84 *Harvard Law Review* 1769 (1971).

49. See J. J. Boddewyn, "The Swedish Consumer Ombudsman System of Advertising Self-Regulation," 19 *Journal of Consumer Affairs* 140 (1985).

defined "advertising injury" as injury arising out of one or more of the following offenses: (a) oral or written publication of material that slanders or libels a person or organization or disparages a person's or organization's goods, products or services; (b) oral or written publication of material that violates a person's right of privacy; (c) misappropriation of advertising ideas or style of doing business; or (d) infringement of copyright, title, or slogan.

One of the policy's coverage exclusions, the "first publication" exclusion, provides that insurance coverage does not apply to "advertising injury . . . arising out of material whose first publication took place before the beginning of the policy period." Additionally, the policy established Heritage's "duty to defend any suit seeking those damages." Under Indiana law, a contract for insurance is subject to the same rules of interpretation as are other contracts. The insured is required to prove that her claims fall within the coverage provisions of her policy, but the insurer bears the burden of proving specific exclusions or limitations to policy coverage.

The insurer's duty to defend, which is broader than its duty to indemnify, is determined by the nature of the claim in the underlying complaint, not its merits. An insurer must defend an action even if only a small portion of the conduct alleged in the complaint falls within the scope of the insurance policy. The intentions of the parties to a contract are to be determined by the "four-corners" of the document. When an insurance contract contains an ambiguity, it should be strictly construed against the insurance company. Yet, when the underlying factual basis of the complaint, even if proved true, would not result in liability under the insurance policy, the insurance company can properly refuse to defend.

Environ, a patent owner, claims that APT willfully infringed on its patents. It also accuses APT of "federal unfair competition" under the Lanham Act by contending that APT made "false and misleading statements as to the creation or ownership" of the piping product "in its application for a patent." The parties have not contended that the patent application constituted an advertisement or an item "in the course of advertising" as required by the Heritage-APT policy. Environ alleges that Defendant APT's marketing of its POLY-TECH piping system as' 'patent pending' creates a cloud on its ownership of the Invention, thereby discouraging investment in or purchase of its products.

We find it implausible that the parties would have intended that direct and induced patent infringement would be covered under the policy without expressly listing those offenses in the phrase "infringement of copyright, title, or slogan." Also, the insurer had no duty to defend the insured since the plaintiff's unfair competition and Lanham Act claims did not qualify as allegations of misappropriation of advertising ideas or style of doing business. The allegation that the insured engaged in unfair competition by misappropriating trade secrets does not allege misappropriation of advertising ideas or styles of doing business as such.

APT claims in abbreviated fashion that Environ's allegations fall within the "disparagement category" of advertising injury offenses. Importantly, Environ never contends that APT's advertisements mention Environ, compare the products of the respective companies, or discredit or denigrate Environ's piping products. While we believe that some direct reference to the competitor's product is necessary to fall within the plain meaning of "disparage," we also do not view Environ's allegations as resulting in a reasonable claim of implied disparagement either. The phrase "patent pending" signifies nothing about the quality or state of Environ's product, as the phrase means exactly what it says—a patent is pending.

Heritage's conduct strikes us as sufficiently reasonable under the circumstances of this case, and, as it turns out, correct as a matter of legal contract interpretation. Heritage retained coverage counsel, who clearly examined the insurance policy provisions at issue and the allegations in the underlying complaint. The reasons supplied for denial of coverage were rational and understandable. We hold that Heritage has no duty to defend its insured because the allegations in Environ's complaint do not constitute advertising injury offenses.

Case Highlights

- Insurance Services Organization (ISO) is a trade association that develops standard insurance forms and clauses.
- "Advertising injury" is a type of insurance coverage provided in standard versions of commercial general liability insurance policies (CGL).
- Under insurance law, the insured is required to prove that her claims fall within the coverage provision of her policy, but the insurer bears the burden of proving specific exclusions or limitations to policy coverage.
- The insurer's duty to defend is broader than its duty to indemnify.
- When an insurance contract contains an ambiguity, it is strictly construed against the insurance company.

Cross-Border Security Offerings

Companies raise capital in a number of ways, including borrowing from banks and accepting investments by venture capitalists. The most common way of raising capital is to sell either debt instruments (bonds) or equity instruments (stock shares). The advantage of selling shares in the company is that it raises capital without incurring a debt obligation. From the investor's perspective, an equity investment, especially in a new company, is made in the hope that the company will be profitable. The internationalization of the capital markets has been one of the major trends in the business world.[50] It is not uncommon for even small or medium investors to allocate a portion of their portfolios to foreign securities. From a legal perspective, this poses questions as to the enforcement and regulation of international securities transactions.

The key issue with the international sale and purchase of securities is how such offerings are to be regulated. Because there is no international policing institution, regulation comes through the enforcement of national regulatory laws. In the United States, the **Securities and Exchange Commission (SEC)** administers federal securities laws. Can the SEC regulate security offerings originating in a foreign country? Can U.S. security laws be applied extraterritorially? It has been deemed fair by U.S. courts "to demand compliance with U.S. laws and regulations of any person or entity who has purposely made a connection with the United States for the sale or purchase of a security, and its conduct has the effect of undermining the stability and fair operation of the securities markets within the United States."[51]

The extraterritorial application of U.S. securities laws follows a standard two-prong test. First, the foreign parties must have had the intent or purpose of selling their securities in the U.S. marketplace. Second, the alleged foreign illegal activities are likely to have an effect within the United States. The second prong is commonly referred to as the **effects test**. The effects test has been used to determine the extraterritorial applicability of many U.S. laws, such as discrimination, antitrust, and tort law. The effects test stands for the principle that the exercise of jurisdiction is appropriate if the illegal activity abroad injures someone within the United States. However, the effects test does not justify the exertion of SEC jurisdiction if no fraud is committed within the United States and the securities are purchased outside the United States.

Offshore security offerings are those in which the offer to sell is not made to a person in the United States or when a security is sold on a foreign stock exchange. To avoid U.S. securities laws, a company can take steps to prevent the solicitation of people within the United States. However, the development of securities transactions over the Internet challenges a company's ability to avoid SEC jurisdiction.

An offering on the Internet not intended for U.S. investors may still be subject to SEC enforcement actions. The global nature of the Internet can lead to the conclusion that such offers are being made "in the United States" and therefore must be registered with the SEC. The SEC has provided guidance, in its "Statement of the Commission Regarding the Use of Internet Web Sites to Offer Securities, Solicit Transactions, or Advertise Investment Services Offshore," for those wanting to avoid U.S. securities laws in offshore offerings.[52] It suggests that the offering

---

50. See Gerald R. Ferrera, Stephen D. Lichtenstein, Margo E. K. Reder, Robert Bird, and William T. Schiano, *Cyberlaw*, at Chapter Eight (2d. ed. 2004).

51. Sharon Drew, "Extraterritoriality of the United States Securities and Exchange Commission," 20 *The Comparative Law Yearbook of International Business* 231, 232 (1998).

52. See U.S. Securities and Exchange Commission, International Series Release No. 1125 (March 1998).

party take reasonable precautions to guard against making sales to U.S. people and to place a disclaimer on the offer, stating that it is not intended for people in the United States.

The **International Organization of Securities Commissions (IOSCO)** has a goal of achieving the comparability of information required under national securities laws in order to facilitate cross-border offerings and listings by multinational securities issuers. To achieve this goal, IOSCO has proposed developing a generally accepted body of disclosure standards that could be used in a uniform disclosure statement for cross-border offerings and listings. In September 1998, IOSCO published its "International Disclosure Standards for Cross-Border Offerings and Initial Listings by Foreign Issuers." A company planning to sell shares internationally should review these standards before preparing required prospectuses and registration statements.

A problem with international standards is that they fail to provide a definition of **materiality**, which is crucial in determining the accuracy of documents and statements. All countries require that a company or issuer disclose all material information. However, the definition of *materiality* varies from country to country. In the United States, the Supreme Court in *TSC Industries, Inc. v. Northway, Inc.*[53] defined *materiality* as follows: "An omitted fact is material if there is a substantial likelihood that a reasonable shareholder or investor would have considered it important."

The definition of *materiality* differs in other countries. For example, the Stock Exchange of Hong Kong's listing rules define *materiality* as the disclosing of information "necessary to enable an investor to make an informed assessment of the activities, assets and liabilities, financial position, management, and prospects of the issuer and of its profits and losses." This definition closely resembles Australia's Corporation Law, which determines materiality based on information that investors would reasonably require for purposes of making an informed assessment of assets, liabilities, financial position, profits and losses, and corporate prospects. In addition, a separate section of the Corporation Law defines a statement or omission as material if it is capable of influencing the decision-making process of a person who commonly invests in securities. Mexican law is similar in defining *materiality* to include any information that investors need to form an opinion of the risk, finances, or operations of a company. However, this definition is more subjective to the extent that Mexican law places responsibility on issuers of securities to determine which information is material, according to this legal definition and in the context of its own business affairs. In contrast, the European Union does not use the concept of "material" and therefore does not provide any definition of *materiality*. Japanese disclosure rules provide numerical guidelines for determining materiality.[54]

INTERNATIONAL

Internationalization of Accounting and Taxation

The internationalization of business has placed pressure on the accounting profession to provide necessary support services.[55] Accounting services, like most professional

---

53.   426 U.S. 438 (1976); see also *Virginia Bankshares, Inc. v. Sandberg*, 501 U.S. 1083 (1991).

54.   See Risk Institute, Materiality, at http://riskinstitute.ch144730.htm.

55.   The importance of liberalizing trade in accounting services has been recognized under the WTO Agreements. The WTO's Working Party on Professional Services (WPPS) has focused its attention on the internationalization of accounting services.

services, can be internationalized on a number of fronts. First, domestic regulations can be modified to take into account the special issues of cross-border transactions. Second, international standards can be enumerated for professional services. Third, countries can recognize each others' professional qualifications and national standards.[56] The adoption of harmonized international standards provides the greatest possibility for increased trade in international accounting services. The areas where international accounting services are needed include transfer pricing, currency translation,[57] and joint venture accounting.

http://
Association of International Accountants: **http://www.aia.org.uk.**

Transfer pricing refers to a method of tax avoidance. In structuring contracts between itself and its foreign subsidiaries, a corporation often attempts to recognize or transfer any profits to subsidiaries located in low-tax countries. The U.S. Internal Revenue Service requires that such intracompany transactions be conducted at arm's length. Contract prices between affiliated companies are to be set at market or reasonable prices. Therefore, multinational corporations need to develop a transfer pricing policy that will be generally accepted in the countries where they do business in order to avoid complicated tax disputes and the potential for double taxation. Tax planning should be done on a country-by-country basis. For example, the social security rates in EU countries range from 20 percent to as high as 40 percent. Some guidance can be obtained through the use of the OECD's guidelines for transfer pricing and documentary requirements.

One approach for taxing multinational corporations or cross-border business transactions is through **unitary taxation**, by which corporate profits are apportioned to the different taxing authorities via a formula based on sales, payroll, and property within each jurisdiction. Transfer pricing issues become more confusing in the growing area of international Internet or electronic commerce. The U.S. policy on Internet commerce, as stated in a 1997 release titled "A Framework for Electronic Commerce,"[58] adopts the following principles regarding the issue of taxation of Internet commerce:

- No tax system should discriminate among types of commerce.
- The system should be transparent.
- The system should accommodate tax systems of other countries.

Currently, the two most influential bodies in the movement to harmonize accounting standards and financial statements are the International Accounting Standards Board (IASB) and the IOSCO. The diversity of accounting practices throughout the world is an encumbrance to the development of truly global capital markets. Companies currently wishing to raise capital in foreign markets have to contend with

---

56. The problem of recognition is especially acute in former nonmarket countries. For example, it was not until 1996 that Russian accountants first received national qualifications. In the substantive area, Russia has adopted international accounting practices, but some idiosyncrasies remain. Russian accounting regulations were intended for use in tax calculation and bookkeeping and were not designed for potential investors to use as a measure of financial performance. Other problems include the use of historical cost in asset valuation rather than economic value, the presentation of revenues on cash and accrual bases, and the widespread use of non-monetary transactions, including barter and setoffs. See Philip H. de Leon, "Russia's Accounting Transition" (1999), at **http://www.bisnis.doc.gov/bisnis/bulletin/9902icar.htm.**

57. Currency translation is the process of expressing amounts denominated in one currency in terms of another currency by use of an exchange rate. Translation adjustments result from the process of translating financial statements from the entity's functional currency (primary currency or currency in which its books are maintained) into the reporting currency. See Statement of Financial Accounting Standards, No. 52 (1981). The translation risk of currency devaluation needs to be addressed on both the management and accounting sides. Translation exposure may result in lower reported earnings. See, e.g., Carol Olson Houston, "Translation Exposure Hedging Post SFAS No. 52," 2 *Journal of International Management and Accounting* 145 (1990).

58. William J. Clinton and Albert Gore, *A Framework for Electronic Commerce* (1997).

costly and complicated national disclosure and reporting requirements. The ability to provide comparable financial statements to be used in cross-border security offerings would significantly decrease the number and types of required filings.

The EU Commission has sought to harmonize reporting requirements at the regional level. At the international level, IASB has developed a number of **international accounting standards (IAS)** and **international financial reporting standards (IFRS)**. IOSCO has deferred to IASB by accepting IAS and has focused its attention on developing a common international prospectus that could be used for listing and filing in all exchanges. These efforts will continue and are essential to further enhance the free flow of capital and related services.

KEY TERMS

advertising injury
agent
agent-distributor searches (ADS)
block exemption
cargo consolidator
commercial agency
consulting contract
Council on Services
Customs Modernization and
    Informed Compliance Act of 1993
dependent agent
duty to defend
effects test
employment as a property right
employment at will doctrine
EU Directive 86/653
EU Directive on Distance Contracts
EU Regulation 2790/1999
European Works Council Directive
evergreen statutes
Federal Trade Commission (FTC)
foreign consultant
foreign sales representative
framework agreement
freight forwarder
French Labor Code

General Agreement on Trade
    in Services (GATS)
goodwill indemnity
ILO Declaration on Fundamental
    Principles and Rights at Work
independent agent
independent contractor
international accounting standards
    (IAS)
international financial reporting
    standards (IFRS)
International Labor Organization
    (ILO)
International Organization of
    Securities Commissions (IOSCO)
key personnel
labor clause
Lanham Act
lifetime employment
materiality
mixed sales
most-favored-nation
multimodal transport
mutual recognition agreements
    (MRA)
national treatment

noncompetition clause
nonpartnership clause
Office of Service Industries,
    Tourism, and Finance (OSITF)
Organization for Economic
    Cooperation and Development
    (OECD)
price-fixing clause
principal
recognition requirements
redundancies
Russian Labor Code
Securities and Exchange
    Commission (SEC)
severance indemnity
sexual harassment policy
termination clause
Termination Protection Act
Trans-Atlantic Business Dialogue
    (TABD)
transfer pricing
transparency
tying clause
unitary taxation
work for hire clause
works council

CHAPTER PROBLEMS

1. This chapter discussed the Japanese tradition of lifetime employment. Research the effects of the prolonged economic recession of the 1990s in Japan, and see how it has affected this tradition. Is the notion of lifetime employment still an apt description of the Japanese employment relationship? If not, how is it different? How does it still differ from the employment-at-will system found in the United States?

2. Review the following consulting agreement. What are the purposes of the different clauses? Would these clauses be enforceable in the United States and in the European Union? How would you improve this agreement? How would you make this agreement more pro-principal or more pro-agent?

CONSULTING AGREEMENT

This Agreement dated April 11, 2005, is made by and between Joe "Hot Shot" Muldune of Menton, France ("Consultant"), and Gator Exporting of

Gainesville, Florida ("Company"). The above parties agree as follows:

1. Services. The company employs the Consultant to perform certain consulting services. The Consultant will consult with the officers and employees of the Company concerning matters relating to the selling, marketing, and advertising of Company's products in the country of France.

2. Term. The agreement shall begin on June 1, 2005, and terminate on May 30, 2008. Either party may cancel this agreement on thirty (30) days' notice to the other party in writing, by certified mail or personal delivery.

3. Time Devoted by Consultant. It is anticipated that the Consultant will spend approximately 35 hours per week in fulfilling his obligations under this agreement. The amount of time may vary from week to week. However, the Consultant will devote a minimum of 100 hours per month to his duties in accordance with this agreement.

4. Place of Services. The Consultant will perform services at a location of Consultant's discretion.

5. Compensation. The Consultant will be paid at the rate of $125 per hour of work performed. However, the Consultant will be paid a minimum of $15,000 per month regardless of the time actually spent. The Consultant will send an itemized statement, on a monthly basis, setting forth the services and time rendered. The Company shall remit payment within 15 days of the receipt of each itemized statement.

6. Independent Contractor. The Company and Consultant agree that the Consultant is being hired as an independent contractor. Accordingly, the Consultant shall be responsible for payment of all taxes arising out of the Consultant's activities, including but not limited to income tax, social security tax, and unemployment insurance taxes.

7. Confidential Information. The Consultant agrees that any information received from the Company which concerns the personal, financial, or other affairs of the Company will be treated in full confidence and will not be disclosed to any other persons or companies.

8. Subcontractors. The Company may from time to time request that the Consultant arrange for the services of third parties. The Company will pay all costs to the Consultant but in no event shall the Consultant employ others without the prior authorization of the Company.

IT IS HEREBY AGREED THIS 5th day of May, 2005

Joe Muldune   Gator Exporting

INTERNET EXERCISES

1. It is estimated that the European Union countries are responsible for 26 percent of the total global trade in services (43 percent if trade between EU members is included). The EU Commission has established a business-driven European services network. Review the EU Web site at **http://www.eurunion.org/partner/transcorpdocs.htm** for information on this network.

2. The most recognized authority on international labor standards is the International Labor Organization (ILO). Review the ILO Web site at **http://www.ilo.org** and become familiar with its standards and its current activities.

3. Review the following Web sites promoting good working conditions and encouraging consumers to boycott companies who allegedly do not respect workers' rights: Corpwatch at **http://www.corpwatch.org**; Maquila Solidarity Network at **http://www.maquilasolidarity.org**; Global Exchange at **http://www.globalexchange.org/economy/corporations/**; and Solidarmonde at **http://www.solidarmonde.fr**.

4. Research some of the following industry organization Web sites for information on exporting services in those specific sectors.

- *Management and Public Relations:* Public Relations Society of America at **http://www.prsa.org**; Society for Human Resources Management at **http://www.shrm.org**.
- *Insurance Services:* American Insurance Association at **http://www.aiadc.org**.
- *Information Technology:* International Federation for Information Processing at **http://www.ifip.or.at**; Society for Information Management at **http://www.simnet.org**.
- *Healthcare:* Healthcare Information and Management Systems Society at **http://www.himss.org/ASP/index.asp**.
- *Franchising:* International Franchise Association at **http://www.franchise.org**.
- *Export Services:* Assist International at **http://www.assist-intl.com**.
- *Environmental Technologies:* National Association of Environmental Professionals at **http://www.naep.org**.
- *Banking and Financial Services:* Financial Management Association International at **http://www.fma.org**; International Society of Financiers at **http://www.insofin.com**.

A company may find that building and protecting international recognition for its brand products are expensive and difficult undertakings. Protection for brand names varies from one country to another, and some developing countries may have barriers to the use of foreign brands or trademarks. In other countries, piracy of a company's brand names and counterfeiting of its products are widespread. To protect its products and brand names, a company must comply with local laws on patents, copyrights, trademarks, and trade secrets. The rights protected under these statutes are generically referred to as intellectual property rights.[1]

Intellectual property refers to a broad collection of rights relating to such matters as:

- Works of authorship protected under copyright law
- Product marks, symbols, and trade names protected under trademark law
- Inventions protected under patent law

Chapter 13

Law of Intellectual Property Rights

- Confidential information and methods of doing business protected as trade secrets or by unfair competition laws
- Specialized creations, such as semiconductor chips and mask works, protected by newer statutory rights[2]

No international treaty completely defines all types of intellectual property, so the intellectual property owner needs to refer to national laws to confirm its rights and the means of protecting those rights.

To best understand the problems of protecting intellectual property internationally, it is important to understand the basic intellectual property principles common to most legal systems. In this chapter, a brief review of the intellectual property law of the United States is the starting point. United States' intellectual property law is the most protective in the world. It provides four general types of intellectual property protection: (1) trademark, (2) copyright, (3) patent, and (4) trade secrets.

Federal statutory law provides the primary protection for the first three, and trade secrets are protected under state laws. **Trademark law** protects words, names, and other symbols used to identify a company's goods and distinguish them from those manufactured by others. Unlike patent and copyright protection, trademark protection can be derived from both federal and state law. For the maximum

http://
General information Web sites on intellectual property law: Emory IP Law at **http://www.law.emory.edu/erd/subject/intellectual.html** and Hieros Gamos International Property Law at **http://www.hg.org/intell.html.**

---

1. Other countries of the world often refer to such property under the term "industrial property rights."
2. Semiconductor mask works or integrated circuit layout design registrations protect the mask works embodied in semiconductor chip products. The Semiconductor Chip Protection Act of 1984 provides the owner of a mask work with the exclusive right to reproduce, import, and distribute such works for a period of ten years. See 17 U.S.C. § 904(b) (2000).

amount of protection, however, the trademark must be registered in the U.S. Patent and Trademark Office. As long as the trademark does not become generic, the trademark may be renewed perpetually.

Federal **copyright law** protects works of original authorship from unauthorized duplication, modification, or distribution. Mere creation of the work results in copyright protection. However, placing a copyright notice on the work and registering it with the Copyright Office provides more complete protection.

Patent law protects inventions that are "novel, useful, and non-obvious." Federal law lists statutory categories of patentable subject matter, including machines, manufactured articles, processes, and compositions of materials.

A **trade secret** is any device or information that is used in a business and gives its owner an advantage over its competitors. Trade secrets law provides for perpetual protection, unless the protected information becomes publicly known. The next section reviews the major tenets of these areas of U.S. law. This section has three purposes. The first is to create awareness of the major issues and concepts found in intellectual property protection. The second is to create a basis of understanding of U.S. intellectual property law for purposes of comparison with similar international and foreign laws. Finally, the shortcoming of intellectual property laws, especially in the international arena, underscores the importance of transfer and licensing agreements presented in Chapter Fourteen.

Intellectual Property Rights in the United States

The United States provides a wide range of protection for intellectual property, including patents, trademarks, service marks, copyrights, trade secrets, and semiconductor mask works. Many businesses, particularly high-technology firms, publishers, chemical and pharmaceutical firms, recording companies, and computer software companies, depend heavily on the protection afforded their creative products and processes. This section reviews the four major areas of protection—trademark, copyright, patent, and trade secrets—found in U.S. law.

Trademark Protection

A trademark is any word, name, symbol, or device or any combination that identifies goods and distinguishes them from those manufactured or sold by others. Trademarks are derived from their commercial use to identify goods and are protected by registration and filing at state and federal levels, as well as through international treaties and conventions. The federal law that deals with trademark issues is the **Lanham Act** or **Trademark Act**.[3]

---

3. The Lanham Act prohibits three forms of unfair competition related to trademark infringement: (1) false advertising, (2) passing off, and (3) false designation of place of origin. The Lanham Act defines "false advertising" as the use of a "false or misleading description of fact, or false or misleading representation of fact in commercial advertising or promotion which misrepresents the nature, characteristics, qualities, or geographic origin of his or her or another person's goods, services, or commercial activities." 15 U.S.C. § 1125(a)(1)(B) (2000). The statement must be literally false or likely to confuse or deceive a purchaser.

    It is not required that a mark be registered to be able to bring a "passing off" or "false designation of origin" claim. To prove "passing off," the plaintiff must prove two things: first, an association of origin by the consumer between the mark and the first user of the product and second, a likelihood of consumer confusion between the trademarked good or service and the infringer's good or service.

A trademark or service mark registered with the U.S. Patent and Trademark Office remains in force for ten years from the date of registration and may be renewed for successive periods of ten years, provided the mark continues to be used and has not been previously canceled or surrendered. A **service mark** is a name, phrase, or other device used to identify and distinguish the services of the provider.

To prove trademark infringement under U.S. law, a party must prove that another's use of the registered mark is likely to cause consumer confusion regarding the source of the product or service. Factors that determine the likelihood of confusion include:

- degree of similarity between the marks
- the intent of the alleged infringer
- the similarity of use of the two products or services
- similarity in the marketing of the goods or services
- the degree of care likely to be exercised by the consumer or purchaser
- evidence of actual confusion
- the strength of the registered mark[4]

The *Best Cellars, Inc. v. Grape Finds at Dupont, Inc.* case explores these factors in making the determination of likelihood of confusion. The case involves the application of trademark protection to **trade dress**. Trade dress refers to the general way a product, service, or business is packaged or presented to the public. The case also serves to highlight the distinction between legally protected trademarks and unprotected **generic marks**.

http://

The Publishing Law Center— "The Nuts and Bolts of Federal Trademark Registration": **http://www.publaw.com/bolts.html.** The Publishing Law Center maintains a database of legal articles giving brief explanations of important intellectual property terms. These articles will be cited often throughout the chapter.

Best Cellars, Inc. v. Grape Finds at Dupont, Inc.
90 F. Supp. 2d 431 (S.D.N.Y. 2000)

Sweet, District Judge. Plaintiff Best Cellars, Inc. ("Best Cellars") has moved for a preliminary injunction to enjoin defendants Grape Finds at Dupont from infringing on various intellectual property rights claimed by Best Cellars under the Lanham Act. This action presents difficult issues, particularly with respect to the law of trade dress protection, itself a complex and shifting field of judicial interpretation. The action involves a unique concept, the retail sale of wine by taste, captured and exemplified in the particular trade dress of the Best Cellars stores. It presents the tension between the protection of certain intellectual property and free and open competition.

Best Cellars operates retail wine stores in New York, Brookline, and Seattle. Joshua Wesson, an internationally recognized wine expert, founded the store. In the early 1990s, he began to think about developing a new kind of retail wine store where people who knew little or nothing about wine could feel as comfortable when shopping as wine connoisseurs, and in which the "wine by style" concept could be implemented. The name "Best Cellars"

came to him in 1993. Wesson spent considerable time before and during the design phase of the first Best Cellars store refining the "wine by style" concept.

Wesson eventually reduced the "world of wine" to eight taste categories: sparkling wines, light-, medium-, and full-bodied white wines, light-, medium-, and full-bodied red wines, and dessert wines. A principal reason Wesson reduced the world of wine to eight taste categories was in order to demystify wine for casual, non-connoisseur purchasers who might be intimidated purchasing wine in a traditional wine store, where wines are customarily organized by grape type and place of origin.

The design for the first Best Cellars retail store—on the Upper East Side in Manhattan—evolved to contain the following elements: (1) For each of the eight taste categories in the Best Cellars system, a corresponding color and a graphic image (an "icon-identifier") both to evoke and to reinforce the sensory associations of each category. (2) A display bottle for each wine stands upright on a stainless-steel wire pedestal so that the label is viewable by

---

4. See, e.g., *First Savings Bank v. First Bank System, Inc.*, 101 F.3d 645 (10th Cir. 1996).

the customer. (3) Under each display bottle, at eye-level, is a "shelf-talker": a $4'' \times 4''$ information card providing the name of the wine, its vintage, a five- or six-line description of its taste, the type of grape from which it is made, its place of origin, the foods which the wine would complement, and its price. (4) The racking system, which is patented by Wesson, is lit from behind, which causes the bottles to glow.

The Grape Finds story begins with Mazur, who while at Columbia Business School discovered the Best Cellars New York store, which he has visited at least ten times. The Grape Finds store opened in Washington, D.C., on December 3, 1999. The store possessed many similarities to the Best Cellars store. The display is organized according to eight taste categories. As with Best Cellars, Grape Finds assigned to each taste category a corresponding color and icon-identifier. Moreover, lights above the racks are directed down causing them to glow. As in Best Cellars, beneath the racks are storage cabinets, creating the same visual look.

Section 43(a) of the Lanham Act provides in pertinent part that:

Any person who in connection with any goods or services, uses any word, term, name, symbol, or device, or any combination thereof, which is likely to cause confusion, or to deceive as to the affiliation or connection, of such person with another person, shall be liable in a civil action.

Trade dress has a broad meaning, and includes "all elements making up the total visual image by which a product is presented to customers as defined by its overall composition and design, including size, shape, color, texture, and graphics." For example, the Supreme Court in the *Two Pesos* case upheld a federal district court's finding that a Mexican restaurant was entitled to protection under § 43(a) for a trade dress consisting of a festive eating atmosphere having interior dining and patio areas decorated with artifacts, bright colors, paintings, and murals.

The public policy rationale for trade dress protection is explained by the Supreme Court as follows: "Protection of trade dress, no less than of trademarks, serves the [Lanham] Act's purpose to secure to the owner of the mark the goodwill of his business and to protect the ability of consumers to distinguish among competing producers." To establish a claim of trade dress infringement under § 43(a), a plaintiff must demonstrate (1) "that its trade dress is either inherently distinctive or that it has acquired distinctiveness through a secondary meaning," and (2) "that there is a likelihood of confusion between defendant's trade dress and plaintiff's."

Best Cellars' Trade Dress Is Inherently Distinctive

Trade dress is classified on a spectrum of increasing distinctiveness as generic, descriptive, suggestive, or arbitrary/fanciful. Suggestive and arbitrary or fanciful trade dress is deemed inherently distinctive. A descriptive trade dress may be found inherently distinctive if the plaintiff establishes that its mark has acquired secondary meaning giving it distinctiveness to the consumer. Under this standard, many trade dresses are likely to be found to be inherently distinctive. The Best Cellars stores look like no other wine stores. The essence of the look is the "wall of wine," with color-coded, iconographic wall signs identifying eight taste categories.

Substantial Likelihood of Confusion

Courts generally apply an eight-factor test to determine the likelihood of confusion between the trade dress of two competitors: (1) the strength of the plaintiff's trade dress, (2) the similarity between the two trade dress, (3) the proximity of the products in the marketplace, (4) the likelihood that the prior owner will bridge the gap between the products, (5) evidence of actual confusion, (6) the defendant's bad faith, (7) the quality of defendant's product, and (8) the sophistication of the relevant consumer group. While the factors are meant to be a guide, the inquiry ultimately hinges on whether an ordinarily prudent person would be confused as to the source of the allegedly infringing product.

First, the strength of a trade dress or trademark is measured in terms of its distinctiveness, "or more precisely, by its tendency to identify the goods sold as emanating from a particular source." For instance, generic marks are not entitled to protection under the Lanham Act. "Marks that are descriptive are entitled to protection only if they have acquired a 'secondary meaning' in the marketplace." Under this standard, Best Cellars' trade dress is quite strong.

Second, as described above, the dominant visual element of both the Best Cellars and the Grape Finds stores is the wall of wine. The evidence demonstrates a significant probability that ordinarily prudent customers in the Grape Finds store will be confused as to whether they are, in fact, in a Best Cellars store.

Third, "the 'proximity-of-the-products' inquiry concerns whether and to what extent the two products compete with each other." The products here are indisputably similar: value-priced bottles of wine. The class of customers is nearly identical.

Fourth, this factor applies when the first user sells its products in one field and the second user sells its products in a closely related field, into which the first user might expand, thereby "bridging the gap." Here, there is no gap to bridge: Best Cellars and Grape Finds sell the same products in the same field.

Fifth, Best Cellars has presented some evidence of actual confusion, but no survey or systematic research was conducted. However, it is black letter law that actual confusion need not be shown to prevail under the Lanham Act, since actual confusion is very difficult to prove and the Act requires only a likelihood of confusion as to source.

Sixth, this factor looks to whether the defendant adopted its dress with the intention of capitalizing on plaintiff's reputation and goodwill. Given the overwhelming evidence of copying of so many aspects of the Best Cellars business, it strains credulity to think that the reproduction of the trade dress—in particular, the "wall of wine"—in the Grape Finds store was not meant to capitalize on the reputation, goodwill, and any confusion between Grape Finds and Best Cellars.

Seventh, no evidence has been presented that Grape Finds' products are inferior to those of Best Cellars. This factor therefore favors Grape Finds.

Eighth, this factor also favors Best Cellars. Both stores are specifically targeting non-sophisticated wine purchasers, and the overwhelming majority of wines sold in each store are priced at the lower end of the spectrum.

As set forth above, in this case seven of the eight factors weigh in favor of Best Cellars. This is not a case requiring a careful balancing of the factors. Some factors weigh more strongly than others, but there is no doubt that, taken together, Best Cellars has made a substantial showing of a likelihood of confusion between its trade dress and that of Grape Finds. Because Best Cellars has demonstrated a substantial likelihood that (1) its trade dress is distinctive, and (2) that there is a likelihood of confusion between its trade dress and the trade dress of Grape Finds, it has demonstrated that it is likely to prevail on the merits of its trade dress claim. Therefore, it has met the requirements for a preliminary injunction. SO ORDERED.

Case Highlights

- Trademark law seeks to balance the protection of intellectual property and the need not to deter free and open competition.
- Protection of trade dress is needed to secure the owner's goodwill in the business and to protect the ability of consumers to distinguish among competing producers.
- To establish a claim of trade dress infringement, a plaintiff must demonstrate (1) "that its trade dress is either inherently distinctive or that it has acquired distinctiveness through a secondary meaning" and (2) "that there is a likelihood of confusion between defendant's trade dress and plaintiff's."
- Generic marks are not entitled to protection under the Lanham Act.

Trademark Dilution

On January 16, 1996, the Lanham Act was amended to include **trademark dilution**. The **Federal Trademark Dilution Act (FTDA)**[5] defines *dilution* as "the lessening of the capacity of a famous mark to identify and distinguish goods or services, regardless of the presence or absence of competition between the owner of the famous mark and other parties, or likelihood of confusion, mistake or deception." Trademark dilution as defined in the FTDA is founded on the premise that the diminution of value of a trademark resulting from its unauthorized use constitutes an invasion of the property rights and good will of the senior user.[6] The **senior mark** or user is the trademark owner bringing the claim of infringement or dilution.

Although the senior user need not show actual loss of sales or profits, the mere fact that customers may associate the junior mark with its senior and famous counterpart is insufficient to establish dilution.[7] The **junior mark** or user referred to here is the party accused of trademark infringement or dilution. A trademark dilution claim entitles the trademark owner to an injunction against another person's commercial use of its mark or trade name.

---

5.   15 U.S.C. § 1127 (2000).
6.   See *World Wrestling Federation Entertainment, Inc. v. Big Dog Holdings, Inc.*, 280 F. Supp.2d 413, 441 (W.D. Pa. 2003).
7.   See *Kellogg Co. v. Toucan Golf, Inc.*, 337 F.3d 616, 628 (6th Cir. 2003).

The two recognized types of dilution are tarnishment and blurring. **Tarnishment** arises when the trademark is linked to products of shoddy quality or is portrayed in an unsavory context likely to evoke unflattering connotations about the product or service or in a manner at odds with the image projected by the trademark.[8] **Blurring** is a diminishing of the selling power and value of the trademark by unauthorized use.[9] An action for blurring pursuant to the FTDA requires use of a mark sufficiently similar to a famous mark to evoke a mental association of the two marks in the minds of consumers, thereby causing economic harm to the famous mark's economic value by lessening its selling power as an advertising agent for goods and services.[10] Relevant factors in determining the existence of blurring include actual consumer confusion and the continued likelihood of such confusion, the duration of the junior use, harm resulting to the junior user as a result of enjoining the use of its mark, and the delay, if any, by the senior user in initiating litigation.[11]

The court in *Nike, Inc. v. Variety Wholesalers, Inc.*,[12] recently stated the requirements for a trademark dilution claim under the FDTA. The trademark owner must establish the following elements:

- The senior mark must be famous;[13]
- The junior user must be a commercial user;
- The commercial use is occurring in interstate commerce;
- Use by the junior user must begin after the senior mark has become famous; and
- Use by the junior user must cause dilution of the distinctive quality of the senior mark.

The U.S. Supreme Court's recent interpretation of the FTDA in *Moseley v. V Secret Catalogue, Inc.* is set forth next. Holders of senior and junior marks also should be aware that individual states have their own antidilution statutes, the elements of which may vary from those set forth in the FTDA.[14] In addition, although they may

---

8. See *Caterpillar, Inc. v. Walt Disney Co.*, 287 F. Supp.2d 913, 921–22 (C.D. Ill. 2003) (use of plaintiff's bulldozers in scene depicting environmental degradation in movie); see also *Tommy Hilfiger Licensing, Inc. v. Nature Labs, LLC*, 221 F. Supp.2d 410, 422–23 (S.D.N.Y. 2002) (use of designations "Tommy Holedigger" and "Timmy Holedigger" for line of pet perfumes).

9. See *Caterpillar, Inc.*, 287 F. Supp.2d at 921; see also *Tommy Hilfiger Licensing, Inc.*, 221 F. Supp.2d at 421–22.

10. See *Planet Hollywood (Region IV), Inc. v. Hollywood Casino Corp.*, 80 F. Supp.2d 815, 895 (N.D. Ill. 1999).

11. See *Times Mirror Magazines, Inc. v. Las Vegas Sports News*, LLC, 212 F.3d 157, 168 (3d Cir. 2000).

12. 274 F. Supp.2d 1352, 1372 (S.D. Ga. 2003).

13. The FDTA sets forth eight nonexclusive factors to consider in determining whether a mark or dress is famous: (1) the degree of inherent or acquired distinctiveness of the mark; (2) the duration and extent of use of the mark in connection with the goods; (3) the duration and extent of advertising and publicity of the mark; (4) the geographical extent of the trading area in which the mark is used; (5) the channels of trade for the goods or services with which the mark is used; (6) the degree of recognition of the mark in trading areas and channels of trade used by the mark's owner and the person against whom the injunction is sought; (7) the nature and extent of the use of same or similar marks by third parties; and (8) whether the mark is registered. See *Planet Hollywood (Region IV), Inc.*, 80 F. Supp.2d at 895; see also *HBP, Inc. v. American Marine Holdings, Inc.*, 290 F. Supp.2d 1320, 1338 (M.D. Fla. 2003) (holding that the mark "Daytona" used in reference to stock car and motorcycle races is not famous against the manufacturer of "Daytona" racing boats because of the extensive use of the term by third parties and its geographic derivation).

14. See, e.g., *Four Seasons Hotels and Resorts, B.V. v. Consorcio Barr, S.A.*, 267 F. Supp.2d 1268, 1333 (S.D. Fla. 2003) (holding that Florida's antidilution statute is not limited to "famous marks" and requires only a likelihood of injury to business reputation or of the dilution of the distinctive quality of the mark).

Moseley v. V Secret Catalogue, Inc.
537 U.S. 418 (2003)

Stevens, Justice. In 1995 Congress amended § 43 of the Trademark Act of 1946 to provide a remedy for the "dilution of famous marks." That amendment, known as the Federal Trademark Dilution Act (FTDA), describes the factors that determine whether a mark is "distinctive and famous," and defines the term "dilution" as "the lessening of the capacity of a famous mark to identify and distinguish goods or services." The question we granted certiorari to decide is whether objective proof of actual injury to the economic value of a famous mark is a requisite for relief under the FTDA.

Petitioners, Victor and Cathy Moseley, own and operate a retail store named "Victor's Little Secret" in a strip mall in Elizabethtown, Kentucky. Respondents are affiliated corporations that own the VICTORIA'S SECRET trademark, and operate over 750 Victoria's Secret stores, two of which are in Louisville, Kentucky, a short drive from Elizabethtown. In 1998 they spent over $55 million advertising "the VICTORIA'S SECRET brand—one of moderately priced, high quality, attractively designed lingerie sold in a store setting designed to look like a woman's bedroom." They distribute 400 million copies of the Victoria's Secret catalog each year, including 39,000 in Elizabethtown. In 1998 their sales exceeded $1.5 billion.

In the February 12, 1998, edition of a weekly publication distributed to residents of the military installation at Fort Knox, Kentucky, petitioners advertised the "GRAND OPENING Just in time for Valentine's Day!" of their store "VICTOR'S SECRET" in nearby Elizabethtown. The ad featured "Intimate Lingerie *for every woman*"; "Romantic Lighting"; "Lycra Dresses"; "Pagers"; and "Adult Novelties/Gifts." An army colonel, who saw the ad and was offended by what he perceived to be an attempt to use a reputable company's trademark to promote the sale of "unwholesome, tawdry merchandise," sent a copy to respondents. Their counsel then wrote to petitioners stating that their choice of the name "Victor's Secret" for a store selling lingerie was likely to cause confusion with the well-known VICTORIA'S SECRET mark and, in addition, was likely to "dilute the distinctiveness" of the mark. They requested the immediate discontinuance of the use of the name "and any variations thereof." In response, petitioners changed the name of their store to "Victor's Little Secret." Because that change did not satisfy respondents, they promptly filed this action in Federal District Court.

Finding that the record contained no evidence of actual confusion between the parties' marks, the District Court concluded that "no likelihood of confusion exists as a matter of law" and entered summary judgment for petitioners on the infringement and unfair competition claims. With respect to the FTDA claim, however, the court ruled for respondents. The court first found the two marks to be sufficiently similar to cause dilution, and then found "that Defendants' mark dilutes Plaintiffs' mark because of its tarnishing effect upon the Victoria's Secret mark." It therefore enjoined petitioners from using the mark "Victor's Little Secret." The Court of Appeals for the Sixth Circuit affirmed.

The VICTORIA'S SECRET mark is unquestionably valuable and petitioners have not challenged the conclusion that it qualifies as a "famous mark" within the meaning of the statute. The relevant text of the FTDA provides that "the owner of a famous mark" is entitled to injunctive relief against another person's commercial use of a mark or trade name if that use "*causes dilution* of the distinctive quality*" of the famous mark. This text unambiguously requires a showing of actual dilution, rather than a likelihood of dilution. This conclusion is fortified by the definition of the term "dilution" itself. The term "dilution" means the lessening of the capacity of a famous mark to identify and distinguish goods or services, regardless of the presence or absence of competition between the owner of the famous mark and other parties, or likelihood of confusion, mistake, or deception.

The contrast between the initial reference to an actual "lessening of the capacity" of the mark, and the later reference to a "likelihood of confusion, mistake, or deception" in the second caveat confirms the conclusion that actual dilution must be established.

Of course, that does not mean that the consequences of dilution, such as an actual loss of sales or profits, must also be proved. At least where the marks at issue are not identical, the mere fact that consumers mentally associate the junior user's mark with a famous mark is not sufficient to establish actionable dilution. Such mental association will not necessarily reduce the capacity of the famous mark to identify the goods of its owner, the statutory requirement for dilution under the FTDA. "Blurring" is not a necessary consequence of mental association. (Nor, for that matter, is "tarnishing.")

The record in this case establishes that an army officer who saw the advertisement of the opening of a store named "Victor's Secret" did make the mental association with "Victoria's Secret," but it also shows that he did not therefore form any different impression of the store that his wife and daughter had patronized. There is a complete absence of evidence of any lessening of the capacity of the VICTORIA'S SECRET mark to identify and distinguish

goods or services sold in Victoria's Secret stores or advertised in its catalogs. The officer was offended by the ad, but
it did not change his conception of Victoria's Secret. His
offense was directed entirely at petitioners, not at respondents. Moreover, the expert retained by respondents had
nothing to say about the impact of petitioners' name on
the strength of respondents' mark.

The evidence in the present record is not sufficient
to support the summary judgment on the dilution count.
The judgment is therefore reversed, and the case is
remanded for further proceedings consistent with this
opinion.

Case Highlights

- The FTDA requires proof of actual dilution of
  a famous mark rather than the mere likelihood
  of dilution.
- Although the senior user of a famous mark need
  not demonstrate actual loss of sales or profits
  to recover for dilution, mental association of the
  marks by consumers is not sufficient where the
  marks are not identical.

result in dilution, some uses may be protected under free speech considerations pursuant to the First Amendment to the U.S. Constitution.[15]

Copyright Protection

http://

The Publishing Law
Center: "Frequently
Asked Questions About
Copyright Law" at
**http://www.publaw.
com/cfaqs.html** and
"The Advantages of
Copyright Registration"
at **http://www.publaw.
com/advantage.html.**

Copyright is a form of protection provided to authors of "original works of
authorship" fixed in a **tangible form** of expression. Works must be fixed in tangible form to receive federal copyright protection; improvisational speeches or
performances that have not been recorded or written are not protected. The
eight generic categories of copyrightable works include literary, dramatic, musical, choreographic, pictorial (including graphic and sculptural works), motion
pictures, sound recordings, and architectural works. These categories are interpreted broadly. For example, computer programs may be registered as "literary
works." Copyright protection is available to both published and unpublished
works. Copyright protection affixes to the work at the time of its creation.
A copyright, as a general rule, has a term that endures for the author's life plus
an additional seventy years after the author's death. In the case of works made
for hire (owned by a business), the duration of the copyright lasts between
95 years from the date of first publication or 120 years from the date of creation,
whichever expires first.[16]

http://

U.S. Copyright Office:
**http://www.copyright.
gov/.** For copyright
application forms see
**http://www.copyright.
gov/forms/.**

Section 106 of the **Copyright Act of 1976** gives the copyright owner the exclusive *right to reproduce* the work in copies; prepare derivative works; to distribute
copies by sale, rental, lease, or lending; and to perform or display the work publicly.
It is illegal for anyone to violate any of these rights. However, the rights are not
unlimited. Sections 107 through 121 of the Copyright Act provide exemptions from
copyright liability. There are three general exceptions to the exclusive rights of

---

15. See, e.g., *Mattel, Inc. v. MCA Records, Inc.*, 296 F.3d 894, 903 (9th Cir. 2002), *cert. denied*, 537 U.S. 1171 (2003) (holding that although the song "Barbie Girl" by the Danish band Aqua diluted the Barbie trademark, the song was not
purely commercial speech and was thus fully protected pursuant to the free speech protections afforded by the
First Amendment); But see *Gideons International, Inc. v. Gideon 300 Ministries, Inc.*, 94 F. Supp.2d 566, 588 (E.D. Pa.
1999) (holding that a nonprofit organization's use of its mark on Bibles was commercial as the organization had
raised money and distributed goods and services to the general public).

16. See 17 U.S.C. § 302(a) & (c) (2000). The constitutionality of these terms was upheld by the U.S. Supreme Court,
which concluded that they did not create perpetual copyrights in violation of the constitutional provision granting copyrights for "limited times." See *Eldred v. Ashcroft*, 537 U.S. 186 (2003).

copyright ownership: (1) first sale doctrine, (2) fair use doctrine, and (3) materials that are part of the public domain.

The **first sale doctrine** terminates the copyright owner's protections over a copy of the copyrighted work once the work is legally sold. The purchaser gains the right to resell the copy.[17] The Copyright Act states that the owner of a copy is entitled to resell the copy without the consent of the copyright owner. The *McDonald's Corporation v. Shop at Home, Inc.* case that follows explores the first sale doctrine in greater detail, including whether sales made in contravention of franchise agreements qualify as "first sales," thereby terminating copyright protection. Although the intellectual property at issue in this case was trademarked,

---

McDonald's Corporation v. Shop at Home, Inc.

82 F. Supp.2d 801 (M.D. Tenn. 2000)

Trauger, District Court Judge. Sports Collectibles, Inc., Classic Collectibles, LLC., and Gary Fillers purchased a large number of Teenie Beanie Baby toys offered in McDonald's 1999 marketing campaign prior to the toys' release date. The Shop At Home television network then offered those toys for sale, giving consumers an opportunity to get the toy while bypassing the "drive through," or avoiding buying a McDonald's Happy Meal. McDonald's has sought and obtained a preliminary injunction from this court and now seeks damages. All defendants have moved for summary judgment. The defendants assert that they are entitled to judgment as a matter of law because the undisputed facts show that they merely re-sold genuine, unaltered McDonald's toys, which does not violate any federal or state trademark or unfair competition laws and is protected by the "first sale doctrine." McDonald's asserts that summary judgment should be denied because the first sale doctrine is inapplicable in this case.

In May 1999, McDonald's ran a marketing campaign that offered a "Teenie Beanie Baby" toy with the purchase of a Happy Meal. The toys were miniature versions of the wildly popular Ty Beanie Baby, and had been a very successful marketing tool for McDonald's in 1997 and 1998. The 1999 toy promotion was to release twelve new toys, four each week throughout May, with the final four figures to be released on May 28. It had entered a license agreement with Ty to supply the toys through what McDonald's refers to as its "supply chain." Simon Marketing ("Simon"), The Marketing Store Worldwide ("TMSW"), Perseco Systems Services L.P. ("Perseco") and Hub 1 Logistics are the various companies within the supply chain. All of these companies in the supply chain act on behalf of McDonald's, but are independent entities, separate from McDonald's corporate empire.

Simon and TMSW contracted with Ty-approved factories located in China to manufacture the 1999 Teenie Beanie Babies on behalf of McDonald's Corp and its licensees. The toys were individually sealed in plastic bags that carried the statement, "Licensed for distribution only by McDonald's restaurants with food purchase. NOT FOR RESALE." The toys were packed in boxes and sealed with a licensing agreement called the shrink wrap agreement attached to the outside. Simon and TMSW paid the Chinese manufacturers for the toys and the two companies took title to the toys. Perseco took possession of the toys when they cleared customs. Perseco shipped the toys to one of four hub warehouses owned by Hub 1 Logistics. Perseco paid Hub 1 Logistics a fee for storing the toys until Perseco shipped the toys to one of 41 distribution centers around the country. The distribution centers paid Perseco for the toys and title passed to the distribution centers. The distribution centers sent the toys to the individual restaurants. Throughout this chain, although McDonald's gave permission for the use of its trademarks, it held neither possession nor title to the toys.

The shrink wrap agreement affixed to the boxes of toys stated that when the franchisees accepted the toy shipments, they were indicating that they agreed to the terms of the shrink wrap agreement. According to the shrink wrap agreement the toys were to be distributed only with food purchases and none of the toys were to be

17.   See 17 U.S.C. § 109(a) (2000).

released before their scheduled release date unless the restaurant ran out of the earlier-released figures. The agreement prohibited selling more than ten toys with any single food purchase and prohibited selling an entire set of all twelve figures in a single transaction. "Title to the intellectual property associated with the Toys is not transferred to you through this License and remains the property of either Ty or McDonald's as applicable," it states. It also states:

This License Agreement becomes effective upon your acceptance of the Toys. You may choose not to enter into this License Agreement by returning for credit all Toys delivered to you. This License Agreement will automatically terminate if you, your employees or agents fail to comply with the Condition of Participation. Upon termination for failure to comply, your supply of Toys for the Promotion will be suspended and if there is a Teenie Beanie Baby promotion in the year 2000, your supply of Toys for that promotion will be limited to one case. Additionally, Ty has agreed to buy back a portion of any undistributed Toys.

McDonald's acts as franchisor and owner of all intellectual property associated with the restaurants, which are operated as independent businesses by the franchisees. The franchisees are allowed to use the McDonald's trademarks under the terms of their franchise agreements, under which they agree to pay McDonald's Corp. a percentage of their gross sales every month. By selling the toys "out the back door" instead of to customers with food purchases, franchisees are depriving McDonald's of the profit from the trademarked toy.

Defendant Gary Fillers apparently began purchasing the toys before they were available to the general public and offered them to the Shop At Home network for sale. Mr. Fillers used relatives to buy as many toys as they could obtain from the restaurants. In so doing, the relatives made purchases that violated not only the shrink wrap agreement, but also the Franchise Agreement between the franchisees and McDonald's. There were purchases of entire sets, of more than ten toys with a single food purchase and some that were made with no food at all. Mr. Fillers provided about 100 sets of the toys to Shop At Home, which distributed them before the authorized release date. The toys were selling for $299.95 for "all Teenie Beanies ever made," or $89.95 for the 1999 set of twelve toys. The "first sale" doctrine, sometimes called the "exhaustion doctrine," is similar to the principle of the same name in copyright law. When considering the doctrine under trademark, a markholder may no longer control branded goods after releasing them into the stream of commerce. After the first sale, the brandholder's control is deemed exhausted. Down-the-line retailers are free to display and advertise the branded goods. Secondhand dealers may advertise the branded merchandise for resale in competition with the sales of

the markholder (so long as they do not misrepresent themselves as authorized agents). It does not matter that the owner of the trademark objects to the use of its mark, as long as one approved sale has already occurred.

McDonald's asserts that because it did not approve of the toys' initial sale until they were sold to those who made food purchases, the sales by the franchisees to the defendants and other third parties were illegitimate, and therefore there could be no "first sale." But here, the toys were "released into the stream of commerce" by the sales up the supply chain numerous times with McDonald's approval. That McDonald's did not approve of the alleged sale between the franchisees and the defendants makes little difference if McDonald's approved of the prior sales of the toys up to and including the sale to the franchisees. In this case, the defendants did nothing to alter the toys, even if agreements with McDonald's were breached. Like the cases cited above, there were no material differences between the product as manufactured and as sold to the consumer. Consumers who bought the toys from Shop At Home would not be deprived of any future rights nor would they be disappointed by receiving a lower quality toy than one purchased with a Happy Meal. They received precisely what they expected to receive and, as such, their goodwill remained intact.

The plaintiff next argues that there was no sale under the first sale doctrine in this case because McDonald's never received its "just reward" for its trademarked goods because it only receives payment through increased food sales brought about by the Teenie Beanie Baby toy promotion. No court has defined the first sale of a trademarked good as taking place only when the trademark owner receives its just reward, and no court has defined trademark rights in the strained manner that is required to reach the conclusion urged by the plaintiff.

Even if it did apply in some trademark cases, it would not apply when the trademark owner consented to the first sale. A first sale takes place when the product has been put on the open market—even if it has not reached the hands of the ultimate consumer. In this case, McDonald's products were on the open market—albeit on their way to the ultimate consumer—long before they reached the hands of Shop At Home or the other defendants. The sale to the franchisees was a first sale to which McDonald's consented. The earlier sales that took place along the supply chain might also qualify as first, second and other sales. Accordingly, McDonald's has no right to seek a just reward after giving consent to these sales.

And McDonald's has other remedies—contained in their agreements—against these entities if, by breaching their agreements with McDonald's, McDonald's is denied its profit. As soon as the franchisees accept shipments from the distribution centers—whether the shipments contain Teenie Beanie Baby toys, hamburger, hot apple pies or ketchup packets—the franchisees have purchased those shipments. The franchisee has an obligation under trademark law not to sell anything other than official McDonald's products under the guise of McDonald's golden arches. However, the franchisee's obligation to make sure the corporation receives its "just reward" is a separate matter protected not by trademark law, but by the franchise and shrink wrap agreements. The Motion for Summary Judgment filed by Shop At Home will be granted.

Case Highlights

- The first sale doctrine provides that the ability of the intellectual property right's holder to control branded goods is exhausted after releasing them into the stream of commerce.
- The first sale doctrine may be invoked when one of many sales is authorized by the intellectual property rights holder.
- The breach of a franchise agreement as a result of the franchisee's misuse of the franchisor's intellectual property rights does not necessarily constitute an actionable breach of intellectual property laws.

rather than copyrighted, novelty goods, the case provides a thorough discussion of the difficulties and risks encountered by a franchisor when violations of its intellectual property rights occur in the supply chain.

Section 107 of the Copyright Act allows for certain "fair uses" of copyrighted material without the consent of the copyrighted owner. The **fair use doctrine** allows others to use small portions of a copyrighted work in the creation of another work. The borrower can legally make unauthorized use of copyright materials in limited contexts. The most common contexts are in connection with a criticism of the work, in the course of news reporting, for teaching purposes, and as part of scholarship or research activities. The determination of whether the use was "fair" is done on a case-by-case basis. The factors analyzed include the purpose or character of the use, such as whether it was of a commercial nature or for nonprofit or educational purposes. The courts also look at the amount of the use in relation to the copyrighted work as a whole and the effect of the use on the value or market of the copyrighted work. These factors are highlighted in the opinion in *Mattel, Inc. v. Walking Mountain Productions* that follows.

Finally, material in the **public domain** is not protected. These materials include government publications and materials whose copyrights have expired. An analogous concept in trademark law is the brand name–generic distinction. A brand name can be protected as a trademark. However, if the name is used widely as a generic name, then it is said to have entered the public domain and is no longer entitled to trademark protection.

Authorship of a copyrighted work determines who holds the copyright. A work created by an individual automatically vests copyright ownership in that individual upon its creation. **Work for hire** is the major exception to this right. Section 101 of the Copyright Act of 1976 contains a two-prong test to determine if a work is for hire. First, a work prepared by employees within the scope of their employment is a work for hire. The Supreme Court in *Community for Creative Non-Violence (CCNV) v. Reid*[18] listed thirteen factors to be used to determine when a third party who is not a regular employee can be considered an

http://

The Publishing Law Center: "The Fair Use Doctrine" at **http://www.publaw.com/work.html** and **http://www.publaw.com/fairuse.html**.

http://

The Publishing Law Center: "Public Domain and the Impact of New Legislation" at **http://www.publaw.com/publicdomain.html**.

http://

The Publishing Law Center: "Copyright Ownership and the Work for Hire Doctrine" at **http://www.publaw.com/work1.html** and **http://www.publaw.com/work2.html**.

18. 490 U.S. 730 (1989).

Mattel, Inc. v. Walking Mountain Productions

353 F.3d 792 (9th Cir. 2003)

Pregerson, Circuit Court Judge. Thomas Forsythe, aka "Walking Mountain Productions," is a self-taught photographer who resides in Kanab, Utah. In 1997, Forsythe developed a series of 78 photographs entitled "Food Chain Barbie," in which he depicted Barbie in various absurd and often sexualized positions. Forsythe uses the word "Barbie" in some of the titles of his works. While his works vary, Forsythe generally depicts one or more nude Barbie dolls juxtaposed with vintage kitchen appliances. For example, "Malted Barbie" features a nude Barbie placed on a vintage Hamilton Beach malt machine. "Fondue a la Barbie" depicts Barbie heads in a fondue pot. "Barbie Enchiladas" depicts four Barbie dolls wrapped in tortillas and covered with salsa in a casserole dish in a lit oven.

Forsythe describes the message behind his photographic series as an attempt to "critique the objectification of women associated with Barbie, and to lambaste the conventional beauty myth and the societal acceptance of women as objects because this is what Barbie embodies." He explains that he chose to parody Barbie in his photographs because he believes that "Barbie is the most enduring of those products that feed on the insecurities of our beauty and perfection-obsessed consumer culture." Forsythe claims that, throughout his series of photographs, he attempts to communicate, through artistic expression, his serious message with an element of humor.

On August 23, 1999, Mattel filed this action in the United States District Court for the Central District of California against Forsythe, alleging that Forsythe's "Food Chain Barbie" series infringed Mattel's copyrights, trademarks, and trade dress. On July 16, 2001, Forsythe moved for summary judgment. On August 22, 2001, the district court granted Forsythe's motion for summary judgment. The district court held that Forsythe's use of Mattel's copyrighted work was fair use. Mattel appeals.

To determine whether a work constitutes fair use, we engage in a case-by-case analysis and a flexible balancing of relevant factors. The four factors we consider are: (1) the purpose and character of the use, including whether such use is of a commercial nature or is for non-profit educational purposes; (2) the nature of the copyrighted work; (3) the amount and substantiality of the portion used in relation to the copyrighted work as a whole; and (4) the effect of the use upon the potential market for or value of the copyrighted work.

The "purpose and character of use" factor in the fair use inquiry asks "to what extent the new work is transformative" and does not simply "supplant" the original work and whether the work's purpose was for- or not-for-profit.

The Supreme Court has recognized that parodic works, like other works that comment and criticize, are by their nature often sufficiently transformative to fit clearly under the fair use exception. The threshold question is whether a parodic character may reasonably be perceived.

A parody is a "literary or artistic work that imitates the characteristic style of an author or a work for comic effect or ridicule." (quoting AMERICAN HERITAGE DICTIONARY 1317 (3d. 1992)). For the purposes of copyright law, a parodist may claim fair use where he or she uses some of the "elements of a prior author's composition to create a new one that, at least in part, comments on that author's works." The original work need not be the sole subject of the parody; the parody may loosely target an original as long as the parody reasonably could be perceived as commenting on the original or criticizing it, to some degree. That a parody is in bad taste is not relevant to whether it constitutes fair use. Mattel, through impressive marketing, has established Barbie as "the ideal American woman" and a "symbol of American girlhood" for many. *Mattel, Inc. v. MCA Records, Inc.*, 296 F.3d 894, 898 (9th Cir. 2002), *cert. denied*, 537 U.S. 1171 (2003). As abundantly evidenced in the record, Mattel's advertisements show these plastic dolls dressed in various outfits, leading glamorous lifestyles and engaged in exciting activities. To sell its product, Mattel uses associations of beauty, wealth, and glamour.

Forsythe turns this image on its head, so to speak, by displaying carefully positioned, nude, and sometimes frazzled looking Barbies in often ridiculous and apparently dangerous situations. His lighting, background, props, and camera angles all serve to create a context for Mattel's copyrighted work that transform Barbie's meaning. Forsythe presents the viewer with a different set of associations and a different context for this plastic figure. In some of Forsythe's photos, Barbie is about to be destroyed or harmed by domestic life in the form of kitchen appliances, yet continues displaying her well-known smile, disturbingly oblivious to her predicament. As portrayed in some of Forsythe's photographs, the appliances are substantial and overwhelming, while Barbie looks defenseless. In other photographs, Forsythe conveys a sexualized perspective of Barbie by showing the nude doll in sexually suggestive contexts. It is not difficult to see the commentary that Forsythe intended or the harm that he perceived in Barbie's influence on gender roles and the position of women in society.

However one may feel about his message—whether he is wrong or right, whether his methods are powerful or banal—his photographs parody Barbie and everything Mattel's doll has come to signify. Undoubtedly, one could make similar statements through other means about society, gender roles, sexuality, and perhaps even social class. But Barbie, and all the associations she has acquired through Mattel's impressive marketing success, conveys these messages in a particular way that is ripe for social comment. By developing and transforming associations with Mattel's Barbie doll, Forsythe has created the sort of social criticism and parodic speech protected by the First Amendment and promoted by the Copyright Act. We find that this factor weighs heavily in favor of Forsythe.

Another element of the first factor analysis is whether the work's "purpose" was commercial or had a non-profit aim. Clearly, Forsythe had a commercial expectation and presumably hoped to find a market for his art. On balance, Forsythe's commercial expectation does not weigh much against him. Given the extremely transformative nature and parodic quality of Forsythe's work, its commercial qualities become less important. The second factor in the fair use analysis "recognizes that creative works are closer to the core of intended copyright protection' than informational and functional works." Mattel's copyrighted Barbie figure and face can fairly be said to be a creative work. However, the creativity of Mattel's copyrighted Barbie is typical of cases where there are infringing parodies. As we have recognized in the past, "this [nature of the copyrighted work] factor typically has not been terribly significant in the overall fair use balancing." The third factor in the fair use analysis asks whether "'the amount and substantiality of the portion used in relation to the copyrighted work as a whole,' are reasonable in relation to the purpose of copying." 17 U.S.C. § 107(3). We assess the "persuasiveness of a parodist's justification for the particular copying done," recognizing that the "extent of permissible copying varies with the purpose and character of the use."

Mattel argues that Forsythe used the entirety of its copyrighted work and that this factor weighs against him. Mattel contends that Forsythe could have used less of the Barbie figure by, for example, limiting his photos to the Barbie heads.

First, Forsythe did not simply copy the work "verbatim" with "little added or changed." A verbatim copy of Barbie would be an exact three dimensional reproduction of the doll. Forsythe did not display the entire Barbie head and body in his photographs. Parts of the Barbie figure are obscured or omitted depending on the angle at which the photos were taken and whether other objects obstructed a view of the Barbie figure.

Second, Mattel's argument that Forsythe could have taken a lesser portion of its work attempts to benefit from the somewhat unique nature of the copyrighted work in this case. Copyright infringement actions generally involve songs, video, or written works. Because parts of these works are naturally severable, the new work can easily choose portions of the original work and add to it. Here because the copyrighted material is a doll design and the infringing work is a photograph containing that doll, Forsythe, short of severing the doll, must add to it by creating a context around it and capturing that context in a photograph. For our purposes, Forsythe's use is no different from that of a parodist taking a basic melody and adding elements that transform the work. In both Forsythe's use of the entire doll and his use of dismembered parts of the doll, portions of the old work are incorporated into the new work but emerge imbued with a different character.

Moreover, we do not require parodic works to take the absolute minimum amount of the copyrighted work possible. As the Supreme Court stated, "once enough has been taken to assure identification, how much more is reasonable will depend, say, on the extent to which the [work's] overriding purpose and character is to parody the original or, in contrast, the likelihood that the parody may serve as a market substitute for the original." We conclude that the extent of Forsythe's copying of the Barbie figure and head was justifiable in light of his parodic purpose and medium used.

The fourth factor asks whether actual market harm resulted from the defendant's use of plaintiff's protected material and whether "unrestricted and widespread conduct of the sort engaged in by the defendant . . . would result in a substantially adverse impact on the potential market" for the original or its derivatives. This inquiry attempts to strike a balance between the benefit the public will derive if the use is permitted and the personal gain the copyright owner will receive if the use is denied. The less adverse effect that an alleged infringing use has on the copyright owner's expectation of gain, the less public benefit need be shown to justify the use.

Mattel argues that Forsythe's work could lead to market harm by impairing the value of Barbie itself, Barbie derivatives, and licenses for use of the Barbie name and/or likeness to non-Mattel entities. Because of the parodic nature of Forsythe's work, however, it is highly unlikely that it will substitute for products in Mattel's markets or the markets of Mattel's licensees. Nor is it likely that Mattel would license an artist to create a work that is so critical of Barbie. The unlikelihood that creators of imaginative works will license critical reviews or lampoons of their own productions removes such uses from the very notion of a potential licensing market.

As to Mattel's claim that Forsythe has impaired Barbie's value, this fourth factor does not recognize a decrease in value of a copyrighted work that may result from a particularly powerful critical work. We recognize, however, that critical works may have another dimension beyond their critical aspects that may have effects on potential markets for the copyrighted work. Thus, we look more generally, not only to the critical aspects of a work, but to the type of work itself in determining market harm. Given the nature of Forsythe's photographs, we decline Mattel's invitation to look to the licensing market for art in general. Forsythe's photographs depict nude and often sexualized figures, a category of artistic photography that Mattel is highly unlikely to license. Forsythe's work could only reasonably substitute for a work in the market for adult-oriented artistic photographs of Barbie. We think it safe to assume that Mattel will not enter such a market or license others to do so. The market for potential derivative uses includes only those that creators of original works would in general develop or license others to develop.

Finally, the public benefit in allowing artistic creativity and social criticism to flourish is great. The fair use exception recognizes this important limitation on the rights of the owners of copyrights. No doubt, Mattel would be less likely to grant a license to an artist that intends to create art that criticizes and reflects negatively on Barbie's image. It is not in the public's interest to allow Mattel complete control over the kinds of artistic works that use Barbie as a reference for criticism and comment.

Having balanced the four § 107 fair use factors, we hold that Forsythe's work constitutes fair use under § 107's exception. We affirm the district court on its grant of summary judgment on Mattel's copyright infringement claims.

Case Highlights

- To determine the existence of fair use, courts will examine (1) the purpose and character of the use, including whether such use is of a commercial nature or is for nonprofit educational purposes; (2) the nature of the copyrighted work; (3) the amount and substantiality of the portion used in relation to the copyrighted work as a whole; and (4) the effect of the use on the potential market for or value of the copyrighted work.
- The purpose and character of the use factor requires a determination of the extent to which the new work is transformative. Parody of the original work has been deemed substantially transformative to constitute fair use.
- The amount of the copyrighted work used must be reasonable in relation to the purpose of the copying; recognizing that the extent of permissible copying varies with the purpose and character of the use.
- Actual market harm or substantially adverse impacts on potential markets resulting from the use of copyrighted material is relevant to the determination of fair use. The lack of shared markets for the original copyrighted material and the "infringing" use may preclude a finding of actual or potential harm to the copyright owner.

"employee" for purposes of copyright ownership (see the following Focus on Transactions feature).

Second, a work is for hire if it was specifically ordered or commissioned for use as a contribution to a collective work or as part of a compilation. The employer or person for whom the work was prepared is considered the author for copyright purposes. In the case of contributions to **collective works**, the contributor of the work retains a copyright for that individual's part, but the creator or producer of the collective work obtains a copyright on the collective work.

Copyright protection is available for all unpublished works, regardless of the nationality of the author. Published works are eligible for copyright protection in the United States if any of the following conditions are met: (1) On the date of first publication, one of the authors is a national or is domiciled in the United States; (2) the work is first published in the United States or in a foreign country that is a party to an international treaty to which the United States is also a party; or (3) the work is a sound recording that was first fixed in a treaty country.

No publication or registration is required to secure a copyright. The mere act of creation and fixing the work in a tangible form automatically creates the copyright.

CCNV v. Reid Factors for "Copyright Employee"

- Hiring party's control over the means and manner by which the work is accomplished
- The level of skill required
- The source of the instrumentalities and tools used in creating the work
- The location of the work
- The duration of the relationship between the parties
- Whether the hiring party has the right to assign additional projects to the hired party
- The extent of the hired party's discretion over when and how long to work
- The method of payment
- The hired party's role in hiring and paying assistants
- Whether the work is part of the regular business of the hiring party
- Whether the hiring party is in business
- The provision of employee benefits
- The tax treatment of the hired party

This is not considered to be an exhaustive list, and no one factor is considered to be determinative.

Publication of the work through distribution of copies, although not required, serves a number of purposes. It is a way of informing the public that the work is protected by copyright. It also provides evidence as to the date of copyright in order to determine the duration of the copyright.

Notice of copyright is no longer necessary in publishing a copyrighted work. Before the 1976 Copyright Act, the law did require the use of a copyright notice for publishing or distributing a copyrighted work. The notice needed to use the copyright symbol, give the year of first publication, and name the owner of the copyright. A standard notice looked as follows: © Jane Doe 2004. In 1989, the notice requirement was eliminated when the United States adhered to the **Berne Convention for the Protection of Literary and Artistic Works**.[19] Notice is still recommended, however, because it removes the infringer's defense of **innocent infringement**. Under the innocent infringement defense, infringers are absolved of liability if they can prove that they did not know the work was protected.

Registration of a copyright with the Copyright Office in Washington, D.C., is not a condition for protection, but registration does provide a number of benefits. First, registration of a copyright establishes a public record. A public record helps the owner prove a claim in future infringement or ownership disputes. Registration establishes a prima facie case of the validity of the copyright and the facts stated in the registration certificate. Second, registration makes available statutory damages and attorney's fees, whereas at common law the copyright owner is limited to actual damages. Third, registration allows the copyright owner to record a duplicate registration with the U.S. Customs Service for protection against the importation of infringing copies. A copyright registration is effective on the date that the Copyright Office receives a properly completed application.

---

19.   Notice is still relevant to maintain the copyright status of older works and still should be used to strengthen the owner's case in a copyright infringement lawsuit.

Patent Protection

U.S. patent law confers on the patent owner the exclusive rights to manufacture, use, and sell the patented product or process within the United States for a period of twenty years. To be fully protected, the patent holder or **patentee** should serve notice by affixing the word *patent* or the abbreviation *pat.*, together with the number of the patent, to the patented item or product. The patent law states that failure to mark the package means "no damages shall be recovered by the patentee in any action for infringement."[20] The patentee will be able to obtain an injunction to prevent further infringement but will not be able to sue for damages for injury caused by the infringement.

The Patent Act defines an infringer as "whoever without authority makes, uses, offers to sell, or sells any patented invention, within the United States or imports into the United States any patented invention."[21] Furthermore, anyone who falsely marks goods with the name of the patentee "with the intent of counterfeiting or of deceiving the public" is liable for damages.[22]

Under the **doctrine of equivalents**, an exact copying of an invention is not necessary to prove a case of patent infringement. The patent owner has to show only that there is "equivalence" between the elements of the patented invention and the infringing product. However, if the second invention is an improvement of the first, then the patent owner is not likely to benefit from the doctrine of equivalents.[23]

In *Warner-Jenkinson Co. v. Hilton Davis Chemical Co.*,[24] the patent owner had developed a process to remove impurities from commercial dyes. Its process operated at pH levels between 6.0 and 9.0. It sought an injunction against the developer of a purification process that worked at a pH of 5.0. The Supreme Court held that the doctrine of equivalents must be applied to the individual elements of the invention or process and not just the invention as a whole. The fact that both parties had developed a process for the purification of dye did not make them equivalent inventions. Instead, it needed to be determined whether a process that operates at a pH level of 5.0 is equivalent to one that works at 6.0. If the two processes were of equivalent quality, then the owner of the first process was entitled to an injunction under the doctrine of equivalents. If a process that works at a lower pH is qualitatively better, then it is to be considered an improvement and, as such, would be protected as a new invention.

Trade Secrets

Unlike a U.S. patent, a trade secret does not entitle its owner to a government-sanctioned monopoly of the invention for a particular length of time. Nevertheless, a trade secret can be a valuable form of protection. Trade secrets are protected

http://
U.S. Patent and Trademark Office: **http://www.uspto.gov.**

http://
Text of Uniform Trade Secrets Act: **http://www.nsi.org/Library/Espionage/usta.htm.**

---

20. 35 U.S.C. § 287(a) (2000).
21. Ibid. § 271(a).
22. Ibid. § 292(a).
23. The doctrine of equivalents also applies to trademarks. In *Enrique Bernat F., S.A. v. Guadalajara, Inc.*, 210 F.3d 439 (5th Cir. 2000), the seller of "Chupa Chups" sued the seller of "Chupa Gurts" for trademark infringement. Guadalajara, Inc., of Mexico, doing business as Dulces Vero USA, sold frozen yogurt cone-shaped lollipops under the name "Chupa Gurts." Chupa Chups, a Spanish company that sold "Chupa Chups," which are ice cream–flavored lollipops, sued for trademark infringement. The appeals court held that there was no infringement because the key term, *chupa*, is a generic Spanish word. Under the foreign equivalents doctrine, courts translate foreign words used as trademarks into what would be their common English meaning in usage to test them for their generic or descriptive meaning. The word *chupa* is a generic Spanish word for lollipop or sucker, so it is due no protection. The court held that there was no likelihood of confusion.
24. 520 U.S. 17 (1997).

under state law and through private contracts. Trade secret protection is a product of state common law, although many states have adopted the **Uniform Trade Secrets Act**, a model law drafted by the National Conference of Commissioners on Uniform State Laws. It prohibits the misappropriation of trade secrets by theft, bribery, or misrepresentation. Companies protect their trade secrets through confidentiality agreements with their employees and by trade secret licensing agreements that prohibit disclosure by licensees.

More recent developments in the area of trade secret law are the passage of the **Economic Espionage Act of 1996 (EEA)**[25] and the designation of customer lists as trade secrets. The EEA makes it a crime to steal not only government secrets but also business trade secrets. One issue recently explored is how to prove a violation of the EAA without first showing that there was a trade secret to be stolen. The court in *United States v. Hsu*[26] held that defendants in a criminal case involving conspiracy to steal trade secrets in violation of the Economic Espionage Act do not have a right to see the trade secrets in question in an effort to prove that there were no trade secrets. In that case, Hsu and others were indicted for violating the EEA by conspiring to steal corporate trade secrets regarding a valuable anticancer drug. The defense maintained that constitutional and procedural requirements of criminal prosecutions dictate full access to the documents so they could establish the defense of legal impossibility (they could not steal trade secrets that did not exist). The court ruled that so long as the defendants believed they were going to steal trade secrets, it does not have to be proven that there were actually trade secrets to steal.

A similar result was reached in *United States v. Yang.*[27] In this case, the defendant, who owned a company in Taiwan, received documents from an agent of Avery Dennison, Inc. The defendant had previously paid the agent to obtain information regarding Avery Dennison's operations. Unbeknownst to the defendant, the agent's activities were discovered, and he agreed to become part of a sting operation directed at the defendant. The agent offered the defendant confidential information regarding Avery Dennison's Asian operations and newly developed emulsion coating product. The defendant was subsequently arrested and charged with violating the EEA for his effort to obtain this information from the agent. The court concluded that, although he did not receive the trade secrets, the defendant was nevertheless properly convicted of an attempt to steal such secrets in violation of the EEA in that he intended to commit the crime and undertook a substantial step toward its commission.

The issue of protecting customer lists as trade secrets was recently examined in *Nowogroski Insurance, Inc. v. Rucker.*[28] The court held that valuable customer lists, which had been reasonably protected by an employer, were protected under the Uniform Trade Secrets Act. An insurance agency sued three former employees for soliciting its clients by using confidential information after they went to work for a competitor. The fact that written forms of the list had not been taken or copied was held to be immaterial. It is the nature of the employment relationship that imposes a duty on employees and former employees not to use or disclose the employer's trade secrets. A valuable customer list, which has been protected by an employer, is due trade secret protection. The fact that the former employee memorized the information, rather than taking it in written form, made no difference.

http://

Text of Economic Espionage Act of 1996 and other U.S. laws. Scroll down to section titled "U.S. Laws Regarding Electronic Surveillance." **http://www.tscm.com/Surveill_Laws.html**

---

25.   18 U.S.C. § 90 (2000).
26.   155 F.3d 189 (3d Cir. 1998).
27.   281 F.3d 534 (6th Cir. 2002).
28.   971 P.2d 936 (Wash. 1999).

Other courts have more recently addressed the issue of customer lists as trade secrets. In *Home Paramount Pest Control Companies, Inc v. FMC Corp. Agricultural Products Group*, the federal district court ruled that a customer list can constitute a trade secret pursuant to the Maryland commercial code.[29] This statute required the court to examine six factors in making this determination: (1) extent to which information is known outside the employer's business, (2) extent to which the information is known to employees and others involved in the industry, (3) extent of measures undertaken by the employer to protect the information, (4) value of the information to the employer and its competitors, (5) amount of money and effort invested by the employer in developing the information, and (6) ease or difficulty with which information could be acquired or duplicated by others. The expenditure of time and money by the employer was of primary importance to the court in *IKON Office Solutions, Inc. v. American Office Products, Inc.*[30] However, in this case, the court found that the customer list was not a protected trade secret pursuant to applicable Oregon law, as the employer's business was conducted in a small market, and any person with a knowledge of the office machine industry could duplicate the customer list by consulting telephone directories and information publicly available from the local Chamber of Commerce.

Extraterritorial Application of United States Law

The Lanham Act[31] allows a claim for false designations of origin.[32] The Court of Appeals in *Scotch Whiskey Association v. Barton Distilling Co.*[33] held that the Lanham Act could be applied extraterritorially where a U.S. producer supplied false labels to a foreign licensee. In that case, the U.S. company supplied labels designating the product as "Scotch Whiskey" to a Panamanian licensee. There was no evidence that the adulterated whiskey was imported into the United States. Nonetheless, the court held that the Lanham Act applied to the U.S. defendant, stating that "no principal of international law bars the United States from governing the conduct of its own citizens."[34]

The court in *Scotch Whiskey Association* relied on the Supreme Court decision in *Steele v. Bulova Watches*.[35] In that case, a U.S. citizen registered the Bulova name in Mexico. He then manufactured watches, using the Bulova name, for sale in Mexico. There was evidence that some of the watches had been imported into the United States. The Supreme Court broadly defined "commerce" in the Lanham Act to include activities of U.S. citizens outside the country. In applying this holding, the court in *Scotch Whiskey Association* held that "the purpose underlying the Lanham Act, to make actionable the deceptive use of false designations of origin, should not be evaded by the simple device of selecting a foreign license."[36]

---

29.   107 F. Supp.2d 684 (D. Md. 2000).
30.   178 F. Supp.2d 1154 (D. Or. 2001), *aff'd*, 61 Fed. Appx. 378 (9th Cir. 2003).
31.   15 U.S.C. §§ 1125 (a) & 1127 (2000).
32.   See ibid. § 1125(a)(1)(A-B).
33.   489 F.2d 809 (7th Cir. 1972).
34.   Ibid. at 812.
35.   344 U.S. 280 (1952).
36.   *Scotch Whiskey Association*, 489 F.2d at 813.

The Gray Market

The importation of counterfeited goods is prohibited under the Lanham Act and the Tariff Act of 1930.[37] The two pertinent sections of the Lanham Act that apply to the area of counterfeited or pirated goods are Sections 32[38] and 43(a).[39] They make it illegal to falsely affix another's trademark to goods or use an improper place of origin designation. The U.S. Customs and Border Protection Service is authorized to seize such goods at the point of entry into the country. To assist the Customs Service, trademark and copyright owners should record their rights with the Service.[40] The Customs Service has established an Intellectual Property Rights Branch to administer the intellectual property components of the U.S. import laws.

The so-called **gray market** problem[41] refers to imports bearing a genuine trademark but imported by a party other than the trademark holder or authorized importer. Also referred to as parallel imports, they include goods produced outside the United States pursuant to an intellectual property right transfer agreement (license) and goods licensed in the United States for export that are subsequently reimported into the United States. In these instances, a U.S. licensor will find its own market territory undercut by identical goods produced under a foreign licensing agreement.

The gray market problem as it pertains to the U.S. domestic market involves goods that are:

- legally produced under a license and that are imported or reimported into the United States
- legally produced by a U.S. foreign subsidiary or affiliated firm and then imported into the United States
- imported into the United States by a foreign firm after it licenses or assigns its U.S. trademark rights to another[42]

The firm that is hurt by gray market imports often seeks to prevent their importation. Section 526 of the Tariff Act provides relief under the first gray market scenario if the license agreement prohibits such importation. The importance of placing restrictions in international licensing agreements to prevent a gray market problem is examined closely in the next chapter.

The Customs Service will not prevent importation in the second scenario because the foreign entity is under the common control of the domestic company. However, Section 42 of the Lanham Act can be used to prevent the importation of foreign-made goods materially different than the same trademarked goods produced in the United States. This is because of the likelihood that the U.S. consumer will be confused into thinking that the goods are identical.

http://

Anti-Gray Market Alliance at **http://www.agmaglobal.org/**

37.   See 15 U.S.C. § 1124 & 19 U.S.C. § 1526(a) (2000).
38.   Section 32 makes it illegal for a person to reproduce or use "any reproduction, counterfeit, copy, or colorable imitation of a registered mark in connection with the sale, offering for sale, distribution, or advertising of any goods or services on or in connection with which such use is likely to cause confusion, or to cause mistake, or to deceive."
39.   Section 43(a) makes it illegal for any person to "affix, apply, or annex, or use in connection with any goods or services, or any container or containers for goods, a false designation of origin, or any false description or representation, including words or other symbols tending falsely to describe or represent the same."
40.   See 19 C.F.R. § 133.1-133.7 (2004).
41.   See Lawrence M. Friedman, "Business and Legal Strategies for Combating Grey-Market Imports," 32 *International Lawyer* 27 (1998).
42.   The Supreme Court attempted to deal with the different gray market scenarios in *Kmart v. Cartier, Inc.*, 486 U.S. 281 (1988).

In general, trademark law does not reach the sale of goods legally produced outside the United States and subsequently imported to compete against the same goods produced domestically. This was the situation in *NEC Electronics v. Cal Circuit Abco*.[43] In that case, the defendant had purchased gray market semiconductor chips from a foreign source and imported them to compete against the trademark owner's California subsidiary. The court held that if the trademark owner "chooses to sell abroad at lower prices than those it could obtain for the identical product in the United States, it cannot look to United States trademark law to insulate the American market or to vitiate the effects of international trade."[44] The onus is on the licensor to provide safeguards in its foreign licensing agreements to diminish the chances of parallel importing.

The first sale doctrine, highlighted in the trademark area by the *NEC Electronics* case, protects the importer of copyrighted products from an infringement action if the goods were purchased from or produced by a licensee of the goods. In *Quality King Distributors, Inc. v. L'anza Research International, Inc.*,[45] the Supreme Court held that under the first sale doctrine, the owner of copyrighted material is entitled, without permission of the copyright owner, to sell or otherwise dispose of purchased copyrighted materials, imported or not. The domestic owner of the copyright had entered in a distribution agreement with an English distributor. The distributor sold large quantities of the goods to the defendant-importer, who resold them at discount prices to unauthorized retailers in the United States. The Supreme Court held that there was no infringement and resale could not be prevented.

The *Columbia Broadcasting System v. Scorpio Music Distributors* case that follows further examines the first sale defense. In that case, the scope of the first sale doctrine was narrowed in relation to the importation of foreign-made phonorecords.

Columbia Broadcasting System, Inc. v. Scorpio Music Distributors, Inc.

569 F. Supp. 47 (E.D. Pa. 1983)

Green, District Court Judge. Plaintiff, Columbia Broadcasting System, Inc. ("CBS"), is a New York corporation which owns United States copyrights to six sound recordings, copies of which comprise the subject matter of this copyright infringement case. On or about January 1, 1981, CBS-Sony, Inc., a Japanese corporation, entered into two written agreements with Vicor Music Corporation ("Vicor"), a Philippines corporation, by which Vicor was authorized to manufacture and sell certain phonorecords exclusively in the Philippines.

On November 2, 1981, CBS-Sony severed its manufacturing and licensing agreements with Vicor. CBS-Sony and Vicor agreed that Vicor would have sixty days following termination of the agreements within which to liquidate its stock. International Traders bought the phonorecords from Rainbow Music, Inc., a Philippines corporation,

which had purchased them from Vicor before Vicor's sixty-day selloff period expired. CBS filed a complaint on February 1, 1982, alleging that without its consent, Scorpio imported the phonorecords to which CBS owns the copyrights and thereby violated § 602 of the Copyright Act which prohibits the importation of phonorecords without consent of the copyright owner.

Scorpio argues that, since the recordings were the subject of a valid first sale from Vicor to Rainbow Music, defendant has not infringed any of CBS' rights. When a work is the subject of a valid first sale, the distribution rights of the copyright owner are extinguished, and title passes to the buyer. Scorpio also argues that it is not an importer within the meaning of § 602. Section 602 provides, in pertinent part: "(a) Importation into the United States, without the authority of the owner of the copyright

---

43. 810 F.2d 1506 (9th Cir. 1987), *cert. denied*, 484 U.S. 851 (1987).
44. Ibid. at 1511. See also *A. Bourjois & Co. v. Katzel*, 260 U.S. 689 (1923); *Olympus Corp. v. United States*, 792 F.2d 315 (2d Cir. 1986), *cert. denied*, 486 U.S. 1042 (1988).
45. 523 U.S. 135 (1998).

under this title, of copies of phonorecords of a work that have been acquired outside of the United States is an infringement of the exclusive right to distribute copies or phonorecords."

The phonorecords at issue were acquired outside of the United States by International Traders and were imported without authorization from CBS, the copyright owner. Nonetheless, Scorpio argues it is not a proper defendant in this matter because it did not import the records from the Philippines; rather, it transacted its business with International Traders, within the United States. However, the question whether defendant was the importer need not be resolved, in view of the law regarding vicarious and contributory infringement and the undisputed fact that International Traders was an importer. Intent is not a necessary element of infringement, and the copyright holder may proceed against any member in the chain of distribution.

Defendant argues that the exclusive rights of a copyright owner, including the right to distribute, are limited by § 109(a). Section 109(a) provides that "the owner of a particular copy or phonorecord lawfully made under this title, or any person authorized by such owner, is entitled, without the authority of the copyright owner, to sell or otherwise dispose of the possession of that copy or phonorecord." I conclude that the section grants first sale protection to the third-party buyer of copies that have been legally manufactured and sold within the United States and not to purchasers of imports such as are involved here. Moreover, declaring legal the act of purchasing from a

United States importer who does not deal directly with a foreign manufacturer, but who buys recordings that have been liquidated overseas, would undermine the purpose of the statute. The copyright owner would be unable to exercise control over copies of the work that entered the American market in competition with copies lawfully manufactured and distributed under this title. This court cannot construe the statute so as to alter the intent of Congress, which has set restrictions on the importation of phonorecords in order that rights of United States copyright owners can be preserved. Accordingly, the defendant's motion to dismiss is DENIED.

Case Highlights

- Generally, when a work is the subject of a valid first sale, the distribution rights of the copyright owner are extinguished.
- Section 602 of the Copyright Act prohibits the importation of phonorecords without consent of the copyright owner.
- Intent is not a necessary element of infringement, and the copyright holder may proceed against any member in the chain of distribution.
- "First sale" protection is available to the third-party buyer of copies of phonorecords that have been legally manufactured and sold within the United States but not to purchasers of imports.

As shown in the *Columbia Broadcasting System* case, there is a history of special statutory protection for music and musical performances. Musicians or performers may enjoy copyright or copyright-like protection in three things, which are important to keep distinct. First, a musical composition itself has been protected by statute under copyright law since 1831. Second, Congress extended copyright protection to sound recordings under the **Sound Recording Act of 1971**.[46] This means that people who make unauthorized reproductions of records or tapes can be prosecuted or face civil liability for copyright infringement. Piracy, which refers to an unauthorized duplication of a performance already reduced to a sound recording and commercially released, is conceptually distinct from "bootlegging," which has been defined as the making of "an unauthorized copy of a commercially unreleased performance."

The Sound Recording Act did not expressly cover "bootlegging." Therefore, in 1994, Congress passed a statute, sometimes referred to as the **Anti-Bootlegging Statute**,[47] criminalizing the unauthorized recording, the transmission to the public, and the sale or distribution of or traffic in unauthorized recordings of live musical performances.

---

46.   See 17 U.S.C. § 102(a)(7) (2000) (including sound recordings on the list of copyrightable "works of authorship").
47.   See 18 U.S.C. § 2319A(a-f) (2000); see also *United States v. Ali Moghadam*, 175 F.3d 1269 (11th Cir. 1999), *cert. denied*, 529 U.S. 1036 (2000).

International Property Rights Protection

The rights granted under U.S. patent, trademark, or copyright law can be enforced only in the United States, its territories, and its possessions. U.S. law confers no protection in a foreign country. Outside the United States, protection is available through international treaties or foreign intellectual property laws. Relevant international treaties establish minimum standards for protection, but individual country laws and practices differ significantly.

http://

World Intellectual
Property Organization:
http://www.wipo.int/.
For full text of international treaties see
**http://www.wipo.int/
treaties/en/.**

The **World Intellectual Property Organization (WIPO)** is the official depository of most international intellectual property conventions. WIPO grew out of the 1883 Paris Convention on patents and trademarks and the 1886 Berne Convention on copyrights. Today, it serves two main purposes. It administers and monitors the enforcement of more than twenty treaties. Second, it promotes the adoption of new intellectual property treaties and conventions. The following Comparative Law feature lists some of the treaties administered by the WIPO and gives the original date of enactment as well as the date of the most recent amendments. Provisions of the World Trade Organization's **Agreement on Trade-Related Aspects of Intellectual Property (TRIPS)** are reviewed in depth later in this chapter. TRIPS has the potential to provide universal protection for intellectual property rights.

Treaties Administered by WIPO

COMPARATIVE LAW

- Convention Establishing the World Intellectual Property Organization, July 14, 1967, amended on September 28, 1979
- Paris Convention for the Protection of Industrial Property, signed March 20, 1883, amended October 2, 1979
- Berne Convention for the Protection of Literary and Artistic Works, amended September 28, 1979
- Madrid Agreement for the Repression of False or Deceptive Indications of Source on Goods, signed April 14, 1891
- Madrid Agreement Concerning the International Registration of Marks, April 14, 1891, amended January 1, 1998
- The Hague Agreement Concerning the International Deposit of Industrial Designs, November 6, 1925, amended January 1, 1998
- Nice Agreement Concerning the International Classification of Goods and Services for the Purpose of the

Registration of Marks, June 15, 1957, amended September 28, 1979
- Lisbon Agreement for the Protection of Appellations of Origin and Their International Registration, October 31, 1958, amended September 28, 1979
- Rome Convention for the Protection of Performers, Producers of Phonograms, and Broadcasting Organizations, October 26, 1961
- Locarno Agreement Establishing an International Classification for Industrial Designs, October 8, 1968, amended September 28, 1979
- Patent Cooperation Treaty, June 19, 1970, regulations enacted on July 1, 1998
- Strasbourg Agreement Concerning International Patent Classification, March 24, 1971, amended September 28, 1979
- Convention for the Protection of Producers of Phonograms Against Unauthorized Duplication of Their Phonograms, signed October 29, 1971

continued

Treaties Administered by WIPO (*continued*)

- Vienna Agreement Establishing an International Classification of the Figurative Elements of Marks, signed June 12, 1973, amended October 1, 1985
- Convention Relating to the Distribution of Program-Carrying Signals Transmitted by Satellite, May 21, 1974
- Budapest Treaty on the International Recognition of the Deposit of Microorganisms for Purposes of Patent Procedure, September 26, 1980

- Nairobi Treaty on the Protection of the Olympic Symbol, September 26, 1981
- Treaty on Intellectual Property in Respect of Integrated Circuits, May 26, 1989
- Trademark Law Treaty, October 27, 1994
- WIPO Copyright Treaty, signed December 20, 1996
- WIPO Performances and Phonograms Treaty, signed December 20, 1996

Paris Convention and Patent Cooperation Treaty

To secure patent and trademark rights outside the United States, a company must apply for patents or register trademarks on a country-by-country basis. U.S. individuals and corporations are entitled to a **right of priority** and to **national treatment** in the 168 countries that are parties to the **Paris Convention for the Protection of Industrial Property**. The Paris Convention, first adopted in 1883, is the major international agreement providing basic rights for protecting industrial property such as patents, designs, and trademarks.

A person who files for a patent or trademark in one member country is given a right of priority for a fixed period of time to file in other countries. The right of priority gives the holder twelve months for patents (six months for trademarks) to file from the date of the first application filed in a Paris Convention country. This right of priority relieves the burden of filing applications in many countries simultaneously. National treatment means that a member country cannot discriminate against foreigners in granting patent or trademark protection. Rights conferred may be greater or less than provided under U.S. law, but they must be the same as the country provides its own nationals.

Article 5 of the Convention sanctions member countries to issue **compulsory licenses** to third parties if the patent or trademark owner does not use the patent or trademark. A compulsory license grants patent or trademark rights to third parties without the consent of the patent or trademark owner. Compulsory licenses can be issued four years after the date of the grant of the patent. A compulsory license is not to be issued if the patentee gives legitimate reasons for its failure to work the patent or trademark. In addition, the parties granted licenses must pay reasonable royalty fees to the patent or trademark owner. U.S. patent law does not authorize the granting of such licenses.

The **Patent Cooperation Treaty (PCT)** addresses procedural requirements, aiming to simplify filing of, searching for, and publication of international patent applications. The PCT entered into force in 1978 and is open to any member of the Paris Convention. To date, 123 countries have become parties to the PCT. The PCT allows companies to file a single (uniform) international application for protection in member states. Individual national applications, however, must follow within thirty months.

http://
Law firm of Covington & Burling: "Compulsory Licensing" at **http://www.cov.com/publications/download/oid55358/473.pdf**

Berne Convention and Universal Copyright Convention

There is no such thing as an international copyright that automatically protects an author's work throughout the world. Protection against unauthorized use depends on the enforcement of national laws on a country-by-country basis. Most national legal systems, however, do recognize foreign works under certain conditions. This recognition of foreign works has been simplified through the enactment of international copyright treaties. Copyright protection has been seen as a moral right of authors and artists in their works. The moral nature of copyrights is inscribed in the cupola above the lobby at WIPO headquarters: "human genius is the source of all works of art and invention. These works are the guarantee of a life worthy of men. It is the duty of the state to protect the arts and inventions with care."

The level and scope of copyright protection available within a country depends on its national laws and treaty obligations. In most countries, the place of first publication is an important criterion for determining whether foreign works are eligible for copyright protection. Works first published in the United States are protected in 155 countries under the **Berne Convention** for the Protection of Literary and Artistic Works. The United States also maintains copyright relations with a number of countries under a second international agreement, the **Universal Copyright Convention (UCC)**.

UCC countries that do not also adhere to the Berne Convention often require compliance with certain formalities to maintain copyright protection. Those formalities require that the copyright be registered and that published copies of a work bear copyright notice, the name of the author, and the date of first publication. The United States also has **bilateral copyright agreements** with a number of countries; the laws of these countries may or may not be consistent with either of the copyright conventions. Before first publication of a work anywhere, it is advisable to investigate the scope of and requirements for maintaining copyright protection for those countries in which copyright protection is desired.

The Berne Convention, originally enacted in 1886, has been amended numerous times. A review of the convention and its amendments illustrates the types of rights protected under the notion of copyright (see Comparative Law: Ten Rights of Authors and Artists Under the Berne Convention). Although created to protect the authors and artists of artistic and literary works directly, the secondary purpose of the Berne Convention has been "to safeguard the large sums of money invested in producing informational goods and services"[48] that are subsequently produced by publishers and others.

The Berne Convention firmly established the rights of authors as a principle of international law but left it primarily to national laws to determine the degree of protection required. For example, it is left to national law to determine what types of works to protect. Once a type of work is afforded protection, then a country is required to extend to foreign authors the same protections granted to national authors. A major limitation on this nondiscrimination principle is that if a country's domestic law grants a longer term of protection than the laws of the author's country of origin, then that country need grant only a term of protection equivalent to the law of the author's country of origin and not the longer term that is given under its own laws.

---

48.   Vincent Porter, *Beyond the Berne Convention* 1 (1991). The coverage of the Berne Convention borrowed heavily from this source.

Ten Rights of Authors and Artists Under the Berne Convention

COMPARATIVE LAW

Moral Right
The right to preserve the integrity of the work, including the right to publish the work. This is an inalienable right that cannot be assigned to an employer or another.

Reproduction Right
The right over all sound and visual recordings and adaptations of the work.

Translation Right
Right over the authorization of translations into other languages except for the limited right of less developed countries to grant compulsory licenses for translations.

Public Performance Right
Right over the performance of dramatic, musical, and literary works.

Broadcasting Right
Right over performances including radio and television broadcasts.

Adaptation Right
Indicates that a broadcaster needs to obtain permission of both the original author and the adapter or arranger.

Recording Right
This right covers recording of musical or dramatic works.

Author's Film Right
The right of the original author to authorize a film of the work.

Rights of Film Creator
Recognizes the separate rights of the owner or creator of the cinematographic work.

Right of Pursuit
Allows national laws to create a right of pursuit to an interest in the secondary and subsequent sales of the work. Thus, if the author or his heirs sell or transfer the rights to the work, they may still claim an interest in the subsequent sale or transfer by the transferee.

Subsequent amendments to the convention expanded the scope of its reach, created additional rights, and recognized new technological developments. These amendments included the Berlin Act of 1908, the Rome Act of 1928, the Brussels Act of 1948, the Stockholm Act of 1967, and the Paris Act of 1971. The **Berlin Act of 1908** recognized for the first time that photographic works (as well as film and sound recordings) were to be given copyright protection. These rights included the right to authorize the adaptation of an original work and the right over subsequent public performances of the work. This was a response to the emerging technologies of sound recording, cinematography, and photography. The Berlin Act authorized for the first time the granting of compulsory licenses by individual countries.

The **Rome Act of 1928** recognized the moral rights of authors and authors' broadcast rights in their works. The moral right allows an author to object to any distortion or other modification of the work. The moral rights of authors are now recognized in Article 6*bis* of the Berne Convention: "independently of the author's economic rights, and even after the transfer of those rights, the author shall have the right to object to any distortion, mutilation, or other modification of or other derogatory action in relation to, the said work, which would be prejudicial to his honor or reputation." Thus, an author could sell the right to reproduce or publicly display the work but retain the ability to reject any modification of it in the reproduction or display. The Rome Act through Article 11*bis* established a broadcast right in response to the development of public radio: "the authors of literary and artistic works enjoy the exclusive right to authorize communication of their works to the public by radio diffusion." Thus, for the first time a right was premised not upon a specific act such as reproduction or performing but on a "process" of communicating the work.

The **Brussels Act of 1948** extended copyright protection to movie films. However, it was left to national law to determine the author or owner of the copyrights to a film. English law places that right with the producer of a film. In contrast, the civil law countries of Europe grant the rights to creative individuals, such as the author of the original story or the writer of the screenplay. The Brussels Act also extended the broadcast right recognized in the Rome Act from sound broadcasting (radio) to television. The **Stockholm Act of 1967** and **Paris Act of 1971** allowed less developed countries to impose compulsory licenses for works out of print or for the translation of works not available in the language of the country.

Agreement on Trade-Related Aspects of Intellectual Property

The Agreement on Trade-Related-Aspects of Intellectual Property (TRIPS) is divided into parts, sections, and articles (See Appendix C). The first three parts provide the general provisions, scope of intellectual property rights, and enforcement provisions. Part I provides "General Provisions and Basic Principles." This part defines the principles of national treatment, most-favored-nation treatment, and the general objective of the agreement. Part II is titled "Standards Concerning the Availability, Scope and Use of Intellectual Property Rights." The articles in each of the five sections in this part make up the operative provisions of intellectual property protections:

Section I: Copyright and Related Rights
Section II: Trademarks
Section III: Geographical Indications (Country of Origin)
Section IV: Industrial Designs
Section V: Patents

Part III explains the type of enforcement mechanisms countries must provide for violations of intellectual property rights. The scope of enforcement mechanisms is shown on the following selected list of articles from Part III:

Article 44: Injunctions
Article 45: Damages
Article 48: Indemnification of the Defendant
Article 51: Suspension of Release by Customs Authorities
Article 57: Rights of Inspection and Information (by rights owner)
Article 61: Criminal Procedures

TRIPS has been described as "the highest expression to date of binding intellectual property law in the international arena." TRIPS became the law of the United States through the enactment of the Uruguay Round Agreements Act of 1994. This framework agreement is to be enforced under the auspices of the World Trade Organization (WTO).[49] With the full force of WTO implementation, TRIPS promises

http://
World Trade
Organization:
http://www.wto.org.

---

49. The constitutionality of TRIPS was challenged in *U.S. v. Moghadam*, 175 F.3d 1269 (11th Cir. 1999), *cert. denied*, 529 U.S. 1036 (2000). The Circuit Court held that the statute enacting TRIPS into the law of the United States was constitutional under the Commerce Clause. The statute was held to be based on a legally ratified treaty "called for by the World Trade Organization whose purpose was to ensure uniform recognition and treatment of intellectual property in international commerce."

to be the best hope for the recognition of minimum standards for national intellectual property law regimes. TRIPS is a comprehensive agreement that has the potential for widespread implementation. It covers the four major areas of intellectual property: patent, copyright, trademark, and trade secrets. The following review not only provides an understanding of TRIPS but also reinforces the reader's knowledge of the basic principles of intellectual property protection.

GENERAL PRINCIPLES

The "general provisions" of TRIPS restate the foundational principles of the GATT-WTO system, including national treatment, most-favored-nation, and transparency. TRIPS requires all signatory countries to apply the national treatment and most-favored-nation principles to the area of intellectual property protection. It restates the national treatment principle by requiring that each signatory "shall accord to the nationals of other Members treatment no less favorable than that it accords to its own nationals with regard to the protection of intellectual property."[50] Article 4 restates the most-favored-nation principle with regard to intellectual property protection as "any advantage, favor, privilege, or immunity granted by a Member to the nationals of any other country shall be accorded immediately and unconditionally to the nationals of all other Members."

The third foundational principle of the WTO, transparency, is mandated in Article 63 of TRIPS. It states that "laws and regulations, and final judicial decisions and administrative rulings of general application, made effective by a Member pertaining to the availability, scope, acquisition, enforcement, and prevention of the abuse of intellectual property rights shall be published."[51] Under the transparency standards of Article 63, countries are required to transmit copies of their laws and regulations to the **Council for Trade-Related Aspects of Intellectual Property**.

To ensure the implementation of the principles, TRIPS established the Council for Trade-Related Aspects of Intellectual Property. Those interested in intellectual property protection should use the Council, along with the WIPO, as a resource. TRIPS instructs the Council to afford members the opportunity to consult on the trade-related aspects of intellectual property rights.

Article 69 implicitly recognizes the problem of "illegal" gray market imports. It requires each country to establish "contact points" in their governments to coordinate with other countries in preventing the importation of goods produced in violation of rights recognized under TRIPS. It specifically instructs customs authorities to cooperate in preventing trade in counterfeit trademark goods and pirated copyright goods.

TRIPS recognizes the current roles of the WIPO and existing intellectual property conventions. Article 3(1) of TRIPS recognizes the continuing roles of existing international conventions, namely, the Paris Convention, Berne Convention, Rome Convention, and the Treaty on Intellectual Property in Respect of Integrated Circuits. Article 8(2) further recognizes countries' rights to limit the grant of intellectual property rights when they are determined to be unreasonable restraints of trade in violation of antitrust laws.

Transitional provisions were incorporated into TRIPS in recognition of the demands TRIPS places on developing countries and former communist countries. These countries were given five years to implement the requirements of TRIPS. The least developed countries are given ten years before TRIPS must be fully

---

50.   TRIPS, art. 3(1).
51.   Ibid. art. 63(1).

implemented. Any other member in the process of transformation from a centrally planned to a free-market economy and undertaking structural reform of its intellectual property system may also benefit from this transitional period. It is imperative for the international licensor of intellectual property rights to check the status of a given country's implementation of TRIPS.

COPYRIGHT AND RELATED RIGHTS

TRIPS requires all WTO members to immediately accede to the Berne Convention. In TRIPS, as in most national laws, copyright protection extends to expressions and not to ideas, procedures, methods of operation, or mathematical concepts. As in the Berne Convention, copyright protection is extended to computer programs, whether in source or object code, as literary works.

Copyright protection is also expressly extended to "compilations of data or other material, whether in machine-readable or other form which by reason of the selection or arrangement of their contents constitute intellectual creations."[52] Thus, databases or customer lists are protected under copyright law. Articles 12 and 14 set forth the minimum **term of protection** for copyright protection. Article 12 provides that, other than with respect to photographic work or a work of applied art, if the term of protection is calculated on any basis other than the life of a natural person, the minimum term of protection shall be "no less than fifty years from the end of the calendar year of authorized publication, or failing such authorized publication within fifty years from the making of the work." Article 14(5) applies specifically to performers and producers of phonograms and provides protection of at least fifty years from the end of the calendar year in which the performance took place.

TRADEMARK PROTECTION

Section Two of TRIPS outlines the parameters for trademark protection. Article 15 of that section provides a broad definition of trademark akin to recent judicial recognition in the United States. It defines a trademark as "any sign, or any combination of signs, capable of distinguishing the goods or services of one undertaking (company) from those of other undertakings. Such signs, in particular words including personal names, letters, numerals, figurative elements, and combinations of colors, as well as any combination of such signs, are eligible for registration as trademarks."[53]

Once recognized as a trademark, the owner of the trademark has the right to prohibit infringement. This right against infringement is defined as "the exclusive right to prevent all third parties not having the consent of the trademark owner from using in the course of trade identical or similar signs for goods or services that are identical or similar to those in respect of which the trademark is registered where such use would result in a likelihood of confusion."[54] Article 17 recognizes the fair use concept found in copyright law and applies it as an exception to trademark protection. The period of protection for trademarks and renewals is set at a minimum of seven years. However, TRIPS states that "the registration of a trademark shall be renewable indefinitely."[55]

TRIPS recognizes the principle that trademark rights can be lost through abandonment or nonuse but rejects the notion of compulsory licensing found in some national laws.[56] Article 19(1) allows a country to cancel a trademark registration if

---

52.   Ibid. art. 10(2).
53.   Ibid. art. 15(1).
54.   Ibid. art. 16(1).
55.   Ibid. art. 18.
56.   See ibid. art. 21.

it is unused for a period of three years. It prohibits such cancellation if the reason for nonuse was due to events outside the control of the registrant (trademark owner or licensee), such as import restrictions or government regulation.

The importance of geographical indications or country of origin designations to the sale of certain products is recognized in Article 22. It notes the rights of others to prevent the false use of geographical indications "where a given quality, reputation, or other characteristic of the good is essentially attributable to its geographical origin."[57] In addition, an entire section of TRIPS is devoted to the protection of "industrial designs." Section Four recognizes "independently created industrial designs" as a separate category of protection. It grants a protection period of ten years for qualifying designs. Article 9(1) recognizes Article 6*bis* of the Paris Convention, giving the owner of a well-known trademark the right to block or cancel an unauthorized registration of its marks in a foreign country.

PATENT PROTECTION

Article 27(1) of TRIPS defines *patentable* as something that is "new, involves an inventive step and is capable of industrial application." For the purposes of this article, "inventive step" and "capable of industrial application" may be deemed synonymous with the "nonobvious" and "useful" requirements found in U.S. patent law. The immediate impact of the TRIPS patent protections for the United States was the extension of the patent period from seventeen to twenty years.

The rights conferred on the patent owner include the right to prevent third parties from the acts of making, using, offering for sale, selling, or importing for these purposes the patented product or process. Interestingly, instead of recognizing integrated circuit designs as patentable, TRIPS recognizes such designs separately and provides for a ten-year period of protection from the date of application or from the date of the "first commercial exploitation."[58] It requires members to agree to provide protection for the layout and design of integrated circuits pursuant to the **Treaty on Intellectual Property in Respect of Integrated Circuits**.

TRADE SECRETS

Trade secrets are recognized under Section Seven of TRIPS. It states that the purpose of recognizing trade secrets is the protection of "undisclosed information." *Trade secret* is defined as information having commercial value that is not commonly known and for which reasonable steps have been taken to maintain secrecy.[59] The owner of the information may prevent the disclosure of such information if disclosure would be contrary to "honest commercial practices." **Commercial practice** is further defined in a footnote as, among other things, "breach of contract, breach of confidence and inducement to breach."[60] Reasonable confidentiality and nondisclosure agreements are considered enforceable commercial practices.

Article 40 is of special importance to licensors of intellectual property rights. Countries are allowed to prohibit certain contractual restrictions that have "adverse effects on trade and may impede the transfer of technology."[61] Article 40(2) allows member states to single out for scrutiny contractual restrictions found in exclusive

---

57. Ibid. art. 22(1).
58. Ibid. art. 38(1).
59. An example of a reasonable step is requiring employees and agents to sign confidentiality agreements.
60. TRIPS, art. 39(2), n. 10.
61. Ibid. art. 40(1).

grantback clauses and clauses that prohibit challenges to the validity of the licensor's rights.[62] These types of clauses will be examined in Chapter Fourteen.

REMEDIES AND PENALTIES

TRIPS provides a menu of penalties and remedies to parties seeking the enforcement and protection of their intellectual property rights. Countries are required to provide civil and criminal remedies, along with procedures for seizing and destroying illegal goods. Civil remedies include damages for lost profits and attorney's fees,[63] along with the granting of injunctions to prevent imported goods from entering "the channels of commerce."[64] Regarding counterfeited goods, Article 59 instructs customs authorities not to permit "the re-exportation of the infringing goods in an unaltered state."

Special provisions are included in TRIPS to prevent the entry of infringing goods. The owner of intellectual property rights may petition the government or customs authority to suspend the importation or exportation of infringing goods.[65] Before granting the suspension, the administrative or judicial authority may require that the petitioner supply security,[66] which can be used to indemnify a party whose goods are wrongfully enjoined or suspended.[67] Article 55 provides for an initial suspension period of ten days. During that period, the petitioner must move forward with a proceeding on the merits or request an additional ten-day suspension. Article 57 gives the petitioner the right to inspect the suspended goods in order to substantiate the claim.

Enforcement of Intellectual Property Rights

After intellectual property owners secure rights in foreign markets, enforcement must be pursued diligently through local law. As a general matter, intellectual property rights are private rights to be enforced by the owner. Enforcement varies from country to country and depends on such factors as the attitude of local officials, substantive requirements of the law, and court procedures. The availability of criminal penalties for infringement, either as the exclusive remedy or in addition to private suits, also varies among countries. U.S. law affords a civil remedy for infringement, including money damages to a successful plaintiff and criminal penalties for more serious offenses.

U.S. exporters with intellectual property concerns should develop a comprehensive strategy for protecting their property. First, they should obtain the available protection provided under U.S. laws covering inventions, trademarks, service marks, copyrights, and semiconductor mask works. Second, before entering into a licensing agreement with a foreign party, licensors should research the intellectual property laws of countries where prospective foreign licensees conduct business. Third, the services of foreign legal counsel should be engaged to file appropriate patent, trademark, or copyright applications within priority periods. Fourth, entry into a foreign licensing agreement should be viewed as only the beginning of

---

62. See Chapter Fourteen (Intellectual Property Licensing).
63. See TRIPS, art. 45(1–2).
64. Ibid. art. 44(1).
65. See ibid. art. 51.
66. See ibid. art. 53(1).
67. See ibid. arts. 48 & 56.

a process. The use of the licensed rights should be monitored for abuse and infringement. The licensor should be prepared to act promptly to protect its rights in case of a foreign infringement. Finally, trade secrets should be protected through appropriate confidentiality provisions in employment, licensing, marketing, distribution, and joint venture agreements.

The importance of utilizing all the sources of intellectual property protection is illustrated in the *Carell v. Schubert Organization* case that follows. The case involves a claim of copyright infringement. The opinion is notable for its references to domestic, foreign, and international copyright laws.

Carell v. The Shubert Organization, Inc.

104 F. Supp.2d 236 (S.D.N.Y. 2000)

Schwartz, District Judge. This action arises out of a dispute concerning the copyright in certain makeup designs created for the cast of the Broadway musical *Cats.* Plaintiff Candace Anne Carell filed this action on July 12, 1999, asserting claims for copyright infringement, false designation of origin, antitrust violations, and an accounting for profits, arising out of defendants' use and publication of her Makeup Designs. The show *Cats* is reportedly "the longest running, most financially successful property" in the history of American theater. There have been over 40 productions of the musical in 27 countries. In addition to her claims brought under the U.S. Copyright Act, plaintiff brings infringement claims under several foreign copyright statutes.

In order for a work to be copyrightable, it must be "an original work of authorship"; that is, it must be (i) original and (ii) fixed in a tangible form. 17 U.S.C. § 102(a). Copyright protection for an original work does not extend to "any idea, procedure, process, system, method of operation, concept, principle, or discovery." The Copyright Act provides that ownership "vests initially in the author or authors of the work." There is no disagreement between the parties that the Makeup Designs are copyrightable, or that the creator of such Designs is entitled to protection even if he or she does not apply the makeup to the show's performers' faces. The Designs contain the requisite degree of originality, and are fixed in tangible form on the faces of the actors.

Domestic Infringement Claims

A complaint based on copyright infringement must allege: (1) which original works are the subject of the copyright claim; (2) that the plaintiff owns the copyrights in those works; (3) that the copyrights have been registered in accordance with the statute; and (4) "by what acts during what time" the defendant infringed

the copyright. A certificate of registration from the United States Register of Copyrights constitutes *prima facie* evidence of the valid ownership of a copyright, although that presumption of ownership may be rebutted.

Foreign Infringement Claims

Plaintiff asserts her copyright infringement claims not only pursuant to U.S. law but also pursuant to several foreign copyright statutes, specifically those of Australia, Canada, Japan, and the United Kingdom, and pursuant to the Berne Convention for the Protection of Literary and Artistic Works ("Berne Convention"). Several courts and authorities support the exercise of jurisdiction over foreign copyright infringement claims. In *Armstrong v. Virgin Records,* 91 F. Supp. 2d 628 (S.D.N.Y. 2000), recently decided in this district, plaintiff, a jazz musician, claimed that defendants violated his copyright in a song recorded by the music group Massive Attack in the United Kingdom, and which was thereafter distributed worldwide. He filed claims for copyright infringement under the Copyright Act and under unspecified international copyright laws. The court held that it could entertain plaintiff's claims under international copyright laws on the basis of diversity jurisdiction, and, potentially, on the basis of pendent subject matter jurisdiction to plaintiff's domestic infringement claims.

Other authorities, while acknowledging that extraterritorial jurisdiction under the Copyright Act is prohibited, have asserted that there may be a basis for jurisdiction in cases similar to the instant matter. As Professor Nimmer has explained: "Even if the United States Copyright Act is clearly inoperative with respect to acts occurring outside of its jurisdiction, it does not necessarily follow that American courts are without jurisdiction in such a case. If the plaintiff has a valid cause of action under the copyright laws of a foreign country, and if personal jurisdiction of the defendant can be obtained in an American court, it is arguable that an action may be brought in such court for infringement of a foreign copyright law. This would be on a theory that copyright infringement constitutes a transitory cause of action, and hence, may be adjudicated in the courts of a sovereign other than the one in which the cause of action arose."

For the reasons set forth above, defendants' motion to dismiss is denied as to plaintiff's copyright infringement and Lanham Act claims. SO ORDERED.

Case Highlights

- Makeup designs are copyrightable as "original works of authorship."
- U.S. copyright law protects works that are "original" and "fixed in a tangible medium."
- U.S. courts will at times exercise jurisdiction over foreign copyright infringement claims.

Foreign Intellectual Property Laws

As stated earlier, *industrial property* and *intellectual property* are interchangeable terms. However, it is important to recognize the increasing use of the latter term at the expense of the former term. The term *industrial property* is disappearing from Anglo-American legal terminology. It used to include the protection of inventions, industrial designs, and trademarks. Many countries have entered the postindustrial era, where the line between goods production and information production is increasingly blurred. Copyright, for example, protects purely utilitarian items, such as computer operating systems, whereas patents may protect quite abstract ideas for ways or methods of doing business.[68] Trademarks have taken on functions quite different from their traditional role of identifying producers of goods. For instance, trademark owners sell their marks as decorations for T-shirts.

The broader and more attractive term *intellectual property* has become the designation for the combination of what used to be industrial property, copyright law, and other related fields.[69] Unification of terminology, however, has not led to a unification of legal institutions. Therefore, researching the different national laws relating to intellectual property is important to see how patent, copyright, and trademark laws interrelate in the foreign country of interest.

Foreign Trademark Law

INTERNATIONAL

In most countries of the world, a trademark is recognized and protected only on the registration of the mark with an appropriate government agency. For example, Articles 2(1) and 8(1) of the **Law of the Russian Federation on Trademarks, Service Marks, and Appellations of Origin (Russian Trademark Law)** state that "legal protection of a trademark in the Russian Federation shall be accorded on the basis of its state registration." A system that allocates rights based on the "first to register" rule is referred to as an **attributive system**. All ownership rights stem from the registration of the trademark or patent. Most countries, however, as required by international trademark conventions, authorize their trademark

---

68.   See generally Larry A. DiMatteo, "The New 'Problem' of Business Method Patents: The Convergence of National Patent Laws and International Internet Transactions," 28 *Rutgers Computer & Technology Law Journal* 1 (2002).

69.   Peter B. Maggs, "Industrial Property in the Russian Federation," in *The Revival of Private Law in Central and Eastern Europe* 377, n. 1 (George Ginsburgs, Donald D. Barry, & William B. Simons, eds., 1996).

offices to reject the registration of internationally recognized trademarks (famous marks) by third parties. This statement is recognized in the Russian Trademark Law. Specifically, Article 7 provides that trademarks of other persons are protected without registration by virtue of international treaties to which the Russian Federation is a signatory.

Brazil first recognized the rights of unregistered foreign trademark owners in revising its industrial property law in 1997. The **Brazilian Industrial Property Law** allows the trademark office to "reject an application to register a mark that wholly or partly reproduces or imitates a well-known mark."[70] In determining whether a trademark is a well-known mark, the law refers to the Paris Convention. Article 126 of the law states that "trademarks that are well known in terms of Article 6*bis* of the Paris Convention for the Protection of Industrial Property shall enjoy special protection, whether or not they have been previously filed or registered in Brazil." However, the window of opportunity to obtain the rights to a trademark is narrow. A contesting party, usually the rightful owner or a licensee, has only sixty days from the time it contests a trademark registration to apply for its own trademark.

INTERNATIONAL

The Brazilian law also allows the trademark owner to sue for damages. Article 210(I-III) provides that the infringer may be sued for lost profits. The lost profit calculation is the one most favorable to the injured party. Thus, the foreign trademark owner can receive the higher of "the profits that would have been obtained by the injured party if the infringement had not taken place; the profits obtained by the infringer or the remuneration that the infringer would have paid to the holder of the infringed rights for a license that would have permitted him to lawfully exploit the subject matter of the rights."[71] Under the former Brazilian law, a foreign holder of a trademark not only had to register the trademark but also had to actively use it within two years of the registration. Because of barriers to investment or lack of interest in doing business in Brazil, many international trademarks lost their protection under Brazilian law.

National trademark laws need to be researched for substantive differences as well. For example, a foreign trademark owner should familiarize itself not only with what is required to register a trademark in a foreign country but also with what is required to preserve the trademark under that national law. Three of the more common areas for concern include:

- the term of the trademark and the requirements for renewal
- pursuing infringement actions to prevent the trademark from being transformed from a brand recognition to generic name or mark
- preventing it from being labeled as an abandoned trademark because of nonuse

Under Russian Law, a registration of a trademark is valid for a period of ten years calculated from the date of receipt of the application. The trademark may be renewed every ten years by filing a renewal request within the last year of the previous registration period. In the event that a registration or a renewal request is rejected, the applicant has three months to appeal the decision to the Chamber for Patent-Related Disputes.

INTERNATIONAL

---

70.   Brazil Industrial Property Law, art. 126(2).
71.   Ibid. art. 210(I-III).

Laws are relatively uniform regarding loss of trademark protection for marks that have generic use. If a trademark or trade name is used to refer to all goods of a certain type and not just to a particular brand name, then trademark rights are expunged. The *Comite Interprofessional du Vin de Champagne* case explores the generic–brand name distinction. This case also demonstrates that, in an international setting, a trademark may be considered generic in one country and a protected brand name in another.

A large number of countries require the owner of a trademark to use the mark or lose protection. The Russian Trademark Law allows the Chamber for Patent-Related Disputes to terminate a trademark registration when there has been uninterrupted nonuse for a period of three years after its registration. The law provides that the registration will not be invalidated in the event that the owner of the trademark shows that its failure to utilize the trademark was for reasons beyond its control. If, for example, the sale of trademarked goods was prevented because of import or export controls, then the owner will retain its trademark rights.

The People's Republic of China views the purpose of intellectual property law in a unique way. Besides the traditional purposes of protecting private property and encouraging technological development, the Chinese see trademark law as a mechanism for quality control and consumer protection. Article 31 of the Chinese Trademark Law

INTERNATIONAL

INTERNATIONAL

Comite Interprofessional du Vin de Champagne v. Wineworths, Ltd.

2 NZLR 432 (1991)

The Comite Interprofessional du Vin de Champagne (CIVC) is a semiofficial body created under French law whose purpose is the protection of the name Champagne. It is disputing with Australian wine interests active in the New Zealand market for sparkling wine that Australian exporters seek to label and sell as champagne. The main dispute is whether the word had in New Zealand crossed the divide from a distinctive word to a generic word. Champagne as we know it is relatively new, having its final development in the 19th century by Dom Perignon of the Benedictine Abbey near Epernay, France. The two features of Champagne of prime importance are the soil and climate in which the grapes are grown, and the method of manufacture by skilled personnel.

The essence of the *methode champenoise* is that the process of second fermentation takes place in the bottle in which it is sold. That requires an operation for shifting the yeast by gradual manipulation down the neck of the inverted bottle for its removal. New Zealanders did not early develop an interest in wines. This was in contrast to Australia where indigenous wine manufacture and drinking became a more integral part of the lifestyle. The plaintiffs recognize that for Australia, like Canada and the United States, there is no legal protection available to them over the use of the appellation *champagne*.

In 1987, Penfolds (Australia) reached an agreement with Wineworths (New Zealand) to export into New Zealand a sparkling wine bearing the label "Australian Champagne." Plaintiffs brought suit claiming that the defendants were guilty of the charge of passing off. It is appropriate to emphasize the plaintiffs' view of what makes the product and name so special. It is avowedly alcoholic and readily capable of producing a pleasurable effect in the stomach. Champagne is appropriate as a wine with which to celebrate; characteristics are that it palpably agitates in the glass, that it is reinforced by exotic origin (France), and its cost.

Is Champagne a Generic Term?

The Court's central task is to determine the overall perception of New Zealanders of the word *champagne*. The following categories of evidence are singled out: (1) dictionaries and linguistic experts, (2) market research, (3) wine expert witnesses, and (4) restaurant wine lists and newspaper advertisements. Based on this evidence, the Court's decision is that the word champagne in New Zealand is not generically used to describe any white sparkling wine.

The Law of Passing Off

The cause of action is not of the classic form whereby one manufacturer seeks to disguise its goods as those of another by imitating name or style of packaging so as to pass off or deceive a buyer as to the true nature of the purchase. This complaint is of a new type of passing off, which is characterized by inconspicuous attachment, and invalid sharing, of a reputation. This new level of passing off makes the identification of the misrepresentation or deceit an indispensable ingredient for liability which is more difficult to prove. The plaintiffs concede that there is no attempt to sell the wine as French wine. They do suggest buyers would think they were buying sparkling wine with all the attractive attributes of Champagne because the product is described by the word.

The essentials of a claim of passing off can be stated within three elements: (1) The case must establish sufficient reputation or goodwill in the name Champagne, (2) The heart of the case is the obligation to show that the challenged actions are likely to cause, or have actually caused, deception, and (3) The plaintiffs suffered or are likely to suffer damage or injury to their business or goodwill. First, there has already been a finding that the word *champagne* retains a distinctive reputation and goodwill and has not become a generic word. Second, the Court's decision is that it is deceptive. Third, the plaintiffs will suffer damage if the word champagne is used on any sparkling wine sold in New Zealand. It follows that the public of New Zealand, by which the Court means the ordinary purchaser without special knowledge of wines and who does not specifically concentrate on differentiation, or is even troubled and carefree about such matters, is likely to be misled. JUDGMENT FOR PLAINTIFFS.

Case Highlights

- "Passing off" is a form of trademark infringement characterized by inconspicuous attachment and invalid sharing of a reputation.
- The crucial factor in passing off is the distinctiveness of the trademark and whether it has become generically used.
- The standard for making the brand name–generic distinction is the perspective of the "ordinary purchaser" or consumer.
- For purposes of conversation at future cocktail parties, note the distinction between champagne that is fermented in "the" bottle versus in "this" bottle. The *methode champenoise* requires that the champagne remain in the bottle while impurities are removed during the second fermentation process. Experts turning the bottle over a prolonged period of time "magically" remove the impurities. This is an expensive process and is referred to as in "this" bottle. The cheaper method involves pumping the champagne out of the bottle, removing the impurities by a machine process, and then returning the future champagne by pumping it into another bottle for the second fermentation. This second method is referred to as in "the" bottle. If used adeptly, this bit of trivia can earn you a cosmopolitan reputation.

---

authorizes the Trademark Office to revoke a registered trademark if a trademarked good is not of reasonable quality. The law is aimed at providing protection only for trademarks for goods of at least average quality. Thus, a trademark owner that produces goods of inferior quality is seen as deceiving consumers. This deception is based on the assumption that if a good is trademarked, then it is of reasonable quality.

Foreign Patent Law

The fundamental difference between the U.S. patent system and most foreign patent systems is the time at which patent rights are created. United States' law incorporates the **first to invent principle**, by which patent rights automatically vest in the inventor at the time of invention. This right is superior to the right of someone who is the first to register the patent with the Patent Office. The inventor has the legal right to have a patent obtained by another party revoked and transferred back to the inventor. The United States and the Philippines are the only two countries that award patents on a first to invent basis. All other countries award patents to the first to file or register a patent application. Under the **first to register principle**, the first party to register an invention will receive a legal patent.

INTERNATIONAL

http://

State Intellectual Property Law of the People's Republic of China: **http://www.sipo. gov.cn/sipo_English/ flfg/default.htm**

INTERNATIONAL

INTERNATIONAL

There is considerable uniformity among national legal systems in the area of what types of inventions are protected under patent law. Chinese patent law mimics U.S. law in defining a "patentable" invention as one that possesses novelty inventiveness, and utility. Article 22 of the **Patent Law of the People's Republic of China** describes novelty as an invention that has previously not been published or publicly used. Inventiveness is defined as substantial progress over existing technology. Utility requires that the invention be capable of being manufactured or producing "effective results."

The **Patent Law of the Russian Federation** defines *patentability* as the invention of something that is novel, inventive, and capable of commercial application. An invention is novel if it is currently unknown, based on the existing level of technology. It is inventive if it does not result from the existing technology in a field. Finally, an invention must be applied commercially meaning it can be employed in industry, agriculture, health, and other spheres of activity. The law further provides that objects of invention include devices, substances, microorganisms, plant and animal cell cultures, and processes. Inventions that are not recognized as patentable under Russian law include articles aimed at meeting aesthetic requirements, scientific theories, and programs for computers.

Russian patent law reserves the right to obtain a patent to the employer and not the employee-inventor. Article 8(2) of the law states that "the right to acquire a patent for an invention, useful model, or industrial design created by an employee in connection with the performance of his official duties or of a specific task set by the employer shall belong to the employer, unless otherwise is envisaged in the contract made between the employer and employee." This is called the work for hire doctrine in the United States. The employee-inventor does have a right to remuneration as agreed between the parties or established by a court. The patent law advises those applying for a patent to use a patent attorney registered with the Patent Authority. The applicant is required to give the patent attorney a certified power of attorney to act on its behalf. The application must be written in the Russian language, provide an adequate description of the invention, and include a certified receipt of the payment of the required patent duties. Temporary protection is given the applicant beginning on the date of the public notice regarding the nature and content of the application. An approved patent is valid for a period of twenty years unless terminated for cause or for nonpayment of duties.

INTERNATIONAL

Chinese patent law adopts the notion of compulsory licensing found in a large number of developing countries but not often used under U.S. law. The Rules on Compulsory License for Exploitation of Patents issued by the State Intellectual Property Office (SIPO) in June 2003 permit the issuance of a compulsory license for a patented invention or utility model when a work unit qualified to exploit the patent has been unable to obtain authorization from the patent holder within a reasonable time, in the event of national emergency or public interest, or when the exploitation of later inventions or models depends on utilization of the earlier invention or model. Compulsory licenses may be issued only by SIPO upon application. SIPO determines the scope and duration of the license, including limitations upon the exploitation of the invention or model by any person other than the applicant and the payment of reasonable fees by the applicant to the patent holder. The applicant or the patent holder may request a hearing before SIPO regarding a request for a compulsory license. Parties dissatisfied with SIPO's decision may seek review in the People's Court within three months of SIPO's decision.

Business Method Patents

In a landmark 1998 decision in *State Street Bank & Trust Co. v. Signature Financial Group, Inc.*[72] the Federal Circuit swept aside the long-standing business methods exception to patentability. The business method in that case involved business software designed to perform financial calculations for an investment system. This broad acceptance of business method patents was underscored a year later by *AT&T Corp. v. Excel Communications, Inc.*,[73] which held that "the scope of [patentable subject matter is] the same regardless of the form, machine, or process in which a particular claim is drafted." The common sense reason given for the exception is that business methods lacked the degree of novelty or nonobviousness on which patent protection is premised. Not providing patent protection to types of business methods that are publicly used, such as business operation techniques, allows them to become part of the public domain and more fully utilized for the benefit of society. Broadening the scope of patent law unleashed widespread criticism and commentary not only in the United States, but also internationally because of the resulting divergence with the patent law systems of Japan and the European Union. The following two excerpts discuss this divergence in the area of **business method patents**.

Business Method Patents in Japan[74]

In November 2000, the **Japanese Patent Office** published draft revisions of its Guidelines for Computer-Software Related Inventions. One impetus for the revision effort was the need to respond to the application of business methods to the Internet. The introduction to the draft states that "as personal computers and the Internet become popular, 'business method-related inventions' utilizing known computers and communication technology come to attract attention from service industries, financial or advertising, which have not formerly been interested in the Patent System." Japanese patent law lists two requirements for patentability: that the invention be "statutory" and that it be "industrially applicable." The crucial determination for computer-related business method patents is whether they fulfill the "statutory" requirement. The Japanese Patent Law defines a statutory invention as a "high grade creation of technical ideas utilizing natural rules."

INTERNATIONAL

There are a number of categories of "inventions" that are considered nonstatutory under Japanese law. One category excludes claims or inventions in which natural laws are not utilized. The Draft Guidelines provide the following explanation: "If a claimed invention [uses] . . . any laws other than natural laws—such as arbitrary arrangements, mathematical methods or mental activities, or *methods for doing business*, for example, the invention is not considered statutory." Although this guideline seems to preclude patents for business methods, a note in the Draft Guidelines suggests otherwise. The note explains that "inventions relating to a method for performing business should be carefully examined, even if a part of it utilizes a physical thing, an apparatus, a device, a system, there are some cases where the claimed invention as a whole does not utilize natural laws but may still

---

72.   149 F.3d 1368 (Fed. Cir. 1998)
73.   172 F.3d 1352 (Fed. Cir. 1999).
74.   DiMatteo, "The New 'Problem' of Business Method Patents" at 28–29.

be patentable." This approach is consistent with the physical transformation standard previously used in U.S. patent law.

The international impact of the United States' embrace of business method patents has been pronounced. The recognition of business method patents is part of a natural process of recognizing the inventive nature of modern technologies. Conceptually, it is increasingly difficult to distinguish between program-related technologies, including Internet business method applications, and the technology with which they interface. If one can say that at least some business methods and their electronic applications are sufficiently inventive, then there is no rational reason to exclude business methods as per se unpatentable. The system instituted by *State Street Bank* overcomes the hazards of attempting to finely quantify classes of patentable and unpatentable inventions by allowing the patent law system to center on improving the quality of patents being granted.

The need for the convergence of the patent law systems of the United States, Europe, and Japan has never been more evident. Despite the initial criticisms of the United States' decision to allow business method patents, there is evidence of movement in Europe and Japan toward future recognition of such patents. The fact that both the Japanese and European Patent Offices continue to study the feasibility of fuller recognition of such patents leaves the door open for more substantial convergence. At the same time, the U.S. Patent Office has moved to quiet criticism of new business method patents by improving the quality of patent grants. The implementation of similar quality improvements by the Japanese Patent Office may be an effort to avoid the issuance of bad patents in the event that the patentability of business methods is liberalized in the future.

The Future of Business Method Patents in Europe[75]

INTERNATIONAL

In its present state, the law regarding the patentability of business methods under the **European Patent Convention (EPC)** leaves much to be desired. There is considerable confusion regarding the scope of Article 52(2)'s exclusion of business methods as patentable subject matter, and national courts and the **European Patent Office (EPO)** have failed to interpret the exclusion uniformly. This confusion has probably been exacerbated the most by the elusive technical contribution requirement.

Follow the United States?

One possibility for harmonization of European patent law would be to simply drop the EPC's business method exception altogether and treat business method claims in the same way as other claims involving patentable subject matter. This is essentially what the United States has done.

Patentability of Business Methods in the United States

The United States has historically fostered a very broad definition of patentable subject matter, illustrated by the much-referenced Supreme Court quote that "anything under the sun that is made by man" is patentable. More specifically, federal law defines patentable subject matter as any "new and useful process, machine,

---

75. Matthew E. Fink, "Patenting Business Methods in Europe: What Lies Ahead?," 79 *Indiana Law Journal* 299, 312–14 (2004).

manufacture, or composition of matter." This definition has been interpreted very broadly; it excludes only "laws of nature, physical phenomena, and abstract ideas."

In sum, business methods are patentable in the United States as long as they produce some useful result. The effect of this is essentially to treat business method patents as per se patentable subject matter—whether claimed independently or as a computer implementation—and to reserve the real inquiry of patentability to the other requirements, namely novelty and nonobviousness. The United States' broad definition of patentable subject matter has been subject to a great deal of scrutiny in Europe. It is not at all clear that business method patents are in fact unworthy of patent protection. Nevertheless, whether Europe ultimately decides to allow business method patents to some degree or to prohibit them altogether, it seems clear that it will not adopt a definition of patentable subject matter as broad as that adopted by the United States.

The **Trilateral (Patent) Office** was formed as a cooperative venture of the United States, European Union, and Japan. It continues to coordinate and provide an avenue for dialogue on the issue of business method patents between the world's three major patent law systems. The Trilateral Office can be assessed through any of the member countries patent office Web sites. See Internet Exercise six at the end of the chapter for the relevant Web sites.

The North American Free Trade Agreement

Regional trade agreements also include intellectual property matters within their scope. Chapter Seventeen of the North American Free Trade Agreement (NAFTA) establishes standards applicable to all forms of intellectual property, as well as specific standards applicable to copyrights, trademarks, patents, and trade secrets. General provisions applicable to all forms of intellectual property require national treatment for nationals of member states (Canada, Mexico, and the United States). The members are also required to provide fair, equitable, and nondiscriminatory procedures with respect to the enforcement of intellectual property rights within their borders. These procedures must provide, among other things, for adequate notice, the opportunity to be heard by an impartial tribunal, the right to counsel, the right to present evidence, the receipt of a timely written decision based on the evidence, and judicial review of administrative decisions. The members are to assure that adequate and effective protection and enforcement of intellectual property rights shall not serve as nontariff barriers to trade. However, member countries may restrict the exercise of intellectual property rights that have an adverse effect on competition in relevant national markets. NAFTA's general provisions also require accession to the Berne and Geneva Conventions, among other international intellectual property agreements.

NAFTA's copyright provisions require the parties to extend protection to works covered by Article 2 of the Berne Convention, including sound recordings, computer programs, and data compilations. Holders of copyrights for such material are granted the right to authorize or prohibit the importation, first public distribution or communication, or commercial rental of these materials. The term of copyright protection for such materials is identical to that provided by parallel provisions contained within TRIPS.

Trademark protection is provided by Articles 1708 and 1712. Article 1708(1) defines a *trademark* as "any sign, or any combination of signs, capable of distinguishing the goods or services of one person from those of another, including personal names, designs, letters, numerals, colors, figurative elements, or the shape of goods or of their packaging." Parties are required to provide the owner of a registered trademark with the right to prevent all persons not possessing the owner's consent from utilizing identical or similar marks for goods or services that are identical to those for which the owner's mark is applied. There must be a likelihood of consumer confusion in order to violate this standard. Parties are free to make registration of trademarks contingent on use, although actual use cannot be a condition for filing a trademark application. Initial registration of a trademark is for a term of ten years, with an unlimited number of additional renewals of ten years. However, registration may be canceled for nonuse for an uninterrupted period of two years. The parties are also authorized to refuse to register or cancel any trademark containing geographical references with respect to goods that do not originate from the indicated territory or region if such reference would mislead consumers as to the origin of the goods.

Patent protections are established by Article 1709. Article 1709(1) provides that inventions, products, and processes are patentable as long as they are "new, result from an inventive step and are capable of industrial application." Member countries may refuse to grant patents for plants and animals and biological processes associated with their production (excluding microorganisms) and under circumstances relating to public order and morality, the health and safety of humans, plants, and animals, or to avoid "serious prejudice" to the environment. The conferral of a patent permits the holder to exclude others from making, using, or selling the patented goods or processes for a term of at least twenty years from the date of filing or seventeen years from the date of the grant of the patent. Patent holders are also free to assign or transfer their patents or conclude licensing agreements. The right of a member country to require compulsory licensing is also recognized in provisions permitting derogation from the exclusive rights associated with the grant of a patent. However, Article 1709(6) requires that such derogation not "unreasonably conflict with the normal exploitation of the patent or unreasonably prejudice the legitimate interests of the patent owner, taking into account the legitimate interests of other persons."

Finally, trade secret protections are established by Article 1711. Article 1711(1) requires the member countries to provide legal means by which trade secrets may be protected from disclosure and exploitation without the consent of the person in lawful control of the information in a manner contrary to "honest commercial practices." Trade secrets subject to protection pursuant to NAFTA are defined by Article 1711(1) as information that is not generally known or readily accessible to people who normally deal with similar bodies of information and possess actual or potential commercial value as a result of its secrecy. In addition, the person claiming trade secret status with respect to designated information must have undertaken reasonable steps to maintain its secrecy. Article 1711 permits the member countries to require a physical manifestation of such information, such as documents, electronic means, optical disks, microfilms, or photographic means, prior to extending trade secret status. Members are prohibited from limiting the duration of trade secrets as long as the conditions for their existence are met.

European Union

The European Union has recognized the importance of uniform laws that transcend national laws on intellectual property rights. The European Union's efforts in this field have been more ambitious than those set forth in NAFTA. In EU countries, the intellectual property owner should make use of means that provide multinational protections.

In the area of trademarks, the EU Trademark Office issues a single trademark that is valid in all EU member states, even though national trademarks continue to coexist with the EU trademark. The following Comparative Law feature provides excerpts from Regulation 2868/95 implementing the **EU Trademark Directive**. This regulation is binding in its entirety and directly applicable in all EU countries. Among other things, it calls for uniform forms for applying for, contesting, and renewing trademarks, along with the option of converting a community trademark application into a national application. The regulation also provides for the registration of licenses.

However, not all of the EU's efforts have met with success. One example of an unsuccessful multinational effort in intellectual property is the Single European Patent. The EU-wide patent was intended to reduce the costs associated with patent applications in the member states, as well as create uniform rules and procedures with respect to licensing and infringement. However, the member states were

http://
For a brief description of the European Community Trademark Act: **http://www. lectlaw.com/filesh/ il-3.htm.**

EU Commission Regulation No. 2868/95 on the Community Trademark

This Regulation contains the necessary provisions for a procedure leading to the registration of a Community trademark, as well as for the administration of Community trademarks.

Rule 22: Proof of Use

Where the party has to furnish proof of use or show that there are proper reasons for nonuse, the Office shall invite him to provide the proof required. If the opposing party does not provide such proof before the time limit expires, the Office shall reject the opposition.

Rule 23: Registration of the Trademark and Rule 85: Community Trade Marks Bulletin

The registration shall be published in the Community Trade Marks Bulletin. The Community Trade Marks Bulletin shall also contain publications of applications.

Rule 29: Notification of Expiry

At least six months before expiry of the registration the Office shall inform the proprietor of the Community trademark and any person having a registered right. Failure to give such notification shall not affect the expiry of the registration.

Rule 34: Special Provisions for the Registration of a License

A license in respect of a Community trademark shall be recorded in the Register as an exclusive license if the proprietor of the trademark or the licensee so request.

Rule 42: Application of Provisions

The provisions of these Rules shall apply to Community collective marks.

Rule 44: Application for Conversion

An application may be made for conversion of a Community trademark application or a registered Community trademark into a national trademark application.

Rule 82: Communication by Electronic Means

Where a communication is sent to the Office by electronic means, the indication of the name of the sender shall be deemed to be equivalent to the signature.

Rule 83: Forms

The Office shall make available free of charge forms for the purpose of filing an application, entering opposition to registration, applying for renewal of a registration, and applying for revocation or for a declaration of invalidity of a Community trademark.

unable to reach agreement with respect to numerous issues, including the languages in which patent applications were to be submitted and the transfer of jurisdiction over disputes from national patent courts to EU institutions. As a result, the EU scrapped plans for the Single European Patent in May 2004. Whether new initiatives emerge from this failure remains to be determined.

Protection in Transitional and Emerging Economies

Protection of intellectual property rights in some emerging economies is hampered by inadequate enforcement of relevant laws and regulations. Foreign companies must be vigilant in protecting their products and associated rights from infringement. In some countries, novel approaches may be needed because of the lack of government or judicial enforcement. One technique used in countries with weak intellectual property law regimes is to track down counterfeiters and sign them as legal licensees. Ultimately, the courses companies take to protect their intellectual property rights will depend on the nature of their products. Some computer software companies, for example, provide free training and sell their software at competitive prices, while warning that copies of their product may contain damaging viruses. Companies with well-known trademarks need to register their marks early and seek the cancellation of any unauthorized registration. In general, a strong local partner or agent can help to protect trademarks and intellectual property.

http://

Office of United States
Trade Representative:
http://www.ustr.gov.

INTERNATIONAL

The **U.S. Trade Representative (USTR)** maintains intellectual property rights "**watch lists**" under Section 301 of the United States Trade Act of 1988.[76] For example, in 2004, the USTR placed thirty-four countries on the watch list, fifteen countries on the priority watch list, and designated one country, Ukraine, as a "priority country." Although the identity of some of these states, such as China, India, Mexico, Russia, and Vietnam, as well as numerous Eastern European countries, may come as no surprise, the list also contains numerous U.S. allies and countries not generally perceived as providing inadequate intellectual property protections including Canada, Israel, and Korea, as well as the European Union. As a result, these lists should be examined prior to making the decision to license in another country.

INTERNATIONAL

The intellectual property law regimes in former Soviet-bloc countries present a special case for scrutiny. The former inventor's certificate system, which gave recognition to an inventor but did not grant a monopoly on profits from the invention, has been mostly abandoned. The now democratic governments have moved to adopt Western-style intellectual property laws. Unfortunately, the commitment to implementation has not been matched with a commitment (or ability) to enforce. Often the laws begin by fully recognizing international conventions like the Paris Convention, Berne Convention, Patent Cooperation Treaty, and Universal Copyright Convention. Because these conventions dictate minimum standards, domestic legislation is needed to upgrade to the higher standards found in developed countries. Most of the former Soviet-bloc countries have enacted such legislation.

The problem has been in the area of enforcement and remedies. The lack of remedies under the old inventor's certificate system has carried over to the system.

76.   See **http://www.ustr.gov** for the most recent edition of the USTR report containing the watch lists.

When an infringement is recognized, the lack of appropriate remedies results in underenforcement. Also, the court system has generally not given harsh penalties to deter intellectual property infringement.

Russian patent law adheres to the "first to register" principle, in which legal rights accrue from the filing of the application.[77] Thus, a U.S. patent holder may find it difficult to prevent infringement unless it takes the necessary steps to obtain a Russian patent. The best approach is to secure the services of a **patent agent**. In fact, Russian patent law requires the appointment of a registered patent agent for any applicant maintaining a residence outside the Russian Federation.[78]

Another issue under Russian patent law is compulsory licensing. If a licensee or a third party makes an improvement on a patent that has not been used for four years, then the law provides that the patent holder must grant the improvement owner a license to use the underlying patent or technology. The "junior" patent holder must show that it cannot use its junior patent without infringing on the rights of the senior patent. The danger of this provision is that "a minor improvement by a second inventor theoretically gives him the right to a license without a reciprocal requirement to grant a license to the first inventor."[79]

Under U.S. law, "if the first inventor refuses to grant a license, the second inventor has no remedy. Russian law provides for compulsory licensing in this situation, thus lessening the value of patent protection."[80] For this reason, it is important to periodically use or "work" the patent to preclude the creation of second inventor rights. One alternative is to retain the property as a trade secret. If the property is retained as a trade secret, all employment contracts should prohibit their post-employment use.

There have been some positive developments aimed at improving the enforceability of Russia's intellectual property law. One positive development was the creation of the **Supreme Patent Chamber** by presidential edict issued on September 11, 1997. This judicial body provides a level of expertise currently lacking in the civil courts. However, its jurisdiction is limited to matters such as the granting of compulsory licenses. Most litigation involving disputes over patent ownership, patent infringement, and licensing contracts remains within the jurisdiction of the lower courts.

Developing an Intellectual Property Protection Strategy

Before entering a foreign market, an intellectual property owner or licensor should develop a strategy or checklist to protect its rights. Protection is especially important in countries with weak intellectual property laws or lax enforcement. A carefully written contract, such as a license, employment, agency contract, franchise, or joint venture agreement, as a mechanism to protect intellectual property will be examined in Chapter Fourteen. The licensor should develop a protection strategy before entering into such an agreement.

77. See Patent Law of the Russian Federation, art. 3(3). Note that Russia is a signatory of the Paris Convention. Therefore, the "true inventor" has twelve months from the filing date in another country to file for a patent in Russia.
78. See ibid. art. 15(2).
79. Marina Portnova, "Ownership and Enforcement of Patent Rights in Russia: Protecting an Invention in the Existing Environment," 8 *Indiana International Comparative Law Review*, 505, 516 (1998).
80. Maggs, "Industrial Property," at 385.

INTERNATIONAL

The following list provides an example of issues to be addressed in such a strategy, using Russia as the target market:

- Explore all protections provided by international conventions. Russia is currently a party to the Patent Cooperation Treaty, Madrid Protocol, Berne Convention, and Universal Copyright Convention, along with the Paris Convention. These treaty commitments supersede its domestic patent law.

- Enlist expert local guidance. Use a patent agent to obtain Russian patents, along with any necessary copyrights and trademarks.

- Determine duties or fees payable during the patent term. After obtaining a Russian patent, it is important to pay periodic maintenance fees. Failure to pay such fees can result in a termination of the patent.[81]

- Learn where and when notice or registrations are due. In Russia, a licensor is required to record any transfer or assignment of property rights. For example, patent transfers or licenses must be registered with the Patent Office.

- Define ownership rights for employees. In Russia, licensees should be required to enter into employment contracts with their employees that clearly delineate ownership of rights to any improvements made to the licensed technology.

- Explore enforcement options. Because of the poor track record of enforcement by the Russian civil court system, entering license agreements with infringing parties may be necessary.

- Protect against compulsory licenses. In Russia, a strong best efforts clause should be incorporated into any transfer agreement requiring the licensee to work the license in order to prevent claims of abandonment and the issuing of compulsory licenses. Chapter Fourteen will discuss the use of best efforts clauses in licensing agreements.

- The **Eurasian Patent Convention** should be utilized when appropriate. This convention allows a Russian patent to be expanded to include other former Soviet republics. The foreign licensor may file an application in the **Eurasian Patent Office** in Moscow.[82]

Finally, the licensor may want to enlist the services of **International Patent Searching Authorities (ISA)** when filing foreign patent applications. A number of national patent offices, including Russia, the United States, and Japan, as well as the European Patent Office, recognize patent search certificates produced by these authorities. ISA will forward the search report and the international patent application authorized under the Patent Cooperation Treaty to signatory countries.

http://

Eurasian Patent Office:
**http://www.eapo.org/
index_eng.html.**

http://

*Volume I of the PCT
Applicant's Guide*
CHAPTER VII: The
International Search
Procedure: Processing
of the International
Application by the
International Searching
Authority: **http://www.
wipo.int/pct/guide/en/
gdvol1/gdvol1–06.htm.**

KEY TERMS

Agreement on Trade-Related Aspects of Intellectual Property Rights (TRIPS)	Berlin Act of 1908	blurring
	Berne Convention for the Protection of Literary and Artistic Works	Brazilian Industrial Property Law
Anti-Bootlegging Statute		Brussels Act of 1948
attributive system	bilateral copyright agreements	business method patent
		collective works

---

81. See Patent Law of the Russian Federation, art. 30.

82. The Eurasian Patent Convention entered into force and effect on January 1, 1996, and provides protection in the Russia Federation, Azerbaijan, Armenia, Belarus, Kazakhstan, Kyrgyz Republic, Moldova, Tajikistan, and Turkmenistan.

commercial practice
compulsory license
Copyright Act of 1976
copyright law
Council for Trade-Related Aspects
    of Intellectual Property
doctrine of equivalents
Economic Espionage Act of 1996
    (EEA)
Eurasian Patent Convention
Eurasian Patent Office
European Patent Convention (EPC)
European Patent Office (EPO)
EU Trademark Directive
fair use doctrine
Federal Trademark Dilution Act
    (FTDA)
first sale doctrine
first to invent principle
first to register principle
generic marks
gray market
innocent infringement
International Patent Searching
    Authorities (ISA)

Japanese Patent Office
junior mark
Lanham Act
Law of the Russian Federation on
    Trademarks, Service Marks and
    Appellations of Origin (Russian
    Trademark Law)
national treatment
Paris Act of 1971
Paris Convention for the Protection
    of Industrial Property
patent agent
Patent Cooperation Treaty (PCT)
patentee
patent law
Patent Law of People's Republic of
    China
Patent Law of the Russian
    Federation
public domain
registration
right of priority
Rome Act of 1928
senior mark
service mark

Sound Recording Act of 1971
Stockholm Act of 1967
Supreme Patent Chamber
tangible form
tarnishment
term of protection
trade dress
Trademark Act
trademark dilution
trademark law
trade secret
transitional provisions
Treaty on Intellectual Property
    in Respect of Integrated
    Circuits
Trilateral (Patent) Office
Uniform Trade Secrets Act
Universal Copyright Convention
    (UCC)
U.S. Trade Representative
    (USTR)
watch list
work for hire
World Intellectual Property
    Organization (WIPO)

CHAPTER PROBLEMS

1. What can a U.S. licensor of intellectual property rights do to prevent a gray market problem? See, e.g., Lawrence M. Friedman, "Business and Legal Strategies for Combating Grey-Market Imports," 32 *The International Lawyer* 27 (1998); Alvin G. Galstian, "Protecting Against the Gray Market in the New Economy," 22 *Loyola of Los Angeles International and Comparative Law Review* 507 (2000); Tait R. Swanson, "Combating Gray Market Goods in a Global Market: Comparative Analysis of Intellectual Property Laws and Recommended Strategies," 22 *Houston Journal of International Law* 327 (2000).

2. What are the basic differences between the U.S. patent system and the patent systems in other countries?

3. *Conflict of law rules* play an important role in the application of national intellectual property laws. Conflict of law rules are applied by courts to determine which national law is to be applied in the case before the court. They are applied when the parties are from different countries or the activities at issue transpired in different countries. The court must decide whether the law of the country of the plaintiff or the defendant, or the law of some other country, should be applied. For example, Itar-Tass Russian News Agency sued *Kurier*, a Russian-language newspaper in New York that copied articles originally published by Itar-Tass, for copyright violation. Itar-Tass claimed *Kurier*'s publications of its

articles violated the Berne Convention and Universal Copyright Convention. Under what law is the ownership of the articles to be determined? Does the Russian copyright owner have standing to sue for infringement in U.S. courts? *Itar-Tass Russian News Agency v. Russian Kurier, Inc.*, 153 F.3d 82 (2d Cir. 1998).

4. Justice Yates stated more than 200 years ago: "Ideas are free. But while the author confines them to his study, they are like birds in a cage, which none but he can have a right to let fly: for, till he thinks proper to emancipate them, they are under his dominion." *Millar v. Taylor*, 4 Burr. 2303 (1769). In 1859, Abraham Lincoln commented further that "the patent system added the fuel of interest to the fire of genius." Using these statements, explain the purpose of intellectual property laws. Also, how do these laws balance the need to protect the property of "creators" through the granting of "monopolies" over their rights and the goal of free competition?

5. L'Oreal applied for a patent on a sun protection factor (SPF) product in Luxembourg on April 13, 1987. It applied in the U.S. on April 12, 1988. Estee Lauder applied for a patent in the U.S. on the same SPF on December 21, 1987. Assuming that the Paris Convention and Patent Cooperation Treaty applied, who is entitled to the U.S. patent? *Estee Lauder Inc. v. L'Oreal, S.A.*, 129 F.3d 588 (Fed. Cir. 1997)

INTERNET EXERCISES

1. Search the United States Copyright Office Web site and report the requirements for filing a copyright registration: **http://www.copyright.gov/.**

2. Research the activities of the World International Property Organization by reviewing its Web site at **http://www.wipo.int.**

3. Review the 2004 Special 301 Report of the United States Trade Representative at **http://www.ustr.gov/Document_Library/Reports_Publications/2004/2004_Special_301/Section_Index.html.** What countries are on the Representative's watch lists? Why are these countries on the list? Be sure to scroll down to the sections titled "Priority Watch list" and "Watch List."

4. Review and compare the texts of the Uniform Trade Secrets Act (**http://nsi.org/Library/Espionage/usta.htm**) and the Economic Espionage Act of 1996 (**http://www.tscm.com/Surveill_Laws.html**). Scroll down to "U.S. Laws Regarding Electronic Surveillance." What types of activities do they prohibit? What types of information are protected? Are there any defenses to claims under these acts? What remedies or penalties are provided for violations?

5. On May 5, 2000, a dispute settlement panel of the World Trade Organization issued its report in the U.S.-Canada dispute over Canada's term of patent protection. The panel essentially agreed with the United States that Canada's seventeen-year patent protection fails to comply with the WTO Agreement on Trade-Related Aspects of Intellectual Property Rights. Article 33 of TRIPS requires WTO members to provide a patent protection term of at least twenty years from filing for all patents existing on January 1, 1996. Canada relied on Article 28 of the Vienna Convention, arguing that there is a presumption against retroactivity for treaties. Review the panel report available on WTO Web site at **http://www.wto.org.**

6. Review the Web sites of the U.S. Patent and Trademark Office (**http://www.uspto.gov/**), European Patent Office (**http://www.european-patent-office.org/**), and Japanese Patent Office (**http://www.jpo.go.jp/**). Also, through these Web sites research the work of the Trilateral Office. The U.S. PTO, EPO, and JPO established the Trilateral offices to facilitate cooperation in the administration of their patent functions (**http://www.uspto.gov/web/tws/gen.htm**).

Chapter Thirteen reviewed some of the shortcomings of foreign and international intellectual property law protections. These shortcomings mean that the licensors of technology and intellectual property rights must negotiate added protections in their international licensing agreements. This chapter analyzes the contractual arrangements used in the field of intellectual property transfer, including common clauses used to protect the rights of the licensor and how best to protect the confidentiality of the licensor's property rights.

An associated issue, introduced in Chapter Thirteen, is the importation of licensed goods into the licensor's market, or what is popularly known as the **gray market problem**. Gray market concerns are addressed in the discussion of the grant clause and termination of licenses. The post-termination rights and duties of the licensees are also covered.

The ability of a licensor to insert contract clauses to best protect its interests is limited by foreign government regulation of restrictive licensing agreements. The law as applied to international intellectual property transfer is

Chapter 14

Intellectual Property Licensing

multilayered and complex. Four areas of applicable law need to be studied:

- Whether home country law (law of licensor) applies extraterritorially
- Whether an international convention can be used to protect the property being transferred
- Whether the foreign host country's laws provide sufficient protection
- Whether host country laws regulate the content of the licensing agreement

The first three areas were reviewed in Chapter Thirteen. The fourth area is addressed in this chapter. This area of law is especially important when the host country has displayed a propensity for not protecting foreign intellectual property rights. In such countries, the restrictions placed in the transfer agreement may be the only means by which a licensor can protect its intellectual property rights. Therefore, it is of paramount importance to determine whether those protective provisions in the transfer or licensing agreement are enforceable in the host country.

Licensing and Intellectual Property Transfer

There are numerous reasons for using licensing or technology transfer agreements to tap into foreign markets. The **licensor** or owner of the technology and intellectual property rights can avoid the costs and time of exporting and importing goods across national borders. Also avoided are the panoply of host country laws, such as tax, labor, and environmental laws, that have to be adhered to when investing directly, and before being able to enter and develop a foreign market.

http://

National Technology
Transfer Center: **http://
www.nttc.edu/default.
asp.** The mission state-
ment of the Center is to
strengthen U.S. indus-
trial competitiveness by
promoting the efficient
identification and
commercialization of
marketable research
and technologies.

Licensing, from the licensor perspective, provides an inviting means of generating revenues without committing large amounts of capital. A technology licensing agreement enables a U.S. firm to enter a foreign market quickly, yet it poses fewer financial and legal risks than owning and operating a foreign manufacturing facility or participating in an overseas joint venture. Licensing also permits U.S. firms to overcome many of the tariff and nontariff barriers that hamper the export of U.S.-manufactured products. For these reasons, licensing can be a particularly attractive method of exporting for small companies or companies with little international trade experience.

Technology transfer arises from agreements to conduct research and development abroad, to provide technical assistance to a subsidiary or joint venture, or to perform other activities under direct commercial licensing agreements between a manufacturer or intellectual property right owner and a foreign entity. Technology licensing is a contractual arrangement in which the licensor's patents, trademarks, service marks, copyrights, or know-how are sold or otherwise made available to a **licensee** for compensation. Such compensation, known as **royalties**, may be a lump sum royalty or an ongoing royalty based on volume of production or sales. U.S. companies frequently license their patents, trademarks, copyrights, and know-how to foreign companies that, based on the technology, manufacture products for sale in a specific country or group of countries.

Technology licensing is not limited to the manufacturing sector. Franchising, discussed in Chapter Three, is also an important form of licensing used in many service industries. In franchising, the franchisor (licensor) permits the franchisee (licensee) to employ its trademark or service mark in a contractually specified manner to market goods or services. The franchisor supports the operation of the franchisee's business by providing advertising, accounting, training, and related services and, in many instances, also products needed by the franchisee.

Intellectual property licensing in the narrowest sense involves the sale or assignment of statutorily recognized rights of patents, trademarks, and copyrights to a foreign licensee or buyer. Intellectual property is usually expanded to include trade secrets, which in the United States are protected under the common law and state statutes. Technology transfer in its widest sense includes more than the licensing of intellectual property rights. It may include the transfer of technical know-how and skills, along with managerial processes and technical services or assistance. This chapter's coverage applies to both licensing and broader transfer scenarios.

Protecting Intellectual Property Rights

http://

Text of Section 337 of
the Tariff Act of 1930:
**http://www.itds.treas.
gov/Sec337.htm.**

As a form of exporting, licensing has certain potential drawbacks. The negative aspects of licensing are (1) weakened control over the rights because they have been transferred to an unaffiliated firm and (2) less profit than would be generated by exporting goods or services. In certain countries, there are also problems of adequately protecting the licensed property from unauthorized use by third parties.

In considering the licensing of intellectual property rights (IPR), remember that foreign licensees may attempt to use the licensed IPR to manufacture products to be marketed in the United States or third countries in direct competition with the licensor or its other licensees. In many instances, U.S. licensors impose territorial restrictions on their foreign licensees if permitted by foreign antitrust and licensing laws. Unauthorized exports to the United States by foreign licensees can sometimes be prevented by filing unfair trade practice complaints with the U.S. International Trade Commission under **Section 337 of the Tariff Act of 1930**.

To facilitate the denial of entry into the United States of unauthorized foreign imports, the licensor should record its copyrights, trademarks, and patents with the U.S. Customs and Border Protection Service. U.S. antitrust law, as a general rule, however, prohibits international IPR licensing agreements that unreasonably restrict imports of competing goods or technology into the United States. The U.S. Department of Justice and Federal Trade Commission's **Antitrust Enforcement Guidelines for International Operations** contains useful advice about the legality of various types of international transactions, including IPR licensing. If significant federal antitrust issues are presented, U.S. licensors can consider applying for a review from the Department of Commerce or request an **opinion letter** from the Department of Justice.

Before entering a foreign licensing agreement, a company must investigate not only the prospective licensee but the licensee's country as well. The government of the host country, at times, will have to approve the licensing agreement before it goes into effect. Some governments, for example, prohibit royalty payments that exceed a certain rate or contractual provisions barring the licensee from exporting products manufactured with or embodying the licensed technology to third countries.

The prospective licensor should review the host country's[1] patent, trademark, and copyright laws; exchange controls; product liability laws; antitrust and tax laws; and attitudes toward repatriation of royalties. The existence of a tax treaty or bilateral investment treaty between the United States and the prospective host country is an important indicator of whether the foreign country is investment and trade-friendly.

Prospective U.S. licensors, especially of advanced technology, should also consider the need to obtain an export license from the U.S. Department of Commerce.[2] Because of the potential complexity of international technology licensing agreements, firms should seek qualified legal advice in the United States before entering into such an agreement. In many instances, U.S. licensors should also retain qualified legal counsel in the host country in order to obtain advice on applicable local laws and to receive assistance in securing the foreign government's approval.

Performing **due diligence** is crucial before entering an international licensing agreement. Due diligence should provide answers to the following questions:

- What formalities are needed to register or protect IPR in the host country?
- Will foreign government authorities need to approve the transfer agreement?
- What types of clauses are likely to be disapproved or violate foreign competition (antitrust) laws?
- Are there other mandatory legal rules specific to a particular country?

The next section reviews some of the due diligence issues that should be addressed by the international licensor of intellectual property.

Preventive Due Diligence

In contemplating the exportation of intellectual property rights, the licensor should undertake a due diligence review. For example, foreign national and international IPR laws need to be reviewed in order to take the necessary steps to best

1. "Host country" in this context means the country of the foreign licensee.
2. See Chapter Six.

http://

For another example of a due diligence checklist see The Publishing Law Center article "Acquisition of Titles and Product Lines: Evaluation, Search, Negotiation, and Due Diligence" at **http://www.publaw.com/acq.html.**

INTERNATIONAL

protect the licensor's rights. In addition, the licensor should review past transfers and infringement actions to determine the types of warranties and protections that it should place in the license agreement. A preventive law checklist should be developed to address these and other concerns (see Focus on Transactions: Checklist for Intellectual Property Transfers). The checklist should be compiled and implemented by an intellectual property review team with input from both legal and technical personnel.

A licensor's due diligence checklist should include determining whether the transfer agreement or license needs to be approved by an agency of the licensee's government. Some countries, unlike the United States, require the **registration** of the license with a government agency. In Russia, for example, licensing agreements with respect to patents must be registered. Failure to register the license results in invalidation of the agreement.[3]

Licensing the right to use a trademark or trade name is one of the more sensitive issues in negotiating a licensing agreement. As indicated in Chapter Thirteen, the

---

Focus on Transactions

Checklist for Intellectual Property Transfers[4]

Intellectual Property Review Team

Assemble an intellectual property review team. This team should include representatives from management; local and foreign legal counsel; technical personnel such as representatives from research and development, engineering, and production; sales and marketing; human resources; and financial.

Patents

- What are the times remaining on the patent terms?
- Have patents been used in countries that require *working*?
- Identify all U.S. and foreign patents associated with the transfer.
- Search U.S. and foreign patent office records for title and payment of all necessary fees.
- Identify procedures for protecting inventions, including procedures for

determining whether an invention should remain a trade secret, foreign filing requirements, and the timeliness of patent filings.

- Identify all markings to be used in conjunction with the production of the licensed product.
- Identify all existing and pending agreements dealing with the patents.
- Are the patents or licenses transferable? Are improvements included in the transfer? Are there any noncompete provisions? What are the termination dates on the patents and licenses?
- Review all correspondence relating to patent disputes, claims of infringement, and letters threatening lawsuits or other notices received by licensor or licensee.
- What steps have been taken to ensure patent rights in the foreign country of the licensee or the geographic area of the license grant? Has the patent been registered under the appropriate foreign national law?

continued

---

3.   See Russian Federation Patent Law, arts. 10(5), 13(5).

4.   Mary Ann Tucker, "Checklist for Due Diligence in Intellectual Property Transactions," 14-1 *Corporate Counsel's Quarterly* 68 (1997). For a more detailed due diligence checklist for business transactions in which intellectual property is involved, see Edward A. Meilman and James W. Brady Jr., "Due Diligence in Business Transactions Involving Intellectual Property Assets," *Intellectual Property Today* 20 (Jan. 2003).

Checklist for Intellectual Property Transfers (*continued*)

Trademarks

- Identify all federal, state, and foreign trademark registrations and pending applications.
- Check title and payment of renewal fees.
- Identify all procedures for protecting trademarks, including procedures for deciding whether to seek registrations.
- Provide licensee with samples of the proper use of the trademarks.
- Review copies of all product advertising and promotional materials.
- Check use of the trademark on the Internet.
- Has there been any period of nonuse of the trademarks?
- Have there been any previous assignments of the trademarks? Have these assignments been recorded?
- Are the trademarks and any licenses pertaining to them transferable or assignable?
- Review renewal dates on trademarks.

Copyrights

- Identify all copyrighted materials associated with the transfer or license.
- Check title to copyrights and payment of renewal fees for copyrights by searching the U.S. Copyright Office.
- Review procedures for identifying "copyrightable" material and the protection of those materials, including procedures for deciding whether to mark or register materials.
- Review all previous agreements dealing with the copyrights.
- Does any action need to be taken in the country of the licensee to protect the copyrights?

Miscellaneous

- What procedures, such as site security, employee access, and monitoring of third parties, should the licensee be required to undertake in order to protect the rights being licensed?
- Review employment agreements relating to intellectual property and confidentiality.
- What procedures and responsibilities should the licensee be required to undertake in relationship to third-party infringements?
- Does country of the licensee require the registration of licenses?

licensor should take all steps to protect its rights to trademarks under the law of the licensee's country. Therefore, before entering any licensing agreement, the licensor should register its trademarks, along with patents and copyrights, under the appropriate foreign national laws. The rights to use the licensor's trademark should be expressly limited to the duration of the agreement. The rights should also be limited to the territory of the license grant and used only in reference to specific products.

Special attention should be given to the protection of **trade names**. In the United States, a company's trade name is protected by state incorporation statutes. In the process of incorporating, a company reserves a corporate name. Such a reservation prevents anyone else from using a similar name when incorporating. The problem is that trade names are not well protected under some foreign incorporation laws. In a number of countries, there is no explicit prohibition against a company using or modifying the name of a preexisting corporation. Therefore, the license agreement should address the issue of the licensee's use or modification of the licensor's trade names. For example, any registration of the trade name should inure to the benefit of the licensor.

Intellectual Property License Registration

National laws determine the formalities of preserving and transferring intellectual property rights. In the United States, even though copyrights and patents are automatically protected at the moment of creation, better protection can be achieved by registering them with the appropriate government office. In the area of licensing or intellectual property transfer, compliance with formalities is especially important. In some countries, failure to register a licensing agreement may render it unenforceable.

The **U.S. Copyright Act** allows the registration of licenses and transfers in the Copyright Office. Doing so gives the licensee important benefits. Section 205(c)(1-2) of the Act provides that the recording of copyright transfers constitutes constructive notice of the facts stated in the recording. This becomes important in the event that the copyright owner transfers two conflicting licenses. Section 205(d) states that the license that is recorded first will prevail, even against licenses that were granted at an earlier date. Section 204(a) of the Copyright Act states that a transfer of copyright ownership is invalid unless the instrument of transfer is in writing and signed by the owner. "Transfer of copyright ownership" is broadly defined in Section 201(d)(1-2) to include the granting of an exclusive license. Thus, both an assignment of all the owner's intellectual property rights and a license of less than total rights need to be in writing.

The formalities of copyright transfers are explored in the *Valente-Kritzer Video v. Pinckney* case that follows. The case also introduces the concept of how U.S. federal intellectual property statutes preempt other causes of action brought by licensees.

Valente-Kritzer Video v. Pinckney

881 F.2d 772 (9th Cir. 1989)

Sneed, Circuit Judge. VKV produces video programming for sale and distribution. Callan Pinckney is the author of a best-selling book entitled Callenetics. VKV offered to produce a home video based on Pinckney's book. VKV alleges that the parties entered into an oral agreement whereby VKV "was given the exclusive right to shop for a home video deal and to negotiate with major home video cassette manufacturer/distributors for the production and distribution of a home video based upon the book."

Pursuant to the agreement, VKV arranged with MCA Home Video, a nationally recognized producer of home videocassettes, to produce the video. Pinckney, however, refused to perform her part of the agreement. Ultimately, Pinckney and MCA agreed to produce the videocassette that was a commercial success. VKV then filed this action for breach of contract, tortious breach of

contract, and fraud. Pinckney moved for summary judgment (dismissal), arguing that the Copyright Act of 1976 preempted all of VKV's claims.

A. Breach of Contract

We first address VKV's action for breach of contract. This claim encounters, as VKV concedes, the requirement that a contract transferring an exclusive license in a copyrighted work be in writing. If an oral transfer of a copyright license is later confirmed in writing, the transfer is valid. The right to prepare a derivative work, such as a videocassette based on a copyrighted book, is one of the exclusive rights comprised in a copyright. Section 204(a) not only bars copyright infringement actions but also breach of contract claims based on oral agreements.

B. Fraud

VKV's final argument is that the district court improperly held that the Copyright Act preempted the claim for fraud. The district court held that VKV's fraud claim is substantially equivalent to the rights afforded to owners and exclusive licensees of copyrighted works under the Copyright Act, and therefore preempted. We believe that the district court carried preemption too far in this instance. Two district courts have held that common law fraud is not preempted by § 301 because the element of misrepresentation is present. In its complaint, VKV does allege the element of misrepresentation that distinguishes this claim from one based on copyright. AFFIRMED in part and REVERSED in part.

> ## Case Highlights
>
> - A transfer of copyright ownership is not valid unless the instrument of transfer is in writing and signed by the owner.
> - "Transfer of copyright ownership" is broadly defined to include the granting of an exclusive license.
> - Certain claims, such as common law fraud, are not preempted by the Copyright Act.

Intellectual Property Licensing Agreement

Once a patent, copyright, or trademark is obtained, the holder is free to assign, transfer, or even mortgage those rights. The licensing agreement is the most common means of transfer. The intellectual property agreement or license takes on added significance in international transfers, and the contract must provide avenues for lawsuits for breach of contract where an infringement claim is unlikely to be sustained under foreign intellectual property laws.

The licensing of technology, intellectual property rights, and know-how creates some of the more complicated and detailed contracts in international business transactions. National laws that restrict the types of clauses that can be incorporated within a licensing agreement further complicate the license-writing process. Some of these restrictions are discussed in the last section of this chapter. The next two sections and the section on reviewing a license agreement discuss the content of such agreements. The issue of the enforceability of these clauses is addressed later in the chapter.

Common Licensing Clauses

Because the licensing of IPR is a private contract, the parties are free to formulate their contract as they like. In case of a subsequent dispute, the courts and arbitration panels will look initially to the contract to determine the respective duties and rights of the parties. However, the licensing agreement is regarded as a *sui generis* contract. Competition (antitrust) laws, for example, will preempt the operation of overly broad territorial restrictions or tying provisions in a licensing agreement.

In most developing countries, certain license clauses are limited by a variety of specific **technology transfer laws**. These laws require approval of the technology transfer agreement by an agency of the government. In essence, the transfer agreement becomes a three-party transaction between the private licensor, the private licensee, and the host (licensee's) government.

Unlike competition law, the aim of technology transfer laws is not to protect competition but to improve the bargaining strength of the licensee and promote local

http://
Yale University Library–
"Liblicence" provides
examples of and commentary on a number
of important licensing
clauses: **http://www.
library.yale.edu/
~llicense/index.shtml**

technological development. The government approval authorities will examine the contract and rewrite the terms to be more licensee-friendly. The clauses that are most closely examined are the confidentiality, grant-back, choice of law, and export restrictions clauses, as well as clauses limiting the licensee's use of the technology after the termination of the license. For example, a **duration clause** often prohibits the use of know-how after the termination of the term of the contract. A technology transfer law may eliminate such a restriction and convert the so-called license into an outright sale.

A **grant-back clause** that requires any improvement of the technology made by the licensee to be assigned back to the licensor is considered invalid under most technology transfer laws, but most countries allow a grant-back clause that is reciprocal or nonexclusive. In a reciprocal grant-back clause, improvements made by either the licensor or licensee are to be shared with the other party.

A **confidentiality clause** restricts access to the technology to a limited number of **key personnel** of the licensee and prohibits any further disclosure of confidential information to third parties. Many licensors require licensees to have all their employees sign separate confidentiality agreements. Most developing countries insist on a broader dissemination of the technology to its citizens and therefore often limit the scope of confidentiality clauses and agreements.

A **choice of law clause** or **forum selection clause** that designates the law of the licensor and the licensor's country as the place of dispute resolution is likely to be disregarded by the courts in a developing country. The approval authority in a developing country generally requires that the transfer agreement be subject to the jurisdiction and law of the host country.

In addition, most licensors desire strict territorial provisions, limiting the licensee to selling only in the territory specified in the license. An export restriction clause is generally inserted to prevent the so-called gray market problem, in which goods are made more cheaply in one country and then exported to compete against the licensor's own goods or those of other licensees. Such restrictions on export may be invalidated under foreign competition laws or under technology transfer laws in many developing countries. Generally, developing countries aggressively promote the export of goods to acquire hard currencies and improve their balance of trade. See Focus on Transactions: Explanations of Common License Clauses for examples and purposes of some other common license clauses.

Foreign competition, technology transfer, and consumer protection laws cannot be avoided through contractual agreement. For example, some foreign contract or consumer laws limit the scope of disclaimers or limitation of liability clauses. Thus, the international licensor must determine what impact such laws, along with differences in customs and trade usage, will have on the operation of their standard licensing agreements. The following sections focus on some of the standard clauses found in intellectual property agreements.[5]

License Grant and Limitations

The single most important clause in any intellectual property, technology, or software licensing agreement is the **grant clause**. It describes the rights and know-how being transferred, along with any restrictions or limitations on their

---

5.   See generally James H. Davis, Kenneth E. Payne & John R. Thomas, "Drafting the Technology License Agreement," *ALI-ABA Course Materials Journal* 13 (Dec. 1996).

use. The licensor should emphasize that the licensee is being granted only the right to use the items being transferred. The grant clause should:

- limit or prohibit the licensee's right to copy the licensed material
- prohibit the licensee from reverse engineering
- state that the licensor retains title to all copyrights, patents, and other proprietary rights
- call for the licensee to cease using the information upon termination and for the return or destruction of all copies

The grant clause should itemize the IPR and know-how being transferred. Referencing exhibits that are attached to the agreement is a common technique. The grant should make clear whether the license is exclusive or nonexclusive. The difference is fundamental to issues regarding the degree of competition that the licensee may expect and in setting the royalty rate. Also, exclusivity is interconnected to issues dealing with infringement. In an **exclusive license**,[6] the licensee should negotiate the right to demand that the licensor sue any third-party infringer or the right to sue in the name of the licensor for any infringements in the license territory.

http://
Licensing Digital
Information—The
Grant Clause: **http://
www.library.yale.edu/
~llicense/usecls.shtml**
and **http://www.
library.yale.edu/
~llicense/usegen.shtml.**

Explanations of Common License Clauses

Focus on Transactions

Compliance with Export Laws

"The licensed products shall not be exported, directly or indirectly, in violation of the export regulations of the United States or be used for any purposes prohibited by the export regulations."

In this clause, the licensee agrees to comply with the export regulations of the licensor's country.

Merger or Integration Clause

"This contract supersedes the terms of any purchase order or ordering document, along with the terms of any unsigned or 'shrinkwrap' license included in any product package."

This clause is especially important where the individual products being transferred come with their own licenses. The licensor would want to supersede such "individual licenses" only if it has provided adequate terms in the master license or transfer agreement.

Limitation of Liability

"The provisions of this Agreement allocate the risks between the licensor and licensee. The licensor's pricing reflects this allocation of risk and the limitation of liability hereto specified."

The parties generally want to exclude liability for indirect, incidental, special, or consequential damages. The licensor may want to limit the extent of its liability to an amount no greater than the total fees paid by the licensee.

Exclusive Remedy Clause

"The licensee's exclusive remedy and the licensor's total liability shall be the correction of defects in the licensed product or the re-performance of services rendered. Upon failure by the licensor to correct the defects within a reasonable period of time, the licensee may terminate the license and recover any fees paid for the product or for the unsatisfactory services."

continued

---

6.   A hybrid of an exclusive license is the sole license in which the licensor retains the right to produce, sell, or use its rights within the licensed territory.

Explanations of Common License Clauses (*continued*)

An ancillary clause to the limitation of liability clause is one that limits the types of remedies available to the parties.

Infringement Indemnity Clause
"Licensor will defend and indemnify licensee against claims of infringement of patent, copyright, or other intellectual property rights provided that (a) the licensee notifies licensor in writing within 45 days of receiving the claim, (b) the licensor shall have full control over the defense of the claim, and (c) the licensee shall assist the licensor in defending the claim. The licensor shall reimburse the licensee for reasonable expenses incurred in providing such assistance. The licensor shall have the option to (a) modify the licensed products to make them non-infringing or (b) obtain a valid license for the licensee. If the licensor determines that it is not commercially reasonable to perform either (a) or (b), then the licensor may terminate this license and refund the license fees. This shall

be licensor's entire liability and the licensee's exclusive remedy for third-party claims of infringement."

The licensee will want assurance that the licensor will defend it against any infringement claims. In turn, the licensor will want to limit its exposure to defending such claims.

Most-Favored-Licensee Clause
"The licensor will notify and offer more favorable terms in the future to ensure that the favored licensee remains on an equal competitive footing with other licensees."[7]

Such a clause requires the licensor to provide the same royalty rate and terms to the licensee that it subsequently gives to another competitive licensee. Such a clause is likely to place the burden in future litigation on the licensor to prove that the most-favored-licensee's competitor was not given a license on more favorable terms or lower royalty rate.

A nonexclusive license grant may include a **most-favored-license** provision in which the licensor is required to amend the license to include more favorable terms negotiated in a subsequent license to another licensee. This ensures that earlier licensees are not placed at an unfair competitive disadvantage.[8] A well-written most-favored-license clause would require the licensor to notify the licensee of any new licenses affecting its territory and to provide a copy of any such licenses so that the licensee can determine if the terms of the other license are more favorable. Finally, the most-favored-license clause should provide that if the licensee demands an amendment to its license in order to incorporate any more favorable terms, it must also accept the incorporation of other less favorable terms included in the subsequent license.

The grant clause should also define the grant in terms of its geographic scope and its duration. If the license is for the right to produce, sell, and use the rights in the United States, then the Patent Act infers that the grant is for the entire United States, along with its possessions and territories.[9] If the license is silent as to duration, then a court may infer that it was intended to grant rights for the entire statutory term of the patent, copyright, or trademark.[10]

---

7. *Carpenter Technology Corp. v. Armco, Inc.*, 800 F. Supp. 215 (E.D. Pa. 1992).
8. Most-favored-license clauses were held to be enforceable in *Carpenter Tech. Corp. v. Armco, Inc.*, 800 F. Supp. 215 (E.D. Pa. 1992).
9. See 35 U.S.C. §§ 100I, 271 (a) (2000).
10. See, e.g., *United States v. Radio Corp. of America*, 117 F. Supp. 449 (D. Del. 1954).

The grant clause may also restrict the nature of the rights being transferred. For example, for technology with different **fields of use**,[11] the grant clause may restrict the type of use for which the transferred rights are to be utilized. The patent owner (licensor) generally has the right to add any other restrictions that it deems appropriate in protecting its interests.

The *Mallinckrodt, Inc. v. Medipart, Inc.* case that follows provides an example of a field of use restriction. It also demonstrates that the licensor has the right to sue not only the licensee for violating a grant restriction but also a third party who assists the licensee in committing the violation. The third party that assists a licensee in the violation of a patent license can be sued for **inducement to infringe**.

The licensor should exercise care not to attempt to obtain benefits beyond the restrictions placed in the license or beyond the scope of its intellectual property rights. For example, in *Monsanto Corporation v. McFarling*,[12] the licensee of genetically modified and patented soybean seeds saved seeds from the resultant crops and used these seeds to produce crops in succeeding years. This use was in violation of the licensing agreement between the parties, which provided that the seeds could be utilized to produce a crop only in a single season and that the licensee could not collect

Mallinckrodt, Inc. v. Medipart, Inc.

976 F.2d 700 (Fed. Cir. 1992)

Newman, Circuit Judge. This action for patent infringement and inducement to infringe relates to the use of a patented medical device in violation of a "single use only" notice that accompanied the sale of the device. Mallinckrodt sold its patented device to hospitals, which after initial use of the devices sent them to Medipart for servicing that enabled the hospitals to use the device again. Mallinckrodt claimed that Medipart thus induced infringement by the hospitals and itself infringed the patent. The device is marked with the appropriate patent numbers, and bears the trademarks "Mallinckrodt" and "UltraVent" and the inscription "Single Use Only." The package insert provided with each unit states "For Single Patient Use Only" and instructs that the entire contaminated apparatus be disposed of in accordance with procedures for the disposal of biohazardous waste. Instead, the hospitals shipped the used manifold/nebulizer assemblies to Medipart, Inc. The "reconditioned" units, as Medipart calls them, are shipped back to the hospitals from whence they came.

Mallinckrodt filed suit against Medipart, asserting patent infringement and inducement to infringe. The district court granted Medipart's motion on the patent

infringement counts, holding that the "Single Use Only" restriction could not be enforced by suit for patent infringement. The court also held that Medipart's activities were permissible repair, not impermissible reconstruction, of the patented apparatus. Mallinckrodt states that the restriction to single patent use is valid and enforceable under the patent law because the use is within the scope of the patent grant, and the restriction does not enlarge the patent grant.

Restrictions on use are judged in terms of their relation to the patentee's right to exclude from all or part of the patent grant, and where an anticompetitive effect is asserted, the rule of reason is the basis of determining the legality of the provision. To sustain a misuse defense involving a licensing arrangement, a factual determination must reveal that the overall effect of the license tends to restrain competition unlawfully in an appropriately defined relevant market.

The district court stated that it intimated no opinion as to whether Mallinckrodt might enforce the restriction on "contract law or property law" or on "equitable grounds." We agree that a patentee may choose among alternate remedies, but to deny a patentee access to statutory remedies is to withhold the protection of the law.

---

11. For example, the patent owner of laser technology may elect to license the technology separately in the fields of medicine, industry, and government armament or defense.

12. 363 F.3d 1336 (Fed. Cir. 2004).

Thus whether Mallinckrodt may also have a remedy outside of the patent law is not before us.

It appears that the Court simply applied the rule of contract law that sale may be conditioned. Private parties retain the freedom to contract concerning conditions of sale. The appropriate criterion is whether Mallinckrodt's restriction is reasonably within the patent grant, or whether the patentee has ventured beyond the patent grant and into behavior having an anticompetitive effect not justifiable under the rule of reason. We conclude that the district court erred in holding that the restriction on reuse was, as a matter of law, unenforceable under the patent law. The grant of summary judgment is REVERSED.

Case Highlights

- A license grant may restrict the licensee to a "single patent use."
- A third party that provides a service that allows a licensee to avoid restrictions found in its patent grant (license) is guilty of "induced infringement."
- A patent owner has the right to exclude others from using its invention. Therefore, it has the right to place use restrictions in licensing the patent, unless the restrictions have an unreasonable anticompetitive effect.

seeds from the crop for use in future planting. In the resultant litigation, the licensee claimed that the restriction constituted misuse of the patent. The court defined **patent misuse** as the imposition of conditions by a patentee (licensor) in a licensing agreement that impermissibly broadens the scope of the patent and imbues it with anticompetitive effects. The issue for resolution is whether the condition is within the reasonable scope of the patent or extends beyond the patentee's statutory right to exclude or restrict use. The court rejected McFarling's claim of patent misuse on the basis that the licensed and patented product (the first-generation seeds) and the good created by the licensee (the second-generation seeds) were identical copies. Thus, the second-generation seeds were within the reasonable scope of the patent. Nevertheless, the misuse defense merits consideration prior to the inclusion of unduly restrictive use limitations in a license agreement.

A major issue that should be addressed in any IPR license is the right of the licensee to export goods from the licensed territory. Of great concern is the licensee's ability to import goods into the country of the licensor. This gray market issue has become hotly contested throughout the world.[13] If the mobility of the goods produced under the license is a concern for the licensor, then it should place restrictions in the license that prevent gray market imports. The World Trade Organization's Agreement on Trade-Related Aspects of Intellectual Property (TRIPS)[14] grants the licensor or intellectual property owner the right to prohibit imports into its home country. Such prohibitions should be clearly delineated in the agreement.

Another method for minimizing gray market risks is for the licensor to negotiate caps on the maximum number of units of the licensed product the licensee can produce in a given year. The licensor could also limit the number of units that the licensee may sell to individual purchasers. In addition, the license should state that the licensee is precluded from selling to anyone who is known to import goods into other markets.

The necessity of the parties reaching specific and detailed agreement with respect to the use of intellectual property is paramount. For example, in *Ulloa v. Universal Music and Video Distribution*,[15] the plaintiff created a spontaneous vocal recording

---

13.   See Chapter Thirteen.
14.   See 35 U.S.C. § 271 (a) (2000).
15.   303 F. Supp.2d 409 (S.D.N.Y. 2004).

while visiting a studio as a guest of another artist recording an album. The plaintiff's vocal performance was recorded and left in the possession of the studio at the end of the plaintiff's visit. The artist recording at the studio at the time of the plaintiff's visit expressed interest in including the plaintiff's vocal performance on her album. However, the studio expressed reservations and advised the plaintiff that it was uncertain whether the recording would appear on the album. The studio and the plaintiff never reached agreement as to the use of the performance. Nevertheless, the performance was subsequently included on the album. In defending the resultant copyright infringement litigation, the studio claimed that the discussions between the parties gave rise to an **implied license** to include the plaintiff's vocal performance on the album. To create an implied license, the court held that the studio had to demonstrate that the vocal performance was created at the request of the studio and relinquished to it with the intent that it be copied and distributed. Despite the fact that the plaintiff left the recording in the possession of the studio, the court held that no implied license was created because the performance was spontaneous (rather than at the studio's request), and the studio advised the plaintiff that it was uncertain whether the performance would be utilized. As a result, there was no meeting of the minds from which the court could imply the creation of a license to include the plaintiff's vocal performance on the album.

In attempting to describe the scope of uses granted by the license, the grant clause may fail to anticipate future unforeseen uses of the intellectual property. This was the issue addressed by the court in *Cohen v. Paramount Pictures Corporation.* In such cases, the court must determine whether the unforeseen use comes within the spirit of the license grant.

http://

Various articles on gray market issues: **http:// asm.sametz.com/ commerce/business_ article_004.shtml**; **http://www.newyork. bbb.org/library/publica- tions/subrep45.html** or **http://www.crn.com/ sections/breakingnews/ dailyarchives. jhtml?articleId = 18838885&_requestid = 821392.**

Cohen v. Paramount Pictures Corp.

845 F.2d 851 (9th Cir. 1988)

Hug, Circuit Judge. This case involves a novel issue of copyright law of whether a license conferring the right to exhibit a film "by means of television" includes the right to distribute videocassettes of the film. We hold it does not. Herbert Cohen is the owner of the copyright in a musical composition entitled "Merry-Go-Round." Cohen granted H & J Pictures, Inc., a "synchronization" license, which gave H & J the right to use the composition in a film called "Medium Cool" and to exhibit the film in theatres and on television. Subsequently, H & J assigned to Paramount Pictures all of its rights, title, and interest in the movie "Medium Cool," including all of the rights and interests created by the license from Cohen to H & J. Sometime later, Paramount furnished a negative of the film to a videocassette manufacturer, who made copies of the film—including a recording of the composition— and supplied the copies to Paramount. Paramount, in turn, sold approximately 2,725 videocassettes of the film, receiving gross revenue of $69,024.26 from the sales.

On February 20, 1985, Cohen filed suit against Paramount in federal district court alleging copyright infringement. Cohen contended that the license granted to H & J did not confer the right to use the composition in a reproduction of the film in videocassettes distributed for home display.

To resolve this case, we must examine the terms of the license, in order to determine whether the license conveyed the right to use the composition in making and distributing videocassette reproductions of "Medium Cool." The document begins by granting the licensee the "authority to record, in any manner, medium, form or language, the words and music of the musical composition and to make copies of such recordings and to perform said musical composition everywhere, all in accordance with the terms, conditions, and limitations hereinafter set forth." It further states: "The license herein granted to perform said musical composition is granted for: (a) The exhibition of said motion picture to audiences in motion picture theatres and other places of public entertainment where motion pictures are customarily exhibited and (b) The exhibition of said motion picture by means of television, including 'pay television,' 'subscription television,' and 'closed circuit into homes' television." Finally, another provision states that the license reserves to the grantor "all rights and uses in and to said musical composition, except those herein granted to the Licensee."

Although the language of the license permits the recording and copying of the movie with the musical composition in it, in any manner, medium, or form, nothing in the express language of the license authorizes distribution of the copies to the public by sale or rental. One of the separate rights of copyright, as enumerated in section 106 of the Copyright Act, is the right "to distribute copies or phonorecords of the copyrighted work to the public by sale or other transfer of ownership, or by rental, lease, or lending." Thus, the right to distribute copies of the videocassettes by sale or rental remained with the grantor under the *reservation of rights provision*.[16]

It is obvious that the distribution of videocassettes through sale and rental to the general public for viewing in their homes does not fit within the purpose of the license grant that is restricted to showing in theatres and other similar public places. Paramount argues that distribution of videocassettes for showing in private homes is the equivalent of "exhibition by means of television." The words of that paragraph must be tortured to expand the limited right granted by that section to an entirely different means of making that film available to the general public—the distribution of individual videocassettes to the general public for private "performances" in their homes. Television and videocassette display have very little in common besides the fact that a conventional monitor of a television set may be used both to receive television signals and to exhibit a videocassette. Moreover,

the license must be construed in accordance with the purpose underlying federal copyright law.

Courts have repeatedly stated that the Copyright Act was "intended definitively to grant valuable, enforceable rights to authors and publishers to afford greater encouragement to the production of literary works of lasting benefit to the world." We would frustrate the purposes of the Act were we to construe this license—with its limiting language—as granting a right in a medium that had not been introduced to the domestic market at the time the parties entered into the agreement.

We hold that the license did not give Paramount the right to use the composition in connection with video-cassette production and distribution of the film "Medium Cool." The district court's award of summary judgment in favor of Paramount is REVERSED.

Case Highlights

- In determining the scope of the grant clause, courts will examine any relevant terms of the license for guidance.
- The Copyright Act reserves all rights, whether or not they existed at the time of the creation of the work, to the creator of the work (copyright owner).
- Expanding a license grant to include the application of the licensed property to a medium that had not been developed at the time of the execution of the license would frustrate the purpose of the Copyright Act (protecting the rights of the creator of works).

Review of Typical License Agreement

The typical license agreement begins with a **preamble** that identifies the parties and the nature of the agreement. The generic licensing agreement will have a number of recitals and a definitions section. The **recitals** are statements of facts pertaining to the parties and the nature of the transaction. They often list the rights being transferred by the licensor. Any untruthful recitals can become the basis for lawsuits asserting breach of warranty or misrepresentation. Because of this, the licensor should verify the status of all its trademarks, copyrights, and patents, along with any patents pending. Definitions explain the meaning of general and technical terms, such as "exclusive" license or "net" sales. Because of differences in language and culture, definitions take on added significance in an international transfer agreement. Extra care should be taken in defining terms in the definition section of an international transfer agreement.

---

16.   See discussion of the reservation of rights clause on page 493.

A number of contract provisions are found in most generic intellectual property licensing agreements.[17] Refer to Doing Business Internationally: License Clause Examples when reading this section. In conjunction with this analysis, keep in mind the following questions:

- What issues are being dealt with in the clauses?
- What issues are being neglected?
- How can the clauses be rewritten for added clarity?
- How can the clauses be made more pro-licensor or pro-licensee?

The materials in this chapter and in Chapter Thirteen 13 address these concerns. The sample clauses provided here are brief and need to be customized for a particular transfer. They are generally written from the perspective of the licensor.

In a **licensed territory clause**, the licensor defines the appropriate sales areas or distribution channels for the licensed product.[18] If the license grants "exclusive" territory, then the licensor cannot grant other licensees the right to sell in the exclusive territory. The licensor will generally want to restrict the licensee's ability to sell products outside the licensed territory.

Another clause that attempts to limit the licensee's ability to compete against the licensor is the **covenant not to compete**. Much like U.S. courts, foreign courts highly scrutinize and limit these types of clauses. The licensor often requires such a clause to prevent the licensee from competing against it after the termination of the license agreement. Article 2596 of the Italian Civil Code typifies the restrictions placed on covenant not to compete clauses. Such clauses are required to be in writing, be limited to a certain geographical area and activity, and not exceed five years in duration. Italian courts generally favor the licensee in narrowing the restrictions pertaining to area and activity.

INTERNATIONAL

In the **reservation of rights clause**, the licensor reserves any intellectual property or contractual rights not expressly transferred by the license. This reservation should always be inserted, even if the license is intended to be exclusive.

The improvements or grant-back clause attempts to reserve to the licensor future rights to any subsequent improvements the licensee makes in the licensed property.[19] The licensor will want to stipulate that any modifications or improvements made by the licensee shall revert to the ownership of the licensor. The clause often requires the licensee to assign to the licensor all its rights to any modification.

The grant-back clause should deal with two distinct issues: (1) ownership of the improvement and (2) the right to use the improvement. A one-sided, nonreciprocal grant-back clause, which gives all rights, title, and the right to use any improvements made by the licensee to the licensor, is not enforceable in some countries.[20] Depending on the country, providing reciprocity or sharing within the grant-back clause may be necessary. As a result, any subsequent improvements made by the licensor may also have to be made available to the licensee.

---

17. See Tucker, "Checklist for Due Diligence." Tucker lists the following clauses as those that should be clearly written: exclusivity or nonexclusivity of license; assignability or nonassignability of license by licensee; rights or cross-licenses for improvements made by licensee or licensor; rights of licensor to terminate license; licensor's warranty of title; confidentiality provision; posttransaction requirements, e.g., due diligence in returning know-how; details for consulting and support necessary to transfer the technology; and a dispute resolution clause.
18. "Licensed product" refers to the products to be produced or sold under the authority granted by the agreement.
19. "Licensed property" refers to the intellectual property rights being transferred under the agreement.
20. In contrast, nonreciprocal grant-back clauses are generally enforced in U.S. courts unless they are held to violate the antitrust laws. See, e.g., *Santa Fe Pomeroy, Inc. v. P. & Z. Co.*, 569 F.2d 1084 (9th Cir. 1978).

One technique for increasing the likelihood that a grant-back clause will be enforced is providing reasonable compensation for the grant back of the licensee's improvements. In addition, the grant back can be made nonexclusive. A nonexclusive grant back allows the licensee to continue to use its improvement within the geographical scope of the license.

The licensee generally pays for the licensed property through royalty payments. The **royalty clause** is negotiated along three general parameters: the royalty rate, guaranteed consideration, and momentum royalties. A generic royalty rate is based on a percentage of sales, determined in one of two ways. The use of *gross sales* generally favors the licensor, and using *net sales* favors the licensee. The distinction between gross sales and net sales is not always significant, however. A net sales definition that allows very few offsets or deductions will result in a figure very close to a gross sales amount. Conversely, a gross sales definition that allows a liberal number of deductions can result in a figure that resembles a net sales figure.

Guaranteed consideration may be a schedule of payments, including a good faith deposit, not connected with sales by the licensee. Guaranteed consideration ensures that the licensee will make reasonable efforts to produce, market, and sell the licensed product. The licensee should negotiate that any advance payments ("guaranteed consideration") are to be credited against future royalties.

Momentum royalties are paid when the licensee sells other product lines. These royalties are based on increases in the licensee's overall sales due to the introduction of the new licensed product. This notion is similar to the rental provisions in commercial leases that base the rent on the tenant's sales. Momentum royalties are negotiated in licenses of marquee products that are likely to draw customers to the licensee's other products.

One type of license that creates special problems in drafting the royalty clause is the **hybrid license**. A hybrid license includes patent use rights, along with some other intellectual property right not of the same type or duration as the patent being licensed. One issue that has been disputed is whether the license may provide for payment of royalties past the expiration of the patent.

The U.S. Supreme Court in *Brulotte v. Thys Company*[21] held that an agreement that extends royalties beyond the life of a patent is per se unenforceable. Therefore, royalty clauses must be carefully written to avoid invalidation because of postexpiration royalties. To avoid invalidation of royalties in a hybrid license, the license should expressly and realistically allocate royalties between the patent right and the other rights. If the license provides for the use of a number of patents or different intellectual property rights, then it should provide for a reduction in royalties upon the expiration of one of the intellectual property rights.

A **best efforts clause** is vital in an exclusive license agreement, because the licensor depends on the licensee to generate sales and royalty payments. Courts have inferred such clauses in exclusive licenses,[22] but the licensor is better served by negotiating a specific best efforts clause with appropriate timetables, benchmarks for production and sales, the amount of monies to be expended by the licensee, and minimum royalty levels. The best efforts clause should provide "penalties" for failure to reach stated goals and for the termination of the license.

---

21.   379 U.S. 29 (1964).
22.   The court in *Shearing v. Iolab Corp.*, 712 F. Supp. 1446 (D. Nev. 1989), extended the implication of best efforts to "improvements." "It is normal and customary in an exclusive licensing arrangement to imply an obligation of the licensee to use its reasonable best efforts with respect to improvements on the invention for which the licensee purchased rights." Ibid. at 1455.

Another purpose of the best efforts clause is to prevent a foreign country from issuing a compulsory license on the licensor's technology to a third party. Some countries require a patent owner to use the patent or lose the exclusive rights to exploit that patent in the country. Granting a license to a national of that country usually satisfies these so-called working requirements. The threat remains, however, that if the licensee fails to work the license the licensor (rights owner) will lose its rights to other parties through the government's granting of compulsory licenses. A best efforts clause should therefore require that the licensee "work" the license.

Transparency in the licensing relationship should be provided for in the license agreement through the insertion of accounting and record-keeping requirements. The accounting provision should call for periodic statements of sales and the royalty payments, as well as some form of certification and audit of the sales amount and royalties owing by an independent accounting firm. The licensor should

---

License Clause Examples

Doing Business Internationally

License Territory

The licensee may not distribute or sell licensed product to grocery stores or super-markets. The licensee may sell the licensed product through the following channels of distribution: gift stores, souvenir stores, and theme parks.

Reservation of Rights

Licensor reserves all rights not expressly conveyed to the licensee. Licensor reserves the right to grant any such reserved rights to other licensees.

Royalties

"Guaranteed Consideration": The sum of $_____ is payable upon the following dates: _____. These sums as set forth above shall be applied against such royalties as become due to the licensor. No part of such Guaranteed Consideration shall be repayable to the licensee. "Royalty Payments": The Royalty Rate shall be five percent (5%). The licensee shall pay a sum equal to the Royalty Rate of all "net sales" by the licensee of the Licensed Product. The term "net sales" shall mean gross invoice price billed customers, less actual quantity discounts and actual returns (actual returns not to exceed 5%).

Accounting

Within thirty (30) days of the end of every month, the licensee shall furnish to licensor complete and accurate statements certified by an officer of the licensee with respect to the number of units sold, their gross sale prices, and itemized deductions from the gross sale prices.

Record-Keeping

The licensee shall maintain and preserve records pertaining to the license at its principal place of business for at least two years following termination or expiration of the license term or any renewals. These records shall include, without limitation, purchase orders, inventory records, invoices, correspondence, banking and financial records, and any other records pertaining to the Licensed Products. Such records and accounts shall be available for inspection and audit at any time during or after the license term during reasonable business hours and upon at least three (business) days written notice by the licensor.

Indemnification

The licensor shall indemnify the licensee and hold it harmless from any loss or

continued

License Clause Examples (*continued*)

liability arising out of any claims brought against the licensee by reason of the breach by the licensor of the warranties and representations stated within this License Agreement. The licensee shall indemnify the licensor and hold it harmless from any loss or liability arising out of any claims brought against the licensor by reason of the licensee's breach of any provision of this License Agreement including any unauthorized use by the licensee, any improper use of trademarks, copyright, patent, design, or process not specifically granted or approved by the licensor, any noncompliance by the licensee with laws or regulations, and for any defects attributable to the licensee's production of the Licensed Products.

Quality Control

The licensee agrees to strictly comply and maintain compliance with the quality standards, specifications, and rights of approval of the licensor in respect to any and all usage of the Licensed Property. Any modification of the Licensed Product must be submitted in advance for the licensor's written approval as if it were a new product.

Licensor Warranties

The licensor warrants that it possesses the right to license the Licensed Products, including any patents, copyrights, or trademarks, in accordance with the provisions of this License Agreement. The making of this License Agreement does not violate any agreements or rights of any other person, firm, or corporation.

Licensee Warranties

The licensee warrants that it will not harm, misuse, or bring in disrepute the Licensed Property. The licensee will manufacture, sell, and distribute the Licensed Products in accordance with the terms of this License Agreement, and in compliance with applicable government regulations and industry standards. Upon reasonable notice, the licensee shall permit the licensor to inspect testing records and procedures with respect to the production and sales of the Licensed Products for compliance with applicable quality standards provided in this License Agreement and for compliance with applicable governmental, regulatory, industry, and certification standards.

Confidentiality

The licensee warrants that it will use its best efforts to maintain the confidential nature of all proprietary information and to prevent unauthorized access, reproduction, use, or disclosure of that information. It will restrict access to key employees on a need-to-know basis. In furtherance of this obligation it shall: (a) maintain all copyright notice, trademark notice, and other proprietary markings and (b) not copy or reproduce the proprietary information except as authorized under this agreement.

Copyright and Trademark Protection (Infringement)

The licensee shall cause to be imprinted on each Licensed Product sold under the License Agreement, and on all advertising, promotional, and packaging material, the proper copyright notices and trademarks as instructed by the licensor. The licensee shall promptly notify the licensor in writing of any infringements by others of the Licensed Property. The licensee shall assist the licensor at the licensor's expense in the procurement, protection, and maintenance of the licensor's rights in the Licensed Property. The licensee agrees to cooperate with the licensor in connection with any claims or suits relating to infringements on the licensor's property rights.

continued

License Clause Examples (*continued*)

Assignment and Sublicensing

This License Agreement is personal to the licensee. The licensee shall not sublicense, franchise, assign, or delegate to third parties any of the rights acquired hereunder. Neither this License Agreement nor any of the rights hereunder shall be sold, transferred, or assigned by the licensee.

Independent Contractor

The licensee is an independent company. Nothing in this agreement is intended to represent that the licensee is to act as an agent or partner of the licensor. The licensee is not granted any rights or authority, express or implied, to bind the licensor in any manner.

Termination

The licensor shall have the right to terminate this Agreement without prejudice to any rights which it may have upon the occur-

rence of any of the following events: (1) The licensee fails to deliver or maintain the required product liability insurance policy, (2) The licensee becomes delinquent on any payments due under this License Agreement, (3) The licensee fails to provide access to the premises or access to the records required to be maintained under this License Agreement, (4) The licensee fails to comply with applicable laws, regulations, or industry standards, (5) The licensee does not commence in good faith to manufacture, distribute, or sell the Licensed Products throughout the Licensed Territory, and (6) The licensee delivers or sells Licensed Products outside the Licensed Territory or knowingly sells Licensed Products to a third party who the licensee knows intends to or reasonably should suspect intends to sell or deliver[23] such Licensed Products outside the Licensed Territory.[24]

---

demand payment of interest on delinquent payments and assurances in case of default. The licensee should be required to retain records pertaining to the license and the sales of the licensed products.

Indemnification clauses work both ways between the licensor and the licensee. The licensee generally wants to be indemnified for any liability stemming from the licensor's title or product warranties. The licensor seeks to be indemnified for any misuse of the license by the licensee.

The licensor should also protect itself through a **disclaimer** or limitation of warranty applicable against the ultimate purchaser or consumer. The licensor will want to insert language requiring the licensee to obtain customer signatures agreeing to the disclaimer or limitation.

The best way to prevent liability for product defects is to require the implementation of quality control measures in the production process. The licensor will want to ensure that the licensee complies with quality standards and specifications. All product modifications should require the licensor's prior approval.

http://

"Licensing Digital Information"— warranties and indemnification: **http://www. library.yale.edu/ ~llicense/warrgen. shtml** and **http:// www. library.yale.edu/ ~llicense/warrcls.shtml.**

---

23. The "reason to know" concept would place a requirement of "due diligence" upon the licensee to investigate a third-party purchaser, especially in large-volume sales.
24. This provision is clearly aimed at preventing a gray market problem for the licensor. In higher-cost products, it would also be prudent to cap the number of units to be produced under the license and the number of units that can be sold to any one purchaser. The overall cap could be determined by calculating an estimate of sales expected for the licensed territory based on its demographics or based on sales figures of similar territories.

The licensor should also negotiate inspection rights and access to the licensee's testing records and reports. In conjunction with the indemnification clause the licensor should require the licensee to obtain a product liability insurance policy.

Warranties and **representations** made in the license are important in liability claims for negligence, misrepresentation, or breach of warranty. The licensor should insert language specifying that only express warranties are enforceable. To further prevent the implication of warranties, the licensor should insert pertinent **negations**. An example of negation includes the statement that the license does not grant the licensee the rights to any subsequent know-how or to additional technical support or information. Another negation may preclude the licensee from using the licensor's trade name. The problem with negation clauses is that a licensor with a U.S. patent cannot be assured that the negation clause will be enforced under foreign law.

The licensee should be required to take all reasonable measures to protect the licensor's copyrights and trademarks. The licensee's duties in this area, detailed in an **infringement clause**, should include affixing the appropriate marks and patent numbers[25] to the products being licensed. The court in *Yarway Corporation v. Eur-Control USA, Inc.*,[26] held that a licensor has a cause of action for damages resulting from the licensee's failure to mark goods as required under the license.

In the area of third-party infringement, the infringement clause places a number of obligations on the licensee. First, the licensee should be made to act as the "eyes and ears" of the licensor because it is in the best position to detect infringement. The licensee should be required to notify the licensor promptly of acts of infringement by third parties. Second, the licensee's cooperation in any infringement proceeding should be required under the transfer agreement.

The license agreement should also detail the rights and duties of the respective parties in the event that a third party sues the licensee for infringement. The most licensee-friendly provision would be an express covenant requiring the licensor to defend and indemnify the licensee against such claims. A licensor-friendly provision, on the other hand, would exclude or limit the licensor's obligations regarding such infringement claims.

One compromise would be to grant the licensee the right to indemnification but limit the indemnity. The licensor can limit its exposure by declaring the option to pay a specified amount to the licensee and terminate the license instead of defending the licensee against an infringement claim. In *Hewlett-Packard Company v. Bausch & Lomb Inc.*,[27] the court upheld such limited indemnification. Another compromise would be an agreement to share the costs of defending any third-party infringement claims.[28]

The licensee's obtaining the right in the license agreement to sue third parties for patent infringement pertaining to the licensed property is not sufficient to give it standing to sue under U.S. patent law. The licensor-patentee must be joined to any such infringement suit.[29] U.S. patent law authorizes infringement actions only

---

25. Failure to affix the patent numbers may prevent the licensor from collecting damages for past infringements unless notice was provided to the infringer and the infringement continued unabated. See 35 U.S.C. § 287(a) (2000).
26. 775 F.2d 268 (Fed. Cir. 1985).
27. 909 F.2d 1464 (Fed. Cir. 1990).
28. See, e.g., *Ortho Pharm. Corp. v. Genetics Institute, Inc.*, 52 F.3d 1026, *cert. denied*, 516 U.S. 907 (1995).
29. See, e.g., *Yarway Corp. v. Eur-Control USA, Inc.*, 775 F.2d 258 (Fed. Cir. 1985) (licensee brought claim of infringement against a holder of another patent under the "doctrine of equivalence," where a patent is filed for something that is the design equivalent of another patented device but in which minor changes have been made in order to avoid an infringement claim).

by the patentee-licensor[30] or the assignee of a patent.[31] The rationale for this rule is that a license grants to the licensee merely a privilege that protects it from a claim of infringement by the owner. The licensee has no property interest in the patent. As such, "the patent owner may tolerate infringers, and in such a case no right of the patent licensee is violated."[32]

The U.S. Supreme Court has long recognized that the patent owner is an indispensable party to an infringement suit.[33] Courts have also held that granting the licensee the right to sue for third-party infringement does not create any obligation on the part of the licensor to assist in such actions. In this regard, it has been held: "There is no implied agreement by a licensor to protect the licensee by suing. In the absence of a covenant to protect the licensee against infringers there is no obligation on the part of the licensor to do so."[34] Courts have, however, recognized the right of an exclusive licensee to demand that the licensor join him as an involuntary plaintiff to an infringement action.[35] This is an indirect way to give the exclusive licensee standing to sue for infringement by third parties of the licensed intellectual property rights of the licensor.

To best protect its interests, the licensee should negotiate a clause requiring the licensor to either sue third-party infringers or to join the licensee in any such actions. The clause should state the repercussions for the licensor's failing to fulfill its obligations under the clause. For example, it may authorize the licensee to sue on behalf of the licensor and require the licensor to reimburse the licensee for the costs of the litigation or provide a discontinuance of the payment of royalty fees. The *Fieldturf, Inc. v. Southwest Recreational Industries, Inc.* case that follows reviews the law regarding whether a licensee has standing to sue for the infringement of intellectual property rights included in its license.

Given the result in the *Fieldturf* case, the parties to the intellectual property licensing agreement must specifically identify the rights that are being transferred to the licensee. If the licensor intends to relinquish the rights to protect the patent and

Fieldturf, Inc. v. Southwest Recreational Industries, Inc.

357 F.3d 1266 (Fed. Cir. 2004)

Mayer, Chief Judge. Fieldturf, Inc. and Fieldturf International, Inc. ("Fieldturf"), the purported exclusive licensees of U.S. Patent No. 4,337,283 ("'283 patent"), appeal the judgment of the United States District Court for the Eastern District of Kentucky dismissing claims alleging violations of the Sherman Antitrust Act, the Lanham Act, the Kentucky Consumer Protection Act, the

common law of Kentucky, and, most relevant here, the Patent Act.

Fieldturf and Southwest Recreational Industries, Inc. ("Southwest") are competitors in the artificial turf market, a market primarily geared toward providing an alternative to natural grass for playing surfaces for athletic games. Southwest manufactures and markets at least two

---

30. See 35 U.S.C. § 281 (2000).

31. See, e.g., *Water Technologies Corp., v. Calco, Ltd.*, 576 F. Supp. 767 (N.D. Ill. 1983). Section 261 of Title 35 of the U.S. Code authorizes such actions by "assignees, grantees, and successors."

32. *Western Electric Co. v. Pacent Reproducer Corp*, 42 F.2d 116, 118 (2d Cir. 1930).

33. See *Waterman v. Mackenzie*, 138 U.S. 252 (1891).

34. *Water Technologies Corp. v. Calco Ltd.*, 576 F. Supp. 767, 772 (N.D.Ill. 1983); see also *Martin v. New Trinidad Lake Asphalt Co.*, 255 F. 93 (1919); *Heidelberg Brewing Co. v North American Service Co.*, 26 F.Supp. 342 (E.D.Ky. 1939).

35. See *Independent Wireless Telegraph Co. v. Radio Corporation of America*, 269 U.S. 459 (1926); see also *Rite-Hite Corp. v. Kelly*, 56 F.3d 1538 (Fed. Cir. 1995), *cert. denied*, 516 U.S. 867 (1995)).

types of artificial turf systems: AstroTurf (R), a carpet-like turf system, and AstroPlay (R), a filled-turf system that more closely resembles the appearance of natural grass. Fieldturf manufactures and markets its own filled-turf system, FieldTurf (R), which is the commercial embodiment of the '283 patent.

Fieldturf claims to possess the right to manufacture and market the embodiment of the '283 patent by virtue of a series of transactions. On December 29, 1980, approximately a year and a half before the '283 patent issued, Frederick T. Haas, Jr., the inventor of record, assigned all rights to the pending patent to a Louisiana partnership, Mod-Sod Sports Surfaces ("MSSS"), owned by Haas and his three children. On March 1, 1994, Mod-Sod Sports Surfaces, Inc. ("MSSSI"), the purported successor in form to MSSS, and Haas entered into an exclusive licensing agreement with SynTenniCo, Inc. ("STC") and Jean Prevost. This gave STC and Prevost the exclusive right to manufacture and market commercial embodiments of the '283 patent, save a limited right retained by MSSSI and Haas to "develop, display, commercialize, and market" to potential customers. In that same document, MSSSI and Haas also retained the right of first refusal to enforce the '283 patent against infringers, enabling STC and Prevost to bring suit only after MSSSI and Haas had declined to do so. On June 19, 1998, Prevost, on behalf of STC, and Haas, on behalf of MSSSI, entered into another exclusive licensing agreement that was deemed to "cancel and replace" the 1994 agreement. On August 17, 1999, STC assigned its rights in the licensing agreement to Fieldturf Holdings, Inc., which in turn assigned its rights to Fieldturf, Inc. on September 14, 1999.

For years Fieldturf and its predecessors in interest consistently have maintained that AstroPlay (R), when installed with infill comprising both sand and rubber, infringes the '283 patent. For example, STC filed suit against Southwest in 1998, in part to prohibit Southwest from manufacturing and marketing AstroPlay® with rubber and sand infill for the duration of the '283 patent. As part of a settlement stemming from that litigation, Southwest agreed to market AstroPlay® with an infill consisting entirely of resilient particles and no sand. In this case, Fieldturf alleges that Southwest resumed infringement of the '283 patent immediately following the execution of the settlement agreement "by manufacturing its AstroPlay (R) grasslike carpets in the United States and then shipping that material overseas, with the understanding that the infringing sand-and-rubber infill would be added abroad." On summary judgment, the district court ruled against Fieldturf on all counts, and

Fieldturf appeals. Southwest asserts that Fieldturf lacks standing to enforce the' '283 patent, and the patent claim should be dismissed for that reason.

Before we can address the merits, we must decide whether Fieldturf has standing to sue on the patent. To bring an action for patent infringement, a party must be either the patentee, a successor in title to the patentee, or an exclusive licensee of the patent at issue. A purported exclusive licensee must show that he possesses "all substantial rights in the patent." Lacking all substantial rights, he may bring suit against third parties only as a coplaintiff with the patentee or a successor in title to the patentee. Otherwise, he lacks standing.

Fieldturf asserts that it has standing to enforce the' '283 patent against third parties not because it is the patentee or a successor in title to the patentee, but rather because it is an exclusive licensee. Consequently, it has the burden to provide evidence endowing it with all substantial rights in the patent. Fieldturf says the 1998 letter agreement between its predecessor in interest STC and MSSSI satisfies this burden.

To determine whether an agreement conveys all substantial rights in the patent, we must ascertain the intention of the parties and examine the substance of what was granted by the agreement. The 1998 agreement is straightforward. In one page, STC, Prevost, MSSSI, and Haas agreed only that in exchange for consideration proffered to MSSSI and Haas, STC "would continue to be the exclusive licensee of the '283 patent except for golf products"; that in exchange for that same consideration, "all past obligations owing by STC and Prevost to MSSSI and Haas would be waived and released"; that STC and Jean Prevost would have a right of first refusal to license any future invention related to the '283 patent; and that the 1998 agreement would "cancel and replace the exclusive license agreement signed in 1994." Notably, the 1998 agreement did not address, as the 1994 licensing agreement had, whether MSSSI and Haas, or STC and Prevost, would have the right to enforce the '283 patent against infringers. The 1998 agreement also did not address, as the 1994 agreement had, whether MSSSI and Haas would retain the right to "develop, display, commercialize, and market" embodiments of the '283 patent. These omissions are significant.

First, without granting STC the right to enforce the patent, either explicitly or impliedly, the document conveys no more than a bare license. See *State Contracting & Eng'g Corp. v. Condotte Am., Inc.*, 346 F.3d 1057, 1062 (Fed. Cir. 2003) (the failure to transfer the right to sue infringers distinguishes a license from an assignment, and the former "generally affords the licensee no right to sue for infringement"); see also *Prima Tek II, L.L.C. v.*

A-Roo Co., 222 F.3d 1372, 1379–80 (Fed. Cir. 2000) ("In evaluating whether a particular license agreement transfers all substantial rights in a patent to the licensee, we pay particular attention to whether the agreement conveys in full the right to exclude others from making, using and selling the patented invention in the exclusive territory."). Second, the licensor's retention of a limited right to develop and market the patented invention indicates that the licensee failed to acquire all substantial rights. Because the 1998 agreement is silent with respect to these important considerations, it is nothing more than an exclusive licensing agreement that fails to convey all substantial interest in the '283 patent. Therefore, Fieldturf lacks standing, and the claim must be dismissed.

> ## Case Highlights
>
> - To bring an action for patent infringement in its own name without the participation of the patentee, a licensee must possess all substantive rights in and to the patent. The failure of an agreement to grant a patentee the right to enforce a patent, either explicitly or impliedly, conveys no more than a bare license.
> - To determine whether an agreement conveys all substantive rights in a patent, a court must ascertain the intention of the parties and examine the substance of what was granted by the agreement.

sue for infringement, this intent should be expressly manifested in the agreement. For example, the agreement could provide that the licensor is transferring its "entire right, title, and interest" in the intellectual property to the licensee, including the right to sue for "past and present infringement." Such language has been held to defeat the allegation of an implied retention of the right to sue by the licensor and permit the licensee to initiate an infringement action on its own behalf.[36]

Another important clause that should be carefully drafted is the termination or default clause. Specific termination rights are detailed in a **termination clause**. The termination clause provides the specific grounds upon which the licensor may unilaterally terminate the license agreement. The licensor should make it clear that the termination of the license also requires the licensee to terminate any sublicenses. Under some foreign laws, the unilateral termination of a licensing agreement by the licensor may require the payment of an indemnity. For this reason, the licensor should specify the types of causes that can automatically trigger a termination without indemnity. For example, the failure of the licensee to meet prescribed sales quotas could result in an automatic termination of the license.

The *Bruce v. Weekly World News, Inc.* case that follows examines the remedies available for infringement of intellectual property rights, in this case, a copyright. The case also examines the various methods used to calculate damage awards in such cases.

Some of the other standard clauses found in licensing agreements include no-challenge, assignment, and independent contractor clauses. Validity or **no-challenge clauses** prohibit the licensee from challenging the exclusiveness or validity of the licensor's intellectual property rights. Such clauses are generally valid in the United States[37] but may be invalid in some foreign countries,[38] where they are considered illegal restrictive trade practices. They are also often prohibited in the transfer-of-technology codes of developing countries.

http://

"Licensing Digital Information"—duration, renewal, and termination: **http:// www. library.yale.edu/ ~llicense/termgen.sht ml** and **http://www. library.yale.edu/~, llicense/termcls.shtml.**

36.   See *State Contracting & Engineering Corp. v. Condotte America, Inc.*, 346 F.3d 1057, 1062–63 (Fed. Cir. 2003).
37.   See, e.g., *Bausch & Lomb, Inc. v. Barnes-Hind/Hydrocurve*, 796 F.2d 443 (Fed. Cir. 1986), *cert. denied*, 484 U.S. 823 (1987); *Shearing v. Iolab Corp.*, 712 F. Supp. 1446 (D. Nev. 1989).
38.   See Chapter Thirteen.

The license agreement should define the licensee's rights to assign or sublicense its license rights through the insertion of **assignment** and **sublicensing clauses**. The license generally provides that the license cannot be sublicensed or assigned.

The **nonpartnership and independent contractor clause** makes clear that the licensee is not acting as an agent or partner of the licensor, hopefully preventing the licensor from being held liable for the actions of the licensee under agency law principles.[39]

Finally, all licenses, especially international ones, should provide for dispute resolution. This is done through choice of law and forum selection provisions. Given the

---

Bruce v. Weekly World News, Inc.

150 F. Supp.2d (D. Mass. 2001)

Stearns, District Court Judge. In March of 1992, Douglas Bruce, a freelance professional photographer, snapped a picture of presidential candidate Bill Clinton in a characteristically affable pose, gripping the hand of an unidentified Secret Service agent. Bruce consigned the photo to the Picture Group, a now defunct Rhode Island photo stock agency. In June of 1992, Susan Chappell, a photo editor at Weekly World News ("WWN"), telephoned Jonathan Yonan, a Picture Group researcher, seeking a photo of Clinton shaking hands. Yonan supplied Chappel with Bruce's photo among others. Chappell told Yonan that she liked the photo and that WWN wanted to manipulate it by cropping the background and superimposing the image of the Space Alien to give the appearance of a tete-a-tete with Clinton. The Space Alien is an extraterrestrial visitor with an avid, if unorthodox, interest in American politics. His exploits have been chronicled for over ten years in the pages of WWN. The Alien first came to WWN's attention in October of 1990 when he was captured by FBI paranormal agents. WWN carried an exclusive account of the Alien's escape a month later. Over the next year, the Alien (to the dismay of an apparently oblivious Secret Service) posed with President George Bush and Reform Party presidential candidate Ross Perot. He then shocked the political world by endorsing Bill Clinton in the 1992 presidential race. Although the Alien facilitated First Lady Hillary Clinton's adoption of an Alien Baby in 1993, in 1994 he became disaffected with the Clintons. After conferring with Rush Limbaugh and Newt Gingrich, he backed Senator Robert Dole in the 1996 presidential contest. The Alien has since remained dependably Republican. He endorsed George W. Bush's presidential bid in early 2000.

After Bruce agreed to the alteration of the photo, Yonan called Chappell to discuss a licensing fee. To Yonan's surprise, Chappell told him that WWN had already retouched the photo. When Yonan and Chappell were unable to agree on a fee, Chappell asked about a buyout. Yonan, unable to reach Bruce, consulted with his superior at the Picture Group, and then quoted Chappell a price of $3,000. Chappell balked and no agreement was reached. A week or two later, Yonan was "shocked" to see the retouched photo on the front page of the August 11, 1992 edition of WWN, paired with the headline "Alien Backs Clinton!" Yonan immediately sent a bill for $500 to WWN, which WWN paid. By contract, half of the fee was shared with Bruce. Until the Picture Group ceased doing business in 1993, Yonan sent a bill each time he saw the retouched photo in WWN. Bruce received a total of $1,775 in fees as a result.

In 1994, while browsing through a current issue of WWN, Bruce saw an advertisement for a t-shirt reproducing the "Alien Backs Clinton" cover. In addition, "Alien Backs Clinton" t-shirts were shown along with other merchandise on WWN's Internet site.

Bruce consulted a New York attorney who sent WWN a cease and desist letter. WWN responded with an offer to pay $500 for a general release, which was not accepted. The matter remained dormant until 1998, when Bruce retained his present attorney.

A prevailing plaintiff in a copyright action is entitled to recover his actual damages, calculated as a measure of the profits lost as a result of the infringement. In addition to actual damages, a plaintiff may also force the infringer to disgorge any nonduplicative profits earned as a result of the copyright violation, that is, "any profits attributable to the infringement that are not taken into account in computing the actual damages." 17 U.S.C. § 504(b). In the context of infringer's profits, the plaintiff must meet

---

39.   The expanded liability of a partner or employee under some foreign laws was detailed in Chapter Twelve.

only a minimal burden of proof in order to trigger a rebuttable presumption that the defendant's revenues are entirely attributable to the infringement; the burden then shifts to the defendant to demonstrate what portion of its revenues represent profits, and what portion of its profits are not traceable to the infringement.

Bruce seeks to recover profits earned by WWN during the infringement period from: (1) sales of the "Alien Backs Clinton" and "Senators Are Aliens" t-shirts; (2) sales of display advertising; and (3) newsstand and subscription sales. As for the t-shirt sales, WWN concedes the right, if not the amount, of Bruce's recovery. During the infringement period, 1,817 units of the "Alien Backs Clinton" t-shirt and 2,207 units of an associated "Senators Are Aliens" t-shirt were sold at $12.95 each, plus a $3.00 surcharge for postage and handling. The average cost of the t-shirts to WWN was roughly $4.25 per unit, yielding a net profit on the Clinton t-shirt of $15,807.90, and on the Senators t-shirt of $19,200.90, for a total of $35,008.80.

Bruce insists that he is entitled to the entire $35,000. Section 504(b) of the Copyright Act, however, permits a defendant to show that some or all of the profits earned from the infringement are "attributable to factors other than the copyrighted work." The defendant can attempt to show that consumers would have purchased its product even without the infringing element. Alternatively, the defendant may show that the existence and amount of its profits are not the natural and probable consequences of the infringement alone, but are also the result of other factors which either add intrinsic value to the product or have independent promotional value.

WWN chose the second route by offering evidence of the conception and development of the Alien character, its resonance with WWN's readership, and its role in a running spoof of American politics. WWN makes the point, and it is a valid one, that no market existed among its readers for a generic photograph of President Clinton shaking hands. Rather its readers were attracted by the oddity of a photograph of President Clinton fraternizing with an alien being. The Alien's "star" power clearly added cachet to Bruce's photo. Under the circumstances, a fair award should recognize that the composite value of the photo is derived from the collaboration of its two "stars," the one facilitated by Bruce, and the other by WWN. This can be achieved by apportioning the Clinton t-shirt profits equally between the two authors, resulting in an award to Bruce of $7,903.95. Applying the same formula to the Senators t-shirt, on which Bruce's photo is one of thirteen represented, a fair apportionment results in an award to Bruce of one-half of one-thirteenth of the profits, or $738.50.

Bruce's estimate of WWN's advertising revenues during the infringement period teeters on speculation. According to Bruce, he took three "representative" issues of WWN, and to the "best of his ability," valued the ads in each issue according to WWN's published rates. Using this method, the plaintiff should recover $511 for all 259 issues that were published during the period whether or not his picture was used, or $132,349 ($511 × 259 issues). Bruce's figures as to WWN's earnings from newsstand and subscription sales are based on WWN's Publishers Statement of Sales. Bruce multiplied the totals of the sales reported during the infringing period by the relevant cover and subscription prices to arrive at gross circulation revenues of $2,765,461, from which amount, using the same formula that he applied to advertising revenues, Bruce calculates he is owed $43,210.

Even if Bruce's estimates are acceptable approximations, the claim for profits from advertising revenues and subscription sales founders on the lack of any showing of a causal relationship between the alleged profits and the misappropriation of the photo. In establishing the infringer's gain, the assessment in every case must be guided by the rule that the statute awards the plaintiff only the "profits of the infringer *that are attributable to the infringement.*" 17 U.S.C. § 504(b). The suggestion that the "Alien Backs Clinton" photo (as opposed to the Alien character) acquired totemic significance as an alter-ego for WWN is not borne out by the evidence. While WWN published the photo often, it did so in comparatively microscopic doses, and as only one of many photos featuring the Alien in the company of various political figures.

Bruce ultimately relies on the literal wording of the Copyright Act that "the copyright owner is required to present proof only of the infringer's gross revenue," thereby shifting to the infringer the burden of proving its "deductible expenses and the elements of profit attributable to factors other than the copyrighted work." 17 U.S.C. § 504(b). We think the term "gross revenue" under the statute means gross revenue reasonably related to the infringement, not unrelated revenues. The statutory term "infringer's gross revenue" should not be construed so broadly as to include revenue from lines of business that were unrelated to the act of infringement.

Bruce identifies his categories of actual damages as follows: (1) four unauthorized editorial uses of the "Alien Backs Clinton" photo; (2) repeated use of the photo on the two infringing t-shirts; (3) 188 unauthorized uses in advertisements for the sale of the t-shirts; (4) forty-eight uses in WWN's subscription advertisements; and (5) sixteen months of unauthorized home page and inside use of the photo on WWN's internet site.

As to the editorial use of the retouched photo in the May 28, 1996 issue of WWN, I conclude that an inflation adjusted fee of $300, based on Bruce's share of the original fee paid to the Picture Group, is a fair award. With respect to the use of the photo on the "Alien Backs Clinton" and the "Senators Are Aliens" t-shirts, I accept the congruent testimony of plaintiffs and defendant's expert witnesses that a fee of $500 for the Clinton use and

$300 for the Senators use is appropriate. The use of the photo in advertising the sale of the t-shirts, I deem non-compensable, as the ads, by generating sales, also generated the profits damages that Bruce has been awarded. I conclude that an award of $1,200 (or $75 a month), a sum more or less consistent with the expert testimony at trial, is appropriate for the unauthorized use of the photo on WWN's website. (Both experts agreed that because the internet is a separate medium, industry practice requires a separate license for internet use). Finally, both experts agreed that a multiple would be applied to fees charged where an infringer made unlicensed use of a photo. Jacobsen pegged the multiple at three, although he conceded that in a case of outright theft, Blaney's suggestion of a multiple of ten would be appropriate. As this case lies somewhere in the middle of the spectrum between a negligent and a larcenous appropriation, I will use a multiple of five to enhance the award of actual damages.

For the foregoing reasons, judgment shall enter for plaintiff Douglas Bruce in the sum of $20,142.45. WWN is hereby ENJOINED from any further sale or distribution of the "Alien Backs Clinton" or "Senators Are Aliens" t-shirts without first obtaining the permission of the plaintiff.

Case Update

On appeal, the U.S. Court of Appeals for the First Circuit increased the damages award relating to licensing fees for the photograph from $1,100 to $5,500. In all aspects, the appellate court affirmed the decision of the district court.

Case Highlights

- A prevailing plaintiff in a copyright action is entitled to recover actual damages, calculated as a measure of the profits lost as a result of the infringement as well as nonduplicative profits earned as a result of the copyright violation and not taken into account in computing actual damages. In any event, the plaintiff is entitled to only those profits of the infringer that are attributable to the infringement.

- There is a rebuttable presumption that an infringer's revenues are entirely attributable to the infringement. The burden thus falls on the infringer to demonstrate what portion of its revenues are not traceable to the infringement. One method the infringer may use to meet this burden is to show that the existence and amount of its profits are not the consequence of the infringement but the result of other factors that either add intrinsic value to the product or have independent promotional value.

- Plaintiffs in copyright infringement cases may recover damages as a result of a wide variety of uses of the protected image, including publication in newspapers, apparel, advertisements (including those seeking subscribers), and reproduction of the image on the Internet.

unevenness of foreign intellectual property law protections, a U.S. licensor should designate U.S. intellectual property law as the law applicable to any dispute.[40]

The most common forum selection clause in international licensing agreements is the arbitration clause.[41] To increase the likelihood of obtaining and enforcing a foreign arbitral award, the place of arbitration should be in a country that has ratified the Convention on the Recognition and Enforcement of Foreign Arbitral Awards ("New York Convention") and where the courts do not have a reputation for interfering with arbitration proceedings.

Law of Licensing

In the event that a licensing agreement fails to resolve a disputed issue, what body of law will be used to interpret and enforce the contract? In the United States, there are two options: the Uniform Commercial Code (UCC) and the Convention for the

---

40.   However, a host country court is unlikely to honor a choice of law that avoids its competition, intellectual property transfer, consumer protection, and termination laws.

41.   For the specifics of negotiating an adequate arbitration clause, see Chapter Four.

International Sale of Goods (CISG). For these laws to apply, the crucial determination is whether the transaction—the sale of software or license of information—is considered to be a sale of goods.

The **mixed sale** articles of the UCC and CISG indicate that software sale contracts are to be considered sales of goods unless a "preponderant part of the obligations of the party who furnishes the goods consists in the supply of labor or other services" or the purchaser supplies "a substantial part of the materials."[42] Under the UCC, "off the shelf" software has been determined to be a good.[43] One view of the licensing of information sees the license as a "sale" of the exclusive rights to use that particular copy of the information. In other cases, however, information licensing seems to fall outside the concept of a "sale of goods" because the licensor retains title to the intellectual property rights and the proprietary information. In such a case, the common law of contracts remains the operative body of law in the United States.

Uniform Computer Information Transactions Act

The most recent attempt at creating a series of rules to apply to licensing transactions is the **Uniform Computer Information Transactions Act (UCITA)**. A brief review of its provisions is useful for two reasons. First, UCITA highlights some of the issues that confront licensors of IPR, technology, and information. Second, its provisions can be used in negotiating and writing a license agreement.[44]

UCITA is a model law adopted in July 1999 in Virginia and Maryland to regulate the formation, performance, and enforcement of computer information transactions. Section 104 of UCITA allows parties to opt in or out of UCITA coverage in mixed transactions. It states that "the parties may agree that UCITA governs the transaction in whole or part." **Computer information transactions** are defined as agreements "to create, modify, transfer, or license computer information or informational rights."[45]

UCITA expressly states that a license of such rights is not a good for purposes of Article 2 of the UCC. Therefore, in states that enact UCITA, it will preempt Article 2 of the UCC in transactions involving the licensing of goods. In UCITA, information is defined as "data, text, images, sounds, mask works or computer programs, including collections and compilations."[46] License means "a contract that authorizes access to, or use, distribution, performance, modification, or reproduction of information or informational rights, but expressly limits the access or uses authorized or expressly grants fewer than all rights in the information, whether or not the transferee has title to a licensed copy."[47] Contracts included within the definition of license include access contracts,[48] lease of a computer program, and a consignment of a copy. Therefore, the licensing of software or intellectual property rights relating

http://

Full text of UCITA:
**http://arl.cni.org/
info/frn/copy/
ucitapg.html.**

---

42. CISG art. 3.

43. See, e.g., *ProCD, Inc. v. Zeidenberg*, 86 F.3d 1447, 1450 (7th Cir. 1996); *i.Lan Systems, Inc. v. NetScout Service Level Corp.*, 183 F. Supp.2d 328, 332 (D. Mass. 2002). But see Lorin Brennan, *Why Article 2 Cannot Apply to Software Transactions, PLI Patents, Copyrights, Trademarks and Literary Property Course Handbook Series* (2001) (demonstrating the judicial trend away from viewing "off the shelf" software as a good subject to Article 2).

44. UCITA will be reviewed again in Chapter Fifteen in conjunction with the "shrinkwrap contract."

45. UCITA, § 102(a)(11).

46. Ibid. § 102(a)(35).

47. Ibid.

48. *Access contract* is defined as "a contract to obtain by electronic means access to, or information from, an information processing system." UCITA § 102(a)(1).

to computer information would be covered under UCITA. UCITA provides rules to deal with legal issues pertaining to contract formation, authentication, duties and rights of performance, breach, remedies, and warranties.

Formation of a License Contract

The formation or offer-acceptance rules in UCITA mimic those found in Article 2 of the Uniform Commercial Code (UCC),[49] with some noticeable variations. The dispatch or **mailbox rule** is modified for electronic acceptance. Under UCITA § 203(4)(A), an electronic acceptance is effective upon receipt. This leads to the question of what is receipt in an electronic transaction. If the electronic acceptance is by e-mail, is the acceptance received when the message is posted in the offeror's e-mailbox or when the offeror opens his or her e-mail? Another model law, the **Uniform Electronic Transactions Act (UETA)**, states that the acceptance is received when it enters the e-mailbox. Section 15 (b)(1-2) of UETA states that "an electronic record is received when it enters an information processing system that the recipient has designated or uses for the purpose of receiving electronic records or information of the type sent and from which the recipient is able to retrieve the electronic record and it is in a form capable of being processed by that system." The obtaining and giving of an e-mail address satisfies the designation requirement.

The next issue raised by UCITA is whether a license contract can be formed between computers or between a human and a computer. UCITA answers in the affirmative on both questions. It defines **electronic agent** as "a computer program, or electronic or other automated means, used by a person to initiate an action, or to respond to electronic messages or performances, on the person's behalf without review or action by an individual at the time of the action or response to the message or performance."[50] Therefore, placing an order through a web page or voice mail creates a contract. Is an offeree able to make a counteroffer when dealing with an electronic agent? The answer to this question is no, because electronic agents are unable to evaluate and respond to counteroffers or to acceptances with additional terms. The counteroffer will be construed as an acceptance if it causes the electronic agent to perform, provide benefits, or allow the use or access that is the subject of the counteroffer.

UCITA handles the "battle of the forms" scenario differently than does UCC Article 2.[51] In the traditional battle of the forms scenario,[52] a contract is formed between merchants, even if the varying or additional terms in the acceptance materially alter the offer. In such a situation, a contract is formed without the additional terms. Under UCITA, additional terms in the acceptance that materially alter the offer prevent the formation of a contract, unless one is formed through the subsequent conduct of the parties.

If the varying terms do not materially alter the offer, then a contract is formed under both UCITA and the UCC. Under UCC Article 2, nonmaterial additional terms in the acceptance become part of the contract. In contrast, UCITA distinguishes between nonmaterial varying terms that conflict with terms in the offer and

---

49. See Chapter Eight.
50. UCITA § 102(a)(27). "Electronic message" is defined as "a record or display that is stored, generated, or transmitted by electronic means for the purpose of communication to another person or electronic agent."
51. See the "battle of forms" discussion in Chapter Eight.
52. See UCC § 2-207.

additional nonmaterial terms that do not conflict with express terms in the offer. In the latter situation, the additional terms do become a part of the contract unless the offeror gives notice of objection within a reasonable period of time.[53] If the nonmaterial additional terms in the acceptance conflict with terms in the offer, then the terms of the offer control.

UCITA also addresses a number of issues pertaining to the writing requirements of the **statute of frauds**. First, it expands the statute of frauds' notion of a "writing" and "signature" to include **electronic records** and **authentication**. An electronic record is information that is inscribed on a tangible medium or that is stored in an electronic or other medium and is retrievable in perceivable form. To "authenticate" or sign an electronic record is to execute or adopt an electronic symbol, sound message, or process referring to, attached to, included in, or logically associated or linked with that record.[54] One method of proving an authentication is through an attribution procedure. This usually entails the use of algorithms or other codes, identifying words or number, encryption, callback, or other acknowledgement.[55]

Foreign Transfer Restrictions

Some foreign countries attempt to regulate or restrict the transfer of technology and intellectual property to its nationals. However, government regulation of licensing agreements is evolving as rapidly as the technology they seek to regulate. One example in this regard is EU Regulation 772/2004, which was adopted in April 2004. This regulation is otherwise known as the **Technology Transfer Block Exemption Regulation (TTBER)**. The other example is regulations adopted by the People's Republic of China in order to bring its intellectual property laws into conformance with the TRIPS Agreement required by China's accession to the WTO. These regulations exemplify restrictions placed upon technology licensing agreements in developed countries and countries with transitional economies. They also demonstrate the rapidly changing nature of regulations applicable to technology transfer agreements. As a result, parties must carefully scrutinize the applicable regulatory environment prior to the initiation of contract negotiations.

INTERNATIONAL

The European Union's TTBER

The EU's TTBER was adopted on April 27, 2004, as part of a larger effort to reform EU competition law.[56] TTBER replaces the previous regulatory regime adopted in 1996, which required parties to notify and seek clearance from the European Commission concerning agreements that restrict competition. TTBER implements Articles 81(1) and 81(3) of the EC Treaty, both of which are applicable to technology licensing agreements. Article 81(1) generally prohibits agreements that restrict competition and trade between member states. Article 81(3) provides an exception to this general prohibition for restrictive agreements whose positive effects on competition

http://
European Patent Office: **http://www. european-patent-office. org/index.en.php.**

INTERNATIONAL

---

53.   See UCITA § 204(d)(2) (Acceptance with Varying Terms).
54.   See ibid. § 201(a)(1) (Formal Requirements).
55.   UCITA § 201(a) sets a licensing fee or price amount of $5,000 before a writing is required. In contrast, Article 2 of the UCC requires a writing for all sale of goods valued at $500.
56.   The following discussion was adapted from Bird & Bird, *The New EU Technology Licensing Rules* (2004).

outweigh their negative effects. TTBER identifies pro-competitive effects as improved economic efficiency, reduction in the duplication of research and development, the strengthening of research and development incentives and innovation, and the generation of product market competition.

Contemporaneous with the enactment of TTBER was the adoption of **Technology Transfer Guidelines (TT Guidelines)**. The TT Guidelines provide greater explanation of TTBER and also a framework for analysis of agreements that are not within TTBER's definition of "technology transfer agreements." Agreements that are not within this definition are not automatically invalid. Rather, these agreements and provisions are analyzed by using the TT Guidelines.

TTBER is applicable to "technology transfer agreements." These agreements are defined to include "a patent licensing agreement, a know-how licensing agreement, a software copyright licensing agreement or a mixed patent, know-how or software copyright licensing agreement."[57] As a result, trademark and copyright licenses are within TTBER only if they are ancillary to patent, know-how, or copyright licensing agreements.

Unlike its predecessor, which listed acceptable (white list) and unacceptable (black list) clauses for inclusion in technology licensing agreements, TTBER adopts an economics-based approach that attempts to determine the impact of the provisions of the licensing agreements on relevant markets. This focus on economics is evident in two aspects. Initially, TTBER distinguishes between agreements between parties ("competitive undertakings") that compete in the relevant technology or product market and noncompeting parties. Second, TTBER grants a "safe harbor" exemption to competitive undertakings and noncompeting parties based on market share. TTBER grants an exemption to technology transfer agreements between "competitive undertakings" if their combined market share does not exceed 20 percent of the relevant technology and product market.[58] This percentage increases to 30 percent for noncompetitors.[59]

Obviously, the calculation of market share is crucial to the validity of technology transfer agreements within the scope of TTBER. Article 8 of TTBER provides that market share shall be calculated on the basis of sales value data. If such data are not available, the calculation of market share shall be based on estimates of "other reliable market information, including market sales volume."[60] Calculations of market share are based on the preceding calendar year. If the parties' market share rises above the thresholds established by TTBER, the exemption for the technology transfer agreement remains in place nonetheless for two consecutive calendar years following the year the threshold was exceeded.

Despite the market share of the parties, TTBER contains a list of so-called **hardcore restrictions** that serve to exclude the entire agreement from exemption to the EU's competition laws.[61] There are separate lists of hard-core restrictions in agreements between competitors and noncompeting parties. Between competitors, the following restrictions are prohibited:

- restrictions of a party's ability to freely set prices
- output limitations

http://

"Recent Developments in EU Competition Law": **http://www. cov.com/publications/ download/oid6006/ 244.pdf.** This article includes checklists for reviewing vertical and horizontal agreements for conformity to EU competition law. It also provides information on popular clauses such as resale price maintenance, territorial, and noncompetition clauses.

---

57. EU Regulation 772/2004, art. 1(1)(b) (2004). The term *know-how* refers to nonpatented information that is secret, substantial (significant and useful), and identified. See ibid. art. 1(1)(i)(i-iii).
58. See ibid. art. 3(1).
59. See ibid. art. 3(2).
60. Ibid. art. 8(1).
61. See ibid. art. 4.

- the allocation of markets and customers except under seven enumerated conditions
- restrictions on the ability of the licensee to exploit its own technology or engage in research and development

Between noncompeting parties, the following restrictions are prohibited:

- restrictions on price setting (although maximum or recommended sales prices are permitted)
- territorial and customer restrictions upon passive sales (except under six enumerated circumstances)

In addition, TTBER provides a list of **excluded restrictions**.[62] The inclusion of these provisions in a technology transfer agreement will be evaluated by utilizing the TT Guidelines. Such provisions do not disqualify the remainder of the agreement from the benefit of TTBER's exemptions. TTBER defines excluded restrictions to include:

- exclusive grant-back obligations with respect to "severable improvement" (defined as "an improvement that can be exploited without infringing the licensed technology")[63]
- no-challenge clauses with respect to the validity of the intellectual property rights
- with respect to noncompetitors, restrictions on the licensee's ability to exploit its own technology or on the parties' ability to conduct research and development

Another difference between TTBER and its predecessor is the identity of the party responsible for making the determination with respect to the impact of the licensing agreement on the marketplace. TTBER replaces the process whereby parties sought the guidance and approval of the European Commission with a self-assessment policy. The parties themselves are now responsible for determining the legality of their agreement and its specific provisions. TTBER grants businesses until March 31, 2006, to conform their agreements to its requirements. Agreements failing to conform to TTBER by this date may be declared null and void and subject the parties to claims for damages and fines. Although the self-assessment feature promotes greater freedom of contract and resultant flexibility in negotiating and drafting license agreements, it also presents significant challenges for businesses. Licensors and licensees are now required to engage in complex legal and economic analyses, including definitions of markets and market shares. Incorrect assessments of these factors may result in the nullification of the agreement in question, liability for damages arising from resultant civil actions, and fines. Thus, the greater freedoms arising from TTBER result in greater risks to businesses.

Finally, TTBER strips the European Commission of its exclusive jurisdiction with respect to compliance with Articles 81(1) and 81(3). The commission no longer possesses the authority to review licensing agreements, grant exemptions, and negotiate provisions with the parties. Rather, enforcement of Articles 81(1) and 81(3) resides with EU competition authorities, as well as the national courts of the member states.

---

62.   See ibid. art. 5.
63.   Ibid. art. 1(n).

Regulations of the People's Republic of China

China has recently revised its intellectual property licensing laws.[64] These revisions were undertaken to conform China's intellectual property laws to the requirements of WTO's TRIPS Agreement. They became effective on January 1, 2002. These revisions consist of four separate regulations. First are the **Regulations on Administration of Technology Imports and Exports (State Council Regulation)** and the **Administrative Measures on Registration of Technology Import and Export Contracts (Registration Measures).** These regulations are applicable to contracts for "technology import and export." Uncertainty with respect to the definition of contracts within the scope of the regulation was subsequently resolved by the **Ministry of Foreign Trade and Economic Cooperation (MOFCOM)** in its Notice on Strengthening the Administration of Technology Import Contracts, issued in February 2002. The notice listed twelve separate contracts to which the State Council Regulation is applicable, including patent transfer, application and implementation contracts, know-how license and transfer contracts, computer software license contracts, and trademark license or transfer contracts to the extent they contain provisions relating to patents and know-how. Trademark licenses not containing associated patents or know-how are governed by a separate trademark law with different rights, restrictions, and procedures.

The State Council Regulation classifies technologies into three categories: prohibited, restricted, and unrestricted for import or export. Any technology not designated as either "prohibited" or "restricted" is deemed to be "unrestricted." Technology classified as "prohibited" may not be imported or exported, and contracts providing for such are null and void. Contracts for the importation or exportation of "restricted" technologies must be approved by the government prior to becoming effective. "Unrestricted" technology contracts must be registered with MOFCOM as well as the local commission on foreign trade and economic relations but are effective nonetheless upon execution. These contracts no longer require government approval, as provided in the former regulatory regime. Registration procedures are set forth in considerable detail in the Registration Measures. Contracts that are subsequently amended or renewed must also be reregistered.

The State Council Regulation also repeals several contractual limitations from the former regulatory regime. The term of the contract may now be set by the parties themselves and is not subject to the ten-year maximum term in the previous law. Furthermore, unlike the previous rules, licensees may be prohibited from using the technology after the expiration of the contract term. The time limit for maintaining confidentiality with respect to the technology or know-how may also exceed the duration of the contract.

However, freedom of contract pursuant to the State Council Regulation is not absolute. Several provisions are prohibited from inclusion in technology import contracts: (1) requiring the licensee to pay for or undertake obligations with respect to patents that have been declared invalid or have expired; (2) restricting the licensee from improving the licensed technology or using such improvements

---

64. The following discussion was adapted from Howard Chao, Aihong Yu & Todd Bissett, "Regulations Governing Technology Transfer to and from China."

(improvements belonging to the improving party); (3) restricting the licensee from acquiring similar technology from other sources; (4) unreasonably restricting sources of raw materials, components, or equipment; (5) unreasonably restricting output, variety, or prices of products produced by the licensee; (6) unreasonably restricting export channels for the licensee's products; and (7) imposing require-ments not closely related to the technology, such as the purchase of unnecessary technology, raw materials, products, equipment, or services. It is uncertain whether such provisions invalidate the entire contract or only the provisions themselves. However, existing contracts previously approved by the government but inconsis-tent with the new regulations remain valid. In addition, the licensor must certify that it is the "lawful holder, licensor or assignor" of the technology and that the technology is "complete, error-free, valid and capable of accomplishing" its repre-sented capabilities.

The third and fourth regulations are **Administrative Measures on Import of Prohibited or Restricted Technology** and **Administrative Measures for Export-Prohibited Technology** or Export-Restricted Technology (collectively the MOFCOM Regulations). With respect to imports, these regulations empower MOFCOM and the State Economics and Trade Commission to approve or deny applications based on whether the technology endangers national security or public interests, life or health, or the environment. Imports consistent with national economic and social development policies are favored. With respect to export contracts, the exporter must receive a license with respect to "restricted technology" from MOFCOM and the Ministry of Science and Technology. Parties dissatisfied with the application of any of the new regulations may apply for administrative review before MOFCOM or initiate appropriate action in the People's Court.

Foreign Registration and Approval

A considerable number of countries, mainly less developed and emerging-economy countries, require some form of government approval of transfer or licensing con-tracts. These transfer regulations can generally be categorized into two types. First, some require a formal government approval (**approval-type transfer law**) before the agreement becomes valid. The Chinese regulatory regime with respect to "restricted" technology falls into this category. Second, there are regulations that require the registration of the agreement (**registration-type transfer law**) with a gov-ernment agency after its execution. Current Chinese regulations with respect to "unrestricted" technology fall into this category. This less onerous type of registra-tion regulation should not be discounted in importance. In some countries, such as Russia, failure to register the agreement may result in severe penalties, including the cancellation of the license or contract. Unfortunately, many licensors do not bother to register their intellectual property rights in the host country or leave it to a licensee to register. The danger of such an approach is illustrated in the follow-ing excerpt on trademark counterfeiting in Brazil:

One of the main causes of trademark counterfeiting in Brazil is a result of association or representation agreements between foreign and local companies. In most cases, when a for-eign company enters into an agreement with a local company to represent its products in Brazil and this foreign company is not registered in the country, the first step taken by the local company is to request that the trademark be registered in its name. In this situation, the

Brazilian company is justified in acting in this manner to protect the trademark which it represents in Brazil. When this is done in good faith, the Brazilian company subsequently transfers the trademark to the company which it represents and this company then licenses it back to the Brazilian company. In many cases, as the foreign company does not immediately request the transfer, not even as a condition in negotiating the representation, such fact is not usually noticed. If there is a misunderstanding between the two for use by the local company of the trademark registration which it registered in its own name, the local company can use this to its advantage in pressuring the foreign company in negotiations.[65]

In those countries that require approval, the type of approval varies in scope and application. In some countries, approval is required only for certain types of technology transfers. When approval is required, the parties have to submit documentation that usually includes the draft agreement, financial statements, and proof of ownership of the technology. Provisions of the contract are generally reviewed with a view to protecting the national licensee. In such circumstances, "Governmental bodies charged with reviewing technology transfer agreements often refer to statutory lists of objectionable business practices (clauses) which must be excised from any agreement as a condition of approval."[66] The most troublesome clauses under approval schemes are those that allow the licensor overly restrictive control, such as one-sided grant-back clauses, and dispute resolution and choice of law clauses that remove all disputes from the host country's courts.

KEY TERMS

Administrative Measures on Import of Prohibited or Restricted Technology
Administrative Measures for Export-Prohibited Technology
Administrative Measures on Registration of Technology Import and Export Contracts (Registration Measures)
Antitrust Enforcement Guidelines for International Operations
approval-type transfer law
assignment clause
authentication
best efforts clause
choice of law clause
computer information transactions
confidentiality clause
covenant not to compete

disclaimer
due diligence
duration clause
electronic agent
electronic records
excluded restrictions
exclusive license
fields of use
forum selection clause
grant-back clause
grant clause
gray market problem
guaranteed consideration
hard-core restrictions
hybrid license
implied license
indemnification clauses
inducement to infringe
infringement clause

key personnel
licensed territory clause
licensee
licensor
mailbox rule
Ministry of Foreign Trade and Economic Cooperation (MOFCOM)
mixed sale
momentum royalties
most-favored license
negations
no-challenge clause
nonpartnership and independent contractor clause
opinion letter
patent misuse
preamble
recitals

65. Mauro J. G. Arruda & Pinheiro Neto-Advogados, "Trademark Counterfeiting and Unfair Competition in Brazil," 21 *Comparative Law Yearbook of International Business* 205, 208 (1999).
66. Alan S. Gutterman, "Regulation of Foreign Inbound Technology Transfers and Direct Investments," 7 *International Quarterly* 599, 600 (1995).

registration
registration-type transfer law
Regulations on Administration of
   Technology Imports and Exports
   (State Council Regulation)
representations
reservation of rights clause
royalties
royalty clause

statute of frauds
sublicensing clause
Tariff Act of 1930
technology transfer
Technology Transfer Block
   Exemption Regulation (TTBER)
Technology Transfer Guidelines
   (TT Guidelines)
technology transfer laws

termination clause
trade names
Uniform Computer Information
   Transactions Act (UCITA)
Uniform Electronic Transactions
   Act (UETA)
U.S. Copyright Act
warranties

CHAPTER PROBLEMS

1. McCoy hired Mitsuboshi to make and supply shrimp knives covered by McCoy's patent and trademarks. When Mitsuboshi produced the knives, McCoy refused to pay for them. Mitsuboshi resold the knives to Admiral Craft. McCoy sued Mitsuboshi Cutlery, Inc., for patent and trademark infringement in violation of U.S. federal law. Is Mitsuboshi guilty of patent and trademark infringement? *McCoy v. Mitsuboshi Cutlery, Inc.*, 67 F.3d 917 (Fed. Cir. 1995), *cert. denied*, 516 U.S. 1174 (1996).

2. "Green River" is the trademark under which Sethness-Greenleaf, Inc., sold to bottlers a soft drink, according to a formula that was Sethness-Greenleaf's trade secret. Sethness-Greenleaf sold the Green River business, including the trademark and the trade secret, to Green River Corp. The purchase price was to be paid in installments. When the price was paid in full, the secret formula for the manufacture of Green River beverage and syrup, till then held in escrow, would be released to Green River Corp. Green River Corp. fell behind in its payments, and Sethness-Greenleaf declared a default, stopped supplying Green River Corp., and demanded the return of the formula from the escrow agent. Unwilling to stop doing business under the "Green River" name, Green River Corp. procured a green soft drink from another producer and sold it under the "Green River" name, precipitating this suit by Sethness-Greenleaf. Green River Corp. counterclaimed that it is not guilty of infringement because Sethness-Greenleaf's failure to continue to supply it with the product was a breach of contract. Assuming that Sethness-Greenleaf is guilty of breach, is Green River Corp. correct? *Green River Bottling Co. v. Green River Corp.*, 997 F.2d 359 (7th Cir. 1993).

3. Your company produces a high-quality component product that is used in the manufacture of high-scale stereo equipment. The component is manufactured through the use of special software developed by your company. The component and associated software are covered under a number of U.S. patents and copyrights. In addition, your company holds a federally registered trademark that stereo manufacturers are allowed to use in the marketing of their products. Your company has made it a strategic goal to expand the production and sale of the components overseas. It is considering licensing the technology in exchange for royalties; however, it wants to protect the market of its domestic manufacturers. What steps should be taken to maximize protection of the company's intellectual property rights? What license terms should your company insist upon?

4. The premier German manufacturer of compact disks decides to export its disks to markets in Eastern Europe. Because of the economic realities of these emerging-economy countries, the manufacturer is forced to sell the disks at a lower price than it sells them for in the German market in order to obtain market share. A wily entrepreneur purchases large quantities of the exported disks and reimports them into the higher priced German market. What is the likely result under European Union law of the German manufacturer's attempt to prevent the importation of the disks?

5. Your technology company, based in the United States, holds a number of patents on Internet-related business applications. It is negotiating a licensing agreement with a major French innovator of Internet technologies. Your company's standard grant-back clause provides a nonreciprocal reversion of all licensee improvements. The French company is refusing to execute the agreement because of the one-sided nature of the clause. Your job is to draft a fair grant-back clause that provides reciprocal rights to the licensor and licensee. How should such a clause deal with the questions of ownership and use? What will be the status of these rights after the termination of the license?

INTERNET EXERCISES

1. Review the Web site of the Cyberspace Law Institute for information on how the Internet interrelates with intellectual property law: **http://www.cli.org.**

2. Review the Web site of the U.S. Copyright Office to determine the requirements for registering a copyright license: **http://www.copyright.gov/.**

3. You own publishing rights to a catalog of popular "do-it-yourself" home and electronic repair manuals. Distributors located in Germany, Italy, and India have approached you. What are your concerns regarding licensing the copyrights to these manuals? Develop a due diligence checklist to use in the negotiation of these licenses. How would your checklist differ for the three countries? Examples of such a checklist can be found at **http://www.publaw.com/acq.html** and **http://www. marklitwak.com/pub_list.htm.** As part of your due diligence research, be sure to see USTR's "priority watch" list and "watch list" noted in Internet Exercise Three at the end of Chapter Thirteen.

The advance of telecommunications, the advent of the information age, the growth of the Internet, and the exploitation of knowledge as a commodity has accelerated the trend toward purely electronic transactions. According to the U.S. Department of Commerce, retail electronic commerce (e-commerce) sales in the United States totaled $15.5 billion in the first quarter of 2004.[1] This total represented 1.9 percent of all retail sales during the quarter. By comparison, during the first quarter of 2000, e-commerce totaled $5.6 billion or 0.8 percent of all retail sales in the United States during that period of time. Despite this growth, the United States ranked sixth in the world behind Denmark, the United Kingdom, Sweden, Finland, and Norway in a study of the prevalence of e-commerce published by *The Economist* in April 2004.

The potential of Internet marketing and sales makes it one of the most important developments in the international marketplace. However, the Internet is within the public domain and, as such, poses risks that have yet to be fully resolved. The scope of e-commerce

Chapter 15

Electronic Business Transactions

EXHIBIT 15.1 *Electronic Transactions (Percentage of All Transactions)*[2]

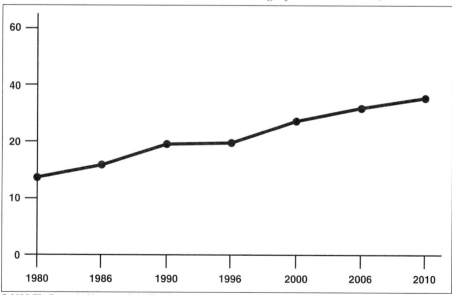

1. See U.S. Department of Commerce, "Retail E-Commerce Sales in First Quarter 2004 Were $15.5 Billion, Up 28.1 Percent from First Quarter 2003, Census Bureau Reports" (May 21, 2004).
2. Source: Adapted from "Technology in Finance," *The Economist* 4 (Oct. 26, 1996).

issues is wide, and these issues touch upon many different areas of business and law. A 1999 EU Council Resolution entitled the "Consumer Dimension of the Information Society" outlined as follows the areas of concern for consumers and the conditions needed for e-commerce to thrive:

- accessibility and affordability
- consumer-friendliness of equipment and applications, as well as the skills necessary to use them
- transparency, including quantity and quality of information
- fair marketing practices, offers, and contract terms
- protection of children against unsuitable content
- security of payment systems, including electronic signature
- which legal rules are applicable to consumer transactions in the new environment, as regards both the choice of law and practicability of existing provisions
- the apportionment of responsibility and liability
- privacy and the protection of personal data
- access to efficient systems of redress and dispute resolution
- information technology as a tool for information and education[3]

http://

Cyberspace law for nonlawyers (Electronic Frontier Foundation): **http://www.eff.org/.** An excellent general Web site for explanations of many of the issues in this chapter. Topics covered include copyright law, trademark law, privacy law, content regulation, dispute resolution, free speech, and libel law.

This chapter surveys a number of these issues, including personal jurisdiction, protection of personal information, and content regulation.

Despite the technological nature of the Internet, the same issues that are found in more traditional international business transactions apply to Internet transactions.[4] For example, does an Internet transaction bring the seller within the scope of the laws and jurisdiction of the country of the buyer? Will the seller be liable for foreign income, sales, and value-added taxes?[5] Is the transaction subject to foreign consumer protection laws?

This chapter begins with a brief look at how questions of jurisdiction are being applied to electronic transactions. It then focuses directly on issues specific to e-commerce, such as trademark infringement, privacy, and database protection. After a brief introduction to electronic data interchange, an analysis of legal issues related to e-contracting is undertaken. The chapter concludes with the topic of e-commerce ethics.

Personal Jurisdiction

A key issue for the person making an initial foray into e-commerce is whether that person will become amenable to the jurisdiction of a foreign court. Does adver-

3. European Union Council Resolution 1999/C 23/01, art. 4(a-k) (Jan. 19, 1999).
4. For problems of applying traditional contract and commercial law constructs to electronic commerce and cyberspace, see Allison Brantley, Shanin T. Farmer, Bacardi L. Jackson, Jana Krupoff, Steven S. List, and Ellen Ray, "The Legal Web of Wireless Transactions," 29 *Rutgers Computer and Technology Law Journal* 53 (2003); Juanda Lowder Daniel, "Electronic Contracting Under the 2003 Revisions to Article 2 of the Uniform Commercial Code: Clarification or Chaos?" 20 *Santa Clara Computer and High Technology Law Journal* 319 (2004); Valerie Watnick, "The Electronic Formation of Contracts and the Common Law 'Mailbox Rule,'" 56 *Baylor Law Review* 175 (2004).
5. The evolving law and issues relating to Internet taxation are beyond the scope of this chapter. See generally Blair Downey, "E-Commerce: The Taxman's Nemesis," 2 *Asper Review of International Business and Trade Law* 53 (2002); "E-Commerce: Mom & Pop v. Dot Com: A Disparity in Taxation Based on How You Shop?" *2002 Duke Law and Technology Review* 28 (2002); John E. Sununu, "The Taxation of Internet Commerce," 39 *Harvard Journal on Legislation* 325 (2002).

tising or processing an order over the Internet provide enough contact with the jurisdiction of the other party to give a foreign court personal jurisdiction? Jurisdiction means the power of a court to hear a case. **Personal jurisdiction** was defined in Chapter Four as the power of the court over the people appearing before it. Under the Due Process Clause of the U.S. Constitution, a court gains personal jurisdiction over a defendant only if the defendant has had **minimum contacts** with the forum state.

Chapter Four discussed the two types of personal jurisdiction exercised by U.S. courts. General personal jurisdiction permits courts to adjudicate any claims against a defendant, regardless of whether the claims have any relation to the selected forum. For a court to exercise general jurisdiction, the defendant must have a significant presence in the forum. This presence may be premised on nationality, residence, or organization within the United States or consist of a "continuous and systematic presence" within the forum.[6] Specific personal jurisdiction permits courts to adjudicate only those claims arising from or relating to the defendant's activities in the forum. For a court to exercise specific personal jurisdiction, the defendant must purposefully avail itself of the protections of the forum.[7] Merely placing a product into the stream of commerce is insufficient unless the defendant designed the product specifically for the forum, provided regular advice to customers in the forum, or maintained a distributor in the forum. Furthermore, the forum must be a reasonable location for the conduct of the litigation. To determine the reasonableness of the forum, the court must balance the burden on the defendant, the interest of the selected forum in resolving the dispute, the plaintiff's interest in obtaining relief in the forum, and applicable foreign policy concerns, if any, arising from the exercise of jurisdiction.

A number of U.S. court decisions offer guidance regarding personal jurisdiction in Internet transactions. These cases are noteworthy for their efforts to apply traditional rules with respect to personal jurisdiction to the Internet. For example, with respect to general jurisdiction, the District of Columbia Court of Appeals held in *Gorman v. Ameritrade Holding Corp.* that the mere use of the Internet for transactions did not justify the abandonment of previous jurisdictional rules or the creation of new rules. Rather, the ability of Ameritrade's customers to open accounts, transfer funds, buy and sell securities, borrow money, and pay on line, when combined with the company's extensive electronic presence, constituted a "continuous and systematic presence" in the District of Columbia.

An example of specific jurisdiction with respect to the Internet is found in the opinion of the Sixth Circuit Court of Appeals in *CompuServe, Inc. v. Patterson*. The *CompuServe* case introduces the method of licensing software known as **shareware**. In that case, Patterson in effect used CompuServe as a distribution center to market his software. Because Patterson had chosen to transmit his product from Texas to CompuServe's system in Ohio, and because that system provided access to his product to others to whom he advertised and sold his product, the court concluded that Patterson purposefully availed himself of the privilege of doing business in Ohio.

http://
Chicago-Kent Law School Project on Internet Jurisdiction: **http://www.kentlaw.edu/cyberlaw/.**

---

6. See *Helicopteros Nacionales de Colombia v. Hall*, 466 U.S. 408.
7. See *Asahi Metal Industries v. Superior Court*, 480 U.S. 102 (1987).

Gorman v. Ameritrade Holding Corp.

293 F.3d 506 (D.C. Cir. 2002)

Garland, Circuit Court Judge. In this case, we consider whether the courts of the District of Columbia may assert general jurisdiction over a defendant that is "doing business" in the District through the medium of the Internet. We hold that they may, although we ultimately affirm dismissal of the complaint because service of process on the defendant was insufficient.

Plaintiff David Gorman is the sole proprietor of Cashbackrealty.com, a real estate broker with its principal place of business in McLean, Virginia. Defendant Ameritrade Holding Corporation is a securities broker-dealer licensed in the District of Columbia with its principal place of business in Omaha, Nebraska. Ameritrade provides online brokerage services through its Internet site to individuals across the country, including District residents. In November 1999, Ameritrade acquired Freetrade.com, Inc., as well as its Internet domain name, "Freetrade.com." Like Ameritrade, defendant Freetrade has its principal place of business in Omaha. Gorman alleges that he had an agreement with the prior owner of Freetrade, under which Cashbackrealty.com was entitled to a front-page link on the Freetrade.com website. According to Gorman, although Ameritrade assumed the obligations of this agreement when it acquired the Freetrade.com domain name, it refused to provide a front-page link for Cashbackrealty.com.

On June 2, 2000, Gorman filed a complaint in the United States District Court for the District of Columbia, alleging that Ameritrade and Freetrade (hereinafter referred to collectively as "Ameritrade") were in breach of contract for refusing to honor the front-page-link agreement. The district court dismissed Gorman's complaint for lack of personal jurisdiction and insufficiency of service of process. With respect to personal jurisdiction, the court held that a "company that acts to encourage or maximize the use by District of Columbia residents of its website does not establish the necessary' 'minimum contacts' with this forum through Internet accessibility," and does not "operate so continuously and substantially within the District that it is fair to allow anyone to sue the enterprise in the District on any claim, without regard to where the claim arose."

Local courts may exercise so-called "specific jurisdiction" over a person for claims that arise from the person's "transacting any business" in the District. However, because Gorman's breach of contract claim against Ameritrade does not arise out of any business transacted between the parties in the District, this font of jurisdiction is unavailable. District of Columbia law also permits courts to exercise "general jurisdiction" over a foreign corporation as to claims not arising from the corporation's conduct in the District, if the corporation is "doing business" in the District. Under the Due Process Clause, such general jurisdiction over a foreign corporation is only permissible if the defendant's business contacts with the forum district are "continuous and systematic."

In his pleadings below, Gorman contended that Ameritrade "sells securities and provides other online brokerage services to residents of the District of Columbia on a continuous basis," and is therefore "continuously doing business in the District of Columbia." Ameritrade concedes that it engages in "electronic transactions" with District residents, and that "Ameritrade undoubtedly derives revenue from those customers." But Ameritrade maintains that those transactions do not occur in the District of Columbia. Rather, the firm declares, Ameritrade's business is conducted "in the borderless environment of cyberspace."

"Cyberspace," however, is not some mystical incantation capable of warding off the jurisdiction of courts built from bricks and mortar. Just as our traditional notions of personal jurisdiction have proven adaptable to other changes in the national economy, so too are they adaptable to the transformations wrought by the Internet. In the last century, for example, courts held that, depending upon the circumstances, transactions by mail and telephone could be the basis for personal jurisdiction notwithstanding the defendant's lack of physical presence in the forum. There is no logical reason why the same should not be true of transactions accomplished through the use of e-mail or interactive websites. Indeed, application of this precedent is quite natural since much communication over the Internet is still transmitted by ordinary telephone lines. Accordingly, the test that we will apply to determine whether the District has general personal jurisdiction in this case is the traditional one: Were Ameritrade's contacts with the District "continuous and systematic"?

Ameritrade concedes that District residents use its website to engage in electronic transactions with the firm. The firm's customers can open Ameritrade brokerage accounts online; transmit funds to their accounts electronically; and use those accounts to buy and sell securities, to borrow from Ameritrade on margin, and to pay Ameritrade brokerage commissions and interest. Using e-mail and web-posting, Ameritrade transmits electronic confirmations, monthly account statements, and both financial and product information back to its customers. As a result of their electronic interactions, Ameritrade and its District of Columbia customers enter into binding contracts, the customers become the owners of valuable securities, and Ameritrade obtains valuable revenue.

What may serve best to take the mystery out of the process—and to demonstrate that nothing about the Ameritrade website need alter our traditional approach to personal jurisdiction—is the fact that Ameritrade also offers its customers the alternative of accomplishing virtually all of the above-described transactions by ordinary mail or telephone. Indeed, if anything, Ameritrade appears susceptible to application of the "doing business" test in a much more literal way than a traditional brokerage firm. Ameritrade's website allows it to engage in real-time transactions with District of Columbia residents while they sit at their home or office computers in the District of Columbia. And by permitting such transactions to take place 24 hours a day, the site makes it possible for Ameritrade to have contacts with the District of Columbia that are "continuous and systematic" to a degree that traditional foreign corporations can never even approach.

In short, on the record before this court, it is quite possible that, through its website, Ameritrade is doing business in the District of Columbia by continuously and systematically "entering into contracts with residents of a foreign jurisdiction that involve the knowing and repeated transmission of computer files over the Internet." *Zippo Mfg. Co. v. Zippo Dot Com, Inc.*, 952 F. Supp. 1119, 1124 (W.D. Pa. 1997).

Ameritrade is quite wrong in treating "cyberspace" as if it were a kingdom floating in the mysterious ether, immune from the jurisdiction of earthly courts. Nevertheless, in this case Ameritrade is saved from the jurisdiction of the district court by a much more mundane problem: the plaintiff simply failed to serve the corporation properly. For that reason, and for that reason alone, the judgment of the district court is *Affirmed.*

Case Highlights

- Courts may exercise general jurisdiction over a foreign corporation as to claims not arising from the corporation's conduct in the forum if the corporation's business contacts with the forum are "continuous and systematic."
- Evidence of a "continuous and systematic" presence in the forum includes the ability to engage in a wide variety of electronic transactions with the defendant corporation and its transmission of electronic confirmations, statements, and product information back to its customers through electronic mail and web postings.

CompuServe, Inc. v. Patterson
89 F.3d 1257 (6th Cir. 1996)

Brown, Circuit Judge. CompuServe is a computer information service headquartered in Columbus, Ohio. CompuServe operates as an electronic conduit to provide its subscribers computer software products, which may originate either from CompuServe itself or from other parties. Computer software generated and distributed in this manner is, according to CompuServe, often referred to as "shareware." Shareware makes money only through the voluntary compliance of an "end user," that is, another CompuServe subscriber who pays the creator's suggested licensing fee if she uses the software beyond a specified trial period. The "end user" pays that fee directly to CompuServe in Ohio, and CompuServe takes a 15 percent fee for its trouble before remitting the balance to the shareware's creator.

Defendant, Richard Patterson, subscribed to CompuServe, and he had placed items of "shareware" on the CompuServe system for others to use and purchase.

When he became a shareware "provider," Patterson entered into a "Shareware Registration Agreement" (SRA). This Agreement expressly provides that both parties entered into the contract in Ohio, and that it is to "be governed by and construed in accordance with" Ohio law. From 1991 through 1994, Patterson electronically transmitted 32 master software files to CompuServe. Patterson's software product was, apparently, a program designed to help people navigate their way around the larger Internet network. CompuServe began to market a similar product, however, with markings and names that Patterson took to be too similar to his own.

CompuServe filed this declaratory judgment action in the federal district court for the Southern District of Ohio. CompuServe sought, among other things, a declaration that it had not infringed any common law trademarks of Patterson. Patterson responded with a motion to dismiss for lack of personal jurisdiction.

The "purposeful availment" requirement is satisfied when the defendant's contacts with the forum state "creates a 'substantial connection' with the forum State," and when the defendant's conduct and connection are such that he "should reasonably anticipate being haled into court there." Patterson chose to transmit his software from Texas to CompuServe's system in Ohio, myriad others gained access to Patterson's software via that system, and Patterson advertised and sold his product through that system. Moreover, this was a relationship intended to be ongoing in nature; it was not a "one-shot affair."

Finally, because of the unique nature of this case, we deem it important to note what we do not hold. We need not and do not hold that Patterson would be subject to suit in any state where his software was purchased or used; that is not the case before us. We also do not have before us an attempt by another party from a third state to sue Patterson in Ohio for, say, a "computer virus" caused by his software; thus we need not address whether personal jurisdiction could be found on those facts. Finally, we need not and do not hold that CompuServe may sue any regular subscriber to its service for nonpayment in Ohio. Because we believe that Patterson had sufficient contacts with Ohio to support the exercise of personal jurisdiction over him, we REVERSE the district court's dismissal.

Case Highlights

- Shareware is a way of selling software whereby the user is permitted to download and use that software for a trial period, after which the user is asked to pay a fee to the author for continued use.
- Due process considerations for purposes of personal jurisdiction are satisfied if the defendant "purposely avails" itself to the laws of the forum state.

By contrast, the *Bensusan Restaurant Corp. v. King* case involved the use of a **passive web page**.[8] In this case, a restaurant operated under the same name as a trademarked nightclub in New York City. The trademark owner brought suit for tortious infringement of trademark in federal court in New York. The court held that the mere creation of a Web site accessible in New York was not enough to prove sufficient intent to do business in New York. The case was dismissed for lack of personal jurisdiction. The court observed that whereas the Internet user in *CompuServe* specifically targeted Ohio by entering into an agreement to sell his software over the Internet to out-of-state

---

Bensusan Restaurant Corp. v. King

126 F.3d 25 (2d Cir. 1997)

Van Graafeiland, Circuit Judge. Plaintiff, Bensusan Restaurant Corp., alleges in its complaint that it is the creator of an enormously successful jazz club in New York City called The Blue Note, which name was registered as a federal trademark for cabaret services on May 14, 1985. Around 1993, a Bensusan representative wrote to King demanding that he cease and desist from calling his club in Missouri The Blue Note. King, at the suggestion of a local Web site design company, permitted that company to create a Web site on the Internet for King's cabaret.

Bensusan then brought the instant action in the Southern District of New York, alleging violations of the Lanham Act and the Federal Trademark Dilution Act of 1995, as well as common law unfair competition. The Web site described King's establishment as "Mid-Missouri's finest live entertainment venue located in beautiful Columbia, Missouri," and it contained the following text: The Blue Note's Web site should not be confused with one of the world's finest jazz clubs, Blue Note, located in the heart of New York's Greenwich Village. Although we realize that attempting to apply established trademark law

---

8. See also *E-Data Corp v. Micropatent Corp.*, 989 F. Supp. 173 (D. Conn. 1997). In this case, the court held that the purchasing of services by downloading material from the Internet was insufficient for purposes of obtaining personal jurisdiction. A key factor in the case was that the accused infringer did not actively advertise its Web site. A user had to obtain its Web address, access it, browse the information, and then download.

in the fast-developing world of the Internet is somewhat like trying to board a moving bus, we believe that well-established doctrines of personal jurisdiction law support the result reached by the district court.

New York law states in pertinent part that a New York court may exercise personal jurisdiction over a non-domiciliary who "in person or though an agent" commits a tortious act within the state. Even if Bensusan suffered injury in New York that does not establish a tortious act in the state of New York. Accordingly, in 1966 the New York Legislature enacted an amendment that provides in pertinent part that New York courts may exercise jurisdiction over a non-domiciliary who commits a tortious act without the state, causing injury to person or property within the state. However, the exercise of jurisdiction is limited to persons who expect or should reasonably expect the tortious act to have consequences in the state and in addition derive substantial revenue from interstate commerce.

Because the alleged facts were not sufficient to establish that substantial revenues were derived from interstate commerce, a requirement that is intended to exclude non-domiciliaries whose business operations are

of a local character, personal jurisdiction can not be determined.

AFFIRMED.

Case Highlights

- The "minimum contacts" standard for establishing personal jurisdiction over a defendant must be applied to Internet activities.
- A long-arm statute grants jurisdiction where a tort (such as trademark infringement) that occurs outside the state causes injury inside the state.
- Mere creation of a Web site containing trademark-infringing material does not satisfy the long-arm statute's requirements for personal jurisdiction.
- Personal jurisdiction does not attach to a tort committed outside a state unless the defendant purposely directed its activities to the state and derived substantial revenue from those activities.

---

purchasers, mere advertising on a passive Web site does not subject one to the jurisdiction of another state's courts.

The *Zippo Manufacturing Co. v. Zippo Dot Com, Inc.*[9] case established a sliding-scale approach to the establishment of personal jurisdiction for Internet activities. In that case, the defendant's Web advertisement was followed by the sale of services to more than 3,000 subscribers in the state of Pennsylvania. The number of contacts and sales within a given state is likely to be considered the major factor in the personal jurisdiction decision. The *Carefirst of Maryland, Inc. v. Carefirst Pregnancy Centers, Inc.* case that follows provides a recent example of applying the *Zippo* sliding-scale approach to personal jurisdiction.

Carefirst of Maryland, Inc. v. Carefirst Pregnancy Centers, Inc.

334 F.3d 390 (4th Cir. 2003)

King, Circuit Judge. In this appeal, we address whether an Illinois organization subjected itself to personal jurisdiction in Maryland by operating an Internet website that allegedly infringed the trademark rights of a Maryland insurance company. Carefirst of Maryland ("Carefirst"), a Maryland corporation with its principal place of business in Maryland, is one of the nation's largest healthcare insurance companies. It is a non-profit

BlueCross BlueShield licensee, primarily in the business of selling prepaid healthcare plans. Carefirst operates exclusively within the mid-Atlantic region of the United States; the majority of its 3.1 million members reside in Maryland and in the nearby states of Pennsylvania and West Virginia. Among the services covered by Carefirst's trademark and service mark in the CAREFIRST name are "educational services, namely, conducting seminars,

---

9.   952 F. Supp. 1119 (W.D.Pa. 1997).

classes, workshops and lectures on nutrition, infant care, prenatal care, fitness, weight reduction, stress management and substance abuse." Carefirst advertises and promotes its products and services extensively via the Internet at www.carefirst.com. Its website includes information on health education classes in pregnancy, child birth, and infant care, and it provides pregnancy-related educational materials.

Carefirst Pregnancy Centers, Inc. ("CPC"), an Illinois corporation with its principal place of business in Illinois, is a non-profit, evangelical, pro-life advocacy organization. CPC's professed mission is to "care for Chicago-area women in pregnancy-related crisis by meeting their emotional, physical and spiritual needs, enabling them to choose life." The organization originally incorporated in 1985 under the name "Loop Crisis Pregnancy Center," but it changed its name in 1999 to "Carefirst Pregnancy Centers, Inc. d/b/a Carefirst."

CPC is headquartered in Chicago, Illinois, and it has no physical presence in Maryland: it has no offices, no telephone listing, no employees, and no agents there. Nor does CPC directly solicit funds from individuals in Maryland. CPC has never even provided counseling services to anyone in Maryland. CPC's sole contact with Maryland springs from its operation of an Internet website, accessible from anywhere in the world through any one of several web addresses.

In 1998, CPC entered into a contract with NetImpact, Inc., a web hosting and web development company incorporated in Delaware and headquartered in Ocean Pines, Maryland. On CPC's behalf, NetImpact purchased several domain names, including "www.carefirstpc.com," "www.carefirstpc.org" and "www.carefirstpc.net." CPC uses its various domain names to direct Internet traffic to CPC's website, throughout which the CAREFIRST name appears. On that website, CPC solicits donations; educates pregnant women about nutrition, infant care, and prenatal care; provides references to Chicago-area medical doctors and hospitals; promotes its counseling services and parenting classes; and advertises the pregnancy tests and ultrasound services that it offers free of charge. The website asserts at several points that the geographic focus of CPC's activities is the Chicago metropolitan area.

In soliciting donations, CPC's website offers prospective donors two methods of contribution: (1) they can call an advertised toll-free number and make a credit card transaction over the phone; or (2) they can make a credit card donation directly through the website. CPC has acknowledged that it received $1,542 in donations (about 0.0174% of its total donation receipts) from Maryland residents between 1991 and September of 2001. Of this amount, only $120 was donated (by nine different Marylanders) after CPC adopted the name "Carefirst Pregnancy Centers, Inc.," in 1999. Apart from a single online donation made by the lawyer for Carefirst in this proceeding, there is no evidence that the Maryland donations were made through the website.

On October 26, 2000, shortly after learning of CPC's use of the CAREFIRST name and mark, Carefirst transmitted a cease-and-desist letter to CPC. After attempting to resolve the dispute, Carefirst, on May 31, 2001, filed suit against CPC in the District of Maryland.

On January 2, 2002, the district court dismissed the action for lack of personal jurisdiction. The court found that CPC's only connections to Maryland arose from the facts that (1) its website could be accessed from anywhere in the world, including Maryland; and (2) the website's "host" was a Maryland corporation. On this basis, the court concluded that CPC did not have sufficient contacts with Maryland to support personal jurisdiction in the Maryland courts. Carefirst timely appealed the dismissal of its complaint.

Our inquiry must focus on the conduct giving rise to the suit, i.e., CPC's alleged infringement of Carefirst's trademark. It is only if (1) CPC purposefully availed itself of the privilege of conducting activities in Maryland, (2) Carefirst's claims arise out of those activities, and (3) the exercise of personal jurisdiction would be constitutionally "reasonable," that CPC can be held subject to specific jurisdiction in Maryland. In conducting this inquiry, we direct our focus to the quality and nature of CPC's Maryland contacts. Even a single contact may be sufficient to create jurisdiction when the cause of action arises out of that single contact, provided that the principle of "fair play and substantial justice" is not thereby offended.

In *Calder v. Jones*, 465 U.S. 783 (1984), the Supreme Court held that a court may exercise specific personal jurisdiction over a nonresident defendant acting outside of the forum when the defendant has intentionally directed his tortious conduct toward the forum state, knowing that that conduct would cause harm to a forum resident. Carefirst contends that, in two distinct ways, CPC expressly aimed its trademark-infringing conduct at the forum state of Maryland: first, CPC set up a semi-interactive website that was accessible from Maryland; and second, CPC maintained a relationship with the Maryland web hosting company, NetImpact.

We begin with our recent decision in *ALS Scan, Inc. v. Digital Service Consultants, Inc.*, 293 F.3d 707, 713 (4th Cir. 2002), in which we addressed "whether a person electronically transmitting or enabling the transmission of information via the Internet to Maryland, causing injury there, subjects the person to the jurisdiction of a court in Maryland." *Id.* at 712. Our *ALS Scan* decision expressly "adopted and adapted" the model for Internet-based specific jurisdiction developed in *Zippo Manufacturing Co. v. Zippo Dot Com, Inc.*, 952 F. Supp. 1119 (W.D. Pa. 1997). *Id.* at 714. In its *Zippo* decision, Judge

McLaughlin of the Western District of Pennsylvania first enunciated that court's influential "sliding scale" model for applying *Calder* principles to cases arising from electronic commerce. The *Zippo* court distinguished among interactive, semi-interactive, and passive websites. When a defendant runs an interactive site, through which he "enters into contracts with residents of a foreign jurisdiction that involve the knowing and repeated transmission of computer files over the Internet," he can properly be haled into the courts of that foreign jurisdiction. *Zippo*, 952 F. Supp. at 1124. If, by contrast, the defendant's site is passive, in that it merely makes information available, the site cannot render him subject to specific personal jurisdiction in a foreign court. *Id.* Occupying a middle ground are semi-interactive websites, through which there have not occurred a high volume of transactions between the defendant and residents of the foreign jurisdiction, yet which do enable users to exchange information with the host computer. "In these cases, the exercise of jurisdiction is determined by examining the level of interactivity and commercial nature of the exchange of information that occurs." *Zippo*, 952 F. Supp. at 1124.

Applying *Zippo*, we held in *ALS Scan* that, as a general matter, "[a] State may, consistent with due process, exercise judicial power over a person outside of the State when that person (1) directs electronic activity into the State, (2) with the manifested intent of engaging in business or other interactions within the State, and (3) that activity creates, in a person within the State, a potential cause of action cognizable in the State's courts." *Id.* at 714. Thus, "a person's action of placing information on the Internet" is not sufficient by itself to "subject that person to personal jurisdiction in each State in which the information is accessed." *Id.* at 712. It is clear that, in order for CPC's website to bring CPC within the jurisdiction of the Maryland courts, the company must have done something more than merely place information on the Internet. Rather, CPC must have acted with the "manifest intent" of targeting Marylanders. Whether CPC intended to target Marylanders can be determined only from the character of the website at issue. First, it is relevant that CPC's sites are "semi-interactive," in that they contain features that make it possible for a user to exchange information with the host computer. When a website is neither merely passive nor highly interactive, the exercise of jurisdiction is determined "by examining the level of interactivity and commercial nature of the exchange of information that occurs." *See Zippo*, 952 F. Supp. at 1126. While the *Zippo* defendant was doing business over the Internet with residents of the forum state, entering into contracts through its website with 3,000 individuals and seven Internet access providers in the forum state, the only concrete evidence of online exchanges between CPC and Maryland residents was

the single donation initiated by Carefirst's counsel (and ostensibly made to bolster the position of her client in this litigation).

Second, we find it pertinent that the overall content of CPC's website has a strongly local character, emphasizing that CPC's mission is to assist *Chicago-area* women in pregnancy crises. Rather than target a Maryland audience, the website states that CPC is a non-profit organization that offers assistance "to more than 46,000 hurting women and families *in the Chicago area*"; that CPC "now operates out of seven different locations *in the city of Chicago and Chicago suburbs*"; and that CPC "teaches abstinence until marriage in public high schools *throughout Chicago's Cook County*." In fact, the only respect in which CPC even arguably reaches out to Marylanders via its Internet website is in its generalized request that anyone, anywhere make a donation to support CPC's Chicago-based mission. Such a generalized request is, under the circumstances, an insufficient Maryland contact to sustain jurisdiction in that forum.

In sum, when CPC set up its generally accessible, semi-interactive Internet website, it did not thereby direct electronic activity into Maryland with the manifest intent of engaging in business or other interactions within that state in particular. Thus, while Maryland does have a strong interest in adjudicating disputes involving the alleged infringement of trademarks owned by resident corporations, it nonetheless remains the case that CPC could not on the basis of its Internet activities have reasonably anticipated being haled into a Maryland court. Consequently, the website fails to furnish a Maryland contact adequate to support personal jurisdiction over CPC in the Maryland courts. For the foregoing reasons, the judgment of the district court is affirmed.

Case Highlights

- A sliding scale may be used to determine if an Internet activity is sufficient to qualify as "minimum contacts" for purposes of attaching personal jurisdiction to a defendant.
- Personal jurisdiction based on an interactive Web site will depend on the level of interactivity and the commercial nature of the site.
- Factors relevant to the application of the sliding-scale approach include the level of activity between residents of the forum and the defendant and whether the Web site at issue was targeted at residents of the forum as distinguished from a local focus.

However, judicial acceptance of the *Zippo* approach has not been universal. The *Hy Cite Corp. v. Badbusinessbureau.com* case that follows is an example of recent criticism of the sliding-scale approach. The opinion in *Hy Cite* represents an attempt to apply traditional jurisdictional rules and repudiate new rules with respect to the Internet. The court rejected the application of the sliding-scale approach on the basis that interactivity of the Web site constitutes an unnecessary and artificially created judicial doctrine without support in traditional jurisdictional jurisprudence. To avoid being amenable to suit in a given jurisdiction, it is advisable to place clear **disclaimers** within a Web site that your intent is not to engage in transactions with residents in that jurisdiction.

Hy Cite Corp. v. Badbusinessbureau.com

297 F. Supp. 2d 1154 (W.D. Wis. 2004)

Crabb, District Court Judge. Plaintiff Hy Cite Corporation is a Wisconsin corporation with a principal place of business in Madison, Wisconsin. Plaintiff markets and sells china and porcelain dinnerware, glass beverageware, cookware and related products under its Royal Prestige trademark.

Defendant badbusinessbureau.com is a limited liability company organized and existing under the laws of St. Kitts/Nevis, West Indies. Defendant does not own any assets in Wisconsin or have any offices or employees in the state. Defendant owns and operates a website, "The Rip-Off Report," located at http://www.badbusinessbureau.com. The website operates primarily as a forum for consumer complaints about various businesses. Consumers submit complaints, or "rip-off reports," about a product or service; defendant posts the complaints on its website. Consumers have submitted at least 61,000 complaints to defendant. Plaintiff's products have been the subject of 30 to 40 of these complaints. Subjects of a consumer complaint may post a rebuttal. Defendant screens the rebuttals and charges a $25 fee to post more than four of them. No Wisconsin company has purchased a rebuttal. Defendant's website serves several functions apart from the consumer complaint and rebuttal forum. First, any company may purchase ad space on defendant's website. No Wisconsin company has purchased any ad space. Second, defendant's website displays a link to purchase a book, Rip-Off Revenge Guide. One Wisconsin resident has purchased the book. Third, defendant solicits donations for the company on its website. Defendant does not recall whether the company has received any donations from Wisconsin. Fourth, defendant's website allows website viewers to enlist as volunteer "rip-off reporters." Finally, defendant offers to contact consumers who post rip-off reports if a class action suit is being considered against the company about which the consumer complained. Defendant has not organized any class action suits in Wisconsin.

Cognizant of the potential dramatic effect that the Internet could have on the law of personal jurisdiction, courts have adopted specialized tests that attempt to place manageable limits on a state's reach over defendants that maintain websites. The most prevalent of these tests was first enunciated in *Zippo Mfg. Co. v. Zippo Dot Com, Inc.*, 952 F. Supp 1119 (W.D. Pa 1997). The court concluded that "the likelihood that personal jurisdiction can be constitutionally exercised is directly proportionate to the nature and quality of commercial activity that an entity conducts over the Internet." Id. at 1124. The court set out a sliding scale of website interactivity to determine whether personal jurisdiction should be exercised. The Zippo test has proved to be influential. Courts across the country have adopted the sliding scale approach, at least nominally, in personal jurisdiction cases involving internet contacts.

I am reluctant to fall in line with these courts for two reasons. First, it is not clear why a website's level of interactivity should be determinative on the issue of personal jurisdiction. As even courts adopting the Zippo test have recognized, a court cannot determine whether personal jurisdiction is appropriate simply by deciding whether a website is "passive" or "interactive." Even a "passive" website may support a finding of jurisdiction if the defendant used its website intentionally to harm the plaintiff in the forum state. Similarly, an "interactive" or commercial website may not be sufficient to support jurisdiction if it is not aimed at residents in the forum state. Moreover, regardless how interactive a website is, it cannot form the basis for personal jurisdiction unless a nexus exists between the website and the cause of action or unless the contacts through the website are so substantial that they may be considered "systematic and continuous" for the purpose of general jurisdiction. Thus, a rigid adherence to the Zippo test is likely to lead to erroneous results.

Second, in Zippo, the court did not explain under what authority it was adopting a specialized test for the internet or even why such a test was necessary. The Supreme Court has never held that courts should apply different standards for personal jurisdiction depending on the type of contact involved. To the contrary, the Court "long ago rejected the notion that personal jurisdiction might turn on 'mechanical' tests." *Burger King Corp. v. Rudzewicz*, 471 U.S. 462, 478 (1985). The purpose of the "minimum contacts" test was to create a standard flexible enough that specialized tests were not needed. Other courts have rejected Zippo while noting that traditional principles of due process are sufficient to decide personal jurisdiction questions in the internet context. See, e.g., *Winfield Collection, Ltd. v. McCauley*, 105 F. Supp. 2d 746, 750 (E.D. Mich. 2000).

Although I decline to adopt the Zippo test as a substitute for minimum contacts, this does not mean that a website's level of interactivity is irrelevant in deciding whether the exercise of jurisdiction is appropriate. The website's level of interactivity may be one component of a determination whether a defendant has availed itself purposefully of the benefits or privileges of the forum state. For example, a finding that a defendant uses its website to engage in repeated commercial transactions may support the exercise of personal jurisdiction, so long as there is a corresponding finding that the defendant is expressly targeting residents of the forum state and not just making itself accessible to everyone regardless of location. See, e.g., *Bancroft & Masters, Inc. v. Augusta National, Inc.*, 223 F.3d 1082, 1087 (9th Cir. 2000) (interactivity is insufficient by itself; there must be "express aiming" at forum state); *B.E.E. International Ltd. v. Hawes*, 267 F. Supp. 2d 477, 484–85 (M.D.N.C. 2003); *Hasbro, Inc. v. Clue Computing, Inc.*, 994 F. Supp. 34 (D. Mass. 1997). However, the ultimate question remains the same, that is, whether the defendant's contacts with the state are of such a quality and nature such that it could reasonably expect to be haled into the courts of the forum state.

To meet the constitutional requirement for general jurisdiction, the defendant must have "continuous and systematic general business contacts" with the forum state. *Helicoptores Nacionales de Colombia, S.A. v. Hall*, 466 U.S. 408, 416 (1984). The defendant's contacts with the forum "must be so extensive to be tantamount" to the defendant's "being constructively present in the state to such a degree that it would be fundamentally fair to require it to answer in a Wisconsin court in any litigation arising out of any transaction or occurrence taking place anywhere in the world."

Plaintiff's argument that general jurisdiction exists in this case borders on the frivolous. Plaintiff has not alleged that defendant has an office in Wisconsin, that defendant does a substantial amount of business in Wisconsin or that agents of defendant spend any time in the state, much less substantial amounts. With the exception of the book sale to one Wisconsin resident and the communication between the parties, all of the activities

identified by plaintiff consist of nothing more than potential contacts. Further, although plaintiff characterizes defendant's internet-based activities as "soliciting" Wisconsin business, plaintiff has not alleged that defendant has done anything to target internet users in Wisconsin.

Defendant's website is accessible to anyone connected to the internet anywhere in the world. Under plaintiff's argument, defendant could be haled into court in any state for any controversy, regardless whether defendant had any contact with a resident of that state. This result would be inconsistent with the Supreme Court's understanding of the requirements of due process. Because plaintiff has not met its burden of proving that defendant has engaged in continuous and systematic contacts with Wisconsin, defendant is not subject to general jurisdiction in this court.

In order to exercise specific jurisdiction, a court must find that the defendant has purposefully established minimum contacts with the forum state, that the cause of action arises out of or relates to those contacts and that the exercise of jurisdiction is constitutionally reasonable. The Court has identified two ways in which minimum contacts may be established for the purpose of specific jurisdiction: (1) purposeful availment by the defendant of the benefits and protections of the forum state's laws, *Asahi Metal Indus. Co., Ltd. v. Superior Court of California*, 480 U.S. 102, 109 (1987); or (2) harm to an individual within the state caused by the defendant when the harm is both intentional and aimed at the forum state.

Plaintiff has failed to show how defendant has made purposeful availment of the benefits of Wisconsin's laws that it could reasonably anticipate being haled into court in this state. As noted above, most of plaintiff's alleged contacts with Wisconsin are only potential contacts. Plaintiff has adduced no evidence that defendant has received any donations from Wisconsin citizens, that any Wisconsin businesses advertise on its website or that it has coordinated any class actions involving people from Wisconsin. No evidence exists to show that defendant has done anything to target Wisconsin consumers. Defendant does not send mailings or unsolicited e-mails to the state. It does not advertise for its site within Wisconsin. The defendant's website is akin to an advertisement in a magazine with a national circulation; the defendant does not control who views it or responds to it. Defendant has had contact with various Wisconsin citizens who have posted consumer complaints on defendant's website. Again, however, plaintiff has not targeted Wisconsin citizens more than the citizens of any other state. More important, plaintiff has not shown what benefit or privilege from Wisconsin has incurred to defendant through the posting of these complaints.

What remains is the one book sale to a Wisconsin resident. Even assuming the one book sale was sufficient by itself, plaintiff would have to show that there was a nexus between the sale and the cause of action. The book sale has no connection with this cause of action. Plaintiff is not suing defendant for breach of contract or fraud but for defamation and trademark infringement arising from the consumer complaints and other references to plaintiff on the website. The only relationship between the sale and the lawsuit is that the sale occurred through the website. Such a tenuous connection is insufficient to show that the lawsuit "directly arose" from this sale.

The effects test is satisfied when the plaintiff alleges that the defendant committed an intentional tort expressly aimed at the forum state; the actions caused harm, the brunt of which was suffered in the forum state; and the defendant knew that the effects of its actions would be suffered primarily in the forum state. Plaintiff fails to allege any facts demonstrating that defendant expressly aimed its activities at Wisconsin. The facts of record do not indicate that defendant creates the text of the consumer complaints. It is the consumers that are using plaintiff's name and making allegedly defamatory statements. If defendant is not creating the text, then defendant is not purposefully directing its activities toward any particular company or state. I agree with the majority of courts that simply placing the name of trademark on a website is not enough to show that a defendant has intentionally targeted the forum state. E.g., *Carefirst of Maryland, Inc. v. Carefirst Pregnancy Centers, Inc.*, 334 F.3d 390, 400 (4th Cir. 2003); *Bensusan Restaurant Corp. v. King*, 937 F. Supp. 295, 301 (S.D.N.Y. 1996). To hold otherwise would subject millions of internet users to suit in the state of any company whose trademarked name they happen to mention on a website.

Even if plaintiff could meet the express aiming requirement, plaintiff has failed to show that it has suffered the brunt of its injury in Wisconsin. Plaintiff suggests that a court may assume that its injury is in Wisconsin because its principal place of business is in Wisconsin. When an injured party is an individual, it is reasonable to infer that the brunt of the injury will be felt in the state in which he or she resides. This is not necessarily the case when the injured party is a corporation. A corporation does not suffer harm in a particular geographic location in the same sense that an individual does. Even if a corporation has its principal place of business in the forum state, it does not follow necessarily that it makes more sales in that state than any other or that harm to its reputation will be felt more strongly in that state. Thus, I agree with the majority of courts that merely identifying the plaintiff's principal place of business is not enough without more to show that the plaintiff has suffered the brunt of an injury in the state. Defendant badbusinessbureau.com's motion to dismiss for lack of personal jurisdiction is GRANTED.

Case Highlights

- The *Zippo* sliding-scale approach to personal jurisdiction with respect to Internet activities has not achieved universal judicial recognition in the United States.
- A court may reject the application of the sliding-scale approach on the basis that interactivity of the Web site constitutes an unnecessary and artificially created judicial doctrine without support in traditional jurisdictional jurisprudence.
- Potential contacts between the operator of a Web site and the forum are insufficient to establish personal jurisdiction over the Web site operator.

INTERNATIONAL

The European Union has taken a somewhat different approach to personal jurisdiction with respect to the Internet. Unlike the United States, the European Union opted for a legislative solution to the jurisdiction issue. In 2000, the European Union adopted Council Regulation 44/2001 on jurisdiction, otherwise known as the **Brussels Regulation**. It was implemented by Civil Jurisdiction and Judgments Order 2001 and came into force on March 1, 2002. The regulation is effective in all member countries except Denmark, which elected to opt out.

The Brussels Regulation provides that, as a general rule, people can be sued in the country in which their principal residence or place of business is located. Lawsuits alleging breach of contract may also be heard in the courts of the country where performance of the obligation at issue was to occur. The parties are free to depart from this rule in their agreement, but such provisions are unenforceable if they conflict with the rights of consumers set forth in Article 15. With respect to consumers, the Brussels Regulation provides that consumers may, as a general rule, bring an action against a business in the consumer's country of domicile. Consumers are entitled to bring such actions in their home courts if the business "pursues commercial activities in the member States of the consumer's domicile or, by any means, directs such activities to that Member State."[10]

The consumer protection provision of the Brussels Regulation raises several issues for businesses operating on the Internet. The regulation provides no detailed rules for determining whether a Web site that offers goods and services to consumers is pursuing commercial activities or directing such activities to the consumer's country of domicile. It is clear from the drafting history of the regulation that the member states did not intend that mere accessibility of a Web site equates with the pursuit or direction of commercial activities. It has been speculated that courts will need to examine the nature of the given Web site to make this determination. For example, a court may conclude that a Web site is pursuing or directing commercial activity in another member state if sales have been made to consumers in the state. In addition, a Web site may be deemed as directed at other member states if it offers a choice of languages or currencies to be utilized in payment. Ultimately, the European Court of Justice will need to resolve the interrelationship of the Internet and the Brussels Regulation.

These jurisdictional rules bring up the crucial issue of whether a court's exercise of personal jurisdiction over a foreign defendant will be recognized and enforced by a foreign court system. A winning plaintiff in international litigation is often forced to seek execution of the judgment in a foreign court system. A defendant may not pay on the judgment voluntarily. In such a case, the judgment holder has to obtain satisfaction of the judgment by taking the assets of the defendant, and doing this requires gaining the cooperation of a foreign court.

Under the international law principle of **comity**, countries are expected to honor the judicial judgments and orders of a foreign court. However, as discussed in Chapter Four, this recognition is sometimes denied. The *Braintech, Inc. v. Kostiuk* case that follows demonstrates that even closely aligned legal systems, such as those of the United States and Canada, will not enforce the judgment of the other if they determine that the exercise of personal jurisdiction was improper. The case is an issue of first instance involving the posting of defamatory information on an Internet bulletin board.

Braintech, Inc. v. Kostiuk

British Columbia Court of Appeals (1999)

Goldie, Justice. The Plaintiff was a technology company incorporated in Nevada and doing business in various United States jurisdictions. It brought an action in Texas against a resident of British Columbia, alleging the Defendant had published defamatory information about the corporation on an Internet bulletin board. The Texas Civil Code deems a nonresident to do business in the jurisdiction if it commits a tort there.

The Plaintiff obtained a default judgment in Texas and commenced an action on that judgment in British Columbia. British Columbia is obligated to recognize foreign judgments according to principles of [reciprocity and] comity. However, there is a constitutional limitation in the United States on the exercise of personal jurisdiction that requires the Defendant to have sufficient minimum contacts with the jurisdiction. Furthermore, the court must consider whether there was a "real and substantial" connection to Texas. The Defendant's only connection to Texas was passive posting on an Internet bulletin board. To enforce recovery

---

10. Brussels Regulation, art. 15.1(c).

of the default judgment would encourage a multiplicity of actions wherever the Internet is available.

The issue in this case is whether there was a real and substantial connection between Texas and the wrongdoing alleged to have taken place. In my opinion, the trial judge erred in failing to consider whether there were any contacts between the Texas court and the parties which could, with the due process clause of the 14th Amendment to the Constitution of the United States, amount to a real and substantial presence. In the circumstances revealed by the record before this Court, British Columbia is the only natural forum and Texas is not an appropriate forum. That being so, comity does not require that the courts of this province to recognize the default judgment in question. DISMISSED.

Case Highlights

- One country is obligated under international law (principle of comity) to recognize the judicial judgments of a foreign court.
- This recognition is not required unless the exercise of personal jurisdiction satisfies the requirements of due process.
- The passive posting of a defamatory statement on an Internet bulletin board does not establish a "real and substantial" connection with a foreign state for purposes of personal jurisdiction.

Trademark Infringement, Dilution, and Cybersquatting

Trademark protection is "the law's recognition of the psychological function of symbols." Two goals of trademark law are reflected in the federal scheme. On the one hand, the law seeks to protect consumers who have formed particular associations with a mark. On the other hand, trademark law seeks to protect the owner's investment in a mark. A recurring problem in Internet commerce has been the misappropriation of names by so-called **cybersquatters**. Cybersquatters are parties that register a famous brand name or trademark as their Internet domain name. The cybersquatter then attempts to extort a payment from the trademark owner for its registered domain name.

The two statutory recourses available in the United States to the trademark owner are the **Lanham Act**[11] and the **Federal Trademark Dilution Act of 1995**.[12] The Lanham Act requires a likelihood of confusion between the junior user's (infringing party) and the senior user's products. Courts have held that when the goods or services are unrelated to the trademark owner's products, such as when the domain name is registered on behalf of no particular product or service, there is no likelihood of confusion. The Federal Trademark Dilution Act, however, does not require proof of a likelihood of confusion.

Courts have held that registering a domain name for the purpose of selling it to a trademark owner is actionable under the Dilution Act.[13] However, simple similarity between the domain name and the trademark is not sufficient in and of itself to permit the trademark owner to prevail in a dilution action. For example, in *Avery Dennison Corp. v. Sumpton*,[14] the U.S. Court of Appeals for the Ninth Circuit reversed a district court decision in favor of the owner of the "Avery Dennison" trademark. The defendants in the case had registered the domain names "avery.net" and "dennison.net." The plaintiff claimed that these registrations infringed upon its interest in the "averydennison.com" mark. With respect to dilution, the court held

http://

The Publishing Law Center—"Trademark Protection in Cyberspace": **http://www.publaw.com/cyber.html.**

---

11.   15 U.S.C. § 1114 (2000).

12.   See ibid. § 1125 (c)(1–4).

13.   See *Panavision Int'l L.P. v. Toeppen*, 945 F. Supp.1296 (C.D. Cal. 1997), *aff'd*, 141 F.3d 1316 (9th Cir. 1998); see also *Intermatic, Inc. v. Toeppen*, 947 F. Supp. 1227 (N.D. Ill. 1996).

14.   189 F.3d 868 (9th Cir. 1999).

that, although distinctive, the Avery Dennison mark was not famous. Also, the marks "avery" and "dennison" had been utilized separately by 1,000 other businesses in a wide range of industries. Furthermore, the defendants were not making commercial use of the Avery Dennison mark, as the domain names they registered were not ".com" but rather ".net" for licensing as electronic mail addresses. This distinction also served to prevent the defendants' activities from being labeled as cybersquatting.

Unlike infringement and unfair competition laws, in a dilution case competition between the parties and a likelihood of confusion are not required to present a claim for relief. Rather, injunctive relief is available under the Federal Trademark Dilution Act if a plaintiff can establish that (1) its mark is famous, (2) the defendant is making commercial use of the mark, (3) the defendant's use began after the plaintiff's mark became famous, and (4) the defendant's use presents a likelihood of dilution of the distinctive value of the mark. The Federal Trademark Dilution Act lists eight nonexclusive considerations relevant to determining whether a mark is famous:

- the degree of inherent or acquired distinctiveness of the mark
- the duration and extent of use of the mark in connection with the goods or services with which the mark is used
- the duration and extent of advertising and publicity of the mark
- the geographical extent of the trading area in which the mark is used
- the channels of trade for the goods or services with which the mark is used
- the degree of recognition of the mark in the trading areas and channels of trade used by the mark's owner and the person against whom the injunction is sought
- the nature and extent of use of the same or similar marks by third parties
- whether the mark was registered on the principal register[15]

In *Panavision International, L.P. v. Toeppen*,[16] it was held that the Federal Trademark Dilution Act was implicated when the defendant registered domain name combinations using famous trademarks and sought to sell the registrations to the trademark owners. Commercial use under the Federal Trademark Dilution Act requires the defendant to be using the trademark as a trademark, thereby capitalizing on its commercial status. In this classic cybersquatter case, the court determined that the infringer's intent was to "arbitrage" the registration that included the plaintiff's trademark.

As discussed in Chapter Thirteen, **blurring** is a type of trademark dilution in which consumers are unlikely to mistake the two companies' products because the products are dissimilar. Nonetheless, the dilutor's use of the mark still may dilute the uniqueness of the more famous mark. The court in *Toys "R" Us v. Feinberg*[17] held that a gun company's use of the domain name "gunsareus" neither infringed nor diluted the senior mark. The court held that any blurring was tenuous because the average consumer would not connect the two names or marks. It confirmed, nonetheless, that dilution is applicable to Internet cases.

In 1999, Congress enacted the **Anti-Cybersquatting Consumer Protection Act (ACPA)**.[18] This act allows the owner of a mark to bring a civil action against a party

---

15.   15 U.S.C. § 1125(c)(1)(A-H) (2000).
16.   141 F.3d 1316 (9th Cir. 1998).
17.   26 F. Supp. 639 (S.D.N.Y. 1998), *rev'd on procedural grounds*, 1999 U.S. App. LEXIS 29833 (2d Cir. Nov. 10, 1999).
18.   15 U.S.C. § 1125(d)(1-4) (2000).

that has a "bad faith intent to profit from that mark" and "registers, traffics in or uses a domain name" that is identical or confusingly similar to a distinctive mark or identical, confusingly similar to, or dilutive of a famous mark. The existence of bad faith may be determined from the following nine nonexclusive factors:

- the trademark or other intellectual property rights of the defendant in the domain name
- the extent to which the domain name is the legal name of the defendant or a name commonly used to identify the defendant
- the defendant's prior use of the domain name in connection with the bona fide offering of goods or services
- the defendant's bona fide noncommercial or fair use of the mark in a site accessible under the domain name
- the defendant's intent to divert consumers from the mark owner's online location to a site accessible under the domain name that could harm the good will represented by the mark for the purpose of commercial gain or with the intent of tarnishing or blurring the mark or creating the likelihood of confusion
- the defendant's offer to transfer the domain name to the mark owner for financial gain without having used or having an intent to use the domain name for the bona fide offering for sale of goods or services
- the defendant's provision of material and misleading false contact information in registering the domain name, as well as failure to maintain accurate contact information or a prior pattern of such conduct
- the registration or acquisition of multiple domain names that the defendant knows are identical or confusingly similar to distinctive marks of others or dilutive of famous marks
- the extent to which the mark incorporated in the domain name is or is not distinctive and famous[19]

Remedies available for domain names registered in violation of the Act include forfeiture and cancellation of the infringing domain name, transfer of the domain name to the owner of the infringed mark, and damages in an amount subject to proof or in a statutory amount ranging from $1,000 to $100,000 per domain name. The *Mattel, Inc. v. Internet Dimensions* case that follows was one of the first cases to apply the ACPA. Note that three types of claims can be made under federal law: trademark infringement, trademark dilution, and violation of ACPA.

Mattel, Inc. v. Internet Dimensions, Inc.

2000 U.S. Dist. LEXIS 9747 (S.D.N.Y. 2000)

Baer, District Judge. Plaintiff Mattel, Inc. ("Mattel"), commenced this action against defendants Internet Dimensions, Inc. ("Internet Dimensions"), and Benjamin Schiff asserting causes of action for (1) trademark infringement under Section 43(a) of the Lanham Act, (2) trademark dilution under Section 43(c) of the Lanham Act, and (3) violation of the Anti-Cybersquatting Consumer Protection Act of 1999 ("ACPA" or "the Act"). Mattel is a publicly held corporation organized and existing under the laws of the State of Delaware. One of its principal products is the trademarked "Barbie" doll.

In 1991, the Second Circuit observed that "the 'Barbie' doll is the best selling toy doll in the world—96 percent of three- to eleven-year-old girls in the United

---

19.   See ibid. § 1125(d)(1)(B)(i)(I-IX).

States own at least one. In the past 30 years 600 million Barbie dolls have been sold—one is sold every two seconds-and, in 1990 alone, 26 million of them were sold, earning gross revenues for Mattel of $740 million."

Internet Dimensions is a corporation organized and existing under the laws of the State of Nevada. Internet Dimensions owns Internet domain names for sites that provide, among other things, "adult" entertainment. One of its domain names is "barbiesplaypen.com."

Mattel's primary claim in this action is that defendants violated the Anti-Cybersquatting Consumer Protection Act. The ACPA, signed into law on November 29, 1999, provides that "a court may order the forfeiture or cancellation of the domain name or the transfer of the domain name to the owner of the mark." It also provides that damages can be awarded for violations of the Act.

The ACPA was passed to "protect consumers and American businesses, to promote the growth of online commerce, and to provide clarity in the law for trademark owners, by prohibiting the bad-faith and abusive registration of distinctive marks as Internet domain names with the intent to profit from the goodwill associated with such marks—a practice commonly referred to as 'cybersquatting.'" The Act provides civil liability for cybersquatting as follows:

A person shall be liable in a civil action by the owner of a mark if that person (i) has a bad faith intent to profit from that mark and (ii) registers, traffics in, or uses a domain name that:

(I) in the case of a mark that is distinctive at the time of registration of the domain name, is identical or confusingly similar to that mark;
(II) in the case of a famous mark that is famous at the time of registration of the domain name, is identical or confusingly similar to or dilutive of that mark;
(III) is a trademark, word, or name.

While there is no particular inherent distinctiveness in the name "Barbie," the mark, as it applies to Mattel, has acquired distinctiveness through four decades of exposure in the American consumer market. The Court concludes that the name "Barbie" and the font normally used to advertise BARBIE products is widely recognized throughout the world on the basis of the marketing efforts that have been undertaken by Mattel over the past four decades. The Court finds that the trademark BARBIE is both "distinctive" and "famous" for purposes of § 1125(d).

The next question is whether the domain name "barbiesplaypen.com" is "identical or confusingly similar to" the BARBIE mark. The similarities between "barbiesplaypen.com" and the BARBIE trademark are as follows: (1) both contain the name "barbie;" (2) the name

"Barbie" on the front page of the Web site and the logo BARBIE both have approximately the same font, slant, size, etc.; (3) both BARBIE and "barbiesplaypen.com" are inextricably associated with the verb "play," in the broad sense of the term. All of the above similarities make the Web site 'barbiesplaypen.com," and its domain name, "confusingly similar," though not "identical" to the BARBIE mark.

I next turn to the issue of whether the defendants registered, used, or trafficked in the domain name "barbiesplaypen.com" with a "bad faith intent to profit" from the Barbie mark. We find that the defendants did engage in a "bad faith attempt to profit" from the BARBIE trademark by maintaining the infringing domain name and Web site. It is clear that the defendants expected the same advertising result as Mattel from the use of the domain name "barbiesplaypen.com." The defendants must have expected that consumers searching under the word BARBIE, or perhaps the words "BARBIE and PLAY," in an Internet search engine would be directed to defendants' pornographic "barbiesplaypen.com" site. The diversion of Internet users to a site containing pornographic images may well *tarnish* the image of Mattel's BARBIE products in the minds of those consumers.

Under the ACPA, Mattel is entitled to an order directing defendants to transfer the registration of the domain name "barbiesplaypen.com" to Mattel. This Court finds that a permanent injunction barring defendants from the commercial use and infringement of any of Mattel's BARBIE trademarks is also warranted. Finally, the plaintiff is also entitled to statutory damages and attorneys' fees.

SO ORDERED.

Case Highlights

- A party can be liable for trademark infringement even if it sells a product dissimilar to the products sold by the trademark owner. For example, if the infringing use of the trademark "tarnishes" the image of the trademark owner, then the user is guilty of trademark dilution.
- Domain names serve to identify the Internet user. Therefore, businesses prefer to use their trade names as part of their domain names.
- Cybersquatting is the bad faith registration of distinctive trademarks as Internet domain names.
- The Anti-Cybersquatting Consumer Protection Act (ACPA) protects trademark owners from the bad faith use of their trade name by others who register infringing domain names.

Internet Privacy and Database Protection

Justice Brandeis once stated that "the right to be left alone is the most comprehensive of rights, and the most valued by civilized persons."[20] The problem of Internet privacy is balancing the individual's right to privacy with the right to develop, transfer, and sell databases compiled with personal data. One issue is the ability of one company to sell its customer list to another company. In this instance, information that an individual believes was submitted confidentially to one party can end up being used by other parties for different purposes.

An example of how databases and privacy interests intersect is the Toysmart.com bankruptcy. Toysmart's bankruptcy filing identified its customer data as a saleable asset. The data consisted of 250,000 customer names, addresses, payment information, and "click stream" histories. The company subsequently received an offer of $100,000 for the database. However, disclosure of the data was in violation of Toysmart's privacy policy, which pledged never to divulge the information contained in the database to third parties.

As a result, the Federal Trade Commission and forty-four state attorneys general intervened to prevent the sale and disclosure. The Federal Trade Commission sought the sale of the database to another online toy seller that maintained the privacy protections promised by Toysmart; however, the state attorneys general sought the destruction of the database. A settlement was reached in January 2001, whereby Toysmart destroyed the customer list and its majority owner, Buena Vista Internet Group, the online subsidiary of the Walt Disney Company, paid $50,000 to creditors. The case demonstrates the difficulty of maintaining customer privacy in the competitive world of electronic commerce. The case also demonstrates the different levels of protection of consumer data acceptable to the states and the federal government. The issues raised by the Toysmart bankruptcy are likely to arise again in future dot-com bankruptcies.

The United States and the European Union (EU) have elected two different approaches to this problem, which is not surprising because ingrained cultural attitudes about personal privacy separate the United States from many European countries. Europeans are more restrictive in regulating the way companies collect and process personal data. The EU has enacted comprehensive legislation to deal with personal privacy on the Internet. In contrast, the United States has not enacted comprehensive data protection legislation, instead electing to allow the Internet industry to largely self-regulate.

Many of today's most popular Web sites serve as data collection instruments. Personal information given by a visitor to a Web site is collected for future use, sometimes covertly through the use of **cookies** or tags. Cookies are used to identify visitors to a Web site. They allow the Web site to obtain the visitor's e-mail address, name, the specific pages of the Web site that were visited, and what electronic transactions were made. This personal information can then be used for future marketing purposes or sold to others by the Web site owners.

Although the United States does not have a comprehensive Internet privacy law, a number of existing statutes offer some protections. The federal statutes focus on specific industries. For example, the **Fair Credit Reporting Act**[21] governs

---

20. *Olmstead v. United States*, 277 U.S. 438, 478 (1928).
21. 15 U.S.C. § 1681-1681v (2000).

the use of data by the credit reporting industry. The **Privacy Act of 1994**[22] restricts government agencies from releasing personal information from its documents and records. The **Telephone Consumer Protection Act**[23] is directed at the abuse of telemarketing activities through telephone solicitations. The **Electronic Communications Privacy Act of 1986**[24] extends federal wiretap requirements to new forms of electronic communications such as e-mail and applies to service providers engaged in the transmission and storage of electronic communications. It does not prevent the recipient of the communication from disclosing the contents to others. The **Telecommunications Act of 1996**[25] restricts telecommunications companies from disclosing information about subscribers' use of their services.

Most recently, the use of bulk e-mail solicitations known as **spamming** was subjected to regulation pursuant to the **Controlling the Assault of Non-Solicited Pornography and Marketing Act of 2003 (Can-Spam Act)**.[26] Among its many provisions, the Can-Spam Act establishes content and procedural requirements for companies initiating e-mail marketing communications and prohibits false or deceptive activities in such communications. The Act grants the Federal Trade Commission regulatory and enforcement authority with respect to such communications and requires it to devise a national "Do Not E-Mail" registry. Civil penalties for violations range from $250 per e-mail to $2 million. Civil penalties may be trebled in the event of willful or knowing violations of the Act. Fraud related to such communications is punishable by prison terms of up to five years.

INTERNATIONAL

Efforts to control spamming in the United States were preceded by similar efforts in the European Union. **Directive 2002/58/EC on Privacy and Electronic Communications** was adopted in July 2002 and was to be implemented by the member states no later than October 31, 2003. This directive was primarily designed to protect the natural person (as opposed to a legal person such as a business) from unwanted communications. The directive requires the sender of an electronic communication to a natural person to have received that person's consent prior to sending direct marketing by electronic mail. Consent must be indicated by "opting in." Specifically, the recipient must agree to accept direct marketing via electronic mail. This varies from the proposed "Do Not E-Mail" list in the United States, which requires recipients to "opt out" of receiving such electronic solicitations. There is an exception to the directive's opt-in requirement for information obtained in the context of an appropriate sale of a good or service in conformance with European Union law, if the same person issues the communication as initiated the sale and the marketing is for the sender's own products or services of a similar nature. Furthermore, recipients may opt out of receiving future communications and solicitations at any time. Any indication that future marketing communications are unwanted constitutes a valid opt out.

In 1995, the European Union enacted the **Directive on the Protection of Individuals with Regard to the Processing of Personal Data and the Free Movement of Such Data (Directive 95/46)**. It states the following standards of data quality:

INTERNATIONAL

22. 5 U.S.C. § 552a (a-v) (2000).
23. 47 U.S.C. § 227(a-f) (2000).
24. 18 U.S.C. §§ 2510-22 (2000).
25. 47 U.S.C. §§ 222-31 (2000).
26. Pub. L. No. 108–187, 117 Stat. 2699 (2003).

- personal data must be "processed fairly and lawfully"
- personal data must be "collected for specific, explicit, and legitimate purposes and not further processed in a way incompatible with those purposes"
- personal data must be "accurate and kept up to date"
- every reasonable step must be taken to ensure that inaccurate or incomplete data are erased or rectified
- personal data that permit identification of the subject should be kept "no longer than is necessary for the purposes for which the data was collected"[28]

The further processing of collected data is limited to where the data subject (consumer) has given "consent unambiguously."[29] An exception is made when the processing of personal data is performed in the public interest or in the exercise of official authority. (See the following Comparative Law feature.)

Directive 95/46 grants the data subject a number of rights. First, every subject has a **right of access** to obtain "confirmation as to whether data relating to him are processed and as to the purposes of the processing, the categories of data being processed, and the recipients to whom the data are disclosed."[30] Second, a **blocking right** and **right of correction** are granted, whereby the subject has the right to "the rectification, erasure, or blocking of data, the processing of which does not comply with this Directive, in particular because of the incomplete or inaccurate nature of the data."[31] Third, there is a limited **right of objection** "on compelling legitimate grounds"[32] to a particular processing of data relating to an individual.

In addition, Article 25 of the directive prohibits the transfer of data outside the EU to a third country that does not provide an adequate level of protection. Therefore, the directive prohibits the transfer of data to the United Sates and other non-EU countries not meeting EU standards for the protection of personal privacy. Even if a third country lacks adequate controls, such transfers are permissible, however, if the subject consents to the transfer or if the transfer is necessary for the performance of a contract between the subject and the data possessor. Article 25 offers the possibility of a severe interruption of data flows from Europe to the United States because the United States has not enacted "adequate" data protection laws.

Initially, the EU continued to permit U.S. companies to export personal data from Europe and entered into negotiations to avert a trade war. In 2000, the United States and the EU completed negotiations on the **safe harbor agreement**. This accord allows for privacy protection that is deemed adequate but not equivalent to that under EU law. If U.S. companies comply voluntarily, they will be given safe harbor from lawsuits by EU countries. A controversial part of the safe harbor principles is that a company can self-certify by filing a letter annually with the Department of Commerce. The certification can be performed through self-assessment or outside review. Any self-assessment should state the company's privacy policy, along with confirming the existence of procedures for conducting periodic reviews, training employees, and disciplining violations. The only specific sanction for misrepresentations in the self-certification letter is by way of an action by the Federal Trade Commission.

http://
Article—"Review of Safe Harbor Agreement after One Year": **http://www.cov.com/ publications/download/ oid6121/254.pdf.**

---

27. Directive 96/9/EC, preamble, ¶ 17.
28. Directive 95/46/EC, art. 6(1)(a-e).
29. Ibid. art. 7(a).
30. Ibid. art. 12(a).
31. Ibid. art. 32(2)
32. Ibid. art. 14(a).

Directive 95/46/EC

European Union Data Privacy Protection (Protection of Individuals with Regard to the Processing of Personal Data)

WHEREAS, cross-border flows of personal data are necessary to the expansion of international trade; the protection of individuals guaranteed in the Community by this Directive does not stand in the way of transfers of personal data to third countries which ensure an adequate level of protection;

WHEREAS, on the other hand, the transfer of personal data to a third country which does not ensure an adequate level of protection must be prohibited;

Principle Relating to Data Quality
Article 6: Member States shall provide that personal data must be:

(a) processed fairly and lawfully;
(b) collected for specified, explicit, and legitimate purposes and not further processed in a way incompatible with those purposes.
(c) adequate, relevant, and not excessive in relation to the purposes for which they are collected and/or further processed;
(d) accurate and, where necessary, kept up to date; every reasonable step must be taken to ensure that data which are inaccurate or incomplete, having regard to the purposes for which they were collected or for which they are further processed, are erased or rectified;

The Data Subject's Right of Access to Data
Article 12: Right of access: Member States shall guarantee every data subject the right to obtain from the controller:

(a) (1) confirmation as to whether or not data relating to him are being processed and information at least as to the purposes of the processing, the categories of data concerned, and the recipients or categories of recipients to whom the data are disclosed,
(2) communication to him in an intelligible form of the data undergoing processing and of any available information as to their source,

The Data Subject's Right to Object
Article 14: Member States shall grant the data subject the right:

(b) to object, on request and free of charge, to the processing of personal data relating to him which the controller anticipates being processed for the purposes of direct marketing, or to be informed before personal data are disclosed for the first time to third parties or used on their behalf for the purposes of direct marketing, and to be expressly offered the right to object free of charge to such disclosures or uses.

Article 23: Liability. Member States shall provide that any person who has suffered damage as a result of an unlawful processing operation or of any act incompatible with the national provisions adopted pursuant to this Directive is entitled to receive compensation from the controller for the damage suffered.

The European Union has enacted comprehensive laws dealing with the protection and use of databases.

Directive 96/9/EC on the Legal Protection of Databases defines the term *database* as "literary, artistic, musical, or other collections of works or collections of other material such as texts, sound, images, numbers, facts, and data systematically or methodically arranged and that can be individually accessed."[27]

The Directive extends protection to databases that are a product of "substantial investment" of human, technical, and financial resources[33] (see Comparative Law: Directive 96/9/EC, Legal Protection of Databases). If a database is a product of such investment, then the directive grants its creator or owner a fifteen-year term of protection.

---

33.   Directive 96/9/EC, art. 7(1).

COMPARATIVE LAW

Directive 96/9/EC

Legal Protection of Databases (March 11, 1996)

1. The making of databases requires the investment of considerable human, technical, and financial resources while such databases can be copied or accessed at a fraction of the cost needed to design them independently;
2. This Directive protects collections, sometimes called compilations, of works, data, or other materials which are arranged, stored, and accessed by means which include electronic processes;
3. No criterion other than originality, in the sense of the author's intellectual creation, should be applied to determine the eligibility of the database for copyright protection, and in particular no aesthetic or qualitative criteria should be applied;
4. Works protected by copyright and subject matter protected by related rights that are incorporated into a database remain, nevertheless, protected by the respective exclusive rights and may not be incorporated into, or extracted from, the database without the permission of the right holder or his successors in title;

Article 3: Object of Protection

1. In accordance with this Directive, databases which, by reason of the selection or arrangement of their contents, constitute the author's own intellectual creation shall be protected as such by copyright.
2. The copyright protection of databases provided for by this Directive shall not extend to their contents and shall be without prejudice to any rights subsisting in those contents themselves.

Article 10: Term of Protection

The right provided for in this Directive shall run from the date of completion of the making of the database and shall expire 15 years from the first of January of the year following the date of completion.

U.S. law, in contrast, does not protect databases, other than by prohibiting the verbatim copying of databases under copyright law. An alternative means of protecting a database in the United States is through trade secrets law. However, it is difficult to maintain a database or customer list as a trade secret if it is accessible by a large pool of employees. It is strategically prudent for U.S. companies to review Directive 96/9/EC to obtain the directive's protection for its European operations.

E-Commerce and E-Contracting

The first generation of electronic contracting was performed through the use of **electronic data interchange (EDI)**. EDI is the computer-to-computer communication of information. The use of EDI for purposes of forming contracts will continue to grow. For example, in the documentary transaction, contracts will be electronically formed, electronic bills of lading will be sent to a third-party record-keeping service, letters of credit will be issued based on preexisting templates, and other necessary documents like insurance certificates will be requested and transmitted by computers. The closed nature of the EDI system allows private parties to create their own law to fill the void created by a lack of legislation.

The rules governing EDI transactions are provided in contracts known as **trading partner agreements** or interchange agreements. This form of contracting makes sense only when one contemplates a long-term contractual relationship with a relatively modest number of contracting parties. (This is in contrast to Internet commerce, which often includes many one-time transactions with relatively unknown purchasers and sellers.) The American Bar Association has developed a **Model Electronic Data Interchange Trading Partner Agreement** that can be tailored to particular types of transactions.

The Internet represents the future of electronic commerce. It has become a powerful tool for marketing and selling products internationally. There are three major commercial effects of the increased use of electronic technologies:

1. Commercial parties have begun to restructure their business practices to use electronic technologies to communicate internally as well as externally.
2. New industries have emerged to provide needed services to companies engaging in electronic commerce.
3. New types of property with commercial value have become commodities for trade domestically and internationally.

The first effect has been reflected in the increasing use of electronic contracting in place of paper transactions. The development of electronic bills of lading and letters of credit is an example of this trend, along with the use of electronic purchase orders and confirmations. The second effect has resulted in the creation of entirely new businesses. Aggregation, discussed later in the chapter, is an example. The final effect pertains to the changing nature or subject matter of business transactions. The creation of new commodities is reflected by the growing business of selling and transferring information.

Framework for Global Electronic Commerce

In 1999, the Clinton White House published **A Framework for Global Electronic Commerce**, in which it set out U.S. policy regarding electronic commerce. The framework's general premise is that regulation of the Internet and e-commerce should be primarily by private and not public means. Specifically, the framework noted: "Governments must adopt a non-regulatory, market-oriented approach to electronic commerce, one that facilitates the emergence of a transparent and predictable legal environment to support global business." The market approach is one in which the parties, through private contract, police their rights and obligations. There will nonetheless be a need for international agreement and governmental regulation in a number of areas.

The paper notes that three areas require international agreement: financial, legal, and market access. In the legal area, the paper calls for a "Uniform Commercial Code for Electronic Commerce," enhanced intellectual property protection, privacy protection, and security initiatives. In the area of developing domestic and international rules and norms, the paper acknowledges the work of the United Nations Commission on International Trade Law (UNCITRAL) in developing its Model Law on Electronic Commerce. Two fundamental principles are given to guide the development of such rules. First, contract and other rules should be technology-neutral. Second, existing rules should be applied or modified before the adoption of new rules for electronic contracting. In addition, the framework advises that these principles are best met internationally through the efforts of organizations like UNCITRAL, the International Institute for the Unification of Private Law (UNIDROIT), and the International Chamber of Commerce in developing model provisions and uniform principles.

In the area of intellectual property, the framework specifically recognizes the problem of trademark infringement and registration of domain names. It poses the preferred solution as the "development of a global market-based system to register Internet domain names." In the area of security, the paper highlights the need to develop "trusted certification services" that permit the secured use of digital signatures.

However, the enactment of a set of comprehensive and generally accepted international rules for governing electronic commerce is unlikely in the foreseeable future. Instead, the law of contracts is likely to remain the governing institution for electronic commerce. The establishment of a contractual relationship in e-commerce generally begins with customer registration. By requiring customers to register, the international vendor is better able to alleviate the concerns for authentication, security, and payment. To place an order, the customer will be required to provide a digital signature. Encryption is used to secure the transmission of the digital signature and credit information. The customer, by clicking at appropriate places, accepts the terms of the contract.

Sales over the Internet that resemble catalog sales are likely to come under the purview of consumer protection laws, and so the e-commerce contract will need to comply with legal disclosure requirements. Within the United States, compliance can be achieved through the use of icons and links. The purchaser needs only to click the appropriate icon or link to obtain the required disclosures. Foreign consumer protection laws will need to be reviewed to determine their applicability to e-commerce.

E-Contracting Law Issues

The open nature of the Internet calls for more proactive government regulation. A legal framework needs to be built to ensure the security and integrity of open network (Internet) transactions. The three major concerns for international electronic contracting are authenticity, enforceability, and confidentiality. Authenticity involves verifying the identity of the party one is dealing with electronically. Enforceability includes the legal scope of the license granted or the warranty given under a national law. It also includes the provability and verification of the contractual terms of an online transaction.

Confidentiality revolves around the protection of sensitive information, such as payment information and trade secrets. The fear is that the public nature of e-commerce makes such information susceptible to fraud and misappropriation by third parties. The minimum level of due diligence pertaining to these three concerns demands a workable knowledge of the legal requirements of forming and proving a contract through the Internet.

Electronic contracting poses a number of questions about the application of contract law to this new medium for transacting business. For example, what communications are considered offers and acceptances? When and where does an electronic acceptance reach the offeror? The answers depend on the type of communications and information being provided. A noninteractive Web page is more like an advertisement or an invitation to make an offer. Conversely, an interactive Web page designed to accept payment information such as credit card numbers could be construed as a standing offer.

The use of e-mail to negotiate contracts opens up the offeror to an acceptance by e-mail. Does the acceptance reach the offeror upon receipt by the service provider and placement in the offeror's mailbox or when the offeror opens the mailbox? The better answer would seem to be the former, because the offeror is inviting acceptance by e-mail and is thus under an implied duty to retrieve the mail in a timely fashion.[34] The next section reviews a model law that attempts to provide answers to these and other formation questions.

Uniform Computer Information Transactions Act

The **Uniform Computer Information Transactions Act (UCITA)**[35] is a model law enacted to cover the creation, transfer, and licensing of computer information and software. UCITA provides rules for sales of software and the licensing of information. A **license** is a contract that grants a licensee limited use of the intellectual and informational property rights of the licensor.[36] The licensor retains ownership of the rights being licensed. Generally, the licensee obtains a right to use a particular copy of the licensor's property.

The formation of a contract under UCITA depends on the receipt of the acceptance by the offeror. This is opposite to the common law's acceptance-upon-dispatch or mailbox rule. Receipt of an electronic notice is defined as "coming into existence in an information processing system or at an address in that system in a form capable of being processed by or perceived from a system of that type by a recipient, if the recipient uses, or otherwise has designated or holds out, that place or system for receipt of notices."[37] Thus, a contract is formed even if the receiving party fails to open or read the message of acceptance. Other offer and acceptance issues addressed by UCITA include:

http://
Text of UCITA:
http://www.law.upenn. edu/law619/f2001/ week07/ucita200a.pdf
or UCITA online at
http://www.webcom. com/legaled/UCITA/.

- Can the downloading of information constitute an acceptance? Alternatively stated, can clicking approval to terms be considered an acceptance? The answer to both of these questions seems to be yes. Both fulfill the fundamental requirement that an acceptance must merely be a definite expression of acceptance.

- In shrink-wrap licensing, how is the additional terms scenario of § 2-207 likely to be handled? UCITA states that the additional terms found in the shrink-wrapped license do become a part of the contract if the purchaser or licensee is able to review them prior to being obligated to pay. After reviewing the license, the purchaser has a right to return the item for a full refund.[38]

---

34. This information was gleaned from Christoph Glatt, "Comparative Issues in the Formation of Electronic Contracts," 6 *Journal of Law and Information Technology* 34, 50–53 (1996).

35. This is a model law published in 1999 that has been enacted by the states of Virginia and Maryland. UCITA was approved by the National Conference of Commissioners on Uniform State Laws in July 1999.

36. UCITA defines a *license* as "a contract that authorizes access to, or use, distribution, performance, modification, or reproduction of information or informational rights." UCITA, § 102(40).

37. Ibid. § 102 (52).

38. Ibid. § 112.

- The use of an **electronic agent**, such as a computer or voice ordering system, to effect a transaction raises a number of legal issues, including: (1) Can contracts be formed through electronic agents? (2) Is a contract formed when a human makes a conditional acceptance to an electronic agent? (3) What if the human attempts to insert additional terms into the contract? Do these additional terms become a part of the contract? UCITA provides rules for such scenarios. Section 206(a-b) states that "a contract may be formed by the interaction of electronic agents" and "a contract may be formed by the interaction of an electronic agent and an individual."[39] The contract is formed if the individual knowingly takes actions or makes statements that cause the electronic agent to perform. Additional terms incorporated into the acceptance do not become a part of the contract if the individual "had reason to know that the electronic agent could not react to the terms as provided."[40]

An additional issue that needs to be addressed is whether statutory warranty laws apply to Internet transactions. U.S. warranty law, as discussed in Chapters Seven and Eight, does pertain to Internet consumer transactions.[41] Therefore, under U.S. law, all warranties for products sold through the Internet must expressly state:

- the parties protected by the warranty
- any limitations on implied warranties
- any limitation of damages
- availability of alternative dispute resolution
- the coverage of the warranty (parts, characteristics of product)
- the responsibility of the seller in case of defect
- the procedure for making a warranty claim
- the commencement and expiration of the warranty period

For sales in other countries, foreign statutory warranty laws would need to be researched.

The "Shrink-Wrap" Contract

Computer software is generally sold encased in plastic wrappers. Inside the wrapper are the terms, including warranty provisions, of the contract intended to govern the sale. Besides a provision triggering the purchaser's acceptance of the **shrink-wrap license** upon opening the package, other common provisions include:

- a clause stating that the customer has not purchased the software itself but has merely obtained a personal, nontransferable license to use the program
- a disclaimer of all warranties, except for a warranty covering physical defects in the diskettes
- a clause purporting to limit the purchaser's remedies to repair and replacement of defective disks and to exclude all consequential or incidental damages caused by the software

---

39. An *electronic agent* is defined as a "computer program, or electronic or other automated means, used by a person to initiate an action, or to respond to electronic messages or performances, on the person's behalf without review or action by an individual at the time of action, or response to a message or performance." UCITA, § 102 (27).
40. Ibid. § 206(c).
41. See, e.g., Magnuson-Moss Act (federal warranty law), 15 U.S.C. § 2301-12 (2000).

- an integration clause providing that the license is the final and complete expression of the agreement
- a provision prohibiting assignment of the program or license without the express prior consent of the licensor

The purchaser does not see the license containing these provisions until after purchasing and taking possession of the software.

Computer equipment and software are also often purchased on line. The purchaser places an order and pays for an item on line but does not see the terms of the sale or license until opening the box at delivery. At issue is whether the parties have actually agreed to the terms provided in the packaged or shrink-wrapped license. U.S. law has increasingly recognized the shrink-wrap license or contract. The agreement found in the package, or sent by the vendor, typically states something to this effect: "Purchaser's receipt of services [or software] constitutes acceptance of all terms and conditions of this Agreement."

Shrink-wrap contracts are generally a U.S. phenomenon. An international seller that hopes to use a shrink-wrap contract should determine if such a contract will be recognized in the country of importation. To protect the seller of software, it may be necessary to require its foreign sales representative or agent to procure a signature on the license agreement from the foreign purchaser.

Another modern form of contracting is the **click-wrap license**. Consumers often purchase software over the Internet. After providing the necessary payment information, the purchaser is allowed to directly download the software; however, the purchaser must first agree to the terms of the software license by clicking the "accept" icon. The problem is that the actual license is embedded in another file that the purchaser can easily ignore. Thus, Web pages can be designed to obtain the purchaser's "acceptance" with very little likelihood that the purchaser will actually view the terms of the offer. (See Focus on Transactions: Key Provisions of UCITA.)

The legal status of shrink-wrap and click-wrap agreements in U.S. courts remains somewhat uncertain. The majority of courts confronted with the issue of enforceability of shrink-wrap licenses have upheld such agreements.[42] These courts have held that shrink-wrap licenses are enforceable if notice is provided on the outside of the box, the terms of the license are set forth on the inside, and the consumer is permitted to reject the license by returning the software. Courts have also upheld click-wrap licenses on similar grounds.[43] However, a small number of courts have refused to enforce click-wrap licenses on the basis of unconscionability and as contracts of adhesion.[44] Perhaps the best approach for licensors, given this uncertainty, is to include shrink-wrap and click-wrap licenses in their software transactions. This approach increases the chances that the licenses will be enforced by providing consumers with two opportunities to opt out of the license terms. There is also judicial support for upholding the terms of licenses extended under such circumstances.[45]

---

42. See, e.g., *Hill v. Gateway 2000*, 105 F.3d 1147 (7th Cir. 1996), *cert. denied*, 522 U.S. 808 (1997); *ProCD v. Zeidenberg*, 86 F.3d 1447 (7th Cir. 1996); *Adobe Systems, Inc. v. Stargate Software, Inc.*, 216 F. Supp.2d 1051 (N.D. Cal. 2002); *Peerless Wall & Window Coverings, Inc. v. Synchronics, Inc.*, 85 F. Supp.2d 519 (W.D. Pa. 2000).

43. See, e.g., *I-Systems, Inc. v. Softwares, Inc.*, 2004 U.S. Dist. LEXIS 6001 (D. Minn., March 29, 2004); *Hughes v. McMenamon*, 204 F. Supp.2d 178 (D. Mass. 2002); *iLan Systems v. Netscout Service Level Corp.*, 183 F. Supp.2d 328 (D. Mass. 2002); *Forrest v. Verizon Communications*, Inc., 805 A.2d 1007 (D.C. 2002); *Caspi v. Microsoft Network, LL.C.*, 732 A.2d 528 (N.J. App. Div. 1999).

44. See, e.g., *Specht v. Netscape Communications Corp.*, 306 F.3d 17 (2d Cir. 2002); *Comb v. Paypal, Inc.*, 218 F. Supp.2d 1165 (N.D. Cal. 2002).

45. See *Mudd-Lyman Sales & Service Corp. v. United Parcel Service, Inc.*, 236 F. Supp.2d (N.D. Ill. 2002).

Focus on Transactions

Key Provisions of UCITA

- UCITA provisions deal directly with software licenses that grant the licensee the right to access information of the licensor. This type of license is referred to as an **access contract**. See UCITA § 611(a-b).
- A contract is formed only when a person has an opportunity to review the terms of the contract. A party's "opportunity to review" the terms of a contract only after paying or beginning performance (as in a shrink-wrap contract) does not form a contract on those terms unless the party has a right to return. UCITA § 112(e)(3).
- A contract may be formed with an electronic agent such as a Web page order system. A contract is formed when an individual acts in a way that he knows will cause the electronic agent to perform. UCITA § 206(b)(1).
- Counteroffers or additional terms are ineffectual against electronic agents. Terms added by an individual do not become a part of the contract if the individual had reason to know that the electronic agent could not react to the terms. UCITA § 206(c).
- A licensor that makes information available by electronic means from its Internet site must give the licensee an opportunity to review the terms of the license (click-wrap contract). The opportunity to review requirement is satisfied if the licensor makes the terms readily available for review before the licensee is obligated to pay, by displaying the terms or a reference to an electronic location prominently and in close proximity to a description of the information or by disclosing the availability of the terms in a prominent place on the site. UCITA § 211.
- UCITA recognizes five warranties: (1) Warranty of Noninterference and Noninfringement (§ 401(a-e)); (2) Express Warranties (§ 402(a-c)); (3) Implied Warranty of Merchantability of Computer Program (§ 403(a-c)); (4) Implied Warranty of Informational Content (§ 404(a-c)); and (5) Implied Warranty of Licensee's Purpose (§ 405(a-d)).
- The Implied Warranty of Informational Content warrants to the licensee that there is "no inaccuracy in the informational content caused by the merchant's failure to perform with reasonable care."
- The licensor has a defense for modification made by the licensee to a computer program, other than by using a capability of the program intended for that purpose. Such a modification invalidates any warranties, express or implied, regarding performance of the modified copy. UCITA § 407.
- A licensor is limited in its ability to use self-help remedies such as *disabling bugs* or *time bombs*. A licensor may use self-help means only on the cancellation of a license if the licensee separately manifested assent to the term. Also, the self-help term must require the licensor to give a fifteen-day notice before exercising the remedy. The notice must give the nature of the licensee's breach and the name, address, and telephone number of a contact person. A wrongful use of electronic self-help makes the licensor liable for the consequential damages of the licensee. UCITA § 816(a-i).

Statute of Frauds Requirements and Authentication

A major obstacle to electronic commerce is the need for a signed writing to form a contract, as is required by the Uniform Commercial Code Article 2 (sale of goods) and Article 5 (letters of credit) and by UCITA (licensing). The Uniform Customs and Practices for Documentary Credits (UCP 500) recognized this problem by replacing the requirement for signatures with a requirement for "**authentication**." Many countries have also attempted to address this problem through the adoption of **digital signature laws**. For example, the Russian Federation recognized the legal validity and enforceability of electronic signatures where appropriate technical safeguards exist for identification and authentication of such signatures.[46] India's Information Technology Act of 2000 recognized the legal status of "secure digital signatures," specifically those subject to verification as unique to the subscriber, capable of identifying the subscriber, and created in a manner or using a means within the subscriber's exclusive control. Egypt adopted a similar law in April 2004. The purpose of these laws is to (1) minimize the incidence of electronic forgeries, (2) foster the reliable authentication of documents in computer form, (3) facilitate electronic commerce, and (4) provide a legal framework for technical standards relating to the authentication of computerized messages.

INTERNATIONAL

The **Electronic Signatures in Global and National Commerce Act (E-Sign Act)**, signed by President William J. Clinton on October 1, 2000, represents the most recent U.S. efforts with respect to the validation of electronic signatures.[47] The E-Sign Act represents federal recognition of legislative efforts in the states, forty-six of which had adopted legislation recognizing the validity of electronic or digital signature technology, and by various groups, including the American Bar Association. The Act provides that, as a general rule, a signature, contract, or record relating to a transaction in or affecting interstate or foreign commerce shall not be denied legal effect on the sole basis that it is in electronic form or that an electronic signature was used in its formation. The term *electronic signature* is defined as "an electronic sound, symbol, or process, attached to or logically associated with a contract or other record and executed or adopted with the intent to sign the record."[48] The E-Sign Act is technology-neutral and does not mandate what type of electronic signature must be used. The Act does, however, allow for digital signatures to serve as a form of electronic signature.[49] The Act also provides for an extensive list of disclosures to be made in the event that the agreement relates to a consumer transaction, including obtaining consent to electronic records and acknowledging that consumer protection standards may be in force and effect regardless of the electronic format of the agreement. State laws relating to electronic signatures are preempted to the extent that they are inconsistent with the E-Sign Act or give greater legal effect to electronic signatures created by using a particular technology. In addition, there are numerous exemptions to the Act, including documents relating to probate and family law matters, credit agreements relating to real property, health and life insurance policies, and recalls of products that endanger public health and safety. The Act also exempts all contracts the terms of which are otherwise governed by the Uniform Commercial Code, with the exception of sales and leases of goods pursuant to Articles 2 and 2A.

The recognition of electronic signatures in the European Union is governed by **Directive 1999/93/EC**. The directive defines an electronic signature as "data in electronic form which are attached to or logically associated with other electronic data and which serve as a method of authentication."[50] Unlike the E-Sign

INTERNATIONAL

46.   See Russian Federation, Federal Act No. 24-FZ (1995).

47.   See 15 U.S.C. §§ 7001-06 (2000).

48.   Ibid. § 7006(5).

49.   A *digital signature* is defined as "an encrypted or mathematically scrambled document that appears as a string of characters appended to the message and serves to identify the sender and establish the integrity of the document. Only someone with the proper software can decode the signature." Daniel W. Uhlfelder, "Electronic Signatures and the New Economy" (Nov. 2000), available at **http://www.gigalaw.com.**

50.   European Union Directive 1999/93/EC, art. 2(1).

Act, the directive recognizes two separate categories of electronic signatures. Article 5(1)(a-b) provides that "Category I Electronic Signatures" are considered the equivalent of handwritten signatures and are admissible as evidence in legal proceedings. To qualify as a Category I Electronic Signature, the signature must be an "advanced electronic signature," defined as an electronic signature that is uniquely linked to the signatory, identifies the signatory, is created using means under the sole control of the signatory, and allows for detection in subsequent changes in data. The signature at issue must also be based on a "qualified certificate" issued by a "certification service provider" and be created with a "secure signature creation device." Such devices are to be designed to reasonably assure the user secrecy and to detect and avoid forgeries. Annexes to the directive set forth the technical specifications required to meet the certification and creation device requirements. Electronic signatures that do not conform to these requirements are deemed "Category II Electronic Signatures." These signatures are not entitled to the degree of protection accorded to Category I signatures. Nevertheless, Article 5(2) provides that such signatures are not to be denied legal effectiveness and admissibility as evidence in legal proceedings on the sole basis that they are in electronic form, are not based on a qualified certificate issued by an accredited certification service provider, or not created by using a secure signature creation device.

International organizations have also issued their own standards for electronic signatures. For example, in 2001 UNCITRAL issued its **Model Law on Electronic Signatures**. Article 6(1) of the Model Law provides that an electronic signature satisfies the requirement of an actual signature if the electronic signature is "as reliable as was appropriate for the purpose for which the data message was generated or communicated in light of all the circumstances."[51] An electronic signature is deemed to be reliable if the signature creation data are linked exclusively to the signatory and under that person's exclusive control and if any alterations of the signature or accompanying data to which it relates are detectable. In a manner similar to the E-Sign Act, the Model Law is technology-neutral as long as the requirements of reliability are met. The Model Law is intended primarily for use in the commercial context and expressly does not override any protections granted to consumers by applicable international conventions or national law.

Until the use of digital signatures becomes more commonplace, other techniques may be used to authenticate the identity of the other party and to confirm the terms of the contractual undertaking. These techniques include acknowledgment, use of independent agents or value-added networks, and encryption. Acknowledgment can be as simple as an e-mail or a facsimile to confirm the online transaction. Private computer networks have become a popular means to broker e-commerce: They provide the vital independent record-keeping function needed to respond to the evidentiary concerns of proving the contract in case of a future breach. Finally, encryption is the strongest vehicle for alleviating concerns about confidentiality.

---

51. UNCITRAL Model Law on Electronic Signatures, art. 6(1) (2001). Article 2(a) defines *electronic signature* as "data in electronic form in, affixed to or logically associated with, a data message, which may be used to identify the signatory in relation to the data message and to indicate the signatory's approval of the information contained in the data message."

International E-Commerce Developments

Developments in e-commerce and Internet law are ongoing at both the national and international levels. The International Chamber of Commerce's guides titled **General Usage for International Digitally Ensured Commerce (GUIDEC I)**, published in 1997, and **GUIDEC II**, published in 2001, address some of the definitional and legal aspects relating to methods of overcoming e-commerce authentication and confidentiality problems. GUIDEC I and II give a general framework for ensuring (authenticating) and certifying digital messages. To do this, they developed some original nomenclature, as well as clear descriptions of the rights and responsibilities of all parties to the electronic commercial transaction. GUIDEC's operative concept of affixing a signature or verifying the author of the data message is referred to as *ensuring*. The stated goals of GUIDEC are, in part, "to enhance the ability of the international business community, to execute secure digital transactions, to establish legal principles that promote trustworthy and reliable digital ensuring and certification practices, and to define and clarify the duties of participants in the emerging ensuring and certification system."[52]

On June 13, 1997, Germany enacted a broad Internet-multimedia law, titled the Federal Act Establishing the General Conditions for Information and Communications Services ("Information and Communications Services Act"). One of the substantive provisions of the Act calls for at least a limited amount of liability for **Internet service providers (ISPs)** for the content of materials accessed through their services. However, this liability extends only if the ISP knew of the content and has the technical means to prevent its use. The law provides a reasonableness standard in determining if the ISP is jointly liable with the creator or provider of the material.[53]

The European Union has made strides to deal with the issues impeding the development of EDI and electronic commerce. In 1997, the European Commission published the "European Initiative on Electronic Commerce" or COM (97) 157. Before that initiative, the EU's first foray into e-commerce was the publication of a **Model EDI Agreement**.[54] The model agreement guides contracting parties on a number of important topics, including the regulation of the processing and acknowledgment of EDI messages, security precautions, operational requirements, and confidentiality protections.

UNCITRAL adopted a **Model Law on Electronic Commerce** on June 12, 1996.[55] The model law merely provides a framework for laws governing electronic commerce and is not comprehensive. The law potentially serves three purposes. Individual governments can use it as a model or guide in drafting national legislation. The law can be used as a source of language for contract-drafting purposes or as a set of default rules incorporated into a contract by reference. Finally, courts and arbitration panels may use it in interpreting existing international conventions and other instruments to the extent that they impede electronic commerce.

http:// "GUIDEC, A Living Document": **http:// www.iccwbo.org/home/ guidec/guidec.asp.**

http:// For more information on the German Internet-multimedia law: **http://www.iid.de**, **http://www.iukdg.de**, or **http://www.bmbf.de.**

INTERNATIONAL

INTERNATIONAL

http:// The European Initiative on Electronic Commerce: **http:// www.cordis.lu/esprit/ src/ecomcom.htm.**

---

52. Guidec II, art. I(2).

53. Similar limitations of liability for ISPs are found in the U.S. Digital Millennium Copyright Act of 1998, Pub. L. No. 105–304, 112 Stat. 2860 (Oct. 28, 1998).

54. The Model Agreement may be accessed through EU Commission Recommendation 94/820/EC and Council Decision 87/499/EEC.

55. The UNCITRAL Model Law on Electronic Commerce was amended in 1998 and may be accessed at UNCITRAL's Web site **http://www.uncitral.org/.**

The model law views the place of dispatch as crucial for determining the important issue of the law of the contract and the appropriate court in which to bring a lawsuit. Under Article 15(4) of the model law, the place of dispatch is the place of business of the sender. Therefore, the contract is concluded at the place of the sender. This is important when there is no express choice of law.

By comparison, as previously noted, the Brussels Regulation establishes the domicile or principal place of business of the defendant as the fundamental ground for jurisdiction. In addition, the place where performance of the obligation at issue was to occur may serve as an alternative ground for jurisdiction. If the contract relates to a consumer transaction, the Brussels Regulation provides that the consumer may bring an action against a business in his or her country of domicile. The application of these rules may lead to a different forum than that contemplated by the model law. Regarding choice of law, the **Rome Convention** on law applicable to contractual obligations provides that the contract, in the absence of a choice of law clause, is to be governed "by the law of the country with which it is most closely connected."[56] Article 4(2) provides a presumption in favor of the performing party's principal place of business.

The notion of incorporation by reference is highlighted in Article 5*bis* paragraph 46–2 of the model law: "incorporation by reference is regarded as essential to the widespread use of EDI, electronic mail, digital certificates, and other forms of electronic commerce. For example, electronic communications are typically structured in such a way that large numbers of messages are exchanged, with each message containing brief information, and relying much more frequently than paper documents on reference to information accessible elsewhere."

National consumer protection laws are major obstacles to such contracting by reference, so incorporation by reference in electronic contracting should be done with the mandatory rules of national laws in mind. In an online contracting environment where reference is made to the "general terms and conditions" of the seller, the application or form contract should clearly reference the terms and conditions document and make it available for review. For first-time users, the site may automatically display the referenced document before allowing the user to complete a transaction.

Electronic Documentation

In the documentary transaction that is central to the exportation of goods, "paper" is becoming less vital. Cost savings generated by electronic transmission are likely to foster increased use of the electronic communication of documents. To generate cost savings, contracts will be electronically formed, electronic bills of lading will be sent to a third-party record-keeping service, letters of credit will be issued based on a preexisting template, and other necessary documents such as insurance certificates will be requested and transmitted by computers. The realization that a bill of lading does not need to be in writing to effect a transfer of title led the Comité Maritime International (CMI) to produce the **Rules for Electronic Bills of Lading**.[57] Article 11 of the Rules provides that electronic data are the equivalent of written forms of such data. In addition, most of the documents involved in the contract formation process (pro forma invoice, purchase order, confirmations) can be transmitted through EDI.

---

56. Ibid. art. 4(1).
57. The CMI Rules for Electronic Bills of Lading may be accessed at **http://www.comitemaritime.org/cmidocs/ rulesebla.html.**

Incoterms 2000 also recognizes the trend toward electronic transmissions. Paragraph A8 of the "Free on Board" provisions of Incoterms states that where the seller and buyer have agreed to communicate electronically, documents may be replaced by an "equivalent electronic data interchange (EDI) message."

Electronic Services Industry

As electronic commerce grows, so does the need for third-party providers and value-added networks to service the industry. These service companies will perform a number of vital functions, including "protocol conversion; storage, transmission, and retrieval services; format translation; message tracing, delivery notification, and integration reports; record retention services; implementation training and consultation; security enhancement; and database development."[58] A first-generation example of the value-added network phenomenon is the Society for Worldwide Interbank Financial Telecommunications (SWIFT) system, which provides a set of rules that govern banks in their telecommunications transactions. The SWIFT system has accelerated the transmission of payments in documentary collections through a private, high-speed communications network among member banks.[59]

The need for Internet security is leading to the development of a growing security service industry. The prevalence of viruses, eavesdropping, hacking, forgery, and interception of messages has led to the creation of an increasingly sophisticated computer security industry designed to secure electronic information and systems. It is estimated that more than $1.6 trillion will be lost as a result of the activities of computer hackers and computer viruses spread through the Internet.

In 2000, the "ILOVEYOU" virus was spread through e-mail and affected more than 45 million files, costing an estimated $2.6 billion in damages, mostly in lost work time. A new industry of Internet security service providers has blossomed to defend against such crimes. Standard security includes the use of firewalls,[60] antivirus software that must be updated weekly, and systems that deny entry to hackers.[61] Custom insurance policies for computer crimes are also now available through Lloyd's of London.

Clearly, the Internet will continue to spawn the development of completely new industries. One example is the currently developing **aggregation** industry. Aggregators amass on a single Web page all information about an individual available on the Internet, including online billings, frequent flyer miles, financial, shopping, and e-mail information. The aggregated information is accessible to the individual with the use of a single password.

Aggregation becomes valuable as individuals' online activities, accounts, and information become more widespread and complicated. Banks have recently begun to affiliate themselves with aggregators to allow customers to review their entire investment and financial portfolio at a single location. Privacy and security concerns need to be resolved for a full flourishing of this new industry.

http://

See the site of a leading aggregator: **http://www.yodlee.com.**

---

58. Amelia Boss, "Electronic Commerce and the Law" in *United Nations, Uniform Commercial Law in the Twenty-First Century* 163 (1992).

59. For more information regarding SWIFT, see **http://www.swift.com;** see also Chapter Eleven.

60. A firewall is a computer barrier between networked computers and the network (Internet). It allows for the denial of access to certain external users. In essence, it allows a company to create its own internal network or intranet, accessible by internal users but not by external users.

61. One cutting-edge tool is the development of biometrics to authenticate users through the use of human characteristic recognition technologies that include the use of human DNA, palm prints, fingerprint and retina scanning, and voice recognition.

Internet Securities Offerings

A recent trend has been to offer investment information and securities over the Internet. This has become possible in the United States because the SEC has relaxed a number of regulatory requirements, openly authorizing **direct public offerings (DPOs)** over the Internet. In its 1995 Release 33–7233, the SEC stated that "the use of electronic media should be at least an equal alternative to the use of paper-based media. Accordingly, issuer or third-party information that can be delivered in paper under the federal securities laws may be delivered in electronic format."[62] Companies may make investment information available directly to prospective investors, prospectuses can be posted on line or delivered on CD-ROM, and sales may be processed over the Internet. The major obstacle to the sale of initial public offerings stock over the Internet is the absence of a secondary market for the resale of the securities. Already, however, there is evidence of the development of an e-marketplace for stocks not sold on the national securities exchanges.

A problem with electronic securities transactions is fraud. Numerous instances of illegal ponzi and pyramid schemes have been reported, as well as more traditional misrepresentations, such as using the opinion of well-known "investment advisors" who are compensated by the offering party.

In 1998, the SEC created the **Office of Internet Enforcement** to investigate and prosecute cases of Internet securities fraud. Since its establishment, the Office of Internet Enforcement has conducted a number of nationwide sweeps of and litigation directed at online investment scams. The most common are the "pump and dump," where promoters make false claims to artificially drive up the price of a stock in order to sell their own shares at a profit; the pyramid, in which participants attempt to make money by recruiting new investors; the "risk-free" fraud that promises substantial profits with no possibility of losses, and fraudulent off-shore investments.[63] The Internet enables scam artists to provide false information to a large audience quickly and anonymously.

E-Commerce Ethics

Along with the need for an adequate legal support structure, electronic commerce carries numerous ethical concerns. The e-commerce industry needs to develop its own self-regulatory code of ethics in order to provide guidance to those using the World Wide Web, Internet, and other electronic networks to transact business. The United Nations Educational, Scientific, and Cultural Organization (UNESCO) has raised a number of themes focusing on the ethical, legal, and societal aspects of e-commerce and the information society, including:

- What is the appropriate role to be played by governmental agencies in providing Internet access to the public?
- What special measures are needed to help developing countries and disadvantaged communities benefit from available knowledge and information?

---

62. The Securities and Exchange Commission has issued several additional interpretive releases relating to securities offerings on the Internet. These releases may be accessed at **http://www.sec.gov/divisions/enforce/internetenforce/interpreleases.shtml.**

63. See U.S. Securities and Exchange Commission, "Internet Fraud: How to Avoid Internet Investment Scams" (2001), available at **http://www.sec.gov/investor/pubs/cyberfraud.html.**

UNESCO has noted that whereas industry and business provide the infrastructure for access to information resources and content, the challenge is to define the concepts of public domain and **universal access** in a global context to promote common public welfare while encouraging private initiative and protecting rightful economic interests.

Another theme addressed by UNESCO is the special plight of developing countries, especially their inability to benefit fully from the new information age. The International Monetary Fund (IMF) has concluded that only 7 percent of the world's population is able to use the Internet and almost 70 percent of all Internet users are located in the United States, Canada, and Europe.[64] Use rates in the developing world pale by comparison. Use of the Internet in Africa constitutes only 0.7 percent of the world total. These percentages are equally dismal in the Middle East (0.5 percent) and Latin America (4.2 percent). The IMF concluded that this **digital divide** magnifies socioeconomic disparities, including educational opportunities, labor productivity, and creativity and ingenuity.[65]

These disparities have caused a number of international organizations to respond. For example, in 2000, the World Economic Forum launched its Global Digital Divide Initiative to develop partnerships between governments and private enterprise to increase the use of information and communications technologies in the developing world. In 2001, UNESCO began a consultative process with countries, international organizations, and other interested stakeholders to promote international cooperation in improving connectivity, increasing access, and lowering the cost of electronic and communications technology. UNESCO's effort was designed to coincide and cooperate with the Digital Opportunities Task Force created by the G-8 countries in 2000 to narrow the technological gap between developed and developing countries. In light of the digital divide and international efforts to bridge it, how should governments balance commercial interests with moral obligations to promote equitable access? To answer this question, it is important to understand the practical obstacles to greater access. For example, what are the most important economic obstacles to information access?

UNESCO asserts that the principle of free access to and free flow of information as defined in Article 19 of the Universal Declaration on Human Rights must include access to digital media. There is also an important concern that greater access may cause unexpected harm to the culture or society of a developing country. UNESCO poses the question, "How can the cultural, artistic, and scientific heritage of developing countries, including traditional and indigenous information, be suitably protected and made fairly available?" UNESCO's plan of action states that the following elements need to be addressed within a global context:

- broader and fairer access to information and communication networks and services
- application of legal exceptions to copyright for developing countries through international conventions
- promotion of freedom of expression while protecting privacy on global networks

---

64. See Ashfaq Ishaq, "On the Global Digital Divide," *Finance and Development* (Sept. 2001).
65. For example, the U.S. Internet Council estimates that information and communications technologies were responsible for 50 percent of the increase in U.S. productivity in the second half of the 1990s.

Advertising and Marketing Ethics

The International Chamber of Commerce has developed **Guidelines on Advertising and Marketing on the Internet (Guidelines)**. Its main philosophical mandate is to encourage advertisers and marketers "to create an electronic environment which all the world's consumers can fully trust." Article 1 states that "all advertising and marketing should be legal, decent, honest, and truthful." Although aspirational in character, the Guidelines do provide some concrete rules:

- Advertisers and marketers should identify themselves and the nature of their connection to any commercial messages placed on the Internet (Article 2).
- The addressees of commercial messages should be clearly informed of the cost of accessing the message or service (Article 3).
- Advertisers and marketers should take reasonable precautions to safeguard the security of their files, post a **privacy policy statement** on their online sites, and disclose the purpose and use of collected data (Article 5).

Another issue of Internet ethics is the obtaining and monitoring of user information without the consent of the user. Current technology allows retailers and others to monitor the activities of Internet users and to collect personal information such as names, addresses, purchasing patterns, and credit card information. For example, when Company X receives an inquiry or order through the Internet, it can insert small text files known as cookies in the user's computer. Cookies store information about the user's Internet use, including frequency and what files and pages are accessed. When the user revisits Company X's Web site, Company X can retrieve the information from the implanted cookie files.

The key fear about cookies is that they give a company the ability to link a user's Internet browsing habits to the user's name and provide that information to other companies. A controversy involving one of the largest Internet advertising companies evolved over this very practice. In April 2002, DoubleClick, Inc. agreed to pay $1.8 million and commit to a series of changes to its business practices in settlement of litigation with respect to its use of cookies. DoubleClick acknowledged its use of cookies to gather information on the habits of Internet users, often without their informed consent. The DoubleClick controversy revolved around its ability to link supposedly anonymous online information to specific individuals through the use of its enormous direct marketing database.

Unlike traditional mass-mailing marketing, sending uninvited bulk e-mails is considered an unethical business practice and violates most "acceptable use policies," as well as applicable U.S. law. Most Internet service providers state acceptable use policies (AUPs) that prohibit users from engaging in bulk e-mail advertising. It is prudent for a prospective user to review the AUP of an Internet access provider before engaging its services.

http://

The Publishing Law Center—"Internet Legal Issues (Spam, Framing, and Linking)":
http://www. publaw.com/spam.html;
http://www.publaw.com/ framing.html; and
http://www.publaw.com/ linking.html.

KEY TERMS

access contract
aggregation
Anti-Cybersquatting Consumer
    Protection Act (ACPA)
authentication

blocking right
blurring
Brussels Regulation
click-wrap license
comity

Controlling the Assault of
    Non-Solicited Pornography
    and Marketing Act of 2003
    (Can-Spam Act)
cookies

cybersquatters
digital divide
digital signature laws
Directive 96/9/EC on the Legal
    Protection of Databases
Directive 1999/93/EC
Directive 2002/58/EC on Privacy
    and Electronic Communications
Directive on the Protection of
    Individuals with Regard to the
    Processing of Personal Data and
    the Free Movement of Such Data
    (Directive 95/46)
direct public offerings (DPOs)
disclaimers
electronic agent
Electronic Communications Privacy
    Act of 1986
electronic data interchange (EDI)
Electronic Signatures in Global
    and National Commerce Act
    (E-Sign Act)

Fair Credit Reporting Act
Federal Trademark Dilution Act of
    1995
A Framework for Global Electronic
    Commerce
General Usage for International
    Digitally Ensured Commerce
    (GUIDEC I)
GUIDEC II
Guidelines on Advertising and
    Marketing on the Internet
    (Guidelines)
Internet service provider (ISP)
Lanham Act
license
minimum contacts
Model EDI Agreement
Model Electronic Data Interchange
    Trading Partner Agreement
Model Law on Electronic
    Commerce
Model Law on Electronic Signatures

Office of Internet Enforcement
passive Web page
personal jurisdiction
Privacy Act of 1994
privacy policy statement
right of access
right of correction
right of objection
Rome Convention
Rules for Electronic Bills
    of Lading
safe harbor agreement
shareware
shrink-wrap license
spamming
Telecommunications Act of 1996
Telephone Consumer Protection Act
trading partner agreement
Uniform Computer Information
    Transactions Act (UCITA)
universal access

CHAPTER PROBLEMS

1. Marobie released copyrighted clip art for use by the fire service industry. The National Association of Fire Equipment Distributors (NAFED) had a Web page on which it placed Marobie's clip art so that any Web user could download it. Marobie sued NAFED and Northwest, the provider of the host computer for NAFED's Web page, for infringement. Is the Internet service provider liable for infringement? *Marobie-FL, Inc. v. National Association of Fire Equipment Distributors*, 983 F. Supp. 1167 (N.D. Ill. 1997).

2. The defendant put up a Web site as a promotion for its upcoming Internet service. The service consisted of assigning users an electronic mailbox and then forwarding advertisements for products and services that matched the users' interests to those electronic mailboxes. The defendant planned to charge advertisers and provide users with incentives to view the advertisements. The defendant argues that the court did not possess personal jurisdiction because the Web site in its current form was a passive provider of information pertaining to future services. What do you think? *Maritz, Inc. v. Cybergold, Inc.*, 947 F. Supp. 1328 (E.D. Mo. 1996).

3. E-Data Corporation ("E-Data") is a Utah corporation with a business office in Connecticut. West Stock, a Washington corporation with its principal place of business in Seattle, Washington, licenses stock photography

to commercial users. It has no offices in Connecticut, owns no property and maintains no financial accounts in this forum, and does not have any employees or other agents in Connecticut. Since December 1995, West Stock has operated "Muse," an Internet-based stock photography service through which purchasers may electronically select a photograph, license its use, pay for that use, and download the image—all via the Internet. E-Data claims that West Stock has infringed on its patent. The patented invention is a system for reproducing information embodied in material objects, such as recordings, video games, motion pictures, books, sheet music, greeting cards, and the like, at point-of-sale locations with the permission of the owner of the information. Specifically, plaintiff claims that defendant West Stock infringes the patent when it offers consumers the opportunity to purchase photography images via the Internet by paying a licensing fee to unlock and instantly download photography images on the consumer's computer. West Stock moves to dismiss contending that the court lacks personal jurisdiction over it in Connecticut. Does the Connecticut court have personal jurisdiction over West Stock? *E-Data Corp. v. Micropatent Corp.*, 989 F. Supp. 173 (D.Conn 1997).

4. Sportsman's is a mail order company that is well known in the aviation field. It began using the logo "sporty" in the 1960s and registered "sporty's" as a trademark in 1985. It spends about $10 million a year advertising its sporty's logo. A competitor, Pilot's Depot, was set up in early 1995 and registered the domain name sportys.com. The competitor then set up another company, Sporty's Farm, which used the domain name sportys.com to advertise the sale of its Christmas trees on that Web site. The question before the court was which company had the right to the domain name. Which company do you think has a right to the domain name? Does Sportsman have to prove that Pilot's Depot acted in bad faith? How does the Anti-Cybersquatting Consumer Protection Act apply to this case? *Sporty's Farm L.L.C. v. Sportsman's Market, Inc.*, 202 F.3d 489 (2nd Cir. 2000), *cert. denied*, 530 U.S. 1262 (2000).

5. Employees may send personal e-mails at work, just as they may have personal phone conversations. Do employees have a right of privacy in the e-mails? Do employers have the right to monitor employee e-mail? Does an employer have to notify its employees of its intent to monitor? Can an employer monitor e-mail after stating that it would not monitor? What would be a proper ethical approach to employer monitoring? *Smith v. Pillsbury Co.*, 914 F. Supp. 97 (E.D. Pa., 1996).

INTERNET EXERCISES

1. (a) Visit the Web site of the CyberSpace Law Center at **http://www.cyberlaw.com.** Prepare a report on recent developments in the area of international piracy and patent infringement. (b) Visit the Web site of Internet Legal Services at **http://www.legalethics.com.** This site covers legal issues dealing with advertising on the Internet and the confidentiality of e-mail. Report on employer and employee rights pertaining to e-mail privacy. (c) Review the directory of firewall and computer security information at **http://www.firewall.com.**

2. (a) Review International Safe Harbor Privacy Principles and report on their requirements: **http://www. ita.doc.gov/td/ecom/shprin.html.** (b) Review the privacy policy of a major online retailer such as Amazon or L.L. Bean. (c) Review industry-based privacy principles and programs such as **http://www.bbbonline.org/** (Council of Better Business Bureaus, Inc., program) or **http://www.truste.org** (TRUSTe is an organization of Web publishers who have agreed to certain privacy principles).

3. The Digital Millennium Copyright Act (DMCA) provides Internet service providers a measure of immunity from liability for illegal content (pornography, defamation). What are the responsibilities of the provider in order to obtain this immunity from prosecution? What are the similarities and differences between DMCA and the German MultiMedia Law discussed in the chapter? For coverage of the DMCA see Educase at **http:// www.educause.edu/Browse/645?PARENT_ID=254** and Association of Research Libraries, "DMCA: Status & Analysis" at **http://www.arl.org/info/frn/copy/dmca.html.** For materials on the German MultiMedia Law see **http:// www.iid.de/contents.html, http://www.iid.de/iukdg/ english.html,** or **http://www.bmbf.de/en/index.php.**

Appendix A

United Nations Convention on Contracts for the International Sale of Goods

(Not Including Sections 91-101 on Ratification)

PART I
SPHERE OF APPLICATION AND GENERAL PROVISIONS

Chapter I
Sphere of Application

ARTICLE 1

(1) This Convention applies to contracts of sale of goods between parties whose places of business are in different States:

    (a) when the States are Contracting States; or

    (b) when the rules of private international law lead to the application of the law of a Contracting State.

(2) The fact that the parties have their places of business in different States is to be disregarded whenever this fact does not appear either from the contract or from any dealings between, or from information disclosed by, the parties at any time before or at the conclusion of the contract.

(3) Neither the nationality of the parties nor the civil or commercial character of the parties or of the contract is to be taken into consideration in determining the application of this Convention.

ARTICLE 2

This Convention does not apply to sales:

(a) of goods bought for personal, family or household use, unless the seller, at any time before or at the conclusion of the contract, neither knew nor ought to have known that the goods were bought for any such use;

(b) by auction;

(c) on execution or otherwise by authority of law;

(d) of stocks, shares, investment securities, negotiable instruments or money;

(e) of ships, vessels, hovercraft or aircraft;

(f) of electricity.

ARTICLE 3

(1) Contracts for the supply of goods to be manufactured or produced are to be considered sales unless the party who orders the goods undertakes to supply a substantial part of the materials necessary for such manufacture or production.

(2) This Convention does not apply to contracts in which the preponderant part of the obligations of the party who furnishes the goods consists in the supply of labour or other services.

ARTICLE 4

This Convention governs only the formation of the contract of sale and the rights and obligations of the seller and the buyer arising from such a contract. In particular, except as otherwise expressly provided in this Convention, it is not concerned with:

(a) the validity of the contract or of any of its provisions or of any usage;

(b) the effect which the contract may have on the property in the goods sold.

ARTICLE 5

This Convention does not apply to the liability of the seller for death or personal injury caused by the goods to any person.

ARTICLE 6

The parties may exclude the application of this Convention or, subject to article 12, derogate from or vary the effect of any of its provisions.

Chapter II
General Provisions

ARTICLE 7

(1) In the interpretation of this Convention, regard is to be had to its international character and to the need to promote uniformity in its application and the observance of good faith in international trade.

(2) Questions concerning matters governed by this Convention which are not expressly settled in it are to be settled in conformity with the general principles

on which it is based or, in the absence of such principles, in conformity with the law applicable by virtue of the rules of private international law.

ARTICLE 8
(1) For the purposes of this Convention statements made by and other conduct of a party are to be interpreted according to his intent where the other party knew or could not have been unaware what that intent was.

(2) If the preceding paragraph is not applicable, statements made by and other conduct of a party are to be interpreted according to the understanding that a reasonable person of the same kind as the other party would have had in the same circumstances.

(3) In determining the intent of a party or the understanding a reasonable person would have had, due consideration is to be given to all relevant circumstances of the case including the negotiations, any practices which the parties have established between themselves, usages and any subsequent conduct of the parties.

ARTICLE 9
(1) The parties are bound by any usage to which they have agreed and by any practices which they have established between themselves.

(2) The parties are considered, unless otherwise agreed, to have impliedly made applicable to their contract or its formation a usage of which the parties knew or ought to have known and which in international trade is widely known to, and regularly observed by, parties to contracts of the type involved in the particular trade concerned.

ARTICLE 10
For the purposes of this Convention:
(a) if a party has more than one place of business, the place of business is that which has the closest relationship to the contract and its performance, having regard to the circumstances known to or contemplated by the parties at any time before or at the conclusion of the contract;

(b) if a party does not have a place of business, reference is to be made to his habitual residence.

ARTICLE 11
A contract of sale need not be concluded in or evidenced by writing and is not subject to any other requirement as to form. It may be proved by any means, including witnesses.

ARTICLE 12
Any provision of article 11, article 29 or Part II of this Convention that allows a contract of sale or its modification or termination by agreement or any offer, acceptance or other indication of intention to be made in any form other than in writing does not apply where any party has his place of business in a Contracting State which has made a declaration under article 96 of this Convention. The parties may not derogate from or vary the effect or this article.

ARTICLE 13
For the purposes of this Convention "writing" includes telegram and telex.

PART II
FORMATION OF THE CONTRACT

ARTICLE 14

(1) A proposal for concluding a contract addressed to one or more specific persons constitutes an offer if it is sufficiently definite and indicates the intention of the offeror to be bound in case of acceptance. A proposal is sufficiently definite if it indicates the goods and expressly or implicitly fixes or makes provision for determining the quantity and the price.

(2) A proposal other than one addressed to one or more specific persons is to be considered merely as an invitation to make offers, unless the contrary is clearly indicated by the person making the proposal.

ARTICLE 15

(1) An offer becomes effective when it reaches the offeree.

(2) An offer, even if it is irrevocable, may be withdrawn if the withdrawal reaches the offeree before or at the same time as the offer.

ARTICLE 16

(1) Until a contract is concluded an offer may be revoked if the revocation reaches the offeree before he has dispatched an acceptance.

(2) However, an offer cannot be revoked:

  (a) if it indicates, whether by stating a fixed time for acceptance or otherwise, that it is irrevocable; or

  (b) if it was reasonable for the offeree to rely on the offer as being irrevocable and the offeree has acted in reliance on the offer.

ARTICLE 17

An offer, even if it is irrevocable, is terminated when a rejection reaches the offeror.

ARTICLE 18

(1) A statement made by or other conduct of the offeree indicating assent to an offer is an acceptance. Silence or inactivity does not in itself amount to acceptance.

(2) An acceptance of an offer becomes effective at the moment the indication of assent reaches the offeror. An acceptance is not effective if the indication of assent does not reach the offeror within the time he has fixed or, if no time is fixed, within a reasonable time, due account being taken of the circumstances of the transaction, including the rapidity of the means of communication employed by the offeror. An oral offer must be accepted immediately unless the circumstances indicate otherwise.

(3) However, if, by virtue of the offer or as a result of practices which the parties have established between themselves or of usage, the offeree may indicate assent by performing an act, such as one relating to the dispatch of the goods or payment of the price, without notice to the offeror, the acceptance is effective at the moment the act is performed, provided that the act is performed within the period of time laid down in the preceding paragraph.

ARTICLE 19

(1) A reply to an offer which purports to be an acceptance but contains additions, limitations or other modifications is a rejection of the offer and constitutes a counter-offer.

(2) However, a reply to an offer which purports to be an acceptance but contains additional or different terms which do not materially alter the terms of the offer constitutes an acceptance, unless the offeror, without undue delay, objects orally to the discrepancy or dispatches a notice to that effect. If he does not so object, the terms of the contract are the terms of the offer with the modifications contained in the acceptance.

(3) Additional or different terms relating, among other things, to the price, payment, quality and quantity of the goods, place and time of delivery, extent of one party's liability to the other or the settlement of disputes are considered to alter the terms of the offer materially.

ARTICLE 20

(1) A period of time for acceptance fixed by the offeror in a telegram or a letter begins to run from the moment the telegram is handed in for dispatch or from the date shown on the letter or, if no such date is shown, from the date shown on the envelope. A period of time for acceptance fixed by the offeror by telephone, telex or other means of instantaneous communication, begins to run from the moment that the offer reaches the offeree.

(2) Official holidays or non-business days occurring during the period for acceptance are included in calculating the period. However, if a notice of acceptance cannot be delivered at the address of the offeror on the last day of the period because that day falls on an official holiday or a non-business day at the place of business of the offeror, the period is extended until the first business day which follows.

ARTICLE 21

(1) A late acceptance is nevertheless effective as an acceptance if without delay the offeror orally so informs the offeree or dispatches a notice to that effect.

(2) If a letter or other writing containing a late acceptance shows that it has been sent in such circumstances that if its transmission had been normal it would have reached the offeror in due time, the late acceptance is effective as an acceptance unless, without delay, the offeror orally informs the offeree that he considers his offer as having lapsed or dispatches a notice to that effect.

ARTICLE 22

An acceptance may be withdrawn if the withdrawal reaches the offeror before or at the same time as the acceptance would have become effective.

ARTICLE 23

A contract is concluded at the moment when an acceptance of an offer becomes effective in accordance with the provisions of this Convention.

ARTICLE 24

For the purposes of this Part of the Convention, an offer, declaration of acceptance or any other indication of intention "reaches" the addressee when it is made orally to him or delivered by any other means to him personally, to his place of business or mailing address or, if he does not have a place of business or mailing address, to his habitual residence.

PART III
SALE OF GOODS

Chapter I
General Provisions

ARTICLE 25

A breach of contract committed by one of the parties is fundamental if it results in such detriment to the other party as substantially to deprive him of what he is entitled to expect under the contract, unless the party in breach did not foresee and a reasonable person of the same kind in the same circumstances would not have foreseen such a result.

ARTICLE 26

A declaration of avoidance of the contract is effective only if made by notice to the other party.

ARTICLE 27

Unless otherwise expressly provided in this Part of the Convention, if any notice, request or other communication is given or made by a party in accordance with this Part and by means appropriate in the circumstances, a delay or error in the transmission of the communication or its failure to arrive does not deprive that party of the right to rely on the communication.

ARTICLE 28

If, in accordance with the provisions of this Convention, one party is entitled to require performance of any obligation by the other party, a court is not bound to enter a judgement for specific performance unless the court would do so under its own law in respect of similar contracts of sale not governed by this Convention.

ARTICLE 29

(1) A contract may be modified or terminated by the mere agreement of the parties.

(2) A contract in writing which contains a provision requiring any modification or termination by agreement to be in writing may not be otherwise modified or terminated by agreement. However, a party may be precluded by his conduct from asserting such a provision to the extent that the other party has relied on that conduct.

Chapter II
Obligations of the Seller

ARTICLE 30

The seller must deliver the goods, hand over any documents relating to them and transfer the property in the goods, as required by the contract and this Convention.

Section I. Delivery of the Goods and Handing Over of Documents

ARTICLE 31

If the seller is not bound to deliver the goods at any other particular place, his obligation to deliver consists:

(a) if the contract of sale involves carriage of the goods—in handing the goods over to the first carrier for transmission to the buyer;

(b) if, in cases not within the preceding subparagraph, the contract relates to specific goods, or unidentified goods to be drawn from a specific stock or to be manufactured or produced, and at the time of the conclusion of the contract the parties knew that the goods were at, or were to be manufactured or produced at, a particular place—in placing the goods at the buyer's disposal at that place;

(c) in other cases—in placing the goods at the buyer's disposal at the place where the seller had his place of business at the time of the conclusion of the contract.

ARTICLE 32

(1) If the seller, in accordance with the contract or this Convention, hands the goods over to a carrier and if the goods are not clearly identified to the contract by markings on the goods, by shipping documents or otherwise, the seller must give the buyer notice of the consignment specifying the goods.

(2) If the seller is bound to arrange for carriage of the goods, he must make such contracts as are necessary for carriage to the place fixed by means of transportation appropriate in the circumstances and according to the usual terms for such transportation.

(3) If the seller is not bound to effect insurance in respect of the carriage of the goods, he must, at the buyer's request, provide him with all available information necessary to enable him to effect such insurance.

ARTICLE 33

The seller must deliver the goods:

(a) if a date is fixed by or determinable from the contract, on that date;

(b) if a period of time is fixed by or determinable from the contract, at any time within that period unless circumstances indicate that the buyer is to choose a date; or

(c) in any other case, within a reasonable time after the conclusion of the contract.

ARTICLE 34

If the seller is bound to hand over documents relating to the goods, he must hand them over at the time and place and in the form required by the contract. If the seller has handed over documents before that time, he may, up to that time, cure any lack of conformity in the documents, if the exercise of this right does not cause the buyer unreasonable inconvenience or unreasonable expense. However, the buyer retains any right to claim damages as provided for in this Convention.

Section II. Conformity of the Goods and Third Party Claims

ARTICLE 35

(1) The seller must deliver goods which are of the quantity, quality and description required by the contract and which are contained or packaged in the manner required by the contract.

(2) Except where the parties have agreed otherwise, the goods do not conform with the contract unless they:

(a) are fit for the purposes for which goods of the same description would ordinarily be used;

(b) are fit for any particular purpose expressly or impliedly made known to the seller at the time of the conclusion of the contract, except where the circumstances show that the buyer did not rely, or that it was unreasonable for him to rely, on the seller's skill and judgement;

(c) possess the qualities of goods which the seller has held out to the buyer as a sample or model;

(d) are contained or packaged in the manner usual for such goods or, where there is no such manner, in a manner adequate to preserve and protect the goods.

(3) The seller is not liable under subparagraphs (a) to (d) of the preceding paragraph for any lack of conformity of the goods if at the time of the conclusion of the contract the buyer knew or could not have been unaware of such lack of conformity.

ARTICLE 36

(1) The seller is liable in accordance with the contract and this Convention for any lack of conformity which exists at the time when the risk passes to the buyer, even though the lack of conformity becomes apparent only after that time.

(2) The seller is also liable for any lack of conformity which occurs after the time indicated in the preceding paragraph and which is due to a breach of any of his obligations, including a breach of any guarantee that for a period of time the goods will remain fit for their ordinary purpose or for some particular purpose or will retain specified qualities or characteristics.

ARTICLE 37

If the seller has delivered goods before the date for delivery, he may, up to that date, deliver any missing part or make up any deficiency in the quantity of the goods delivered, or deliver goods in replacement of any non-conforming goods delivered or remedy any lack of conformity in the goods delivered, provided that the exercise of this right does not cause the buyer unreasonable inconvenience or unreasonable expense. However, the buyer retains any right to claim damages as provided for in this Convention.

ARTICLE 38

(1) The buyer must examine the goods, or cause them to be examined, within as short a period as is practicable in the circumstances.

(2) If the contract involves carriage of the goods, examination may be deferred until after the goods have arrived at their destination.

(3) If the goods are redirected in transit or redispatched by the buyer without a reasonable opportunity for examination by him and at the time of the conclusion of the contract the seller knew or ought to have known of the possibility of such redirection or redispatch, examination may be deferred until after the goods have arrived at the new destination.

ARTICLE 39

(1) The buyer loses the right to rely on a lack of conformity of the goods if he does not give notice to the seller specifying the nature of the lack of conformity within a reasonable time after he has discovered it or ought to have discovered it.

(2) In any event, the buyer loses the right to rely on a lack of conformity of the goods if he does not give the seller notice thereof at the latest within a period of two

years from the date on which the goods were actually handed over to the buyer, unless this time-limit is inconsistent with a contractual period of guarantee.

ARTICLE 40

The seller is not entitled to rely on the provisions of articles 38 and 39 if the lack of conformity relates to facts of which he knew or could not have been unaware and which he did not disclose to the buyer.

ARTICLE 41

The seller must deliver goods which are free from any right or claim of a third party, unless the buyer agreed to take the goods subject to that right or claim. However, if such right or claim is based on industrial property or other intellectual property, the seller's obligation is governed by article 42.

ARTICLE 42

(1) The seller must deliver goods which are free from any right or claim of a third party based on industrial property or other intellectual property, of which at the time of the conclusion of the contract the seller knew or could not have been unaware, provided that the right or claim is based on industrial property or other intellectual property:

   (a) under the law of the State where the goods will be resold or otherwise used, if it was contemplated by the parties at the time of the conclusion of the contract that the goods would be resold or otherwise used in that State; or

   (b) in any other case, under the law of the State where the buyer has his place of business.

(2) The obligation of the seller under the preceding paragraph does not extend to cases where:

   (a) at the time of the conclusion of the contract the buyer knew or could not have been unaware of the right or claim; or

   (b) the right or claim results from the seller's compliance with technical drawings, designs, formulae or other such specifications furnished by the buyer.

ARTICLE 43

(1) The buyer loses the right to rely on the provisions of article 41 or article 42 if he does not give notice to the seller specifying the nature of the right or claim of the third party within a reasonable time after he has become aware or ought to have become aware of the right or claim.

(2) The seller is not entitled to rely on the provisions of the preceding paragraph if he knew of the right or claim of the third party and the nature of it.

ARTICLE 44

Notwithstanding the provisions of paragraph (1) of article 39 and paragraph (1) of article 43, the buyer may reduce the price in accordance with article 50 or claim damages, except for loss of profit, if he has a reasonable excuse for his failure to give the required notice.

Section III. Remedies for Breach of Contract by the Seller

ARTICLE 45

(1) If the seller fails to perform any of his obligations under the contract or this Convention, the buyer may:

    (a) exercise the rights provided in articles 46 to 52;

    (b) claim damages as provided in articles 74 to 77.

(2) The buyer is not deprived of any right he may have to claim damages by exercising his right to other remedies.

(3) No period of grace may be granted to the seller by a court or arbitral tribunal when the buyer resorts to a remedy for breach of contract.

ARTICLE 46

(1) The buyer may require performance by the seller of his obligations unless the buyer has resorted to a remedy which is inconsistent with this requirement.

(2) If the goods do not conform with the contract, the buyer may require delivery of substitute goods only if the lack of conformity constitutes a fundamental breach of contract and a request for substitute goods is made either in conjunction with notice given under article 39 or within a reasonable time thereafter.

(3) If the goods do not conform with the contract, the buyer may require the seller to remedy the lack of conformity by repair, unless this is unreasonable having regard to all the circumstances. A request for repair must be made either in conjunction with notice given under article 39 or within a reasonable time thereafter.

ARTICLE 47

(1) The buyer may fix an additional period of time of reasonable length for performance by the seller of his obligations.

(2) Unless the buyer has received notice from the seller that he will not perform within the period so fixed, the buyer may not, during that period, resort to any remedy for breach of contract. However, the buyer is not deprived thereby of any right he may have to claim damages for delay in performance.

ARTICLE 48

(1) Subject to article 49, the seller may, even after the date for delivery, remedy at his own expense any failure to perform his obligations, if he can do so without unreasonable delay and without causing the buyer unreasonable inconvenience or uncertainty of reimbursement by the seller of expenses advanced by the buyer. However, the buyer retains any right to claim damages as provided for in this Convention.

(2) If the seller requests the buyer to make known whether he will accept performance and the buyer does not comply with the request within a reasonable time, the seller may perform within the time indicated in his request. The buyer may not, during that period of time, resort to any remedy which is inconsistent with performance by the seller.

(3) A notice by the seller that he will perform within a specified period of time is assumed to include a request, under the preceding paragraph, that the buyer make known his decision.

(4) A request or notice by the seller under paragraph (2) or (3) of this article is not effective unless received by the buyer.

ARTICLE 49

(1) The buyer may declare the contract avoided:

   (a) if the failure by the seller to perform any of his obligations under the contract or this Convention amounts to a fundamental breach of contract; or

   (b) in case of non-delivery, if the seller does not deliver the goods within the additional period of time fixed by the buyer in accordance with paragraph (1) of article 47 or declares that he will not deliver within the period so fixed.

(2) However, in cases where the seller has delivered the goods, the buyer loses the right to declare the contract avoided unless he does so:

   (a) in respect of late delivery, within a reasonable time after he has become aware that delivery has been made;

   (b) in respect of any breach other than late delivery, within a reasonable time:

      (i)   after he knew or ought to have known of the breach;
      (ii) after the expiration of any additional period of time fixed by the buyer in accordance with paragraph (1) of article 47, or after the seller has declared that he will not perform his obligations within such an additional period; or
      (iii) after the expiration of any additional period of time indicated by the seller in accordance with paragraph (2) of article 48, or after the buyer has declared that he will not accept performance.

ARTICLE 50

If the goods do not conform with the contract and whether or not the price has already been paid, the buyer may reduce the price in the same proportion as the value that the goods actually delivered had at the time of the delivery bears to the value that conforming goods would have had at that time. However, if the seller remedies any failure to perform his obligations in accordance with article 37 or article 48 or if the buyer refuses to accept performance by the seller in accordance with those articles, the buyer may not reduce the price.

ARTICLE 51

(1) If the seller delivers only a part of the goods or if only a part of the goods delivered is in conformity with the contract, articles 46 to 50 apply in respect of the part which is missing or which does not conform.

(2) The buyer may declare the contract avoided in its entirety only if the failure to make delivery completely or in conformity with the contract amounts to a fundamental breach of the contract.

ARTICLE 52

(1) If the seller delivers the goods before the date fixed, the buyer may take delivery or refuse to take delivery.

(2) If the seller delivers a quantity of goods greater than that provided for in the contract, the buyer may take delivery or refuse to take delivery of the excess quantity. If the buyer takes delivery of all or part of the excess quantity, he must pay for it at the contract rate.

Chapter III
Obligations of the Buyer

ARTICLE 53

The buyer must pay the price for the goods and take delivery of them as required by the contract and this Convention.

Section I. Payment of the Price

ARTICLE 54

The buyer's obligation to pay the price includes taking such steps and complying with such formalities as may be required under the contract or any laws and regulations to enable payment to be made.

ARTICLE 55

Where a contract has been validly concluded but does not expressly or implicitly fix or make provision for determining the price, the parties are considered, in the absence of any indication to the contrary, to have impliedly made reference to the price generally charged at the time of the conclusion of the contract for such goods sold under comparable circumstances in the trade concerned.

ARTICLE 56

If the price is fixed according to the weight of the goods, in case of doubt it is to be determined by the net weight.

ARTICLE 57

(1) If the buyer is not bound to pay the price at any other particular place, he must pay it to the seller:

    (a) at the seller's place of business; or

    (b) if the payment is to be made against the handing over of the goods or of documents, at the place where the handing over takes place.

(2) The seller must bear any increases in the expenses incidental to payment which is caused by a change in his place of business subsequent to the conclusion of the contract.

ARTICLE 58

(1) If the buyer is not bound to pay the price at any other specific time, he must pay it when the seller places either the goods or documents controlling their disposition at the buyer's disposal in accordance with the contract and this Convention. The seller may make such payment a condition for handing over the goods or documents.

(2) If the contract involves carriage of the goods, the seller may dispatch the goods on terms whereby the goods, or documents controlling their disposition, will not be handed over to the buyer except against payment of the price.

(3) The buyer is not bound to pay the price until he has had an opportunity to examine the goods, unless the procedures for delivery or payment agreed upon by the parties are inconsistent with his having such an opportunity.

ARTICLE 59

The buyer must pay the price on the date fixed by or determinable from the contract and this Convention without the need for any request or compliance with any formality on the part of the seller.

Section II. Taking Delivery

ARTICLE 60

The buyer's obligation to take delivery consists:

    (a) in doing all the acts which could reasonably be expected of him in order to enable the seller to make delivery; and

(b) in taking over the goods.

Section III. Remedies for Breach of Contract by the Buyer

ARTICLE 61

(1) If the buyer fails to perform any of his obligations under the contract or this Convention, the seller may:

(a) exercise the rights provided in articles 62 to 65;

(b) claim damages as provided in articles 74 to 77.

(2) The seller is not deprived of any right he may have to claim damages by exercising his right to other remedies.

(3) No period of grace may be granted to the buyer by a court or arbitral tribunal when the seller resorts to a remedy for breach of contract.

ARTICLE 62

The seller may require the buyer to pay the price, take delivery or perform his other obligations, unless the seller has resorted to a remedy which is inconsistent with this requirement.

ARTICLE 63

(1) The seller may fix an additional period of time of reasonable length for performance by the buyer of his obligations.

(2) Unless the seller has received notice from the buyer that he will not perform within the period so fixed, the seller may not, during that period, resort to any remedy for breach of contract. However, the seller is not deprived thereby of any right he may have to claim damages for delay in performance.

ARTICLE 64

(1) The seller may declare the contract avoided:

(a) if the failure by the buyer to perform any of his obligations under the contract or this Convention amounts to a fundamental breach of contract; or

(b) if the buyer does not, within the additional period of time fixed by the seller in accordance with paragraph (1) of article 63, perform his obligation to pay the price or take delivery of the goods, or if he declares that he will not do so within the period so fixed.

(2) However, in cases where the buyer has paid the price, the seller loses the right to declare the contract avoided unless he does so:

(a) in respect of late performance by the buyer, before the seller has become aware that performance has been rendered; or

(b) in respect of any breach other than late performance by the buyer, within a reasonable time:

(i) after the seller knew or ought to have known of the breach; or

(ii) after the expiration of any additional period of time fixed by the seller in accordance with paragraph (1) of article 63, or after the buyer has declared that he will not perform his obligations within such an additional period.

ARTICLE 65

(1) If under the contract the buyer is to specify the form, measurement or other features of the goods and he fails to make such specification either on the date

agreed upon or within a reasonable time after receipt of a request from the seller, the seller may, without prejudice to any other rights he may have, make the specification himself in accordance with the requirements of the buyer that may be known to him.

(2) If the seller makes the specification himself, he must inform the buyer of the details thereof and must fix a reasonable time within which the buyer may make a different specification. If, after receipt of such a communication, the buyer fails to do so within the time so fixed, the specification made by the seller is binding.

Chapter IV
Passing of Risk

ARTICLE 66
Loss of or damage to the goods after the risk has passed to the buyer does not discharge him from his obligation to pay the price, unless the loss or damage is due to an act or omission of the seller.

ARTICLE 67
(1) If the contract of sale involves carriage of the goods and the seller is not bound to hand them over at a particular place, the risk passes to the buyer when the goods are handed over to the first carrier for transmission to the buyer in accordance with the contract of sale. If the seller is bound to hand the goods over to a carrier at a particular place, the risk does not pass to the buyer until the goods are handed over to the carrier at that place. The fact that the seller is authorized to retain documents controlling the disposition of the goods does not affect the passage of the risk.

(2) Nevertheless, the risk does not pass to the buyer until the goods are clearly identified to the contract, whether by markings on the goods, by shipping documents, by notice given to the buyer or otherwise.

ARTICLE 68
The risk in respect of goods sold in transit passes to the buyer from the time of the conclusion of the contract. However, if the circumstances so indicate, the risk is assumed by the buyer from the time the goods were handed over to the carrier who issued the documents embodying the contract of carriage. Nevertheless, if at the time of the conclusion of the contract of sale the seller knew or ought to have known that the goods had been lost or damaged and did not disclose this to the buyer, the loss or damage is at the risk of the seller.

ARTICLE 69
(1) In cases not within articles 67 and 68, the risk passes to the buyer when he takes over the goods or, if he does not do so in due time, from the time when the goods are placed at his disposal and he commits a breach of contract by failing to take delivery.

(2) However, if the buyer is bound to take over the goods at a place other than a place of business of the seller, the risk passes when delivery is due and the buyer is aware of the fact that the goods are placed at his disposal at that place.

(3) If the contract relates to goods not then identified, the goods are considered not to be placed at the disposal of the buyer until they are clearly identified to the contract.

ARTICLE 70

If the seller has committed a fundamental breach of contract, articles 67, 68 and 69 do not impair the remedies available to the buyer on account of the breach.

Chapter V
Provisions Common to the Obligations of the Seller and of the Buyer

Section I. Anticipatory Breach and Instalment Contracts

ARTICLE 71

(1) A party may suspend the performance of his obligations if, after the conclusion of the contract, it becomes apparent that the other party will not perform a substantial part of his obligations as a result of:

    (a) a serious deficiency in his ability to perform or in his creditworthiness; or

    (b) his conduct in preparing to perform or in performing the contract.

(2) If the seller has already dispatched the goods before the grounds described in the preceding paragraph become evident, he may prevent the handing over of the goods to the buyer even though the buyer holds a document which entitles him to obtain them. The present paragraph relates only to the rights in the goods as between the buyer and the seller.

(3) A party suspending performance, whether before or after dispatch of the goods, must immediately give notice of the suspension to the other party and must continue with performance if the other party provides adequate assurance of his performance.

ARTICLE 72

(1) If prior to the date for performance of the contract it is clear that one of the parties will commit a fundamental breach of contract, the other party may declare the contract avoided.

(2) If time allows, the party intending to declare the contract avoided must give reasonable notice to the other party in order to permit him to provide adequate assurance of his performance.

(3) The requirements of the preceding paragraph do not apply if the other party has declared that he will not perform his obligations.

ARTICLE 73

(1) In the case of a contract for delivery of goods by instalments, if the failure of one party to perform any of his obligations in respect of any instalment constitutes a fundamental breach of contract with respect to that instalment, the other party may declare the contract avoided with respect to that instalment.

(2) If one party's failure to perform any of his obligations in respect of any instalment gives the other party good grounds to conclude that a fundamental breach of contract will occur with respect to future instalments, he may declare the contract avoided for the future, provided that he does so within a reasonable time.

(3) A buyer who declares the contract avoided in respect of any delivery may, at the same time, declare it avoided in respect of deliveries already made or of future deliveries if, by reason of their interdependence, those deliveries could

not be used for the purpose contemplated by the parties at the time of the conclusion of the contract.

Section II. Damages

ARTICLE 74

Damages for breach of contract by one party consist of a sum equal to the loss, including loss of profit, suffered by the other party as a consequence of the breach. Such damages may not exceed the loss which the party in breach foresaw or ought to have foreseen at the time of the conclusion of the contract, in the light of the facts and matters of which he then knew or ought to have known, as a possible consequence of the breach of contract.

ARTICLE 75

If the contract is avoided and if, in a reasonable manner and within a reasonable time after avoidance, the buyer has bought goods in replacement or the seller has resold the goods, the party claiming damages may recover the difference between the contract price and the price in the substitute transaction as well as any further damages recoverable under article 74.

ARTICLE 76

(1) If the contract is avoided and there is a current price for the goods, the party claiming damages may, if he has not made a purchase or resale under article 75, recover the difference between the price fixed by the contract and the current price at the time of avoidance as well as any further damages recoverable under article 74. If, however, the party claiming damages has avoided the contract after taking over the goods, the current price at the time of such taking over shall be applied instead of the current price at the time of avoidance.

(2) For the purposes of the preceding paragraph, the current price is the price prevailing at the place where delivery of the goods should have been made or, if there is no current price at that place, the price at such other place as serves as a reasonable substitute, making due allowance for differences in the cost of transporting the goods.

ARTICLE 77

A party who relies on a breach of contract must take such measures as are reasonable in the circumstances to mitigate the loss, including loss of profit, resulting from the breach. If he fails to take such measures, the party in breach may claim a reduction in the damages in the amount by which the loss should have been mitigated.

Section III. Interest

ARTICLE 78

If a party fails to pay the price or any other sum that is in arrears, the other party is entitled to interest on it, without prejudice to any claim for damages recoverable under article 74.

Section IV. Exemptions

ARTICLE 79

(1) A party is not liable for a failure to perform any of his obligations if he proves that the failure was due to an impediment beyond his control and that he could

not reasonably be expected to have taken the impediment into account at the time of the conclusion of the contract or to have avoided or overcome it or its consequences.

(2) If the party's failure is due to the failure by a third person whom he has engaged to perform the whole or a part of the contract, that party is exempt from liability only if:

   (a)   he is exempt under the preceding paragraph; and

   (b)   the person whom he has so engaged would be so exempt if the provisions of that paragraph were applied to him.

(3) The exemption provided by this article has effect for the period during which the impediment exists.

(4) The party who fails to perform must give notice to the other party of the impediment and its effect on his ability to perform. If the notice is not received by the other party within a reasonable time after the party who fails to perform knew or ought to have known of the impediment, he is liable for damages resulting from such non-receipt.

(5) Nothing in this article prevents either party from exercising any right other than to claim damages under this Convention.

ARTICLE 80

A party may not rely on a failure of the other party to perform, to the extent that such failure was caused by the first party's act or omission.

Section V. Effects of Avoidance

ARTICLE 81

(1) Avoidance of the contract releases both parties from their obligations under it, subject to any damages which may be due. Avoidance does not affect any provision of the contract for the settlement of disputes or any other provision of the contract governing the rights and obligations of the parties consequent upon the avoidance of the contract.

(2) A party who has performed the contract either wholly or in part may claim restitution from the other party of whatever the first party has supplied or paid under the contract. If both parties are bound to make restitution, they must do so concurrently.

ARTICLE 82

(1) The buyer loses the right to declare the contract avoided or to require the seller to deliver substitute goods if it is impossible for him to make restitution of the goods substantially in the condition in which he received them.

(2) The preceding paragraph does not apply:

   (a)   if the impossibility of making restitution of the goods or of making restitution of the goods substantially in the condition in which the buyer received them is not due to his act or omission;

   (b)   if the goods or part of the goods have perished or deteriorated as a result of the examination provided for in article 38; or

   (c)   if the goods or part of the goods have been sold in the normal course of business or have been consumed or transformed by the buyer in the course of normal use before he discovered or ought to have discovered the lack of conformity.

ARTICLE 83

A buyer who has lost the right to declare the contract avoided or to require the seller to deliver substitute goods in accordance with article 82 retains all other remedies under the contract and this Convention.

ARTICLE 84

(1) If the seller is bound to refund the price, he must also pay interest on it, from the date on which the price was paid.

(2) The buyer must account to the seller for all benefits which he has derived from the goods or part of them:

    (a) if he must make restitution of the goods or part of them; or

    (b) if it is impossible for him to make restitution of all or part of the goods or to make restitution of all or part of the goods substantially in the condition in which he received them, but he has nevertheless declared the contract avoided or required the seller to deliver substitute goods.

Section VI. Preservation of the Goods

ARTICLE 85

If the buyer is in delay in taking delivery of the goods or, where payment of the price and delivery of the goods are to be made concurrently, if he fails to pay the price, and the seller is either in possession of the goods or otherwise able to control their disposition, the seller must take such steps as are reasonable in the circumstances to preserve them. He is entitled to retain them until he has been reimbursed his reasonable expenses by the buyer.

ARTICLE 86

(1) If the buyer has received the goods and intends to exercise any right under the contract or this Convention to reject them, he must take such steps to preserve them as are reasonable in the circumstances. He is entitled to retain them until he has been reimbursed his reasonable expenses by the seller.

(2) If goods dispatched to the buyer have been placed at his disposal at their destination and he exercises the right to reject them, he must take possession of them on behalf of the seller, provided that this can be done without payment of the price and without unreasonable inconvenience or unreasonable expense. This provision does not apply if the seller or a person authorized to take charge of the goods on his behalf is present at the destination. If the buyer takes possession of the goods under this paragraph, his rights and obligations are governed by the preceding paragraph.

ARTICLE 87

A party who is bound to take steps to preserve the goods may deposit them in a warehouse of a third person at the expense of the other party provided that the expense incurred is not unreasonable.

ARTICLE 88

(1) A party who is bound to preserve the goods in accordance with article 85 or 86 may sell them by any appropriate means if there has been an unreasonable delay by the other party in taking possession of the goods or in taking them back or in paying the price or the cost of preservation, provided that reasonable notice of the intention to sell has been given to the other party.

(2) If the goods are subject to rapid deterioration or their preservation would involve unreasonable expense, a party who is bound to preserve the goods in accordance with article 85 or 86 must take reasonable measures to sell them. To the extent possible he must give notice to the other party of his intention to sell.

(3) A party selling the goods has the right to retain out of the proceeds of sale an amount equal to the reasonable expenses of preserving the goods and of selling them. He must account to the other party for the balance.

PART IV
FINAL PROVISIONS

ARTICLE 89
The Secretary-General of the United Nations is hereby designated as the depositary for this Convention.

ARTICLE 90
This Convention does not prevail over any international agreement which has already been or may be entered into and which contains provisions concerning the matters governed by this Convention, provided that the parties have their places of business in States parties to such agreement.

Appendix B

Agreement Establishing the World Trade Organization

(Selected Provisions)

ARTICLE I
ESTABLISHMENT OF THE ORGANIZATION

The World Trade Organization (hereinafter referred to as "the WTO") is hereby established.

ARTICLE II
SCOPE OF THE WTO

1. The WTO shall provide the common institutional framework for the conduct of trade relations among its Members in matters related to the agreements and associated legal instruments included in the Annexes to this Agreement.

2. The agreements and associated legal instruments included in Annexes 1, 2 and 3 (hereinafter referred to as "Multilateral Trade Agreements") are integral parts of this Agreement, binding on all Members.

3. The agreements and associated legal instruments included in Annex 4 (hereinafter referred to as "Plurilateral Trade Agreements") are also part of this

Agreement for those Members that have accepted them, and are binding on those Members. The Plurilateral Trade Agreements do not create either obligations or rights for Members that have not accepted them.

4. The General Agreement on Tariffs and Trade 1994 as specified in Annex 1A (hereinafter referred to as "GATT 1994") is legally distinct from the General Agreement on Tariffs and Trade, dated 30 October 1947, annexed to the Final Act Adopted at the Conclusion of the Second Session of the Preparatory Committee of the United Nations Conference on Trade and Employment, as subsequently rectified, amended or modified (hereinafter referred to as "GATT 1947").

ARTICLE III
FUNCTIONS OF THE WTO

1. The WTO shall facilitate the implementation, administration and operation, and further the objectives, of this Agreement and of the Multilateral Trade Agreements, and shall also provide the framework for the implementation, administration and operation of the Plurilateral Trade Agreements.

2. The WTO shall provide the forum for negotiations among its Members concerning their multilateral trade relations in matters dealt with under the agreements in the Annexes to this Agreement. The WTO may also provide a forum for further negotiations among its Members concerning their multilateral trade relations, and a framework for the implementation of the results of such negotiations, as may be decided by the Ministerial Conference.

3. The WTO shall administer the Understanding on Rules and Procedures Governing the Settlement of Disputes (hereinafter referred to as the "Dispute Settlement Understanding" or "DSU") in Annex 2 to this Agreement.

4. The WTO shall administer the Trade Policy Review Mechanism (hereinafter referred to as the "TPRM") provided for in Annex 3 to this Agreement.

5. With a view to achieving greater coherence in global economic policy-making, the WTO shall cooperate, as appropriate, with the International Monetary Fund and with the International Bank for Reconstruction and Development and its affiliated agencies.

ARTICLE IV
STRUCTURE OF THE WTO

1. There shall be a Ministerial Conference composed of representatives of all the Members, which shall meet at least once every two years. The Ministerial Conference shall carry out the functions of the WTO and take actions necessary to this effect. The Ministerial Conference shall have the authority to take decisions on all matters under any of the Multilateral Trade Agreements, if so requested by a Member, in accordance with the specific requirements for decision-making in this Agreement and in the relevant Multilateral Trade Agreement.

2. There shall be a General Council composed of representatives of all the Members, which shall meet as appropriate. In the intervals between meetings of the Ministerial Conference, its functions shall be conducted by the General Council. The General Council shall also carry out the functions assigned to it by this Agreement. The General Council shall establish its rules of procedure and approve the rules of procedure for the Committees provided for in paragraph 7.

3. The General Council shall convene as appropriate to discharge the responsibilities of the Dispute Settlement Body provided for in the Dispute Settlement Understanding. The Dispute Settlement Body may have its own chairman and shall establish such rules of procedure as it deems necessary for the fulfilment of those responsibilities.

4. The General Council shall convene as appropriate to discharge the responsibilities of the Trade Policy Review Body provided for in the TPRM. The Trade Policy Review Body may have its own chairman and shall establish such rules of procedure as it deems necessary for the fulfilment of those responsibilities.

5. There shall be a Council for Trade in Goods, a Council for Trade in Services and a Council for Trade-Related Aspects of Intellectual Property Rights (hereinafter referred to as the "Council for TRIPS"), which shall operate under the general guidance of the General Council. The Council for Trade in Goods shall oversee the functioning of the Multilateral Trade Agreements in Annex 1A. The Council for Trade in Services shall oversee the functioning of the General Agreement on Trade in Services (hereinafter referred to as "GATS"). The Council for TRIPS shall oversee the functioning of the Agreement on Trade-Related Aspects of Intellectual Property Rights (hereinafter referred to as the "Agreement on TRIPS"). These Councils shall carry out the functions assigned to them by their respective agreements and by the General Council. They shall establish their respective rules of procedure subject to the approval of the General Council. Membership in these Councils shall be open to representatives of all Members. These Councils shall meet as necessary to carry out their functions.

6. The Council for Trade in Goods, the Council for Trade in Services and the Council for TRIPS shall establish subsidiary bodies as required. These subsidiary bodies shall establish their respective rules of procedure subject to the approval of their respective Councils.

7. The Ministerial Conference shall establish a Committee on Trade and Development, a Committee on Balance-of-Payments Restrictions and a Committee on Budget, Finance and Administration, which shall carry out the functions assigned to them by this Agreement and by the Multilateral Trade Agreements, and any additional functions assigned to them by the General Council, and may establish such additional Committees with such functions as it may deem appropriate. As part of its functions, the Committee on Trade and Development shall periodically review the special provisions in the Multilateral Trade Agreements in favour of the least-developed country Members and report to the General Council for appropriate action. Membership in these Committees shall be open to representatives of all Members.

8. The bodies provided for under the Plurilateral Trade Agreements shall carry out the functions assigned to them under those Agreements and shall operate within the institutional framework of the WTO. These bodies shall keep the General Council informed of their activities on a regular basis.

ARTICLE VI
THE SECRETARIAT

1. There shall be a Secretariat of the WTO (hereinafter referred to as "the Secretariat") headed by a Director-General.

2. The Ministerial Conference shall appoint the Director-General and adopt regulations setting out the powers, duties, conditions of service and term of office of the Director-General.

3. The Director-General shall appoint the members of the staff of the Secretariat and determine their duties and conditions of service in accordance with regulations adopted by the Ministerial Conference.

4. The responsibilities of the Director-General and of the staff of the Secretariat shall be exclusively international in character. In the discharge of their duties, the Director-General and the staff of the Secretariat shall not seek or accept instructions from any government or any other authority external to the WTO. They shall refrain from any action which might adversely reflect on their position as international officials. The Members of the WTO shall respect the international character of the responsibilities of the Director-General and of the staff of the Secretariat and shall not seek to influence them in the discharge of their duties.

ARTICLE IX
DECISION-MAKING

1. The WTO shall continue the practice of decision-making by consensus followed under GATT 1947.[1] Except as otherwise provided, where a decision cannot be arrived at by consensus, the matter at issue shall be decided by voting. At meetings of the Ministerial Conference and the General Council, each Member of the WTO shall have one vote. Where the European Communities exercise their right to vote, they shall have a number of votes equal to the number of their member States[2] which are Members of the WTO. Decisions of the Ministerial Conference and the General Council shall be taken by a majority of the votes cast, unless otherwise provided in this Agreement or in the relevant Multilateral Trade Agreement.[3]

ARTICLE X
AMENDMENTS

2. Amendments to the provisions of this Article and to the provisions of the following Articles shall take effect only upon acceptance by all Members:

    Article IX of this Agreement;
    Articles I and II of GATT 1994;
    Article II:1 of GATS;
    Article 4 of the Agreement on TRIPS.

ARTICLE XI
ORIGINAL MEMBERSHIP

1. The contracting parties to GATT 1947 as of the date of entry into force of this Agreement, and the European Communities, which accept this Agreement and the Multilateral Trade Agreements and for which Schedules of

---

1   The body concerned shall be deemed to have decided by consensus on a matter submitted for its consideration, if no Member, present at the meeting when the decision is taken, formally objects to the proposed decision.

2   The number of votes of the European Communities and their member States shall in no case exceed the number of the member States of the European Communities.

3   Decisions by the General Council when convened as the Dispute Settlement Body shall be taken only in accordance with the provisions of paragraph 4 of Article 2 of the Dispute Settlement Understanding.

Concessions and Commitments are annexed to GATT 1994 and for which Schedules of Specific Commitments are annexed to GATS shall become original Members of the WTO.

2.   The least-developed countries recognized as such by the United Nations will only be required to undertake commitments and concessions to the extent consistent with their individual development, financial and trade needs or their administrative and institutional capabilities.

ARTICLE XII
ACCESSION

1.   Any State or separate customs territory possessing full autonomy in the conduct of its external commercial relations and of the other matters provided for in this Agreement and the Multilateral Trade Agreements may accede to this Agreement, on terms to be agreed between it and the WTO. Such accession shall apply to this Agreement and the Multilateral Trade Agreements annexed thereto.

2.   Decisions on accession shall be taken by the Ministerial Conference. The Ministerial Conference shall approve the agreement on the terms of accession by a two-thirds majority of the Members of the WTO.

3.   Accession to a Plurilateral Trade Agreement shall be governed by the provisions of that Agreement.

3.   In the event of a conflict between a provision of this Agreement and a provision of any of the Multilateral Trade Agreements, the provision of this Agreement shall prevail to the extent of the conflict.

ARTICLE XVI
MISCELLANEOUS PROVISIONS

4.   Each Member shall ensure the conformity of its laws, regulations and administrative procedures with its obligations as provided in the annexed Agreements.

5.   No reservations may be made in respect of any provision of this Agreement. Reservations in respect of any of the provisions of the Multilateral Trade Agreements may only be made to the extent provided for in those Agreements.

DONE at Marrakesh this fifteenth day of April one thousand nine hundred and ninety-four, in a single copy, in the English, French and Spanish languages, each text being authentic.

LIST OF ANNEXES

ANNEX 1

ANNEX 1A: MULTILATERAL AGREEMENTS ON TRADE IN GOODS
General Agreement on Tariffs and Trade 1994
Agreement on Agriculture
Agreement on the Application of Sanitary and Phytosanitary Measures

Agreement on Textiles and Clothing

Agreement on Technical Barriers to Trade

Agreement on Trade-Related Investment Measures

Agreement on Implementation of Article VI of the General Agreement on Tariffs and Trade 1994

Agreement on Implementation of Article VII of the General Agreement on Tariffs and Trade 1994

Agreement on Preshipment Inspection

Agreement on Rules of Origin

Agreement on Import Licensing Procedures

Agreement on Subsidies and Countervailing Measures

Agreement on Safeguards

ANNEX 1B: General Agreement on Trade in Services and Annexes

ANNEX 1C: Agreement on Trade-Related Aspects of Intellectual Property Rights

ANNEX 4 PLURILATERAL TRADE AGREEMENTS

Agreement on Trade in Civil Aircraft

Agreement on Government Procurement

International Dairy Agreement

International Bovine Meat Agreement

Appendix C

Agreement on Trade-Related Aspects of Intellectual Property Rights

(Selected Provisions)

PART I:
GENERAL PROVISIONS AND BASIC PRINCIPLES

ARTICLE 2—INTELLECTUAL PROPERTY CONVENTIONS
2.   Nothing in Parts I to IV of this Agreement shall derogate from existing obligations that Members may have to each other under the Paris Convention, the Berne Convention, the Rome Convention and the Treaty on Intellectual Property in Respect of Integrated Circuits.

ARTICLE 3—NATIONAL TREATMENT
1.   Each Member shall accord to the nationals of other Members treatment no less favourable than that it accords to its own nationals with regard to the protection 3 of intellectual property, subject to the exceptions already provided in, respectively, the Paris Convention (1967), the Berne Convention (1971), the Rome Convention and the Treaty on Intellectual Property in Respect of Integrated Circuits.

ARTICLE 4—MOST-FAVORED-NATION TREATMENT

With regard to the protection of intellectual property, any advantage, favour, privilege or immunity granted by a Member to the nationals of any other country shall be accorded immediately and unconditionally to the nationals of all other Members. Exempted from this obligation are any advantage, favour, privilege or immunity accorded by a Member:

ARTICLE 7—OBJECTIVES

The protection and enforcement of intellectual property rights should contribute to the promotion of technological innovation and to the transfer and dissemination of technology, to the mutual advantage of producers and users of technological knowledge and in a manner conducive to social and economic welfare, and to a balance of rights and obligations.

PART II:
STANDARDS CONCERNING THE AVAILABILITY, SCOPE AND USE OF INTELLECTUAL PROPERTY RIGHTS

Section 1: Copyright and Related Rights

ARTICLE 9—RELATION TO BERNE CONVENTION

1. Members shall comply with . . . the Berne Convention (1971).
2. Copyright protection shall extend to expressions and not to ideas, procedures, methods of operation or mathematical concepts as such.

ARTICLE 10—COMPUTER PROGRAMS AND COMPILATIONS OF DATA

1. Computer programs, whether in source or object code, shall be protected as literary works under the Berne Convention (1971).
2. Compilations of data or other material, whether in machine readable or other form, which by reason of the selection or arrangement of their contents constitute intellectual creations shall be protected as such. Such protection, which shall not extend to the data or material itself, shall be without prejudice to any copyright subsisting in the data or material itself.

ARTICLE 12—TERM OF PROTECTION

Whenever the term of protection of a work, other than a photographic work or a work of applied art, is calculated on a basis other than the life of a natural person, such term shall be no less than fifty years from the end of the calendar year of authorized publication, or, failing such authorized publication within fifty years from the making of the work, fifty years from the end of the calendar year of making.

Section 2: Trademarks

ARTICLE 15—PROTECTABLE SUBJECT MATTER

1. Any sign, or any combination of signs, capable of distinguishing the goods or services of one undertaking from those of other undertakings, shall be capable of constituting a trademark. Such signs, in particular words including personal

names, letters, numerals, figurative elements and combinations of colours as well as any combination of such signs, shall be eligible for registration as trademarks. Where signs are not inherently capable of distinguishing the relevant goods or services, Members may make registrability depend on distinctiveness acquired through use. Members may require, as a condition of registration, that signs be visually perceptible.

3.   Members may make registrability depend on use. However, actual use of a trademark shall not be a condition for filing an application for registration. An application shall not be refused solely on the ground that intended use has not taken place before the expiry of a period of three years from the date of application.

4.   The nature of the goods or services to which a trademark is to be applied shall in no case form an obstacle to registration of the trademark.

5.   Members shall publish each trademark either before it is registered or promptly after it is registered and shall afford a reasonable opportunity for petitions to cancel the registration. In addition, Members may afford an opportunity for the registration of a trademark to be opposed.

ARTICLE 16—RIGHTS CONFERRED

1.   The owner of a registered trademark shall have the exclusive right to prevent all third parties not having his consent from using in the course of trade identical or similar signs for goods or services which are identical or similar to those in respect of which the trademark is registered where such use would result in a likelihood of confusion. In case of the use of an identical sign for identical goods or services, a likelihood of confusion shall be presumed. The rights described above shall not prejudice any existing prior rights, nor shall they affect the possibility of Members making rights available on the basis of use.

2.   Article 6bis of the Paris Convention (1967) shall apply, mutatis mutandis, to services. In determining whether a trademark is well-known, account shall be taken of the knowledge of the trademark in the relevant sector of the public, including knowledge in that Member obtained as a result of the promotion of the trademark.

ARTICLE 18—TERM OF PROTECTION

Initial registration, and each renewal of registration, of a trademark shall be for a term of no less than seven years. The registration of a trademark shall be renewable indefinitely.

ARTICLE 19—REQUIREMENT OF USE

1.   If use is required to maintain a registration, the registration may be cancelled only after an uninterrupted period of at least three years of non-use, unless valid reasons based on the existence of obstacles to such use are shown by the trademark owner. Circumstances arising independently of the will of the owner of the trademark which constitute an obstacle to the use of the trademark, such as import restrictions on or other government requirements for goods or services protected by the trademark, shall be recognized as valid reasons for non-use.

2.   When subject to the control of its owner, use of a trademark by another person shall be recognized as use of the trademark for the purpose of maintaining the registration.

ARTICLE 20—OTHER REQUIREMENTS

The use of a trademark in the course of trade shall not be unjustifiably encumbered by special requirements, such as use with another trademark, use in a special form or use in a manner detrimental to its capability to distinguish the goods or services of one undertaking from those of other undertakings. This will not preclude a requirement prescribing the use of the trademark identifying the undertaking producing the goods or services along with, but without linking it to, the trademark distinguishing the specific goods or services in question of that undertaking.

ARTICLE 21—LICENSING AND ASSIGNMENT

Members may determine conditions on the licensing and assignment of trademarks, it being understood that the compulsory licensing of trademarks shall not be permitted and that the owner of a registered trademark shall have the right to assign his trademark with or without the transfer of the business to which the trademark belongs.

Section 3: Geographical Indications

ARTICLE 22—PROTECTION OF GEOGRAPHICAL INDICATIONS

1. Geographical indications are, for the purposes of this Agreement, indications which identify a good as originating in the territory of a Member, or a region or locality in that territory, where a given quality, reputation or other characteristic of the good is essentially attributable to its geographical origin.

2. In respect of geographical indications, Members shall provide the legal means for interested parties to prevent:

    (a) the use of any means in the designation or presentation of a good that indicates or suggests that the good in question originates in a geographical area other than the true place of origin in a manner which misleads the public as to the geographical origin of the good;

    (b) any use which constitutes an act of unfair competition within the meaning of Article 10bis of the Paris Convention (1967).

3. A Member shall, ex officio if its legislation so permits or at the request of an interested party, refuse or invalidate the registration of a trademark which contains or consists of a geographical indication with respect to goods not originating in the territory indicated, if use of the indication in the trademark for such goods in that Member is of such a nature as to mislead the public as to the true place of origin.

4. The provisions of the preceding paragraphs of this Article shall apply to a geographical indication which, although literally true as to the territory, region or locality in which the goods originate, falsely represents to the public that the goods originate in another territory.

Section 4: Industrial Designs

ARTICLE 25—REQUIREMENTS FOR PROTECTION

1. Members shall provide for the protection of independently created industrial designs that are new or original. Members may provide that designs are not new or original if they do not significantly differ from known designs or combinations of known design features. Members may provide that such protection shall not extend to designs dictated essentially by technical or functional considerations.

ARTICLE 26—PROTECTION

1. The owner of a protected industrial design shall have the right to prevent third parties not having his consent from making, selling or importing articles bearing

or embodying a design which is a copy, or substantially a copy, of the protected design, when such acts are undertaken for commercial purposes.

3. The duration of protection available shall amount to at least ten years.

Section 5: Patents

ARTICLE 27—PATENTABLE SUBJECT MATTER

1. Subject to the provisions of paragraphs 2 and 3 below, patents shall be available for any inventions, whether products or processes, in all fields of technology, provided that they are new, involve an inventive step and are capable of industrial application. 5 Subject to paragraph 4 of Article 65, paragraph 8 of Article 70 and paragraph 3 of this Article, patents shall be available and patent rights enjoyable without discrimination as to the place of invention, the field of technology and whether products are imported or locally produced.

2. Members may exclude from patentability inventions, the prevention within their territory of the commercial exploitation of which is necessary to protect public order or morality, including to protect human, animal or plant life or health or to avoid serious prejudice to the environment, provided that such exclusion is not made merely because the exploitation is prohibited by domestic law.

3. Members may also exclude from patentability:

    (a) diagnostic, therapeutic and surgical methods for the treatment of humans or animals;

    (b) plants and animals other than microorganisms, and essentially biological processes for the production of plants or animals other than non-biological and microbiological processes. However, Members shall provide for the protection of plant varieties either by patents or by an effective sui generis system or by any combination thereof. The provisions of this subparagraph shall be reviewed four years after the entry into force of the Agreement Establishing the WTO.

ARTICLE 28—RIGHTS CONFERRED

1. A patent shall confer on its owner the following exclusive rights:

    (a) where the subject matter of a patent is a product, to prevent third parties not having his consent from the acts of: making, using, offering for sale, selling, or importing for these purposes that product;

    (b) where the subject matter of a patent is a process, to prevent third parties not having his consent from the act of using the process, and from the acts of: using, offering for sale, selling, or importing for these purposes at least the product obtained directly by that process.

2. Patent owners shall also have the right to assign, or transfer by succession, the patent and to conclude licensing contracts.

ARTICLE 29—CONDITIONS ON PATENT APPLICANTS

1. Members shall require that an applicant for a patent shall disclose the invention in a manner sufficiently clear and complete for the invention to be carried out by a person skilled in the art and may require the applicant to indicate the best mode for carrying out the invention known to the inventor at the filing date or, where priority is claimed, at the priority date of the application.

2.   Members may require an applicant for a patent to provide information concerning his corresponding foreign applications and grants.

ARTICLE 31— OTHER USE WITHOUT AUTHORIZATION OF THE RIGHT HOLDER

Where the law of a Member allows for other use of the subject matter of a patent without the authorization of the right holder, including use by the government or third parties authorized by the government, the following provisions shall be respected:

(a)   authorization of such use shall be considered on its individual merits;

(b)   such use may only be permitted if, prior to such use, the proposed user has made efforts to obtain authorization from the right holder on reasonable commercial terms and conditions and that such efforts have not been successful within a reasonable period of time. This requirement may be waived by a Member in the case of a national emergency or other circumstances of extreme urgency or in cases of public non-commercial use. In situations of national emergency or other circumstances of extreme urgency, the right holder shall, nevertheless, be notified as soon as reasonably practicable. In the case of public non-commercial use, where the government or contractor, without making a patent search, knows or has demonstrable grounds to know that a valid patent is or will be used by or for the government, the right holder shall be informed promptly;

(c)   the scope and duration of such use shall be limited to the purpose for which it was authorized, and in the case of semi-conductor technology shall only be for public non-commercial use or to remedy a practice determined after judicial or administrative process to be anti-competitive.

(d)   such use shall be non-exclusive;

(e)   such use shall be non-assignable, except with that part of the enterprise or goodwill which enjoys such use;

(f)   any such use shall be authorized predominantly for the supply of the domestic market of the Member authorizing such use;

(g)   authorization for such use shall be liable, subject to adequate protection of the legitimate interests of the persons so authorized, to be terminated if and when the circumstances which led to it cease to exist and are unlikely to recur. The competent authority shall have the authority to review, upon motivated request, the continued existence of these circumstances;

(h)   the right holder shall be paid adequate remuneration in the circumstances of each case, taking into account the economic value of the authorization;

ARTICLE 33—TERM OF PROTECTION

The term of protection available shall not end before the expiration of a period of twenty years counted from the filing date.

Section 6: Layout-Designs (Topographies) of Integrated Circuits

ARTICLE 35—RELATION TO IPIC TREATY

Members agree to provide protection to the layout-designs (topographies) of integrated circuits (hereinafter referred to as "layout-designs") in accordance with

Articles 2-7 (other than paragraph 3 of Article 6), Article 12 and paragraph 3 of Article 16 of the Treaty on Intellectual Property in Respect of Integrated Circuits and, in addition, to comply with the following provisions.

ARTICLE 38—TERM OF PROTECTION

1. In Members requiring registration as a condition of protection, the term of protection of layout-designs shall not end before the expiration of a period of ten years counted from the date of filing an application for registration or from the first commercial exploitation wherever in the world it occurs.

Section 7: Protection of Undisclosed Information

ARTICLE 39

1. In the course of ensuring effective protection against unfair competition as provided in Article 10bis of the Paris Convention (1967), Members shall protect undisclosed information in accordance with paragraph 2 below and data submitted to governments or governmental agencies in accordance with paragraph 3 below.

2. Natural and legal persons shall have the possibility of preventing information lawfully within their control from being disclosed to, acquired by, or used by others without their consent in a manner contrary to honest commercial practices so long as such information:

   is secret in the sense that it is not, as a body or in the precise configuration and assembly of its components, generally known among or readily accessible to persons within the circles that normally deal with the kind of information in question;

   has commercial value because it is secret; and

   has been subject to reasonable steps under the circumstances, by the person lawfully in control of the information, to keep it secret.

PART III:
ENFORCEMENT OF INTELLECTUAL PROPERTY RIGHTS

ARTICLE 41

1. Members shall ensure that enforcement procedures as specified in this Part are available under their national laws so as to permit effective action against any act of infringement of intellectual property rights covered by this Agreement, including expeditious remedies to prevent infringements and remedies which constitute a deterrent to further infringements. These procedures shall be applied in such a manner as to avoid the creation of barriers to legitimate trade and to provide for safeguards against their abuse.

2. Procedures concerning the enforcement of intellectual property rights shall be fair and equitable. They shall not be unnecessarily complicated or costly, or entail unreasonable time-limits or unwarranted delays.

3. Decisions on the merits of a case shall preferably be in writing and reasoned. They shall be made available at least to the parties to the proceeding without undue delay. Decisions on the merits of a case shall be based only on evidence in respect of which parties were offered the opportunity to be heard.

4. Parties to a proceeding shall have an opportunity for review by a judicial authority of final administrative decisions and, subject to jurisdictional provisions in national laws concerning the importance of a case, of at least the legal aspects of initial judicial decisions on the merits of a case. However, there shall be no obligation to provide an opportunity for review of acquittals in criminal cases.

ARTICLE 42—FAIR AND EQUITABLE PROCEDURES

Members shall make available to right holders civil judicial procedures concerning the enforcement of any intellectual property right covered by this Agreement. Defendants shall have the right to written notice which is timely and contains sufficient detail, including the basis of the claims. Parties shall be allowed to be represented by independent legal counsel, and procedures shall not impose overly burdensome requirements concerning mandatory personal appearances. All parties to such procedures shall be duly entitled to substantiate their claims and to present all relevant evidence. The procedure shall provide a means to identify and protect confidential information, unless this would be contrary to existing constitutional requirements.

ARTICLE 44—INJUNCTIONS

1. The judicial authorities shall have the authority to order a party to desist from an infringement, inter alia to prevent the entry into the channels of commerce in their jurisdiction of imported goods that involve the infringement of an intellectual property right, immediately after customs clearance of such goods. Members are not obliged to accord such authority in respect of protected subject matter acquired or ordered by a person prior to knowing or having reasonable grounds to know that dealing in such subject matter would entail the infringement of an intellectual property right.

ARTICLE 45—DAMAGES

1. The judicial authorities shall have the authority to order the infringer to pay the right holder damages adequate to compensate for the injury the right holder has suffered because of an infringement of his intellectual property right by an infringer who knew or had reasonable grounds to know that he was engaged in infringing activity.

Section 4: Special Requirements Related to Border Measures

ARTICLE 51—SUSPENSION OF RELEASE BY CUSTOMS AUTHORITIES

Members shall, in conformity with the provisions set out below, adopt procedures to enable a right holder, who has valid grounds for suspecting that the importation of counterfeit trademark or pirated copyright goods may take place, to lodge an application in writing with competent authorities, administrative or judicial, for the suspension by the customs authorities of the release into free circulation of such goods.

ARTICLE 53—SECURITY OR EQUIVALENT ASSURANCE

1. The competent authorities shall have the authority to require an applicant to provide a security or equivalent assurance sufficient to protect the defendant and the competent authorities and to prevent abuse. Such security or equivalent assurance shall not unreasonably deter recourse to these procedures.

ARTICLE 57—RIGHT OF INSPECTION AND INFORMATION

Without prejudice to the protection of confidential information, Members shall provide the competent authorities the authority to give the right holder sufficient opportunity to have any product detained by the customs authorities inspected in order to substantiate his claims. The competent authorities shall also have authority to give the importer an equivalent opportunity to have any such product inspected. Where a positive determination has been made on the merits of a case, Members may provide the competent authorities the authority to inform the right holder of the names and addresses of the consignor, the importer and the consignee and of the quantity of the goods in question.

PART V: DISPUTE PREVENTION AND SETTLEMENT

ARTICLE 63—TRANSPARENCY

1. Laws and regulations, and final judicial decisions and administrative rulings of general application, made effective by any Member pertaining to the subject matter of this Agreement (the availability, scope, acquisition, enforcement and prevention of the abuse of intellectual property rights) shall be published, or where such publication is not practicable made publicly available, in a national language, in such a manner as to enable governments and right holders to become acquainted with them.

2. Members shall notify the laws and regulations referred to in paragraph 1 above to the Council for Trade-Related Aspects of Intellectual Property Rights in order to assist that Council in its review of the operation of this Agreement.

ARTICLE 66—LEAST-DEVELOPED COUNTRY MEMBERS

1. In view of their special needs and requirements, their economic, financial and administrative constraints, and their need for flexibility to create a viable technological base, least-developed country Members shall not be required to apply the provisions of this Agreement, other than Articles 3, 4 and 5, for a period of 10 years from the date of application as defined under paragraph 1 of Article 65 above. The Council shall, upon duly motivated request by a least-developed country Member, accord extensions of this period.

ARTICLE 68—COUNCIL FOR TRADE-RELATED ASPECTS OF INTELLECTUAL PROPERTY RIGHTS

The Council for Trade-Related Aspects of Intellectual Property Rights shall monitor the operation of this Agreement and, in particular, Members' compliance with their obligations hereunder, and shall afford Members the opportunity of consulting on matters relating to the trade-related aspects of intellectual property rights.

Appendix D

Excerpts from International Convention for the Unification of Certain Rules of Law Relating to Bills of Lading

("Hague Rules")

ARTICLE 1

In this Convention the following words are employed with the meanings set out below:

(a) "Carrier" includes the owner or the charterer who enters into a contract of carriage with a shipper.

(b) "Contract of carriage" applies only to contracts of carriage covered by a bill of lading or any similar document of title, in so far as such document relates to the carriage of goods by sea, including any bill of lading or any similar document as aforesaid issued under or pursuant to a charter party from the moment at which such bill of lading or similar document of title regulates the relations between a carrier and a holder of the same.

(c) "Goods" includes goods, wares, merchandise and articles of every kind whatsoever except live animals and cargo which by the contract of carriage in stated as being carried on deck and is so carried.

(d) "Ship" means any vessel used for the carriage of goods by sea.

(e) "Carriage of goods" covers the period from the time when the goods are loaded on to the time they are discharged from the ship.

ARTICLE 2

Subject to the provisions of Article 6, under every contract of carriage of goods by sea the carrier, in relation to the loading, handling, stowage, carriage, custody, care and discharge of such goods, shall be subject to the responsibilities and liabilities, and entitled to the rights and immunities hereinafter set forth.

ARTICLE 3

1. The carrier shall be bound before and at the beginning of the voyage to exercise due diligence to:

    (a) Make the ship seaworthy.

    (b) Properly man, equip and supply the ship.

    (c) Make the holds, refrigerating and cool chambers, and all other parts of the ship in which goods are carried, fit and safe for their reception, carriage and preservation.

2. Subject to the provisions of Article 4, the carrier shall properly and carefully load, handle, stow, carry, keep, care for, and discharge the goods carried.

3. After receiving the goods into his charge the carrier or the master or agent of the carrier shall, on demand of the shipper, issue to the shipper a bill of lading showing among other things:

    (a) The leading marks necessary for identification of the goods as the same are furnished in writing by the shipper before the loading of such goods starts, provided such marks are stamped or otherwise shown clearly upon the goods if uncovered, or on the cases or coverings in which such goods are contained, in such a manner as should ordinarily remain legible until the end of the voyage.

    (b) Either the number of packages or pieces, or the quantity, or weight, as the case may be, as furnished in writing by the shipper.

    (c) The apparent order and condition of the goods.

    Provided that no carrier, master or agent of the carrier shall be bound to state or show in the bill of lading any marks, number, quantity, or weight which he has reasonable ground for suspecting not accurately to represent the goods actually received, or which he has had no reasonable means of checking.

4. Such a bill of lading shall be prima facie evidence of the receipt by the carrier of the goods as therein described in accordance with paragraph 3(a), (b) and (c).

5. The shipper shall be deemed to have guaranteed to the carrier the accuracy at the time of shipment of the marks, number, quantity and weight, as furnished by him, and the shipper shall indemnify the carrier against all loss, damages and expenses arising or resulting from inaccuracies in such particulars. The right of the carrier to such indemnity shall in no way limit his responsibility and liability under the contract of carriage to any person other than the shipper.

6. Unless notice of loss or damage and the general nature of such loss or damage be given in writing to the carrier or his agent at the port of discharge before or at the time of the removal of the goods into the custody of the person entitled to delivery thereof under the contract of carriage, or, if the loss or damage be not apparent, within three days, such removal shall be prima facie evidence of the delivery by the carrier of the goods as described in the bill of lading.

If the loss or damage is not apparent, the notice must be given within three days of the delivery of the goods.

The notice in writing need not be given if the state of the goods has, at the time of their receipt, been the subject of joint survey or inspection.

In any event the carrier and the ship shall be discharged from all liability in respect of loss or damage unless suit is brought within one year after delivery of the goods or the date when the goods should have been delivered.

In the case of any actual or apprehended loss or damage the carrier and the receiver shall give all reasonable facilities to each other for inspecting and tallying the goods.

7. After the goods are loaded the bill of lading to be issued by the carrier, master, or agent of the carrier, to the shipper shall, if the shipper so demands, be a "shipped" bill of lading, provided that if the shipper shall have previously taken up any document of title to such goods, he shall surrender the same as against the issue of the "shipped" bill of lading, but at the option of the carrier such document of title may be noted at the port of shipment by the carrier, master, or agent with the name or names of the ship or ships upon which the goods have been shipped and the date or dates of shipment, and when so noted, if it shows the particulars mentioned in paragraph 3 of Article 3, shall for the purpose of this Article be deemed to constitute a "shipped" bill of lading.

8. Any clause, covenant, or agreement in a contract of carriage relieving the carrier or the ship from liability for loss or damage to, or in connexion with, goods arising from negligence, fault, or failure in the duties and obligations provided in this Article or lessening such liability otherwise than as provided in this Convention, shall be null and void and of no effect. A benefit of insurance in favour of the carrier or similar clause shall be deemed to be a clause relieving the carrier from liability.

ARTICLE 4

1. Neither the carrier nor the ship shall be liable for loss or damage arising or resulting from unseaworthiness unless caused by want of due diligence on the part of the carrier to make the ship seaworthy and to secure that the ship is properly manned, equipped and supplied, and to make the holds, refrigerating and cool chambers and all other parts of the ship in which goods are carried fit and safe for their reception, carriage and preservation in accordance with the provisions of paragraph 1 of Article 3. Whenever loss or damage has resulted from unseaworthiness the burden of proving the exercise of due diligence shall be on the carrier or other person claiming exemption under this Article.

2. Neither the carrier nor the ship shall be responsible for loss or damage arising or resulting from:

    (a)   Act, neglect, or default of the master, mariner, pilot, or the servants of the carrier in the navigation or in the management of the ship.

(b)   Fire, unless caused by the actual fault or privity of the carrier.

(c)   Perils, dangers and accidents of the sea or other navigable waters.

(d)   Act of God.

(e)   Act of war.

(f)   Act of public enemies.

(g)   Arrest or restraint or princes, rulers or people, or seizure under legal process.

(h)   Quarantine restrictions.

(i)   Act or omission of the shipper or owner of the goods, his agent or representative.

(j)   Strikes or lockouts or stoppage or restraint of labour from whatever cause, whether partial or general.

(k)   Riots and civil commotions.

(l)   Saving or attempting to save life or property at sea.

(m) Wastage in bulk or weight or any other loss or damage arising from inherent defect, quality or vice of the goods.

(n)   Insufficiency of packing.

(o)   Insufficiency or inadequacy of marks.

(p)   Latent defects not discoverable by due diligence.

(q)   Any other cause arising without the actual fault or privity of the carrier, or without the actual fault or neglect of the agents or servants of the carrier, but the burden of proof shall be on the person claiming the benefit of this exception to show that neither the actual fault or privity of the carrier nor the fault or neglect of the agents or servants of the carrier contributed to the loss or damage.

3.   The shipper shall not be responsible for loss or damage sustained by the carrier or the ship arising or resulting from any cause without the act, fault or neglect of the shipper, his agents or his servants.

4.   Any deviation in saving or attempting to save life or property at sea or any reasonable deviation shall not be deemed to be an infringement or breach of this Convention or of the contract of carriage, and the carrier shall not be liable for any loss or damage resulting therefrom.

5.   Neither the carrier nor the ship shall in any event be or become liable for any loss or damage to or in connection with goods in an amount exceeding 100 pounds sterling per package or unit, or the equivalent of that sum in other currency unless the nature and value of such goods have been declared by the shipper before shipment and inserted in the bill of lading.

This declaration if embodied in the bill of lading shall be prima facie evidence, but shall not be binding or conclusive on the carrier.

By agreement between the carrier, master or agent of the carrier and the shipper another maximum amount than that mentioned in this paragraph may be fixed, provided that such maximum shall not be less than the figure above named.

Neither the carrier nor the ship shall be responsible in any event for loss or damage to, or in connection with, goods if the nature or value thereof has been knowingly misstated by the shipper in the bill of lading.

6. Goods of an inflammable, explosive or dangerous nature to the shipment whereof the carrier, master or agent of the carrier has not consented with knowledge of their nature and character, may at any time before discharge be landed at any place, or destroyed or rendered innocuous by the carrier without compensation and the shipper of such goods shall be liable for all damage and expenses directly or indirectly arising out of or resulting from such shipment. If any such goods shipped with such knowledge and consent shall become a danger to the ship or cargo, they may in like manner be landed at any place, or destroyed or rendered innocuous by the carrier without liability on the part of the carrier except to general average, if any.

ARTICLE 5

A carrier shall be at liberty to surrender in whole or in part all or any of his rights and immunities or to increase any of his responsibilities and obligations under this Convention, provided such surrender or increase shall be embodied in the bill of lading issued to the shipper.

The provisions of this Convention shall not be applicable to charter parties, but if bills of lading are issued in the case of a ship under a charter party they shall comply with the terms of this Convention. Nothing in these rules shall be held to prevent the insertion in a bill of lading of any lawful provision regarding general average.

ARTICLE 6

Notwithstanding the provisions of the preceding Articles, a carrier, master or agent of the carrier and a shipper shall in regard to any particular goods be at liberty to enter into any agreement in any terms as to the responsibility and liability of the carrier for such goods, and as to the rights and immunities of the carrier in respect of such goods, or his obligation as to seaworthiness, so far as this stipulation is not contrary to public policy, or the care or diligence of his servants or agents in regard to the loading, handling, stowage, carriage, custody, care and discharge of the goods carried by sea, provided that in this case no bill of lading has been or shall be issued and that the terms agreed shall be embodied in a receipt which shall be a non-negotiable document and shall be marked as such.

Any agreement so entered into shall have full legal effect.

Provided that this Article shall not apply to ordinary commercial shipments made in the ordinary course of trade, but only to other shipments where the character or condition of the property to be carried or the circumstances, terms and conditions under which the carriage is to be performed are such as reasonably to justify a special agreement.

ARTICLE 7

Nothing herein contained shall prevent a carrier or a shipper from entering into any agreement, stipulation, condition, reservation or exemption as to the responsibility and liability of the carrier or the ship for the loss or damage to, or in connexion with, the custody and care and handling of goods prior to the loading on, and subsequent to, the discharge from the ship on which the goods are carried by sea.

ARTICLE 10

The provisions of this Convention shall apply to all bills of lading issued in any of the contracting States.

Index